# Major Problems in the
# History of Imperial Russia

Major Problems in European History Series

# Major Problems in the History of Imperial Russia

Edited by

**James Cracraft**
University of Illinois, Chicago

**D. C. Heath and Company**
Lexington, Massachusetts    Toronto

*Address editorial correspondence to:*

D. C. Heath and Company
125 Spring Street
Lexington, MA 02173


Acquisitions Editor: James Miller
Developmental Editor: David Light
Managing Editor: Sylvia Mallory
Production Editor: Elizabeth Gale
Designer: Judith Miller
Photo Researcher: Mary Stuart Lang
Production Coordinator: Charles Dutton
Permissions Editor: Margaret Roll


Cover: "Revue passée par le Czarevitch" painting by Eugene Detaille. Giraudon/ Art Resource, NY.

Credits:
Photographs: p. 1, The Bettman Archive; p. 79, The Granger Collection; p. 253, The Granger Collection; p. 439, Bildarchiv Preussischer Kulturbesitz.
Maps: Ortelius Design

Published simultaneously in Canada.

Printed in the United States of America.

International Standard Book Number: 0-669-21497-3

Library of Congress Catalog Number: 93-70549

10 9 8 7 6 5 4 3 2 1

# Preface

This book provides a unique array of essays and documents relating to the history of Imperial Russia. It is intended for the use primarily of college and university students. Given the more general historical importance of the Russian Empire and its Soviet successor, the volume should also be useful to anyone seriously interested in modern European or world history. Indeed, in light of the collapse of the Empire's Soviet successor, this volume should interest anyone seeking to understand the more durable factors in Russian history and such alternatives as there were in 1917 to the imposition of Soviet rule.

The Imperial period of Russian history began in the reign of Peter the Great (1689–1725), the first emperor, and ended with the reign of Nicholas II (1894–1917), who proved to be the last. It was a most eventful as well as clearly demarcated era. These two centuries witnessed, among other crucial developments, the establishment of the Russian Empire as a great power in Europe and the world; the gradual Europeanization (or Westernization) of Russian institutions and culture; the formation of a distinctive Imperial elite; the continual expansion and buildup of the Empire itself, until it occupied roughly one-sixth of the land surface of the earth; the coming of the Industrial Revolution; and the tentative foundation, late in the period, of a modern legal system designed to order an increasingly complex, pluralist society. At the same time, Imperial Russia was the scene of repeated and often deadly conflict between peasants and landlords, officials and reformers, workers and employers, Russians and non-Russians, policemen and revolutionaries. By 1905, indeed, virtually the whole of this complex, fractious society stood in opposition to the Imperial regime, and revolution ensued. These are some of the major problems or themes dealt with in this book.

The volume contains thirty essays by historians, each concerned with one or more such major problem or theme, and some forty-nine illustrative primary sources (or documents). The essays and related documents, grouped in fourteen chapters, are introduced and connected by explanatory commentaries, and each chapter concludes with suggestions for further reading. The volume can thus serve either as the main resource for appropriate courses or as supplementary reading. It does not include excerpts from any of the standard textbooks on Russian history, and there is little or no overlap with the few available collections of essays or documents.

Part I (Chapters 1 and 2) consists of introductory material. The essays in Chapter 1 offer distinctive overviews of Russian history that focus on two critical problems: the influence of the generally harsh natural environment on Russia's historical development, and Russia's relationship to Europe (or "the West"). The essays and documents in Chapter 2 concern the more immediate historical—or Muscovite—background, and particularly the fundamental institutions of autocracy and serfdom linking Muscovite with Imperial Russia.

The bulk of the book, then, is devoted to the history of Imperial Russia proper. Part II (Chapters 3–6) is concerned with the eighteenth century, and gives special emphasis to the reigns of Peter the Great and Catherine the Great. Part III (Chapters 7–10) covers the nineteenth century, particularly the era of reform and counter-reform (1855–1905). Part IV (Chapters 11–14) is devoted to the last decades of the Imperial period, especially economic and social developments. Two entire chapters (Chapters 6 and 10) discuss the buildup of the Empire itself in the eighteenth and nineteenth centuries, and Chapter 14 relates the collapse of the Imperial regime in the midst of World War I.

Thus readers will find that internal developments have been emphasized in these readings at the expense of foreign affairs; that social and economic history are given more space than purely administrative or, alas, cultural history; and that considerable attention is paid to legal and constitutional questions, which are usually neglected in Russian histories in favor of more sensational topics. The fact that the Russian Empire was just that—an empire of disparate peoples in which the Russians themselves became a minority—is also emphasized. And throughout the book an effort has been made to portray the Empire as a living *polity*: as a vast and heterogeneous political organism the like of which had not been seen in the world since the days of the Roman Empire.

The Imperial period of Russian history has attracted the attention of numerous scholars, and in compiling this volume I could choose from a large body of first-rate work in English. Yet that attention has not been evenly distributed. Political history (including diplomatic and administrative affairs) fills many more pages of the literature than does strictly social, economic, or cultural history. Much more work has been done on the period from 1855 to 1917 than on earlier times; on elite or secular culture than on religion or popular culture; on radical and revolutionary groups than on the liberal or constitutional movement; on Russians rather than indigenous or subject peoples; and on men rather than women. Impressive efforts have been made to fill out the historical record in these and other respects, to be sure; and, drawing on these efforts, I have tried in this book to provide a broader or more balanced coverage of topics than is found in the few existing textbooks or collections. Unfortunately, I have had to slight urban, cultural, and non-Russian ethnic history—in part because of ever-pressing space limitations, in part because of the state of the respective fields. Specialized studies in these areas are available in English, however, as the further reading suggestions indicate.

Considerations of time and expense as well as space limitations restricted the number of selections that could be newly translated from Russian (or other foreign languages), as did the shortcomings of most Soviet scholarship. Nevertheless, three of the essays and many of the documents appear here in English for the first time, joining the numerous selections that were previously translated and published elsewhere. The documents have been chosen to illustrate major points made in the preceding essays and to convey some sense of the source-base of Imperial Russian history. The further reading suggestions listed at the end of each chapter, culled from the scholarly literature in English, include both books and journal articles, and editions of documents as well as works by historians. These suggestions are intended to assist students at various levels of knowledge and interest, and with access to libraries or bookstores of varying size and scope. A list of works relevant to the whole of Imperial Russian history is appended to this Preface (see p. viii).

Apart from necessary abridgment, the essays and documents have been slightly edited to achieve greater consistency in terminology and transliteration. The latter follows the modified Library of Congress system used by the *Slavic Review*, the journal of the American Association for the Advancement of Slavic Studies, with the further simplifications normally employed in history books intended for a broad readership. All dates in this volume are given in accordance with the Julian or Old Style calendar adopted by Peter the Great for use in Russia beginning in January 1700 (see Documents, Chapter 3). In the eighteenth century, this calendar was eleven days behind the Gregorian or New Style calendar that was steadily superseding it in Europe and beyond; in the nineteenth century, twelve days behind; in the twentieth, thirteen days. The New Style calendar was finally adopted in Russia in February 1918.

For their help in seeing this book into print, I would like to thank Catherine Prygrocki and Mary Parks of the staff of the History Department, University of Illinois at Chicago; and James Miller, David Light, Margaret Roll, and Elizabeth Gale of D. C. Heath and Company, the publishers. For helpful advice in developing the project I am grateful to Marc Raeff, the distinguished Russian historian whose vast *oeuvre* is modestly represented here, and to my colleague Jonathan Daly, fresh from his doctoral studies at Harvard. Six reviewers commissioned by D. C. Heath—anonymous at the time—made helpful suggestions regarding my draft tables of contents: Seymour Becker, Rutgers University; Peter Czap, Amherst College; Stephen Hoch, University of Iowa; David McDonald, University of Wisconsin-Madison; Samuel Ramer, Tulane University; and Richard Wortman, Columbia University. I thank them all—even though, I would assure them, I know not who suggested what.

Finally, I wish to dedicate the book to my many students over the years at UIC; to my colleagues in the History Department; and to my wife, Nancy. They have sustained me in ways that I cannot fully repay.

J.C.

**FURTHER READING** (works relevant to the whole of Imperial Russian history)

Basil Dmytryshyn, ed., *Imperial Russia: A Source Book, 1700–1917*, 3rd edn. (1990) (documents)

William C. Fuller, Jr., *Strategy and Power in Russia, 1600–1914* (1992)

Neil M. Heyman, *Russian History* (1993) (handbook)

David MacKenzie and Michael W. Curran, *A History of Russia, the Soviet Union, and Beyond* (1993) (textbook)

Charles A. Moser, ed., *The Cambridge History of Russian Literature* (1989)

Marc Raeff, *Understanding Imperial Russia: State and Society in the Old Regime*, trans. (from French) Arthur Goldhammer (1984) (essays)

Nicholas V. Riasanovsky, *A History of Russia*, 5th edn. (1993) (textbook)

Hugh Seton-Watson, *The Russian Empire, 1801–1917* (1967, 1988)

Andrzej Walicki, *A History of Russian Thought from the Enlightenment to Marxism*, trans. (from Polish) Hilda Andrews-Rusiecka (1979)

Joseph L. Wieczynski, ed., *The Modern Encyclopedia of Russian and Soviet History*, 55 vols. to date (1976–   )

# Contents

## 4   From Peter the Great to Catherine the Great

## 5 The Age of Catherine

## 6 Empire-Building: The Eighteenth Century

## PART III   THE NINETEENTH CENTURY

## 7 Apogee of Empire

## 13   Opposition to the Imperial Regime

## 14   Crisis and Collapse

*Major Problems in the*
*History of Imperial Russia*

# PART I

# *Introduction*

Monument to Peter the Great, *The Bronze Horseman*, in St. Petersburg.

# Chapter 1

# *Historical Overviews*

The essays in this chapter raise some of the biggest "problems" that historians of Russia have had to face. In the first, Richard Pipes of Harvard University discusses the influence of geography on Russia's historical development, a factor he sees as crucial; indeed, in adducing major economic, demographic, social, and even political consequences from Russia's physical environment, Professor Pipes comes close to a kind of geographical determinism, which many other historians would reject in principle. Nevertheless, his essay is highly informative as well as stimulating, and it introduces many of the main topics to be dealt with in this book.

The next two essays address the fundamental question of Russia's relation to Europe (or "the West"). Prince N. S. Trubetzkoy (1890–1938), member of an old and devoutly religious Russian noble family, studied linguistics at the universities of Moscow and Leipzig, a field to which he later made distinguished scholarly contributions. Following the Communist Revolution he left Russia, and from 1922 until his death Trubetzkoy lectured at Vienna University on Slavic history and literature as well as linguistics. Around 1920 he joined several other émigré Russian scholars in founding the "Eurasian movement," a subsequently influential school of thought which saw the essential Russia, beneath its imposed Imperial and then Communist regimes, as a world apart, one utterly distinct from "Romano-Germanic" Europe in particular and an entity that was truly unique from geographical, historical, and even psychological points of view. In 1925 he published *The Legacy of Genghis Khan: A Perspective on Russian History Not from the West but from the East,* a short book exemplifying the Eurasian approach, from which the excerpts printed below, in a new English translation, are taken. Although scholars today may dispute various details in the work of Trubetzkoy (and other Eurasianists), the Eurasian perspective continues to challenge fundamentally the prevailing Eurocentric approach to Russian history.

The third essay, by Thomas G. Masaryk (1850–1937), is a classic example of the Eurocentric approach. A prominent Czech nationalist and the first president of the Czechoslovak Republic (1918–1935), Masaryk rose to fame as a teacher and writer. In 1882 he became professor of philosophy at the Czech university of Prague, where he specialized in both British and German thought while pursuing a longstanding interest in Russia, which he first visited in 1892. His initial study of Russian literature broadened into a more general investigation of Russian history, on which he lectured at the University of Chicago in 1902 and back at Prague in 1906–1907. Perceiving by this time that the Russian Empire had entered a period of crisis, he undertook another extended visit in 1910. In 1913 he published his magisterial two-volume cultural history of Russia entitled *Russland und Europa* (*The Spirit of Russia,* in its English edition), which immediately attracted widespread attention and was to remain influential in forming Western and even Russian views of Russia for decades to come. Masaryk's own introduction to this work is reprinted below. In it he adumbrates his famous thesis that, as viewed in about 1913, "Russia has preserved the childhood of Europe." Like Prince Trubetzkoy, Masaryk saw Russia and Europe as distinct entities and, like Trubetzkoy, he understood that Russia since the time of Peter the Great had been undergoing intensive Europeanization. But Masaryk, unlike Trubetzkoy, considered Europeanization a largely positive as well as inevitable process, one marking Russia's progress in civilization, though the process was still far from complete. Russia at the end of the Imperial period was definitely part of Europe, in Masaryk's perspective; but Russia, in her church and peasant masses, was also still living in Europe's Middle Ages. "When I contrast Russia and Europe, I contrast two epochs."

Is Russia totally unique? Or is Russia simply a backward part of Europe, struggling to catch up with "the West"? "Slavophiles," insisting on Russia's uniqueness, and "Westerners," insisting that Russia had to follow the West, initiated this debate in Russia itself in the 1840s. In one form or another the debate has continued to this day.

# The Environment and Its Consequences

## RICHARD PIPES

The contemporary western reader has little patience for physical geography, . . . and understandably so, because science and technology have to an unprecedented degree liberated him from dependence on nature. But even that relative freedom from vagaries of the environment which modern western people have come to enjoy is an event of very recent date and narrowly confined in scope. As far as conditions of pre-modern life are concerned, the notion of independence from nature is irrelevant. To understand human life prior to the Scientific and Industrial Revolutions as well as outside the relatively limited part of the world directly affected by them, it is necessary to allow the natural environment a role much greater than that of decorative backdrop. Men living in the pre-scientific

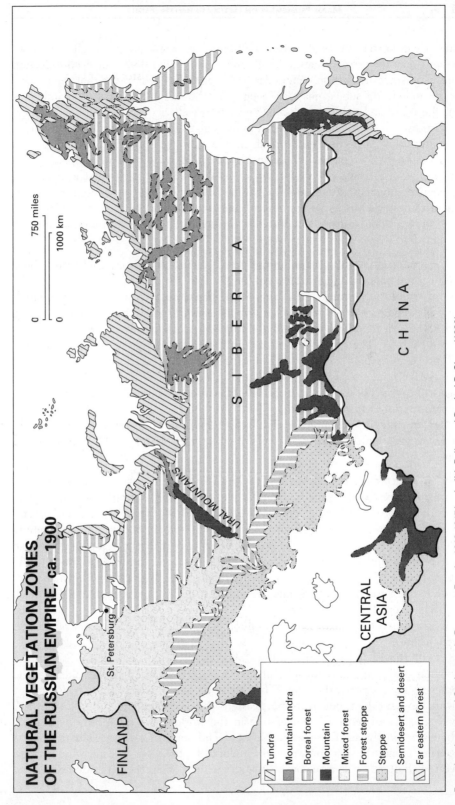

# NATURAL VEGETATION ZONES
# OF THE RUSSIAN EMPIRE, ca. 1900

FINLAND

St. Petersburg

URAL MOUNTAINS

S I B E R I A

C H I N A

CENTRAL
ASIA

0 — 750 miles
0 — 1000 km

**Legend:**
- Tundra
- Mountain tundra
- Boreal forest
- Mountain
- Mixed forest
- Forest steppe
- Steppe
- Semidesert and desert
- Far eastern forest

From *Landscape and Settlement in Romanov Russia, 1613-1917* by Judith Pallot and Denis J.B. Shaw (1990).
Reprinted by permission of Oxford University Press.

and pre-industrial phases of history had and continue to have no choice but to adapt themselves to that nature which provides them with all they need to sustain life. And since adaptation implies dependence, it is not surprising that the natural environment, the subject-matter of geography, should have had a decisive influence on the mind and habits of pre-modern man as well as on his social and political institutions. It is only when he began to feel emancipated from total subordination to nature that man could fantasize about being master of his own fate.

In the case of Russia the geographic element is particularly important because . . . the country is inherently so poor that it affords at best a precarious existence. This poverty gives the inhabitants little latitude for action; it compels them to operate within a very narrow band of options.

In terms of *vegetation*, Russia can be divided into three main zones, which run, in belt-like shape, from east to west:

1. the tundra: this region, north of the Arctic Circle, is covered with lichens and cannot support organized human life;

2. south of the tundra lies an immense forest, the largest in the world, which occupies much of the northern half of Eurasia from the Arctic Circle to between 45 and 50 degrees northern latitude. This forest can be further subdivided into three parts: A. The needle-leaved taiga in the northern regions, composed mainly of spruce and pine; B. The mixed forest, partly needle-leaved, partly broad-leaved: *this is the central area of Russia, where stands Moscow and where the . . . Russian state had its beginning* [italics added]; and, C. The wooded steppe, a transitional region separating forest from grassland;

3. the steppe, an immense plain stretching from Hungary to Mongolia: here no trees grow unless planted and cultivated; of itself, nature yields only grass and brush.

As concerns cultivable *soil*, Russia can be divided into two principal zones, the border between which roughly coincides with the line separating forest from steppe:

In the forest zone, the predominant type of earth is *podzol*, a soil short of natural plant food; what there is of the latter lies in the subsoil and requires deep ploughing to be of use. In this region there are numerous bogs and marshes, as well as large stretches of sand and clay. In part of the wooded steppe and through much of the steppe proper the prevailing soil is the fertile black earth (*chernozem*), which owes both its color and fertility to humus, the product of decayed grass and brush. The black earth has from 2 to 16 per cent humus spread in a layer two to six feet deep. Its surface covers approximately a quarter of a billion acres, which are the center of Russian agriculture.

The *climate* of Russia is of the so-called Continental type, that is, hot in the summer and very cold in the winter. The winter weather grows colder as one proceeds in an easterly direction. The coldest regions of Russia are to be found not in its most northern but in its most eastern parts: Verkhoiansk, the Siberian city with the lowest recorded temperature in the world has a less northerly latitude than Narvik, the ice-free port in Norway. The reason for this peculiarity of the Russian climate is that the warm air produced by the Gulf Stream, which warms western Europe, cools as it moves inland and away from the Atlantic coast. One of the consequences of this fact is that Siberia, potentially an inexhaustible reservoir of agricultural land, is in its major part unsuited for farming; in its eastern regions, lands located at the same latitude as England cannot be tilled at all.

*Precipitation* follows a pattern different from that prevailing in the distribution of the vegetation and soil. It is heaviest in the north-west, along the coast of the Baltic Sea, where it is brought in by the warm winds, and decreases as one moves in the opposite direction, towards the south-east. In other words, it is the most generous where the soil is the poorest. Another peculiarity of precipitation in Russia is that the rain tends to fall heaviest in the second half of the summer. In the Moscow region, the two rainiest months of the year are July and August, when nearly a quarter of the entire annual precipitation occurs. A small shift in the timetable of rain distribution can mean a drought in the spring and early summer, followed by disastrous downpours during the harvest. In western Europe the rainfall distributes itself much more evenly throughout the year.

Finally, the *waterways*. Russia's rivers run in a north-south direction; none of the major rivers runs east-west. However, the lateral branches of the great rivers do just that; and because Russia is flat (no point in its European part exceeds 1,400 feet) and its rivers originate not in mountains but in swamps and lakes formed by swamps they have gentle gradients. As a result, Russia possesses a unique network of navigable waterways, composed of large rivers and their numerous branches linked with one another by means of easy portages. Even with primitive modes of transport it is possible to navigate across Russia from the Baltic to the Caspian seas, and to reach by water a high proportion of the land lying in between. In Siberia, the water network happens to be so excellently meshed that in the seventeenth century Russian fur trappers succeeded in traversing in a very short time thousands of miles to the Pacific and inaugurating regular commerce between Siberia and the home country by means of river transport. Were it not for these waterways, life in Russia would have been hardly feasible above the mere subsistence level until the advent of railways. The distances are so great and the costs of maintaining roads under the prevailing extremes of temperature so high that land transport was practicable only in the winter, when snow provided a smooth surface for sleighs. This fact accounts for the great reliance of Russians on water transport. Until the second half of the nineteenth century the bulk of merchandise moved on boats and barges.

Like the other Slavs, the ancient Russians were primarily a pastoral people; and like them, upon settling down in their . . . territories, they slowly made the transition to agriculture. Unfortunately for them, the area which the [ancient Russians] penetrated and colonized happens to be uniquely ill suited for farming. The indigenous Finns and Turks treated farming as a supplementary occupation, concentrating in the forest zone on hunting and fishing, and in the steppe on livestock breeding. The Russians chose otherwise. Their heavy reliance on farming under adverse natural conditions is perhaps the single most basic cause of the problems underlying Russian history.

Some of these difficulties have been alluded to already: the indifferent quality of the soil in the north, and the vagaries of the rainfall, which is heaviest where it does the least good, and has a tendency to come down too late in the agricultural season. The peculiar topographical and seasonal distribution of the rainfall is a major reason why, over the course of its recorded history, Russia has averaged one bad harvest out of every three.

But the gravest and least soluble problems derive from the extreme northern location of the country. Together with Canada, Russia is the northernmost state in the world. It is true that modern Russia [controlled] large territories with semi-tropical climates (the Crimea, the Caucasus and Turkestan), but these were acquired late, mostly in the mid-nineteenth century, in the course of imperial expansion. The cradle of the Russian state, . . . lies in the zone of mixed forests. Until the middle of the sixteenth century, Russians had been virtually confined to this area, because the steppe with its coveted black earth was under the control of hostile Turkic tribes. Russians began to penetrate the steppe in the second half of the sixteenth century, but they became masters of it only towards the end of the eighteenth when they at long last conclusively defeated Turkish power. During the formative period of their statehood they had to live between 50 and 60 degrees of northern latitude. This is approximately the latitude of Canada. In drawing comparisons between the two countries, however, several differences must be kept in mind. The bulk of the Canadian population has always resided in the southern-most part of the country, along the Great Lakes and the St. Lawrence River, . . . which in Russia corresponds to the latitudes of the Crimea and the central Asian steppe. Nine-tenths of the Canadian population lives within two hundred miles of the United States border. North of the 52nd parallel Canada has little population and hardly any agriculture. Secondly, throughout its history Canada has enjoyed friendly relations with its richer southern neighbor, with which it has maintained close economic relations. . . . And finally, Canada has never had to support a large population; those of its people whom the economy could not employ have been in the habit of moving, seasonally or permanently, to the United States. None of these advantages exists in the case of Russia: its neighbors have been neither rich nor friendly, and the country has had to rely on its own resources to support a population which already in the middle of the eighteenth century was larger than Canada's is today.

The principal consequence of Russia's location is an exceedingly short farming season. In the taiga, around Novgorod and St. Petersburg, it lasts a mere four months in the year (from mid-May to mid-September). In the central regions, near Moscow, it stretches to five and a half months (mid-April to end of September). In the steppe, it lasts six months. The remainder of the Russian year is altogether unsuitable for agricultural work, because the soil is as hard as rock and the land is covered by a deep blanket of snow.

In western Europe, by contrast, the growing season lasts eight to nine months. In other words, the western farmer has at his disposal anywhere from 50 to 100 per cent more time for field work than the Russian. Furthermore, in parts of Europe where the winter is mild, the winter months can be employed for occupations other than field work. The economic and social consequences of this simple climatic fact will be elucidated below.

The brief growing season, and its corollary, a long and hard winter, create an additional difficulty for the Russian peasant. He must confine his livestock indoors two months longer than the western farmer. His cattle thus misses out on the early spring grazing, and when finally set free in the meadow it is in a thoroughly emaciated condition. Russian livestock has always been of an inferior quality, notwithstanding attempts by the government and enlightened landlords to improve it; imported western breeds have promptly degenerated to the point where they became indistinguishable from the miserable domestic variety. The difficulties in raising livestock have discouraged efficient meat and dairy farming in the forest zone. They have affected adversely the quality of the draught animals and caused perennial shortages of manure, especially in the north, where it is most needed.

The consequence of Russia's poor soil, unreliable rainfall and brief growing season have been low yields.

Agricultural yields are most meaningfully measured in terms which indicate how many times the seed reproduces itself: when, for example, one grain cast at sowing time gives five grains at harvest, we speak of a yield ratio 1:5. The typical yield ratio in medieval Europe was 1:3 or at best 1:4, the minimum yields which make agriculture worth while and create conditions capable of sustaining life. A 1:3 ratio, it must be noted, means an annual doubling rather than tripling of the sown seed, because each year one of every three grains harvested must be set aside for seed. It also means that one acre of arable out of every three has to be devoted to seed production. In the second half of the thirteenth century, west European yields began to experience a significant rise. The principal cause of this phenomenon was the growth of cities, whose trading and manufacturing population had given up growing food, buying it from farmers instead. The emergence of a rich urban market for cereals and other produce encouraged western landlords and peasants to raise a surplus by more intensive use of labor and heavier manuring. In the late Middle Ages, western yields rose to 1:5, and then, in the course of the sixteenth and seventeenth centuries, they improved further to 1:6 and 1:7. By the middle of the nineteenth century, countries with advanced farming, headed by England, regularly obtained yields of 1:10. Such a dramatic improvement had an even greater economic significance than might appear at first glance. Where the soil can be depended upon regularly to return ten grains for each grain sown, the farmer needs to set aside for seed only a tenth of the land and a tenth of the harvest, instead of a third of each, as he must do under a 1:3 yield. The net return on a 1:10 yield is 4½ times what it is on a 1:3 yield, making it theoretically possible to sustain in a given area that many more inhabitants. The cumulative effect of such a surplus over a number of years can be readily appreciated. It may be said that civilization begins only where one grain of seed multiplies itself at least five times; it is this minimum surplus which determines (assuming no food imports) whether a significant proportion of the population can be released from the necessity of raising food to pursue other occupations. [As one expert has stated,] "In a country with rather low yield ratios highly developed industry, commerce and transport are impossible." And so, one may add, is highly developed political life.

Like the rest of Europe, Russia averaged in the Middle Ages ratios of 1:3, but unlike the west, it did not experience any improvement in yield ratios during the centuries that followed. In the nineteenth century, Russian yields remained substantially the same as they had been in the fifteenth, declining in bad years to

1:2, going up in good ones to 1:4 and even 1:5, but averaging over the centuries 1:3 (slightly below this figure in the north and slightly above it in the south). Such a ratio generally sufficed to support life. The picture of the Russian peasant as a creature [forever] groaning under oppression and grubbing to eke out a miserable living is simply untenable. . . . Recent computations of the incomes of Novgorod peasants in the fifteenth century, and of the Belorussian–Lithuanian peasants in the sixteenth (both inhabitants of northern regions with the inferior, *podzol,* soil) do indeed indicate that these groups had managed to feed themselves quite adequately. The trouble with Russian agriculture was not that it could not feed its cultivators but that it never could produce a significant surplus. The productivity lag of Russia behind western Europe widened with each century. By the end of the nineteenth century, when good German farms regularly obtained in excess of one ton of cereals from an acre of land, Russian farms could barely manage to reach six hundred pounds. In Russia of the late nineteenth century, an acre of land under wheat yielded only a seventh of the English crop, and less than a half of the French, Prussian or Austrian. Russian agricultural productivity, whether calculated in grain yields or yields per acre, was by then the lowest in Europe.

The low productivity of the Russian soil, however, cannot be blamed entirely on the climate. Scandinavia, despite its northern location, attained already by the eighteenth century yield ratios of 1:6, while the Baltic provinces of the Russian Empire, where the land was in the hands of German barons, in the first half of the nineteenth century had yields from 1:4.3 to 1:5.1, that is, of a kind which made it possible to begin accumulating a surplus.

The other cause of low agricultural productivity in Russia, besides the natural factors already enumerated, was the absence of markets. Here, as is the case with most historical phenomena, cause and effect confronted each other in reciprocal fashion: the cause produced the effect but then the effect became a force of its own which in turn influenced and transformed its original cause. Unfavorable natural conditions made for low yields; low yields resulted in poverty; poverty meant that there were no buyers for agricultural produce; the lack of buyers discouraged yield improvements. The net effect was the absence of incentives. A vicious circle of this kind could be broken only by the intervention of some external force, in this case the opening of commercial contacts with other countries or major scientific or technical innovations.

Clearly, an agricultural surplus must be disposed of not to other farmers but to people who themselves do not grow food, and this means, in effect, the inhabitants of cities. Where an urban market is absent, little can be done with the excess grain except to distill it into spirits. As noted above, the improvement in the yield ratios of medieval Europe was originally associated with the growth of cities; the emergence of sizeable trading and artisan groups both encouraged improvements in farming and was made possible by them. Now in Russia cities have never played a significant role in the nation's economy; and paradoxically, over the centuries, their role tended to decline rather than grow. As late as the eighteenth century, Russia's urban inhabitants comprised only 3 per cent of the total population, and even this figure is deceptive because the majority of Russian city dwellers traditionally have consisted of landlords and peasants who grew their own food. Nor could Russia dispose of its grain abroad because there were for it no foreign markets until the middle of the nineteenth century at which time countries with advanced industrial economies decided it was cheaper for them to import food than to grow it. Russia is too remote from the great routes of international trade to have developed a significant urban civilization on the basis of foreign commerce. [At various] times in its history she was pulled into the mainstream of international trade; each time the result was the sprouting of cities; but each time, too, the urban flowering proved short-lived. . . . Russia's cities, few in number and, except for Moscow, small in population, came to serve primarily military and administrative purposes, and as such would not provide a significant market for food.

There were thus no economic incentives present to try to overcome nature's handicaps. The Russian landlord and peasant looked upon the soil primarily as a means of subsistence, not of enrichment. Indeed, no major fortunes in Russia were ever made from agriculture. Little money was invested in it, because the yields were meager and the market exceedingly narrow. Well into the nineteenth century, the basic instrument of the Russian farmer was a primitive plough called *sokha*, which scratched the soil instead of turning it over . . . but which had the advantage of requiring little pulling power and being ten times as fast as the plough. The basic crop was rye. It was chosen because of its hardiness and adaptability to the northern climate and poor soil. It also happens to be the cereal crop with the lowest yields. The prevalent pattern of cultivation from the sixteenth to the nineteenth centuries was the three-field system which required that one third of the land always lie fallow to regain its fertility. The system was so uneconomical that in countries with advanced agriculture like England it had been abandoned in the late Middle Ages. The whole stress in Russia was on getting the most out of the land with the least possible investment of time, effort and money. Every Russian sought to extricate himself from the land: the peasant desired nothing better than to abandon the fields and become a pedlar, artisan or usurer; the rural merchant, to join the nobility; the noble to move into the city or make a career in the state service. The proverbial rootlessness of Russians, their "nomadic" proclivities so often noted by western travelers accustomed to people seeking roots, whether in the soil or in social status, have their main source in the marginal quality of Russian farming, i.e., in the inability of the land, the chief source of national wealth, to furnish much beyond sustenance. . . .

It is because the soil offered so little and dependence on it was so precarious, that Russians of all classes have learned from the earliest to supplement agricultural income with all kinds of "industries" or *promysly*. In its virgin state, the Russian forest zone teemed with what appeared an inexhaustible supply of wildlife: deer and elk, bears, and an immense variety of fur-bearing rodents. These were hunted and trapped by peasants working for princes, landlords, [and] monasteries as well as for themselves. Honey was plentiful; it was not even necessary to build hives, because the bees deposited honey in the trunks of dead trees. The waters abounded in fish, including sturgeon which made its way upstream from the Caspian. This abundance of wildlife allowed early Russian settlers to raise their standards of life above the bare subsistence level. How important such forest commodities where in the Russian budget may be seen from the fact that in the seventeenth century income derived from the sale of furs (mostly to foreign merchants) constituted the single largest item in the revenues of the [tsar's] treasury. As the forests were cleared to make way for agricultural land and pastures, and overhunting and overtrapping depleted the supply of wildlife, especially the more valuable varieties of fur-bearing animals, Russians increasingly shifted their attention from the exploitation of natural resources to manufacture. In the middle of the eighteenth century there emerged in Russia a peculiar form of cottage industry (*kustarnaia promyshlennost'*), employing both free and serf labor, and working for the local market. This industry supplied Russia with a high proportion of its farming and household needs, simple cloth, silver, icons, musical instruments and so forth. Much of the relative prosperity of both landlord and peasants between the middle of the eighteenth and middle of the nineteenth centuries derived from such manufacture. Towards the end of the nineteenth century, the growth of factory industry undercut the market for the unsophisticated products of cottage industry, and deprived peasants, especially in the northern provinces, of vital supplementary income.

Promysly, however, vital as they were, could not of themselves support the national economy: the latter, in the end, depended on farming. The rapid exhaustion of the soil under conditions of Russian agriculture compelled the peasant to be continually on the move in search of virgin land or land which had regained its fertility from a long rest. Even had the population of the country remained constant, Russia would have always experienced an unusual amount of peasant movement. The rapid growth of population in modern times gave this tendency a powerful added stimulus.

In so far as imperfect demographic records allow one to judge, until the middle of the eighteenth century the population of Russia remained relatively small. The most generous estimates place it at 9–10 million in the middle of the sixteenth century, and 11–12 million towards its end; other, more conservative estimates, put it at 6 and 8 million, respectively. These figures compare with a sixteenth-century population of 20 million in Austria, 19 in France, and 11 in Spain; Poland in the seventeenth century had some 11 million inhabitants. In Russia, as in the rest of Europe, the demographic spurt began around 1750. Between 1750 and 1850, the population of the Russian Empire quadrupled (from 17–18 to 68 million). Some of this growth, perhaps as much as 10 million, can be accounted for by conquest; but even when allowance has been made for expansion, the natural growth remains impressive. After 1850, when territorial expansion virtually ceased (the only major area conquered after that date, Turkestan, did not have many inhabitants), the population of Russia increased at a staggering rate: from 68 million in 1850 to 124 million in 1897 and 170 million in 1914. If during the second half of the sixteenth century, Russia's population had increased perhaps by 20 per cent, in the second half of the nineteenth it doubled. Russia's rate of population growth during the second half of the nineteenth century was the highest in Europe—and this at the very time when its grain yields were Europe's lowest.

Unless the population were to perish from mass starvation—which until the Communist regime it did not, despite recurrent harvest failures and occasional regional famines—the food to feed these additional mouths had to come from somewhere. Imports were out of the question, for Russia had little to sell abroad with the proceeds of which to buy food; and those who did the selling—the tsar and the richest landlords—preferred to import luxuries. Indeed, cereals constituted Russia's own largest export item: Russia kept on exporting cereals in the nineteenth century even when she had not enough for her own people. Intensification of productivity through heavier manuring, use of machinery, and other methods conducive to rationalization was not feasible either, partly because the returns were too meager to justify the necessary investments, partly because the rigid social organization of the peasantry resisted innovation. Capital was invested in land mainly on those southern farms which grew food for export to England and Germany; but on this land improvements of production did not benefit the peasant. The solution therefore was to put more and more fresh land under cultivation, that is, to practice extensive, in lieu of intensive, agriculture. Statistical records indicate that the acreage under cultivation in Russia expanded steadily in response to this need, increasing between 1809 and 1887 by 60 per cent (from 197 to 317 million acres). The availability of virgin land discouraged efforts to raise productivity; it was cheaper and easier to put new land to use than to improve the old. But even this steady expansion of the sown area did not suffice, for rapid as it was the population grew faster while yields remained constant. In the 1880s, there was virtually no virgin land left in central and southern Russia, and agricultural rents rose spectacularly. At the same time . . . the growth of modern industry deprived the peasants of the main source of supplementary income by preempting the market for the simple products of his cottage industry. Here, in a nutshell, is the root of the celebrated "agrarian crisis" which so convulsed Russia during the late imperial period and contributed so greatly to its collapse.

However, so long as the frontier remained infinitely expandable, the Russian peasant pressed outward, leaving behind him the exhausted soil and seeking soil that no human hand had touched. Colonization is so fundamental a feature of Russian life that Kliuchevsky considered it to be its very essence: "The history of Russia," he wrote . . . "is the history of a country which colonizes itself."[1]

Until the middle of the sixteenth century, Russian colonization had to be confined to the western portion of the forest zone. Attempts to gain a foothold in the black earth belt were invariably beaten back. The steppe, where the black earth lay, provided ideal conditions for livestock grazing, the principal occupation of the nomadic Turks, and they annihilated any agricultural settlements which tried to establish themselves on it. The road leading to the east, to Siberia, was barred first by the Golden Horde, and then, after its dissolution in the fifteenth century, by its successor states, the khanates of Kazan and Astrakhan [see Chapter 6]. The only

---

1. On V. O. Kliuchevsky, the famous Russian historian, see Chapter 3.—Ed.

area open to Russian colonization in the first six or seven centuries of Russian history was the far north. Some colonists, spearheaded by monasteries, did indeed venture beyond the upper Volga, but this inhospitable area could not absorb much population.

A dramatic change in the history of Russian colonization occurred after the conquest in [1552–1556] of the khanates of Kazan and Astrakhan. Russian settlers immediately began to pour towards the mid-Volga, ejecting the indigenous Turks from the best lands; others pushed beyond, crossing . . . the Urals, into southern Siberia where lay large stretches of pure, virgin black earth. But the main migratory push then and subsequently proceeded in the southern and south-eastern direction, towards the so-called Central Black Earth Zone. In the 1570s the government constructed a chain of stockades facing the steppe from the Donets to the Irtysh rivers, and under its protection, peasants ventured into what had been always a nomad preserve. The movement, once inaugurated, progressed with an elemental force. Each major economic or political upheaval in the center of Russia produced migratory outpourings. In this colonist expansion sometimes the peasant preceded the government, sometimes the government led the way; sooner or later, however, the two elements were certain to meet and fuse. One of the basic reasons for the tenacity with which Russians have managed to hold on to conquered territories lies in the fact that their political absorption was and to this day continues to be accompanied by colonization.

It is estimated that in the seventeenth and eighteenth centuries more than two million settlers migrated southward from Russia's central regions, penetrating first the wooded steppe and then the steppe proper. During these two centuries, some 400,000 settlers also migrated into Siberia. The greatest migratory wave struck the black earth belt after 1783, the year the Russians annexed the Crimea and subjugated the raiders who . . . for centuries had harassed their settlements. In the nineteenth and early twentieth centuries 12–13 million migrants, most of them natives of the central provinces, moved south, with another four and a half or five million migrating into southern Siberia and the steppes of central Asia. The latter movement involved a wholesale dispossession and ejection of the Asian natives from their ancestral grazing lands.

In the earlier period (1552–1861), the mass of Russian migrants consisted either of free peasants or of runaway serfs, or else serfs forcibly transferred from the center to work on the estates of military men serving on the frontier. After the emancipation of the serfs in 1861, the migrants were free peasants, now sometimes resettling with the assistance of the government which was eager to ease rural overpopulation in the central provinces. Over the centuries, the geographic pattern of Russian population distribution assumed the shape of a wedge, whose base has come to rest in the western part of the forest zone and the tip of which points south-east. This demographic wedge has continued to elongate over time, its changing shape reflecting a steady shift of the center of the Russian population from its original homeland in the forest towards the steppe. In modern times, the heaviest concentration of the Russian population is in the black earth belt. The Revolution [of 1917] changed nothing in this respect. Between 1926 and 1939 over four million persons migrated eastward, mostly into the Kazakh steppe. The census of 1970 [indicated] that the movement [had] not ceased, the central regions continuing to lose population to the borderlands. A major secular process in progress for four hundred years has been carrying the Russian population outward from the central forest zone, mostly towards the east and south, causing them to inundate areas inhabited by nations of other races and cultures, and producing serious demographic dislocations in the path of their movement.[2]

Having surveyed the economic and demographic consequences produced by Russia's environment, we can now turn to the consequences of a social character.

The first fact to note is that the geography of Russia discourages individual farming. A general rule seems to exist which holds that northern climates are conducive to collective farm work. . . . There are many reasons why this should be so, but in the ultimate analysis all of them have to do with the brevity of the agricultural season. . . . The unalterable fact that all the field work in Russia must be completed between four and six months (instead of the eight to nine months available to the western farmer) calls for work being performed with great intensity, and induces the pooling of resources, human as well as animal and material. An individual Russian peasant, farming with his wife and minor children and a horse or two simply cannot manage under the climatic conditions prevailing in the forest zone; he needs help from his married children and neighbors. In the southern zone of Russia the pressure to work collectively diminishes somewhat, which explains why in pre-Revolutionary Russia most of the individual farmsteads, called *khutora*, were to be found in the Ukraine and the Cossack regions.

The collective character of farming in Russia influenced the structure of the peasant family and the village.

The traditional type of peasant family in Russia, prevalent until a century ago, was of the so-called joint type; it consisted of father, mother, minor children and married sons with their wives and offspring. The head of this group was called *bol'shak* ("the big one" or "boss"). He was most commonly the father. Upon his death the family usually broke up; but sometimes it happened that after the father had died or become incapacitated the joint family continued together under one of the brothers whom it elected to serve as bolshak. The bolshak, a kind of paterfamilias, had final say in all family matters; he also set the schedule for field work and performed the sowing. His authority, originally derived from customary law, was given legal status in the 1860s by the rural courts which recognized his verdict as binding in disputes occurring within the family. All the property was held in common. The joint family was economically very advantageous. It was widely acknowledged by persons with expertise in rural life that field work in Russia was best done by large family teams, and that the quality of the peasants' performance depended in large measure on the bolshak's intelligence and authority. Both the

---

2. Since the end of the Second World War, there has been significant Russian migration westward as well, into areas . . . populated by Poles, Jews, Germans and the Baltic nationalities. This colonization, in contrast with those of the past, [was] heavily urban. It [was] occasionally accompanied by mass expulsions and deportations of the indigenous peoples on charges of "nationalism."

government and landlords did all in their power to preserve this institution, not only because of its demonstrable influence on productivity but also because of its political and social benefits to them. Officials and landlords alike preferred to deal with the head of the household rather than with its individual members. Furthermore, they liked the assurance that a peasant who for some reason (illness or alcoholism, for example) could not work would be taken care of by his relatives. The peasants themselves had more ambivalent feelings. They undoubtedly recognized the economic advantages of the joint family since they had developed it spontaneously. But they disliked the tensions which were bound to arise where several married couples lived under the same roof; they also preferred to hold property individually. After gaining personal freedom in 1861, the one-time serfs broke up the joint families into their constituent units with precipitous speed, much to the detriment of Russian agriculture and their own well-being.

The basic social unit of the ancient Slavs was a tribal community, estimated to have consisted of some fifty or sixty people, all related by blood and working as a team. In time, the communities based on blood relationship dissolved, giving way to a type of communal organization based on joint ownership of arable and meadow, called in Russian *mir* or *obshchina*. The origin of this famous institution has been a subject of intense debate for more than a century. The debate began in the 1840s when a group of romantic nationalists known as Slavophiles became aware of the peasant commune as an institution confined to Russia, and extolled it as proof that the Russian people, allegedly lacking in the acquisitive "bourgeois" impulses of western Europeans, were destined to solve mankind's social problems. Haxthausen popularized this view in his book, published in 1847 [see Chapter 7]. . . . In 1854, however, this whole interpretation was challenged by Boris Chicherin, a leading spokesman of the so-called Westerner camp, who argued that the peasant commune as then known was neither ancient nor autochthonous in origin, but had been introduced by the Russian monarchy in the middle of the eighteenth century as a means of assuring the collection of taxes. Until then, according to Chicherin, Russian peasants had held their land by individual households. Subsequent researches blurred the lines of the controversy. [Opinion today] holds that the commune of the imperial period was indeed a modern institution, as Chicherin claimed, there being no solid evidence of its existence before the eighteenth century. It is also widely agreed that pressure by the state and landlord played a major part in its formation. At the same time, economic factors seem also to have affected its evolution to the extent that there exists a demonstrable connection between the availability of land and communal tenure: where land is scarce, the communal form of tenure tends to prevail, but where it is abundant it is replaced by household or even family tenure.

Whatever the merits of the case, in the imperial period the vast majority of the Russian peasants held their land communally; in the central provinces the commune was virtually universal. The arable was divided into sections corresponding to the quality of the soil and distance from the village. Each household had the right to claim in every such section one or more strips corresponding to the number of its adult members; the latter were typically defined as all men between the ages of 15 or 17 and 60–65, and all married women under the age of 48. The strips were extremely narrow, measuring between nine and twelve feet in width and several hundred yards in length. A household might have had thirty to fifty or more such strips scattered in a dozen different locations around the village. The principal purpose of this arrangement was to enable every peasant to pay his share of rents and taxes. Since households grew or diminished over time, every so often (e.g., at nine-, twelve-, or fifteen-year intervals) the commune took its own census, on the basis of which it carried out a "black repartition" (*chernyi peredel*), resulting in a re-allotment of the strips. The system was meant to guarantee every peasant an equitable share of the land, and every household enough land to support itself and to meet its responsibilities to the landlord and state. In reality, peasants were loath to part with the strips in which they had invested time and effort, especially if from an increase of the village population the repartition caused their allotments to be diminished. The authorities therefore had to step in repeatedly to enforce redistribution by decree. . . .

[Nevertheless,] unlike the joint family, imposed on them by a combination of economic necessity and pressure from above, the commune enjoyed peasant loyalty. It provided a high degree of security without seriously inhibiting freedom of movement. It also allowed common access to meadow as well as co-ordination of field work which was highly desirable under the prevailing climatic conditions and the open field system. The latter was done by a council of the mir, composed of all the bolshaks. The peasants ignored the criticism levied at the commune by economists, who saw it as a millstone around the neck of the more enterprising among them, and tenaciously clung to it. In November 1906, the imperial government introduced easy procedures for the consolidation of strips into individual farmsteads. The legislation had a limited measure of success in the borderlands of the empire; in central Russia, the peasants simply ignored it.

In so far as the political system of Russia is [concerned,] the influence of the natural environment [may] be delineated [here] in the most general terms.

On the face of it, nature intended Russia to be a decentralized country formed of a multitude of self-contained and self-governing communities. Everything here militates against statehood: the poverty of the soil, remoteness from the main routes of international trade, the sparsity and mobility of the population. And Russia might well have remained a decentralized society, with many scattered centers of localized power, were it not for geopolitical factors which urgently demanded firm political authority. The extensive, highly wasteful nature of Russian rural economy and the need for ever fresh land to replace that exhausted by overcultivation and undermanuring compelled Russians at all times to push outward. As long as their colonization had been confined to the taiga, the process could unroll spontaneously and without military protection. But the rich and desirable soil lay in the steppe, under the control of nomadic Turkic and Mongol tribes which not only did not tolerate any agricultural settlements on their grazing territories, but themselves frequently carried out raids into the forest in search of slaves and loot. Until the end of the eighteenth century, when their superior political and military organization gave them an upper hand, the Russians were unable to penetrate the black earth zone in any significant numbers, and indeed were often themselves victims of aggression on the part of their steppe neighbors. In the sixteenth and seventeenth centuries there was scarcely a year when Russians did not fight along their southern and south-eastern frontiers. Although Russian historians tend to depict these wars as defensive in nature, they were as often as not instigated by Russian colonist pressure. In the western parts, where Russians bordered on Poles, Lithuanians, Swedes and Germans, the situation was somewhat calmer, but even here, during this period, there was war approximately one year out of every two. Sometimes it was the westerners who pushed eastward; sometimes it was the Russians who took the initiative in their quest for access to ports or to the rich lands of the Polish–Lithuanian Commonwealth. Military organization thus was a necessity, for without it Russian colonization, so essential to its economic survival, could not have been carried out.

This being the case, one might have expected Russia to develop early in its history something akin to the bureaucratic regime of the "despotic" or "Asiatic" kind. The logic of things, indeed, impelled Russia in this direction, but for a variety of reasons its political development took a somewhat different route. The typical regime of the "Oriental Despotic" kind seems to have come into being not to meet military exigencies but from the need for effective central management capable of organizing the collection and distribution of water for irrigation. Thus arose what Karl Wittfogel calls the "agro-despotism" common to much of Asia and Central America.[3] Now in Russia there was no need for authority to assist in the extraction of wealth from the land. Russia was traditionally a country of widely scattered small farms, not one of latifundia, and it knew nothing of central economic management until the imposition of War Communism in 1918. But even if such management had been required, the country's natural conditions would have prevented its introduction. One need only consider the difficulties of transport and communication in Russia before the advent of railroads and telegraphs to realize that the kind of control and surveillance essential to an "Oriental Despotism" was entirely out of the question here. The immense distances and the climate with its severe winters and spring floods precluded in pre-modern Russia the construction of a regular road network. In Persia of the fifth century B.C. a messenger of King Darius traveled along the Royal Road at a rate of 380 kilometers in 24 hours; in Mongol Persia of the thirteenth century government couriers covered some 335 kilometers in the same period of time. In Russia, *after* regular postal services had been introduced by Swedish and German experts in the second half of the seventeenth century, messengers crawled at an average rate of 6–7 kilometers an hour; and since they traveled only by daytime, with luck and in the right season they might have made 80 or so kilometers in a 24-hour period. It required approximately 8 to 12 days for a dispatch from Moscow to reach one of the principal border towns of the empire, such as Archangelsk, Pskov and Kiev. For an inquiry to be answered, therefore, 3 weeks were needed. Towns and villages lying at some distance from the principal roads, especially those along the eastern frontier, were for all practical purposes

---

3. Karl A. Wittfogel, *Oriental Despotism* (1957).

incommunicable. This factor alone made it impossible to institute in Russia a tightly organized bureaucratic regime before the 1860s when railways and telecommunications were introduced.

The resultant situation presented an antinomy: its economic conditions and external situation required Russia to organize militarily and therefore politically in a highly efficient manner, and yet its economy inhibited such organization. There was a basic incompatibility between the country's possibilities and its needs.

The manner in which this predicament was resolved provides the key to Russia's constitutional development. The state neither grew out of the society, nor was imposed on it from above. Rather it grew up side by side with society and bit by bit swallowed it. The locus of original political authority was the private domain of the prince or tsar, his *oikos* or *dvor*. Within this domain the prince reigned absolute, exercising authority in the double capacity as sovereign and proprietor. Here he was in full command, a counterpart of the Greek *despotes*, the Roman *dominus*, and the Russian *gosudar'*, that is lord, master, outright owner of all men and things. Initially, the population of the princely domain consisted mainly of slaves and other persons bonded in one form or another to the proprietor. Outside his domains, where the population was free and exceedingly mobile, the Russian ruler exercised very little authority at first, his power being confined largely to the collection of tribute. This kind of dyarchy established itself in the forest zone during the twelfth and thirteenth centuries, at the same time when in England, France and Spain the modern western state was beginning to take shape as an entity separate from the ruler. From the solid base of authority furnished by their private domains, the Russian princes—gradually and only after having overcome massive resistance—spread their personal power over the free population living outside these domains. The princely dynasty of Moscow . . . , which emerged as the country's leader, transferred the institutions and practices which it had initially worked out in the closed world of its oikos to the realm at large, transforming Russia (in theory, at any rate) into a giant royal estate. However, even after it had laid formal claim to all Russia being its private domain or *votchina* (sixteenth to seventeenth centuries), the Russian government lacked the means to make the claim good. It had no alternative, therefore, but to continue the old dyarchic arrangement, farming out the bulk of the country to the landed gentry, clergy and bureaucracy in return for fixed quotas of taxes and services. But the principle that Russia belonged to its sovereign, that he was its *dominus*[,] was firmly established; all that was lacking to enforce it were the financial and technical means, and these were bound to become available in due course.

Since Aristotle, political thinkers have distinguished a special variant of "despotic" or "tyrannical" governments characterized by a proprietary manner of treating the realm, although no one seems to have worked out a theory of such a system. In Book III of his *Politics*, Aristotle devotes a brief paragraph to what he calls "paternal government" under which the king rules the state the way a father does his household; but he does not develop the theme. . . . In Hobbes's *Elements of Law*, governments are divided into two basic types, the Commonwealth, formed by mutual consent for the purpose of protection from external enemies, and Dominium or "Patrimonial Monarchy" created as a result of conquest and submission "to an assailant for fear of death."[4] But Hobbes, too, having stated the issue, let the matter drop. The term "patrimonial regime" was revived and introduced into current usage by Max Weber. In his [famous] threefold division of types of political authority, distinguished mainly by their administrative character, Weber defined the "patrimonial system" as a variant of personal authority based on tradition (the other variant being "charismatic"). "Where authority is primarily oriented to tradition but in its exercise makes the claim of full personal powers, it will be called 'patrimonial authority'." In its extreme form, "Sultanism," it entails complete ownership of land and mastery over the population. Under a patrimonial regime, the economic element absorbs, as it were, the political. "Where the prince organizes his political power—that is, his non-domainial, physical power of compulsion *vis-à-vis* his subjects outside his patrimonial territories and people, his political subjects—in the same essential manner as he does his authority over his household, there we speak of a *patrimonial state* structure." "In such cases, the political structure becomes essentially identical with that of a gigantic landed estate of the prince."[5]

There is considerable advantage in retaining the term "patrimonial" to define a regime where the rights of sovereignty and those of ownership blend to the point of becoming indistinguishable, and political power is exercised in the same manner as economic power. "Despotism," whose root is the Greek *despotes,* has much the same etymological origins, but over time it has acquired the meaning of a deviation or corruption of genuine kingship, the latter being understood to respect the property rights of subjects. The patrimonial regime, on the other hand, is a regime in its own right, not a corruption of something else. Here conflicts between sovereignty and property do not and cannot arise because, as in the case of a primitive family run by a paterfamilias they are one and the same thing. A despot violates his subjects' property rights; a patrimonial ruler does not even acknowledge their existence. By inference, under a patrimonial system there can be no clear distinction between state and society in so far as such a distinction postulates the right of persons other than the sovereign to exercise control over things and (where there is slavery) over persons. In a patrimonial state there exist no formal limitations on political authority, nor rule of law, nor individual liberties. There can be, however, a highly efficient system of political, economic and military organization derived from the fact that the same man or men—kings or bureaucracies—dispose of the country's entire human and material resources.

Classic examples of patrimonial regimes are to be found among the Hellenistic states which emerged from the dissolution of the empire of Alexander the Great, such as Egypt of the Ptolomies (305–30 B.C.) and the Attalid state in Pergamum (c. 283–133 B.C.). In these kingdoms, founded by Macedonian conquerors, the ruler controlled all or nearly all the productive wealth. In particular, he owned the entire cultivated land which he exploited partly directly, through his personal staff using his own labor force, and partly indirectly, by distributing estates on service tenure

4. Thomas Hobbes (1588–1679), English political philosopher.—Ed.
5. Max Weber, *The Theory of Social and Economic Organization* (1947).

to his nobility. The Hellenistic king was often also the country's principal industrialist and merchant. The primary purpose of this kind of arrangement was to enrich its sovereign proprietor. Rather than seeking to maximize resources, the emphasis lay on stabilizing income, and to this purpose the government often set fixed quotas of goods which it expected to receive, leaving the remainder to the inhabitants. In extreme cases, such as Hellenistic Pergamum, something close to a planned economy seems to have come into being. Because there was no free market, social classes in the customary sense of the word could not arise; instead there were social estates organized hierarchically to serve the king and tending to ossify into castes. There was no nobility with defined rights and privileges, but only ranks of servitors, whose status depended wholly on royal grace. The bureaucracy was powerful but it was not permitted to become hereditary. Like the nobility, it owed its status and privileges to the king.

The patrimonial system best defines the type of regime which emerged in Russia between the twelfth and seventeenth centuries and which, with certain lapses and modifications, has survived until the present. . . .

# The Legacy of Genghis Khan

## N. S. TRUBETZKOY

In historical perspective the present-day state that is called Russia was once part of the Mongolian Empire founded by Genghis Khan. But one cannot equate Russia with the empire of Genghis Khan. Almost all of Asia was incorporated into the empire of the great Mongolian conqueror and his immediate heirs. But no matter how much Russian influence has penetrated China, Persia, and Afghanistan, these countries have not become parts of Russia, and if Russia were to incorporate them into herself, she would indeed alter her historical physiognomy. Russia's historical heritage includes only the fundamental nucleus of Genghis Khan's empire, not its entirety. This nucleus is characterized by specific geographical features that distinguish it from the remaining parts of the former Mongolian Empire.

Geographically, the territory of Russia, understood as the nucleus of the Mongolian Empire, can be defined in the following manner. A long, more or less uninterrupted zone of unforested plains and plateaus stretches almost from the Pacific Ocean to the mouth of the Danube. This belt can be called the "steppe system." It is bordered on the north by a broad zone of forests, beyond which lies the tundra. In the south, the steppe system is bordered by mountain ranges. Thus there are four parallel zones stretching from west to east: the tundra, the forests, the steppes, and the mountains. In the meridional direction (i.e., from north to south or south

From Nikolai Sergeevich Trubetzkoy, *The Legacy of Genghis Khan and Other Essays on Russia's Identity*, ed. Anatoly Liberman, 1991, pp. 163–66, 178–83, 189–94, trans. by Kenneth Brostrom. Reprinted by permission of The University of Michigan Slavic Publications.

to north) this system of four zones is intersected by a system of great rivers. This then is the essence of the geographical configuration of the land mass under discussion. It lacks both access to the open sea and the ragged coastline so characteristic of Western and Central Europe and East and South Asia. With regard to climate, this land mass is distinguished from both Europe and Asia proper by a set of characteristics associated with the term "continental climate": extreme variations between summer and winter temperatures, a distinct isotherm and wind direction, and so on. This land mass differs from both Europe and Asia proper and constitutes a separate continent, a separate part of the earth, which in contrast to Europe and Asia can be called *Eurasia*.

The population of this part of the earth is not homogeneous and comprises several races. The difference between the Russians and the Buryats or the Samoyeds is very great. But a series of intermediate, transitional links exists between these extremes. With regard to anthropological facial type and build, there are no striking differences between the . . . Russian and the Mordvin or the Zyryan. Likewise, no striking transition exists between the Mordvin and Zyryan and the Cheremiss or the Votyak; as representatives of a type, the Volga-Kama Finns (the Mordvins, Votyaks, and Cheremiss) are very similar to the Volga Turks (the Chuvash, Tatars, and Meshcheryaks). The Tatar type gradates into the Bashkir and Kirghiz type, from which, by way of similar gradual transitions, we pass to what is, properly speaking, the Mongolian-Kalmyk-Buryat type.

Eurasia represents an integral whole, both geographically and anthropologically. The presence within it of geographically and economically diverse features, such as forests, steppes, and mountains, and of natural geographical connections between them makes it possible to view Eurasia as a region that is more or less self-sufficient economically. By its very nature, Eurasia is historically destined to comprise a single state entity.

From the beginning the political unification of Eurasia was a historical inevitability, and the geography of Eurasia indicated the means to achieve it. In ancient times only the rivers and steppes served as paths of communication. The forests and mountains were not suited to this, while the tundra was a region inhospitable to the development of any human activity. We have already seen that the numerous great river systems within the territory of Eurasia are oriented in a north-south direction, while the single steppe system passes across the entirety of Eurasia from east to west. Consequently, there was only one path of communication between east and west, while there were several between north and south (all the riverways between north and south intersect the steppe road between east and west at some point). Therefore, a people that gained control over one of the river systems became the master of only one specific part of Eurasia, but a people that gained control of the steppe system became the master of Eurasia. In mastering the segments of the river systems located in the steppes, they subjugated each of these systems in its entirety. Only a state that controlled the entire steppe system could unite all Eurasia.

Within the territory of Eurasia there were originally tribes and states with a settled life style along the rivers, and steppe tribes with a nomadic life style. Conflict between river and steppe was inevitable, and it is indeed a predominant feature of the . . . history not only of [Russia], but of the other Eurasian river states (e.g., the [medieval kingdoms] of the Khazars and of Khorezm). In the beginning the nomads were divided into many tribes, each of which remained within a defined area of the steppe; only when some tribe penetrated an adjacent area would conflict break out between neighboring tribes. At that time the river states were able to oppose the steppe people quite successfully. The constant threat of nomadic raids on the river settlements and the never-ending danger that trade along the rivers would be interrupted made normal development impossible for the river states. But they continued to exist and to struggle with the nomads, although not always successfully.

The situation changed radically when Genghis Khan [1167?–1227] subjugated the nomadic tribes of the Eurasian steppe and transformed the Eurasian steppe system into a single, all-encompassing nomad state with a superb military organization. Nothing could resist such power. All the organized states within the territory of Eurasia lost their independence and became subject to the ruler of the steppes. Thus Genghis Khan was successful in accomplishing the historical task set by the nature of Eurasia, the task of unifying this entire area into a single state, and he accomplished this task in the only way possible—by first unifying the entire steppe under his power, and through the steppe, the rest of Eurasia. . . .

. . . Genghis Khan was the bearer of an important, positive idea, and the desire to create and organize, not the desire to destroy, was predominant in his activities. This must be remembered when we approach Russia as the historical heir to Genghis Khan's state.

[Now,] let us return to a question of fundamental interest to us, the origins of the Russian state. It is not enough to state that the geographical territory of Russia more or less coincides with the nucleus of Genghis Khan's empire, for it still remains unclear how the empire of the great Mongolian conqueror came to be replaced by the Russian state.

The destruction of the independent feudal principalities of *Rus'* by the Mongolian invasion [1237–1242] and their incorporation into the Mongolian state undoubtedly caused a profound upheaval in the hearts and minds of the Russian people.[1] Their anguish and their keen awareness of the humiliation suffered by Russian national pride merged with a strong new impression engendered by the grandeur of a foreign conception of the state. All Russians were disoriented, the abyss seemed to yawn before them at every step, and they began to search desperately for some solid ground. An eruption of acute spiritual tumult and turmoil was the result—complex processes whose significance is generally undervalued.

The hallmark of this period was the extraordinarily vigorous development of religious life. For ancient Rus' the period of Tatar rule was above all else an epoch of religion. The foreign yoke was perceived by the religious mind as God's punishment for past sins; the reality of the punishment reinforced the consciousness of the reality of the sin and the reality of a vengeful Divine Providence, and it confronted every person with the problem of individual repentance and purification

---

1. *Rus'*—pronounced "Roose"—was the medieval name for the lands of the East Slavs, ancestors of the Ukrainians and Belorussians as well as the Russians.—Ed.

through prayer. The flight to monasticism and the creation of new monasteries and convents took on the character of mass movements. The intense religious orientation of the inner life of Russians suffused every product of the spirit, especially art, with its colors. This period is associated with feverish creative activity in all areas of religious art; icon painting, church music, and religious literature reached new heights (the oldest specimens of religious folk poetry appeared at this time). This powerful upsurge in religious life was a natural accompaniment to that revaluation of values, to that disillusionment with life, which were caused by the calamity of the Tatar [Mongolian] invasion.[2]

At the same time, a fiery devotion to the national ideal arose as a reaction against the depressing awareness of national humiliation. The Russian past began to be idealized—not the recent past of the feudal principalities, the darker sides of which had led to . . . defeat . . . and were thus all too obvious—but a more distant past. This idealization is evident in such works as "The Tale of the Destruction of the Russian Land" and in the *byliny* [heroic songs], which, as we now know, were reworked during this very period. In the folk consciousness, this idealization of Rus' and of ancient Russian heroism transformed minor princes and their retainers into all-Russian heroes, and their adversaries—unimportant leaders of Cuman raids—into Tatar khans commanding numberless hordes; such idealization strengthened the national pride that was swelling in opposition to the foreign yoke. Together with the emergence of this spirit of national military heroism there developed another conception of heroism fostered by the religious revival, a heroism that was ascetic and sacrificial, that found real embodiments in Russian monks and in the martyrs executed by the [Tatars]. This contemporary and local Russian heroism merged in the Russian mind with traditions of ancient, non-Russian, Christian heroism. Thus, in reaction to the despair occasioned by total defeat at the hands of the Tatars, a wave of heroism—primarily religious but also nationalistic—was growing and gaining strength in Russian hearts and minds. . . .

[T]he religious and national revival of [the Tatar] period became a universal social phenomenon and a powerful factor in the development of a national identity and a national culture.

Such was the spiritual and psychological atmosphere created in Old Rus' by the Tatar Yoke. It was in this atmosphere that the underlying historical direction of the epoch was defined—the absorption of the Tatar conception of the state and its application to the conditions of Russian life. Historians usually pass over or ignore this process. They describe Russia during the period of the Tatar Yoke as if no Tatar Yoke existed. The fallacy of this perspective in historical writing is obvious. . . .

. . . [T]here exist undeniable historical connections between the Russian and Mongolian state systems in such important branches of state activity as the organization of finance, the mails, and the means of communication[;] . . . it is natural to

---

2. Tatars and Mongols originated as different though related tribes in Inner Asia (Móngolia), and the Mongols of Genghis Khan (a title meaning "Universal King") actually conquered the Tatars in forming their empire. But for reasons unknown the Mongolian conquerors became more generally known as Tatars, particularly in Russia. Historians of Russia use the names interchangeably.—Ed.

assume the existence of such connections in other areas—in the structure of the administrative apparatus, in the organization of the military, and so on. If Russian historians would only abandon their preconceived and absurd indifference to the fact of Russia's participation in the Mongolian state and examine the history of Russia from another perspective, the origins of many aspects of the state *mores* of so-called "Muscovite Rus'" would present themselves in an entirely new light. Russia's inclusion in the Mongolian state system could not be a matter of form only, simply the extension to Russia of the system of government as it existed in the other provinces and regions of the Mongolian Empire; the spirit of the Mongolian state system must also have been absorbed by Russia to some degree.

It is true that, for reasons to be discussed below, the ideational foundations of this state system gradually began to crumble and disappear after the death of Genghis Khan. It is also true that the Tatar rulers and officials with whom the Russians had to deal were in most cases very far from measuring up to the ideals of Genghis Khan. Nevertheless, certain traditional ideas continued to exist within the Mongolian state system, and beyond the imperfections of its implementation there glimmered the state ideal, the fundamental design created by the great founder of the nomad state. And the spirit of Genghis Khan associated with the Mongolian state system, a spirit permeating and audible within it like a musical overtone, could not remain unnoticed and was certain to touch the souls of the Russians. In comparison with the extremely primitive notions of the state typical of pre-Mongolian Rus', the Mongolian conception developed by Genghis Khan was grand, and its grandeur was bound to impress the Russians deeply.

Thus the Tatar Yoke gave rise to a rather complex situation. As Russia acquired the techniques of the Mongolian state system, she also appropriated its spirit, its underlying design. Although this state system and its fundamental ideas were perceived as foreign and hostile, their grandeur, especially in comparison with the primitive insignificance of pre-Mongolian Russian conceptions of the state, made such a powerful impression that reactions of one sort or another were inevitable. The fainthearted simply bowed down and tried to find a personal niche for themselves. But bolder spirits could not reconcile themselves to this situation; the unprecedented religious revival and the birth of a new national self-awareness, of a heightened sense of national dignity, did not permit them to bow down before the might of a foreign state or before a foreign idea of the state. Yet this idea attracted them irresistibly and often filled their thoughts. It was necessary to find a way out of this painful dilemma. And find it they did, thanks to the religious revival.

The Tatar conception of the state was unacceptable to the extent that it was foreign and hostile. But the great idea possessed an irresistible power of attraction. Consequently, the Russians had to do away with what was unacceptable, what made it foreign and hostile. In other words, it had to be separated from its Mongolianism and associated with Orthodoxy, so it could be heralded as one's own, as Russian. In doing this, Russian national thought turned to Byzantine-Greek political ideas and traditions that provided material useful in the religious appropriation and Russification of the Mongolian state system. The ideas of Genghis Khan, obscured and eroded during the process of their implementation but still glimmering within the Mongolian state system, once again came to life, but in a completely new, unrecognizable form after they had received a Byzantine Christian foundation. In the Russian mind they acquired all the intensity of the religious fervor and national self-affirmation that distinguished the spiritual life of this era. They acquired unprecedented vividness and freshness, and with such contours they had become genuinely *Russian*. This is how the miraculous transformation of the Mongolian conception of the state into the Orthodox Russian conception occurred.[3]

This miracle is so out of the ordinary that many would prefer to deny it. Nevertheless, it is a fact, and the psychological interpretation of this miracle offered above provides it with a satisfactory explanation. In any case, let us remember that Russia had come to know Orthodox Byzantium long before the Tatar Yoke and that during the time of the Yoke the grandeur of Byzantium was in eclipse. Yet for some reason it was during the period of Tatar rule that Byzantine state ideologies, which formerly had no particular appeal in Russia, came to occupy a central place in the Russian national consciousness. It follows that the grafting of these ideologies onto Russia was not motivateod by the prestige of Byzantium, and that they were needed only to link an idea of the state, Mongolian in origin, to Orthodoxy, thereby making it Russian. So it was that this idea was absorbed, an idea which Russians had encountered in real life after their land was incorporated into the Mongolian empire and became one of its provinces.

The center of the process of inner rebirth was Moscow. All the phenomena brought into existence by the Tatar Yoke resonated there with exceptional force. It was in Moscow and in the Moscow region that the positive and the negative spiritual processes characteristic of this era were most strikingly evident. Instances of moral degradation, unprincipled opportunism, humiliating servility vis-à-vis the Tatar regime, and careerism stained by treason and crime were not unusual there. But it was also in the Moscow region that religious feelings were afire and at white heat. The embodiment of this fervor was Sergius of Radonezh, founder of the [Trinity-St. Sergius] Monastery, the principal center of the religious revival during the Tatar rule. The assimilation of the techniques of the Mongolian state system and of the Tatar life style proceeded at an especially rapid pace in Moscow. This is why Russians in this area assimilated more easily and quickly the spirit of the Mongolian state, that is, the ideational legacy of Genghis Khan. It was also Moscow and the Moscow region that exhibited particular interest in Byzantine state ideologies. Every manifestation of the complex psychological process that culminated ultimately in the transformation of the Mongolian state system into the Russian had its center in Moscow.

The Grand Princes of Moscow gradually became the living bearers of the new Russian state spirit. It is difficult now to judge to what degree they were conscious "gatherers of the Russian land." Initially they may have simply adapted themselves to the Tatar regime as they strove to extract as much personal profit as possible

---

3. The lands of Rus' were Christianized, beginning in the tenth century, by missionaries of the Eastern or Greek Orthodox Church centered in Byzantium (Constantinople, later Istanbul). By the mid-fifteenth century, when Mongol rule over Russia had greatly weakened, an autonomous Russian Orthodox Church, centered in Moscow, had been established.—Ed.

from it; they may have been governed by self-interest and not by any patriotic considerations. Then, after assimilating a larger vision of the state but perhaps still viewing Russia as merely a province of the Mongolian Empire, they began to work with the Tatars. Finally, they began to work with conscious intent against the Khan of the Golden Horde, striving to usurp his place—first, with regard to Russia, and later, with regard to other lands under the control of the Golden Horde.[4] Certain centralist traditions doubtlessly existed in the house of the Suzdal princes from which the Muscovite princes sprang, but they would not have been sufficient to transform the Muscovite princes into the "Tsars of all Rus'." This transformation became possible owing to the psychological process which, as we have seen, led to the emergence of the Russian state ideology. In addition, the Muscovite princes (to the extent that they were loyal servants) enjoyed the full patronage and support of the Horde, which could only welcome the administrative centralization of its Russian province. Whatever the case, the political unification of Russia under the power of Moscow was a direct result of the Tatar Yoke.

The expression "the overthrow of the Tatar Yoke," which occurs in old textbooks of Russian history, is conventional and imprecise. There never was, strictly speaking, a genuine overthrow of the Horde by military force. After the battle of Kulikovo Field [1380], Russia continued to pay tribute to the Tatars for a long time and so remained a part of the Mongolian Empire. It would be more accurate to call Ivan III's refusal [in 1480] to pay tribute to the Tatars the "overthrow of the Yoke," but this event attracted little attention and had no military consequences. Nor was the title of Tsar, which Ivan III [sometimes] assumed, considered anything out of the ordinary by the Tatars; the rulers of some of the larger areas within the Mongolian Empire had long since assumed the title of khan or tsar while preserving their political connections with the empire. The important historical moment was not the "overthrow of the Yoke" nor the separation of Russia from the power of the Horde, but the extension of Moscow's power over a large part of the territory once under the control of the Horde—in other words, *the replacement of the Tatar khan by the Muscovite tsar, together with the transfer of the center of political power to Moscow*. This took place during the reign of Ivan the Terrible, after the conquests of Kazan, Astrakhan, and Siberia [see Chapter 6]. . . .

Thus, the external history of the "rise of Moscow," or of the beginnings of the Russian state, can be depicted in the following manner. The Tatars looked upon the Russia they had conquered as a single province. From the perspective of the Tatar state system, the financial and administrative unification of the Russian province was much to be desired. The Muscovite princes took this task upon themselves, and in doing so they were champions of the Horde's political strategy and agents representing the central Tatar government. The Muscovite princes prospered greatly in these endeavors, and they won the unswerving trust of the

---

4. The Khanate (Kingdom) of the Golden Horde, with its capital of Sarai at the lower Volga River, was the division of the Mongolian Empire to which, after about 1240, the conquered lands of Rus' were subject. The lands of Rus' united—or "gathered"—by the grand princes of Moscow formed Muscovite Rus', or Russia.—Ed.

Tatars and made themselves indispensable to them. They were transformed into the permanent, hereditary governors of the Russian province of the Tatar Empire, the equals of the other provincial khans and rulers, from whom they differed only in their nonnomadic origins and their non-Islamic faith.[5] Gradually all these provincial rulers who called themselves tsars and khans (including the Muscovite tsar) became so emancipated that their connections with the central government became purely nominal or disappeared altogether, while the central government had ceased to exist. But the consciousness of a state entity lived on, as did an awareness of the need to reunify the uncoordinated provinces of the former Tatar state, now separated into independent kingdoms.

This task had to be accomplished by one or another of the provincial rulers. The Tatars failed to do so, and it was completed by the only non-Tatar provincial overlord, the Muscovite tsar. From that moment he ceased to be the ordinary ruler of a single, independent province; he ceased to be a separatist and became the representative of central state power, the restorer of the unity of the Tatar state system. The phrase "gatherers of the Russian land" does not capture the importance of the Muscovite tsars. While they were "gathering" (i.e., while they were restricting themselves to the unification of *Russian* lands administratively and financially, while they were collecting tribute from them for the Tatar treasury and imposing on them the Tatar state system), they were merely provincial governors, local agents of the central Tatar government. Even when they revolted against this power, they did not overstep the boundaries of provincialism. They became genuine rulers of a state only when they abandoned the "gathering of Russian land" for the "gathering of Tatar land," that is, when they decided to subjugate the separate, uncoordinated parts of the northwest *ulus* [division] of the Mongolian Empire.

However, the external history of the formation of the Muscovite state system becomes comprehensible only in the light of its internal, psychological, and ideological history. Without the profound spiritual rebirth that swept over the Russian nation as one product of its reaction to the Tatar Yoke, Russia would have been completely assimilated and would have remained one of the many fragments of Genghis Khan's empire. If among the provincial rulers of the Mongolian Empire *only* the Muscovite tsars aspired to control the entire Eurasian territory once united by Genghis Khan, if they alone had both the external and the internal strength to realize this aspiration, and if in assimilating the legacy of Genghis Khan Russia retained her national identity and even strengthened it, then this occurred because . . . it was in Russia alone that the spirit and ideas of Genghis Khan underwent a religious transformation and emerged in a revitalized and genuinely Russian form. It was in this crucible of national religious feeling that the northwest *ulus* of the Mongolian Empire was fused into the Muscovite state, replacing the Mongolian khan with the Orthodox Russian tsar. . . .

The national and religious revival, which intensified in Russia during the Tatar

---

5. The Tatars of the Golden Horde converted from their primitive nature religion—with admixtures of Christianity and Buddhism—to Islam in the fourteenth century.—Ed.

rule and led to the emergence of a religiously sanctioned concept of a national state, was contemporaneous with the opposite psychological process in the ruling circles of the Tatars—the weakening of the ideological and moral foundations of the Mongolian state system. And when the separate provinces of the erstwhile Mongolian Empire (among them Russia) began to acquire an ever-increasing degree of independence, only in the Russian province ruled by Moscow had the idea of the state acquired a new religious, moral, and national foundation. It is therefore not surprising that the Prince of Moscow began to enjoy a certain moral prestige among the Tatars themselves, and this long before the so-called overthrow of the Tatar Yoke. Tatar nobles and highly placed officials living among the Russians gradually ceased to treat them with contempt; they were then inspired by the national religious revival themselves, and converted to Orthodoxy. Instances of the conversion of representatives of the Tatar ruling circles to the Russian faith and of their entry into Russian service became commonplace, and the Russian ruling class began to admit Tatars in great numbers. The importance of this phenomenon is usually underestimated. Historians lose sight of the fact that every such "conversion" presupposes a profound spiritual upheaval. Only the extraordinary force of the religious fervor everywhere present in Russian society at that time could induce a Moslem, and a Tatar into the bargain, to change his faith. The newly converted Tatars who joined the ranks of the Russian ruling class had immense importance for Russia: they were representatives of the noble nomad type that Genghis Khan regarded as the backbone of his state; they contributed greatly to the formation of this new state and became reliable supports for the emerging Russian state system. They brought with them the traditions and practices of the Mongolian state system and strengthened in their own persons the Russian state's connection as heir apparent with the Mongolian state. Thus the transformation of the Muscovite Grand Prince into the successor of the Khan of the Golden Horde and the replacement of the Mongolian state system by the Russian were the results of two parallel psychological processes, one occurring in a Russian milieu and the other in the Tatar ruling circles. . . .

One important problem unknown to the Mongolian Empire confronted the Muscovite state system—defense against the West. All of the Ukraine and Belorussia, which had belonged to Eurasia . . . from time immemorial, was under the control of Catholic Poland, Europe's outpost in the East; and it was only with the greatest difficulty that a part of these lands was reunited with the Eurasian world under the control of Moscow. But Poland was not without competitors. In the northwest, there was increasing danger of a Swedish invasion, while other European countries not immediately bordering on Russia were greedily reaching out for the wealth of Russia-Eurasia through maritime trade. National defense was a necessity, but one that implied another—the need to acquire Western military and industrial technology. The situation was complex and difficult. Russia had to borrow and learn certain things from Europe but avoid falling into a state of cultural and spiritual dependence. Inasmuch as the peoples of Europe were not adherents of Orthodoxy but called themselves Christians (i.e., from the Russian point of view they were heretics), the spirit of Europe and of European civilization was perceived by Russians as heretical, sinful, anti-Christian, and satanic. Contamination by this spirit was a very great danger.

The Muscovite tsars were aware of the complexity of this situation, and they turned away from the path of technological apprenticeship. They limited themselves in this direction to half measures; they invited European specialists, craftsmen, and instructors to work in Russia, but kept them isolated and watched them closely to prevent excessive fraternization with Russians. This certainly was no solution to the problem. Sooner or later it would be necessary to begin borrowing European technology in earnest, while taking decisive measures against contamination by the European spirit.

It was Peter I [reigned 1689–1725] who decided to borrow European technology. But he was so carried away by this undertaking that it became almost an end in itself for him, and he took no measures against contamination by the spirit of Europe. The task was accomplished in the worst way possible, and with catastrophic results: external power was purchased at the cost of Russia's complete cultural and spiritual enslavement by Europe. In borrowing Western technology to strengthen Russia's external power, Peter I subjected Russian national sensibilities to the most terrible humiliations and destroyed the foundations on which Russia's internal power and might rested. . . .

It is true that Peter's grand design was born of patriotism, but a patriotism that was unique and unprecedented in Russian experience. He did not care about the genuine, historical Russia, because he had a passionate dream of creating from Russian material a great European power that would resemble other European countries in every way, but surpass them in territorial size and military might. His attitude toward the Russian material from which he had to create this great power reflected hostility, not love, for he had to wage a never-ending, stubborn war against this material, which naturally resisted his efforts to squeeze it into the mold of an alien ideal. This explains the paradox characteristic of all Peter's activities: his fiery, self-sacrificing love for his country . . . was inseparable from his conscious, malicious desire to humiliate national sensibilities and to mock traditions sacred to every Russian.

The borrowing of European technology was historically inevitable because of the need for a national defense, but the forms it took during Peter's reign did not correspond to this need and even contradicted it. No foreign conquest could have destroyed the national culture of Russia to the extent that Peter's reforms did, even though they were originally intended to protect Russia from foreign conquest. The explanation for the disastrous direction taken by these reforms resides not in histori-cal necessity but in Peter's character. His activities inevitably promoted to the highest civil and military offices the type of individual who was hostile to the genuine national element in Russian life; this corrupted the upper strata of society, making a change in course impossible even after his death. There were too many people with a personal stake in the new regime, and the military and the government were in their hands.

Thus, Peter set the tone for the entire course of Russia's subsequent history. He initiated a new period, the era of antinational monarchy. The bases of Russian life were radically altered. Since the ideological foundations of the former Russian state system had been overturned and trampled upon, the new state system had to depend exclusively upon power. Serfdom and military organization had existed in Russia previously, but she became a genuinely feudal and militarist nation only after the beginnings of Europeanization. The new ideology was one of unadulterated imperialism in all matters, including culture; while an alien civilization was being implanted in Russia, in foreign policy enthusiasm for foreign conquest reigned supreme. Thus, the paradox that characterized all of Peter's activities was preserved in this ideology. . . .


## Russia and Europe

### THOMAS G. MASARYK

A general survey of Russian development since the days of Peter the Great shows the country divided into two halves, consisting respectively of an Old Russia with a [pre-Petrine] civilization and a New, European Russia.

An alert observer traveling through Russia will gain a vivid perception of the nature and evolution of this cultural divergence. One entering Russia from Europe (it must be remembered that the Russian crossing the western frontier speaks always of "going to Europe") has first to traverse a [non-Russian] province or territory. He must pass through Poland, the Baltic provinces, or Finland, through lands annexed from Europe, whose inhabitants are Catholic or Protestant, and who have a European civilization of old date. The connection of these regions with Orthodox Russia is still comparatively superficial. But the further eastward we go, the further do we find ourselves from Europe, until at length Europe is represented only by the railway, the refreshment rooms at the stations, and isolated hotels furnished and managed in European style. The same contrast strikes us between [St. Petersburg] and Moscow. In Moscow, and also in [St. Petersburg], it strikes us between the modern portions of the city and the old town which is purely Russian. Odessa, on the other hand, is a new town, quite European.[1]

When compared with the two capitals, and especially when compared with [St. Petersburg], the rural districts, the villages, are Russian. The great landowners, aristocrats, furnish their country-seats in European style. Similarly, many factories in country districts are European oases. Things technical, things practical, are for the most part European: railways, factories, and banks; commerce to some extent (including internal trade); army and navy; in part, also, the bureaucratic machine of state. It is true that any one whose first impression of this machine is derived from the Warsaw post office will find it extremely disagreeable. I need hardly say

Excerpted from: Thomas G. Masaryk, *The Spirit of Russia: Studies in History, Literature and Philosophy* (London: George Allen and Unwin Ltd., 1919), vol. 1, pp. 2–6. Translated from German by Eden and Cedar Paul.

1. Odessa, on the Black Sea, was founded in 1794.—Ed.

that European elements are everywhere intermingled with Russian, and after a little practice we learn to distinguish the transitional stages and the manifold combinations. Close observation and increasing knowledge enable us to detect the difference between that which has been directly imported from Europe and the native imitation or adaptation, so that we come to recognize how Russia and Europe merge in great things and in small.

After a time we shall obviously learn to detect the same contrasts in men as well as in things. European and Russian thought and feeling present themselves in the most diversified combinations. Before long the conviction is forced upon us that the Europeanization of Russia does not consist solely in the adoption of isolated ideas and isolated practical institutions, but that we [are dealing] with a characteristic historical process in virtue of which the Old Russian essence, civilization, and modes of life are being transformed and destroyed by the inroad of the European essence, civilization, and modes of life. The individual Russian undergoing Europeanization experiences this contrast in his own intimate personality. Since the human being cannot live disintegrated, there is forced upon him the attempt to secure an organic connection between the Russian that he is by inheritance and the European that he is by acquirement, to secure as far as possible a unification of the two. The task is difficult! Try to picture to yourself vividly the contrast between the Russian peasant (and the peasant is still Russia), on the one hand, and the writer, the officer, the landowner, or the skilled technician, on the other—men who have been educated in Paris, Berlin, or Zurich, and who are familiar with the life of these cities. People differing thus widely have not merely to live side by side, but must think and work with one another and for one another!

The spiritual contrast between Russia and Europe is displayed in its fullest significance in the Russian monastery. Here we find the most genuine and the oldest Russian life, the feeling and thought of Old Russia. We see this already in the monasteries of [St. Petersburg], but we see it yet more clearly in remoter monasteries and hermitages. Russia, Old Russia, is the Russian monk. During my first visit to Russia [ca. 1892] I had a vivid experience of this. In Moscow I was moving in circles where intellectual development was most advanced, but withdrawing one day from this Europeanized environment, I paid a visit to the [Trinity-St. Sergius] monastery. With its institutions, its treasures, and its relics, this monastery takes us back into fourteenth-century Russia; but in the dependent monastery Bethany, and yet more in the hermitage of Gethsemane, we find ourselves in an even remoter historical epoch. In the center of the forest stands the hermitage, with an ancient wooden church—a veritable Gethsemane! The contrast was all the more striking seeing that the previous day I had been debating religious problems with Tolstoi and his friends.[2] . . . Now I found myself at the hermitage of Gethsemane, with its catacombs, its wonder-working relics, and its icons! One of Tolstoi's friends, a man of position, had given me a letter of introduction to the head of the monastery, so that I was able to see everything. Never shall I forget the man who showed me

2. Masaryk refers to Leo Tolstoi (1828–1910), the famous writer.—Ed.

round the hermitage. This monk was about twenty-five years old. He had grown up in and for the monastery, and his mind was entirely dominated by its Orthodox ideas. To him the world seemed something altogether foreign, whilst I was an emissary from, [and] a part of, the outer world, from which he was a refugee. Now he was to accompany me through the catacombs and to explain what I saw. The things which to him were objects of the most devout contemplation were to be elucidated to the [non-Russian], the European, the heretic, the mere sightseer! I could not fail to note and to be sorry for my guide's distress, but I must admit that his uneasiness was a trifle irritating to the European in me. He genuflected before every relic and every icon, at least before the principal ones; he was continually crossing himself; kneeling down he touched the holy precincts with forehead and lips. As I watched him closely I perceived that alarm was gaining on him, that he was obviously terrified, momentarily expecting that Heaven would punish me for my wickedness and unbelief. But punishment was withheld, and almost without his knowledge and understanding, into the depths of his soul there crept a shadow of doubt. This was obvious in his earnest request that I would at least bow before the chief relic. It was plain that he was no longer anxious about the safety of the heretic, but that the Almighty's failure to send due punishment was troubling him. . . . After we had finished with the catacombs I wished to return alone, but my guide would not leave me. Before long I realized that the monk on his side wanted to acquire knowledge. He gave free rein to his curiosity, to his eager desire to learn something of the world, of Europe. His world-hunger sparkled in his eyes, and I could not satisfy his appetite for narrative and explanation. At length he, a Russian, began to ask me, a [non-Russian], about Moscow, [St. Petersburg], Russia. Several times we paced the distance between the hermitage and the margin of the forest. My companion never wearied in his interrogations. Hitherto he had known the world in the light of the Bible and the legends of the saints, but now he was listening to the unheard of and unsuspected. At length I had to make my way back to the principal monastery. Despite my repeated and cordial thanks, the monk accompanied me to the very gate; there he continued to stand, and would not take his homeward path after my last words of farewell had been uttered—what on earth did the man want? Did he expect a gratuity? The thought had been worrying me for some little time. I was ashamed of it; it hurt me to entertain it; but in the end I found it impossible to doubt that this strictly religious contemner of the world was accustomed to receive tips! My head was whirling with thoughts about Russia and Europe, belief and unbelief; and I blushed as I slipped a note into the extended palm of the guardian of Gethsemane. . . .

This experience and many similar ones, especially those gained during a pilgrimage to another leading monastery, and during my intercourse with the "old believers" and the sectaries—in a word, the observation and study of the religious life of the churches, afford ample insight into Old Russia of the days before Peter the Great. To understand European and Europeanized Russia, it is necessary to know what Moscow . . . has been and still is for Russia in matters of civilization.

I owe to Tolstoi my introduction to the old believer wonderland. One of the best old believer curio dealers in Moscow gave me his personal guidance through the length and breadth of this Old Russia.

Old Russia, Russia in contrast to Europe! Yet the monk in Gethsemane, the pilgrims, the Orthodox, the peasantry—they all carried me back in memory to childhood, when my primitive faith was undisturbed. Such were my own beliefs and such were my own actions when I went on pilgrimage in boyhood; such are still the beliefs and actions of the children and the wives of our Slovak peasants when they visit the shrine of the miracle-working virgin on Mt. Hostein; such were the beliefs and such was the teaching of my own mother. But this childhood has passed away for ever, simply because childhood must yield place to maturity. . . .

Russia has preserved the childhood of Europe; in the overwhelming mass of its peasant population it represents Christian medievalism and, in particular, Byzantine medievalism. It was but a question of time when this middle age would awaken to modernity, and the awakening was in large part due to Peter and his successors.

I am acquainted with a fair proportion of the civilized and uncivilized world, and I have no hesitation in saying that Russia was and is the most interesting country known to me. Slav as I am, a visit to Russia has involved many more surprises than a visit to any other land. In England and America, for example, I had no feeling of surprise. The latest novelty seemed to me nothing more than an obvious development of something with which I was already familiar at home. Yet in Russia, although as a Slav I am competent, I believe, to grasp in Russian literature what is termed the spirit of the language and of the nation; although Russian life, as revealed in the creative works of Russian authors, is intimately congenial to my own moods, in so far as these are Slav, and arouses harmonious echoes in my own Slav nature—yet in Russia I ever and anon feel surprise! The European, one who lives in the present, has the current of his thought involuntarily directed towards the future, and anticipates the conclusions that will follow from the given historic premises. But in Russia he finds himself back in the past, often in the Middle Ages, finds himself in a life utterly different from that of the modern and progressive west. In the [non-Christian] lands of Asia and Africa we do not receive this general impression in anything like the same strength, because the customs differ so utterly from ours; but Russia is of our own kind, exhibits our own quality, is what Europe has been. . . .

Russia is—Europe as well. When, therefore, I contrast Russia and Europe, I contrast two epochs. Russia does not differ essentially from Europe; but Russia is not yet essentially one with Europe.

# FURTHER READING

James H. Bater and R. A. French, *Studies in Russian Historical Geography*, vol. 1 (1983)

Peter K. Christoff, *An Introduction to Nineteenth-Century Russian Slavophilism*, 4 vols. (1961, 1972, 1982, 1991)

Abbott Gleason, *European and Muscovite: Ivan Kireevsky and the Origins of Slavophilism* (1972)

Charles J. Halperin, "George Vernadsky, Eurasianism, the Mongols, and Russia," *Slavic Review* 41 (1983), 477–483

——, *Russia and the Golden Horde* (1985)

Michel Hoang, *Genghis Khan* (1990)

Anatoly Liberman, "N. S. Trubetzkoy and His Works on History and Politics," in *Nikolai Sergeevich Trubetzkoy, The Legacy of Genghis Khan and Other Essays on Russia's Identity*, ed. Anatoly Liberman (1991), 295–375

Paul E. Lydolph, *Geography of the U.S.S.R.: Topical Analysis* (1979)

David Morgan, *The Mongols* (1987)

Judith Pallot and Denis J. B. Shaw, *Landscape and Settlement in Romanov Russia, 1613–1917* (1990)

Paul Ratchnevsky, *Genghis Khan: His Life and Legacy* (1992)

Nicholas V. Riasanovsky, "The Emergence of Eurasianism," *California Slavic Studies* 4 (1967), 39–72

———, *Russia and the West in the Teachings of the Slavophiles* (1952)

Teodor Shanin, *Russia as a "Developing Society": The Roots of Otherness*, vol. 1 (1986)

Leslie Symons, ed., *The Soviet Union: A Systematic Geography* (1983)

Andrzej Walicki, *The Slavophile Controversy: History of a Conservative Utopia in Nineteenth-Century Russian Thought*, trans. Hilda Andrews-Rusiecka (1989)

CHAPTER 2

# The Muscovite
# Heritage

The "Muscovite period" is the name conventionally given by historians to the several centuries of Russian history immediately
preceding the Imperial period. The name arises from the fact
that during these centuries the city of Moscow (*Moskva,* in Russian)
and its ruler (called grand prince or, after 1547, *tsar',* meaning king)
came to dominate the lands and peoples of Russia. Hence historians
also refer to Muscovite Russia or "Muscovy," to Muscovite culture and
institutions, and so forth, as we saw in Chapter 1.

    This chapter is devoted to the Muscovite background to the Impe-
rial period and particularly to the fundamental Muscovite institutions
of autocracy (absolute monarchy) and serfdom, both of which survived almost to the end of the Imperial period itself.


## ESSAYS

In the first essay, Nancy Kollmann of Stanford University proposes that the Muscovite
autocracy, contrary to the traditional view, was in fact a "façade," the creation of a
religious-political ("theocratic") ideology and court ceremonial that vaunted the grand
prince or tsar of Moscow as the sovereign head of God's family on earth. This conservative ideology and especially its enactive ceremonial naturally grew more elaborate as
the Muscovite state grew in power, wealth, and extent; and both served the crucial
political and social functions first of uniting the ruling "boyar" elite within itself and
then of uniting that elite with the rest of Muscovite society, with the grand prince or
tsar as the unifying center. Meanwhile, behind this façade the boyars—heads of the
leading clan-patronage networks—got on with the business of managing the Muscovite
state and exploiting the country's wealth. Professor Kollmann thus warns us against
taking too literally the claims to absolute power of the "Great Sovereign Tsar and
Autocrat of Moscow and All Russia," as the ruler came to be called, and urges us to
see Muscovite court politics as a continuous personal competition among members of
the elite for enhanced social status, official position, material advantage, and "honor."
It was, she insists, a *patrimonial* system of politics ruling what was still, from top to
bottom, a strongly patrimonial society. The system, medieval by European standards,
survived the Time of Troubles (1598–1613) in Russia; and right down to the reign of

Peter the Great it worked remarkably well to provide political stability in a steadily expanding state and frequently turbulent society.

A major implication of Professor Kollmann's work is that the real assertion of absolute monarchy in Russia, drawing both on patrimonial principles and on newly imported political theories, first occurred under Peter the Great. While not necessarily disagreeing with this thesis, Richard Hellie of the University of Chicago stresses the enormous, even "hypertrophic" power the Muscovite government had acquired by the sixteenth century to intervene radically in society in the interests of the "magnates" who controlled that government. As Professor Hellie argues in the second essay, this power was used, in successive stages, to enserf the Russian peasantry, the vast majority of the population. It was a particularly harsh form of serfdom, he points out, especially for peasants living on land belonging to current or former state servicemen (the nascent nobility), to magnates (or boyars), and to leading churchmen and monasteries: such peasants, perhaps half of the total, came to be little better than slaves. Hellie also shows that the enserfment was not planned as such or historically predetermined but rather resulted from the government's response to a series of fortuitous events and changes in military technology; moreover, he suggests that it was part and parcel of an increasingly rigid stratification of Muscovite society as a whole. What remains unexplained here is how the "hypertrophic" power of the Muscovite state itself came into being. One explanation, emphasizing geographical location and adaptation to the natural environment, was attempted by Professor Pipes in Chapter 1. Prince Trubetzkoy, also in Chapter 1, traced this power to Mongolian and Byzantine origins.

## Muscovite Patrimonialism

### NANCY SHIELDS KOLLMANN

In each generation an inner circle of boyars dominated the [Muscovite ruler's] court; these boyars enjoyed greater prestige and additional benefits of rule. As a group, boyars shared real authority with the sovereign, and the inequities of power among them gave rise to fierce competition. Ideology and ceremony, however, do not reflect these realities of hierarchy, conflict, and what one might call the patrimonial pluralism of court politics. Muscovy is depicted in contemporary sources as apolitical. Only the sovereign is presented as having political power; the boyars are treated as equals in their powerlessness. Although this interpretation is at variance with reality, it reveals certain principles of politics: a normative code governing political relationships and the formation of political groups; a set of values that prompted outbreaks of violence among the boyars and that provided ways to control it. If we can successfully identify and trace these underlying principles of Muscovite politics, we may be able to distinguish between ideology and reality concerning events that occurred during times of political crisis. . . .

Reprinted from *Kinship and Politics: The Making of the Muscovite Political System, 1345–1547* by Nancy Shields Kollmann, pp. 146–51, 181–87 with the permission of the publishers, Stanford University Press. © 1987 by the Board of Trustees of the Leland Stanford Junior University.

The court was immensely successful in concealing the dynamism of its politics from the outside world and in convincing foreigners that Muscovy was ruled literally by an autocrat. Sigismund von Herberstein, an envoy of the Hapsburg [Austrian] court in the early sixteenth century, declared: "In the sway which he holds over his people, he surpasses all the monarchs of the whole world." It comes as some surprise that the ideology and public ceremony of court politics diverged so radically from the reality that we have seen. There was constant sparring of ambitious men at court, yet Muscovite ideology denies that political interaction occurred. The sovereign is depicted as a literal autocrat; neither the boyars nor other individuals or social groups share authority with him. To some extent this political ideology developed from the theocratic vision of the churchmen who wrote chronicles, but it should not be dismissed for that reason. Not only churchmen promoted the façade of autocracy—the boyars themselves accepted it, which suggests that it was grounded in political reality.

The sovereign was routinely described in chronicles and other ideological writings as the sole decision maker, regardless of his age or abilities. . . . Ceremony was an especially effective communicator of this ideology. During the reign of Ivan III [1462–1505], the Daniilovichi [Muscovite ruling dynasty] began to stage increasingly elaborate court rituals, such as coronations, public processions, formal audiences, and pilgrimages. This ceremonial activity should be interpreted as a new emphasis on old principles, not as a break with tradition, since the themes that were stressed in these ceremonies—the sovereign's omnipotence and his paternal relationship with the boyars—had been enunciated extensively in writings and court ritual since before Ivan III's reign.

In these ceremonies and in written sources, Muscovite political interaction was presented as essentially moral and personal; thus it was denied what might be called public or constitutional legitimacy. Authors of written sources, lacking a term for the collectivity of the boyars, referred to them by name or simply as "the boyars." What modern observers would consider political relationships the sources referred to as personal ties: political conflict and amibition were explained by loyalty, friendship, and kinship. The political realm was depicted as being ruled over by the sovereign alone; therefore, court politics was not characterized by pluralism, conflict, or compromise—all of which are fundamental to politics as generally understood. In ideology Muscovite politics had no dynamism; the state was a harmonious family, each member obediently playing his role in the community of God on earth.

The sovereign was at the center of a theocratic vision of government: court ceremony presented him as separate from and superior to the boyars. When he held audiences, he was seated on a throne raised above the level where the boyars sat; he was surrounded by splendid bodyguards who were regally garbed in white and carried ceremonial axes. The sovereign's omnipotence was demonstrated by the immensity and splendor of his entourage. On festive occasions, the sovereign flaunted jewel-encrusted golden drinking cups, crowns, orbs, and scepters; sovereign and boyars alike were decked out in jewel-encrusted robes. (Much of this finery can still be seen in the Kremlin Armory Museum.) Even when (or perhaps especially when) the sovereign was incompetent and the boyars were managing the state, court ceremony maintained the fiction that Moscow was ruled by its sovereign. When Ivan IV was six years old [1536], he held audiences with two parties of foreign ambassadors but told them that he could not host a banquet for them because he was "still of minor age and sitting at table would be too tiring." When he was twelve, the sovereign did carry out the elaborate ritual of such a banquet, greeting the guests and distributing food to them in the proper hierarchical order. Throughout, the implicit message was the centrality of the sovereign and the total subservience of others to him.

Political disgrace reinforced the centrality of the sovereign; exile from the presence of the sovereign was the symbolic expression of such disgrace, which also included more tangible punishment, such as incarceration and confiscation of wealth. Unfortunates were said to have been deprived of the sight of the tsar's "bright eyes." The boyars were portrayed as passive and weak, implying that they recognized and accepted their subservience. As we have seen, . . . they were passive spectators of the tsar's marriage making. The [tsar's] custom of holding public "viewings" of potential brides indicates that the boyars themselves participated in rituals that contradicted some of the most fundamental principles of court politics—in this case, the primacy of the sovereign's marriage in determining the boyars' hierarchy of power. Foreign travelers expressed dismay at what they perceived as the humiliation of the great men of the realm, who called themselves "slaves" and prostrated themselves before the sovereign. Olearius noted: "In addressing the Tsar the magnates must unashamedly not only write their names in the diminutive form, but also call themselves slaves, and they are treated as such."[1] Although these descriptions are inconsistent with reality, they evidence a concern for controlling the potentially powerful and ambitious boyars.

Some ceremonies and written sources stressed the omnipotence of the sovereign, others elaborated a complementary and more complex theory of political relationships. According to presentations of the latter sort, political interaction was constrained by the tsar's autocracy, but his friendship with his advisers personalized and modulated politics. The sovereign was depicted as a man of great piety, by means of whose virtue God's blessings were bestowed on the people. Sovereigns confirmed that image by marching in religious processions through Moscow's streets bearing icons on festival days, and by making frequent pilgrimages to distant monasteries. On special occasions the tsar and his family distributed alms and granted amnesties. Acting out ideology, these processions had symbolic significance, for they communicated the ideal of Moscow's social order; they also gave the populace an opportunity to affirm its unity as a community. In this ideological view of Muscovite politics, boyars were given legitimacy as advisers, reflecting in some measure their real power. Just as the metropolitan [chief bishop] oversaw moral and religious matters, the boyars oversaw secular affairs. These men thus acted as liaisons between the grand prince and his people. That boyars had a traditional

---

1. Adam Olearius, a learned German observer of mid-seventeenth-century Russia (see Further Reading).—Ed.

right to rule jointly with the sovereign is reflected in contemporary illustrations of court ceremony, where the tsar is depicted associating with his boyars, not dominating over them. It is also shown in descriptions of the grand prince's attitude of comradely loyalty toward his boyars. Vasily III, for example, entreated his boyars to defend his kingdom and his minor son after his death as follows: "I [literally, we] am your born sovereign, and you are my eternal boyars; and you, brothers, stand firm so that my son may be made the sovereign of the state and so that there may be justice in the land."

Through the prism of an idealized ideology, these sources reveal the court's desire that politics be conducted in unanimity without strife. In addresses to the "Hundred Chapters" (*Stoglav*) Church Council attributed to Ivan IV [reigned 1533–1584], the sovereign pleaded with the boyars to forget their "prior disputes" and be reconciled. He urged his prelates, boyars, and all his advisers to "help me, assist me, all of you together and in unanimity" in accomplishing the work of the council. The sovereign told the prelates: "Do not hesitate to speak in unanimity words of piety concerning our Orthodox Christian faith. . . . For it is with great zeal and joy that I agree to be your coservant and defender of the faith. . . . This is why, by [my] command, henceforth all disagreement shall be dispelled and total agreement and harmony shall be maintained among us." This too was the theme of the "council of reconciliation" of 1549: Ivan IV summoned his boyars and forgave them transgressions they had committed during his minority; he urged them to be reconciled and in the future to rule "as one."

The ubiquity of the theme of harmony and unanimity compels us to take it seriously as a principle of Muscovite politics. It is not consistent with the reality of court politics, which was marked by dissension, but it hints at limits on such fractious disputes. One such constraint was expressed ideologically by the assertion that all boyars were equal—equal in subservience to the sovereign, equal in their degree of access to him, equal in status and power. Implicit in their equality was harmony: the boyars should not disrupt their unity by contentiousness. Unanimity was the implicit way for boyars to prevent and resolve political conflicts. The expectation of rule by unanimity, or consensus, constrained individual boyars, regardless of their personal eminence. Boyars could not rule or aspire to rule. In keeping with the ideology's emphasis on affinitive relations in politics, boyar ambition that caused strife was regarded as a moral defect, not as an unavoidable part of political interaction. Boyars were condemned in moral terms: for giving bad advice, for being corrupted by the devil, or for "not wishing well for the grand prince." A virtuous boyar was a man who "truly wished well for the grand prince, serving him in faith and justice." Boyars were criticized for taking action without first informing the sovereign, as well as for seeking power independently and thus threatening society's welfare. The following condemnation of the boyars at the 1551 *Stoglav* Church Council is attributed to the tsar: "The boyars and magnates, faithful and loving toward my forefathers, did not give me good counsel. For I considered them well disposed towards me, but instead they usurped independent power for themselves. . . . I was orphaned, and the tsardom was made a widow. And so our boyars seized the opportunity for themselves . . . and no one prohibited them from their totally unseemly undertaking."

Muscovite ideology made it very clear that boyars were supposed to act as a unified group. One boyar was harshly criticized for refusing to attend upon the sovereign or to "counsel with the boyars on the affairs of the sovereign and state." Boyars were also criticized for having too exclusive a relationship with the sovereign, for aspiring to excessive power, and for seizing goods beyond their proper share. . . . In all these examples, containment of the boyars' ambitions for the good of the court is implicit but is stated metaphorically: political interaction—conflict, compromise, and competition—is equated with moral turpitude. The overriding theme of political ideology is the pursuit of static harmony. Such ideological tenets suggest some rules of politics: the sovereign shall act as a unifying center; political relations shall be based on such ties as loyalty, dependence, and kinship; the boyars may participate in government but should restrain their competition to maintain stability ("unanimity" was the chroniclers' term).

It was the constant threat of instability—resulting from foreign wars, a fragile economy whose functioning was in part dependent upon a hostile climate, the administration of a large state by a small bureaucracy, and the boyars' ambitions for power—that gave rise to such a conservative set of values. The ideology expressed the deepest concerns of Muscovy's political actors; a façade of autocracy was necessary to prevent chaos. The primary purpose of the ideology of autocracy described here was to impose limits on the boyars' political competition. In theory, designation of the sovereign as the only legitimate political figure prevented boyars' competition from threatening the state's stability. Boyars fought to gain a greater share of power but not to replace the sovereign. They sought higher status but did not attempt to prevent others from seeking it. But in 1598, when the dynasty died out, boyar factions ignored all limits on competition and struggled to become sovereign. The result was the state of anarchy that Muscovy's ideology and political controls had been specifically designed to prevent.[2] Typically, however, boyars were guided by this ideology and thus stabilized their potentially volatile political system. . . .

This analysis of political activity at the Muscovite court between the fourteenth and mid-sixteenth centuries, like the sources on which it is based, emphasizes family and affinitive relationships. It has been founded on a prosopographical study of the Muscovite boyar elite, on an analysis of Muscovite history in the given period, and, finally, on an interpretation of Muscovite political ideology. It is in some ways an anthropological analysis of politics, for it focuses attention on relationships among individuals and factions, rather than on classes or political institutions. Political conflict is viewed here as a balancing of interests, not as a collision of contradictory ideologies; political groups are considered to have been formed on the basis of family, marriage, patronage, and personal loyalties. Political competition was moderated by the pursuit of stability, for stability gave the Muscovite political system power to accomplish its goal of territorial expansion and strength to prevail against threats from outside.

---

2. This "state of anarchy," traditionally called the Time of Troubles, lasted from 1598 until the establishment of a new ruling dynasty in Moscow—the Romanov—in 1613.—Ed.

Social classes and institutions did exist in Muscovy, but they were not politically potent. Muscovite boyars and their clans did constitute a small, privileged estate, an "aristocracy," but it was an aristocracy only in social terms. It did not wield power as a corporate estate. Similarly, Muscovy had institutions that were becoming increasingly complex—ministries, a central and territorial administration—but they also had no power of their own in politics. Those agencies that did possess political power wielded it as a single unit. The ruler did not act politically as the "monarchical" branch of government, continually battling the corporate estates or institutions; rather he ruled through his charisma, commanding total loyalty and favoring selected men with personal relationships as advisers to him. Together with these counselors, the boyars, the sovereign ruled patrimonially; Muscovy's grand princes and boyars concerned themselves with the public good only inasmuch as it was consistent with their own self-interest.

Even in studies of . . . European history, where categories of public authority, corporate rights, and constitutional development are more applicable than in studies of Russian history, scholars are taking an approach similar to the one employed here. Influenced by the new social history, . . . by prosopography, and by numerous other trends and methods of analysis, scholars of medieval and early modern European history have been finding that the heralded "rational" institutions and attitudes of Western politics . . . were modulated in practice by the continued importance of loyalty to family, patrons, friends, and dynasty. Such patrimonial means of forming relationships—once considered pertinent only to the "private" sphere of life—are coming to be seen as important parts of the "public" sphere, including politics, in premodern settings. . . . [H]istorians of Muscovy have been generally unable to resolve the tension between rational and patrimonial factors in their interpretations of court politics. This work has attempted to develop an analysis of court politics that is consistent with the patrimonial nature of Muscovy's politics and society well into the sixteenth century.

An essential facet of Muscovite court politics was the exclusivity in power of the grand prince and his boyars. They appeased nonpolitical classes by offering them social and economic benefits, while denying them decision-making roles in leadership. They used a service land grant system and ultimately enserfment to compensate the expanding servitor class without yielding it power as a group. Grand princes maintained control over localities, and derived significant income from them, without conceding autonomy to local governments. The grand prince and his boyars granted scribes landholding rights and privileges, such as access to the judicial system that the boyars themselves used; by the seventeenth century, the sovereign was even awarding court rank to selected scribes. But the bureaucracy as an institution was not enfranchised. Neither was the merchantry: Moscow's merchants, a potential middle-class political force, were bought off with economic benefits and privileges. The moral authority of the church was essential to Muscovite political ideology and social cohesion; consequently, the sovereign and his boyars rewarded the church with land grants and treated its hierarchs with honor. But neither they nor the church's other officials held decision-making power.

The Muscovite court's social exclusivity gave it a stability that allowed the state to rise to regional dominance by the mid-sixteenth century. Extensive territorial expansion continued in the seventeenth century. . . . The state then had to contend with occasional uprisings—by the citizens of conquered Kazan, by Cossacks,[3] by disgruntled peasants—but no serious challenges to Moscow's power were leveled. The state's outward stability was matched by strong continuity in its political system. For the most part, the court—grand prince, boyars, and their allies—preserved order by disciplining its own disruptive members, as in the 1490's . . . [and] in numerous incidents of disgrace. The court imposed restraints on political conflict, restraints that were evident in the mid-fifteenth-century dynastic war and that contributed to a resolution of the bitter struggles of the 1530's and 1540's.

Starting in the second half of Ivan IV's reign, however, the political system suffered assaults that might have destroyed it. Ivan IV himself seems to have tried to dismantle the political order—by creating a new elite [the so-called *Oprichnina*], by marrying many times, and even by killing his eldest son, if contemporary rumors . . . are to be believed. Ivan's creation of the Oprichnina incited factional struggles among the boyars that resulted in the execution of many boyars and the eventual amalgamation of the Oprichnina's new elite into the established Muscovite boyar elite. But the court political system was not thereby destroyed; the composition of the elite was changed and enlarged, but many of the same great families . . . maintained power under the next tsar, Fedor Ivanovich (ruled 1584–1598).

Although outwardly politics and government in the seventeenth century seem to have abrogated most of the principles of Muscovy's patrimonial political order, this impression is false. The number of central Muscovite ministries expanded, as did the number of high ranks at court and the number of men to whom such ranks . . . were awarded. But the bureaucracy as an institution continued to be excluded from decision making, and ironically, as the number of men in the top four court ranks increased, their power as a group diminished. Muscovy was still ruled primarily by a small number of powerful boyars in the inner circle. The peasants were enserfed in the seventeenth century, but that act does not indicate the rise of the lesser servitor class [a proto-nobility] to political potency. Rather, petitions by servitors for enserfment complemented the government's needs in the mid-seventeenth century for better local administration and tax collection. Enserfment furthered the gradual transformation of the landed cavalry into Muscovy's local administrative apparatus, but it did not represent a step toward political pluralism. Similarly, [Polish] and eventually [other] European etiquette, art, and literature were brought to the court, but they were not immediately accompanied by Westernization of court politics.

Some of the same key principles governed court politics even in the seventeenth century. The restoration of the boyar elite by the Romanovs in the first decades of the seventeenth century, after the Time of Troubles, favored sixteenth-century families and gave power to men from both winning and losing factions. Consensus remained the means to settle political conflicts. The Time of Troubles, for example,

---

3. Cossacks were frontiersmen who lived in self-governing communities and supported themselves by animal husbandry, brigandage, and occasional military service.—Ed.

came to an end in 1613 only when all boyars agreed on a new distribution of power arranged around the primacy of the Romanov family. Marriage remained important in determining status hierarchy: just as the marriage of Boris Godunov's sister to Tsar Fedor Ivanovich had been the crucial link with the Daniilovich family that established the balance of power among boyars in the generation after the Oprich-nina, the marriage of Boris Ivanovich Morozov to Tsar Aleksei Mikhailovich's sister-in-law in 1648 confirmed his status as the leading boyar of his time. Political conflict continued to be generated by factional ambitions and set off by succession crises. The clashes that occurred during Peter I's youth (1682–1689) between the Miloslavskie and Naryshkiny, kinsmen of [his father] Tsar Aleksei Mikhailovich's two wives, for example, are as good a textbook case of court political struggles as those of Ivan IV's minority [in the 1530s and 1540s].

Some political traditions were modified in the seventeenth century. Tsars began to choose women from obscure families for their brides, for example, rather than selecting members of leading boyar families. This prevented an ambitious boyar clan from gaining too much power. In such circumstances, members of the inner circle intermarried with the sovereign's new kinsmen, perpetuating the principle that the most powerful boyars shared a kinship link of some sort with the tsar. Although the Muscovite administration was becoming larger and more elaborate, although the organization of the army and of the servitor classes was gradually changing, . . . and although Muscovy's preeminence in East European politics was rapidly expanding, politics at the pinnacle of power continued to observe traditional principles. The vehemence of Peter I's attack on the vestiges of the political system described here suggests their endurance.

These reflections on Muscovite court politics might be applied fruitfully to considerations of other aspects of Muscovite political structure, such as political integration. All governments must establish effective links with the societies they rule. Government by coercion would not have resulted in the stability that Muscovy obviously enjoyed. How did the grand princes and boyars gain societal acceptance of so exclusive a political system? At first glance, one-way communication from the central government to the masses would seem to have characterized Muscovite government. Central and local administrators executed policy made by the grand prince and boyars; the central government maintained the national defense and oversaw a unified monetary and judicial system. But these central functions did not give rise to a more broadly concerned government apparatus; involvement of the central government in provincial matters was minimal. Local communities governed themselves in areas such as the maintenance of public order, the upkeep of community property, and the allocation of the tax burden. In doing so they used traditional methods, relying on cooperation among families in the village commune and applying customary law to settling disputes.

Despite their tenuous ties with the localities, grand princes and the boyar elite achieved some degree of societal acceptance of their political order. To some extent the church provided a unifying cultural influence; its presence throughout the Muscovite state complemented the political centralization promoted by the court and gave Muscovy some degree of cultural homogeneity. The court itself furthered the development of political cohesion by sponsoring events and supporting customs that linked the center with privileged social groups (servitors, merchants, scribes). Some of these events have been misconstrued as being more modern and more Western than they actually were: in reality, they reveal the ingenious way in which Moscow's traditional society confronted the problem of political integration.

The Councils of the Land (*zemskie sobory*), the most formal of the events promoted by the court, developed the grand prince's and boyars' contacts with privileged social strata in a way consistent with the themes of Muscovite political ideology. The councils are frequently considered a protoparliamentary institution, which they were not. In many Western nations, the establishment of parliaments was accompanied by a movement to ensure regularity of meetings, permanence of composition and size, and division into chambers representing constituent social estates. But Moscow's Councils of the Land met irregularly . . . and had no fixed membership or statehouse; their members were not elected but selected, were expected to vote unanimously in a mass assembly, and had no right of initiative. The councils' agendas were fixed by court leaders; their members merely rubber-stamped government policies. Nevertheless, these assemblies seem to have served an important function.

Councils of the Land aroused support among the nontaxpaying [elite] social groups on important issues, such as the selection of a new dynasty, the declaration of war, and the making of peace. They allowed communication between the untaxed populace and the government, albeit through informal channels. Councils of the Land created tangible bonds between central and provincial servitor, between center and merchantry, scribes and church hierarchs. They thus embodied physically the theocratic community that Muscovy's political ideology postulated Muscovy to be and furthered political integration.

The Muscovite central government entertained another means by which social groups, most frequently the servitor classes and the urban estates, communicated their desires to the government. Such groups did not enlist the help of their enfranchised legislators (for they had none), nor did they sue the government in the courts. Rather, they petitioned the sovereign directly. The wording of the petition (the petitioner describes himself as a lowly "slave" and seeks the ruler's "favor") reflects not so much the literal autocracy of the sovereign as the nature of the political system. Since political ideology tolerated no intermediary institutions between the central government and society, servitors and members of other social groups could only address the sovereign in a personal manner. Such requests also reflected the reality of politics; individuals sought favors not from representative bodies, but from the personal source of all power and benefits. At the same time petitions allowed privileged classes to make effective contact with the government.

Family honor was greatly venerated among families in the Mucovite elite; the concept was used, like Councils of the Land and petitions, to connect the court with the broader community in a way consistent with patrimonial social norms. Honor was the measuring stick by which the servitor class determined status in precedence litigation; the custom of awarding compensation to individuals whose family honor had been insulted . . . similarly maintained social hierarchy among the servitors and in other nontaxed groups. The use of honor as the ordering principle of the elite complements Muscovy's patrimonial political relationships because honor, like consensus and petition, focuses on the individual's personal dependence on the social group. Muscovy used it, rather than institutional mechanisms, to maintain stability in the elite broadly defined.

These reflections suggest that Muscovite court politics was merely a part of a larger, integrated polity that derived its structure from personal connections—in this case, family ties, patron-client dependencies, and affinitive networks among groups—and that centered its ideology on these themes. Muscovy was not a "well-ordered police state," a bureaucratically organized commonwealth whose ruler and officials served the public good. Muscovy was a minimally governed society in most ways, far more similar to medieval European states than to its European contemporaries. Muscovy's historical writing and political ideology in the period from the fourteenth to the mid-sixteenth centuries were medieval in their ideal of a godly community and their naive explanation of historical causation. Despite its overarching central administration, the state was medieval in its tolerance of regional loyalties and local autonomy. It was medieval in its legal attitudes and practices, even though rulers from Ivan III on attempted to inculcate more complex judicial practices and to make the application of written law codes more widespread. The emphasis on the ruler's charismatic sovereignty that symbolically united Muscovite society into a single, theocratic community was similarly traditional. Court politics, with its emphasis on family, loyalty, and consensus, likewise reflected the patrimonial traditions of Muscovite society.

# Enserfment in Muscovite Russia

## RICHARD HELLIE

The enserfment [of the Russian peasantry] developed in three or four stages. During the quarter-century-long civil war in the reign of Vasily II (1425–1462), selected monasteries which had grown into large economic enterprises needing much manpower were granted the right by the state power to curtail the movement of their peasants to the period around St. George's Day (November 26). This was a political concession in a period of labor disruption for services rendered by a particular monastery; or it was done to gain a monastery's support. The civil war began because no principle existed to decide who should be [grand] prince, whether accession was lateral or vertical. In the past the khan had resolved such issues, but this was no longer realistic with the Tatar hegemony in its decline.[1] The contesting sides could only fight it out. In the process Vasily II's side gave away some peasant freedom to gain support.

---

From Richard Hellie, *Enserfment and Military Change in Muscovy*, pp. 235–50, 262–64. Copyright © 1971, reprinted by permission of The University of Chicago Press.

1. Reference is to the period of Mongol or Tatar rule in Russian history (ca. 1240–1480).—Ed.

For reasons difficult to determine, this curtailment was applied to all peasants by the law code (*Sudebnik*) of 1497. After 1497 most peasants could move at only one time of year, upon payment of a small fee to the landlord. This by no means enserfed the peasants, who seem not to have protested against the minor restriction and who continued to move freely until the 1570s and even into the 1580s. It can hardly be accidental that peasant mobility was not curtailed completely at this time, for there was no organ to enforce such edicts. So long as free land was accessible, curtailing mobility became possible only with the progressive development of the central administration in the sixteenth century. Lacking an effective centralized system of courts and a developed system of record-keeping, the government could hope to curtail peasant mobility only to the time most convenient for all parties concerned—peasant, lord, and tax collector. Nevertheless, the government was becoming accustomed to the idea that it could limit peasant mobility.

At the end of the fifteenth century the middle service class was forming. It was a new military force of cavalrymen equipped with bows and arrows who were given conditional land grants by the government for their support. In order for this group to function, their lands had to be populated with rent-paying peasants. By the middle of the sixteenth century the middle service class had become the major military force of the Muscovite state. This resulted in a general elevation of the status of the middle service class, whose members came to adopt the values of the magnates [boyars] along with some of their prerogatives.

In the second half of the reign of Ivan IV (1533–1584) a number of disasters befell Muscovy. The major ones were Ivan's Livonian War (1558–1583) and his Oprichnina (1565–1572). The result was great hardship for the peasants, who deserted certain key areas, particularly the lands assigned to the members of the middle service class. This in turn proved to be a disaster for the middle service class, which could not serve unless the peasant labor force was stabilized. Members of the middle service class had just begun to acquire control over and a personal interest in their service landholdings. The average member of the middle service class had only a half dozen peasant households for his support, and any loss of these dues-payers was a serious financial blow. Had the serviceman not been given a vested interest in six specific peasant households and had some other way been discovered to finance the army, such as on a cash basis, . . . [their] reaction to the labor shortage on [their] lands might have been different, or even might not have occurred.

The government, accustomed to regulating peasant mobility, did the only thing it could: it forbade peasants to move at all. This was a "temporary" measure initiated in 1581 in some areas. These "forbidden years," as they were called, spread throughout the 1580s. In 1592 (or 1593) Boris Godunov, who was seeking support in his bid for the throne, promulgated a decree forbidding all peasants to move until further notice. The country's economy was still in a state of disorder, and doubtlessly the middle service class wanted all movement from their lands curtailed, so Boris obliged. As a result, the cavalrymen became even less interested in rendering military service and more concerned with their economies.

Not all groups wanted mobility curtailed, for peasants had a tendency to move to the large estates belonging to the great boyars and the monasteries. Boris also needed their support in his drive for the throne, so he agreed (also in 1592) to place a five-year time limit on the recovery of peasants who moved in violation of the interdiction. This meant that a fugitive peasant who could escape detection by his rightful lord for five years (not too difficult in Russia) became a free man.

The traumatic Time of Troubles had little influence on the enserfment. . . . While many individuals and institutions were hard hit by the dislocations of the Troubles, two of the wealthy monasteries which had been in the center of the holocaust seem to have been the ones which brought up the peasant question after 1613. The [Trinity-St. Sergius Monastery] was granted an extraordinary nine-year time limit to recover fugitives. This was the same institution which within the next decades was to benefit significantly from a short time limit to sue for the return of runaways. Had the superiors of the monastery possessed any memory or foresight, they would have realized that the long-term peasant flow was in their direction, that they would soon recover their laborers, and that the extraordinary privilege they were requesting could only work to their ultimate disadvantage. However, a long time-horizon was not common among Muscovites.

The Smolensk War (1632–1634), with its concomitant high taxes, caused turmoil in the peasant community, and the agriculturalists began to move in violation of the Forbidden Years. Also important [were] the fortuitous capture of Azov, the revival of Tatar attacks on the Ukraine, and the rebuilding of the system of fortified lines. The high taxes at the center, combined with the possibility of lower rents and even complete freedom on the frontier, stimulated southward migration. In fortifying the frontier, the government was contributing to a situation leading to the binding of the population to the poor podzolic soils of the center and thus delaying the development of the better chernozem lands further south. Having secured the southern frontier lands, the government found itself unable to let them be populated as rapidly as it would have desired. This deprived the army of manpower to garrison the frontier and the treasury of the additional revenue which taxes on the better farm land would have produced.

The middle service class asked several times in the dozen-year period after the Smolensk War for the time limit on the recovery of fugitive peasants to be repealed. The magnates running the government refused, for in the chronically labor-short economy they valued the movement of peasants to their own estates. No crisis intervened to force them to act contrary to their personal inclinations.

In this period two developments occurred which further undermined the peasants' position and elevated that of the middle service class. For one thing, the peasant's civil status was being degraded so that he began to resemble a slave in the eyes of the law. The importance of the existence of slavery as a model for developing serfdom should be stressed. The legal abasement of the peasantry, originating in the sixteenth century, was particularly noticeable in the 1620s, and continued at a slower pace thereafter. It created a distinction between the peasant and the rank-and-file cavalryman which had been lacking before, and serfdom became an automatic status-elevator in the Russian social edifice. It was also at this time that a purge was begun of some of the grandsons of peasants, slaves, and cossacks who had joined the middle service class in the sixteenth century.

In the same era the gunpowder revolution finally overtook Muscovy almost completely. By this time the Tatars had ceased to be the major threat to the Muscovite state. The result was that, in warfare for the control of huge fortresses, the middle service class cavalryman with his bow and arrow was technologically obsolete in the face of infantry outfitted with firearms. In the Smolensk War the Russian government introduced a new, Western-style army equipped with hand firearms, but disbanded the army after the war. This meant that the middle service class in the relatively peaceful years of the 1630s and 1640s was still the major military force at the disposal of the Muscovite government.

These two developments must have made a dramatic impression on the middle service class. There is an obvious risk in making cross-cultural assumptions, but the following analysis provides a good explanation of some of the phenomena observed in this period. The cavalrymen were conscious of their technological obsolescence and frightened by the gunpowder revolution. On the basis of their social utility alone they would have little right to social prestige. They were also aware of their rising, protected status in society and of the ever-increasing gap between them and the peasantry. Their rise in social position was slow and probably largely accidental while the middle service class was useful; the rise was faster and deliberate when obsolescence began to set in. Beginning in the reign of Boris, the servicemen took advantage of the tsar's weak position to get the government to restrict access to their increasingly privileged position. They also had the government expel individuals of recent lowly origin from their ranks. Multiplying rapidly in peacetime and thus becoming less scarce themselves, they were a group with no technical skill or genuine specialization to support claims to exclusiveness, so they built on their historically legitimate base to achieve privilege. In the dawning era of massive infantry armies using gunpowder technology, the trained peasant or slave infantryman armed with a flintlock handgun under the command of a foreign officer had more intrinsic worth and genuine skill than the archer on horseback from the supposedly elite military caste. This caste had to rule out competition artificially, by having the government codify the caste's privileged position in the law. Only when pressed would the *pomeshchik* [service landholder] join the new army, and then, aping the haughty Poles, only as a cavalryman, in spite of the fact that the day of the cavalry was waning.

For his psychological security the serviceman needed to have the peasant beneath him and, if possible, under his control. When peasants fled, the serviceman lost not only financial support, but also the presence of degraded people under his authority who reminded him daily that he was superior. The loss of prestige must have been particularly poignant when the peasant fled south and joined the frontier forces on the Belgorod *cherta* [line], which was contributing to the obsolescence of the old cavalry against the Tatars. A closed society, then, was of crucial importance if the middle service class was to preserve its prestige, its limited authority and power, and its perquisites, particularly its claim to the bulk of the peasant labor force.

This also helps to explain the resort to *mestnichestvo* [the system of court precedence] in the 1640s, which previously had been a privilege of the elite, and the frantic petition campaign to make sure the peasantry remained abased. As a gulf began to develop between the peasantry and the middle service class, the latter's views on the lower classes became increasingly more like those of the magnates. In turn, as will be shown below, the peasantry failed to distinguish between the ruling magnates, who set the tone and policies of Russia, and the petty gentry, who had a few serfs each. Having been created by the government, the middle service class grew to proportions certainly never initially envisaged and in time acquired perquisites and an accompanying cast of mind which initially had been the property solely of the magnates of the upper upper-service class. This development was certainly one of the reasons for the continuation of serfdom in the second half of the seventeenth century.

In 1648 civil disorders broke out in Moscow and a dozen other towns. By this time the middle service class was very conscious of its military obsolescence, particularly as [Boyar Boris] Morozov had begun to modernize the army again—which helped stimulate the discontent which caused the uprising. This class knew that it had no technical competence which would either justify its privileges or distinguish it from the mass of the peasantry. Nevertheless the obsolete cavalrymen placed a high value on their authority over the peasants (from whom they were legally and socially becoming ever more separate) and desired to preserve their status in society and their continued dominance over the recently degraded peasantry. In 1648 the frantic middle service class again demanded the repeal of the time limit, a move which would consolidate the class's privileges and elevated social status and, its members hoped, alleviate its economic plight. The reluctant government, fearing the disorders and hoping to purchase the support of the middle service class in the time of crisis, granted the request in the law code (*Ulozhenie*) of 1649. Heretofore the repeal of the right to move on St. George's Day had been assumed to be temporary. Without explicitly saying so, the *Ulozhenie* in fact made it permanent. As a result, the peasants, unable to move legally and forever subject to return if they moved illegally, were enserfed [see Documents].

The government was able to create by legislative initiative a rigidly stratified society because of the hypertrophy of the state power in Russia. It was not mainly a fear of a possible peasant uprising which had inhibited the government from consummating the enserfment earlier, but rather the fact that the magnates were looking out for their own best interests, which experience had led them to believe lay in a mobile peasantry.

During the Thirteen Years War (1654–1667) with Poland and Sweden the obsolete middle service class military organization was phased out and then abolished in favor of the new Western-style army. As far as I can determine, the members of the middle service class, in large numbers, ceased to serve in the army and took on no new functions in the course of the rest of the seventeenth century. The middle service class was becoming a privileged [nobility]. The peasants remained enserfed and continued to support a military class which had lost its central position in Muscovy. After 1662 the mutuality of obligations which had featured the peasant–middle service class relationship broke down: the peasants ceased to have rights, and their lords had significantly reduced obligations. Serfdom was seemingly an anachronism. The institution had been created as a political concession to favor selected monasteries and to help support the [middle-servicemen] cavalry, but in the 1660s the monasteries were prospering and the [cavalry] ceased to make up the backbone of the army.

While the peasants were being enserfed, the rest of society was becoming rigidly stratified as well. Clearly, the conversion of the townsmen into a closed caste followed in the wake of the enserfment. Prior to the Time of Troubles there had been little concern with the status of the townsmen, although there had been some legislation in the 1590s. The cataclysm had a drastic impact on the towns. Many were destroyed, most were severely depopulated. Servicemen and church institutions with tax privileges had moved in and taken over many towns by 1613. The condition of the towns continued to deteriorate into the 1620s.

The government relied extensively on the towns for revenue to pay for the increasingly expensive military forces required by advancing technology. This was true after 1613, in spite of the destruction of much of urban life during the [Time of Troubles]. The government tried to collect the taxes on the basis of the old records. The townsmen could not pay, and after 1613 demanded the return to the tax rolls of all who had fled. The government did not object, and methods developed for dealing with fugitive peasants were applied to absent urban taxpayers. By the 1620s the time limit for forcing return to the town tax rolls was ten years. At this time the limit for recovering peasants was five years, which throws additional light on the attitude toward the peasant question of the magnates running the government. Few townsmen were going to work for the magnates (although some townsmen would, the so-called *zakladchiki*, a form of urban slave), so they let the time limit on recovering fugitive urban dwellers run far ahead of that for runaway peasants. Later, in the 1630s, the gap became even more dramatic: townsmen could be recovered for up to twenty-five years, a statute of limitations never attained by the middle service class in the quest for its peasants. In 1642 the time limit for recovering those who had fled from [the town of] Pskov was abolished completely. [This] principle was overturned in the *Ulozhenie*. Townsmen were not to be returned to their old places of residence, but were bound where they were at the moment. The government was indifferent to where townspeople lived because they could be taxed anywhere. The same principle, incidentally, applied to the peasantry: it is time to discard the notion that seignorial peasants [peasants on noble estates] were enserfed to aid the [tsar's treasury]. By 1649 the townsmen also achieved a near monopoly on urban activities, largely trade and manufacturing, and on the ownership of town property. Thus, at their own request, they became a closed caste.

[Boyar] B. I. Morozov made these concessions to the townsmen because he wanted their support in the summer and autumn of 1648. He could yield to most of the townsmen's requests because they cost his faction practically nothing. The only exception was Patriarch Iosif [head of the church], who had 710 houses in seven Moscow "settlements" and was upset by the confiscation of church property in and around the towns. Morozov and the rest of his supporters had very little of this type of tax-exempt property. They were also relatively unaffected by the forcing of the tax-exempt *zakladchiki* on to the tax rolls, and by the granting of monopolies on trade and industry to the townsmen. The magnates were hardly concerned by the migration of townsmen because the latter rarely moved from the towns to [their] estates. . . .

The tide in the direction of a rigidly stratified society was strong. Caught up were nearly all segments of society—the service classes, the townsmen, the peasantry. The *Ulozhenie* of 1649 codified and made more strict the previous governmental pronouncements on social structure. Contemporaries were aware of what had occurred, as revealed in a petition of 1657. The writers noted that there were four basic, rigidly distinct groups in society: the clergy, servicemen, merchants, and the peasants. Each had its assigned place, functions, and duties in the social organism. Nevertheless, the peasant question was the central issue, and the closing off of other social groups followed and was determined by the fate of the mass of the agriculturalists. Throughout the Muscovite period the fate of the peasantry was the crucial variable, chiefly, of course, because the peasants formed the vast majority of the population. . . .

. . . Serfdom became a solidly entrenched institution. A decade after the *Ulozhenie* the middle service class, essential no longer, was eclipsed; within five years more it no longer existed as a military force. Even the landholding servicemen began to rely more on cash payments from the government for their subsistence and military needs, and less on their service lands. The service land system, which the peasants had been enserfed to support, was in the process of being converted into the heritable property of its owners and proved no more capable of supporting them than had the *pomest'e* [service estate] prior to 1649. In many ways the enserfment turned out not to be the panacea the middle service class thought it would be.

The general course of Russian military development lay in the direction of an army paid for entirely by the state treasury. Logically this would have meant a radical cancellation of the service land system and the conversion of all dues into state taxes to be paid by the government to the servicemen. Such a step had been advocated . . . in the middle of the sixteenth century. Had [this] advice been followed, the Russian peasant conceivably might have escaped enserfment. Increased taxes for support of the army played a role in the enserfment, but only secondarily; the turmoil ensuing from peasant flight to escape onerous levies played havoc with the middle service class's ability to support itself, with the consequences which have been shown. The government, however, was nearly always able to levy taxes, regardless of where the populace lived. . . . Moreover, had the real inequality of demands on the peasantry associated with the *pomest'e* system not existed, the agriculturalists would have moved much less [often] in their search for temporary relief from the oppressive exactions. . . .

Muscovy had an opportunity to turn away from the *pomest'e* method of financing the army during the Thirteen Years War. Peasants on conquered territory were ordered to pay their traditional dues in cash and kind to the Russian government for distribution to the troops. The plan failed, however, because it ran head-long into customary beliefs about the political role of land-ownership in occupied territory as well as the fact that one of the goals of warfare in the Muscovite period was the seizure of populated land to support the middle service class cavalry. Beginning at least as early as the annexation of Novgorod at the end of the fifteenth century, Moscow had developed the practice of ensuring an area's loyalty and rewarding its own troops by deporting the indigenous landowners and replacing them with Muscovite servicemen. The same procedure was repeated after the annexation of Pskov, Kazan, and Baltic lands. Therefore it is not at all surprising that during the Thirteen Years War Moscow soon parcelled out conquered territories to its own servitors and to indigenous servicemen who were willing to pledge allegiance to the tsar. This may have been strategically and politically wise, but Russia lost an opportunity to enter a wedge into the *pomest'e* system.

Not all Russians were oblivious of the contradictions inherent in the privileged position of the gentry [nobility] after the Thirteen Years War. In the 1680s and 1690s Charles XI of Sweden confiscated many estates for the crown (his "reduction"). V. V. Golitsyn, who ran the Russian government from 1682 to 1689 for Tsarevna Sophia, learned of Charles's acts of 1680, 1682, and 1683, and contemplated emulating the northern monarch. He drafted a proposal for the creation of a regular army containing both the gentry and other categories of servicemen. All would receive only cash pay from a peasant head-tax. The gentry were to lose both their land and serfs. Whether a realization of Golitsyn's project would have signified the end of serfdom is debatable, but it certainly would have reduced drastically the number of peasants subject to seignorial [noble] control and increased proportionately those who were taxpaying . . . peasants. The project was not realized because Golitsyn was soon deposed by Peter [I] and those representing traditional Muscovy.

The middle service class itself was treated by the government in a more high-handed manner in the second half of the seventeenth century, in sharp contrast to 1648. Petitions for relief were sometimes rejected out of hand. The members of the middle service class were ordered around after 1648 in a fashion hardly conceivable earlier. The gentry's [nobility's] weak condition, embodied in its minimal social utility, did not allow it to protest such treatment or the consolidation of power by the magnates, for the latter always could simply threaten to free the serfs and thereby divest the *dvoriane* and *deti boiarskie* [nobility] of their economic support and social status. This weak condition was the consequence of the government's creation of the new army, which prepared the way for the eventual triumph of the Moscow magnates over the rest of society.

Another sign of the decline of the middle service class can be seen in the disappearance of the [Council] of the Land [*Zemskii Sobor*] after the commencement of the Thirteen Years War. The Zemskii Sobor after 1613 had developed into one of the forums where the middle service class could express its interests with the assurance that the government would be listening. After the 1648 experience, when the government was forced to make numerous concessions to the elected delegates to the Zemskii Sobor, the power elite, one can be quite sure, desired to get rid of the consultative institution. During the Thirteen Years War this became possible. The central government's information-gathering system was perfected to the point that it did not have to summon representatives from the provinces to learn the condition of the country. This ability stemmed from the development of the *voevoda* provincial administration at the expense of the decaying *guba* system.[2] The fiscal system was organized so that the autocracy was sure it could raise no more revenue by consulting the townsmen and leading merchants of the realm. Also, the government did not have to consult with the foreign mercenary officers or with the troops of the new formation regiments about whether they wanted to fight, as had become customary with the middle service class. Therefore, after 1653, the state power never again convoked the [Council] of the Land, and Russia lost its chance to have an extended parliamentary experience.

The [Council] of the Land was not the only thing that seemed vital in 1648 but was soon fated to disappear. Along with that institution went many of the concessions which had been granted under duress during the crisis. Probably only their promoters took many of the new laws seriously, and even at the time of their promulgation the government probably had no intention of enforcing many of them. A few examples will suffice. In 1648 all peasant lands in the western Pomore region which had been sold were ordered confiscated from the buyers and returned to their former owners. In September of 1649 the government cancelled the provisions for retroactive confiscations. The *Ulozhenie* prescribed that all towns be granted a certain area around them for garden plots and pasture. The lands were to be confiscated for the town or exchanged for court lands elsewhere. After being enforced rigorously for a short while, these provisions were soon emasculated, then ignored. Another major concession to the townsmen was a decree that no tax-exempt party would be allowed to keep properties in town. Endless litigation vitiated much of the effectiveness of this measure. A decree of 1681 reversed this law and allowed tax-exempt parties to keep taxable properties in towns. The monopoly of the townsmen on trade proved to be ephemeral [, as did] the stricture against additional land acquisition by the church. . . . The Monastery Chancellery, created under pressure from the delegates to the [Council] of the Land to bring most of the church and its secular subjects under lay control, was abolished at the request of the patriarch and clergy in 1677. . . .

It is apparent that many of the concessions granted under duress in 1648 were soon annulled, but serfdom was not. I am sure that the government, had the resolve been present, could have abolished serfdom after 1649, but it did not. Why?

The seignorial [noble] peasantry remained enserfed until 1861 (or even to the beginning of the twentieth century) for several reasons. Inertia was only a minor factor, as revealed by the fact that the government deliberately undid many of the other 1648 concessions. The causes for the continuance of serfdom in the reign of Aleksei and later must be sought elsewhere.

Initially the . . . Miloslavsky government had to get used to ruling,[3] and any abrupt change on the peasant question would have aroused the instant ire of the middle service class. Then the Thirteen Years War preoccupied the government

---

2. The *voevoda*, or governor, was sent by the tsar from Moscow, whereas the old *guba* (district) system was locally based.—Ed.
3. Miloslavsky was the family name of Tsar Aleksei's first wife, Maria, whom he married in 1648; she died in 1669.—Ed.

until the Truce of Andrusovo in 1667. As usual, the combatants exhausted each other, and Russia was forced to sue for a peace significantly less favorable than might have been anticipated after the war had been under way only a few years. This peripeteia, along with the plague of the 1650s and the developing church schism and its represesion, consumed most of the energy of the ruling elite.

The truce itself was forced at least partly by peasant disorders, which [were followed by the great uprising of 1667–1671 led by Stenka Razin]. After 1649 serfdom had become increasingly more degrading and severe. While the *pomest'e* [service estate] was not to be merged completely with the *votchina* [hereditary estate] until 1714, the service landholders took increasing liberties with the persons of their serfs, even occasionally moving them illegally from the former kind of holding to the latter. In 1658 peasant flight had been made a criminal offense and the apprehended runaway was supposed to be beaten with the knout. In the years [1658–1663], a period which saw the phasing out of the middle service class, the government ceaselessly had conducted investigations throughout the territory of Muscovy to discover and return the tens of thousands of serfs who had fled south and east from their lords after the *Ulozhenie* to escape the plague and crop failure, recruiting, mounting taxes, and general oppression. Unprecedented numbers had fled after the outbreak of the Thirteen Years War. Peasants had been returned who had moved as much as fifty years prior to their discovery.

The Razin rebellion, unlike the Time of Troubles with its slave and peasant uprisings at the beginning of the century, was definitely a class war, with the peasants on one side against—indiscriminately—the lords on the other. The peasants were not revolting against the entire system, but against some of its manifestations. They did not possess sufficient political insight to understand what caused their discontent, which in fact was largely the product of the enserfment. Many of the rebels were runaways from the center, further agitated because their rapid accumulation had caused a famine in the Don region. The spark which lit the Razin uprising was a refusal by the bankrupt government to pay the cossacks what they considered their due. As a result, much of the uprising had economic manifestations—the starving rebels tried to make ends meet. Although the rebels' primary purpose was not to overthrow the system, contemporaries in the upper and middle service classes, frightened by the rebels' rhetoric, cannot be blamed for not having appreciated this fact.

In the Time of Troubles, when the prohibition of peasant movement was considered by all to be "temporary," members of both the upper and middle service classes had at one time or another been on the side of the revolting peasants and slaves under Bolotnikov. During the Smolensk War a few members of the middle service class joined the Balash rebellion. In 1648 *deti boiarskie* [petty noblemen] were to be found among the rebels against the government in Moscow. However, the *Ulozhenie* served as a watershed, with the result that in 1650 and 1662 members of the middle service class participated in those uprisings only on the government side—that is, by repressing them. The new law code created a closer identity of interest between the magnates running the government and the middle service class; both were privileged groups performing less and less necessary state service while simultaneously exploiting the increasingly abased, oppressed, and angry masses. The code also contributed to the opening of the ultimately notorious chasm between the upper and lower classes in Russia.

By the time of the Razin uprising, the peasants had a generalized feeling that serfdom was definitely their lot and the cause of many of their woes. While they did not fully understand the institution and its complexities, the rebels' proclaimed goals were to attain freedom and to kill first the boyars and then all the lords plus all the military officers. This type of talk, plus the rebels' actions, hardened the elite against all the peasants and forged an alliance between the members of the upper and middle service classes (the magnates and gentry [nobility]) for the common purpose of survival in a new hostile environment. The rebels also brought the wrath of the church on themselves (the Patriarch's anathema, church funds to pay loyal troops who suppressed the rebellion) by mutilating and drowning priests whenever they were encountered.

After the rebellion, in which the political fabric of Muscovy seemed to have been challenged by the peasantry, any actions which might have amounted to concessions to the serfs were out of the question. The *Razinshchina* [Razin rebellion] upset the peasantry wherever it occurred, causing the massive peasant flights which typically accompanied any form of rural chaos in Russia. Certainly most landowners in such a situation would not have tolerated any legal measures which might have caused more unrest in the serf community, as would have happened had the peasants been given the right to move. As in 1607, when the . . . government crushed the Bolotnikov uprising, in the late 1660s and 1670s the government was in a mood only for repression. Like so many others, this rebellion for freedom backfired.

The Razin revolt set off a chain of uprisings leading to the 1682 disturbances in Moscow and other towns. This in turn stimulated serf uprisings in the countryside. The result was that the government saw only uprisings and thought only of repression for much of the time after the introduction of the new army, when logic alone would have dictated rolling back the enserfment. The ruling elite devoted its attention to suppressing the unrest rather than to solving its causes. . . .

In time the mutual interest of the magnates and the gentry [nobility] in the maintenance of serfdom developed to such an extent that the autocracy felt serfdom to be [the] "twin pillar" [along with the nobility itself] upon which the whole political and social structure was based. The roots of these late eighteenth- and early nineteenth-century sentiments can be traced back to the Razin uprising. By the end of the seventeenth century the common interest of the upper and middle service classes in the peasant question was embodied in the fact that only they (plus church bodies) could own serfs. With this went a near monopoly on the right to own land, a true tenure, which kept the urban castes out of the countryside.

The personalities of the leaders of Muscovy help explain why serfdom flourished after 1649. Most of them were weak, venal individuals incapable of understanding what would really be in Russia's best interest; or else they were strong-minded men concerned with issues other than serfdom. . . .

. . . V. V. Golitsyn can be included with this [latter] group. To enhance his independence from the traditional powers of Muscovy, he gave thought to the problem of the army and serfdom, but he had no opportunity to effect his reforms because he was purged as a result of his . . . vainglory and corruption. Understanding of the Muscovite period is impossible until one comprehends that most policies, particularly internal ones, but also external ones, were conceived and executed almost exclusively in the interests of the magnates. The rare exceptions had to be coerced from the government by the interested parties. . . .

[To sum up:] In the Muscovite period of Russian history the enserfment of the peasantry was a governmental reaction to labor dislocation at times of crisis and a second-order consequence of technological change. The catalysts, or immediate causes, of this development were the civil war of the fifteenth century, Ivan IV's Oprichnina and Livonian War, the dynastic crisis after the death of Ivan IV, the Smolensk War, and the civil disorders of 1648. All of the immediate causes were catalysts which, injected into the Muscovite situation, caused the rigidification and severe stratification of Russian society.

One ultimate cause was the general underpopulation of the country, which resulted, during times of disruption, in glaring labor shortages for certain kinds of landholders. Also crucial were the lengthy frontiers, which had to be defended by increasingly expensive armed forces, which in turn had to be supported by a sparse population subsisting on very low-level agriculture. While the new taxes to pay for the gunpowder revolution did not cause the stratification of Russian society, they did accelerate it because the peasants fled the imposts and then their lords demanded that they be returned. In times of political disruption the government, often headed by less than ideal rulers, usually felt it needed support, which regularly could be purchased by granting concessions to powerful interest-groups. There were many concessions which the hypertrophic government could give, as we have seen, but a major one involved control over the peasantry. This concession was attractive both for economic and sociopsychological reasons. Almost all wealth was produced by the peasantry, so that those who were not primary producers had to live indirectly off agriculture, or not at all. Also, Russian society was very status conscious and placed a high value on dominance and authority. This attitude loomed particularly important when the middle service class became aware of its military obsolescence. The series of deliberate concessions granted by the state power to satisfy the economic demands and psychic needs of its constituents resulted in the enserfment, [certainly unintended,][4] of the peasantry.

Concessions to the lower classes as a response to chaos and disorder never seem to have occurred to any Russian rulers. . . . Rather than solve the problems of peasant discontent, the ruling group, probably because of limited ability and perception coupled with commitments other than to what we in the twentieth century think of as social justice, preferred to team up with the service class and church to keep the lid on by repression. Mainly because there were few cracks in the upper and middle service class–church alliance, lower-class rebellion had little chance of success. . . .

---

4. brackets in original

Once serfdom was consolidated, nearly all forces at work favored its retention in the face of peasant opposition—even in face of the fact that the gunpowder revolution created an army consisting largely of peasant draftees commanded by foreign officers and thus made the old middle service class cavalry, which had demanded the enserfment, obsolete. When the government wanted to, it could simply ignore the enserfment, as in the case of fugitives to the frontier or in urban areas, and even occasionally when runaways appeared on the magnates' own estates. . . . As it happened, the *Ulozhenie* proved not to cost the magnates much and aided the gentry [nobility] little in their quest for a larger share of the country's wealth. On the other hand, the enserfment served as social cement between the great and small lords in the hostile peasant environment. While progress in the government administration and tax-collection system as well as in the economy was insufficient to permit a total discarding of the traditional natural support of the army, it was adequate to permit adoption of the new technology and the tactics of gunpowder warfare, enabling Muscovy to survive as a political entity. The continuation of serfdom permitted a peaceful, radical reform of the army in spite of the fact that this reform dispossessed the potentially troublesome and powerful middle service class. The tsar and his favorite oligarchs were able to rule without challenge. The restriction the enserfment placed on their ability to enrich themselves by recruiting additional labor was a small price to pay for the power to rule. In this way part of the groundwork was laid for the autocratic rule in Russia which continued to the [end of the Imperial period].

# Documents

The *Ulozhenie* (law code) of 1649 provided in its Chapter 11 for the enserfment of the Russian peasantry. But as readers of Chapter 11, printed below, will see, the enserfment was not enacted in a direct or positive way. Rather it was a matter of abolishing all time restrictions on the recovery of runaway peasants and their families (and of any grain they might have grown or personal property they might have taken with them). In effect, Chapter 11 of the *Ulozhenie* lent the Muscovite government's powerful support to the efforts of landholders to stop their peasants from moving away. Thus peasants officially registered in one of the government's census books as resident on such and such a piece of land (or estate), which effectively meant all peasants, could not legally leave that land and take up residence elsewhere without the permission (manumission) of whoever controlled that land—be it officers of the tsar's court or government department, a bishop, the head of a monastery, or a landlord by right of military service or personal inheritance; and regardless, too, of whether that landlord was Russian or "foreign" (for example, a Tatar or a German who had served the tsar and been granted an estate). Moreover, no landholder "ever shall receive others' peasants and shall not retain them under himself" under pain of heavy fines, public beatings, and imprisonment (Articles 9, 10, 27). Children of enserfed peasants who attempted to escape serfdom by denying their parentage, and were caught, were to be tortured (Article 22). With few restrictions (Articles 30 and 31), peasants could be legally bought, sold, mortgaged, or otherwise transferred to new masters along with the land on which they were officially resident (that is, to which they were now permanently bound). The effectiveness of this blanket prohibition of free peasant movement in the years after 1649 would vary, depending on a given landlord's determination to recover runaway peasants and the current government's willingness or ability to assist him in doing so. (For purposes of colonization and state security, for instance, the government might prefer to leave runaway peasants settled in frontier zones—something which did in fact happen.) Yet serfdom as prescribed in Chapter 11 of the *Ulozhenie* of 1649 remained in force until 1861, by which time it was widely recognized as a major factor in Russia's economic and social backwardness.

The second of these documents is intended to indicate how religion permeated late Muscovite society, and to convey something of the everyday reality of Muscovite life. It is taken from the *Life* of Archpriest Avvakum, which is considered a rare monument of Muscovite Russian literature. Avvakum (Russian for Habakkuk, the Biblical prophet) was born about 1621 in a village near Nizhnii Novgorod, the important market town on the upper Volga well east of Moscow. His father was the local priest and "given to hard drink," as Avvakum tells us in his *Life*; but his mother "fasted and prayed zealously and was ever teaching me the fear of God." In 1638, at her behest, he married the daughter of the village blacksmith and prepared to follow his father into the church. He was ordained deacon of a nearby village church at the age of twenty-one, priest at twenty-three, and archpriest sometime before March 1652. In the 1640s he became active in a movement for moral and religious reform which had emerged primarily among the parish clergy of the upper Volga region and whose members were known as the "lovers of God" or "zealots of piety." In the early years (1645–1652) of the reign of Tsar Aleksei Mikhailovich the influence of this movement reached into the court itself, where Avvakum was introduced in 1647. In 1652 another "zealot" from the upper Volga region, the monk Nikon, was named patriarch of Moscow. Patriarch Nikon proceeded to order certain reforms of Russian religious practice aimed at conforming it with that of the Greek church, historically the preeminent church of the Eastern Orthodox world (the world of the former Byzantine Empire, which had fallen to the Ottoman Turks in 1453). The arbitrary manner in which Nikon promoted his reforms, as well as his implicit condemnation of traditional Russian religious practice, soon led to a break with other prominent "zealots" including Avvakum, who considered that the Greek church had become corrupt under Turkish rule.

Nikon's religious reforms of the 1650s have been seen by historians as one manifestation of the Muscovite government's ambition to assume leadership of the entire Eastern Orthodox world; while the opposition of Avvakum and his friends and their followers, who came to be known collectively as the "Old Believers," has been described as a conservative, puritanical, populist, and even nationalist reaction to the imposition of those reforms by the rulers of church and state acting under the influence of foreign (mainly Greek) clerics. In any case, the deepening break or schism (*raskol*) in the Russian church between the two sides, formalized at the Moscow church council of 1666–1667, had far-reaching consequences. It has been estimated for instance that as many as one million people fled Russia in the ensuing century to escape persecution as Old Believers, and that by the end of the nineteenth century as much as a fourth or more of the Russian population belonged to Old Believer and other sects.

Avvakum spent fourteen years in various forms of exile and imprisonment for his opposition to the Nikonian reforms, and in 1682, in the remote northern settlement of Pustozersk, he and three other recalcitrant clergy were executed by fire. His *Life*, written or dictated during these years, polemical and didactic though it is, also includes numerous lively narrative and descriptive passages of great interest. In the version pexcerpted here, dating to about 1673, Avvakum recounts the end of his exile among Russian colonists in the "new land of Dauriia" east of Lake Baikal, in far eastern

Siberia, about 5,000 miles from Moscow; his journey back to Russia proper; his continued refusal to accept the reforms; and his final banishment to Pustozersk.

## Enserfing the Russian Peasantry: The *Ulozhenie* (Chapter 11) of 1649

### CHAPTER 11. —THE JUDICIAL PROCESS FOR PEASANTS. IN IT ARE 34 ARTICLES.

1. Concerning the sovereign's peasants and landless peasants of court villages and rural taxpaying districts who, having fled from the sovereign's court villages and from the rural taxpaying districts, are now living under the patriarch, or under the metropolitans, and under the archbishops, and the bishop [sic]; or under monasteries; or under boyars, or under [any other courtiers and nobles], and under foreigners, and under all hereditary estate owners and service landholders; and in the cadastral [census] books, which books the census takers submitted to the Service Land Chancellery and to other chancelleries after the Moscow fire of the past year 1626, those fugitive peasants or their fathers were registered [as living] under the sovereign: having hunted down those fugitive peasants and landless peasants of the sovereign, cart them [back] to the sovereign's court villages and to the rural taxpaying districts, to their old allotments as [registered in] the cadastral books, with their wives, and with their children, and with all their movable peasant property, without any statute of limitations.

2. Similarly, if hereditary estate owners and service landholders proceed to petition the sovereign about their fugitive peasants and about landless peasants, and they testify that their peasants and landless peasants, having fled from them, are living in the sovereign's court villages, and in rural taxpaying districts, or as townsmen in the urban taxpaying districts, or as musketeers, or as cossacks, or as gunners, or as any other type of servicemen in the trans-Moscow or in the frontier towns; or under the patriarch, or under the metropolitans, or under the archibishops and bishops; or under monasteries; or under boyars, and under [other courtiers and nobles], and under foreigners, and under any hereditary estate owners and service landholders: return such peasants and landless peasants after trial and investigation on the basis of the cadastral books, which books the census takers submitted to the Service Land Chancellery after the Moscow fire of the past year 1626, if those fugitive peasants of theirs, or the fathers of those peasants of theirs, were recorded [as living] under them in those cadastral books, or [if] after those cadastral books [were compiled] those peasants, or their children, were recorded in new grants [as living] under someone in books allotting lands or in books registering land transfers.

From Richard Hellie, ed. and trans. *The Muscovite Law Code* (Ulozhenie) *of 1649*, Part I: *Text and Translation*, pp. 85–94. Reprinted by permission of Charles Schlacks, Jr., Publisher.

Return fugitive peasants and landless peasants from flight on the basis of the cadastral books to people of all ranks, without any statute of limitations.

3. If it becomes necessary to return fugitive peasants and landless peasants to someone after trial and investigation: return those peasants with their wives, and with their children, and with all their movable property, with their standing grain and with their threshed grain. Do not impose a fine for those peasants [on their current lords] for the years prior to this present Law Code. . . .

4. If fugitive peasants and landless peasants are returned to someone: chancellery officials of the sovereign's court villages and the rural taxpaying districts, and estate owners, and service landholders shall get from those people [to whom the fugitives are returned] inventory receipts, signed by them, for those peasants and landless peasants of theirs and their movable property in case of dispute in the future.

Order the town public-square scribes to write the inventory receipts in Moscow and in the provincial towns; in villages and hamlets where there are no public-square scribes, order the civil administration or church scribes of other villages to write such inventories. They shall issue such inventory receipts signed by their own hand. . . .

5. Concerning the vacant houses of peasants and landless peasants, or [their] house lots, registered in the cadastral books with certain estate owners and service landholders; and in the cadastral books it is written about the peasants and landless peasants of those houses that those peasants and landless peasants fled from them in the years prior to [the compilation of] those cadastral books, but there was no petition from them against anyone about those peasants throughout this time: do not grant a trial for those peasants and landless peasants on the basis of those vacant houses and vacant lots because for many years they [the landlords] did not petition the sovereign against anyone about those peasants of theirs.

6. If fugitive peasants and landless peasants are returned from someone to plaintiffs after trial and investigation, and according to the cadastral books; or if someone returns [fugitives] without trial according to [this] Law Code: on the petition of those people under whom they had lived while fugitives, register those peasants in the Service Land Chancellery [as living] under those people to whom they are returned.

Concerning those people from whom they are taken: do not collect any of the sovereign's levies [due from the peasants] from such service landholders and hereditary estate owners on the basis of the census books. Collect all of the sovereign's levies from those estate owners and service landholders under whom they proceed to live as peasants upon their return.

7. If, after trial and investigation, and according to the cadastral books, peasants are taken away from any hereditary estate owners and returned to plaintiffs from their purchased estates; and they purchased those estates from estate owners with those peasants [living on them] after [the compilation of] the cadastres; and those peasants are registered on their lands in the purchase documents: those estate owners, in the stead of those returned peasants, shall take from the sellers similar peasants with all [their] movable property, and with [their] standing grain and with [their] threshed grain, from their other estates.

8. Concerning those estate owners and service landholders who in the past years had a trial about fugitive peasants and landless peasants; and at trial someone's [claims] to such fugitive peasants were rejected, prior to this decree of the sovereign, on the basis of the statute of limitations on the recovery of fugitive peasants in the prior decree of the great Sovereign, Tsar, and Grand Prince of all Russia Mikhail Fedorovich of blessed memory [reigned 1613–1647]; and those fugitive peasants and landless peasants were ordered to live under those people under whom they lived out the years [of the] statute of limitations; or certain service landholders and hereditary estate owners arranged an amicable agreement in past years, prior to this decree of the sovereign, [and] someone ceded his peasants to someone else, and they confirmed it with registered documents, or they submitted reconciliation petitions [to settle court suits]: all those cases shall remain as those cases were resolved prior to this decree of the sovereign. Do not consider those cases anew and do not renegotiate [them].

9. Concerning peasants and landless peasants registered under someone in the census books of the past years 1645/46 and 1646/47; and after [the compilation of] those census books they fled from those people under whom they were registered in the census books, or they proceed to flee in the future: return those fugitive peasants and landless peasants, and their brothers, and children, and kinsmen, and grandchildren with [their] wives and with [their] children and with all [their] movable property, and with [their] standing grain and with threshed grain, . . . to those people from whom they fled, on the basis on the census books, without any statute of limitations. Henceforth no one ever shall receive others' peasants and . . . retain them under himself.

10. If someone after this royal Law Code proceeds to receive and retain under himself fugitive peasants, and landless peasants, and their children, and brothers, and kinsmen; and hereditary estate owners and service landholders demand those fugitive peasants of theirs from them [in a trial]: after trial and investigation, and according to the census books, return those fugitive peasants and landless peasants of theirs to them with [their] wives and with [their] children, and with all their movable property, and with [their] standing grain, and with [their] threshed grain, and with [their] grain still in the ground, without any statute of limitations.

Concerning the length of the time they live under someone as fugitives after this royal Law Code: collect from those under whom they proceed to live 10 rubles each for any peasant per year for the sovereign's taxes and the service landholder's incomes. Give [the money] to the plaintiffs whose peasants and landless peasants they are.

11. If someone proceeds to petition the sovereign against someone about such fugitive peasants and landless peasants; and those peasants and their fathers are not registered in the cadastral books under either the plaintiff or the defendant, but those peasants are registered under the plaintiff or the defendant in the census books of the past years 1645/46 and 1646/47: on the basis of the census books, return those peasants and landless peasants to that person under whom they are registered in the census books.

12. If a peasant's daughter of marriageable age flees from someone, from an hereditary estate or from a service landholding, after this royal decree; and while

a fugitive she marries someone's limited service contract slave or a peasant; or after this royal decree someone entices a peasant's daughter of marriageable age, and having enticed [her], marries her to his own limited service contract slave, or peasant, or landless peasant; and that person from whom she fled proceeds to petition the sovereign about her; and it is established . . . conclusively at trial and investigation that that unmarried young woman fled, or was enticed away: return her to that person from whom she fled, along with her husband and with her children, which children she bore by that husband. Do not return her husband's movable property with her.

13. If that fugitive unmarried young woman marries someone's slave or peasant who is a widower; and prior [to his marriage] to her, that husband of hers had children by his first wife: do not return those first children of her husband to the plaintiff. They shall remain with that person in whose possession they were born into slavery or into peasantry.

14. If a plaintiff proceeds to sue for stolen property along with that fugitive unmarried young woman [which she allegedly stole when she fled]: grant him a trial for that. After trial compile the decree that is necessary.

15. If a peasant widow flees from someone; and her husband had been registered in the cadastral or allotment books, and in extracts [from them], or in any other documents among the peasants or the landless peasants [living] under that person from whom she fled; and having fled, that peasant woman marries someone's limited service contract slave or peasant: return that peasant widow with her [new] husband to that service landholder under whom her first husband had been registered in the cadastral or census books, or in the extracts, and in any other documents.

16. If the first husband of that widow is not registered [as living] under that person from whom she fled in the cadastral and census books and in any other documents: that widow shall live under that person whose slave or peasant she marries.

17. If a peasant or landless peasant flees from someone; and in flight he marries his daughter of marriageable age or a widow to someone's limited service contract slave, or to a peasant, or to a landless peasant [living under] that person to whom he flees; and later on after trial it becomes necessary to return that fugitive peasant with [his] wife and with [his] children to that person from whom he fled: return that fugitive peasant or landless peasant to his former service landholder, together with his son-in-law to whom he had married his daughter [while] in flight. If that son-in-law of his has children by his first wife: do not hand over those first children of his to the plaintiff.

18. If such a fugitive peasant or landless peasant, while in flight marries his daughter to someone's limited service contract slave, or hereditary slave, or peasant, or landless peasant [registered under] another service landholder or hereditary estate owner: return that peasant's daughter who was married while in flight, along with her husband, to the plaintiff.

19. If a service landholder or estate owner proceeds to discharge from his service landholding or from his hereditary estate, or someone's bailiffs and elders proceed to discharge, peasant daughters of marriageable age or widows to marry someone's slaves or peasants: they shall give such peasant daughters, women of

marriageable age and widows, manumission documents signed by their own hands, or by their spiritual fathers [local clergy], in case of a future dispute.

Collect the fee for permitting such peasant daughters to marry peasants of another lord by mutual agreement. Concerning that which someone collects for the marriage departure fee: write that explicitly in the manumission documents.

20. If any people come to someone on [his] hereditary estate and service landholding and say about themselves that they are free; and those people desire to live under them as peasants or landless peasants: those people whom they approach shall interrogate them—what kind of free people are they? And where is their birth place? And under whom did they live? And whence did they come? And are they not someone's fugitive slaves, and peasants, and landless peasants? And do they have manumission documents?

If they say that they do not have manumission documents on their person: service landholders and hereditary estate owners shall find out about such people accurately, whether they really are free people. Having investigated accurately, bring them in the same year for registration to the Service Land Chancellery in Moscow; Kazan-area residents and residents of Kazan by-towns shall bring them to Kazan; Novgorodians and residents of the Novgorodian by-towns shall bring them to Novgorod; Pskovians and residents of the Pskov by-towns shall bring them to Pskov. [Chancellery officials] in the Service Land Chancellery and governors in the provincial towns shall interrogate such free people on that subject and shall record their testimonies accurately.

If it becomes necessary to give those people who are brought in for registration, on the basis of their testimony under interrogation, as peasants to those people who brought them in for registration: order those people to whom they will be given as peasants to affix their signatures to the testimonies of those people after they have been taken.

21. If an estate owner or a service landholder brings in for registration the person who approached him without having checked accurately, and they proceed to take such people in as peasants: return such people as peasants to plaintiffs after trial and investigation, and according to the census books, along with [their] wives, and with [their] children, and with [their] movable property.

Concerning [what shall be exacted] from those people who take in someone else's peasant or landless peasant without checking accurately: collect for those years, however, many [the peasant] lived under someone, 10 rubles per year for the sovereign's taxes and for the incomes of the hereditary estate owner and service landholder because [of this rule]: without checking accurately, do not receive someone else's [peasant].

22. Concerning peasant children who proceed to deny their fathers and mothers: torture them.

23. If people of all ranks, desiring to bind under themselves others' fugitive peasants and landless peasants as their own, take loan documents or loan notes on them for a large [crop] loan; and those fugitive peasants and landless peasants are returned to someone after trial and investigation; and they [who gave the loans] proceed to petition against those people [to whom the peasants were returned] for that [crop] loan on the basis of those loan notes and loan documents: reject those people who have such [crop] loan notes and loan documents. Do not grant them

a trial on the basis of those [crop] loan documents or of any other documents. Do not believe those loan documents and [crop] loan notes.

Take those notes and loan documents from them to the chancellery and register [them] in the books. Return those fugitive peasants and landless peasants with the entire [crop] loan to [their] old estate owners and service landholders.

Concerning those people from whom those fugitive peasants or landless peasants are taken: reject [their claims] for that [crop] loan [because of this rule]: do not receive others' peasants and landless peasants, and do not give them a [crop] loan.

24. Concerning brothers, and children, and kinsmen of their peasants [living on the lands] of hereditary estate owners and service landholders who are registered in the census books in households together with their fathers and kinsmen; and after the census they split up and proceeded to live by themselves in their own households: do not place those households in the category of concealed households, and do not call them additional households, and do not register them in the Service Land Chancellery, because they are registered together with their fathers and kinsmen in the census books. . . .

25. Concerning people of all ranks who proceed to sue someone for their own fugitive peasants and for their peasant movable property, and they demand sums of 50 rubles and more in their claim[s] for such peasant movable property; and someone proceeds to sue someone for his own fugitive peasants, but he does not state the peasant movable property precisely in the plea, how much of what kinds of property, and the price of it; and the defendant does not testify that those peasants are [living] under him, and it becomes necessary [to resolve the case by] an oath: place [under the cross] 4 rubles per head for those peasants, as [demanded in] the plea; and for unspecified movable property, [place] 5 rubles for each [lot]; for large quantities of movable property, resolve [the case] by a trial.

26. If a defendant does not deny [that fugitive] peasants [are living under him], but testifies about the movable property that that peasant came to him without any movable property; but the plaintiff testifies that his peasant came to that defendant of his with movable property; but he does not state in his plea how much of what kinds of movable property that peasants of his had, or the value of that peasant movable property; and it also becomes necessary [to resolve the case by] an oath: place 5 rubles per lot of undescribed peasant movables under the cross. Having taken the peasants from the defendant, return them to the plaintiff.

27. If someone at a trial denies [retaining] someone's peasant and takes an oath on the matter; but later on that peasant, whom he denied under oath, appears on his property: having taken that peasant from him, return him to the plaintiff with all the movable property as [demanded] in the plea. Inflict a severe punishment on him for the offense that he kissed the cross not in accordance with the truth, beat him with the knout around the market places for three days so that it will become known to many people why the decreed punishment is being inflicted on him. Having beaten him with the knout around the market places for three days, imprison him for a year. Henceforth do not believe him in any matter, and do not grant him a trial in any cases against anyone.

28. Concerning defendants who do not deny having possession of peasants at trial, and after trial it becomes necessary, having taken such peasants from the defendant, to return them to the plaintiff: return such peasants as peasants to the

plaintiffs with [their] wives and with [their] children, even though the children of those fugitive peasants are not registered in the cadastral books, but are living together with their father and mother, and not in separate households.

29. Concerning defendants who at a trial proceed to deny [having possession of] fugitive peasants and their peasant movable property; and later on they testify under oath that they do have those peasants; and they proceed to return them to the plaintiffs, but as previously they deny having the movable property: order that peasant movable property exacted from them and give it to the plaintiffs without taking an oath because at trial they denied everything concerning both people and property, but later they returned the peasants, but they want to reap the benefits from their property themselves.

30. Concerning peasants and landless peasants who are registered in the cadastral books, or in allotment books, or in records of land transfers, and in extracts [from these books as living] under service landholders and hereditary estate owners separately on their service lands and hereditary estate lands: those service landholders and hereditary estate owners shall not move their peasants from their service lands to their hereditary estate lands. They shall not thereby lay waste their service landholdings.

31. If some service landholders and hereditary estate owners proceed to move their peasants from their service lands to their hereditary estate lands; and subsequently their service landholdings are given to any other service landholders; and those new service landholders proceed to petition the sovereign about those peasants who were moved from the service lands to the hereditary estate lands [and they ask] that such peasant be returned from the hereditary estate lands to the service lands from which they were moved: return those peasants from the hereditary estate lands to the service lands for those new service landholders with all their peasant movable property, and with [their] standing grain and with [their] threshed grain.

32. If someone's peasants and landless peasants proceed to hire themselves out to labor for someone: those peasants and landless peasants shall hire themselves out to labor for people of all ranks voluntarily with written documents or without written documents.

Those people to whom they hire themselves out to labor shall not take indentures, and [crop] loan notes, and limited service slavery contracts on them, and shall not bind them to themselves by any means.

When those hirelings have completed laboring for them, they shall release them . . . without any restraint.

33. Concerning slaves and peasants who flee across the frontier from service landholders and from hereditary estate owners of all ranks and from the border towns; and, having been across the frontier and returning from across the frontier, they do not want to live with their own old service landholders and hereditary estate owners, [and] they proceed to request their freedom: having interrogated those fugitive slaves and peasants, return them to their old service landholders and hereditary estate owners from whom they fled. Do not grant them freedom.

34. Concerning slaves and peasants who flee across the frontier to the Swedish and [Polish-] Lithuanian side from any hereditary estate owners and service landholders who have been granted service landholdings in the frontier towns; and

across the frontier they marry similarly fugitive older women and young women of marriageable age [who belong to] different service landholders; and having gotten married, they return from across the frontier to their own old service landholders and hereditary estate owners; and, when they return, those old service landholders of theirs proceed to petition the sovereign, one about the young woman of marriageable age or about the older woman, [stating] that his peasant woman married that fugitive peasant; and his defendant proceeds to testify that his peasant married that fugitive young woman or the older woman across the frontier while a fugitive: at trial and investigation, grant them lots [that is, flip a coin] on the question of those fugitive slaves and peasants of theirs. Whoever gets the lot, that one [shall get the couple and] shall pay a 5-ruble marriage departure fee for the young woman, or for the older woman, or for the man because they were both fugitives across the frontier.

## Archpriest Avvakum Describes His Struggle for the Lord, ca. 1673

We journeyed out of Dauriia, and the food ran low. And with the brethren . . . I entreated God, and Christ gave us a Siberian stag, a huge beast. With this [for food] we managed to sail [down river] to Lake Baikal. Sable hunters, Russians, had gathered in a camp by the lake; they were fishing. The good souls were glad to see us. . . . Looking at us they wept, the dear souls, and looking at them we wept too. They heaped us with food, as much as we needed; they carted up about forty fresh sturgeon in front of me, and themselves said, "There you are, Father, God put them in our seines for you; take them all!" Bowing to them and blessing the fish, I commanded that they take them back again: "What do I need so many for?"

We stayed with them awhile and then, taking a small provision near our need, we fixed the boat, rigged up a sail, and set out across the lake. The wind quit us on the lake, so we rowed with oars—the lake's not so almighty wide there, maybe eighty or a hundred versts.[1] When we put into shore, a squall blew up and it was a hard pull finding a place to land because of the waves. Around it the mountains were high and the cliffs of rock, fearfully high; twenty thousand versts and more I've dragged myself, and I've never seen their like anywhere.[2] Along their summits are halls and turrets, gates and pillars, stone walls and courtyards, all made by God. Onions grow there and garlic, bigger than the Romanov onion and uncommonly

---

From K. N. Brostrom, trans. and ed. *Archpriest Avvakum: The Life, Written by Himself*, Michigan Slavic Translations No. 4, 1979, pp. 76–94. Reprinted by permission of The University of Michigan Slavic Publications.

1. A Russian *versta* is equivalent to .66 of a mile or 1.06 kilometers.—Ed.
2. "Twenty thousand versts and more": Avvakum refers to the whole length of his journey from Moscow into Siberia and back between 1653 and 1664, a total of more than 13,000 miles!—Ed.

sweet. Hemp grows there too in the care of God, and in the courtyards are beautiful flowers, most colorful and good-smelling. There's no end to the birds, to the geese and swans—like snow they swim on the lake. In it are fish, sturgeon and taimen salmon, sterlet and amul salmon, whitefish, and many other kinds. The water is fresh, but huge seals and sea lions live in it. . . . The lake swarms with fish. The sturgeon and taimen salmon are fat as can be; you can't fry them in a pan—there'd be nothing but fat left! And all this has been done for man through Jesus Christ our Light, so that finding peace he might lift up his praise to God. "But man is like to vanity; his days are as a shadow that passeth away."[3] He cavorts like a goat, he puffs himself out like a bubble, he rages like a lynx, he craves food like a snake; gazing at the beauty of his neighbor he neighs like a colt; he deceives like a devil; when he's gorged himself he sleeps, forgetting his office; he doesn't pray to God; he puts off repentance to his old age and then disappears. I don't know where he goes, whether into the light or into the darkness. Judgment Day will reveal it for each of us. Forgive me, I have sinned worse than all men.

After this I sailed into Russian towns, and I meditated about the Church, that I "could prevail nothing, but that rather a tumult was made." Sitting there feeling heavy at heart, I pondered: "What shall I do? Preach the Word of God or hide out somewhere? For I am bound by my wife and children." And seeing me downcast, the Archpriestess approached in a manner most seemly, and she said unto me, "Why are you heavy at heart, my lord?" And in detail did I acquaint her with everything: "Wife, what shall I do? The winter of heresy is here. Should I speak out or keep quiet? I am bound by all of you!" And she said to me, "Lord a'mercy! What are you saying, Petrovich? I've heard the words of the Apostle—you were reading them yourself: 'Art thou bound unto a wife? seek not to be loosed. Art thou loosed from a wife? seek not a wife.' I bless you together with our children. Now stand up and preach the Word of God like you used to and don't grieve over us. As long as God deigns, we'll live together, and when we're separated, don't forget us in your prayers. Christ is strong, and he won't abandon us. Now go on, get to the church, Petrovich, unmask the whoredom of heresy!" Well sir, I bowed low to her for that, and shaking off the blindness of a heavy heart I began as before to preach and teach the Word of God about the towns and everywhere, and yet again did I unmask the Nikonian heresy with boldness.

I wintered in Eniseisk [1662–1663], and after a summer of sailing, I again wintered in Tobolsk [1663–1664]. And on the way to Moscow, in all the towns and villages, in churches and marketplaces I was ashouting, preaching the Word of God, and teaching, and unmasking the mummery of the godless. Then I arrived in Moscow. Three years I journeyed from Dauriia, and going there I dragged along five years against the current. They carried me ever to the east, right into the middle of native tribes and their camps. There's much could be said about this! Time and again I was even in the natives' hands. On the Ob, that mighty river,

---

3. From Psalm 144:4. Avvakum frequently quotes from or paraphrases the Bible; references will not be identified hereafter.—Ed.

they massacred twenty Christians before my eyes, and after thinking over me some, they let me go altogether. Again on the Irtysh River a group of them was lying in ambush for a [boatful] of our people from Berezov. Not knowing this I sailed toward them, and drawing near I put in to shore. They leaped around us with their bows. Well sir, I stepped out and hugged them like they were monks, and myself said, "Christ is with me, and with you too." And they started acting kindly towards me, and they brought their wives up to my wife. My wife likewise laid it on a bit, as flattery happens in this world, and the womenfolk warmed up too. We already knew that when the womenfolk are pleasant, then everything will be pleasant in Christ. The men hid their bows and arrows and started trading with me. I bought a pile of bearskins, yes and then they let me go. When I came to Tobolsk I told about this; people were amazed, since the Tatars and Bashkirs were warring all over Siberia then. And I, not choosing my way and hoping in Christ, I had journeyed right through the middle of them. I arrived in Verkhoturie [on the border of Russia and Siberia], and my friend Ivan Bogdanovich Kamynin was amazed at me: "How did you get through, Archpriest?" And I said, "Christ carried me through, and the most immaculate Mother of God led me. I fear no one; only Christ do I fear."

Afterwards I journeyed to Moscow; like unto an angel of the Lord was I received by the Sovereign and boyars—everyone was glad to see me. I dropped in on Fedor Rtishchev [a pious boyar]; he leaped out of his chamber to greet me, received my blessing, and started talking on and on—three days and nights he wouldn't let me go home, and then he announced me to the Tsar. The Sovereign commanded that I be brought then and there to kiss his hand, and he spoke charitable words: "Are you living in health, Archpriest? So God has ordained that we see one another again." And in answer I kissed and pressed his hand and said myself, "The Lord lives and my soul lives, my Sovereign and Tsar, but what's ahead will be as God deigns." And he sighed, the dear man, and went where he had to. And there were some other things, but why go on and on? That's all past now. He ordered me put in the monastery guest house in the Kremlin, and when his train passed my lodging, often he'd bow nice and low to me, and himself say, "Bless me and pray for me." And another time on horseback he took his cap off to me . . . and he dropped it. He used to lean out of his carriage to see me. Later all the boyars after him started bowing and scraping too: "Archpriest, bless us and pray for us!" How, sir, can I help but feel sorry for that Tsar and those boyars? It's a pity, yes it is! You see how good they were. Yes, and even now they're not wicked to me. The devil is wicked to me, but all men are good to me. They were ready to give me a place wherever I wanted, and they called me to be their confessor, that I might unite with them in the faith. But I counted all this as dung and I gain Christ, being mindful of death, even as all this doth vanish away.

For lo, most terribly was it announced to me in Tobolsk, in a light sleep: "Beware, lest thou be sundered from me." I leaped up and fell down before the icon in great fear, and myself said, "O Lord, my God, I won't go where they chant in the new way." I had been at Matins in the Cathedral Church . . . and there, in that church, I had played along with their fool's tricks before lords of the realm. What's more, after my arrival in Moscow I had watched the division of the Host two or three times while standing by the credence table in the sanctuary, and I had cursed them, but as I got used to going I left off cursing.[4] I was just about stung by that stinger, the spirit of the Antichrist! And that's why Christ our Light scared me, and said unto me, "After so great a suffering, dost thou wish to perish? Take heed lest I cut thee asunder!" So I didn't go to the service, but was served dinner at a prince's instead, and I acquainted them with all this in detail. . . . [T]hat good soul Prince Ivan Andreevich Khilkov, started to weep. And was it for me, accursed man, to forget the abundance of God's benefactions?

Once during the winter in Dauriia I was hurrying . . . across the ice of a lake toward a fishing spot, to my children.[5] Snow's not found there, but the great frosts thrive, and the ice freezes thick, close to the thickness of a man. I was thirsty, and so almighty wearied was I from thirst I couldn't walk any more. It was in the middle of the lake—about eight versts wide it was—and no way to get any water. Lifting my eyes to Heaven I began to speak: "O Lord, who brought forth water from a rock in the desert for thy people, for thirsting Israel, then and now thou art! Give me to drink by those means which thou knowest, my Master and my God!" Ah, woe is me! I don't know how to pray! For the sake of the Lord, forgive me! Who am I? A dead dog! The ice started to crack in front of me; it parted this way and that across the entire lake, and then came back together again. A great mountain of ice rose up, and as everything was settling down I stood in the customary place, and lifting my eyes to the east I bowed down twice or thrice, calling upon the name of the Lord in sparing words from the depths of my heart. God left me a small hole in the ice, and falling down I drank my fill. And I wept and rejoiced, thanking God. Then the icehole closed and I arose, bowed to the Lord, and again hurried off across the ice where I had to go, to my children.

And it was often that way with me at other times during my wanderings. On the move, whether I was dragging a dogsled, or fishing, or cutting firewood in the forest, or doing something else, at those times I still recited my Office, Vespers and Matins or the Canonical Hours—whatever. But if it was awkward around other people and we had made camp, and my comrades weren't getting along with me and didn't like my rule, and I hadn't managed it on the move, I'd step away from them, down a mountain or into a forest, and do it short and sweet. I would strike the earth with my head, and sometimes there were tears, and that's how I supped. But if the others were getting along with me, I'd place the folding icons against their props and say a short little Office; some prayed with me, others boiled their porridge. And traveling by sledge on Sabbath days I chanted the entire church service at resting places, and on ordinary days I chanted riding in a sledge. And there were times I chanted while riding on the Sabbath too. When it was most awkward, I still grumbled some, if only a bit. For as the hungering body desireth to eat and the thirsting body to drink, so doth the soul desire spiritual sustenance, my Father Epifany.[6] Neither famine of bread nor thirst for water destroys a man; but a great famine it is for a man to live, not praying to God.

---

4. Avvakum refers to the preparation of the communion elements, a rite that had been altered by the Nikonian reforms.—Ed.
5. Avvakum and Anastasiia had at least eight children, two of whom died as babies in Siberia.—Ed.
6. Epifany was Avvakum's loyal companion and confessor in Pustozersk.—Ed.

There was a time in the land of Dauriia, Father—if you . . . will not be wearied by the listening, sinner that I am, I will acquaint you with these things—there was a time that I broke down in my rule from feebleness and terrible hunger. Hardly any was left, only the evening psalms and the Compline and the Prime. But more than that there wasn't. So I dragged along like a little old beast, grieving about my rule but not able to hold to it. You see how weak I'd got! Once I went to the forest for firewood, and with me gone my wife and children sat on the ground by the fire, my daughter with her mother—both were weeping. Agrafena, my poor, suffering darling, was still a little girl then. I came back out of the forest. The babe was crying her heart out. Her tongue was tied, she couldn't got a word out, just sat there mewling at her mother. Her mother was looking at her and weeping. I caught my breath and with a prayer stepped up to the child, and said unto her: "In the name of the Lord I command you: speak with me. Why are you weeping?" And jumping up and bowing she started speaking plainly: "I don't know who it was locked up inside me, Father, a bright little thing, but he held me by the tongue and wouldn't let me talk to Mommy, and that's why I was crying. But he said to me, 'Tell your father that he'd better keep his rule like before, so you'll all journey back to Russia. But if he doesn't start keeping his rule—and he's been pondering this himself—then you'll all die here, and he'll die with you.'" Yes, and a few other things were said to her at that time too: how there'd be an edict about us, and how many of our old friends we'd find in Russia. And thus did it all come to pass.
. . .

I will speak again about my life in Moscow. They saw that I was not joining them, so the Sovereign ordered [boyar] Rodion Streshnev to convince me to keep quiet. I eased his mind: "The Tsar is invested by God, and here he's been good as gold to me"—I expected he might come around little by little. And lo and behold, on St. Simeon's Day they vowed I would be placed in the printing house to correct books. And I was mighty happy; for me this was needful, better even than being a confessor. He showed his favor and sent me ten rubles, the [Tsaritsa] likewise sent ten rubles. . . . Rodion Streshnev sent ten rubles too, while our great and good old friend Fedor Rtishchev, he ordered his treasurer to slip sixty rubles into my bonnet. About others there's nothing more to say—everyone pushed and pulled something or other over. I lived all this time in the household of my light, my dear Feodosia Prokopevna Morozova, as she was my spiritual daughter; and her sister Princess Evdokiia Prokopevna was also my spiritual daughter. My lights, Christ's martyrs! And I was always visiting the home of our dear departed Anna Petrovna Miloslavskaia.[7] And I went to Fedor Rtishchev's to wrangle with the apostates.

And so I lived this way near half a year, and I saw that these ecclesiastical triflings "could prevail nothing but that rather a tumult was made," so I started grumbling again, and even wrote a little something to the Tsar, that he should seek after the ancient piety and defend from heresies our common mother, the Holy Church, and that he should invest the patriarchal throne with an Orthodox

---

7. The Morozova sisters, both of the high nobility, eventually were executed for following the Old Belief. Anna Miloslavskaia was related to Tsar Aleksei's first wife.—Ed.

shepherd instead of that wolf and apostate Nikon, the villainous heretic! And when I had prepared the letter, I fell grievously ill, so I sent it to the Tsar in his carriage by my spiritual son Fedor, the fool in Christ, [who was later] hanged . . . on the gallows. With boldness he stepped up to the Tsar's carriage with the letter, and the Tsar ordered him locked up . . . , still with the letter. He didn't know it was mine. But later, after taking the letter from him, he ordered him released. And Fedor, our dear departed, after staying with me awhile, he came before the Tsar again in a church, and there that blessed fool started in with his silly pranks. And the Tsar, being angered, ordered him sent to the Chudovskii Monastery [in the Kremlin]. There Pavel the Archimandrite [abbot] put him in irons, but by God's will the chains on his legs fell to pieces, before witnesses. And he, our light, our dear departed, he crawled into the hot oven in the bakery after the bread was taken out and he sat there, his bare backside against its bottom, and gathered the crumbs and ate them. So the monks were in terror, and they told the Archimandrite, who is now the Metropolitan Pavel. And he acquainted the Tsar with this, and the Tsar came to the monastery and ordered him set free in honor. And again he came back to me.

And from that time the Tsar started grieving over me. It wasn't so nice now that I had started to speak again; it had been nice for them when I kept quiet, but that didn't sit right with me. So the bishops started to buck and kick at me like goats, and they schemed to banish me from Moscow again, as many servants of Christ were coming to me, and comprehending the truth they stopped going to their worship with its seductive snares. And there was a judgment from the Tsar for me. "The bishops are complaining about you," he said, "you've started to empty the churches. Go into exile again!" The Boyar . . . Saltykov told me this. And so we were taken off to Mezen.[8] Good people started to give us a plenty of this and that in the name of Christ, but it was all left behind. They only took me with my wife and children and the help. But passing through towns I again taught the people of God, and those others I exposed for what they are, the motley beasts! And they brought us to Mezen [in the fall of 1665].

After keeping us there a year and a half, they took me to Moscow again alone. My two sons Ivan and Prokopy also journeyed with me, but the Archpriestess and the rest all stayed at Mezen. After bringing me to Moscow [in 1666] they took me under guard to the Pafnutev Monastery. And a message came there; over and over they kept saying the same thing: "Must you go on and on tormenting us? Join with us, dear old Avvakum!" I spurned them like devils, but they wouldn't stop plaguing me. I blistered them good in a statement I wrote there and sent along with Kozma, the Deacon of Iaroslavl and a scribe in the patriarchal court. But Kozma, I don't know of what spirit that man is. In public he tried to win me over, but on the sly he encouraged me, speaking so: "Archpriest! Don't abandon the ancient piety! You'll be a great man in Christ when you endure to the end. Don't pay attention to us, we are perishing!" And I said in answer that he should come again to Christ. And he said, "It's impossible. Nikon's tied me hand and foot!" Putting it simply, he'd renounced Christ before Nikon and just that fast he couldn't stand on his

---

8. A settlement located about halfway between Moscow and Pustozersk.—Ed.

own two feet, poor man. I wept and blessed him, the miserable soul. More than that there was nothing I could do for him. God knows what will become of him.

After keeping me in Pafnutev for ten weeks in chains, they took me again to Moscow, and in the Chamber of the Cross [in the patriarch's palace, in the Kremlin] the bishops disputed with me, then led me into the great cathedral, and after the Transposition of the Host they sheared the Deacon Fedor and me, and then damned us, but I damned them in return.[9] Almightly lively it was during that Mass! And after keeping us awhile in the Patriarch's Court, they carried us away at night to . . . the Monastery of St. Nikola. And those enemies of God cut off my beard. But what do you expect? They're wolves for a fact, they don't pity the sheep! Like dogs they tore at it, leaving me one tuft on my forehead like a Pole. They didn't take us to the monastery by the road but through marsh and mire so no one would get wind of it. They saw themselves they were acting like fools, but they wouldn't abandon their folly. Befogged by the devil they were, so why grumble at them? If they hadn't done it, someone else would have. The time of which it is written has come; according to the Gospel: "It must needs be that offenses come." And another apostle hath said: "It is impossible but that offenses will come; but woe unto him through whom they come!" Look you, listener: Our misery is unavoidable; we cannot pass it by! To this end doth God suffer the visitation of offenses, so there might be an Elect, so they might be burned, might be purified, so those tested by tribulation might be made manifest among you. Satan besought God for our radiant Russia so he might turn her crimson with the blood of martyrs. Good thinking, devil, and it's good enough for us—to suffer for the sake of Christ our Light!

They kept me at St. Nikola's for seventeen weeks in a freezing cell. There I had a heavenly visitation; read of it in my letter to the Tsar, you'll find it there. And the Tsar came to the monastery. He walked around my dungeon some, groaned, and left the monastery again. It seems from this he was sorry for me, but God willed it so. When they sheared me, there was great turmoil between them and the late [Tsaritsa].[10] She stood up for us then, the dear soul, and later on she saved me from execution. Much could be said about this! God will forgive them! I'm not asking that they answer for my suffering now, nor in the age to come. It behooves me to pray for them, for the living and for those resting in eternity. The devil set the breach between us, but they were always good to me. Enough of this! . . .

Later they bore me away again to the Pafnutev Monastery, where they kept me locked up in a dark cell and in fetters nigh onto a year [September 1666–May 1667]. Here the cellarer Nikodim was good to me at first. But then, it seems the poor man used some of that tobacco . . . afterwards seized in the house of the Metropolitan of Gaza, along with a domra and other secret monastic doodads used in merrymaking. Forgive me, I have sinned, it's none of my business. . . .[11]

---

9. Shearing the hair of Deacon Fedor and Archpriest Avvakum symbolized their loss of clerical status.—Ed.

10. Tsaritsa Maria Miloslavskaia, first wife of Tsar Aleksei, died in 1669.—Ed.

11. The "Metropolitan of Gaza" (Paisios Ligarides), a visiting Greek cleric of dubious reputation, was among those who voted to condemn Avvakum at the Moscow church council of 1666–1667.—Ed.

On Easter I begged respite for the festival from this cellarer Nikodim, that he order the doors opened for me to sit a spell on the threshold. But he heaped curses on me and refused savagely, for no reason. Afterwards, coming into his cell, he was taken mortally ill. He was anointed with oil and given the Sacrament, and once and for all he stopped breathing. That was on Easter Monday. During the night, towards Tuesday, a man in my image and in radiant vestments came to him with a censer and censed him, and taking him by the hand raised him up, and he was healed. And that night he rushed to me in the dungeon with the servitor, and as he came he was saying, "Blessed is this cloister, for such are the dungeons it possesses! Blessed is this dungeon, for such are the sufferers it possesses! And blessed are the fetters!" And he fell down before me, clutched my chain, and said, "Forgive me! For the sake of the Lord, forgive me! I have sinned before God and before you: I gave you offense, and God punished me for it." And I said, "How punished? Tell me of it." And he again, "But you yourself came and censed me, you showed me your favor and raised me! Why hide it?" The servitor standing there too said, "My lord and father, I led you out of the cell by the arm and then bowed down to you, and you came back this-away." And I charged him not to tell people of this mystery. And he asked of me how he should live henceforth in Christ: "Or do you order me to abandon everything and go into the desert?" I chastened him a bit and didn't order him to abandon his stewardship, only that he should keep the ancient traditions of the Holy Fathers, even if on the sly. And bowing he went away to his own cell, and in the morning at table he told all the brethren. Fearlessly and boldly did people trudge over to visit me, and they begged for my blessings and prayers. But I taught them from Holy Writ and healed them with the Word of God. At that time some few enemies made peace with me there. Alas! When will I leave this age of vanity? It is written: "Woe unto you when all men shall speak well of you." In truth I do not know how to live to the end; there are no good works in me, but God glorified me! But this he knows, it's as he wills.

Our dear departed Fedor, my poor strangled one, journeyed to me there on the sly with my children, and he asked of me, "How do you say I should go about, the old way in a long shirt, or should I don other clothes? The heretics are hunting for me and want to put me to death. I was in Riazan, under guard in the court of the Archbishop," he said, "and he, Ilarion, he tortured me no end—it was a rare day he didn't flog me with whips; he kept me fettered in irons, forcing me toward that new Sacrament of the Antichrist.[12] I got weak, and at night I'd weep and pray, saying, 'O Lord, if thou dost not deliver me, they will defile me and I will perish. What then wilt thou do for me?'" And much did he weep as he talked. "And lo," he said, "suddenly, Father, all the irons fell from me with a crash, and the door unlocked and opened of itself. So I bowed down to God and got out of there. I came up to the gates, and the gates were open! And I headed along the highroad straight for Moscow. When it started to get light, here came the hunters on horses!

---

12. Ilarion, archbishop of Riazan, a town east of Moscow, required that Fedor take communion according to the reformed (Nikonian) rite.—Ed.

Three men raced past, but they didn't catch sight of me. I was hoping in Christ and kept trudging along. Pretty soon they came riding back toward me barking, 'He took off, the son of a whore! Where can we nab him?' And again they rode past without seeing me. So now I've trudged over here to ask whether I should go on back there and be tortured or put on other clothes and live in Moscow?" And I, sinner that I am, I directed him to put on the clothes. But I didn't manage to bury him outside the reach of the heretics' hands; they strangled him at Mezen, hanging him on the gallows. Eternal remembrance to him. . . . You have suffered for Christ! . . .

Uncommonly stern was the ascetic life of that Fedor. During the day he played the blessed fool, but all night long he was at prayer with tears. I knew many a good person, but never had I seen such an ascetic! He lived with me about half a year in Moscow—I was still feeble—the two of us stayed in a little back room. Most the time he'd lie down an hour or two, then get up; he'd toss off a thousand prostrations and then sit on the floor, or sometimes stand, and weep for maybe three hours. But even so I'd be lying down, sometimes asleep, but sometimes too feeble to move. When he had wept his fill and even more, he'd come over to me: "How long are you going to lie there like that, Archpriest? Get your wits about you, you're a priest, you know! How come you're not ashamed?" And I was very feeble, so he'd lift me up, saying, "Get up, sweet Father of mine, well come on, just drag yourself up somehow!" And he'd manage to stir some life into me. He'd tell me to recite the prayers sitting down, and he'd make the prostrations for me. A friend of my heart for certain! . . . [He] became my spiritual son as I was coming back from Siberia. In the church vestry, he'd come running in for prayer and say, "When you first come out of that frost into the warm, Father, it's no end burdensome just then." And his feet clattered across the bricks like frozen blocks. But by morning they didn't hurt once again. He had a Psalter from the new printings in his cell then; he still knew only a little bit about the innovations. And I told him about the new books in detail.[13] He grabbed the book and tossed it into the stove then and there, yes, and he damned all innovation. No end fiery was that faith of his in Christ! But why go on and on? As he began, so he ended. He didn't pass his radiant life in story-telling, not like me, accursed man. There's why he passed away in the odor of sanctity.

A fine man too was dear Afanasy, the good soul. My spiritual son he was; as a monk he was called Avraamy. The apostates baked him in their fire in Moscow, and like sweet bread was he yielded up to the Holy Trinity. Before he took the cowl he wandered about both summer and winter barefoot, wearing just a long shirt. Only he was a little gentler than Fedor, and a wee bit milder in his asceticism. He was a great lover of weeping—he'd walk and he'd weep. And if he was talking with someone, his words were quiet and even, like he was weeping. But Fedor was most zealous and active no end in the business of God. He endeavored to destroy

---

13. Eight editions of the Psalter (book of Psalms) containing Nikon's revisions were published between 1653 and 1663.—Ed.

and expose untruth no matter what. But leave them be! As they lived, so they passed away in our Lord Jesus Christ.

I will chat with you some more about my wanderings. When they brought me from the Pafnutev Monastery to Moscow [May 1667], they put me in a guesthouse, and after dragging me many a time to the Chudovskii Monastery, they stood me before the Ecumenical Council of Patriarchs.[14] And all of ours [senior Russian clergy] were sitting there too, like foxes. Much from Holy Writ did I say to the patriarchs; God opened my sinful lips and Christ put them to shame! They said to me at last, "Why are you so stubborn? All ours from Palestine—the Serbs, and Albanians, and Rumanians, and Romans, and Poles[15]—they all cross themselves with three fingers, but you stand there all alone in your stubbornness and cross yourself with two fingers. This is not seemly!" But in Christ did I answer them, after this manner: "Teachers of Christendom! Rome fell long ago and lies never to rise. The Poles perished with her; to the end were they enemies of Christians. And Orthodoxy has become motley in color even with you, from violation by Mahmet the Turk. We can't be surprised at you, you are enfeebled. Henceforth, come to us to learn! By the Grace of God we have autocracy. In our Russia before Nikon the Apostate, the Orthodox faith of devout princes and tsars was always pure and spotless, and the Church was not mutinous. That wolf Nikon, in league with the devil, betrayed us through this crossing with three fingers. But our first shepherds, just as they crossed themselves with two fingers, so did they bless others with two fingers according to the tradition of our Holy Fathers, Meletius of Antioch, and Theodoret the Blessed, Bishop of Cyrrhus, and Peter of Damascus, and Maksim the Greek. What is more, the wise Moscow Council [of 1551] during the reign of Tsar Ivan [IV] charged us to cross ourselves and to bless others by conforming our fingers in the manner taught by the Holy Fathers of the past, Meletius and the others. At that council in the time of Tsar Ivan were the Bearers of the Sign Gury and Varsonofy, the miracle workers of Kazan, and Filipp, and Abbot of Solovki—all Russian saints!"

And the patriarchs fell to thinking, but like a bunch of wolf whelps our Russians bounced up howling and began to vomit on their own Holy Fathers, saying, "They were stupid, our Russian saints had no understanding! They weren't learned people—why believe in them? They couldn't even read or write!" O holy God, how didst thou bear such great mortification of thy saints? As for me, poor man, it was bitter, but nothing could be done. I blistered them, I blistered them as much as I could, and at last I said unto them: "I am clean, and I shake off the dust clinging to my feet before you; according to that which is written: 'Better one who works the will of God than a multitude of the godless!'" So they started shouting at me even worse: "Seize him! Seize him! He has dishonored us all!" And they started

---

14. The church council of 1666–1667, meeting in a hall in the Kremlin, was attended by the Greek patriarchs of Antioch and Alexandria as well as other Greek and Russian senior clergy; Tsar Aleksei and the new patriarch of Moscow (replacing the deposed Nikon), Joasaph II, presided.—Ed.

15. Throwing in "Romans and Poles," both of course Roman Catholic, Avvakum seeks further to discredit his opponents.—Ed.

to shove me around and beat me—even the patriarchs threw themselves on me. There were about forty of them there, I expect—a mighty army for the Antichrist had come together! Ivan Uarov grabbed me and dragged me around some, and I shouted, "Stop it! Don't beat me!" So they all jumped back. And I began to speak to the Archimandrite interpreter: "Say to the [Greek] patriarchs: the Apostle Paul writes, 'For such an high priest became us, who is holy, harmless,' and so on; but you, after beating a man, how can you perform the liturgy?" So they sat down. And I walked over toward the doors and flopped down on my side: "You can sit, but I'll lie down," I said to them. So they laughed, "This archpriest's a fool! And he doesn't respect the patriarchs!" And I said to them, "We are fools for Christ's sake! Ye are honorable, but we are despised! Ye are strong, but we are weak!" Then the bishops again came over to me and started to speak with me about the Alleluia.[16] Christ gave me the words; I shamed the whore of Rome within them. . . . And Evfimei, the Cellarer of the Chudovskii Monastery, said, "You're right. There's nothing more for us to talk to you about." And they led me away in chains.

Afterwards the Tsar sent an officer with some musketeers, and they carried me off to the Sparrow Hills. There too they brought the priest Lazar and the monk and elder Epifany. Shorn and abused like peasants from the village they were, the dear souls! Let a man with sense take a look and he'd just weep looking at them. But let them endure it! Why grieve over them? Christ was better than they are, and he, our Light, he got the same from their forefathers Annas and Caiaphas. There's no reason to be surprised at men nowadays—they've got a pattern for acting so! We should grieve a bit for them, poor souls. Alas! you poor Nikonians! You are perishing from your wicked, unruly ways!

Then they led us away from the Sparrow Hills to the Andreevskii Monastery, and later to the Savvin Settlement [June 1667]. The troop of musketeers guarded us like brigands, even went with us to shit! Remember it, and you don't know whether to laugh or cry. How Satan had befogged them! Then to St. Nikola [monastery, again]; there the Sovereign sent Captain Iury Lutokhin to me for my blessing, and we talked much about this and that.

Afterwards they brought us again to Moscow . . . and took still more statements from us concerning Orthodoxy. The gentlemen of the bedchamber Artemon and Dementy were sent to me many a time, and they spoke to me the Tsar's words: "Archpriest, I know your pure and spotless and godly life, and I with the [Tsaritsa] and our children beg your blessing. Pray for us!" The messenger said this, bowing the while. And I will always weep for the Tsar; I'm mighty sorry for him. And again he said, "Please listen to me. Unite with the ecumenical [Greek] bishops, if only in some little thing." And I said to him, "Even if God deigns that I die, I will not unite with the apostates! You are my Tsar," I said, "but what business do they have with you? They lost their own tsar,[17] and now they come dragging in here to swallow you whole. I will not lower my arms from the heights of heaven,"

16. Avvakum refers to another of Nikon's innovations.—Ed.
17. Avvakum refers to the fall of Byzantium/Constantinople to the Turks, in 1453.—Ed.

said I, "till God gives you over to me!" And there were many such messages. This and that was said. Finally he said, "Wherever you may be, don't forget us in your prayers!" Even now, sinner that I am, I entreat God on his behalf as much as I can.[18]

Later, after mutilating my brethren but not me, they banished us to Pusto-zersk. . . .


## FURTHER READING

Samuel H. Baron, trans. and ed., *The Travels of Olearius in Seventeenth-Century Russia* (1967)

Paul Bushkovitch, *Religion in Seventeenth-Century Russia* (1992)

Robert O. Crummey, *Aristocrats and Servitors: The Boyar Elite in Russia, 1613–1689* (1983)

———, *The Formation of Muscovy 1304–1613* (1987)

———, *The Old Believers and the World of Antichrist, 1694–1855* (1970)

Nancy Shields Kollmann, *Kinship and Politics: The Making of the Muscovite Political System, 1345–1547* (1987)

———, "The Seclusion of Elite Muscovite Women," *Russian History* 10 (1983), 170–187

Richard Hellie, *Enserfment and Military Change in Muscovy* (1971)

———, *Slavery in Russia, 1450–1725* (1982)

Lindsey Hughes, *Sophia, Regent of Russia [1682–1689]* (1990)

Edward L. Keenan, "Muscovite Political Folkways," *Russian Review* 45 (1986), 115–181; 46 (1987), 157–197

Donald G. Ostrowski, "Church Polemics and Monastic Land Acquisition in Sixteenth-Century Muscovy," *Slavonic and East European Review* 64 (1986), 357–379

Daniel Rowland, "Did Muscovite Ideology Place Limits on the Power of the Tsar (1540s–1660s)?" *Russian Review* 49 (1990), 125–155

Serge Zenkovsky, ed., *Medieval Russia's Epics, Chronicles and Tales* (1974)

# The Eighteenth Century

The young tsarina, Catherine II.

CHAPTER 3

# The Era of
# Peter the Great

Imperial Russian history—the period of the Russian Empire—may be said to have begun formally on October 22, 1721, when in an elaborate public ceremony in St. Petersburg, the city he had founded (in 1703), Tsar Peter I formally accepted from his Senate (which he had founded in 1711) the title "Father of the Fatherland, All-Russian Emperor, Peter the Great" (see Documents below). Thereafter in all official documents the Russian ruler was styled "Emperor" or "Empress," "His" or "Her Imperial Majesty," and the state over which he or she ruled was called the "All-Russian Empire." Gradually such usage was adopted in their diplomatic relations by all the other states of the world, although in everyday usage both at home and abroad the Russian ruler was still often referred to by the traditional titles of "Tsar" or "Tsaritsa."

Behind these formalities lay substantive changes of enormous historical importance. In fact, the Senate's official act of 1721 conferring the Imperial title on Peter was inseparably linked with the simultaneous celebration of the end of the Northern War (1700–1721) with Sweden, then a major power in Europe. The war had begun badly for Russia; and in order to withstand Swedish invasion and then to secure control of the Baltic coastlands conquered from Sweden, Peter's government had been obliged to reform, sometimes radically, Russia's armed forces, economy, and state administration. The result was extensive political, economic, social, and even cultural modernization—that is, Europeanization (or Westernization)—in Russia, a program of sweeping change that was embodied in St. Petersburg itself, Russia's new capital and seaport built in European style on conquered Baltic land and inhabited from the beginning by numerous non-Russians (especially Finns and Germans) as well as Russians.

Historians differ on the nature, causes, and consequences of the Petrine reforms in Russia. Yet virtually all agree that Russia under Peter I became a major European power; that Petrine Russia underwent radical internal change; that Peter himself was a truly extraordinary ruler; and that Peter's reign (1689–1725) had a lasting impact on Russia and, indeed, the world.

## Essays

The first essay is by a leading Russian historian of the Petrine era, Evgeny Viktorovich Anisimov, a research scholar of the St. Petersburg branch of the Institute of History of the Russian Academy of Sciences (also founded by Peter I; see Documents). While conceding that much that Peter undertook in reforming Russia was necessary and even positive, at least in the short term, Dr. Anisimov focuses on how Peter's measures worked to inhibit the development of capitalism in Russia and to create a "totalitarian, military-bureaucratic, police state." He compares the ruler cult established or refurbished under Peter with the twentieth-century cult of Stalin, and suggests that Peter laid the foundations of the imperialist policies followed by all of his successors. Anisimov's overall analysis would seem to reflect visceral hostility to the recent Communist regime in Russia and may well be regarded by other historians as excessively negative. He largely ignores, for example, the beneficial aspects of Peter's promotion of European science, technology, art, and architecture in Russia, a point touched on in various of the documents printed below. Nevertheless, Anisimov's account of the Petrine achievement is solidly based in the factual history of the reign.

    In his essay, Anisimov also draws heavily on the classic account of Vasily Osipovich Kliuchevsky (1841–1911), who was professor of Russian history at Moscow University for more than thirty years. Kliuchevsky is still considered the single most influential historian of Russia, and his major writings, republished in the 1930s and the 1950s in the Soviet Union, are appearing again in a massive new Russian edition. The second essay, by an American specialist, discusses critically Kliuchevsky's influential interpretation of Peter the Great and offers something of an antidote to Anisimov's more recent essay.

## Peter I: Birth of the Empire

### E. V. Anisimov

We of the late twentieth century cannot fully grasp the disruptive effect of the Petrine reforms in Russia. In the nineteenth century, however, people saw this point more clearly. Here is what the historian M. P. Pogodin wrote (1841) about the importance of Peter the Great: "In his hands are gathered together all the threads of our national existence. Wherever we look we encounter this colossal figure, who casts his long shadow over our entire past and in fact blocks from view our earlier history, who at this very moment still holds us in his grasp, and who, it seems, will never fade from our view however far we progress into the future." Indeed, what Peter had created in Russia outlasted Pogodin's generation, as it did the generations following his. We need only think of the last general levy of military recruits in 1874—some 170 years after the first, ordered by Peter in 1705. Peter's

From E. V. Anisimov, "Petr I: Rozhdenie Imperii," Voprosy istorii, 1989 no. 7 (July), pp. 3–20. Translated by James Cracraft.

Senate lasted from 1711 until December 1917, or 206 years; the Synodal administration of the Orthodox church remained as he had established it for 197 years (1721 to 1918); the soul tax was abolished only in 1887, 163 years after he had introduced it (1724).

In other words, we can find few consciously created institutions in Russian history which lasted as long and which exercised as much influence on all aspects of the life of the people as those created by Peter. Still more, certain political principles and stereotypes elaborated or decisively confirmed under Peter endure to this day. . . . It therefore behooves succeeding generations of historians to consider anew the Petrine reforms in an effort to understand their impact on Russia's destiny.

I might begin by noting that among the many symbols of the Petrine era familiar to us from literature and art, that of the ship under sail with the skipper [Peter] standing on the bridge is especially apt—"that glorious skipper," in the words of the poet [Alexander] Pushkin [1799–1837], "who seized so powerfully the rudder of our ship of state." For Peter himself, such a ship represented more than a structure organized and thought out to the last detail, a material embodiment of rational thought. It symbolized, too, the ideal society, the best of the organizations so far devised by man in his eternal struggle with the elements. Here converged much of the thinking of the so-called Age of Reason, thinking which permeated the very air breathed by the European scholars and statesmen of Peter's time. These new ideas affirmed that science or experimental knowledge provided mankind with the most reliable means for mastering the forces of nature, and that the state was a purely human institution which rational beings could alter as they saw fit in pursuit of goals which they themselves had set.

The state is built like a house, taught Hobbes. Like a ship, we might add. This idea of the human, not divine, origin of the state gave birth to the notion that the state was an ideal instrument for the transformation of society, for the formation of virtuous subjects; that it was itself an ideal institution and one which could achieve the "common good." . . . Of course, it would be an exaggeration to say that Peter founded his empire on the ideas of the Age of Reason. Rather was it a matter of the powerful influence such ideas exerted on the practical policies of the great reformer. But neither should we ignore the fact that the tsar was personally acquainted with Leibniz, and knew well the works of Grotius and Pufendorf.[1] He ordered that Pufendorf's treatise *On the Duties of Man and the Citizen* be translated into Russian. All such details must be taken into account if we are adequately to appraise both the Petrine reforms and the tsar-transformer himself.

During Peter's active reign [1689–1725] Russia's economy took a great leap forward. Industry in particular advanced at an unprecedented pace: by 1725, at least 200

---

1. Gottfried Wilhelm von Leibniz (1646–1716) was a German philosopher and mathematician whom Peter personally met (1711) and with whom he corresponded on various projects. Hugo Grotius (1583–1645) was a Dutch jurist and statesman whose works laid the basis of international law. Samuel Pufendorf (1632–1699) was an influential German jurist, historian, and political theorist of the time.—Ed.

individual manufactories had arisen by comparison with the 15 to 20 in existence at the end of the seventeenth century. The most characteristic feature of this process was the leading role played by the autocratic state: its active involvement in all spheres of economic life. Such a role was conditioned by many factors.

The economic ideas of mercantilism, widespread in Europe and Russia at this time, taught that the survival of the state was dependent on the accumulation of capital through a favorable balance of trade—that is, by maximizing exports while minimizing imports. This doctrine in itself required state intervention in the econ-omy. Encouraging "beneficial" or "necessary" forms of industry and trade, from the state's point of view, went hand in hand with prohibiting or limiting "harmful" or "unnecessary" ones. Hoping to increase his country's might, Peter was scarcely indifferent to the ideas of mercantilism. And the notion of compulsion in economic policy coincided with the general principles of "forced progress" that he practiced in all his reforms.

Indeed, in Russian conditions the ideas of mercantilism served to ground the characteristic direction of domestic policy as a whole. Russian losses at the beginning of the Northern War [against Sweden, 1700–1721] powerfully stimulated state industrial construction and the state's intervention, more generally, in the economy. The buildup of numerous manufactories mainly of a military nature was undertaken not out of abstract economic considerations but in response to the immediate and dire necessity of providing for the army and navy. The extreme situation obtaining after the [Russian] defeat at Narva in 1700, which entailed the loss of Russia's artillery, necessitated the rearming and expansion of the army and dictated the character, tempo, and specific forms of industrial growth under Peter and of, more widely, his entire economic policy.

At the basis of his policy lay the notion of the state's directive role in the life of society as a whole, in the economy in particular. Disposing of huge financial and material resources, enjoying monopoly rights over the land and its natural wealth, and disregarding the property rights of the various social estates [sosloviia], the state took it upon itself to initiate the necessary industrialization. Proceeding from clearly understood interests and aims, the state dictated everything that was connected with the production and marketing of goods. The new state industrial system soon generated principles and methods of running the economy that were unknown to the Russia of earlier times and would remain in force for years to come.

A similar situation arose with respect to trade. While establishing its own industry the state also created (or, more exactly, greatly strengthened) its own commercial system, one that strove to maximize profits from goods destined both for sale within Russia and for export. The state thus took control of trade by primitive but very effective means: a monopoly on the procurement and marketing of certain goods was introduced while the range of such goods (salt, flax, leather, hemp, grain, tallow, wax, etc.) was constantly broadened. State monopolies, more-over, promoted arbitrary price rises for goods sold on the internal market and, more importantly, both limited and regulated the activities of merchants, since in the overwhelming majority of cases the right to sell the monopolized goods was given to a specially designated agent [otkupshchik]. This agent paid a large sum of money directly into the treasury and then strove to turn a profit at the expense of both suppliers and consumers, thus inflating prices and eliminating his possible competitors.

Indeed, the Petrine era was truly extortionate in the history of the Russian merchantry. A sharp increase in the direct taxes and various services due the treasury from the most prosperous sector of the urban population, like the forced formation of trading companies (judged by Peter the most suitable form of commercial organization for Russia), were only two of the exactions he imposed on the merchantry with the aim of raising as much money as possible for the state. Other such measures included the forced resettlement of merchants in St. Petersburg—for years it remained a poorly built frontier town—and the administrative regulation of when merchants could sell their goods, which goods they could sell and at which ports, and where, conversely, they were forbidden to do so. . . .

Such was the price paid by Russia's entrepreneurs for Peter's military victories. But the cost of these victories was shared by the rest of the population, too, with the greatest burden falling on the shoulders of the peasantry. The weight of dozens of taxes in money and kind, of military recruitment, of levies of laborers and horses, of heavy transport and quartering obligations, and of other such impositions destabilized the mass economy, leading to the impoverishment and flight of hundreds of thousands of peasants. An upsurge of brigandage and armed resistance, and the rebellion along the Don led by Bulavin [1707–1708], were among the consequences of the unremitting fiscal pressure on the peasantry.

Beginning in 1719, when the military threat had definitely receded in the west and Russia's successful conclusion of the Northern War was no longer in doubt, Peter significantly altered his economic policy. All monopolies on goods for export were de facto liquidated, and private industrial enterprise was encouraged. Mining rights were extended to everyone, native and foreigner alike, even if they infringed on feudal claims to the land where the minerals were found. The practice of transferring state enterprises, particularly those operating at a loss, to individual owners or to specially created companies now became common. The new owners were given numerous state incentives: interest-free loans, tax exemptions, and so on. Vital assistance to entrepreneurs came with the establishment in 1724 of a protective tariff—simultaneously lighter on exported goods of native manufacture, heavier on goods imported from abroad. . . .

There is, however, no reason to think that in changing his economic policy Peter intended to weaken the state's influence on the national economy, or that he thus unwittingly facilitated the development of the capitalist forms and means of production then widespread in western Europe. In essence, Peter changed his emphases, not his principles. Manufactories were in fact leased to individual entrepreneurs or companies on strictly defined terms, terms that could be altered as needed by the state, which retained the right to confiscate an enterprise if the terms were not carried out. The main obligation of entrepreneurs was the timely fulfillment of treasury orders; only such surpluses as remained thereafter could be sold on the open market. Then there were the central state organs created by Peter [beginning in 1718] to manage trade and industry: the College of Mines, the College of Manufactures, the College of Commerce, and the Main Municipal Council. These were bureaucratic institutions designed for state regulation of the economy:

instruments of the autocracy's commercial and industrial policies, which were based on mercantilism.

In Sweden, whose state institutions served as models for the Petrine reforms, similar administrative colleges, generally speaking, carried out royal policy on the same theoretical basis. But conditions in Russia differed from those in Sweden because of their respective sizes, political customs and cultures, [stages of] industrial development, resources, and, above all, because of the extraordinarily severe state regulation of the economic life of Russia's inhabitants. . . . [In Russia after 1718] private enterprise was tightly harnessed to the state chariot by a system of governmental orders mainly of a military nature. The system provided a steady income for the manufacturers, who were guaranteed the sale of their goods to the treasury. On the other hand, it closed off technological improvement and sharply curtailed competition, the eternal engine of free enterprise. Attempts to raise the level of production were thus of little avail. . . .

The state's active intervention in the economy was only one aspect of the problem [of retarded development in Russia]. Established social relations, long since guided by the state, were in effect transferred to the new manufactories, greatly lessening their potential as capitalist enterprises. I refer above all to certain peculiarities in the exploitation of labor. Throughout the years of the Northern War—a time of rapid economic buildup—workers of various backgrounds were recruited by enterprises: both the state and private owners employed "assigned" peasants (living on lands not claimed by private landlords, these peasants discharged their obligations to the state by working in the enterprises to which they were now "assigned"), ordinary criminals, and hired hands. The last category of workers derived from the presence in society of numerous petty nontaxpayers and fugitive peasants as well as from the existence of completely legal means of escaping servitude or taxation, conditions which created a contingent of "freemen and wanderers" in the country. The authorities winked at the exploitation of fugitive labor. But beginning in about 1720 important social measures were introduced [by Peter's government]: an intensified campaign to recover fugitive peasants, who were to be returned to their former masters; a universal census, connected with Peter's tax reform, which fixed all peasants [and townsfolk] to the place where they were inscribed in the tax rolls; and a reduction of "freemen and wanderers" to the status of fugitive criminals.

This sudden change in governmental policy was immediately reflected in industry. Owners of manufactories and managers of state enterprises complained of the catastrophic situation created by the exodus of fugitives and by the prohibition, under pain of fines, on thereafter hiring such people. Deliveries to the treasury became uncertain. At this juncture a law appeared that was to have the most serious consequences. By a decree of January 18, 1721 [see Documents], enacted for the benefit of the state, Peter permitted private manufacturers to purchase peasants [from the state or from private landlords] for work in their enterprises. Thus a decisive step was taken towards converting such enterprises, ostensibly nascent capitalist structures, into serf manufactories.

This reversion to feudal norms took no account of a new social reality: the emergence in Russia of both private manufacturers and industrial workers. No room was made for them [in the traditional social structure]: they were treated only as variants of the established order [the manufacturer as a kind of feudal landlord, the industrial worker as a kind of bondsman or serf]. A decree of May 28, 1723, then regulated the procedures for employing persons who did not belong to the owner of an enterprise or were not "assigned" to it: all such persons had to have their landlord's permission (a passport) to work [in a given enterprise] or they would be subject to arrest and immediate return to the place where they were inscribed in the tax rolls. Thenceforth industry could develop only as a form of serfdom. The role of free labor was constrained, treasury enterprises employed only "assigned" labor, and the institution of the "recruit"—the lifetime "industrial soldier"— emerged. Even workers in private enterprises who had belonged to nobody in particular came to be considered bondsmen [of the enterprise]. Whole branches of industry went over almost exclusively to serf labor. This victory of [one or another form of] forced labor in industry foreordained that economic backwardness of Russia which became increasingly evident in the nineteenth century.

Similarly, serfdom impeded the formation of a bourgeoisie in Russia. The privileges granted by the state to manufacturers bore a feudal character. It was easier and more profitable for them to buy "peasant lads" than to hire workers on the free market. Yet labor so bought entailed an unproductive use of capital: it has been estimated that no more than half of these serfs were fit to work in industry. In such conditions one can scarcely envisage the expansion and improvement of production. Industrial monopolies, including the preferential sale of certain goods, and exclusive rights to raw materials—these and other such privileges [granted by Peter to selected manufacturers] were not in essence capitalist but only variations of medieval practices.

Serfdom also deformed social attitudes. As serf-owners, manufacturers did not develop their own social identity or corporate consciousness. At a time when in western Europe the bourgeoisie was already loudly advancing its claims against monarch and nobility, in Russia low-born manufacturers were aspiring to share the privileges, and the fate, of the noble estate. The conversion into aristocrats of the Stroganovs and Demidovs [industrial entrepreneurs ennobled by Peter and his successors] is the clearest case in point.

So the Petrine state's vigorous industrial drive created the economic base necessary for the nation's development while simultaneously deflecting it from the capitalist course on which other European countries had embarked. It is natural to ask whether there might have been another path—ways and means to achieve the economic take-off other than those chosen in Peter's time. If we accept that Russia's conquest of the Baltic littoral was essential to her full development, and that a peaceful negotiation with Sweden of access to the Baltic Sea was impossible, then much that Peter undertook was necessary, including the creation of industry in the shortest possible time. Still, the historical path taken does not seem to have been the only one available even in his time.

The decree of 1721 and subsequent acts permitting the purchase and exploitation of enserfed peasants by industrial entrepreneurs had, as we can now see, the most fateful consequences. Perhaps the only alternative would have been the abolition of serfdom itself. Did such a possibility exist, in principle, under Peter? His older contemporary, the Swedish king Charles XI, undertook in the 1680s the so-called Great Reduction. State lands were created [from aristocratic as well as royal domains] and leased to peasants, thus freeing them from serf dependence. No such alternative existed for Peter. Serfdom was established in Russia long before his birth and had permeated the entire life of the country, including the consciousness of its people. In Russia, as distinct from western Europe, serfdom played a peculiar, all-encompassing role. Its destruction would have undermined the autocracy itself, crowning as it did a pyramid of slavery in various forms. Thus the decree of 1721 stood like a signpost on the main road of Russian history, at the end of which stood the decree of 1861 [emancipating the serfs].

Pursuing the comparison of Petrine Russia with a ship, let us now consider its upper structure, above the waterline, beneath which lay hidden the economic basis of society.

The transformation of the governmental apparatus which began at the end of the seventeenth century proceeded apace in the early years of the eighteenth. Prosecuting the Northern War entailed the creation of a modern army and the construction of a navy, which led to an enormous increase in governmental activity. The *prikaz* [departmental] system inherited by Peter from his predecessors could not cope with the increasingly complex tasks of governing. New departments were needed, and so-called chancelleries [*kantseliarii*] appeared. But they were few in number and limited in scope, and from early in the war it was clear that the governmental machine of central *prikazy* and local districts [*uezdy*] could not keep pace with the autocrat's urgent initiatives. This lag manifested itself in shortages of money, personnel, food, and other supplies for the army and fleet.

There followed the local-government reform of 1707–1710: provinces [*gubernii*] appeared, each combining several of the former *uezdy*, and a system of military commissioners [*krigskomissary*] was instituted. The main purpose of this reform was to bring order to the provisioning of the army, and direct links were established between the new provinces and the regiments assigned to them. The reform thus responded to the pressing needs of the autocracy. But it also advanced the already well-developed tendency toward bureaucracy. Peter proposed to solve all state problems precisely by strengthening the bureaucratic element of his government. The local-government reform led not only to the concentration of financial and administrative power in the hands of a few provincial governors representing the center, but to the creation in the localities of a uniform network of hierarchical bureaucracies each staffed with a large number of officials [*chinovniki*]. The system was further developed by the local-government reform of 1719. And similar notions had inspired the foundation of the Senate [1711]. In fact, the bureaucratic tendency in government, which had emerged long before Peter, received decisive confirmation under him. Meetings of the Boyars' Duma—the traditional council of the high nobility—came to an end early in the eighteenth century and its directive role in central and local government was taken over by a so-called Council of Ministers [*Konsiliia ministrov*], a provisional committee of the most important department heads, whose actions clearly reveal the tendency to bureaucratic regulation. . . .

Here again we see the enormous role played by the state, a factor that must be taken into account if we are to understand a wide range of phenomena in

Russian history. Public opinion did not define legislation but rather the other way around: legislation was the most important means of forming (and deforming) public opinion as well as social consciousness. Proceeding from both rationalist principles and traditional conceptions of the role of autocracy in Russia, Peter accorded enormous significance to written legislation, believing that "correct" laws, enacted in timely fashion and fully carried out, could achieve everything from the provision of bread for the people to a reformation of manners. The exact fulfillment of the law Peter considered a panacea for all of life's problems. Doubts about the adequacy of law in this respect never really occurred to him.

Law was to be actualized only through a system of bureaucratic institutions. A veritable cult of administration grew up under Peter. The mind of Russia's great reformer was first of all directed to enacting legislation that would as far as possible seize and regulate the entire life of his subjects—whether in commerce or the church, in the barracks or the private home. Secondly, Peter dreamed of creating a state apparatus as complete and perfect as a clock, and by means of which he could actualize his legislation. He got the idea of creating such an apparatus early on, but it was only when a break occurred in his war with Sweden that he moved to implement it. Around 1720 he began to abandon unvarnished coercion in various spheres of domestic policy in favor of regulation by means of bureaucracy.

The model Peter chose for his reforms was, as mentioned, the Swedish state structure, which was founded on functional principles and characterized by a division of authority and a uniform hierarchical apparatus. But in generalizing and systematizing administrative law in Russia Peter went much further than the European exponents of "camaralism."[2] Combining Swedish experience with certain aspects of Russian reality Peter created, in addition to a whole series of individual regulations [reglamenty], a regulation of regulations without precedent in Europe: the General Regulation [General'nyi reglament] of 1719–1724. The Regulation of the Admiralty College [1720], in particular, spelled out the 56 duties of officials from the president of the college down to a "provost" who was to ensure that "in the Admiralty nobody relieves himself except in the designated places; and should somebody relieve himself elsewhere, he is to be whipped and ordered to clean it up."

The reform of the Senate [from 1718] was crucial here. In it were now concentrated judicial, administrative, and legislative functions, and it was given supervision of both the [new central administrative] colleges and the [new] provincial governments. Nominating and confirming officials was also an important prerogative of the Senate. Its unofficial head [from 1722] was the procurator-general [general-prokuror], who was endowed with special powers and subordinate only to the monarch. To carry out his duties a whole procuracy was created (on the French model): procurators of varying rank were to ensure the legality and correctness of administration throughout the central and in much of local government. This pyramid of overt supervision was duplicated in a pyramid of secret surveillance by officials

2. Camaralism, a version of mercantilism worked out in Austria and other German states beginning in the later seventeenth century, was a distinctive theory of government and economy, an entire administrative "science" which placed heavy emphasis on the interest and role of the sovereign (or state) in a country's economy.—Ed.

called fiscals [*fiskaly*], whose duty to inform was unlimited and hence wide open to abuse. From Peter's time in Russia "fiscality" [*fiskal'stvo*] became synonymous among the people with despicable informing.

The creation of a bureaucratic machine in place of the medieval system of governance based on custom was a natural process: bureaucracy is an indispensable element of the modern state. But in Russian conditions, where the unbounded will of the monarch served as the sole source of law and officials were responsible to nobody except their own superiors, the creation of a bureaucratic machine constituted a kind of "bureaucratic revolution." The machine managed to consolidate itself regardless of whether its ongoing motive force—the ruler on the throne—was intelligent or stupid, industrious or lazy. An invulnerable caste of bureaucrats thus came into being. . . .

Peter's ship of state, quite obviously, was a warship first and foremost. His world outlook was such that he viewed the state apparatus as a subdivision of the military. This was not simply a matter of his personal militarism, or of the fact that he had grown accustomed to military operations: in 28 of the 36 years of his active reign he was at war. Peter was also convinced that the army represented a model social structure, one worthy of application to the whole of society, one that had been tested in battle. Military discipline could help instill in the people love of order, industriousness, social awareness, and Christian morality. The transfer of military principles to the civil sphere is evident in the extension of military regulations to state institutions as well as in the texts of the military statutes themselves. Thus by Peter's personal decree the Military Statute of 1716, the basic law of the armed forces, was to be regarded as a fundamental legislative act operative at all levels of government. Not all of its norms were applicable to the civil sphere, so specially compiled extracts were to be used. As a result, military forms of punishment were meted out in civil cases: never before nor after in Russian history was such a huge number of decrees promulgated promising the death penalty for transgressions of duty. In 1723 Peter divided all crimes into two kinds: "private" and "state," the latter to designate all "transgressions of duty." Peter thought that the transgressions of the bureaucrat harmed the state even more than treason on the battlefield.

The regular army raised by the great reformer came to occupy the leading place in the life of Russian society. It is no exaggeration to say that in Russia in the eighteenth and nineteenth centuries the state was subordinate to the army, not the other way around. St. Petersburg would have reverted to wasteland had all the monuments, buildings, and structures linked with military affairs and military victories somehow disappeared. The "palace revolutions" of the eighteenth century became possible thanks in large part to the outsized importance of the military, especially the [elite] guards regiments [founded by Peter], in the public life of the Empire.

The Petrine reforms were marked by a growing use of professional soldiers in the civil administration. Military personnel, especially guards officers, often served as emissaries of the tsar with extraordinary powers. Even such an undertaking as the "revision" [*reviziia*: census of the population, 1718–1723] was entrusted to the armed forces, an effort that required the services of nearly half of the officer corps; after Peter the government would frequently resort to this practice. The army was reorganized and quartered [around the country] in accordance with the census, imposing a permanent obligation on the people. This system of supporting the army, borrowed by Peter from Sweden and adapted to Russian conditions, was extremely burdensome. Thenceforth the most effective means of punishing rebellious peasants was to quarter soldiers in their homes, while freedom from this obligation came to be considered a privilege earned for special services by certain villagers and townsfolk.

The laws on quartering troops—especially the *Plakat* of 1724—were supposed to regulate relations between the people and the military. In actual practice, however, the authority of the regimental commander exceeded that of the local civil administration. Not only did his troops collect the new [1724] soul tax [levied on all male peasants and townsfolk] in the region assigned to their regiment, a matter in which they had a direct interest, but they also carried out such political functions as arresting fugitive peasants, suppressing popular resistance, supervising population transfers, and enforcing the passport system. . . .

The Petrine era in Russia is also notable for an attempt to provide a theoretical basis for autocracy. In elaborating his conception of unlimited monarchy, Feofan Prokopovich [1681–1736] drew on both Muscovite royal tradition and European theories of "natural law." His work, exhibiting an eclectic mixture of Scriptural citations and extracts from the latest treatises propounding the "contractual" theory of the origin of the state, sought to convince Russian readers that the autocratic power was based on both divine and natural law. This appeal to reason, characteristic of the contractual and natural-law line of thought [current in Europe], was no doubt novel in the ideology of Russian autocracy, supplemented as it was by an idealized "model" of the tsar's own service to the throne.

This notion of the monarch's "duty" or "obligation," formulated here for the first time in Russian political thought, outlined the limits—more exactly, recognized the limitlessness—of his power, which was considered indispensable for the effective dispatch of the "royal business." The ideas of rationalism—the principles of "reason" and "order"—loomed large in the mind of Peter. Yet when speaking of his democratic outlook and capacity for hard work, of the selflessness of the great reformer, we must remember a major difference between the "service" of the tsar and the service of his subjects: for the latter, it was service *to* the monarch, which merged with service to the state. In other words, in his daily labors Peter provided a model of service to himself, to the Russian autocrat.

To be sure, service to the fatherland, to Russia, a notion that drew on traditional patriotism, was a most important element of the political culture of the Petrine era. But at its basis lay the medieval identification of the power and person of the autocrat with the state itself. Conflating representations of statehood and fatherland sacred to every citizen and symbolized by an independent national existence, on the one hand, with representations of the bearer of that statehood—an utterly real, far from faultless, mortal human being: such a conflation tended to confer on the latter, the ruler, by reason of the position he occupied, the sacred attributes of statehood. (In more recent history the clearest such identification of the person of the ruler with the state and fatherland is to be found in the cult of Stalin.)

All of this had, in the subsequent political history of Russia, as is well known, the most serious consequences. For *any* step taken against the bearer of power, be it the supreme ruler or a petty bureaucrat, would be treated as a step against the statehood personified in him, against Russia, against the people, and as such considered treason, its perpetrator an enemy of the fatherland, of the people. The idea of identifying an offense against the person of the monarch with an offense against the state can be traced back to the law code [*Ulozhenie*] of 1649; but the apotheosis of this idea was reached under Peter, when references to "the fatherland" and even to "the land" disappeared from military and civil oaths, leaving only the autocrat as the embodiment of statehood.

Paternalism was the most important element of Peter's political doctrine, and it was personified in the figure of the wise, visionary monarch, the father of the fatherland and of the people. In [the treatise entitled] *The Right of the Monarch's Will* [1722] we find the assertion, paradoxical at first glance but logical enough in the paternalist context, that if the monarch, by reason of his supreme power, is father to his own father, then he, the son-sovereign, is by the same token father to all of his subjects. It should be noted that the paternalist idea is close to Max Weber's notion of the "charismatic leader" intermediate between the traditional and the democratic leader. Such a [charismatic/intermediary] leader may comport himself democratically, scorn material interests, repudiate the past, and in this sense represent a "specific revolutionary force." Yet there could be only one "father of the fatherland," only one "father of the nation." Charismatic authority bears an exclusively personal character and cannot be passed on, like the throne, to an heir.

In assuming the official title "Father of the Fatherland" [see Documents, Act of October 22, 1721], Peter doubtless was aware of the charismatic aspect of his power, based as it was less on a claim to divine origin than on a recognition of its purely personal features, especially his pedagogical, exemplary fulfillment of "duty." Simplicity in his personal life and a democratic mixing with people of various social ranks were joined in Peter with an open disdain for many of the traditional honors accorded the autocrat and a constant striving to break with social stereotypes. True, that leaves open the question of the outcome of the "revolutionary break" that occurred in Russia under Peter . . . a break that led in the final analysis to the consolidation of a kind of political bondage derived from serfdom.

His reforms were conceived by Peter as a permanent school, as instruction which corresponded naturally with his typically rationalist perception of the world. In a time of stormy change, of instability, of general uncertainty (typical features of crucial moments in history); a time when the goals of reform, except the most obvious, were not apparent or understood by many people and even met with open or, more often, covert opposition: in this situation the idea took root in Peter's mind of the wise Teacher and his ignorant, often stubborn student-subjects who could be instructed only with the aid of force, by use of the cane. Of course, the notion of coercion as the most effective means of governance was hardly new with Peter. But he was the first [Russian ruler] to employ compulsion, the "pedagogical cudgel," with such persistence. A contemporary recalled Peter once telling his entourage: "Foreigners say I rule over unwilling slaves. I rule subjects, who obey my decrees. These decrees contain good, and are not harmful to the state. English liberty has no more place here than do peas on a knife. One needs to know the people, how to rule them. . . . Malevolence and villainy against me and the fatherland cannot succeed—the law will rein them in. A free man is one who does not do evil but serves the good."

This hymn to dictatorial rule (in effect, to tyranny) is confirmed both by Peter's sympathy for Ivan the Terrible and by his frequently expressed opinion that resort to compulsion was the only way to success in Russian conditions. In a decree of the College of Manufactures of 1723 concerning the difficulty of developing industry in the country, Peter wrote: "There are few volunteers, it is true, because our people are like ignorant children who never learned the alphabet, who were not compelled [to do so] by their masters and to whom at first it seems most vexing; but when they have learned [it], then they are grateful. It is clear that not everyhing is done voluntarily; but already much gratitude is heard, which has already borne fruit."

Peter's reign demonstrated that countless appeals and threats could not compel people to do what Peter wanted done swiftly, precisely, and spontaneously. Few among the tsar-reformer's associates felt confident enough to risk acting without his orders. Indeed, such was inevitable, as Peter had set himself an unrealizable task. As the historian V. O. Kliuchevsky wrote, Peter "hoped by his terrible power to stimulate initiative in an enslaved society, and through a slave-owning nobility to establish European learning and popular enlightenment in Russia as the indispensable condition of social development; he wished that the slave, while remaining a slave, should act consciously and freely. The combination of depotism and freedom, of enlightenment and slavery—this political squaring of the circle, this riddle, delivered to us from the time of Peter, is still unsolved." Reading the letters of his associates, who experienced feelings of helplessness and even despair when they did not have exact instructions from the tsar, Peter had good grounds for believing that without him nothing would get done. Together with this sense of his own indispensability, which was far from vain, went a sense of isolation, especially in his last years: a sense that while his associates feared him, they did not understand.

So we see before us not simply a ship, but a galley—a galley on whose deck strolls a nobility dressed in military uniform while the other estates are chained, like so many oarsmen, to the benches below. Peter, most assuredly, reformed not only the state, military, and economic structures [of Russia], but the social as well. And here I refer not just to the indirect social consequences of various reforms, but also to the immediate social changes that resulted directly from his reform of the estate system.[3]

In the Petrine era, the once unitary estate of "servicemen" disintegrated. Its upper level—the servitors "by inheritance"—were converted into the kind of

---

3. "Estate," here as throughout Anisimov's essay, means social estate (*soslovie*), not landed estate. —Ed.

noblemen [*dvoriane*] familiar to us from later times while the lower levels of servitor—whether "by inheritance" (mainly "single-homestead men" [*odnodvortsy*] settled in the southern regions) or "by enlistment"—became state peasants.

The formation of the noble estate, which subsequently enjoyed exclusive serf- and land-owning rights, was the result both of a gradual division [of the old service estate] into upper and lower strata and of deliberate action by the state power. New criteria of service were introduced [by Peter] for the upper level. The principle of personal merit replaced that of heredity, which had permitted the leading servitors to monopolize the highest positions in society, the army, and the court. Peter's seemingly democratic initiative here opened the way to the top for the most capable men in service. Codified in the famous Table of Ranks of 1722 [see Documents], the new system also strengthened the nobility at the expense of newcomers from the other estates. But this was not the ultimate aim of the reform. Employing the principle of personal merit as strictly laid down in the Table of Ranks, where a ladder of ranks from ensign or clerk at the bottom was provided which even the highest official had to climb, Peter converted the rather amorphous mass of servicemen "by inheritance" into a military-bureaucratic corps totally subordinate to, and completely dependent on, himself.

To be sure, the noble estate came to be seen as a corporate body distinguished by its special rights and privileges and by its corporate consciousness, principles, and customs. But Peter had striven to bind the conception of noble status as closely as possible to the obligation of permanent state service, with its requisite knowledge and practical skills. All nobles were assigned to the various state institutions and military units and their sons had to go to school. They were sent abroad to study, forbidden by the tsar to marry should they refuse to be educated, and deprived of their lands if they evaded his service.

In short, Peter's policy regarding the nobility was very strict; and it is only by stretching the point that this bureaucratized, regulated nobility, obliged to study and then to serve and serve again, could be called a ruling class. It was to stress the primacy of service that the law on entail was introduced in 1714 [see Documents], whereby the nobility was forbidden to sell or mortgage landed property, including inherited land, under pain of confiscation by the state—something that did in fact happen. The law thus compelled the nobility to think of state service as the principal source of their livelihood. It is hard to imagine what the Russian nobility might have become had Peter's principles been followed after his death. The nobility's actual emancipation [from state service] and its development as a corporate estate took place under the banner of "liberation" between the 1730s and the 1760s, when, successively, Peter's law on entail was abolished, the period of state service was restricted, and, finally, the Manifesto of 1762 was proclaimed—a document whose title, "On Granting Freedom and Liberty to All the Russian Nobility," speaks for itself [see Documents, Chapter 4]. But in Peter's time the nobility was considered above all a bureaucratic and military caste closely tied to the chariot of state.

The social category of state peasants arose as a by-product of the tsar's plan to unite various categories of Russia's unbonded population into a single estate liable to the soul tax. Such folk included the single-homestead men of the south, the black-earth peasants of the north, and the non-Russian peasants of the middle and lower Volga regions: together they would constitute some 18 percent of the population obligated [from 1724] to pay the soul tax. Thenceforth the most notable mark of the single-homestead men, erstwhile servitors "by inheritance" or "by enlistment," was their liability to taxation, which thus closed to them forever the door to noble status—this even though some of them still held serfs and lands by right of service. Indeed, thenceforth generally speaking attachment to the taxpaying estates was a mark of the unprivileged; and Peter's policy toward those who had become state peasants was to restrict as far as possible any privileges they might enjoy as persons who were not formally enserfed.

Peter also decided to reform the social structure of the towns of Russia by implanting institutions that had deep roots in the medieval towns of Europe. So one fine day Russian tradesmen and merchants awoke to find themselves members of corporations and guilds, while the remaining minority of townsfolk were investigated to determine who among them were fugitive peasants to be returned to their former places of residence. The creation of guilds was the purest fiction, however, as the military enumerators of the census were committed to maximizing the number of persons liable to pay the soul tax [on which the military depended]. Fiscal concerns, not the stimulation of industry and trade, took first place. Equally important, Peter left unchanged the system of assessing [urban] taxes on "goods and chattels" [zhivoty], so that the most substantial townsfolk were obliged to pay for dozens and even hundreds of their indigent neighbors. Thus were medieval social forms strengthened in Russian towns, which in turn hampered the development of capitalist relations.

Peter's new system of urban government was also little more than a formality. All local town councils were subordinated [from 1720] to a Main Municipal Council [in St. Petersburg] and none of these offices bore any relation to those of western Europe, which were genuine organs of urban self-government. Townsfolk who became members of the local councils were regarded in essence as officials of the central government, and their duties were even enumerated in the Table of Ranks. The administration of justice, collection of taxes, and maintenance of order in urban Russia were the basic functions entrusted to the new town councils, and nothing more.

Social reform under Peter extended to the serfs and slaves [kholopy], who were merged into a single estate. Slavery [in Russia] had a long history and well-developed legal tradition, and the extension of slave law to serfdom paved the way for their merger, a process that was reinforced by the Law Code of 1649, which gave juridical expression to serfdom. Nevertheless, important differences persisted into the Petrine era: slaves working their masters' fields or as domestic servants were not subject to taxation, and a significant portion of them—the so-called indentured [kabal'nye] slaves—traditionally had the right to freedom after their masters' death. At first under Peter the opportunities for slaves to achieve freedom were sharply curtailed, and they were made liable by law to military conscription. Then, by means of a succession of harsh decrees [as mentioned earlier], the traditional category of "freemen and wanderers" was in effect liquidated: this category had been the main source of slaves and their refuge if and when they were freed. Finally, between 1719 and 1724 slaves were enrolled to pay the soul tax. Having thus lost their tax-exempt status, slaves became equal to serfs, who had long ago lost their right to freedom. By a stroke of the pen the age-old institution of slavery had been suppressed, and with consequences that would last far into the future. The remarkable increase in feudal labor dues [barshchina] in the middle of the eighteenth century was owed in no small measure to the disappearance of slavery, as serfs now had to shoulder the full burden of working their masters' fields.

Similarly, the status of the clergy and their dependents was regularized under Peter, with the result that distinctions among ecclesiastical peasants were eliminated and all were made liable to taxation. At the same time, ecclesiastical servitors who could not claim clerical status were made liable to taxation, military service, or service in almshouses. Indeed, the estate structure of Russia underwent in the Petrine period a kind of drastic simplification, the process consciously directed by the reformer with the aim of creating a so-called regular [or regularized, reguliarnoe] state, one that might also be characterized as a totalitarian, military-bureaucratic, police state.

Restrictions such as those on movement within the country, on choice of occupation, on transferring from one "social order" [chin] to another, were typical of the established regime in Russia; all were traditional elements of the government's estate policy before Peter. . . . But in pre-Petrine times the moderating influence of custom was strong, estate boundaries were permeable, and the variegation of a medieval society gave its members—especially those who were not bound by service, taxation, or serf law—infinitely more scope for personal fulfillment than did Peter's regularized society. His legislation is distinguished by its much starker regulation of the rights and duties of each estate and, correspondingly, by its much stricter control of social mobility.

Peter's tax reform was enormously important in this regard. With the introduction of the soul tax [1724], which was preceded by a census of all male souls, every taxpayer was fixed to the place where he had been enrolled—which for peasants (the vast majority) meant his home village or commune [obshchina]. This in itself impeded any change in status. Not wishing to paralyze the urban economy, Peter's government allowed serf peasants (decree of April 13, 1722), on payment of a huge fee, to settle in towns, though they would remain subject to their landlords. The law thus permitted the peasant to trade even as it guaranteed his master's power over him; the serf, lengthening so to speak his chain, became a so-called trading peasant. A similar arrangement was made for serfs to work in manufactories [as noted earlier]. The social-economic significance of this "Solomonic" solution is obvious: such a "serf on leave" [otkhodnik], his labor exploited by the industrial enterprise, received his pay, which was then converted into the quit-rent [obrok] owed his landlord. This was a dead-end sort of [socioeconomic] development.[4]

---

4. The legal restrictions on "trading peasants," like the laws permitting industrial enterprises to purchase serfs and exploit state peasants, were in effect repealed under Catherine II.—Ed.

Major, longlasting police measures were also characteristic of the Petrine period. The most serious of these were the assignment in 1724–1725 of regular army
regiments to permanent quarters in the localities where the soul tax was collected
for their support, and the bestowal of police powers on the commanders of these
units. Another such measure was the introduction of the internal passport system.
Without a passport no peasant or townsman had the right to leave home. Trans-
gressing the passport system (lost or expired passport, going beyond the permitted
limits of travel) automatically made one a criminal liable to arrest and deportation
to one's former place of residence. Such measures were a product not so much of
the tsar's suspicious nature as of his peculiar understanding of rationalist ideas,
according to which their concrete application to Russia required that the reformer
intensify his tutelage of society by enlarging the state's role in the life of the country
as a whole, in that of each estate, and in that of every individual. All of this imbued
Peter's regime with the aspect of a police state, provided we understand by this
term not just a repressive organization but one that, more importantly, undertakes
to "regularize" the life of its subjects in everything from the construction of their
houses following specified plans to the meticulous control of their moral and even
spiritual behavior.

I neither exaggerate here nor intend to be ironical. It is well known that Peter
launched a church reform, one embodied in his establishment [1721] of a collegial
(synodal) form of ecclesiastical government to replace the patriarchate. The suppression of the latter was another instance of how Peter eliminated any remnants of
"princely" (or appanage) power as inconsistent with autocracy. Having assumed in
effect the headship of the church, he suppressed its autonomy. Moreover, he made
extensive use of the church to carry out his policy of policing his subjects. The
latter were obliged, under pain of heavy fines, to attend services and to confess
their sins to a priest. The priest in turn, also by force of law, was obliged to inform
the authorities of any legal transgressions he had learned of while hearing confession.

This rude intrusion of the state into ecclesistical and religious matters had a
most baneful effect on the spiritual development of society and on the history of
the church itself. The conversion of the church into a bureaucratic office protective
of the interests of the autocracy and subservient to its requirements signaled the
triumph of statism [etatizm] and the suppression, for the people, of a spiritual
alternative to the regime and to ideas emanating from the state. The church, with
its age-old traditions of protecting those oppressed and abased by the state; the
church, whose ministers had comforted the condemned and had publicly censured
tyrants: the church had become a dutiful instrument of authority and thus largely
lost the respect of the people, who one day would view with indifference its collapse
in the wreckage of the autocracy [1917] and the subsequent destruction [under
communism] of its houses of worship.

So much for the crew of Peter's ship. The question now arises, whither did she sail
under her royal skipper? What were his destinations?

Russia's external political position underwent fundamental change in the course
of the Northern War. The [Russian victory at the] battle of Poltava [1709] sharply
divided the war into two phases: from 1700 to 1709, and from 1709 to [the Peace

of Nystadt in] 1721. In the first phase, following its victorious defense of Narva [1700], Sweden held the military initiative: its forces occupied Poland and Saxony, and invaded Russia. Peter resolved accordingly to maintain and reform his army and to build up the military potential of his country. He also tried, unsuccessfully, to revive the Northern Alliance (Denmark, Saxony, Russia), which had been paralyzed by Charles XII's victories.[5] In this first phase of the war, taking advantage of the absence of major Swedish forces in the eastern Baltic area, Peter was able to occupy [the province of] Ingria and lay the foundations of St. Petersburg and [offshore fortress of] Kronshtadt.

The Poltava victory enabled Peter to take the initiative, which he did, consolidating his hold on Ingria and also Karelia, occupying Livonia and Estonia, and then invading Germany, where with the help of Denmark and Saxony and to some degree of Prussia and Hanover he began joint operations against Swedish Pomerania. In less than six years the allies ousted the Swedes from all of their Baltic possessions. Thus ended, in 1716, the Swedish empire. But in the division of its territories Russia suddenly made new claims, claims that were backed by its brilliant victories on land and sea.

First, Peter refused to be bound by previous assurances to his allies that he would limit himself to [recovering] the old Russian territories taken by the Swedes after Russia's Time of Troubles in the early seventeenth century, namely Ingria and Karelia. Estonia and Livonia, conquered by Russian forces in 1710, were incorporated into Russia, whose greatly strengthened army and navy would guarantee these conquests. Secondly, since 1712 Peter had been involved in German affairs—first in the struggle against Sweden in Pomerania, Holstein, and Mecklenburg and then, after Sweden's ouster from these territories, in the effort to establish Duke Charles Leopold as absolute ruler of Mecklenburg, which entailed military operations and treaty talks with Holstein, a hostile neighbor of Denmark.

The "Mecklenburg question," that of Holstein, and that also of Courland became the source of heightened tensions in the concluding phase of the Northern War, and even after it; for Peter, having forcefully intruded into German affairs, now had to contend with the influence, unfriendly to him, of England, France, and Denmark. In 1709 he launched his peculiar "marital invasion" of Europe: that year his niece, Anna Ivanovna, became duchess of Courland and her sister, Catherine, duchess of Mecklenburg. Peter's son Aleksei later married Princess Charlotte Sophie of Wölfenbuttel, while his elder daughter Anna was betrothed to—and after his death married—Duke Charles Frederick of Holstein.

The Peace of Nystadt of 1721 legally affirmed not only Russia's victory in the Northern War and acquisition of the eastern Baltic region, but also the birth of a new empire: the link between Russia's celebration of the Peace and Peter's formal acceptance of the title of Emperor is obvious [see Documents]. His government used its rising military power to enhance its influence over the entire Baltic area. The conclusion of a treaty of alliance with Sweden was an undoubted diplomatic

---

5. Charles XII, king of Sweden (1697–1718).—Ed.

triumph, while the "Holstein question" permitted Peter to influence affairs both in Sweden itself, whose royal dynasty was linked with Holstein, and in Denmark, from whom Russia obtained abrogation of the tolls levied on ships passing through the sound. After Peter's death Russia's growing involvement in Holstein brought her to the verge of war with Denmark.

Peter was motivated here not only by the political goal of augmenting his influence in the Baltic world, but by economic interests as well. His mercantilist philosophy required him to seek a favorable balance of trade; in fact, it could be said that after the Peace of Nystadt commercial considerations dominated Russia's foreign policy. This distinctive conjunction of the military-political and commercial interests of the Russian Empire gave rise to the Russo-Persian War of 1722–1723, which was supplemented by forays into central Asia. Peter's knowledge of international commerce induced him to seize the routes carrying the trade in the rarities of India and China. His conquest of the southern coast of the Caspian Sea was not meant to be temporary [as it proved to be]. Having annexed this important Persian territory to Russia [1723] and built fortresses there, Peter proceeded with a plan to deport its Muslim population and settle it with neighboring Orthodox peoples [mainly Armenians]. A staging point was thus created on the Caspian Sea in preparation for an Indian campaign—the peculiar "Indian syndrome" that has possessed numerous conquerors, Peter among them (there could be no true empire without the riches of India). And from there the idea was to launch an adventurous attempt to conquer Madagascar, as indicated by secret [Russian] preparations in 1723.

In sum, the reign of Peter witnessed a metamorphosis in Russia's foreign policy: resolving urgent national problems was superseded by the pursuit of typically imperial goals. The Petrine reforms led to the creation of a military-bureaucratic state ruled by a strongly centralized autocratic power based on a serf economy and mighty armed forces (whose numbers continued to grow after the Northern War). That Peter's ship of state should sail off to India followed naturally from the internal development of his empire. Peter laid the foundations of Russia's imperial policy of the eighteenth and nineteenth centuries. The process of forming Russia's Imperial image had begun.

## Kliuchevsky on Peter the Great

JAMES CRACRAFT

Eleven of the sixteen lectures of Part 4 of V. O. Kliuchevsky's famous *Course in Russian History* are devoted to the person and reign of Peter I, the remaining five to the "fate of Peter the Great's reform" from his death in 1725 to the accession

From "Kliuchevsky on Peter the Great" by James Cracraft from *Canadian-American Slavic Studies*, Vol. 20, nos. 3–4 (Fall-Winter 1986), pp. 367–81. Reprinted by permission of Charles Schlacks, Jr., Publisher.

of Catherine II in 1762. Unlike the four other parts—or volumes—of the *Course*, which are based on students' lecture notes dating back to the 1880s, Part 4 was considerably rewritten by Kliuchevsky himself between August 1907 and December 1909, when it was sent to press, less than a year and a half before his death. It was the master's last recorded word on the historical significance for the Russians of their first emperor.

Kliuchevsky's Soviet biographer, Academician Nechkina, insists that in rewriting his lectures on Peter I the old man was deeply influenced by current events, particularly the Revolution of 1905. The direct evidence for this view is slight, a matter of a few words. For example, in a notebook of the time Kliuchevsky wrote: "Peter I. He acted like an Old-Russian tyrant but in him glimmered for the first time the idea of the popular good, after him extinguished for a long time, a very long time." This jotting, says Nechkina, encapsulated "one of Kliuchevsky's basic conclusions about Peter"; became, indeed, the "dominant thesis of his entire interpretation"; and shows, in his use of the word "popular" rather than the standard "common" or "general," which is also found in Petrine documents, the "historical lesson of 1905." Be that as it may, the length and contents of the lectures themselves leave no doubt that Kliuchevsky labored mightily to explain how, as he saw it, Peter's achievement was at once great but not exactly revolutionary, accidental but in some degree planned, terrible for the masses and yet marvelous for Russia, the work of a ruler who was to be feared, even hated, but always admired—especially by comparison with nearly all of his successors, and most especially the present one, the unmentionable Nicholas II. Nechkina says as much, too, while classifying the second of the lectures in question, Kliuchevsky's character-study of Peter I, as nothing short of "brilliant."

As portrayed by Kliuchevsky, Peter was essentially the *velikii khoziain*, the typical tightfisted, autocratic "big boss-landlord" of Muscovite Russia except that, unlike his predecessors, he was not a "stay-at-home boss with soft hands" but a "worker-boss, self-taught, a tsar-of-all-trades." This difference was a result of Peter's irregular upbringing, personal predilections, and mentality: "in his mental makeup one of those simple, straightforward people who can be read at a glance." It meant that in military affairs he was rather the quartermaster and shipbuilder than the active commander and strategist; at home, a "guest in his own house," leading to the tragic conflict with his son [Aleksei]; and in politics, a "ruler without rules." A "kind man by nature," "honest and sincere" in his personal dealings, "fair," even "benevolent" in outlook, he was nevertheless "boorish," even cruel, as tsar; devoid of political principle or any sense of social obligation and "instinctively arbitrary"; irreverent to the point of blasphemy, given to fits of rage, and respectful of nobody, "not even himself"; above all, "more a doer than a thinker" and always and everywhere the "big boss." It is a compelling portrait, somber, even haunting; the picture, perhaps, of a tragic hero: of a well-meaning tyrant whose glimpse of a better life for his people died with him.

Kliuchevsky's explanation of the nature and sequence of the Petrine reforms is equally memorable, and revolves around that extended military and diplomatic struggle known to contemporary Russians as the "Swedish War" but in Europe as the "Northern War," a convention followed by Kliuchevsky. The War, he says, decreed the order of the reforms, determined their tempo and the very methods of reform. Reforming measures followed one another in the sequence called forth by the needs of the War. The latter dictated in the first instance reform of the country's military forces. . . . The military reform was the first of Peter's reformative acts, the most protracted and the most burdensome, both for himself and for the people. . . . The Northern War and its alarums, its early defeats and later victories, defined Peter's way of life, determined the direction and the tempo of his reforms. . . . His tireless labors in this regard, continuing for nearly three decades, formed and confirmed his outlook and feelings, his tastes and habits. . . . Peter became the reformer so to speak unconsciously, even unwillingly: the War led him on and to the end of his life pulled him towards reform.

Kliuchevsky's insistence on the explanatory importance of the Swedish War in the history of the Petrine period approached the dogmatic, as we see; and it is reflected in his notebooks. "So war was the true perpetrator of reform," he wrote at one point, or again: "Not military affairs but military successes and the situation created by them for Russia were the source of reform"; and again: "Conduct of reforms from the War; before [the great victories of 1708–1709] by letter and through persons; afterwards by decree and through institutions."

Yet if Kliuchevsky is emphatically clear on the military motive of the Petrine reforms, and on their essentially military and fiscal nature, he is a good deal less than lucid on their longer-term consequences. The question of the overall significance in Russian history of the Petrine period he obviously found both complex and deeply troubling, yet one that had to be answered: "Peter's reform is the central point of our history, at once the sum of the past and the making of the future." Indeed, "the question of the significance of the Petrine reform is in large degree the question of the development of our historical consciousness," so often and so extensively had it been debated by Russians since Peter's own time. It is strange to reflect that notwithstanding the revolutionary and cataclysmic events in Russia since Kliuchevsky's time, much the same could be said today.

As Kliuchevsky points out, with evident pride, Peter's military victories won for Russia the status and prestige of a recognized European power, a status best symbolized perhaps in the new capital city, St. Petersburg, which by 1725 "had become the diplomatic capital of the European East," no less. These victories and the new status they brought with them had been made possible by Peter's military and associated administrative reforms, by his creation of a navy and reform of the tax system, by the hiring of numerous foreign experts and the founding of technical schools, by the reorientation and expansion of Russia's foreign trade, by a new burst of industrial development. Yet the whole enterprise was enormously costly; quite simply, "After Peter the state became stronger, but the people poorer." At the same time, it was accomplished not only "amidst a persistent and dangerous war," but against the opposition of the people, in a mighty struggle with "popular apathy and indolence, a rapacious bureaucracy and boorish landowning gentry, a struggle with prejudice and fear, with the ignorant reproofs of the clergy." So

the reform, modest and organic in its original design, directed to a restructuring of the armed forces and a broadening of the state's financial resources, gradually turned into a stubborn internal struggle, stirring up the stagnant mold of Russian life and agitating all classes of society. Initiated and led by the supreme power, by the customary leader and director of the nation, it took on the character and methods of a forced upheaval, of a kind of revolution.

It was a "revolution," Kliuchevsky explains, not by reason of its aims or results, which neither envisaged nor produced fundamental political, economic, or social change, "but only because of its methods and of the impact it made on the minds and nerves of contemporaries," causing a great "shock" that was the "unforseen consequence of the reform but not its intended aim."

> Peter's reform was a struggle of despotism with the people, with their lethargy. He hoped by his terrible power to stimulate initiative in an enslaved society, and through a slaveowning nobility to establish European learning and popular enlightenment in Russia as the indispensible conditions of social development; he wished that the slave, while remaining a slave, should act consciously and freely. The combination of despotism and freedom, of enlightenment and slavery—this political squaring of the circle, this riddle, delivered to us from the time of Peter, is still unresolved.

In this last remark, surely, the portentous events of Kliuchevsky's last years are at least faintly reflected (as Nechkina has insisted)—there, and in the Chekhovian mood of the famous concluding simile, where Kliuchevsky asks his readers to reconcile themselves with the legacy of the self-sacrificing despot as one "reconciles oneself with a violent spring storm, which, uprooting the ancient trees, freshens the air, and by its downpour assists the growth of the new crop."

First published in 1910, Kliuchevsky's lectures on Peter I enjoyed an enormous success. His "image of Peter the Great," writes Nicholas Riasanovsky, soon became the "best known and the most admired among educated Russians, or at least the best known and most admired after Pushkin's hero" of the epic poems "Poltava" and especially "The Bronze Horseman." The comparison to Pushkin is apt, since Kliuchevsky's was a "magnificent artistic image," as Professor Riasanovsky goes on to say; "an image so effective that it tended to obscure its own contradictions." Both orally and in print, moreover, in the successive Moscow editions of Kliuchevsky's *Course*, his image of Peter "remains strong among Russian and Soviet intellectuals" to this day, as Riasanovsky also notes, providing several examples.[1]

We might pause to consider why, in spite of its "contradictions," Kliuchevsky's account of the Petrine period in Russian history should have been, and remained, so influential among Russians. Riasanovsky's reference to its "magnificent" art is an obvious clue. At the time of Kliuchevsky's death one of his pupils, M. M. Bogoslovsky, a distinguished Petrine specialist, eulogized precisely the master's style for its "artistic beauty and the acuity of its comparisons and epithets." Yet it was

---

1. Nicholas V. Riasanovsky, *The Image of Peter the Great in Russian History and Thought* (1985).

more than a matter simply of style: "The secret of his synthetic power," Bogoslovsky declared, "is to be sought in his vivid artistic talent, in the force of his imagination and feelings," a talent or force which impelled him at times "to depart from the accepted norm. . . . The brush of the painter gave no rest to his hand, and amidst the sociological formulations he would suddenly paint as it were a live portrait of [among others] Peter the Great." Indeed, Kliuchevsky belonged "among the great Russian artists," to that tendency or school "which flourished in the second half of the nineteenth century and included Repin among the painters and in literature, above all, Tolstoi. Like these great representatives of Russian art, he was a Realist"; or again, in sum, both a "sociologist-historian and a realist-artist."

It surely is difficult, if not impossible to convey in English the quality of Kliuchevsky's prose, at once dense, biting, and mellifluous. Yet for Russian readers the prose itself of Kliuchevsky's *Course* is one of its main attractions. This point leads to another, also raised by Bogoslovsky, when celebrating the *Course* as a "splendid monument of our national consciousness. . . . The *Course* has already become the bedside book of every educated Russian," he observed [in 1912], while predicting that when translated it would "open the eyes of foreigners to the truth of our history." The deep patriotism of Kliuchevsky's *Course*, a matter also of its essential pedagogical function, whereby the voice of the teacher is clearly heard addressing his students, with a liberal use of personal pronouns, arresting aphorisms, and homely similes: this patriotic, personal, and pedagogical element is obviously another source of its initial, and continuing, appeal. Indeed Kliuchevsky's *Course*, with the reign of Peter as its "central point," may be considered, at one level, a masterpiece of Russian nationalist rhetoric.

In making this second point a third must quickly be added. Bogoslovsky compared the *Course* to the paintings of Repin, a comparison which suggests that Kliuchevsky shared the populist outlook as well as the "realist" style of Repin. This point was confirmed by another of his eulogists and former pupils (and distinguished Petrine specialist), P. N. Miliukov. Kliuchevsky's "populism," according to Miliukov, was the "democratic" populism of the 1860s and 1870s as distinct from the "constitutional-liberal current" of later times; and it drew for its sustenance ultimately on his own childhood, as the son of a poor village priest, the source of his lifelong attachment to the "old Russian way of life." This basic feeling for the "good folk of old *Rus'* " is reflected in the *Course*, says Miliukov, particularly in Kliuchevsky's evident sympathy for seventeenth-century Muscovy; thus we need only compare his depiction of that "fine Russian soul" and "best representative of the old Russia," Aleksei Mikhailovich, father of Peter I, to his portrait of Peter himself. *Svoi-chuzhoi:* "If in the world of Muscovite *byt* [mores] he felt at home [*svoim*], then in that of Petersburg he was a stranger [*chuzhoi*]."

> Muscovite *Rus'* was closer to him, dearer and, I think, more comprehensible. . . . [The eighteenth century] was not sympathetic to him. He looked on this period with something less than favor, and a gentle irony, gradually losing his good-natured outlook; and the further he went the sharper he became, even malicious. The century of Europeanization he spied and eavesdropped on like a stranger, one to whom "his own" will always be dear and in whom the foreign will never cease to arouse feelings of a certain enmity.

It is an exacting appreciation, one feels, but fair, on the evidence of the relevant lectures themselves; and it certainly helps in assessing Kliuchevsky's assessment of the Petrine reforms.

Before proceeding to such an assessment, however, we might consider certain intrinsic or inevitable limitations in Kliuchevsky's account of Peter I. The first of these is the lecture form, which, while helpful in a pedagogical setting, and even necessary, is not well suited to the sober transmission of knowledge to wholly or largely uninformed readers. This obvious limitation, the reverse of a main attraction of the *Course*, need not be dwelled on. A second such point, involving the fundamental historiographical problem of sources, does require further comment; as does a third that should be raised here, touching on certain of Kliuchevsky's underlying assumptions.

The lectures on Peter I, dating to the 1880s, are based primarily on the relevant volumes of S. M. Soloviev's very detailed *History of Russia from the Earliest Times*, which had been published by 1872. This fact is attested to by the archeographical efforts of Kliuchevsky's Soviet editors, by the secondary authorities, and by various of the master's students, quoting Kliuchevsky himself. Apart from Soloviev, these same sources indicate, Kliuchevsky drew on the *Complete Collection of Laws of the Russian Empire from the Year 1649*, familiar to every historian, the equally familiar miscellanies of Golikov and Ustrialov, the better known memoirs of the period, and monographs published in his later years, particularly those by his students Bogoslovsky and Miliukov on respectively Peter's local government reforms and on the Petrine economy—the latter of which, with its thesis that Peter attained for Russia the status of a European power at the cost of ruining the country, seems greatly to have disturbed Kliuchevsky as he revised his lectures for publication.

Kliuchevsky's lectures on Peter I, in short, are not based on original research in any very strict sense of the term. Nor are they based—nor could they have been—on the monographs and documentary collections that have appeared since his death. To the built-in limitation regarding their sources (or "data-base"), in other words, must be added the inevitable problem of obsolescence. It is all the more remarkable, therefore, that Kliuchevsky's analysis of the Petrine reforms is so often penetrating, his emphasis, at times, still so fresh. Nor has the very complexity of his "very complex assessment of the Petrine reforms" (Academician Nechkina's phrase) been superseded among serious historians, the various attempts to simplify matters notwithstanding.

This brings us to the somewhat elusive question of Kliuchevsky's underlying assumptions; assumptions, or preconceptions, which may appear questionable now if not obsolete, or at least *more* questionable now than they did then. I have in mind his crucial nationalist and statist preconceptions and his notion of Russia as always and inseparably a part of Europe. It is clear from virtually every page of the *Course* that for all of his "democratic populism" Kliuchevsky was as committed to the absolute value in history of the nation state—here, the Russian state—as were any of his predecessors or contemporaries; a commitment which permitted, even required him seriously to distort the earlier centuries of Russian history (in which "Russia" should perhaps rather be seen as at best a linguistic-cultural community supporting a number of states or quasi-states, tribal leagues, and so forth), to deny to the Ukraine any claim to a national identity, and to temper his criticisms of Peter I—to mention only three of its effects. It may be that particularly in his treatment of Peter Kliuchevsky came as close as any Russian historian has ever come to questioning the absolute value of the state. Still, a miss in a matter so important, as Kliuchevsky himself might have said, finding an equivalent Russian saying, is as good as a mile.

At the same time, Kliuchevsky's notion of Russia as Europe, while perhaps typical of most educated Russians of his day, is curiously at odds both with his devotion to Old Russia and with his hostility to Peter's reforms and their aftermath. The resulting confusion is to be seen (for example) in his alternating use of the terms "Europe" and "Western Europe." Referring to Peter's famous Grand Embassy of 1697–98 across the Baltic territories to north Germany, Holland, and elsewhere, we read that he thus, at the age of twenty-five, "finally caught sight of Western Europe"; but shortly thereafter we are told that at the north German courts Peter "first entered the big European world." Kliuchevsky quotes Peter as saying: " 'We need Europe for several decades and then must turn back from her to home,' " with the comment: "thus the rapprochement with Europe was in Peter's eyes only a means to an end"—this when we have just read that it was "Western Europe" that Peter had need of, and so forth. Kliuchevsky's notebooks are more directly revealing, in this as in other respects: ". . . out of a big and disdained semi-Asiatic state Peter made a European power"; "Peter was fascinated by Europe's technical and financial, not political and moral, sides"; St. Petersburg was a "gigantic work of despotism, equal to the Egyptian pyramids." In short, the unquestioned assumption that Russia somehow was always a part of Europe not only adds confusion to Kliuchevsky's analysis; it also accounts, in part, for the ambivalence of his assessment of the Petrine reforms and for his deflation, if not denial, of their revolutionary character.

This essay concludes with specific criticisms of Kliuchevsky's portrayal of Peter I, his explanation of the nature and sequence of the Petrine reforms, and his assessment of the overall significance of the Petrine period in Russian history. In doing so it does not pretend to offer a consensus of more recent Petrine scholarship, only this writer's views.

Kliuchevsky's thesis that Peter I was "one of those simple, straightforward people who can be read at a glance" is, in a sense, impossible to refute, since its truth seems to depend on the observer's acuity and perhaps also on the state of psychology in the observer's own culture. I tried to make this point elsewhere, in a study of certain dream-records of Peter I which first came to light in 1884 and were thereafter entirely ignored by historians, Kliuchevsky included. The study pointed out the rare, even unique nature by contemporary European standards of Peter's action in recording his dreams and suggested possible interpretations of some of them—interpretations indicating among other things ambivalence towards Moscow (rather than hatred of it) on Peter's part, his deep admiration for Turkey (rather than

Europe), and a fundamental conflict waging within him between his baser and nobler selves (rather than the simple, good-natured, essentially harmonious personality posited by Kliuchevsky). I also suggested that even taking this evidence seriously was not possible before the Freudian revolution in psychology had been absorbed by historians.[2]

Yet a close reading just of Kliuchevsky's character-study of Peter I reveals inconsistencies suggestive of a more complex personality than his own conclusions allow. His treatment of Peter's lifelong indulgence in drunken, public, often elaborately staged parodies, usually of ecclesiastical rites and authorities, is a case in point. Describing these "oppressive, exhausting festivities" as "indecent to the point of cynicism," and rejecting attempts by European observers—both contemporary and later—to divine in them a calculated political and educational motive (discrediting the Russian church), Kliuchevsky reduces the matter to a question of temperament. "It is hard to say whether the cause was a need for vulgar dissipation after a hard day's work, or Peter's habit of not reflecting on his conduct"; but Kliuchevsky is certain that nothing more was involved, reminding us that Peter's father displayed a taste for buffoonery, too, and that mocking the church indeed was a "Russian custom in moments of jollity." Thus in spite of their elaborate indecency and scandalous public display—which elicited extensive comment, surprise, and even shock among contemporary observers, both Russian and European—Peter's drunken parodies reflect only an "urge to play the fool." If he and his accomplices "mocked everything, sparing neither national tradition nor popular sentiment nor their own dignity," they were nevertheless "like children who in their games parody the words, gestures, even facial expressions of adults without ever thinking to censure or anger them." Besides, says Kliuchevsky in so many words, the church deserved it. Yet apart from the fact that Peter's conduct in this regard had precisely the effect of arousing prolonged, passionate, and widespread opposition to his rule, as Peter well knew, the activities of what he called his "Most Extravagant, All-Joking and Most Drunken Council," planned by him in minute detail, with the mandatory participation of dozens, even hundreds of people, men and women, of high station and low, in mockery not only of ecclesiastical but of royal—his own—authority, and carried out to the extremes of debauchery: all of this, surely, points to a complex, in part morbid, personality.

Equally, Kliuchevsky's emphasis on Peter the doer, the craftsman, the soldier and "boss-landlord" obscures both the fact of what he himself refers to in passing as Peter's "strong aesthetic sense" and "taste for architecture," and the consequences of this undoubted fact. This aspect of Peter's life and work has been investigated in detail only by specialists in art and architecture, particularly in more recent years; and their findings, confined to the specialized literature, have been largely overlooked by general historians. That literature documents among other things Peter's sustained interest in the graphic arts, in the arts of painting and sculpture,

---

2. J. Cracraft, "Some Dreams of Peter the Great: A Biographical Note," *Canadian-American Slavic Studies* vol. 8 no. 2 (Summer 1974), 173–197.

in tapestry and various of the applied arts, in all aspects of architecture, including design: an interest which in most cases, especially that of architecture, resulted in a sophisticated knowledge thereof—not to mention the eventual foundation of an Academy of Fine Arts in Russia, the formation of the first major art collections in the country, the creation of Russia's first museums, ornamental parks, and picture galleries, the building of St. Petersburg in the "new style," and so on. These are not the interests, let alone the achievements, of a simple mind, of a mere craftsman, even when they are not combined with his better known interests and achievements in science and technology.

Similarly, in his depiction of Peter I's character Kliuchevsky chooses to empha-size the assessments of European observers of the younger, rather than of the mature, tsar. For instance, the Anglican Bishop Burnet's recollection of the "boorish, ungovernable" Peter as he appeared in England in 1698 is cited—"designed by nature rather to be a ship carpenter than a great prince," said Burnet—in preference to Leibniz's awestruck observation, after talking with Peter at length in 1716, of "the vivacity and judgment of this great Prince . . . ; he summons experts to him and in conversation astounds them with the knowledge he shows of their affairs . . . all the mechanical sciences . . . seafaring . . . astronomy and geography." Or the remarks of John Perry, the English engineer who worked for Peter for fourteen years, and was greatly taken by his "genious and curiosity to enquire into the reason and causes of things, which method . . . he uses with indefatigable application in the minutest things." Peter, Perry added, was "very curious in observing the eclipses that happen, and in describing and discoursing of the natural cause of them . . . and of the motions of those other heavenly bodies within the system of the sun, according as the great Sir Isaac Newton has indisputably demonstrated to the modern world." This was not a simple man. Nor was the Peter who impressed Thomas Consett, the Russian-speaking Anglican chaplain in Russia (1717–1725), as "an impartial and excellent judge of any controverted points in religion"; nor the tsar whose inquiries about the "polytheism of the pagans, and if there were a pagan work on the subject," in the words of a learned local divine, resulted in the translation and publication for the first time in Russia of a book on Classical mythology.

Kliuchevsky's portrayal of Peter I, in sum, is too restricted with regard to the evidence as well as too positive in some respects, too negative in others. Yet more objectionable is his thesis that in one way or another the Swedish War explains virtually everything of significance that occurred at the time. It was to expedite the War, it is true, that various military, fiscal, and administrative reforms were introduced. In each case, though, the reforms in question were either not the first to be introduced or not necessarily the most important to be undertaken, contrary to Kliuchevsky's explicit assertions. The earliest military reforms, for example, particularly those in siegecraft and fortification, were implemented in the 1680s and 1690s—well before the Swedish War began (1700)—and in connection first with the youthful Peter's war games and then with his campaigns against the Turks. His earliest administrative reforms also date to the 1690s, particularly the creation of the Preobrazhenskii Prikaz, which was given sweeping jurisdiction over political offenses in connection with what appears to have been a rising tide of opposition to Peter's early rule, an opposition fueled, be it noted, by Peter's irregular—i.e., scandalous—public behavior as exemplified in the activities of his "Most Drunken Council." His tax reform, which brought with it the first universal census in Russia as well as numerous administrative and other changes, went well beyond the requirements of the Swedish War, as it clearly was intended to do; and the same may be said for the introduction of the collegial administrative system and associated local governmental and judicial reforms. Nor can Peter's Church reform be explained simply as a matter of administrative convenience based primarily on fiscal considerations prompted by the War, if only because it constituted, with its abolition of the patriarchate and other drastic changes, such a sharp break with the past. Here again the spreading internal opposition to Peter, spreading for reasons that had little to do with the War, provides the key. Kliuchevsky devotes considerable attention to this opposition but never links it, in a directly causal way, with anything of importance that happened in the Petrine period. The "war thesis," presumably, stood in the way.

As for Kliuchevsky's thesis that Peter's regime was revolutionary only in its methods and in its impact on contemporaries, I must, again, demur. To the extent that these methods were arbitrary, coercive, impetuous, or drastic, we should begin by noting, they were scarcely novel in Russian—Muscovite—history; even the use of foreigners and of foreign patterns or models had, in principle, ample precedent. Similarly, the cumulative impact or "shock" on contemporaries of the Nikonian reforms and the ensuing Great Schism of the time of Peter's father, or of the so-called Time of Troubles of the early seventeenth century, are surely comparable to that of the Petrine reforms. The difference here, like the difference in methods employed by Peter I and any of his predecessors, can only be a matter of degree. This would be consistent with Kliuchevsky's overall periodization of Russian history, whereby the reign of Peter I constitutes but one phase of a "fourth period" extending from 1613 (end of the Time of Troubles, advent of the Romanov dynasty) to 1855 (accession of Alexander II, advent of the Great Reforms). On the other hand, it would seem *not* to be consistent with his characterization of the Petrine era, quoted earlier in this essay, as the "central point of our history."

Kliuchevsky correctly pointed out that the Petrine reforms did not result in fundamental political, economic, or social change in Russia, at least not in the nearer term. It does not follow from this, though, that fundamental change was not intended, or that the seeds of such change were not deliberately sown. Arcadius Kahan, the economic historian, depicts the Petrine era as one of "rapid growth" and "extreme effort" in both industry and trade, for example. It was an era in which "the economic resources of the nation were strained to the utmost, when the burden of taxation grew heavier, the losses in human life and labor were large, and a large part of the country's output was consumed in prolonged wars." Yet it was also, Kahan says, "a period during which large investments were made whose gestation was destined to be long and whose returns were to be reaped later. This was particularly true for the investments in overhead capital or infrastructural projects such as roads and canals." The development of St. Petersburg under Peter I Kahan calls "the single most massive investment of the century": one which produced, "in a short time," the "most significant center of Russian foreign trade"; a trade whose growth in the eighteenth century was nothing less than spectacular, having increased, "in real terms, approximately fifteen-fold."[3]

St. Petersburg embodies, indeed, the Petrine achievement. By January 1725, when Peter I died, it had already become Russia's leading city, as he demonstrably had intended it to become virtually from its founding (in 1703). As well as Russia's main port and a major industrial center, it was now the chief residence of the ruler of the newly named Russian Empire, the principal seat of his government, and the headquarters of the Russian church: all of which institutions, in their titles, administrative procedures, even personnel; their dress, furnishings, and architecture, had been more or less Europeanized. From St. Petersburg European artistic and architectural norms and techniques, fashions in clothing and entertainment, notions of science and education, standards of justice and morality, would be more or less rapidly imposed on the rest of the country. One concrete result of these converging developments was the inundation of the Russian language with as many as 3,000 new words of Latin, German, Italian, Dutch, English, Swedish, and French origin, a lexical invasion of wholly unprecedented proportions. Visiting the city in 1739, the Italian Count Algarotti called St. Petersburg "this great window recently opened in the north through which Russia looks on Europe." The image is too passive. St. Petersburg was also the main channel through which Europeans, their goods, their words, and their ways poured into Russia.

What had happened in Russia by the end of Peter's reign was a kind of cultural revolution. A process of intensive Europeanization, for which certain precedents could be found in seventeenth-century Muscovy, was irreversibly, as it proved, set in motion. The Russian Empire had become a major component of the European state system and its economy interlinked with Europe's at a time when Europe was coming rapidly to dominate the world; and after 1725 every major movement in European science, art, religion, or manners would in time produce its Russian variant, until in due course Russian high culture entered the European mainstream (say, around 1850). These obviously were longer-term developments of immense historical significance, whether for good or for ill (Kliuchevsky tended to stress the latter). They can be traced back to the energy and will, above all others, of one man: Peter I "the Great."

My criticisms notwithstanding, nor the limitations mentioned earlier, Kliuchevsky's lectures on Peter I remain the classic work on the subject, the standard and point of departure for all later historians.

## DOCUMENTS

This section begins with a selection of legal enactments taken from the *Complete Collection of Laws of the Russian Empire from the Year 1649* (*Polnoe sobranie zakonov Rossiiskoi Imperii s goda 1649*, hereafter abbreviated PSZ), which was published in 1830

---

3. Arcadius Kahan, *The Plow, the Hammer and the Knout: An Economic History of Eighteenth-Century Russia* (1985).

in 45 volumes. The legislation printed here, as edited and translated for this volume, illustrates both the comprehensive content and the didactic style of the various Petrine reforms. It also illustrates Peter's preoccupation with state, especially military, concerns and his striving to catch up with the more advanced European countries. These documents are followed by excerpts from Peter's legislation of 1721 enacting his reform of the Russian church, whereby the autonomous office of patriarch was abolished and replaced by a Holy Synod appointed by the tsar.

The main author of Peter's church reform was Feofan Prokopovich (1681–1736), a Ukrainian divine from the Kiev Academy who had studied in the West and in 1715 had been called to St. Petersburg to assist the tsar in various projects. His speech at Peter's funeral in 1725, praising the first emperor in terms that were to become part of the official Petrine myth, comes next.

# Petrine Reform Legislation

## PETER CHANGES THE CALENDAR, 1699

It is known to the Great Sovereign [Peter] that not only in many European Christian countries, but also among the Slavic peoples who are in full accord with Our Eastern Orthodox Church . . . [as well as among] the Greeks, from whom we received our faith: that all of these peoples count their years from eight days after the birth of Christ, that is, from January 1 [rather than September 1, as did the Russians], and not from the creation of the world [as did the Russians, the present year by this method being 7208]; wherefore there is a great difference in these [two calendars]. It is now 1699 years since the birth of Christ, and this coming January 1 will begin the new year 1700 and a new century. So the Great Sovereign has decreed, for this good and beneficial matter, that henceforth in all government offices beginning this January 1 the year is to be counted as 1700 from the birth of Christ. And in recognition of this good beginning and of the new century [there shall be] in the royal city of Moscow, after solemn prayers of thanksgiving to God, appropriate festivities. . . .

## PETER'S DECREE ON WEARING GERMAN CLOTHES, 1701

[All ranks of the service nobility, leading merchants, military personnel, and inhabitants of Moscow and the other towns, except the clergy] are to wear German clothes and hats and footwear and to ride in German saddles; and their wives and children without exception are also so to dress. Henceforth nobody is to wear [traditional] Russian or cossack clothes or to ride in Russian [i.e., Tatar-style] saddles; nor are craftsmen to make such things or to trade in them. And if contrary to this the Great Sovereign's decree some people wear such Russian or cossack clothes and

The laws of Peter I printed here are taken from the *PSZ*, in this order: vol. 3 no. 1736; vol. 4 nos. 1887, 2015; vol. 5 nos. 2789, 3151; vol. 6 nos. 3711, 3770, 3840, 3890, 3893; vol. 7 nos. 4378, 4443. Translated by James Cracraft.

ride in Russian saddles, the town gatekeepers are to exact a fine from them, [so much] for those on foot and [much more] from those on horseback. Also, craftsmen who make such things and trade in them will be, for their disobedience, severely punished.

## PETER'S DECREE ON SHAVING, 1705

All courtiers and officials in Moscow and all the other towns, as well as leading merchants and other townsmen, except priests and deacons, must henceforth by this the Great Sovereign's decree shave their beards and mustaches. And whosoever does not wish to do so, but to go about with [traditional Russian] beard and mustache, is to pay a [hefty] fine, according to his rank. . . . And the Department of Land Affairs [in Moscow] is to give [such persons] a badge in receipt, as will the government offices in the other towns, which badges they must wear. And from the peasants a [small] toll is to be exacted every day at the town gates, without which they cannot enter or leave the town. . . .

## PETER'S DECREE ON ENTAIL, 1714

We Peter the First, All-Russian Tsar and Autocrat, etc., etc., etc., promulgate this decree to all subjects of Our State, of whatever rank and dignity they may be.

Whereas by the division of immovable property [real estate] among children after [the death of their] fathers great harm is done in Our State, both to State interests and to the ruin of subjects and the families themselves. . . .

[And whereas] should the immovable property pass to one son alone and the others [inherit] only the movable property [furniture, clothes, etc.], state revenues would be more regular . . . [noble] families would not decline . . . [and] the other sons would have to earn their bread through state service, education, trade, or something else . . . which would be beneficial to the State. . . .

We therefore ordain

1. that all immovable properties, that is, family, service, and purchased estates as well as homesteads and shops, are not to be sold or mortgaged but retained by one family member, in such manner:

2. Whoever has sons is to bequeath the immovable property to one of them alone, whomever he wishes, and that one will inherit [the said property]; the other children of both sexes will be awarded the movable properties, which their father or mother is to divide among them as he or she sees fit, leaving out the one who will inherit the immovable. And if somebody does not have sons, but does have daughters, he must do likewise. And if no such designation is made in his lifetime, then the immovable is to be designated by [government] decree the inheritance of the big son by primogeniture [po pervenstvu], and the movable will be divided in equal portions among the others; and the same is to be understood about daughters.

3. Whoever is childless may leave the immovable to one of his family [or clan, rod], as he wishes, and give the movable as he wishes to his relatives or even to strangers. But if he does not do so during his lifetime, then all of his property will be divided by decree among his family [or clan]: the immovable to a near [the nearest] one, and the rest to the others, as appropriate, in equal fashion. . . .

16. And should some matter henceforth arise that cannot be settled by this decree, it is to be reported in writing to the Senate, where special points [clarifications or additions] will be made and published, as with this decree. And without such a further decree no action is to be taken, under pain of loss [confiscation] of all one's goods and banishment. . . .

## MANIFESTO DEPRIVING TSAREVICH ALEKSEI
### OF THE THRONE, 1718

We [Peter I] hope that the great part of Our loyal subjects . . . know with what diligence and care We tried to raise Our firstborn son, Aleksei. To which end [We] gave him from his childhood tutors both Russian and foreign, and ordered them to instruct him not only in the fear of God and Our Christian faith of the Greek confession, but in the best of military and political (or civil) knowledge and foreign affairs, and to read in other languages History and all the military and civil sciences appropriate to a worthy ruler, so that he might be a worthy heir to Our All-Russian throne.

But We have seen that all Our above-mentioned efforts for the upbringing and education of Our said son were in vain, for he was ever disobedient to Us and paid no attention to what is proper for a good heir, and neither studied nor listened to the tutors assigned to him by Us, but rather went about with certain useless people from whom no good could have come to him. And though We treated him repeatedly with warmth and tenderness, and sometimes with paternal punishment, and took him with Us on many military campaigns, so as to teach him the military business, which is the first of the secular matters [needed] for the protection of his fatherland, but always withdrew him from harsh battles for the sake of the succession, though We did not spare Ourselves, and sometimes left him in Moscow, entrusting to him the governance of certain State affairs, for his instruction; and then sent him into foreign lands, believing that the sight of such regular States would inspire him and incline him to goodness and industry. Yet all this Our zeal availed nothing, and these seeds of learning fell on stone. For not only did he fail to act in this, but he hated it, and showed no inclination whatsoever for either military or civil affairs. Rather did he ceaselessly cavort with useless and base persons of coarse and disgusting habits. . . .

And though Our son, for his hostile deeds over many years against Us, his father and Sovereign . . . deserves to lose his life, nevertheless in paternal love We deeply sympathize with him, and forgive him his transgressions, and free him from punishment. Yet in consideration of his unworthiness and of all the above-mentioned useless behavior We cannot, in good conscience, leave him heir after us to the Russian throne, knowing that through this dishonorable conduct he would forfeit all the glory of Our people and benefit to the State acquired by God's mercy and Our unceasing labors. . . .

We therefore . . . by paternal authority . . . and as Autocratic Sovereign, for the good of the State, deprive him, Our son Aleksei, because of his faults and crimes, of the succession after Us to Our All-Russian throne, even if not one person of Our family should survive Us. . . . [Note: Peter I's baby son by his second wife, also named Peter, who was born in 1715, is then proclaimed heir; but the child died in 1719, leaving Peter I with two daughters. See further below, Peter's succession law of 1722.]

### PETER'S DECREE ON THE PURCHASE OF PEASANT VILLAGES FOR FACTORIES, 1721

Whereas by former decrees it was forbidden to merchants to buy [peasant] villages because such persons, except for their commercial ventures, had no other enterprises of benefit to the State; so now, following Our decrees, as all can see, many merchants have companies and many especially have founded various industrial works augmenting the State's benefit, namely silver, copper, iron, coal, and such like as well as silk, linen, and wool factories, many of which are already in operation. Therefore it is permitted by this Our decree, for the increase of such factories, for both nobles and merchants to buy [peasant] villages for these factories with the permission of the College of Manufactures [a government department recently created by Peter; see below the College's "Regulation" of 1723], but only on this condition: that these villages should remain permanently assigned to these factories. Therefore neither nobles nor merchants may sell or mortgage these villages to anybody without the factories, nor by any schemes enserf or redeem [these peasants]; except that in cases of dire necessity these villages may be sold with the factories with the permission of the College of Manufactures. And should anybody act contrary to this [decree], everything will be confiscated. . . .

### DECREE ON THE SALE OF SERFS, 1721

It was customary in Russia, and still is, that the petty nobility [*melkoe shliakhetstvo*] sells peasants and workers and domestics separately, like cattle, to whoever wants to buy [them]; which is not done in the whole world, and especially when the landlord sells father or mother, son or daughter [separately] from the [rest of the] family, whence comes much grief. His Majesty the Tsar has ordered a halt to this selling. But if a complete halt is impossible, then they should be sold as needed by whole families, and not separately. This [matter] is to be clarified in the compilation of the new law code [*Ulozhenie*], as the High-Ruling Lord Senators judge right. [Note: no new law code was ever issued under Peter I.]

### PETER ACCEPTS THE IMPERIAL TITLE, 1721

On the 20th day of this October, after council in the Senate together with the Holy Synod, the intention was adopted to beg His Majesty, in the name of the whole Russian people, in proof of their due gratitude for His high mercy and the Paternal care and pains which He has been pleased to show throughout His most glorious Reign, and especially during the war with Sweden; and [to acknowledge that] through His leadership alone, as is well known to all, He has brought the All-Russian State to such a strong and good condition and His subject people to such glory before the whole world: that He be pleased to accept from them, on the example of other [rulers], the title Father of the Fatherland, All-Russian Emperor, Peter the Great. . . .

Thereupon His Imperial Majesty was pleased to reply in short but very strong words . . . : "(1) I very much wish that all Our people clearly recognize what the Lord God by the late war and conclusion of this peace [with Sweden] has done for us. (2) It is right to thank God with all [our] strength; nevertheless, hoping for peace, it is not right to slacken in military matters, so that what happened to the Greek [Byzantine] Monarchy [it fell to the Ottoman Turks in 1453] does not happen to Us. (3) It is right to labor for the general benefit and profit, as God lays it before Our eyes, both inside [Russia] and outside, whence the people will gain relief."

And the Senate, with most humble bows, thanked His Majesty for such Imperial mercy and paternal admonition. . . .

## THE TABLE OF RANKS, 1722

The Table of Ranks [*Tabel o rangakh*] of all the ranks [*chinov*] Military, Civil [*Statskikh*] and Court, [indicating] which ranks are in which class [*klasse*] and which of those in one class have seniority according to time of entrance into rank, although the Military are above the others, even if they [the others] were promoted into said class earlier. . . .

[The Table follows, divided into three vertical columns headed "Military," "Civil," and "Court" (meaning the ruler's court), with the Military column subdivided into "Land Forces," "Guards," "Artillery," and "Naval." Each column contains 14 "Classes": for example, Class 1 under Military/Land Forces contains the rank "General-Fieldmarshal" while the corresponding rank in the Civil column is "Chancellor." Class 8 in the same two columns begins with "Major" and "Senate Secretary" respectively, each followed by the several other ranks in this class ("Lieutenant-Captain of the Fleet," "College Assessor," etc.). The lowest class in the two columns, Class 14, includes the rank of "Ensign" under Military/Land Forces and "College Commissar" under Civil. Thus all officer ranks and civil or court positions of any importance are listed, hierarchically, in the 14 classes of the Table of Ranks. One oddity of the Table is that officers of the Guards regiments consistently rank higher than officers in the Land, Artillery, or Naval services: thus a colonel of Guards (Class 4) is equivalent to a major general in the Land Forces or the Artillery and to a rear admiral in the Navy. At the same time, as indicated above, all military officers take precedence over civil or court officials of equivalent rank.]

[The following 19] points are appended to the above-instituted Table of Ranks so that everybody knows how to act regarding these ranks.

1. Princes of Our [Peter's] Blood and those married to Our Princesses have in all cases precedence and rank above all other Princes and high servitors of the Russian State.

2. Naval and Land [officers] are appointed to command in the following manner: when they are of the same rank, although one is senior in service, the Naval commands the Land [officer] at sea, and the Land the Naval on land.

3. Whoever shall demand honor higher than his rank, or take a position higher than the rank given to him, shall be fined two months' pay for each offense. . . .

4. Under [pain of] the same fine, nobody is to demand a rank for himself who cannot show the appropriate patent.

5. So also nobody is to assume rank according to a character which he received in foreign services so long as We have not confirmed said character, which confirmation We will be glad to grant to each according to his merit.

6. Without a patent, a document of release [from service] does not give rank to anybody, unless the said release shall be signed by Our hand.

7. All married women assume rank according to their husbands'; and should they do so contrary to this [Table and supplementary points], they are to pay the same fine as would their husbands for the same offense.

8. Although We grant free entry to public assemblies where the Court is present to sons of Princes, Counts, Barons, and the most distinguished Nobility and servitors of the Russian State before others of lower station, and gladly wish to see that on all occasions they are distinguished from such others by [their filial] dignity, nevertheless We do not thereby grant any rank to anybody so long as they do not render any service to Us and the Fatherland and receive a character for said service. . . .

11. All Russian or foreign [state] servitors who are or actually were in the first eight [classes of] ranks [i.e., from major in the Land Forces to general-fieldmarshal, and their civil and court equivalents, inclusive], their legitimate children and descendants in perpetuity, are to be considered equal to the best old Nobility though they might be of low birth, and were never promoted to Noble status by Crowned Heads nor granted a coat of arms. . . .

15. Military officers not from the Nobility who achieve senior rank [major or above] shall thereupon become Noblemen, as shall their children born thereafter; but if they had children before [said promotion], one son only may be granted Nobility upon the father's petition. Civil or court officials who achieve such rank but are not from the Nobility, their children are not [to be] Nobles. . . . [Thus non-noble military officers are granted special access to hereditary noble status, with its associated right to own serfs.]

## STATUTE ON THE SUCCESSION
## TO THE THRONE, 1722

We Peter the First, Emperor and All-Russian Autocrat, etc., etc., etc.

Whereas Our Son Aleksei's sin of Absalom [detailed above in the Manifesto of February 3, 1718; Peter here refers to Abalom's betrayal of his father, King David, as related in the Bible] is known to all [and then citing various precedents from Muscovite times as well as Peter's own decree on entail of March 23, 1714, also printed above, which supposedly was designed to prevent "private houses from coming to ruin from unworthy heirs"]. . . . We therefore establish this statute: that it should always be in the will of the Ruling Sovereign to designate whomever he chooses as heir, and moreover, perceiving some inadequacy, to set the designated one aside; this so that His children and descendants should not fall into such evil as [did Aleksei], having this restraint upon them. We therefore command all Our loyal subjects, clerical and lay without exception, to affirm this Our statute before God and His Gospel [according to the form of oath attached]. And whosoever shall be opposed to this or misinterpret it shall be considered a traitor liable to capital punishment and ecclesiastical excommunication.

## Peter Establishes the College of Manufactures, 1723

His Imperial Majesty most mercifully ordains this Regulation [*Reglament*] of the College of Manufactures, in accordance with which it shall administer its affairs.

Whereas His Imperial Majesty, for the creation and increase of manufactures and factories, has been pleased to establish this special College. . . . He has therefore been pleased to grant it guidance according to the following points. . . .

1. The College of Manufactures has supreme direction over all manufactures and factories and other matters relating to its administration throughout the Russian Empire, and must act in loyalty and zeal as it is here laid down. . . .

6. Whereas His Imperial Majesty has sought diligently to establish and disseminate in the Russian Empire, for the common good and profit of His subjects, various manufactures and factories such as are found in other states, the College is hereby ordered diligently to seek ways in which to introduce these and other curious arts into the Russian Empire, especially those for which materials can be found within the Empire; and to introduce the appropriate privileges for those people who want to create places of manufacture.

7. His Imperial Majesty permits everybody, of whatever rank and quality, in any and all positions, to found manufactories wherever they find it right. This [permission/invitation] is to be published everywhere. . . .

8. The College must be careful, when granting privileges to somebody to found a factory, that others who might later want to found such are not excluded; for from the zeal [competition] between manufacturers can come not only growth, but quality, and the manufactured goods will be sold at a moderate price, which would benefit His Majesty's subjects. Nevertheless, the College is to see that where [existing] factories are sufficient, the creation of other such factories does not corrupt manufacturing, especially by the making of [goods of] poor quality, even though they be sold cheaply.

9. The College must diligently inspect manufactories that are formed into [joint stock] companies, that they be maintained in good condition. . . .

10. Factories founded or henceforth to be founded at His Majesty's expense, having been brought to a good condition, are to be made over to private persons; the College is to be diligent in this endeavor. . . .

17. [This point repeats Peter's decree of January 18, 1721, printed above, on the purchase of peasant villages for factories.] . . .

23. So that master craftsmen of all sorts should voluntarily come to the Russian Empire from other States and establish manufactories as they wish at their own expense, the College is to send Manifestos to His Majesty's Ministers at foreign Courts inviting such craftsmen to settle in Russia. And whoever wants to come is to be assisted, with both free entry into Russia and free exit with his properties, and to bring needed materials and instruments without payment of customs [etc.]. . . .

## Peter Founds an Academy of Arts and Sciences, 1724

His Imperial Majesty has decreed the formation of an Academy in which languages would be studied, also other sciences and fine arts, and books would be translated.

On January 22, being in the Winter Palace [in St. Petersburg] and having heard a Project about the formation of this Academy, His Imperial Majesty was pleased to note on it with His own hand: "Designate for its support the revenues from the customs and excise duties collected from the [conquered Baltic] towns of Narva, Dorpat, Pernau and Arensburg, [an annual sum of] 24,912 rubles"; and in this decree of His Imperial Majesty the Ruling Senate concurred. . . . [The text of the Project follows:]

For the disposition of the arts and sciences two kinds of institution are usually used: the first kind is called a University; the second, an Academy or society of arts and sciences.

1. A University is an assemblage of learned people who teach the high sciences like Theology and Jurisprudence, Medicine and Philosophy, to young people, to the level, that is, that such [sciences] have now reached. An Academy is an assemblage of learned and expert people who not only know these sciences to their present level, but through new inventions (publications) strive to perfect and increase them; and they have no care for the teaching of others.

2. Although an Academy comprises the same sciences and the same members as a University, nevertheless in other states these two institutions have no connection between them, as there are numerous learned people from which various [such] assemblages can be formed. And [this is so] in order that the Academy, which strives only to conduct the arts and sciences to the best level by speculation (reflection) and investigation, whence both professors in Universities and students derive benefit, is not distracted by teaching; and [in order that] the University is not deflected from teaching by clever investigations and speculations, and the young people are thus neglected.

3. Whereas in Russia an institution for promoting the arts and sciences is now to be founded, it is impossible to do so after the example of other States; rather the situation in this State must be considered regarding both those teaching and those to be taught, and an institution formed that by the growth of the sciences [through research] would not only spread the glory of this State at the present time, but through teaching and disseminating them [these sciences] would benefit the people in the future.

4. Both of these intentions will not be fulfilled by the establishment alone of an Academy of sciences, for although it would promote and disseminate the arts and sciences, they would not soon take root among the people; still less [would they be fulfilled] by the establishment of a University, for when you consider that there are still no [secular] primary or secondary schools [in Russia], in which young people could learn the basics and then move on advantageously to the higher levels of science: in such a situation a University would be of no benefit.

5. Thus what is needed most of all [in Russia] is the establishment of an institution in which some of the most learned people would do the following: (a) Conduct and perfect the sciences, but in such a way that (b) Young people (those who can profit from it) could be publicly taught by them, and (c) Some people could be trained by them to teach the fundamentals of all the sciences to [other] young people.

6. In this way one institution with minimal losses would do as great a benefit [in Russia] as do three different ones in other states [secondary school, university, and academy]. . . .

7. And since this institution is similar to the Academy which is in Paris (except for this difference and advantage, that this Academy is also to do what is appropriate to a University or College), I [Peter] therefore would hope that this institution could most conveniently be called an Academy.

The sciences which could be done in this Academy can be freely divided into three classes: (1) all the Mathematical sciences and those that depend on them; (2) all the parts of Physics; (3) the Humanities, History, and Law. . . .

The duties of the Academicians [members of the Academy] are: (1) to investigate everything already done in the sciences; to promote what is needed for their correction and growth; to report anything found in such an event and give it to the Secretary, who must record it as appropriate. . . . (5) If His Imperial Majesty requires that an Academician investigate some matter [that lies] within his science, then he must do it with all diligence, and report on it in due course. . . . (6) Every Academician is obliged to prepare a system or course in his science for the benefit of students. . . . (8) Lest the Academicians lack the necessary facilities, a Library and a cabinet [museum] of natural objects should be opened. . . . [Note: The St. Petersburg Academy of Sciences, with its library and museum, and staffed mainly by German scholars, opened for business in August 1725, some six months after Peter's death.]

## Reforming the Church

### MANIFESTO CREATING THE HOLY SYNOD, 1721

We, Peter the First, Tsar and All-Russian Autocrat, etc. Among the heavy responsibilities We bear, in virtue of the authority bestowed on Us by God, for the reformation [*ispravlenie*] of Our people and those others subject to Our rule, Our attention has been drawn to the ecclesiastical order [*chin:* the clergy]; and having observed therein much irregularity and great deficiency in its affairs, We should indeed be anxious lest We appear ungrateful to the Most High if, having received such great assistance from Him in reforming both the military and the civil orders, we should neglect to reform the ecclesiastical; anxious lest when the Impartial Judge shall demand an accounting of His Trust to us, We shall have no reply.

Reforming the Church: from *PSZ*, vol. 6 no. 3718, compared with draft texts in P. V. Verkhovskoi, *Uchrezhdenie Dukhovnoi Kollegii i Dukhovnyi Reglament* [Establishment of the Ecclesiastical College and the Ecclesiastical Regulation] (Rostov-on-Don, 1916), vol. 2, pp. 6–11, 27–33. Translated by James Cracraft.

Therefore, mindful of the example of the pious kings in both the Old and the New Testaments, and having assumed responsibility for reforming the ecclesiastical order, and seeing no better means to this end than government by council, because this [governing the church] is too great a burden for a single person [that is, the patriarch] whose power is not hereditary: We hereby establish an Ecclesiastical College, that is, an ecclesiastical governing council which shall have authority, by the Regulation [*Reglament*] here following, over all spiritual affairs in the All-Russian Church. And We command all our loyal subjects of both the ecclesiastical and secular orders to consider this an important and powerful body; to bring to it their most serious spiritual concerns for direction, resolution, and conclusion; to be content with its decisions and judgments; and to obey its decrees in all things under pain of the severe punishment dealt those who defy or disobey the other Colleges [recently established by Peter in the state administration, namely the colleges of War, Foreign Affairs, Manufactures, etc.].

The Ecclesiastical College must hereafter supplement its Regulation with new rules, as shall be required by the varying circumstances of different cases; however, the College must not do so without Our consent.

We further determine that this Ecclesiastical College shall be composed [like the state colleges] of one president, two vice-presidents, four councillors, and four assessors. . . . And upon taking office [they] must make an oath or promise on the Holy Gospels according to the attached form. [Note: At its formal opening, on February 14, 1721, the Ecclesiastical College was officially renamed "Most Holy Governing Synod." The president and other members of the Holy Synod, all appointed by Peter, were all clergymen of various ranks and included, as second vice-president, Archbishop Feofan Prokopovich.]

## OATH OF THE HOLY SYNOD

I, the undernamed, hereby promise and swear by Almighty God and on His Holy Gospels that I am in duty bound, and by my duty wish, and in every way shall endeavor, always to seek in the counsels and judgments and all business of this ecclesiastical governing council the very essence of truth and justice, and to conform in all things to the rules prescribed in the Ecclesiastical Regulation or hereafter decreed by agreement of this council with the consent of His Majesty the Tsar. In all this shall I act out of sincere love of God and neighbor, according to my conscience and without hypocrisy, envy, malice, or obstinacy, suffering naught but the fear of God for having always in mind His incorruptible judgment. I am resolved that the glory of God, the salvation of souls, and the edification of the entire Church shall be the end of all my thoughts, words, and deeds; that I shall labor not for myself but for the Lord Jesus. . . . In case of doubt I shall not feign ignorance but shall diligently seek knowledge and right understanding in Holy Scripture, in the decrees of the church councils, and in the teachings of the holy fathers.

I swear by Almighty God that I wish to be, as I am in duty bound to be, a loyal, true, obedient, and devoted servant of my natural and true Tsar and Sovereign Peter the First, All-Russian Autocrat, etc.; and after Him to His Majesty's august and lawful successors, who by the will and autocratic power of His Majesty have been or hereafter shall be decreed worthy to assume the throne. All powers, rights, and prerogatives (or privileges) belonging to the Supreme Sovereignty of His Majesty the Tsar which have been or hereafter shall be enacted I shall guard and defend unsparingly, to the utmost limits of mind and body, even unto death, should events so require. I shall enthusiastically and to the last measure seek to promote everything that in any way might contribute to the faithful service and employ of His Majesty; and immediately I discover any damage, harm, or injury to His Majesty's interests, I shall strive not only to expose it in timely fashion but in every way to remedy it. And when in the service and employ of His Majesty or the Church some secret matter of whatever kind is entrusted to me, I shall keep it in complete secrecy and reveal it to nobody who has no need to know about it or to whom I am not commanded to reveal it. [Note: This paragraph of the Synod's oath of office follows almost verbatim that taken by all senior officials of Peter's government, as prescribed in the General Regulation of 1720.]

In conclusion to this my oath I kiss the words and cross of my Savior. Amen.

## The Ecclesiastical Regulation, Part I

This Regulation is divided into three Parts . . . namely: I. The grave reasons for [establishing] such an administration [the Ecclesiastical College/Holy Synod], and a description of it. II. Matters subject to its jurisdiction. III. The duties, procedures, and powers of the members themselves.

## Part I

What is an Ecclesiastical College [Holy Synod], and what are the grave reasons for [establishing] it?

An administrative college is nothing else than an administrative body in which certain matters are subject to the control not of a single person but to that of the several qualified persons appointed by the Supreme Authority. . . . And such colleges, varying according to the business and needs of the State, the Most Potent All-Russian Tsar, the Most-Wise Peter the First, has established for the good of the Fatherland beginning in the year 1718.

And as a Christian Sovereign, Guardian of Orthodoxy and all good order in the Holy Church, and having observed the needs of the ecclesiastical order and desiring that it should be better administered, He has deigned to establish an Ecclesiastical College. . . .

Lest anybody imagine, however, that this kind of administration is unsuitable [for the Church] and that the spiritual affairs of an entire society might be better directed by a single person [the patriarch], as the affairs of a particular diocese are directed by its bishop, we here put forth [nine] weighty reasons to prove that government by council is indeed the best, and better than one-man rule, especially in a Monarchical State such as our Russia.

1. In the first place, truth is more surely discovered by a council than by a single person. An old Greek proverb says that second thoughts are wiser than first;

thus how much more wisely will many thoughts, rather than one, resolve some issue. . . . In government by council proposals are examined by many minds . . . so that a doubtful matter is more surely elucidated and quickly explained, and what is required to resolve it is seen without difficulty.

2. And so far as there is more certain knowledge, there is great power to do things. For people are more inclined to accept and obey the decision of a council than the decree of a single person. The power of monarchs is autocratic, which God Himself commands us to obey in good conscience; yet monarchs have their advisors, not only for the sake of better ascertaining the truth but in order that disobedient subjects should not slander them by saying that they rule by force and caprice rather than by justice and truth. How much more so, then, should this be the case in church government, where the authority is not monarchical and the person governing is forbidden to lord it over the clergy. When only one person rules, his adversaries may slander him alone and so detract from the force of his decisions. But this is not possible when decisions proceed from a council.

3. And this is especially true when an administrative college is founded by the Monarch and is under His authority. For a college is not some faction secretly joined to promote its own interest but rather is composed of persons gathered together for the common good by order of the Autocrat after consultation with His advisors.

4. This is also important: when one person rules, procrastinations and interruptions in business often occur because of the overwhelming demands made upon him or because of his sickness or infirmity; and when he dies, business stops altogether. It is otherwise with government by council: if one member is absent, say even the chief person, the others carry on, and business continues its uninterrupted course.

5. But what is particularly advantageous, in such a College there is no room for partiality, intrigue, or bribery. . . . Should one member be partial to or adversely prejudiced against a person on trial, the second, third, and so on will be free of any such prejudice. How could bribery prevail when matters are decided not arbitrarily but only after regular and serious consideration? For any individual member will be wary lest he be unable to show good cause for his opinion and so be suspected of having taken a bribe. This would be particularly true if the College were composed of persons who could not possibly conspire together in secret, that is, of persons of different rank and station—bishops, abbots, and members of the secular clergy who are in positions of authority. In truth it cannot be seen how such persons could dare to reveal to one another a nefarious plot, let alone conspire in wrongdoing.

6. Similarly, a college enjoys greater freedom of mind to administer justice, for unlike a single governor it need not fear the wrath of the mighty. To put pressure on many persons, and moreover persons of different rank, is not so easy as pressuring one person.

7. And this is most important: the Fatherland need not fear from a counciliar government the sedition and disorders that proceed from the personal rule of a single church leader. For the common folk do not perceive how different is the ecclesiastical power from that of the Autocrat, but, dazzled by the great honor and glory of the Supreme Pastor [the patriarch], they think him a kind of second

Sovereign, equal to or even greater than the Autocrat Himself, and imagine that the ecclesiastical order is another and better State. Thus the people are accustomed to reason among themselves, a situation in which the tares of seditious talk by ambitious clerics multiply and act as sparks which set dry twigs ablaze. Simple hearts are perverted by these ideas, so that in some matters they look not so much to their Autocrat as to the Supreme Pastor. And when they hear of a dispute between the two, they blindly and stupidly take sides with the ecclesiastical ruler rather than the secular one, and dare to conspire and rebel against the latter. The accursed ones deceive themselves into thinking that they are fighting for God Himself, that they do not defile but hallow their hands even when they resort to bloodshed. Criminal and dishonest persons are pleased to discover such ideas among the people: when they learn of a quarrel between their Sovereign and the Pastor, because of their animosity toward the former they seize on the chance to make good their malice, and under pretense of religious zeal do not hesitate to take up arms against the Lord's Annointed; and to this iniquity they incite the common folk as if to the work of God. And what if the Pastor himself, inflated by such lofty opinions of his office, will not keep quiet? It is difficult to relate how great are the calamities that thereby ensue.

These are not mere inventions: would to God that they were. But in fact this has more than once occurred in many States. One need only investigate the history of Constantinople since Justianian's time to discover much of this. Indeed the Pope by this very means achieved so great a preeminence, and not only completely disrupted the Roman Empire, while usurping a great part of it for himself, but more than once has profoundly shaken other States and almost completely destroyed them. Not to mention similar threats which have occurred among us.

In government by an ecclesiastical council there is no room for such mischief. For here the president himself enjoys neither the great glory which dazzles the people nor excessive lustre and notoriety; there can be no lofty opinions of him; nor can flatterers exalt him with inordinate praises, because what is well done by such an administrative council cannot possibly be ascribed to the president alone. The very name President is not a proud one, for it means nothing more than "he who presides," and neither can he think highly of himself nor can others extol him. Moreover, when the people see that this administrative council [the Ecclesiastical College/Holy Synod] has been established by decree of the Monarch with the concurrence of the Senate, they will remain meek and put away any hope of receiving aid in their rebellions from the ecclesiastical order.

8. Church and State will further benefit from such an administrative council since not only each of its members, but the President himself, is liable to the judgment of his brothers, that is of the College itself, in case of notable transgression. This is not what happens when one Supreme Pastor rules, for he is unwilling to be tried by his subordinate bishops. And should he be compelled thus to stand trial, the common folk, who are ignorant of the processes of law and judge blindly, would be suspicious of such a trial and subject it to abuse. Hence it would be necessary to summon a general council to try such a Pastor, which can only be managed at great trouble and expense for the entire country. And at the present time (when the Eastern patriarchs live under the Turkish yoke, and the Turks are

more than ever wary of our State), it would seem impossible. [Note: Here and in the preceding point (7) the authors of the Ecclesiastical Regulation, mainly Peter I and Feofan Prokopovich, seem to have in mind events during the reign of Peter's father, Tsar Aleksei Mikhailovich, when the reforms of Patriarch Nikon produced a schism in the Russian church, as discussed in Chapter 2 in connection with the reading from the *Life* of Archpriest Avvakum, a leading opponent of the reforms. The schism was only resolved, at least superficially, by the Moscow church council of 1666–1667, which was attended by the other four patriarchs of the Eastern Orthodox church—of Constantinople, Jerusalem, Antioch, and Alexandria—and/ or their representatives.]

9. Finally, such an administrative council [the Ecclesiastical College/Holy Synod] will become a kind of school of ecclesiastical government. For in the exchange of the many different opinions, counsels, and sound arguments required by current business each member can be conveniently instructed in ecclesiastical administration and, by daily practice, learn how best to administer the House of God. Hence the most suitable members of the College will deservedly advance to the episcopal [bishop] rank. And thus in Russia, with God's help, grossness [*grubost'*] will soon disappear from the ecclesiastical order, and the best results may be hoped for.

## Feofan Prokopovich Eulogizes Peter the Great, 1725

What is this? Oh Russians, what have we lived to witness? What are we doing? We are burying Peter the Great! Is it not a dream, an apparition? Alas, our sorrow is real, our misfortune certain! Contrary to everybody's wishes and hopes he has come to his life's end, he who has been the cause of our innumerable good fortunes and joys; who has raised Russia as if from among the dead and elevated her to such heights of power and glory; or better still, he who—like a true father of the fatherland—has given birth to Russia and nursed her. Such were his merits that all true sons of Russia wished him to be immortal; while his age and solid constitution gave everyone the expectation of seeing him alive for many more years; he has ended his life—o, horrible wound!—at a time when he was just beginning to live after many labors, troubles, sorrows, calamities, and perils of death. Do not we see well enough how much we have angered Thee, O Lord, and abused Thine patience[?] O, we are wretched and unworthy, our sins are immeasurable! He who does not see it is blind; he who sees it and does not confess his cruelty is obdurate. But why intensify our complaints and pity which we ought to assuage. How can we do it? For if we recall his great talents, deeds, and actions we shall feel the wound from the loss of such a great good, and we shall burst into tears.

Text by Feofan Prokopovich in Marc Raeff, ed. *Peter the Great Changes Russia* (2nd. ed., 1972), pp. 39–43, trans. by Marc Raeff. Reprinted by permission of D. C. Heath and Company.

Alone a kind of lethargy or a death-like sleep can make us forget this truly great loss.

What manner of man did we lose? He was your Samson, Russia. No one in the world expected his appearance among you, and at his appearance the whole world marveled. He found but little strength in you, and on the model of his name he made your power strong like a rock and diamond. Finding an army that was disorderly at home, weak in the field, the butt of the enemy's derision, he created one that was useful to the fatherland, terrible to the enemy, renowned and glorious everywhere. In defending his fatherland he at the same time returned to it lands that had been wrested from it and augmented it by the acquisition of new provinces. Destroying those who had arisen against us, he at the same time broke and destroyed those who had evil designs on us; and closing the mouth of envy, he commanded the whole world to glorify him.

Russia, he was your first Japhet! He has accomplished a deed heretofore unheard of in Russia: the building and sailing of ships, of a new fleet that yields to none among the old ones. It was a deed beyond the whole world's expectation and admiration, and it opened up to thee, Russia, the way to all corners of the earth and carried thine power and glory to the remotest oceans, to the very limits set by thy own interests and by justice. Thine power which had been based on land he also has established on the sea, firmly and permanently.

He was your Moses, o Russia! For are not his laws like the strong visor of justice and the unbreakable fetters of crime[?] And do not his clear regulations illuminate your path, most high governing Senate, and that of all principal and particular administrations established by him[?] Are they not beacons of light in your search for what will be useful and what will avoid harm, for the security of the law-abiding and the detection of criminals[?] In truth, he has left us wondering wherein he has been best and most deserving of praise; was he loved and caressed more by good and honest men than hated by unrepentant sycophants and criminals?

O Russia, he was your Solomon, who received from the Lord reason and wisdom in great plenty. This is proven by the manifold philosophic disciplines introduced by him and by his showing and imparting to many of his subjects the knowledge of a variety of inventions and crafts unknown to us before his time. To this also bear witness the ranks and titles, the civil laws, the rules of social intercourse, propitious customs, and codes of behavior, and also the improvement of our external appearance. We see and marvel then at our fatherland; it has changed externally and internally, and it has become immeasurably better than it had been previously.

And he was your David and your Constantine, o Russian Church! The synodal administration is his work, and oral and written exhortations, too, have been his concern. The heart saved from the path of ignorance heaves a sigh of relief! What . . . zeal he has displayed in combatting superstition, adulatory hypocrisy, and the senseless, inimical, ruinous schism nesting in our midst. How great his desire and his endeavor to find the best pastoral talent, the truest divine wisdom, and the best improvement in everything.

Most distinguished man! Can a short oration encompass his immeasurable glory? Yet our present sad and pitiful state—moving us to tears and sighs—does not permit us to extend the discourse. Probably, in course of time, the thorns that butt our heart will dull, and then we shall speak of his deeds and virtues in fuller detail, even though we shall never be able to praise him adequately enough. But at this time, even remembering him but briefly, as if only touching the edges of his mantle, we see, my poor and unfortunate hearers, we see who has left us and whom we have lost.

Russians, it is not in vain that we feel exhausted by sadness and pity, not in vain, even though this great monarch, our father, has left us. He has gone—but he has not left us poor and wretched: his enormous power and glory—manifested in the deeds I spoke of before—have remained with us. As he has shaped his Russia, so she will remain: he has made her lovable to good men, and she will be loved; he has made her fearful to her enemies, and she will be feared; he has glorified her throughout the world, and her glory will not end. He has left us [ecclesiastical], civil, and military reforms. For if his perishable body has left us, his spirit remains.

Moreover, in departing forever he has not left us orphaned. How can we call ourselves orphans when we behold his sovereign successor, his true companion in life and the identically minded ruler after his death, our most gracious and autocratic sovereign, great heroine and monarch, mother of all Russians![1] The world bears witness that the female sex is no hindrance to Your being like Peter the Great. Who does not know Your God-given, natural sovereign wisdom and maternal charity! And these two qualities have arisen and developed firmly, not merely because of Your cohabitation with such a ruler—for he cared little to have merely a companion for his bed—but by dint of Your sharing in his wisdom, labors, and misfortunes; so that over many years—like the gold refined in the crucible—he has formed an heir to his crown, power, and throne.

We can but expect that You will consolidate what he has done and complete what he has left unfinished, that You will preserve everything in good order! Courageous soul, only endeavor to overcome Your insufferable pain, a pain compounded by the loss of Your most beloved daughter;[2] Yours is like a cruel wound that has been exacerbated by a new blow. And in this most bitter loss endeavor to be the way everybody has seen You alongside the active Peter, his companion in all labors and misfortunes.

And you, sons of Russia of all ranks and title, most noble estate, console your monarch and your mother by your loyalty and obedience; also console yourselves with the certain knowledge that in your monarch you see Peter's spirit—as if not all of Peter had withdrawn from you. For the rest, we bow before God our Lord who has thus visited us. Let merciful God, Father of all consolation, wipe the unquenchable tears of our sovereign Lady and her most beloved kin—daughters, grandchildren, nieces, and the whole imperial family; and let His merciful care sweeten the bitterness of their hearts and give us consolation. O Russia, seeing who and what manner of man has departed from you, behold also whom he has left to you. Amen.

---

1. Catherine I, second wife of Peter the Great, Empress of Russia from 1725 to 1727.—Ed.
2. Reference is to the death [March 4, 1725] of Nathalie, daughter of Peter and Catherine, . . . at the age of seven. (Peter himself . . . died January 28, 1725.)

# F U R T H E R   R E A D I N G

M. S. Anderson, *Peter the Great* (1978)

Evgenii V. Anisimov, *The Reforms of Peter the Great: Progress Through Coercion in Russia*, trans. John T. Alexander (1993)

Valentin Boss, *Newton and Russia: The Early Influence, 1698–1796* (1972)

James Cracraft, *The Church Reform of Peter the Great* (1972)

———, ed., *Peter the Great Transforms Russia* (1991)

———, *The Petrine Revolution in Russian Architecture* (1988)

Max J. Okenfuss, ed. and trans., *The Travel Diary of Peter Tolstoi: A Muscovite in Early Modern Europe* (1987)

Claes Peterson, *Peter the Great's Administrative and Judicial Reforms: Swedish Antecedents and the Process of Reception* (1979)

Nicholas V. Riasanovsky, *The Image of Peter the Great in Russian History and Thought* (1985)

A. P. Vlasto and L. R. Lewitter, eds. and trans., *Ivan Pososhkov: The Book of Poverty and Wealth* (1987)

# CHAPTER 4

# From Peter the Great to Catherine the Great

F ollowing the death of Peter I "the Great" in 1725 the Russian Empire was ruled, at least nominally, by a succession of his male and female relatives: by his second wife, Catherine I (1725–1727); his grandson, Peter II (1727–1730); his niece, Anna Ivanovna (1730–1740); a great-grandnephew, Ivan VI (1740–1741); his daughter, Elizabeth (1741–1761); and another grandson, Peter III (1761–1762). All of these rulers came to the throne in the midst of a political crisis that can be traced in large part to the confusion engendered by Peter's new succession law (see Documents, Chapter 3). Two of the reigns—those of Ivan VI and Peter III—were abortive, and two others—those of Catherine I and Peter II—were brief and ineffectual. The ten-year reign of Empress Anna became notorious in Russian history owing to the dominance of the St. Petersburg court by her German favorites, who allegedly had little interest in Russia's welfare. Peter III, himself half-German by birth and mostly German by upbringing and outlook, was overthrown and then assassinated by politicians and troops acting on behalf of his wife, Catherine, herself a German who went on to rule as Empress Catherine II "the Great" (1762–1796).

Thus between them Peter the Great and Catherine the Great ruled Russia for considerably more than half of the eighteenth century. Of the monarchs who reigned between them, only Empress Elizabeth, who also came to the throne as the result of a palace coup, has drawn much attention from historians, mainly because of the relative length and stability of her reign.

## ESSAYS

First, the Russian historian E. V. Anisimov, author of the essay on Peter I in Chapter 3, describes in an excerpt from his history of Elizabeth's reign how "restoring" her father's "legacy" after the rule of "alien" cliques at court became the declared policy of her government. In reality, as Dr. Anisimov argues here, Elizabeth's court was also dominated by corrupt favorites who helped further the emergence of the landowning nobility as the dominant class in Russia. This dominance, as he also grimly makes clear, was based on exploitation of the enserfed peasantry, who continually resisted, often violently. Moreover, Anisimov argues, this exploitation was "feudal" in character and thus hampered the development of capitalism in Russia, returning to a main theme of his earlier essay. Meanwhile Russian high culture, centered at the Imperial court in St. Petersburg and at the "nobility's capital" in Moscow, became steadily more European. It was under Empress Elizabeth that Moscow University and the St. Petersburg Academy of Fine Arts, both destined to become world-class institutions of their kind, were founded.

In the second essay, the late Professor Nadejda Gorodetzky of Liverpool University in England concludes her study of the Russian monk, bishop, religious writer, and later saint known as Tikhon Zadonsky (1724–1783) by assessing Tikhon's historical significance. Her work reminds us that during the Imperial (or Synodal) period of Russian church history, often excoriated by critics as a time of ecclesiastical abasement and religious malaise, loyal Russian churchmen were doing their best to raise the religious, moral, and educational standards of both clergy and people while earning reputations for piety, learning, and charity. The corruption and "free thinking" of the court and much of the nobility, along with the cosmopolitan and secular nature of Imperial Russian culture, have tended to blind historians to this other Russian reality.

Timofei (Timothy) Savelich Sokolovsky (later abbreviated to Sokolov) was born in the Novgorod region, the sixth child of a minor village cleric, and was trained at the Novgorod Seminary founded by the Archbishop Amvrosy mentioned in Dr. Anisimov's essay. On becoming a monk (1758) he took the name Tikhon; and as a scholar and ascetic of growing distinction he rose rapidly in the church, being appointed bishop of Voronezh in 1763 by direct action of Catherine II. Voronezh was an important city on the Don River (figuring largely in Catherine's plans for further Russian expansion south), in an area settled by numerous cossacks and Old Believers. There Bishop Tikhon labored for the Lord until 1767, when because of illness he retired to a monastery located east of the Don (hence his more common surname Zadonsky—that is, Tikhon from "beyond the Don"). Frail but never entirely reclusive, he lived at the monastery until his death in 1783, now famous locally for his work among the poor and for his spiritual counseling. His collected writings were first published in five volumes by the Synod in 1836, and he was canonized in 1861. The Russian writer Fedor Dostoevsky was deeply impressed by the spiritual legacy of St. Tikhon, on whom he based the famous character Father Zosima in his novel *The Brothers Karamazov* (1880).

## Empire of the Nobility

### E. V. ANISIMOV

Having successfully conspired to seize power [the coup of November 25, 1741], Empress Elizabeth had no definite program in either domestic or foreign policy. She and her entourage had no constructive ideas that might have signaled a fundamental change in the socioeconomic course of the country. The new empress

From E. V. Anisimov, *Rossiia v seredine XVIII veka: Bor'ba za nasledie Petra* (Moscow: Mysl', 1986), pp. 43–78, 224–226. Translated by John T. Alexander.

began her reign only with rather vague notions about the necessity of restoring the "principles" of Peter the Great that had been trampled on by the German favorites [of her predecessor, Empress Anna], of reintroducing the governmental institutions abolished after Peter's death, and of reestablishing Peter's forgotten laws. Neither Elizabeth nor her counselors conceived of the scope of the basic problems of Peter's great legacy—of the empire that stretched from the shores of the Baltic to the Pacific Ocean.

On this huge expanse in the 1740s and 1750s lived in all some 19 million people of both sexes. They were distributed extremely unevenly over the country's territory. While the population of the central industrial region encompassing the Moscow province and those adjoining it totaled no less than 4.7 million, the population of all of Siberia and northern Russia was no more than 1 million. No less peculiar was Russia's social structure at this time. The great majority of the country's inhabitants were peasants. The peasant population was divided into two basic groups: proprietary peasants (belonging to individual landlords, the Imperial court, and monasteries) and state peasants, whose suzerain was the state. Of the peasant population counted in the census of 1744–1747 (7.8 million souls of the male sex), landlords' peasants comprised 4.3 million souls or 50.5 percent of the total. The serf [proprietary] population as a whole constituted almost 70 percent of all peasants and 63.2 percent of the country's total population. Such a sizable preponderance of serfs quite eloquently attests to the character of Russia's economy in the mid-eighteenth century.

The Petrine reforms had facilitated the country's industrial development. In the first half of the eighteenth century outstanding successes were achieved in ferrous metal production. Back in 1700 Russia had smelted five times less pig-iron than England, the leader of the time (2,500 tons versus 12,000 tons). But by 1740 the output of pig-iron in Russia had already reached 25,000 tons and she had left England (17,300 tons) far behind. Subsequently the disparity continued to grow, and by 1780 Russia smelted 110,000 tons of pig-iron to England's 40,000 tons. At the end of the eighteenth century the industrial revolution that had begun in England put an end to the economic power of Russia, a power built largely on the semi-serf organization of labor. But in the mid-eighteenth century there was no reason to speak of a Russian economic crisis, and in these same years other branches of industry as well as trade were developing, too. . . .

The peculiar way in which Elizabeth came to power defined to a large extent the peculiarities of her domestic policy. Her very first decrees proclaimed that Petrine "principles" would provide the basis of governmental activity. In fact, one may confidently state that Elizabeth's coming to power signaled the onset of an unprecedented propaganda campaign. Its purpose was to cultivate a public opinion well disposed to the new monarch and to persuade as broad a circle of her subjects as possible of the legality of her power as Peter I's daughter, of the immutability of her rights to the throne. . . . Moreover, this notion of Elizabeth's succession to Peter's "principles" was combined with two concepts that would prove to exert much influence on the subsequent historiographical tradition. The first was that with Elizabeth's coming to power the political canonization of Peter the Great was completed. His person and deeds were evaluated unequivocally as a heaven-sent good for Russia. Archbishop Amvrosy vividly formulated this concept of Peter's greatness in a sermon of December 18, 1741, which elaborated on ideas expressed in Feofan Prokopovich's famous sermon of 1725 on the occasion of Peter's death [see Documents, Chapter 3]. Astonished by what had been accomplished under Peter, Amvrosy exclaimed: "How was it possible at one and the same time to establish the articles of war, to make war without rest for several decades, to journey through various countries and states, to found a navy, to reform the ecclesiastical and civil orders, and to do all of this with extreme difficulty and almost in danger of losing one's own most precious life! Oh, truly did Peter manifest therein extreme zeal for the Fatherland; sped along by God, he was able to do what in other states had been done over many centuries. When he made war, he taught the warriors how to do it; while teaching the warriors, he promoted the wellbeing of the citizenry; while promoting the wellbeing of the citizenry, he did not cease to think about his clergy."[1]

The second of these concepts advanced an extremely negative view of the period of Russian history stretching from the death of Catherine I [Peter's second wife, Elizabeth's mother] in 1727 to Elizabeth's own accession in 1741. These fourteen years were condemned as a time of darkness and decline for the country. In a sermon of March 25, 1742, Archimandrite [Abbot] Dmitry Sechenov of the Sviiazhsk Bogoroditsky monastery declared that with the burial of Peter and Catherine "our prosperity was buried; after their deaths the Lord punished us for our lawlessness and injustice with frequent changes [in government], and in such harmful changes Russia underwent such evil and such indecency that in recalling them sickness pierces the belly." In the sermon of Archbishop Amvrosy already quoted Elizabeth is made to say, as she rallies the soldiers for her coup: "My parents . . . toiled, established a regular army, acquired great treasure by many labors, yet now it is all dissipated and furthermore, even my life is in danger. But I sorrow not so much for myself as for the most dear Fatherland, which, ruled by aliens, is being ruined. . . ."

It is not accidental that we pay so much attention to the sermons of the beginning of Elizabeth's reign. In the eighteenth century, as earlier too, the pulpit was a tribune from which the decisions of the authorities were made known to the broad mass of the people, who were required to attend church. This tribune was also widely used for the propagation and explanation of official ideas. Hence the huge public significance of sermons is understandable. Delivered quite often by the most brilliant orators of their time, they were received as works of literature, and could produce an exceptionally profound impression on a flock that was almost completely illiterate. . . .

In the sermons of the 1740s the palace coup of November 25, 1741, was depicted as a civic and religious feat of Elizabeth personally, who, like some messiah

---

1. Amvrosy (Ambrose) Iushkevich (ca. 1690–1745), another Ukrainian graduate and former teacher of the Kiev Academy, was at this time (1741) archbishop of Novgorod, a member of the Synod, and Court Preacher. He was to crown Elizabeth in Moscow in April 1742, and in 1744 would formally receive the future Catherine II, German-born and a Lutheran, into the Orthodox church.—Ed.

inspired by Providence and the image of her great father, had resolved [in the words of her coronation program] "to cast out the night owls and bats seated in the nest of the Russian eagle, to capture and defeat the perfidious despoilers of the Fatherland, to tear out of alien hands the legacy of Peter the Great, to liberate the sons of Russia from captivity and lead them to the utmost felicity. . . ." And these ideas passed into the literature and art of the era.

Thus the ideological doctrine of Elizabeth's reign. The foremost task she envisaged was the restoration of state institutions and legislation to their status under Peter I. By a decree of December 12, 1741—the central enactment of a restorationist character—it was stated that, having "discovered the order of state administration of internal affairs altered from what it had been under Our father . . . and mother," the Senate was to take back "its former power of all kinds in said administration" and all of Peter's decrees and regulations were to be "most strictly maintained and followed without fail in all the departments of Our state." The Cabinet of Ministers—the highest governmental organ under Elizabeth's immediate predecessors—was liquidated and the Cabinet of Her Imperial Majesty, the monarch's personal office, was reinstated. Following the decree of December 12 a whole series of enactments restored the Colleges of Mines and of Manufactures, the Main Municipal Council, the Provisions Chancellery. . . . Proclaiming her "intention and desire . . . that all Our Empire be ruled according to the laws of Our most dear parent the Sovereign Emperor Peter the Great," Elizabeth condemned (decree of February 25, 1742) the favoritism of the preceding reigns and proclaimed that henceforth promotion in rank would proceed exclusively by seniority and merit. All promotions made in the reign of Ivan VI [1740–1741] were abrogated.

Of course, this did not stop Elizabeth herself from constantly violating the Petrine principle of advancement through service. . . . When she felt the need, she changed without blinking even fundamental Petrine laws. In February 1742 an adjustment was introduced into the Table of Ranks whereby the court rank of gentleman of the bedchamber was made equal to that of brigadier general, an adjustment motivated by the empress's wish to recognize the merits of persons who had helped her ascend the throne (Peter and Alexander Shuvalov, Mikhail Vorontsov, and others). Meanwhile the many petitions of scholars of the Academy of Sciences about raising their service status, which might have improved their position in the bureaucracy, went unrequited under Elizabeth. . . .

Practice showed rather soon that to restore the past, even if recent and glorious, and to live according to its rules, was impossible. On coming to power Elizabeth had put before the Senate the task of reviewing all decrees issued since Peter's death and of abrogating those that contradicted Peter's legislation. The Senate embarked on the work and by 1750 had managed to review only the decrees issued from 1725 to 1729. Ahead lay a gigantic task (the *Complete Collection of Laws [PSZ]* alone includes 3,000 decrees for the years 1729–1741), while the fruits of this work were minimal. In 1754 Peter Shuvalov delivered a speech in the Senate in Elizabeth's presence, and said that review of the decrees of the past ten years would in itself yield little and would scarcely facilitate the correction of deficiencies. In his opinion, it would be desirable to direct the effort toward devising a new code of laws—a new *Ulozhenie*—and to create a commission for that purpose. Under the influence of palpable necessity Elizabeth felt compelled to agree with Shuvalov and to admit that "manners and customs have been changing with the passage of time, so change in the laws is also necessary." A commission for the compilation of a new law code was created. . . .

The failure of Elizabeth's "restorationist" policies was no doubt predetermined by the fact that she followed not the spirit but the letter of Petrine legislation, blindly copying his system of administration. This inevitably robbed her government in the 1740s of the necessary dynamism. Having abolished the Cabinet of Ministers, she reinstituted the importance of the monarch's personal participation in state affairs. Through her personal office (the Cabinet of Her Imperial Majesty) she could control a huge amount of business. The abundance of personal decrees characteristic of the beginning of Elizabeth's reign testifies to the formal strengthening of the monarch's personal participation in government. Like Peter, Elizabeth thus concentrated all authority in her own hands. But the resemblance to Peter ended there. Neither in personal qualities nor in working habits could the daughter match the father. Peter's creative, strenuous labor, inspired by a definite system of ideas, was unknown to Elizabeth. Fearing anything new and unfamiliar, she stubbornly chained herself to the Petrine legacy; and if she did not find in it answers to a current problem, she became flustered and let matters take their course, putting off for months or even years the resolution of questions that required the slightest initiative, or delegating them to her advisors.

It is not surprising that, try as we might, we will not find fresh ideas in the laws issued in the 1740s, ideas that would allow us to describe the domestic policies of Elizabeth's government as either original or purposeful. . . . Nor should we forget the elements of demagoguery inherent in those policies. The constant declarations of fidelity to Peter's "principles" served the end, above all, of strengthening the empress's authority. In fact, her "fidelity" shows forth clearly in her attitude to Peter's favorite child, the navy. In 1733 Russia had in the Baltic thirty-seven ships of the line and fifteen frigates, but in 1757 the number of ships had decreased to twenty-seven and of frigates to only eight, while their condition was pitiful. For years the squadrons did not put to sea, and the first sea campaign of the Seven Years' War [1756–1763, in which Russia fought against Prussia] showed the almost total disrepair of the fleet, which feared a fresh wind more than the foe. Ships lost rotted spars, sprang leaks, and sank.

And in Elizabethan times amazingly little was done to immortalize the memory of the great transformer of Russia. The papers of the Cabinet of Peter the Great rotted away unattended. Voltaire was commissioned to write the history of Peter's reign only at the end of the 1750s.[2] Although in 1743 Elizabeth approved the project of a great equestrian statue of Peter the Great by Carlo Bartolomeo Rastrelli, the monument, which was finished in 1747 by the sculptor's son, did not see the

---

2. Voltaire did however promptly complete the work, based on documents sent him by Elizabeth's government: his *Histoire de l'Empire de Russie sous Pierre le Grand [History of the Russian Empire under Peter the Great]*, first published in two volumes in 1765, rapidly became an international best-seller.—Ed.

light of day until well after her reign. The empress had lost interest in it and halted the financing.

Yet objectively, it must be noted, the open proclamation by Peter the Great's daughter that his principles were fundamental to her own rule held great significance for Russia's future. Peter and everything connected with his personality and concerns symbolized a great break, the advent of a new epoch in the country's life. During Elizabeth's reign the process of Europeanizing Russia became irreversible. To a large extent this was due to her recognition of the magnitude of the changes achieved at the start of the eighteenth century, and to her conscious desire to continue the work begun by Peter. . . .

[Thus] Elizabeth rather quickly convinced everybody that she did not intend to drive the foreigners out of Russia. Like Peter, she embraced the idea of using foreign specialists, of whom Russia had great need, but under the supervision of native Russians. This approach remained constant throughout her reign and could not fail to bear fruit. Hundreds of top-grade foreign specialists—seamen, army officers, engineers, scholars, artists, and musicians—found a second home in Russia and made their contributions to her economy, culture, and science. To the ranks of such foreigners belong the Rastrellis father and son [architects and sculptors], the composer Francesco Araja, the painter Giussepe Valeriani, the historian Gerhard Friedrich Müller, and many others.

If the excesses of the beginning of Elizabeth's reign may be explained chiefly by a wave of nationalism born of the years of "alien" rule [under Empress Anna], then the reactions of the upper ranks of the Russian clergy had deeper roots. Her coming to power, following the overthrow of the "foreign minions," raised their hope that under the pressure of anti-German public opinion the empress would not only expel all the foreigners but would, if not return Russia to pre-Petrine times, then at least weaken state supervision of the church and be stricter in handling heterodoxy and atheism. . . .

Elizabeth could not ignore the opinions of churchmen who had given her support in her first days in power. Nor were her own religious views distinguished by toleration. Thus among the first acts of her government was a whole series of laws aimed at stopping the spread in Russia of other faiths besides Orthodoxy (decrees on dismantling Armenian churches and Muslim mosques, on combating the Quakers, on expelling Jews, and so forth) as well as at increasing Orthodox missionary activity among her pagan subjects. Thus began, too, the next stage of the autocracy's struggle with the Schism, which bound together broad circles of the peasantry discontented with the religious and social policies of absolutism.[3] Under Elizabeth there would be no thought of compromise: by decrees of October 1742 and February 1743 all the punitive regulations of Peter I and Catherine I, perhaps the most severe in the autocracy's long struggle with the Schism, were

---

3. The seventeenth-century origins of the Great Schism in Russia were discussed in Chapter 2, in connection with the *Life* of Avvakum.—Ed.

confirmed. Research has shown that Elizabeth's decrees did not remain on paper; in the reign of Peter's daughter, persecution of schismatics [or Old Believers] was intensified throughout the Urals region and in Siberia. . . .

Still, concerned no less than the Synod with maintaining the purity of the "true faith" as well as good order in church, Elizabeth remained Peter's daughter. Along with decrees strengthening the importance of the church in the life of the country came the decree of February 19, 1743, showing the empress's fidelity to Peter's policy of secularization. In the imperative form characteristic of Peter, this decree confirmed all his enactments prescribing that "all Russian people of whatever rank, except the clergy and farming peasants, are to wear German clothes like that of the foreigners and to shave their beards and mustaches; and nobody is to wear [traditional] Russian or cossack clothes or other illegal dress, or to sell them in the market, under pain of severe punishment" [see Documents, Chapter 3]. The practical and symbolic significance of this decree is difficult to overestimate, considering the complexity of the situation—the resurgent nationalism—at the beginning of Elizabeth's reign.

Further, the hope had also arisen in the first years of the reign among the most conservative of the higher clergy that the Synod might be abolished altogether and the patriarchate reestablished. The initiator of the movement was the metropolitan of Rostov, Arseny Matseevich. He was supported by many members of the Synod headed by that Archbishop Amvrosy who was quoted above. Elizabeth's frequent meetings with the hierarchs of the church in the first half of the 1740s permit us to assume that the proposal to restore the patriarchate was known to the express; yet in this question, so important to the churchmen, she did not intend to make concessions. Neither in these years nor later was the proposal seriously discussed in government circles. To be sure, in the 1740s members of the Synod persuaded Elizabeth to go along with some changes in the administration of the church's immovable property (the College of Economy, founded in 1726 to supervise this property, was liquidated). But this did not change the trend towards secularization begun under Peter and completed in 1764 under Catherine II, with the full transfer of the church's landed wealth to the state. . . .

Overall, Elizabeth's internal policies in the 1740s are not notable for their integrity. One prominent move by her government at this time was the second census of the taxpaying population. It was conducted in 1744–1747 on the model of Peter's first census [1722–1724] but it encompassed more territory. In the course of this second census a grand total of 9.1 million male souls was registered, or 17 percent more than the total of Peter's census (7.8 million). This was a great success for the government, as before taking the census it had been informed that since the first census more than 2.1 million souls had disappeared from the tax rolls. Now, after compiling the new cadastral books, the government could count on an increase in collections from direct taxes—the most important source of state revenue. And remittances to the treasury actually did increase. But this was due in great measure to one circumstance.

Among the first propaganda measures of the new monarchy was a decree "forgiving" the taxed population for arrears in tax payments in all seventeen years of the existence of the soul tax [1724–1741]. In December 1741 the Arrears Chancellery was liquidated: it had been the main organ for extracting taxes due, which by then already exceeded 5 million rubles or the amount of one year's total take from the soul tax. In 1752 arrears were "forgiven" to 1746 inclusive, for a total forgiven of 2.5 million rubles. These measures coincided with taking the second census and collecting taxes according to the new tax rolls. The government's calculation had proved accurate. The extraction of arrears accumulated over many years had always been ineffective, provoking constant complaints, embittering indigent taxpayers, and—most important—complicating (or making impossible) the successful collection of current taxes. Following the remission of almost all arrears, collection of the soul tax according to the new rolls proceeded much more expeditiously than before, and despite the traditional covert and sometimes even overt resistance of the taxpayers. Furthermore, in 1742 and 1743 the annual amount of the soul tax was temporarily reduced from 70 to 60 copecks [100 copecks to the ruble].

A decrease in the soul tax was also enacted in 1749–1751, 1753–1754, and 1757–1758. But in these years it was connected with the implementation of a program proposed, very likely, by one of the brightest statesmen of Elizabeth's reign, Peter Ivanovich Shuvalov [1700–1762]. His activities are linked with a new stage in the domestic policies of Russian absolutism. Therefore it is appropriate to discuss Shuvalov's more important projects in greater detail.

In the polemical and political documents of the second quarter of the eighteenth century it had become commonplace to recognize the huge significance of the taxpaying peasantry whether for the defense of the state or for its general wellbeing (we should note that nobles and clergy did not pay the soul tax, while ordinary townsmen as well as the peasants did). Arguing in favor of proposals for lightening the peasants' tax burden, several senior officials had written in a memorandum of 1727: "The army is so vital that without it the state cannot stand, and therefore it is necessary to care for the peasants; for the soldier is linked to the peasant like the soul to the body; if there be no peasant, then there will be no soldier either." Virtually the same thought occurred to Peter Shuvalov: "State functionaries of every quality: nobility, clergy, and all sorts of proprietors, all draw their sustenance in everything from them [the peasants]." But from these unoriginal observations Russia's richest dignitary made quite original deductions.

Stating that the soul tax provided the lion's share of state revenue, Shuvalov directed his readers' attention to its "extreme inconvenience" for the taxpayer, which led, on the one hand, to the ruination of the peasantry and, on the other, to the growth of arrears. The point was that the soul tax, which Peter had introduced in 1724, was assessed on the entire male population without distinction as to age, physical condition, and economic position. The tax-censuses of male "souls" were carried out rarely, so that for extended periods rural and urban communities were obligated to pay the tax not only for the elderly and the under-age but also for those who had fallen off the tax rolls: the dead, fugitives, army recruits, and so forth. This evoked constant complaints from the peasants and townsmen, exacerbated their impoverishment and flight, and, as a result, the payment of the soul tax fell into arrears. There the matter stood by the mid-1740s. Meanwhile the treasury was confronting a sharply increased demand for more revenue. For the growth of the army alone not less than 1.2 million rubles were urgently needed, and by 1749 the budget deficit had reached 3.6 million rubles.

Peter Shuvalov understood that to increase the rate of the unpopular soul tax would be shortsighted, and therefore he put forward the proposal, extremely bold for that time, of reorienting budget revenues from direct to indirect taxation. Specifically, in projects of 1745 and 1747 he proposed gradually to raise the price on salt sold by the state (geared to increased salt extraction) and proportionately to lower the soul tax. In persuading Elizabeth to follow this course, Shuvalov wrote: "The sale [of salt], however high the price is set, cannot harm revenue because salt is essential to sustain human life, and thus revenue from salt is not dependent on free choice." In a supplement to the project of 1747 Shuvalov submitted a proposal for raising the price of spirits, with part of the anticipated profit also to be earmarked as compensation for lowering the soul tax. Although both proposals pursued the aim of the "profitmakers" [pribyl'shchiki: officials first appointed by Peter I to invent new taxes]—namely, increased revenue for the treasury—Shuvalov's notion of replacing direct taxation by indirect was undoubtedly quite progressive for the time. The finances of the leading countries of Europe had been developing precisely in this direction (intensifying commercial-monetary relations). For example, out of 575 million livres of income in the budget of contemporary France, 300 million (52 percent) came from the salt tax and 60 million (10 percent) from the excise on spirits. Of course, in the final accounting the salt tax, like any other, weighed on the shoulders of the people no less heavily than the soul tax, for salt was indeed "essential to sustain human life." But the shrewd semantic camouflage of this measure in combination with the lowering of the soul tax by an annual average of three copecks "per census soul" over a six-year period (and amid the Seven Years' War) allowed the government to introduce the reform without too much controversy. In sum, the price of salt was raised by 120 percent while remittances to the treasury from the salt tax grew from 801,000 rubles in 1749 to 2.2 million rubles in 1761, that is, by a factor of three. Receipts to the treasury from raising the price of spirits following Shuvalov's proposal almost tripled, too: from 1.2 million rubles in 1749 to 3.4 million rubles in 1761.

In 1752 and 1753 Shuvalov submitted projects for the reform of customs duties. He proposed in general to abolish all internal taxes on commerce while increasing import and export duties by 13 copecks per ruble. This reform was implemented by a decree of December 1753. And it, too, was crowned with success for the treasury. In 1753 the customs had yielded only 1.5 million rubles whereas in 1761 the total was 2.7 million rubles—and this in a time of war [Seven Years' War, 1756–1763]!

Yet it was not its fiscal aspect that distinguished Shuvalov's customs reform. As we know, in the eighteenth century the complex economic process of forming a national market was occurring: economic specialization was increasing in various regions of the country, the number of fairs was growing, and internal commercial ties were becoming more intensive. The huge country was beginning to function more and more as a single economic organism. Nevertheless, many obstacles stood in the way of the rapid development of national economic ties, among which the most serious were internal customs duties. They hampered the development of trade, and under Peter I taxes on internal commerce had actually increased. Now, as a result of Shuvalov's customs reform, this vestige of the Middle Ages had been brought to an end. I do not exaggerate. As late as the nineteenth century the economies of many European countries suffered from the internal customs barriers inherited from the period of feudal divisions. In France, internal customs duties were liquidated only with the monarchy itself, in the course of the French Revolution, while in Germany they were abolished only in the 1830s. These facts underscore the boldness and novelty of the Shuvalov project: its author's unconventional thinking.

Now let us review the internal background to Peter Shuvalov's economic reforms, excluding at the outset such superficial causes as his concern for the "state interest" as well as the personal stake of this new "mogul" in the financial aspect of each of his projects. But in order to do this—to bring out the social mechanism that led to these reforms—it is essential to go back twenty or thirty years and touch on the Petrine reforms or, more precisely, their short-term results. For thanks to those reforms, Russia had achieved remarkable successes in economic and political development and in the course of a single generation had entered the ranks of leading world powers, all of which had tremendous significance for the country's subsequent development.

On whose account had these successes been achieved and who, in the final reckoning, reaped their fruits? The facts permit us to affirm that the Petrine era witnessed a fundamental strengthening of the feudal exploitation of the peasantry, a consolidation of the serf regime in all its manifestations, and, as never before, a solidifying of the noble estate's domination of all spheres of the country's life. . . .

The introduction of the soul tax in 1724 had led only to the stabilization of the state dues of the peasants: over several decades the amount levied "per census soul" remained 70 copecks a year. The law did *not* determine the scope of the landlord dues owed by the peasants. On the contrary, given the stability of the soul tax landlords could increase the rent at will without worrying that the state would tax away the surplus product that they counted on. In this way, the introduction of the soul tax stimulated a significant, uninterrupted growth in the labor and money dues owed by peasants to their noble masters. Nor did the latter confine themselves to receiving such dues. The success of Peter I's economic development had suggested to the nobility the quite long-term and, as it then seemed, easy option of making money from commercial and industrial enterprises. Between the 1740s and the 1760s noble entrepreneurship became especially marked in the metallurgical industry, a development directly connected with the rising profitability of this industry. In 1750 the demand for Russian iron reached an unprecedented level: 100 percent of all production. This gave birth to a peculiar industrial boom.

The first to beat a path to the metal industries were the brothers Peter and Alexander Shuvalov, who appropriated the most profitable state enterprises located in the Urals and in the European center of the country. The industrial undertakings of titled entrepreneurs like them, like Mikhail and Roman Vorontsov, like Ivan Chernyshev, Sava Iaguzhinsky, and others, stemmed from such exceptionally favorable circumstances as allow us to label them hothouse plants. First, they all received from the treasury on extremely favorable terms enterprises that were already profitable. Second, they had at their disposal unlimited quantities of raw materials (ores most of all), forest and water resources, and, most importantly, an unpaid labor force: either serfs, or state peasants assigned for months at a time to work off their soul tax. The state did everything possible to insure that the new owners did well. It gave them loans, offered special debt repayment terms, made exceptions in the law. Industrial entrepreneurs from other social estates and the state's remaining enterprises were put in an unequal competitive position in all respects.

Still, noble entrepreneurship in metallurgy (as in other branches of industry) sooner or later met with failure. Why? A comprehensive answer to this question has been given by the historian N. I. Pavlenko. . . . In his opinion, noble entrepreneurship can be understood only in the context of the then prevailing feudal relations, since merely acquiring factories did not make their owners capitalists but rather "in essence continued the tradition of feudal grants." If the noble factory owner did achieve success (temporary, as a rule), he did so only as a result of applying *extensive* methods of managing his economy: more factories or forges were built, more state peasants were assigned to the factories than the law permitted, the industrial exploitation of his own serfs was stepped up. Yet in receiving an industrial enterprise in the form of a feudal grant, he had received something qualitatively different from a feudal estate; "and all noble entrepreneurs managed their industrial economies with the same primitive, rapacious devices that they used to manage their serf estates. Their wasteful management is demonstrated by the fact that nobles who received such basic resources as factories to supplement their income not only failed to improve their financial affairs, but even made them worse. All noble factory owners ended up hopelessly in debt to the treasury and private creditors." However, for us now the outcome of their enterprise is less important than the phenomenon of serfowners adapting themselves to a developing capitalist structure with a view to receiving feudal rent on an expanded scale.

Of course, not every nobleman was wealthy enough to dabble in metallurgy. Many nobles were content to distill spirits on their estates. Surplus grain from his own *demesne* [home estate] as well as from his peasants in the form of natural *obrok* [dues in kind], the unpaid toil of his serfs, whose obligations were expanded to include "sitting with the wine" along with work in the fields: all this made distilling in the eyes of the nobility a seductive source of supplementary income. Between 1730 and 1770 distilling became one of the most popular enterprises on serf estates. In a project of 1741, Andrei Osterman [a senior official] remarked on the development of private distilling and the slackness of the [government's] battle against the contraband commerce in spirits. He wrote that for landowners living in St. Petersburg (even "those who possess the smallest hamlets"), their peasants brought to town "from 100 to 300 pails of spirits, such a great amount that not only could they not drink it up themselves, but even if they used it instead of water it would last for a year!" Osterman's derisive perplexity reflects his lack of understanding of the fundamental interests of the dominant class. In the same project he even proposed to restrict distilling by the nobility. Elizabeth's government, detecting no humor in the situation, anxiously moved to meet the nobles' needs. Although she did not abolish the treasury's extremely lucrative monopoly on the trade in spirits, she actively fostered the development of distilling by the nobility, her most radical measure in this direction being the decree of 1755 forbidding all non-nobles to engage in distilling. Thereafter non-noble distilleries were subject to liquidation or sale, and the nobility monopolized one of the most lucrative branches of industry. . . .

It should be emphasized that in the first half of the eighteenth century and especially after Peter's death in 1725 the Russian economy was increasingly marked by wholesale use of the involuntary labor of serfs or assigned state peasants. Entrepreneurs, including non-nobles, did not have to rely on the free labor market which, with the strengthening of the state's campaign against fugitives and "freemen and wanderers," had anyway substantially declined. The more certain and cheaper method of providing factories with a work force was to purchase or assign whole villages to them.

The essentially protectionist policy pursued by Peter I and his successors provided for the assignment and sale of peasants and of whole peasant villages primarily to the owners of manufactories who supplied the treasury with products necessary for defense (iron, woolen cloth, saltpeter, hemp, etc.). By a decree of Empress Anna of 1736 all workers, including those freely hired, were acknowledged to be serfs of the owners of the enterprise. Empress Elizabeth in 1744 reconfirmed Peter's enactment of January 18, 1721 [see Documents, Chapter 3] permitting private manufacturers to purchase villages for their enterprises. Thus it is not surprising that in Elizabeth's time entire branches of industry, if not almost all of Russian industry, were based on involuntary labor. Most of the industrial works belonging to the Stroganovs and the Demidovs, for example, employed exclusively the labor of serfs and assigned peasants, while the woolen industry in general did not know about hired labor: the state, interested in the delivery of woolens to the army, liberally gave away state peasants to the millowners. . . . True, entrepreneurs who did not enjoy the treasury's protection (in the linen, silk, and other "nonstrategic" branches of industry) mostly made do with freely hired labor. Yet on the whole, to repeat, serf forms of production predominated, which could only affect the country's economic development in the most negative way. In the second half of the eighteenth century and especially in the first half of the nineteenth, manufacturing based on feudal forms of exploitation outranked in aggregate all other factors causing Russia to lag behind the European powers in many vital respects.

To return to the nobility, we should note that industry, whether in metallurgy or distilling, had not become its basic source of nonagricultural income. Commerce was regarded as the most profitable and safest business for a nobleman. The basic articles of trade were raw materials—grain, pitch, hemp—which went for export and were bought in Europe in practically unlimited quantities. The nobility received income from commerce in two ways. On the one hand, noble merchants obtained permission to export huge shipments of grain while, on the other, they encouraged the development of trading by their peasants, among whom highly independent and resourceful dealers arose.

In the mid-1750s Vice-Chancellor Mikhail Vorontsov submitted a petition in which he asked the empress to grant him a monopoly on the export of grain. In the explanatory part of the petition he put forth ideas of a noneconomic character that enable us to see how a nobleman and high official reconciled the "general state benefit" with his own narrow class interests. Vorontsov championed protectionism, extensive foreign trade, and an active trade balance while positing that the state's wealth was based on the "products which grow in it," products which furnished the main items of trade. Such a typically physiocratic approach would offer, in his opinion, many advantages.[4] With the disappearance of surplus cheap grain, which would be sold abroad, the peasantry in its pursuit of gain would forget its inherent "sloth and the poverty stemming therefrom," bring new fields under cultivation, and engage in the transport of grain to ports. If one considers that serfs constituted almost 70 percent of the peasantry while their landlords, Vorontsov above all, aspired to monopolize the grain trade, it will become clear that the wealth to be gained from more active peasant grain cultivation would go into the pockets of those same landlords.

Now let us recall the projects of Peter Shuvalov, which had envisaged a decrease of the soul tax, for their true social significance is revealed precisely in the concrete socioeconomic situation that had taken shape in Russia by the mid-eighteenth century. The soul tax on the peasantry, responsibility for the payment of which was borne by the serfowners themselves, had continually provoked objections from the nobility. Behind this discontent stood a transparent calculation: the money taken by the state in the form of the soul tax came out of the general pool of rents extracted from the peasants by their owners. In his analysis of noble petitions of 1767, the historian V. N. Latkin found that almost all of them sought a lessening of peasant state dues "by showing how hard life was for the *muzhik* [peasant] and how crucial it was to lighten his load. One may smile at the platonic love for less fortunate brethren wafting from these petitions. Unfortunately, there is nothing at all platonic in any of this, inasmuch as such a defense of peasant interests stemmed from purely practical considerations. The fewer state duties the muzhik fulfilled and the fewer taxes he paid, the less was he depressed economically: one can get more out of a *rich* muzhik. Here in a nutshell is the simple philosophy prompting the noble petitioners' defense of peasant pockets against exploitation by the state."

Contemporaries already understood the real background of such a "defense." The anonymous author of "A Note about Salt" in the 1760s observed: "It is true that the nobility, perhaps sympathizing with their peasants, consider an increase of the soul tax to be an unbearable thing for the common folk; yet for the increase of their own incomes they think nothing of imposing [annual] dues of two rubles or even three and more on their own peasants instead of the 40 copecks per soul recommended by Sovereign Peter the First." The Note's author accurately indicated the general rise of peasant dues to their lords in the eighteenth century, which was

---

4. The Physiocratic School was a group of economists in eighteenth-century France who stressed agriculture as the source of wealth and attempted to formulate a natural law of economic life.—Ed.

directly linked to the curtailment of state taxes on privately held peasants. The 70-copeck soul tax set soon after Peter's death remained unchanged, except for a few special years, until the end of the century, whereas the value of the ruble over the same period declined by a factor of no less than five. So in contrast to the sharp rise in landlord rent the state tax sharply declined. And in this light one must reconsider Peter Shuvalov's proposals about replacing direct taxes by indirect ones. If nobles attracted into commercial activity were to be given the most favorable terms, this could best be done not by countless exceptions to the commercial and customs laws but by a fundamental reform. In short, the abolition of internal customs duties as proposed by Shuvalov was a response to the needs of the nobility. . . .

It is likewise instructive that the abolition of internal customs duties did not bring in its train the removal of other barriers to free trade, namely the various monopolies and franchises that were quite profitable for the nobility. The greatest "monopolist" and franchiser of the Elizabethan period was none other than Peter Shuvalov. In the 1740s and 1750s he obtained franchises on several trades that previously had fed whole generations of fishermen and artisans. He received monopoly rights on the hunting of walruses, whales, and fish in northern Russia, in Lake Ladoga, and even in the Caspian Sea. These trades brought him huge revenues practically unsupervised by the treasury. Other wealthy landlords and courtiers, like the greatest landowner of Russia, Peter Borisovich Sheremetev, did not hesitate to deprive the merchants of even petty franchises. In 1758 the chancellor's brother, Roman Vorontsov, and Chamberlain A. I. Kurakin received a monopoly on all "oriental" commerce for a term of thirty years.

State support of the commercial and industrial ventures of the nobility also found expression in the new tariff of 1757, which was blatantly protectionist in character. Barriers were erected to the importing of foreign industrial goods which might compete with the products of native manufactories, whose owners included noblemen. At the same time, comparatively low export duties were assessed on processed goods and raw materials. Moreover, recognizing the nobility's extensive involvement in the sale of grain abroad, the government permitted grain to be exported free of customs duties.

To be sure, the tariff of 1757 was on the whole favorable to the development of Russia's trade and industry. But banking policy was oriented mainly towards satisfying the needs of the nobility. In 1756 Peter Shuvalov began submitting projects dedicated to monetary matters. One such project led to the creation of the Copper Bank, which he headed himself. Of the 20.5 million rubles in profit the state received from the reminting of copper money, Shuvalov proposed to earmark 6 million rubles as the capital of the Copper Bank. The aim of the bank was to make large loans (50,000 to 100,000 rubles at a time), at 6 percent annually for terms of as long as eighteen years, to nobles, factory owners, and big merchants. According to Shuvalov's way of thinking, state credit on easy terms would enable the nobility to avoid domination by private creditors (with their ruinously high interest rates) as well as to establish mills and manufactories. "Debt will oblige us," proclaimed the ideologue of the nobility, "to concern ourselves with the welfare of all of society, but especially of our fellow nobles." As the historian S. M. Troitsky has justly remarked, the substance of Shuvalov's project undoubtedly attests to "its author's desire to use the state budget as a means not so much of developing trade and industry in the interest of the bourgeoisie that was then in formation or for new opportunities to increase revenues to the treasury, as of mending the finances of ruined noblemen and helping them to adapt to the growth of commercial-monetary relations in the country." We should note that in 1759–1761 huge loans from the Copper Bank went to the Grandmaster of the Hunt, S. K. Naryshkin, and to Chamberlain S. P. Iaguzhinsky (150,000 rubles each); to Gentleman of the Bedchamber P. I. Repnin and Baron S. G. Stroganov (100,000 rubles each); to Count I. G. Chernyshev and General Lieven (50,000 rubles each); and to many other representatives of the high nobility. After Peter Shuvalov's death in 1762 it was discovered that the organizer and leader of the whole business had himself taken out a loan of 473,000 rubles. By the middle of 1762 the Copper Bank had advanced loans of 3.2 million rubles, the greater part of which—2 million rubles—went into the pockets of noblemen.

The foregoing demonstrates quite convincingly the actual domination of Russia's economy by the nobility. This objective factor was bound to be reflected in the sphere of politics, ideology, and law. Indeed, the first half of the eighteenth century witnessed the formation of a noble corporate consciousness and ethos and the development of a noble ideology.

The most important feature of this world view was the nobility's new conscious-ness of a commonality of interests and of a certain privileged isolation, as a kind of "corps," from the other social estates. The term "the corps of the nobility" is first encountered in the instructions submitted by delegates of the nobility to the Legislative Commission of 1767.[5] These instructions are extremely interesting for us, as the ideas expressed therein had matured in Elizabethan times or even earlier. As one historian of the Commission (V. N. Latkin) has written: "The view that all hereditary nobles constituted in aggregate some single whole, that they were, in a word, a single 'corps' endowed with special rights and privileges, the constituent elements of which corps were also imbued with an awareness of common estate interests: this view was a product of the new, Petrine Russia and was expressed both before and during the reign of Catherine II. . . ." In Elizabeth's time this corporate consciousness found expression in a series of concrete demands that the nobility served on the absolute monarch.

As was mentioned earlier, on Peter Shuvalov's initiative a commission had been organized in 1754 for drafting a new law code (*Ulozhenie*). By the end of 1761 the commission had completed the most important, third part of the future code: "On the Status of Subjects in General." Analysis of its contents shows that it met all the noble demands voiced in the mid-eighteenth century. Elizabeth's death and then the overthrow of Peter III [1761–1762] prevented completion of the code, and so its third part was not published. Nevertheless it and the other surviving

5. The Legislative Commission convened in 1767 in Moscow by Catherine II is discussed in the fol-lowing chapter.—Ed.

materials of the commission possess great historical value, permitting us to establish clearly the policy of Elizabeth's government regarding the nobility. . . . The Elizabethan Law Code, in Latkin's words, was capable of "significantly satisfying the wishes" of only one estate. Indeed, its decidedly pro-nobility character becomes obvious by comparing it with Catherine II's legislation. In a whole series of instances Elizabeth had intended to grant the nobility even more privileges—at the expense of general state interests—than were provided by Catherine, whose reign came to be known as the "Golden Age" of the Russian nobility. . . .

We know that in the first half of the eighteenth century the nobility had actively pressed for the consolidation of its exclusive position in the social system of the country. Most of all it had sought to limit access to its ranks by newcomers from the other estates. The most conservative part of the nobility had championed the abolition of Peter's Table of Ranks, which had opened for non-nobles the possibility of earning sufficient rank in state service to become noblemen. The other, more moderate nobles had sought a division of their estate into hereditary and ranked nobility, insisting as they did on the introduction of genealogical books, a mass verification of the authenticity of proofs of nobility, and the exclusion of imposters from the "estate of the well-born." These ideas had preoccupied noblemen in the succession crisis of 1730; and the same ideas would preoccupy their sons when compiling the noble instructions for Catherine II's Legislative Commission of 1767. In the draft of Elizabeth's Law Code they became the juridical norm. The first six paragraphs of its Chapter XXII "On Nobles and Their Preferment" are literally pervaded by a noble caste spirit. Here noble preferment is based on the notion that noblemen were distinguished "from other citizens by their prudence and bravery" and because they had demonstrated "extraordinary art, zeal, and eminent service to the Fatherland and to Us [the ruler]." The nobility is then divided into several categories according to degree of eminence. . . .

The compilers of the Elizabethan Law Code practically abolished the Petrine Table of Ranks on the grounds evidently that its original objective had been met: enough noblemen had achieved and continued to achieve success in "science, navigation, and the military art" that it was no longer necessary to goad them into doing so by granting the "special advantages of noblemen alone" to persons from other estates (*raznochintsy:* commoners) who merited promotion in state service. Indeed, the compilers of Elizabeth's Code went so far as to abolish compulsory state service for the nobility. This provision was given the force of law by Peter III on February 18, 1762, in his "Manifesto Granting Liberty and Freedom to All the Russian Nobility" [see Documents below]. We need not recount in detail this treasured dream of nobles since the time of Peter I, who had compelled them to train for service and to serve for life. The provision of "liberty and freedom" to all nobles was a direct response to their longstanding wish for an end to compulsory state service, a wish that had been only partly satisfied by a decree of 1736 curtailing such service to twenty-five years.

The draft Elizabethan Law Code also guaranteed noblemen privileged terms for resuming state service [after leave or retirement], the right to travel abroad, freedom from participation in any "affairs of the land," and so forth. It introduced, moreover, several quite important privileges which the nobility had long and stubbornly pressed for and which it was to demand in the instructions of 1767. Section

15 of Chapter XXII envisaged that in contrast to other subjects noblemen could not be arrested (unless caught redhanded), tortured, subjected to corporal punishment of any kind, or banished to hard labor. Perhaps the most vital provision of the paragraph on punishment prohibited the ruler from confiscating the estates of noblemen found guilty of crimes. In 1785 all of these privileges would be granted to the nobility by Catherine II. . . .

But more: a provision of the draft Code against non-nobles buying populated land was obviously motivated in large part by the nobility's aspiration to monopolize the most important source of economic wellbeing and of labor for factories—the serf village—and thus to control the most profitable branches of industry. Thus Section 7 of Chapter XXIII of the Code, entitled "The Rights of Merchants," flatly states that merchants are authorized "to establish and to own manufactories and workshops—except distilleries, glassworks, and all sorts of other enterprises for metals and minerals, which all belong to noblemen." In other words, Elizabeth's Code introduced monopoly rights for the nobility to the entire metallurgical industry and confirmed its monopoly on distilling granted in 1754. . . .

Let me emphasize that the right freely to own souls and to exploit the enserfed peasantry belonged completely and indivisibly to the nobility alone. Without exaggeration one may state that Section 1 of Chapter XIX of the Elizabethan draft Code, "On the Authority of Nobles," marks the real apotheosis of serfdom: "The nobility possess full authority without exception over its people and peasants of the male and female sex and over their property, except for the taking of life and whipping with the knout and applying torture to them. And so each nobleman is free to sell and to mortgage his people and peasants, to give them as dowries and as recruits and to indenture them, to free them to work a trade on subsistence for a time, to give widows and maidens in marriage to outsiders, to transfer them from village to village . . . to teach them various arts and crafts, to allow them to marry and, at his wish, to use them in [domestic] service, [hard] labor, and on missions; and to apply any and all punishments except those above excluded, or to present them in court for punishment, or, at his discretion, to grant pardon and thus freedom from punishment."

Mark this quotation carefully, reader! Before you is a document rare in its candor, its cynical exposure of the essence of serfdom. It contains not a word about the rights of the peasant; it speaks of him only as living property. And this document was supposed to become the basic law of the land! In this sense Section 1 of Chapter XIX of the draft Code of 1754–1761 is unique, for it differs both from the norms of the Law Code of 1649, which had left the peasant some, albeit formal, rights [see Documents, Chapter 2] and from the ensuing legislation of the second half of the eighteenth century, which would make every effort to mask this same unlimited authority of one person over the life, property, freedom, and dignity of another: this domination of one class by another.

In sum, the draft of the Elizabethan Law Code reflects the nobility's extraordinary rise to importance in the life of the country by the 1760s. Although the draft did not become law, its norms were revived in the nobles' instructions of 1767 and most would be enacted by Catherine II, thus juridically consolidating the nobility's authority for years to come. . . .

After the Petrine reforms, the only path of development for the Russia of modern times was that taken by Peter. An active foreign policy, a powerful standing army and navy, a developed commerce and industry that focused above all on defense needs, promotion of a national culture and educational system: all these aspects of Peter's political doctrine became acknowledged aims of post-Petrine governments. But there were shades or nuances which in practice influenced the consistency and tempo of attaining these aims. These nuances, which often depended on the personality of the ruler and of his or her advisors, became in the final analysis an important factor in the country's general development.

The Elizabethan period was undoubtedly propitious for movement along the path blazed by Peter, as manifested in many spheres of the country's life. Elizabeth's foreign policy, in contrast to that of her immediate predecessors, was more consistent in achieving the national objectives that Peter had considered most important. This feature of Russian policy was reflected with special clarity in Russia's successful participation in the Seven Years' War. The War, whatever its ultimate results, became a test not only of the might of the Russian army, but also of the solidity of the foreign-policy system laid down by Peter and developed under Elizabeth.[6]

Obvious, too, were Russia's economic successes in the Elizabethan period. Statistical data speak clearly about the huge potential of Russian industry and commerce and about their intensive growth. In this period the feudal mode of production had still not exhausted itself and the momentum imparted by Peter had not only not run down but, thanks to his daughter's protectionist policy, had gathered greater force.

The period under review also favorably affected the development of Russian national culture. Lomonosov worked most fruitfully precisely in the decades from 1740 to 1760 [see Documents, Chapter 6]. In creatively mastering the values that had been introduced in the course of the Petrine cultural reform, Russian literature, painting, theater, architecture, and music produced in these years many masterpieces that stand on a par with the treasures of other periods. The flowering of Russian national culture in the next period [under Catherine II] drew on developments of the 1740s and 1750s, and we can state with assurance that in this respect these were not lost decades.

Elizabeth's government came to power with the slogan of restoring Petrine "principles" in both foreign and domestic policy. While in the commercial-industrial sphere as well as in those of culture and foreign policy this goal was realized to a considerable degree, in other spheres of policy Elizabeth's government suffered failure. This was caused not only by the thoughtless pursuit of ideals of the past that were not in themselves clearly conceived and could not by themselves have

---

6. The Seven Years' War (1756–1763) in Europe found Russia allied with Austria and France against the Prussia of Frederick the Great. Russian military successes against Prussia were negated, however, with the death late in 1761 of Empress Elizabeth and the accession of Peter III, who was a great admirer of Frederick and withdrew Russia from the war. Resentment of Peter's action within the Russian political and military establishment is considered by historians one major factor in Peter's overthrow (June 1762) in favor of his wife, who became Empress Catherine II.—Ed.

brought success, but also by the fact that the general Petrine concept of service in the "common good" by all subjects up to and including the tsar (which for the nobility had meant onerous lifetime service to the state) could no longer be realized in practice. The consolidation of the nobility's socioeconomic position, building on the gains of the preceding years [1725–1741], had borne its fruit. The nobility emerged under Elizabeth as a cohesive corporation acutely aware of its dominant position and determined to exploit it to maximum benefit. One consequence of this development came in the form of demands that the autocracy guarantee the nobility favorable conditions of life at the expense of the other classes and estates. There were even noble pretensions to supreme political power, although the significance of this last tendency should not be exaggerated, since the regime of absolute monarchy as a whole corresponded to the interests of the nobility.

In sum, the power of this huge state, gaining strength year by year, rested on the foundation of serfdom. The Empire's flowering meant the flowering of the power of the noble estate, which comprised an insignificant fraction of the population but which concentrated in its hands the country's basic wealth. In the Elizabethan period, the landowners' uncontrolled enrichment of themselves by raising rents led naturally and inevitably to the exhaustion of the peasant economy. It was to a considerable extent precisely during this period that the system took shape which later became widely known in the classics of Russian literature: the system which gave rise to criminal landlords, serf orchestras, harems of "shepherdesses," and the routine buying and selling of human beings. It was a system founded on human abasement, the abuse of personality, and the nearly total paralysis of the political and public life of the bulk of the absolute monarch's subjects. The reigning political regime of autocracy closed the path to supreme power not only to public forces other than the nobility, but frequently even to able representatives of this, the dominant class. Favoritism, corruption, ignorance, fear of making a decision and taking responsibility for its execution, stultifying bureaucratism: all these and other vices of the rule of absolute monarchy cost the country dearly, as did the exorbitant luxury of the court of its spoiled sovereign, who had inherited neither talent nor energy from her father and who was incapable of resolving the problems of a great state.

## St. Tikhon Zadonsky

NADEJDA GORODETZKY

In the history of the Russian church Tikhon is neither an innovator nor the head of some school or party. He did not fight theological battles or direct important movements of ecclesiastical learning and policy, . . . he did not open new vistas to Russian monasticism, . . . nor was he a great ecclesiastic and statesman. . . . The popularity of his *Works* bears witness to his influence, but it was a spiritual and

From Nadejda Gorodetzky, *Saint Tikhon Zadonsky: Inspirer of Dostoevsky* (London: S.P.C.K., 1951), pp. 190–94.

moral influence of a non-combative, non-spectacular, silent type. One can only guess to what genuine heart-searchings his booklets stimulated many a parish priest or simple Russian layman.

Though he had absorbed all the cultural treasures available in his epoch, Tikhon could have repeated the words of a sixteenth-century monk, Philotheus of Pskov:

> I am a villager. I have learned to read and to write but I have not examined Greek subtleties. I have not read the rhetors and astronomers. I was not born in Athens and have not conversed with the philosophers, but I have read the books of the Sacred Law.

Tikhon was simply a monk and a bishop who had read the books of the sacred law, who pointed to the need of having the Bible in Russian translation, and who took it as the substance of his own thought and action. These are the features which determine his place in the history of Russian religious thought.

One can define him as a religious reformer grounded in the Scriptures. For he certainly belongs to the current of reformers of the Russian Church. . . . In the "non-reformed" Russian Church not a century has passed without producing some ecclesiastical reformer who has left his mark and whose efforts have borne some fruit. Even the [Ecclesiastical] Regulation [of Peter I], in spite of its dangerous and polemical spirit, contained elements of truthful criticism. There is a risk, in the modern reaction against the eighteenth century, of forgetting altogether that the thought of this epoch, though in many ways limited and superficial, also contained true and progressive features in the best sense of the word. Tikhon belonged to his epoch and to the eighteenth-century reforming current which inspired the Synodal Russian Church in the persons of her best representatives.

Accordingly, his place in the Orthodox world is not in the metaphysical line of the great Alexandrians, nor in that of the desert fathers or the Byzantine mystics; his place is among the bishops of the "humanistic" and evangelical school of St. Basil and St. John Chrysostom.[1] With St. Basil, he believed in the "reasonable sacrifice" of an asceticism which respects and sanctifies the entire human person. He sought salvation not in dogmatical speculation or through certain techniques of contemplation, through ritualism or unusual deeds of asceticism, but through meditation, prayer, love and the practice of the gospel of Jesus Christ. And like St. John Chrysostom, he was a bishop—that is, a dispenser of the word and of the sacrament—and a pastor who applied himself to the teaching, the social and individual reform and guidance of his flock. His denunciation of social evils has a lasting value.

Nor is this all. Together with the . . . liturgical doctors of the Orthodox Church, St. Tikhon goes back to the fullness of the New Testament doctrine of the Church and to a lofty sacramental teaching. A modern reader familiar with the development of mystical ecclesiology and with literature on the Church as the Body of Christ is in danger of under-estimating the value and importance of Tikhon's teaching on this subject. One must keep his background in mind. The doctrinal controversies

---

1. Reference is to various of the classical fathers of the Eastern (Greek) Orthodox Church.—Ed.

of the seventeenth and early eighteenth centuries undoubtedly won a place in the general history of Russian religious thought and expressed a certain development in doctrinal teaching. They still remain of interest and importance for students of theology. . . . [B]ut from Peter I onwards attention was focused on the relationship of Church and State. In the period of the . . . [Ecclesiastical] Regulation, Tikhon's words come with a refreshing vigor. His scriptural doctrine of the Church transcends the polemics of the time. It enables an individual steeped in his teaching on Christ to incorporate this ideal into the life of the whole Christian body. Therefore, too, his writings on the sacraments of baptism and of the eucharist have a living appeal, and remain to this day one of the best Russian exhortations on the subject. A liturgical revival in the Russian Church . . . would be justified in claiming Tikhon as its patron saint.

St. Tikhon was not a dogmatist. Yet he has made a definite doctrinal contribution. It must not be forgotten that as late as the [1830s] some of his books were used in the seminaries as doctrinal text-books. He claimed no originality; he wrote what belonged to the tradition. But he was the first to attempt to produce an accessible and integral presentation of Christian dogma in its application to the life of the individual and of society. Thus an intellectual approach to Christianity was intimately united with moral theology. The difficulty of appreciating and analyzing Tikhon's thought lies precisely in his unified presentation of doctrine, morals and mystical life. The novelty and strength of his writings were all the more striking in that he did not use the language of the seminaries—theological terms couched in a heavy style, and often tedious, owing to the latinized forms of words and the polonisms of the previous generation—he wrote in a beautiful and picturesque language accessible to any reader.

Fr. G. Florovsky writes:

> St. Tikhon was a great writer. His books fascinate by their light yet plastic images. His *True Christianity* in particular has a historical significance. It is not a dogmatic system; it is rather a work on mystical ethics or asceticism. But it was a first attempt to formulate living theology and experimental theology in distinction, and as a counterbalance, to the schools devoid of authentic experience.[2]

This experimental aspect of theology links St. Tikhon, as we have seen in studying his sources, with the pietists. One cannot lay too much stress on his insistence that personal feeling and a personal act of faith are necessary for one to become a real Christian. He is a true contemporary of the eighteenth-century secular and religious western writers, by the place he gives to feeling and to religious experience. The Slavophiles, who so strongly advocated integrity of mind, feeling and will, and believed Russia to be the embodiment of such "existential" religious philosophy, could have found their best example in St. Tikhon.

---

2. Quoting Georges Florovsky (1893–1979), a leading Russian Orthodox theologian of the twentieth century, whose *Collected Works* have been published (6 vols., 1972–1987) in English translation.—Ed.

Dostoevsky was right when he turned for this integrity to St. Tikhon. He found in him the emphasis on freedom and beauty which was so dear to both of them. One might say that Tikhon is the first Russian ecclesiastical writer who can be called "modern." His language, style, thought and feeling are not only those of their century; they foreshadow developments of the future.

St. Tikhon was a living reply to the anti-religious ideas generated in eighteenth-century Russia. Dostoevsky must have felt this when he so persistently tried to portray him as an answer to and refutation of the denial of God. . . . His appreciation was particularly true when he added that "the most important thing about Tikhon is Tikhon."

For not only is Tikhon linked by every fiber of his being with the Russian tradition so that he could be identified with the piety of his people; it is his personality which is most striking. There is in him that solid and natural character, that nearness to nature, that "soil" for which Dostoevsky himself expressed his longing through the tortuous and passionate minds and destinies of Ivan or Dimitry Karamazov, and of so many others. The Russian novelists had often found such integrated characters among the people. A modern writer, Boris Zaitzev, insists on the calm naturalness of St. Sergius of Radonezh; and, to use his metaphor, we find the same "odor of freshly planed wood" in St. Tikhon.

This would not, however, have been enough to make a lasting impression. Neither during his lifetime nor after his death could Tikhon pass unnoticed. His personality could not but influence others through the sheer force of his generous, disinterested love and his truly holy poverty, which overflowed into the lives of his fellowmen in the continual giving of his possessions and in his endless compassion. Love of God and love of man were the motives of his reforming zeal. Without violence, though with vigor, without striving to break or change any systems, he said simply and sincerely what he wished to say, instructing and edifying rather than protesting and demanding. Symbolically, the leaflets which he circulated in his diocese were for display not in public places, but inside churches, for the use of his clergy and people. His reforming spirit and ideas were based on humility, on personal repentance, all the more deep in that it emanated from a life wholly reformed according to the Word of God.

Tikhon's pastoral teaching is quite outstanding. In a land where spiritual progress was mainly conceived in the form of monastic life, he revived the Christian appeal to men of all conditions, and he enlivened it by examples of failure and virtue within his own Russia. Tikhon's teaching on true Christianity in each walk of life opened new vistas before every struggling soul. He left no precise spiritual method, but he was the first Russian writer to deal with the obstacles and progress of the Christian soul in its bearing upon everyday life. His readers cannot fail to recognize throughout his works the personal experience of one totally given to God. They are the revelation of the supernatural life of a soul, with its trials, despondency and fear, and with its triumph, "the token here on earth of eternal life."

Christians of all traditions can recognize in his experience and writings the essential values of their faith, striven after, lived and loved by him with utter sincerity. The Catholic may be attracted by his faithfulness to the tradition of the

Church, his sacramental mysticism, his devotional emphasis on the Crucified. The Protestant may appreciate his love of the Bible, his freedom, his social Christianity and his message for everyday life. Perhaps it is exactly this blending of many-sided experience that makes the person of St. Tikhon a living expression of Orthodoxy at its best. In spite of historical and national differences, one can hardly fail to recognize in him, transcending his human difficulties and history, that "gift from above," which, coming from the One Source, remains in all its diversity one: saintliness.

# D OCUMENTS

E. V. Anisimov refers in his essay above (as he does in his essay in Chapter 3) to Emperor Peter III's Manifesto of February 18, 1762, abolishing compulsory state service for the Russian nobility. Dr. Anisimov sees this act as the culmination of a long campaign by the nobility for release from the obligation of lifetime service imposed by Peter the Great. Other historians, notably Marc Raeff and Robert E. Jones (see Further Reading), have suggested rather that the state was thus freeing *itself* from the necessity of employing numerous unqualified, unwilling, or otherwise unwanted noblemen and that it was thus *strengthening* the Petrine (bureaucratic) principle of merit and seniority for retention or promotion in service over the (aristocratic) principle of class or birth. To be sure, the two interpretations are not mutually exclusive: the interests of the Imperial state and the Russian nobility frequently coincided. Moreover, the Manifesto—printed below as the first document—clearly encouraged *voluntary* state service by noblemen, just as their release from compulsory service was somewhat conditional. And it remains incontestable that the Manifesto of 1762, which would be confirmed and extended by Catherine II, was a landmark in the process of legally establishing the nobility as a uniquely privileged estate in Russia, one which retained its dominant position in society and the economy (a position based on its exclusive right to own serfs) while being freed from the obligation of state service.

The second of these documents is taken from Prince M. M. Shcherbatov's tract *On the Corruption of Morals in Russia*, which was written in 1787. Shcherbatov (1733–1790) appears in the tract as a veteran and critical observer of life at the Imperial court. His main theme is the Russian nobility's moral decline in the eighteenth century, a decadence expressed in the selfish individualism and unrestrained materialism (or "voluptuousness") that had replaced, as he saw it, the patrician sense of responsibility and restraint characteristic of the old, Muscovite aristocracy (from which he himself was descended). Viewing pre-Petrine Russia as a nation just emerging from primitive simplicity, Shcherbatov was both positive and negative about Peter himself, praising him for his civilizing program of Europeanization while condemning its violent, excessively rapid, and superficial aspects. Among Peter's unworthy successors, Shcherbatov was particularly critical of the reign and court of Empress Elizabeth, having been, as he says here, "an eye-witness of the way of life and voluptuousness of those days."

## Peter III's Manifesto Emancipating the Russian Nobility, 1762

Not only all of Europe, but the greater part of the world, bear witness to how burdensome and difficult was the labor of Our Beloved Sovereign Grandfather, Peter the Great, eternally glorious, all-wise Monarch and All-Russian Emperor, for the prosperity and benefit of His fatherland, leading Russia to perfection whether in military, civil, or political affairs.

But in so doing it was necessary, first of all, to instruct the well-born Nobility, as the main Part [*Chlen*] of the State, and to show [it] how great is the advantage of enlightened Powers in human wellbeing over the countless peoples sunk in the depths of ignorance. And therefore, given the extreme situation at that time, [Peter] was impelled to order the Russian Nobility, as a mark of his special favor, to enter the military and civil services; and more, in order to teach well-born youth not only the various liberal sciences, but also the many useful arts, [he] sent them to European States, and to the same end established various schools within Russia, so as to produce as soon as possible the desired fruit.

It is true that in the beginning these dispositions often seemed burdensome and unbearable to the Nobility, depriving [it] of peace and quiet, taking [it] from home, and [requiring it] to continue in military and other service against its own will, and to enroll its sons in service; whence some [nobles] sought to escape, incurring thereby not only fines but deprivation of their estates, to the detriment of themselves and their heirs.

Yet the aforesaid requirement, though in the beginning sometimes accompanied by force, was most beneficial, and was followed by all occupants of the Russian Throne from the time of Peter the Great and especially by Our Beloved Aunt of blessed memory, the Sovereign Empress Elizabeth daughter of Peter, who, imitating Her Sovereign Parent, spread and increased under Her protection knowledge of political affairs and the various sciences in the Russian Realm. And We look with satisfaction on what has come from all of this; and every true son of his fatherland must acknowledge that innumerable benefits have ensued from it, [namely] extirpation of the crudeness harmful to the general good, transformation of ignorance into sound judgment, useful knowledge and diligence in service, an increase in military affairs of skillful and brave generals, the appointment of suitable persons in civil and political affairs: to conclude, in a word, lofty thoughts have penetrated the hearts of all true patriots of Russia [as seen] by the unlimited loyalty to and love of Us, the great zeal and fervor for Our service. And therefore We do not find it necessary to require service, such as was done up to this time.

And so We, in consideration of the foregoing, and by the power given to Us by the Most High, grant from Our High Imperial grace liberty and freedom henceforth and forever to all the Russian well-born Nobility and [its] heirs, that they might continue service in Our Empire or in other European Powers allied with Us on the basis of the following legislation:

From *PSZ*, vol. 15 no. 11, 444. Translated by James Cracraft.

1. All Nobles currently in Our various services may continue therein as long as they wish and their condition permits them; although military [servicemen] should not request discharge from service or leave either during a campaign or three months before one. . . .

2. All Nobles who have served Us well and honorably are to be promoted one rank upon retirement, provided they have been in their previous rank more than a year; but those who wish to enter the civil service from the military, and there is a vacancy, should be promoted only if they have served three years in their previous rank.

3. Those [nobles] who have been retired for some time, or have left the military for another of Our services, and wish to enter again into military service: they will be accepted, provided they show themselves worthy of their rank and are not promoted higher than those who were at the same rank when they were discharged. . . . We ordain this so that serving [officers] shall have advantage and benefit before those not in service; also, that someone retired from the civil service and wishing to return may be able to do so according to his suitability.

4. Whoever, discharged from Our service, wishes to travel to another European State, is to be given the necessary passports at once by Our Foreign College, with this condition: that should the need arise, those Noblemen located outside Our State will return to their fatherland as soon as they are notified, and take up service with all possible speed according to Our will, under pain of sequestration of their estates.

5. Russian Nobles serving other European Sovereigns may return to their fatherland and as they wish freely enter Our service, if there is a vacancy, and at the same rank for which they have [foreign] patents. . . .

6. And since by this Our Most Gracious ordinance no one of the Russian Nobility shall continue in service unwillingly, nor be required to attend to any business in Our government departments, except in special cases, and then only by a Personal decree signed by Our own hand; We command that the contrary decree of the Sovereign Emperor Peter the First, specifying that in the Senate in St. Petersburg and in its Office in Moscow retired Nobles shall serve as needed, be amended, so that henceforth 30 persons for the Senate and 20 for its Office shall annually be elected by the Nobles themselves in the provinces concerned. . . .

7. Although by this Our Most Gracious ordinance all well-born Russian Nobles . . . shall enjoy liberty forever, Our fatherly concern for them still obtains as well as for their young sons, who henceforth at the age of 12 years shall be registered at the most convenient office of the Master Herald . . . with information about their upbringing and where they wish to continue their education, whether in the various schools established in our State or in those of other European Powers or in their own homes with skilled and knowledgeable teachers, as may suit the parents. However, let no one of the well-born Nobility dare to raise his children without appropriate education under pain of Our anger. Therefore We command all Nobles with no more than 1,000 peasant souls under them to register their sons at Our Noble Cadet Corps [school in St. Petersburg, founded in 1730], where they will learn everything appropriate to the well-born Nobility . . . ; and after [completing his] education each according to his dignity may assume the privileges of his station, and by the same token enter and continue in service as provided above.

8. Nobles now serving in Our military service as soldiers and in other lower ranks [who] have not attained Officer status, will not be discharged until they have served for 12 years.

9. But since We in this Our Most Gracious ordinance to all the well-born Russian Nobility lay down for all time a fundamental and unalterable law; We affirm in conclusion by Our Imperial word, in the most solemn manner, always to maintain it inviolably; and Our lawful Successors shall not alter it in any way, but preserve this Our ordinance as an unshakable support of the Autocratic All-Russian Throne. And in return We hope that all the well-born Russian Nobility, sensible of Our liberality to them and their heirs, will remain in their most submissive loyalty and devotion to Us, and not seek to escape from service, but rather enter it willingly and zealously, and continue to serve honorably and proudly as long as possible; no less will they diligently and eagerly educate their sons in the beneficial sciences. For all those who never serve will not only spend all their time in sloth and idleness, but will not educate their sons in any useful sciences for the benefit of their fatherland; and these We command all Our faithful subjects and true sons of the fatherland to despise and reject as persons harmful to the general good; nor will they be permitted access to Our Court, or to public assemblies and celebrations.

## M. M. Shcherbatov Laments Corruption at Court, 1730–1762

Empress Anna [reigned 1730–1740] liked a magnificence and stateliness in . . . keeping with her rank, and so the court, which was still not officially organized, was set on an official footing. The number of court ranks was increased, silver and gold glittered on all the courtiers, and even the royal livery was covered with silver. The Court Equestrian Chancellery was established, and the court carriages had all the glitter possible at the time. Italian opera was introduced, and such spectacles as orchestral- and chamber-music began. There were formal, crowded gatherings at court; balls, triumphs and masquerades.

The . . . above description shows what advances were made by evil ways, through the circumstances of the reign and the example of the court. The severity of the régime took away from the subjects all courage to express their thoughts, and the grandees became not councillors, but yes-men of the monarch and her favorites, in all cases where they had reason to fear causing displeasure by their contradiction. Patriotism diminished, and selfishness and the desire for rewards increased.

The magnificence introduced at court compelled the grandees, and by example, others too, to increase their own magnificence, which already in clothes, tableware and other forms of decoration, was beginning to exceed all bounds; the excessive

From M. M. Shcherbatov, *On the Corruption of Morals in Russia*, ed. and trans. by A. Lentin, 1969, pp. 191–235. Reprinted by permission of Cambridge University Press magnificence was noticed by the Empress Anna herself, and a decree was issued, forbidding the wearing of gold and silver in dress; it was permitted to continue wearing such clothes until they wore out, and these clothes were actually docketted. But this order was in vain, when the court itself had fallen into this luxury . . . .

This luxury was not only seen on the ceremonial clothes of the courtiers and other ranks; it was even to be seen on the uniforms of the officers of the Guard, especially the uniforms of the Horse Guards, which were then blue with red cuffs, set with loops, and with broad gold galoon along the seams. Many eminent men began to keep open tables, such as Field-Marshall Count Münnich and Vice-Chancellor Count Ostermann (though he lived very modestly in other respects); Gavrilo Ivanovich Golovkin; Admiral of the Fleet Count Nikolai Fyodorovich Golovin, and others.

The number of different wines now increased, and champagne, burgundy and cape-wine, previously unknown, began to be imported and taken at table. Instead of furniture made of plain wood, none other was now used but English furniture, made of red-wood mahogany. Houses were increased in size, and instead of a small number of rooms, now began to contain whole suites, as is attested by the buildings erected at the time. These houses began to be upholstered in cloth and other upholsteries; for it was considered improper to have a room without upholsteries. Mirrors, of which there had been very few at first, now began to be used in all rooms, and large mirrors at that.

Carriages were also magnificent: rich, gilt carriages with polished glass panes, upholstered in velvet, with gold and silver fringes; costly thoroughbred horses; costly heavy gilt and silver harnesses, with silk caparisons and gold and silver. Rich liveries also came into use. . . .

Every luxury brings pleasure and a certain degree of comfort, and hence is eagerly accepted by all; and the more agreeable it is, the further it spreads. So it was that spreading from great to small, it began to appear everywhere: the grandees, living beyond their means, became increasingly dependent on the court, as a source of favors, while the lower orders became increasingly dependent on the grandees, for the same reason.

Resoluteness, justice, nobility, moderation, family-loyalty, friendship, loyalty, attachment to religion and the civil law, and patriotism—all this disappeared, and its place began to be taken by contempt of duties to God and man, envy, ambition, avarice, ostentation, cunning, servility and flattery, by which everyone proposed to make his fortune and gratify his desires.

However, among the people at large there remained a large number of men who, not being so close to the court, still preserved the old austerity of morals; and justice was administered, if not from inclination, then at least from fear of punishment, and still kept her scales quite evenly balanced.

Such were the circumstances in which Princess Elizabeth, daughter of Peter the Great and the Empress Catherine, ascended the throne of Russia. . . .

Passing over the way in which her accession to the throne of all [Russia] was brought about . . . , I turn to a description of her character, as indicative of the causes of the dissolution of morals.

In her youth, this monarch had been a woman of remarkable beauty. She was devout, kindhearted, compassionate and generous. By nature she was endowed with adequate intelligence, but she had no enlightenment whatever; I was assured by [her secretary] that she was unaware that Great Britain is an island. By nature she was of a cheerful disposition and a woman who sought greedily after amusements; she was conscious of her beauty and was passionately fond of enhancing it with various adornments. She was lazy, and impatient of any task requiring any assiduity; so that through her laziness, not only domestic state papers sometimes lay for many years without her signature, but even foreign state papers, such as treaties, lay by her side for several months, through her delay in signing her name. Luxurious and voluptuous, she placed much confidence in her favorites, but always in such a way that she retained her regal authority over them.

In the course of her accession to the throne of all [Russia] she had promised before [an icon] of the Miraculous Savior, that if she should accede to her father's throne, then no one should be put to death at her order throughout her reign. However, once on the throne, she had many of the grandees put on trial. Upon what charge? On the charge that they had been loyal to the monarchs previously reigning; that they had failed to acknowledge her as heir to the throne, and that through fear of her father's name and her birth they had given advice prejudicial to her in the interest of those monarchs. These men were sentenced to death. They were brought to the scaffold, and although reprieved from death, were sent into exile.

Such a man was Admiral-of-the-Fleet Count Ostermann, a man of distinguished intellect who, by his administration of ministerial affairs, had brought Russia many advantages. Another such was Field Marshal Count Münnich, many times victor over the Turks, and first of the European generals to quell the pride of that anti-Christian nation. These men and several others were sent into exile for their zeal to the Empress Anna and Prince Ivan [Ivan VI].

But were they the only ones who showed them zeal, and served them faithfully? For fourteen years the whole of Russia had been guilty of that same crime, and the courtiers, following the whims of the Empress Anna, had shown scant respect indeed for Princess Elizabeth. Consequently everyone had good reason to fear her vengeance in the form of exile if not execution. . . .

Such was the state of fear in which the whole Court found itself, and where there is fear there is no resoluteness.

The first to come to power was Prince Nikita Trubetskoy, who had not been much in favor at the Court of [Empress] Anna. A clever man, ambitious, subtle, malicious and vindictive, he was promoted to Procurator-General. In order to flatter the new Empress, and possibly with his own ends in mind, he suggested the restoration of all the laws of Peter the Great. Empress Elizabeth, who revered her father's memory, agreed to this; and all the laws of Empress Anna which had been issued contrary to the decrees of Peter the Great (apart from the Law of Primogeniture in Entail), were repealed. These included many extremely useful measures.

While flattering the monarch, it was also necessary to flatter her favorite, who at this time was Aleksei Razumovsky, later Count. This man, of Circassian Cossack [Ukrainian] origin, had been brought to the court of Princess Elizabeth as a choirboy, and became her lover. He was a good man at heart but of small intellect, and like all Circassians, addicted to drink; and so it was through this passion of his that men tried to humor him.

Stepan Apraksin, also a generous and goodhearted man but little versed in affairs, was cunning, luxurious and ambitious; and, moreover, though he was not a drunkard, he was not averse to indulging this excess on occasion. Then there was Count Aleksei Bestuzhev, who was recalled from exile, having been a Cabinet Minister under the Empress Anna . . . , for which reason indeed he had been exiled. He was a clever man, versed in political affairs through long experience, a friend of the national interest, but cunning, malicious and vindictive, voluptuous, luxurious, and with his own passion for drink. This pair, Apraksin and Bestuzhev, used to drink together with Razumovsky, and to pander to this passion of his. They comprised the party at court hostile to Prince Nikita Trubetskoy.

There were others too who enjoyed the monarch's favor. These included the Empress's kinsmen. . . .

Next to enjoy particular respect at court were those who had known of the Empress's plans to ascend the throne. . . .

The Empress's gratitude also extended to those who had served her faithfully at her court, and these included the two brothers, Alexander and Peter Shuvalov (the latter's wife . . . was a favorite of the Empress)—I shall have occasion to mention this pair later on. . . .

All these people received various rewards, and men of no fortune were enriched. Since birth alone and ranks received for long years of service no longer afforded pre-eminence at court, the social classes were intermingled; and whatever a rich man of base extraction or risen from the minor [nobility] did out of ostentation, a man of rank, noble birth or meritorious service but who had not been rewarded, regarded it as a disgrace not to do likewise.

As the social classes were intermingled, as ranks began to lose their prestige, while there was no equality of income, some, who received a great deal from the monarch's generosity, could afford to spend a great deal; while others, with only birth, service and a small income to their name, aspired to equality with them. Then, of course, luxury and voluptuousness began to spread from top to bottom and to ruin the lower orders. And since voluptuousness never sets bounds to its excesses, the very grandees began to seek ways of increasing voluptuousness in their homes.

The Court, copying, or rather humoring, the Empress, arrayed itself in cloth-of-gold. The grandees sought all that is richest in dress, all that is rarest in drink. As far as servants were concerned, they restored the traditional large number of retainers and added luxury in their dress. Carriages glittered with gold. Costly horses became necessary to pull the gilt carriages, not so much because they were really needed but simply for show. Houses began to be decorated with gilt, with silk upholsteries in all rooms, expensive furniture, mirrors, and so forth. All this brought pleasure to the house-owners, taste increased, imitation of the most luxurious nations grew, and a man was respected in proportion to the magnificence of his way of life and furnishings.

Being an eye-witness of the way of life and voluptuousness of those days, I shall try and set forth some examples. Count Aleksei Bestuzhev had such a large wine-cellar that it realized a considerable sum, when after his death it was sold to the Counts Orlov. The pavilions which were erected at his country-seat on Kamenny Island [in St. Petersburg] had ropes of silk. Stepan Apraksin always kept a grand table, his wardrobe contained many hundred sorts of rich coats. When he commanded the Russian Army in the campaign against the King of Prussia, all the comforts and pleasures of a thriving commercial city, together with every luxury, followed in his train, amid the clash of arms and turmoil of the march. His tents covered the area of a town; his luggage was borne by over 500 horses, and for his personal use he had fifty richly caparisoned post-horses.

Count Peter Sheremetev, first Chamberlain and then Commander-in-Chief and Adjutant-Genral, was then the richest man in Russia . . . .

A man of extremely mediocre intellect, lazy, ignorant of affairs and, in a word, a man who dragged down rather than bore his name, and only took pride in his riches, he lived with all possible magnificence, and always with the monarch's approval. His clothes weighed him down with gold and silver, and dazzled the eyes with their brilliance. His carriages, in which he takes no interest, were not only in the best taste, but were ordered from France, and were the most expensive. His table was magnificent, his retinue enormous, and in a word, his scale of living was such that it happened more than once that when the Empress arrived unexpectedly at his house with no small number of courtiers, he could entertain them to dinner as readily as if he had prepared for them. This stood him in good stead and he was held in particular esteem at court at all times, irrespective of the various changes of personnel there.

Count Ivan Chernyshev, at first a gentleman-in-waiting, and then Chamberlain, was not so much a man of intellect, as quick, cunning and prompt, a man who, in a word, combined all the necessary qualities of a courtier. He provided many examples of every kind of voluptuousness. Unfortunately for Russia, he had spent no little time traveling abroad. He had seen all the most attractive aspects of voluptuousness and luxury at the other European courts. All this he had adopted, all this he brought to Russia, and all this he tried to install in his own country.

His clothes were particularly tasteful and costly, and he had so many of them that he once ordered twelve coats at a time. His table, tastefully and expensively provided, appealed . . . to taste, smell and sight. His carriages glittered with gold, and the very livery of his pages was embroidered with silver. The wines at his table were the best and most expensive.

And indeed, he acquired a certain eminence through this as a man of taste, he was always held in particular respect at court, he married a wealthy bride . . . a kinswoman and favorite of the monarch. Then he became a friend of the favorite, Ivan Shuvalov. The latter was instrumental in acquiring for him the ribbon of the White Eagle of Poland, which was then held in particular veneration. Under the same patronage, he received from the Senate, at negligible cost, that is, no more than 90,000 rubles, certain copper works, containing over a hundred thousand rubles' worth of ready copper. Several years later, having brought these works into a state of ruin, he entered a large claim on them, and sold them back to the Treasury for 700,000 rubles.

Taking root, such luxury also penetrated to classes of men who, by their rank and circumstances, should have had no need of it. Prince Boris Golitsyn (who began by deserting from the Army as a Lieutenant or Captain, and later retired as a Major), made the greatest possible display of luxury in Moscow. His rich clothes and those of his wife, his livery, his carriages, his table, wines, servants and so on—all was magnificent. Such a luxurious scale of living brought him respect of a certain kind, but exhausted his fortune and, indeed, he died ruined from his public and private debts, and his wife was long to suffer and endure need, as a result of her husband's folly, in order to pay back his debts.

Thus voluptuousness everywhere took root, to the ruination of noble houses and the corruption of morals. But where did it have its most harmful effects? And where, combined with ostentation and love of power, did it, as it were, win its victory over sound morals? This was in the person of Count Peter Shuvalov. The name of this man is remembered in Russia, not only for all the harm which he himself caused, but also for the examples which he left for men to follow.

The Shuvalov family had never held high rank in Russia, and the father of this Shuvalov . . . was, in his youth, a [familiar] at the house of Prince Fedor Shcherbatov, brother to my grandfather . . . . Having entered the service, he finally reached the rank of Major-General after many years there, and was Governor at the town of Archangel, where my father took over from him. From there he was promoted to Governor either at Riga or at Reval, where he died.

A wise and honest man, he had two sons, Alexander and Peter, whom he gave a decent education, and entered for service at the court of [Princess] Elizabeth. During the reign of the Empress Anna, they strove to fill the Princess's court with men who had neither noble birth nor riches, and so from pages they reached the rank of gentlemen-in-waiting.

Peter Shuvalov was a clever man, quick, ambitious, covetous and luxurious. He was married to . . . a woman full of vices, but a favorite of the Empress. Shuvalov, relying on his record of service at her court when . . . he had shared her oppression, and also relying on the Empress's friendship for his wife, began to wield exceptional power from the very accession of the Empress Elizabeth. He was soon promoted to Chamberlain, and through his intellect, well suited to politics and flattery, increased his power. He was promoted to Lieutenant-General and was given a seat in the Senate.

Here, to all the subtlest stratagems of courtly cunning—that is, not merely flattery, humoring the monarch, fawning before the favorite, Razumovsky, bribing all the base and dissolute women who surrounded the Empress (some of these sat up with her at night, others massaged her feet)—to all this he added a pompous grandiloquence which meant little. He realized that the state revenues were not properly organized, while the Empress was luxurious and voluptuous. While the Senate, having no information concerning what sums were available, and where, was always complaining of the lack of funds, Shuvalov always said that there were plenty, and was able to find the sums necessary to satisfy the Empress's luxury.

In order to have enough money for the increase in voluptuousness, at a time when others did not dare to impose any taxes in view of the nation's poverty, Shuvalov, with his own ostentation and advantages in mind, increased the revenues from the leases on [spirits] by his own efforts, and to satisfy his own avarice, made himself a leaseholder.

He strove to introduce monopolies, and personally took out a lease on tobacco, the fishing industry in the White Sea and the Arctic Ocean, and the Forests of Olonetsk, making a profit on all this for himself. Under a most merciful monarch, he set up a kind of inquisition to investigate the illegal trade in spirits, and stained the Russian provinces with the blood of those who were tortured and lashed with the knout, and filled the wastes of Siberia and the mines with those who were sent into exile and forced labor. It is estimated that up to 15,000 people suffered such a punishment.

Turning to trade, he increased the duties on goods indiscriminately; and by thus forcing up expenditure at a time of rising voluptuousness, he forcibly brought many people to ruin. He raised the price of salt, and thereby brought about poverty and sickness among the people.

Turning to the currency, he raised then lowered its value: he reduced the five-copeck copper coin to the value of two copecks, and poor subjects who lived on a capital of copper coin ultimately lost three-fifths of their capital. At his suggestion, a copper currency was minted at the rate of eight rubles to the pood, and then reminted at sixteen rubles to the pood.[1] None of these measures was taken without a profit on the side for Shuvalov.

Having already reached the rank of Grand Master of the Ordnance, and supported by his kinsman, Ivan Shuvalov, whom he introduced as a lover for the licentious Empress—at a time when everywhere in Europe artillery was being increased, and Russia, having thousands of cannons, might have equipped her army and fleet simply by recasting them—Shuvalov had a large number of the old cannons minted into copper currency, and considered it to his credit that he had converted an allegedly unknown and perished treasure into current treasure.

Unable to conceal his covetousness, by means of his power and authority, and availing himself of a law of Peter the Great, whereby mines were to be transferred into private hands, he acquired ownership of some important factories, including the finest in the country, . . . and that with such unscrupulousness, that when this factory, which was capable of yielding a profit of many hundred thousand rubles, was valued at 90,000 rubles, he was not ashamed to complain to the Senate that it had been valued too highly. After a revaluation, where neither justice nor the national interest were considered, out of fear of his authority, he received it for no more than 40,000 rubles—a factory, at which as many as 20,000 serfs were registered, and which afterwards yielded him up 200,000 rubles, and which was later taken back by the treasury in order to cover his debts for a negligible sum, namely 75,000 rubles.

---

1. "pood": an old Russian unit of weight equal to about 36 pounds.—Ed.

Leases, monopolies, bribe-taking, his own administration of trade, and embezzle-
ment of State property, however, could not satisfy his greed and voluptuousness.
He founded a bank, which clearly might have been useful to the subjects. It dealt
in copper currency; the borrower was obliged to repay at a rate of two per cent,
and after some years to bring in a capital in silver.

But who made use of this bank? He himself, by taking out a million rubles;
[the man] who took over from him his lease on the forests of Olonetsk, and gave
him the money which he had borrowed from the bank; the Armenians, who took
out a monopoly on the Astrakhan trade, and gave him most of the money which
they borrowed; Prince Boris Golitsyn, who spent . . . little of the money he borrowed
on himself[:] . . . it is averred that of 20,000 rubles . . . borrowed, he spent only
4,000 . . . .

His [Peter Shuvalov's] love of power, like his avarice, knew no bounds. Not
content with being Grand Master of the Ordnance, Adjutant-General and Senator,
he conceived the desire of forming a private army for himself. This suggestion of
his, like every suggestion he made, was accepted, and he created an army, consisting
of 30,000 infantry men, divided into six legions or regiments . . . responsible to no
one but him.

In Russia it seems that the fate of such otiose schemes is to come quickly into
being, and still quicker to fail. This army, composed of the best soldiers of the state,
took the field against the Prussian forces, suffered many casualties, and achieved
nothing. Part of it was converted into fusilier regiments, again under his command,
and later was completely disbanded. . . .

Among his many such corrupt undertakings, however, the following two were
begun at his suggestion, namely, the National Land Census and the drawing up of
a new Code of Laws. But it must be taken as an indisputable truth that a corrupt
heart brings with it a corrupt reason, which is redolent of corruption in all things.

Although it cannot be said that the idea of a National Land Census was not
useful to the state, and that the Instruction for this census did not contain many
good measures, yet there were also many measures which were drawn up, not in
accordance with justice, but, either through his own shrewdness or that of his
followers, for their own ends.

The carrying out of the Census was still worse. A man corrupt at heart, he
chose corrupt men to carry out the various duties. These, looking not to society's
benefit but to their own profit, also gave their approval to corrupt men. Hence a
large number of abuses resulted at this time, and this Census became not an
advantage to society but a sure means of enriching those in authority at the people's
expense.

The drawing up of the Code of Laws had no better success. For to this most
useful measure of state were assigned not men who, by their profound knowledge
of the condition of the country and the old laws, together with a knowledge of
logic and moral philosophy and an unimpaired record of many years' service, might
have deserved the name of lawgivers and benefactors of their country: but [rather
a certain] Emme, a learned man, but coarse and inhuman by nature; Divov, a stupid
man, quick to invent laws, but understanding little of their meaning, and avaricious
in addition; Iushkov, a good man and not a bribe-taker, who at any rate was familiar

with the laws of Russia, but lazy, idle, and an unreliable judge; Kozlov, a clever man who knew the laws, but had only just emerged from an investigation for bribe-taking and peculation; Glebov, a toady of Count Shuvalov, a seemingly clever man, but one who combined all the vices of Count Peter himself.

Such were the men, and such was their work. They filled their Code of Laws with a mass of biased articles, in which each sought to settle his own law-suits, or, having entered on new ones, to take the opportunity to annul other law-suits. They filled it with such unheard-of cruelties by way of torture and punishment, that when, at its completion, without having been read by the Senate and other organs of state, it was presented to the monarch to sign, this good-hearted sovereign was ready to sign without reading it. Suddenly, glancing through the pages, she came upon the chapter containing the tortures. She glanced at it, and, horrified at its tyranny, refused to sign, ordering it to be revised. In this remarkable fashion Russia was saved from this inhuman piece of legislation.

But I have digressed too far from my subject, interesting though such a digression may be. I only expanded it in order to show the character of this notorious man. The grandee's corruption, by its example, also brought corruption to the lower orders.

And indeed, though bribe-taking, injustice and corruption certainly existed before his rule, yet it was always at the risk of incurring the severity of the laws; and the people, though they might have to pay some small sum, could not justly complain that they were ruined by the judges. But with his rise, injustice was brazenly committed, laws fell into disrepute, and bribe-taking was openly practiced. For the favor and protection of Count Shuvalov, his mistresses, or his favorites . . . [were] a sufficient guarantee of impunity to commit any injustice and to ruin the people by exacting bribes.

The very Senate feared his power, and was obliged to submit to his wishes, and he was the first to expel justice from this, the supreme organ of government. . . .

I cannot omit to mention one law of this Count Peter Shuvalov, which was drawn up for his own profit, and which loosened the bond of matrimony, which was hitherto held sacred in Russia. Among other things, uniting husbands and wives and, in accordance with God's Law, subordinating women to their husbands, there was a law forbidding a woman to sell or mortgage her property without her husband's consent; and the husband was always obliged to signify his permission by signing the title-deeds.

Count Peter Shuvalov needed to buy an estate, belonging to a certain Countess Golovin . . . , who lived apart from her husband, and hence could not secure his consent. Shuvalov suggested that this sign of female subjection should be abolished. At his suggestion—he being all-powerful in the state—a decree was drawn up. He bought the estate and thus gave occasion for women to leave their husbands at will, to ruin their children, and having left their husbands, to ruin themselves.

I think I have adequately described the various enterprises of Count Shuvalov, tending to his own profit. They angered me at the time, not only for the actual evil that was then done, but also for the example which was being set. I prophesied at the time that he would find many imitators.

And this, indeed, has happened. . . .

I must now mention his morals and luxury. In his schemes and enterprises, he could not constantly keep an open house, and demonstrate his luxury through a magnificent scale of living. But in his private life he was voluptuous and luxurious. His house was decorated in the finest style possible at the time. His buffet was laden with all that is most precious and tasty. His dessert was most magnificent for those days, for at a time when many people lived their whole lives without knowing the taste of pineapples, and had never even heard of bananas, he had both of these in abundance, and was the first private person to install a large pineapple-orchard.

The wines taken by him were not merely the best, but, not content with those that are usually imported and consumed, he produced a pineapple-wine in his own home. His carriage glittered with gold, and he was the first man to have a team of English horses, which were then very expensive. His clothing was also ostentatious: it glittered with gold, silver, lace and embroidery; and he was the first, after Count Aleksei Razumovsky, to have diamond buttons, star, medals and epaulettes—the only difference was that Shuvalov's diamond ornaments were the more costly.

In order to gratify his licentiousness, he always had many mistresses, whom he showered unstintingly with money, and in order that his bodily powers might match up to such luxury, he took strong medicines every day, which finally brought about his death.

In a word, although he then had an income of over 400,000 rubles, yet this was not enough to cover his luxury, licentiousness and gifts for the Empress's followers, and he died over a million rubles in debt to the treasury.

Such examples could not fail to spread to the whole nation, and luxury and voluptuousness everywhere increased. Houses began to be magnificently furnished, and people were ashamed not to have English furniture. Meals became magnificent, and cooks, who were not originally considered the most important servant in the household, began to receive large salaries. . . .

Oranges and lemons could not be expensive at St Petersburg, where they are imported by ship, but in Moscow they were so rare that they were only bought for an invalid or for a particularly grand table; now they were in abundance even in Moscow.

Costly and hitherto unknown wines came into use, and not only in the houses of the great; but even the lower orders started to take them; and it was considered elegant to serve various different kinds at table. Many people even placed lists of the various wines under the guests' plates at table, so that each could request whichever wine he wanted. English beer, never taken until now, was introduced by Countess Anna Vorontsov, who loved it. It began to be taken daily, and not only at the tables of the great; but even the common people, forsaking Russian beer, began to get drunk on it.

The candles hitherto in use were mainly tallow candles; and whenever wax candles were used in noble houses in the presence of guests, even these were of yellow wax. Now candles came into use everywhere, and in most cases they were of white wax.

Luxury in dress exceeded all bounds: there was brocade, velvet with gold and silver, clothes embroidered with gold, silver and silk (for galoon was already considered paltry stuff), and these in such quantities that the wardrobe of some courtier or fop was sometimes equal to the rest of his fortune; and even people of modest means had large wardrobes.

And indeed, how could this have been otherwise, when the monarch herself applied all her efforts to adorning her person, when she made it a rule to put on a new dress every day, and sometimes two or three a day? I am ashamed to state the number, but it is averred that after her death she left several tens of thousands of different dresses. Uniforms were then not worn by anyone of means, apart from in the service, and it was even forbidden to attend the court dances in uniform.

Carriages were of a magnificence commensurate with all the rest. A carriage of Russian make was now held in contempt, and it was necessary to have a French carriage with polished glass panes, at a cost of several thousand rubles, with harnesses and horses to match, and so on. . . .

Under a voluptuous and luxurious monarch, it is not surprising that luxury made such advances; but it is surprising that under a devout monarch there were so many infringements of God's Law as far as morals were concerned. I refer to the preservation of the sanctity of marriage, which is a sacrament according to our faith. So true it is that one vice and one false step lead to others. We can count this time as the beginning of the period when women began to desert their husbands.

I do not know the exact circumstances of the first extraordinary divorce, but the facts were these: Ivan Buturlin . . . had a wife, Anna. She fell in love with Stepan Ushakov, and leaving her husband, married her lover. After publicly contracting this adulterous and unlawful marriage, they lived together openly.

Then Anna Borisovna, . . . born Princess Golitsyn, who was married to Count Peter Apraksin, left him. I am not going into the reasons why she left her husband, who certainly led a dissolute existence. But I know that this divorce was decided by a civil, not an ecclesiastical, authority. Her husband, for an alleged attempt to do her some insult in a German play, was placed under arrest and kept in confinement for a long time. Finally the order came that she was to be given a specified portion of her husband's property during his lifetime, and to be known by her maiden name as Princess Golitsyn. And so, casting off her husband's name and causing him to be placed under arrest, she became heiress to part of his property, for no other reason than that her father . . . enjoyed a certain favor at Court, and that later, in connection with her divorce, she became a friend of Countess Elena Kurakin, Count Shuvalov's mistress.

The example of such divorces was soon followed by many other women. I have only named two from the reign of the Empress Elizabeth, but today [ca. 1787] they can be reckoned in hundreds. . . .

Such was the condition of morals at the time of the death of this Empress. She died, leaving the throne to her nephew, Peter, the son of her elder sister, Anna, who married the Duke of Holstein. Peter III was endowed with a good heart, if this is possible in a man who had neither intellect nor morals: for in other respects he not only had a very weak intellect, but was apparently actually insane; he was steeped in all the vices, voluptuousness, luxury, drunkenness and licentiousness. This man who now ascended the throne of all [Russia] with its corrupt morals, was himself excessively corrupt—both by nature and because throughout the reign of the Empress Elizabeth, men had tried to corrupt his morals even more—and therefore could do nothing to improve this situation.

The monarch had as his chief favorite Lev Naryshkin, a quite intelligent man, but with the sort of mind that never concentrates on anything; cowardly, greedy for honors and gain, prone to every luxury, a joker, and, in a word, from his behavior and his love of joking, more fit to be a court-jester than a grandee. He ministered to all the monarch's passions.

Having ascended the throne of [Russia], unsound in mind, and ignorant of all political affairs, the monarch conceived the desire of enhancing the prestige of the army by his liberal conduct towards it. All his Holstein officers, of whom he had a small corps, together with the officers of the Guard, often had the honor of sharing his table, to which ladies too were always invited. What were these parties like?

Idle chatter was combined with immoderate drinking; the punch served after the meal, the pipes that were provided, the protracted drinking-bouts and tobacco-smoke suggested some ale-house rather than the monarch's residence. A short-coated and loud-mouthed officer won preference over one who merely knew his duty.

To praise the King of Prussia, who had only just ceased to be our enemy, and to belittle the courage of the Russian troops, brought the honor of gaining the monarch's affection; and Count Zakhar Chernyshev, for . . . proving, in a test between Russian artillery and captured Prussian artillery, that the Russian artillery was more efficient, failed to receive the ribbon of St Andrew, which was then being generously awarded.

The monarch had a mistress, the ugly and stupid Countess Elizabeth Vorontsov; but once on the throne, he was no longer satisfied with her, and soon all the good-looking women were subjected to his lust. It is averred that Alexander Glebov, who was then Procurator-General and had also been promoted by him to Commissary General for War, offered him his stepdaughter . . . ; and the aforementioned Princess Elena Kurakin was brought to him for the night by Lev Naryshkin. I myself have heard from him that her brazenness was such that after the night was over, and he was conveying her home early in the morning, and wanted to travel with the carriage-blinds closed, in order to protect her honor . . . , she, on the contrary, opened the blinds, wishing to show everyone that she had spent the night with the monarch.

This was a remarkable night for Russia, as I was told by Dmitry Volkov, who was then his [Peter III's] Secretary. In order to hide from Countess [Vorontsov] the fact that he would be making merry that night with his newly arrived mistress, Peter III told Volkov, in her presence, that he was going to spend the night with *him* working out a certain important scheme known to him in connection with the good government of the state.

Night fell. The monarch went off to enjoy himself with Princess Kurakin, having told Volkov to have some important piece of legislation written by morning. Volkov was locked up in an empty room together with a Great-Dane [dog]. Not knowing the reason for this or what the monarch had in mind, Volkov did not know what to begin writing. But write he must. Being an enterprising man, he remembered the frequent exhortations made by Count Roman Vorontsov to the monarch, concerning the freedom of the nobility. Sitting down, he wrote out the manifesto concerning this. In the morning he was released from confinement, and the manifesto was approved by the monarch and promulgated [as printed above].

It was not only the monarch who indulged his licentiousness by thus using well-born women for his own pleasure; the whole Court had reached such a state that almost everyone kept a mistress openly; and women sought lovers for themselves without hiding the fact from their husbands or kinsmen.

Shall I enumerate, to their shame, the names of those women who were not ashamed to fall into such licentiousness, scorning modesty and decency, which is one of women's chief virtues? No, let their names be hidden from posterity, and let not their families be dishonored by a reminder of the crimes of their mothers and grandmothers. And so, content to describe the climate of depravity, I shall not go into details of their licentiousness or mention their names. For indeed, it is only with great reluctance that I force myself to mention the names of such people at all, even where it is absolutely necessary, for the sake of this work [tract], which is destined to remain hidden in my family.

And so dissoluteness in women's morals, humoring of the monarch, and every kind of luxury and drunkenness now comprised the characteristic features of the Court. From here some of them had already spread to other classes of society in the reign of the Empress Elizabeth, and the rest had begun to spread, when the wife of this Peter III, [Catherine,] born the Princess of Anhalt-Zerbst, had him deposed and ascended the throne of Russia. . . .

## FURTHER READING

J. L. Black, G.-F. Müller and the Imperial Russian Academy [of Sciences] (1986)

Gregory L. Freeze, The Russian Levites: Parish Clergy in the Eighteenth Century (1977)

Robert E. Jones, The Emancipation of the Russian Nobility, 1762–1785 (1973)

Arcadius Kahan, "Continuity in Economic Activity and Policy during the Post-Petrine Period in Russia," Journal of Economic History 25 (1965), 61–85; and Kahan, "The Costs of 'Westernization' in Russia: The Gentry [Nobility] and the Economy in the Eighteenth Century," Slavic Review 25 (1966), 40–66; both in Michael Cherniavsky, ed., The Structure of Russian History: Interpretative Essays (1970), 191–211, 224–250
———, The Plow, The Hammer, and the Knout: An Economic History of Eighteenth-Century Russia (1985)

John P. LeDonne, Absolutism and Ruling Class: The Formation of the Russian Political Order, 1700–1825 (1991)

Carol S. Leonard, Reform and Regicide: The Reign of Peter III of Russia (1992)

Gary Marker, Publishing, Printing, and the Origins of Intellectual Life in Russia, 1700–1800 (1985)

Marc Raeff, "The Domestic Policies of Peter III and His Overthrow," American Historical Review, 75 (1970), 1289–1310

Hans Rogger, National Consciousness in Eighteenth-Century Russia (1969)

# The Age of Catherine II

C atherine II dominated Russia as no ruler had since Peter I, a feat all the more remarkable in that, unlike Peter, she had no legitimate claim to the throne. But, in politics here as so often elsewhere in history, nothing succeeds like success. From the moment she seized the throne from her hapless husband, Peter III (1762), until her death (1796), she ruled the Russian Empire with spectacular success. Whether her long reign actually benefited the great majority of her subjects, or even most of the tiny noble elite, is another question.

Catherine was born (1729) Sophia Augusta Fredericka ("Figchen"), princess of Anhalt-Zerbst, which was a very minor German principality subordinate to the king of Prussia, for whom her father worked. In 1744 she went to Russia, where a marriage had been arranged between her and Grand Duke Peter, heir to the Russian throne and a distant relative. She converted from Lutheranism to Russian Orthodoxy, taking the name Catherine, and in 1745, on marrying Peter, became the Grand Duchess Catherine. The marriage appears to have been singularly unhappy, and as spouse of the boorish heir to the throne Catherine's life seems to have been lonely and even dangerous. But she never looked back. Over the next seventeen years she read extensively in the political literature of the day, learned Russian, and gave birth to the Grand Duke (and future emperor) Paul. Most important for her own and Russia's future, Catherine spent her years as grand duchess mastering the murky politics of the court of Empress Elizabeth, thus positioning herself to become empress in her own right when her unloved husband, after six months of inept rule, was overthrown in the palace coup of June 28, 1762. (Eight days later, he was murdered by officers supporting Catherine, evidently out of fear that he might try to regain the throne.) It should be noted that sooner or later Catherine adroitly enacted or confirmed all of her late husband's basic policies, including "emancipation" of the nobility, secularization (confiscation) of church lands, military reform, and even the alliance with Prussia.

# ESSAYS

In foreign affairs, Catherine II's great achievements included the outright annexation to Russia of the duchy of Courland and of much of Ukraine, Belorussia, and Lithuania (resulting from the three Partitions of Poland—in 1772, 1793, 1795—executed in alliance with Prussia and Austria) as well as the annexation of Crimea (1783), formerly a Tatar khanate under the Ottoman (Turkish) Empire. These diplomatic-military successes firmly established Russia as a Great Power in Europe and the world. At home, again deliberately following the lead of Peter the Great, Catherine concentrated on administrative and legal reform and on promoting the development of Russian high culture, especially art and education. Her reign came to be seen by some as a "Golden Age" in the history both of the Russian nobility and of Russian culture—in the history, it might be said, of the educated, autonomous, morally responsible individual in Russia. The reign has also been subjected to quite hostile and negative criticism by historians expressing populist, Marxist, Russian nationalist, and/or sexist views. These and other matters are raised in the essay that follows by Isabel de Madariaga, retired professor of Russian history at London University who has devoted much of her scholarly life to Catherine's reign, producing the single most important book on the subject (see Further Reading) as well as the shorter book for students from which this essay is excerpted.

In the second essay, another distinguished specialist, Marc Raeff, retired professor of Russian history at Columbia University, discusses in depth the Pugachev Rebellion of 1773–1775, which is widely viewed as a major crisis of Catherine's reign—perhaps *the* major crisis—and which Raeff sees as a mass protest against the coming to Russia of the modern, European, Petrine state and culture.

## Catherine as Woman and Ruler

### ISABEL DE MADARIAGA

Catherine ruled Russia from 1762 to 1796. "In an absolute monarchy, everything depends on the disposition and character of the Sovereign," the British Envoy to Russia, Sir James Harris, observed in 1778. The ruler sets the tone in every field far more than in a limited monarchy, as Great Britain was at the time, or in a democracy, as the United Kingdom is today. Peace or war, prosperity or poverty, a free and easy intellectual and social life, or a society isolated from outside influences and dragooned into conformity, all this depended to a great extent on the character of the individual ruler.

The personality of Catherine thus merits some attention. Inevitably it changed a good deal over the thirty-four years of her reign. Yet some features of her character remained present throughout. She was to begin with a woman of an optimistic and cheerful temperament, looking on the bright side of things, not easily depressed or downhearted. This shows clearly in her letters to Potemkin, who, on the contrary,

From Isabel de Madariaga, *Catherine the Great: A Short History*, pp. 203–218. Copyright © 1990 by Yale University Press. Reprinted with permission of the publisher.

was subject to formidable bouts of despondency, for instance at the beginning of the second Turkish war in 1787, when after the loss of his precious fleet in a storm on the Black Sea he was prepared to throw up his command and evacuate the Crimea. Catherine wrote letters to him full of encouragement, urging him to believe that a bold spirit would overcome failures, advising him about his indigestion, which she was sure contributed to his depression. "Goodbye, my friend," she concluded one letter in 1788, "neither time, nor distance, nor anyone on earth will change my thoughts of you and about you."[1]

It was this same positive temper which enabled her to steer her way through the shoals at the Russian court while she was still grand duchess and gave her the courage to embark on the *coup d'état* which brought her to the throne. Its success should not conceal from one how dangerous failure might have been. Imprisonment in a convent would have been the mildest penalty she might have had to suffer. Throughout her life Catherine showed very strong and steady nerves at moments of crisis: during the early plots against her; during the Pugachev Revolt, when she had to be dissuaded by her ministers from going herself to Kazan to restore morale after the sacking of the city by Pugachev. But her health did not remain unaffected by these crises and she suffered from frequent headaches and digestive disorders.

By the standards of her time Catherine was a well-read woman of considerable breadth of interest and intellectual curiosity. She was interested in politics, history, education, literature, linguistics, architecture, painting. In her literary as in her legislative production she was pragmatic in her approach, pedantic in her execution, and eclectic as regards her sources. She seemed to feel that if the law described down to the last detail precisely how its provisions were to be implemented, better results would be achieved. In the Russian context, no doubt she was right to think that the careful drafting of laws would prevent misinterpretation. In her Instruction of 1767, she had quoted Montesquieu's dictum that you cannot change customs by means of laws but only by means of other customs; but her faith in the power of law to change conduct survived and shows through in her major legislative innovations [see Documents below].

A hard-working woman, Catherine rose early, lit her fire, made her black coffee and settled down at her desk to indulge in her "scribbling." A blank sheet of paper made her fingers itch to start writing. After a few hours devoted to her literary or political activities, she would see her secretaries and ministers, withdraw to perform her toilette in private and only appear in her dressing room for her hair to be dressed. She did not go in for the elaborate court ritual of the *lever* and the *coucher* (receptions on getting up and going to bed) still practiced at the French court. In private Catherine dressed simply in a loose silk gown, but on state occasions she was richly dressed and wore splendid jewels. Dinner was usually at 2 P.M. and, since the Empress was not interested in food, it was notoriously bad. Catherine was also very abstemious, and did not drink even wine unless her Scottish physician, Dr. Rogerson, prescribed it.

---

1. Grigory A. Potemkin (1739–1791), a leading soldier and politician of Catherine's reign, is further identified later in this essay.—Ed.

The afternoon was devoted to reading or working, or seeing specially invited guests, such as Diderot or Grimm.[2] The Empress would then play for a while with her grandchildren, and adjourn to spend the evening at the theater or at her private parties in the Hermitage [her private palace in St. Petersburg]. These were completely informal. It was forbidden to rise when the Empress stood up, and those who had the right to attend talked, gambled, played paper games or went in for theatricals until about 10 P.M. when the Empress, who never took any supper, withdrew attended by her current favorite, and the guests dispersed in search of a well-provided table and a better cook than Catherine's.

All those who ever attended the court bear witness to the grace and dignity with which Catherine conducted herself, to the ease and charm of her manners. Claude Carloman de Rulhière, who was attached to the French Embassy in St. Petersburg at the time of Catherine's *coup d'état*, described her appearance in 1762:

> She has a noble and agreeable figure; her gait is majestic, her person and deportment [are] full of graces. Her air is that of a sovereign. All her features proclaim a superior character. . . . Her brow is broad and open, her nose almost aquiline. . . . Her hair is chestnut colored and very beautiful, her eyebrows brown, her eyes brown [they were in fact blue] and very beautiful, acquiring a bluish tint in certain lights; her complexion is dazzling. Pride is the principal feature of her physiognomy. The pleasantness and kindness of her expression are, to the eye of a keen observer, rather the consequence of a great desire to please. . . .

George Macartney, British Envoy in 1766, was even more impressed:

> I never saw in my life a person whose port, manner and behavior answered so strongly to the idea I had formed to myself of her. Tho' in the thirty seventh year of her age, she may still be called beautiful. Those who knew her younger say they never remembered her so lovely as at present. . . . It is inconceivable with what address she mingles the ease of behavior with the dignity of her rank, with what facility she familiarizes herself with the meanest of her subjects, without losing a point of her authority, and with what astonishing magic she inspires at once both respect and affection. Her conservation is brilliant, perhaps too brilliant for she loves to shine in conversation. . . .

The desire to impress, not only by her physical presence but by her intellectual qualities, is noted by many observers of Catherine, beginning with the adventurer Count Casanova, and it explains the well-merited reputation she had for vanity. To Sir James Harris it appeared that:

> she has a masculine force of mind, obstinacy in adhering to a plan and intrepidity in the execution of it; but she wants the more manly virtues of deliberation, forbearance in prosperity and accuracy of judgment, while she possesses in a high degree the weaknesses vulgarly attributed to her sex—love

---

2. Denis Diderot (1713–1784), French Enlightenment thinker and editor of a famous 34-volume encyclopedia, corresponded regularly with Catherine and visited Russia, for six months, in 1773. Baron Friedrich Melchior von Grimm (1723–1801), a well-connected German intellectual based in Paris, also regularly corresponded with Catherine and also visited Russia in 1773.—Ed.

of flattery and its inseparable companion, vanity; an inattention to unpleasant but salutary advice; and a propensity to voluptuousness, which leads her to excesses that would debase a female character in any sphere of life.

The Chevalier de Corberon, who was not admitted to Catherine's small court circle and was therefore somewhat jaundiced, regarded Catherine as a "comédienne," always acting a part.

Whether she was acting a part or not, Catherine throughout her life showed her ability to get on with people in all ranks of life. Her servants adored her and remained with her for years; her secretaries were well treated, and the diary kept by A. V. Khrapovitsky, himself a poet and writer, who was her private secretary in the years 1782 to 1793 and also helped her with her literary works, illustrates her kindness, her consideration for his health and welfare. She was always well received by the common people on her various travels throughout Russia, and it was the aristocracy, not the people, who cold-shouldered her in Moscow. Of course personal access to the palace and to the presence of the Empress was much easier in those days than it is today to the presence of kings, presidents and ministers, for she did not have to be protected against terrorists, journalists or photographers. Catherine drove about the streets of St. Petersburg in an open sledge at night, with just a few attendants, in perfect security. The public—decently dressed—was admitted to the imperial parks, and wherever she traveled Catherine gave receptions to which the local nobility and townspeople were invited. The French Ambassador, Ségur, describes how after one such lengthy reception the Empress emerged with her cheeks colored bright pink with rouge from having kissed so many of the painted faces of the merchants' ladies.

Life was also made easier for her ministers by her commonsensical and unpretentious approach to work. Ministers did not have to stand in her presence like Disraeli or Gladstone before Queen Victoria. The letters and notes she wrote asking for advice, and the letters she received with advice, reflect a genuine partnership in the search for a solution to a particular legislative or administrative problem. Where her correspondence over a particular legislative project can be followed, as with Count Sievers over the Statute of Local Administration of 1775, it is clear that her advisers and ministers had no hesitation in countering her ideas and expressing their own. The minutes of the meetings of the Council of State frequently reflect the vigorous debate which took place. On the other hand Catherine could also write stinging rebukes to officials who failed her.

Within the mental climate of her time and of her position as ruler, Catherine also showed more originality than any previous ruler of Russia and than most rulers at the time in Europe, except perhaps the Grand Duke Leopold of Tuscany, in her thoughts about changing the nature and the structure of Russian central government by altering the relationship of the central power and the corporate forces in Russian society, forces to which she had herself given legal form. It is here that the influence of William Blackstone's *Commentaries on the Laws of England* (in a French translation) is so noteworthy. Catherine made over 700 pages of notes from Blackstone and wrote various drafts at different times of the changes in the constitutional structure she proposed to introduce.

*Plans for constit. reform*

In a manner typical of her industrious nature, she hoped to begin to draw up her final plans in the course of her journey to the Crimea in 1787, and ordered her secretary to collect all her notes on Blackstone to take with her, as well as a copy of her Instruction, which she wished to compare with her notes on Blackstone. Familiar with her plans and never at a loss for a compliment, Khrapovitsky exclaimed that one day Russians would treasure her work as the English treasured their Magna Carta. Throughout her journey Catherine continued to work on her plans for constitutional reform. From what one can tell of her intentions, she viewed her project as as means of consolidating absolute government in Russia by making it more responsive to the various estates and more efficient. The most novel feature she drew from her reading of Blackstone was her plan for a high court, which seemed to have some of the legislative features of the British Parliament and some of its judicial elements. The separate chambers into which the proposed High Court was to be divided would have appointed councilors, but also assessors, elected by the local nobles, townspeople and state peasants.

Though Catherine never completed even a draft law, these papers show that as late as 1787 she could still contemplate fundamental reform, which associated elected representatives of the free estates with the machinery of central government in a way which was not even to be thought of again until the reign of Alexander II [1856–1881]. It is not possible to tell what inspired her to think such institutions necessary or advisable in Russia. Did something remain of her lengthy conversations with Diderot in 1774, who had urged her to keep the Legislative Commission in being and who had warned her, "All aribtrary government is bad, even the arbitrary government of a good, strong, just and wise master. . . . He deprives the nation of the right to deliberate, to wish, or not to wish to oppose, to oppose even that which is good. In a society of men, the right of opposition seems to me a natural right, inalienable and sacred." The best of depots "is a good shepherd who reduces his subjects to the condition of animals; he makes them lose the sense of liberty. . . ."

It is unfortunately also not possible to tell on the evidence available at present whether Catherine abandoned her projects because of the outbreak of war with Turkey in 1787, or because she was feeling old and discouraged, or because of her dismay at the use made of their power by elected "representatives" of the people in the French Revolution. As Marc Raeff, the historian who has done most to illuminate Blackstone's influence on Catherine, points out, there is a direct line between her plans and those of M. M. Speransky in 1809 and those of the liberal reformers of the late 1870s. The secretariat of Catherine's Legislative Commission of 1767 continued in being, and worked on attempts at codification throughout her reign. There is no doubt that later reformers drew on the various projects and studies which were produced by this secretariat (most of which remain unpublished) and that later on the codification of Russian law undertaken in the reign of Nicholas I by Speransky also drew on its resources. Hence the continuity of ideas between the eighteenth and the nineteenth centuries.

It was Catherine's private life which really exercised the gossipmongers of the time (and later). By twentieth-century standards there was nothing abnormal about it until her breach with Grigory Orlov in 1772—he had been her lover for twelve years and was the father of her son, A. Bobrinskoy, never legitimized, but known to be hers, and recognized as his brother by Paul I. (The rumor that she had five daughters by Orlov is quite unsubstantiated.) During their liaison Orlov seems to have conducted himself in such a way as not to arouse violent hostility. He was brave, lazy, good-natured, neither very intelligent nor very cultured. He played a prominent part in court functions and festivities. But he was a liberal-minded man and he should be remembered for two initiatives: he invited the [celebrated] philosopher Rousseau, who quarreled with everybody, to settle in Russia (presumably with Catherine's consent); and he sponsored a number of projects on his estates to find an alternative to serfdom for the establishment of peasants on the land, also with Catherine's knowledge and approval.

Catherine was induced to dismiss Orlov in 1772 because of his unfaithfulness, and she chose a new lover, whom she did not love and who was given no government post, simply because she could not live alone. Something of her emotional life at this time is known, for she described it in moving terms in a letter to Grigory Potemkin with whom the great love affair of her life began in December 1773. Potemkin was already a lieutenant-general in the army, and had distinguished himself in the war against the Turks. He was probably thirty-four years old—ten years younger than Catherine and a bold, enterprising, imaginative, moody, arrogant, witty and intelligent man. He ceased to be Catherine's lover in 1776, but he kept his official positions to the surprise of many at court, who expected him to be dismissed when Catherine took a new lover, P. V. Zavadovsky. But he remained the most powerful figure at court, and continued as Catherine's principal adviser and confidant. It is possible that he was her husband—there were rumors that a religious ceremony had taken place—at any rate she trusted him absolutely. His role at her side can be compared to that of Leicester beside Elizabeth I of England. A woman ruler, however able, needs someone very reliable indeed to command her armies, someone who will not turn against her (as Essex did against Elizabeth). Catherine found her helpmate in Potemkin, who continued to dominate the scene at her side until his death in 1791.

Potemkin was a favorite, since his power originated in his personal relationship with Catherine. But he was not only a favorite, he was also a statesman. Nevertheless, other senior ministers and officials were bound to resent his seemingly boundless power and authority, the fact that he, above anyone else, had the ear of the Empress, that he could overrule and dominate, that he could draw on the Treasury for his private and public needs. Courtiers might fear him, they might hate him, but they could not despise him. (He was also a man of considerable culture, who had the complete works of Rousseau in his library, and yet preserved close links with the Russian Church, and loved all exotic peoples and religions.) From her letters to Grigory Potemkin, and to Peter Zavadovsky, it is evident that Catherine was passionately in love with both of them (and they with her) but that for reasons which no one can really at this date fathom, the relationships did not last.

But the favorites who followed Zavadovsky (who was dismissed in 1778) did nothing to increase Catherine's reputation. She needed their companionship both as lovers and as partners in her intellectual and cultural activities, but only two of them, A. D. Lanskoy (1780–1784) and A. Dmitriev Mamonov (1786–1789), seem to have been reasonably well educated and capable of providing Catherine the woman with the affection and friendship she craved. . . . But the first died in her arms, possibly of diphtheria, in 1784 leaving Catherine absolutely heartbroken. She poured out her grief to Baron Grimm:

> When I began this letter on June 7, 1784 I was happy and gay . . . but things have changed on July 2. . . . I am sunk in the deepest sorrow, my happiness is over. I thought I too would die at the irreparable loss of my best friend I suffered just eight days ago . . . my room has become an empty cave in which I drag myself around like a shadow. . . . I can neither eat nor sleep. . . .

The death of Lanskoy shows Catherine at her most human; she continued to work, but she could not bear to spend the rest of the summer in Tsarkoe Selo, or to resume normal court life.[3] Finally, after some months, she found a new lover.

Later, A. Dmitriev Mamonov betrayed Catherine's affection in a different way, by falling in love with one of her maids of honor. Deeply hurt, Catherine dismissed him and arranged his marriage. As the Empress grew older, her favorites became younger, and though they were not given prominent political positions, their closeness to Catherine meant that they were the channel by which private and even corrupt influence could be brought to bear. Catherine was now beginning to feel her age. She had grown very stout, though according to the French painter, Mme. Vigée Lebrun, she remained very charming, with her white hair framing a noble face, and beautiful, very white hands. But she no longer had the energy, or perhaps the discrimination, to judge the harm Platon Zubov did to her reputation, though her impatience with his incompetence in the fulfillment of his public duties is duly noted by the somewhat biased diarist Khrapovitsky. The future Alexander I, who was often in the company of his grandmother, made quite clear his hatred and contempt for her favorite.

The great Russian historian N. M. Karamzin, though critical particularly of the corruption and neglect of the public interest in the last years of Catherine II, nevertheless wrote in a memorandum he drew up for Alexander I in 1811 that "should we compare all the known epochs of Russian history, virtually all would agree that Catherine's epoch was the happiest for Russian citizens; virtually all would prefer to have lived then than at any other time." This verdict is in striking contrast to the judgments of some late-nineteenth-century Russian historians which have influenced historians in the west. Soviet historians unanimously [claimed] that peasants, and the serfs in particular, were more and more severely exploited in the reign of Catherine II to the extent that one wonders that any remained alive. And many contemporary western historians have echoed these judgments without examining the evidence on which they are based.

There was of course opposition both to Catherine's usurpation of the throne and to some of her policies. There were those who, like the Vorontsov brothers, Alexander, the President of the College of Commerce, and, even more so, Simon,

---

3. Tsarskoe Selo, today a public park and museum near St. Petersburg, was the favorite retreat of Catherine, who greatly expanded and beautified its palace and grounds.—Ed.

the long-serving Ambassador to England, had supported Peter III in 1762, and had never forgiven Catherine for usurping the throne and dislodging their sister Elizabeth, who had been Peter III's mistress. There were others who had hoped that Catherine would merely be regent for her eight-year-old son Paul. This was the case above all with Count Nikita Panin, who had hoped to benefit from his position as governor of the young Grand Duke to achieve a position of considerable power in a regency council.

It is essential to realize how little opposition there was to the form of government, absolutism, in Russia. The bulk of the population accepted the legitimacy of the regime however much some people might disagree with some policies. Government operated largely as a partnership between the nobility, the townspeople and the Crown, and the political class in a largely illiterate and materially still very primitive country was minute. Individuals might criticize specific policies, but the Russian political system provided no channels for groups to form with common programs. There were only small patronage and clientele circles around specific magnates. This explains the importance of the favorites and of high-ranking ministers like Prince A. A. Viazemsky or Alexander Vorontsov. They all became rich (or richer) and Catherine's favorites were given high rank. Nobles anxious for promotion gravitated towards one or other of the magnates as long as their favor lasted.

The most important clientele group, as long as he lived, formed around Potemkin. Another very influential group, deeply opposed to Potemkin, formed around Count Nikita Panin, Foreign Secretary and governor of the Grand Duke [Paul] until his dismissal in 1781 (he died in 1783). It continued to some extent around the Grand Duke after Panin's dismissal. At one time some members of this group of courtiers and high officials, notably the playwright Denis Fonvizin, even drafted plans for constitutional changes in Russia, to be implemented by the Grand Duke on becoming emperor, changes which would turn Russia into a proper monarchy, as distinct from a despotism, namely a state in which the ruler abided by principles laid down in "fundamental laws" which he would himself be unable to alter. In the event, Paul proved to be one of the most despotic rulers Russia has ever known, and these plans only came to light much later, in Alexander I's reign. This kind of clandestine constitutional criticism of Catherine's rule tended rather to be expressed either in odes to the Grand Duke, or in fables such as that of *Callisthenes* published by Fonvizin in 1786, in which Alexander the Great is made to choose between the virtuous advice of a moral philosopher and the capricious and arbitrary whims of a favorite and ends up by choosing the latter and condemning the philosopher to a cruel death. At this stage Catherine seems to have been indifferent to such indirect criticism of her rule but it cannot have helped Fonvizin when he attempted to launch a periodical in 1788.

The two most serious plots, aimed against Catherine as a usurper and at placing the ex-Emperor Ivan VI on the throne [took place early in her reign]. In the following years there were several noble conspiracies, mainly among officers in the Guards Regiments. Some originated among officers who had expected Paul to be proclaimed emperor with Catherine as regent; some represented a reaction to the rumor that she intended to marry Grigory Orlov. Several more alleged plots were investigated by the Secret Chancery between 1762 and 1772, some of them originating among common soldiers wanting to prolaim Paul emperor—many of them merely incoherent ranting by very young men who had drunk too much. Nevertheless Catherine took such plots very seriously, and most of those involved ended up in Siberia condemned to hard labor or settlement.

What was particularly disturbing for Catherine was that anyone plotting against her had a pretender to hand in the person of her son [Paul]. These fears all came together in the early 1770s. Some loose talk among the Guards who complained about rumors that freedom was to be given to the serfs ("and then how shall we live?") and that an officer had been arrested for beating a sergeant ("previously officers were not arrested without a personal order from the tsar") and several other incidents of a similar nature seemed to indicate a seditious temper among the minor nobility serving in the Guards. The plotters had not failed to remark in their confused speeches that Paul was now of age (he was eighteen years old in 1772), and Catherine could well be expected to step down from the throne and let him reign. The use of Paul's name by Pugachev in 1773–1774 was also alarming, though since Pugachev was rebelling on behalf of the restoration of "Peter III" Paul was not a real threat in that context.

Catherine dealt with the situation in several ways. In the first place she acknowledged Paul's maturity by arranging his marriage, which took place in September 1773. The bride was a princess of Hesse Darmstadt; she did not learn Russian; she flirted, she intrigued and she got into debt. Two years after the wedding she died in childbirth and a second wife was soon found for the Grand Duke. But with Paul's marriage Catherine was able to sever the ties which linked him to Count Nikita Panin, who had continued to be governor and Master of the Court of the Grand Duke. Panin now ceased to live in the palace and see his charge daily. He was no longer able systematically to disparage Catherine's policies nor to direct Paul's political judgment, though he had already sown the seeds of an unbounded admiration for Frederick II of Prussia in his young pupil.

At the same time Catherine, in 1773, this time together with Panin, was able to complete the transfer of the Duchy of Holstein Gottorp, which Paul had inherited from his father, to the King of Denmark. Denmark had always had claims on the duchy, and Catherine had been glad to negotiate a treaty by which her son lost the duchy which might provide him with a territorial base outside Russia in which he might seek refuge and from which he could mount an attack in the event of a breach with his mother. The treaty had been negotiated in 1767, but its ratification had to wait for Paul's majority. Holstein Gottorp was now exchanged for the duchies of Oldenburg and Elmenhorst, which went to a minor branch of the Holstein family. At this very moment, however, Catherine was faced with a plot to urge Paul to demand his rights, this time led by the man who was negotiating the Holstein exchange on her behalf, Count Saldern. The details of the plot have never been made clear, and though Saldern was undoubtedly largely bribed by the Danes, he seems to have been acting on his own behalf. He left Russia never to return. In fairness to Paul, it must be added that though he was often very critical orally of his mother's policies, and sometimes countered her plans in foreign policy, he never actually encouraged any attempt to dethrone her.

Looking back, the historian may well be tempted to think that the years 1771–1777 were the most difficult and dangerous of Catherine's whole reign. Had the plague continued to ravage Moscow in 1771; had Pugachev succeeded in setting the center of Russia ablaze; above all had the Russian army been defeated by the Turks, she might well have been overthrown in favor of Paul. But her luck held, and in the middle of this tremendous crisis she found the man—Potemkin—who inspired her with self-confidence as a woman and as a ruler. From the peace of Kuchuk-Kainardji [ending favorably the war of 1768–1774 against Turkey] in July 1774 Catherine's authority as Empress was unchallenged.

There were probably more critics of Catherine's policies than we have any means of knowing. The absence of a free press, indeed of any kind of press other than the government gazettes, makes it very difficult to assess the nature of public opinion, and one must rely on memoirs, letters and diplomatic dispatches written by foreigners who were often prejudiced or ill-informed. In general, opposition to Catherine's policy, apart from that arising among disgruntled courtiers passed over in the race for what they considered well-deserved promotion, seems to have centered on foreign policy, particularly war, which many opposed, and on the role of Catherine's favorites in government, more particularly that of Grigory Potemkin, accountable only to the Empress in all that they did.

Bezborodko and some of Catherine's other ministers fully supported the annexation of the Crimea. In the 1780s and 1790s there was certainly a war party, which supported the acquisition of the steppes in the south and of territory in Poland. Many nobles saw in these Russian acquisitions opportunities to acquire estates or land for themselves. But quite apart from considerations of whether Russia needed to grow larger, or whether expansion for the sake of expansion fitted in with the moral precepts of a just war, as some nobles thought they should, many nobles resented the loss of manpower consequent on the conscription of serfs in wartime, and the policy of Potemkin of offering a refuge to fugitive serfs in order to people the empty lands of the south. One cannot, of course, tell to what extent the opposition to Catherine's expansionist policies was really a disguised form of opposition to the personality and power of her favorite, and to the reforms which he was inaugurating in the army. There is some evidence that this was the case because the person around whom this opposition crystallized was again the Grand Duke Paul. He hated Potemkin, and he disapproved of the former's policy as President of the College of War, of increasing the number of lightly armed cavalry regiments, and of simplifying the soldier's uniforms to make them more comfortable. It has been argued by one historian that Radishchev's *Journal from St. Petersburg to Moscow* for which he was sentenced to ten years' exile in Siberia should be regarded much more as an attack on the incompetent and corrupt conduct of the war of [1787–1791] by Potemkin than as an attack on serfdom. Radishchev, it is argued, was tried in fact for sedition in time of war rather than for his revolutionary opinions on serfdom [see Documents].

One can fairly assume the existence of other critics of the role of favorites and of Catherine's policies. But they did not make their criticism public. Prince M. M. Shcherbatov wrote *On the Corruption of Morals in Russia* in 1787, but it was published for the first time by Alexander Herzen in 1859 in London. Shcherbatov was a disgruntled aristocrat who felt that he had not achieved the rank which should have been his, though Catherine was very generous to him. In his book he attacked the materialism, corruption and immorality of the Russian court from the time of Peter I and compared it unfavorably with the simplicity of seventeenth-century Russia. He accused the Empress of arbitrary and despotic conduct, and "although she is in her declining years, although grey hair covers her head and time has marked her brow with the indelible signs of age, yet her licentiousness does not decline." It certainly would not have been possible to publish Shcherbatov's extremely frank criticism of the public and private lives of eighteenth-century Russian rulers during the reign of one of them. Indeed even today such an attack on a living person would undoubtedly fall foul of the laws of libel.

On the other hand the rising of the assigned peasants in the Urals in 1763–1764 and the rising led by Pugachev in 1773–1774 are clear indications of popular dissatisfaction with specific government policies among Cossacks, state peasants, industrial serfs and privately owned serfs. But the discontented did not normally coalesce into one single, massive opposition; they usually formed single-issue groups among the peasantry, anxious to escape from the tyranny of a particular landowner. Moreover the dissatisfaction felt by the peasants was part of a widespread, formless hatred of and revolt against the modern state, which taxed them, called them up to serve in the army (or, worse, the navy), instead of leaving them in peaceful occupation of all the land, without any officials, officers or landowners intervening between them and a benevolent tsar.

There is one aspect of the opposition to Catherine which has so far been much less well documented. The example which the Empress so glaringly provided of total disregard for the rules of domestic mortality—acceptable at that time in a man, totally unforgivable in a woman—turned many of the Church hierarchy, such as Metropolitan Platon of Moscow, and of the more straitlaced nobles, of which there were many, and the Moscow freemasons against her. Catherine's private life was contrasted with the apparent domestic happiness of Paul (he was more discreet). She was accused of corrupting young people and family life by her example, and the Russian court, particularly in its later years, rivaled French society, or the grand Whig society of England, in its dissoluteness, though high standards of decorum were always maintained in public.

Lower down the social scale, there was considerable opposition to Catherine's secularization of Church lands, to the widespread closure of monasteries and convents, and the concentration of monks and nuns in a smaller number of larger establishments. Local minor nobles and townspeople appealed to be allowed to keep open at their own expense small convents which they had often endowed in the past and which acted as refuges for their wives and sisters—requests which were sometimes granted. Unofficially, women's groups in provincial towns set up self-supporting "women's communities," in which women could live a disciplined and religious life, and undertake good works without being officially rated as nuns. What one might call the conservative opposition to Catherine's "enlightenment policies" needs further study.

It is still too early today to make a considered judgment on the impact of Catherine's reign in Russia, and to interpret her policies with any certainty. Research on her reign [was] so neglected in the USSR for so many years that there are many aspects of the government of Russia which remain totally unstudied. To mention but a few, almost nothing is known about the operations of the law courts set up in 1775; about the operation of the noble provincial assemblies and the town assemblies; about the activities of the treasury chambers; about the activities of the land commissars and the social class they were actually drawn from; about the exploitation of small agricultural estates belonging to nobles and about the state peasant villages. Some of these topics have been touched on in more general works, but there has been no systematic study of how particular institutions actually worked. There are very few biographies of the statesmen and ministers who worked with Catherine, and none of them reach the standard expected in the west. . . . There are no studies of merchant dynasties which might illustrate the development of trade and industry.

The traditional view for a long time has been that Catherine was so badly in need of noble support to keep the throne that she deliberately increased the power of the nobles over their serfs, and governed in such a way as to consolidate noble domination and exploitation of the human and material resources of the country. This theory is still found in some modern histories of her policies, but it no longer commands general agreement. In the light of the work that has been done mainly by British and American historians it is now more possible to see both what the Empress tried to achieve and what obstacles faced her. By temperament, as well as because she was aware that she had no legitimate claim to the throne, Catherine wished to prove herself a reformer, in the spirit of German cameralism as modified by the enlightenment. Her policies were presented to the Russian (and to the European) public clothed in the language of the enlightenment. But there was a considerable discrepancy between her aims and her achievements. It is this discrepancy between the rhetoric in which she expressed her aims and hopes and the actual performance of the institutions she created which has left her open to the charge of hypocrisy. But she was no hypocrite. She believed in her reforms, but she had to use the human tools to hand, and there is no doubt that, while she found many great administrators, most of the officials on whom she had to rely did not live up to her expectations. Was she informed of these inadequacies? Did she turn a blind eye? We cannot tell at this stage. What remains true however is that Catherine was the first ruler of Russia to conceive of drawing up legislation setting out the corporate rights of the nobles and the townspeople, and the civil rights of the free population of the country. The nobility, the townspeople and the free peasants were given a legal framework within which these rights could be pressed. She was also the first ruler ever to establish special courts to which the state peasants had access and in which they could and did sue merchants and nobles. During her reign the individual—other than the serf or the soldier—was allowed more space, more responsibility, more security, more dignity. For a while an increasingly diversified Russian society escaped from the overwhelming pressure of the militarization imposed on it by Peter I and restored by Paul I [reigned 1796–1801].

Catherine did not increase the power of the nobles over the serfs, nor did she turn large numbers of Russian state peasants into private serfs. She did not, as we

know, free the serfs, or even attempt to regulate relations between serfs and landowners by law. Her hold on the throne was not strong enough to enable her to put
through a policy which would have been opposed by the whole of the Russian
political elite, both the nobility and the townspeople. She did not have the power
of coercion necessary to enforce a policy which would have to be put through by
the very people who benefited from the *status quo*. But that should not be the sole
criterion by which she is judged.

Catherine was not a revolutionary like Peter I, who forced his policies on a
reluctant society without counting the human cost. She paid attention to public
opinion; as she said to Diderot, "what I despair of overthrowing I undermine." Her
absolute authority rested, as she well knew, on her sensitivity to the possible.

After the death of Potemkin in 1791 and the disappearance of many of Catherine's
long-serving ministers in the late 1780s and early 1790s, the Empress was surrounded
by lesser men. There were still many remarkable governors active in the provinces,
but the new men who took up posts in the center were inexperienced and lacking
in character. Catherine herself was suffering by now from the shrinking of horizons
which comes with age, just when the storms of the French Revolution were being
unleashed all over Europe. She was tired and she could no longer control events
and people. In September 1796 the young King of Sweden, Gustav IV Adolf, broke
off the negotiations for his marriage with Catherine's granddaughter over her
conversion to Lutheranism. The insult was public and the Empress suffered a slight
stroke. It was followed by a more serious stroke which surprised her in her closet
on November 16. She died on November 17 without recovering consciousness. In
the words of a contemporary American historian, [John P.] LeDonne, she "remains
the finest gift of the German lands to her adopted country."

## Pugachev's Rebellion

### Marc Raeff

What aggravated the situation in Russia before 1773 was the persistence of a
few conditions which had been sources of irritation and conflict since the
beginning of the century. As the repeated complaints of deputies to the Codification
[Legislative] Commission of 1767 testify, security and protection of property and
person were woefully inadequate in the Russian empire. The complaints came
mostly from nobles who had been spoliated and browbeaten by richer and influential
neighbors, attacked by brigands, and cheated by unscrupulous merchants. But anything that worsened the condition of these nobles also directly affected their peasant

From Robert Forster and Jack P. Greene, eds., *Preconditions of Revolution in Early Modern Europe*,
The Johns Hopkins University Press, Baltimore/London, 1970, pp. 167–200.

serfs, who in the final analysis had to make up for their masters' losses and who bore the brunt of the brutality directed at their owners.

A major source of lawlessness and dissension was the frequent lack of set and recognized boundaries between estates, peasant allotments, Church property, and state lands. Hence the general demand for a comprehensive land survey. After a false start under Elizabeth, it really got under way with the issuance of revised instructions in 1765. As badly needed as it was, however, the survey did have undesirable consequences for some groups of the population. Indeed, Catherine's instructions of 1765 directed that the surveyors register and validate all existing boundaries unless they were being contested in court by the parties concerned. These instructions meant in effect that the state acquiesced to previous seizures of state lands and empty tracts, and ratified the spoliations of free peasants and petty serf owners by rich and influential nobles. Among the main victims were the *odnodvortsy* (owners of one homestead), about whom more will be said in connection with the Pugachev revolt itself. Along the same lines, the third general census, begun in 1762, not only counted and registered the taxable population but also immobilized it. As it had done since the sixteenth century, the process of counting drove to flight those who did not wish to be tied down permanently.

To round out the picture of disarray and insecurity which contributed to the peasantry's forebodings of the traditional world's crumbling and of worse times to come, we should note the frequent recurrence of crop failures, plagues, and epidemics. Among the latter the most dramatic was the 1771 epidemic in Moscow, which brought to the surface all the unconscious and unfocused fears and panics of the populace. In a way, it was a prelude and dress rehearsal for the Pugachev revolt. That is why, on the eve of the rebellion, the report of drought in the Ural area sounded ominous indeed.

Government policies with respect to Church matters further contributed to the unsettling atmosphere which permeated the Russian body social in the early 1770s. Since the sixteenth century the Muscovite state had followed a policy which aimed at putting under secular control all lands owned by the Church (monasteries, dioceses). Peter the Great pursued the same goal, but shifted the focus of attention to the political and fiscal control of the Church hierarchy. The latter was saddled with new obligations, while its administration was assimilated to a department of the secular state. But the Church's resources—or the means of collection—were inadequate to meet the new obligations imposed on it. As a consequence, its serfs were among the most exploited and poorly administered of the peasantry. Little wonder that discontent and unrest were endemic among Church peasants, so much so that Catherine II estimated that about fifty thousand were in open revolt at the time of her accession. Elizabeth had laid the ground for a new administrative setup by transferring Church (primarily monastic) peasants from the direct control of ecclesiastic institutions to that of local noblemen and tax farmers. However, this arrangement did not prove very successful either, because the tax farmers and local nobles used their new function to their exclusive personal advantage.

The legislation of Peter III with respect to the Church aroused some of those rumors and hopes which played no small part in the Pugachev uprising. Following perhaps his personal anti-Orthodox inclinations, as well as his unreflecting impetu-osity, Peter decreed on February 16 and March 22, 1762, that all Economy Peasants (i.e., serfs on monastic and diocesan lands) be removed from the direct administra-tion of the College of Economy and, in return for the payment of a yearly quitrent of one ruble per soul, have the free use of all the land they worked. This act was naturally interpreted as a freeing of the Church peasants and as the first step toward a general emancipation of all serfs. The peasants "interpreted" the decrees to mean that they were free to discontinue their payments and obligations to church authorities, and the government had to intervene with clarifications restricting the implications of the law.

To assuage the Church hierarchy, as well as to provide a firm basis for new legislation, Catherine II annulled the act of Peter III upon her accession. This annulment aroused the peasants' suspicion of her as an evil, illegitimate ruler enthroned to cheat them of the freedom granted by their "true" tsar. Eventually, Catherine promulgated her own, more moderate act of secularization in 1764, which eliminated any hopes for general emancipation the peasants may have entertained. The confusion and tergiversations of the government in this matter led to rumors and disturbances, all of which came into the open during the Pugashev uprising, when many Church peasants revolted in support of their own "true" emperor, who had given them freedom, a freedom of which the evil nobles and unlawful empress had robbed them.

Peter III had also made himself quite popular with the Old Believers and other dissenters through a series of measures which improved their status, permitted freer exercise of their rites, and encouraged those who had fled beyond the borders of the empire to return to Russia. The resettling of Old Believers from Poland in the eastern provinces—e.g., the valley of the Irgiz—made of Peter III's name a virtual password into the ranks of that peculiar freemasonry which was the Old Believers and of which Pugachev made good use in the earlier stages of his career.

Often we read in general histories that Peter III's granting freedom from service to the nobility led the peasants to expect a similar act freeing them from serfdom; and the failure of such an act to materialize was ascribed to the conspiracy of the nobility to which Peter himself fell victim. This interpretation is hard to document, and it is doubtful that such reasoning, if it did occur, played a decisive role in the *Pugachevshchina*. But, to the extent that Peter's manifesto of February 18, 1762, made it possible for many nobles to leave service and return to their estates, it resulted in increasingly closer supervision and greater exploitation of the serfs. The fact that this was indeed sometimes the case and a direct cause of peasant discontent and rebellion is well documented in our sources.

With the peasants agitated by various rumors of freedom relating to the short reign and mysterious demise of Peter III, it is little wonder that the people believed he had not died, that he would return to complete the emancipation of his people. Hence the dozen or so pretenders—familiar company in times of trouble in Rus-sia—who are known to have appeared between 1762 and 1774. Without going into the fascinating story of this phenomenon it may suffice to note here that the legendary pretender appears as the suffering and wandering tsar or prince-redeemer, the savior; the false Peter III also appeared in this saintly form. In the case of the Old Believers the myth was reinforced by their mystical conceptions of the Second Coming of Christ. Thus the founder of the Skoptsy sect (castrators) claimed to be both Christ and Peter III. Nor was it an accident that Pugachev's claim to be Peter III was suggested to him and promoted by Old Believer hermits in the Iaik region.

In summary, Russia was undergoing the travails and disarray that accompanied its adaptation to the innovations introduced by Peter the Great earlier in the century. With respect to social structure, the nobility and the peasantry had undergone a transformation that had changed their mutual relationship as well as the relation of each to the state; but their estate character still needed to be defined more clearly by legislation. The legislation had been promised but had not yet been fulfilled.

To the population the role of the state appeared particularly ambiguous. On the one hand, it had spread its grip geographically and administratively: many areas and activities that earlier had been left to communal and individual action were now within its direct purview. On the other hand, the state aimed at promoting novel trends in the economy and society which would make for entrepreneurial modernity. At the same time it had also taken the seemingly paradoxical step of eliminating direct connection with the people by allowing the serf-owning nobles to become a barrier between peasantry and ruler. The decree of 1767, which completely prohibited direct petitions to the empress from the peasantry, was only the final act of a trend that had shattered the traditional concept of the sovereign held by the people.

Let us now turn to an examination of the specific conditions that prevailed in the region where the Pugachev revolt took place—i.e., the middle Volga valley (the area between the Volga and the Ural watershed) and the open plains between the southern slopes of the Ural Mountains and the Caspian Sea. The mere enumeration of these constituent parts gives an idea of the area's variety, a variety of landscapes and economic resources which was reflected in the social makeup of the region. We shall therefore describe and discuss the specific regional circumstances that formed the background of the rebellion, and were sometimes a direct cause of it, in terms of groups and classes of inhabitants.

In the absence of reliable detailed local studies, it is difficult to generalize about the conditions of Russian peasants in the areas of agricultural settlement, i.e., the provinces of Penza, Perm, Saratov, and the eastern fringe of Voronezh. Yet, on the basis of studies that treat this area roughly as a unit, the dominant impression is that the peasant was better off in this eastern frontier than in the central provinces around Moscow. An area of relatively recent settlement and development, the peasants' land allotments were not only adequate but even plentiful, although in truth much of it was not used to the full. Balanced against these positive aspects was the fact that because of the recent date of their settlement the peasants were not quite attuned to the local geographical and climatic conditions, so that we observe greater fluctuations in harvest yields than occurred in the old central provinces.

But, in the eighteenth century, land had not yet become the scarce commodity and sore spot of the peasants' economy which it was to be in the late nineteenth century. More vital to their prosperity were the serfs' dues and obligations to their masters and to the state. The quitrent payments [obrok] had risen considerably in the . . . eighteenth century; yet from all evidence they had remained lower in the east than in the central agricultural regions of Russia. On the basis of our present knowledge it is more difficult to determine the extent of conversions to *corvée* [*barshchina*: labor dues], . . . one of the significant trends, during the second half of the eighteenth century. There are indications that it took significant proportions in the Province of Penza, which more and more produced for export beyond its own confines, taking advantage of transportation facilities offered by the waterways of the Volga system. A similar trend is to be observed in Saratov Province. [We should note that] a change to *corvée* was perceived as a new, rigid, and particularly burdensome form of "exploitation"—even though in strict economic terms the *corvée* was not necessarily worse than the *obrok* [dues in cash or kind]. This feeling was especially strong in "new" areas of settlement, where the peasants had generally enjoyed greater leeway than their counterparts in the central regions.

The extent of the steady increase in hired help on noble and peasant lands and of social stratification within the village, emphasized by Soviet historians as a factor in rural ferment, is difficult to determine. The mere presence of landless agrarian workers naturally contributed to the lack of cohesion in the village and may have made for acute conflicts, but it need not have resulted in open revolt. Quite clearly, however, with its peasant organization and life resting on traditional forms and fixed customs, the village would react strongly to any sudden change, and such a reaction could take the form of disobedience, open revolt, and anarchy. For instance, a change in ownership might trigger a revolt if the new owner attempted to change—not to mention increase—the dues and obligations of the peasants. While not confined to Russia, such a situation was more frequent there in the eighteenth century—and the effects more dramatic—because the inheritance laws and customs led to a considerable redistribution and splintering of estates which radically transformed their character.

All in all, the condition of the serfs and the state of agriculture in the areas of Russian settlement were no worse in the east than in the center; as a matter of fact, all things considered (including the greater likelihood of the landlord being far away in the capitals), it was probably better. . . . But the circumstances of the other social groups reveal a few important differences from those of the Russian peasantry.

The Volga valley had for a long time been the haven for escaped serfs from the central provinces. Although gradually superseded by regions farther east (and south), in the eighteenth century the middle course of the "Mother River" still attracted many loose-footed elements of the Russian people. These escapees *(beglye)* either established their own villages or joined existing households and estates. Most of them were runaways from state lands in the central provinces; only a minority had escaped from privately owned estates, because individual owners, or their agents, apparently managed to control their serfs better than did state officials. Beginning in the 1730s, however, a new trend may be discerned in the pattern of settlement of these escapees from the center. In the first quarter of the eighteenth century most of the peasants who had fled settled down in their own households, forming new villages of their own. After the 1730s they tended to become landless, hired agricultural help on the estates of local nobles (or Cossack elders) or in other peasants' households. Obviously, this development meant that the more restless, as well as impoverished, element was on the increase in the region. The escaped peasants settling along the middle Volga were the object of a double squeeze. The free land they worked as squatters was coveted by estate-owning nobles moving from the north and northwest who were grabbing all the land they could lay their hands on, by means fair or foul—state grants, purchase, or outright seizure. On the lands they acquired these nobles settled their own serfs, whom they moved from the old estates in central Russia, or they took in the landless laborers mentioned above and virtually turned them into their bondsmen. A similar squeeze was exercised from the south. The Cossack elders (*starshina*, i.e., officers) from the Don Cossack Host had become landowners (an act in 1775 was to equate them in status with the Russian service nobility) and were expanding their holdings beyond the territory of the Host, where their opportunities were restricted by the privileges of the Cossack Host and the absence of serf peasants. They, too, settled their new estates with serfs moved from the central provinces or with landless *beglye*, whom they attached to the land. Thus from both north and south the formerly free "frontier" of the Volga valley was nibbled away by the advance of the estate using serf labor.

In the westernmost part of the region swept by the Pugachev rebellion, the right bank of the middle Volga (administratively part of Voronezh [Province]), were a number of *odnodvortsy* (single homesteaders). These were the descendants of petty military servicemen who had settled on what in the sixteenth and early seventeenth centuries had been the military frontier protecting Moscow from Crimean Tartars and Ottoman Turks. With the end of their military function, they had declined to the status of small, but free, peasants who tilled their own lands, in some cases with one serf family to help them out. A high proportion of them also were Old Believers, so that they felt particularly alienated from the state established by Peter the Great—an alienation which an extra heavy fiscal burden did nothing to relieve. Having lost their military [function], the *odnodvortsy* were no longer subject to the state's concern and protection. As they occupied lands that lay directly athwart the path of the nobility's agricultural expansion into the fertile black-soil steppe, they were hard-pressed by landowners from the central provinces who by hook or by crook were acquiring land and settling their serfs on it.

Impoverished as they were, the *odnodvortsy* were defenseless against the encroachments of nobles who had connections in the capitals and the means to bribe officials. The poorest among them lost their land and sank to the level of hired laborers and sometimes even became serfs. At the same time, they continued to claim privileged status, their right, as servicemen and freemen, to own serfs themselves. Because of their own economic weakness they resisted and mistrusted everything that tended to modernize the economy and to change the traditional pattern of self-sufficiency into production for a market. . . . [T]he *odnodvortsy* reacted to their sense of loss and alienation from the new trends by pinning their hopes on the providential leader or ruler who would bring them salvation by restoring them to their former function and status. It is from their ranks that several of the pretenders arose; and Pugachev, who claimed to be Peter III the tsar-savior and restorer, found ready support among the *odnodvortsy* of Voronezh *guberniia* [Province].

If the *odnodvortsy* represented a native social group that had lost its traditional military, political, and economic functions, the foreign colonists who had been settled on the Volga in the reign of Elizabeth were a new and alien element. The foreigners were not too numerous, about 23,000 souls, but they occupied lands on the lower middle course of the Volga, neighboring on the Kalmyk and Don Cossak territories, where the last act of the Pugachev rebellion was to take place. Although one might expect their situation to have been better than that of the Russian peasantry, it was not. In the first place, not all foreign colonists had the same legal status or were treated alike. Indeed, about half of them had been brought there by individual recruiters and were obliged to turn over to the latter one-tenth of all their produce, as well as to submit to their authority in all administrative and police matters. The recruiters' power, however, was more arbitrary and direct than that of the regular provincial administration. Many of the colonists had been recruited hastily, only to satisfy the greed of the recruiters, and they were not prepared for agricultural work—at any rate, not under Russian conditions. The yield of their labor was therefore quite small, for they suffered profoundly from crop failures and famine. In addition, they were much exposed to raids and incursions by their nomadic neighbors, which added physical insecurity to their hardships. In 1764 new regulations improved their status by placing them under the special supervision of regular state organs. But this compromise did not satisfy the settlers, because they wanted to be state peasants and completely free of control by their recruiters or special officials.

Northeast European Russia traditionally had been a region of large Church landholdings. Between the Volga and the northern massif of the Urals there were several large monasteries with huge amounts of land and numerous peasant serfs attached to them. It was to be expected that the confusion which resulted from the fitful attempts at secularization—Catherine's retreat from Peter III's legislation and then her own compromise settlement—would excite the peasants, whose hopes for freedom had been raised high only to be belied by subsequent events. The remoteness of the area from the capital and the nearest episcopal sees (Kasan and Nizhnii Novgorod) prevented the local authorities from adequately coping with peasant discontent; by the 1760s thousands of peasants belonging to monasteries were in open rebellion.

The longest and most dramatic revolt was at the Dalmatovo Monastery in the Urals, the so-called *dubinshchina* in 1762–1764. General A. Bibikov (future commander of the forces against Pugachev) and Prince A. Viazemsky (future procurator-general of the Senate) were dispatched to investigate the causes of the revolt, put it down, and suggest reforms to prevent its repetition. Obviously, these high officials succeeded in coping with only the outward manifestations of discontent, for we find the peasants of the Dalmatovo Monastery at the center of the Pugachev rebellion in the Urals in 1773–1774.

Besides the regular monasteries there were also numerous small monasteries and hermitages of Old Believers in the region east of the Volga. They constituted another element that was receptive to Pugachev's appeals. As a matter of fact, the network of Old Believer *startsy* ("holy men") and hermitages served to propagandize the appearance of Peter III—Pugachev—and his successes, and they also helped him recruit his first followers from among the Old Believer Cossacks of the Iaik.

In the middle of the eighteenth century the Urals were Russia's major mining and industrial region. The area had developed at a rapid pace since Peter the Great had allowed factory and mine owners to attach and ascribe (*pripisat'*) serfs to their enterprises. Serfs so ascribed [assigned] were compelled to work in the mines and factories at those times when they were not needed in the fields. In fact, their obligations were particularly burdensome and intolerable because the time spent in traveling to and from the factory or mine (sometimes as far away as several hundred miles) was lost. Naturally, the serfs' aspiration was to return to their villages for good and be freed from the horrible work in the factories and mines. In the course of the century it had become evident that such compulsory labor was quite unsatisfactory. A decree of Peter III, which prohibited the further ascription of villages and peasants to factories until such time as a new code of laws would settle their status definitely, had raised the expectation among ascribed peasants that their freedom was near and that they would be allowed to return to their homes. The appearance of Pugachev (whom they also believed to be Peter III) was naturally interpreted by them as a signal to rise, leave the factories and mines, and return to their native villages.

In the 1770s, however, the mainstay of the Ural labor force was the workers who belonged to the factories—industrial serfs, we might call them. As everywhere in Europe at the time, such labor was the lowest of the low, at the bottom rung of society and the economy. Needless to say, the working conditions, with heavy reliance on child and female labor, were appalling by any standards. In addition, the workers had to carry a heavy burden of taxation and various dues. Their quitrent payments rose from one ruble to one ruble seventy kopecks in the middle of the eighteenth century, but their wages did not increase. By the middle of the eighteenth century many of the factory hands and miners were children of the original factory serfs and frequently held the status of hired laborers, who were paid wages. But the pay scale was very low, and working conditions were not good in their case either. Because they no longer tilled the soil they were particularly hard hit by the rise in prices on such vital commodities as salt and grain.

The situation of many workers worsened when in the reign of Elizabeth a number of state-owned factories were turned over to private owners (in fact given away to such favorites as the Shuvalov brothers). The new owners, interested only in obtaining high benefits rapidly, intensified the exploitation of their labor force (and plant facilities) without regard for the future. At the same time, like landowners with respect to the serfs, they stood as a solid barrier between their workers and the government, precluding appeals to, and intervention by, the state for improvement of conditions. With the loss of Russia's competitive advantage on the world market (due mainly to high transportation costs and technological rigidity) the production of the Ural mines and iron-smelting factories declined, hitting hardest the workers who had no other place to go or no other skill to market. Quite clearly, then, there was enough material to support rebellion against the system. By and large the factories supported Pugachev, some voluntarily continuing to produce artillery and ammunition for the rebels (a significant factor in Pugachev's success).

The workers' support of Pugachev frequently had another motive as well: their need of protection against Bashkir raids on factories in the southern Urals. (In the north, where this danger was minimal, the factories were more divided in their loyalties.) The Bashkirs had been pushed from their traditional winter camps and summer grazing lands as dams were built, flooding encampments and pastures, and forests were cut down to meet the needs of the expanding mining and industrial enterprises. The Bashkirs had to yield their lands, grazing grounds, and fishing places under duress and at derisive prices, much like the American Indians selling Manhattan Island. Not surprisingly, they hated the factories and took their revenge whenever possible by raiding them or attacking their workers. That is why some factories appealed to Pugachev, whom the Bashkirs supported, for protective charters and in return worked for him.

The conflict between the factory population and the Bashkirs highlighted the fact that the region affected by the Pugachev revolt comprised many non-Russian, non-Christian native peoples. Such a heterogeneous population created special problems for the government, and it provided opportunities for those opposing the state and seeking support among the discontented, as yet unassimilated natives. Instead of considering separately each one of the many non-Russian peoples caught up in the revolt, let us look at three major "problem areas" . . . that were the sources of discontent and opposition to the central Russian government and its agents.

In those areas which had been under Russian control for a long time and whose native population was primarily sedentary, the major problem was conversion to Orthodox Christianity. This was the case in the upper valley of the Volga and its northeastern tributaries, a territory dependent upon the archdiocese of Kazan, the native population of which consisted of Tatar Muslims and primitive groups of hunters, fishermen, and tillers such as the Cheremys, Mordvinians, and Chuvash. Initiated by Empress Anna and continued under Elizabeth, an active program of conversion had been promoted under the aggressive aegis of the archbishops of Kazan. With respect to the Tatar Muslims the results had been disappointing, and the conversion campaign only resulted in the destruction of many mosques, the digging up of cemeteries, and various economic and social hardships determined by the whims of local officials and landowners. In any event, it seems that the Tatar Muslims did not play an active part in the Pugachev uprising, even though large numbers of them lived in and around Kazan.

But the people and tribes which practiced various forms of paganism, shamanism, and animism offered much less resistance to conversion. Allured by promises of tax advantages . . . and quick to bow to the pressure of local authorities, they converted—at least formally—in large numbers in the eighteenth century. But the act of conversion itself became the source of further exactions and a shameless abuse of their trust. With the full support and active participation of provincial officials, local clergies collected "gifts" and the tribute in kind under various pretexts; noticing (or deliberately planting) evidence of inadequate fulfillment of ritual and dietary prescriptions on the part of the newly converted, they would impose heavy fines or exact bribes. Confused and impoverished by such illegal collections and exactions, the natives became restless. They tried to bring their plight to the attention of the central government; elections of deputies and the meetings of the Codification [Legislative] Commission of 1767 afforded them the long-sought opportunity to voice their grievances. But their last hopes were shattered when their petitions were turned back, their access to the sovereign being impeded by local officials. They were ready to join a movement of discontent or rebellion.

While conversion was not a major issue for the natives farther east—Muslim and Buddhist nomads in the open steppes beyond the Volga—the advance of agricultural settlement brought in its wake serious and far-reaching conflicts. Throughout the eighteenth century the imperial government consistently pursued a policy which aimed at changing the nomads' way of life by transforming the cattle raisers into sedentary tillers of the soil (which in the long run would bring about their cultural and social Russification as well). The successful outcome of such a policy would make it possible for greater numbers of Russians to move onto new arable lands without fear of raids from neighboring nomads. Thus the grazing lands of the Bashkirs and Kirghiz were relentlessly whittled away. The Kirghiz were hard pressed on the lower Volga and the Irgiz [rivers], while the Bashkirs were gradually dispossessed of their summer grazing spots on the southern slopes of the Urals. At the same time, the nomads were pressured into abandoning their traditional ways and taking up sedentary agricultural pursuits.

The Bashkirs were the main target of this conversion effort: their elders and tribal chiefs were promised rewards of rank, money, gifts, and medals if they would lead their people into social and economic change. The effort was not fruitless, for some chieftains and their clans began to settle down and till the land. Not surprisingly, however, this development caused considerable tension within Bashkir society, and the breakup of traditional links and solidarities resulted in friction and unrest. In addition, the turn to agriculture frequently required the settlement of a new, alien element—non-Russians of various origin, known as *tepteri*, who provided a landless agricultural labor force for the richer, settled Bashkirs. Friction was great between these exploited and scorned *tepteri* and the Bashkirs among whom they lived, so that when the latter rose in revolt the *tepteri* remained loyal to the Russian government, in whom they saw a protector. The Russian state was also using fiscal policy to tighten its control over the Bashkirs and to push them onto a new path of social and economic development. Indeed, the basis of taxation was changed from the tribute in kind, normally levied on all non-Christian peoples of the east, to compulsory purchases of salt in state-owned stores at fixed prices. Eventually the Bashkirs were put on the *obrok*, albeit at a low rate. All these measures tended to introduce the elements of a market and money economy by government fiat, and they were bound to upset the traditional equilibrium.

There was, of course, also the usual conflict between nomadic peoples and their settled neighbors, a conflict heightened by national, religious, as well as political, rivalries. The Cossacks on the Don clashed with Kalmyk and Kirghiz nomads, and the foreign colonists were frequently the object of ruinous raids by Kirghiz tribes. We have commented on the conflict that pitted Bashkirs against factory workers; in addition, there were clashes between Bashkirs and Russian agricultural settlers branching out from the regional center, Orenburg. Finally, old rivalries between nomadic peoples (Kalmyks versus Kirghiz, Kirghiz versus Bashkirs) were cleverly exploited by the Russians (especially by I. I. Nepliuev, the governor-general of Orenburg from 1742 to 1758). All of these developments kept the region seething with discontent, and pretexts for defection from the central government were never lacking.

The third and final aspect of what in modern parlance would be called the nationality question involved the relationship between the natives and the central government. This relationship was no longer a live issue along the banks of the Volga, because the central government was well in command there and the adminis-trative setup followed the usual Russian pattern. Where central control was a more recent development, however, the areas of friction were numerous. The establishment of Orenburg [1743] had been viewed by the Bashkirs as a symbol of the physical presence and control of the Russians, and this view was confirmed by the colonization drive and the protection given to Russian settlers by the governors of Orenburg. (Pugachev's promise to abolish the *guberniia* [Province] of Orenburg was designed to arouse the Bashkirs, who indeed would join him enthusiastically in besieging the hated city.) But the Russians had not only built the fortress of Orenburg and settled and administered its territory, they had also imposed service obligations (frontier guards, auxiliary troops against the Turks) on the Bashkirs and had levied large numbers of horses for their own military needs. These policies provoked bitter and long-lasting revolts (1735–1741, 1755–1757) that required a great military effort before they were quelled; but each repression was followed by heavy levies of horses, fines, and more stringent service obligations. Undaunted, in 1773 the Bashkirs were once more ready to shake off the most burdensome aspects of Russian rule, and they listened with favor to Pugachev's promise to restore to them the right to "be [free] like steppe animals." Their antagonism toward the government explains why they joined the revolt, in spite of their own quarrels with the Iaik Cossacks and their profound aversion to everything Russian. They would provide Pugachev with some of his best and most loyal lieutenants.

Several times in the preceding pages passing reference was made to the Cossacks. It is time now to turn our attention to them, because they triggered the revolt and provided the mainstay of Pugachev's military power to the very end of the uprising. Since the middle of the seventeenth century (when the [Dnieper] and Don Cossacks came under Moscow's sovereignty), Cossack societies had been undergoing a dual process of transformation. Their social organization, political autonomy, and military function steadily yielded to pressures from the central government in Moscow and St. Petersburg, and by the middle of the eighteenth century the latter was asserting complete and direct control. The Cossacks' right to elect their chiefs (*ataman* and *starshina*) and to follow their "democratic" traditions was steadily eroded and restricted. In the case of the Don Cossacks, from whose midst Pugachev had come, *Ataman* S. Efremov tried in the 1760s to stem the tide and obtain a loosening of controls by St. Petersburg. His attempt failed (1772), and the way was opened for the complete incorporation of the Don Cossack Host into the regular framework of the military organization of the empire, which was completed in 1775 by G. Potemkin. Other aspects of St. Petersburg's growing control were the increases in the number of Cossacks obliged to serve on the border and the formation of new Cossack regiments to be held in constant readiness. In this way the Volga Cossack Host was formed in 1732. In 1770 a special regiment was detached from this Host and sent to the Kuban frontier for permanent military duty. In short, the fear was ever present that the loose and traditional Cossack organization would be changed to the rigid regimentation of the regular army. It was a constant cause of agitation that easily turned into open rebellion.

But the traditional Cossack pattern was also eroded from within. Indeed, a process of economic and social differentiation was taking place: the *starshina* [elders, or "officer" group] was becoming more prosperous, more influential, and it increasingly identified with the way of life, ideals, and aspirations of the regular Russian elite. The Cossack elders were accumulating land, estates on which they settled serfs (or used their poorer fellow Cossacks like virtual bond labor). They petitioned for and received ranks from the central government which gave them the status of regular noblemen and at times secured for them political advantages as well. Obviously, such developments in the midst of what at one time had been a "military democracy" brought friction and discontent in their wake. The ever-present antagonism between the government-oriented *starshina* and the rank and file erupted into open conflict at the slightest provocation. Only shortly before the appearance of Pugachev, the Dnieper Cossacks had been shaken by a rebellion of the lower and foot-loose elements.

Of the several Cossack hosts in existence in the eighteenth century, that of the Iaik was most directly and completely involved in the Pugachev revolt. This particular Cossack society was an offshoot of the Don Host: most of its members were Old Believers who had settled along the Iaik (now Ural) River. . . . They guarded the empire's borders primarily against the Kirghiz nomads that roamed the steppes beyond the Iaik; on occasion they were also called to participate in other temporary operations, particularly against the Turks. Their main occupation and source of revenue was fishing in the plentiful Iaik River. In the reign of Peter the Great the fishing rights had been farmed out to the Cossacks, the Host having to pay a fixed annual sum. The collection of this payment was the responsibility of the *ataman*.

The Iaik Cossacks had still other causes for discontent. To increase the revenues the government received from the Iaik Host, the fishermen were ordered to purchase state-owned salt at set prices. Salt was essential to preserve the catch, and forced purchase at high prices heavily burdened the Cossacks. As the war against Turkey [1768–1774] dragged on, causing heavy losses in manpower, the College of War suggested the formation of an auxiliary "Moscow Legion" from the ranks of the smaller Cossack Hosts, each of which would furnish a set number of recruits for the legion (1769). The proposal was greeted with deep suspicion because it aroused the fear that through this indirect method the government would try to assimilate the Cossacks to the regular army. . . . It was a clear threat to the Cossacks' autonomous and traditional organization; the implied subjection to drilling, the use of unfamiliar weapons, the wearing of regular uniforms, and the shaving of beards and cutting of hair were anathema to a Cossack Host, whose members were mostly Old Believers. Finally, the government planned to control the Host's membership, to prevent escaped serfs from hiding in its ranks, and to keep accurate accounts for purposes of taxation and military service. To this end the Cossacks had to be registered, and the accession of new members became almost impossible. The role of the Cossack assembly also was drastically reduced, to the benefit of the *ataman* and appointed officers.

In short, as the Petrine state threatened to eradicate most of their old privileges and traditions, the Cossacks' temper rose to the boiling point. With their petitions and requests disregarded in St. Petersburg (and even in Orenburg) and with the official commissions of investigation apparently siding with the *ataman* and the *starshina,* the Iaik Cossacks revolted. In 1772, provoked by the way General von Traubenberg was carrying out his investigation, they rioted. They murdered von Traubenberg and several subaltern officers. The revolt was put down by a military detachment from Orenburg, but the tension remained.

The Iaik Host was prepared to follow any leader promising the return of the good old times, especially if he claimed to be the "legitimate" sovereign, Peter III. In due course such a pretender did appear—he was the Cossack Bogomolov. But Bogomolov did not have a chance to make much of a stir; he was seized and deported to Siberia (and died en route). Naturally, when Pugachev "revealed" himself as the true Peter III he immediately found support among the Iaik Cossacks. They not only were his first followers, but they also staffed his headquarters and provided him with his most loyal combat force and personal guard.

While the deep involvement of the Iaik Cossacks with Pugachev may have been due in large part to the accident of their geographical location and to the particular troubles that immediately preceded Pugachev's appearance, there is no doubt that in general the Cossacks were a major factor in the revolt. The Don Cossacks, it is true, did not support Pugachev in the last phase of his revolt, when he was seeking their help after his flight from Kazan. (They may have been reluctant to join someone whose success was then very much in doubt, but more important, their combativeness had been pretty much broken after *ataman* Efremov's attempt a few years earlier, and they were under close government surveillance.) But Pugachev himself had stemmed from their ranks, and in the earlier period of his career as a rebel he did find some support among them. The Iaik and Volga Cossacks, of course, did follow him. What is even more interesting is the fact that all the Cossacks idealized his memory and his rebellion, weaving much of their folklore around it. They exemplified the discontent and rebelliousness of a traditional group in the face of transformations wrought (or threatened) by a centralized absolute monarchy. . . . [T]he Cossacks opposed the tide of rational modernization and the institutionalization of political authority. They regarded their relationship to the ruler as a special and personal one based on their voluntary service obligations; in return they expected the tsar's protection of their religion, traditional social organization, and administrative autonomy. They followed the promises of a pretender and raised the standard of revolt in the hope of recapturing their previous special relationship and of securing the government's respect for their social and religious traditions.

As our brief survey of the difficulties experienced by the government with respect to the Cossacks, Bashkirs, and monastery peasants must have indicated, local administration left much to be desired in the eastern frontier regions. Inadequate local government was characteristic of the empire as a whole, but the deficiency was greater and fraught with more dangerous consequences in the east, where the population was sparse and diversified ethnically, the distances great, and the territory still open to incursions from the outside. We read with astonishment and almost disbelief that the Kazan [region], with six provinces and a population of about 2.5 million, was administered by only eighty regular officials. The towns were sadly underpopulated, in most cases little more than walled-in villages, and their officials were ill-prepared to meet any serious challenge. They panicked and fled rather than take decisive measures, as seen in the numerous cases of *voevody* and other functionaries who deserted their posts at the first rumor of Pugachev's approach. We might add that prior to and during the revolt the governors of Orenburg and Kazan . . . were of low caliber. Given these circumstances, the weak and inefficient response of the authorities to the first signs of the rebellion becomes understandable and its rapid spread comprehensible.

It is only fair to point out that the few and inadequately prepared officials had little military power they could rely on. The garrisons of provincial fortresses (with the exception of such centers as Orenburg and Tsaritsyn) were ridiculous both in number and in quality. There is no need to insist; we have only to read the description of a small provincial garrison in the east as accurately and vividly drawn by [Alexander] Pushkin in [his story] *The Captain's Daughter*. In the east only a few landowners actually resided on their estates; the majority of the peasant serfs were supervised by unreliable and corrupt managers and a few government officials.

To summarize, the eastern borderlands shared the general features we have noted for the empire as a whole, with a double dynamic pattern. . . . On the one hand, we have a shrinking of the "frontier," the extension of direct state control over regions and social groups that heretofore had lived in a traditional and autonomous framework (Cossacks, natives). On the other hand, this same "rationalizing" and centralizing state was removing itself from the exercise of direct control over the common people by allowing the "interposition" of serf- and landowning nobles. In so doing the state gave inadequate protection and security to those forces which might have made for economic and social modernization. In view of this basic ambiguity and disarray, it was natural for the people to seek a sense of security and order by escaping from the present and, with the help of a "true ruler," to try to restore their direct personal connection with the source of political authority. The first goal, therefore, was the elimination of what [has been called] the new "priesthood" of the secular state. In Russia this priesthood was not so much the bureaucracy of the king's men (as in Western Europe) as it was the serf-owning state servitors, who lacked authority in the government but had complete and arbitrary control over their peasant serfs. In short, the main enemy was the serf-owning noble, who exercised evil power without bearing its moral burden as did the tsar, the saintly, suffering prince.

Without going into an account of the revolt itself, which would throw little light on its causes and background, we may, however, note a few of its characteristic features in an effort to understand better its dynamics and impact. The history of the revolt may be divided into three phases whose specific traits should be noted briefly. The first period, the fall and winter of 1773–1774, was characterized by the revolt of the Iaik Cossacks, who, with the assistance of the Bashkirs, attacked Orenburg, the seat of government authority in the region. The siege, which lasted several months, ended in failure; Pugachev could not take the city and was forced to withdraw into the Ural Mountains and the Bashkir region. There he remained until late spring, 1774, when the second phase of the revolt began. Having replenished his arsenal in the Ural factories, and expecting support from the peasants attached to factories and monasteries, Pugachev sallied forth westward from the Urals in the late spring or early summer of 1774. Most Bashkirs refused to follow him, and at first his support was limited to the Cossacks and some factory workers and peasants. But as he emerged from the Urals and turned toward the Volga he was well received by small towns, as well as by state and monastery peasants. He managed to capture Kazan but failed to hold it. Forced to retreat, he first went north, then crossed to the right bank of the Volga and turned southward down the river toward the region of the Don Cossack Host. At this point, after Pugachev had crossed to the western shore of the great river, the serfs rose *en masse* in the adjoining regions. The uprising became general: landowning nobles were killed or put to flight, and their estates were burned; bands of serfs roamed the countryside almost to the gate of Nizhnii Novgorod, striking fear and panic into the hearts of landowners in and around Moscow. This phase of the revolt had a flavor strongly reminiscent of [events] in France fifteen years later, except that in Russia the rising was sparked not by fear of bandits but by the actual forays of peasant gangs invoking the authority of the "true" Tsar Peter III, Pugachev.

It has been argued that, had Pugachev properly understood the dynamics of the peasant uprising he helped to provoke, he would not have turned south but would instead have marched west; with the help of the widespread and spontaneous serf uprising he would have been able to conquer the center of Russia and even Moscow. But like his Cossack forerunner in the seventeenth century, Stenka Razin, Pugachev was not interested in the fate of the peasants and preferred to recoup his forces by arousing the Don Cossacks (or perhaps merely to take refuge there). But he failed to capture Tsaritsyn; and in the manner typical of primitive rebellions his own Cossack lieutenants turned him over to the imperial troops who were pursuing him.

We should note that, in the first place, Pugachev failed to hold any major urban center; his movement was confined to the open countryside, especially in the territory of Cossacks and natives. In the second place, we ought to keep in mind that the real serf and peasant revolt started only after Pugachev's defeat at

Kazan; it was an anticlimax, even though it turned out to be the bloodiest phase of the rebellion as well as the greatest threat to the social status quo. The Cossacks thus were the permanent, solid core of the movement; the other groups and regions were involved only through the accidents and fortunes of Pugachev's struggle with the imperial army.

These facts raise the question about the nature of the revolt that has much agitated Russian and Soviet historiographers: Was it a "conscious" effort to change the social and political systems, or was it merely a spontaneous, violent outbreak of anger and discontent? The Soviets [believed] that it was a regular peasant war; but this interpretation hardly seems justified in the light of what we have seen of the background and causes. At best it is a simplification which applies only to the last phase of the rebellion. The movement, it seems to me, was primarily a "frontier" and Cossack affair, and its leadership never understood the possibilities offered by the serf uprising and a direct move against Moscow. This fact may also help to explain why the Pugachev rebellion was the last large-scale peasant rebellion not limited to a locality.

As pretender, Pugachev endeavored to project himself in the image of the ideal ruler. The folkloristic tradition has emphasized this image by providing the typical medieval validation: he was the real tsar as long as he was successful; his very failure destroyed his claim and opened the way for a new pretender (there were several of them after 1774). He could not be defeated in open combat, but, once his success had been questioned, his own closest followers turned against him, rejected him, and delivered him to those authorities whose success had proved their legitimacy.[1]

According to folk memory and contemporary legends (confirmed both by Pugachev and his followers at their interrogation), Pugachev appeared as the pretender-liberator. He was Christlike and saintly because he had meekly accepted his dethronement by his evil wife and her courtiers. He had not resisted his overthrow, but had left sadly to wander about the world. He had come to help the revolt, but he did not initiate it; the Cossacks and the people did that. The image, therefore, is that of a passive leader, strongly reminiscent, of course, of the image of the saintly meekness of . . . medieval Russian ideals of kingship. The pretender's wanderings, in truly holy fashion, took him to Jerusalem and Constantinople first; he then returned to Russia which he crisscrossed as a pilgrim. Wandering about the Russian land he learned of its condition and needs; he helped his people through his counsel and prayers before he accepted again the leadership to restore rightful authority. But how did one know that he was the rightful tsar? He had the imperial magic signs, like stigmata, on the chest and on the head. Pugachev uncovered them to prove his identity to the doubters. With a ceremonial that reminds one of the Muscovite and Byzantine tradition, he made himself awesome and difficult of access. As head of the movement, he acted primarily as ultimate judge, punishing and

---

1. Following his capture in the field, Pugachev was taken to Moscow, secretly tried, and publicly executed on January 10, 1775.—Ed.

pardoning at will. The very arbitrariness of his actions was a sign of his regal sovereignty and nature. He intervened only when called on to make a final decision or render a verdict of justice. Under the circumstances one may wonder how the people accounted for his failure. Interestingly enough, they did it in terms of God's law: Pugachev failed because he appeared before his time; he allowed himself to be tempted by human considerations (of pity and mercy) rather than abide by the will of God, Who had ordained that twenty years elapse between his dethronement and his return. In addition, he sinned by marrying a Cossack girl while his own lawful wife (whatever her crimes) was still alive; these acts of hubris predetermined his ultimate failure.

Yet the image projected by Pugachev was not entirely medieval or traditional, as the legends and folklore might lead us to believe. There were also clearly elements of the modern Petrine notions of political authority. Like Peter the Great, the pretender had gone abroad to learn; like the first emperor, he was of foreign birth (here both positive and negative elements of the popular image of Peter I merge in a curious fashion). Pugachev tried to appear as . . . "Sovereign Emperor." The medals struck for him show him in neoclassical profile, in armor. Some presumed portraits make him look very much like Peter the Great, with the cat-like mustache and wild eyes. Finally, in some of his proclamations he had his name written in Latin (he was illiterate, of course); he was also alleged to have said that after he regained his throne he would make *Iaitskii gorodok* [the Iaik Cossack headquarters] his "Petersburg."

More significant than these externals were Pugachev's attempts at reproducing the St. Petersburg bureaucracy, the Petrine state. He established his own College of War with quite extensive powers and functions. He . . . appointed to the rank of general, conferred titles, granted estates in the Baltic regions, and even gave away serfs. He accepted and approved petitions for retirement from government service. Yet he also appointed a *dumnyi diak* (secretary of the tsar's council in the seventeenth century) to act as his main secretary—an interesting amalgam of old and new titles similar to what was practiced even by the immediate successors of Peter the Great. Particularly striking for someone who is alleged to have risen against the burdens of the state, Pugachev in his proclamations did not promise complete freedom from taxation and recruitment. He granted only temporary relief, similar to the gracious "mercies" dispensed by a new ruler upon his accession.

We have here perhaps the main clue to Pugachev's and his followers' concept of the state. They believed that the basis of political organization of society was service to the state (sovereign) by commoner and noble alike. . . . Thus all soldiers were changed into Cossacks—i.e., free, permanent military servicemen—and so were all other military personnel, even the nobles and officers who joined Pugachev's ranks (voluntarily or under duress). Symbolically, in pardoning a noble or officer who had been taken prisoner, Pugachev's first act was to order that the prisoner's hair be cut in Cossack fashion (paralleling the "shaving of the forehead" which signified conscription into the emperor's regular army). All peasants also should be servants of the state: they were to become state peasants (instead of serfs of private owners or of monasteries) and serve as Cossacks, i.e., militia. (Note, they were not to be given personal freedom.) The nobles in turn were no longer to be estate-

and serf-owners, but were to revert to their [Muscovite] status as the tsar's service-men. . . .

Was there no concept of freedom in this movement? There was: freedom from the nobility, which implied the natural freedom to be what God had made one to be—a tiller of the soil, who was free to work and possess the land he had made productive, or cattle-raising nomads, who were free "like steppe animals." Naturally, too, old religious practices were to be tolerated, for Pugachev "granted beards and the cross," i.e., the freedom to be an Old Believer. He talked about the nobles as traitors to himself and to the people, and of his intention to restore the natural direct bonds between himself and the people—there need not be any intermediaries, any "secular priesthood" of nobles. . . .

The ideal of Pugachev's followers was essentially a static, simple society where a just ruler guaranteed the welfare of all within the framework of a universal obligation to the sovereign. The ruler ought to be a father to his people, his children; and power should be personal and direct, not institutionalized and mediated by land- or serf-owner. Such a frame of mind may also account for the strong urge to take revenge on the nobles and officials, on their modern and evil way of life. This urge manifested itself with particular force, of course, in the last phase of the revolt: the serfs destroyed the estates of the nobility especially their most modern features (e.g., glass panes, windows, and mantlepieces), for these were symbols of the new, alien, secular civilization; there were also some instances of "Luddite" actions [smashing machinery] on the part of factory workers in the Urals.

Taking these features of the movement's ideology and symbolism as indications of its participants' basic attitudes and aspirations, it is quite clear that they felt disarray stemming from a sense of crisis of the old and traditional order. Somehow they were aware that there could be no going back to the old forms, but neither could they accept the dynamic implications of the new. They were particularly frightened by apparent economic and social changes, and they rejected the individu-alistic dynamics implicit in them; they wished to recapture the old ideals of service and community in a hierarchy ordained by God. Most significantly, it seems to me, they were not able to come to terms with the functional organization and impersonal institutionalization of authority. In this inability they were not alone, nor the last, as the Decembrist movement [1825] and the history of the intelligentsia have shown. Pugachev and his followers needed a palpable sense of direct relationship with the source of sovereign power and ultimate justice on this earth. The Cossacks were, of course, most keenly aware of the loss of their special status and direct contact with the tsar and his government; but so were the serfs and, in an inchoate way, some of the non-Russian natives as well. The movement was thus "reactionary" in the etymological sense, with its predominance of negative-passive ideological elements; at times it seemed a childlike desire to return to the quiet and security of the protective family.

Not surprisingly, in view of this childlike urge to return to the protective family, we detect on the part of the rebels a naïve desire to be loved by their elders, i.e., the true tsar and his good boyars. Was this not the mirror image of the ambivalence the upper class felt, vis-à-vis the common people, which became noticeable at about the same time? Both the peasants and upper class dimly perceived that they had become alien to each other, that they had ceased to be members of the same God-ordained, harmonious order. This realization may go a long way in explaining the excessive panic and fear that the last phase of the rebellion aroused in the nobility of Moscow and St. Petersburg. Little wonder that the educated nobles reacted by trying to create a new image of the peasant which would emphasize those very qualities that could put their fears to rest. Instead of the view of the serf as an uncouth half-beast who could be kept down only by force, we observe the emergence of the notion of the peasant as a child, a child who has to be protected against himself and carefully guided into the new "civilization." While this reaction was clearly defensive, it also bespoke a subconscious and correct understanding of the psychic mechanism that had driven the people to rebellion. The dim awareness that for the peasant—as with children—feelings of justice and the need for personified authority outweighed the possible advantages of rationalized and institutionalized power not only started a new trend in Russian literature but also helped to shape the basic attitudes of the elite: a feeling of ambivalence toward, and alienation from, the people, coupled with an almost overpowering sense of social responsibility and moral guilt. These were to be the driving forces in creating modern Russian culture, with its double aspect of guilt and distance with respect to both the state and the people. . . .

## D OCUMENTS

Catherine II saw herself primarily as a legislator in the mold of Peter the Great, and indeed in the first five years of her reign (1762–1767) she issued an average of twenty-two decrees a month. She was well aware, however, that this legislation only added to the chaotic state of Russian law. Since the *Ulozhenie* (law code) of 1649 had been compiled (Chapter 2), thousands of new laws had been promulgated often without any clear reference to previous laws on the same subject, with the result that neither courts nor people knew what the law in force actually was, a situation that produced endless lawsuits and bureaucratic chicanery. Peter himself as well as Empress Elizabeth had appointed commissions to draw up a new code, but neither finished the job. In 1766 Catherine announced for the same purpose the convening of a grand Legislative Commission made up this time not of appointed officials but of elected representatives of the various social estates and groups (except the enserfed peasants). She herself drew up a lengthy "Great Instruction" (*Velikii nakaz*) which was to guide the Commission in its work and which she later described as the projected "foundation" of a whole new legal system for Russia. In the event, some 580 deputies chosen by government institutions (29, including one deputy from the Holy Synod), the nobility (142), registered townspeople (209), and state (or "free") peasants and other social groups (200, including 54 deputies from the non-Russian tribes of the Empire) met in Moscow, heard Catherine's Instruction, and then debated their concerns between July 1767 and October 1768, when with the outbreak of war with Turkey Catherine prorogued the full Commission, leaving a number of sub-commissions to continue working until the early 1770s, when they too gave up. No new law code had been approved and promulgated. Nevertheless, as Isabel de Madariaga has written, "the debates in the full assembly, the discussions in the sub-commissions, the draft codes of the rights of nobles, townspeople, cossacks, and peasants, and the material included in the lists of grievances brought by the deputies provided the Empress (and subsequent historians) with a vast amount of information about the needs, wishes, and opinions of local people upon which she was able to draw in later legislation." As for the Instruction itself, in which Catherine drew liberally on the works of Montesquieu, the Italian jurist Cesare Beccaria, Adam Smith, and other influential thinkers of the time, it "brought before the deputies ideas on law, justice, and humane and civil behavior such as had never been publicly proclaimed in Russia."

Below are excerpts from the Instruction as translated into English by a learned Russian gentleman and published in London in 1768. These are followed by excerpts from one of Catherine's major legislative acts: her lengthy charter of 1785 to the nobility, which together with her charter to the towns of the same year constitute, again quoting Isabel de Madariaga, "the coping stone [capstone] of Catherine's program of giving corporate status to the social estates." (A third charter, designed to give such status to the state peasants, was drafted under Catherine but never issued.) The personal civil rights of the members of the noble and urban estates are set out in the two documents, as are a limited number of *corporate* political rights: *politically* Russia was to remain, in Catherine's scheme, an absolute monarchy, but one which would now be solidly based on law and a corporately structured society of largely self-governing estates. (Her overall model seems to have been pre-Revolutionary France; we note also that approximately 50 percent of her subjects, the enserfed peasants, were left out of the scheme altogether.) The "Charter on Rights and Advantages to the Towns of the Russian Empire" also introduced an elaborate system of urban self-government, extending in this respect Catherine's earlier "Statute on Local Administration" of 1775, which was issued in the wake of the Pugachev Rebellion and intended to strengthen the power of government in newly defined provinces (sing. *guberniia*).

But the nobility, again, were the big winners. Confirming and greatly extending Peter III's Manifesto of 1762, Catherine's "Charter on the Rights, Liberties, and Privileges of the Well-Born Russian Nobility," excerpted below, provided that nobles could not be deprived of their lives, noble status, property, or "honor" without trial by their peers; could not be subjected to corporal punishment; were not obligated to pay the soul tax or to quarter troops, nor to serve in the armed forces or the bureaucracy; were free to travel abroad and enter foreign service, to establish manufactories and to exploit the subsoil (mines and quarries) as well as the forests on their lands; and retained the right to "purchase villages" (that is, to own and acquire serfs, this being, the charter implied, their *exclusive* right). Furthermore, self-governing elected noble assemblies were to be set up in all districts and provinces, with the right to address the Senate and Empress directly about local needs and grievances (bypassing the Imperial bureaucracy). All nobles were divided into a hierarchy of six categories according to whether they were titled (prince, count, baron), ancient (proofs going back a hundred years or more), foreign, had received their patents directly from Catherine or other rulers, or had merely been promoted in the Table of Ranks, whether as military officers or as civil servants. The Russian nobility would now more closely resemble European nobilities, since official recognition of noble status with all its privileges was now based on proof of noble birth as well as distinguished state service. Whether the Russian nobility was now also a fully fledged ruling class, as the historian John P. LeDonne has argued (see Further Reading), is a question that has yet to be fully resolved.

The third document in this section is very different in character. Both E. V. Anisimov (in Chapter 4) and Isabel de Madariaga (above) have indicated that although Catherine herself was opposed to serfdom, representatives of the serf-owning nobility in her entourage quickly made it clear to her that they would tolerate no alteration of this fundamental Russian institution. Other educated noblemen came to deplore serfdom on moral and economic grounds, however. Yet few went so far as Alexander Radishchev, who wrote a semifictional travel book condemning the whole Russian system of autocracy, nobility, bureaucracy, and serfdom. For this he suffered arrest, imprisonment, loss of noble status, trial for treason, and the death sentence; Catherine commuted the sentence to banishment for ten years to Siberia. The book, *A Journal from St. Petersburg to Moscow*, was printed by Radishchev on his own press in May 1790. A selection appears below.

Alexander Radishchev was born in Moscow in 1749, the son of an educated nobleman who owned land (and peasants) in Saratov province, well to the east and south of Moscow; a relative of his mother was the first curator of Moscow University. After education at home he was appointed to the Corps of Pages in St. Petersburg (1762–1766), where he seems to have incurred his intense dislike of the Imperial court. Between 1766 and 1771 he studied law and philosophy at the University of Leipzig, in Germany, on a state scholarship, and then entered government service, first on the civil side, later on the military, from which he was honorably discharged in 1775 as a second major. During the next two years he married and spent time at the family estate in Saratov province, which had been in the swath of the Pugachev Rebellion, from which his father had been saved by his own peasants. In 1777 he reentered the civil service, in 1785 was made a knight of the Order of St. Vladimir, and by 1790 had risen to be head of the St. Petersburg Customs House. Meanwhile, taking advantage of the relatively liberal climate of opinion in Catherine's Russia (and of his noble and official status), Radishchev continued to read widely in French, German, and English literature and to write poetry as well as prose, including an *Ode to Liberty* in which he praised George Washington as the embodiment of liberty and commended the American people: "Your example has set a goal for us—we all wish for the same." In the *Ode* he also pronounced his own epitaph: "He who was born here [in Russia] under the yoke of tyranny and bore gilded fetters was the first to proclaim liberty to us." Unfortunately for Radishchev, by 1790, when he published his *Journey*, Empress Catherine had grown old in power and was greatly alarmed by the opening phases of the French Revolution. She immediately read the book herself, and noted: "Its purpose is clear on every page: its author, infected and full of the French mania, is trying in every possible way to break down respect for authority and for the authorities, to stir up in the people indignation against their superiors and against the government." The Empress's private secretary put it more bluntly in his diary: "She was pleased to say that he [Radishchev] was a rebel worse than Pugachev." In fact, few Russians of the time could even have read, much less been stirred up by, such a stylized literary work as the *Journey*, privately printed in a few hundred copies most of which Radishchev himself destroyed. But then Catherine, something of an author herself, had always had great respect for the printed word. Ironic, too, is the fact that Radishchev was just the kind of enlightened official that Catherine had been striving for decades to multiply.

Radishchev was released from Siberian exile by Emperor Paul soon after Catherine's death, but not fully restored to his status, rank, and honors until 1801, when Paul's son and heir, Emperor Alexander I, appointed him to yet another commission on revising the laws. In this position Radishchev formally proposed the extensive reforms hinted at in his *Journey*, including abolition of serfdom and establishment of an English-style constitutional monarchy in Russia. Evidently frightened by what he took to be a hostile reaction to his reform proposals by the commission's chairman, Count P. V.

Zavadovsky, and no doubt depressed by his experiences, Radishchev committed suicide by poisoning on September 12, 1802. The *Journey* was published in London in 1859 by Alexander Herzen, the "father of Russian socialism" (see Chapter 8), but not in Russia until after the Revolution of 1905. It circulated in manuscript, however, among the "intelligentsia" of the first decades of the nineteenth century, for whom Radishchev provided both a program and a martyr. Indeed, some historians trace the origins of the modern Russian revolutionary movement to Radishchev and his *Journey*.

## Catherine Instructs the Legislative Commission, 1767

1. The Christian Law teaches us to do mutual good to one another as much as we possibly can.

2. Laying this down as a fundamental rule prescribed by that religion which has taken or ought to take root in the hearts of the whole people; we cannot but suppose that every honest man in the community is, or will be, desirous of seeing his native country at the very summit of happiness, glory, safety, and tranquillity.

3. And that every individual citizen in particular must wish to see himself protected by laws which should not distress him in his circumstances but, on the contrary, should defend him from all attempts of others that are repugnant to this fundamental rule.

4. In order therefore to proceed to a speedy execution of what we expect from such a general wish, we . . . ought to begin with an inquiry into the natural situation of this Empire. . . .

6. Russia is a European state.

7. This is clearly demonstrated by the following observations: the alterations which Peter the Great undertook in Russia succeeded with greater ease because the manners which prevailed at that time, and had been introduced amongst us by a mixture of different nations and the conquest of foreign territories, were quite unsuitable to the climate. Peter the First, by introducing the manners and customs of Europe among the *European* people in his domains, found at that time such means [success] as even he himself did not expect.

8. The possessions of the Russian Empire [are so vast that they] extend upon the terrestrial globe to 32 degrees of latitude and 165 of longitude.

9. The Sovereign is absolute; for there is no other authority but that which centers in his single person that can act with a vigor proportionate to the extent of such a vast Dominion. . . .

From *The Grand Instruction to the Commissioners Appointed to Frame A New Code of Laws for the Russian Empire. Composed by Her Imperial Majesty Catherine II* . . . , translated by Michael Tatischeff (London, 1768), pp. 69–73, 81–85, 123, 144–145, 159–161, 178–181, 193–195.

11. Every other form of government whatsoever would not only have been prejudicial to Russia, but would even have proved her entire ruin. . . .

13. What is the true end of Monarchy? Not to deprive people of their natural liberty but to correct their actions, in order to attain the Supreme Good. . . .

15. The intention and end of Monarchy is the glory of the Citizens, of the State, and of the Sovereign. . . .

18. The intermediate powers, subordinate to and depending on the supreme power, form the essential part of monarchical government.

19. . . . [Yet] in the very nature of things the Sovereign is the source of all imperial and civil power.

20. The laws, which form the foundation of the state, send out certain courts of judicature through which, as through smaller streams, the power of the Government is diffused.

21. The laws allow these courts of judicature to remonstrate [to the Legislator] that such and such an injunction is unconstitutional, prejudicial, obscure, or impossible to be carried into execution, and to direct which injunction [citizens] ought to obey and in what manner. These laws undoubtedly constitute the firm and immovable basis of every state. . . .

61. There are means of preventing the growth of crimes, and these are the punishments inflicted by the laws. . . .

63. In a word, every punishment which is not inflicted through necessity is tyrannical. The Law has its source not merely from Power [but also from] Nature. . . .

66. All laws which aim at the extremity of rigor, may be evaded. It is moderation which rules a people, and not excess of severity.

67. Civil liberty flourishes when the laws deduce every punishment from the peculiar nature of every crime. The application of punishment ought not to proceed from the arbitrary will or mere caprice of the Legislator, but from the nature of the crime. . . .

68. Crimes are divisible into four classes: against religion, against manners [morality], against the peace, against the security of the citizens. . . .

74. I include under the first class of crimes [only] a direct and immediate attack upon religion, such as sacrilege, distinctly and clearly defined by law. . . . In order that the punishment for the crime of sacrilege might flow from the nature of the thing, it ought to consist in depriving the offender of those benefits to which we are entitled by religion; for instance, by expulsion from the churches, exclusion from the society of the faithful for a limited time, or for ever. . . .

76. In the second class of crimes are included those which are contrary to good manners.

77. Such [include] the corruption of the purity of morals in general, either publick or private; that is, every procedure contrary to the rules which show in what manner we ought to enjoy the external conveniences given to man by Nature for his necessities, interest, and satisfaction. The punishments of these crimes ought

to flow also from the nature of the thing [offense]: deprivation of those advantages which Society has attached to purity of morals, [for example,] monetary penalties, shame, or dishonor . . . expulsion from the city and the community; in a word, all the punishments which at judicial discretion are sufficient to repress the presumption and disorderly behavior of both sexes. In fact, these offenses do not spring so much from badness of heart as from a certain forgetfulness or mean opinion of one's self. To this class belong only the crimes which are prejudicial to manners, and not those which at the same time violate publick security, such as carrying off by force and rape; for these are crimes of the fourth class.

78. The crimes of the third class are those which violate the peace and tranquillity of the citizens. The punishments for them ought also to flow from the very nature of the crime, as for instance, imprisonment, banishment, corrections, and the like which reclaim these turbulent people and bring them back to the established order. Crimes against the peace I confine to those things only which consist in a simple breach of the civil polity.

79. The penalties due to crimes of the fourth class are peculiarly and emphatically termed Capital Punishments. They are a kind of retaliation by which Society deprives that citizen of his security who has deprived, or would deprive, another of it. The punishment is taken from the nature of the thing, deduced from Reason, and the sources of Good and Evil. A citizen deserves death when he has violated the public security so far as to have taken away, or attempted to take away, the life of another. Capital punishment is the remedy for a distempered society. If publick security is violated with respect to property, reasons may be produced to prove that the offender ought not in such a case suffer capital punishment; but that it seems better and more comfortable to Nature that crimes against the publick security with respect to property should be punished by deprivation of property. And this ought inevitably to have been done, if the wealth of everyone had been common, or equal. But as those who have no property are always most ready to invade the property of others, to remedy this defect corporal punishment was obliged to be substituted for pecuniary. What I have here mentioned is drawn from the nature of things, and conduces to the protection of the liberty of the citizens. . . .

209. Is the punishment of death really useful and necessary in a community for the preservation of peace and good order?

210. Proofs from fact demonstrate to us that the frequent use of capital punishment never mended the morals of a people. . . . The death of a citizen can *only* be useful and necessary in *one* case: which is, when, though he be deprived of liberty, yet he has such power by his connections as may enable him to raise disturbances dangerous to the publick peace. This case can happen only when a People either loses or recovers their liberty, or in a time of anarchy, when the disorders themselves hold the place of laws. But in a reign of peace and tranquillity, under a Government established with the united wishes of a whole People, in a state well fortified against external enemies and protected within by strong supports, that is, by its own internal strength and virtuous sentiments rooted in the minds of the citizens, and where the whole power is lodged in the hands of a Monarch: in such a state there can be no necessity for taking away the life of a citizen. . . .

294. There can be neither skillful handicraftsmen nor a firmly established commerce where Agriculture is neglected, or carried on with supineness and negligence.

295. Agriculture can never flourish where no persons have any property of their own.

296. This is founded upon a very simple rule: Every man will take more care of his own property than of that which belongs to another; and will not exert his utmost endeavors upon that which he has reason to fear another may deprive him of.

297. Agriculture is the most laborious employment a man can undertake. The more the climate induces a man to shun this trouble, the more the laws ought to animate [encourage] him to it. . . .

348. The rules of Education are the fundamental institutes which train us up to be citizens. . . .

350. It is impossible to give a general education to a very numerous people, and to bring up all the children in schools; for that reason, it will be proper to establish some general rules which may serve by way of advice to all parents.

351. Every parent is obliged to teach his children the fear of God as the beginning of all Wisdom, and to inculcate in them all those duties which God demands from us in the Ten Commandments and in the rules and traditions of our Orthodox Eastern Greek religion.

352. Also to inculcate in them the love of their Country, and to ensure they pay due respect to the established civil laws, and reverence the courts of judicature in their Country as those who, by the appointment of God, watch over their happiness in this world.

353. Every parent ought to refrain in the presence of his children not only from actions but even from words that tend to injustice and violence, as for instance, quarreling, swearing, fighting, every sort of cruelty, and such like behavior; and not to allow those who are around his children to set them such bad examples.

354. He ought to forbid his children, and those who are around them, the vice of lying, even in jest; for lying is the most pernicious of all vices. . . .

356. [In sum,] Everyone ought to inculcate the fear of God in the tender minds of children, to encourage every laudable inclination and to accustom them to the fundamental rules suitable to their respective situations; to incite in them a desire for labor and a dread of idleness, as the root of all evil and error; to train them up to a proper decorum in their actions and conversation, civility, and decency in their behavior; and to sympathize with the miseries of poor unhappy wretches; and to break them of all perverse and froward humors; to teach them economy and whatever is most useful in all affairs of life; to guard them against all prodigality and extravagance; and particularly to root a proper love of cleanliness and neatness as well in themselves as in those who belong to them: in a word, to instill all those virtues and qualities which join to form a good education; by which, as they grow up, they may prove real citizens, useful members of their community, and ornaments to their country.

447. Every subject, according to the order and place to which he belongs, is to be inserted separately in the Code of Laws—for instance, under judicial, military, commercial, civil, or the police, city or country affairs, etc. etc.

448. Each law ought to be written in so clear a style as to be perfectly intelligible to everyone, and, at the same time, with great conciseness. For this reason explanations or interpretations are undoubtedly to be added (as occasion shall require) to enable judges to perceive more readily the force as well as use of the law. The Maritial Law [i.e., the lengthy, detailed *Military Statute* first issued by Peter the Great in 1716] is full of examples of the like nature, which may easily be followed.

449. But the utmost care and caution is to be observed in adding these explanations and interpretations, because they may sometimes rather darken than clear up the case; of which there are many instances [in the existing laws].

450. When exceptions, limitations, and modifications are not absolutely necessary in a law, in that case it is better not to insert them; for such particular details generally produce still more details.

451. If the Legislator desires to give his reason for making any particular law, that reason ought to be good and worthy of the law. . . .

452. Laws ought not to be filled with subtile distinctions, to demonstrate the brilliance of the Legislator; they are made for people of moderate capacities as well as for those of genius. They are not a logical art, but the simple and plain reasoning of a father who takes care of his children and family.

453. Real candor and sincerity ought to be displayed in every part of the laws; and as they are made for the punishment of crimes, they ought consequently to include in themselves the greatest virtue and benevolence.

454. The style of the laws ought to be simple and concise: a plain direct expression will always be better understood than a studied one.

455. When the style of laws is tumid and inflated, they are looked upon only as a work of vanity and ostentation. . . .

457. The style of the Code of Laws of Tsar Aleksei Mikhailovich [*Ulozhenie* of 1649; see Documents, Chapter 2], of blessed memory, is in general clear, simple, and concise. We listen with pleasure when extracts are quoted from it; no one can mistake the meaning of what he hears; the words in it are understood even by persons of middling capacities. . . .

511. A Monarchy is destroyed when a Sovereign imagines that he displays his power more by changing the order of things than by adhering to it, and when he is more fond of his own imaginations than of his will, from which the laws proceed and have proceeded.

512. It is true there are cases where Power ought and can exert its full influence without any danger to the State. But there are cases also where it ought to act according to the limits prescribed by itself.

513. The supreme art of governing a State consists in the precise knowledge of that degree of power, whether great or small, which ought to be exerted according to the different exigencies of affairs. For in a Monarchy the prosperity of the State depends, in part, on a mild and condescending government.

514. In the best constructed machines, Art employs the least moment, force, and fewest wheels possible. This rule holds equally good in the administration of government; the most simple expedients are often the very best, and the most intricate the very worst.

515. There is a certain facility in this method of governing: It is better for the Sovereign to *encourage*, and for the Laws to *threaten*. . . .

519. It is certain that a high opinion of the glory and power of the Sovereign would increase the strength of his administration; but a good opinion of his love of justice will increase it at least as much.

520. All this will never please those flatterers who are daily instilling this pernicious maxim into all the sovereigns on Earth, that *Their people are created for them only*. But We think, and esteem it Our glory to declare, that "We are created for Our people." And for this reason, We are obliged to speak of things just as they ought to be. For God forbid that after this legislation is finished any nation on Earth should be more just and, consequently, should flourish more than Russia. Otherwise, the intention of Our laws would be totally frustrated; an unhappiness which I do not wish to survive.

521. All the examples and customs of different nations which are introduced in this work [the Instruction] ought to produce no other effect than to co-operate in the choice of those means which may render the people of Russia, humanly speaking, the most happy in themselves of any people upon the Earth.

522. Nothing more remains now for the Commission to do but to compare every part of the laws with the rules of this Instruction.

## Catherine's Charter to the Nobility, 1785

With the new gains and the expansion of Our Empire, now that We . . . everywhere enjoy complete domestic and external tranquillity, We increasingly direct our attention to the ceaseless task of providing Our faithful subjects with firm and stable enactments in all the requisite areas of civil administration, for greater prosperity and order in times to come. And to that end We have seen fit, first of all, to extend Our solicitude to Our faithful and loyal Russian Nobility, being mindful of its afore-mentioned services, ardor, zeal, and unswerving fidelity to the Autocrats of [All Russia], which it has rendered unto Us and Our Throne in the most turbulent of times, in wartime as well as in the midst of peace. And, following the examples of justice, mercy and grace set by Our late predecessors who adorned and glorified the Russian Throne, and moved by Our own Maternal

From David Griffiths and George E. Munro, eds. and trans., *Catherine II's Charters of 1785 to the Nobility and the Towns*, 1991, pp. 4–9, 11, 15–16. Reprinted by permission of Charles Schlacks, Jr., Publisher.

love for, and special gratitude toward, the Russian Nobility, We do in keeping with Our Imperial will and pleasure vouchsafe, declare, ordain, and confirm for the recollection of future generations, the following articles, for the benefit of the Russian Nobility, Our service and the Empire, immutably and for all time to come.

## Concerning the Personal Privileges of Nobles

1. The title of Nobility is a consequence of the quality and virtue of men who in times past commanded, distinguishing themselves by [their] services, whereby, transforming service itself into dignity, they acquired for their posterity the designation of well-born.

2. It is not only beneficial to the Empire and the Throne but also just that the respected station of the well-born Nobility be preserved and confirmed immutably and inviolate. And to that end the well-born Nobility's dignity, as it was in times past and is presently, shall henceforward and forever be inalienable, inheritable and hereditary for those honorable family lines that enjoy it, and therefore:

3. A Nobleman imparts his noble dignity to his wife.

4. A Nobleman transmits his well-born noble dignity to his children by inheritance.

5. A Nobleman or Noblewoman shall not be deprived of noble dignity unless they [sic] deprive themselves thereof by a crime irreconcilable with the principles of noble dignity.

6. Crimes that transgress and are irreconcilable with the principles of noble dignity are the following: 1) violation of an oath; 2) treason; 3) brigandage; 4) robbery of any kind; 5) deceitful conduct; 6) crimes that by law entail deprivation of honor and corporal punishment; 7) if it be proved that [he] attempted to induce or instruct others to commit such crimes.

7. But inasmuch as noble dignity may not be taken away except for a crime; and as marriage is honorable and instituted by God's law: therefore a well-born Noblewoman who marries a non-noble shall not be deprived of her station; but she does not impart nobility to her husband and children.

8. A well-born [nobleman] shall not be deprived of noble dignity without trial.

9. A well-born [nobleman] shall not be deprived of honor without trial.

10. A well-born [nobleman] shall not be deprived of life without trial.

11. A well-born [nobleman] shall not be deprived of property without trial.

12. A well-born [nobleman] shall not be tried except by his peers.

13. The case of a well-born [nobleman] who has committed a criminal act, and who according to the laws is subject to deprivation of noble dignity, or honor, or life, shall not be concluded without being presented to the Senate and [the verdict] confirmed by the Imperial Majesty.

14. We vouchsafe that all crimes of any sort [committed] (by a well-born) [nobleman] [at least] ten years in the past, which have not been uncovered for that long time, and for which proceedings have not been instituted, henceforward be consigned to eternal oblivion, even if somewhere persons calling [him] to account, plaintiffs or informants should come forward.

15. Corporal punishment shall not extend to the well-born [nobleman].

16. Nobles serving in the lower ranks of Our armed forces are to be treated in all cases of punishment just as those with commissioned officer rank are treated by Our military regulations.

17. We confirm that the well-born Russian Nobility is to enjoy freedom and liberty [now and] in future generations for all time to come.

18. We confirm to well-born [nobles] now in service permission to continue service or else to petition for discharge from service, in keeping with established regulations.

19. We confirm to well-born [nobles] permission to enter into the service of other European powers allied with Us, and to travel abroad.

20. But inasmuch as the well-born noble title and dignity have in times past been, are [now], and shall henceforward be acquired by service and industry beneficial to the Empire and throne, and as the very station of the Russian Nobility depends upon the security of the fatherland and the throne: therefore at any time when the Russian Autocracy has want of him, when the service of the Nobility to the common good is necessary and needful, each well-born Nobleman is obligated at the first summons of the Autocratic Power to spare neither labor nor even life itself in State service.

21. A well-born [nobleman] has the right to style himself in writing proprietor of his service landholdings as well as owner of his ancestral and inherited estates and [those] granted [him].

22. A well-born [nobleman] has the authority and freedom to give away, or to bequeath, or to confer either as dowry or as a maintenance allotment, or to transfer or to sell to whomsoever he deems fit, any estate he is the first to acquire; but an inherited estate may be disposed of only in the manner prescribed by law.

23. In the event of his conviction of even the most serious crime, the inherited estate of a well-born [nobleman] shall be passed on to his legal heir or heirs.

24. Inasmuch as Our wish and desire has been, is, and with God's help will inalterably be, that the Empire of [All Russia] be ruled by legislation and enactments promulgated by Our Autocratic Power, for the confirmation of justice, righteousness and the security of the estate and property of each: We consider it proper once more to forbid and strictly to reaffirm the ancient prohibition [to the effect] that no one presume arbitrarily to confiscate the estate of a well-born [nobleman], or lay it waste, without trial and verdict according to the laws of those judicial instances to which trials are assigned.

25. The administration of justice and retribution for a crime are entrusted solely to the judicial instances created for that purpose. . . . They hear the complaints of the plaintiffs and the defendant's defense, and render their decisions on the basis of the laws that everyone, of whatever birth and lineage, is obligated to obey. And if in this regard the well-born [nobleman] has a legal claim, or if one is lodged against a well-born [nobleman], it must be adjudicated by the judicial instances established for and having jurisdiction in such a case, in keeping with prescribed procedure; for it would be unjust and incompatible with public order if each [person] were to take it into his head to be judge in his own case.

26. The right of well-born [nobles] to purchase villages is confirmed.

27. The right of well-born [nobles] to sell wholesale whatever is grown in their villages or produced by handicraft [therein] is confirmed.

28. Well-born [nobles] are permitted to maintain factories and [other] industrial works in their villages.

29. Well-born [nobles] are permitted to establish trading settlements on their hereditary estates, and to hold markets and fairs at them in accordance with State legislation, with the knowledge of the Governors-General and the Provincial Boards, taking care that the times set for fairs in their trading settlements be compatible with the times [of those] in neighboring localities.

30. The right of well-born [nobles] to own or to build or to purchase houses in towns and to maitnain handicraft industries therein is confirmed.

31. If any well-born [nobleman] wishes to avail himself of municipal law, he is also subject to it.

32. Well-born [nobles] are permitted to sell wholesale or to export by sea from designated ports whatever commodities are grown [on their estates] or subsequently produced in accordance with the law; for they are not forbidden to own or to construct factories, handicraft industries and [other] industrial works of any kind.

33. The right of well-born [nobles] to private property, granted by [Our] gracious decree of June 28, 1782, not only in [whatever is to be found on] the surface of the land belonging to each of them but also in all the hidden minerals and vegetation [found] both in the bowels of that land and in the waters belonging to him, and in all the metals produced therefrom, is confirmed in full strength and meaning, as explained in that decree.

34. The right of well-born [nobles] to the ownership of forests growing on their lands, and to their free utilization in full strength and meaning, as set forth in [Our] gracious decree of September 22, 1782, is confirmed.

35. The manor house in the village is to be free from quartering [of soldiers].

36. A well-born [nobleman] is to be personally exempt from personal taxes.

*Concerning the Assembly of Nobles, the Establishment of the Noble Corporation in the Province, and Concerning the Benefits of the Noble Corporation*

37. We grant Our faithful Nobles permission to assemble in that province in which they maintain their residency, to form a noble corporation . . . , and to avail themselves of the rights, benefits, distinctions, and privileges set forth below.

38. The Nobility assembles in the province every three years in the winter time, at the summons and with the permission of the Governor-General or Governor, both for the elections entrusted to the Nobility and for hearing the proposals of the Governor-General or Governor.

39. The Assembly of the Nobility . . . is permitted to elect a Provincial Marshal of the Nobility for that province. And to that end the Assembly of the Nobility is to submit every three years [the names of] two of the County Marshals of the

Nobility . . . ; and whichever of these the Governor-General or Governor shall designate is to be Provincial Marshal of the Nobility for that province.

40. By authority of articles 64 and 211 of the [Statute of 1775 on Local Administration], the County Marshal of the Nobility is elected by ballot every three years by the Nobility of that county.

41. By authority of article 65 of the [Statute of 1775 on Local Administration], the ten Assessors of the Superior Land Court and the two Assessors of the Court of Conscience are elected every three years by the Nobility of those counties that come under the jurisdiction of that Superior Land Court, and [their names] are submitted by it to the Administrator, or the Governor when there is no Governor-General [in place]. And if they have no apparent vice, . . . the Nobiliary choice [is confirmed].

42. The ten Assessors (of the Superior Land Court and the Assessors of the Court of Conscience, the County Court and the Lower Land Court) are elected every three years by the Nobility of those counties that come under the jurisdiction of that Superior Land Court from among the Nobles living locally or from among those who are inscribed in the list of Nobles of that province, providing they are not absent because of service and duties.

43. By authority of article 66 of the [1775 Statute], the County or District Judge and the Land Officer or Captain are elected by the Nobility every three years, and [their names] are to be submitted. . . . And if they have no apparent vice, the Governor confirms the Nobiliary choice.

44. By authority of article 67 of the [1775 Statute], the Assessors of the County Court and the Noble Assessors of the Lower Land Court are elected by the Nobility every three years, and [their names] are submitted. . . . And if they have no apparent vice, the Governor confirms the Nobiliary choice.

45. If election by ballot covering the whole Nobility seems to the Assembly of the Nobility to be protracted and inconvenient, the Assembly of the Nobility is then permitted to present candidates for the balloting.

46. In the event of proposals to the Nobility by the Governor-General or Governor, the Assembly of the Nobility of the province shall take the proposals into consideration, and shall either respond properly thereto or else consent [thereto], according to the circumstances, conformable to both legislation and the common good.

47. The Assembly of the Nobility is permitted to submit representations to the Governor-General or Governor regarding its corporate needs and interests.

48. Permission is confirmed for the Assembly of the Nobility to submit representations and complaints through its Deputies both to the Senate and to the Imperial Majesty, in accordance with legislation. . . .

64. A Nobleman who has never served or, having served, failed to achieve commissioned officer rank (even if commissioned officer rank was bestowed upon him at retirement), may attend the Assembly of the Nobility; but he must not sit with those who have served honorably, nor may he have a vote in the Assembly of the Nobility, nor is he suitable to be elected to those duties that are filled by election by the Assembly of the Nobility.

65. The Assembly of the Nobility is permitted to exclude from the Assembly of the Nobility a Nobleman who has been disgraced by a court, or whose patent and dishonorable vice is known to all, even if he has yet to be judged, until he is acquitted.

66. We renew the edicts issued by Our Predecessors of blessed memory that destroyed (in accordance with the petition of the Nobles themselves thereupon) the system of preference and rank based on place in the family and family service, which proved harmful to the State. And for the recollection by future generations, We once more command that a heraldry book of the Nobility be compiled in every province, in which the Nobility of that province is to be inscribed, so that each well-born Noble family line be particularly enabled thereby to perpetuate its dignity and title hereditarily, from generation to generation, uninterruptedly, immutably, and safely, from father to son, to grandson, to great-grandson, and to legitimate posterity, as long as God deigns to grant it issue.

67. In order to compile the heraldry book of the Nobility . . . , the Nobility of each county elects by ballot one Deputy every three years, so that those Deputies together with the Provincial Marshal of the Nobility of that province assume responsibility for the actual compilation and maintenance of that heraldry book of the Nobility, in keeping with the instructions therefor given to them.

68. The given name and family name of every Nobleman possessing immovable property in that province, and able to confirm his nobility with proofs, are to be inscribed in the heraldry book of the Nobility. . . .

69. If anyone is not inscribed in the heraldry book of the Nobility of that province, he not only shall not belong to the Nobility of that province, but also does not enjoy the general privileges of the Nobility of that province.

70. Every well-born Nobleman . . . inscribed in the heraldry book of the Nobility has the right, when he attains his majority, to attend the Assembly of the Nobility of that province.

71. We vouchsafe to grant to the Nobility of each [province] a charter signed by Us, with the State seal affixed, in which are spelled out word for word these nobiliary corporate and personal privileges recorded here above and below. . . .

89. Upon reading the heraldry book in the Assembly of the Nobility, the Provincial Marshal of the Nobility and the [District] Deputies of the Nobility, after making two exact copies of the heraldry book of that province, sign the heraldry book and both copies, deposit the heraldry book of that province in the archives of the Assembly of the Nobility, and send both copies to the Provincial Board, which will deposit one copy in the archives of the Provincial Board and send the other copy to the Senate for preservation in the Heraldry Office.

90. If henceforward someone receives by inheritance, or by mortgage deed, or by purchase deed, or by grant, any hereditary estates or villages in that province, he must petition at the next session of the Assembly of the Nobility to be entered in the heraldry book [of the nobility]. And if the Assembly of the Nobility has knowledge [of the matter], and entertains no doubts about his well-born condition, he shall be entered in the heraldry book without [further] inquiry. If he is [already] included in the heraldry book of another province, and presents to the Assembly

of the Nobility a charter to that effect signed by the Provincial Marshal and the County Deputies of the Nobility, and bearing the seal of the Assembly of the Nobility; that serves as sufficient proof for [his] entry in the heraldry book of that province.

### Proofs of Well-Born Condition

91. The well-born [nobles] are comprehended to be all those who either are born of well-born forefathers, or have been granted the dignity by Monarchs. As for proofs of well-born condition, they are numerous, and depend more on the test of antiquity and the careful examination and review of the proofs than on new prescriptions. The diverse origins of noble families by themselves create difficulties for the prescription of rules. Strict justice does not permit the exclusion of even a single proof [of station], whatever its nature, except in those instances in which the letter of the law rejects such proof. Given such a delicate and difficult situation with regard to this important matter, Our usual gracious solicitude had led Us to decide upon a just means of extending the hand of assistance to Our beloved, loyal, Russian, well-born Nobility, by confirming the following proofs of well-born condition, without however excluding such legitimate and incontrovertible proofs of a given family line as can be found over and above these, although they be not prescribed here.

92. Incontrovertible proofs of well-born condition are:

1. Diplomas of Noble dignity bestowed by Our predecessors, or by Us, or by other crowned Heads.

2. Coats of arms bestowed by Sovereigns.

3. Patents of rank that carry with them Noble dignity.

4. Proofs that a Russian order of knighthood has graced a personage.

5. Proofs by way of letters patent or charters of commendation.

6. Decrees granting lands or villages.

7. [Service estates granted] for noble service.

8. Decrees or charters transforming service [estates] into hereditary estates.

9. Decrees or charters for villages and hereditary estates bestowed, even if those have since been alienated from the family line.

10. Decrees or instructions or charters given to a Nobleman to serve as an ambassador, an envoy or [perform] some other mission.

11. Proofs of Noble service by ancestors.

12. Proofs that one's father and grandfather led well-born lives, or maintained [appropriate] station or [performed] service consonant with the Noble title, and attestation thereto by twelve people of well-born station, of whose Nobility there is no doubt.

13. Deeds of purchase, mortgage deeds, marriage contracts, and wills involving a Noble estate.

14. Proofs that one's father and grandfather possessed villages.

15. Proofs of lineage and heredity descending to son from father, grandfather,

great-grandfather, and as far back as they wish or are able to trace, sufficient for inscription in a given part of the heraldry book along with their family.

Decrees containing proofs of Nobility [follow]. . . .


# Alexander Radishchev Excoriates
# Russia's Social System, 1790

. . . [Village of Liubani.] . . . A few steps from the road I saw a peasant ploughing a field. The weather was hot. I looked at my watch. It was twenty minutes before one. I had set out on Saturday. It was now Sunday. The ploughing peasant, of course, belonged to a landed proprietor, who would not let him pay [dues in money or kind (obrok)]. The peasant was ploughing very carefully. The field, of course, was not part of his master's land. He turned the plough with astonishing ease.

"God help you," I said, walking up to the ploughman, who, without stopping, was finishing the furrow he had started. "God help you," I repeated.

"Thank you, sir," the ploughman said to me, shaking the earth off the plough-share and transferring it to a new furrow.

"You must be a Dissenter [Old Believer], since you plough on a Sunday."

"No, sir, I make the true sign of the cross," he said, showing me the three fingers together. "And God is merciful and does not bid us starve to death, so long as we have strength and a family."

"Have you no time to work during the week, then, and can you not have any rest on Sundays, in the hottest part of the day, at that?"

"In a week, sir, there are six days, and we go six times a week to work on the master's fields; in the evening, if the weather is good, we haul to the master's house the hay that is left in the woods; and on holidays the women and girls go walking in the woods, looking for mushrooms and berries. God grant," he continued, making the sign of the cross, "that it rains this evening. If you have peasants of your own, sir, they are praying to God for the same thing."

"My friend, I have no peasants, and so nobody curses me. Do you have a large family?"

"Three sons and three daughters. The eldest is nine years old."

"But how do you manage to get food enough, if you have only the holidays free?"

"Not only the holidays: the nights are ours, too. If a fellow isn't lazy, he won't starve to death. You see, one horse is resting; and when this one gets tired, I'll take the other; so the work gets done."

---

Reprinted by permission of the publishers from A Journey from St. Petersburg to Moscow by Aleksandr Nikolawvich Radishchev, pp. 46–48, 151–54, 158–60, 187–91, 219–221, Cambridge, Mass.: Harvard University Press, Copyright © 1958 by the President and Fellows of Harvard College.

"Do you work the same way for your master?"

"No, sir, it would be a sin to work the same way. On his fields there are a hundred hands for one mouth, while I have two for seven mouths: you can figure it out for yourself. No matter how hard you work for the master, no one will thank you for it. The master will not pay our head [soul] tax; but, though he doesn't pay it, he doesn't demand one sheep, one hen, or any linen or butter the less. The peasants are much better off where the landlord lets them pay a commutation tax [obrok] without the interference of the steward. It is true that sometimes even good masters take more than three rubles a man; but even that's better than having to work on the master's fields. Nowadays it's getting to be the custom to let villages to tenants, as they call it. But we call it putting our heads in a noose. A landless tenant skins us peasants alive; even the best ones don't leave us any time for ourselves. In the winter he won't let us do any carting of goods and won't let us go into town to work; all our work has to be for him, because he pays our head tax. It is an invention of the Devil to turn your peasants over to work for a stranger. You can make a complaint against a bad steward, but to whom can you complain against a bad tenant?"

"My friend, you are mistaken; the laws forbid them to torture people."

"Torture? That's true; but all the same, sir, you would not want to be in my hide." Meanwhile the ploughman hitched up the other horse to the plough and bade me good-bye as he began a new furrow.

The words of this peasant awakened in me a multitude of thoughts. I thought especially of the inequality of treatment within the peasant class. I compared the [state] peasants with the [proprietary] peasants. They both live in villages; but the former pay a fixed sum, while the latter must be prepared to pay whatever their master demands. The former are judged by their equals; the latter are dead to the law, except, perhaps, in criminal cases. A member of society becomes known to the government protecting him, only when he breaks the social bonds, when he becomes a criminal! This thought made my blood boil.

Tremble, cruelhearted landlord! on the brow of each of your peasants I see your condemnation written. . . .

. . . [T]o return to our more immediate concern with the condition of the agriculturists, we find it [serfdom] most harmful to society. It is harmful because it prevents the increase of products and population, harmful by its example, and dangerous in the unrest it creates. Man, motivated by self-interest, undertakes that which may be to his immediate or later advantage, and avoids that from which he expects no present or future gain. Following this natural instinct, everything we do for our own sake, everything we do without compulsion, we do carefully, industriously, and well. On the other hand, all that we do not do freely, all that we do not do for our own advantage, we do carelessly, lazily, and all awry. Thus we find the agriculturists in our country. The field is not their own, the fruit thereof does not belong to them. Hence they cultivate the land lazily and do not care whether it goes to waste because of their poor work. Compare this field with the one the haughty proprietor gives the worker for his own meager sustenance. The worker is unsparing in the labors which he spends on it. Nothing distracts him from his work. The savagery of the weather he overcomes bravely; the hours intended for rest he spends at work; he shuns pleasure even on the days set aside for it. For he looks after his own interest, works for himself, is his own master. Thus his field will give him an abundant harvest; while all the fruits of the work done on the proprietor's demesne will die or bear no future harvest; whereas they would grow and be ample for the sustenance of the citizens if the cultivation of the fields were done with loving care, if it were free.

But if forced labor brings smaller harvests, crops which fail to reach the goal of adequate production also stop the increase of the population. Where there is nothing to eat, there will soon be no eaters, for all will die from exhaustion. Thus the enslaved field, by giving an insufficient return, starves to death the citizens for whom nature had intended her superabundance. But this is not the only thing in slavery [serfdom] that interferes with abundant life. To insufficiency of food and clothing they have added work to the point of exhaustion. Add to this the spurns of arrogance and the abuse of power, even over man's tenderest sentiments, and you see with horror the pernicious effects of slavery, which differs from victory and conquest only by not allowing what victory cuts down to be born anew. But it causes even greater harm. It is easy to see that the one devastates accidentally and momentarily, the other destroys continuously over a long period of time; the one, when its onrush is over, puts an end to its ravages, the other only begins where the first ends, and cannot change except by upheavals which are always dangerous to its whole internal structure.

But nothing is more harmful than to see forever before one the partners in slavery, master and slave. On the one side there is born conceit, on the other, servile fear. There can be no bond between them other than force. And this, concentrated in a small range, extends its oppressive autocratic power everywhere. But the champions of slavery, who, though they hold the sharp edge of power in their hands, are themselves cast into fetters, become its most fanatical preachers. It appears that the spirit of freedom is so dried up in the slaves that they not only have no desire to end their sufferings, but cannot bear to see others free. They love their fetters, if it is possible for man to love his own ruination. I think I can see in them the serpent that wrought the fall of the first man. The examples of arbitrary power are infectious. We must confess that we ourselves, armed with the mace of courage and the law of nature for the crushing of the hundred-headed monster that gulps down the food prepared for the people's general sustenance—we ourselves, perhaps, have been misled into autocratic acts, and, although our intentions have always been good and have aimed at the general happiness, yet our arbitrary behavior cannot be justified by its usefulness. Therefore we now implore your forgiveness for our unintentional presumption.

Do you not know, dear fellow citizens, what destruction threatens us and in what peril we stand? All the hardened feelings of the slaves, not given vent by a kindly gesture of freedom, strengthen and intensify their inner longings. A stream that is barred in its course becomes more powerful in proportion to the opposition it meets. Once it has burst the dam, nothing can stem its flood. Such are our brothers whom we keep enchained. They are waiting for a favorable chance and time. The alarum bell rings. And the destructive force of bestiality breaks loose with terrifying speed. Round about us we shall see sword and poison. Death and fiery desolation will be the meed for our harshness and inhumanity. And the more procrastinating and stubborn we have been about the loosening of their fetters, the more violent they will be in their vengefulness. Bring back to your memory the events of former times. Recall how deception roused the slaves to destroy their masters. Enticed by a crude pretender [Pugachev], they hastened to follow him, and wished only to free themselves from the yoke of their masters; and in their ignorance they could think of no other means to do this than to kill their masters. They spared neither sex nor age. They sought more the joy of vengeance than the benefit of broken shackles.

This is what awaits us, this is what we must expect. Danger is steadily mounting, peril is already hovering over our heads. Time has already raised its scythe and is only awaiting an opportunity. The first demagogue or humanitarian who rises up to awaken the unfortunates will hasten the scythe's fierce sweep. Beware!

But if the terror of destruction and the danger of the loss of property can move those among you who are weak, shall we not be brave enough to overcome our prejudices, to suppress our selfishness, to free our brothers from the bonds of slavery, and to re-establish the natural equality of all? Knowing the disposition of your hearts, I am sure that you will be convinced more readily by arguments drawn from the human heart than by the calculations of selfish reason, and still less by fears of danger. Go, my dear ones, go to the dwellings of your brothers and proclaim to them the change in their lot. Proclaim with deep feeling: "Moved to pity by your fate, sympathizing with our fellow men, having come to recognize your equality, and convinced that our interests are mutual, we have come to embrace our brothers. We have abandoned the haughty discrimination which for so long a time has separated us from you, we have forgotten the inequality that has existed between us, we rejoice now in our mutual victory, and this day on which the shackles of our fellow citizens are broken shall become the most famous day in our annals. Forget our former injustice to you, and let us sincerely love one another."

Such will be your utterance; deep down in your hearts you already hear it. Do not delay, my dear ones. Time flies; our days go by and we do nothing. Let us not end our lives merely fostering good intentions which we have not been able to carry out. Let not our posterity take advantage of this, win our rightful crown of glory, and say contemptuously of us: "They had their day." . . . [1]

The story of a certain landed proprietor proves that man for the sake of his personal advantage forgets humanity towards his fellow man, and that to find an example of hardheartedness we need not go to far-off countries nor seek miracles through thrice-nine lands; they take place before our eyes in our own country.

A certain man who, as they say in the vernacular, did not make his mark in the government service, or who did not wish to make it there, left the capital, acquired a small village of one or two hundred souls, and determined to make his living by agriculture. He did not apply himself to the plough but intended most

---

1. Radishchev is addressing his fellow noblemen, of course; or, at least, his fellow educated noblemen.—Ed.

vigorously to make all possible use of the natural strength of his peasants by applying them to the cultivation of the land. To this end he thought it the surest method to make his peasants resemble tools that have neither will nor impulse; and to a certain extent he actually made them like the soldiers of the present time who are commanded in a mass, who move to battle in a mass, and who count for nothing when acting singly. To attain his end he took away from his peasants the small allotment of plough land and the hay meadows which noblemen usually give them for their bare maintenance, as a recompense for all the forced labor which they demand from them. In a word, this nobleman forced all his peasants and their wives and children to work every day of the year for him. Lest they should starve, he doled out to them a definite quantity of bread, known by the name of monthly doles. Those who had no families received no doles, but dined . . . together, at the manor, receiving thin cabbage soup on meat days, and on fast days bread and kvas [light beer made from old bread], to fill their stomachs. If there was any real meat, it was only in Easter Week.

These serfs also received clothing befitting their condition. Their winter boots, that is, bast shoes, they made for themselves; leggings they received from their master; while in summer they went barefooted. Naturally these serfs had no cows, horses, ewes, or rams. Their master did not withhold from these serfs the permission, but the means to have them. Whoever was a little better off and ate sparingly, kept a few chickens, which the master sometimes took for himself, paying for them as he pleased.

With such an arrangement it is not surprising that agriculture in Mr. So-and-So's village was in a flourishing condition. Where the crops were a failure elsewhere, his grain showed a fourfold return; when others had a good crop, his grain had a tenfold return or better. In a short time he added to his two hundred souls another two hundred as victims of his greed, and, proceeding with them just as with the first, he increased his holdings year after year, thus multiplying the number of those groaning in his fields. Now he counts them by the thousand and is praised as a famous agriculturist.

Barbarian! You do not deserve to bear the name of citizen. What good does it do the country that every year a few thousand more bushels of grain are grown, if those who produce it are valued on a par with the ox whose job it is to break the heavy furrow? Or do we think our citizens happy because our granaries are full and their stomachs empty? Or because one man blesses the government, rather than thousands? The wealth of this bloodsucker does not belong to him. It has been acquired by robbery and deserves severe punishment according to law. Yet there are people who, looking at the rich fields of this hangman, cite him as an example of perfection in agriculture. And you wish to be called merciful, and you bear the name of guardians of the public good! Instead of encouraging such violence, which you regard as the source of the country's wealth, direct your humane vengeance against this enemy of society. Destroy the tools of his agriculture, burn his barns, silos, and granaries, and scatter their ashes over the fields where he practiced his tortures; stigmatize him as a robber of the people, so that everyone who sees him may not only despise him but shun his approach to avoid infection from his example. . . .

[Village of Mednoe.] . . . Twice every week the whole Russian Empire is notified that N. N. or B. B. is unable or unwilling to pay what he has borrowed or taken or what is demanded of him. The borrowed money has been spent in gambling, traveling, carousing, eating, drinking, etc.,—or has been given away, lost in fire or water, or N. N. or B. B. has in some other way gone into debt or incurred an obligation. Whatever the circumstances, the same story is published in the newspapers. It runs like this: "At ten o'clock this morning, by order of the [District] Court, or the Municipal Magistrate, will be sold at public auction the real estate of Captain G., Retired, viz., a house located in — Ward, No. —, and with it six souls, male and female. The sale will take place at said house. Interested parties may examine the property before the auction."

There are always a lot of customers for a bargain. The day and hour of the auction have come. Prospective buyers are gathering. In the hall where it is to take place, those who are condemned to be sold stand immovable. An old man, seventy-five years of age, leaning on an elmwood cane, is anxious to find out into whose hands fate will deliver him, and who will close his eyes. He had been with his master's father in the Crimean Campaign, under Field Marshal Münnich. In the Battle of Frankfurt he had carried his wounded master on his shoulders from the field.[2] On returning home he had become the tutor of his young master. In childhood he had saved him from drowning, for, jumping after him into the river into which he had fallen from a ferry, he had saved him at the risk of his own life. In youth he had ransomed him from prison, whither he had been cast for debts incurred while he was a subaltern of the Guards. The old woman, his wife, is eighty years of age. She had been the wet-nurse of the young master's mother; later she became his nurse and had the supervision of the house up to the very hour when she was brought out to this auction. During all the time of her service she had never wasted anything belonging to her masters, had never considered her personal advantage, never lied, and if she had ever annoyed them, she had done so by her scrupulous honesty. The forty-year-old woman is a widow, the young master's wet-nurse. To this very day she feels a certain tenderness for him. Her blood flows in his veins. She is his second mother, and he owes his life more to her than to his natural mother. The latter had conceived him in lust and did not take care of him in his childhood. His nurses had really brought him up. They part from him as from a son. The eighteen-year-old girl is her daughter and the old man's granddaughter. Beast, monster, outcast among men! Look at her, look at her crimson cheeks, at the tears flowing from her beautiful eyes. When you could neither ensnare her innocence with enticements and promises nor shake her steadfastness with threats and punishments, did you not finally use deception, and, having married her to the companion of your abominations, did you not in his guise enjoy the pleasures she scorned to share with you? She discovered your deception. Her bridegroom did not touch her couch again, and since you were thus deprived of the object of your lust, you employed force. Four evildoers, your henchmen, holding her arms and

---

2. Radishchev refers to the war service of the peasant (serf) up for auction.—Ed.

legs—let us not go on with this. On her brow is sorrow, in her eyes despair. She is holding a little one, the lamentable fruit of deception or violence, but the living image of his lascivious father. Having given birth to him, she forgot his father's beastliness and her heart began to feel a tenderness for him. But now she fears that she may fall into the hands of another like his father. The little one—. Thy son, barbarian, thy blood! Or do you think that where there was no church rite, there was no obligation? Or do you think that a blessing given at your command by a hired preacher of the word of God has established their union? Or do you think that a forced wedding in God's temple can be called marriage? The Almighty hates compulsion; He rejoices at the wishes of the heart. They alone are pure. Oh, how many acts of adultery and violation are committed among us in the name of the Father of joys and the Comforter of sorrows, in the presence of His witnesses, who are unworthy of their calling! The lad of twenty-five, her wedded husband, the companion and intimate of his master. Savagery and vengeance are in his eyes. He repents the service he did his master. In his pocket is a knife; he clutches it firmly; it is not difficult to guess his thought—. A hopeless fancy! You will become the property of another. The master's hand, constantly raised over his slave's head, will bend your neck to his every pleasure. Hunger, cold, heat, punishment, everything will be against you. Noble thoughts are foreign to your mind. You do not know how to die. You will bow down and be a slave in spirit as in estate. And if you should try to offer resistance, you would die a languishing death in fetters. There is no judge between you. If your tormentor does not wish to punish you himself, he will become your accuser. He will hand you over to the governmental justice. Justice! Where the accused has almost no chance to justify himself! Let us pass by the other unfortunates who have been brought out for sale.

Scarcely had the dreadful hammer come down with its dull thud, and the four unfortunates learned their fate, when tears, sobs, and groans pierced the ears of the whole gathering. The most stolid were touched. Stony hearts! Of what use is fruitless compassion? O ye Quakers! If we had your souls, we would take up a collection, buy these unfortunates, and set them free. Having lived together for many years heart to heart, these unfortunates in consequence of this abominable auction will feel the anguish of parting. But if the law, or rather, the barbarous custom, for nothing is said about it in the law, permits such contempt for humanity, what right have you to sell this child? He is an illegitimate child. The law sets him free. Stop! I will denounce this violation of the law; I will deliver him. If I could only save the others with him! O fortune! Why have you given me so miserably inadequate a portion? Today I long to enjoy your sweet favor, for the first time I begin to feel a passion for wealth. My heart was so troubled that, rushing away from the gathering and giving the last dime in my purse to the unfortunate people, I ran away. On the staircase I met a foreigner, a friend of mine.

"What's happened to you? You're weeping."

"Turn back," I said to him, "and do not be a witness to this shameful spectacle. You once cursed the barbarous custom of selling black slaves in the distant colonies of your country. Go away," I repeated, "and do not be a witness of our benightedness, lest, in talking to your fellow citizens about our customs, you have to report our shame."

"I cannot believe it," my friend replied. "It is impossible that in a land where everyone is allowed to think and to believe what he pleases, such a shameful custom should exist."

"Do not be amazed," I answered; "the establishment of religious freedom offends only the priests and monks, and even they would rather acquire a sheep for themselves than for Christ's flock. But freedom for the peasants offends, as they say, against the right of property. But all those who might be the champions of freedom are great landed proprietors, and freedom is not to be expected from their counsels, but from the heavy burden of slavery itself. . . .

[Village of PESHKI.] However much I was in a hurry to finish my journey, hunger, which according to the proverb, breaks stone walls, compelled me to step into the post hut; and, since I could not get any ragout, fricassee, paté, or other French food invented to bring on indigestion, I had to make a meal out of an old piece of roast beef which I carried with me for an emergency. After I had thus dined much worse than many a colonel (not to speak of generals) on distant campaigns, I followed the laudable popular custom and filled my cup with coffee freshly prepared for me, and thus satisfied my squeamish appetite with the fruit of the sweat of unfortunate African slaves.

Seeing the sugar in front of me, the landlady, who was mixing some dough, sent her little boy to me, to ask for a small piece of this lordly food. "Why lordly?" I said to her, as I gave the child what was left of my sugar; "can't you use it, too?"

"It is lordly because we have no money to buy it with, while the gentry [nobility] use it because they do not have to earn the money for it. It's true that our bailiff buys it when he goes to Moscow, but he too pays for it with our tears."

"Then do you mean that anyone who uses sugar makes you weep?"

"Not all, but all the noblemen. Aren't you drinking your peasants' tears when they have to eat such bread as we eat?" Saying this, she showed me what her dough was made of. It consisted of three-fourths chaff and one-fourth of unsifted flour. "And with the crops failing this year, we can thank God even for this. Many of our neighbors have a worse time of it. What good does it do you noblemen to eat sugar when we are starving? The children are dying, and so are the grownups. But what can we do about it? You worry and worry, and then have to do what the master orders." And she began to put the bread into the oven.

This reproach, not uttered in anger or indignation, but with a profound feeling of sorrow in her soul, filled my heart with grief. For the first time I looked closely at all the household gear of a peasant hut. For the first time I turned my heart to things over which it had only glided heretofore. The upper half of the four walls, and the whole ceiling, were covered with soot; the floor was full of cracks and covered with dirt at least two inches thick; the oven without a smokestack, but their best protection against the cold; and smoke filling the hut every morning, winter and summer; window holes over which were stretched bladders which admitted a dim light at noon time; two or three pots (happy the hut if one of them each day contains some watery cabbage soup!). A wooden bowl and round trenchers called plates; a table, hewn with an axe, which they scrape clean on holidays. A trough to feed the pigs and calves, if there are any. They sleep together with them, swallowing the air in which a burning candle appears as though shrouded in mist or hidden behind a curtain. If they are lucky, a barrel of kvas that tastes like vinegar, and in the yard a bath house in which the cattle sleep if people are not steaming in it. A homespun shirt, the footwear given them by nature, and leggings and bast shoes when they go out. Here one justly looks for the source of the country's wealth, power, and might; but here are also seen the weakness, inadequacy, and abuse of the laws: their harsh side, so to speak. Here may be seen the greed of the gentry [nobility], our rapaciousness and tyranny; and the helplessness of the poor. Ravening beasts, insatiable leeches, what do we leave for the peasants? What we cannot take from them, the air. Yes, and nothing but the air. We frequently take from them not only the gifts of the earth, bread and water, but also the very light. The law forbids us to take their life—that is, to take it suddenly. But there are so many ways to take it from them by degrees! On one side there is almost unlimited power; on the other, helpless impotence. For the landlord is to the peasant at once legislator, judge, executor of his own judgments, and, if he so desires, a plaintiff against whom the defendant dare say nothing. It is the lot of one cast into fetters, of one thrown into a dismal dungeon: the lot of the ox under the yoke.

Hard-hearted landlord, look at the children of the peasants subject to you! They are almost naked. Why? Have you not imposed upon those who bore them—in pain and sorrow—a tax, in addition to all their work on your fields? Do you not appropriate the linen to your own use even before it is woven? And of what use to you are the stinking rags which your hand, accustomed to luxury, finds loathsome to touch? They will scarcely do for your servants to wipe your cattle with. You collect even that which you do not need, in spite of the fact that the unprotected nakedness of your peasants will be a heavy count against you. If there is no judge over you here, you will be answerable before the Judge Who is no respecter of persons, Who once gave you a good guide, conscience, whom, however, your perverse reason long ago drove from his dwelling place, your heart. But do not imagine that you will escape punishment. The sleepless watcher of your deeds will surprise you when you are alone, and you will feel his chastising strokes. Oh, if only they could be of some good to you and those subject to you!—Oh, if man would but look into his soul more frequently, and confess his deeds to his implacable judge, his conscience! Transformed by its thunderous voice into an immovable pillar, he would no longer dare to commit secret crimes; destruction and devastation would become rare. . . .

# FURTHER READING

John T. Alexander, *Bubonic Plague in Early Modern Russia: Public Health and Urban Disaster* (1980)

——, *Catherine the Great: Life and Legend* (1989)

——, *Emperor of the Cossacks: Pugachev and the Frontier Jacquerie of 1773–1775* (1973)

Roger Bartlett and Janet Hartley, eds., *Russia in the Age of Enlightenment: Essays for Isabel de Madariaga* (1990)

J. L. Black, *Citizens for the Fatherland: Education, Educators, and Pedagogical Ideals in Eighteenth-Century Russia* (1979)

Wallace L. Daniel, *Grigorii Teplov: A Statesman at the Court of Catherine II* (1991)

Gregory L. Freeze, ed. and trans., *From Supplication to Revolution: A Documentary Social History of Imperial Russia*, Part One (1988)

Robert E. Jones, *The Emancipation of the Russian Nobility* (1973)

———, *Provincial Development in Russia: Catherine II and Jakob Sievers* (1984)

———, "Urban Planning and the Development of Provincial Towns in Russia during the Reign of Catherine II," in J. G. Garrard, ed., *The Eighteenth Century in Russia* (1973), 321–344

John P. LeDonne, *Ruling Russia: Politics and Administration in the Age of Absolutism, 1762–1796* (1984)

A. Lentin, ed. and trans., *Voltaire and Catherine the Great: Selected Correspondence* (1974)

Isabel de Madariaga, "Catherine II and the Serfs: A Reconsideration of Some Problems," *Slavonic and East European Review* 52 (1974), 34–62

———, *Catherine the Great: A Short History* (1990)

———, "The Foundation of the Russian Educational System by Catherine II," *Slavonic and East European Review* 57 (1979), 369–395

———, *Russia in the Age of Catherine the Great* (1981)

Allen McConnell, "Catherine the Great and the Fine Arts," in Ezra Mendelsohn and Marshall S. Shatz, eds., *Imperial Russia, 1700–1917: Essays in Honor of Marc Raeff* (1988), 37–57

Marc Raeff, *The Well-Ordered Police State: Social and Intellectual Change in the Germanies and Russia, 1600–1800* (1983)

Hugh Ragsdale, "Evaluating the Traditions of Russian Aggression: Catherine II and the Greek Project," *Slavonic and East European Review* 66 (1985), 97–117

David L. Ransel, *The Politics of Catherinian Russia: The Panin Party* (1975)

CHAPTER 6

# Empire-Building:
# The Eighteenth Century

Although the formal foundation of the Russian Empire dates to the reign of Peter the Great (more precisely, to his assumption of the title of Emperor in October 1721), Russia had become a vast, multiethnic, Eurasian state well before Peter's time. The origins of the Russian Empire in this informal sense may be traced to the warfare and diplomacy, and the settlement and assimilation policies, of Grand Prince Ivan III "the Great" (reigned 1462–1505) and Tsar Ivan IV "the Terrible" (1533–1584). The Empire's origins may also be traced to the spontaneous actions of countless individual Russian peasants, monks, fur-trappers, and cossacks, who in the sixteenth and seventeenth centuries moved in growing numbers into the sparsely populated lands east and south of the Muscovite heartland in search of fresh fields to cultivate (free of exacting landlords), space for new monasteries, heathen folk to baptize, animal skins for the lucrative fur trade with Europe, adventure, or booty. In the process, the relatively primitive indigenous peoples of the huge Volga and Don river valleys, of the Ural mountain region, and of that continental ocean known vaguely as Siberia (*Sibir*), were beaten by Russians in battle, driven away, converted to Russian Orthodoxy, bought off or co-opted (local elites), and, sooner or later, numerically overwhelmed. Historically the whole process has been compared to the roughly contemporaneous European and especially Spanish colonization of the Americas.

The most dramatic moments in the story of Russia's "prelude to empire" came with the conquest of the Muslim Tatar (or Mongol) khanates (kingdoms) of Kazan and Astrakhan. In the 1420s the once powerful khanate of the Golden Horde, which since about 1240 had ruled from afar the lands that came to form the Muscovite heartland, began to break up into a series of successor states, the most important of which were the khanates of Kazan, Astrakhan, and Crimea (which became a vassal state of the Ottoman Empire in 1475). In 1476–1480 Ivan III of Moscow refused to pay any more tribute to the rump khanate of the Golden Horde, and got away with it; hence the year 1480 has been considered to mark the formal end of the "Mongol Yoke" in Russian history. But the other khanates remained, threatening Russian lands and commercial interests and posing obstacles to further Russian expansion south and east. Thus Ivan IV's conquest in the 1550s of the Tatar cities of Kazan and Astrakhan was a most important victory, as it gave Moscow dominion over the entire middle and lower Volga river with adjacent lands (the upper Volga lay in the Muscovite heartland) and complete control, therefore, of major trade routes with the Persian, central Asian, and Chinese worlds. The conquest of Kazan also opened the door to Russian colonization of Siberia, which thereafter proceeded steadily—a process reflected, as we saw, in the *Life* of Archpriest Avvakum (Documents, Chapter 2).

By the end of the seventeenth century the Russian advance into Siberia had reached the Pacific Ocean, and Russia's borders now abutted on China (Treaty of Nerchinsk, 1689) as well as the Persian and Ottoman empires, the domains of various central Asian powers, and, in the west, the Baltic empire of Sweden and the sprawling Polish-Lithuanian state. Indeed, the tsardom that Peter I inherited from his father and brothers was a vast, multiethnic, Eurasian empire; just as the foreign enemies against whom he made war—Crimea and Ottoman Turkey, Sweden, Poland-Lithuania, Persia—were inherited from his predecessors. In decisively defeating Sweden, Peter acquired for Russia lands inhabited by Finns, Latvians, Estonians, and Germans of the Lutheran and Roman Catholic confessions, thus adding still further ethnic and religious dimensions to the Empire he ruled.

# ESSAYS

The Muscovite conquest of Kazan and Astrakhan, like the ongoing Russian colonization of Siberia, were essentially matters of power, land, and wealth. At the same time, as Prince Trubetzkoy pointed out (Chapter 1), the Muscovite state and church explained and justified these endeavors in terms of a Christian crusade against Muslims and assorted pagan folk. (Moscow's famous Church of Basil the Blessed, on Red Square, was built to commemorate the conquest of Kazan, the victory of Christianity over Islam.) But such a justification could scarcely be applied to the Russian annexation under Peter I (and under his father, Tsar Aleksei) of Ukrainian, Belorussian, and Baltic lands—lands inhabited by Christian peoples including fellow Orthodox Slavs. The first of these essays discusses the attempts by Peter's government to work out a secular theory of empire sufficient to explain and justify, to both foreign and domestic audiences, the more complex reality that Russia had become. In doing so, the essay considers traditional Muscovite dynastic claims as well as the question of a nascent Russian nationalism (or national consciousness), and indicates how Europeanization under Peter influenced a budding Russian identity that was imperial, rather than narrowly national, in scope. This "imperialist tendency" of Petrine political theory, with the doctrine of absolutism at its core, received fuller formulation under Catherine II—as was suggested at various points in Chapter 5 and as Professor Raeff makes clear in the second of these essays. Catherine's warfare and diplomacy added substantially to her "vastly diversified and multi-ethnic polity," in Raeff's words; and his essay concentrates on her efforts to integrate the peoples of the Russian Empire by means of more "enlightened" administrative ideas and practices. Raeff is describing, in other words, the emergence of an Imperial Russian elite and culture.

# Empire Versus Nation: Russian Political Theory Under Peter I

## JAMES CRACRAFT

If "nationalism" by any commonly accepted definition of the term was not a force in Russian history before the nineteenth century, when did a "national consciousness" arise? One historian, Michael Cherniavsky, has detected "flashes" of such an "individual and collective self-identification" in early modern Russia, and particularly in the time of Peter the Great. Actually, Cherniavsky found "two national consciousnesses" active in Russia then: one, that of the Europeanizing Peter I and his gentry ("for if they, the ruling class, defined 'Russia,' then everything they did was, by definition, Russian"); the other, that of the Old Believers and the "peasants in general, [who] began to insist on beards, traditional clothes, and old rituals—creating, in reaction, their own Russian identity." These two national consciousnesses—elite and popular—were thus in conflict with one another from the beginning, a conflict, Cherniavsky left us to suppose, that was never resolved.[1]

While agreeing that the Petrine period was a critical one in the evolution of political culture in Russia (assuming both national consciousness and political theory to be aspects of political culture), I propose a quite different hypothesis. It is that the emergence of national consciousness in Russia was preempted almost at once by the imposition under Peter I of an absolutist ideology that was imperialist, not nationalist, in tendency. This imperialist tendency of Petrine absolutist ideology, which I will call Petrine hegemony theory and discuss with reference to the annexation by the Petrine state of certain non-Russian territories, was vague in its requirements, fairly tolerant (at least initially) of diversity, and open-ended. It drew on foreign as well as local sources. It helped to determine the subsequent development of Russian national consciousness in the eighteenth century and contributed its share, historically, to the formation of both Russian nationalism and Russian imperialism in the nineteenth century. In short, Petrine hegemony theory expressed the dominant form of Russian national consciousness in the Petrine period, and is not to be seen as in fundamental opposition to some other, allegedly popular but still unproven reserve of *national* sentiment.

Indeed, considering the apparent deficiency of appropriate source material as well as the problem of definition, it is doubtful that the existence of a pre-Petrine *popular* Russian national consciousness will ever be demonstrated. Rather, it is likely that the emergence of national consciousness at the popular or mass level in Russia

---

From "Empire Versus Nation: Russian Political Theory under Peter I" by James Cracraft reprinted from *Harvard Ukranian Studies*, vol. 10 no. 3/4 (December 1986), pp. 524–540. Reprinted with permission of the publisher.

1. Michael Cherniavsky, "Russia," in Orest Ranum, ed., *National Consciousness, History, and Political Culture in Early-Modern Europe* (1975), pp. 118–143.

will continue to be seen as a nineteenth-century phenomenon, a product of such factors as the Napoleonic invasion and the development among an articulate elite of Russian forms of the spreading European movement of, precisely, nationalism.

Yet more, it could be argued that the scattered reflections of national feeling to be found in the memorials of the pre-Petrine Russian elite, mainly a clerical elite, do not constitute evidence of a national consciousness, either. This argument turns in the main on the generally acknowledged centrality of history in the development of nationalism and even of national consciousness: on the concept of history itself, and then of national history. Medievalist chronicles and chronographies, for the most part never printed or printed only later by scholars, are not lacking among the written remains of pre-Petrine Russia, of course; nor are historical tales, boastful genealogies, regal tables and dynastic accounts, and highly stylized biographies—all with a sizable legendary, not to say fictive, component. But this is not what we mean by "history." In Moscow in the 1630s Adam Olearius [the German scholar and diplomat] was struck by the fact that the Russians he met were "little interested in memorable events or the history of their fathers and forefathers," something he found to be particularly true of the "great boyars." About forty years later the anonymous author of a Russian history commissioned by Tsar Fedor Alekseevich— possibly the first such history ever attempted—complained in his preface that among the peoples of the world only the Muscovites lacked a proper account of their past. In fact, it was only under Peter I and his daughter Empress Elizabeth that both modern historiography and national history began to be cultivated in Russia, the work for the most part of immigrant Ukrainian and German scholars.

This is not to say, recalling Cherniavsky, that the Petrine regime failed to arouse widespread opposition in Russia. Nor is it to deny that the focus of much of this opposition was Peter himself—the man and his policies, not his office. Nor is it to deny that in expressing their opposition some of Peter's opponents called him, among other things, a "servant of Antichrist" or "Antichrist" himself, a "Latinizer," a "German" or a "Swede," even a "Musulman," in disguise. But I would not agree, all considered, that such epithets can be construed as evidence of "xenophobia," let alone of the kind of xenophobia which constitutes, in turn, "a true confirmation of national consciousness."[2] The widespread and persistent opposition to the Petrine regime in Russia was political, economic, personal, religious and/or cultural in motivation. And insofar as it was directed against Peter himself, it was against the tsar's perpetual, public, and seemingly unconcerned display of his own many follies, vices, and frailties (drunken cavorting with common sailors and workmen, typically shabby dress, mocking of the church, and so on). It was an anguished opposition to a pattern of behavior which did great violence to a world view that was still essentially religious. But expressions of religious

---

2. Cherniavsky, "Russia," in Ranum, *National Consciousness*, p. 140; "xenophobia," it might be asked, by comparison with the situation in what contemporary state or society?

community, of a religious outlook, of a religious identity, cannot be taken as manifestations of *national* consciousness. To do so, surely, is only to cloud the matter at hand.

Finally, it is surely also anachronistic to call the Russian state before Peter I (or even after him) a "nation-state,"[3] the term to mean, presumably, a political entity regarded by its subjects, conscious of a common nationality, as identical with their collective self and hence deserving of their highest loyalty. On the contrary, the Russian state of pre-Petrine times was a patrimonial-dynastic state of pronounced theocratic aspect. Its subjects thought to owe their primary loyalty to the father-ruler (*tsar'* or "king," etc.) who lived in the "royal city" of Moscow, and whose dominion over the kingdoms, principalities, towns, and lands enumerated in his full title was his both by hereditary right and "by the grace of God." This dominion was supported and even shared, somewhat ambiguously, by the head—patriarch—of a coterminous Orthodox Christian church to whom the tsar's faithful subjects also owed allegiance (as did the tsar himself). "Russia"—*Rosiia* or *Rossiia*, the term which in official documents had now largely replaced the older *Rus'*—was delineated not by the nationality of its inhabitants, but primarily by their subjection to the Orthodox ruler of "all Russia" or, after the treaty of 1654 with the Ukrainians, of "all Great and Little Russia" (or again, after the conquest of Vilnius in 1656, of "all Great, Little, and White Russia"). To be sure, as the seventeenth century wore on these patrimonial, dynastic, theocratic, and personalist (or anthropomorphic) notions of ultimate political authority in Russia were challenged and even contra-dicted by religious schism and the infiltration of more abstract ideas from the West. But there is nothing in the sources to suggest a sense as yet of either belonging to, or presiding over, a nation-state.

Petrine absolutist ideology was a fusion of recent European theories of sovereignty, monarchy, and law with established Russian notions of patrimony (*otchina/votchina*), autocracy (*samoderzhavstvo*), and dominion (*gosudarstvo*). The ideology was formu-lated, usually at the explicit direction of Peter I himself, in response to specific events of the time, particularly the challenge to monarchical absolutism posed by rival theories of ecclesiastical or aristocratic power, theories that were both domestic and foreign in origin. The formulation of the new ideology—new in the Russian context and new in its Russian shadings—was entrusted by Peter I to various learned outsiders in his service, none of his native-born subjects, evidently, having been judged adequate to the task. These outsiders were Greek, German, Ukrainian, or, in one outstanding case (P. P. Shafirov's), Ukrainian-Jewish in background; and in varying degrees they drew on European sources, as mentioned, as well as on their knowledge of the local scene. The results are to be read in writings directly attributable to one or another of these men; in major pieces of Petrine legislation, usually collective efforts in which Peter himself lent a hand; in Peter's own papers;

---

3. Ranum, introduction, *National Consciousness*, pp. 1ff.; Cherniavsky, in ibid., pp. 118ff.; Jaroslaw Pelenski, *Russia and Kazan: Conquest and Imperial Ideology* (1974), pp. 8, 10, and passim.

and in the extended treatise entitled (in short form) *Pravda voli monarshei* [The Right of the Monarch's Will].

Peter's order to his troops on the eve of the battle of Poltava (June 27, 1709) provides a fair sample of the element of national sentiment in Petrine absolutist ideology (there is some doubt as to whether Peter himself composed the order, none that it issued from his immediate entourage):

> Let the Russian army know that the hour has drawn nigh in which the very existence of the whole fatherland is placed in their hands; either Russia will perish completely or she will be reborn for the better. They must know that they have been armed and drawn up in battle array not for the sake of Peter, but for that of the realm [*gosudarstvo*: dominion] entrusted to him, for their kinsfolk, and for the all-Russian people. . . . And let them know for certain that [Peter's] life is not dear to him, if only Russia and Russian piety, glory, and prosperity survive.

A passage of the *Military Statute* of 1716 clearly exposes the absolutist element in Petrine political ideology:

> His Majesty [Peter I] is a sovereign monarch who need not account for his acts to anyone on earth, but has the power and authority to govern his Dominions and lands as a Christian Ruler, in accordance with his own will and good judgment.

This passage, it seems, was derived directly from a Swedish source.

An attempt to root the ruler's absolute power in natural law as well as in Scripture and church law is manifest in the "Sermon on Royal Authority and Honor" preached by Feofan Prokopovich, the Ukrainian divine who became Peter's leading apologist, on Palm Sunday (April 6), 1718, in what was now styled "royal St. Petersburg":

> And behold, might not there be in the number of natural laws this one, that there are to be authorities holding supreme power among the peoples? There is indeed! And of all the laws this is the chief one. For because the ill will of a depraved race does not hesitate to break nature's command to love ourselves and not to do unto others what we would not wish for ourselves, always and everywhere a guardian has been wanted, a protector and strong upholder of the law; and this is the ruling authority. . . . For we hold it certain that supreme authority receives its beginning and cause from nature itself. And if from nature, then from God himself, the creator of nature. . . . Therefore we cannot help but call God himself the cause of the ruler's authority; whence it is also clear that nature, too, instructs us in the submission owed to [him]. . . . The authority of the ruler is necessary to natural law.[4]

Petrine absolutist ideology in its fullness is perhaps best represented in the celebrated treatise *Pravda voli monarshei vo opredelenii naslednika derzhavy svoei* ["The Right of the Monarch's Will in Designating the Heir to His Power"], a work first published in 1722 which is also attributed to Prokopovich and which certainly was

---

4. On Prokopovich, see Documents, Chapter 3.—Ed.

composed, on Peter's direct orders, by one or more of those learned outsiders who assisted him in matters of propaganda and state policy. The treatise advanced a justification of absolute monarchy and particularly of the monarch's right to designate his own successor should he have been "so unfortunate in his sons as to think none of them capable and fit to govern." It was written, as Peter himself states in its preface, to refute the "contradictions of certain enemies learned in political thought" and those equally of certain "hotheads among our people . . . [who] sow the tares of sedition in our country and bring the Russian people into disrepute among foreigners." At issue were two Petrine decrees, the first of February 1718 excluding his elder son Aleksei from the succession, the second of February 1722 ordaining that the reigning monarch "should always have the power to designate his heir, and, having once designated him, to set him aside should he notice that he is in any way unfit" [Documents, Chapter 3]. The "learned enemies" referred to by Peter were authors of pamphlets published in Europe attacking these decrees, while the seditious "hotheads" in question were domestic opponents of the tsar who condemned his treatment of his son.

In advancing its arguments *Pravda voli monarshei* invokes Scripture, the Code of Justinian, certain classical authors, decrees of Peter I, and, interestingly, Hugo Grotius's *De jure belli et pacis* [On the Law of War and Peace].

> Among the peoples, Slavic and others, the title of majesty is used to designate the highest and unsurpassable honor; it is applied to supreme rulers alone. The title signifies not only their transcending dignity, than which, after God's, there is no higher on earth, but also [their] supreme legislative power—the power to judge without appeal and to issue incontrovertible orders while not being itself subject to any laws whatever. It is thus that the most eminent jurists define majesty; among others, Hugo Grotius says precisely this: "the highest power (termed majesty) is one whose actions are not subject to the control of another power, so that they cannot be rendered void by any other human will save his own."[5]

Later, discussing various forms of government, the *Pravda* states that the form in which "all power is held in the hands of a single person is called Monarchy, that is, Autocracy." Monarchy, then, was either elective or, as in the Russian case, hereditary. Moreover it was clear that every form of government, hereditary monarchy included, had "its inception in a primary consensus among this or that people, always and everywhere acting wisely by the direction of Divine Providence." Thus

> In a hereditary monarchy, the popular will was expressed in this way to the first monarch, if not in words, then in deeds: "We desire unanimously that for our common good you should rule over us forever; that is, since you are mortal, you yourself must leave us a successor after you [are gone].

---

5. Grotius, in the original work quoted here, clearly refers to the sovereign state—to the sovereignty of the state; the author or authors of the *Pravda*, inserting the phrase "(termed majesty)," make Grotius refer more precisely to the ruler himself.

As for their part,

> The people must obey all the orders of the Autocrat without contradiction or murmur, as was shown above from the word of God and has now been clearly shown from this explanation of the popular will; for since the people have divested themselves of their general will and have given it up to their Monarch, they must obey his orders, laws, and statutes without objection.

The secular as well as the thoroughly absolutist character of this theory of Russian government, which in both respects was without precedent in Muscovite, East Slavic, or Byzantine thought, deserves emphasis. It was a theory which did not allow for the independent existence of any other institution, and which granted the ruler priority, in both time and importance, over the church in particular. The tsar was now a vaguely "Christian" rather than a specifically Orthodox ruler: a supra-confessional "Majesty" possessed of a power over his subjects that was limited only by his own will. Not even his children had independent rights, and most emphatically not the right of succession: "For an Autocratic Ruler," to quote *Pravda voli monarshei* one last time, "is Ruler not only to the subject people, but to his own children as well."

Expressions of the imperialist tendency of Petrine absolutist ideology—what I call Petrine hegemony theory—are to be found in various broadsides or manifestos issued by the tsar in the course of a military or diplomatic campaign, in the treaties or instruments of capitulation which he concluded with non-Russian rulers or local elites, and, most fully, in P. P. Shafirov's lengthy *Discourse* of 1717 explaining Peter's reasons for his prolonged war against Charles XII of Sweden.

Peter's reaction to the defection in 1708 of the Ukrainian hetman (prince), Ivan Mazepa, to the side of Charles XII provides a good case in point. First, he repeatedly invoked the bond of Orthodox Christianity in his effort to contain the effects of Mazepa's defection, and in so doing drew on established Russian and, indeed, Ukrainian conventions. Yet in his proclamations and decrees to the local authorities following Mazepa's flight, Peter's religious appeal was more negative than positive: more an attempt to arouse or to play on local religious antipathies by depicting the "heretic" Swedes as bent on desecrating Orthodox churches and monasteries or on converting them, in collusion with their Polish allies, into Catholic or Uniate institutions. Moreover, the religious was only one element of Peter's overall appeal—of his public justification for why he condemned Mazepa as a "betrayer of his people" and had ordered the convening of a *rada* (Ukrainian council) to elect a new hetman, one whose loyalty to the tsar was tried and true. For Peter portrayed himself now not only as "one with you [the Ukrainians] in faith," as their "Orthodox ruler," but also as the "ruler and protector" by hereditary right of the "Little-Russian people and land": he was, invoking the tsar's title as adapted in the 1650s, "Autocrat of all Great, Little, and White Russia" as well as, in another older version of his title to be found in these same documents, "hereditary ruler and grand prince" of the "Kiev" and "Chernihiv" lands, among others. In Peter's eyes, not only had Mazepa gone over to the common enemy, the Swedes and the Polish anti-king—Stanisław Leszczyński—whom they had placed on the throne; and not only did Mazepa intend thereby to "enslave" his countrymen to the Swedes and/or to "subjugate" them to the Poles, but Mazepa aspired (Peter somewhat inconsistently claimed) to set himself up as "sovereign prince in the Ukraine."

This was the heart of the matter. There could be only one "sovereign prince" in any land claimed or acquired by the Russian ruler. Moreover, given what we know already of Petrine political theory, we can see that Peter's promises in these same documents to respect the (Ukrainian) Cossack "liberties, rights, and privileges" guaranteed by his father were largely—one might say necessarily—meaningless. Subjects could have no such rights. At a more personal level, there is also evidence here that Peter was stunned by the hetman's defection, that he refused to believe that Mazepa could have had any legitimate reason for renouncing his allegiance to the tsar, and that he persisted, therefore, in blackening the old man's character. That Mazepa perceived himself as an autonomous prince who had voluntarily and, as it turned out, temporarily accepted the tsar's suzerainty, seems utterly to have escaped Peter's understanding.

Following Mazepa's defection and subsequent defeat at Poltava (1709), the Petrine notions of undivided sovereignty and unlimited monarchy began to take hold in the Left-Bank (eastern) Ukraine—took hold, it might be added, with the help of a part of the Ukrainian elite, who saw their own best future and that of "Little Russia" in submission to the "all-Russian" tsar. In Poland-Lithuania, by contrast, where Peter attempted to protect the local Orthodox population, to claim the rest of his assumed Ukrainian inheritance, and to dominate central politics, no such thing happened. This was because, at least in part, Polish ideas of limited monarchy, of confederation and of *szlachta* (noble) democracy, were too firmly rooted. It has been shown, for instance, that in allying itself with Peter against Charles XII and Leszczyński between 1706 and 1709, the Confederation of Sando-mierz [alliance of Polish noblemen] in no way surrendered traditional Polish interests to the tsar. On the other hand, while Peter's attempt to dominate Polish central politics was based on simple *Machtpolitik*, his claims to a protectorate over the local Orthodox population and to possession of the Right-Bank (western) Ukraine were grounded in continuing Russian assumptions—now more forcefully expressed—of ethno-religious homogeneity and monarchical hereditary right. And this boded ill for Poland's future as a viable, sovereign state. As for the Right-Bank Ukraine itself, events later in the eighteenth century would also show that no less than in the case of Kiev, which had enjoyed a measure of civic autonomy under Polish rule, or in that of the Left-Bank Ukraine, with its tradition of Cossack democracy, would the Russian government tolerate diversity within unity: this in part because, I would now argue, any divergence from the Russian model in what were coming to be regarded as "Russian" lands—in this case, "Little Russian"—was literally incon-ceivable.

In the Baltic territories annexed by Peter I in the course of his war with Sweden the Russian ruler could not, to be sure, invoke the Orthodox faith or the heritage of old *Rus'* as claims on his new subjects' loyalty. On the contrary: in his universal of August 16, 1710, in German, to the inhabitants of Estonia, Peter frankly acknowledged that the Evangelical religion prevailed throughout the country and, eschewing any intention of introducing innovations here, pledged not only to preserve intact the local church's liberties, rights, and privileges, but to expand them. This was the same Lutheran religion which scarcely two years before Peter had reviled in his campaign to arouse Ukrainian resistance to the "heretic" Swedes. Similarly, Peter promised to maintain intact the liberties, rights, and privileges of the nobility of Livonia and the magistracy of Riga in the several accords and instruments of capitulation that he concluded with them, just as he agreed to leave the civil administration of these territories in the hands of Germans "because the inhabitants are of the German nation."

Obviously, the motives behind Peter I's concessions to the churches and leading classes of Livonia and Estonia were largely pragmatic: the need to pacify and to secure control of these newly won and valuable lands while the war against the Swedish king, their erstwhile master, went on. Clearly, too, Peter's assumption in victory of the vanquished Swede's position as overlord of these territories and protector of their dominant Lutheran religion encouraged the development in Russia itself of that new, more secular, indeed supra-confessional idea of monarchy which was discussed above. We notice that in these documents of accord, capitulation, and pacification the tsar is titled, officially for the first time, "emperor" (*imperator*), with the distinctly universalist as well as secularist connotations that this title bore. Yet we should also notice in these documents that any concessions regarding local rights, liberties, or privileges were always granted conditionally: (1) on condition that the concessioners, so to speak, maintained in the future perfect loyalty to the tsar; and (2) because the concessioners had already sworn, unconditionally, to be the tsar's most faithful subjects. And we know what that meant. In other words, these concessions by Peter to the local elites of the newly conquered Baltic territories represented pragmatic adaptations of basic Russian notions governing the relations of ruler and subject, not any fundamental redefinition of same. The anomaly, as time would show, remained just that: an anomaly.

Peter's annexation of Livonia and Estonia was at first publicly justified—again in the documents just mentioned—only by right of conquest in a war both caused and perpetuated by the Swedish king. It was also represented as a "liberation" of these territories from the "Swedish yoke." There appear to have been some grounds for the latter view and some actual support for it in the "liberated" territories themselves. But the Russian annexation of Livonia and Estonia and, earlier, of Karelia and Ingria, as well as the long and difficult Swedish war itself, seemed to require, for both foreign and domestic consumption, some fuller, more theoretical justification. This task Peter entrusted to P. P. Shafirov, a seasoned diplomat in his service, who by 1717 had produced, under Peter's personal supervision, the *Discourse* already mentioned [see Documents below].

In the *Discourse* the Russian annexation of the Baltic territories was defended not only by right of conquest in a just war—Russian victories being evidence, incidentally, of divine favor—but on alleged historical and legal grounds as well. It was argued that these territories "did of old make part of the Russian Empire."

That was to say, at one time or another in the past these "provinces" had been acknowledged as "under the jurisdiction and protection of the Russian crown"—a claim that was true only with respect to Ingria—and that they were thus among the tsar's "hereditary lands." These lands had been given up, moreover, only in adversity, and in gaining or regaining control of them now the Russian side had behaved with perfect legality, in accordance with both natural and civil law. Indeed, it was argued here that as the "Father of the Fatherland"—a title he was formally to assume in 1721—Peter had been obliged to recover by war these "hereditary provinces" which had been "unjustly wrested from his Crown." For as the "potentates in this world have no superior over them but Almighty God, . . . every Monarch is bound to defend with arms and force his right and dominions, which he holds of God, and to oppose force with force at opportune times, as has been the practice in the whole world from its beginning, and will be until its end." It was also argued, still at the more theoretical level, that Peter had justifiably gone to war against Sweden "for the advantage and interest of his own Realm," a principle which meant in practice, as it was further explained, developing Russia's commerce with Europe by securing control of "this side of the Baltic."

Shafirov's treatise has been described as a "legal-historical brief, officially inspired but unofficial in character, written by an individual well versed in the theory and practice of early eighteenth-century international law and diplomacy." But for our purposes now the treatise is interesting for what it added to the Russian justification for annexing the Baltic territories in particular, and for what it reveals—or confirms—about Petrine hegemony theory in general. Employing current, wholly secular notions of legality and of what came to be called *Realpolitik*, concepts which frequently required the use—in Russian—of new words, Shafirov (and Peter I) had provided an elaborate rationalization for Russia's original aggression against Sweden, for Russia's continued prosecution of the war, and for the Russian takeover of the lands in question. The rationalization was intended primarily to gain European approval of (or at least acquiescence to) Russia's conduct here, to calm critics of the war at home, and to set the stage for negotiations with Sweden. But nowhere in this lengthy work are any rights or peculiarities of the inhabitants themselves of the occupied territories ever mentioned, while at the same time, as noted, the rights and powers of the Russian monarch are often adduced.

This leaves the reader to infer that as against the rights of the sovereign his subjects even here had none, and that his acknowledgment in practice of their peculiarities was at best a temporary concession of his power. Most probably this was not a matter of oversight or of deliberate *legerdemain* [sleight of hand; trickery] but of, again, an unwillingness or even an inability to alter fundamental Russian conceptions of the relation of sovereign and subject, the peculiarities of a new situation or the possible implications of new ideas notwithstanding. In Shafirov's treatise, as in *Pravda voli monarshei*, contemporary European thought is mined in support of the Russian monarchy while the tendencies in European thought hostile to monarchical absolutism are ignored. It is also remarkable that in Shafirov's treatise, written just a few years after Mazepa's downfall, the office of the Ukrainian hetman is referred to as that of the tsar's "general," the Cossacks are termed his "subjects," the Ukraine is called his "dominion" and the unfortunate Mazepa himself, simply a "traitor."

Thus, hegemony theory under Peter, such as it was, was essentially an extension or adaptation of Petrine absolutist ideology to new or different conditions, and little more. Like the latter, it was a mixture of tradition and innovation, but a mixture in which the new subsumed and advanced, rather than modified, the old. The thrust of Petrine hegemony theory was clearly to strengthen the center at the expense of the "province"; to subordinate local liberties, rights, or privileges to the undivided, unlimited, undiluted dominion of the tsar-emperor. An "empire" indeed had come into being, but as an assemblage of provinces grouped around the sovereign's Russian realm and awaiting "Russification," using that term now in a narrowly political sense. Or so the theory inclined. Perhaps the historical importance of the justifications for Russian annexation of non-Russian territories advanced under Peter I lies in the fact that they imposed no legal or moral restraints whatever on the practitioners of Russian imperial policy.

In conclusion, the element of national sentiment infusing both Petrine absolutist ideology and its imperailist tendency—what I have called Petrine hegemony theory—might be emphasized. For it was, ostensibly, on behalf of the "Russian" people that the Petrine wars were waged, new territories were annexed, and, in an unprecedented exercise of royal power, the new succession law was laid down. It was, after all, in an effort to enhance the glory and prosperity of the "all-Russian realm" that the government was further centralized, the church subordinated to the monarch by the institution of the Holy Synod, and a new capital city, St. Petersburg, built on conquered land. Indeed, these and other political and military accomplishments of the Petrine regime gave rise, there is plenty of evidence to show, to a surge of what must be called national pride. The sentiment is unmistakably present, for example, in the act of October 1721 of the newly founded Senate and Synod conferring the imperial and other new dignities on Peter [see Documents, Chapter 3]:

> To show due gratitude to His Majesty for his gracious and paternal care and exertions for the welfare of the realm during the whole of his most glorious reign, and especially during the recent Swedish war; moreover [to acknowledge that] through his guidance alone, as is well known to everyone, he has brought the all-Russian realm into such a strong and prosperous condition and his subject people into such glory before the whole world: it is resolved to beg His Majesty, in the name of the whole Russian people, to accept from them the title of Father of the Fatherland, All-Russian Emperor, Peter the Great.

Nor did it end with Peter I. Here is Lomonosov, in a panegyric to Peter's memory delivered in April 1755 to commemorate the coronation (in 1743) of his daughter, Empress Elizabeth [see Documents below]:

> Our Monarch is robed in purple, is annointed for imperial rule, is crowned and receives the Scepter and Orb. Russians rejoice, filling the air with applause and acclamation. Enemies blanch and quail. . . . Following the example of

her great progenitor [Peter I], she [Elizabeth] gives crowns to Sovereigns, calms Europe with peaceful arms, consolidates the Russian inheritance. . . . The far-flung Russian state, like a whole world, is surrounded by great seas on almost every side. On all of them we see Russian flags flying. . . . Here new Columbuses hasten to unknown shores to add to the might and glory of Russia [etc.].

Or here is Potemkin, in the later 1770s, urging Catherine II that it was her "duty to exalt the glory of Russia" by annexing the Crimean Khanate [Documents, below]. This was the same Catherine "the Great" who a dozen years before, in her famous "Instruction" to the Legislative Commission [see Documents, Chapter 5], had declared that in Russia

> The sovereign is absolute; for no other authority except that which is concentrated in his person can act appropriately in a state whose expanse is so vast. The expanse of the state requires that absolute power be vested in the person who rules over it. . . .

Or here, finally, is Prince Bezborodko in a memorandum of 1799 to Catherine's son, Emperor Paul:

> Russia is an autocratic state. Its size, the variety of its inhabitants and customs, and many other considerations make it the only natural form of government for Russia. All arguments to the contrary are futile, and the least weakening of the autocratic power would result in the loss of many provinces, the weakening of the state, and countless misfortunes for the people.

> Is it too much to suggest that both absolutism and imperialism were inherent in Russian nationalism virtually from the beginning, and that in studying the origins and development of the one we cannot ignore the others?

## Imperial Policies of Catherine II

### MARC RAEFF

Since the beginnings of its history Russia was—and still is—a vastly diversified and multi-ethnic polity. Yet its historiography has barely reflected this fact, leaving not only a gap in our knowledge but also influencing the views and actions of the ruling elites. It is, therefore, both of interest and importance to see how the cultural-human diversity and the physical size were dealt with administratively by the imperial government. In the present article I shall focus my attention on the reign of Catherine II, which was a significant period in this respect, as in so many others.

From Marc Raeff "Imperial Policies of Catherine II" in Hans Lemberg et al., eds., *Osteuropa in Geschichte und Gegenwart: Festschrift fur Gunter Stokl zum 60 Geburtstag* (Cologne and Vienna: Bohlau Verlag, 1977) pp. 97–113. Reprinted by permission of the author.

An important factor in the ways newly acquired territories and their peoples were dealt with by the central authorities, in Moscow or St. Petersburg, was the time and manner of their acquisition. As I have argued elsewhere, the fact that the first conscious and significant "imperial" expansion occurred in the 16th century, as if continuing the so-called "gathering of Russian lands," played no mean role in the elaboration of the outlook and methods of Russian administrators. Some new elements were introduced with the "modern" incorporation of the Baltic provinces by Peter the Great; but even these innovations were implemented in the spirit and with the means that had been developed by previous generations under different circumstances. In dealing with the period of Catherine II we should, therefore, remember that basic attitudes and many practices had a long history. But her reign did witness the development among the governing elites of an awareness of the basic issues involved in the empire's diversity. This heightened consciousness stemmed from the greater cultural and political sophistication developed by the Russian elites, but also from Russia's integration into the [European] world, so that contemporary European ideas and practices were purposefully applied to the solution of administrative and political problems.

First, let us briefly consider the intellectual framework within which Catherine II and her advisors operated. The underlying conceptual and methodological assumptions were derived from [the] cameralist theory and practice of [early modern Europe]. We may recall that Catherine II herself received her first education in the cameralist environment of a petty German court in the first half of the 18th century, and that whatever secular education was imparted formally or informally to the leading personalities of Russia was patterned on the prevailing European models. Furthermore, the Russian administration was generously sprinkled with officials of foreign background and training, either specially hired by the state or issued from the westernized elites of the Baltic and western provinces.

The prevailing political and administrative notions of continental Europe in the late 17th and the first half of the 18th century were what we call, in short hand fashion, cameralism and mercantilism. We need not differentiate between the two, for in essence they were only two facets of one system. Developed in the world of petty German territorial principalities following the Thirty Years War (although its roots go back to the theologians and political practitioners of the Reformation), cameralism views the state as a single and self-contained unit. The ruler and his administration are the driving force of an active and interventionist policy covering all facets of public life within the territorial limits of the state, whether large or small. The dynamic quality of the regime derives from a voluntaristic conception of its political function: to maximize society's economic and cultural potential, so as to expand its wealth and power to maintain independence and extend its influence within a system of equally sovereign, autarkic, and dynamic states. Little wonder that these regimes' main concern was fiscal, and that their principal administrative goal was to increase the productive capacity and resources of the nation.

Applied to administration proper, this political conception resulted in the . . . "well ordered police state," whose working principle and goal [were] well stated by J. H. G. von Justi in a popular and influential treatise which Catherine II read early in her career. . . . Of course, such an orientation paved the way for the administration's involvement in the supervision, control, direction, and promotion of all facets of public—and frequently also of private—life as they seemed to affect the goal of expanding welfare and progress. . . . It also resulted in the state's active and energetic involvement in educational and cultural policy. The ruler's, or state's, task was to maximize the potential for greater prosperity and happiness by eliminating conflicts and frictions through a firm anchoring of security of person and property, and by seeing to it that each estate, class, or group in society make its proper contribution.

The practical effectiveness of the system rested on the preservation of existing social structures, for the corporate bodies, estates, and classes had to be used as instruments in achieving the goals we have described. To be sure, these traditional bodies were not sufficient and the positive role of the state could be performed adequately only with the help of a body of officials organized along bureaucratic lines as the willing instruments of the ruler. But the two went hand in hand, and in the successful cameralist absolutisms the ruler's bureaucracy cooperated effectively with the traditional leadership (with which it frequently had common social roots) in the pursuit of new policy goals which, in fact, transmuted the original social structure in favor of a dynamic, modern one. Significantly, social change and social mobility were to be kept within bounds and the traditional framework was to be preserved; but not too rigidly, perhaps, so as to permit select individuals, who by their capacity and dynamic enterprise had contributed to the overall purpose, to rise in status and eventually merge with the ruling elites of the polity.

The basic assumption of political and economic harmony, and of social and cultural uniformity, points to some paradoxes or contradictions in the cameralist approach to administration and state policy.

There is a contradiction between reliance on positive state direction and controls and the maximizing of the productive (creative) potential of individuals and groups. We also observe an antinomy between expanding wealth, welfare, and happiness and the preservation of social stability. Finally there is scope for conflict in the reliance on the activity of autonomous groups and estates, the free role of "*pouvoirs intermédiares* [intermediary powers]," on the one hand, and the *dirigisme* [control] of the central state bureaucracy, on the other.

In a sense these contradictions were immanent to the philosophical and anthropological preconceptions of 17th and 18th century cameralist administrators. The absolutist *Polizeistaat* ["police state"] was based squarely on Cartesian rationalism which—besides its mechanistic conception of nature—posits the uniformity of human nature operating within a stable universe. Thus laws and other human arrangements should basically be the same everywhere since man's nature is uniform. Differences are differences in developmental level and are thus the object of guidance and informed action by the state that aims at overcoming them. Yet it was precisely in the 16th and 17th centuries that Europeans discovered cultural relativism; a realization that men are different in their ways and ideals entered the consciousness of the educated European and was beginning to be taken into account, however inadequately, by administrators of colonial empires. The apparent discrepancy between the two insights about man—uniformity of nature and variety of culture—were reconciled in the notion of levels (stages) of development within a general uniform pattern of evolution and progress in man's way of life. A people's way of life becomes the criterion of achievement on the developmental scale; and the necessary transformation in a way of life can be fostered, helped along, or in some cases even imposed, by the intervention of the paternalistic state through "police" legislation.

These general considerations should be kept in mind as we turn to an examination of the concrete policies pursued in the reign of Catherine II with respect to the empire's economic, ethnic, [and] cultural diversity. The view that the empire was a single economic unit had been given legislative form by [Empress] Elizabeth when she abolished internal tariffs. The final sanction came in the first years of the reign of Catherine II. The incorporation of the provinces acquired at the first partition of Poland [1772] gave rise to the advocacy of an expansion of the empire's economic borders by abolishing custom posts between the Ukraine, Russia proper and the former Polish lands. [Russians noticed, too], that trade itself could be a means for furthering and expanding political control and increasing the potential of the empire. This was especially true if this became the preliminary for agrarian settlement.

With the promotion of agricultural settlement, and especially the furtherance of agriculture, we are in the realm of classical cameralist concerns and the problem of handling ethnic and cultural variety. The state's furtherance of agriculture through foreign settlements and internal migration corresponded exactly to the basic cameralist goal of maximizing society's resources [in order] to make the state self-sufficient and foster population growth. This consideration led Catherine II to support and promote the settlement of the southern steppe regions, especially after the elimination of Turkish and Crimean threats to the area's security. The policy had, of course, diplomatic and . . . imperialistic aspects which only reinforced the state's direct concern and intervention. But what is more interesting and important for us here is to note the manner in which Catherine and her main advisor, Potemkin, dealt with the problem of ethnic and cultural variety in the settlement policy [she] fostered.

First was the belief, based on the notion implicit in 17th century rationalism, that the highest stage of human socio-economic development was settled agriculture combined with active trade (and some manufacturing). To promote agricultural settlement, therefore, was to extend the area of this high stage of social development. And in so doing the state was setting an example and preparing the ground for those populations that had not yet reached this stage. The government would help with various incentives, but these incentives were predicated on the other equally important aspect of the policy: the standard used to gauge the level of development and which also provided the institutional framework was the Great Russian peasant, or those foreigners—i.e., Germans—who had the same high level and even higher institutional forms. Thus the administration endeavored to draw non-settled natives into the orbit of the Russian agricultural population. This aim was pursued with special energy in the newer frontier regions—i.e., Siberia, east of Astrakhan—where the help of the native elites was actively enlisted to his end. The success was mixed, and on the whole not significant, in the absence of an adequate density of Russian agricultural settlement to provide a model and invite emulation through more or less amicable persuasion. The best documented instance, besides the earlier expansion of Russian peasant settlement beyond the Volga and into the South, was the case of the Buriat region in Siberia at the end of the 18th century and in the early years of the 19th. It goes without saying that such a policy helped to disrupt and even change traditional patterns, which in turn produced those very conflicts which the government aimed at avoiding. In any event, the policy's thrust was clear: to bring about uniformity and full integration by eliminating social and economic differences and by bringing all subjects to share a similar way of life—a way of life which 18th century enlightened rationalism considered the height of social development.

Most important for the imperial administration, the settlers and their advanced institutions offered the basis for the extension to the new frontiers the legal and administrative ways and norms of the central core lands. That this was indeed the intention of the imperial administrators is made clear in the fiscal and administrative provisions for different treatment of these regions: all advantages were to be strictly temporary, to be eliminated gradually as the region's population became more and more alike to that of the central provinces in its way of life.

The *Gleichschaltung* [policy of unification] went beyond the fiscal domain, for the final step was to come when the native population would be equalized with the Russian peasantry with respect to recruiting duties and obligations.

The implicit belief in economic and social uniformity meant that the imperial administration would endeavor as much as possible to develop and promote manufacturing and trade, not only out of purely cameralist considerations of maximizing resources and securing autarky for military requirements, but also to promote lateral social mobility. Indeed, the cameralist conception implied a belief in the social division of labor along estate lines, each estate—or corporate entity—having its specific function in the polity. The balance and harmony of functions assured the state's wealth and power while promoting the subjects' welfare, progress, and prosperity. Therefore, in the absence of such estates or corporate groups it behooved the state, i.e., the administration, to foster their development. Thus Catherine endeavored to promote European style estate structures for the Russian population, in particular to foster the middle class of merchants, tradesmen, and small manufacturers that was still lacking in spite of the efforts of Peter I. This the imperial government did not only within the confines of traditional Russia, but also in the frontier regions where the native populations had a very different social makeup and institutional traditions. Here, too, the purpose was to generate the basic social uniformity that was considered necessary for harmony and to assure security and stability.

More significant still, and more successful, was imperial policy in fostering the integration of the non-Russian economic elites into the all-Russian imperial framework. Wherever . . . a class of native traders [existed,] efforts were made to guarantee them security of person and property, along [with] their traditional customs, and to give them a stable role in the pattern of economic and social relations in their home areas. This was to be achieved by laws that maintained traditional behavior and organizations while separating these economically active elites from the masses of their fellow subjects. The privileged position of these elites paved the way for their integration into the Russian pattern: gradually the special privileges were eroded as they were forced to give way to Russian norms when native and local elite organizations were assimilated to the Russian estate institutions. Thus pressure for the full integration and russification of the native economic elites increased.

From an administrative—or rather political—point of view, the empire was considered a unit. Of course its enormous expanse, especially in view of contemporary techniques of transportation and communication, created the need for regional or local deconcentration, i.e., the delegation of some functions to local-level institutions. But in the Russian case we encounter even in this respect a basic uniformity which is striking when compared with contemporary France and Prussia, not to speak of the Habsburg monarchy. This high degree of uniformity had its roots in the very process of the "gathering of Russian lands" and it had received renewed impetus in the mechanistic and rational approach of Peter the Great. Functions could be delegated, but only on the assumption that the government was paternalistic and performed a didactic role, so that functions of administration were the same everywhere, that they would be implemented in a [socially and culturally] uniform environment, and that the means available for their implementation would also be basically identical. This implied making use of uniform bureaucratic techniques, for variations affected only superficial differences which would, in most cases, be temporary, until the economic and social forces of integration and assimilation we have mentioned earlier had produced their effect.

[Starting with] Peter I's measures on local government, we can trace a consistent and conscious policy of eliminating traditional, historically conditioned administrative units in favor of a pyramidal structure of identical subdivisions. The policy reached a first stage of fulfillment in the reign of Catherine II. The old, large *gubernii* [provinces] were split up and reshuffled and the empire was divided into new provinces based on a roughly identical number of population (between 200,000 and 300,000), with little regard for geography, historic social bonds, or effective economic connections. In order to provide the necessary administrative centers, new "cities" were created by *fiat* [decree] out of villages, though some lip service was given to their potential economic functions as trade centers. But this economic potential was evaluated from the point of view of imperial connections, not on the basis of local and regional patterns of trade. The large provincial units in turn were subdivided into a number of districts (*uezdy*) also on the basis of population, . . . and they were endowed with uniform institutions. With this went uniform administrative procedures and personnel. Of course, distinctions between regions could not be fully ignored; but Catherine acknowledged only such broad distinctions as north, center, south, [and] east. The local officials, both elected and appointed, were given identical uniforms [of] different color[s] . . . corresponding to these regions. . . .

The perennial Russian shortage of qualified personnel to take care of the new local institutions forced the government to rely on local participation. But it made sure that this participation [was] uniform in terms of forms and procedures, and especially in terms of recruitment from comparable social groups. Wherever local forces were absent or inadequate, the [government] continued to rely on the regular bureaucracy. In case of need, personnel were sent from the capitals [St. Petersburg or Moscow] and an effort was made to create new bureaucratic cadres locally. These new cadres were recruited from the traditional strata of Russian society so as to insure their continued predominance in the empire. For instance, an effort was made to recruit subaltern officials and clerks from the clerical estate whose Great Russian tradition was firmly rooted in uniform education and culture.

At the same time the government also endeavored to create or develop the local forces that its institutions required. This was accomplished by means of the integration of native local elites through cultural and political russification. The process received renewed impetus from the legislation of 1775 (Statute on Local Administration) and 1785 (Charters to the Nobility and to the Towns): in an apparent paradox, while promoting greater reliance on local forces and extending the areas of administrative deconcentration, the statutes also intensified the pressures for russification on the part of the native elites and their integration into the all-Russian estate structure. In the end, the policy suffered failure because opposition and difficulties were dealt with through harsh centralization and forcible integration—but this was to be the story of the 19th century which brought about insuperable strains and open conflict.

The goal of integration and uniformity which was implied in the cameralist belief in the uniformity of human nature and a universal pattern of social progress was never achieved with respect to the Old Believers, especially the extreme sects whose members were persecuted and kept out of public regular institutions. A policy of active discrimination against religious extremism was pursued in the reign of Catherine II who considered all forms of religious exaltation (including Free Masonry and mysticism) dangerous to government and society—which only resulted in their retreating to the borders of the empire. . . . But in other cases religion proved a convenient vehicle for the achievement of cultural and social integration. Russian Orthodoxy was favored, of course, as the state religion. Efforts were made to attract new members, although missionary activity was normally not encouraged by the state. More important, recognized minority churches and denominations were put under state administrative control similar to that of the Russian church, while their governing bodies were at times [moved] nearer to the central authorities.

In line with the hallowed experience that family bonds were one of the most effective means to fasten ties and secure loyalties, the imperial government endeavored to foster such family alliances among the local elites as would integrate them more easily into the Great Russian nation. On the other hand the state's administrative apparatus and influence were brought to bear to discourage family ties with non-Russians. It was an old policy, for *mutatis mutandis* it had been followed with respect to Tatar elites in the 16th century, and it had not been forgotten when it came to integrate the Crimea and the Southern steppe regions. An even more blatant instance may be found in the Ukraine where the local elite experienced the strong cultural pull of neighboring Poland, a pull that St. Petersburg felt [it] imperative to break. In the reign of [Empress] Anna [1730–1740] already a secret instruction had been issued to influence marriages. Catherine pursued a similar policy with respect to education, especially after the first partition of Poland, to steer the elites into local or Russian schools and prevent them from going to Polish, particularly Jesuit, institutions of learning. Not quite so openly, because of the need for their skills, was the effort to orient the Baltic noble elites towards Russia and to reduce their studying in Germany. Eventually it led to the reopening of a German university at Dorpat (Iuriev) in the early 19th century and making it a tool of Russian cultural integration.

Another traditional method to cope with ethnic and cultural variety was to "russify" the elites in the hope that they would lead or drag their fellow subjects to integration into Russian culture and society. For the achievement of this goal the imperial government had a particular effective tool at its disposal: the Table of Ranks. Indeed, the Table permitted [the government] to reward all services to the state with ranks that could lead to ennoblement and assimilation to the Russian ruling elite. Reward with ranks was particularly effective in creating a single imperial ruling elite, for it conferred equal rights and privileges with respect to ownership of serfs, control of mineral resources on the private estate, security of person and property. The system had been used with good results in the case of the Ukrainian elite . . . culminating in the integration of the [cossacks] in 1775. Of course, other forms of official reward and distinction might lead to similar benefits, for example bestowal of military and civil orders. Characteristically, the imperial government was prepared to make allowance for native cultural and religious traditions to enable their leaders to accept these awards: for instance, a special form of the order of St. George was designed for Tatars, so as not to hurt their [Muslim] susceptibilities. The cooption of local leaders for subaltern administrative services and offices led to their integration into the bureaucratic hierarchy whose forms and procedures had to be followed; and this in turn might lead to [promotion] and social and cultural russification. These methods proved particularly effective in the Crimea and later on the Southeastern frontier and in Siberia.

In view of the "modernizing," goal-directed, active nature of the cameralist state, its elite and bureaucracy had also to share a common outlook, values, and language, which resulted in assigning a leading role to education. At issue was a westernized education, but an education that was carried on in a Russian form [which] implied integration into the emerging imperial Russian culture. We need not belabor the frequently amusing or pathetic existential aspects of the process which are to be found in numerous memoirs. The result is well known: a modern Russian culture open to all members of the educated classes, from whatever background, and which served as the foundation and matrix for the astoundingly creative and vital literary, artistic, and scientific achievements of the 19th century, achievements that in turn served as a pole of attraction to the new leadership from both the lower classes and non-Russian peoples. The educational process resulted in a cultural and linguistic uniformity which became the royal road of access to the leading positions in Russia, attracting thereby the ambitious elites of the subject peoples in the empire. It served to weaken, if not actually erode, the cultural identity of these elites and thus undermined their peoples' ability to resist russification. Early and effective results along this line had become apparent among the Ukrainian leadership. These elites became largely russified and were coopted into the imperial bureaucracy. It [would] require newcomers from the lower classes to revive effectively the national and cultural traditions of the Ukraine [in the nineteenth century]. In the case of politically and culturally strong ethnic groups the result was a bi-cultural and bi-lingual elite as illustrated by the German-Russian society of the capital

[St. Petersburg,] which made signal contributions to both the administrative and scientific lives of the empire in the 19th century. On a more modest scale we observe a similar development among the Greek and Armenian communities whose settlement in newly acquired Southern Russia, especially in the Crimea and Odessa, was actively promoted by Catherine II.

Special arrangements and privileges granted to individual groups to cope with particular local problems and conditions were never regarded as permanent. . . . The imperial government viewed them strictly as temporary and transitional [on] the way to full integration, in fact to what we must call, for want of a better term, full russification. The intention as well as the cameralist form of the process were made explicit in Catherine's well known secret instruction [of 1764] to Count Rumiantsev upon his appointment to the governor-generalship of the Ukraine.

A similar observation may be made about all special provisions to respect native legal traditions; they were temporary and served to smooth the path to eventual integration—social, economic, and cultural. Not only were customs always to be superseded by Russian law whenever a Russian was one of the parties to a legal dispute, but also Russian legal norms were to be applied in all cases not specifically covered by customary law. The application of Russian norms, however, entailed the introduction, however gradual or indirect, of Russian institutional and organizational patterns. This was good cameralist, *Polizeistaat* [police state] tradition which, basing itself on the priority of abstract reason, also gave precedence to royal edicts and law over custom. Another step was taken in Russia as well; the customary law was collected and codified, and in the process subjected to further russification in substance, if not always in form. If there was acceptance of cultures and norms considered high on the Enlightenment scale of values, for example in the Baltic provinces, it was only in the expectation of assimilating them, too, into the imperial fabric once economic progress, education, and culture had raised Russia proper to conform to the higher level of development. The other peoples deemed to be at an inferior stage had to be integrated by transforming their way of life to conform to the higher level of the Russians. There was rather little effective resistance to this policy since the material advantages were great, Russian power overwhelming, and the national consciousness of the non-Russian, as well as Russian, populations [was] still far from developed. In such a situation the state could find ample scope for its didactic and leading role and it did not fail to take advantage of it.

The pattern, therefore, was clear: temporary recognition of local and cultural differences but only as a step in the process of integration; integration was to lead to uniformity, first administrative and economic, then institutional and social, and finally cultural. In fact, the goal may be termed institutional russification, though it was not seen as such by contemporaries . . . , partly because of their low sophistication, partly because its effects had not become apparent. The Russian government and administrative elites did not perceive it because modification and "modernization" involved no compulsory change in language and religion. As a matter of fact, to the political writers and practitioners of the day, issues of language and religion were secondary matters, and they were surprised when they triggered violent discontent or general national opposition. To a cosmopolitan elite language was but a convenient instrument and [a member of such an elite was] ready to accept another [language] if it seemed more effective or desirable. If the Russian elites were prepared to acquire German or French for this reason, why should not other peoples in the empire switch to [Russian] as a better instrument of communication and a cultured way of life? The imperial government was blind to the problems of cultural autonomy and identity and their relationship to administrative, economic, and social uniformity. Catherine's ideal was that of the rationalist cameralist autocrat whose duty it was to bring enlightened progress to all [her] peoples. . . .

In conclusion we should take note and emphasize—as it is in contrast to what was to happen [in] Russia . . . from the middle of the 19th century on—the great flexibility in the means resorted to by Russian administrators in the 18th century in paving the way for integration and uniformity. Emphasis was on gradualism, and generally mild tolerance, so as to preserve stability and peace. But precisely this emphasis on—and belief in—maintaining harmony and stability blinded Russian officials to the contradictions and potential dangers inherent in their policies. It was difficult to square social stability based on estates and corporate bodies with the dynamic expansion and maximizing of the productive potential of society. Fraught with greater hazards still [was] the myopia [regarding] the religious, cultural, and socio-psychological dimensions of [the various peoples'] sense of identity. These blind spots came to haunt the government of St. Petersburg in the 1860s and they endowed the emerging Russian and national intelligentsias with much of their strength.

# DOCUMENTS

The first document is excerpted from P. P. Shafirov's *A Discourse Concerning the Just Reasons which His Majesty Tsar Peter I had for Beginning the War against King Charles XII of Sweden in the Year 1700*, which was published in Russian at St. Petersburg in 1717 and soon thereafter in German, English, and two more Russian editions. As mentioned in the first of the essays above, Peter Shafirov (1669–1739) was a seasoned diplomat in Russian service whom Peter appointed to draw up a theoretical justification of his war against Charles XII and annexation of Baltic lands formerly ruled by Sweden, lands which included the site of his new capital, St. Petersburg. In doing so, Shafirov adduces supposed linguistic and historical evidence as well as Russian dynastic claims, recounts at length an alleged insult to Peter by the Swedish governor of Riga in 1697 (while Peter, incognito, was visiting the city), draws on the developing field of international law, and appeals to Russian pride and self-interest. Shafirov thus provided not only a rationalization of Peter's war against Sweden, but also a Russian version of what might be called the contemporary European "right of empire." It might be stressed that he never once mentions the rights, interests, or wishes of the inhabitants of the territories disputed by the rulers of Sweden and Russia.

Shafirov's relatively modest rhetorical effort is followed by the full-blown classical oratory of Mikhailo Vasilevich Lomonosov (1711–1765), whose career is indicative of important cultural developments in eighteenth-century Russia. Lomonosov, the son of peasants from the Kholmogory region near the White Sea, received a primary education in local church schools and then, pretending to be the son of a priest, in 1731 entered Moscow's Slavonic-Greek-Latin Academy, a Jesuit-like college of liberal arts and theology founded in the 1680s. In 1736 he became a student of the "university" run by the St. Petersburg Academy of Sciences (see Documents, Chapter 3), and was sent to Marburg in Germany to study mining and chemistry. But at Marburg and then at Freiburg he also pursued his study of classical Greek and Roman authors, read contemporary German literature, and traveled extensively, returning home in 1741 with an education that was, for a Russian, truly formidable. Appointed a fellow of the St. Petersburg Academy, he successfully conducted scientific research and rose to become professor of chemistry and a member of the academy's governing board. He also made important contributions to the development of Russian literary scholarship, history, geography, and even art (mosaic), and helped to found Moscow University. Throughout his career he exhibited a strong streak of nativist Russian patriotism, particularly in his frequent polemics with his German colleagues in the St. Petersburg Academy. Perhaps most important in the long range, Lomonosov contributed significantly to the establishment of a standard Russian literary language, one which would subsume and transcend the various idioms and dialects spoken and written in the country. This development—crucial to the emergence of a modern Russian culture and polity—is usually considered to have culminated in the earlier nineteenth century, as exemplified by the works of Alexander Pushkin or N. M. Karamzin (see Documents, Chapter 7).

Lomonosov's career was greatly assisted by the friendship and protection of Ivan Shuvalov, the favorite of Empress Elizabeth mentioned in Chapter 4 (Anisimov essay) and a rich and powerful patron of learning. The speech excerpted here—formally a panegyric in memory of Peter the Great—was delivered by Lomonosov on April 26, 1755, to commemorate Elizabeth's coronation (in 1743). The speech powerfully evokes the official myth of Peter the Great (to whom Lomonosov personally had good reason to be grateful), celebrates Elizabeth's resumption of her father's legacy, and otherwise exudes Russian imperialist nationalism, which is why we include it here.

The last documents of the chapter are connected with the Russian annexation under Catherine II of the Khanate of Crimea, that remnant of the Golden Horde which had been a vassal state of the Ottoman Empire (Turkey) since 1475 and the object of Russian designs since the 1680s. By the Treaty of Kuchuk-Kainardji, marking Russia's victory in the war of 1768–1774 against Turkey, various smaller territories in the Black Sea region were ceded outright to the Russian Empire while the Crimean Khanate, at Russian insistence, became nominally independent. In 1783, on Catherine's orders to Grigory Potemkin, commander of Russian forces in the region and developer of the "New Russia" on the Black Sea, Crimea was simply annexed. With its extensive Black Sea coast (where the Russian naval base of Sevastopol was soon established), balmy climate, vineyards, and old urban centers, Crimea—renamed Taurida to evoke its ancient Greek connections—was a major acquisition for Russia (Catherine rewarded Potemkin himself with the title Prince of Taurida). Its Muslim Tatar inhabitants, who had been emigrating by the thousands to Turkish territory since 1774, were replaced by Russian settlers; remaining Muslims were granted freedom of worship while the Tatar elite was absorbed into the Russian nobility; and the Russian system of local administration as laid down in Catherine's Statute of 1775, with its representative component, was extended to the new province. These developments are reflected in the two documents excerpted below, as is the imperialist thinking of Catherine II and her chief agent in the south.

## P. P. Shafirov
## Justifies the Empire, 1717

. . . The Swedes themselves cannot deny that the [Baltic] provinces of Karelia and Ingria, with all the territories, towns, and places thereto belonging, did of old make part of the Russian Empire; an assertion that is evident from the treaties established and the correspondence maintained from long ago between the Crowns of Russia and Sweden. There is particularly a Treaty kept to this day in the Russian Chancellery [of Foreign Affairs] which was made in the time of Tsar Ivan IV of glorious memory concerning a truce for forty years agreed on between the Governor of Novgorod, according to the custom of those times, and Gustavus I King of Sweden: for in ancient times the kings of Sweden were obliged to negotiate all treaties and to have correspondence only with the governors of Novgorod, the Russian monarchs never deigning to correspond directly with the kings of Sweden, a thing which was first granted in the year 1564. Several other treaties made with Kings Eric, John, and Charles IX [of Sweden] not only prove that the tsars of Russia had the property and possession of the abovesaid provinces, but also that the greater part of the provinces of Livonia and Estonia were under the jurisdiction and protection of the Russian Crown. A plain proof of which is, among other things, that the city of Dorpt (in the Russian language *Iuriev Livonskii*) situated in Livonia was built in the year 1026, according to the testimony of credible Russian chronicles, by the Russian Grand Prince Iaroslav (or George) and called after his name Iuriev, which is as much as to say "George's Town." In the like manner the city of Reval [in Estonia] is called in the Russian chronicles *Kolivan*, which may be interpreted as "Ivan's Town" after the name of a Russian Grand Prince Ivan, who lived in ancient times. . . . Another evident mark of this are the Russian churches of the Grecian [Orthodox] confession in the two cities of Dorpt and Reval, which have been preserved there for many centuries. And though the said provinces sometimes, in troublesome conjunctures, departed from their Russian obedience, yet they were reunited to Russia either by treaties or by force of arms. For instance, in the reign of the Russian Grand Prince Alexander (who was surnamed *Nevskii* on account of a great victory which he obtained [in 1240] on the river *Neva* over King Magnus of Sweden) the province of Livonia, which had thrown off their obedience to him, was reduced to their former allegiance and a yearly tribute was imposed on them.
. . .

But [owing to Russian weakness in the Time of Troubles, 1598–1613] the Tsar's ambassadors then saw themselves under an absolute necessity, in order to save their own country from utter ruin, to consent to a prejudicial and forced peace by which they yielded up to the King of Sweden the abovesaid provinces of Ingria and Karelia with the fortresses and territories thereto belonging, as also the islands at the mouth of the Neva [where St. Petersburg was now located] . . . and to pay

From F. C. Weber, *The Present State of Russia*, vol. 2 (London, 1722), pp. 241–43, 268–74, 296–97, 342, 349–51.

besides to the Crown of Sweden a considerable sum of money. The Swedes by the like unjust means wrested from Russia the provinces of Livonia and Estonia, which formerly had belonged in part to the dominions of the Tsars of Russia and in part had been under their protection and paid tribute to them; they stipulated in this treaty, and made the Russian ambassadors consent to it, that Russia should resign all its pretensions to the said provinces. . . .

In this manner the Crown of Sweden became possessed of the aforesaid provinces contrary to all equity and charity, and against so many pacifications [peace agreements] and defensive alliances, to the irreparable damage of the Russian Empire and the whole nation, not only with relation to trade but, what was of the greatest importance, cutting them [Russia] off from communication with all the states of Europe. After which the Swedish Crown, as a perpetual and inveterate enemy of Russia, has at all times endeavored to keep this nation in perpetual blindness and ignorance with regard to military as well as civil arts and sciences, and to hinder them from attaining any experience by the intercourse with other European nations. . . .

Everyone who is not blinded by passion and animosity will easily conclude and confess that His Majesty Tsar Peter I has in truth had rightful cause, supported by all the laws of the world, to recover those provinces which, with the greatest injustice and in breach of all the pacifications and defensive alliances confirmed by solemn oaths, had been torn off and extorted from his Empire, and by forcible possession withheld for near one hundred years; and that in due satisfaction to the damage thereby occasioned, and for the revenues and contributions drawn out of them for so many years, he was entitled to seize on other provinces likewise unlawfully taken in possession by Sweden. . . .

Should anybody object in justification of Sweden that the said provinces having been yielded up to Sweden by a formal treaty with Russia, it was not just to take the same back from them in violation of said treaty, I answer that, even supposing His Majesty the Tsar had no new causes weighty enough for beginning a war with Sweden, yet there were ancient causes for it sufficiently justifiable for the Laws of Nature and Nations beyond all reproaches of conscience. Nay, he even was obliged, as the Father of his Country, to recover at a fair opportunity the hereditary dominions wrested from his Crown in so unjust a manner. . . ; he was obliged to reunite to his Crown by his just arms a property of which it had been robbed by fraud and all sorts of unfair means, at a time when the Russian Empire was at a very low ebb and on the brink of ruin; more, he was obliged to carry his pretensions beyond that, to obtain satisfaction for the damage and injuries his Crown had suffered. . . . For as great Princes in this world have no superior over them but Almighty God, the great and supreme judge, who, according to his long-suffrance, commonly punishes in the other world transgressions committed here below; every Monarch is bound to defend with arms and force his right and dominions, which he only holds of God, and to oppose force to force on proper occasions, as has been observed ever since the beginning of the world and will be to the end of it. . . .

Now, though all the ancient causes above related would have been weighty and urgent enough for Russia to begin a war with the Crown of Sweden, yet His Majesty the Tsar's equitable mind did not permit him to do it had not Sweden given *new* causes . . . and blown up the fire of old offenses and injuries . . . by a new insult offered to His Majesty's own high Person, which happened [in Riga in March 1697]. . . .

[Moreover, once the war had begun Peter frequently proposed peace.] But the King of Sweden not only refused to hearken to those proposals, his ministers even returned a haughty and insolent answer: the King their master, said they, would not make peace before he had entered the city of Moscow and dethroned His Majesty the Tsar; then he would divide his whole Empire into small principalities and provinces; and in order to weaken the power of Russia, he would oblige them by a treaty to abolish the regular forces and military discipline which [Peter] had introduced after the example of the rest of Europe, to forsake the new fashioned dress introduced by [Peter] for the glory of his nation after the custom of Europe, and to resume their old-fashioned clothes and long beards. . . . The King of Sweden was even so confident his designs could not fail that he already began to dispose of many appointments in the Russian Empire in favor of his generals, in reward for their services. A plain instance of this was General Spar, when he was at Berlin at the house of [a certain Polish officer] in a numerous company, and boasted that he had just received from the King his master letters patent appointing him governor of the city of Moscow, which he actually produced; some of the company indeed congratulated him on that account, but others gave him to understand that the long way to Moscow and the Tsar's numerous army might prove powerful obstacles to his taking possession of that appointment. But he replied, with that haughtiness which at that time was usual to them and made them on all occasions break out into opprobrious language, that they were able to drive the Russian rabble not only out of their own country but even out of the world with no other weapons but their whips. Such scandalous expressions His Majesty the Tsar and the whole Russian nation were obliged not only to hear, but also to read in publick writings. . . .

And so we are persuaded that the gentle reader will have been sufficiently informed by this short treatise for what reasons the war was begun and why it has continued so long, as also who was the cause of it and what conduct has been observed on both sides. But as a war, as long as it lasts, is not very pleasing in itself, and is generally attended with all sorts of hardships and inconveniences, there are many persons found in this country [Russia] who complain of it, and appear malcontent. . . . But we who have been raised to this pitch of glory chiefly by the help and assistance of the Almighty, and next by the wise administration and indefatigable cares of our most gracious Tsar and Lord, who not only has put his land forces on a regular foot and inured them to all the arts of war, but has also raised a fleet of ships and galleys, of which hardly anything was known before in Russia: we, I say, ought not to murmur and show discontent on account of the continuance of the war, but rather bear the weight of it with patience and magnanimity, and use our incessant and utmost efforts, with the help of the Almighty, to bring this war to a period, and to obtain an advantageous and lasting peace.

At the same time let us consider: if by restoring certain places to this enraged neighbor [Sweden] we suffer him to re-establish himself on this side of the Baltic, and to settle in the midst of us, what good can we reasonably expect from him for the future? . . . Should we, without any regard to the glory, honor, and advantages we have obtained, make peace (as the malcontents would have it), what tranquillity can we promise to ourselves? Certainly none at all; we must rather expect all sorts of troubles, calamities, and even the ruin of our own country. . . .

And here I conclude, desiring the gentle reader to give a kind reception to this Discourse which I have drawn up according to my small talent without any show of learning or Oratory, and to be persuaded that every particular in it has been represented according to Truth, as taken from credible authorities and records.

## M. V. Lomonosov Extolls Russian Greatness, 1755

My listeners, as we commemorate the most holy anointing of our most gracious Autocrat [Empress Elizabeth] and Her coronation as Sovereign of the All-Russian state, we behold God's favor to Her and to our common fatherland, favor like unto that at which we marvel in Her birth and in Her coming into possession of Her patrimony. Her birth was made wonderful by omens of empire; Her ascension to the throne is made glorious by courage protected from on high; Her acceptance from the Lord's hand of Her Father's crown and splendid victories is infused with reverential joy. It may be that there are still those who are in doubt whether Rulers are set up on earth by God or whether they obtain their realms through chance; yet in itself the birth of our Great Sovereign compels conviction here, inasmuch as even at that time She had been elected to rule over us. Not the dubious divinations of astrology, based on the position of the planets, nor yet other manifestations or changes in the course of nature, but clear signs of God's Providence shall serve as proof of this. PETER's most glorious victory over His foes at Poltava [1709] took place in the same year as the birth of this Great Daughter of His, and the Conqueror riding in triumph into Moscow was met by the coming into the world of ELIZABETH. Is this not the finger of Providence? Do we not hear a prophetic voice in the mind's ear? Behold, behold the fruition of that bliss promised to us in auguries. PETER triumphed in victory over external enemies and in the extirpation of traitors; ELIZABETH was born for similar triumphs. PETER, having returned the crown to the lawful Sovereign, made His entry into His Father's city; ELIZABETH entered the human community in order that Her father's crown should afterward revert to Her. PETER, having protected Russia from pillage, brought joy, secure and serene, in place of gloomy fear; ELIZABETH saw the light of day that She might pour the sunshine of happiness over us and free us from the gloom of sorrows. PETER led in His train numerous captives, conquered no less by His magnanimity than by His courage; ELIZABETH was delivered from the womb that She might thereafter captivate the hearts of Her subjects with philanthropy, gentleness, and generosity. What wondrous destinies ordained by God do we behold, O ye who hearken to me! Victory together with birth, the delivery of the fatherland with the delivery of the

From Marc Raeff, ed., *Russian Intellectual History: An Anthology* (New York: Harcourt, Brace & World, Inc., 1966), pp. 32–35. Translated by Ronald Hingley.

child from the Mother, the extraordinary triumphal procession and the ordinary rites of birth, swaddling clothes together with triumphal laurels, a baby's first cry mingled with joyous applause and acclamation! Were not all these things an earnest of Her Father's virtues and of Her Father's realm to the child ELIZABETH who was then born?

How much Almighty Providence did lend aid to Her own heroism on the path to the throne is a matter whereof joyous memories shall not grow silent throughout the ages. For it was moved by the power and spirit of Providence that our Heroine brought salvation and renewal to the All-Russian state, to its observed glory, to the great deeds and designs of Peter, to the inner satisfaction of our hearts, and to the general happiness of a large part of the world. . . .

Our Monarch is robed in purple, is anointed for imperial rule, is crowned and receives the Scepter and the Orb. Russians rejoice, filling the air with applause and acclamation. Enemies quail and blench. They slip away, turning their back on the Russian army, hide beyond rivers, mountains, swamps; but everywhere the strong hand of crowned ELIZABETH hems them in; from Her magnanimity alone do they receive relief. How clear are the auguries of Her blessed rule, which we see in all that has been said above, and how we joyously marvel at their longed-for realization! Following the example of Her great progenitor [Peter], she gives crowns to Sovereigns, calms Europe with peaceful arms, consolidates the Russian inheritance. Gold and silver flow out of the bowels of the earth, giving pleasure to Her and to the community; subjects are relieved of their burdens; neither within the realm nor beyond its bounds is the soil stained with Russian blood; the people multiply and revenues increase; magnificent buildings arise; the courts are reformed; the seeds of learning are planted in the state, while everywhere there reign dearly loved peace and quiet and an age which resembles our Monarch Herself.

And so, since our incomparable Sovereign has raised up Her Father's realm as presaged by birth, gained by courage, confirmed by Her triumphant coronation, and adorned by glorious deeds, She is in justice the true Heiress of all His deeds and praise. Therefore in praising PETER we shall praise ELIZABETH. . . .

## Russia Annexes Crimea

### POTEMKIN'S MEMORANDUM TO CATHERINE II
### URGING ANNEXATION, 1780

The Crimea, by its [geographical] position, creates a breach in our borders. Whether the Turks have to be watched along the Bug [river] or on the Kuban [river] side, we always have to worry about the Crimea. Here we can clearly see why the present khan [of the Crimea] does not please the Turks: it is because he will not let them enter through the Crimea into our very heart, so to speak. Now, just imagine that the Crimea is yours and no longer a thorn in your side; suddenly our frontier situation becomes splendid: along the Bug the Turks adjoin us directly and therefore have to deal with us themselves and not use others as a cover. Here we can see every step they take. And as for the Kuban side, in addition to a dense series of forts, manned with garrisons, the numerous Don [Cossack] Host is always in readiness. The security of the population of [New Russia] will then be beyond doubt; navigation on the Black Sea will be free; as it is now, your ships have difficulty in leaving port and find it still harder to enter. In addition, we shall rid ourselves of the difficulties of maintaining the forts we now have in remote outposts in the Crimea. Most Gracious Sovereign! My unbounded devotion to you compels me to speak out: disregard envy, which is powerless to hinder you. It is your duty to exalt the glory of Russia. Look what others have acquired without opposition: France took Corsica; the Austrians, without war, took more from the Turks in Moldavia than we did. There are no powers in Europe that would not divide Asia, Africa, and America among themselves. The acquisition of the Crimea can neither strengthen nor enrich you, but it will give you security. It will be a heavy blow, to be sure, but to whom? To the Turks! a still more compelling reason for you to act. Believe me, you will acquire immortal fame such as no other sovereign of Russia ever had. This glory will open the way to still further and greater glory: with the Crimea will come domination of the Black Sea; it will be in your power to blockade the Turks, to feed them or to starve them. To the [Crimean] khan you may grant anything you choose in Persia; it will keep him happy. He will offer you the Crimea this winter; the population will gladly submit a petition to this effect. Just as the annexation will bring you glory, so will posterity shame and reproach you if continued disturbances lead it to say: "She had the power to act but would not or let the moment slip by." If gentle is thy rule, then Russia needs a paradise. Taurida [Crimea]! [B]ehold how Catherine II shall again bring you the peace of a Christian rule.

## CATHERINE'S MANIFESTO
### PROCLAIMING THE ANNEXATION, 1783

The active experience of many years has given abundant proof that just as the former submission [of the Tatar peoples of the Crimea and Kuban] to the [Ottoman] Porte led to coolness and disputes between the two powers [Russia and Turkey], similarly their reorganization into a free territory, given their inability to enjoy the fruits of this freedom, serves as a constant source of disturbances, losses, and difficulties for our troops. . . .

But now, on the one hand, we must take into consideration the great expenditures consumed on the Tatars and for the Tatars, totaling, by accurate calculation, over twenty million rubles, without counting the loss in human lives which cannot be measured in money; and on the other hand, it has become known to us that the Ottoman Porte is beginning to exercise supreme authority in Tatar territory, to wit, on the island [actually a peninsula] of Taman, where an [Ottoman] official, who had come with troops, ordered to be publicly beheaded an envoy sent to him by [Khan] Shagin-Girei to inquire as to the reason for his arrival, and proclaimed the local inhabitants to be Turkish subjects. This act has nullified our former mutual obligations concerning the freedom and independence of the Tatar peoples; it makes us all the more certain that our assumption at the time of the peace treaty, in making the Tatars independent, is not enough to eliminate all occasions that might arise for disputes over the Tatars; and it restores to us all those rights which we acquired by our victories in the last war and which existed in full force up to the conclusion of peace. And therefore, in keeping with the solicitude incumbent upon us for the welfare and majesty of our fatherland, striving to assure its welfare and security, and likewise looking upon this as a means of eliminating forever the unpleasant causes that disturb the eternal peace concluded between the Russian and Ottoman empires, which we sincerely wish to maintain forever, and no less as compensation and satisfaction for the losses we have suffered, we have decided to take under our dominion the Crimean Peninsula, the island of Taman, and the entire Kuban region [the right bank of the Kuban River].

In proclaiming to the inhabitants of these regions, through this our imperial manifesto, this change in their way of life, we make a sacred and unshakable promise on behalf of ourselves and our successors upon the throne to maintain them on a basis of equality with our hereditary subjects [and] to preserve and defend their persons, property, temples, and ancestral faith, and may the unhindered practice of this faith, with all its lawful ceremonies, remain inviolable; [and we promise] finally, to allow each class among them all those rights and privileges enjoyed by the corresponding [classes] in Russia; in return for which we require and expect from the gratitude of our new subjects that, in their happy change from unrest and confusion to peace, tranquillity, and lawful rule, they will make very effort to liken themselves to our ancient subjects in loyalty, zeal, and moral conduct and to merit alongside of them our monarchical favor and bounty.

## FURTHER READING

Terence Armstrong, *Russian Settlement in the North* (1965)
———, *Yermak's Campaign in Siberia* (1975)
Glynn Barratt, *Russia in Pacific Waters, 1715–1825* (1981)
Roger P. Bartlett, *Human Capital: The Settlement of Foreigners in Russia, 1762–1804* (1979)
Basil Dmytryshyn, E. A. P. Crownhart-Vaughan, and Thomas Vaughan, eds. and trans., *To Siberia and America: Three Centuries of Russian Eastward Expansion* [1558–1867], 3 vols. (collection of documents; vol. 1 covers period 1558–1700; vol. 2, 1700–1797) (1985–1989)
Alton S. Donnelly, *The Russian Conquest of Bashkiria, 1552–1740: A Case Study in Imperialism* (1968)
Alan Fisher, *The Crimean Tatars* (1978)
———, *The Russian Annexation of the Crimea, 1778–1783* (1970)
Charles J. Halperin, *Russia and the Golden Horde* (1985)
Henry R. Huttenbach, "Muscovy's Conquest of Muslim Kazan and Astrakhan" and "Muscovy's Penetration of Siberia," chapters in Michael Rywkin, ed., *Russian Colonial Expansion to 1917* (1988), pp. 45–102

Michael Khodarkovsky, *Where Two Worlds Met: The Russian State and the Kalmyk Nomads, 1600–1771* (1992)

Walther Kirchner, ed. and trans., *A Siberian Journey: The Journal of Hans Jakob Fries, 1774–1776* (1974)

John D. Klier, *Russia Gathers Her Jews: The Origins of the Jewish Question in Russia, 1772–1825* (1986)

Zenon E. Kohut, *Russian Centralism and Ukrainian Autonomy: Imperial Absorption of the [Ukrainian] Hetmanate, 1760s–1830s* (1988)

George V. Lantzeff and Richard A. Pierce, *Eastward to Empire: Exploration and Conquest on the Russian Open Frontier, to 1750* (1973)

Janet Martin, *Treasure of the Land of Darkness: The Fur Trade and Its Significance for Medieval Russia* (1986)

David Morgan, *The Mongols* (1987)

Jaroslaw Pelenski, *Russia and Kazan: Conquest and Imperial Ideology (1438–1560s)* (1974)

Stanford Shaw, *History of the Ottoman Empire and Modern Turkey*, vol. 1: *Empire of the Gazis: The Rise and Decline of the Ottoman Empire, 1280–1808* (1976)

# The Nineteenth Century

Peasants in their village, probably a few years
after the abolition of serfdom by Alexander II.

# Apogee of Empire

R ussia was ruled in the first half of the nineteenth century by
two sons of Emperor Paul, who was assassinated in 1801: Emperors Alexander I (1801–1825) and Nicholas I (1825–1855). The period of their remarkably long and stable rule is considered by most
historians the apogee of the Russian Empire: a period of great international power and prestige, thanks to Russia's leading role in the defeat of Napoleon (1812–1815), and of relative domestic peace and
prosperity. But appearances are often deceiving, as the essays that follow make clear. And Russia's defeat in the Crimean War (1854–1855)
would reveal how far the Empire had fallen behind its European rivals, not only in military terms but in political, economic, and social
development as well.

## E SSAYS

Alexander Radishchev, as mentioned in Chapter 5, was severely punished by the
government of Catherine II for advocating an end to autocracy in Russia and the
establishment of an English-style constitutional monarchy. Catherine's grandson, Alexander I, liberally educated under her personal direction, came to the throne with similar
ideas. Or did he? Professor Raeff addresses this question in the following excerpt from
his classic study of the enigmatic Alexander's "most outstanding" advisor and assistant
(and sometime friend of Radishchev), Michael (Mikhail M.) Speransky (1772–1839).
Although little concrete reform actually resulted from Speransky's labors for Alexander
I, this son of a village priest, in Raeff's words, "left a profound mark on the attitudes
and practices of the Imperial administration and helped to create the framework
within which the social, economic, and administrative changes of the 1860s [the Great
Reforms] were to take place." Moreover, one of Speransky's projects, the codification—at last—of existing Russian law, *was* completed under Nicholas I, in 1830: this
was the *Complete Collection of Laws of the Russian Empire* (or PSZ), various extracts
from which were printed in the preceding chapters of this book. We should also note
that a more recent study of Speransky's *draft* proposals to Alexander (see article by John
Gooding, Further Reading below) suggests that he was not the believer in enlightened
absolutism depicted by Raeff but a genuine constitutionalist who had to disguise his
liberal views as he struggled to convince Alexander, ultimately without success, of the
need for fundamental reform. Speransky, in short, was a covert Decembrist.

The Decembrists were Russian army officers who conspired to stage an uprising in December 1825, at the time of Nicholas I's accession, in the name of peasant emancipation and the founding of a constitutional order in Russia with basic civil rights for all. The uprising was a miserable failure; 579 officers were arrested, of whom 426 were punished (five were executed). But the whole affair made a profound impression on the new emperor, a point emphasized by Nicholas V. Riasanovsky in these excerpts from his book on the ideology behind the rigid and reactionary "Nicholaevan system." Professor Riasanovsky, of the University of California at Berkeley, provides here both a lively portrait of Nicholas himself and a succinct assessment of his reign, which is generally considered to mark the apogee of the Russian autocracy.

# The "Constitutionalism" of Alexander I

## Marc Raeff

Rarely had an Emperor's death been greeted with more unabashed joy and happiness than the sudden end of Paul I on the night of March 11–12, 1801. While the Imperial family (in particular Paul's widow and his son, Alexander, the new Emperor) experienced a grief that was inextricably mixed with the pangs of a bad conscience,[1] the capital celebrated exuberantly. The four years of Paul's reign had been well-nigh and uninterrupted nightmare for Russian "society" in general, and for the officers and officials in the capital in particular. The Emperor's odd caprices, manias, inconsistencies, and his outbursts of uncontrolled rage had kept the country trembling with fear. Getting ready for their tour of duty, officers always took extra money with them, for Paul's dissatisfaction or sudden impulse might turn into an order to march off to Siberia directly from the Parade Grounds. The Monarch's suspiciousness in regard to his imperial and personal dignity (too long kept insecure by his mother, Catherine II), knew no bounds and manifested itself in the most obnoxious and silly ways. At his approach in the street, everybody was required to dismount or step off the carriage and curtsy; to underscore the distance between himself and other mortals, Paul forbade the inhabitants of St. Petersburg to harness more than two horses to their carriages. His hatred of the French Revolution led to a meticulous regulation of dress: round hats, long trousers, various feminine clothing accessories, reminiscent of French innovations in the domain of fashion, were banned under heavy penalties. To prevent the spread of harmful ideas from entering his realm, Paul closed the borders to printed material, including musical scores, forbade the use of certain foreign words, and kept his subjects from traveling abroad.

From Marc Raeff, *Michael Speransky, Statesman of Imperial Russia* (The Hague: Martinus Nijhoff, 1957), pp. 29–46. Reprinted by permission of the author.

1. Paul had been murdered—evidently with Alexander's knowledge, if not approval.—Ed.

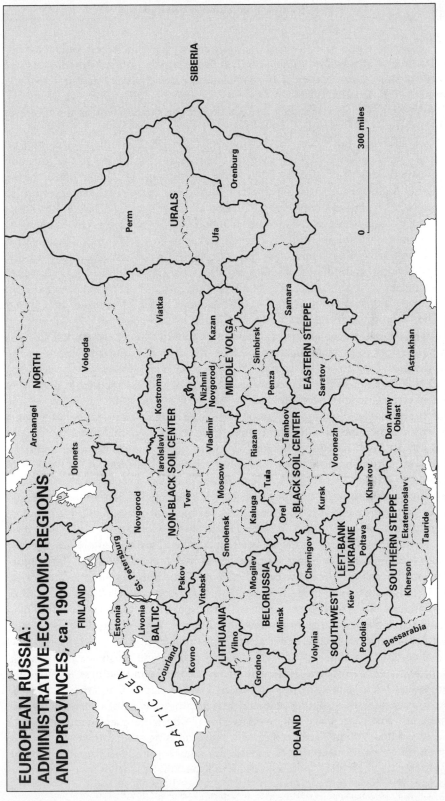

Map of European Russia drawn by B. Nelson for Seymour Becker's *Nobility and Privilege in Late Imperial Russia.*
©1985 by Northern Illinois University Press. Used with permission of the publisher.

These and other bothersome petty restrictions would have been only a superficial source of annoyance or grievance had Paul's regime satisfied the interests and needs of the various classes of the population, particularly the nobility. But the Emperor was so much taken up with the minutiae of military life (paradomania, Prince Adam Czartoryski called it) that he left the government at the mercy of ill-chosen and often changed favorites. . . . Foreign policy was conducted with a cavalier disregard for what, in the reign of Catherine II, had been considered Russia's vital national interests, and diplomacy was subordinated to the romantic infatuations and caprices of the Emperor (as for instance, his championship of the Order of Malta). Paul's actions, especially in the first years of his reign, seemed to be dictated less by any purposeful conception of policy than by his intense personal craving to undo whatever his mother had done. This spirit of contradiction, raised to the status of "statesmanship," resulted in an even greater disorder in affairs than had been usual in Russia up to that time. It completely undermined the continuity, purposefulness, and stability of policy which Catherine II had finally succeeded in bringing about by a judicious use of "public opinion" and of the force of tradition. Oblivious and scornful of the feelings of his subjects, Paul I revoked the Charter of the Nobility [and] the Charter of the Towns, and inflicted serious damage [on] Russian trade by his break with England on account of Malta, which in truth was of no concern to Russia. Emperor Paul had at least one good intention, to set the maximum of the corvé [barshchina: labor dues] at three days a week. However, incapable and unwilling to enforce this measure, he did not succeed in improving the wretched condition of the serfs, while at the same time he increased the nobility's anger and sulking opposition. It seemed that Paul had a talent for doing everything to displease and harm those who counted in the state. In fact, he distrusted a "free" nobility residing in its estates, away from his immediate supervision and running its own affairs without government direction and control. Paul wanted to return to an earlier tradition which saw in the nobleman exclusively a servant of the state. To the Emperor's mind, every ablebodied nobleman should serve in the army, and if physically disabled, in the civil government. He therefore forcibly impressed noblemen into service, in direct violation of the Charters of 1761 and 1785 which had "forever" freed the nobility from compulsory state service. Naturally, having once tasted the benefits of freedom from service, the nobility was unwilling to see the clock turned back half a century. The nobles would not easily let go their hard-won privileges and "corporate status." Paul's disregard of the interests of the nobility, coupled with the superficial annoyances with which he beset his officers and courtiers, proved too much. By 1800 already, the violent end of the reign was a foreseeable conclusion.

The four years of imperial terror served as catalytic agent for the political maturation of the Russian nobility. The seeds of political consciousness, in a Western sense, had been planted in their minds by the policies of Catherine II and the penetration of French philosophic and literary works. It is, of course, quite true that Catherine's engoûment [infatuation] with the Enlightenment and liberalism à la Diderot and Voltaire had been mere window dressing and propaganda. Yet, her intention to give Russia a clear and orderly administration, consistent with the requirements of progress and civilization and the Empire's newly won position in Europe, had been genuine enough. In any case, both the propaganda and the practical efforts at "modern" legislation had greatly influenced the educated portions of the nobility. The glory and prosperity of her reign had enhanced the prestige of the tenets of the Enlightenment, and it established in many minds a direct connection between the country's progress and the implementation of Western ideologies in Russia. The excesses of the French Revolution turned many a Russian "liberal" aristocrat from the radical consequences of the [Enlightenment], but they could not, and did not, destroy the newly gained beliefs and social consciousness. Repelled by the extremism and brutality of the French course, the Russian nobility turned to the example provided by England. In England the "progressive" aristocracy of Russia found an impressive respect for a gentleman's liberty and dignity, and it could also observe how the "best" men participated in the administration of county and country.

At the time of Catherine's death in 1796, the educated nobleman who served and lived in St. Petersburg or Moscow was thoroughly conscious of his dignity and worth as an individual; he had come a long way from the timidity and cringiness of his forebears, the servants—*kholopy* [literally, "slaves"]—of the Tsars of Moscow. Now, he expected the government to treat him like a human being; he believed that he was entitled to feel secure in his life and property. But not alone as an individual had the educated Russian nobleman achieved self-respect and dignity, he also considered himself a member of the first "estate" (*soslovie*) of the realm—an estate that had earned a privileged position by its distinguished services to the crown. By the Charter of 1785 the nobility had received some degree of autonomy in the management of its [corporate] affairs, and the Statute on the Provinces [Local Administration] of 1775 had assigned it an important role. . . . Was this not telling proof of the monarch's recognition of the nobility's ability to take care of itself, to attend to the needs of its estate without harm to the interests of the state? And it does not really matter for our present purposes whether this privileged status had been wrung from the state by the nobility's own efforts or whether Catherine II had given it as a "sop" to insure the government's centralized and bureaucratic control of all really important matters of national policy.[2] Whatever its origin, the nobles interpreted their new status as evidence of their social and political maturity. Paul's regime presented a mortal danger to this newly gained social consciousness and individual self-esteem.

In the light of this situation, the almost indecent joy which greeted the news of Paul's violent demise becomes quite understandable. The exhilaration reached a higher pitch yet when Alexander's proclamation of accession promised a return to the principles of his grandmother, the great Catherine. All shared the belief that Paul's course of arbitrariness and despotism was abandoned forever, and this belief found its strongest and most articulate expression among the upper ranks of the nobility. The old dignitaries of Catherine's time, supported by the aristocracy—the greatest and perhaps exclusive beneficiaries of the policy pursued by the Empress—wished to secure firmly the privileges of the first estate of the Empire. In their opinion, the principles of the Enlightenment—in their English form—should

---

2. As he indicates elsewhere, Raeff favors the latter explanation.—Ed.

be put into practice for the benefit of the upper rungs of the nobility. The catchword which summarized and symbolized these aspirations was the term "constitution," or, in more careful mouths, "fundamental laws" and "fundamental institutions." The future for the realization of these aspirations looked very bright and hopeful indeed, for did not the young ruler, Alexander I, share these desires and did he not intend to give "fundamental laws" which would put Russia on an equal footing with the civilized nations of Western Europe and prevent the recurrence of the despotism of a madman? In Russia where everything depended on the will and preference of the ruler, Alexander's alleged sympathy with these aims was a good omen. Strengthened by his "people's" enthusiastic love and loyalty, the young Emperor could lead his country to a new future in satisfying the aspirations and desires of his subjects.

Alexander's charm, youth, and sincere idealism held out the promise that the optimistic hopes of even the most ardent and enthusiastic advocates of fundamental reforms would not be disappointed. The approval he had apparently given to the removal, although not the murder, of his despotic father was viewed as a pledge of his loyalty to the interests of Russian society. The young sovereign's seeming liberalism did not come as a surprise, for Catherine had entrusted the education of her preferred grandchild to the liberal, enlightened, and virtuous Swiss republican, La Harpe. Young Alexander's confidences to La Harpe and to his friends, the Polish "hostage" Adam Czartoryski and Count Victor Kochubei, soon became known, at least in their general tenor. To Kochubei Grand Duke Alexander had confided that his only ambition was to give a constitution to Russia and then spend the remainder of his days in rustic retirement on the banks of the Rhine. To the astonished Czartoryski the heir presumptive of the most autocratic state had declared his "hatred of despotism, wherever and by whatever manner it was exercised and that he loved liberty, that liberty was owed equally to all men." At another time the Grand Duke surprised, and embarrassed, his Polish friend by asking him to write the draft of a proclamation of accession which would embody their liberal ideals. One of Alexander's first acts when he acceded to the throne was to recall to his side his "liberal" friends whom Paul's suspicion and dislike had driven from St. Petersburg. With these friends the young Emperor regularly consulted on the problems of government. Although they were not appointed to any official position, they formed an "Unofficial Committee" to consider, discuss, and work on a reorganization of the administration. All this seemed to justify the country's hopeful optimism that Russia was about to enter a new era.

How sincere was Emperor Alexander about his constitutional plans? This question has been the subject of much debate and agrument among historians. A definitive solution of the debate cannot be our purpose here. But for a proper understanding of the setting in which Speransky was to work, we must obtain some knowledge of the Emperor's attitude toward governmental reforms. . . . [And] we must first make sure that we have a proper understanding of the term "constitution" as it was used by Alexander and his friends. Did this key word have the same meaning for them as it did for the high dignitaries of Catherine's time, or for the Decembrists, or for the "progressive" and liberal scholars who wrote the history of this period? The most convenient way of determining Alexander's "definition" is to analyze his reaction to some of the plans of administrative reorganization and reform that were submitted to him in the first years of his reign.

No sooner had Paul I been laid to rest than many high officials and dignitaries from Catherine's times voiced their views on Russia's political organization. In spite of some variations of detail, these voices belonged to a rather homogeneous group composed of "elder statesmen" whose thinking revolved around a reform of the Senate. For the sake of brevity we might call this the "senatorial party." The group commanded the young Emperor's attention and respect not only because its members were influential and experienced administrators, but also because it had the support of the most active participants in the palace revolution of March 11, 1801 [which brought Alexander to power]. The senatorial party advocated the return to the traditions of Catherine II, as promised in [Alexander's] Proclamation of Accession and enthusiastically welcomed by the nobility. The senatorial group could, therefore, claim to speak with the authority of a "public opinion" whose support the young ruler needed and craved. Prodded by it, Alexander asked the Senate to redefine its powers and functions and to present a plan for its reorganization. The Senate complied readily, and several of its members drafted proposals whose contents were eventually consolidated into one paper . . . and submitted to the Emperor. At the same time, several high dignitaries close to the Senate . . . drafted a charter to the Russian people which they intended to have promulgated at the coronation of Alexander I.

In spite of some differences in detail, the members of the senatorial party pursued the same aims. They proposed to give the dominant role in the government to the higher nobility by reestablishing the Senate (or . . . an enlarged Council of State) as the highest executive organ and by granting it a consultative voice and limited power of initiative in the legislative process. In addition, the Charter for the Russian People guaranteed to the Emperor's subjects, and specifically to the nobility, legal safeguards which would protect their life and property against the arbitrary caprices of the monarch's bureaucracy. The Senators (or Councillors of State) were to be selected among the high dignitaries of the realm; and, in addition, perhaps—at a later stage—a few noblemen from each province might be appointed by the government upon recommendation of the Governor. The important function assigned to the Senate was the supervision of the administration and the execution of the decrees and edicts, seeing to it that no bureaucrat violated the basic laws and privileges of the nation. The actual task of legislation remained, as in the past, in the hands of the Emperor and his immediate advisers, but the Senate would have a "droit de remontrance" [right of appeal]. In this manner, without specifically restricting the absolute power of the monarch, the Senate would obtain effective means for safeguarding the "fundamental laws" of the realm; that is, the rights and privileges of the various classes of the Russian people, most particularly of course, those of the nobility. These proposals were quite clearly the basis for an aristocratic, oligarchic, "constitution."

Although these projects did not abolish absolutism in Russia outright, they were frankly following the example of those Western European states where by securing a dominant political position, the nobility had been successful in checking the excesses of a monarchy's bureaucratic absolutism. The implicit reasoning of the

Senatorial party was that the security and liberty of a *Rechtsstaat* [state of laws] could best be brought about in Russia by first securing intangible rights and privileges for one class of the nation. Eventually these rights and privileges—legally guaranteed and protected by the Senate—could be extended to other classes as well. The history of England, and perhaps Sweden, seemed to them a telling example of the benefits of such an evolution.

We should not dismiss these proposals as merely unabashed selfish "class" legislation. Undeniably, compared to the direction political thought and practice had taken in the West since 1789, the program of the Senatorial party does seem "reactionary," designed to protect a social class that appeared on its way out. But we should not forget that Russia was behind Western Europe in its political and social evolution. And at least we can recognize that the Senatorial party had "historical logic," if there be such a thing, on its side. The *Rechtsstaat* and representative institutions had originated in the West in a way that was not unlike that suggested by the [Senatorial party]; political and legal privileges had first been granted, or won, to one "estate," the nobility, and circumstances later forced their extension to other groups of society. In the meantime, the rights and privileges of one class kept monarchical absolutism and bureaucratic arbitrariness within bounds; the monarchy had been weakened in its ability to resist the extension of these rights and privileges; and an important segment of the population had had the experience of political responsibility. The classical illustration of such an evolution was of course England; but even France under the Ancien Régime [before the 1789 Revolution] had partaken of this trend, and so had Sweden and Prussia. All of this, naturally, does not mean to say that the program of the Senatorial group was the only or even the best approach to Russia's political and social problems. But inasmuch as Russia's most pressing need was the establishment of a firm rule of law, this approach promised success in a country where only the upper nobility was prepared to participate actively in political life.

Emperor Alexander, however, either rejected the proposals out of hand . . . or restricted their scope to such an extent that he rendered them practically meaningless (for example, the decree on the powers of the Senate, 1802). This reaction did not come as a result of the Emperor's realization of the true meaning and potential implications of the proposals. He had neither the necessary theoretical knowledge nor sufficient political experience for that. The projects of the Senatorial party were distasteful to Alexander for three main reasons. In the first place, imbued with the "esprit de système" of the 18th century, he had a fundamental dislike of anything that might give exceptional status to a group or a class. For this reason he was unreceptive to any suggestion which was not derived from abstract general principles and which would not result in a clear, logical and neat system of organization. He was not to be impressed by appeals to historical traditions and precedents and hoped to base all his actions on grounds of natural reason alone. In this sense, and in spite of his later emotional and religious development, Alexander remained faithful to 18th century anti-historicist rationalism. In the second place, and subjectively this was a more weighty reason, he was naturally suspicious of an aristocracy which had just overthrown an Emperor [Paul] and might do it again if given the power and opportunity. Lastly, and most important of all, despite his professed liberalism and republicanism, Alexander was very jealous of his autocratic power and prerogatives.

The Emperor's jealousy of his power took numerous and varied forms as Alexander was very quick to detect and react to anything that might be interpreted as a challenge to his position and will. As early as the times of the Unofficial Committee (1801–1803), the "honeymoon" of the young sovereign's liberalism, Count Stroganov noted that Alexander became very stubborn as soon as anyone disagreed with his preferences, so that it was best not to try to convince him by direct argument and open discussion, but rather bring up the subject later in an indirect way. Every time a concrete plan for the reorganization of the government along more "constitutional" lines was proposed, Alexander delayed his decision, refused to implement it, and eliminated everything that might even remotely constitute a restriction of his prerogatives. [An incident] in the Senate [in 1802] was a very clear and dramatic illustration of Alexander's [inconsistent] attitude to a . . . literal implementation of the rights he himself had granted to the Senate [earlier] in 1802. And later still, after he had given a constitution to the Kingdom of Poland in 1815, he refused to conform to it and constantly violated its provisions and principles. . . . In 1816, when a group of high dignitaries and noblemen dared to request permission to coordinate their actions in liberating their serfs, under provisions of the law on Free Agriculturists (1803), the Emperor bluntly reminded them that he alone would decide if any coordinated action was to be taken and that he did not need anyone's advice on how to rule. Alexander's suspicion of anyone who might conceivably oppose his autocratic will was almost pathological. He had all dignitaries and even members of his own family shadowed by the police; to make sure of the police, his personal secret agents spied on the police. Anyone as concerned about the preservation of his power and prestige was not very likely to accept constitutional limitations on his will. And as a matter of record, he never did.

And yet, all his life and throughout his reign, Alexander talked about giving a constitution to his peoples; he established commissions and committees to draft constitutional reforms, he asked his friends and his ministers to submit proposals of constitutions. If the projects of the Senatorial party were not due to the initiative of the Emperor, almost all others were. Besides discussing reforms with the Unofficial Committee, Alexander sought suggestions and advice from [Thomas] Jefferson and [Jeremy] Bentham [the English liberal philosopher]. In 1814 he ordered the Baltic German Baron Rosenkampf, newly arrived in St. Petersburg, to write a constitution—much to Rosenkampf's surprise and against his will and better judgment. A similar offer made to Freiherr vom Stein was rejected by the Prussian statesman; in 1809 came Speransky's plan. This interest in constitutions did not disappear during the so-called "reactionary" period of Alexander's reign, i.e., after 1812 and the Congress of Vienna [1815]. At the opening of the Polish Sejm [parliament] in 1818, the Emperor expressed his hope that he still would be able to give a constitution to his Russian lands too. And after General Balashev's experiment with a reform of the regional administration (1816) came the project of a Charter written by Novosiltsev (1820). To the very end of his life, Alexander kept thinking about constitutional reforms and projects, as witness his words [to this effect] to Karamzin on the eve of his departure to Taganrog in August 1825.[3] This consistent interest which verges on obsession goes a long way to disprove the opinion held by some historians that his constitutionalism was only a youthful infatuation, a romantic pipe dream which evaporated soon after his accession. It further provides evidence that, contrary to the belief held by many in the 1820's, the Emperor had not turned away from his earlier intentions of reform under the influence of mysticism, the reactionary counsels of [the Austrian minister, Prince] Metternich, or the brutal militarism of [his assistant] Arakcheev.

    Was then Alexander's persistent toying with constitutional changes a hypocritical sham? Or perhaps was it only due to his meek yielding to the pressures of public opinion and the stronger wills of his advisers? Historians have now discredited the legend, which originated in his own lifetime, that Alexander was a weak person, easily influenced by his entourage. As a matter of fact, modern research and the publication of new documents at the beginning of this century have clearly shown that some of the policies which had been attributed to outside influences . . . had been Alexander's own. More often than not, the Emperor pursued their implementation in the teeth of the most stubborn resistance and opposition of his family, ministers, and even favorite friends.[4] If Alexander was not an influenceable weakling, can we explain the apparent contradiction by pointing to his duplicity, his habit of "wearing" a different face for each one who approached him? At times it is asserted in the literature on the subject that the Emperor wore a mask of liberalism to conciliate "public opinion" and to gain popularity. But we have pointed out that too often he went against this opinion and that he did not fear loss of popularity. To believe in Alexander's duplicity about constitutionalism is to read his entire reign in the light of the "reactionary" measures of the 1820's and to forget that even then he was still thinking of constitutional reform. If we must speak of Alexander's duplicity, we should first get away from the dichotomy of liberal vs. reactionary. From his earliest days the Emperor had been put in a situation which required tactful diplomatic maneuvering, caught as he was between the demands of his grandmother and the duty he owed to his father. To hide his thoughts and to evade direct answers became second nature to him; even as autocratic ruler, when he met with strong opposition to his plans, he rarely met the issue head on, but preferred to reach his ends in a roundabout way. This went well with his jealous concern for his power, his desire to appear friendly and well disposed to all. Rather than defend openly his position, rather than show his dislike or distrust of a person

---

3. Alexander died in faraway Taganrog, on the Black Sea, in November 1825.—Ed.
4. Reference to two instances may suffice here. . . . Alexander followed his own policy of "friendship" with Napoleon . . . in spite of the strong opposition of his own mother, most of his ministers, the Court, the nobility, and the people. [However] in 1812 he refused to negotiate with Napoleon as long as the French [invaders] were on Russian territory, and resisted all pleas for peace [from] his mother, his brother, and courtiers. And after 1815, Alexander I was alone responsible for the creation and operation of the military colonies [in Russia]. He insisted on their establishment and continuation even though Arakcheev advocated their abolition after the high cost and difficulties of the project had become apparent.

frankly, he resorted to back-stage intrigues and maneuvers. This evasiveness and indirectness coupled with suspicious distrust for his closest advisers created the impression of vacillation, [of] weakness. The Emperor seemed to pursue different, contradictory policies one after another. And while it is quite true that Alexander rarely had the patience and energy to apply his mind to the exacting task of implementing his plans completely and well, he did not waver as much in his basic principles as might appear from a superficial acquaintance with the facts of his reign. Behind the changeability and indirectness of means, there was a stubborn persistence of purpose. Duplicity and weakness are not the answer, and to discover the meaning the concept of constitution had for Alexander we must look in another direction.

The answer lies in the very contents the Emperor put into the term constitution. His idea of what "constitution" should imply was shared by many other personalities of the time—the . . . members of the Unofficial Committee, for one example—although they were at times willing to carry its implications further than was the monarch. As Alexander and his friends were neither experienced jurists nor learned in political philosophy, they did not state their definition of the term anywhere explicitly, unambiguously, or fully. However, the meaning they attached to the term can be inferred from scattered comments and the "twist" they gave their reform proposals. It will perhaps be easier to begin with what they did *not* mean by the term constitution [italics added]. They did not have in mind that meaning of the term which gained currency after 1815, particularly in the 1820's, and which substantially is the meaning we still give it today. When about 1820 the future Decembrists, for instance, spoke of constitution, they referred to the concepts and traditions which had their origin in English parliamentarism and which found formal and extreme expression in the written constitutions of the American and French revolutions. Constitution then meant a written document clearly stating the sources and character of political sovereignty, guaranteeing the basic rights of all citizens, establishing the mechanism of a representative parliamentary government, and, most important, confining the executive to a position subordinate to that of the elected legislative power. Neither Alexander I nor the members of the Unofficial Committee subscribed to this definition of constitution.

What they called constitution should perhaps be termed "fundamental principles of administrative organization." The term constitution conveyed to them the idea of an orderly system of government and administration, free from the caprices and demoralizing tyranny of arbitrariness. To give Russia a constitution, therefore, implied bringing clarity and order to the administration and basing the relationship between the government and the individual subject on the rule of law. The issues of popular sovereignty, "no taxation without representation," the doctrine of separation and balance of powers were of no direct concern to the Autocrat of [All Russia] and his chosen advisers. And while they spoke in terms of the concepts that had gained popularity and currency in the latter part of the 18th century, they applied them to a different situation and gave them a different twist from that in Western Europe or America. The most striking instance of this change was their use of the idea of separation of powers. Montesquieu and other 18th-century writers, following Aristotle, and on the basis of their interpretation of the English "constitution," had maintained that the executive, legislative and judiciary had to be kept separate in terms of personnel, authority, [and] jurisdiction, so that none of them could monopolize all the political power in the state. But while using the same terms, the Unofficial Committee and Alexander meant only the mechanical division of functions of government for the sake of more efficient and orderly administration.

The primordial concern for order and clarity in the administrative machinery becomes quite evident when we read Count Stroganov's notes of the meetings of the Unofficial Committee and the various proposals for reform discussed there. This excessive stress on clarity and mechanistic harmony of the administration was far greater than the objective situation of the Russian government demanded; after all, the Senatorial party also aimed at improving the administration and yet in their projects there was never so much emphasis on order and clarity. The reason for this stress on mechanical harmony is to be sought in the intellectual habits of the Emperor and his entourage. True to the *esprit de système* and the belief in mechanical laws of nature, no institutional structure appeared good to them unless it was composed of discreet, separate elements which functioned according to laws based on the dictates of logic and natural reason. Everything not essential to such a simple and orderly structure had to be eliminated, for it stifled the efficient working of the *machine* of government. In this respect Alexander and his friends were not so much the disciples of Montesquieu and Blackstone (as in a sense Catherine II had been) but of Bentham and the authors of the several French constitutions. In a sense too, this approach facilitated the development of an enlightened absolutism helped by a responsible and well controlled bureaucracy. . . .

In regard to the Emperor himself, an additional personality trait contributed to his insistence on orderliness, clarity and a well defined mechanical hierarchy of government institutions. Alexander I, as well as his younger brothers, had inherited his grandfather's and father's worship of the external trappings of army life. . . . Whatever the sincerity of Alexander's filial feelings, in one respect he was a convinced and admiring son of his father: the minutiae of army administration, daily drill, military ceremonial and parades, [and] uniforms absorbed Alexander's interest as much as they had Paul's. Throughout his adult life Emperor Alexander preferred to devote his time to military details, even to the neglect of his other duties. He could spend hours on end drilling the regiments of the guard in preparation for a parade; in St. Petersburg he never missed the daily ceremony of the relief of the guard at the palace; often did a courier or minister wait with an urgent message or report until the Emperor had finished studying the details of a new uniform. Admittedly, not all of this concern was vain and useless[;] Alexander did a great deal to modernize the army and make it into a more efficient fighting force. His mania for military regulations and detailed prescriptions found its most complete expression in the notorious Military Colonies which he established in the 1820's under the supervision of Count Arakcheev. No doubt, this predilection for detailed regimentation, order, and hierarchical organization also influenced his approach to the problems of government. Infatuated with the perfect discipline, mechanical simplicity, [and] orderly hierarchy of military organization, he wanted to see the same traits prevail in the administration of his Empire.

The Emperor's understanding of the term constitution implied the rejection of all those features of a nation's life rooted in historical tradition and precedent, which did not develop in a very orderly or logical way and whose manifestations were not amenable to rigid bureaucratic control. In a sense, his mechanistic approach, directly derived from the precepts of Enlightened Absolutism, stood in direct contrast to the "organistic," historical approach of the Senatorial party, with its emphasis on the autonomous development of estates and institutions. Alexander and his friends were, therefore, receptive to borrowings from Napoleonic models and such imitation in turn served to reinforce the elements of enlightened bureaucratic absolutism contained in their plans. The results of their labors illustrated this bureaucratic bent very clearly: they rejected the principle of collegiate rule, which under Russian conditions—as even Speransky admitted later—had a great deal to recommend itself, and they gave their preference to monocratic ministries (1802). [This] paved the way to a more intensive bureaucratization of the Russian government on the model of the army. The ministers, like staff officers of a commander, were responsible to their chief, the Emperor, only individually. On the provincial level, the governors, directly appointed by the Emperor, were subordinated to the ministers, and became the local agents of execution of a highly centralized, paramilitary hierarchy. Quite naturally, throughout the reign of Alexander I, we witness an increasing monopolization of power and influence by governors and ministers, at the expense of the few institutions which could claim to represent the estates of the realm, as for example, the Senate, the marshals of the nobility, assemblies of the nobility, city assemblies and mayors. In turn, reliance on a centralized and hierarchical bureaucracy led the Unofficial Committee to stress the need of preserving the autocratic power of the Emperor. Indeed, only the absolute power of a well-meaning, enlightened autocrat could bring about the necessary reforms in the face of a passive, or even unfriendly, nation. . . .

[A] negative attitude towards the nobility as an "estate" gave further grounds for Alexander's belief in the leadership of a bureaucracy expressing the autocratic power and will of an enlightened sovereign. It points to a fundamental conception of political power, a conception which . . . runs as a guiding thread through the actions of the imperial government during the period of Speransky's activity. . . .

In passing, let us note two further characteristic traits of the Unofficial Committee's method. . . . First of all, the Committee laid down as an intangible rule and principle that all reforms were to be introduced in such a manner that there could be no doubt of their expressing only the will of the Emperor, and not that of any "party" or private interest. Secondly, the measures of reorganization were to be prepared in strict secrecy, without the participation of "society" and "public opinion" and issued all at once as the new and intangible law of the realm. A far cry from the truly "liberal" and constitutional approach in the West! It is interesting to observe also that in spite of their alleged partiality for things English, the Unofficial Committee found the best expression of their aims and the clearest statement of their purpose in the "constitution" of Prussia: an absolute monarchy ruling with the help of an efficient bureaucracy according to clearly defined laws which assured the security, life, property and freedom of economic action of the individual citizen.

The answer to our question, what was the meaning of Alexander's constitution-alism, is therefore quite clear. The Emperor and his close advisers in the Unofficial Committee defined constitution as the rule of law, and the clear, logical, hierarchical organization of the administration. Law, order, [and a] clear structure [for] the political machine were the contents they put into such words as constitution, fundamental laws, etc. At no time did they mean representative institutions, checks and balances, abolition of the autocracy—even though these might have been the long-range dream, to come true for other generations; this conception and definition prevailed throughout the entire government career of Speransky.

True enough, such an approach might conceivably have brought about a true constitutional—in the modern sense—development. In this belief many "progres-sive" and truly liberal individuals in the 19th century in Russia spent all their energies in the service of an autocratic government. But today—with the superior benefit of hindsight—we can say that the hopes for such an evolution were doomed to failure as long as Russia's political transformation was directed by an all-powerful bureaucracy and at the mercy of the whim of an absolute ruler, with no social group or class strong enough to put a check on their despotism.

## The Supreme Commander: Nicholas I

### Nicholas V. Riasanovsky

Two images stand out in the numerous [contemporary] descriptions of Nicholas I: his physical beauty and his majestic bearing, the two blending perfectly to produce one overwhelming impression. Friend and foe alike were affected by the powerful presence of the emperor, and some were smitten by it. A lady in waiting spoke of him as a "terrestrial divinity." A Prussian officer extolled his physical qualities. The great poet [Alexander] Pushkin compared Nicholas to Moses. La Ferronnays, the French ambassador, could not control his enthusiasm after his first audience with the emperor, this new and "educated Peter the Great." A Polish enemy recorded how he was overcome by the stunning majesty of the Russian tsar, "the ruler of the world in appearance," and how he was unable to meet the imperial gaze. The Marquis de Custine, who gained a lasting literary reputation by his violent and brilliant denunciation of the Russia of Nicholas I [see Documents below], was nevertheless strongly attracted by the figure of its ruler "whose head dominates all other heads . . . Virgil's Neptune . . . one could not be more emperor than he."

Custine's opinion was the general opinion. Nicholas I came to represent autoc-racy personified: infinitely majestic, determined and powerful, hard as stone, and relentless as fate. The emperor himself believed in this image, as did most of his contemporaries and most of the subsequent historians. In the annals of mankind,

"The Supreme Commander" excerpted from Nicholas V. Riasanovsky, *Nicholas I and Official Nation-ality in Russia, 1825–1855*, pp. 2–22, 266–270. Copyright © 1959 The Regents of the University of California Press. Reprinted by permission of the University of California Press.

few pictures have come down to us so simple, sharp, and clear as this portrait of the despotic Russian ruler.

Yet, better acquaintance changes this image. The empress, as her diary and letters testify, found many things about her husband which did not fit the general view. Close collaborators with the emperor and other people who lived long at court also discovered new facets of his personality. Historians, too, as they studied their subject more closely, came up with some unexpected results. The most meticulous of them, Professor Theodore Schiemann, produced a fine, many-sided narrative of the emperor's behavior which, unfortunately, he failed to understand or interpret in an entirely satisfactory manner.[1] Another prominent investigator reached the conclusion that the impression left by Nicholas I was a result of his historical role, not of his personal attributes.[2] Still others note "failings," "exceptions," and "contradictions" in the character of the emperor.

Those who became well acquainted with Nicholas I were struck by the disclosure of the other side of his allegedly monolithic personality. Furthermore, and very few went deep enough to see it, this second side of the emperor's character, far from being transitory or secondary, was as fundamental as the first. In fact, the two were indissolubly linked and were always in operation together. Nicholas I's insistence on firmness and stern action was based on fear, not on confidence; his determination concealed a state approaching panic, and his courage fed on something akin to despair. The two elements of his personality were invariably present, but they could be seen best in a time of crisis, such as that in 1848. When the news of the revolution in France reached Russia, the emperor's reactions were, characteristically, first, extreme nervousness and excitement verging on panic, and, second, a demand for immediate and drastic action. As he tried to convince his brother-in-law, the king of Prussia: "Act *firmly and promptly*, or, I am telling it to you, I am repeating it, *all is lost*." The emperor's boiling emotions could not be restricted to personal correspondence. In the same month of March he issued a resounding manifesto, which he had composed himself, refusing to accept the modifications proposed by his chief advisers. This remarkable document began with a brief account of the new "disturbances" which had arisen in the West, first in France, then also in the neighboring German states until "insolence, recognizing no longer any limits, is in its madness threatening even our Russia entrusted to us by God." Nicholas I continued:

> But let this not be!
> Following the sacred example of our Orthodox forefathers, after invoking the help of God Almighty, we are ready to meet our enemies, wherever they may appear, and, without sparing ourselves, we shall, in indissoluble union with our Holy Russia, defend the honor of the Russian name and the inviolability of our borders.

---

1. Reference is to Theodore Schiemann, *Geschichte Russlands unter Kaiser Nikolaus I*, 4 vols. (Berlin, 1904–19).—Ed.
2. A. E. Presniakov, *Emperor Nicholas I of Russia: The Apogee of Autocracy* (1974; first published Leningrad, 1925).—Ed.

We are convinced that every Russian, every loyal subject of ours will respond gladly to the call of his monarch; that our ancient battle cry: "for faith, tsar, and fatherland" will now once more show us the way to victory, and that then with feelings of reverent gratitude, as now with feelings of sacred trust in Him, we shall all exclaim:

God is with us! Understand this, O nations, and submit, for God is with us!

This manifesto which, in the words of Baron Korff who helped the emperor draft it, contained a challenge to combat, referred to external threats which did not exist, and expressed hopes of victory while no hostilities were as yet in prospect, produced a great impression both in Russia and, especially, abroad. Count Nesselrode, Nicholas I's minister of foreign affairs, hastened to explain in a special article in the quasi-official *Journal de St. Petersburg* that the imperial proclamation should not be misinterpreted and that Russia wanted peace and had no intention whatsoever of fighting anybody, provided she were not attacked first. But international suspicion proved hard to dispel. And even, long after 1848 became history, scholars were still trying to discover the arcane political, diplomatic, or strategic reasons which made the Russian emperor issue his unaccountable manifesto.

Nervous fear and outbursts of aggressiveness characterized Nicholas I from childhood. The future emperor was a self-willed boy who found it difficult either to study with his teachers or to enjoy himself with his playmates. Often withdrawn and shy, he insisted on having his way, refused to recognize mistakes, and flew into a rage at every obstacle. . . . In addition to this general irritability, Nicholas I was subject to phobias. In his early childhood he dreaded officers, fireworks, thunder, and cannons. As a fully grown man and emperor he developed, following the great fire of the Winter Palace in 1837, a nervous fear of flames and smoke. And he had always to avoid heights because of the resulting dizziness. There is also considerable evidence of Nicholas's persistent horror at the sight of blood which may have influenced his behavior on the day of the Decembrist uprising [December 14, 1825] and again in the Russo-Turkish war of 1828–1829.

The intensity of the emperor's nervousness was such that it gradually began to affect his excellent health and his magnificent physique. Medically Nicholas I had a good record, being almost free of serious illness, but his powerful organism began to crumble under the continuous strain: he became subject to frequent nervous ailments, usually connected with political or personal crises; he had periods of depression; he became more and more pessimistic in his outlook; and he found it increasingly difficult to control his temper. He lost his hair early, and his appearance indicated, more and more, tension and fatigue rather than his former fitness and strength. A number of the emperor's contemporaries speak of a disastrous break in his health between the years of 1840 and 1845. It was then, in their opinion, that Nicholas I aged suddenly and lost much of his former vigor and resilience. Nicholas's death at the age of fifty-eight marked, in a sense, the culmination of this process. The emperor succumbed to an aggravated cold which his tired body refused to fight.

The heavy burden of an empire lay all the heavier on the shoulder of Nicholas because of his deep emotional involvement in his task and, in fact, in everything around him. The detachment and the superior calm of an autocrat, which Nicholas I tried so often and so hard to display, were merely a false front, and frequently they failed to perform even that function. In reality, the emperor was usually seething with passions, especially with rage and with fear, but also with a kind of exultation when he felt that he was striking telling blows against the enemy. He was given to sentimentality and to tears which coursed down his cheeks, for example, when he was preparing his strange 1848 manifesto. Nicholas's violent hatred concentrated apparently with equal ease on an individual, such as the French king Louis-Philippe, a group, such as the Decembrists, a people, such as the Poles, or a concept, such as Revolution. Much has been written about the emperor's tremendous emotional involvement in the Decembrist affair, an involvement which ceased only with his death. But Nicholas I had the same general attitude in all his other relations as well, assailing with equal vehemence "the King of the French," a corrupt minor official, or a delinquent sergeant in one of his regiments. His impulse was always to strike and keep striking until the object of his wrath was destroyed.

Aggressiveness, however, was not the emperor's only method of coping with the problems of life. Another was regimentation, orderliness, neatness, precision, an enormous effort to have everything at all times in its proper place. Nicholas I was by nature a drill master and an inspector general. The army became his love, almost an obsession, from childhood to the end of his life. Toy soldiers and military games constituted the devouring passion of Nicholas's boyhood, as well as of that of his younger brother Michael. Attempts to turn his attention in other directions proved singularly unsuccessful. Typical is the story of one assignment. In 1810 the fourteen-year-old boy was told to write a theme on the subject that military service was only one of the careers open to a nobleman, and that he could also enter other occupations which were equally useful and honorable. The future emperor failed to produce any essay at all, and his teacher finally dictated one to him.

As he grew older, Nicholas's enchantment with the army retained its full force, while his activity in that field increased greatly. He became a most devoted and enthusiastic officer and a lifelong expert in such things as the field manual, drill of every sort, and playing the drum. When Emperor Alexander I put Nicholas in charge of the army engineers, the younger brother finally obtained a large military establishment which he could drill, inspect, and supervise continuously. Then, in 1825, he became the supreme commander of all the Russian armed forces, and of all of Russia besides. The new emperor eagerly took up his vastly expanded military functions, but he remained a junior officer at heart. His great attachment remained the minutiae of army life: the physical appearance of his troops, small unit drill, uniforms with their buttons, ribbons, and colors which he proceeded to rearrange with a most painstaking devotion to duty. As emperor, Nicholas continued to participate personally in as many military reviews and exercises as possible. Indeed this kind of army life represented "as he himself admitted, his one true delight."[3] It was also observed that the Russian emperor could not restrain his joy when he

---

3. This typical comment was made by Count A. Benckendorff, one of Nicholas's closest associates.

received honorary ranks and appointments in Prussian or Austrian regiments, and that he insisted on having appropriate uniforms made immediately and on drilling his new troops. Time and again he surprised Prussian and Austrian officers by his perfect knowledge of their field manuals.

It was especially at large-scale military reviews that Nicholas I experienced rapture, almost ecstasy, that he felt a violent swelling of his emotions and sensed the proximity of God. For instance, his letter to the empress describing the great military celebration arranged in 1839 on the field of Borodino is a remarkable combination of precise technical information about the ceremony and of powerful religious feeling.[4] "From the depth of my soul I prayed to God for you, for our children, for the well-being of our entire great Russian family." At another huge military review, with the Austrian ambassador in attendance, the emperor, his eyes filled with tears, placed his hand over his heart, lifted his gaze to heaven and prayed loudly: "God, I thank Thee for making me so mighty, and I beg Thee to give me the strength never to abuse this power."

Regimentation was not limited to the army. Nicholas made every effort to regulate minutely and precisely all phases of his own life, and he treated other people in the same manner. Everything had to be in its proper order, nothing was to be left to chance. The emperor's personality was rigid and austere, strikingly deficient in spontaneity and warmth. To quote a contemporary of Nicholas:

> . . . the usual expression of his face has something severe and misanthropic in it, something that does not put one at all at one's ease. His smile is a smile of civility which is not at all a result of gaiety or of spontaneity. The habit of repressing these feelings has become so inseparable from his very being that you see in him no awkwardness, no embarrassment, nothing studied; and yet all his words, as all his movements, follow a cadence as if he had a sheet of music in front of him. . . . There is nothing in the tone of his voice or in the construction of his sentences that indicates pride or dissimulation; and yet you feel that his heart is closed, that the barrier is impassable, and that one would be mad to hope to penetrate the privacy of his thought.

It is not surprising that, as grand duke, Nicholas never attracted the love of his subordinates. When he ascended the throne, his passion for regimentation and regulation became government policy, affecting in manifold ways every single Russian and leaving a special impress on his whole reign.

This minute and perfectionist ordering of everything apparently served the emperor as a defense mechanism. He needed it because all his life he was on the defensive. Incessantly he struggled against his own emotions, against the Decembrists and other enemies in Russia, against corruption and other surrounding evils, against world revolution. Order, precise, complete order, was necessary to keep all of these opponents down, and Nicholas I would fly into a panicky rage not only at a report of a new uprising in Paris, but also when a soldier was not properly groomed for a review or a student failed to be attentive to a classroom.

---

4. Borodino, near Moscow, was the site of the major battle during Napoleon's invasion of Russia in 1812.—Ed.

Custine remarked aptly: "The emperor of Russia is a military commander, and each one of his days is a day of battle."

The military emphasis of Nicholas was, again, mainly defensive. Even as a child "whenever he built a summer house, for his nurse or his governess, out of chairs, earth, or toys, he never forgot to *fortify* it with guns—*for protection*."[5] He grew to be the chief military engineer of his country, specializing in fortresses, and still later, as emperor, he staked all on making the entire land an impregnable fortress.

Life, for Nicholas, was full of strife and frustration, and he found it difficult to endure. Fortunately, he could obtain solace from several sources, one of which was his extremely highly developed sense of duty. As the weary emperor wrote to his wife in July, 1849:

> How remarkable really is my fate. I am told that I am one of the mightiest rulers of the world, and one must say that everything, that is, everything that is permissible, should be within my reach, that, within the limits of discretion, I should be able to do what I please and where. But in fact just the opposite is the case as far as I am concerned. And if one asks about the basic cause of this anomaly, there is only one word: Duty! Yes, this is no empty word for those who have become accustomed from their youth to understand it as I have. This word has a *sacred meaning* which makes all personal considerations retreat, everything must keep silent in front of this one feeling, everything must step back, until one, together with this feeling, disappears into the grave. That is my key word. It is hard, I admit it, I suffer more from it than I can tell—but I have been created to suffer. [Italics in original.]

Duty, then, was the answer to the tragedy of life, and the emperor continued to do his duty, to perform his obligations, working indefatigably all the time, often almost in a frenzy, working to stifle the pain which threatened to become unbearable. If this principle of duty took no account of the personal wishes of the emperor, it proved to be equally despotic toward his people. As Nicholas I declared concerning his Polish subjects: "They must be made *happy* in spite of themselves."

Nicholas was completely devoted to his duties, and he expected the same degree of devotion from his subordinates. As soon as he became the chief of army engineers, he issued the following typical order, written in his own hand:

> Obeying the high will of the emperor [Alexander I] I assumed, on the twentieth day of this month of January, the position of the inspector general of the engineers. In informing the corps of engineers of this fact, I consider it my duty to confirm to all the members of the corps that, by diligent performance of one's duties, zeal for the interests of the state, and good conduct, everyone will earn imperial favor and will find in me an eager intercessor before His Majesty. But in the opposite case, for the slightest negligence, which will never and under no circumstances be pardoned, one will be treated according to the full severity of the laws. I expect to have perpetual satisfaction from the zeal and firmness of the commanders and from

---

5. Author quotes from a contemporary Russian source; italics in the original.—Ed.

the enthusiasm and complete obedience of the lower ranks. Trusting in that, I assure each and every one that I know how to appreciate the kindness of the emperor who made me the commander of such a distinguished corps. 20th January, year 1814. The inspector general of the engineers, Nicholas.

When Nicholas succeeded Alexander as emperor he continued to demand unfailing service from his subjects, and he refused to excuse anybody "ever and under any circumstances." This attitude was all the more natural for the new autocrat because, from childhood, he had exhibited a certain ruthlessness, a lack of consideration for others, and an inability to see any point of view but his own. Nicholas took himself and his work very seriously indeed. And he had virtually no sense of humor. The emperor's ceaseless efforts to make everybody follow his example—a subject to be discussed later in this study—ranged from his reorganization of much of the administrative procedure of the state and his appointment of numerous high-level committees which were to consider and reconsider ways to eliminate abuses and to establish more efficient government in Russia, to early morning personal visits of various government offices intended to find out whether their occupants were at their desks on time. Punishment swiftly followed transgression. Even as a boy Nicholas came to the conclusion that Louis XVI of France [executed in 1793 by revolutionaries] had failed in his duty because he had been lenient with evildoers. Much later he stated the matter succinctly to a Polish delegation: "I am willing to forget all the evil that you have done me personally, but the emperor does not forget."

Nicholas carried through his determination not to be soft like his unfortunate French fellow ruler and never to forget. Relentless harshness became the outstanding characteristic of his reign, and was so noted by virtually all of his contemporaries. . . . Once the emperor even issued an order meant to punish a warship. The occasion was the surrender of the frigate "Raphael" to the Turks in the war of 1828–1829. The edict, addressed to Admiral Greig, ended as follows: "Trusting in the help of the Almighty I persevere in the hope that the fearless Black Sea fleet, burning with the desire to wash off the shame of the frigate 'Raphael,' will not leave it in the hands of the enemy. But, when it is returned to our control, considering this frigate to be unworthy in the future to fly the flag of Russia and to serve together with the other vessels of our fleet, I order you to burn it."

In the trials and tribulations of life, Nicholas was supported not only by his powerful sense of duty, but also by his firm religious convictions. The two were intrinsically connected. Duty meant in the last analysis duty to God, the ultimate supreme commander. In relation to Providence, the Russian autocrat remained a subordinate officer determined to execute his orders well and to occupy an honorable place in the great military review to be held in the next world. Many of his efforts failed, but his conscience remained clear as long as he did not cease to try his best. And he never ceased.

God, however—so Nicholas believed—had many functions: in addition to being the last link in the chain of command and the final judge, he was an ever-present influence in the life of an individual and also his consoler. It is remarkable to what extent the emperor felt the hand of God in his day-to-day existence. As he asserted in a letter to his brother Constantine: ". . . I am firmly convinced of divine protection which manifests itself in my case in too perceptible a manner for me not to be able to notice it in everything that happens to me, and here is my strength, my consolation, my guiding light in all matters." The emperor's messages to his military commanders were full of expressions of gratitude to God for His intercession and help in war, coupled with admonitions to be humble and modest in the realization that victory was a divine gift, not a human achievement. Providence served this purpose too for Nicholas: it enabled him to bow his head with the lowly and divested him, if only for fleeting moments, of the pride and the burden of an autocrat.

On another occasion, the emperor wrote to Count P. Tolstoi on August 9, 1831: "God rewarded me for my journey to Novgorod for, several hours after my return, He granted my wife to be delivered successfully of a son Nicholas." The same day, in another letter, he discussed this event as follows: "God blessed my wife granting her yesterday a happy deliverance of a son Nicholas. Our joy is great and one cannot fail to recognize, from the depth of one's soul, the mercy of God Who, through all the grief and misfortunes, sustained the health of my wife in such a marvelous manner." The journey to Novgorod which the emperor mentioned as his special merit was occasioned by a revolt in that district among the so-called military colonists. The ensuing reprisals included severe corporal punishment for some two thousand six hundred rebels, one hundred and twenty-nine of them dying in the course of the chastisement. The horror of it all notwithstanding, Nicholas felt that he deserved a reward because he had performed his hard duty with courage, firmness, and dispatch.

The Russian ruler was well-nigh perfect in the execution of his wearisome religious obligations. He assiduously attended long church services and in his numerous visits to the provincial centers of his sprawling empire he invariably began at the cathedral where he was received with proper, often extensive, ceremony, and which he entered devoutly and with many genuflections. All this was, of course, a matter of protocol which Nicholas would not eliminate or even curtail. But beyond that, he found reassurance, tranquillity, and joy in Orthodox church services which formed a part of his life from childhood. Nicholas loved church singing, and at times sang with the choir. He prayed, apparently with ardor and with conviction, and he followed closely every part of the ritual. In the few spare moments of his crowded schedule he read the Bible, especially the Gospels and the Epistles, daily, at least so some of his biographers assert. There is even evidence that the emperor was interested in contemporary theological writing, which is all the more noteworthy because he was not at all intellectually inclined.

Nicholas was fully Orthodox in that he was devoted to the Orthodox Church in the same complete and unquestioning manner in which he was devoted to his country or to his regiment. He had none of the spiritual restlessness and cosmopolitan religious seekings of his immediate imperial predecessor [Alexander I]. Nevertheless he appreciated Christian denominations other than his own and was keenly aware of the distinction between Christendom and the non-Christian world. He even developed a special liking for Lutheranism, the faith of his numerous Prussian relatives. Indeed, such German historians as Schiemann have noted that the emperor's religious attitude was, in certain particulars, Protestant rather than Orthodox.

Nicholas's religious convictions deserve attention for several reasons. They were all-pervasive, affecting every phase of his life in an important manner. They were applied consistently and thoroughly by the emperor to many complex personal and political problems. Yet apparently he was never led to doubt these fundamental assumptions, either in youthful revolt, or in mature despair. Nicholas's faith remained always simple, blunt, and unswerving. In his own words, he believed "in the manner of a peasant." The emperor fully recognized the value of religion in maintaining morality, order, and stable government, in his state as in any other. But, at least as far as his personal beliefs were concerned, the reverse relationship was the more important one: discipline, law, autocratic rule, with all their burdens and all their pains, had to go on functioning because they had been ordained by God, a superior officer from whose decision there could be no appeal. The state was to serve God, not God the state.

The emperor's sense of duty and his straightforward religious convictions were closely connected to the general sincerity and honesty of his character. His admirers presented Nicholas I as a knight in shining armor; his critics marvelled at his directness and bluntness. But even the antagonists of the Russian despot often had to admit his integrity and his truthfulness. To cite the opinion of Custine: "I do not believe that there is today on any throne a prince who detests falsehood so much and who lies so little as this one." Historians have on the whole confirmed this verdict. It may be added that Nicholas I considered honesty essential even when it involved the protection of something he hated. Thus he censured the violation of the constitutions in their countries by both Charles X of France and Ferdinand II of the Kingdom of the Two Sicilies, because the two rulers had previously accepted these fundamental documents.

Nicholas's behavior was strongly affected by the Christian ethic, and also by the aristocratic code in which he was brought up. The first influence represented often an ideal to be sought, actual performance falling far short of it. But it did provide a basic frame of reference for the emperor's moral values and judgments, and it may have accounted for such aspects of his behavior as his leniency towards the Turkish prisoners of war and his insistence on the humane treatment of the population in occupied territories. The code of a gentleman emphasized honesty, honor, and proper manners. It made Nicholas react very sharply to the news that one of his generals had struck a captive enemy, and, on a larger scale, it led to his depending too much in his foreign policy on personal meetings between rulers and on verbal promises. In ethics as in everything else the emperor was an absolutist: the same true moral principles held sway everywhere and at all times, and nobody had the right to escape their compelling power.

Religion, morality, duty all played their part in supporting Nicholas I in his life of continuous struggle. His family contributed to the same end in a somewhat different manner, by allowing the tsar to express certain emotions and to develop certain sides of his personality which remained otherwise completely repressed. Nicholas enjoyed his family very much, and on most counts he was a good husband and a good father. His marriage to the Prussian princess who later became the Russian Empress Alexandra was a love match as well as a dynastic arrangement, and the couple remained very close to each other for many happy years. Their correspondence offers an impressive testimonial of their mutual affection as well as of the fullness with which the ruler kept his wife informed of the affairs of state and of everything else that interested him. Nicholas was, of course, the master of his family and of his household as much as of his empire, but Alexandra acquired the position of a trusted and loved companion in all matters. The emperor became similarly devoted to his children and later, as they began to grow up, he maintained his attachment to them, building them palaces, arranging appropriate marriages, and generally playing the role of paterfamilias on a grand scale. Family meant simplicity, peace, and quiet for Nicholas, and these gifts were extremely welcome after the enormous formality and strain of his exalted office. But his close relationship to his wife was particularly important. As Nicholas wrote her in 1836, after nineteen years of marriage:

> God has given you such a happy character that it is no merit to love you. I exist for you, yes, you are I—I do not know how to say it differently, but I am not your salvation, as you say. Our salvation is over *there yonder*, yonder where we shall all be admitted to rest from the tribulations of life. I mean, if we earn it down here by the fulfillment of our duties. Hard as they may be, one performs them with joy when one has a beloved being at home near whom one can breathe again and gain new strength. If I was now and then demanding, this happened because I look for everything in you. If I do not find it, I am distressed, I say to myself, no, she does not understand me, and these are unique, rare, but difficult moments. For the rest, happiness, joy, calm—that is what I seek and find in my old Mouffy [Nicholas's nickname for his wife]. I wished, as much as this was in my power, to make you a hundred times happier. . . .

Yet even this imposing declaration of Nicholas's love for his wife indicated that all was not well in the imperial household. In truth, the emperor was in some ways an exacting and a harsh husband. He found it difficult to accept the fact that his wife often failed to keep up with his restless activity, especially as her health declined with the years. He could hardly bear separation from her, even for brief periods of time. The crisis in the summer of 1845 illustrated well the attitude of the emperor, although at the same time it represented an extreme case of his neurotic behavior toward his wife. Trouble arose when the empress accepted medical advice to spend some time in the sunshine of Sicily. Nicholas, who had expected that his wife would not have to go any further away than the Crimea, was seized by one of his attacks of panic and rage. For days the imperial family and those around them were in extreme nervous turmoil. . . .

The emperor's fidelity to his wife and the very close attachment of the imperial couple did not last all the way to Nicholas's death. Many reasons can be advanced for this change in the emperor's behavior. He was not only the ruler of a great empire as well as "the most handsome man in Europe," but also a charmer who enjoyed feminine company and was often at his best with the ladies. Nicholas's aristocratic code of behavior included the principle of gallantry. Time and again in the course of imperial voyages the Russian autocrat would forego various personal comforts so that female members of his wife's retinue could be better accommodated. Moreover, the emperor was extremely responsive to physical appearance, especially to feminine beauty, and he has often been described as a sensuous and passionate man. Perhaps more to the point is the probability that Nicholas was seeking in a new relationship more of the reassurance and support which he needed so badly throughout his life but which kept constantly evading him.

The emperor's choice fell on Mademoiselle Nelidov, a lady in waiting. But although observers noted Nicholas's great interest in her as early as the autumn of 1841, it took the Russian ruler several years to overcome his, and possibly her, moral scruples and establish a liaison with her. Characteristically, the intervening period was for Nicholas a time of bitter inner struggle, and one can appreciate the remark of Countess Nesselrode, the wife of the foreign minister, to the effect that she wished that the emperor would simply make Mademoiselle Nelidov his mistress and be done with it. The liaison, once established, proved to be a permanent one, and it was not a secret at court. The position of the empress was all the more painful because she had to tolerate the new favorite in her entourage. Later Nicholas apparently acquired one more mistress, again a lady in waiting, Mademoiselle Kutuzov.

The emperor treated his numerous children much as he treated his wife. The relationship was a close and a warm one, Nicholas being invariably an interested and solicitous father. But, here again, the unfortunate personality of the emperor contributed to certain acute crises and tensions, for example, when the romance of his elder son and heir to the throne, Alexander, with a Polish girl threatened to spoil a projected dynastic marriage.

Nicholas I had a number of artistic and aesthetic interests. He passionately admired nature, particularly beautiful southern landscapes. He became a specialist in architecture, both military and civil, and he loved to apply his knowledge of this field in practice. The emperor was brought up to appreciate art, and he developed great enthusiasm for the paintings of the Renaissance, especially those by Raphael and Titian, and for statues of classical antiquity. In music too he profited from both native ability and training. He sang well, and he played the horn in a good palace quartet which the empress accompanied on the piano. Famous musicians, including Franz Liszt, were invited to give "house" concerts for the imperial family. As ruler, Nicholas did much to promote art and architecture in Russia. As to literature, his tastes ran generally to the sentimental and the second-rate. The emperor read much, trying in fact to acquaint himself with everything published in Russia and with many items produced abroad, but he had little appreciation of writing as a form of art. His judgments of books were consistently moral and political rather than aesthetic, and he missed most of the glory of the Russian literature of his day.

It has been noted that Nicholas's artistic preferences formed a close parallel to his other interests and inclinations. One historian [Presniakov] wrote: "His aesthetics is permeated with militarism as its best incarnation. His politics and his aesthetics are in a remarkable harmony: everything in line. He loved uniformity, straight lines, a severe symmetry, the regularity of design." It may be added that the bay of Naples, St. Peter's, and the statues of the Vatican gallery inspired the emperor with much the same rapture which he felt at the sight of well-aligned military formations or when inspecting a mighty fortress.

Life was burdensome and painful to Nicholas I. Yet, instead of rebelling violently against his surroundings, he achieved a certain adjustment by means of emphasis on the concept of duty, on religion, and on the sad lot of the Christian in this vale of tears. He also found some relief in a close relationship with his wife and with a few other people, although these human contacts in turn often led to new difficulties. It was natural for the emperor to develop a pessimistic and fatalistic outlook. His associates noted that he took little care of himself, refusing, for instance, to postpone his trips at the news of assassination plots, with this typical remark: "God is my guardian, and if I am no longer needed for Russia, He will take me to Himself."

As political misfortunes piled on unresolved personal conflicts, the emperor's attitude became more and more that of hopelessness and resignation. The Crimean War came as the crowning blow. When Nicholas's diplomatic system collapsed, and Russia was left alone against a hostile coalition, the weary tsar remarked: "Nothing remains to me but my duty as long as it pleases God to leave me at the head of Russia." "I shall carry my cross until all my strength is gone." "Thy will be done." . . .

The marvel—and the mistake—of Nicholas I's long rule is to be found in its extraordinary doctrinaire rigidity and consistency. The steadfast monarch governed his vast empire and participated in the destinies of the world on the basis of a few simple principles which he held with passionate conviction. The ideology of the reign, known as Official Nationality, deserves more attention that it has hitherto received.[6] Far from being mere propaganda or empty talk, it represented the conscious orientation of the Russian government in the course of thirty eventful years. Its roots lay deep in Russian history, most especially in the creation of the modern Russian state by Peter the Great, as well as in the subsequent development of that state. The doctrine of Official Nationality also faithfully reflected a stage in general European evolution, marked by the defeat of Napoleon and the joint effort of victorious powers to restore something like the old order on the continent. As theory, the Russian teaching constituted a typical philosophy of the age of restoration and reaction. In practice it meant a way of managing the enormous and relatively backward Russian state. And while one can easily criticize Nicholas I's desperate effort personally to set everything straight in his far-flung realm, one should at least try to appreciate the difficulties of his position.

The emperor's stubborn loyalty to his convictions taxed the understanding of many of his contemporaries and of numerous subsequent historians. Time and again they have tried to explain Nicholas I's actions more "realistically," notably on the basis of the immediate interests of Russia rather than of the tsar's professed principles. For example, some specialists have maintained that Russian intervention in Hungary in 1849 resulted from the fear of Polish rebels who took an active part in the Hungarian movement, not from the desire to crush revolution, come to the aid of Austria, or honor the treaty of 1833. Even Schiemann, who is in many ways the

---

6. The ideology of "Official Nationality," as Riasanovsky makes clear in the rest of his book, proclaimed absolute dedication to the principles of Orthodoxy (the institution and teachings of the Russian Orthodox church), Autocracy (as established by Peter the Great), and Nationality (or "Russianness," meaning Russian traditions and culture).—Ed.

leading authority on the reign of Nicholas I, argued that the Russian autocrat wanted to manipulate Austria and Prussia so they would serve as a shield against liberalism and revolution and do his fighting for him—this in spite of the fact that the German scholar also repeatedly pointed out in his work the tsar's eagerness for combat and the reluctance of his allies. In fact, this contrast between the recognition of the extremely rigid and doctrinaire nature of the tsar's policy and the attempts, which nevertheless persist, to ascribe its various manifestations to "practical" reasons, constitutes one of the peculiarities of historical writing dealing with this period. A dismissal of "realistic" interpretations does not indicate, however, that Nicholas I ignored Russian interests. Rather he saw these interests in terms of his fundamental beliefs, not apart from them; the effectiveness of the autocrat's service to his native land depended thus largely on the soundness of the beliefs.

Similarly the extreme regimentation and repression of Nicholas I's reign have to be considered in the light of the emperor's convictions and of the aims which he attempted to achieve. While many specific instances of censorship or police interference must be judged ridiculous and stupid, the system as a whole makes good sense provided one accepts the dogma of Official Nationality and the need to impose it upon Russia. Once more Nicholas I stands vindicated or convicted primarily on the basis of his beliefs.

It is necessary to understand the doctrine of Official Nationality in order to comprehend the reign of Nicholas I. But understanding does not imply endorsement. The government ideology of autocracy and of the absolute control of the life of the country by the monarch represented at best one narrow approach to statecraft. It could be called progressive in the age of Peter the Great, in particular in Russia where the mighty sovereign undertook sweeping reforms in the face of an overwhelming popular opposition and indifference. It became increasingly less forward-looking with the passage of time and the social, political, economic, and intellectual evolution of Europe, turning into something of an anachronism in the nineteenth century. The rigid iron rule of Nicholas I tended to obscure the fact that even during his reign, and perhaps especially during his reign, Russia was undergoing fundamental change. The serf economy of the country steadily declined in favor of freer labor, monetary exchange, distant markets, and, in short, the rise of capitalism. Socially too, in spite of all government efforts, new forces were coming to the fore, the Russian intelligentsia of the 1840s being already much more democratic in origin than that of the 1820s. Russian culture, literature in particular, blossomed out in new splendor. . . . [A] number of leading Russian writers contributed in one way or another to the official doctrine [; but] the main currents of this cultural renaissance ran in other directions. The Russia of Pushkin, of Lermontov, of the young Turgenev and Dostoevsky, or, indeed, of Gogol had little in common with the official version.[7]

---

7. Reference is to the leading writers of the first "golden age" of Russian literature: Alexander Pushkin (1779–1837), Mikhail Lermontov (1814–41), Ivan Turgenev (1818–83), Fedor Dostoevsky (1821–81), and Nikolai Gogol (1809–52).—Ed.

Ideas also changed. Educated Russians . . . espoused views different from and often antagonistic to the teaching of their government. The Slavophiles, the Westernizers, the members of the Brotherhood of Cyril and Methodius, [and others] all saw visions of their native land and made plans for its future which did not fit the prescribed model. The extremist . . . and the moderate . . . religious thinkers of the Slavophile camp and atheists . . . liberals and socialists, constitutionalists and federalists, found themselves in opposition to the Russia of Nicholas I. The revolutionary ideas of the age, notably romantic nationalism, penetrated the official doctrine itself, contending for allegiance with the older dynastic interpretation. Of still greater significance was the fact that the reign of Nicholas I marked not only the flowering but also the beginning of the waning of romanticism in Russia. The romantic emphasis on religion, authority, uniqueness, history, and tradition gradually gave ground to a secular, materialistic, and positivist outlook which the tsar correctly considered the deadly foe of his system. It is worth noting that the revolutionary movement of the Decembrists, inspired by the ideas of the Age of Reason and by Jacobin [French revolutionary] practice, had no militant successor in Russia until the 1870s, after the end of the romantic epoch and the advent of realism and the cult of science.

While the split between government and society in Russia continued to increase during the thirty long years of Nicholas I's reign, the gulf between the empire of the tsars and the West widened even more perceptibly. For the leading countries of the West, propelled by the industrial revolution, were undergoing a still more rapid transformation than the state of the Romanovs. Yet the autocrat's only answer to all the change at home and abroad remained a reaffirmation of his old principles, a heroic effort to turn the clock back. Following the revolutions of 1848, government and life in Russia acquired a certain nightmarish quality which forced even many supporters of the existing regime to cry out in despair. The debacle of the Crimean War came both as logical retribution and as liberation.

The historical significance of the reign of Nicholas I and the system of Official Nationality can be judged in several contexts. In the evolution of Russia it meant an attempt, for three decades, to freeze growth and impose stagnation. The liberal hopes of the time of Alexander I, already betrayed by that monarch himself, gave place to outspoken reaction. Abroad, Russia, the recent liberator of Europe, turned definitely into its gendarme. In fairness to Nicholas I it is right and proper to emphasize that his problems were great and his choices limited. Most critics of the emperor knew less about the condition of Russia than he did, and none of them had the awesome responsibility of translating theory into practice. Still, the sovereign's total refusal to consider any other way but his own led to a dead end, all the more so because the existing system was constantly becoming more obsolete and less workable. Although Russia certainly was not Great Britain or France and although it had to find a solution based on its own capabilities, it seems presumptuous to argue that the great reforms of the 1860s could not have been enacted in the fifties and the forties, or that the liberal hopes of the reign of Alexander I were bound to be doomed even if the successor to that emperor believed in constitutionalism, not autocracy. While numerous circumstances delimited the area within which the government system could operate, the fundamental rigidity lay in the system itself.

In a sense Russia never recovered the thirty years lost under Nicholas I. Alexander II instituted reforms; Alexander III appealed to the nationalist sentiment which his grandfather had spurned; in the reign of Nicholas II the country obtained even a shaky constitutional machinery. But all these new departures remained somehow tentative and incomplete. And it was still largely the old order of Nicholas I, the antiquated *ancien régime*, that went down in the conflagration of 1917. . . .

# D o c u m e n t s

The challenge to absolutism (autocracy), the dominance of the nobility, and the persistence of serfdom in Russia posed in their different ways by Alexander Radishchev, Michael Speransky, and the Decembrists naturally evoked a conservative response. An early and notably articulate example of this reaction is the lengthy memorandum to Alexander I written in 1810–1811 by Nicholas Karamzin (1766–1826), who was at the time the official historian of the Russian Empire. A son of the serf-owning nobility of the middle Volga region whose father (unlike Radishchev's) had nearly been killed by his peasants in the Pugachev Rebellion, Karamzin was educated privately in both French and German as well as Russian, served for a year in one of the elite guards regiments, and traveled extensively in western Europe (at the height of the French Revolution) before settling down in Moscow to become a writer, editor, and historian of distinction. Alarmed by the "liberalism" of the earlier years of Alexander's reign and especially by Speransky's constitutional projects and talk of peasant emancipation, Karamzin wrote his *Memoir on Ancient and Modern Russia* (as it is called in its English translation, excerpted below), hoping to persuade Alexander that preserving the autocracy and even serfdom was essential to Russia's survival as a great state. Drawing on his knowledge of Russian history, Karamzin insisted on the special position and inviolable property rights of the nobility, and invoked dire consequences should their serfs be liberated. It is not known whether Alexander actually read the *Memoir*. But from the 1830s it circulated widely in Russian society in both printed and manuscript versions, its arguments becoming the stock in trade of opponents of emancipation and constitutional reform.

    Karamzin's forebodings are followed by the observations of a French aristocratic visitor to Russia in 1839, the Marquis de Custine (1790–1857). Custine's extended account of his visit, excerpted here, was first published in Paris in 1843 and promptly thereafter in numerous editions and translations. Custine often appears in his account as a snobbish gossip and would-be philosopher (or historian); but in his firsthand descriptions of Nicholas I and his court, he has left an unforgettable picture of the "apogee of autocracy."

    Quite different is the account of another aristocratic visitor to Russia at about the same time, Baron August von Haxthausen (1792–1866). A German landowner with a deep interest in agriculture, Haxthausen trained as a social scientist at the University of Göttingen and held various positions in the Prussian civil service which drew on his expertise. He became interested in agriculture in the Russian Empire as early as 1837, and published an article on the subject that caught Emperor Nicholas's eye, who invited him to pursue his studies in the country itself. This he did for an entire year (1843–1844), concentrating his attention on peasant life in the Russian heartland, where he was astonished to discover that the medieval agricultural commune (as he understood it) had survived intact. His somewhat romantic descriptions of the

Russian peasant commune became a main attraction of his *Studies on the Interior of Russia*, which appeared in German in three volumes in 1847–1852 and were quickly translated into French and English (an authoritative Russian edition was published in Moscow in 1870). A generation and more of Russian Slavophiles, populists, socialists, and others drew liberally for their different reasons on Haxthausen's depiction of that other Russia, away from St. Petersburg and the Imperial elite, which was embodied in the peasant commune. That Haxthausen's influence persists to this day will be evident to close readers of this book (Chapter 1, essay by Pipes).

## N. M. Karamzin Defends the Established Order, 1811

At this point [in Russian history] Peter appeared . . . [and] he seized hold of the helm of state with a mighty hand. He strove toward his destination through storms and billows. He reached it—and everything changed!

His goal was not only to bring new greatness to Russia, but also to accomplish the *complete* assimilation of European customs. . . . Posterity has praised passionately this immortal sovereign for his personal merits as well as for his glorious achievements. He was magnanimous and perspicacious, he had an unshakable will, vigor, and a virtually inexhaustible supply of energy. He reorganized and increased the army, he achieved a brilliant victory over a skillful and courageous enemy, he conquered Livonia, he founded the fleet, built ports, promulgated many wise laws, improved commerce and mining, established factories, schools, the academy, and, finally, he won for Russia a position of eminence in the political system of Europe. And speaking of his magnificent gifts, shall we forget the gift which is perhaps the most important of all in an autocrat: that of knowing how to use people according to their ability? Generals, ministers, or legislators are not accidentally born into such and such a reign—they are chosen. . . . To choose good men one must have insight; only great men have insight into men. Peter's servants rendered him remarkable assistance on the field of battle, in the Senate, and in the Cabinet. But shall we Russians, keeping in mind our history, agree with ignorant foreigners who claim that Peter was the founder of our political greatness? . . . Shall we forget the princes of Moscow, Ivan I, Ivan III, who may be said to have built a powerful state out of nothing, and—what is of equal importance—to have established in it firm monarchical authority? Peter found the means to achieve greatness—the foundation for it had been laid by the Moscow princes. And, while extolling the glory of this monarch, shall we overlook the pernicious side of his brilliant reign?

Let us not go into his personal vices. But his passion for foreign customs surely exceeded the bounds of reason. Peter was unable to realize that the national spirit

Reprinted by permission of the publishers from *Karamzin's Memoir on Ancient and Modern Russia: A Translation and Analysis*, pp. 120–27, 130–34, 147–48, 155–56, 163–67, 204–05, translated and edited by Richard Pipes, Cambridge, Mass.: Harvard University Press, Copyright © 1959 by the President and Fellows of Harvard College.

constitutes the moral strength of states, which is as indispensable to their stability as is physical might. This national spirit, together with the faith, had saved Russia in the days of the Pretenders. It is nothing else than respect for our national dignity. By uprooting ancient customs, by exposing them to ridicule, by causing them to appear stupid, by praising and introducing foreign elements, the sovereign of the Russians humbled Russian hearts. Does humiliation predispose a man and a citizen to great deeds? The love of the fatherland is bolstered by those national peculiarities which the cosmopolite considers harmless, and thoughtful statesmen beneficial. Enlightenment is commendable, but what does it consist of? The knowledge of things which bring prosperity; arts, crafts, and sciences have no other value. The Russian dress, food, and beards did not interfere with the founding of schools. Two states may stand on the same level of civil enlightenment although their customs differ. One state may borrow from another useful knowledge without borrowing its manners. These manners may change naturally, but to prescribe statutes for them is an act of violence, which is illegal also for an autocratic monarch. . . .

Human life is short, and the rooting of new customs takes time. Peter confined his reform to the gentry [nobility]. Until his reign all Russians, from the plough to the throne, had been alike insofar as they shared certain features of external appearance and of customs. After Peter, the higher classes separated themselves from the lower ones, and the Russian peasant, burgher, and merchant began to treat the Russian gentry [nobility] as Germans, thus weakening the spirit of brotherly national unity binding the estates of the realm.

Over the centuries the people had become accustomed to treat the boyars with the respect due to eminent personages. They bowed with genuine humbleness when, accompanied by their noble retinues, with Asiatic splendor, to the sound of tambourines, the boyars appeared in the streets on their way to church or to the sovereign's council. Peter did away with the title of boyar. He had to have ministers, chancellors, presidents! The ancient, glorious Duma gave way to the Senate, the *prikazy* were replaced by colleges, the *diaki* by secretaries, and so it went. Reforms which made just as little sense for Russians were introduced into the military hierarchy: generals, captains, lieutenants took the place of *voevody, sotniki, piatidesi-atniki,* and so forth. Imitation became for Russians a matter of honor and pride.

Family customs were not spared by the impact of the tsar's activity. The lords opened up their homes; their wives and daughters emerged . . . ; men and women began to mingle in noise-filled rooms at balls and suppers; Russian women ceased to blush at the indiscreet glances of men, and European freedom supplanted Asiatic constraint. . . . As we progressed in the acquisition of social virtues and graces, our families moved into the background; for when we have many acquaintances we feel less need of friends, and sacrifice family ties to social obligations.

I neither say nor think that the ancient Russians who had lived under the grand princes or the tsars were in all respects superior to us. We excel them not only in knowledge, but also in some ways morally; that is to say, we are sometimes overcome with shame by things which left them indifferent, and which indeed are depraved. However, it must be admitted that what we gained in social virtues we lost in civic virtues. Does the name of a Russian carry for us today the same inscrutable force which it had in the past? No wonder. In the reigns of Michael

[Mikhail] and of his son [1613–1676] our ancestors, while assimilating many advantages which were to be found in foreign customs, never lost the conviction that an Orthodox Russian was the most perfect citizen and *Holy Rus'* [Holy Russia] the foremost state in the world. Let this be called a delusion. Yet how much it did to strengthen patriotism and the moral fiber of the country! Would we have today the audacity, after having spent over a century in the school of foreigners, to boast of our civic pride? Once upon a time we used to call all other Europeans *infidels*; now we call them brothers. For whom was it easier to conquer Russia—for *infidels* or for *brothers*? That is, whom was she likely to resist better? Was it conceivable in the reigns of Michael and Fedor for a Russian lord, who owed everything to his fatherland, gaily to abandon his tsar forever, in order to sit in Paris, London, or Vienna, and calmly read in newspapers of the perils confronting our country? We became citizens of the world but ceased in certain respects to be the citizens of Russia. The fault is Peter's.

He was undeniably great. But he could have exalted himself still higher, had he found the means to enlighten Russians without corrupting their civic virtues. Unfortunately, Peter, who was badly brought up and surrounded by young people, met and befriended the Genevan Lefort. This man, whom poverty had driven to Moscow, quite naturally found Russian customs strange, and criticized them in Peter's presence, while lauding to high heaven everything European. The free communities of the German settlement [outside Moscow], which delighted the untrammeled youth, completed the work of Lefort, and the ardent monarch with his inflamed imagination, having seen Europe, decided to transform Russia into Holland.

National inclinations, habits, and ideas were still sufficiently strong to compel Peter, in spite of his theoretical liking for intellectual liberty, to resort to all the horrors of tyranny in order to restrain his subjects, whose loyalty, in fact, was unquestionable. The Secret Chancery of the Preobrazhenskoe operated day and night. Tortures and executions were the means used to accomplish our country's celebrated reform. Many perished for no other crime than the defense of the honor of Russian caftans and beards, which they refused to give up, and for the sake of which they dared to reproach the monarch. These unfortunates felt that by depriving them of their ancient habits Peter was depriving them of the fatherland itself.

The extraordinary efforts of Peter reflect all the strength of his character and of autocratic authority. Nothing frightened him. The Russian church had had since time immemorial its head, first in the person of the Metropolitan, and lastly in that of the Patriarch. Peter proclaimed himself the head of the church, abolishing the Patriarchate as dangerous to unlimited autocracy. But, let us here note, our clergy had never contended against secular authority, either princely or tsarist. Its function had been to serve the latter as a useful tool in affairs of state, and as a conscience at times when it occasionally left the path of virtue. Our primate had one right: not to act, not to rebel, but to preach the truth to the sovereigns—a right which carries blessings not only for the people, but also for the monarch whose happiness consists in justice. From Peter's time on the Russian clergy had deteriorated. Our primates [bishops] turned into mere sycophants of the tsars, whom they eulogized in biblical language from the pulpits. . . .

Shall we close our eyes to yet another glaring mistake of Peter the Great? I mean his founding a new capital [St. Petersburg] on the northern frontier of the state, amidst muddy billows, in places condemned by nature to barrenness and want. Since at that time he controlled neither Riga nor Reval, he might have founded on the shores of the Neva a commercial city for the import and export of merchandise; but the idea of establishing there the residence of our sovereigns was, is, and will remain a *pernicious* one. How many people perished, how much money and labor was expended to carry out this intent? Truly, Petersburg is founded *on tears and corpses*. A foreign traveler, upon entering a country, usually looks for its capital in localities which are most fertile and most propitious for life and health. In Russia, he sees beautiful plains, enriched with all the beauties of nature, shaded by groves of linden trees and oaks, traversed by navigable rivers whose banks please the eye and where, in a moderate climate, the salutary air favors long life. He sees all this, and regretfully turning his back on these beautiful regions, enters sands, marshes, sandy pine forests, where poverty, gloom, and disease hold sway. This is the residence of the Russian sovereigns, who must strive to the utmost to keep the courtiers and guards from starving to death, as well as to make good the annual loss of inhabitants with newcomers, future victims of premature death! Man shall not overcome nature!

But a great man demonstrates his greatness with his very errors. They are difficult if not impossible to undo, for he creates the good and the bad alike forever. Russia was launched on her new course with a mighty hand; we shall never return to bygone times! It would have taken another Peter the Great at least twenty or thirty years to establish the new order much more firmly than all the successors of Peter I up to the time of Catherine II had done. Notwithstanding his marvelous diligence, Peter left much to be finished by his successors. . . .

. . . Catherine II was the true inheritor of Petrine greatness, and the second architect of the new Russia. The main achievement of this unforgettable queen was to soften autocracy without emasculating it. She flattered the so-called *philosophes* of the eighteenth century, and admired the character of the ancient republicans, but she wished to command like a terrestrial goddess—and she did. Peter, having violated national customs, had to have recourse to cruel methods. Catherine could do without them, to the satisfaction of her gentle heart: for she required of Russians nothing contrary to their conscience or civil tradition, and endeavored only to exalt either the fatherland, given her by heaven, or her own fame—and this she tried to achieve by victories, laws, and enlightenment. Her proud, noble soul refused to be debased by timid suspicion, and so vanished the dread of the Secret Chancery. With it left us also the spirit of slavery, at any rate among the upper classes. We accustomed ourselves to pass judgment, to praise in the actions of the sovereign what was praiseworthy, and to criticize what was not. Catherine listened to our opinions, and there were times when she struggled within herself, but she always overcame the desire for revenge—a virtue of great excellence in a monarch! Catherine was confident of her greatness, and firm, unshakable in her declared purposes. Constituting the sole spirit of all the political movements in Russia, and holding firmly in her hands the reins of power, she eschewed executions and tortures, and imbued the hearts of ministers, generals, and all state officials with a most lively fear of arousing her displeasure, and with a burning zeal to win her favor. For all these reasons Catherine could scorn idle gossip; and when sincerity spoke words of truth, the queen thought—"I have authority to demand silence of this generation of Russians, but what will posterity say? And shall thoughts, confined by fear to the heart, be less offensive to me than the spoken word?" This manner of thought, demonstrated by the actions of a reign which lasted for thirty-four years, distinguished her reign from all those which had preceded it in modern Russian history. That is to say, Catherine cleansed autocracy of the stains of tyranny. This calmed men's hearts, and led to the development of secular pleasures, knowledge, and reason.

Having raised throughout her realm the moral value of man, Catherine reexamined all the inner parts of our body politic, and left none unimproved. She emended the statutes of the Senate, the *gubernii* [provinces], the courts, as well as those of the economy, army, and commerce. Special praise is due to the foreign policy of her reign. Under Catherine Russia occupied with honor and glory one of the foremost places in the state system of Europe. In war we vanquished our foes. Peter had astounded Europe with his victories—Catherine made Europe accustomed to them. Russians began to think that nothing in the world could overcome them—a delusion which brought glory to this great queen! Although a woman, she knew how to choose commanders as well as ministers and administrators. Rumiantsev and Suvorov were equals of the most illustrious generals in the world. Prince Viazemskii earned for himself the reputation of a worthy minister with his prudent political economy and the preservation of order and integrity. Shall we reproach Catherine for her excessive love of military glory? Her triumphs assured the external security of the realm. Let foreigners condemn the partition of Poland—we took what was ours. The queen followed the policy of noninterference in wars which were of no concern to Russia and of no use to herself, yet she succeeded in maintaining in the empire the martial spirit which victories had bred.

In his endeavor to please the gentry, the weak Peter III had granted them the freedom to choose whether or not to enter state service. The sagacious Catherine did not abrogate this law, but she was able to neutralize its politically harmful consequences. The queen wanted to supplant the love of Holy Rus', weakened by the reforms of Peter the Great, with civic ambition. To achieve this end she combined new attractions and benefits with service ranks, and devised symbols of distinction, the value of which she endeavored to maintain by bestowing them only on people of merit. The Cross of St. George could not produce valor, but it did bolster it. Many served in order to keep their seat and the right to speak at Assemblies of the Nobility; many, notwithstanding the spread of luxury, greatly preferred titles and ribbons to material gains. All these factors strengthened the necessary dependence of the gentry on the throne.

But we must admit that the most brilliant reign of Catherine was not without its dark side. Morals continued to deteriorate ever more in the palaces as well as in the cottages—in the former from the example set by the dissolute court, in the latter from the spread of taverns, which brought income to the treasury. . . . We must regretfully concede that while zealously praising Catherine for the excellencies of her soul, we unwillingly recall her foibles, and blush for mankind. We must also note that justice did not flourish at that time. . . . The very political institutions devised by Catherine reveal more sparkle than substance; the choice fell not upon the best in content, but the prettiest in form. . . . Catherine sought in laws theoretical perfection, but she failed to consider how to make them function most smoothly and most usefully. She gave us courts without having trained judges; she gave us principles but without the means with which to put them into practice. Many of the harmful consequences of the Petrine system also emerged more clearly in the reign of this queen. Foreigners secured control over our education; the court forgot how to speak Russian; the gentry sunk into debt from the excessive emulation of European luxury; dishonest deals, inspired by a craving for fancy were more common; the sons of Russian boyars dispersed abroad to squander their money and time on the acquisition of a French or English appearance. We possessed academies, institutions of higher learning, popular schools, wise ministers, a delightful society, heroes, a superb army, an illustrious fleet, and a great queen—but we lacked decent upbringing, firm principles, and social morality. The favorite of a great lord, even though of low birth, was not ashamed to live in splendor; the lord himself was not ashamed of corruption. People traded in truth and ranks. Catherine—a great statesman at principal state assemblies—proved a woman in the minutiae of royal activity. She slumbered on a bed of roses, she was deceived or else deceived herself. She either did not see, or did not wish to see many abuses, perhaps considering them unavoidable, and she felt satisfied with the overall successful, glorious progress of her reign. Yet when all is said and done, should we compare all the known epochs of Russian history, virtually all would agree that Catherine's epoch was the happiest for Russian citizens; virtually all would prefer to have lived then than at any other time. . . .

Let us now turn to [the] internal policies [of Alexander I]. Instead of reverting at once to the order established by Catherine, an order affirmed by thirty-four years of experience, and vindicated, so to speak, by the disorders of Paul's reign; instead of abolishing only that which was superfluous and introducing that which was indispensable; in short, instead of first examining and then merely correcting, the counselors of Alexander developed a fancy to introduce novelties into the principal organs of royal authority. In so doing they ignored the wise precept which teaches that all novelty in the political order is an evil to which recourse is to be had only of necessity; for time alone gives statutes the requisite firmness, since we respect more that which we have respected for a long time, and do everything better from habit. . . . Prudent legislators of the past, when compelled to introduce changes into the political systems, tried to depart as little as possible from the old. "If you have no choice but to alter the number of officials and their authority," says the sage Machiavelli, "then, for the sake of the people, do at least keep their titles unchanged." We do quite the opposite: leaving the thing itself unchanged, we invent titles, and contrive different methods to produce the same effect! An evil to which we have grown accustomed bothers us much less than a new evil, while new benefits do not wholly inspire confidence. The reforms accomplished so far give us no reason to believe that future reforms will prove useful; we anticipate them more with dread than with hope, for it is dangerous to tamper with ancient political structures. Russia, after all, has been in existence for a thousand years, and not as a savage horde, but as a great state. Yet we are being constantly told of new institutions and of new laws, as if we had just emerged from the dark American forests! We require more preservative than creative wisdom. Peter's excesses in imitating foreign powers are justly condemned by history, but are they not worse yet in our own time? Where, in what European country, do the people prosper, where does justice flourish, where does good order prevail, where are hearts content and minds at rest? [W]here do we find a civil society fulfilling its true mission—in the Russia of Catherine II, or in the France of Napoleon? Where do we find more arbitrary power and absolutist whim? Where are the affairs of state handled with greater legality and order? We perceive in Alexander's beautiful soul a fervent desire to institute in Russia the rule of law. He could have attained this aim more readily, and made it more difficult for his successors to deviate from the lawful order, had he left the old institutions intact but imbued them, so to say, with a constant zeal to serve the public interest. It is far easier to change new things than old ones. Alexander's successors are much more likely to be impressed with the power which is heightened in the Senate than that which is attributed to the present Council. Novelties breed novelties, and encourage despotic licentiousness.

Let us say once and let us say again that one of the main reasons for the dissatisfaction of Russians with the present government is its excessive fondness for political changes, changes which shake the foundations of the empire, and the advantages of which are still an open question. . . .

[We] are told that the present government had the intention of emancipating proprietary [landlord, or seignorial/seigneurial] serfs. One must know the origins of this bondage. . . . [From all this it] follows: 1) that the present day proprietary serfs were never landowners; that is, they never had land of their own, which is the lawful, inalienable property of the gentry [nobility]; 2) that the serfs who are descended of the *kholopy* [slaves] are also the lawful property of the gentry and cannot be personally emancipated without the landlords receiving some special compensation; 3) that only the free peasants who were bound to their masters by Godunov [Tsar Boris Godunov, reigned 1598–1605] may, in justice, demand their previous freedom; but since 4), we do not know which of them are descended of the *kholopy*, and which of free men, the legislator faces no mean task when he tries to untie this Gordian knot [serfdom], unless he is bold enough to cut through it by proclaiming all to be equally free: the descendants of war captives, purchased, lawful slaves, as well as the descendants of enserfed peasants, the former being freed by virtue of the law of nature, and the latter by virtue of the power of the autocratic monarch to abrogate the statutes of his predecessors. I do not want to pursue this controversy further, but I should like to point out that as far as the state is concerned, natural law yields to civil law, and that the prudent autocrat abrogates only those laws which have become harmful or inadequate, and which can be replaced by superior ones.

What does the emancipation of serfs in Russia entail? That they be allowed to live where they wish, that their masters be deprived of all authority over them, and that they come exclusively under the authority of the state. Very well. But these emancipated peasants will have no land, which—this is incontrovertible—belongs to the gentry. They will, therefore, either stay on with their present landlords, paying them quitrent, cultivating their fields, delivering bread where necessary—in a word, continuing to serve them as before; or else, dissatisfied with the terms, they will move to another, less exacting, landlord. In the first case, is it not likely that the masters, relying on man's natural love for his native soil, will impose on the peasants the most onerous terms? Previously they had spared them, seeing in the serfs their own property, but now the greedy among them will try to exact from the peasants all that is physically possible. The landlords will draw up a contract, the tiller will renege—and there will be lawsuits, eternal lawsuits! In the second case, with the peasant now here, now there, won't the treasury suffer losses in the collection of the [soul tax] and other revenues? Will not agriculture suffer as well? Will not many fields lie fallow, and many granaries stay empty? After all, the bread on our markets comes, for the most part, not from the free farmers but from the gentry. And here is one more evil consequence of emancipation: the peasants, no longer subjected to seignorial [landlord] justice from which there is no appeal and which is free of charge, will take to fighting each other and litigating in the city—what ruin! . . . Freed from the surveillance of the masters . . . , the peasants will take to drinking and villainy—what a gold mine for taverns and corrupt police officials, but what a blow to morals and to the security of the state! In short, at the present time, the gentry, dispersed throughout the realm, assist the monarch in the preservation of peace and order; by divesting them of this supervisory authority, he would, like Atlas, take all of Russia upon his shoulders. Could he bear it? A collapse would be frightful. The primary obligation of the monarch is to safeguard the internal and external unity of the state; benefitting estates and individuals comes second. Alexander wishes to improve the lot of the peasants by granting them freedom; but what if this freedom should harm the state? And will the peasants be happier, freed from their masters' authority, but handed over to their own vices, to tax farmers, and to unscrupulous judges? There can be no question that the serfs of a sensible landlord, one who contends himself with a moderate quitrent or with labor . . . , are happier than state peasants, for they have in him a vigilant protector and defender. Is it not better quietly to take measures to bridle cruel landlords? These men are known to the governors. If the latter faithfully fulfill their obligations, such landlords will promptly become a thing of the past; and unless Russia has wise and honest governors, the free peasants will not prosper either. I do not know whether Godunov did well in depriving the peasants of their freedom since the conditions of that time are not fully known. But I do know that this is not the time to return it to them. Then they had the habits of free men—today they have the habits of slaves. It seems to me that from the point of view of political stability it is safer to enslave men than to give them freedom prematurely. Freedom demands preparation through moral improvement—and who would call . . . the dreadful prevalence of drunkenness a sound preparation for freedom? In conclusion, we have this to say to the good monarch: "Sire! history will not reproach you for the evil which you have inherited (assuming that serfdom actually is an unequivocal evil), but you will answer before God, conscience, and posterity for every harmful consequence of your own statutes." . . .

The gentry [nobility] and the clergy, the Senate and the Synod as repositories of laws, over all—the sovereign, the only legislator, the autocratic source of authority—this is the foundation of the Russian monarchy, which the principles followed by the rulers can either strengthen or weaken.

States, like human beings, have their definite life spans: thus believes philosophy, and thus teaches history. As a sensible mode of life prolongs a man's age, so a sensible political system prolongs the age of states. Who will estimate the years which lie ahead of Russia? I hear the prophets of imminent disaster, but my heart, thank God, refuses to believe them. I see danger, but not as yet destruction!

Russia is still forty million strong, and the autocrat is a sovereign inspired with zeal for the public good. If, being human, he commits errors, he undoubtedly does so with good intentions—this itself is an indication that they will probably be corrected in the future.

If, in general, Alexander should in the future be more cautious in introducing new political institutions, striving above all to strengthen those already in existence, and paying more attention to men than to forms; if, applying severity judiciously, he should induce the lords and officials zealously to fulfill their obligations; if he should conclude peace with Turkey and save Russia from a third, most dangerous war with Napoleon, even at the cost of so-called honor—a luxury only strong states can afford, and one which is by no means identical either with their basic interests or with their self-preservation; if, without further multiplying paper notes [money], through the application of prudent economy, he should reduce the expenditures of the treasury, and devise some means of raising the pay of impoverished military and civil officials; if, through the strict enforcement of custom regulations, he should create a balance between the import and export of merchandise, and if, as must needs follow from these premises, high prices should gradually fall—then Russia would bless Alexander, uncertainty would come to an end, disaffection would evaporate, habits useful to the state would emerge, the progress of things would become more even and regular, the new and the old would blend into one, the past would be recalled ever less frequently, and evil gossip, though present, would lose a sympathetic ear! . . . The fate of Europe does not at present depend on us. Whether France will change her dreadful system, or whether God will change France, no one can tell, but storms do not last forever! The day when we perceive clear skies over Europe, and Alexander enthroned over an *integral* Russia, we shall extol that good fortune of Alexander which he well deserves by virtue of his uncommon kindness!

Loving the fatherland, loving the monarch, I have spoken frankly. I now revert to the silence of a loyal subject with a pure heart, praying to God: may he protect the Tsar and the Russian Empire!

## The Marquis de Custine Is Dazzled
## by the Imperial Court, 1839

I have just returned from the palace [the Winter Palace, in St. Petersburg], after having witnessed, in the Imperial chapel, all the Greek [Orthodox] ceremonies of the marriage of the Grand Duchess Maria [daughter of Nicholas I] with the Duke de Leuchtenberg.

I will endeavour to describe [it] in detail, but in the first place I must speak of the Emperor [Nicholas I].

The predominant expression of his countenance is that of a restless severity, which strikes a beholder at the first glance; and, in spite of the regularity of his features, conveys by no means a pleasant impression. Physiognomists pretend, with much reason, that the hardness of the heart injures the beauty of the countenance. Nevertheless, this expression in the Emperor Nicholas appears to be the result of experience rather than the work of nature. By what long and cruel sufferings must not a man have been tortured, when his countenance excites fear, notwithstanding the voluntary confidence that noble features inspire.

A man charged with the management and direction, in its most minute details, of some immense machine, incessantly fears the derangement of one or other of its various parts. He who obeys suffers only according to the precise measure of the evil inflicted: he who commands, suffers first as other men suffer, and afterwards that common measure of evil is multiplied a hundred fold for him by the workings of imagination and self-love. Responsibility is the punishment of absolute power.

If he be the *primum mobile* [prime mover] of all minds, he becomes the center also of all griefs: the more he is dreaded the more he is to be pitied.

He to whom is accorded unlimited rule sees, even in the common occurrences of life, the specter of revolt. Persuaded that his rights are sacred, he recognizes no bounds to them but those of his own intelligence and will, and he is, therefore, subject to constant annoyance. An unlucky fly, buzzing in the Imperial palace during a ceremony, mortifies the Emperor: the independence of nature appears to him a bad example: every thing which he cannot subject to his arbitrary laws becomes in his eyes as a soldier, who in the heat of battle revolts against his officer. The Emperor of Russia is a military chief, and every day with him is a day of battle.

Nevertheless, at times, some gleams of softness temper the imperious looks of this monarch, and then the expression of affability reveals all the native beauty of his classic features. In the heart of the husband and the father, humanity triumphs for a moment over the policy of the prince. When the sovereign rests from his task of imposing the yoke upon his subjects, he appears happy. This combat between the primitive dignity of the man and the affected gravity of the sovereign appears

From Marquis de Custine, *Empire of the Czar: A Journey Through Eternal Russia*, trans. anon. (London: Longman, 1843; reprinted New York: Doubleday, 1989), pp. 135–38; 142–44; 155–62; 179–85; 195–96.

to me worthy the attention of an observer: it occupied mine the greater part of the time I passed in the chapel.

The Emperor is above the usual height by half a head; his figure is noble, although a little stiff: he has practiced from his youth the Russian custom of girding the body above the loins to such a degree as to push up the stomach into the chest, which produces an unnatural swelling or extension about the ribs, that is as injurious to the health as it is ungraceful in appearance. . . .

The Emperor has a Grecian profile—the forehead high, but receding; the nose straight, and perfectly formed; the mouth very finely cut; the face, which in shape is rather a long oval, is noble; the whole air military, and rather German than Slavonic. His carriage and his attitudes are naturally imposing. He expects always to be gazed at, and never for a moment forgets that he is so. It may even be said that he likes this homage of the eyes.

He passes the greater part of his existence in the open air, at reviews, or in rapid journeys. During summer the shade of his military hat draws across his forehead an oblique line, which marks the action of the sun upon the skin. This line produces a singular effect, but it is not disagreeable, as the cause is at once perceived.

In examining attentively the fine person of this individual on whose will hangs the fate of so many others, I have remarked with involuntary pity that he cannot smile at the same time with the eyes and the mouth, a want of harmony which denotes perpetual constraint; and which makes one remember with regret that easy natural grace, so conspicuous in the less regular but more agreeable countenance of his brother, the Emperor Alexander. The latter, always pleasing, had yet, at times, an assumed manner. The Emperor Nicholas is more sincere; but he has an habitual expression of severity, which sometimes gives the idea of harshness and inflexibility. If, however, he is less fascinating, he is more firm than his late brother: but then it must be added, that he has also a proportionately greater need of firmness. Graceful courtesy insures authority, by removing the desire of resistance. This judicious economy in the exercise of power is a secret of which the Emperor Nicholas is ignorant; he is one who desires to be obeyed, where others desire to be loved.

The figure of the Empress is very elegant; and, though she is extremely thin, I find an indefinable grace about her whole person. Her mien, far from being haughty, as I had been informed, is expressive of an habitual resignation. On entering the chapel she was much affected, and I thought she was going to faint. A nervous convulsion agitated every feature of her face, and caused her head slightly to shake. Her soft blue, but rather sunken, eyes, told of deep sufferings supported with angelic calmness. Her look, full of feeling, has the more power, from its seeming unconscious of possessing any. Faded before her time, and so weak, that it is said she cannot live long, her appearance gives the idea of a passing shadow, or of something that belongs no more to earth. She has never recovered from the anguish she had to undergo on the day of her assession to the throne,[1] and conjugal duty has consumed the rest of her life.

---

1. A reference to the Decembrist uprising.—Ed.

She has given too many idols to Russia,—too many children to the Emperor. . . .

Every one sees the state of the Empress, but no one mentions it. The Emperor loves her: when [she is] ill in bed he attends her himself, watches by her bed-side, and prepares and administers her food or medicine. No sooner is she better, than he destroys her health with the excitement of fêtes and journeys; but the moment that danger is again apprehended, he renounces all his projects. Of the precautions that might prevent evil he has a horror. Wife, children, servants, relations, favorites,—all in Russia must follow in the imperial vortex, and smile on till they die. All must force themselves to conform to the wish of the sovereign, which wish alone forms the destiny of all. The nearer any one is placed to the imperial sun, the more he is a slave to the glory attached to his situation. The Empress is dying under the weight of this slavery. . . .

The Greek marriage rites are long and imposing. Every thing is symbolical in the Eastern church. It seemed to me that the splendors of religion shed a luster over the solemnities of the court.

The walls and the roof of the chapel, the [vestments] of the priests and of their attendants, all glittered with gold and jewels. There are riches enough here to astonish the least poetical imagination. The spectacle vies with the most fanciful description in the Arabian Nights; it is like . . . that Oriental poetry in which sensation prevails over sentiment and thought.

The imperial chapel is not of large dimensions. It was filled with the representatives of all the sovereigns of Europe, and almost of Asia; by strangers like myself, admitted in the suite of the diplomatic corps; by the wives of the ambassadors, and by the great officers of the court. A balustrade separated us from the circular enclosure, within which the altar was raised. This altar is like a low square table. Places in the choir were reserved for the imperial family: at the moment of our arrival they were vacant.

I have seen few things that could compare with the magnificence and solemnity which attended the entrance of the Emperor into this chapel, blazing with gold and jewels. He appeared, advancing with the Empress, and followed by the court retinue. All eyes were immediately fixed upon him, and his family, among whom the betrothed pair shone conspicuously. A marriage of inclination [love] celebrated in broidered habiliments [costumes], and in a place so pompous, was a novelty which crowned the interest of the scene. This was repeated by every one around me; for my own part I cannot give credit to the marvel, nor can I avoid seeing a politic motive in all that is said and done here. The Emperor perhaps deceives himself, and believes that he is performing acts of paternal tenderness, while in the bottom of his heart he may be secretly influenced in his choice by the hope of personal advantage.

It is with ambition as with avarice; misers always calculate, not excepting even the moment when they believe they are yielding to disinterested sentiments.

Although the court was numerous, and the chapel small, there was no confusion. I stood in the midst of the *corps diplomatique*, near the balustrade which separated us from the sanctuary. We were not so crowded as to be unable to distinguish the features and movements of each of the personages, whom duty or curiosity had there brought together. No disorder interrupted the respectful silence that was maintained throughout the assembly. A brilliant sun illuminated the interior of the chapel, where the temperature had, I understood, risen to thirty degrees [centigrade, or 84 degrees F]. We observed in the suite of the Emperor, habited [dressed] in a long robe of gold tissue, and a pointed bonnet, likewise adorned with gold embroidery, a Tatar Khan, who is half tributary and half independent of Russia. This petty sovereign had come to pray the Emperor of all the Russians to admit among *his pages* a son, twelve years old, whom he had brought to Petersburg, hoping thus to secure for the child a suitable destiny. The presence of this declining power, served as a contrast to that of the successful monarch, and reminded me of the triumphal pomps of Rome.

The first ladies of the Russian court, and the wives of the ambassadors of the other courts . . . graced with their presence the circumference of the chapel. At the lower end, which terminated in a brilliant, painted rotunda, were ranged the whole of the imperial family. The gilded ceiling, reflecting the ardent rays of the sun, formed a species of crown around the heads of the sovereigns and their children. The attire and diamonds of the ladies shone with a magic splendor in the midst of all the treasures of Asia, which beamed upon the walls of the sanctuary, where royal magnificence seemed to challenge the majesty of the God whom it honored without forgetting its own.

All this gorgeous display is wonderful, especially to us, if we recall the time, not distant, when the marriage of the daughter of a Tsar would have been scarcely heard of in Europe, and when Peter I declared, that he had a right to leave his crown to whomsoever he pleased. How great a progress for so short a period!

When we reflect on the diplomatic and other conquests of this power, which not long since was considered as of but little importance in the civilized world, we are led to ask ourselves if that which we see is not a dream. The Emperor himself appeared to me not much accustomed to what was passing before him; for he was continually leaving his prayers, and slipping from one side to the other, in order to remedy the omissions of etiquette among his children, or the clergy. This proves that, in Russia, even the court has not yet finished its education. His son-in-law was not placed quite conveniently, whereupon he made him shift his position by about two feet. The Grand Duchess, the priests themselves, and all the great functionaries of the court seemed to be governed by his minute but supreme directions. I felt that it would have been more dignified to leave things as they were, and I could have wished that when once in the chapel, God only had been thought of, and each man had been left to acquit himself of his functions, without his master so scrupulously rectifying each little fault of religious discipline, or of court ceremonial; but in this singular country the absence of liberty is seen everywhere: it is found even at the foot of the altar. Here the spirit of Peter the Great governs the minds of all. . . .

Yesterday at seven o'clock I returned to the palace with several other foreigners, in order to be presented to the Emperor and Empress [at a court ball].

It is easy to perceive that the former cannot for a single instant forget what he is, nor the constant attention which he excites; he studies attitude incessantly,—from whence it results that he is never natural, not even when he is sincere. He has three expressions, not one of which is that of simple benevolence. The most habitual appears to be that of severity. Another, though rarer expression, suits perhaps better his fine face—it is that of solemnity; a third is that of politeness, in which are mixed some shades of gentleness and grace, that serve to temper the chill produced by the two former. But notwithstanding this grace, there is still something which injures the moral influence of the man; it is, that each expression is assumed or cast off at will, without the least trace of one remaining to modify the one next adopted. For such change we are not prepared, and it therefore appears like a mask, that can be put on or off at pleasure. Let not my meaning of the word mask be misunderstood,—I employ it according to its strict etymology. In Greek, *hypocrite* means an actor: the hypocrite was a man who masked himself to perform a play. I would only say, then, that the Emperor is always engaged in acting his part.

[Nor do I say] that the physiognomy of this prince lacks candor, but it lacks natural expression. Thus, the chief evil under which Russia suffers, the absence of liberty, is depicted even on the countenance of its sovereign: he has many masks, but no face. Seek for the man, and you still always find the Emperor.

I believe this remark may be turned to his praise: he acts his part conscientiously. He would accuse himself of weakness were he to be for a single moment plain and simple, or were he to allow it to be seen that he lived, thought, and felt as do common mortals. Without seeming to partake of any of our affections, he is always governor, judge, general, admiral, prince,—never anything more,—never anything less. He will surely grow weary of all this effort as he advances in life; yet it will place him high in the opinion of his people, and perhaps of the world, for the multitude admire the efforts which astonish them,—they pride themselves in seeing the pains that are taken to dazzle them.

Those who knew the Emperor Alexander, eulogize that prince on entirely different grounds. The qualities and the faults of the two brothers were altogether opposite; there was no resemblance, and likewise no sympathy between them. In this country, the memory of a defunct emperor is little honored, and in the present instance inclination accords with the policy that would always have the preceding reign forgotten. Peter the Great is more nearly resembled by Nicholas than by Alexander, and he is more the fashion at the present day. If the ancestors of the emperors are flattered, their immediate predecessors are invariably calumniated.

The present Emperor never lays aside the air of supreme majesty except in his family intercourse. It is there only that he recollects that the natural man has pleasures independent of the duties of state; at least, I hope that it is this disinterested sentiment which attaches him to his domestic circle. His private virtues no doubt aid him in his public capacity, by securing for him the esteem of the world; but I believe he would practice them independently of this calculation.

Among the Russians, sovereign power is respected as is a religion the obligations and authority of which stand independently of the personal merit of its priests: the virtues of the prince being superfluous, are so much the more sincere.

If I lived at Petersburg I should become a courtier, not from any love of place or power, nor from any puerile vanity, but from the desire of discovering some road that might reach the heart of a man who differs from all others. Insensibility is not in him a natural vice, it is the inevitable result of a position which he has not chosen, and which he cannot quit. . . .

The Emperor is, by extraction, more a German than a Russ. The fineness of his features, the regularity of his profile, his military figure, his bearing, naturally a little stiff, all remind one of Germany rather than of Muscovy. His Teutonic temperament must have been long schooled and fettered ere he could have become, as he now is, a thorough Russian. Who knows?—he was perhaps born a plain good-natured man! If so, what must he not have endured before he could appear only as the chieftain of the Slavonians? The obligation of achieving a continual victory over himself in order to reign over others, will explain much in the character of the Emperor Nicholas.

Far from inspiring me with dislike, these things attract me. I cannot help viewing with interest one feared by the rest of the world, and who is, in reality, only so much the more to be commiserated.

To escape as much as possible from the constraint which he imposes on himself, he is as restless as a lion in a cage, or a patient in a fever; he is constantly moving on foot or on horseback; reviewing, carrying on little wars, sailing, maneuvering his fleet, giving and receiving fêtes. Leisure is that which is most dreaded at this court; whence I conclude that no where else is ennui [boredom] so much felt. The Emperor travels incessantly; he journeys over at least 1500 leagues every season, and he has no notion that others have not the strength to do as he does. The Empress loves him, and dreads leaving him; she therefore follows him as well as she can, and is dying of the fatigues and excitement consequent upon this life. . . .

I was presented this evening, not by the French ambassador, but by the grand master of the court ceremonies. Such was the order of the Emperor, of which I was previously informed by our ambassador. I cannot tell whether this is the usual proceeding, but it was the manner in which I was presented to their imperial majesties.

All the foreigners admitted to the honor of approaching their persons, were assembled together in one of the saloons which they would have to cross in proceeding to open the ball. We arrived at the appointed hour, and had to wait a long time for the appearance of the illustrious personages.

There were with me two or three French, a Pole, a Genevese, and several Germans. The opposite side of the saloon was occupied by a row of Russian ladies, assembled there to pay their court.

The Emperor received us with a refined and graceful politeness. At the first glance it was easy to recognize a man who, notwithstanding his power, is obliged and accustomed to humor the self-love of others.

In order to intimate to me that I might, without displeasing him, survey his empire, his majesty did me the honor of saying that it was at least necessary to see Moscow and Nizhnii Novgorod before a just idea of the country could be formed. "Petersburg is Russian," he added, "but it is not Russia."

These few words were pronounced in a tone of voice that could not be forgotten, so strongly was it marked by authoritativeness and firmness. Everybody had spoken to me of the imposing manners, the noble features, and the commanding figure of the Emperor, but no one had prepared me for the power of his voice: it is that of a man born to command. In it there is neither effort nor study, it is a gift developed only by habitual use.

The Empress, on a near approach, has a most winning expression of countenance, and the sound of her voice is as sweetly penetrating as that of the Emperor is naturally imperious.

She asked me if I came to Petersburg with the simple object of traveling. I replied in the affirmative. "I know that you are a curious observer," she continued.

"Yes Madame," I answered, "it is curiosity which brings me to Russia; and this time, at least, I do not regret having yielded to a passion for travel."

"You really think so?" she replied with a gracefulness of manner that was very charming.

"It appears to me that there are such wonderful objects in this country, that to believe them requires that we should see them with the eyes."

"I should wish you to see much and to view favorably."[2]

"This wish of your majesty's is an encouragement."

"If you think well of us, you will say so, but it will be useless; you will not be believed: we are ill understood, and people will not understand us better."

These words in the mouth of the Empress struck me, on account of the preoccupation of idea which they discovered [revealed]. It seemed to me also that she meant to manifest a kind of benevolence towards me, which was expressed with a politeness and a simplicity that are rarely seen.

The Empress, the moment she speaks, inspires confidence as well as respect. Through the reserve which the language and usages of court render compulsory, it is easy to see that she has a heart. This misfortune imparts to her an indefinable charm. She is more than an Empress, she is a woman.

She appeared to be suffering from extreme fatigue. The thinness of her person is quite shocking. The agitation of the life she leads is consuming her, and they say that the ennui of a life more calm would be equally injurious.

The fête which followed our presentation was one of the most magnificent that I have ever seen. The admiration and astonishment with which each saloon of this palace (rebuilt in a year) inspired the whole court, imparted a dramatic interest to the formal pomp of the usual ceremonies. Every hall and every painting was a subject of surprise to the Russians themselves, who now for the first time saw the marvelous abode which the word of their Deity had caused to spring from its ashes.[3] What an effort of human will, thought I, as I contemplated each gallery, sculpture and painting. The style of the ornaments calls to mind the age in which the palace was originally founded [under Empress Elizabeth], and what I saw appeared already ancient. They copy everything in Russia, not excepting even the effects of time. These wonders inspired the crowd with an admiration that was contagious, and my internal indignation at the means by which the miracle was created, began

---

2. Custine's conversations with the Imperial couple were, of course, in French.—Ed.
3. The Winter Palace was rebuilt under Nicholas after a fire in 1837 nearly destroyed it.—Ed.

to diminish. If I could feel such an influence after only two days' abode here, what allowance should not be made for the men who are born, and who pass their life, in the air of the Russian court!—that is in Russia; or it is the air of the court which is breathed from one end of the empire to the other. Even the serfs, through their relations with their lords, feel the influence of that sovereign will which alone animates the country: the courtier who is their master, is for them the image of the Emperor, and the court is present to the Russians wherever there is a man to command, and men to obey. . . .

I must now describe [one] of the magic fêtes at which I am present every evening. With us [in Paris] the balls are disfigured by the somber attire of the men, whereas the varied and brilliant uniforms of the Russian officers give an extreme brilliancy to the saloons of Petersburg.

In Russia the magnificence of the women's apparel is found to accord with the gold of the military dress. . . .

[On this occasion the] whole length of the garden front of the Michael Palace [in St. Petersburg] is ornamented by an Italian colonnade. Yesterday they availed themselves of a temperature of twenty-six degrees [C., or 79 degrees F.] to illuminate the spaces betwixt each pillar of this exterior gallery with clusters of small lamps, arranged in a manner that had a very original effect. The lamps were formed of paper in the shape of tulips, lyres, vases, etc. Their appearance was both tasteful and novel.

The light that proceeded from the groups of lamps was reflected in a picturesque manner upon the pillars of the palace, and among the trees of the garden. The latter was full of people. In the fêtes at Petersburg the people serve as an ornament, just as a collection of rare plants adorns a hot-house. Delightful sounds were heard in the distance, where several orchestras were executing military symphonies, and responding to each other with a harmony that was admirable. The light reflected on the trees had a charming effect. Nothing is more fantastically beautiful than the golden verdure of foliage illuminated during a fine night.

The interior of the grand gallery in which they danced was arranged with a marvelous luxury. Fifteen hundred boxes of the rarest plants in flower formed a grove of fragrant verdure. At one of the extremities of the hall, amid thickets of exotic plants, a fountain threw up a column of fresh and sparkling water: its spray, illumined by the innumerable wax lights, shone like the dust of diamonds, and refreshed the air, always kept in agitation by the movement of the dance. It might have been supposed that these strange plants, including large palms and bananas, all of whose boxes were concealed under a carpet of mossy verdure, grew in their native earth, and that the groups of northern dancers had been transported by enchantment to the forests of the tropics. It was like a dream; there was not merely luxury in the scene, there was poetry. The brilliance of the magic gallery was multiplied a hundred-fold by a greater profusion of enormous and richly gilded pier and other glasses than I had ever elsewhere seen. The windows ranged under the colonnade were left open on account of the excessive heat of the summer night. The hall was lofty, and extended the length of half the palace. The effect of all this magnificence may be better imagined than described. It seemed like the palace of the fairies: all ideas of limits disappeared, and nothing met the eye but space, light, gold, flowers, reflection, illusion, and the giddy movement of the crowd, which crowd itself seemed multiplied to infinity. Every actor in the scene was equal to ten, so greatly did the mirrors aid the effect. I have never seen any thing more beautiful than this crystal palace; but the ball was like other balls, and did not answer to the gorgeous decorations of the edifice. . . .

. . . [B]efore the banquet, the Empress, seated under her canopy of exotic verdure, made me a sign to approach her; and scarcely had I obeyed, when the Emperor also came to the magic fountain, whose shower of diamonds was giving us both light and a freshened atmosphere. He took me by the hand; and led me some steps from the chair of his consort, where he was pleased to converse with me for more than a quarter of an hour on subjects of interest; for this prince does not, like many other princes, speak to you merely that it may be seen he does so.

He first said a few words on the admirable arrangements of the fête; and I remarked, in reply, that in a life so active as his, I was astonished that he could find time for every thing, including even a participation in the pleasures of the crowd.

"Happily," he replied, "the machine of government is very simple in my country; for, with distances which render every thing difficult, if the form of government was complicated, the head of one man would not suffice for its requirements."

I was surprised and flattered by this tone of frankness. The Emperor, who understands better than any one that which is felt, though not expressed, proceeded—replying to my thought—"If I speak to you in this manner, it is because I know that you can understand me: we are continuing the labors of Peter the Great."

"He is not dead, sire; his genius and his will still govern Russia."

When any one speaks in public with the Emperor, a large circle of courtiers gathers at a respectful distance, from whence no one can overhear the sovereign's conversation, though all eyes continue fixed upon him.

It is not the prince who is likely to embarrass you when he does you the honor of conversing; it is his suite.

The Emperor continued:—"It is not very easy to prosecute this work: submission may cause you to believe that there is uniformity among us, but I must undeceive you; there is no other country where is found such diversity of races, of manners, of religion, and of mind, as in Russia. The diversity lies at the bottom, the uniformity appears on the surface, and the unity is only apparent. You see near to us twenty officers, the two first only are Russians; the three next to them are conciliated Poles; several of the others are Germans; there are even the Khans of the Kirguises [Kirgiz, a Turkic people of the steppe], who bring me their sons to educate among my cadets. There is one of them," he said, pointing with his finger to a little Chinese monkey, in a whimsical costume of velvet all bedizened with gold.

"Two hundred thousand children are brought up and instructed at my cost with this child."

"Sire, every thing is done on a large scale in this country—every thing is colossal."

"Too colossal for one man." . . .

"I can truly say, sire, that one of the chief motives of my curiosity in visiting Russia was the desire of approaching a prince who exercises such power over men."

"The Russians are amiable; but he should render himself worthy who would govern such a people."

"Your majesty has better appreciated the wants and the position of this country than any of your predecessors."

"Despotism still exists in Russia: it is the essence of my government, but it accords with the genius of the nation."

"Sire, by stopping Russia on the road of imitation, you are restoring her to herself."

"I love my country, and I believe I understand it. I assure you, that when I feel heartily weary of all the miseries of the times, I endeavor to forget the rest of Europe by retiring towards the interior of Russia."

"In order to refresh yourself at your fountainhead?"

"Precisely so. No one is more from his heart a Russian than I am. I am going to say to you what I would not say to another, but I feel that you will comprehend me."

Here the Emperor interrupted himself, and looked at me attentively. I continued to listen without replying, and he proceeded:—

"I can understand republicanism: it is a plain and straightforward form of government, or, at least, it might be so; I can understand absolute monarchy, for I am myself the head of such an order of things; but I cannot understand a representative monarchy: it is the government of lies, fraud, and corruption; and I would rather fall back even upon China than ever adopt it."

"Sire, I have always regarded representative government as a compact inevitable in certain communities at certain epochs; but like all other compacts, it does not solve questions—it only adjourns difficulties."

The Emperor seemed to say, Go on. I continued:

"It is a truce signed between democracy and monarchy, under the auspices of two very mean tyrants, fear and interest; and it is prolonged by that pride of intellect which takes pleasure in talking, and that popular vanity which satisfies itself on words. In short, it is the aristocracy of oratory, substituted for the aristocracy of birth: it is the government of the lawyers."

"Sir, you speak the truth," said the Emperor, pressing my hand: "I have been a representative sovereign, and the world knows what it has cost me not to have been willing to submit to the exigencies of *this infamous* government (I quote literally). To buy votes, to corrupt consciences, to seduce some in order to deceive others; all those means I disdained, as degrading those who obey as much as those who command, and I have dearly paid the penalty of my straightforwardness; but, God be praised, I have done for ever with this detestable political machine. I shall never more be a constitutional king. I have too much need of saying all that I think ever to consent to reign over any people by means of strategem and intrigue."[4]

The name of Poland, which presented itself incessantly to our thoughts, was not once uttered in this singular conversation.

---

4. Nicholas refers to his experience as constitutional king of Poland according to the charter granted by Alexander I in 1815, an arrangement Nicholas "modified" following the Polish revolt of 1830–1831 against Russian rule.—Ed.

The effect it produced on me was great. I felt myself subdued. The nobleness of sentiment which the emperor displayed, and the frankness of his language, seemed to me greatly to temper his omnipotence.

I confess I was dazzled! A man who could, notwithstanding my ideas of independence, make himself forgiven for being absolute monarch of sixty millions of fellow-beings, was, in my eyes, something beyond our common nature; but I distrusted my own admiration. . . .

## August von Haxthausen Discovers the Russian Peasant Commune, 1844

The Russians first entered the great European family of nations in the eighteenth century. The very fact that they belong to the Eastern church separated them more sharply from the West than one would imagine, since there is no essential difference in the teachings of Roman and Greek Catholicism. More important in isolating them from European cultural development was the Tatar and Turkish rule, which lasted for so many centuries. However, this did help to preserve the original quality of their social organization; almost no foreign elements penetrated the social institutions, particularly to the level of the populace. To our modern conception of things, they thus appear underdeveloped and in many respects rude. Yet these institutions are better suited to the character of these peoples than are those of the western Slavs [Poles and Czechs].

Within the past 150 years the Russians have begun to adopt the civilization of the West. Although this endeavor has been successful among the upper classes and in the governmental institutions, Western culture has hitherto failed to penetrate to the populace. The Russian church and the rigidity of Russian popular institutions have offered unusually strong resistance. Recently, however, a significant change has come about in this respect, above all in the church. The rapid advancement of industry has also begun to corrode the core of Russian national life, the customs, practices, and conceptions of the people. Whether this impulse was a natural outgrowth of the internal development of the nation, whether it was encouraged or merely guided by the government, whether it will redound to the advantage or detriment of the people—these are frivolous questions at the present time, for this movement is an accomplished fact, and no human power can arrest its progress. We can only urge an understanding government to endeavor to preserve the nobility and beauty of the national character, customs, and institutions. . . .

Like their Polish and Bohemian colleagues, the Russians, too, must cope with their language. Until 150 years ago Western culture, thought, and legal concepts had little influence on Russia, so that the inner core of the entire social order could

Text by August von Haxthausen *Studies on the Interior of Russia*, ed. S. Frederick Starr, translated by Eleanore L. M. Schmidt, pp. 275–79, 280–85, 288–93. Copyright © 1972, reprinted by permission of The University of Chicago Press.

evolve almost independently. In the past 150 years, however, when culture in Russia has been exclusively foreign, the language, in particular, adopted a great many alien concepts, and words took on new meanings. Since the educated classes departed from national customs and viewed them instead through foreign glasses, they confused their indigenous institutions with analogous foreign ones. Furthermore, because the language of the educated in everyday life as well as in scholarly studies and in commerce is imbued with foreign concepts, the vocabulary necessary to express genuinely national conditions is often wanting. To restore the original meaning of those words relating to indigenous institutions by divesting them of the secondary meanings which crept in with foreign concepts is one of the greatest tasks confronting Russian scholars.

To clarify our point, let us take as an example the Russian word *mir*. Out of the Latin word *communitas* and the German term *Gemeinde* there developed a specific legal concept, which in all the western European countries has only slightly different nuances of meaning. In each of these languages the corresponding term has a specific juridical and constitutional meaning which is wholly comprehensible to the educated and the uneducated. The Russian word *mir*, on the other hand, as it is used in commercial and legal language or in the colloquial speech of the educated, differs from its meaning in the language of the common people. Among the former this term is synonymous with the French *commune*; it designates a group of people who simply happen to live in the same place, or the administrative district of a city, a borough, or a village. Among the populace its connotation is totally different. Literally the word *mir* implies something sacred; it means both *commune* and *universe* and is best translated by the Greek *cosmos*. We recall no proverb in the German or Romance languages in which the authority, the law, and the sanctity of the commune are recognized. Russian, however, contains a vast number of these:

> God alone directs the *mir*.
> The *mir* is something vast.
> The *mir* is a surging wave.
> The *mir* has a broad neck and nape.
> Cast everything on the *mir*, for the *mir* will carry it away.
> The tear of the *mir* is liquid, but caustic.
> The *mir* sighs, and the cliff explodes.
> The *mir* simply sighs, and it echoes in the forest.
> One chops wood in the forest, and the chips fly about in the *mir*.
> A thread from the *mir* will make a shirt for a naked man.
> No one on earth can dissociate himself from the *mir*.
> What belongs to the *mir* belongs also to the mother's darling.
> Whatever the *mir* decides must come to pass.
> When the entire *mir* sighs, the contemporary generation suffers a miserable death.
> The *mir* is the nation's rampart.

. . . Because the Russian commune or *mir* constitutes in our opinion the real foundation of the entire social order, we should like to sketch its principal features. . . .

To understand the nature of the *mir*, one must carefully examine the fundamental character of the Slavs in general and the Russians in particular. . . . Nowhere are the ties of the blood relationship, the unity of the family and its natural extension, the commune, so clearly revealed as in the Russian people. Family unity and the common ownership of property represented the original character of Slavic society. Among the western Slavs, however, this feature is not as well developed or as strictly preserved as among the Russians.

The family found its unity in its head, the father. Without a father, the family simply could not exist. Because absolute equality prevailed in the family, anarchy would have broken out immediately had there been no common leader. If the father died, his eldest brother or son took his place, assuming absolute paternal authority. Indeed, if the natural succession of paternal authority was interrupted by the insanity of the eldest or his entrance into a religious order, the remaining members of the family elected a leader. Even if the youngest was chosen, he nevertheless became the senior, the father, who was obeyed without question. This custom, which acquired the force of law, has found expression in many proverbs. For example, "The opinion of the eldest is always right." "Where there is age, there is also law." "The younger brothers must respect the eldest like a father." The Russian princes also followed this principle. The grand duke was always called the eldest even if he was younger than the petty princes. . . . In Slavic families organized in this manner, no member possessed an individual fortune; rather, everything was considered to be common property which each adult member would have been entitled to dispose of freely had he not been subordinated to the absolute authority of his natural or elected father. Whoever wanted to withdraw from the unity of the family with its collective ownership of property in order to establish his own independent family (which, however, has always been considered to be a calamity, a *chernyi peredel*), forfeited his share of the communal property and consequently his right of inheritance.

In the course of time the members of the family became so numerous that it was no longer possible to maintain the unity of the communal household. Several members, together with their wives and children, began to establish individual households. They built separate homes and farmsteads but preserved the communal organization with its patriarchal rule. This represents the original Slavic village-community (a family commune) under the authority of its elder (*starik, starshii, starshina, starosta*). The property was not divided into private holdings, but the land was cultivated in common and the harvest equally distributed among all the households. The very same conditions are said to exist today in many regions of Serbia, Bosnia, and Bulgaria. Even in Russia, in the depths of the forest, one finds similar communes among the Raskolniki [Old Believers].

It is clear that these social conditions are incompatible with cultural and in particular agricultural advancement. Throughout Russia proper there nevertheless has developed out of these social conditions a rural organization in which the principle of communal property has been fully retained. The forests and pasture land always remain undivided; the plowlands and meadows are apportioned to the various families in the commune, who, however, do not own the land but have only the right to use it temporarily. Formerly the lots may have been redistributed annually among the married couples of the community, each receiving a share equal to all the others in terms of quality. Today, however, in order to avoid expenses and great inconveniences the land is reapportioned after a certain number of years. If, for example, a father should die and leave six sons who are not of age, the widow generally continues to manage the farm until her sons marry. Then, however, they do not divide among themselves the plot which their father had cultivated; instead this land reverts to the commune, and all six sons receive a share equal to that held by the other members of the community. All together they might hold five to six times the amount of land which their father had held. If the six sons should marry when their father is still alive, then he claims for each one of them an equal allotment of the communal land. Since the sons continue to live in the same household with their father, he does not have to worry about establishing them. On the contrary, a marriage is fortunate for the family. Even if she has no dowry, the arrival of a daughter-in-law means an additional share of the communal property. The marriage and establishment of his daughters is thus the least of a Russian peasant's worries. . . .

In my opinion it is highly probable that the Russians were originally a pastoral people who gradually settled down and adopted farming. Only this hypothesis explains many of the peculiarities in the character, the way of life, and the customs of the Russian people.

The entire social and even political life of the nomadic or pastoral peoples rests on the patriarchal principle. The family subordinated to its father and the tribe headed by its chief represent a natural hierarchy. Only in time of need, peril, or war do the tribes unite. In conformance with the patriarchal principle the senior member of the oldest tribe will step to the head of this alliance. As soon as the danger had ceased to exist, the alliance generally dissolves. A new doctrine, a prophet like Mohammed . . . or the call to conquer the world, as in the case of Genghis Khan, may fire the tribes with enthusiasm. As though driven by instinct, they follow their leader to victory or death. Despotism rests on power; a monarchy, an aristocracy, and a democracy are based on the idea of law. In a patriarchal state the principle of organization and authority is rooted in instinct and custom. The father or patriarch governs with absolute power because nature and custom summon him to rule; the children obey without questioning for the same reason. There are no rights, only duties. It is the father's duty to rule and to provide for his family, that of the children to obey. Since the nomadic peoples own no real property, the basis for the concept of law with all of its intricacies is lacking. Movable property gives rise to and employs only the simplest legal relationships.

The establishment of permanent homes over the past fifteen centuries, the introduction of agriculture, of Christianity, of the European concept of monarchy, and modern civilization gradually produced a political organism which is nearly identical to that found among the other agricultural peoples of Europe. Nevertheless, the fundamental principles of the original nomadic society are still manifest in the character, the customs, and the entire history of the Russians. . . .

The mother's command over the daughters is just as absolute as the father's authority over all his children. The same respect and obedience are shown to the communal authorities, the *starosta* and the white-heads and above all to their common father, the tsar. A Russian has one and the same word for addressing his natural father, the *starosta*, his master, the emperor, and finally, God, namely, "father" or "little father" (*batushka*). Similarly he calls every fellow Russian "brother" (*brat*), whether he knows him or not!

The common Russian (*muzhik*) knows absolutely no servile fear, but only a childlike fear or awe in the presence of his tsar, whom he loves with a devoted tenderness. He enters the military reluctantly, but once a soldier he harbors no resentment or ill will, serving the tsar with the greatest loyalty and devotion. The famous Russian word *prikazano* (it is ordered) has a magical effect on him. It goes without saying that whatever the tsar commands must be done. The Russian would never resist or defy the tsar's order; indeed, the impossibility of its execution would never occur to him. Even in the case of mere police proscriptions, the Russian does not say "it is forbidden" (*zapreshcheno*) but rather "it is not ordered" (*ni prikazano* or *nevoleno*). The profound reverence shown the tsar is evidenced above all in the Russian's attitude toward everything regarded as belonging to the monarch. He has the greatest respect for the *kazennye*, the state lands or the tsar's property. A Russian proverb says: "The *kazennye* do not die, are not consumed by fire and do not drown in water."

There is almost no case of persons responsible for collecting taxes ever having been attacked or robbed, even though they travel long distances alone and often carry considerable sums of money. In northern Russia, in the province of Vologda, where the customs are untainted and the inhabitants very honest, the tax collector, upon arriving in a village, knocks on every window and cries "kassa." Everyone brings him his tax for the year and drops it into a sack. Knowing he will never be cheated, the collector does not bother to check the amount. When night falls, he enters the first good house and places the sack of money under the icon of the saint. He then looks for lodging and sleeps without a care, confident that the next morning he will find everything just as he had left it! . . .

Who would be so bold as to venture a plausible conjecture about the origin of the Russian or indeed of the entire Slavic race? Probably after having wandered about the Asiatic and European steppes for many centuries, several nomadic tribes began to settle in the fertile river valleys. . . . It is likely that the Slavs first settled in the areas around Valdai and Lake Ilmen, with Novgorod later their center. At any rate, this is what their oldest chronicler, Nestor, has stated. Branching out in all directions from this common center, the colonies which they founded were located primarily along the rivers. . . . They established a community which cannot properly be called a city in the western European sense of the word. The distinction between a city and a village was unknown to the ancient Russians, who merely differentiated between mother and daughter communities. As long as the supply of food was adequate, they dwelled together in the same place, but, when it became impossible to extract the necessary food supplies from the soil, the commune sent out colonies in all directions. Individual families never established isolated farms; rather, small communities founded villages. These daughter communes maintained very close ties with the mother commune which governed them, and they even called it mother. Hence we find ancient Mother Suzdal, Mother Vladimir, Mother Novgorod, and Mother Pskov. It was in this way that territories arose. This is undoubtedly the meaning of the expression "land" [*zemlia*], which is used in all the Slavic countries and whose historical origin is so enigmatic. . . .

The mother commune governed the daughter communes of the land and also offered them protection and refuge when an enemy approached. Although the family and communal organization of the mother and the daughter communes was not essentially different, they were nevertheless gradually distinguished by their different means of livelihood. In the mother commune, commerce and industry began to assume a major role, with agriculture declining in importance. The structures erected for its own defense and that of the land gradually gave a different appearance. Because the contacts with civilized nations resulted in an imitation of the external forms of foreign culture, the mother communes took on the features of western European cities. It was primarily the citadel located in the center of the community which gave it an urban appearance. The genuinely Slavic city is always comprised of three parts. In the center is the citadel (*gorod*) with its walls, towers, and battlements. Surrounding the fortress is the industrial city with a circumvallation. The industrial city is encircled by the agricultural city, which, like our European suburbs, is generally divided into several districts. This layout is so basic that even today Moscow's police precincts are not located next to one another but rather around each other.

Although in principle and in appearance there was originally no distinction between the urban and rural communities in Russia, in the course of time a significant difference emerged. The larger municipalities of Novgorod, Kiev, Moscow, and Iaroslavl have become cities as we know them in western Europe. A middle class has come into being which, to be sure, is basically different from its western European counterpart. While the culture, customs, and views of the Russian middle class do not contrast sharply with those of the rural population, they nevertheless have a particularistic local coloration. The history of Novgorod with its rebellions, divisions, and internal wars offers sufficient evidence of this. It should not be forgotten that Novgorod's contacts with the German Hanseatic cities, which extended over a long period of time, probably brought it the ideas of the medieval German bourgeoisie. Moreover, the history and orientation of Novgorod is unique, and its particularism is alien to the Russian character. Hence these peculiarities are not to be found at all, or only to a very minor degree, in the history of the other cities.

This particularism issues from a local patriotic sentiment which is, as we have already mentioned, alien to the Russian character. But in this particularism one can discern the vestiges of the primitive nomadic nature of the people. The nomad knows no attachment to his place of birth or the land which he has inherited from his ancestors. Born in the tent of the horde, he is forever moving about, using the pastures here and there, but he does not claim ownership to a specific piece of property; all the land belongs to him. His family, his horde, and his tribe are the surroundings to which he is devoted and in them he senses his native land, should he be with them in one place today and somewhere else tomorrow. The only places on earth to which he feels bound are the shrines of his tribe and the graves of his ancestors.

Even today one finds in the Russian little attachment to the soil which he temporarily cultivates. His real existence is wandering about on all the highways and byways. Like a nomadic horde he moves about in large caravans with his companions. At home in his village it is only his family, his neighbors, the entire community, above all the individuals to whom he is deeply attached, and not the soil. . . . Without a moment's hesitation he will move to remote areas to establish colonies, if all or even half of the commune takes part and provided only his family and neighbors are among the settlers. The only regret he may have is that he will never again see his village church or the graves of his ancestors. The Russians are imbued with the feeling that the entire country, all Russia, as far as it is inhabited by the Russian race, belongs to all the people and therefore to each member of the tribe. As master of the community, the tsar distributes the land among the various classes of the population with each person being entitled to the use of a share.

To repeat, the Russian feels no profound allegiance to the place of his birth but is imbued with an ardent patriotism. The country of one's ancestors, Holy Russia, the fraternity of all Russians united under the tsar, a common religion, the ancient shrines and the burial places of one's ancestors—all three elements form a vital and harmonious whole which embraces and pervades the Russian's soul. Within this whole everything is personified. Just as every Russian is a brother to every other Russian, in contrast to the foreigner . . . and just as he has special names and affection for his most distant relatives, he also regards the inanimate objects of nature as being kindred and gives them the sacred names of kin. He designates God, the tsar, the priest, and every old man as father and calls the church his mother. He always speaks of Russia as the Holy Mother Russia. The capital of the empire is the Holy Mother Moscow and the mightiest river the Mother Volga. The Don River springing from Lake Ivan is addressed as "You, Don, son of Ivan." He even calls the road from Moscow to Vladimir, "Our dear mother, the Vladimir highway" (nasha matushka Vladimirsha). Even domestic animals and horses in particular are given the names of kin, such as "little mother," "little brother," etc. The center of all remembrance and Russian history is Moscow, the holy mother of the nation, which all Russians love and revere. Throughout his life every Russian cherishes the desire to visit the mother city, to see the spires of the holy churches and to pray at the tombs of Russia's patron saints, for Mother Moscow has always suffered and shed her blood for Russia, just as the Russian people have always sacrificed their lives for her. . . .

Let us now turn our attention to the general character of the Russian people. The sense of unity in the nation, in the commune, and in the family is the foundation of Russian society. Every form of individualism and nearly every form of property, especially land, coalesces in each of these three unities. Except for the nation itself and its representative, the tsar, no one owns real property. All of the property held by the communes and the families is merely granted to them temporarily and thus is not based on the principle of permanent ownership. In every aspect of life the idea of communal property is evident. It constitutes the basic principle of Russian society, whereas among other peoples, the Germanic for example, the principle of communal property applies only in families related by blood or marriage. Among the Russians the family itself is not limited by blood. The servant who raises the son of an aristocrat loves him more than his father and is always considered a member of the family. He is given the specific national name of "uncle." Anyone who has not understood this most fundamental principle of

Russian social life cannot appreciate the profound intimacy of these relationships. Blood is a part of parenthood, to be sure, but not everything. As the peasant commonly says: "Why should I worry about the steer? The calf is mine." He loves and takes as good care of the cuckoo as his own child.

Several sects, specifically the Skoptsy (eunuchs) offer the most unusual example of this. They have wives and children whom they love and care for as if they were their own. Paternal authority, the most absolute of all authority, is not limited exclusively to blood relationship. The adoptive father, the eldest brother, the eldest member of the commune, the *starosta*, and the leader chosen by the *artel* [craft workshop], are obeyed with the same respect. Kinship through baptism and the church is considered to be the equivalent of consanguinity. . . . The tsar is the father of the Russian people, but the land of his birth is of no importance. . . . Empress Catherine II, even though a woman and a foreign princess, found the same respect and affection as the native Russian princes. Upon becoming tsaritsa she belonged to the nation. This profound respect for authority is accorded every person who, by the grace of God, assumes this office.

While the Russian humbly obeys and holds all his superiors in the real or fictive family hierarchy in great esteem, he still feels that everyone is equal. He honors and obeys every father, but he considers himself to be the peer of all his brothers. The sense of equality is most clearly evidenced when the muzhik, the peasant, stands in the presence of the tsar. Knowing that everyone is equal before the tsar, he speaks to him naturally, easily, and without reserve, which a member of the upper classes can seldom do. We can best observe the manifestation of this feeling of equality during all religious celebrations and in church. The peasant has the greatest respect for the *chinovnik* or official; he trembles in the presence of a general, but in church he considers himself to be his equal and even crowds ahead of him. In a Russian church one always sees the peasants huddled together in the front and the persons of rank in the rear. During a special celebration in one of the churches in Moscow an aristocratic gentleman wanted to go to the front of the church. His servant, a Russian-speaking German, said to one of the peasants standing before him: "Don't you see that the general would like to move forward?" The peasant, however, calmly replied: "Brother, we are standing before God, and in His presence we are all equal."

There is a peculiar instability and mobility in the Russian national character. Nowhere do we encounter rigid forms. The Russian does not like rules or a specific regimentation, nor does he want a fixed position in his life or in his profession. He demands the greatest independence; he wants to be able to move about freely, to remain at home or to take to the road as he pleases. He does not want to be subjected to strict discipline or thrift. The Russian is hospitable and prodigal regarding food and drink, never conserving his provisions. He loves risk, gambling, and speculation. Because a great deal of money passes through his hands, he disregards the copeck. In his family life he will not tolerate sharply defined relationships between parent and child, father and son, husband and wife. He does not permit outsiders to mingle in his domestic affairs. He has no property which is permanently his. Rich today, poor tomorrow! A family's wealth hardly lasts two generations. . . . In his relationship to his superiors, however, he does not want to be free, perferring to be ruled. He loves the authoritarianism of a father, of a *starosta*, of the tsar, and of his master every now and then. Indeed, he would seek this subordinate status if he did not already have it. He does not even mind being squeezed now and again, for oppression awakens and steels his faculties so that he can shrewdly escape unjust treatment. He demands that his superiors be firm and severe, but he does not want to be governed by rigid laws or lifeless constitutions. He loves human arbitrariness. He wants a personal tsar whose authority is limited neither by written laws nor by estates. Just as primitive Christianity had no written word or constitution but was merely based on the practice of a Christian life, the Russian, too, desires that secular life be based on this very principle. Each individual should carry his constitution within, for he then will know his place and his vocation. . . .

By means of a highly formalistic system in all the official organs and activities of the state, the government since the reign of Peter I has sought to counteract this flighty and unstable quality in the national character, which endangers the stability of society throughout. So numerous are the governmental controls, laws and ordinances that this system is unparalleled in all of Europe. Outwardly there appears to exist an order, uniformity, and security which the most perceptive critic could not hope to improve upon. But we do not intend to extol this system. The best actions undertaken by the various administrative bodies do not follow these regulations. Charlemagne traveled widely to observe conditions first hand and executed his own projects. Where he was unable to go personally, he sent reliable and experienced emissaries, his *missi,* who submitted an exact account to him. After seeing what had to be done, they took the proper measures in his name. Emperor Nicholas also follows this procedure.

Russian national life resembles the land. It is a vast open plain where everything moves about freely and joyfully. But the government constructed a wall around it and left several gates open.

Every impartial Russian who is familiar with his country and his people will acknowledge the accuracy of our comments on the Russian national character and its embodiment in the organization of the family, the commune, and society. It is clear that many traits may have been exaggerated and others not sufficiently emphasized. Furthermore many features are lacking for a truly comprehensive portrayal. The reasons for this deficiency can be attributed to the fact that this book is to the best of our knowledge the first attempt to describe the Russian character based on these principles and also to the fact that this task has been undertaken by a foreigner.

The foundation as well as the entire edifice of the Russian social order constitutes too sharp a contrast to the principles and ideas of modern Western civilization, which are dominant in the educated classes, not to have been sharply criticized. Hitherto these Russian institutions have not been actively defended. But their passive resistance is so strong and they are rooted so deeply . . . in the national life that superficial attacks are incapable of putting this solid edifice out of joint. Furthermore, no Russian can totally free himself from the inbred inclinations of Russian national character. Western European culture, which will always be merely an adopted culture, cannot eradicate these tendencies. The profound attachment which the Russian still has toward indigenous institutions thwarts every attempt to modify them in their essence. We hope that this foreign, unnational culture will never succeed in seriously threatening or destroying this sanctuary of the Russian people. . . .

In Russia there is no national or family bond without a coordinating focus, a leader, a father, or a master. A leader is absolutely indispensable in the Russian's life. The Russian selects a father if God has taken his natural father from him. Even the free commune chooses an elder (*starosta*) and obeys him unconditionally. He is not the delegate of the community, but rather its father with full paternal authority. One must keep this point clearly in mind if one is to understand the position of the tsar. Russian society is very much like a colony of bees, in which royalty is a natural necessity. Just as the colony would cease to exist without its queen, so, too, would Russian society cease to exist without the tsar. In Russia the tsar is neither the delegate of a sovereign people nor the first servant of the state nor the legitimate lord of the land. He is not even a sovereign ruling by the grace of God. He is simultaneously the unity, the leader, and the father of the people. He holds no office; rather, he occupies the position of a parent. He is simply the father in whom the nation recognizes the unity of its blood. This feeling is as much a part of the common man as the awareness of his own being! Hence, the tsar can never err, in the people's opinion. Whatever he does is always deemed right. Every reduction or limitation of his power, even in the well-intentioned sense of the Germanic organization of the estates, appears to be utter nonsense in the Russian's eyes. Ivan IV could thus commit atrocities and the people remained loyal to him and loved him as before. He is still the favorite of the common people and the hero of folk legends and popular ballads!

At the present time in particular, the organization of the Russian commune is of immense political value to Russia. All the western European nations are suffering from an evil which threatens to destroy them and for which no cure has been found: pauperism and "proletarianism." Protected by its communal organization, Russia escapes this evil. Every Russian has a home and his share of the communal land. Should he personally relinquish his allotment or lose it in some way, his children still have the right as members of the commune to claim their own share. There is no *mob* in Russia, only a *people*. This will continue to be the case as long as new, unnational institutions do not create an unpropertied mob, which we hope is no longer to be feared.

Precisely because it is rooted in the basic character of the entire Slavic race and because it developed spontaneously out of the Russian people, the principle of communal organization is the same throughout Russia. To destroy this principle or even to modify it essentially would be, in my opinion, extremely dangerous. The drawbacks of this organization in regard to agricultural progress are too evident to require an explanation. But the political value of this institution outweighs the disadvantages so greatly that they never could be placed on the same scale. Furthermore, I do believe that the detrimental effects can be offset or modified in various ways without eliminating the principle—for example, by restoring the original system of cultivating the land, particularly in the smaller communes or in the subdivisions of the larger communes. This could be accomplished by abolishing the distribution of land and by reintroducing communal agriculture. In my opinion these proposals can be realized among a people so accustomed to obeying authority. I am certain that agriculture could be carried on much more efficiently in this manner and that no one would be at a disadvantage if, instead of dividing the land, the harvest were equally distributed.

# Further Reading

J. R. Black, *Nicholas Karamzin and Russian Society in the Nineteenth Century: A Study in Russian Political and Historical Thought* (1975)

David Christian, "The Political Ideals of Michael Speransky," *Slavonic and East European Review*, 54 (1976), 192–213

John S. Curtiss, *The Russian Army under Nicholas I, 1825–1855* (1965)

———, *Russia's Crimean War* (1979)

Marquis de Custine, *Letters from Russia*, ed. and trans. Robin Buss (1991)

George F. Kennan, *The Marquis de Custine and His "Russia in 1839"* (1971)

W. Bruce Lincoln, *Nicholas I, Emperor and Autocrat of All the Russias* (1989)

Allen McConnell, *Tsar Alexander I: Paternalistic Reformer* (1970, 1993)

Roderick E. McGrew, *Paul I of Russia, 1754–1801* (1992)

Alan Palmer, *Alexander I, Tsar of War and Peace* (1974)

A. E. Presniakov, *Emperor Nicholas I of Russia: The Apogee of Autocracy*, trans. Judith C. Zacek (1974; originally published Leningrad, 1925)

Marc Raeff, *The Decembrist Movement* (1966)

———, *Michael Speransky, Statesman of Imperial Russia*, 2d ed. (1969)

Hugh Ragsdale, ed., *Paul I: A Reassessment of His Life and Reign* (1979)

———, *Tsar Paul and the Question of Madness* (1988)

Nicholas V. Riasanovsky, *Nicholas I and Official Nationality in Russia, 1825–1855* (1959, 1961)

———, *A Parting of Ways: Government and the Educated Public in Russia, 1801–1855* (1976)

D. B. Saunders, "Historians and Concepts of Nationality in Early Nineteenth-Century Russia," *Slavonic and East European Review*, 60 (1982), 44–62

Elise Kimerling Wirtschafter, *From Serf to Soldier* (1990)

C H A P T E R  **8**

# Emancipation and the Great Reforms

I n the 1860s and 1870s the government of Emperor Alexander II
(reigned 1855–1881) undertook a series of "Great Reforms" in Russia, the most fundamental of which was peasant emancipation. Reform of local administration (at the provincial, district, and town levels) soon followed, and was aimed at establishing new organs of
representative government—particularly the so-called *zemstvo,* or
elected council—at these local levels while stimulating local initiative
in such matters as elementary education and public health. At the
same time, the archaic Russian judicial system was overhauled, universal military conscription (with a much reduced term of service) was introduced, a central state bank was created, and government control
of the universities as well as official censorship were curtailed. Factors
such as the growing influence of Western ideas on educated Russians
and public disgust with an often arbitrary, inefficient, and corrupt bureaucracy no doubt played their part in convincing the Imperial government of the need for reform—as did manifestations of peasant unhappiness with the burdens of serfdom. Yet historians generally agree
that Russia's defeat in the Crimean War was the key factor, as it persuaded Alexander II and his principal advisors that without basic internal change the Russian Empire could not hope to maintain its hard-
won position as a major world power. There is much less agreement,
however, regarding the overall results of the Great Reforms. Some historians stress the degree to which they succeeded in modernizing Russia by western standards, while others point to their more or less
serious flaws. One thing is certain: politically the Russian Empire
remained, after the Great Reforms as before, a top-heavy autocracy,
with all executive, legislative, and judicial power ultimately concentrated in the hands of the emperor. And if the emperor, for whatever
reason, should change his mind about reform . . . ?

# Essays

To emancipate the Russian peasantry from the "Gordian knot" of serfdom was an immense undertaking for the Imperial government, as it would directly affect the lives of some 22,700,000 male serfs (seigneurial peasants) and their at least equally numerous female relatives, who together constituted about 47 percent of the peasant population of the Russian Empire or some 40 percent of the Empire's total population. (Figures from the Imperial census of 1858–1859; another 23,500,000 male "rural residents" were classified as "state peasants," and nearly 2,000,000 more were designated "appanage peasants"—that is, peasants living on lands assigned to members of the Imperial family.) The state and appanage peasants, representing respectively 49 and 4 percent of the peasant population, were the subjects of separate legislation enacted later in the 1860s. The famous Emancipation of 1861 was directed first and foremost at the 22,700,000 seigneurial peasants or serfs proper (including approximately 1,500,000 household serfs, or domestic servants) and their nearly 104,000 noble landlords.

Peasant emancipation in some form or another had been discussed in Russian government circles for decades, and under Nicholas I committees had been formed to draw up concrete proposals. But these initiatives had little effect until 1857–1858, when Alexander II created a powerful Main Committee on Peasant Affairs and various intergovernmental Editing Commissions charged with hammering out the principles and language of the emancipation legislation. The resulting statutes, which were nothing if not complex, were clear on two basic points: the peasants should be freed of landlord control, and there should be some sort of land settlement. The rest was a welter of confusing and even contradictory conditions and clauses. The sometimes wavering autocrat, Alexander II, assisted by "enlightened bureaucrats," had done battle against all but a small minority of the serf-owning nobility; but the nobility's resistance as well as urgent financial concerns had complicated and watered down the Emancipation's provisions regarding peasant land allotments and redemption payments. The Emancipation also left intact the traditional peasant commune, with its antiquated agricultural methods, and did little to alleviate peasant poverty. Indeed, the problems and flaws of the Emancipation, seen in the longer term, are emphasized by historians as much as its basic achievements. The first essay below, by Francis William Wcislo of Vanderbilt University, is a case in point.

Wcislo's essay is followed by excerpts from Richard Wortman's study of the Judicial Reform of 1864, on whose success depended so much on Russia's future development. Professor Wortman, who teaches Russian history at Columbia University, also sees this reform as the culmination of a process going back decades, tracking it to the gradual emergence within the Imperial government of a group of legal experts who aspired to create an independent judiciary and legal profession in Russia. But the fate of the Judicial Reform, Wortman further shows, was also highly problematic, as it ran counter to the government's ingrained habits of autocracy and bureaucracy, which ultimately subverted it.

# The Dilemmas of Emancipation

## FRANCIS WILLIAM WCISLO

The abolition of serfdom was a triumph of bureaucratic reform. It was also a victory fraught with consequences for the future. A decade before this event, the social and political order shaped by the institution of serfdom had seemed immutable, its alteration a possibly dangerous and apparently impossible task. Moreover, because the threads of the Gordian knot [serfdom] bound mentalities as well, both officials in the government and members of the nobility found it easier to dabble with the servile *status quo* than contemplate its elimination. Ten years later, rural society had been lifted off its servile foundations and placed down again within economic and administrative structures of the state's own making: a herculean act seldom rivaled in previous or subsequent Russian history.

Much of the responsibility for this achievement belonged to a handful of enlightened officials, whose influence was magnified by the uncompromising belief in legality, rationalism, and state power that education and service had inspired in them. Ensconced in ministerial institutions and sheltered by the most traditional trappings of personalized autocratic power . . . and [supported by] the commitment of the sovereign tsar Alexander II, these officials maneuvered the state toward a goal that had eluded the preceding generation. And they strengthened, if not created altogether, the example and tradition of statist reform for those who succeeded them.

Yet the emancipation also left a range of unresolved dilemmas for which these officials also bore ultimate responsibility. First, many of the administrative reforms that the Editing Commissions had assumed would accompany abolition were not realized—although here the growing reluctance of Alexander II to pursue the far-reaching changes he had patronized earlier must be acknowledged as well. General administrative reform was never achieved during the reign of Alexander II. And state and appanage peasants, the other half of Russia's peasant population, received their emancipation under separate legislative acts only later in the 1860s. Local self-administration, created by the zemstvo statute of 1864 to address important administrative concerns and involve the provincial nobility in local affairs, was an appendage grafted onto the state apparatus. Its institutional relations to government authority were never defined, and its role in local government was constrained from the outset.

Second, although officials of the Editing Commissions had struggled to change these patterns, the results of their work also strengthened the superordinate bureaucratic and police hegemony that had been—and after 1861 increasingly continued to be—a characteristic feature of Russian administration. Assuming supervision of the land redemption operation greatly expanded the arena of government fiscal concerns and provided a powerful economic rationale for intensifying the supervision of the state's "debtor," the peasant commune. The commissions created a new

From Francis William Wcislo, *Reforming Rural Russia: State, Local Society, and National Politics, 1855–1914* (Princeton University Press, 1990), pp. 43–45.

network of peasant self-administration, which, although intended as a vehicle for civil order and progress, was burdened with police and fiscal obligations and which, in turn, saddled the state with an echelon of peasant officialdom. The emancipation legislation also solidified the estate structure of society by extending administration and law to the seigneurial peasantry. As we shall have occasion to see, this institutional and legal isolation of a peasantry that enlightened officials had hoped to incorporate eventually into rural civil society rigidified the institutional separation dividing peasants from it and created grounds for what contemporaries soon would begin to call "the estate segregation of the peasants."

Third, the emancipation statute posed a number of other intractable problems for future relations between state and educated society. A reform conducted by the state in the interests of the state largely ignored the interests of a society that itself had experienced the invigorating years of the later 1850s. While the rise of the radical intelligentsia lies outside this discussion, one certainly can point to the disillusionment of noble provincial deputies in 1859–1860, the disaffection generally evident among educated strata before the Polish rebellion of 1863–1864, and the spurt of oppositionist, at times overtly constitutionalist sentiment, which between 1861 and 1865 became evident among some provincial noble and zemstvo assemblies. Indeed, after 1866 zemstvo self-administration itself became a festering reminder of the distance separating state and society in the emancipation's aftermath.

Perhaps the final and most critical consequence of emancipation was the responsibility that the state had assumed for *krest'ianskoe delo*—"the peasant matter." In his final report to Alexander, Rostovtsev [General Ia. I. Rostovtsev, the leading official in the emancipation process] had assured the tsar that the emancipation statute would effect an orderly and impartial resolution of serfdom, guarantee the economic interests of the nobility, and assure the future prosperity of the peasantry. In order to accomplish these sweeping goals, the government would broaden its administrative and legal presence in rural society, tying the very legitimacy of autocratic authority to the order and prosperity it had promised to secure. The stakes of this game were quite high, indeed, and the round to be played of very long duration.

## Towards the Rule of Law

### RICHARD S. WORTMAN

The reform of 1864 created a modern judicial system and introduced the necessary preconditions to a rule of law in Russia. The new courts enjoyed complete discretion in civil suits, bringing to an end the intervention of administrative authorities in disputes between individuals. Protecting property rights and the interests of creditors, they provided elements of legal security in Russian life. Though

From Richard S. Wortman, *The Development of a Russian Legal Consciousness*, pp. 269–70, 275–80, 282–89. Copyright © 1976, reprinted by permission of The University of Chicago Press.

the guarantees for the accused in criminal prosecution were far from complete, the statutes established rules against arbitrary arrest and other denials of personal liberty. They made legal defense a regular part of criminal trials. The police continued to enjoy rights of preliminary detention and immunities from official responsibility, but they usually observed the rules of the statutes in nonpolitical cases. It is clear that whatever their deficiencies, the independent courts made available remedies and means to safeguard personal rights that were unattainable in the past.

The judges in the new courts developed a sense of the competence and the integrity of the judicial system. While the *Digest of Laws* continued to be the law of the land, they evolved their own body of legal norms and precedents that relied increasingly on western principles of jurisprudence. They created the beginnings of a Russian common law. Those who attained high governmental office fought attempts to abridge the independence of the judiciary. In the last two decades of the nineteenth century the large number of former legal officials in the State Council resisted attempts to cripple or eliminate the jury system and to restore the "unity" of state institutions by reinstating administrative control of the courts.[1] With the reform, a Russian bar arose with high professional standards and established itself during the next half-century as a group working to defend and extend the rights of the individual in Russia.

The officials in the new judiciary assumed authority over areas of the law that had previously been within the purview of the administration. They enjoyed the authority that accrues to technical expertise, what Talcott Parsons describes as "the specificity of function," which allows the professional to enjoy authority, but only in his special field. Such authority disregards the hierarchical principles upon which authoritarian government is based. . . . This specialization gives rise not only to new authority, but to an ethos that endows the professional with a sense of his own responsibilities, goals, and importance. In Russia, where legal professionals were faced with a general sense of lawlessness and an incomprehension of the law, this ethos grew into a sense of mission. They regarded the dispensation of justice as their own special responsibility, thus claiming an authority that had been viewed as the monarch's prerogative.

Specialization, it is likely, proceeded in other branches of the [Imperial] administration as well after the Great Reforms. Undoubtedly, in other ministries the level of education of personnel continued to rise during the second half of the nineteenth century, and specialized expertise became more common. But until we have detailed monographic studies on other institutions, we cannot assess the extent of these tendencies and the nature of their impact on the operation of autocracy. It appears, however, that nowhere did it proceed as far as in the judiciary during the decades after the reform. . . . Alexander II's notion of unlimited power, as a "tangible personal possession," placed a limit on the rationalizing tendencies the tsar would allow. The concessions to judicial expertise, as we have seen, were a result of the

---

1. The State Council, a body of experts appointed to assist the sovereign in legislation, was created by Alexander I in 1810.—Ed.

economic exigencies of the reform era, and the particularly grievous state of the courts. Thus, while it is probable that professional competence rose generally in the administration, nowhere would the sense of professional consciousness be as articulate as it was in the judiciary.

But the specialized authority of the new judiciary fit uncomfortably into the traditional patterns of autocratic attitudes. The sacrifice of part of sovereign author-ity might lead to the loss of supreme prerogatives. The ruler feared that legal interpretation could not be kept within bounds, that once a judiciary began to interpret the law, interpretation could pass imperceptibly into rulings on law that would have the semblance of legislative enactment. It was this misgiving that had made Catherine the Great and Alexander I so wary in their dealings with the Senate, and that underlaid Nicholas I's general attitudes toward judicial authority.

The new judiciary introduced an element of disruption into Russian institutions that would split the Russian polity into mutually antagonistic and uncomprehending parts. The clashes took place at a high level—where the officials responsible for the defense of the interests of administration and judiciary confronted each other, and often proved incapable of fathoming each other's mentalities or goals. On the one side were the administrators, beholden to the power of the executive as the instrument of the autocratic will; on the other, the legal officials who regarded the judiciary as the only guarantor of justice. The administrators feared legal expertise, which seemed to introduce doubts and the snares of legal reasoning when forceful action was called for. The legal officials feared the government, which seemed, as always, to regard the judiciary as a nuisance thwarting its political designs.

The traditional fears of the autocrat were immediately given substance by the efforts of Minister of Justice [D. N.] Zamiatnin. Hardly was the ink dry on the statutes of 1864, when Zamiatnin sought to aggrandize the Ministry of Justice at the expense of the other branches of the administration. . . .

The minister of interior represented the forces of self-defense within the autoc-racy. While an independent judiciary encouraged the flourishing of autonomous and dynamic forces in society, the autocracy had traditionally been suspicious of all independent groups as bearers of opposition and sedition. The suspicion persisted through the reforms, and would seek the first signs of threat to burst forth once again, now in new circumstances, when increased social activity raised untold possibilities of loss of autocratic control. Karakazov's attempt on the life of the tsar [in 1866] and the articles in liberal journals were immediate sources of distress. But any disturbance of the placidity of the system, inevitable in the postreform condi-tions, would have been enough to reawaken the feelings of insecurity and direct the tsar to his primary concern, the preservation of the autocratic system. . . .

In their first years, the new courts threatened lower levels of the administration as well. Independent courts placed a limit on administrative authority that neither governors nor police officials were accustomed to, and both complained loudly. Police chiefs felt it humiliating to appear before court investigators at court hearings. The Kazan governor complained . . . that the procurators had the right to issue warnings to the police and even to drag them into court. "That means they have two superiors? They won't think me worth a cent. What kind of head of the province am I after this?" The Orel governor found that the police were refraining from preparing reports to avoid the chagrin of appearing in court. They felt especially humiliated by the authority justices of the peace enjoyed to issue warnings to them, and the procurators to initiate disciplinary procedures against them. Prince [V. F.] Odoevsky wrote in September 1866 that the Moscow police were complaining that the courts hindered their work: "They don't let them hit or yell at people, or, even worse, let them take money from anyone and everyone."

The governors, too, felt humiliated by the new practices. They objected to the prohibition against their official visits to the courts. They regretted the loss of authority to supervise the lower ranks of judicial personnel and their inability to influence appointments of justices of the peace. The Riazan and Orel governors wanted the right to receive information on criminal investigations, from which they were now excluded. Judicial . . . officials refused to yield to pressures to appoint governors' protégés.

Many aspects of the new system affronted the governors. At special commissions, they were distressed to find themselves only second in rank to the chairmen of the Judicial Chambers. . . . Many judicial officials refused to appear before governors when summoned. . . . In 1870, a crisis developed in Kherson province, when the entire judicial corps defied an order by a newly appointed governor to appear before him. In retaliation, the governor ordered the police not to cooperate with the courts. The police chief began composing reports accusing an assistant-procurator of drunken conduct. That assistant-procurator, it turned out, was in charge of a case involving illegal actions by a police officer. The police chief also accused a judge in the Circuit Court of robbery and abduction.

Filled with pride in their new station, some judicial officials felt emboldened to make open shows of disrespect. The chairman of the Orel Circuit Court returned a notice from the governor that invited the members of the judiciary to prayers for forthcoming holidays. The chairman informed him that "members of the court, by the force of law itself are placed beyond dependence on the Governor." The Olonets governor submitted a list of impertinences committed by members of the courts. A court investigator had appeared before him in a sheepskin coat, claiming that he did not have to wear a uniform. Other court investigators sent careless reports to him written on scraps of paper. Judges appeared at committee meetings in casual jackets rather than uniforms. The uncertainty of the relations allowed the members of the judiciary [said one] to "make direct ridicule of the administration." [Indeed,] the courts seemed hostile to the needs of the administration. . . .

Between New Year's Day and Easter 1867, Zamiatnin's position [as Minister of Justice] became untenable. The tsar felt himself increasingly uncomfortable with the independent courts, and Zamiatnin would not let him forget the new limits to his authority. . . . In April 1867, Zamiatnin was relieved as minister. His passing went unlamented in the upper ranks of the administration. His commitment to the judiciary lost him . . . imperial favor. He remained in the State Council, but the respect he received was formal and cursory. On the anniversary of his fiftieth year in the imperial administration in 1873, the government withheld the customary recognition for long service. Congratulations came only from the judiciary. A delegation arrived from the Moscow courts, and he received thirty telegrams from various officials in courts across Russia.

The fall of Zamiatnin brought to an end the brief period of assertive leadership by a minister committed to the judiciary. Prince Sergei Urosov served as acting minister for six months, then Count Constantine Ivanovich Pahlen became minister of justice. Pahlen, while not opposed to the independence of the judiciary, worked to ensure that it would not arrogate to itself a position above its station in the Russian state system. A [graduate] of Petersburg University, the thirty-four-year-old Pahlen was the first minister of justice to hold a law degree. But his rapid rise had occurred entirely through the Ministry of Interior. The heir to an estate of three thousand *desiatiny* [about 8,100 acres], he had associated himself with the conservative group of large landowners in the government and was a protégé of its leaders. . . . He had served as vice-director of the Department of Police, then as governor of Pskov province. In these positions, he had openly defended the interests of the police and administration against the threat of a new judiciary. When Zamiatnin had visited Pskov to select officials for the new courts, Pahlen had made a point to be out of town on a tour of the province. His appointment struck the judicial cadres as an openly hostile act.

Pahlen early was apprehensive of the menace posed by the judiciary to administrative hegemony. He shared the sense that judicial authority could not be limited unless subordinated. Even before the new courts had appeared in Pskov, he warned, in 1865, that "the influence of the police will weaken as a result of the full dependence of the political authority on the judicial." As minister, he became a defender of the governors and the police in their squabbles with the independent judiciary. He supported a project, sponsored by Petersburg Police Chief Trepov, which would have allowed the police to issue their own administrative rulings, making them responsible only to the governor. This plan . . . was forestalled by strong opposition in the State Council. But during the 1870s Pahlen was able to secure approval for individual measures enhancing the role of the police.

The chief aim of Pahlen's policy in his first years as minister was to make the agencies of prosecution an effective arm of the government. The procurators of the 1860s regarded themselves as impartial defenders of the law, and were not, in Pahlen's mind, sufficiently concerned with securing convictions. He had in common with Zamiatnin a friendliness and ability to associate with subordinates, and tried to win them over to his point of view by persuasion. But when this did not work, he could use more direct methods. Most prominent of these in the late sixties was his effort to end the independence of the court investigators. The new investigators, introduced in 1860, had developed before the reform into a cadre with high morale that worked together with the procurators and felt a common esprit with them. Pahlen changed all investigators' appointments to acting investigators, and made them completely dependent on the whim of their superiors and the ministry. The effect on their morale was devastating: They lost the standing and independence they enjoyed as members of the judiciary, and became petty *chinovniki* holding inferior, insecure positions. Pahlen succeeded in destroying the spirit uniting procurators and investigators that had helped to promote an independent, professional view of the role of prosecution. . . .

Once reliable and loyal leadership was ensured for the new judiciary, the government attempted to make use of the courts to answer the challenge presented by the revolutionary movement. The tsar and his advisors had expected the new sense of legality engendered by the reform to promote the respect for law in the population and to align the interests of the population more closely with those of the regime. Pahlen was the chief proponent of the view that court prosecution could stigmatize the revolutionaries as outlaws and neutralize their appeal. He tried to use the courts to dispense political justice. . . .

But the political justice of the 1870s did not achieve its appointed goals. The [public] trials [of accused—or self-proclaimed—revolutionaries] proved serious miscalculations that only revealed the gulf between the principles animating the autocracy and its judiciary. The public would watch the prosecution clumsily fumbling to bring in convictions, often on weak or nonexistent grounds. Conservatives, like Aleksei Tolstoi and Pobedonostev [see Chapter 9], would see in the trials a dangerous concession of the autocracy's power of punishment to popular judgment. By 1878, Pahlen's brash self-confidence appeared a tragicomic self-delusion that pointed to the need for a more ruthless policy toward the judiciary.

The refusal of the courts to deal harshly with the revolutionaries was in part the result of the sharp division that had grown up between state and society in Russia. The reformers, when prescribing public jury trials in 1862, had presumed a government "not rejecting any useful transformations for the perfection of the state administration and the social order." They had predicated their recommendation of the jury system upon "a certain degree of harmony between the strivings of the government and society." Then the momentum of reform gradually diminished, and the censorship and police continued to be active in suppressing free thought, all of which left aspirations unsatisfied and created bitter resentments toward the government.

Judges in political trials, despite their image of Olympian impartiality, often are influenced by their social sympathies and opinions. But many of the judges who dismayed the government with their impartiality or leniency were not sympathetic to the revolutionaries. . . . The verdicts and sentences were at least in part the result of the way the government approached the problems of prosecution. The administration's contempt for the legal process ensured an ignorance of the problems of dealing with the courts. Pahlen, carrying the administrative mentality into the judicial system, treated the organization of the prosecution with nonchalance and even apathy. He tried to remain above demeaning clashes in the legal arena, where the state had to play the role of equal adversary. He scorned issues of jurisprudence. "Akh, all of that is theory," was his customary reply to opinions on legal questions. But this fashionable *hauteur* [arrogance] would leave the government at the mercy of those who could exercise legal expertise.

The most extraordinary feature of the trials of the 1870s was not the government's cynical use of the courts for political purposes, which is the usual function of the political justice, but its unwillingness to comprehend what was involved in prosecuting these cases. . . . So confident was Pahlen that the judges would respond sympathetically to the government's case, that he took no care to have the prosecution conducted effectively. . . .

Yet the failure of his approach did not change Pahlen's mind. Rather it drove him to try harder to win approval for the government's struggle against the revolutionaries. His last attempt to use the courts as an instrument of autocratic policy was the trial of Vera Zasulich [in 1878]. Zasulich had shot and wounded Trepov, the

Petersburg governor-general, in retaliation for his striking a revolutionary prisoner, Bogoliubov. There was no doubt about the shooting; Zasulich herself openly admitted it. Pahlen now committed what was perhaps his greatest miscalculation. Since there was no doubt about the act, he decided to turn the case into a jury trial, hoping, as the reformers had promised, to use the jury as a means of branding the revolutionaries for what they were. Accordingly, he decided to try the case not as a political trial but as a simple attempted murder, requiring a jury, and he had evidence of Zasulich's revolutionary associations withheld.

Pahlen again assumed an attitude of indifference toward the prosecution. After two procurators refused to take the case, and resigned their positions, the ministry settled for Kessel, a mediocrity who had only recently been promoted to his position. Pahlen's own efforts were limited to a clumsy attempt to influence Koni, the presiding judge in the Petersburg Circuit Court. He repeatedly asked Koni to guarantee him a verdict of guilty. When Koni refused, he threatened to tell the tsar or remove the case from the jurisdiction of the jury. "The prosecutor is not so important," he told Koni. "We are relying more on you. . . . What's a prosecutor?" When informed that Kessel was a poor prosecutor, Pahlen replied, according to Koni, "It doesn't matter, it is such an open and shut case."

The verdict of not guilty sent the audience into a tumult. "Cries of uninhibited joy, hysterical sobbing, desperate applause, the stamping of feet, cries: *Bravo! Ura! Molodtsy! Vera! Verochka! Verochka!*" Many crossed themselves, many in the upper "more democratic section" embraced each other. But enthusiastic applause also came from the section reserved for judges. The press greeted the decision with a similar acclaim. It was seen as the triumph of public opinion, an open protest of "public conscience" against the oppression of autocracy, the sign of an awakening of the forces of society. But the Zasulich verdict taught other lessons as well, and, as has been so often the case, the voice of the future proved to be the voice of the past. Pobedonostev wrote to his pupil [the future Alexander III], in horror, that the response of the audience was "just like at the end of a drama in the Mikhailovskii Theatre."

> Most important, how can this attempt be regarded as not political! And these people resolved out of a faint-hearted fear to offend public opinion, out of a wish to strut before the intelligentsia and even Europe, to show respect for the jury system. The state interest connected with this case was so great and important that it should have been defended at all costs, with full certainty, without the slightest thought of the possibility of excusing the crime.

The jury's acquittal of Zasulich dealt the final blow to Pahlen's policy. The judgment, taken in what appeared as flagrant disregard of the facts, merely confirmed the lingering fear that, rather than impartial tribunals, the courts represented a political element, a forum for antigovernment sentiments menacing to the autocratic power. Pahlen shortly submitted his resignation. His successors . . . were officials who had come out of the judicial system and could speak for its interests. But the judicial system itself had shown its unreliability and their influence in the government was small.

After the Zasulich trial, the government gave up its pretense of legality in its struggle against the revolutionaries. It dealt with them through the administrative order—direct police punishment or by summary military justice.[2] This tendency culminated in the law of 14 August 1881, which provided for siege conditions with broad executive authority for summary justice in political crimes [see Chapter 9]. The strained tolerance the autocracy had shown toward its judiciary now turned into open animosity. Official publicists issued vitriolic attacks on the independent judiciary and the jury system. Legislative efforts were launched to cripple or eliminate the jury system and to restore the "unity" of state institutions by reinstating administrative control of the courts. The result was a state at war with its own court system, a fatal rift between the traditional and the legal bases of the autocrat's authority.

The inability to deal with the judicial process cost the government dearly not only in the political arena. . . . The state proved clumsy and incompetent in the defense of its interests in civil cases against the treasury as well. The plaintiffs would hire the best lawyers, while the fiscal interests received at best perfunctory and weak defenses. Nor did the government appear concerned to protect its legal position. Rather, it held to the old conceptions of power, even when they no longer worked. Thus the form of official contracts and agreements, often of emormous length, did little to secure the state's interest, but the officials of the treasury administration retained the old view. They regarded themselves "not as contracting parties, obliged to observe the conditions of agreements, but an authority whose commands must be obediently accepted."

A separate judiciary raised difficulties for the Russian autocracy that it did not for other states that had followed absolutist patterns. The Prussian administration—Russia's model of institutional effectiveness, order, and power—possessed a tradition of working with jurists and officials who had an understanding of the law, and was able to adapt to an independent court system. In the face of threats from revolutionaries, the courts and the administration shared common goals in striving to protect the regime against its enemies. This basic agreement continued under the [German] empire [after 1870], so that while the courts did not always act according to the government's plans, they were not thought to harbor an alien system of law.

The experience of Japan, which borrowed the Prussian judicial system in the last decades of the nineteenth century, is also in striking contrast to Russia's. In Japan, too, the judiciary had traditionally been held in low regard and had no existence separate from the administration; litigation was viewed as an evil. But the reforms of the second half of the nineteenth century that established separate courts in Japan did not create a conflict between courts and monarchy. The judiciary did not raise threats to the emperor's supremacy. The great security of the ruler's authority, the greater harmony between administration and society, permitted a separate judiciary to be introduced without the conflict and trauma that accompanied it in Russia.

---

2. Of 73 trials of members of the People's Will (revolutionary group) in the 1880s, 42 were heard by military courts, seven by a special session of the Senate. Only the least significant cases were left to the regular court system.—Ed.

For the Russian autocracy to accept an independent judiciary required that it betray its essence and cease to be the Russian autocracy. The judicial function had received little homage in the political culture of Russian autocracy. The exertion of untrammeled executive power had been the flair of autocracy, providing its magnetic appeal and making possible its greatest triumphs. Through forceful direct action, it had achieved the consolidation of a centralized state authority and the conquests that had first united the Russian lands and then made the Muscovite prince an emperor.

The chief virtues in such a state were military. The Russian nobility was preponderantly a class of military servitors and lacked both the feudal rights and the traditions of service in local judicial institutions inherited by most European nobilities. When they became owners of the serfs, they shared their sovereign's executive predispositions and regarded themselves as little potentates in the image of the tsar. A sense of the importance of their legal rights came only in the late eighteenth century, and then as a result of the efforts of the autocracy itself to emulate western political systems.

The image of a patriarchal tsar dispensing a personal justice maintained its hold in the eighteenth and early nineteenth century and fed a distrust of formal institutions that might dilute the monarch's power to extend personal grace, benefits, and privilege. Personal connections, access to high individuals close to the tsar, gave the Russian nobility a way to avoid submitting themselves to the demeaning rule of petty officials. Though noblemen staffed judicial institutions in the eighteenth century, they left the technical work to clerks, who carried on their work in secret and almost without responsibility. As a result of these attitudes, an awareness of the need for judicial understanding, legal literature, and education came late to the Russian nobility.

It was in this setting that the Russian autocracy took on the aspirations of European absolutist monarchies. It buttressed its traditional appeals of legitimacy with new claims to be the guarantor of the well-being of the nation and the rights of the population. The means it used were those of the European police states of the seventeenth and eighteenth centuries: the rational will of the sovereign legislator would be enforced by well-organized institutions, closely supervised by special organs to minimize error and dishonesty. A rationalized administrative structure could induce lesser officials, including the judges, to apply laws precisely, according to their letter. The antilegalist bias of western absolutism, with its faith in the supreme wisdom of the legislator, fit in well with the traditional Russian suspicion of the judiciary. It was this absolutist vision, in one or another form, that guided Russian statecraft down to the Great Reforms.

By the early nineteenth century, the experience of absolutist government, as well as the challenge posed by liberal and revolutionary doctrines, made the leaders of the autocracy increasingly aware of the need for expertise in applying and understanding the law. The attempts to centralize and rationalize the bureaucracy, undertaken by Alexander I and Nicholas I, led to the creation of specialized, functional branches of the administration, which in turn demanded a greater training and specialization of personnel. An expansion of higher education accompanied the administrative reforms, as the government endeavored to prepare officials capable of understanding the law. The goal was to produce officials trained in the law who would be loyal and technically proficient servants of the executive.

But the new officials differed from the old not only in the extent of their knowledge about the laws. Introducing men knowledgeable in the law involved the end of the hegemony of eminent noblemen, whether retired officers or aristocrats enjoying sinecures, over the legal system. They were replaced by members of the middle or lower nobility, who used the advantages conferred by education to rise quickly to important positions. For the first time, high judicial posts were filled by men who had spent most or all of their service in the judicial administration. They formed a group of legal officials with common social characteristics, education, and career experiences. They worked in an official world that assigned a great, though ill-defined importance to their expertise and ability.

The new contingent also brought different attitudes and goals into the administration. Educational and cultural currents exerted a decisive influence on the outlook of Russian officials, providing them with an ethos that would govern their relationship to their peers and their work. Many officials barely knew their fathers, and carried little in the nature of social commitment or goals away from their homes. They found their values in the intellectual world and institutions they entered as youths. When these values changed, the mentalities of officials changed as well, permitting significant discontinuities of viewpoint between succeeding generations of officials. In Nicholas I's reign, cadres of officials trained to respect the law and the universal norms of legal science entered an administration geared to subordinate the judicial function and exclude legal expertise.

Thus in the first half of the nineteenth century, the Russian autocracy, following the model of the absolutist state, introduced a new element into its officialdom. The judicial experts came from a stratum of the nobility that had previously sought to rise through the military. Its members had little in common with either the military traditions of their families or the institutional traditions of the earlier officialdom. Unguided by traditional values, they sought their own way. Abandoning the separation between personal and public lives sought by their sentimentalist predecessors, they found personal meaning in their work and cherished a genuine professional commitment to the law. They regarded the law as their own province and not the monopoly of the autocrat and his favorites. For the first time a sense of the calling of the legal official appeared in the Russian state.

As we have seen, the circumstances of the reform era allowed the legal experts to triumph and embody their ideas in new judicial institutions that vested authority over the interpretation and application of the law in a professional judiciary. But the members of this judiciary, imbued with an idealist sense of the mission of the law and a romantic sense of personal commitment, remained a world apart from the Russian state system. More traditional bureaucrats, who had learned to see all authority emanating from the tsar, regarded alternative sources of law with growing qualms. Two mutually hostile intellectual universes thus existed side by side in the Russian state. When issues of conflict arose, the traditional antagonism to the judiciary resurfaced, creating an atmosphere that was antipathetic to the basic values of the new courts and breeding conditions that would stunt their further development.

The new judicial system expanded in the decades after the reform. It was extended to the western Ukraine, the Baltic provinces, Siberia, and the Caucasus. The number of officials in the new courts increased threefold from 1870 to 1900 and continued to rise in the first years of the twentieth century. The budget of the [M]inistry [of Justice] also grew, increasing about threefold from 1869 to 1894 and almost twofold again by 1914. Despite this expansion, hereditary noblemen continued to play a dominant, if diminishing, role in the system. In 1900 all the members of the Senate's Criminal Cassation Department, 70 percent of all the members of the [Judicial] Chambers, and 58 percent of the members of the Circuit Courts were hereditary noblemen. By 1913, the proportions had fallen to 58 percent of the chamber members and 42 percent of the circuit court members.

The growth of the system, however, indicated no change in the basic antipathy that administrative authorities felt toward it. Unable to abolish the independence of the courts, the government acted in insidious and demoralizing ways that were injurious to their development. It favored politically loyal and submissive officials for appointment to high judicial positions. During the 1870s and 1880s, the [Imperial] School of Jurisprudence turned into a training ground for elite mediocrities, attentive to the needs of the executive authority. Their preeminence was a constant grievance to university graduates. Judges' salaries were raised little after the 1860s, and with the rise in the cost of living, complaints were heard again that judges were receiving salaries that were low and even inadequate.

The government showed itself hostile or indifferent to the basic principles and concerns of the court system. It introduced minor but troublesome abridgments of the independence of judges. It strove to undermine public confidence in the jury system and curtail its competence. It proved inattentive to the legislative needs of the new judiciary. In postreform Russia, the old *Digest of Laws* became increasingly cumbersome and outdated, but the government again pursued the goal of codification desultorily, like some kind of necessary but distasteful charade. Corps of legal experts completed a criminal code in 1903 and a civil code in 1913, but except for parts of the criminal code, they remained on paper in 1917. Reform of the police, a precondition to the proper operation of criminal justice, was never undertaken seriously after the 1860s. The government remained averse to the reforms in credit and commercial law necessitated by the new industrial economy. The autocracy thus kept itself apart from the forces of change it had stimulated and, as the Russian economy developed and expanded, ensured its own obsolescence.

As before the reform [Judicial Reform of 1864], the dominant attitudes in society came to mirror official attitudes. The intelligentsia shared the government's absorption with political goals and contempt for the judicial process, Kistiakovskii [a jurist] lamented in 1909. This had led to a general debasement of legal institutions. "Here 'judge' is not an honorable calling that attests to impartiality, selflessness, and high service to the law alone, as it does among other peoples." Only in the first decades after the reform, he claimed, had there been high-minded and distinguished judges. Writers like Leo Tolstoy and [Fedor] Dostoevsky expressed a common distaste for members of the judicial profession as officials cold and un-Russian in their rational adherence to legal science. The intelligentsia saw true justice as emanating from a just political, social, or ethical order—the creations of better legislators—and not from a legal process guided by principles of jurisprudence.

Legal modernization did not bring an element of stability to Russia. Imbued with a consciousness of its own worth and mission, the new legal profession had impugned the autocrat's claim to be the source and protector of legality. It represented an alien system that did not share the preoccupations and fears of the ruler and his entourage. As such, it only added to the inimical forces the government found beyond its power to direct or curb.

The independent courts defended standards of legality that the autocrat, in the midst of bitter political struggle, could not observe. The tsarist government resorted to increasingly brutal and extralegal methods to deal with the revolutionary movement at the close of the nineteenth and the beginning of the twentieth century. In such circumstances, it was difficult for the ruler to maintain his former image as champion of the law. Shedding the guise of absolute ruler, guardian of the rights and welfare of the population, the last two tsars [Alexander III, Nicholas II] tried instead to resume the role of patriarch, personal and religious leader of the nation. They appealed to national feeling and tried to appear close to the common people. But these products of the international culture of royalty were poor candidates for personal or charismatic leadership. Rather, their reactions to threats were defensive and retaliatory. Embattled, the Russian autocracy in sure and fatal steps took leave of its legal system and relied increasingly on force. Elevating itself beyond legality, it subverted the claims to obedience upon which its power ultimately rested.

## D OCUMENTS

Alexander Herzen (1812–1870) has been called the father of Russian socialism. The illegitimate son of a rich, eccentric Russian nobleman and his German mistress (hence his German surname), Herzen was early exposed to German Romanticism, an interest he pursued as a student at Moscow University (from 1829), where he helped form a discussion group—a "circle"—devoted to the study of western philosophy and literature. The circle was eventually broken up by agents of Nicholas I, who considered it subversive; Herzen was imprisoned for a year and then banished to the provinces (1835–1839). There he saw firsthand the poverty and backwardness of rural Russia—while himself living comfortably on his father's allowance and holding several positions in local government. He was also developing as a writer, and in 1840–1841 published the first installments of his memoirs, which eventually filled several volumes (under the title My Past and Thoughts) and are considered a masterpiece of their kind. Here Herzen stressed the moral obligation of educated Russians to serve their country and its people (Radishchev and the Decembrists were among his heros), though not necessarily in government. Arrested again on a spurious charge in 1841 and once more banished to the provinces, he immersed himself in the works of Hegel, finding there "the algebra of revolution." He also read George Sand and became a proponent of women's liberation. On returning to Moscow he quickly emerged as a leader of the "Westerners," a group of young intellectuals who insisted that to advance in the modern world Russia should adopt western values and institutions as well as western technology.

But Herzen himself retained a strong measure of sympathy for the rirval doctrines of Slavophilism (see Chapter 1), with their emphasis on the special character of the Russian peasantry. In these years he also imbibed European socialism (moving from the theories of Saint-Simon to those of Fourier, Proudhon, and others), eventually declaring himself a fully fledged socialist, materialist, and atheist. After inheriting a small fortune from his father, he left Russia for western Europe (1847). Although he was never to return, his homeland and its problems remained at the forefront of his concerns as a writer, self-styled propagandist, and publisher.

Life in France, Italy, and then in England considerably moderated Herzen's earlier "westernism"—though he retained a lifelong admiration for the individualism and freedom of expression that he found especially in England. Between 1849 and 1853 he expounded in a series of writings his theory of a special Russian socialism based on the peasant commune (his idyllic picture thereof owed much to Haxthausen): the theory would inspire two generations of radical youth in Russia, until supplanted by Marxism. In London in 1853 Herzen founded the Free Russian Press, which was to publish (in Russian) some 70 titles, including a periodical—*The Bell*—that was dedicated to exposing official arbitrariness, corruption, persecution, and ignorance in Russia and was, for about eight years, immensely influential among educated Russians. In *The Bell* and in letters and other writings Herzen specifically advocated serf emancipation, an end to censorship, reform of the courts, and abolition of corporal punishment. In all these ways he contributed greatly to creating the liberal climate of opinion in Russia that in turn helped produce the Great Reforms. Apart from his memoirs (published in English in 1924–1927 and again in 1968), Herzen's best known work is a book of essays on philosophy and politics entitled *From the Other Shore* (English edition of 1963; this volume also includes his influential work, "The Russian People and Communism"). Various of his main themes are characteristically expressed in his open letter of 1851—printed below—to Jules Michelet, the famous French historian who earlier that year had published an essay containing derogatory remarks about the Russia of Emperor Nicholas I and its repressive role in European affairs. Here Herzen also describes the emergence under Nicholas I of that radical Russian intelligentsia of which he himself was a leading member. As he saw it, the intelligentsia, along with the communal—or "communistic"—peasantry, would someday liberate Russia from the alien, oppressive Imperial government and nobility.

The second document is Alexander II's Manifesto of February 19, 1861, announcing the emancipation of the Russian serfs (compare Peter III's Manifesto of 1762 emancipating the nobility, in Chapter 4, and the *Ulozhenie* of 1649 enserfing the peasantry, in Chapter 2). Alexander's Manifesto pretty much speaks for itself. In establishing at last a broad new social estate, that of "free rural inhabitants" and then, in due course, of "free peasant proprietors [or landowners]," the Emperor clearly saw himself as finishing the work of his predecessors. The seigneurial as well as the state peasantry would now join, in stages, "the higher and middle estates" already defined in law; and the enlightened absolute monarchy based on law and a corporately structured society of largely self-governing estates envisioned by Catherine II (see Documents, Chapter 5) would be completed. The essentially conservative motivation of Alexander's Emancipation—as of the Great Reforms generally—is clear.

The third document is written by another well-informed foreign observer, Donald Mackenzie Wallace (1841–1919), who first visited Russia near the end of the Reform era. A Scottish scholar and journalist, Wallace initially became interested in Russia by reading Baron Haxthausen (Documents, Chapter 7). He arrived in St. Petersburg in March 1870 intending to stay for a few months, "but unexpectedly found so many interesting subjects of study that I remained [in Russia] for nearly six years—till December, 1875." He had excellent local connections, learned Russian well, and traveled widely in the country. His lengthy account of his stay—a solid book of 600 pages—is especially valuable for his firsthand observations of social life and the early progress of the Great Reforms. In these extracts he discusses Emancipation and the peasantry, and the local government—or *zemstvo*—reform.

## Alexander Herzen
## Defends the "Hidden Russia," 1851

DEAR SIR [Jules Michelet],—You hold so high a position in the general estimation, and every word which comes from your noble pen is received by European democracy with such complete and deserved confidence, that I cannot keep silent in a matter that touches upon my deepest convictions. I cannot leave unanswered the description of the Russian people which you have [recently published].

This answer is necessary for another reason also. The time has come to show Europe that when they now speak about Russia they are not speaking of something absent, far away, deaf and dumb.

We who have left Russia only that free Russian speech may at last be heard in Europe, we are on the spot and deem it our duty to raise our voice when a man wielding a great, well deserved authority [Michelet] has said that he "asserts, swears and will prove that Russia does not exist, that Russians are not men, that they are devoid of moral sense."

Do you mean by this official Russia, the *façade*-Tsardom, the Byzantine-German Government? Then we agree beforehand with everything that you will tell us; it is not for us to play the part of defender. The Russian Government has so many literary agents in the press of Paris that it will never lack for eloquent apologies.

But it is not official society alone that is dealt with in your work; you have stirred the question to its lowest depths: you have spoken of the people.

Poor Russian people! There is no one to raise a voice in its favor! Judge for yourself, Monsieur, whether I can, without poltroonery, be silent on an occasion such as this.

The Russian people does exist, Monsieur, is alive and it is not even old; it is very young. Men do die in youth, without having lived; it does happen, but it is not the normal thing.

The past of the Russian people is obscure, its present is frightening, but it has nevertheless some claims on the future. It does not *believe* in its present situation; it has the temerity to hope, and it hopes the more, the less it possesses.

The most difficult period for the Russian people is drawing to its close. A frightful conflict awaits it; its enemy is making ready.

From *My Past and Thoughts* by Alexander Herzen, pp. 1648, 1659–79. Copyright © 1968 by Chatto and Windus Ltd. Reprinted by permission of Alfred A. Knopf, Inc.

The great question, "to be or not to be," will soon be decided for Russia, but one has no right to despair of the result before the fight has begun.

The Russian question is assuming dimensions which are grave and disturbing; it is the object of intense preoccupation to all parties; but I think that too much attention is paid to the Russia of the Tsar, to official Russia, and too little to the Russia of the people, to hidden Russia. . . .

With what crime, after all, Monsieur, do you reproach the Russian people? What is the foundation of your accusation?

"The Russian," you say, "is a liar and a thief; he is lying and always stealing, and quite innocently, for it is his nature."

I shall not stop to call attention to the sweeping nature of this observation, but should like to be allowed to put to you this simple question: who, now, is the deceived, the robbed, the dupe? Heavens above, it is the landowner, the government official, the steward, the judge, the police officer: in other words, the sworn foes of the peasant, whom he looks upon as apostates, as traitors, as half-Germans. Deprived of every possible means of defense the peasant resorts to cunning in dealing with his oppressors; he deceives them, and he is perfectly right in doing so. Cunning, Monsieur, is, in the words of a great thinker [Hegel], the irony of brute force.

Through his horror of private property in land, as you have so well observed, through his listless, careless temperament, the Russian peasant, I say, has seen himself gradually and silently caught in the toils of the German bureaucracy and of the landowners' power. He has submitted to this humiliating yoke with the resignation of despair, I agree, but he has never *believed* in either the rights of the landowner, or the justice of the law-courts, or the fair-dealing of the administration. For nearly two hundred years the peasant's whole life has been nothing but a dumb, passive opposition to the existing order of things. He submits to oppression, he endures it, but he dips his hand in nothing that goes on outside the village communes.

The idea of the Tsar still enjoys prestige among the peasants; it is not the Tsar Nicholas that the people venerates; it is an abstract idea, a myth, a providence, an avenger, a representative of justice in the people's imagination.

After the Tsar, only the clergy could possibly have a moral influence on Orthodox Russia. The higher clergy alone represent old Russia in governing spheres; the clergy have never shaved their beards, and by that fact have remained on the side of the people. The people listen with confidence to a monk. But the monks and the higher clergy, occupied exclusively, as they say, with life beyond the grave, care little for the people. The *Pop* [priest] has lost all influence through his cupidity, his drunkenness, and his intimate relations with the police. Here, too, the peasants respect the idea but not the person.

As for the sectaries,[1] they hate both person and idea, both *Pop* and Tsar.

Apart from the Tsar and the clergy every element of government and society is utterly alien, essentially antagonistic to the people. The peasant finds himself in

---

1. In the Russian version this is *raskolniki,* schismatics [or Old Believers].

the literal sense of the word an outlaw. The law-court takes good care not to protect him, and his share in the existing order of things is entirely confined to the twofold tribute that lies heavily upon him and is paid in his sweat and his blood. Poor disinherited man, he instinctively understands that the whole system is ordered not for his benefit but to his detriment, and that the whole problem of the government and the landowners is to wring out of him as much labor and as much money as possible. Since he understands this and is gifted with a supple and resourceful intelligence, he deceives them all and in everything. It could not be otherwise; if he spoke the truth it would already be an assent on his side, an acceptance of their power over him; if he did not rob them (observe that to conceal part of the produce of his own labor is considered theft in a peasant) he would thereby be fatally recognizing the lawfulness of their exactions, the rights of the landowners and the justice of the law-courts.

To understand the Russian peasant's position fully you must have seen him in the law-courts; you must have seen with your own eyes his bleak, dismayed expression, his utter muteness, his watchful eyes, in order to understand that he is a civilian prisoner of war before a court-martial, a traveler facing a gang of brigands. From the first glance it is clear that the victim has not the slightest trust in the hostile, pitiless, implacable creatures who are questioning, tormenting and fleecing him. He knows that if he has money he will be acquitted; if not, he will be condemned without respite.

The Russian people speak a Russian that is somewhat archaic; the judges and the clerks write in the modern, bureaucratic language, vitiated and barely intelligible; they fill whole folios with ungrammatical jargon, and retail this mummery as fast as possible to the peasant. It is his own business to understand this unaccentuated snuffling and muttering if he can, and find his way out of the affair if he knows how. The peasant knows this, and he is on his guard. He does not say one word too much, he conceals his uneasiness and stands dumb and dazed, like a ninny.

The peasant who has been acquitted by the court is no more elated than if he had been condemned. In either case the decision seems to him the result of arbitrariness or chance.

In the same way, when he is summoned as a witness he will perjure himself and deny everything, deny again and again, even in the face of incontestable proof. Being found guilty by a law-court carries no stigma in the eyes of the Russian peasant. Exiles and convicts with him go by the name of *unfortunates*.

The life of the Russian peasantry has hitherto been confined to the commune. It is only in relation to the commune and its members that the peasant recognizes that he has rights and duties. Outside the commune he recognizes no duties and everything seems to him to be based upon violence. The baneful side of his nature is his submitting to that violence, and not his refusing in his own way to recognize it and his trying to protect himself by guile. There is much more uprightness in lying before a judge set over him by unlawful authority than in a hypocritical show of respect for the verdict of a jury packed by a prefect, whose revolting iniquity is as clear as daylight. The people respect only those institutions which reflect their innate conception of law and right.

There is a fact which no one who has been in close contact with the Russian peasantry can doubt. The peasants rarely cheat each other. An almost boundless good faith prevails among them; they know nothing of contacts and written agreements.

The problems connected with the measurement of their fields are inevitably complicated, owing to the everlasting sharing out of the land in accordance with the number of workers in the family; yet the Russian countryside never resounds with complaints or lawsuits. The landowners and the government ask nothing better than to intervene, but neither opportunity nor motive is given to them. The petty disputes which arise are promptly decided by the elders or by the commune, and the decision is accepted by everyone. It is just the same thing in the *artels* (mobile associations of working men). There are associations of masons, carpenters and others, consisting of several hundred individuals belonging to different communes, who group themselves together for a given time—for a year for instance—and thus form the *artel*. At the expiration of the year the workmen divide their profit in accordance with the work done by each and with the decision of all the associates. The police never have the satisfaction of meddling in their accounts. Almost always the *artel* makes itself responsible for every one of its members.

The bonds between peasants belonging to the same commune are even closer when they are not Orthodox but sectaries. From time to time the government organizes a savage raid on some sectarian commune. Peasants are imprisoned and banished, and it is all done with no preconcerted plan, no consistency, no necessity or provocation, simply in answer to the injunctions of the clergy and reports from the police. The real nature of the Russian peasant, the solidarity that binds him to his brothers, is displayed during these hunts after sectaries. One should see them at such times, I say, deceiving the police, saving their co-religionists, concealing their holy books and vessels, and enduring the most inhuman tortures without uttering a word. I challenge anyone to bring forward a single case in which a sectarian commune has been betrayed by a peasant, even by an Orthodox one.

The nature of a Russian makes police inquiries extremely difficult. I congratulate him with all my heart. The Russian peasant has no morality except what naturally, instinctively flows from his communism; this morality is deeply rooted in the people; the little they know of the Gospel supports it; the flagrant injustice of the government and the landowner binds the peasant still more closely to his customs and to his commune.[2]

---

2. A peasant commune belonging to Prince Kozlovsky bought their freedom by paying a sum agreed to by the owner. The land was divided among the peasants in proportion to the sum contributed by each to the purchase money for freedom. This arrangement was apparently most natural and just. The peasants, however, thought it so inconvenient and inconsistent with their habits that they decided to divide out among them the total of the redemption money as simply a debt incurred by the commune and to proceed to divide the land according to their accepted custom. This fact is vouched for by Baron von Haxthausen. The author himself [Herzen] visited the commune in question.

In a book recently published in Paris and dedicated to the Emperor Nicholas, the writer, a member of the Russian Council of State, says that this system of the division of land seems to him

The commune has saved the man of the people from Mongol barbarism and civilizing Tsarism, from the landlords with a veneer of Europe and from German bureaucracy. The communal system, though it has suffered violent attacks, has stood firm against the encroachments of the authorities; it has successfully survived up to the development of socialism in Europe.

This is a providential fact for Russia.

The Russian autocracy is entering upon a new phase. Having grown out of [the] anti-national revolution [of Peter the Great], it has accomplished its mission. It has created a colossal empire, a numerous army, a centralized government. Without principles, without tradition, it has no more to do; it is true that it undertook another task—to bring Western civilization into Russia; and it was to some extent successful in doing that while it still persisted in its fine role of civilizing government.

That role it has now abdicated.

The government, which had broken with the people in the name of civilization, has lost no time a hundred years later in breaking with civilization in the name of absolutism.

It did so as soon as the tri-colored specter of liberalism began to be visible through its civilizing tendencies: it tried then to return to nationalism, to the people. That was impossible—the people and the government had nothing in common any longer; the former had grown away from the latter, while the government thought it could discern rising from deep within the masses the still more terrible specter of the Red Cock.[3] All things considered liberalism was still less dangerous than another Pugachev, but the panic and distaste of liberal ideas had become such that the government was no longer capable of making its peace with civilization.

---

unfavorable to the development of agriculture (as though the object of it were the success of agriculture!); he adds, however: "It is difficult to escape these disadvantages, because this system of land divisions is bound up with the organization of our communes, which it would be *dangerous to touch*; it rests on the fundamental idea of the unity of the commune, and the right of every member of it to a proportional share in the communal soil, and so it consolidates and fortifies the communal spirit, which is one of the most conservative elements in the social order. At the same time it is the best defense against the spread of the proletariat and the diffusion of communistic ideas." (We may well believe that for a people in actual fact possessing their property in common, communistic ideas present no danger.) "The good sense with which our peasants themselves modify, according to the local conditions, the inconveniences of their system where such are inevitable is extremely remarkable; so is the ease with which they agree over the compensation for inequalities arising from differences of soil, or the confidence with which everyone accepts the decisions of the elders of the commune. It might be expected that the continual re-divisions would give rise to numerous disputes, and yet the intervention of the higher authorities is only necessary in the very rarest cases. This fact, *very strange in itself,* can only be explained by the sole fact that the system, with all its disadvantages, has so grown into the morals and conceptions of the peasants that its drawbacks are accepted without a murmur." "The idea of the commune is," says the same author, "as natural to the Russian peasant, and as fully embodied in all the aspects of his life, as the corporate municipal spirit that has formed the nucleus of the *bourgeoisie* of Western Europe is distasteful to his character."

3. To "let fly the Red Cock" is the popular Russian phrase for arson.

Since then the sole aim of Tsarism has been Tsarism. It governs in order to govern: its immense powers are employed to support each other for their reciprocal neutralization, to win a factitious repose. But autocracy for the sake of autocracy in the end becomes impossible; it is too absurd, too barren.

This has been felt, and work is being sought in Europe. Russian diplomacy is the most active; agents, advice, threats, promises and spies are sent in all directions. The Russian Emperor regards himself as the natural protector of the German Princes; he meddles in the least intrigues of their little courts; it is he who settles their disputes, scolding some, giving Grand Duchesses [the Emperor's daughters] to others. But this is not a sufficient outlet for his energy. He undertakes the duty of chief gendarme of the world; he is the supporter of every reaction, every barbarism. He poses as the representative of the monarchical principle in Europe, assumes the airs and graces of the [European] aristocracy. . . .

Unhappily there is nothing in common between [Western] feudal monarchism with its definite basis, its past and its social and religious idea, and the Napoleonic despotism of Petersburg, which has in its favor nothing but a deplorable historic necessity, a transitory usefulness, but no principle.

And the Winter Palace [of the Emperor, in St. Petersburg], like a mountaintop towards the end of autumn, is more and more thickly covered with snow and ice. The sap artificially raised to these social heights is withdrawing; nothing is left them but material power, and the hardness of the rock which can still resist for some time the onslaught of the waves of revolution that are shattered at the foot of it.

Nicholas, surrounded by his generals, his ministers, his officers and his bureaucrats, defies his isolation, but grows visibly gloomier, more morose, more preoccupied. He sees that he is not loved; he discerns the bleak silence that surrounds him and gives free access to the distant bellowing which seems to be coming nearer. The Tsar wishes to forget himself; he proclaims aloud that his aim is the aggrandizement of the Imperial power.

There is nothing new in these professions of faith; for the last twenty years he has labored unwearyingly, unrestingly for that sole object; he has spared neither tears nor blood.

He has succeeded in everything: he has destroyed Polish nationalism; in Russia he has extinguished liberalism.

What more does he want, indeed? Why is he so somber?

The Emperor feels very well that Poland is not dead. In place of the liberalism which he has persecuted with a shabby intolerance, for that exotic flower could not take root in Russian soil, since it has nothing in common with the people, he sees another question arising like a cloud big with storms.

The people is beginning to shudder and stir beneath the yoke of the landowners; local insurrections are constantly breaking out; you yourself, Monsieur, quote a terrible instance of this.

The party of progress demands the emancipation of the peasants; it is ready to be the first to sacrifice its own privileges. The Tsar hovers, undecided; he loses his head: he desires emancipation and puts hindrances in its way. He has grasped that freeing the peasants involves freeing the land; that this in its turn would be the beginning of a social revolution, would sanction rural communism. To dodge the question of emancipation seems to me impossible; to defer its solution to the next reign is easier, but it is a cowardly resource, and only amounts to the respite of a few hours wasted at a wretched posting-station that has no horses. . . .

Now you can see, Monsieur, how fortunate it is for Russia that the village commune has not been dissolved, that personal ownership has not split up the property of the commune; how fortunate it is for the Russian people that it has remained outside all political movements, even outside European civilization, which would necessarily have undermined the commune, and which to-day is itself reaching by means of socialism its own negation.

Europe, as I have said in another place, has not solved the antinomy between the individual and the State, but has put [posed] the problem; Russia has not found the solution either. It is in the face of this problem that our equality begins.

At the first step towards the social revolution Europe is confronted with this people which presents it with a solution, half-savage and rudimentary, but still a solution, that of the continual sharing out of the land among its cultivators. And observe, Monsieur, that this great example is given us not by educated Russia, but actually by the people itself, by its inner life. We Russians who have passed through European civilization are no more than a means, a leaven, interpreters between the Russian people and revolutionary Europe. The man of the coming Russia is the *muzhik* [peasant], just as in regenerated France it will be the workman.

But, if this is so, have not the Russian peasantry rather more claim on your indulgence, Monsieur?

Poor peasant! So intelligent, so simple in his ways, content with so little, he has been chosen as the sighting point [target] for every possible injustice. The Emperor decimates him with conscription, the landowner steals his third days which belong to him, the official abstracts his last ruble. The peasant endures in silence; but he does not despair: he still keeps his commune. If a member is torn from it, the commune draws its ranks closer. One would have thought the peasant's fate deserved compassion, yet he is not stirred up; and instead of pitying him men upbraid him.

You refuse him, Monsieur, even the last refuge that remains to him, where he feels himself a man, where he loves and is not afraid; you say: "His commune is not a commune, his family is not a family, his wife is not a wife; before she is his, she is the property of the landowner; his children are not his children—who knows who is their father?"

So you abandon this luckless people not to scientific analysis but to the contempt of other nations, who will read your fine legends trustingly and with pleasure.

It is my duty to say a few words on this subject.

Family life among all the Slavs is very highly developed; it may be the one conservative element in their character, the point at which their destructive criticism stops. The family owning its possessions in common is the prototype of the commune.

The rural family is reluctant to split itself up into several homes; not uncommonly three or four generations go on living under the same roof under the patriarchal authority of a grandfather or great-uncle. The woman, commonly oppressed, as is always the case in the agricultural class, begins in Russia to be treated with respect when she is the widow of the elder of the family.

It is by no means rare to see the whole management of affairs entrusted to a white-haired grandmother. Is this a proof that the family does not exist in Russia?

Let us pass to the landowner's relationship to the family of his serf; but for the sake of clearness let us distinguish the rule from its abuses, right from crimes.

*Le droit du seigneur* has never existed among the Slavs.[4]

The landowner cannot legally demand the "first-fruits" of a marriage or a breach of conjugal fidelity. If the law were carried out in Russia, he would be equally punished for the violation of a serf-woman as for an assault on a free woman, namely, by penal servitude or relegation to Siberia, with the loss of all rights, according to the gravity of the circumstances. Such is the law: let us look at the facts.

I do not pretend to deny that, with the social position given by the government to the landowners, it is very easy for them to debauch the wives and daughters of their serfs. By oppression and punishment the landowner can always bring his serfs to a pass in which some will offer him their wives or daughters. . . .

It is no matter for wonder, either, that the most honorable fathers and husbands can find no redress against the landowners, thanks to the fine judicial system of Russia. . . . All these filthy abuses are perfectly possible, I admit; one has but to appeal to the memory of those who know the coarse, depraved manners of some of the Russian nobility to be certain of it; but as far as the peasant is concerned he is far indeed from being indifferent to the brazen licentiousness of his masters.

Allow me to cite a proof of it.

Half of the landowners murdered by their serfs (the statistics give their number as sixty to seventy a year) fall victims to their erotic exploits. Legal proceedings on such grounds are rare; the peasant knows that the judges are invariably deaf to his complaints; but he has an axe; he is master of the use of it, and knows that he is.

Having said so much about the peasants, I shall ask you, Monsieur, to follow me in a few reflections about Russia.

Your view of the intellectual movement in Russia is no more indulgent than your opinion of the character of the people; with one stroke of the pen you have struck out all the work done by our fettered hands!

One of Shakespeare's characters, not knowing how to humiliate a despised opponent, says to him: "I even doubt of your existence!" You have gone further, Monsieur, for it is not even a matter of doubt to you that Russian literature does not exist. I quote from your own words:

"We are not going to amuse ourselves by looking down scornfully if a few clever people in Petersburg, exercising themselves in the Russian language as though it was a learned language, have amused Europe with a pale presentation of a supposed

---

4. Reference is to the supposed feudal right of lords to have sexual relations with the brides of their dependents. —Ed.

Russian literature. If it were not for my respect for Mickiewicz [famous Polish poet] and his saintly aberrations, I should really censure him for the indulgence, one might even say charity, with which he has had the goodness to speak seriously of this trifling."

I search in vain, Monsieur, for the reason for the disdain with which you greet the first cry of pain of a people that is waking up in its prison-house, an outburst which the hands of its jailer is doing its utmost to stifle at birth.

Why have you been unwilling to lend an ear to the harrowing notes of our sad poetry, of our chants through which a sob can be heard? What curtain has blinded you to our hysterical laughter, the perpetual irony behind which hides the deeply ulcerated heart, and at bottom is only the fatal consciousness of our impotence?

Oh, how I should like to be able to make you a worthy translation of some lyrics of Pushkin or Lermontov, or some of the people's songs of Koltsov! Then you would hold out to us a friendly hand, Monsieur; you would be the first to beg us to forget what you have said!

Next to the communism of the peasants nothing is more characteristic of Russia, nothing is such an earnest of her future, as her literary movement.

Between the peasantry and literature there looms the monster of official Russia, of "Russia the lie," or "Russia the cholera," as you call her. This Russia extends from the Emperor and passes from soldier to soldier, from petty clerk to petty clerk, down to the smallest assistant to a commissary of police in the remotest corner of the Empire. So it unfolds and so, at every step of the ladder, . . . it gains a new power for evil, a new degree of corruption and tyranny. This living pyramid of crimes, abuses and extortions, of the batons of policemen, of heartless German administrators everlastingly famished, ignorant judges everlastingly drunk and aristocrats everlastingly servile; all this is soldered together by complicity, by the sharing of the plunder and gain, and supported at its base on six hundred thousand animated machines with bayonets. The peasant is never defiled by contact with this world of governing cynicism; he endures it—that is the only way in which he is an accessory.

The camp opposed to official Russia consists of a handful of men who are ready to face anything, who protest against it, fight it, expose and undermine it. From time to time these isolated champions are thrown into dungeons, tortured, relegated to Siberia, but their place does not long remain empty, for fresh combatants come forward; it is our tradition, the inheritance entailed upon us.

The terrible consequences of human speech in Russia necessarily give it added power. The voice of a free man is welcomed with sympathy and reverence, because with us to lift it up one absolutely must have something to say. One does not so lightly decide to publish one's thoughts when at the end of every page one sees looming a gendarme, a troika, a *kibitka* [cart] and, in prospect, Tobolsk or Irkutsk [cities in Siberia]. . . .

The Russian people do not read. You know, Monsieur, that it was not the country-folk, either, who read the Voltaires and Diderots: it was the nobility and part of the Third Estate [townspeople]. In Russia the enlightened part of the Third Estate belongs to the nobility and gentry, which consists of all that has ceased to be the peasantry. There is even a proletariat of the nobility which partly merges into the peasantry, and another, an emancipated proletariat, mounts on high and is ennobled. This fluctuation, this continual exchange, stamps the Russian nobility with a character which you will not find in the privileged classes in the rest of Europe. In a word the whole history of Russia, since the time of Peter I, is only the history of the nobility and gentry and of the influence on them of European civilization. I shall add here that the Russian nobility and gentry equal in numbers at least half the electorate of France established by the law of May 31, 1850.

During the eighteenth century the neo-Russian literature continued to elaborate the rich sonorous, magnificent language that we write to-day: a supple, powerful language capable of expressing the most abstract ideas of German metaphysics and the light sparkling wit of French conversation. This literature, which flowered under the inspiration of the genius of Peter I, bore, it is true, the impress of the government—but in those days "government" meant reform, almost revolution.

Till the moment of the great [French] Revolution of 1789 the Imperial throne complacently draped itself in the finest vestments of European civilization and philosophy. . . . In the Hermitage [of Catherine II] there was continual talk about Voltaire, Montesquieu and Beccaria. You, Monsieur, know the reverse of the medal.

Yet the triumphal concert of . . . the Court began to be disturbed by a strange, unexpected note. This was a sound vibrant with irony and sarcasm, with a strong tendency towards criticism and skepticism, and this sound, I say, was the only one susceptible of vitality, of external development. The rest, the temporary and exotic, had necessarily to perish.

The true character of Russian thought, poetical or speculative, develops in its full force after the accession of Nicholas to the throne. Its distinguishing feature is a tragic emancipation of conscience, an implacable negation, a bitter irony, a painful self-analysis. Sometimes this all breaks into insane laughter, but there is no gaiety in that laughter.

Cast into oppressive surroundings and endued with great sagacity and a fatal logic, the Russian frees himself abruptly from the religion and morals of his fathers. The emancipated Russian is the most independent man in Europe. What could stop him? Respect for his past? . . . But what serves as a starting point of the modern history of Russia, if not an absolute denial of nationalism and tradition?

Could it be that other "past indefinite," the Petersburg period perhaps? That tradition lays no obligation on us; on the contrary, . . . [it] sets us free, but it imposes on us no belief.

On the other hand, the past of you Western European peoples serves us as a lesson and nothing more; we do not regard ourselves as the executors of your historic testament.

Your doubts we accept, but your faith does not rouse us. For us you are too religious. We share your hatreds, but we do not understand your devotion to what your forefathers have bequeathed to you: we are too downtrodden, too wretched, to be satisfied with a half-freedom. You are restrained by scruples, and held back by reservations. We have neither reservations nor scruples; all we lack at the moment is strength. . . .

It is from this, Monsieur, that we get the irony, the fury which exasperates us, which preys upon us, which drives us forward, which sometimes brings us to Siberia, torture, banishment, premature death. We sacrifice ourselves with no hope, from distaste, from tedium. . . . There is indeed something irrational in our life, but there is nothing vulgar, nothing stagnant, nothing *bourgeois*.

Do not accuse us of immorality because we do not respect what you respect. Since when has it been possible to reproach foundlings for not venerating their parents? We are independent because we are beginning from our own efforts. We have no tradition but our structure, our national character; they are inherent in our being, they are our blood, our instinct, but by no means a binding authority. We are independent because we possess nothing. We have hardly anything to love. All our memories are filled with bitterness and resentment. Civilization and learning were held out to us at the end of a knout [a Russian whip].

What have we to do with your traditional duties, we younger brothers robbed of our heritage? And how could we honestly accept your faded morality, unchristian and inhuman, existing only in rhetorical exercises and indictments of the prosecution? What respect can be inspired in us by your Roman-barbaric system of law, those heavy, crushing vaults, without light or air, repaired in the Middle Ages and whitewashed by the newly enfranchised Third Estate? I admit that the tricks of the Russian law-courts are even worse, but who could prove to us that your system is just?

We see clearly that the distinction between your laws and our *ukazy* [decrees] lies principally in the formula with which they begin. *Ukazy* begin with a crushing truth: "The Tsar commands"; your laws are headed with the insulting lie of the threefold republican motto [Liberty, Equality, Fraternity] and the ironical invocation of the name of the French people. The code of Nicholas is directed exclusively against men and in favor of authority. The Code Napoleon does not seem to us to have any other quality. We are dragging about too many chains that violence has fastened on us to increase the weight of them with others of our choice. In this respect we stand precisely on a level with our peasants. We submit to brute force. We are slaves because we have no means of freeing ourselves; from the enemy camp, none the less, we accept nothing.

Russia will never be Protestant. Russia will never be *juste-milieu* ["moderate"].

Russia will not make a revolution with the sole object of getting rid of the Tsar Nicholas and gaining, as the prize of victory, other Tsars: parliamentary representatives, judges, police officials and laws. We are asking for too much, perhaps, and shall achieve nothing. That may be so, but yet we do not despair; before the year 1848 Russia could not, and should not, have entered the phase of revolution; she had only her education to get, and she is getting it at this moment. The Tsar himself perceives it, so he bludgeons the universities, ideas, the sciences; he is striving to isolate Russia from Europe, to kill culture. He is practicing his vocation.

Will he succeed? As I have said elsewhere, we must not have blind faith in the future; every fetus has its claim to development, but for all that not every fetus does develop. The future of Russia does not depend on her alone but is bound up with the future of the whole of Europe. Who can foretell what the fate of the Slav world will be when reaction and absolutism shall have vanquished the revolution in Europe?

Perhaps it will perish: who knows?

But in that case Europe too will perish. . . .

And history will continue in America. . . .

## Alexander II's Manifesto Emancipating the Serfs, 1861

Called by Divine Providence and the sacred law of succession to Our ancestral All-Russian Throne, in response to which call We vowed in Our heart to embrace in Our Royal love and Solicitude all Our faithful [subjects] of every rank and estate . . . ; [and] investigating the condition of [said subjects] who comprise the State, We saw that State law, while actively promoting the welfare of the higher and middle estates [by] defining their obligations, rights, and privileges, has not equally favored the bonded people [serfs], [who are] so called because as a matter partly of old laws and partly of current custom they have been hereditarily bound to the authority of landlords, who are obliged accordingly to see to their welfare. Hitherto the rights of the lords were broad and not precisely defined in law, wherefore tradition, custom, and the lord's good will prevailed. At best this [system] produced good patriarchal relations of sincere solicitude and benevolence on the part of the lords and good-natured submission from the peasants. But owing to the decline of morals [literally, a lessening of the simplicity of manners], an increase in the variety of [landlord-peasant] relationships, and a lessening of the lords' direct paternal relations with their peasants, whereupon landlord rights some-times fell into the hands of persons seeking only their own advantage [bailiffs, stewards, overseers]: [for all these reasons] good relations weakened, and the way was opened to an arbitrariness [proizvol] that has been burdensome for the peasants and not conducive to their welfare, whence they have shown indifference to any improvement in their lives.

Such was perceived by Our Predecessors of worthy memory, and they took steps to improve the condition of the peasantry. But these steps [by Alexander I and Nicholas I] were only partly successful, depending as they did on the good will and voluntary action of landlords and applicable as they were only to certain localities, as required by special circumstances or [introduced] by way of experiment. . . .

We were therefore convinced that the task of improving the condition of the bonded people [serfs] is a legacy to Us from Our Predecessors, and a destiny conferred upon Us in the course of events by the hand of Providence.

---

From *PSZ*, 2nd series, vol. 36 pt. 1 (St. Petersburg, 1863), no. 36,650. Translated by James Cracraft.

We began this task by an act of trust in the Russian Nobility, knowing of its great proofs of loyalty to the Throne and of its readiness to make sacrifices for the good of the Fatherland. We left it to the Nobility Itself to assemble and consider a new arrangement of peasant affairs, whereupon it was proposed to the Nobles to limit their rights over peasants and to bear the difficulties of a transformation that would entail losses to themselves. And Our trust was justified. Through its representatives in the Provincial Committees chosen by the whole Nobility of every province, the Nobility voluntarily renounced any rights to the person of the bonded ones. These Committees, after collecting the needed information, drew up proposals regarding a new order for people living in bondage and [new] relations with [their] lords.

These proposals were quite varied, as could have been expected from the very nature of the task. They were checked, collated, put in proper form, corrected and supplemented in the Main Committee appointed to this task. And the new Statutes [Polozheniia] on seigneurial peasants and domestic folk [household serfs] thus compiled were [then] examined in the State Council [the highest organ of the Imperial government, created by Alexander I].

Having called on God for assistance, We are resolved to complete this task.

Pursuant to these new Statutes, the bonded people [serfs] are to receive in due course the full rights of free rural inhabitants.

The landlords, preserving their right of ownership of all lands belonging to them, are to grant to the peasants, in return for a certain obligation, perpetual use of their homestead [usadebnaia osedlost'] as well as such quantity of plowland and other goods as is provided in the Statutes, so that they may be secure in their livelihood and fulfill their duties to the Government.

In taking advantage of this land allotment, the peasants are thereby required to fulfill the obligations to [their] lords specified in the Statutes. In this condition, which is transitional, the peasants are temporarily obligated.

They are also to be given the right to buy their homestead; and with their lord's agreement they may acquire ownership of the plowland and other goods assigned to their perpetual use. On acquiring ownership of said land, the peasants are freed of any duties owed on it to the lord, and thus enter the well-defined estate of free peasant proprietors [or landowners].

A Special Statute defines the transitional status of domestic folk [household serfs], as appropriate to their duties and needs. Two years after publication of this Statute, they will receive complete freedom and certain temporary privileges.

In accordance with these general principles of the said Statutes, the future status of peasants and domestic folk is to be defined; a system for administering peasant affairs is to be established; and the rights granted to the peasants and domestic folk, as well as their obligations to the Government and the lords, are to be specified in detail.

Although these Statutes, [as well as] the General, Local, and Supplementary Rules for certain special localities, for small landowners, and for peasants working in their lords' factories or industries, have [all] been adapted as far as possible to local economic needs and practices; nevertheless, to preserve the customary order where it is mutually advantageous We leave it to the lords to reach voluntary understandings with [their] peasants and to conclude agreements [with them] regarding the extent of the peasants' land allotments and corresponding obligations, observing therein the rules laid down for preserving the inviolability of such agreements.

As this new arrangement, given the inescapable complexity of the changes required by it, cannot be introduced at once, but rather needs time for that, meaning not less than two years: so in the course of this time, to avoid confusion, and to maintain the public and private good, the order hitherto existing on seigneurial estates should be preserved until, on completion of the necessary preparations, the new order will begin.

For the proper realization of this, We have seen fit to command that:

1. A Provincial Office of peasant affairs be opened in every province, to which is to be entrusted oversight of the affairs of peasant communes settled on seigneurial lands.

2. Mediators [Mirovye Posredniki] be appointed in all districts to resolve all misunderstandings and disputes arising in the execution of the new Statutes, and District Mediation Centers formed of them.

3. Then to form mediation offices on the lords' estates, which offices, while leaving the rural communes in their present state, will open local [volost'] administrations in major settlements and bring small villages under one such administration.

4. To compile, verify, and register a statutory charter for every rural commune or estate, in which charter shall be specified, on the basis of the applicable Statute, the quantity of land to be granted to the peasants in perpetual use and the extent of the obligations owed by them to the lord in return for the land and any other goods granted by him.

5. The terms of these statutory charters are to be carried out on each and every estate during the two years following the day of publication of this Manifesto.

6. During this time the peasants and domestic folk are to remain in their former submission to the lords, and fulfill without fail their former obligations.

7. The landlords will continue to keep order on their estates, with judicial and police powers, until the formation of the local [volost'] administrations and opening of the local [volost'] courts.

Considering the inescapable difficulties involved in this transformation, We place Our hope first of all in the surpassing goodness of Divine Providence, which protects Russia.

Then do We rely on the valiant zeal for the common good of the Well-born Noble estate, to whom We cannot fail to express, on behalf of Ourselves and the whole Fatherland, well-deserved recognition of [their] unselfish execution of Our designs. Russia will not forget that, prompted only by respect for human dignity and Christian love of neighbor, they voluntarily renounced the law of bondage [serfdom] and laid the basis of a new economic future for [their] peasants. We assuredly expect that with like nobility they will exhibit the utmost care in seeing that the new Statutes are carried out in good order, and in a spirit of peace and benevolence; that every landowner will complete, on his own land, the great civic act of his entire estate [the estate of the nobility]; and that, having arranged the affairs of the peasants settled on his land and of his domestic folk on terms advantageous to both sides, he will thus give a good example to the rural people and an incentive to [their] exact and conscientious fulfillment of State regulations.

Mindful of [such] examples of the landowners' generous solicitude for the good of [their] peasants, and of the peasants' recognition of same, We are confirmed in Our hope that mutual voluntary agreements will resolve most of the difficulties that are unavoidable when general rules are applied to the varying circumstances of individual estate lands. In this way the transition from the old order to the new will be alleviated, and mutual trust, good accord, and a unanimous aspiration for the common good will be strengthened in the future.

To facilitate the execution of those agreements between landowners and peasants by which the latter will acquire ownership of plowland as well as their homesteads, the Government will provide the means, on the basis of special rules, to pay the loans and transfer the debts encumbering estates [this refers to the so-called redemption payments that millions of peasants would thus owe the government for years to come].

And We place Our hope in the good sense of Our people.

When word of the Government's plan to abolish the law of bondage [serfdom] reached peasants unprepared for it, there arose a partial misunderstanding. Some [peasants] thought about freedom and forgot about obligations. But the general good sense [of the people] was not disturbed in the conviction that anyone freely enjoying the goods of society correspondingly owes it to the common good to fulfill certain obligations, [a conviction held] both by natural reason and by Christian law, according to which "every soul must be subject to the governing authorities" (Romans 13:1) and "pay all of them their dues," in particular "labor, tribute, fear, and honor" (Romans 13:7). [Similarly strong is the popular conviction] that rights legally acquired by the landlords cannot be taken from them without a decent return or [their] voluntary concession; and that it would be contrary to all justice to make use of the lords' land without bearing the corresponding obligations.

And now We hopefully expect that the bonded people, as a new future opens before them, will understand and accept with gratitude the important sacrifice made by the Well-born Nobility for the improvement of their lives.

They will understand that, receiving the advantages of ownership and the freedom to conduct their own affairs, they owe it to society and to themselves to realize the beneficence of the new law by a loyal, judicious, and diligent exercise of the rights granted to them. The most beneficent law cannot make people happy if they do not themselves labor to build their happiness under the protection of the law. Prosperity is acquired and increased only by hard work, the judicious use of strength and resources, strict economy, and, overall, by an honest, God-fearing life.

The executives [officials] who prepared the new way of life for the peasantry and will manage its realization must be vigilant that this is done legally, calmly, and in a timely way, so that the peasants are not distracted from their indispensable farmwork. May they carefully work the land and gather its fruits, so that from a well-filled granary they may take the seeds for sowing the fields which they will now use in perpetuity or someday own outright.

Make the sign of the cross, Orthodox people, and invoke with Us God's blessing on thy free labor, the pledge of thine own prosperity and of the public good.

Given at St. Petersburg in the year of Our Lord one thousand eight hundred sixty-one, and of Our Reign the seventh.

[signed] Alexander

## Donald Mackenzie Wallace Explains the *Mir* and the *Zemstvo*, 1877

On my arrival at Ivánofka, my knowledge of the [*mir*] was of that vague, superficial kind which is commonly derived from men who are fonder of sweeping generalizations and rhetorical declamation than of serious, patient study of phenomena. I knew that the chief personage in a Russian village is the *Selski starosta*, or the Village Elder, and that all important Communal affairs are regulated by the *Selski Skhod*, or Village Assembly. Further, I was aware that the land in the vicinity of the village belongs to the Commune, and is distributed periodically among the members in such a way that every able-bodied peasant possesses a share sufficient, or nearly sufficient, for his maintenance. Beyond this elementary information I knew little or nothing.

My first attempt at extending my knowledge was not very successful. Hoping that my friend Ivan might be able to assist me, and knowing that the popular name for the Commune is *Mir*, which means also "the world," I put to him the direct, simple question, "What is the Mir?"

Ivan was not easily disconcerted, but for once he looked puzzled, and stared at me vacantly. When I endeavored to explain to him my question, he simply knitted his brows and scratched the back of his head. This latter movement is the Russian peasant's method of accelerating cerebral action; but in the present instance it had no practical result. In spite of his efforts, Ivan could not get much further than the "Kak vam skazat'?" that is to say, "How am I to tell you?"

It was not difficult to perceive that I had adopted an utterly false method of investigation, and a moment's reflection sufficed to show me the absurdity of my question. I had asked from an uneducated man a philosophical definition, instead of extracting from him material in the form of concrete facts, and constructing therefrom a definition for myself. These concrete facts, Ivan was both able and willing to supply; and as soon as I adopted a rational mode of questioning, I received an abundant supply of most interesting information. This information, together with the results of much subsequent conversation and reading, I now propose to present to the reader in my own words.

From Donald Mackenzie Wallace, *Russia* (New York: Henry Holt and Company, 1877), pp. 120–37, 213–18.

The peasant family of the old type is, as we have just seen, a kind of primitive association, in which the members have nearly all things in common. The village may be roughly described as a primitive association on a larger scale.

Between these two social units there are many points of analogy. In both there are common interests and common responsibilities. In both there is a principal personage, who is in a certain sense ruler within, and representative as regards the outside world: in the one case called Khozain, or Head of the Household, and in the other Starosta, or Village Elder. In both the authority of the ruler is limited: in the one case by the adult members of the family, and in the other by the heads of households. In both there is a certain amount of common property: in the one case the house and nearly all that it contains, and in the other the arable land and pasturage. In both cases there is a certain amount of common responsibility: in the one case for all of the debts, and in the other for all the taxes and Communal obligations. And both are protected to a certain extent against the ordinary legal consequences of insolvency, for the family cannot be deprived of its house or necessary agricultural implements, and the Commune cannot be deprived of its land, by importunate creditors.

On the other hand, there are many important points of contrast. The Commune is, of course, much larger than the family, and the mutual relations of its members are by no means so closely interwoven. The members of a family all farm together, and those of them who earn money from other sources are expected to put their savings into the common purse; whilst the households composing a Commune farm independently, and pay into the common treasury only a certain fixed sum.

From these brief remarks the reader will at once perceive that a Russian village is something very different from a village in our sense of the term, and that the villagers are bound together by ties quite unknown to the English rural population. A family living in an English village has little reason to take an interest in the affairs of its neighbors. The isolation of the individual families may not be quite perfect, for man, being a social animal, takes, and ought to take, a certain interest in the affairs of those around him, and this social duty is sometimes fulfilled by the weaker sex with more zeal than is absolutely indispensable for the public welfare; but families may live for many years in the same village without ever becoming conscious of common interests. So long as the Jones family do not commit any culpable breach of public order, such as putting obstructions on the highway or habitually setting their house on fire, their neighbor Brown takes probably no interest in their affairs, and has no ground for interfering with their perfect liberty of action. Jones may be a drunkard and hopelessly insolvent, and he may some night decamp clandestinely with his whole family and never more be heard of; but all these things do not affect the interests of Brown, unless he has been imprudent enough to entertain with the delinquent more than simply neighborly relations. Now, amongst the families composing a Russian village, such a state of isolation is impossible. The Heads of Households must often meet together and consult in the Village Assembly, and their daily occupations must be influenced by the Communal decrees. They cannot begin to mow the hay or plow the fallow field until the Village Assembly has passed a resolution on the subject. If a peasant becomes a drunkard, or takes some equally efficient means to become insolvent, every family in the village has a right to complain, not merely in the interests of public morality, but from selfish motives, because all the families are collectively responsible for his taxes. For the same reason no peasant can permanently leave the village without the consent of the Commune, and this consent will not be granted if all his actual and future liabilities are not met. If a peasant wishes to go away for a short time, in order to work elsewhere, he must obtain a written permission, which serves him as a passport during his absence; and he may be recalled at any moment by a Communal decree. In reality he is rarely recalled so long as he sends home regularly the full amount of his taxes—including the dues which he has to pay for the temporary passport—but sometimes the Commune uses the power of recall for the purpose of extorting money from the absent member. If it becomes known, for instance, that an absent member receives a good salary in one of the towns, he may one day receive a formal order to return at once to his native village, and be informed at the same time, unofficially, that his presence will be dispensed with if he will send to the commune a certain amount of money. The money thus sent is generally used by the commune for convivial purposes. Whether this method of extortion is frequently used by the Communes, I cannot confidently say, but I suspect that it is by no means rare, for one or two cases have accidentally come under my own observation, and I know that the police of St. Petersburg have been recently ordered not to send back any peasants to their native villages until some proof is given that the ground of recall is not a mere pretext.

In order to understand the Russian village system, the reader must bear in mind these two important facts: the arable land and the pasturage belong not to the individual houses, but to the Commune, and all the households are collectively and individually responsible for the entire sum which the Commune has to pay annually into the Imperial Treasury.

In all countries the theory of government and administration differs considerably from the actual practice. Nowhere is this difference greater than in Russia, and in no Russian institution is it greater than in the Village Commune. It is necessary, therefore, to know both theory and practice; and it is well to begin with the former, because it is the simpler of the two. When we have once thoroughly mastered the theory, it is easy to understand the deviations that are made to suit peculiar local conditions.

According, then, to theory, all male peasants in every part of the Empire are inscribed in census lists, which form the basis of the direct taxation. These lists are revised at irregular intervals, and all males alive at the time of the "revision," from the newborn babe to the centenarian, are duly inscribed. Each Commune has a list of this kind, and pays to the Government an annual sum proportionate to the number of names which the list contains, or, in popular language, according to the number of "revision souls." During the intervals between the revisions the financial authorities take no notice of the births and deaths. A Commune which has a hundred male members at the time of the revision may have in a few years considerably more or considerably less than that number, but it has to pay taxes for a hundred members all the same until a new revision is made for the whole Empire.

Now in Russia, so far at least as the rural population is concerned, the payment of taxes is inseparably connected with the possession of land. Every peasant who pays taxes is supposed to have a share of the arable land and pasturage belonging to the Commune. If the Communal revision lists contain a hundred names, the Communal land ought to be divided into a hundred shares, and each "revision soul" should enjoy his share in return for the taxes which he pays.

The reader who has followed my explanations up to this point may naturally conclude that the taxes paid by the peasants are in reality a species of rent for the land which they enjoy. So it seems, and so it is sometimes represented, but so in reality it is not. When a man rents a bit of land he acts according to his own judgment, and makes a voluntary contract with the proprietor; but the Russian peasant is obliged to pay his taxes whether he desires to enjoy land or not. The theory, therefore, that the taxes are simply the rent of the land, will not bear even superficial examination. Equally untenable is the theory that they are a species of land-tax. In any reasonable system of land-dues the yearly sum imposed bears some kind of proportion to the quantity and quality of the land enjoyed; but in Russia it may be that the members of one Commune possess six acres, and the members of the neighboring Commune seven acres, and yet the taxes in both cases are the same. The truth is that the taxes are personal, and are calculated according to the number of male "souls," and the Government does not take the trouble to inquire how the Communal land is distributed. The Commune has to pay into the Imperial Treasury a fixed yearly sum, according to the number of its "revision souls," and distributes the land among its members as it thinks fit.

How, then, does the Commune distribute the land? To this question it is impossible to give a definite general reply, because each Commune acts as it pleases. Some act strictly according to the theory. These divide their land at the time of the revision into a number of portions or shares corresponding to the number of revision souls, and give to each family a number of shares corresponding to the number of revision souls which it contains. This is from the administrative point of view by far the simplest system. The census list determines how much land each family will enjoy, and the existing tenures are disturbed only by the revisions which take place at irregular intervals. Since 1719 only ten revisions have been made so that the average length of these intervals has been about fifteen years—a term which may be regarded as a tolerably long lease. But, on the other hand, this system has serious defects. The revision list represents merely the numerical strength of the families, and the numerical strength is often not at all in proportion to the working power. Let us suppose, for example, two families, each containing at the time of the revision five male members. According to the census list these two families are equal, and ought to receive equal shares of the land; but in reality it may happen that the one contains a father in the prime of life and four able-bodied sons, whilst the other contains a widow and five little boys. The wants and working power of these two families are of course very different; and if the above system of distribution be applied, the man with four sons and a goodly supply of grandchildren will probably find that he has too little land, whilst the widow with her five little boys will find it difficult to cultivate the five shares allotted to her, and utterly impossible to pay the corresponding amount of taxation—for in all cases, it must be remembered, the Communal burdens are distributed in the same proportion as the land.

But why, it may be said, should the widow not accept provisionally the five shares, and let to others the part which she does not require? The balance of rent after payment of the taxes might help her to bring up her young family.

So it seems to one acquainted only with the rural economy of England, where land is scarce, and always gives a revenue more than sufficient to defray the taxes. But in Russia the possession of a share of Communal land is often not a privilege, but a burden. In some Communes the land is so poor and abundant that it cannot be let at any price. Witness, for instance, many villages in the province of Smolensk, where the traveler may see numerous uncultivated strips in the Communal fields. In others the soil will repay cultivation, but a fair rent will not suffice to pay the taxes and dues.

To obviate these inconvenient results of the simpler system, some communes have adopted the expedient of allotting the land, not according to the number of revision souls, but according to the working power of the families. Thus, in the instance above supposed, the widow would receive perhaps two shares, and the large household, containing five workers, would receive perhaps seven or eight. Since the breaking-up of the large families, such inequality as I have supposed is, of course, rare; but inequality of a less extreme kind does still occur, and justifies a departure from the system of allotment according to the revision lists.

Even if the allotment be fair and equitable at the time of the revision, it may soon become unfair and burdensome by the natural fluctuations of the population. Births and deaths may in the course of a very few years entirely alter the relative working power of the various families. The sons of the widow may grow up to manhood, whilst two or three able-bodied members of the other family may be cut off by an epidemic. Thus, long before a new revision takes place, the distribution of the land may be no longer in accordance with the wants and capacities of the various families composing the Commune. To correct this, various expedients are employed. Some Communes transfer particular lots from one family to another, as circumstances demand; whilst others make from time to time, during the intervals between the revisions, a complete re-distribution and re-allotment of the land.

The system of allotment adopted depends entirely on the will of the particular Commune. In this respect the Communes enjoy the most complete autonomy, and no peasant ever dreams of appealing against a Communal decree. The higher authorities not only abstain from all interference in the allotment of the Communal lands, but remain in profound ignorance as to which system the Communes habitually adopt. Though the Imperial Administration has a most voracious appetite for symmetrically-constructed statistical tables—many of them formed chiefly out of materials supplied by the mysterious inner consciousness of the subordinate officials—no attempt has yet been made to collect statistical data which might throw light on this important subject. In spite of the systematic and persistent efforts of the centralized bureaucracy to regulate minutely all departments of the national life, the rural Communes, which contain about five-sixths of the population, remain in many respects entirely beyond its influence, and even beyond its sphere of vision!

But let not the reader be astonished overmuch. He will learn in time that Russia is the land of paradoxes; and meanwhile he is about to receive a still more startling bit of information—a statement that should be heralded in by a flourish of trumpets. In "the great stronghold of Caesarian despotism and centralized bureaucracy," these Village Communes, containing about five-sixths of the population, are capital specimens of representative Constitutional government of the extreme democratic type!

When I say that the rural Commune is a good specimen of Constitutional government, I use the phrase in the English, and not in the continental sense. In the continental languages a Constitutional government means a government which possesses a long, formal document, composed of many successive paragraphs, in which the functions of the various institutions, the powers of the various authorities, and all the possible methods of procedure are carefully defined. Such a document was never heard of in Russian Village Communes. Their Constitution is of the English type—a body of unwritten, traditional conceptions, which have grown up and modified themselves under the influence of ever-changing practical necessity. If the functions and mutual relations of the Village Elder and the Village Assembly have ever been defined, neither the Elders nor the members of the Assembly know anything of such definitions; and yet every peasant knows, as if by instinct, what each of these authorities can do and cannot do. The Commune is, in fact, a living institution, whose spontaneous vitality enables it to dispense with the assistance and guidance of the written law.

As to its thoroughly democratic character there can be no possible doubt. The Elder represents merely the executive power. All the real authority resides in the Assembly, of which all Heads of Households are members.

The simple procedure, or rather the absence of all formal procedure, at the Assemblies, illustrates admirably the essentially practical character of the institution. The meetings are held in the open air, because in the village there is no building—except the church, which can be used only for religious purposes—large enough to contain all the members; and they almost always take place on Sundays or holidays, when the peasants have plenty of leisure. Any open space, where there is sufficient room and little mud, serves as a Forum. The discussions are occasionally very animated, but there is rarely any attempt at speech-making. If any young member should show an inclination to indulge in oratory, he is sure to be unceremoniously interrupted by some of the older members, who have never any sympathy with fine talking. The whole assemblage has the appearance of a crowd of people who have accidentally come together, and are discussing in little groups subjects of local interest. Gradually some one group, containing two or three peasants who have more moral influence than their fellows, attracts the others, and the discussion becomes general. Two or more peasants may speak at a time, and interrupt each other freely—using plain, unvarnished language, not at all parliamentary—and the discussion may become for a few moments a confused, unintelligible noise, "a din to fright a monster's ear"; but at the moment when the spectator imagines that the consultation is about to be transformed into a promiscuous fight, the tumult spontaneously subsides, or perhaps a general roar of laughter announces that some one has been successfully hit by a strong *argumentum ad hominem*, or biting personal remark. In any case there is no danger of the disputants coming to blows. No class of men in the world is more good-natured and pacific than the Russian peasantry. When sober they never fight, and even when under the influence of alcohol they are more likely to be violently affectionate than disagreeably quarrelsome. If two of them take to drinking together, the probability is that in a few minutes, though they may never have seen each other before, they will be expressing in very strong terms their mutual regard and affection, confirming their words with an occasional friendly embrace.

Theoretically speaking, the Village Parliament has a Speaker, in the person of the Village Elder. The word Speaker is etymologically less objectionable than the term President, for the personage in question never sits down, but mingles in the crowd like the ordinary members. Objection may be taken to the word on the ground that the Elder speaks much less than many other members, but this may likewise be said of the Speaker of the House of Commons. Whatever we may call him, the Elder is officially the principal personage in the crowd, and wears the insignia of office in the form of a small medal suspended from his neck by a thin brass chain. His duties, however, are extremely light. To call to order those who interrupt the discussion is no part of his functions. If he calls an honorable member Durák (blockhead), or interrupts an orator with a laconic "Moláchi!" (hold your tongue!), he does so in virtue of no special prerogative, but simply in accordance with a time-honored privilege, which is equally enjoyed by all present, and may be employed with impunity against himself. Indeed, it may be said in general that the phraseology and the procedure are not subjected to any strict rules. The Elder comes prominently forward only when it is necessary to take the sense of the meeting. On such occasions he may stand back a little from the crowd and say, "Well, Orthodox, have you decided so?" and the crowd will probably shout, "Ladno! ladno!" that is to say, "Agreed! agreed!"

Communal measures are generally carried in this way by acclamation; but it sometimes happens that there is such a decided diversity of opinion that it is difficult to tell which of the two parties has a majority. In this case the Elder requests the one part to stand to the right and the other to the left. The two groups are then counted, and the minority submits, for no one ever dreams of opposing openly the will of the "Mir." . . .

In the crowd may generally be seen, especially in the northern provinces, where a considerable portion of the male population is always absent from the village, a certain number of female peasants. These are women who, on account of the absence or death of their husbands, happen to be for the moment Heads of Households. As such they are entitled to be present, and their right to take part in the deliberations is never called in question. In matters affecting the general welfare of the Commune they rarely speak, and if they do venture to announce an opinion on such occasions they have little chance of commanding attention, for the Russian peasantry are as yet little imbued with the modern doctrines of female equality, and express their opinion of female intelligence by the homely adage: "The hair is long, but the mind is short." According to one proverb, seven women have collectively but one soul, and according to a still more ungallant popular saying, women have no souls at all, but only a vapor. Woman, therefore, as woman, is not deserving of much consideration, but a particular woman, as head of a household is entitled to speak on all questions directly affecting the household under her care. If, for instance, it be proposed to increase or diminish her household's share of the land and the burdens, she will be allowed to speak freely on the subject, and even to indulge in a little personal invective against her male opponents. She thereby exposes herself, it is true, to uncomplimentary remarks; but any which she happens to receive she will probably repay with interest—referring, perhaps, with pertinent virulence to the domestic affairs of those who attack her. And when argument and invective fail, she is pretty sure to try the effect of pathetic appeal, supported by copious tears—a method of persuasion to which the Russian peasant is singularly insensible.

As the Village Assembly is really a representative institution, in the full sense of the term, it reflects faithfully the good and the bad qualities of the rural population. Its decisions are therefore usually characterized by plain, practical common sense, but it is subject to occasional unfortunate aberrations in consequence of pernicious influences, chiefly of an alcoholic kind. An instance of this fact occurred during my sojourn at Ivánofka. The question under discussion was whether a *kabák*, or gin-shop [tavern], should be established in the village. A trader from the district town desired to establish one, and offered to pay to the Commune a yearly sum for the necessary permission. The more industrious, respectable members of the Commune, backed by the whole female population of the locality, were strongly opposed to the project, knowing full well that a kabak would certainly lead to the ruin of more than one household; but the enterprising trader had strong arguments wherewith to seduce a large number of the members, and succeeded in obtaining a decision in his favor.

The Assembly discusses all matters affecting the Communal welfare, and, as these matters have never been legally defined, and there is no means of appealing against its decisions, its recognized competence is very wide. It fixes the time for making the hay, and the day for commencing the plowing of the fallow field; it decrees what measures shall be employed against those who do not punctually pay their taxes; it decides whether a new member shall be admitted into the Commune, and whether an old member shall be allowed to change his domicile; it gives or withholds permission to erect new buildings on the Communal land; it prepares and signs all contracts which the Commune makes with one of its own members or with a stranger; it interferes, whenever it thinks necessary, in the domestic affairs of its members; it elects the Elder—as well as the Communal tax-collector, and watchman, where such offices exist—and the Communal herd-boy; above all, it divides and allots the Communal land among the members as it thinks fit.

Of all these various proceedings, the English reader may naturally assume that the elections are the most noisy and exciting. In reality this is a mistake. The elections produce little excitement, for the simple reason that, as a rule, no one desires to be elected. Once, it is said, a peasant who had been guilty of some misdemeanor was informed by an Arbiter of the Peace—a species of official of which I shall have much to say in the sequel—that he would be no longer capable of filling any Communal office; and instead of regretting this diminution of his civil rights, he bowed very low, and respectfully expressed his thanks for the new privilege which he had acquired. This anecdote may not be true, but it illustrates the undoubted fact that the Russian peasant regards office as a burden rather than as an honor. There is no civic ambition in those little rural Commonwealths, whilst the privilege of wearing a bronze medal, which commands no respect, and the reception of a few rubles as salary, afford no adequate compensation for the trouble, annoyance, and responsibility which a Village Elder has to bear. The elections are therefore generally very tame and uninteresting. . . .

Far more important than the elections, is the redistribution of the Communal land. It can matter but little to the Head of a Household how the elections go, provided he himself is not chosen. He can accept with perfect equanimity Alexei, or Ivan, or Nikolai, because the office-bearers have very little influence in Communal affairs. But he cannot remain a passive, indifferent spectator, when the division and allotment of the land come to be discussed, for the material welfare of every household depends to a great extent on the amount of land and of burdens which it receives.

In the southern provinces, where the soil is fertile, and the taxes do not exceed the normal rent, the process of division and allotment is comparatively simple. Here each peasant desires to get as much land as possible, and consequently each household demands all the land to which it is entitled—that is to say, a number of shares equal to the number of its members inscribed in the last revision list. The Assembly has, therefore, no difficult questions to decide. The Communal revision list determines the number of shares to be allotted to each family. The only difficulty likely to arise is as to which particular shares a particular family shall receive, and this difficulty is commonly obviated by the custom of casting lots. There may be, it is true, some difference of opinion as to when a re-distribution should be made, but this question is easily decided by a simple vote of the Assembly.

Very different is the process of division and allotment in many Communes of the northern provinces. Here the soil is often very unfertile, and the taxes exceed the normal rent, and consequently it may happen that the peasants strive to have as little land as possible. In these cases such scenes as the following may occur.

Ivan is being asked how many shares of the Communal land he will take, and replies in a slow, contemplative way, "I have two sons, and there is myself, so I'll take three shares, or somewhat less if it is your pleasure."

"Less!" exclaims a middle-aged peasant, who is not the Village Elder, but merely an influential member, and takes the leading part in the proceedings. "You talk nonsense. Your two sons are already old enough to help you, and soon they may get married, and so bring you two new female laborers."

"My eldest son," explains Ivan, "always works in Moscow, and the other often leaves me in summer."

"But they both send or bring home money, and when they get married, the wives will remain with you."

"God knows what will be," replies Ivan, passing over in silence the first part of his opponent's remark. "Who knows if they will marry?"

"You can easily arrange that!"

"That I cannot do. The times are changed now. The young people do as they wish, and when they do get married they all wish to have houses of their own. Three shares will be heavy enough for me!"

"No, no. If they wish to separate from you, they will take some land from you. You must take at least four. The old wives there who have little children cannot take shares according to the number of souls."

"He is a rich Muzhik (peasant)!" says a voice in the crowd. "Lay on him five souls!" (that is to say, give him five shares of the land and of the burdens).

"Five souls I cannot! By God, I cannot!"

"Very well, you shall have four," says the leading spirit to Ivan; and then, turning to the crowd, inquires, "Shall it be so?"

"Four! four!" murmurs the crowd; and the question is settled.

Next comes one of the old wives just referred to. Her husband is a permanent invalid, and she has three little boys, only one of whom is old enough for field labor. If the revision list were taken strictly on the basis of distribution, she would receive four shares, but she would never be able to pay four shares of the Communal burdens. She must therefore receive less than that amount. When asked how many she will take, she replies with downcast eyes, "As the Mir decides, so be it!"

"Then you must take three."

"What do you say, little father?" cries the woman, throwing off suddenly her air of subservient obedience. "Do you hear that, ye Orthodox? They want to lay upon me three souls! Was such a thing ever heard of? Since St. Peter's Day my husband has been bed ridden—bewitched, it seems, for nothing does him good. He cannot put a foot to the ground—all the same as if he were dead; only he eats bread!"

"You talk nonsense," says a neighbor; "He was in the [tavern] last week."

"And you!" retorts the woman, wandering from the subject in hand, "what did you do last parish fête? Was it not you who got drunk and beat your wife till she roused the whole village with her shrieking? And no further gone than last Sunday—pfu!"

"Listen!" says the old man sternly, cutting short the torrent of invective. "You must take at least two shares and a half. If you cannot manage it yourself, you can get some one to help you."

"How can that be? Where am I to get the money to pay the laborer?" asks the woman, with much wailing and a flood of tears. "Have pity, ye Orthodox, on the poor orphans! God will reward you"; and so on, and so on.

I need not weary the reader with a further description of these scenes, which are always very long and sometimes violent. All present are deeply interested, for the allotment of the land is by far the most important event in Russian peasant life, and the arrangement cannot be made without endless talking and discussion. After the number of shares for each family has been decided, the distribution of the lots gives rise to new difficulties. The families who have manured plentifully their land strive to get back their old lots, and the Commune respects their claims so far as these are consistent with the new arrangement; but often it happens that it is impossible to conciliate private rights and Communal interests, and in such cases the former are sacrificed in a way that would not be tolerated by men of Anglo-Saxon race. This leads, however, to no serious consequences. The peasants are accustomed to work together in this way, to make concessions for the Communal welfare, and to bow unreservedly to the will of the Mir. I know of many instances where the peasants have set at defiance the authority of the police, of the provincial governor, and of the central Government itself, but I have never heard of any instance where the will of the Mir was openly opposed by one of its members.

In the preceding pages I have repeatedly spoken about "shares of the Communal land." To prevent misconception, I must explain carefully what this expression means. A share does not mean simply a plot or parcel of land; on the contrary, it always contains at least four, and may contain a large number of distinct plots. We have here a new point of difference between the Russian village and the villages of Western Europe.

Communal land in Russia is of three kinds: the land on which the village is built, the arable land, and the meadow or hay-field. On the first of these each family possesses a house and garden, which are the hereditary property of the family, and are never affected by the periodical re-distributions. The other two kinds are both subject to re-distribution, but on somewhat different principles.

The whole of the Communal arable land is first of all divided into three fields, to suit the triennial rotation of crops already described, and each field is divided into a number of long narrow strips—corresponding to the number of male members in the Commune—as nearly as possible equal to each other in area and quality. Sometimes it is necessary to divide the field into several portions, according to the quality of the soil, and then to subdivide each of these portions into the requisite number of strips. Thus in all cases every household possesses at least one strip in each field; and in those cases where subdivision is necessary, every household possesses a strip in each of the portions into which the field is subdivided. This complicated process of division and subdivision is accomplished by the peasants themselves, with the aid of simple measuring-rods, and the accuracy of the result is truly marvelous.

The meadow, which is reserved for the production of hay, is divided into the same number of shares as the arable land. There, however, the division and distribution take place not at irregular intervals, but annually. Every year, on a day fixed by the Assembly, the villagers proceed in a body to this part of their property, and divide it into the requisite number of portions. Lots are then cast, and each family at once mows the portion allotted to it. In some Communes the meadow is mown by all the peasants in common, and the hay afterwards distributed by lot among the families; but this system is by no means so frequently used.

As the whole of the Communal land thus resembles to some extent a big farm, it is necessary to make certain rules concerning cultivation. A family may sow what it likes in the land allotted to it, but all families must at least conform to the accepted system of rotation. In like manner, a family cannot begin the autumn plowing before the appointed time, because it would thereby interfere with the rights of the other families, who use the fallow field as pasturage.

It is not a little strange that this primitive system of land tenure should have succeeded in living into the nineteenth century, and still more remarkable that the institution of which it forms an essential part should be regarded by many intelligent people as one of the great institutions of the future, and almost as a panacea for social and political evils. . . .

Very soon after my arrival in Novgorod [old city in northwestern Russia] I made the acquaintance of a gentleman, who was described to me as "the president of the provincial Zemstvo-bureau," and finding him amiable and communicative I suggested that he might give me some information regarding the institution of which he was the chief representative. With the utmost readiness he prepared to be my Mentor with regard to the Zemstvo, at once introduced me to his colleagues, and invited me to come and see him at his office as often as I felt inclined. Of this invitation I made abundant use. At first my visits were discreetly few and short, but when I found that my friend and his colleagues really wished to instruct me in all the details of Zemstvo administration, and had arranged a special table for my convenience, I became a regular attendant, and spent daily several hours in the bureau, studying the current affairs, and noting down the interesting bits of statistical and other information which came before the members, as if I had been one of their number. When they went to inspect the hospital, the lunatic asylum, the seminary for the preparation of village schoolmasters, or any other Zemstvo institution, they invariably invited me to accompany them, and made no attempt to conceal from me the defects which they happened to discover. . . .

The Zemstvo [created by the local-government reform of 1864] is a kind of local administration which supplements the action of the rural communes, and takes cognizance of those higher public wants which individual communes cannot possibly satisfy. Its principal duties are to keep the roads and bridges in proper repair, to provide means of conveyance for the rural police and other officials, to elect the justices of peace, to look after primary education and sanitary affairs, to watch the state of the crops and take measures against approaching famine, and in short to undertake, within certain clearly-defined limits, whatever seems likely to increase the material and moral well-being of the population. In form the institution is parliamentary—that is to say, it consists of an assembly of deputies which meets at least once a year, and of a permanent executive bureau elected by the assembly from among its members. If the assembly be regarded as a local parliament, the bureau corresponds to the ministry. In accordance with this analogy my friend the president was sometimes jocularly termed the prime minister. Once every three years the deputies are elected in certain fixed proportions by the landed proprietors, the rural communes, and the municipal corporations. Every province and each of the districts into which the province is subdivided has such an assembly and such a bureau.

Not long after my arrival in Novgorod I had the opportunity of being present at a District Assembly. In the ball-room of the "Club de la Noblesse" ["Club of the Nobility"] I found thirty or forty men seated round a long table covered with green cloth. Before each member lay sheets of paper for the purpose of taking notes, and before the president—the Marshal of Noblesse [Nobility] for the district—stood a small hand-bell, which he rang vigorously at the commencement of the proceedings and on all occasions when he wished to obtain silence. To the right and left of the president sat the members of the executive bureau, armed with piles of written and printed documents, from which they read long and tedious extracts, till the majority of the audience took to yawning and one or two of the members positively went to sleep. At the close of each of these reports the president rang his bell—presumably for the purpose of awakening the sleepers—and inquired whether any one had remarks to make on what had just been read. Generally some one had remarks to make, and not unfrequently a discussion ensued. When any decided difference of opinion appeared, a vote was taken by handing round a sheet of paper, or by the simpler method of requesting the Ayes to stand up and the Noes to sit still.

What surprised me most in this assembly was that it was composed partly of nobles and partly of peasants—the latter being decidedly in the majority—and that no trace of antagonism seemed to exist between the two classes. Landed proprietors and their ci-devant [former] serfs evidently met for the moment on a footing of equality. The discussions were always carried on by the nobles, but on more than one occasion peasant members rose to speak, and their remarks, always clear, practical, and to the point, were invariably listened to with respectful attention by all present. Instead of that violent antagonism which might have been expected considering the constitution of the assembly, there was a great deal too much unanimity—a fact indicating plainly that the majority of the members did not take a very deep interest in the matters presented to them.

This assembly was held in the month of September. At the beginning of December the Assembly for the Province met, and during nearly three weeks I was daily present at its deliberations. In general character and mode of procedure it resembled closely the District Assembly. Its chief peculiarities were that its members were chosen, not by the primary electors, but by the assemblies of the ten Districts which compose the Province, and that it took cognizance merely of those matters which concerned more than one District. Besides this, the peasant deputies were very few in number—a fact which somewhat surprised me, because I was aware that, according to the law, the peasant members of the District Assemblies were eligible, like those of the other classes. The explanation is that the District Assemblies choose their most active members to represent them in the Provincial Assemblies, and consequently the choice generally falls on landed proprietors. To this arrangement the peasants make no objection, for attendance at the Provincial Assemblies demands a considerable pecuniary outlay, and payment to the deputies is expressly prohibited by law.

To give the reader an idea of the elements composing this assembly, let me introduce him to a few of the members. A considerable section of them may be described in a single sentence. They are commonplace men, who have spent part of their youth in the public service as officers in the army, or officials in the civil administration, and have since retired to their estates, where they gain a modest competence by farming. Some of them add to their agricultural revenues by acting as justices of the peace. A few may be described more particularly.

You see there, for instance, that fine-looking old general in uniform, with the St. George's Cross at his button-hole—an order given only for bravery in the field. That is Prince S——, a grandson of one of Russia's greatest men. He has filled high posts in the administration without ever tarnishing his name by a dishonest or dishonorable action, and has spent a great part of his life at Court without ceasing to be frank, generous, and truthful. Though he has no intimate knowledge of current affairs, and sometimes gives way a little to drowsiness, his sympathies in disputed points are always on the right side, and when he gets to his feet he always speaks in a clear soldier-like fashion.

The tall gaunt man, somewhat over middle age, who sits a little to the left is Prince W——. He, too, has a historical name, but he cherishes above all things personal independence, and has consequently always kept aloof from the Administration and the Court. The leisure thus acquired he has devoted to study, and he has produced several very valuable works on political and social science. An enthusiastic but at the same time cool-headed abolitionist at the time of the Emancipation, he has since constantly striven to ameliorate the condition of the peasantry by advocating the spread of primary education, the establishment of rural credit associations in the villages, the preservation of the communal institutions, and numerous important reforms in the financial system. Both of these gentlemen, it is said, generously gave to their peasants more land than they were obliged to give by the Emancipation law. In the Assembly Prince W—— speaks frequently, and always commands attention; and in all important committees he is a leading member. Though a warm defender of the Zemstvo institutions, he thinks that their activity ought to be confined to a comparatively narrow field, and thereby he differs from some of his colleagues, who are ready to embark in hazardous, not to say fanciful, schemes for developing the natural resources of the province. His neighbor, Mr. P——, is one of the most able and energetic members of the assembly. He is president of the executive bureau in one of the Districts, where he had founded many primary schools, and created several rural credit associations on the model of those which bear the name of Schultze-Delitsch in Germany. Mr. S——, who sits beside him, was for some years an arbitrator between the proprietors and emancipated serfs, then a member of the Provincial Executive Bureau, and is now director of a bank in St. Petersburg.

To the right and left of the president—who is Marshal of Noblesse for the province—sit the members of the bureau. The gentleman who reads the long reports is my friend "the prime minister," who began life as a cavalry officer, and after a few years of military service retired to his estate; he is an intelligent, able administrator, and a man of considerable literary culture. His colleague, who assists him in reading the reports, is a merchant, and director of the municipal bank. His neighbor is also a merchant, and in some respects the most remarkable man in the room. Though born a serf, he is already, at middle age, an important personage in the Russian commercial world. Rumor says that he laid the foundation of his fortune by one day purchasing a copper caldron in a village through which he was passing on his way to St. Petersburg, where he hoped to gain a little money by the sale of some calves. In the course of a few years he amassed an enormous fortune; but the cautious people think that he is too fond of hazardous speculations, and prophesy that he will end life as poor as he began it.

All these men belong to what may be called the party of progress, which anxiously supports all proposals recognized as "liberal," and especially all measures likely to improve the condition of the peasantry. Their chief opponent is that little man with close-cropped, bullet-shaped head and small piercing eyes, who may be called the leader of the opposition. That gentleman opposes many of the proposed schemes, on the ground that the province is already overtaxed, and that the expenditure ought therefore to be reduced to the smallest possible figure. In the District Assembly he preaches this doctrine with considerable success, for there the peasantry form the majority, and he knows how to use that terse, homely language, interspersed with proverbs, which has far more influence on the rustic mind than scientific principles and logical reasoning; but here, in the Provincial Assembly, his following composes [comprises] only a respectable minority, and he confines himself to a policy of obstruction.

The Zemstvo of Novgorod has—or at least had at that time—the reputation of being one of the most enlightened and energetic, and I must say that in the assembly of 1870 the proceedings were conducted in a business-like, satisfactory way. The reports were carefully considered, and each article of the annual budget was submitted to minute scrutiny and criticism. In several of the provinces which I afterwards visited I found that affairs were conducted in a very different fashion: quorums were formed with extreme difficulty, and the proceedings, when they at last commenced, were treated as mere formalities and dispatched as speedily as possible. The character of the assembly depends of course on the amount of interest taken in local public affairs. In some districts this interest is considerable; in others it is very near zero.

The reader may perhaps imagine that the Zemstvo has, like the rural commune, grown up slowly in the course of centuries, and is in its present form a remnant of ancient liberties, which has successfully resisted the centralizing tendencies of the autocratic power. In reality it is nothing of the sort. It is a modern institution, created by the autocratic power about ten years ago, and represents the most recent attempt to lighten the duties and correct the abuses of the Imperial administration by means of local self-government. . . .

# FURTHER READING

Edward Acton, *Alexander Herzen and the Role of the Intellectual Revolutionary* (1979)

John W. Atwell, "The Russian Jury," *Slavonic and East European Review*, 53 (1975), 44–61

E. Willis Brooks, "Reform in the Russian Army, 1856–1861," *Slavic Review*, 43 (1984), 63–82

Terence Emmons, *The Russian Landed Gentry and the Peasant Emancipation of 1861* (1968)

———— and Wayne S. Vucinich, eds., *The Zemstvo in Russia: An Experiment in Local Self-Government* (1982)

Daniel Field, *The End of Serfdom: Nobility and Bureaucracy in Russia, 1855–1861* (1976)

————, *[Peasant] Rebels in the Name of the Tsar* (1976)

Stephen P. Frank, "Popular Justice, Community and Culture Among the Russian Peasantry, 1870–1900," The Russian Review, 46 (1987), 239–65

Gregory L. Freeze, ed. and trans., *From Supplication to Revolution: A Documentary Social History of Imperial Russia*, Part Two (1988)

C. A. Frierson, "Rural Justice in Public Opinion: The Volost' Court Debate [1861–1912]," *Slavonic and East European Review*, 64 (1986), 526–45

Abbott Gleason, *Young Russia: The Genesis of Russian Radicalism in the 1860s* (1983)

Gary M. Hamburg, "Peasant Emancipation and Russian Social Thought: The Case of Boris N. Chicherin," *Slavic Review*, 50 (1991), 890–904

Steven L. Hoch, "The Banking Crisis, Peasant Reform, and Economic Development in Russia, 1857–1861," *American Historical Review*, 96 (1991), 795–820

———, *Serfdom and Social Control in Russia: Petrovskoe, a Village in Tambov* (1986)

John L. H. Keep, *Soldiers of the Tsar: Army and Society in Russia, 1462–1874* (1985)

Peter Kolchin, *Unfree Labor: American Slavery and Russian Serfdom* (1987)

W. Bruce Lincoln, *The Great Reforms: Autocracy, Bureaucracy, and the Politics of Change in Imperial Russia* (1990)

———, *In the Vanguard of Reform: Russia's Enlightened Bureaucrats 1825–1861* (1982)

Martin Malia, *Alexander Herzen and the Birth of Russian Socialism* (1961)

Martin McCauley and Peter Waldron, eds. and trans., *The Emergence of the Modern Russian State, 1855–1881* (1988)

Bruce W. Menning, *Bayonets before Bullets: The Imperial Russian Army, 1861–1914* (1992)

Martin A. Miller, *The Russian Revolutionary Emigres, 1825–1870* (1986)

W. E. Mosse, *Alexander II and the Modernization of Russia* (1958, 1992)

Derek Offord, *Portraits of Early Russian Liberals* (1985)

Daniel T. Orlovsky, *The Limits of Reform: the Ministry of Internal Affairs in Imperial Russia, 1802–1881* (1981)

N. G. O. Pereira, *Tsar-Liberator: Alexander II of Russia, 1818–1881* (1983)

Geroid Tanquary Robinson, *Rural Russia Under the Old Regime* (1932, 1967)

S. Frederick Starr, *Decentralization and Self-Government in Russia, 1830–1870* (1972)

George Vernadsky et al., eds. and trans., *A Source Book for Russian History from Early Times to 1917*, vol. 3 (1972)

Aurele J. Violette, "The Grand Duke Konstantin Nikolayevich and the Reform of Naval Administration, 1855–1870," *Slavonic and East European Review*, 52 (1974), 584–601

Richard S. Wortman, *The Development of a Russian Legal Consciousness* (1976)

———, "Rule by Sentiment: Alexander II's Journeys through the Russian Empire," *American Historical Review*, 95 (1990), 745–71

Judith E. Zimmerman, *Mid-Passage: Alexander Herzen and European Revolution, 1847–1852* (1989)

CHAPTER 9

# Reaction and Counter-Reform

The later years of the reign of Alexander II saw a waning of reform in Russia, as officials opposed to any further change (or to any change at all) regained ascendancy in the Imperial government and the Emperor himself wavered. In part it was the natural reaction of an essentially conservative establishment to the wave of peasant uprisings, student disturbances, and general unrest that accompanied the introduction of the Great Reforms. The nationalist rebellion of 1863–1864 in Poland, after Alexander had restored a large degree of local autonomy, added Russian nationalist fervor to the gathering forces of reaction, as did the growth of radical and revolutionary agitation in Russia proper. In 1866 a deranged student attempted to assassinate the Emperor, an event which appears to have cemented Alexander's decision to abandon reform. Later that year he appointed a well-known reactionary, Count Dmitry Tolstoi, to the influential post of minister of education, and Tolstoi proceeded to clamp down on the universities and in other ways to restrict public education. Censorship was also reintroduced; the financial authority of the new organs of local self-government—the zemstvos—was curtailed; and, as indicated by Professor Wortman in the preceding chapter, the government began to subvert its own Judicial Reform of 1864. On the other hand, new forms of municipal self-rule were introduced on schedule (1870) and important military reforms were enacted as late as 1874. Yet the government's reactionary drift was unmistakable, as was the growing discontent of nearly every sector of public opinion. By 1878, in the judgment of the leading Soviet historian of the period (P. A. Zaionchkovsky), the autocracy had reached a point of crisis.

To appease the public and resolve the crisis, Alexander resumed a more moderate policy. He dismissed Tolstoi, appointed several prominent liberals or moderates to the government, and named an able general and provincial governor, Count M. T. Loris-Melikov (1825–1888), to head a special commission charged with suppressing revolutionary terrorism. In August 1880 Alexander appointed Loris-Melikov to the crucial position of minister of the interior, where he was to draft further reforms as well as continue to suppress opposition. Early in 1881 Loris-Melikov cautiously proposed to this end that Alexander convoke in stages an informal national assembly ("General

Commission") composed of officials appointed by him and of delegates elected by the zemstvos and towns. Loris-Melikov's stated aim was to upstage the radicals and combat sedition by involving in the legislative process, in an "exclusively con-sultative capacity," the disaffected but still loyal liberal and moderate elements of Russia's educated and economic elite. He explicitly assured the Emperor that his proposal had "nothing in common with Western constitutional forms." Yet Loris-Melikov's General Commission might well have become, in the words of a contem-porary English observer (journalist Charles Lowe), a kind of "baby parliament" such as had led to the establishment of a constitutional monarchy in the neigh-boring German Empire. Alexander, by all accounts, perceived that this was so and was ready to sign the necessary decree. But on March 1, 1881, while riding in his carriage in St. Petersburg, he was assassinated by a bomb thrown by a member of a revolutionary organization called the "People's Will." In retrospect, it was a moment of supreme tragedy in Russian history and a shock comparable to that caused by President Lincoln's assassination in the United States in 1865.

The assassination of Alexander II confirmed his badly shaken son and heir, Al-exander III, in a policy of "faith in the strength and truth of autocratic power." (On the original of Loris-Melikov's proposal, Alexander III wrote: "Thank God this criminal and hasty step toward constitution was not taken.") His reign (1881–1894) and that of *his* son and successor, Nicholas II, down to the Revolution of 1905, were a period of continuous reaction in Russia. Not only was any further reform rejected by Alexander III and then by Nicholas II (until he was forced by revolution to reconsider), but between 1881 and 1905 the Imperial government sought by means of "counter-reforms" to limit or undo the changes that had al-ready been made. In the short term, under the strong if narrow-minded Alexan-der III, this policy worked to preserve the autocracy, promote economic develop-ment, and maintain the Russian Empire's standing as a world power. In the longer run, under the weak and fatalistic Nicholas II, it was nothing short of disastrous.

# Essays

First, Richard Pipes argues that in the 1880s, overreacting to revolutionary terrorism, the government of Alexander III created a "proto-police state" whose activities only succeeded in radicalizing Russian society, thus precipitating the Revolution of 1905. Obviously overstated at times and intentionally provocative, Professor Pipes's account of this period nevertheless compellingly evokes the sinister and even absurd ways in which the autocratic system sought to preserve itself against the forces of change. Thomas S. Pearson of Monmouth College (New Jersey) then offers a more complex picture of the background to the 1905 Revolution. He suggests that among its major causes were the persistent failings of government at the *local* level; also, that Alexander III's "counter-reforms" of 1889–1890, the "legislative cornerstone" of his reign, at-tempted to "renovate" local government "without relinquishing political authority." In other words, Alexander III (followed by Nicholas II) tried to make local government more effective in Russia particularly in stimulating the economy while curtailing if not abolishing the elements of local self-rule granted by Alexander II's reform of 1864. Yet neither on their own terms, Pearson concludes, nor on any other, can Alexander III's measures here be considered successful. Compared with its main European rivals,

Russia at the turn of the twentieth century remained a vastly underdeveloped country administratively as well as economically, and the autocracy lurched once more into crisis.

Before reading Pearson's essay, it might be noted again that the zemstvos (councils) created by the local government reform of 1864 were elected by qualified voters at the district (*uezd*, or county) as well as the provincial (*guberniia*) levels, and tended to be dominated by members of the local landed nobility (whose own organs of estate self-government, going back to Catherine II, continued to function at the district and provincial levels as well). The *volost'* (canton, township) administrations, created by the Emancipation of 1861, had jurisdiction over one or more peasant villages (or communes), and were organs exclusively of *peasant* self-rule. Or so, it seems, they were supposed to be—until Alexander III's "land captains" (*zemskie nachal'niki*) came on the scene.

# Towards the Police State

## RICHARD PIPES

The murder of Alexander II saved the bureaucracy from that which it had dreaded the most: the participation of society in political decision making. After momentary hesitation, Alexander III decided that order would be best restored not by further concessions but by more stringent measures of repression. Reform projects ceased; N. P. Ignatev, the new Minister of the Interior, who had the bad judgement to propose to Alexander III the convocation of estates on the model of Muscovite Land Assemblies, was promptly dismissed from his post. The patrimonial principle, held in disfavor since the middle of the eighteenth century, surfaced once again. The "state," as henceforth understood, meant the tsar and his official-dom; internal politics meant protecting both from the encroachments of society. A quick succession of emergency measures completed the subjection of society to the arbitrary power of the bureaucracy and police.

On August 14, 1881, Alexander III signed into law the most important piece of legislation in the history of imperial Russia between the abolition of serfdom in 1861 and the October Manifesto of 1905, and more durable than either. This document, which codified and systematized the repressive legislation issued in the preceding years, has been the real constitution under which—brief interludes apart—Russia has been ruled ever since. In a manner characteristic of Russian legislative practices, in the official Collection of Statutes and Ordinances this momentous piece of legislation is casually sandwiched between a directive approving minor alterations in the charter of the Russian Fire Insurance Company and one concerning the administration of a technical institute in the provincial town of

Reprinted with the permission of Macmillan Publishing Company, a Division of Macmillan, Inc. from *Russia Under the Old Regime* by Richard Pipes, pp. 305–316. Copyright © 1974 by Richard Pipes. (Originally published by Charles Scribner's Sons)

Cherepovtsy. Its full title reads "Regulation concerning measures for the protection of the [established] system of government and of public tranquillity, and the place-ment of certain of the Empire's localities under a state of Reinforced Safeguard." In its opening paragraphs, the decree asserted that ordinary laws had proved insuffi-cient to preserve order in the Empire so that it had become necessary to introduce certain "extraordinary" procedures. In its operative parts, the decree fully concen-trated the struggle against subversion in the hands of the Ministry of the Interior where it has largely remained since. Two kinds of special situations were provided for: "Reinforced Safeguard" and "Extraordinary Safeguard," corresponding to what in western practice was known as Minor and Major States of Siege. The power to impose Reinforced Safeguard in any part of the Empire was entrusted to the Minister of the Interior and Governors General acting with his concurrence. Extraordinary Safeguard required the approval of the tsar and cabinet. The conditions under which either state could be imposed were not clearly specified.

Under "Reinforced Safeguard," the milder of the two states, Governors General, ordinary governors, and governors of cities could do any or all of the following: imprison any resident up to a period of three months and fine him up to 400 rubles; forbid all social, public, and private gatherings; close down all commercial and industrial enterprises either for a specified period or for the duration of the emer-gency; deny individuals the right to reside in their area; and hand over troublemakers to military justice. They were furthermore empowered to declare any person em-ployed by the zemstvos, city governments or courts as "untrustworthy" and to order his instantaneous dismissal. Finally, organs of the local police and gendarmerie were authorized to detain for up to two weeks all persons "inspiring substantial suspicion" from the point of view of state security. When it deemed it necessary to have recourse to Extraordinary Safeguard, the government appointed a Commander-in-Chief who, in addition to all the powers enumerated above, enjoyed the right to dismiss from their posts elected zemstvo deputies (as distinct from hired employees) or even to shut down the zemstvos entirely, as well as to fire any civil servants below the highest three ranks. The latter provision was not casually inserted. Ignatev, the Minister of the Interior when this decree came out, considered bureau-crats and their children to harbor some of the most subversive elements in the country, and suggested periodic "purges" of unreliable elements from the civil service. Under Extraordinary Safeguard, the Commander in Chief could also suspend periodical publications and close for up to one month institutions of higher learning. He could jail suspects for up to three months and impose fines of up to 3,000 rubles. The same edict also substantially increased the powers of the gendarmes in areas under either Reinforced or Extraordinary Safeguard.

The significance of this legislation can perhaps be best summarized in the words of a man who, as head of the Department of the Police from 1902 to 1905, had a great deal to do with its enforcement, namely A. A. Lopukhin. After his retirement he published a remarkable pamphlet in which he stated that the decree of August 14, 1881 caused the fate of the "entire population of Russia to become dependent on the personal opinions of the functionaries of the political police." Henceforth, in matters affecting state security there no longer were any objective criteria of guilt: guilt was determined by the subjective impression of police officials. Ostensibly "temporary," with a validity of three years, this law was regularly renewed every time it was about to expire until the very end of the imperial regime. Immediately upon the promulgation of the Decree of August 14, ten provinces, including the two capital cities of St. Petersburg and Moscow, were placed under Reinforced Safeguard. The number was increased after 1900, and during the Revolution of 1905 some localities were placed under Extraordinary Safeguard. After the suppression of the revolution, under the prime ministership of P. Stolypin, in one form or another the provisions of this Decree were extended to all parts of the Empire, with the result that the laws pertaining to civil rights contained in the October Manifesto [of 1905] and in subsequent Duma [parliamentary] legislation were effectively nullified.

After August 14, 1881, Russia ceased to be an autocratic monarchy in any but the formal sense. . . . The paradox was that the steady encroachment on the rights of individual subjects carried out in the name of state security did not enhance the power of the crown; it was not the crown that benefited but the bureaucracy and police to whom ever greater latitude had to be given to cope with the revolutionary movement. And the absurdity of the situation lay in the fact that the challenge was entirely out of proportion to the measures taken to deal with it. In February 1880, at the height of terror, when Loris-Melikov was given dictatorial powers, the police knew of fewer than 1,000 active cases of anti-state crimes—this in an Empire with nearly 100 million inhabitants!

The extent of police interference in everyday life of late imperial Russia is difficult to convey. One of the most powerful weapons in the hands of the police was its authority to issue certificates of "trustworthiness" which every citizen was required to have before being allowed to enroll at the university or to assume a "responsible" post. To have been refused such a certificate, condemned a Russian to the status of a second-rate citizen, and sometimes virtually forced him to join the revolutionaries. Furthermore, a vast range of activities was impossible without prior permission of the police. As listed in 1888–1889 by a knowledgeable American observer, George Kennan[1], . . . a Russian citizen of the late 1880s was subject to the following police restrictions:

> If you are a Russian, and wish to establish a newspaper, you must ask the permission of the Minister of the Interior. If you wish to open a Sunday-school, or any other sort of school, whether in a neglected slum of St. Peters-burg or in a native village in Kamchatka, you must ask the permission of the Minister of Public Instruction. If you wish to give a concert or to get up tableaux for the benefit of an orphan asylum, you must ask permission of the nearest representative of the Minister of the Interior, then submit your programme of exercises to a censor for approval or revision, and finally hand over the proceeds of the entertainment to the police, to be embezzled or given to the orphan asylum, as it may happen. If you wish to sell newspapers

---

1. George Kennan (1845–1924) traveled extensively in Russia and Siberia in the 1880s, detailing his experiences in a series of magazine articles and in his famous two-volume work, *Siberia and the Exile System* (1891), a work that was extremely critical of the Russian government's treatment of political offenders in prison and exile.—Ed.

on the street, you must get permission, be registered in the books of the police, and wear a numbered brass plate as big as a saucer around your neck. If you wish to open a drug-store, a printing-office, a photograph-gallery, or a book-store, you must get permission. If you are photographer and desire to change the location of your place of business, you must get permission. If you are a student and go to a public library to consult Lyell's *Principles of Geology* or Spencer's *Social Statics*, you will find that you cannot even look at such dangerous and incendiary volumes without special permission. If you are a physician, you must get permission before you can practice, and then, if you do not wish to respond to calls in the night, you must have permission to refuse to go; furthermore, if you wish to prescribe what are known in Russia as "powerfully acting" medicines, you must have special permission, or the druggists will not dare to fill your prescriptions. If you are a peasant and wish to build a bath-house on your premises, you must get permission. If you wish to thresh out your grain in the evening by candle-light, you must get permission or bribe the police. If you wish to go more than fifteen miles away from your home, you must get permission. If you are a foreign traveler, you must get permission to come into the Empire, permission to go out of it, permission to stay in it longer than six months, and must notify the police every time you change your boarding-place. In short, you cannot live, move, or have your being in the Russian Empire without permission. . . .

Another important source of police power was the right granted it by a decree of March 12, 1882, to declare any citizen subject to overt surveillance. An individual in this category had to surrender his personal documents in exchange for special police papers. He was not allowed to move without police authorization and his quarters were liable to be searched at any time of day or night. He could not hold any government job or any public post, belong to private associations, or teach, deliver lectures, operate typographies, photographic laboratories or libraries, or deal in spirits; he could practice medicine, midwifery and pharmacology only under licence from the Ministry of the Interior. The same ministry decided whether or not he was to receive mail and telegrams. Russians under overt surveillance constituted a special category of sub-citizens excluded from the operations of law and the regular administration and living under direct police rule.

The security measures outlined above were reinforced by criminal laws which tended to weigh Russian jurisprudence overwhelmingly in favor of the state. Kennan made the following observations, all of them readily verifiable, concerning the Criminal Code of 1885:

> In order to appreciate the extraordinary severity of [the] laws for the protection of the Sacred Person, the Dignity, and the Supreme Authority of the Tsar it is only necessary to compare them with the laws for the protection of the personal rights and honor of private citizens. From such a comparison it appears that to injure a portrait, statue, bust, or other representation of the Tsar set up in a public place is a more grievous crime than to so assault and injure a private citizen as to deprive him of eyes, tongue, an arm, a leg, or the sense of hearing. To organize or take part in a society which has for its object the overthrow of the Government or a change in the form of the Government, even although such society does not contemplate a resort to violence nor immediate action, is a crime of greater gravity than to so beat,

maltreat, or torture a human being as partly to deprive him of his mental faculties. The making of a speech or the writing of a book which disputes or throws doubt upon the inviolability of the rights or privileges of the Supreme Authority is as serious an offense as the outraging of a woman. The mere concealment of a person who has formed an evil design affecting the life, welfare, or honor of the 'Tsar, or the affording of refuge to a person who intends to bring about a restriction of the rights or privileges of the Supreme Authority, is a more serious matter than the premeditated murder of one's own mother. Finally, in the estimation of the penal code, the private citizen who makes or circulates a caricature of the Sacred Person of the Tsar, for the purpose of creating disrespect for his personal characteristics or for his management of the Empire, commits a more heinous crime than the jailer who outrages in a cell until she dies an imprisoned, helpless, and defenseless girl fifteen years of age.

The system of political repression included exile. This could be imposed either by a court sentence or by administrative decision, and could take one of several forms ranging widely in severity. The mildest form was to be sent out of the country or into the provinces for a specified length of time to live under overt police surveillance. More severe was a sentence of exile for settlement to Siberia (western Siberia was considered a much milder place of punishment than eastern). Such "settled exiles" were essentially free men allowed to work gainfully and have their families with them. If they had money to supplement the small government allowance, they could live in considerable comfort. The harshest form of exile was hard labor (*katorga*, from the Greek *katergon*, meaning galley). This type of penal servitude had been introduced by Peter the Great who used criminals to build ships, work mines, help construct St. Petersburg and furnish free labor wherever else it was necessary. Hard labor convicts lived in prison barracks and performed menial work under guard. Dostoevsky, who spent time doing *katorga*, left an unforgettable picture of it in his *Notes from the House of the Dead*. After 1886, the exploitation of forced labor (including prison labor) was governed by special regulations designed to assure that the government made money on it. In 1887, for instance, it brought the Ministry of the Interior a gross income of 538,820 rubles out of which, after expenses, there remained a net profit of 166,440 rubles.

Because so many different officials had the power to impose sentences of exile, statistics of this type of punishment are hard to come by. [One] usually reliable source estimates that in the 1890s there were in Siberia 300,000 exiles of all sorts, forming 5.2 percent of the population, as well as 14,500 prisoners serving sentences of hard labor. However, as had been the case in the first half of the century, only a small fraction of these exiles were committed for political crimes. Zaionchkovsky, who had access to the pertinent archives, cites official reports to the effect that in 1880 there were in the whole Russian Empire only about 1,200 people under sentences of exile for political crimes; of these, 230 resided in Siberia and the rest in European Russia; a mere 60 served terms of hard labor. (These figures do not include over 4,000 Poles exiled for participation in the 1863 uprising.) In 1901, the total number of political exiles of all sorts, both those sentenced by courts and administrative procedures, increased to 4,113, of which 3,838 were under overt police surveillance, and 180 on hard labor.

To complete the picture of restrictive measures imposed by the government of Alexander III, mention must be made of policies subsumed under the term "counter-reforms," whose avowed aim it was to emasculate the Great Reforms of Alexander II. Among them were limitations on the competence of the zemstvos, abolition of the office of justice of the peace, and introduction of "Land [Captains]," local officials with much discretionary authority over the peasants. The Jews, who were considered particularly prone to subversion, were subjected in the reign of Alexander III to the full force of disabling laws which, though long on the statute books, in the past had not been strictly applied.

Thus, in the early 1880s, all the elements of the police state were present in imperial Russia. These may be summarized as follows:

1. Politics was declared the exclusive preserve of the government and its high functionaries; any meddling in them on the part of unauthorized personnel, which included all private citizens, was a crime punishable by law;

2. The enforcement of this principle was entrusted to a Department of Police and a Corps of Gendarmes whose exclusive concern was with crimes against the state;

3. These organs of state security had the power
   a. to search, arrest, interrogate, imprison, and exile persons either guilty of political activity or suspected of it;
   b. to refuse any citizen a certificate of "trustworthiness," lacking which he was prevented from engaging in a great variety of activities, including attendance at institutions of higher learning and employment in public institutions, governmental or other;
   c. to supervise all kinds of cultural activities of citizens and to certify the statutes of public associations;

4. In the fulfilment of its duties, the Department of the Police and the Corps of Gendarmes were not subject to supervision by the organs of the judiciary; they were also exempt from the jurisdiction of the regular civil administration on whose territory they operated;

5. By a variety of means at its disposal, such as overt surveillance, Siberian exile, and hard labor, the political police apparatus could partly or fully isolate dissidents from the rest of society;

6. No literature could be published in Russia or enter it from abroad without the censor's permission;

7. The Minister of the Interior had the authority to declare any region of the Empire under Reinforced Safeguard, in which event normal laws and institutions were suspended and the entire population became subject to martial law; top provincial administrators likewise had the power, with the Minister's approval, to turn dissidents over to courts martial. . . .

Yet, when all is said and done, it would be difficult to maintain that imperial Russia was a full-blown police state; it was rather a forerunner, a rough prototype of such a regime, which fell far short of its full potential. The system had too many loopholes. Most of these resulted from the assimilation by the Russian ruling elite of Western institutions and Western values which, though incompatible with the patrimonial spirit, they were unwilling to give up. Such loopholes quite vitiated the elaborate set of repressive measures introduced in the 1870s and 1880s.

Of these counterforces perhaps the most important was private property. The institution came late to Russia, but once introduced it soon made itself thoroughly at home. While harassing its subjects for the slightest political offences, the imperial regime was very careful not to violate their property rights. When publishing in London *The Bell*, that powerful irritant to the authorities, Alexander Herzen had his rents regularly forwarded to him from Russia by an international bank. Lenin's mother, even after one of her sons had been executed [1887] for an attempt on the tsar's life and two of her other children had been jailed for revolutionary activity, continued until her death to draw the government pension due to her as a civil servant's widow. The existence of private capital and private enterprise nullified the many police measures intended to cut off "untrustworthy" elements from their means of livelihood. Political unreliables could almost always find employment with some private firm whose management was either unsympathetic to the government or politically neutral. Some of Russia's most radical journalists were subsidized by wealthy eccentrics. Zemstvos openly engaged radical intellectuals as statisticians or teachers. The Union of Liberation, a clandestine society which played a critical role in sparking off the 1905 Revolution, was likewise supported from private resources. Private property created all over the Empire enclaves which the police was powerless to trespass in so far as the existing laws, cavalier as they were with personal rights, strictly protected the rights of property. . . .

Another loophole was foreign travel. Granted to dvoriane [the nobility] in 1785, it was gradually extended to the other estates. It survived even during the darkest periods of repression. Nicholas I tried to limit it by threatening to deprive dvoriane [nobles], who between the ages of ten and eighteen studied abroad, of the right to enter state service. In 1834 he required dvoriane to confine their foreign residence to five years, and in 1851 he reduced it further to two years. In the Criminal Code [of 1885], there were provisions requiring Russian citizens to return home from abroad when so ordered by the government. But none of these measures made much difference. Russians traveled in western Europe frequently and stayed there for long periods of time; in 1900, for instance, 200,000 Russian citizens spent abroad an average of 80 days. In Wilhelmian [contemporary] Germany, they constituted the largest contingent of foreign students. To obtain a passport valid for travel abroad one merely had to send an application with a small fee to the local governor. Passports were readily granted even to individuals with known subversive records, evidently on the assumption that they would cause less trouble abroad than at home. It is not in the least remarkable that the revolutionary party which in October 1917 took control of Russia had had its leader and operational headquarters for many years in western Europe.

Thirdly, there were powerful factors of a cultural nature inhibiting the full use of the existing machinery of repression. The elite ruling imperial Russia was brought up in the western spirit, and it dreaded disgrace. It hesitated to act too harshly for fear of being ridiculed by the civilized world. It was embarrassed to appear even in its own eyes as behaving in an "Asiatic" manner. The imperial elite certainly was psychologically incapable of applying violence regardless of its consequences. There exists a touchingly prim note from Nicholas II, a kind of epitaph of his reign, which he sent late in 1916 to relatives who had interceded on behalf of a Grand Duke implicated in the assassination of Rasputin: "No one is permitted to engage in murders." Such an ethic simply did not go with police rule.

The result of the conflict between the old patrimonial psychology and modern western influences, was to yield a police force that was ubiquitous, meddlesome, and often brutal, but on the whole inefficient. The powers given to the political police were entirely out of proportion to the results achieved. We have seen some statistics bearing on political offences: the small number of people under surveillance or in exile, and the insignificant proportion of books intercepted by censorship. In the decade of the 1880s, there were only seventeen persons executed for political crimes, all of them perpetrators of assassination or assassination attempts. During the reign of Alexander III—a period of severe repression—a total of four thousand persons were detained and interrogated in connection with political offences. These are very insignificant figures when one considers Russia's size and the massiveness of the machinery set up to deal with subversion.

The principal if unintended accomplishment of the proto-police regime was to radicalize Russian society. Its definition of political crimes was so comprehensive that the far-flung nets of security precautions caught and united people who had next to nothing in common with one another. From the legal point of view, hardly any distinction was drawn between conservative, nationalist, liberal, democratic, socialist and anarchist forms of discontent. A monarchist landlord outraged by the incompetence or corruption of the bureaucracy in his district became in the eyes of the law and the gendarmerie an ally of the anarchist assembling bombs to blow up the imperial palace. With its proscriptions, the government actually pushed its citizens into opposition ranks, where they became receptive to extremist appeals. For example, the laws in force in the 1880s forbade university students to form corporate organizations of any kind. Given the loneliness, poverty and natural social inclinations of young men it was inevitable that they would seek each other out and, in contravention of the law, form associations; these by their very existence acquired clandestine status and as such were easily infiltrated and taken over by radicals. It was the same with labor legislation. Stringent prohibitions against the formation of worker associations transformed even the most harmless labor activities into anti-state crimes. Workers whose sole interest might have lain in self-education or economic betterment were driven into the arms of radical students whom they actually mistrusted and disliked. Thus it was the government itself which helped accomplish the seemingly impossible, namely an alliance of all shades of public opinion, from the Slavophile right to the socialist-revolutionary left, which under the name "Liberation Movement" in 1902–1905 at long last wrung a constitution out of the government.

# The Failure of Reform

## THOMAS S. PEARSON

Beleaguered by famine, workers' strikes, student unrest, and military defeat
. . . [in the Russo-Japanese War of 1904–1905], the [Imperial] regime stumbled
into the revolution of 1905 and came perilously close to losing its power. Although
many causes lay behind this event, the administrative shortcomings of tsarism in
the late nineteenth century were undoubtedly among the most important. These
failings were particularly noticeable in the government's policy on local self-government, for here Russia's rulers confronted the centuries-old problem of governing a
uniquely huge, underdeveloped empire with inadequate human and economic resources and with largely uneducated social classes who, for various reasons, regarded
self-government with indifference. . . .

The problem of local self-government . . . warrants special attention because
postreform Russia came under unusual pressures as [both] a great power and a
developing state, and because self-government provided a critical link between
[the] autocracy and Russian society. Faced with unprecedented demographic growth
and the need for economic change in his realm, Tsar Alexander II abolished serfdom
and in 1861–1864 introduced a series of Great Reforms, among them a system of
elected self-government that was to become the most significant local administrative
reform in Russian history between the Petrine era and 1905. Although these changes
put Russia in the ranks of European states that had established a decentralized
system of public self-government at midcentury to harness new social forces and
perpetuate monarchical rule, the Russian experiment with self-government proved
exceptional in two respects. On the one hand, the creation of elected peasant [*volost'*]
and zemstvo self-government compounded tensions in the tsarist government—for
instance, between central and local concerns and between local public and state
officials—that were unmatched in their extent and gravity elsewhere in Europe.
This was largely because a strong and active system of public self-government
in Russia potentially provided the basis for the development of civil liberties,
constitutional government, and religious and national freedom—forces antithetical
to the tsarist order. On the other hand, the Russian experience with local self-
government stands out because the tsarist empire was the only European state to
reverse its course of decentralization so abruptly in the late nineteenth century,
with the same purpose of perpetuating imperial rule and consolidating its social
support.

This [study] focuses on the Russian government's efforts to direct local self-
government and its reform from its introduction in 1861 to its bureaucratization
under the land captains and zemstvo counterreforms of 1889 and 1890. It seeks to
answer two interrelated questions: Why did the Russian government introduce

From Thomas S. Pearson, *Russian Officialdom in Crisis: Autocracy and Local Self-Government,*
*1861–1900,* 1989, pp. vii–ix, xv–xvi, 245–60. Reprinted by permission of Cambridge University
Press.

these counterreforms in local self-government? and What does our case study of the administrative reasons for these counterreforms and the bureaucratic politics surrounding them tell us about the nature and viability of the imperial government on the eve of the twentieth century? . . .

By and large, historians agree that the autocracy was in crisis in the late 1870s and early 1880s, as illustrated by terrorist attacks on its officials and its reliance on extralegal means to suppress opposition. The 1890s have also been called a period of crisis because of the outbreak of famine and cholera in the provinces and burgeoning strike activity in the cities. However, the term "crisis" is also warranted in a wider sense, as used here, to characterize the government's increasing futility at managing rural administrative development with its paternalistic bureaucracy and traditional corporate institutions, and its inability to renovate local government with its ministerial apparatus. In this sense, Russian officialdom experienced what some scholars have called a crisis of "penetration," which entailed the extension of government control over its territories and social groups and the development of bureaucratic efficiency. To be sure, bureaucratic inefficiency alone does not constitute a crisis. Yet in autocratic Russia, as perhaps nowhere else in Europe, state attempts at rural control through the Great Reforms bred public disillusionment and administrative and economic problems for Russian officials far beyond the routine type. When an activist state (such as Russia following the Crimean defeat) is unsuccessful in managing its broader, more complex responsibilities effectively, the result is often social alienation and bureaucratic rigidity—especially when there is no basis for meaningful public participation in government. These conditions make the regime more vulnerable to political challenges [to] its legitimacy, such as occurred in Russia during the revolutionary years 1905 and 1917.

Along these lines I contend that the land captain and zemstvo counterreforms, like the local self-government established in the 1860s, were designed to meet specific rural needs and were a product of a ministerial system of government that Alexander II developed with his Great Reforms. This compartmentalized arrangement promoted more professional administration and bureaucratic penetration in the provinces and left the tsar's personal power intact by allowing the autocrat to choose from different ministerial approaches and ideologies of local development. Unfortunately, it also produced ministerial fragmentation and confusion at all levels and helped put state institutions into conflict with the new zemstvo and peasant institutions. Besides generating reverberations in the provincial bureaucracy, these conflicts impeded the work of local self-government and complicated state efforts to modify, not to mention overhaul, the legislation of the 1860s.

Nonetheless, Russian officialdom pressed on and devised the counterreforms for practical statist reasons. I maintain that the government did so following the autocratic crisis of the late 1870s because it was convinced that elected peasant and zemstvo institutions, as established in the 1860s, were mismanaged, insolvent, and politically troublesome to autocracy. Indeed, that crisis revealed that the administrative and fiscal order of the state ultimately hinged on the work of elected institutions outside the government's strict control. Put another way, the state's efforts to control the provinces in the Great Reform era were shown to be inadequate by the political crisis of 1878–1882. Yet in the 1880s, as two decades earlier, the state had few options for overhauling local administration owing to shortages of personnel and funds, its distrust of elected officials, and sporadic tensions between local state and public institutions.

Viewed against this backdrop, the counterreform proposals of Minister of Internal Affairs Dmitry Andreevich Tolstoi and his role in their enactment merit reevaluation. We shall show how throughout the 1880s he insisted that local self-government be depoliticized and bureaucratized in order to fulfill its administrative functions. However, the prospect of all local self-government concentrated under his ministry challenged the ministerial power equilibrium established under Alexander II and violated the principles of Alexander II's reform officials who sat in the State Council. Tolstoi's peers recognized that the balance of power between the capital and localities was a key to state security, administrative order, and their own political status, and thus most of them joined forces and employed various strategies, with some success, to blunt the counterreform measures. By the end of the nineteenth century, . . . public self-government had been repudiated but not fully bureaucratized, leaving a tangled, confused local administration and divided ministerial hierarchy that would come under attack at the turn of the century. . . .

In enacting the Land Captain and Zemstvo statutes of 1889 and 1890, the government formally concluded more than twelve years of systematic work on rural self-government reform.[1] Likewise, the legislation closed a chapter in postreform Russian history that saw the introduction of self-government in the countryside in the early 1860s and the first serious state efforts to reorganize it over the next quarter century. During this period and increasingly in the 1890s, the Russian government faced a rural crisis marked by acute land and grain shortages, the breakup of traditional patriarchal ties, and the rapid swelling of tax and redemption arrears; in the latter case, direct tax arrears rose from 22 percent of the anticipated collection in 1876–1880 to 119 percent in the years 1896–1900, and in 1903 redemption dues arrears hit 138 percent. Amid these developments, Russian officialdom exhibited many characteristics of a government in crisis as it grappled with the problem of local self-government and other matters connected with state penetration of the provinces. Overwhelmed by the many tasks of rural administration and development and short of personnel and funds, the government nevertheless distrusted the self-governing institutions that it had created to assist it. Seeking an ideology of administration that could provide the right combination of local initiative and political control, the state repeatedly sought to reorganize local self-government. Yet each time its efforts at institutional renovation became bogged down in interest group politics, particularly when the debates reached the highest circles in St.

---

1. In 1892 the government also adopted a new Municipal Statute; its major provisions adhered to the guidelines of the 1890 zemstvo counterreform. The "land captains," appointed by the central government to serve at the local level, were given extensive authority over peasant affairs. The "Zemstvo statute" drastically curtailed the fiscal and other powers of the elected zemstvos in favor of centrally appointed officials, particularly the provincial governors.—Ed.

Petersburg. Without imperial intervention, for better or for worse, the proposed legislation was buried under the weight of official opposition and inertia. . . .

In this respect, our study points up a fateful irony of the government of late Imperial Russia that other accounts, focusing primarily on capital city politics or on rural administration, have overlooked. As the government grew more knowledgeable and concerned about its local self-governing institutions, and rural conditions generally in the 1870s and 1880s, it proved less capable of reforming them by legislative means. In essence, both administrative and political factors must be kept in mind in assessing autocracy's record on local self-government reform and its implications for the survival of the old order. Local self-government, as introduced in elected peasant, zemstvo, judicial, and municipal institutions, was no luxury for the tsars. Rather, it was necessary to compensate for the inadequacies of prereform administration and the lack of state personnel and fiscal resources to govern the provinces alone. But local self-government had important political and administrative ramifications for the entire government. Not only did it become a topic of ideological conflict between elite officials who advocated *zakonnost'* [legality] and greater public responsibility on the local level versus those who preferred more state control, but local self-government discharged administrative functions vital to the state ministries, which had their own local bureaucracies and sense of institutional mission in the countryside. Hence, the state repeatedly sought to balance local administrative initiative and political order—a challenge that [particularly] frustrated . . . [V. K.] Pleve, . . . minister of internal affairs, who in the period [1902–1904] sought to reduce "excessive centralization" by decentralizing (deconcentrating) local administration while elevating the governors' leadership in local affairs.

This perennial quest to activate public self-government and neutralize it politically proved in fact to be a curse of autocratic power. This was because in introducing administrative decentralization and public self-government, Alexander II—in what we have called his ministerial system—diffused responsibility for local administrative and economic development among numerous ministries. Besides promoting more effective and specialized ministerial activity at the local level, this arrangement established a ministerial power structure that left his personal authority intact. For political reasons as well, he left the traditional social estates fundamentally in place as he introduced public self-government, thereby ensuring that the experienced landed gentry [nobility], despite their past failings in local administration, would play the leading role in peasant and zemstvo self-government. Unfortunately, this policy that favored political control over public initiative had a number of adverse consequences for tsarism from 1861 to 1900. Besides failing to define local self-government as a truly public or state enterprise—in effect, leaving it unprotected by law or government authority—the policy also tied local self-government reform to ministerial government. Thus, local self-government reform served as a battleground for rival ideologies and interests and concerned many ministers, not merely successive ministers of internal affairs (the focus of most studies of the counterreforms). For similar reasons, it evoked intense conflict among zemstvo, gentry, and other rural spokesmen anxious to use the principles of decentralization and self-government to their own advantage. Hence, reform, never an easy process in tsarist

Russia, became even more complicated and cumbersome under Alexander II and Alexander III, as special interests frequently transcended administrative needs of state.

More immediately, however, this system of public self-government bred administrative confusion and political dissatisfaction in the provinces and St. Petersburg. By the late 1870s, the state had compelling practical reasons for overhauling local self-government. The autocratic crisis, with its backdrop of revolutionary attacks on tsarism, had its roots in the breakdown of peasant and zemstvo administration, and it awakened top officials to the political dangers of mismanaged rural administration, sporadic zemstvo–bureaucratic conflict, and rapidly rising absenteeism in peasant and zemstvo assemblies. Significantly, from the late 1870s on elite officials were preoccupied with these problems because, unlike revolutionary terrorism, they did not diminish even temporarily following the end of the "crisis of autocracy" in 1882. Although reports of rural anarchy, administrative confusion, official corruption, and apathy during this period were probably exaggerated—given the tendency of some conservative officials to equate "democracy" with "anarchy"—still, coming from many different sources and pinpointing many specific examples, they dispelled official illusions about the inherent democratic tendencies of peasants. They [officials] understood the ineffectiveness of peasant customary law in maintaining rural order and the inability of the *volost'* administration to handle peasant, zemstvo, and state needs. Faced with nearly uniform criticism of peasant self-government, top officials naturally concluded that peasants left unsupervised by the district bureaus might lose their respect for all authorities. In this context, the sudden, massive growth in tax arrears disturbed the ministers and Alexander II, because such arrears, which were due to mismanaged tax collection and poor harvests, crippled zemstvo and state work and because, more than any other aspect of local self-government, they were the subject of peasant complaints.

Under these circumstances, the government began the process of local government reform [or counterreform] in 1879–1880. . . . In tracing the development of the land captains legislation, we see that *all* factions in the reform debate from 1881 to 1890 favored establishing personal supervisory authority over peasant self-government and using the landed gentry in some fashion (elected, appointed) in this capacity. More important, this evidence of a rural administrative crisis, although by no means a complete or even true picture in all cases, convinced the government in 1880–1881 that it could no longer afford to leave the provinces unsupervised, in the hands of elected officials who acted according to local custom or personal interest. True, Tolstoi later used the rural authority crisis and reports of zemstvo–government friction in the late 1870s and early 1880s to consolidate his political power and the social support of autocracy, but this should not obscure the main point.[2] Even before the reaction following Alexander II's assassination began, the government committed itself to some basic concepts in local self-government reform that were introduced in the legislation of 1889–1890.

---

2. Count Dmitry A. Tolstoi (1823–1889), the reactionary minister of education (1866–1880) under Alexander II, was appointed minister of the interior (internal affairs) by Alexander III in 1882.—Ed.

Given these priorities and the recurrent shortage of qualified local personnel and funds, the government debate focused on ideologies of administration, and not gentry interests, to the dismay of [leading reactionaries]. As in the early 1860s, the reform discussions of the 1880s concentrated on the relationship between state and local public institutions and provided expression for two conflicting ideologies of state building—decentralization and centralization (which in its extreme form meant bureaucratization). There were two reasons for this. On the one hand, both ideologies could be modified to fit the current political environment and the aspirations of various officials. Like other European nations in the late nineteenth century, the Russian government was neither completely centralized nor decentralized, but contained aspects of both centralization and decentralization. Thus, the decentralists favored ending peasant self-government and separate state and zemstvo institutions in the belief that the decentralization of the 1860s was too limited for the 1880s.

In their plans to reorganize local self-government, the decentralists and centralists not only put forth conflicting ideologies, but as the discussions at all levels of government revealed, they brought political issues concerning autocracy and the estates order to the forefront. Although both factions proclaimed their support for autocracy and gentry leadership in local self-government, they had very different views on Russia's political future and the state–gentry relationship. For administrative reasons, the . . . decentralists . . . advocated comprehensive local government reform and a devolution of political authority beyond the Great Reforms, because they assumed that Russia belonged to the community of Western nations and should emulate their political evolution. Their proposals to give the zemstvo executive authority over peasant administration and to create zemstvo-controlled district bureaus revealed their commitment to the principles of Alexander II's reforms and the public service ideal that they embodied. They were convinced that the gentry, freed from bureaucratic interference in their roles as zemstvo officials and supervisors in an all-estate village and *volost'* administration, would educate peasants and establish genuine public self-government at all levels—a prospect that left the future of the traditional estates order in doubt. It was precisely that possibility that made this proposal so objectionable to [the conservative] gentry marshals that Tolstoi invited to the . . . debates.

Yet Tolstoi was even more determined to use the gentry as a vehicle in his administrative and political designs. . . . Certainly, Alexander III's government reaffirmed its support for the traditional estates and Tolstoi, conservative that he was, viewed autocracy and the estates order as inseparable. But it is misleading to conclude that the land captains and zemstvo counterreforms were due primarily to Tolstoi's desire for a new "pro-gentry course" or to gentry class pressure or interests. Such an interpretation not only overlooks the statist reasons for the legislation but, as an explanation for the counterreform, it is flawed in three ways. First, . . . the gentry was not being displaced as leaders in local self-government by nongentry in the early 1880s, as Tolstoi and other officials readily acknowledged. The gentry indeed maintained its dominant role in local self-government as peace arbitrators, elected justices of the peace, permanent members of the district bureaus, and zemstvo assembly chairmen and executive officials. As Tolstoi saw it, the problem was that some gentry officials put their concept of public service above the state's welfare, while petty gentry and nongentry landowners ignored the needs of the state and local population in making careers out of elected office.

Second, although the *soslovie* [estate] system was remarkably durable as a legal order that allowed social groups to interact with state agencies, under Alexander III the elite bureaucracy developed more and more into a separate caste in Russian society with its own income, ethos, and ideologies. Even Tolstoi, who was not one of the arrivés [newcomers] who worked his way into the ministries from the 1860s on, was renowned for subordinating all interests (even personal ones) to the needs of state. Heeding the advice of his governors, in 1883–1884 he aimed to transform local gentry officials from elected rural guardians into his state agents, in effect impressing them into a distinct rural bureaucratic corps. True, Tolstoi wanted his officials to have wide discretionary powers to operate effectively in the villages, unencumbered by excessive regulation and intrusive supervision. But as Tolstoi and his opponents all recognized, the main issue in local self-government reform was the relationship between the state and local self-government, not whether the gentry would continue to play the leading role in this area. This point is substantiated by a third factor that challenges the view that the counterreforms were introduced mainly to suit the gentry. Far from signaling a new faith in the landed gentry, the legislation, with its bureaucratic regimen for land captains and its attack on previous gentry leadership, impressed . . . Prince Obolensky and others as an assault on the traditional *soslovie* system.

In essence, Tolstoi intended to have the gentry serve on his terms to restore administrative order and build rural support for autocracy. This distinguished him from such other conservatives as Pobedonostsev [see Documents] . . . who merely spoke of a bond between tsar and *narod* [people]. Although Tolstoi's program hinged on attracting the necessary gentry volunteers to hold these offices . . . , it was no throwback to the prereform era of local gentry control. Nor was it a plan for the systematic mobilization of rural support and the modernization of rural society, a process that hit its stride with Stolypin's reforms (1906–1911) and Soviet collectivization two decades later. Rather, Tolstoi's plan of bureaucratized local self-government gambled on harnessing rural society and, through his Ministry of Internal Affairs, on putting the state in control of rural development. Judging by the results of the 1890s, the plan (to the extent that it was introduced) failed to do either. . . .

Indeed, if we look back at state efforts to reform local self-government from 1861 to 1900, it is clear that by the end of the century the Imperial government suffered from three serious, if not fatal, weaknesses. First, the government arguably had less rural social support than it did in the 1860s, when it imposed a broad, and not altogether popular, program of reforms in the countryside that also aimed at propping up the traditional social order. At the time the enlightened bureaucrats were quite optimistic that local self-government would provide a vehicle to mobilize the support of the progressive landed gentry for the regime. Twenty-five years later, however, the situation was different. Given the diminishing numbers of landed gentry and the problems that gentry-led local self-government created for the state, Tolstoi decided to bureaucratize self-government in order to build peasant support for autocracy. In other words, fifteen years before the more celebrated and radical agrarian reforms of Stolypin, the government saw the peasantry as its most important and permanent base of rural support.

From the state's vantage point, there were some initial signs that land captains were succeeding in introducing law (*zakonnost'*) into the peasant village. By 1990, peasants were bringing increasing numbers of cases to the reorganized *volost'* courts, which, under the land captain's supervision, operated on the basis of the civil code rather than local customary law. Yet such trends do not tell us much about peasant reaction to bureaucratization. On the contrary, published accounts largely suggest that the peasants viewed the land captains as state agents who acted according to personal authority rather than law. The intrusion of land captains into the villages did little to rekindle peasant enthusiasm for elected office; in fact, peasants and their officials regarded them as unwelcome interlopers much as colonized peoples have resented foreign protection. Like peasants in developing nations they saw little connection between the taxes they paid and the state services provided, perhaps because in 1894 over 80 percent of all *volost'* expenditures went to administrative costs, versus 12 percent for public health and charity and only 3 percent to peasant agriculture. In short, although it is risky to generalize about peasant attitudes toward the state, it is clear that the counterreforms did not have the administrative and political effect on the peasants that Tolstoi had in mind. In 1902, Minister of Internal Affairs Sipiagin admitted as much in attacking the corruption and collusion of peasant officials and village police and in contending that such officials occasionally participated in mass disorders. Yet, significantly, the ministry's plan for peasant administrative reform consisted mainly of strengthening the punitive authority and bureaucratic duties of the village elder.

If Tolstoi's bureaucratization of local self-government as a rule failed to generate peasant support for autocracy, it even more critically alienated and polarized the landed gentry. The traditionalist faction, still bitter about and critical of the Great Reforms, in many instances attacked the counterreforms as they retreated to the strongholds of their corporate institutions, thereby adding to the fragmentation of local administration. They coalesced briefly with their liberal counterparts in the 1905 Revolution out of a common hatred for officialdom. After 1905, the traditional gentry, feeling betrayed by the counterreform experience, did its best to derail . . . [any] further extension of the bureaucracy into the countryside. Meanwhile, the liberals' campaign for genuine public self-government, zemstvo autonomy, a zemstvo at the *volost'* level, and constitutional reform circa 1900 drew from gentry ranks along with urban professionals and [others]. It pointed to the archaic nature of Tolstoi's bureaucratic paternalism, given the increasing urbanization, industrialization, and erosion of traditional class distinctions. In effect, the counterreforms did mold public opinion, but not in the manner that Tolstoi envisioned. Rather, Russian officials, more isolated than ever, were in the precarious position of deriving little visible support from the countryside, and as such Russian officialdom in the late nineteenth century found itself reduced to small deeds in matters of rural administration and economic development—measures unlikely to build rural support in the short run.

Ministerial fragmentation constituted a second important weakness of the late Imperial regime and one directly connected, as we have seen, to the process of ministerial expansion in the provinces through local self-government reform. In tracing the crisis of late tsarist officialdom, we recognize that bureaucracies by nature have their conflicts, stress points, and professional identities. This was particularly true in tsarist Russia because all power revolved around the person of the emperor and because as an autocratic society the government functioned as the only legally sanctioned political arena up to the 1905 Revolution. Moreover, ministerial fragmentation was not a new phenomenon in Russia at the end of the nineteenth century. It existed in the prereform era, and clashes between the ministers of justice and of internal affairs in the 1860s were commonplace. . . .

Nonetheless, as this study shows, by the time of the counterreforms the central government was not only fragmented on ideological and institutional grounds, with the latter particularly dividing Alexander III's ministers; even more important, this absence of unity and direction in central policy making had critical ramifications for state efforts to direct rural development and mobilize rural support. By the 1880s, Alexander III's ministers, firmly rooted in the ministerial system and balance of power ethos inherited from their predecessors, proved quite effective in the tactics of procrastination, petty criticism, counterprojects and intrigue in their attempts to oppose Tolstoi's counterreforms. Accountable only to an autocrat who remained passive in most administrative matters, these ministers repeatedly resisted any changes and pressed for a quick return to normal bureaucratic routine following periods of national emergency, for instance, 1878–1882. Such bureaucratic behavior in the aftermath of a government crisis was by no means unique to Russia in the 1880s. The increase in specialized administrators, the turnover in elite personnel, the emphasis on discipline and careerism, the intense fighting between top officials, and the desire to close off bureaucratic ranks to outsiders had many of the earmarks of the power struggle in the Prussian bureaucracy following the 1848 Revolution. Whereas the Prussian bureaucracy of the 1850s and 1860s surrendered its corporate identity and autonomy and allied itself with the junkers, in Russia elite officials became more isolated from landed society and more dependent on the tsar. Each of the ministries involved with local administration and, ipso facto, local self-government, developed its own priorities for rural administrative and economic development. For these reasons, Tolstoi's counterreform projects, which attested to his "primacy" in ministerial circles and proposed to give him control over local administrative, fiscal, and judicial matters, came under attack as deviant impulses that invited severe sanctions from his bureaucratic peer group. These ministers all realized that Tolstoi's plan to create his own corps of paternalistic state agents jeopardized their own power and that of their field agents.

Such ministerial fragmentation had adverse consequences in the provinces, too, not only in blocking other reform measures . . . , but also in adding to the burdens of provincial officialdom. At the end of the nineteenth century, the twenty or so collegial bureaus representing the various ministries at the provincial level had no standardized procedures or integrated functions. In practice more than ever, the responsibility for ministerial policy execution fell on the governors and provincial administration became the scene of power struggles, especially between the ministers of finance and of internal affairs. . . .

Indeed, the ministerial conflict over local self-government reform from 1861 to 1900 shows that tsarist officials joined forces in opposing reform proposals much more readily than in supporting any measure, whatever its objective. Although other works on the institutional and ideological limits of reform have reached a similar conclusion, our study illustrates how much ministerial conflict over local self-government reform over the long haul inhibited the development of rural administration and central policy making. There were two reasons for this. First, more than other areas (labor policy, agriculture, peasant resettlement) that produced interministerial conflict, the expansion of ministerial power into the provinces in the nineteenth century limited opportunities for public participation in local administration, especially given the state's determination to monopolize political power. Second, local self-government suffered because [ministerial adversaries] used [it] as a means of protecting their own local authority or defending the principles of the Great Reforms while doing little to promote its development. Personality politics and ideological conflict, not ministerial order, dictated reform legislation in Russia. Such compartmentalized government and the attitudes it bred posed great difficulties for tsarism in years when, challenged by rapid population growth, the appearance of new social groups, industrialization and agrarian crises, and public criticism, the state had to make far-reaching changes in administrative personnel and procedures to survive.

Even with the expansion of ministerial power, rural Russia remained seriously undergoverned. This fact constituted a third weakness of the tsarist system in the late nineteenth century, and it was closely related to Russia's crisis of "bureaucratic penetration" and to the personalized nature of autocratic authority. On the one hand, Russia's "undergovernment," like that of nineteenth-century Spain and post-Risorgimento [united] Italy, was the result of the country's economic backwardness. The tsarist government consistently lacked adequate resources to regulate social and economic affairs and provincial/regional administration. For instance, in 1900, . . . the Ministry of Internal Affairs had only 1,582 constables and 6,874 police sergeants to administer a rural population of roughly 90,000,000, and personnel shortages were even more the rule in other branches of government. By contrast, the more industrialized European states (Britain, France) had long established rural administrative networks, so that in the late nineteenth century they had fewer conflicts over rural jurisdictions of local state, corporate, and public institutions.

On the other hand, unlike Italy and Spain, Russia owed much of its "underinstitutionalized" status to the distinct nature of autocratic rule, which favored personal authority and discretionary action over formal regulations and a vastly increased bureaucracy. The personalized, paternalistic nature of autocracy had its champions in postreform Russia, who claimed that such rule was especially suited to governing the countryside with a minimum of personnel. The autocrat, his ministers, governors, and land captains could cut through red tape, circumvent "irrelevant" laws and procedures, and get to the heart of rural administrative problems. Unfortunately, however, such personalized authority without any organization to coordinate or prioritize policy invited ministerial infighting on major reform issues, especially because elite officials were more dependent than ever on retaining special imperial favor. On the local scene, such personal authority did little to promote cooperation between state and public officials, as zemstvo difficulties with rural police officials illustrated. In this respect, the assassination of Alexander II in 1881 did not produce the abrupt turnabout in tsarist administration that historians usually assume. Rather, both Alexander II and his successor refused to relinquish any personal power and instead made government decisions on what they considered to be the best interests of autocracy. In Alexander II's case, this meant reorganizing the ministerial power structure (initially at the expense of the Ministry of Internal Affairs), introducing comprehensive administrative reforms, and providing a greater role in the reform process for subordinate institutions (the ministries and State Council). The tsar's reliance on a variety of state agencies for initiative made such an impact on officials involved in reform preparations during his reign that, not surprisingly, twenty years later in the State Council debate over the land captains and zemstvo projects, many of these same officials exaggerated their role in policy making. They forgot that by the late 1870s the Ministry of Internal Affairs, with Alexander's firm backing, had begun to assert its own control over local officials from other ministries (for instance, the justices of the peace).

Unlike his father, Alexander III at first believed that no change at all would be in the best interests of autocracy, and that the tsar had a sacred duty not to be bound by law or to rely on subordinate agencies. When his anachronistic views failed to curb rural administrative conflicts and disorder, the tsar turned to Tolstoi's program of centralization (bureaucratizing local self-government), and to counterreforms in education and the judiciary. Yet even then Alexander III did not display the commitment to see the reform through to its conclusion, as did Alexander II, and with Tolstoi's death in 1889, the impulse for reforming local self-government slackened noticeably. In part, this irresolution had its roots in the way the tsars manipulated their ministers, for both Alexander II and his son flattered themselves as better judges of men than of proposals. Generally distrusting their officials, they never allowed any one minister to direct state policy (as primus inter pares) for more than several years, and ministers took advantage of that tendency. Although this system left the emperor in control of his court, it spread feelings of insecurity, powerlessness, and pessimism among ministers, who hesitated to propose controversial reforms that could embroil them in conflict with their colleagues and possibly lead to their dismissal. In view of the evidence, it is clear that the tsar and his ministers were both manipulators and victims of this system of personalized authority.

In short, by the time of Nicholas II's reign (and indeed up to 1906) Russia remained an autocratic state in principle and fact, with all of the problems that such rule entailed. Like its prereform counterparts, the late Imperial regime was overburdened with routine work, isolated from its subjects, and "had no time and energy left to think, plan, and conceive policies *de longue haleine*."[3] The government, as illustrated by the history of local self-government reform, suffered because of the

---

3. The phrase is Marc Raeff's in *Well-Ordered Police State*, p. 217.

absence of an institution (a cabinet, for instance) or a permanent ministerial hierarchy to plan long-term administrative policy, set priorities, and coordinate state initiatives. As evident from the reigns of Alexander II and Alexander III, the tsar was not able to handle these extensive, weighty responsibilities alone; indeed, top officials . . . made precisely this point in the 1870s and 1880s in calling for an institution/hierarchy to provide direction in central policy making and local administration. The turnover in imperial "favorites" in postreform Russia, each of whom had his own plan of local self-government reform, proved that no lasting reorganization of local government (or control over the steady development of rural society and economy) was possible without a fixed ministerial hierarchy or institutional structure in the capital to set policy priorities for officials.

In a wider sense, the problems that the Russian government had with local self-government and local self-government reform seem relevant to transitional societies undergoing modernization, especially where autocratic regimes are involved. Although historical circumstances by their very nature are unique, the tsarist experience supports the argument that local self-government is vital to "developing" states, even if it had proved more successful in industrialized societies. As this study suggests, the greatest immediate problem with local self-government for autocracies is not the political risks that it poses but rather the difficulty of mobilizing rural support for it, especially in conditions of material poverty, illiteracy, and village parochialism. In tsarist Russia, such traditional problems had roots in the *soslovie* [estate] organization that the government religiously defended up to the twentieth century. But Russia's experiment with local self-government likewise shows that unified central government and a clear delineation of the identity, role, and limits of local self-government are vital preconditions for the development of public self-government. In transitional societies, bureaucratic institutions provide the catalyst for rapid economic and social development; where boundaries between local state and public institutions are not clearly defined, jurisdictional conflict and public disenchantment are likely to follow. At the same time, this study points up the political risks that regimes face in bureaucratizing local self-government, particularly when the process is undertaken haphazardly, or as part of a political reaction. Under such conditions, local self-government may well become a vehicle of political opposition (as happened in Russia after 1900), especially if bureaucratized self-government should fail to deliver effective administration in return for its rural costs. As the tsarist state discovered early in the twentieth century, the failure to mobilize public support and preserve rural order would open the door to more revolutionary approaches in matters of rural development and governance.

# DOCUMENTS

Alexander II was assassinated by members of a revolutionary group called the People's Will (*Narodnaia volia*). This group was a terrorist offshoot formed in 1879 of the party of "Land and Liberty" (*Zemlia i volia*), itself the first formal organization—founded in 1862, disbanded, refounded in 1876—of that "populist" movement (*narodnichestvo*) among the radical intelligentsia which was originally inspired by the writings of Alexander Herzen and others (see Documents, Chapter 8). The Land and Liberty party arose out of a perception that the Emancipation of 1861 had not improved the lot of the peasantry and that economic prosperity for all and universal civil rights could be achieved in Russia only by representative government—meaning popular democracy—at the national level. Yet for this to happen the masses needed enlightenment, a perception that prompted the "to the people movement" of 1873–1874, when thousands of enthusiastic young populists fanned out into the countryside only to meet a highly skeptical and hostile reception from the peasantry: eventually some 4,000 would-be enlighteners were detained by the government on suspicion of sedition. The failure of this direct recourse to the people precipitated the split of 1879 among disillusioned party members into two main factions: one, the party of Black Repartition (*Chernyi peredel*), continued to agitate among the peasants, urging them to seize seigneurial and state land and divide it among themselves; the other, the party of the People's Will, while still dedicated to "populism and socialism," waged a terrorist campaign aimed at destabilizing the Imperial government as a prelude to seizing power themselves and establishing a revolutionary state. The People's Will, which never seems to have counted more than thirty active members, concentrated on attempts to assassinate the Emperor, which it succeeded in doing on March 1, 1881. Thereafter, under intense police pressure, both it and the Black Repartition collapsed (leaders of the latter would soon found, in European exile, the first Russian Marxist group). But populism as a general ideology of land reform and popular democracy survived, and resurfaced formally, thanks to the Revolution of 1905, in the Russian Socialist Revolutionary Party (see Chapter 13).

Vera Nikolaevna Figner (1852–1942) was a high-minded, self-sacrificing member of the People's Will. Like so many populists, she came from a privileged background and early in life committed herself to serving the masses of poor people in Russia—in her case by pursuing a medical career. She had almost completed her medical degree, in Switzerland, when, owing to the Russian government's continuing discrimination against women and the gathering crisis at home, she responded to the pleas of her radical friends and went back to Russia (1876). There she joined the Land and Liberty party and was a founding member (1879) of the People's Will. Though she did not directly participate in the assassination of Alexander II, she was arrested for complicity in planning it (which she did not deny), tried, and condemned to death—a sentence commuted to life in prison, where she remained until released in 1904. In her *Memoirs*, written much later, Figner concentrates on her work as a revolutionary and on her years in prison, and somewhat obfuscates her commitment to political violence (not only was Alexander II horribly mangled before dying, but various bystanders and assassins themselves were killed in the several attempts on his life and that of other high officials). Thus Figner quotes with approval the September 1881 declaration of the Executive Committee of the People's Will (of which she was a member) condemning the recent assassination of U.S. President James Garfield as a "manifestation of that despotic spirit which we aim to destroy in Russia. Personal despotism [the assassination of a popularly elected president] is as condemnable as group despotism, and violence may be justified only when it is directed against violence." In the excerpts from her *Memoirs* printed below she describes the day of Alexander's assassination, and appends an open letter to his successor written by her Executive Committee a few days later. The letter attempts to justify the assassination and then spells out the party's revolutionary demands, warning that if they are not met, Russia will inevitably suffer a terrible revolution.

On April 29, 1881, Alexander III responded to these and other radical (or even moderately liberal) demands with a manifesto announcing his faith in autocracy and confirming his policy of reaction. The manifesto—the second document here—was written for him by Constantine (K. P.) Pobedonostsev (1827–1907), a legal scholar and sometime official who had been his tutor. Alexander II had appointed Pobedonostsev chief procurator of the Holy Synod (that is, lay administrator of the Russian Orthodox church) in 1880, a position he held until 1905 and in which among other things he greatly expanded the role of the church—with its message of submission to authority—in primary education throughout Russia. He became known as the "high priest of reaction," a role amply reflected in his various writings and pronouncements, which are remarkable for their pervasive pessimism, even cynicism, about the human condition. Our third document is excerpted from a well-known collection of Pobedonostsev's essays first published in Moscow in 1896, essays in which he attacks such hallowed democratic principles as a free press, the separation of church and state, and, here, parliamentary government based on popular sovereignty.

## | Vera Figner Defends Assassination in the | Name of the People, 1881

By order of the [Executive] Committee [of the People's Will, hereafter "the party"] I was to remain at home until two o'clock on that first day of March [1881], to receive the Kobozevs, for Bogdanovich was to leave the shop an hour before the Tsar's party should pass that way, and Yakimova was to leave directly after the signal that the Tsar had made his appearance on the Nevsky [avenue]. A third person (Frolenko) was to switch on the electric current, and then leave the shop as a casual customer, in case he should escape perishing in the ruins from the explosion wrought by his own hand.[1]

At ten o'clock Frolenko came to see me. With astonishment I saw him take from a package that he had brought with him, a bottle of red wine and a sausage, which he put on the table, preparing to have a little lunch. In my state of intense excitement, after our decision and the sleepless night spent in preparations, it seemed to me that to eat and drink was impossible.

"What are you doing?" I asked, almost with horror, as I beheld this matter-of-fact procedure on the part of a man who was destined to an almost certain death under the ruin caused by the explosion.

"I must be in full possession of my strength," calmly replied my comrade, and he imperturbably began to eat.

---

From Vera Figner, *Memoirs of a Revolutionist* (New York: International Publishers Co., Inc., 1927; facsimile reprint Northern Illinois University Press, 1991), pp. 98–100, 307–312. Reprinted with permission of International Publishers Co. Inc.

1. The names are of various fellow members—men and women—of People's Will. "The shop" was a fake cheese shop set up by the revolutionaries along the Emperor's customary route in St. Petersburg.—Ed.

I could only bow in silent admiration before this disregard of the thought of possible death, this all-absorbing realization that, in order to fulfil the mission which he had taken upon himself, he must be in full possession of his strength.

Neither Bogdanovich nor Yakimova came to the apartment. Isayev returned, and with him a few members of the party, with the news that the Tsar had not passed the shop, but had gone home [in another direction]. Forgetting entirely that they had not followed the return route of the Tsar, and also had not been informed of the last decision of the [Executive] Committee, to act, whatever might occur, though it be only with bombs, I left the house thinking that for some unforeseen reasons the attempt had not taken place.

And indeed, the Tsar did not pass through the Sadovaya; but it was at this point that Sofia Perovskaya displayed all her self-possession. Quickly concluding that the Tsar would return by way of the quay along the Ekaterininskaya Canal, she changed the entire plan of action, deciding to employ only the bombs. She made the rounds of the bomb-throwers and instructed them to take new positions, after they had agreed that she was to give the signal by waving her handkerchief.

Shortly after two o'clock, two detonations that sounded like shots from a cannon, thundered out, one after another. Rysakov's bomb wrecked the Tsar's carriage, while Grinyevitsky's struck the Tsar. Both the Tsar and Grinyevitsky were mortally wounded, and died within a few hours.

When I left the house after Isayev's return, everything was quiet, but half an hour after I had made my appearance at Gleb Uspensky's, Ivanchin-Pisarev came to him with the news that there had been some explosions and that a rumor was circulating to the effect that the Tsar had been killed, and that in the churches the people were already swearing allegiance to the heir.

I rushed home. The streets hummed with talk, and there was evident excitement. People were speaking of the Tsar, of his wounds, of blood and death. When I entered my own dwelling and saw my friends who as yet suspected nothing, I was so agitated that I could hardly utter the words announcing the death of the Tsar. I wept, and many of us wept; that heavy nightmare, which for ten years had strangled young Russia before our very eyes, had been brought to an end; the horrors of prison and exile, the violence, executions, and atrocities inflicted on hundreds and thousands of our adherents, the blood of our martyrs, all were atoned for by this blood of the Tsar, shed by our hands. A heavy burden was lifted from our shoulders; reaction must come to an end and give place to a new Russia. In this solemn moment, all our thoughts centered in the hope for a better future for our country.

Shortly afterwards Sukhanov joined us, joyful and excited, and embraced and congratulated us all in the name of that future. The letter to Alexander III [reprinted below] drawn up a few days later, is characteristic of the general state of mind of the members of the party in St. Petersburg, during the period that followed the first of March. The letter was composed with a moderation and tact that won the sympathetic approval of all Russian society. Upon its publication in the West, it produced a sensation throughout all the European press. The most moderate and conservative periodicals expressed their approval of the demands of the Russian

Nihilists, finding them reasonable, just, and such as had in large measure been long ago realised in the daily life of Western Europe. . . .

## THE LETTER OF THE EXECUTIVE COMMITTEE OF THE WILL OF THE PEOPLE TO TSAR ALEXANDER III

Your Majesty:—

Fully comprehending the sorrow which you are experiencing during these present moments, the Executive Committee does not, however, feel it right to yield to the impulse of natural delicacy, which demands, perhaps, a certain interval of waiting before the following explanation should be made. There is something higher than the most legitimate emotions of a human being: that is one's duty to his native land, a duty for which every citizen is obliged to sacrifice himself and his own feelings, and even the feelings of others. In obedience to this primal duty, we have determined to address you at once, without any delay, since that historical process does not wait, which threatens us in the future with rivers of blood and the most violent convulsions.

The bloody tragedy [assassination of Alexander II] which was played on the shores of the Ekaterininsky Canal [in St. Petersburg] was not accidental, and surprised no one. After all that has passed in the course of the last decade, it was absolutely inevitable, and in this lies its profound meaning—a meaning which must be understood by the man whom fate has placed at the head of the state power. To interpret such facts as being the evil plots of separate individuals, or even of a band of criminals, would be possible only to a man who was quite incapable of analyzing the life of nations. In the course of ten years we have seen how, notwithstanding the most severe persecutions, notwithstanding the fact that the government of the late Emperor sacrificed everything, freedom, the interests of all classes, the interests of industry and even its own dignity, everything, unconditionally, in its attempt to suppress the revolutionary movement, that movement has nevertheless tenaciously grown and spread, attracting to itself the best elements of the nation, the most energetic and self-denying people of Russia, and for three years now has engaged in desperate, partisan warfare with the government. You know well, your Majesty, that it is impossible to accuse the government of the late Emperor of lack of energy. They have hanged our followers, both guilty and innocent; they have filled the prisons and distant provinces with exiles. Whole dozens of our leaders have been seized and hanged. They have died with the courage and calmness of martyrs, but the movement has not been suppressed, it has grown and gained strength. Yes, your Majesty, the revolutionary movement is not such as to depend on individual personalities. It is a function of the national organism, and the gallows, erected to hang the most energetic exponents of that function, is as powerless to save this outworn order of life, as was the death of the Savior on the cross, to save the corrupt, ancient world from the triumph of reforming Christianity.

Of course, the government may continue to arrest and hang a great multitude of separate individuals. It may destroy many revolutionary groups. Let us grant that it will destroy even the most important of the existing revolutionary organizations.

This will not change the state of affairs in the least. The conditions under which we are living, the general dissatisfaction of the people, Russia's aspiration towards a new order of life, all these create revolutionists. You cannot exterminate the whole Russian people, you cannot therefore destroy its discontent by means of reprisals; on the contrary, discontent grows thereby. This is the reason that fresh individuals, still more incensed, still more energetic, are constantly arising from the ranks of the people in great numbers to take the place of those who are being destroyed. These individuals, in the interests of the conflict, will of course organize themselves, having at hand the ready experience of their predecessors, and therefore the revolutionary movement in the course of time must grow stronger, both in quality and quantity. This we have actually seen in the last ten years. What did the death of the adherents of Dolgushin, Tchaikovsky, the agitators of the year 1874, avail the government? The far more determined populists arose to take their place. The terrible reprisals of the government called forth upon the stage the terrorists of '78 and '79 [1878 and 1879]. In vain did the government exterminate such men as the adherents Kovalsky, Dubrovin, Osinsky, and Lizogub; in vain did it destroy dozens of revolutionary circles. From those imperfect organizations, by the course of natural selection there developed still hardier forms. There appeared at last [1879] the Executive Committee, with which the government has not yet been able to cope.

Casting a dispassionate glance over the depressing decade through which we have lived, we can accurately foretell the future progress of the movement if the political tactics of the government do not change. The movement must go on growing, gaining strength; terroristic acts will be repeated in ever more alarming and intensified forms. A more perfect, stronger revolutionary organization will take the place of the groups that are wiped out. In the meantime, the number of malcontents in the land will increase, popular faith in the government will lapse, and the idea of revolution, of its possibility and inevitability, will take root and grow more and more rapidly in Russia. A terrible outburst, a bloody subversion, a violent revolutionary convulsion throughout all Russia, will complete the process of the overthrow of the old order.

What evokes this terrible perspective, what is responsible for it? Yes, your Majesty, a terrible and sad perspective. Do not take this for a mere phrase. We understand better than any one else, how sad is the perishing of so much talent, such energy, in a labor of destruction, in bloody conflicts, when, under different conditions, these forces might be directly applied to creative work, to the progress of the people, the development of their minds, and the well-being of their national life. Whence comes this sad necessity for bloody strife?

From the fact, your Majesty, that there exists among us now no actual government, in the true meaning of the word. A government, according to its fundamental principle, should express only the aspirations of the people, should accomplish only the Will of the People. While in Russia, pardon us for the expression, the government has degenerated into a veritable camarilla, and deserves to be called a band of usurpers far more than does the Executive Committee.

Whatever may have been the intentions of the Sovereign, the acts of the government have had nothing in common with the popular welfare and desires.

The Imperial Government has subjugated the people to the state of bondage, it has delivered the masses into the power of the nobility; and now it is openly creating a pernicious class of speculators and profiteers. All its reforms lead to but one result, that the people have sunk into ever greater slavery, into a state of more complete exploitation. It has brought Russia to such a point that at the present time the popular masses find themselves in a state of utter beggary and ruin, not free even at their own domestic firesides from the most insulting surveillance, powerless even in their own communal village affairs. Only the spoiler, the exploiter, is favored by the protection of the law and the government. The most revolting depredations remain unpunished. But what a terrible fate awaits the man who sincerely thinks and plans for the public welfare! You know well, your Majesty, that it is not only the socialists who are exiled and persecuted. What kind of a government is this, then, which protects such an "order"? Is it not rather a band of rascals, an absolute usurpation?

This is the reason why the Russian government has no moral influence, no support in the people; this is why Russia gives birth to so many revolutionists; this is why even such a fact as regicide awakens joy and sympathetic approval in an enormous part of the population. Yes, your Majesty, do not deceive yourself with the declarations of fawners and flatterers. Regicide is very popular in Russia.

There are two possible escapes from this situation: either a revolution, quite inevitable, which cannot be averted by any number of executions, or a voluntary turning to the people on the part of the Supreme Authority. In the interests of our native land, in the desire to avoid those terrible calamities which always accompany a revolution, the Executive Committee turns to your Majesty with the advice to choose the second course. Believe us that as soon as the Supreme Authority ceases to be arbitrary, as soon as it firmly determines to accomplish only the demands of the nation's consciousness and conscience, you may boldly drive out the spies who defile your government, send your convoys into their barracks, and burn the gallows which are depraving your people. The Executive Committee itself will cease its present activity, and the forces organized around it will disperse and consecrate themselves to cultural work for the benefit of their own people. A peaceful conflict of ideas will take the place of the violence which is more repugnant to us than to your servants, and which we practice only from sad necessity.

We turn to you, casting aside all prejudices, stifling that distrust, which the age-long activity of the government has created. We forget that you are the representative of that power which has so deceived the people, and done them so much harm. We address you as a citizen and an honorable man. We hope that the feeling of personal bitterness will not suppress in you the recognition of your duties, and the desire to know the truth. We too might be embittered. You have lost your father. We have lost not only our fathers, but also our brothers, our wives, our children, our best friends. But we are ready to suppress our personal feelings if the good of Russia demands it. And we expect the same from you also.

We do not lay conditions upon you. Do not be shocked by our proposition. The conditions which are indispensable in order that the revolutionary movement shall be transformed into peaceful activity, have been created, not by us, but by history. We do not impose them, we only recall them to your mind.

In our opinion there are two such conditions:

1. A general amnesty for all political crimes committed in the past, inasmuch as these were not crimes, but the fulfilment of a civic duty.

2. The convocation of an assembly of representatives of all the Russian people, for the purpose of examining the existing forms of our state and society, and revising them in accord with the desires of the people.

We consider it necessary to mention, however, that in order that the legality of the Supreme Authority may be confirmed by popular representation, the process of selecting delegates must be absolutely unrestricted. Therefore the elections must be held under the following conditions:

1. The deputies must be sent from all ranks and classes alike, and in numbers proportionate to the population.

2. There must be no restrictions imposed upon either the electors or the deputies.

3. Electioneering, and the elections themselves, must be carried out in complete freedom, and therefore the government must grant as a temporary measure, prior to the decision of the popular assembly:

a. Complete freedom of the press,
b. Complete freedom of speech,
c. Complete freedom of assembly,
d. Complete freedom of electoral programs.

This is the only way in which Russia can be restored to a course of normal and peaceful development. We solemnly declare before our native land and all the world, that our party will submit unconditionally to the decision of a Popular Assembly which shall have been chosen in accord with the above-mentioned conditions; and in the future we shall offer no armed resistance whatever to a government that has been sanctioned by the Popular Assembly.

And so, your Majesty, decide. Before you are two courses. On you depends the choice; we can only ask Fate that your reason and conscience dictate to you a decision which will conform only to the good of Russia, to your own dignity, and to your duty to your native land.

(Signed)   THE EXECUTIVE COMMITTEE.

March 10, 1881.

# Manifesto of Alexander III Affirming Autocracy, 1881

It has pleased God, in His inscrutable judgment, to bring a martyr's end to the glorious reign of Our beloved father and to lay upon Us the sacred duty of autocratic power.

Acknowledging the will of Providence and the law of Imperial succession, We accepted this burden in a terrible hour of public grief and horror, before Almighty God, trusting that, foreordained as it was that We should assume power at such a dangerous and difficult time, He would not refrain from granting Us His assistance. We trust also that the fervent prayers of Our devoted people, known throughout the whole world for their love of and devotion to their sovereigns, will draw God's blessing upon Us and the labor of government to which We have been appointed.

Our father, deceased in God, having received the autocratic power from God for the good of the people entrusted to him, remained faithful to his sworn duty unto death, and sealed his great service with his blood. Not so much by the strict commands of authority, as by beneficence and gentleness, did he accomplish the great work of his reign: the emancipation of the bonded peasants [serfs], having secured the cooperation of the landed nobility, ever receptive to the voice of goodness and honor; he established justice in the realm and made all his subjects forever free, calling them to share in local government and the country's economy. May his memory be blessed for all time!

The base and wicked murder of the Russian sovereign in the midst of his loyal people, prepared to lay down their lives for him, by worthless scum, is a terrible, shameful, unheard of thing in Russia, and has darkened the whole land with grief and horror.

In the midst of Our great grief, the voice of God commands us to rise courageously to the business of government, with hope in Divine Providence and faith in the strength and truth of autocratic power, which We have been called upon to affirm and protect for the people's good against any encroachment upon it.

So also let courage animate the troubled and horrified hearts of Our Faithful subjects, of all who love the Fatherland and have been devoted from generation unto generation to the hereditary royal power. Under its shield, and in unbroken union with it, our Land has more than once survived great troubles, and with faith in God has risen in power and glory from grievous trials and tribulations.

Consecrating Ourselves to Our great service, We call upon all Our Faithful subjects to serve Us and the state in fidelity and truth, for the eradication of the vile sedition disgracing the Russian land, for the strengthening of faith and morality, for the proper upbringing of children, for the extermination of falsehood and theft, and for the introduction of truth and good order in the operations of the institutions given to Russia by her benefactor, Our beloved father.

[Alexander]

From K. P. Pobedonostsev i ego korrespondenty: Pis'ma i zapiski, ed. M. N. Pokrokskii, vol. 1 (Moscow, 1932), pp. 51–52. Translated by James Cracraft.

## Constantine Pobedonostsev
## Attacks Democracy, 1896

What is this freedom by which so many minds are agitated, which inspires so many senseless actions, so many wild speeches, which leads the people so often to misfortune? In the democratic sense of the word, freedom is the right of political power, or, to express it otherwise, the right to participate in the government of the state. This aspiration of each and everyone for a share in government has so far found no fixed boundaries nor true end, but incessantly grows. . . . Forever extending its base, the new democracy now aspires to universal suffrage—a fatal error, and one of the most remarkable in the history of mankind. By this means, the political power so passionately demanded by democracy would be shattered into innumerable pieces, of which each citizen acquires a single one. What will he do with it then? How will he employ it? It has undoubtedly been shown that in the attainment of this aim democracy violates its sacred formula of "freedom indissolubly joined with equality." It has been shown that this apparently equal distribution of "freedom" among all involves the total destruction of equality. Each vote, representing an inconsiderable fragment of power, by itself signifies nothing; an aggregation of votes alone has a relative value. The result may be likened to the general meetings of shareholders in public companies. By themselves individuals are powerless; but he who controls the largest number of these fragmentary forces is master of all, and therefore controls the government. We may well ask, what constitutes the superiority of democracy? Everywhere the strongest man becomes master of the state; sometimes a fortunate and resolute general, sometimes a monarch or administrator with knowledge, dexterity, a clear plan of action, and a determined will. In the democratic form of government the real rulers are the dexterous manipulators of votes, with their placemen, the mechanics who so skillfully operate the hidden springs which move the puppets in the arena of democratic elections. Men of this kind are ever ready with loud speeches lauding equality; in reality, they rule the people as any despot or military dictator might rule it. The extension of the right to participate in elections is regarded as progress and the conquest of freedom; democratic theorists hold that the more numerous the participants in political rights, the greater is the probability that all will employ this right for the common good of all, and to establish universal freedom. Experience proves a very different thing. The history of mankind bears witness that the most essential, fruitful, and durable reforms emanated from the supreme will of statesmen or from a minority enlightened by lofty ideas and deep knowledge; and that, on the contrary, the extension of the electoral principle is accompanied by an abasement of political thought and the vulgarization of opinion in the mass of the electors. It shows that this extension—in great states— was inspired by secret aims to concentrate power,

From K. P. Pobyedonostseff, *Reflexions of a Russian Statesman*, trans. R. C. Long (London: Grant Richard & Co., 1898), pp. 26–44, revised by James Cracraft. Cf. K. P. Pobedonostsev, *Moskovskii sbornik*, 5th edn. (Moscow, 1901), pp. 25–49.

or led directly to dictatorship. In France, universal suffrage was suppressed with the cessation of the Terror, and was re-established twice merely to affirm the despotism of the two Napoleons. In Germany, the establishment of universal suffrage served merely to strengthen the central authority of a famous statesman [Bismarck] who had acquired popularity by the success of his policy. What will come after him, Heaven only knows!

The manipulation of votes under the banner of democracy is a common occurrence today in most European states, and its falsehood, it would seem, has been exposed to all; yet few dare to rise openly against it. The unhappy people must bear the burden, while the Press, herald of an imaginary public opinion, stifles the cry of the people with its [slogans vaunting democracy]. But to an impartial mind, all this is nothing better than a struggle of parties, and a shuffling with numbers and names. The voters, by themselves inconsiderable individuals, acquire value in the hands of clever agents. This value is realized by many means—mainly, by bribery in innumerable forms, from gifts of money and trifling goods to the distribution of lucrative posts in the financial departments and the administration. Little by little a class of electors has been formed which lives by the sale of its votes to one or other of the political organizations. So far has this gone in France, for instance, that serious, intelligent, and industrious citizens in immense numbers abstain from voting, considering it impossible to contend with the gangs of political agents. With bribery go violence and threats, and reigns of terror are organized at elections, by the help of which the respective gangs advance their candidates; hence the stormy scenes at electoral demonstrations, in which firearms have been used, and the field of battle strewn with the bodies of the killed and wounded.

An organized party and bribery—these are the two mighty instruments which are employed with such success for the manipulation of the mass of voters. Such methods are not new. Thucydides depicts in vivid colors their employment in the ancient republics of Greece. The history of the Roman Republic presents monstrous examples of bribery as the chief instrument of parties at elections. But in our time a new means has been found of working the masses for political aims and of joining numerous people in adventitious alliances, giving rise to an imaginary consensus. This is the art of rapidly and dexterously spreading ideas, of composing phrases and formulas disseminated with the confidence of burning conviction, as the last word of science, as dogmas of political science, as infallible descriptions of events, personalities, and institutions. At one time it was believed that the faculty of analyzing facts and deducing general principles belonged to a few enlightened minds and deep thinkers; now it is considered a universal attainment, and, under the name of convictions, common political phrases have become a sort of popular coin minted by newspapers and political orators.

The faculty of seizing and assimilating on faith these "convictions" has spread among the masses, and become infectious, especially among people insufficiently or superficially educated, who constitute the great majority everywhere. This tendency of the masses is exploited with success by politicians who seek power; the art of creating generalizations serves for them as a most convenient instrument. All generalization proceeds by the path of abstraction; from a number of facts the irrelevant are eliminated, the suitable gathered up, and general formulas deduced.

It is plain that the justice and value of these formulas depend upon what facts have been judged irrelevant and unsuitable. The speed and ease with which general conclusions are arrived at today are explained by the extremely casual way in which suitable facts are selected and then generalized. Hence the great success of political orators and the extraordinary effect of the abstractions which they throw to the masses. The crowd is easily attracted by commonplaces and generalities invested in sonorous phrases; it cases nothing for proof which is inaccessible to it; thus is formed unanimity of thought, a unanimity that is imaginary and illusory, but in its consequences real enough. This is called the "voice of the people," with the addition, the "voice of God." It is a deplorable error. The ease with which men are drawn by commonplaces leads everywhere to the extreme demoralization of public thought, to a weakening of the political sense of the whole nation. Of this, France to-day presents a striking example, and England has not escaped the infection. . . .

That which is founded on falsehood cannot be right. Institutions founded on false principles cannot be other than false themselves. This truth has been demonstrated by the bitter experience of ages and generations.

Among the falsest of political principles is the principle of popular sovereignty, the principle that all power issues from the people and is based upon the popular will—a principle which, unfortunately, has become more firmly established since the time of the French Revolution. Thence proceeds the theory of parliamentarism, which hitherto has deluded much of the so-called intelligentsia and has infatuated, unhappily, certain foolish Russians. It continues to maintain its hold on many minds with the obstinacy of a narrow fanaticism, although every day its falsehood is exposed more clearly to the whole world.

In what does the theory of parliamentarism consist? It is supposed that the people in popular assemblies make laws themselves and elect responsible officers to execute their will. Such is the ideal conception. Its direct realization is impossible. The historical development of society necessitates that local groupings increase in numbers and complexity; that separate tribes be assimilated into one people or, retaining their languages, unite under a single state flag; and that the state's territory extend indefinitely: under such conditions direct government by the people is inconceivable. The people must, therefore, delegate its right of sovereignty to a certain number of elected persons and invest them with governmental autonomy. These representatives in turn cannot govern directly but are compelled to elect a still smaller number of trustworthy persons—ministers—to whom they entrust the preparation and execution of the laws, the apportionment and collection of taxes, the appointment of subordinate officials, and the disposition of the armed forces.

In the abstract this mechanism is quite harmonious; but for its proper operation many conditions are essential. The working of the machine is based on the constant and completely balanced interaction of impersonal forces. It may act successfully only when the delegates of the people abdicate their personalities; when on the benches of parliament sit mechanical executors of the instructions given to them; when the ministers of state also remain impersonal, absolute executors of the will of the majority; when the elected representatives of the people are always capable of understanding precisely, and executing conscientiously, the program of action, expressed with mathematical precision, which has been given to them. Under such conditions the machine would work correctly and accomplish its purpose. The law would actually embody the will of the people; administrative measures would actually emanate from parliament; the house of state would actually rest on the elective assemblies, and each citizen would directly and consciously participate in the management of public affairs.

Such is the theory. Let us look at the practice. Even in the classic countries of parliamentarism it would satisfy not one of the conditions enumerated. The elections in no way express the will of the voters. The popular representatives are in no way restricted by the opinions of the voters but are guided by their own arbitrary judgments and calculations, as modified by the tactics of the opposing party. In reality, ministers are despotic, and they rule, rather than are ruled by, parliament. They attain power, and lose power, not by virtue of the will of the people but through immense personal influence or the influence of a strong party, which places them in power or drives them from it. They dispose of all the forces and resources of the nation at will; they grant privileges and favors; they maintain a multitude of idlers at the expense of the people; and they fear no censure as long as they enjoy the support of the majority in parliament, a majority which they maintain by the distribution of bounties from the rich tables that the state has put at their disposal. In reality, the ministers are as irresponsible as the representatives of the people. Mistakes, abuse of power, and arbitrary acts are daily occurrences, yet how often do we hear of the grave responsibility of a minister? It may be once in fifty years a minister is tried, with a result that is nothing when compared with the celebrity gained by the solemn procedure.

Were we to attempt a true definition of parliament, we should say that parliament is *an institution serving for the satisfaction of the personal ambition, vanity, and self-interest of its members*. The institution of parliament is indeed one of the greatest illustrations of human delusion. Enduring in the course of the centuries personal despotism and oligarchical government, and ignoring [the fact] that the defects of absolute rule are the defects of the society which lives under it, men of intellect and knowledge have laid the responsibility for their misfortunes on their rulers and on the defects of government; and they have imagined that by adopting the form of popular sovereignty or representative government, society would be delivered from its misfortunes and from the violence it has endured. What is the result? The result is that, despite a change in name, all has remained essentially as before, and men, retaining the weaknesses and defects of their nature, have transferred to the new form all their former habits and tendencies. As before, they are ruled by personal will, and in the interests of privileged persons; only this personal will is no longer embodied in the monarch, but in the leader of a party; and privilege no longer belongs to an aristocracy of birth, but to the majority that controls parliament and the government.

On the pediment of this edifice is inscribed: "All for the Common Good." This is no more than a deceitful formula: parliamentarism is the triumph of egoism—its highest expression. Everything here is calculated to serve the ego. In the parliamentary fiction, the representative, as such, surrenders his personality and serves as the embodiment of the will and opinions of his constituents; in reality, the constituents in the very act of election surrender all their rights in favor of their representative. In his program and speeches the candidate for election lays constant emphasis upon this fiction; he reiterates his phrases about the common good; he is nothing but a servant of the people; he will forget himself and his interests in the interest of society. But these are words, words, only words—temporary steps of the staircase by which he climbs to the height he aspires to and then casts aside when he needs them no longer. Thus, so far from beginning to work for society, society becomes the instrument of his aims. For him his constituents are a herd, an aggregation of votes, and he, as their possessor, resembles those rich nomads whose flocks constitute their whole capital—the foundation of their power and eminence in society. Thus is developed to perfection the art of playing on the instincts and passions of the masses, in order to attain the personal ends of ambition and power. The masses lose all importance for their representative until it is time for them to be played upon again; then false and flattering and lying phrases are lavished as before; some are suborned by bribery, others terrified by threats—the endless chain of maneuvers which are essential to parliamentarism. Yet this electoral farce continues to deceive humanity, and to be regarded as an institution which crowns the house of state. Poor humanity! In truth may it be said: *mundus vult decipi, decipiatur* [the world wishes to be deceived, let it be deceived].

This is how the representative principle works in practice. The ambitious man comes before his fellow-citizens and strives by every means to convince them that he more than any other is worthy of their trust. What motives impel him to this quest? It is hard to believe that he is impelled by disinterested zeal for the common good.

In our time, nothing is so rare as men imbued with a feeling of solidarity with the people, ready for labor and self-sacrifice for the common good. This is the ideal; but such natures are not inclined to come into contact with the baseness of everyday life. He who, in the consciousness of duty, is capable of disinterested service of the community does not descend to the soliciting of votes, or to crying his own praise at election meetings in loud and vulgar phrases. Such a man manifests his strength in his own work, in a small circle of likeminded men, and scorns to seek popularity in the noisy market-place. If he approaches the crowd, it is not to flatter it or to pander to its instincts but to expose its follies and vices. To men of duty and honor the procedure of elections is repellent; the only men who regard it without abhorrence have selfish, egotistical natures, and wish thereby to attain their personal ends. To acquire popularity such men have little scruple in assuming the mask of ardor for the public good. They cannot and must not be modest, for with modesty they would not be noticed or spoken of. By their positions, and by the role which they have chosen, they are *forced to be* hypocrites and liars. They must cultivate, fraternize with, and be amiable to their opponents to gain their favor; they must lavish promises, knowing that they cannot fulfill them; and they must pander to the basest tendencies and prejudices of the masses in order to acquire majorities for themselves. What honorable nature would accept such a role? Describe it in a novel, and the reader would be repelled; but in elections the same reader gives his vote to the living actor playing this very same role.

Elections are a matter of art, having, like the military art, their strategy and tactics. . . . In theory, the elected candidate must be the favorite of the majority; in fact, he is the favorite of a minority, sometimes very small, but representing an organized force, while the majority, like sand, has no coherence, and is therefore powerless before the clique or the party. In theory, the election favors the intelligent and capable; in reality, it favors the pushing and impudent. It might be thought that education, experience, and conscientiousness in work would be essential requirements in the candidate; in reality, whether these qualities exist or not, they are not needed in the electoral struggle, where the essential qualities are audacity, a combination of self-assurance and oratory, and even some vulgarity, which often arouses the masses. Modesty in union with delicacy of feeling and thought, is worth nothing.

Thus comes forth the representative of the people, thus he acquires his mandate. How does he employ it? How will he turn it to advantage? If energetic by nature he will attempt to form a party; if he is of an ordinary nature, then he joins one party or another. The leader of a party above all things requires a strong will. This is an organic quality, like physical strength, and does not by any means inevitably accompany moral excellence. With extremely limited intellect, with infinite egoism, and even wickedness, with base and dishonest motives, a man with a strong will may become the leader of a party and thus control men far surpassing him in moral and intellectual worth. Such may become the ruling force in parliament. To this should be joined another decisive force—eloquence. This also is a natural faculty, involving neither moral character nor high intellectual culture. A man may be a deep thinker, a poet, a skillful general, a subtle jurist, an experienced legislator, and at the same time may not enjoy the gift of fluent speech, while, on the contrary, one with the most ordinary intellectual capacity and knowledge may possess a special gift of eloquence. The union of this gift with a plentitude of intellectual power is a rare and exceptional phenomenon in parliamentary life. The most brilliant improvisations, which have brought glory to orators and influenced great decisions, seem as colorless and contemptible, when read, as descriptions of scenes enacted in former times by celebrated actors and singers. Experience shows that in great assemblies decisive action does not follow the reasonable speech, but rather the bold and brilliant one; that the arguments most effective on the masses are not the clearest and best constructed—those that most truly penetrate to the heart of the matter—but those expressed in sounding words and phrases, artfully selected, constantly reiterated, and calculated to play on the instinct of baseness always dominant in the masses. The masses are easily drawn by outbursts of empty declamation, and under such influences often make sudden decisions, which they later regret on cold-blooded consideration of the matter.

Therefore when the leader of a party combines with a strong will the gift of eloquence, he assumes his role on the open stage before the whole world. If he does not possess this gift he stands, like a stage manager, behind the scenes and directs from there all the acts of the parliamentary spectacle, allotting their roles to others, appointing orators to speak for him, employing all the subtle but irresolute intellects of his party to do his thinking for him.

What is a parliamentary party? In theory, it is an alliance of men with common convictions who join forces for the realization of their views in legislation and in government. But this description applies only to small parties; the large party, which alone is an effective force in Parliament, is formed under the influence only of personal ambition, and centers itself on one commanding personality. By nature, men are divided into two classes—those who tolerate no power over them, and therefore of necessity strive to rule themselves; and those who by their nature dread the responsibility inseparable from decisive action, and who shrink from any decisive act of will. The latter were born for submission, and together constitute a herd, which follows the men of will and resolution, who form the minority. Thus the most talented persons submit willingly, and gladly entrust to stronger hands control of their affairs and the moral responsibility for their direction. Instinctively they seek a leader and become his obedient instruments, inspired by the conviction that he will lead them to victory—and, often, to the spoils. Thus all the essential actions of parliament are controlled by party leaders, who inspire all decisions, who lead the struggle, and profit from victory. The public sessions are no more than a spectacle for the public. Speeches are delivered to sustain the fiction of parliamentarism; seldom does a speech by itself affect the decision of parliament in an important matter. Speech-making serves for the glory of orators, for the increase of their popularity, and the making of their careers; only on rare occasions does it affect the distribution of votes. Majorities and minorities are usually decided before the session begins.

Such is the complicated mechanism of the parliamentary farce; such is the great political lie which dominates our age. By the theory of parliamentarism, the rational majority must rule; in practice, it is five or six party leaders who rule. In theory, decisions are controlled by clear arguments in the course of parliamentary debates; in practice, they in no wise depend on debates but are determined by the will of the leaders and the promptings of personal interest. In theory, the representatives of the people consider only the people's welfare; in practice, their first consideration is their own advancement and the interests of their friends. In theory, they must be from the best citizens; in practice, they are the most ambitious and impudent. In theory, the elector votes for his candidate because he knows him and trusts him; in practice, the elector votes for a man whom he hardly knows but who has been forced on him by the speeches of an interested party. In theory, parliamentary business is directed by experience, good sense, and unselfishness; in practice, the chief motive powers are a firm will, egoism, and eloquence.

Such in essence is the institution exalted as the summit and crown of the edifice of state. It is sad to think that even in Russia there were and are men who aspire to the establishment of this falsehood among us; that our professors still preach to their young listeners about representative government as the ideal political institution; that our newspapers exalt it in their pages under the banner of justice and order without troubling to look closer, to examine without prejudice the parliamentary machine in action. Yet even there, where centuries have sanctified its existence, faith is already waning; there, while the liberal intelligentsia still vaunts it, the people groan under the yoke of this machine and recognize the falsehood hidden within it. We may not see, but our children and grandchildren assuredly will, the overthrow of this idol, which contemporary thought in its self-deception continues to worship. . . .

## FURTHER READING

Robert F. Byrnes, *Pobedonostsev, His Life and Thought* (1968)

Terence Emmons and Wayne S. Vucinich, eds., *The Zemstvo in Russia: An Experiment in Local Self-Government* (1982)

Daniel Field, "Peasants and Propagandists in the Russian Movement to the People of 1874," *Journal of Modern History*, 59 (1987), 415–38

Gregory L. Freeze, *The Parish Clergy in Nineteenth-Century Russia: Crisis, Reform, Counter-Reform* (1983)

G. M. Hamburg, *Politics of the Russian Nobility, 1881–1905* (1984)

Deborah Hardy, *Land and Freedom: The Origins of Russian Terrorism, 1876–1879* (1987)

Hans Heilbronner, "Alexander III and the Reform Plan of Loris-Melikov," *Journal of Modern History* 33 (1961), 384–397

Edward H. Judge, *Plehve: Repression and Reform in Imperial Russia, 1902–04* (1983)

David A. J. Macey, *Government and Peasant in Russia, 1861–1906: The Prehistory of the Stolypin Reforms* (1987)

Robert E. MacMaster, *Danilevsky: A Russian Totalitarian Philosopher* (1967)

Norman Naimark, *Terrorists and Social Democrats: The Russian Revolutionary Movement under Alexander III* (1983)

Derek Offord, *The Russian Revolutionary Movement in the 1880s* (1986)

Philip Pomper, *Sergei Nechaev* (1979)

Donald Rawson, "The Death Penalty in Late Tsarist Russia: An Investigation of Judicial Procedures," *Russian History*, 11 (1984), 29–52

Richard G. Robbins, Jr., *Famine in Russia, 1891–92: The Imperial Government Responds to A Crisis* (1975)

Charles A. Rudd, *Fighting Words: Imperial Censorship and the Russian Press, 1804–1906* (1982)

David Saunders, *Russia in the Age of Reaction and Reform, 1801–1881* (1992)

Frederick F. Travis, *George Kennan and The American-Russian Relationship, 1865–1924* (1990)

Franco Venturi, *Roots of Revolution: A History of the Populist and Socialist Movements in Nineteenth-Century Russia*, trans. (from Italian) Francis Haskell (1960, 1983)

Heide W. Whelan, *Alexander III & the State Council: Bureaucracy & Counter-Reform in Late Imperial Russia* (1982)

Peter A. Zaionchkovsky, *The Russian Autocracy in Crisis, 1878–82*, ed. and trans. Gary M. Hamburg (1979)

# Empire-Building:
# The Nineteenth Century

We return in this chapter to the Russian Empire as empire—as a vast and ever growing assemblage of peoples and places stretching from the Baltic Sea to the Pacific Ocean and ruled from St. Petersburg by the autocratic emperor through his Imperial government and subordinate bureaucracy, military, and police. In the nineteenth century, this growth took place primarily to the south and east: into and across the Caucasus mountains, where Georgian, Armenian, Turkic, and other lands were annexed, and on into Central Asia and the territories of the Far East, where numerous other peoples were subdued. But in the northwest, too, the Grand Duchy of Finland was wrested from Sweden (1808–1809) and, in the southwest, the province of Bessarabia was taken from the Ottoman Empire (1812). Indeed, by the end of the nineteenth century Russians were a minority within the Russian Empire (about 47 percent of the total population) while the Empire itself had become by far the largest continuous—or overland—state in the world.

## E S S A Y S

The two relatively brief essays here—by Professors Andreas Kappeler of Cologne University in Germany and Edward C. Thaden of the University of Illinois at Chicago—discuss the Russian Empire as it stood in the late nineteenth century, stressing its multiethnic character (Kappeler) and the complexities of its policy of "Russification" (Thaden). Neither essay makes it sufficiently clear, perhaps, that the Russian Empire was dominated by a multi-ethnic Imperial elite—an elite of Baltic-German, Polish, Ukrainian, Georgian, Armenian and other nobles, officials, officers, academics, wealthy merchants and industrialists who, along with Russians, had voluntarily adopted that Imperial or "All-Russian" culture which, like the elite itself, dated back to the reforms of Peter the Great. In the course of the nineteenth century, as Thaden indicates, local nationalist movements arose—in tandem with a narrower Russian or "Great Russian" nationalism—to challenge the hegemony of this Imperial culture and elite. Such local nationalisms—in Poland, Finland, Ukraine, the Baltic provinces and elsewhere, as well as in Russia proper—were the product of foreign influences (nationalism was in the European air) as well as indigenous factors (including reactions to Russification or, in the case of Russians, reaction to the rise of the other nationalisms and fears engendered by such external events as the emergence of the German Empire). Economic factors—for example, Russian poverty versus the relative prosperity of the western (non-Russian) provinces—also played a part. And gradually these nationalisms would constitute a powerful centrifugal force pulling the Empire apart.

# The Multi-Ethnic Empire

## ANDREAS KAPPELER

A t the end of the nineteenth century, the Russian Empire was marked by a pronounced heterogeneity of economic, social, and cultural patterns. Whereas in the eighteenth century it had expanded far into Europe, in the nineteenth century its center of gravity moved back towards Asia, owing to its eastward expansion. The proportion of Russians diminished, that of Muslims and nomads increased. Although thinkers like the Panslavist Nicholas Danilevsky stressed the Russian Empire's unique Eurasian position,[1] in the view of the Imperial government and elite it remained a European state. Indeed, government-initiated modernization during the second half of the nineteenth century overcame Russia's relative backwardness vis-à-vis the rest of Europe and achieved an at least partial parity with the advanced countries of the West. This was, in short, a further push towards Europeanization.

Peasant emancipation, industrialization, urbanization, the commercialization of agriculture, and the expansion of formal education energized multi-ethnic Russia and changed its character. Social mobility permeated new layers of the population, while modernization advanced the economic integration of the borderlands as well as standardizing administrative and social structures. Migrating Russians increased their demographic proportion especially in the steppelands, which previously had supported pastoral nomads, as well as in certain industrial sites on the periphery. Russian military and administrative elites now occupied leading positions in all the borderlands except Finland. The Russian language and Russian culture as well as Russian Orthodoxy increasingly became instruments of homogenization [or Russification]. At the same time, social and national mobilization reached numerous non-Russian ethnic groups, which gradually evolved into modern nations with new elites, literary languages, and high cultures. These contradictory trends of homogeni-

---

From Andreas Kappeler, *Russland als Vielvolkerreich: Entstehung, Geschichte, Zerfall* (Munich: Verlag C. H. Beck, 1992), pp. 262–66. Translated by Leo Schelbert. Reprinted with permission from C. H. Beck'sche.

1. Danilevsky's book *Russia and Europe*, first published in 1869, became a sort of bible for conservative Russian nationalists in the 1880s and 1890s.—Ed.

zation and diversification intensified the political and social tensions in the late
tsarist multi-ethnic Empire.

Modernization, however, differed widely in the Russian Empire by region and
sector. Not only did the core of the Empire's political system remain unchanged,
but also its socioeconomic base, which was agrarian. The majority of its people
lived in rural areas, preserved traditional economic patterns, and remained illiterate.
The dynastic autocracy and traditional order of social estates remained important
bonds and, despite secularization, religion maintained its significance for culture
and ethnic identity.

The structure of the late tsarist multi-ethnic Empire was shaped by this mixture
of new and traditional elements. The same holds true for the position occupied by
the non-Russian elites who in the course of the Empire's expansion had been
coopted into the Imperial nobility. Although, as a result of peasant emancipation,
the Polish, Georgian, Azerbaizhan, and Baltic-German nobilities had lost their
special political position (except in Finland) and, in large numbers, had suffered
social decline, a numerically diminished noble elite was still able to retain its social
and economic dominance in the various regions. Owing to the growth of an educated
Russian upper class, the Russian state had become less dependent on the nobility
than in previous centuries; yet it still could not function without the nobility's
cooperation. Thus Baltic-Germans, Germans, Finns, Poles, and Caucasians continued to fill important posts not only in local government, but in the military and
administrative elites of the center. The especially numerous Polish nobility took
on new tasks in scholarship, technology, and culture.

Social and national mobilization also brought pressure to bear on those mobile
groups of their respective diasporas—Jews, Germans, and Armenians—who in the
pre-modern Russian Empire had been active in economic, administrative, scholarly,
and cultural pursuits. Their specific capabilities especially in languages and their
special networks of communication had made them invaluable to the state while
keeping them dependent on the state. Although, as the nineteenth century neared
its end, the lower social strata of the Empire and the various nationalists intensified
their hostility towards these groups, and the government abdicated its traditional
role as their protector, they continued to work as before. Jews, Germans (Baltic-
Germans and Germans in other urban centers), and Armenians, but also Greeks
and Tatars, remained especially numerous in cities and towns, where they were
overrepresented in commerce, credit, and the crafts. They also appeared among
the entrepreneurs, though not as often as foreigners. Jews continued to be active
in the western provinces of the Empire [the notorious Pale of Settlement], Germans
in the northwest, Armenians and Greeks in the south, Tatars in the east. In
the center, various Germans including numerous recent immigrants furthered the
Empire's modernization as scholars, physicians, and engineers. Jews played an important role in banking despite being forced to reside in designated areas [see Docu-
ments]. Yet these mobile diaspora-groups had already passed the zenith of their
importance. Russians—especially the socially mobilized lower groups—increasingly
took over their tasks, while the emergence of nationalism destroyed the government's confidence in their loyalty and intensified prejudice against them as alien

ethno-religious bodies. The growth of anti-Semitism as well as anti-Armenian and anti-German sentiments indicates that in Russia's modernization these groups were to play the role of scapegoats.

The capital, St. Petersburg, remained a mirror of the multi-ethnic Empire whereas Moscow was more demonstrably Russian. In the second half of the nineteenth century, the relative size of the non-Russian groups among St. Petersburg's inhabitants remained fairly constant while their absolute numbers increased markedly along with the increase in the general population. In 1869, 16.8 percent of the 667,000 inhabitants were non-Russian; in 1900, it was 17.8 percent of a total of 1.4 million inhabitants. The Germans, the largest group after the Russians, had fallen from 6.8 to 4 percent of the total and the Finns from 2.7 to 1.4 percent, while the percentage of Poles had risen from 2.3 to 3.5, of Belorussians from 0.4 to 2.9, of Estonians from 0.6 to 1.3, and of Jews from 1.0 to 1.4. Yet in numerous sectors of the economy the non-Russian inhabitants of St. Petersburg—among them many women—were proportionately overrepresented. Germans were especially prominent among the city's mechanics, bakers, and watchmakers as well as its entrepreneurs, merchants, physicians, teachers, and engineers. Many Finns worked in the jewelry business, in factories, and as domestic servants; most Estonians and Belorussians were also workers or servants. Traditionally the Poles of St. Petersburg were military officers, officials, and students, but by the end of the century they were also members of the intelligentsia and factory workers. The Jews were mainly merchants and artisans, increasingly also army surgeons, physicians, and lawyers. On the whole, non-Russians were significantly more numerous in the higher professions than Russians. Thus the special skills of the non-Russian ethnic minorities were utilized in the modernization of St. Petersburg. Although the importance and magnetism of the Russian language and of Russian culture were intensifying in St. Petersburg as well as throughout the Empire, the various non-Russian communities maintained their religious and cultural enclaves in the capital.

On the whole, therefore, the structure of the multi-ethnic Russian Empire remained complex and diverse. Modernization sharpened its colonial character, as the economic development of some regions became increasingly dependent on the center and its industries [that is, a relatively large central industrial zone, including Moscow and St. Petersburg]. The scholarly literature thus differentiates between a classic overseas colonialism and a "European" or "internal" form. With the intense promotion of cotton agriculture, the Central Asian area of the Russian Empire became the very prototype of a classic colony. Moreover, with the increasing migration of Russian peasants into the area, their colonial settlements expanded, which led to the further dislocation of various pastoral nomads, mountain peoples, and hunters who in turn became increasingly dependent on the center. Russia's Asian territories, accordingly, may be labeled colonies without qualification—not only because of their role as providers of raw materials and markets, but also because of their peoples' relatively low socio-economic and socio-cultural levels of development and limited juridical status. Although the Transcaucasian region also became dependent, colony-like, on the center, especially after the production of oil was stepped up, it does not quite fit the classic colonial model because of its Imperial aristocracy, economically influential Armenian middle class, and the relatively high educational level of its Christian population.

Ukrainian scholars have viewed Ukraine as an internal colony. The development of heavy industry in southern Ukraine had colonial features, to be sure, owing to the way in which it was oriented to the production of raw materials and was directed from the outside. Nevertheless, the relationship of Russia to Ukraine may be labeled colonial only in a limited sense, since modernization benefited the region itself and its socio-economic level of development remained higher than that of Russia. Admittedly, the majority of the Ukrainian people became ever more economically disadvantaged. Yet to speak of this as Russian colonialism is further complicated by the fact that Russia itself remained economically backward at the end of the nineteenth century and was dependent on foreign capital, know-how, and enterprise.

Nor can the northwestern periphery of the Empire be considered colonially dependent on Russia. Although the Russian center, especially its two main cities, had experienced turbulent economic, social, and cultural growth, Poland, Finland, and the Baltic provinces maintained their socio-economic and socio-cultural lead. While these regions became more closely tied to the center, their economies profited from the Russian market and the importation of raw materials from Russia. As for agricultural development, most western and southern regions were ahead of the Russian center and the lands to the east.

Even if one considers ethnic groups instead of regions, it becomes clear that the Russians were in no way the privileged "master race" or *Herrenvolk* of the Empire. They had indeed narrowed the gap of the pre-modern age, but they were behind a whole range of other ethnic groups in urbanization and literacy. A broadly based "Russian" intelligentsia had emerged, yet even here Germans, Poles, and Jews were better represented than ethnic Russians. The mass of Russian peasants continued to live far below the level of most peasants in the other parts of the Empire, although the landless rural proletariat was proportionately larger among some ethnic groups in the western provinces. If one considers average life expectancy as one measure of a group's standard of living, the Russians were not only behind the Latvians, Estonians, Lithuanians, and Jews, but also the Ukrainians, Belorussians, Tatars, and Bashkirs. The modernization of Russia itself and of the Russians was therefore regionally as well as socially behind that of most other regions and ethnic groups. Although the tsarist government promoted the Russian center and the Russian power elite, the mass of provincial Russians remained a neglected majority. . . .

So who benefited from the expansion of the Russian Empire? Most non-Russians and many Russians complained (and still complain) that they were subjugated and exploited by the center. But then as later only the state and the largely Russian power elite in the bureaucracy and army reaped advantages from the Imperial system. It cannot be doubted that for centuries the politics of continued expansion and the task of safeguarding the Imperial system had demanded immense human and material resources, had led to the neglect of Russia's internal social, economic, and political development, had furthered extensive rather than intensive growth, and had thus prolonged Russia's backwardness. Rousseau's remark about Russia being unable to digest Poland proved to be prophetic.[2] Neither the tsarist Empire nor the Soviet Union that succeeded it was able to digest the numerous pieces it had all too quickly swallowed.

# Russification

### EDWARD C. THADEN

National liberation movements in the borderlands of the Russian Empire around 1900 have seldom been viewed in the perspective of the [Imperial] government's actual nationality policy. Too often historians have seen this policy as some form of russification resulting from Panslavism, Great Russian chauvinism, or the ultra-nationalism of such journalists as M. N. Katkov and I. S. Aksakov. The term "russification" is not, however, necessarily one that is to be rejected for the purposes of serious discussion of tsarist nationality policy. Catherine II used the verb "russify" as early as 1764 in a secret instruction that she sent to Prince Alexander Viazemsky. In Catherine's context, russification meant the centralization and unification of the Empire's administrative and legal structure in order to promote the interests of the Russian state and to assure government control of society and the welfare of the Empress' subjects [see Chapter 6]. It is in this sense that the term "russification" will be used in this essay.

Tsarist nationality policy was only partly successful. It succeeded in areas where the local nobility's institutions of self-government were weakly developed—e.g., in the left-bank Ukraine and in the eastern borderlands. In the western borderlands [that is, Finland and the Baltic and Polish provinces], as such statesmen as M. M. Speransky and N. A. Manasein have pointed out, the local legal, administrative, and social institutions seemed in many ways to be superior to those of the rest of pre-reform Russia. Because Russian law was neither uniform nor codified before the 1830's and because there was a shortage in Russia of trained and competent jurists and officials, it was difficult to justify the introduction of Russian institutions into the western borderlands. Furthermore, serfdom and various Russian social tensions produced by serfdom also made the tsarist state very dependent on those responsible for maintaining social order in the countryside, namely, the landowning nobility. For example, in the Baltic provinces Russian officials usually hesitated to exploit social unrest among Estonian and Latvian peasants as a pretext to weaken the position of the Germans [landlords] in the Baltic countryside. To be sure, Russian

---

2. Reacting to the First Partition of Poland (1772), the philosopher Jean-Jacques Rousseau advised the Poles, "If you cannot prevent your enemies from swallowing you, at least you can prevent them from digesting you."—Ed.

From *American Contributions to the Seventh International Congress of Slavists, Warsaw, August 1973*, vol. 3: History, ed. Anna Cienciala, (The Hague-Paris: Mouton, 1973), pp. 69–78. Reprinted by permission of Mouton de Gruyter, a division of Walter de Gruyter & Co.

pressure helped produce emancipation by 1819 and a number of other agricultural reforms at a later date, but these reforms were always made on terms acceptable to the Baltic nobles.

In this essay the examples of Finland and the Baltic provinces will be used to illustrate the close connection between russification and reform in the practice of tsarist nationality policy in the western borderlands. The case of Poland will not be considered here, because the uprising of 1863 made reform a secondary issue in Poland, despite the efforts of Iu. F. Samarin and N. A. Miliutin [Imperial officials] to use agricultural reform as a means of winning Polish peasant support for Russia. In Finland, work on coordinating the codification of Finnish and Russian law began in the thirties [1830s]. It was, however, abandoned in the forties [1840s], when Nicholas I only needed to be reminded . . . of Finland's tranquillity and social stability to decide that it was still premature to codify Finnish law in preparation for the introduction of Russian law into the Grand Duchy. During the sixties [1860s] additional concessions were made to the Finns; however, in the following decade Minister of War D. A. Miliutin saw the incompatibility of a "completely separate independent [Finnish] army within the Empire's borders," with general military reform and the integration of the Finnish armed forces into the Russian army. Other ministers soon came to similar conclusions, resulting in a general re-orientation of Russian policy in Finland toward the end of the nineteenth century.

In the Baltic provinces Nicholas I's attempts at administrative and religious russification were for the most part abandoned after the outbreak of revolution in Europe in 1848. His son Alexander [Emperor Alexander II] continued to follow a conciliatory policy toward the Baltic-Germans by being relatively tolerant toward the Lutheran Church, and by refusing to follow the advice of those who advocated undermining German social and political control in the Baltic region through the introduction of Russian *zemstvo* and peasant reforms. Alexander II and his principal advisers believed, however, no less than did Russian nationalistic journalists, in the necessity of merging the Baltic provinces with the rest of the Empire; therefore, they worked systematically to introduce Russian institutions into this area. Thus, in 1862 Alexander II, in approving the basic principles of legal reform in Russia, affirmed the necessity of extending these principles to "all regions governed under special institutions." Governors of such areas were instructed to indicate what modifications had to be made in the new judicial reform to adapt it to the particular conditions of their respective regions. In 1866 Alexander confirmed the opinion of the Department of Laws of the State Council that the police institutions of the Baltic provinces should conform as closely as possible to those of other parts of the Empire. In 1867 he approved the recommendation of the Committee of Ministers to enforce a law of 1850 that required the use of Russian for the official business of all branches of the state bureaucracy in the Baltic provinces. In 1877 the Russian municipal reform of 1870 was extended to Baltic towns. In 1880 one feature of the judicial reform of 1864, namely, the institution of the justice of the peace, was introduced in the Baltic provinces. Later that same year the State Council recommended that the Minister of Justice should take further measures to extend the entire 1864 legal system to the Baltic area.

In 1881, Alexander III departed somewhat from the previous pattern of cautious and gradual russification in the western borderlands, for he then became the first Russian tsar to refuse to confirm the privileges and special rights that Peter the Great had granted to the Baltic German nobility and townsmen some 170 years earlier. In the following year he decreed that work should begin on the codification of Finnish laws. Both acts indicated that officials in St. Petersburg were reconsidering a well-established Russian policy of allowing the German and Swedo-Finnish upper classes in the western borderlands privileges and a degree of autonomy unknown in other parts of the Empire. Yet both Alexander III and his successor Nicholas II made their respective concessions to the requests and wishes of Baltic-Germans and Swedo-Finns. Their nationality policy in the western borderlands, therefore, represented a peculiar combination of reform, russification, and compromise. It was indeed the complexity and contradictions of this policy, as the following examination of its application in the Baltic provinces and Finland between 1881 and 1914 should reveal, that made it so difficult for national liberation movements to organize effectively against the authority of the tsarist state around 1900.

Alexander III's Slavophile and chauvinistic tendencies and antipathy for the Baltic-Germans are well known. Some of the measures undertaken in the Baltic provinces during his reign are certainly to be understood in these terms, e.g., russifying elementary education for Estonians and Latvians, and attempting to separate them from the German upper classes and Lutheran clergy through missionary and proselytizing activities, and also the official encouragement of conversion to Orthodoxy. At the same time, the instructions that Senator N. A. Manasein received in 1882 clearly reveal the desire of Alexander III and his ministers to extend to the Baltic provinces the reforms introduced in the central parts of the Empire during the sixties [1860s]. Manasein, in the report presented to Alexander III in 1884, emphasized the benefits which would accrue to the benefit of both Russia and of the majority of Latvians and Estonians with the establishment of Russian laws, *zemstvos*, courts, and police and peasant institutions in the Baltic provinces. Interested in improving the lot of the Estonian and Latvian peasants, Manasein especially recommended action to enforce existing legislation protecting peasant rights, and to prepare for the fundamental reform of Baltic agriculture.[1]

Russian officials in St. Petersburg—including Manasein, who became Minister of Justice in 1885—succeeded only to a limited extent in their self-proclaimed role as Baltic reformers. There is, of course, little question that the introduction of Russian laws, courts, and police institutions in 1889 did produce positive results for the majority of Estonians and Latvians inhabiting the three Baltic provinces. Interest in Baltic social reform tended, however, to diminish in the second part of the eighties [1880s], when Russian officials began to consider the [project of introducing land captains]. Since this project assured gentry [noble] control of the

---

1. Manasein, as his name indicates, was himself of Baltic origin.—Ed.

*zemstvos*, its introduction into the Baltic provinces after it became law in 1889 would have meant bringing Estonian and Latvian peasant representatives together with German landowners in common organs of self-government which would have remained effectively under the control of the Germans. Such an arrangement was even more objectionable than exclusive German control of local self-government, for such control at least had the virtue of separating the Estonians and Latvians from the Germans. At the same time, official irritation with German nobles tended to decrease as the government intensified its efforts to reinforce the position of the nobility in Russian society toward the end of the nineteenth century.

Russification in the Baltic provinces was undeniably pushed to counterproductive extremes, especially in regard to elementary education and religion. Official Baltic policy also had its positive sides, but it was difficult for the government to act meaningfully in the general area of social reform. The very structure of Russian society and the attitudes of the political elite, especially during the period of counterreform after 1881, almost precluded the possibility of promoting the social and economic interests of the Estonian and Latvian peasants—a worthy cause pleaded not only by several Slavophiles but even by such influential persons as N. A. Manasein and Emperor Alexander III himself.

During the 1860's the case of Finland illustrated very well that Alexander II had no comprehensive or fixed plan for the russification of the Empire's western borderlands. In the last fifties [1850s] and early sixties [1860s] Alexander and his principal advisers [were] inclined to accept the status quo in the Baltic provinces, and to make concessions to the Poles and Finns which assured them a considerable degree of autonomy within the Empire. In Poland and the Baltic provinces, however, either rebellion or serious social problems soon suggested to St. Petersburg officials that Russian laws and institutions should perhaps be introduced, in order to assure the control of the government over the affairs of these two areas. At the same time, however, they allowed the Finnish Diet to meet in 1863 for the first time since 1809, and considerably extended its rights and functions in the Diet Act of 1869. This was the point of departure for the further development of Finnish autonomy during the following several decades.

As has already been pointed out, Russian officials first perceived the disadvantages of growing Finnish autonomy in connection with the preparation of the military reforms of the sixties and seventies [1860s and 1870s]. Soon, the question of Finnish military service became inextricably connected with a protracted discussion of the relation of Finnish legislation to general Imperial legislation. In 1881 the problem of reconciling conflicts between Finnish and Russian law came to the attention of the Finnish Governor-General F. L. Heiden, for at that time he discovered that local Finnish legislation prevented the Russian authorities from arresting a Finnish citizen involved in the activities of Russian revolutionists residing in Helsingfors [the Finnish capital, now Helsinki]. This trivial episode marked the resumption of Russian efforts, temporarily abandoned by the beginning of the fifties [1850s], to make Finnish law conform more closely with general Imperial legislation. Finnish law codification projects prepared by the Finns during the [1880s] soon revealed to Russian legal specialists and officials in the Ministry of Justice and in the Codification Section of the State Council the full extent of the differences separating Finnish and Russian views on the nature of Finland's legal relationship with other parts of the Russian Empire, for the Finns believed that commitments made at the beginning of the nineteenth century formally bound the Russian monarch to recognize the validity of existing Finnish fundamental laws and to work through the Finnish Diet in preparing new legislation. Russian legal experts rejected this Finnish view of the relationship of Finland to the rest of the Empire in a number of memoranda, articles, and books. The Russian position was summarized in a memorandum to Alexander III prepared in 1891 by Governor-General Heiden, who argued that the Russian Emperor had the right to issue laws for Finland in all cases involving mutual Russo-Finnish interests. For Heiden it was clear that the interests of Finland had to be subordinated to those of Russia, and that the Russian Emperor did not necessarily have to consult the Finnish Diet about legislation that affected the interests of both Finland and the Empire as a whole. As [the historian] B. E. Nolde has pointed out, this was the essential argument of innumerable Russian committees, articles, and books on Finland during the next two decades.

The excesses of russification in Finland and the extent to which Russians encroached upon Finnish liberties have been exaggerated by many historians and publicists. Several "crusades" against Finland did take place in the Russian national-ist press, and Governor-General N. I. Bobrikov undeniably did display extraordinary tactlessness in his dealings with the Finns between 1898 and 1904. The actual measures introduced by the Russian [Imperial] government were, however, scarcely extreme, and seem to have been motivated more by a desire to defend legitimate Russian interests in Finland than by some form of Russian nationalism or great power chauvinism. After all, even Bobrikov's extremism was largely confined to such measures as introducing Russian conscription into Finland, making Russian the language of the Finnish Senate, founding an official Russian language newspaper in Finland, and increasing the number of inspectors and the hours of Russian-language instruction in Finnish schools. What preoccupied the Russian official mind more than anything else in regard to Finland during these years was a problem then referred to as the "Order of Promulgating Laws of General State Significance Concerning Finland." Six committees discussed this problem between 1891 and 1910, and their affirmation of the principle formulated by Governor-General Heiden in 1891 found formal expression in the Tsar's manifesto of February 3, 1899, and the Law of June 17, 1910. Neither the manifesto of 1899 nor the law of 1910 questioned the validity of purely local Finnish laws, but they clearly limited the authority and jurisdiction of the Finnish Diet and Senate by placing the ultimate lawmaking authority for Finland in the hands of Russian officials in St. Petersburg. This was especially the case for the law of June 17, 1910, which not only determined fully and comprehensively the extent of Imperial authority, but also specifically listed nineteen categories of laws of general state interest concerning Finland.

In regard to both the Baltic provinces and Finland, it is not acceptable to dismiss russification as being simply an illustration of brutal tsarist oppression of borderland nationalities. Russification was also an expression of the desire of the Russian government to impose a uniform and "systematic legal-administrative order"[2] on all parts of the Empire. Prior to the Crimean War [1853–1856], centralizing officials failed in their efforts to integrate the relatively advanced western borderlands with the rest of Russia because of the shortcomings of Russia's society, legal system, and administrative structure. After the [Great Reforms] this situation changed somewhat, for, at least in the opinion of many Russian reformers, the new *zemstvos*, courts, municipal institutions, peasant legislation, and educational system, placed the Russian center of the Empire on a higher level of social, legal, and political development than that of the western borderlands. Thus, such an advocate of unification and reform in the borderlands as Iury Samarin expected not only the abolition of the "medieval" privileges of borderland nobles but also a concerted effort on the part of the Russian government to "elevate the people, to assure its economic welfare, and to give it hope and an impartial court in quarrels with the nobles. . . . In Finland, to be sure, what nineteenth-century tsarist officials had actually done to promote Finnish social and economic welfare was not universally appreciated around 1900. In any case, defenders of Russian policy in Finland could and did argue that the interests of the entire Empire necessarily had to be given priority over those of its constituent parts. Also, they repeatedly pointed out that Russia had no intention of encroaching upon Finnish autonomy but only wished to safeguard the general welfare of the Empire's inhabitants, including the Finns, who had prospered and flourished during a century of Russian rule.

In the Baltic provinces there can be little question that the introduction of Russian courts, municipal institutions, and police institutions during the 1870's and 1880's did improve the position of the Latvian and Estonian majority of the population vis-à-vis the privileged German minority. Russian officials, however, always found administrative reforms easier to introduce than social ones. Thus, they hesitated to challenge the position of the Baltic landowners and did little to improve the lot of landless peasants in the countryside, or that of workers in the cities. The attraction of Russia for the lower classes was therefore diminished. However, no systematic attempt was made to prevent Latvians and Estonians from developing their own native cultures, which made great progress during the era of russification despite the official educational and cultural policies of the tsarist government.

The examples of Finland and the Baltic provinces suggest many of the difficulties encountered by national liberation movements in resisting russification between 1881 and 1914. Had russification been limited to the harsh national oppression so often depicted by anti-Russian publicists, the task of forming effective and united opposition movements to tsarist authority would have been greatly simplified. Russification was, however, a complex policy that did not affect all nationalities and different social strata within these nationalities in the same way. Thus, in Finland,

---

2. This phrase is taken from George Yaney, *The Systematization of Russian Government: Social Evolution in the Domestic Administration of Imperial Russia, 1711–1905* (1973).

the Constitutionalists who had opposed Bobrikov and the subordination of Finnish law to Russian law suffered a crushing defeat in the election of 1907, the first one held in Finland under the democratized election procedures approved by the tsar and the Finnish estates in the preceding year. Clearly, resistance to russification was not necessarily the key to understanding Finnish political behavior at the beginning of the twentieth century.

Nor is such resistance probably the only key to understanding the history of other national liberation movements in the Russian Empire during the same period. Many people in all parts of the Empire benefited from the reforms and the consolidation of Russia as a modern national state that followed the Crimean War. The extent to which russification, in the sense that this term has been used in this paper, actually benefited each individual nationality inhabiting the Empire's borderlands is, of course, a subject that needs further investigation [see Further Reading, works by Thaden and others]. But it is from such an investigation that we are likely to obtain a more sophisticated and differentiated understanding of the Russian Empire's national liberation movements during the generation preceding World War I and the 1917 Revolution.

## D OCUMENTS

The first document is the circular letter to the European powers issued by Prince Alexander M. Gorchakov (1798–1883), Alexander II's longtime foreign minister (1856–1879), on November 21, 1864. The letter contains the first public justification of Russian imperialist policy in Central Asia, a policy Gorchakov himself initially opposed as a reckless and dangerous diversion of Russian attention away from Europe and urgent home affairs (the Great Reforms). Nevertheless, Gorchakov's circular clearly reflects the ideological distance official Russia had traveled since the eighteenth century (see Documents, Chapter 5): Russia, now conceived of as a fully European—that is, "civilized"—power, had, like the other European powers (and later the United States), a civilizing mission in the non-European parts of the world, which in Russia's case meant "barbarous" Asia. And Gorchakov himself, with his thoroughly European education and command of several European languages, his years of service in diplomatic posts in Europe and sense of himself as a European Russian statesman (Bismarck regarded him as a mentor): Gorchakov personally embodied the European aspirations of the Imperial Russian elite of the later nineteenth century.

Next comes a description by James Bryce of the capital of Russian Transcaucasia, Tiflis (now Tbilisi, capital of Georgia), as he found it in 1876, on the eve of the military campaigns of 1877–1878 against Ottoman Turkey and its local allies which completed Russia's conquest of the region. Bryce (1838–1922), the English historian and diplomat who became famous in the United States as ambassador from Britain (1907–1913) and author of *The American Commonwealth* (first published 1888), made an extended trip through the Russian Empire and on into Turkey in 1876–1877. The following is excerpted from his published impressions of the journey, which illustrate well the multi-ethnic and imperial character of this southern city, and mirror, of Emperor Alexander's burgeoning realm.

The third document provides an extended and largely self-explanatory account of official and unofficial Russian antisemitism particularly in the southwestern province of Bessarabia, which was first acquired from Turkey in 1812. (Southern Bessarabia was lost to Turkey in 1856, a consequence of Russia's defeat in the Crimean War, but was regained in 1878.) The author of the account, Prince S. D. Urusov, was governor of Bessarabia in 1903–1904. Born in 1862 into a distinguished old Russian family, he was a conscientious Imperial official until he resigned from the service in 1904 in protest against the punitive measures of the current government. After the 1905 Revolution he was elected an independent deputy to the first Duma (parliament), which convened in 1906 only to be dissolved by Nicholas II after little more than two months. Urusov retired to his estate to complete the memoirs excerpted here, which were published in Moscow in 1907. The memoirs expose the dark underside of the Imperial government's policies in the reactionary period 1881–1905 and especially those directed against Jews, who suffered more official discrimination than any of the Empire's other non-Russian subjects.

## The Gorchakov Circular on Russia's Mission in Central Asia, 1864

The position of Russia in Central Asia is that of all civilized states which are brought into contact with half-savage nomad populations possessing no fixed social organization.

In such cases, the more civilized state is forced in the interest of the security of its frontier, and its commercial relations, to exercise a certain ascendancy over their turbulent and undesirable neighbors. Raids and acts of pillage must be put down. To do this, the tribes on the frontier must be reduced to a state of submission. This result once attained, these tribes take to more peaceful habits, but are in turn exposed to the attacks of the more distant tribes against whom the State is bound to protect them. Hence the necessity of distant, costly, and periodically recurring expeditions against an enemy whom his social organization makes it impossible to seize. If, the robbers once punished, the expedition is withdrawn, the lesson is soon forgotten; its withdrawal is put down to weakness. It is a peculiarity of Asiatics to respect nothing but visible and palpable force. The moral force of reasoning has no hold on them.

In order to put a stop to this state of permanent disorder, fortified posts are established in the midst of these hostile tribes, and an influence is brought to bear upon them which reduces them by degrees to a state of submission. But other more distant tribes beyond this outer line come in turn to threaten the same dangers, and necessitate the same measures of repression. The State is thus forced to choose between two alternatives—either to give up this endless labor, and to abandon its frontier to perpetual disturbance, or to plunge deeper and deeper into barbarous countries, when the difficulties and expenses increase with every step in advance.

From A. Krausse, *Russia in Asia: A Record and a Study* (New York: Henry Holt & Co., 1899), pp. 224–25.

Such has been the fate of every country which has found itself in a similar position. The United States in America, France in Algeria, Holland in her Colonies, England in India; all have been forced by imperious necessity into this onward march, where the greatest difficulty is to know where to stop.

Such have been the reasons which have led the Imperial Government to take up, first, a position resting, on one side, on the Syr-Daria [river], on the other, the Lake of Issik Kul, and to strengthen these lines by advanced forts.

It has been judged indispensable that our two fortified lines, one extending from China to the Lake of Issik Kul, the other from the Sea of Aral, along the Syr-Daria, should be united by fortified points, so that all posts should be in a position of mutual support leaving no gap through which nomad tribes might make their inroads and depredations with impunity.

Our original frontier line along the Syr-Daria to Fort Perovsky, on the one side, and on the other, to Lake Issik Kul, had the drawback of being almost on the verge of the desert. It was broken by a wide gap between the two extreme points; it did not offer sufficient resources to our troops, and left unsettled tribes over the back with which any settled arrangement became impossible.

In spite of our unwillingness to extend our frontier, these motives had been powerful enough to induce the Imperial Government to establish this line between Issik Kul and the Syr-Daria by fortifying the town of Khemkend, lately occupied by us. This line gives us a fertile country, partly inhabited by Kirghiz tribes, which have already accepted our rule, and it therefore offers favorable conditions for colonization, and the supply of provisions to our garrisons. In the second place, it puts us in the neighborhood of the agricultural and commercial population of Kokand.

Such are the interests which inspire the policy of our august master [Emperor Alexander II] in Central Asia.

It is needless for me to lay stress on the interest which Russia evidently has not to increase her territory, and, above all, to avoid raising complications on her frontiers, which can but delay and paralyze her domestic development. Very frequently of late years the civilization of these countries, which are her neighbors on the Continent of Asia, has been assigned to Russia as her special mission.

## James Bryce Describes "Wonderfully Picturesque" Tiflis, 1876

Tiflis:—The capital of Transcaucasia is a type of the country. It is a city of contrasts and mixtures, a melting-pot into which elements have been poured from half Europe and Asia, and in which they as yet show no signs of combining.

From James Bryce, *Transcaucasia and Ararat: Being Notes of a Vacation Tour in 1876*, 4th ed. (London, Macmillan and Co., Ltd., 1896), pp. 142–60, 163–68.

It stands on the Kura which is here a swift, turbid stream, just above the point where it emerges from the upland country into the great steppe that stretches away to the Caspian. High hills of a shaly limestone and schist enclose it on all sides, those on the south rising some 800 to 1200 feet above the river. They are not very picturesque hills, especially after May, when the herbage on them is utterly burnt away by heats, and they stand out bare, brown, and stern, with no color except when the setting sun bathes them for a moment in a purple glow. Even so, however, they give the city a character one would not like to miss. Besides, they shelter it from the cold blasts that rush down in the winter from the Caucasus, so that the winter climate is one of the pleasantest in these latitudes, warm and equable, yet not nearly so damp as that of the Black Sea coast. While the steppe of the Lower Kura is covered with snow and swept by bitter north-easters, consumptive patients can here go out all the winter through. The mean temperature of the year is a little lower than that of Rome, which is in the same latitude, while the mean of the adjoining steppe is that of Northern France. On the other hand, Tiflis is intolerably hot and close in summer. Down in this hollow, where not a breath of air can reach you from the mountains you descry, where the sun's rays are reflected from bare slopes and white houses, where often not a shower will fall for months together, one gasps and pants, one is not merely scorched, but stifled. I have repeatedly seen thunderstorms play all round the town, sheets of rain desending a few miles off, and the streets lit up at night by the flashes, when scarcely a drop would fall in Tiflis itself. Add to this that the water is scarce and indifferent, and the dust truly Oriental, and it is easy to understand that summer is not the time to enjoy the Transcaucasian capital. So in summer, pretty nearly every one who can afford it, and can get free from his official duties, makes off to the hills. The court, that is to say, the Grand Duke [Grand Duke Michael, brother of Alexander II and commander-in-chief of Russian forces in the Caucasus], who is the sun of this system, and his attendant planets, the adjutants, go to Borzhomi, a charming spot among wooded mountains eighty miles to the west-north-west, in the upper valley of the Kura. Others cross the Caucasus to Piatigorsk or Kislovodsk, favorite watering-places at the northern base of [Mount] Elbruz; a few go by way of Odessa to Europe. Towards the middle of September they begin to return, and by November society is again in full swing.

The hills which I have mentioned break down pretty steeply towards the river, and it is chiefly on the lower slope of those lying on its right or south-western bank, which are much the higher, that the town [Tiflis] is built, descending in terraces towards the river, whose course is here (speaking generally) south-east. At the east end of the city two rocky spurs almost meet, the Kura forcing its way in rapids and eddies between them. On the north-east side stands the citadel, which is now also the prison, and the ancient Georgian cathedral; behind it, on a sort of terrace, are the enormous barracks. The opposite rocks are crowned by the picturesque ruins of a Persian fortress, whence we discover the long wooded line of the outermost mountains of Daghestan, and, in clear weather, the glittering snows of Kazbek, rising over the watershed which divides Europe from Asia. These irregularities of surface, with the swift stream rushing through between precipitous banks, give a great charm to Tiflis, and make it look much larger than it really is. The views over it are very striking, not that the individual buildings are fine, for they are nearly all modern, and, like so much modern Russian work, handsomely uninteresting; but the mass of houses with groves and gardens interspersed, the stern brown setting of hills, the motley throng just visible upon the bridges, the glimpses of far-away mountains, make up a *coup d'oeil* [stunning view] not easily forgotten. I cannot recall any European city that resembles it. . . .

Seen from above, Tiflis is one continuous city, interrupted only by public or private gardens here and there. But in reality it consists of three perfectly distinct towns, unlike in their origin, their buildings, their population. First, there is the Russian town, all new, bright, showy, and, externally at least, clean. It is on the south-west bank of the river, rising steeply towards the hills, and is, of course, the fashionable residential quarter, as well as the region of the best shops, the opera-house, public offices, and so forth. The streets are wide and straight; the houses high, all new-looking, and all as like one another as in Paris or Chicago. Rows of trees are planted in front of European shops with plate-glass windows. This part, indeed, has only grown up within the last sixty years. Here live the court—the Grand Duke has a handsome palace fronting to the principal street, called, in St. Petersburg fashion, Golovinski Prospekt [Avenue]—and, indeed, pretty nearly all the officials, besides a certain number of rich Armenians. You might fancy yourself in Odessa, or one of the newer and better suburbs of Moscow.

To the east of this Russian town, and lying deep down in the hollow along the river, is old Tiflis, a genuine Eastern city, with its narrow crooked streets, ill-paved or not paved at all, and houses of one or two stories only, the whole horribly dirty, yet incomparably more picturesque than the smart propriety of the modern town. Each of the principal trades has a street or streets, or a covered arcade in the bazaar, entirely to itself: thus in one street you find the dealers in arms, in a second the leather-sellers, in a third the jewelers, in a fourth the carpet merchants, in a fifth the furriers, on whose walls hang the skins of Caucasian bears and Hyrcanian [Persian] tigers. The ground-floor room of the house is open to the street, from which it is generally raised a step or two; here the dealer squats on a piece of matting, surrounded by his assistants, with his wares hung or stowed round the walls behind and in the room which is visible at the back. If he practices a handicraft, he works at it here in the sight of all men, just as in some old-fashioned English villages the shoemaker may still be seen sitting in his front room open to the air, and hammering away at a solid boot sole, much more solid than anything that comes from an Eastern last. Thus, as you pick your way down the lanes, jostled into the middle by the crowd, and in the middle nearly run over by the impetuous droshkies [Russian carts], you can see the whole industry of the place in full swing: bread is being baked in one street, swords forged in another, cloth woven in a third. There is no department in which the artisans are particularly strong, except perhaps in the making of ornamental arms, such as pistols and daggers, and of silver cups and flagons, the designs on which are often very beautiful. . . . The value of the old silver goods is well known; it is little use hoping for a bargain where so many Russian buyers are about, and where the sellers are mostly Armenian. Pretty things, especially belts, are still made in what is called niello work. The jewelry rather disappointed us. So near Persia one expects to see splendid turquoises at least, not to speak of gold work, emeralds and rubies, quite abundant. Though we spent hours in the jewelers' street, it is possible we may have missed the best shops, for out of the great number of turquoises shown us, though some were big, very few were of a specially fine color. It is true that the small ones were considerably cheaper than in St. Petersburg; perhaps the finest are bought up in Persia to be sent direct thither or to Constantinople. The settings are mostly very simple and uniform. What pleased us best were the great dark rooms, running away back from the streets, in which the carpet dealers, most of whom are Persians or Tatars, keep their goods stocked, the darkness being not only pleasant in summer, but a sensible advantage to the seller. Here a wonderful variety of all kinds of rugs, mats, and carpets may be seen, the best, perhaps, Persian from Tabriz and Khorassan, and Tekke Turkman from Merv, but plenty of other kinds. . . . A considerable trade is also done in lamb-skins (those called in England Astrakhans) and in silks and embroideries from Bokhara.

The crowd, noise, and bustle of this Eastern town are at their highest on the bridge which in the middle of it spans the Kura, whose waves, breaking against the cliffs that enclose it, are hardly heard over the din of voices, loud and harsh as the voices of Orientals usually are. Hard by is the road leading to the neighboring eastern gate, through which all the traffic flows in from Armenia, Persia, and the steppe; now a string of camels, now troops of donkeys laden with fruit or charcoal, now the rough, slow, solid-wheeled bullock carts of the country, now a party of mounted Cossacks clattering over the pavement. Piles of fruit from the German gardens strew the ground, mixed with huge bullock-skins full of Kakhitian [Georgian] wine. From the rocks above the grim walls of the citadel frown down, and beside them appears the gray cupola of the most ancient among the Georgian churches; nearer, and half-hidden by the confused mass of houses, you see the domes and minarets of the rival mosques of the Sunni Tatars and the schismatic Persian Shias. One can hardly believe that a Russian Paris is only half a mile away.

Quitting this district, ascending the southern bank of the river, and crossing it by the principal bridge, which is adorned by a statue of Prince Voronstov, the famous governor of Transcaucasia [1844–1856], one enters a third quarter, equally unlike either of the two I have just been trying to describe. You forget Russia, you forget Asia: you fancy yourself on the banks of the Swabian Neckar. This is the German settlement, still called by everybody "The Colony," which was originally quite a distinct town, and has only in the recent growth of Tiflis become united to it by a continuous line of houses. It is inhabited by Germans, the descendants of emigrants who came hither from Würtemberg sixty years ago, driven from their homes by a new hymn-book which their prince insisted on forcing upon his subjects, and which they considered too lax in its statements of doctrine. The Russian Government, always delighted to secure industrious and peaceable colonists, received them warmly, placed them first near Odessa, and ultimately, at their own wish, transferred them hither. Here they have dwelt ever since, not increasing much in numbers, though some few have joined them from Germany, preserving all their old ways and habits, cherishing their Protestant faith, and singing out of their dear old hymn-book. Rows of trees run along the principal street; breweries and beer-gardens border it, where the honest burgher sits at night and listens over his supper to a band, as his cousins are doing at the same hour in the suburbs of Stuttgart. Tidy little *Fraus* come out in the evening-cool to the doorsteps, and knit and chat among their fair-haired Karls and Gretchens. They have their own schools, far better than any which Russian organization produces; they are nearly all Protestants, with a wholesome Protestant contempt for their superstitious Georgian and Armenian neighbors. They speak nothing but German among themselves, and show little or no sign of taking to Russian ways or letting themselves be absorbed by the populations that surround them. It was very curious to contrast this complete persistency of Teutonism here with the extraordinarily rapid absorption of the Germans among other citizens which one sees going on in those towns in the Western States of North America, where—as in Milwaukee, for instance—the inhabitants are mostly German, and still speak English with a markedly foreign accent. But of course, when one thinks about it, the phenomenon is simple enough. Here they are exiles from a higher civilization planted in the midst of a lower one; there they lose themselves among a kindred people, with whose ideas and political institutions they quickly come to sympathize. . . .

The German population of Tiflis may, at present, amount to some five or six thousand souls. Most of them are artisans, or gardeners—gardening is almost entirely abandoned to them by the lazy Georgians—only a few are shopkeepers or merchants. Of course, most of the men of science, and a pretty good proportion of government *employés* [officials], belong to the *Culturvolk* [are Germans]; but these are mostly stray wanderers from the Baltic Provinces, or from old Germany itself, not home-bred colonists. They are friendly, pleasant people, among whom an Englishman soon feels himself at home, and who are ready to show him every kindness. I should be ungrateful indeed not to acknowledge the help and advice we received from several among them, and which in some cases were given by persons to whom we had not brought introductions.

Although there are but three distinct towns in Tiflis, there are at least six distinct nations. Besides the Russians and Germans, of whom I have spoken already, the Georgians, Armenians, Tatars, and Persians all contribute sensibly large elements to the population. The Georgians are at home, and may probably be the most numerous; amongst the motley faces in the streets their type seemed the most common. Most of them are nobles, . . . and most of them are poor; they form probably one-third of the day laborers and servants. As the men generally wear European coats and trousers in the town, though in the country a dress much like the Circassian is common among the better class, they are not so easily recognized for Georgians as the women, whose singular head-gear—a square cloth cap ornamented with a kind of crown, from which there hangs down over the shoulders a long white gauze veil—makes them wonderful ornaments of the streets. . . . They are certainly a splendid race to look at, these Georgians, both men and women, but I doubt if they are anything more. They have produced comparatively little literature and not much art (except in the way of ecclesiastical decoration). They fell into the hands of the Russians because they could not resist, bravely as they fought, the effete despotism of Persia; and now though they do not really like the Russians, and will give you to understand as much on the sly, I do not suppose they would ever raise a finger against them. Perhaps their spirit has been broken by the long and unequal struggle which they, always a small nation, had to maintain against such bitter foes as Turks and Persians, and in judging them one ought to remember not only that they were a small nation exposed to the attacks of much larger ones, but also that to the south-east they had no natural frontier behind which they could shelter themselves. And it may well be that they have mended since the Persian yoke was broken, and will mend still further. . . .

The most conspicuous figures in the streets, next to the Georgian ladies, are the clerics, whose jolly faces are surmounted by huge cylindrical hats, from which depend long veils of a sort of black crape, while a robe of black serge, with immense sleeves, covers the body to the ankles. It is curious to any one who remembers France, Italy, or Spain, to see so many ecclesiastical countenances in which there is neither asceticism nor priestcraft, nor indeed any professional expression except a sort of vacuous and self-complacent good-humor, the good-humor of a lazy man who has plenty to eat and drink. When there meets you a keener or more restless glance, you may be sure that it comes from an Armenian eye.

The Armenians are a large and apparently an increasing element of the population, easily known by their swarthy complexion and peculiar physiognomy. They are the most vigorous and pushing people in the country, and have got most of its trade into their hands, not only the shop-keeping, but the larger mercantile concerns. A good many, too, are in the Russian service, and have thriven in it; in fact, more than half the *employés* [officials] in Transcaucasia are said to be Armenians. Like most successful people, they are envied and ill-spoken of, possibly calumniated by their less energetic neighbors. Sharp men of business they certainly are, thrifty, able to drive a hard bargain, and sticking wonderfully together. Among them there are several persons of learning and ability, and as their education improves and their wealth increases, the number of such persons is likely to grow; so that altogether one seems to see a considerable future before them. Although they get on well enough with the Russians, they do not much mix or intermarry either with them or the Germans, but have a society of their own, which is quite self-sufficing.

The Persians in Tiflis are said to number 10,000, all of whom live in the older part of the city, to whose picturesqueness those of the better sort add a good deal by their long dark or yellowish brown robes and pointed hats of black lamb's-wool. Tiflis was once under direct Persian rule, and for a much longer time under Persian supremacy, so that one may believe this Iranian population has remained here ever since, and need not suppose any recent immigration. A few are merchants, driving a trade in carpets, silks, and the other goods of their country; the rest are handicraftsmen. Some trades they have almost appropriated, particularly that of masons, in which they are said to excel all the other workmen of these countries. They live upon next to nothing, are steady workers, and have not yet learnt to organize strikes.

The Tatars are probably about as numerous as the Persians, but as many of them are carriers coming to and fro from the Caspian coast and Persia, they are more a floating than a settled population. They are all poor people, have a good name for industry and sobriety, do a good deal of the unskilled labor, and keep all the baths, an important profession in an Eastern city. All are of course Mohammedans

[Muslims], some of the Sunni persuasion; but a probably larger number, especially of those from the Persian border, are Shias.

Besides these six leading races, Tiflis is full of all sorts of nondescript people from different parts of the Caucasus. The nurses are all, one is told, Osetes [Ossetes, or Ossetians]—Georgian women object to domestic service—and thus many children grow up able to speak that interesting language. . . .

Imeritians, Mingrelians, and even Abkhasians from the Black Sea coast, not unfrequently come here looking for work; occasionally one recognizes the delicate aquiline features and keen eyes of a Lezghian, armed to the teeth, from the mountains of Daghestan. Even Europe is not wholly unrepresented, for although there are very few Italians or English . . . there are, besides Poles, plenty of Frenchmen[:] hotel-keepers, upholsterers, dyers and cleaners of cloth, confectioners, and, above all, hairdressers. So strangely mixed a population it would be hard to find anywhere, even in the East. You never can guess what language the men who pass you in the street are talking; it may be any one of some eight or nine that are spoken almost equally. We, of course, could only distinguish French and German, and sometimes Russian, but the friends who walked beside us would say from time to time: "These fellows are talking Armenian, or Tatar, or Georgian, or Ossete, or Persian," as the case might be. The commonest is Russian, not that they are the most numerous class, but because, being the official language, it is the second language most frequently learned by persons of every nation in addition to their own. Thus pretty nearly all the Germans, at least the men, speak Russian, and I fancy most of the Armenians also, as they are excellent linguists, and more ambitious to rise than the Georgians. On the front shops are seen names written in Russian, French, German, Armenian, and Georgian, more rarely in Persian. There are very few Jews; perhaps the Armenians leave no room for them.

Tiflis, whose native name, Tbilisi, is said to be derived from a Georgian word meaning hot, and to refer to the warm springs, is a place of some historical note. Tradition says that the first fort was erected here by a lieutenant of the Sassanid kings of Persia in A.D. 380, and that at it, seventy-five years later, the reigning monarch of Georgia, Vaktang Gurgaslan, founded a city, to which, in the beginning of the following century, his son Datchi transferred the seat of government, attracted by the hot sulfurous baths. Compared, however, to the antiquity of the former capital Mtzkhet (twelve miles to the north-west), which was founded by a great-great-great-grandson of Noah, Tiflis appears a settlement of yesterday. Like most cities in these countries, it has been so often destroyed in the war that hardly anything remains from primitive times; nothing, indeed, except the old cathedral on the citadel hill, already mentioned, called the Melekhi, which is attributed to King Vaktang. Of these devastations, the most ruinous were those which it suffered from Timur in the fourteenth century, and from the savage Persian Aga Mohammed Khan in 1795, in the invasion which led the last Georgian king to cede to the Tsar the country he could not defend. When the Russians came, it was a very small place, confined to the region round the lowest bridge, of which I have spoken already; even in 1834 it had but 25,000 inhabitants. Latterly, what with the general growth of the country, and with the concentration of trade at this particular point, where several lines of road meet the railway to the Black Sea, it has grown very fast, and may now have a population of 80,000 or more. Building still goes on, and house rents are inordinately high.

Its newness gives the city one merit, which most travelers, whatever they may say, will secretly appreciate. It has no sights. You have no picture galleries, churches, monuments, manufactories, arsenals, Green Vaults, and so forth, duly noted in your guide-book, which a sense of duty—a sad presentiment that when you have returned home, you will be ashamed not to have done them—drives you to see. It is a place where you may settle down in your hotel and do just as you please, saunter forth in the morning to buy grapes, and mingle with the many-tongued throngs in the meat and fruit market, doze away in the sultry afternoon upon a sofa, and in the evening-cool drive out to call on some friend, or sit in the public garden, under the mellow southern moon, and hear the band discourse military music till near midnight. As there are no buildings older than the seventeenth century, always excepting the little old Melekhi church, and nothing at all remarkable since then, no collections, except a museum, which is interesting, so far as it goes, and very nicely arranged and kept, but small when one considers the resources of the country in the way of minerals, animals, and antiquities; and a botanic garden, also well managed by a German botanist, but languishing for want of funds, there is really nothing for the visitor to do except lounge and amuse himself by watching the dresses and manners of the motley crowd. In fact, the town itself is a museum; the inhabitants are the sight of Tiflis, quite sufficient to keep curiosity alive for days and weeks together. . . .

It was too hot for walks or drives in the outskirts of the city, even had there been anything to see—which there is not, for, once beyond the houses, you are in an utterly bare and dreary land, especially dreary at this season [September], when the crops have been lifted from the brown soil. There is but one walk which is really worth taking,—a short walk which, as a guide-book would say, no traveler ought to omit. The lofty ridge of hills which rises behind Tiflis on the south-west sends down a steep spur to the river in the form of a long, narrow, rocky ridge, called the Sololaki hill, whose north side is turned to the town, while its back slopes down to the valley of a small stream called the Tsavkissi. Its bed is dry in summer, what little water there is being drawn off for the botanic garden and the supply of the town. One of the highest and best isolated tops of this ridge is crowned by the ruins of the Persian fortress which dominated the city: broken round and square towers connected by a line of walls, that stand picturesquely up against the sky. On another point are the remains of what local antiquaries pronounce to be a Persian shrine, a temple to the Sun or to Fire, dating from the times of the Sassanid kings, before the crescent of Islam were heard of. One climbs to the top of this ridge through the shady walks of the botanic garden, which lies on the declivity of it away from the town, looking across the dry and desolate glen of the Tsavkissi, on the farther side of which a multitude of tombstones stuck in the ground, unfenced and uncared for, shows where the Persians of Tiflis bury their dead. An ascent, which grows steeper when one has left the trees of the garden, ends suddenly at a sort of portal in the rocky ridge, and through this one sees all Tiflis lying at one's feet: the Oriental crowd on the bridge, the Russian sentries at the Grand Duke's palace in the Golovinski boulevard, the orchard-embowered houses of the Swabian colony beyond the river, the rush of whose waters one seems to hear amid the mixed hum and stir that rises from the busy streets. Behind are the wooded hills through which the Dariel road descends from the valley of the Aragva, and, still farther, ridge beyond ridge rising towards the central line of the Caucasus, where the snows of Kazbek glitter over all.

The mass of hills from which this Sololaki height is an offset rises farther to the west into a sort of upland plateau, where lies the pleasant little summer retreat of Kajori, the nearest to Tiflis of all those hill-stations to which its people retire during the heats. We went there—it was the only excursion we had time to make—to present ourselves to the general who was then acting as military adjutant to the Grand Duke Michael (the Lieutenant of the Caucasus), and who was therefore practically commander-in-chief and war minister for the Caucasian provinces. It was a drive of some eight or nine miles; so, in order that we might travel with proper dignity, our hostess procured for us a phaeton, which is the name in Tiflis for a two-horse vehicle, those with one horse being merely droshkies. . . . The road winds in a succession of curves up the hills south of the city, and then turns to the west along a gently rising table-land, broken here and there by valleys in which dwarf oaks shelter themselves, but mainly covered by large corn-fields, where teams of twelve or sixteen oxen were ploughing up the stubble. The air grew fresher and fresher as we mounted out of the oven where Tiflis lies, till in a couple of hours we reached Kajori, where, at 5000 feet above the sea and 3700 feet above Tiflis, we were reveling in a climate like that of the middle slopes of the Alps, keen cool breezes making even the powerful sun enjoyable. There is a good deal of wood about, which adds to the sense of coolness, and . . . [a] more delightful spot to be idle in can hardly be imagined than this grassy upland, with its invigorating breezes and prospects stretching over two hundred miles of forest, dale, and mountain.

The prince Adjutant-General, however, to whom we presented ourselves in his pretty little wooden villa, was not idle. Mounted Cossacks were galloping up with despatches, waiting outside, and galloping off again down the steep road to Tiflis with that air of important haste which the bearer of despatches loves to assume. However, this did not prevent us from receiving a cordial welcome, and enjoying a long and leisurely conversation, resumed after dinner in the open air, in which our host showed a mastery not only of European politics generally, but even of English party politics and the views and sympathies of our leading statesmen, which few of our own soldiers or diplomatists could have equalled. . . .

I seem to have given in these few pages but a meager account of the sights of the Transcaucasian capital, wanting both in the practical precision of Baedeker and the wealth of illustrative learning and disquisition and quotation which is the glory of our great English series of guide-books. Even the picturesque side of the place suffers in the hands of a traveler who must own that he has little eye for costume. My excuse is that in Tiflis it is not the particular things to be seen in the city that impress themselves on one's memory: it is the city itself, the strange mixture of so many races, tongues, religions, customs. Its character lies in the fact that it has no one character, but ever so many different ones. Here all these peoples live side by side, buying and selling, and working for hire, yet never coming into any closer union, remaining indifferent to one another, with neither love, nor hate, nor ambition, peaceably obeying a government of strangers who annexed them without resistance and retain them without effort, and held together by no bond but its existence. Of national life, or municipal life, there is not the first faint glimmering: indeed, the aboriginal people of the country seem scarcely less strangers in its streets than do all the other races that tread them. It is hard to say what the future has in store for such a town; meantime it prospers, delivered for ever from the fear of Persian devastation, and, in spite of bran-new [sic] boulevards and stuccoed shop-fronts, it is wonderfully picturesque.

# S. D. Urusov Explains Russian Antisemitism, 1907

The real cause of the Kishiniev pogrom [of 1903] remains obscure.[1] Those April riots gave rise to an agitation and burning interest in Russia and abroad not weakened by the subsequent massacres of Jews that took place in various cities and towns in 1905 and afterwards, in 1906. Judging by the emotional storm aroused by this first pogrom, it will not be forgotten, and will occupy a place of marked interest in Russian history of the beginning of the twentieth century. I must, therefore, speak of the impressions made upon me by the background to the disorders of Easter, 1903, which deprived the Kishinev Jews of forty-two lives and inflicted on them a loss of at least a million rubles.

But in spite of every effort to give a clear account of the entire matter, and notwithstanding my wish to detail impartially my impressions, I can but faintly sketch the events that preceded the pogrom, which itself took place before my arrival. These I was not able thoroughly to investigate.

First, I must say that in examining, before going to Bessarabia, the secret papers of the Kishinev case in the Central Police Bureau at St. Petersburg, I found not a thing to justify the assumption that the Ministry of the Interior thought it expedient to permit a Jewish massacre or even an anti-Jewish demonstration in Kishinev. Indeed, such a sinister policy on the part of that ministry is inconceivable; for A. A. Lopukhin, formerly prosecuting attorney at the courts of Moscow and St. Petersburg and the Kharkov Court of General Sessions, was at that time the head of this department. He was invited by Plehve [also Pleve, minister of the interior 1902–1904] to reform the police according to a broad plan worked out in general outlines by Lopukhin, and submitted by him to the Minister, upon assuming office. Whenever he was charged with being a reactionary, Plehve liked to point to the

---

From Prince S. D. Urussov, *Memoirs of a Russian Governor*, ed. and trans. Herman Rosenthal (New York: Harper & Brothers Publishers, 1908), pp. 77–83, 142–65, 168–70, revised by James Cracraft. Cf. Russian original: Kn. S. D. Urusov, *Ocherki Proshlago*, vol. 1: *Zapiski Gubernatora: Kishinev 1903–1904 g.* (Moscow, 1907), pp. 155–69, 293–332, 335–43, 348–54.

1. Urusov arrived in Kishinev, capital of Bessarabia, after the pogrom had occurred.—Ed.

new department head to show that he, Plehve, was seeking men with broad views and irreproachable names. Lopukhin, indeed, enjoyed a high reputation with the judiciary, and much was expected of him. He became the victim of the Minister's policy of constantly postponing constructive work, and was dragged, against his will, into Plehve's sphere of action. The latter's moto was, "Pacification first, then reforms." Nevertheless, Lopukhin's influence more than once toned down and set within legal bounds the Minister's iron will and dictatorial ways. Plehve regarded him as a liberal, yet continued to respect him and often gave in to him. My intimacy with Lopukhin, based on our blood relationship and close friendship, enables me to assert that it is entirely inadmissible to suspect his department of engineering pogroms at that time.

I also entertain grave doubts of the authenticity of a letter alleged to have been addressed by the Minister of the Interior to the Governor of Bessarabia, and published in the English papers. This letter, guardedly but transparently, nonetheless suggested an indulgent attitude towards any active warfare carried on by the Christian populace against their oppressors, the Jews. I read this apocryphal letter only once, and that quite a while ago, and therefore report its contents with hesitation and, at any rate, only approximately. But I am deeply convinced of its spurious character. Plehve was incapable of such an unguarded act, and would in no case have ventured to leave the proof of his instigations in the hands of a governor almost unknown to him, and in whom he had but little confidence. Even had he wanted to launch a pogrom policy, he would hardly have ventured on any such step. But, setting aside the last consideration as due to my personal bias, one must keep in mind that Raaben [Urusov's predecessor] was not the proper agent to carry out any such projects. He was a very decent man, did not aspire to anything, did not court his superior's favor, and, moreover, was quite tolerant towards the Jews. He himself, losing his official position, suffered from the pogrom. For a long time he could not return to office despite the fact that the Tsar was favorably disposed towards him, and he received the opportunity of partly rehabilitating himself only after Plehve's death. Confidential agents carrying out delicate commissions do not get such treatment.

Was not the pogrom, then, a sudden and irresistible outburst of animosity accumulated long ago: retribution exacted for old wrongs, the manifestation of the spontaneous force of the common people, the mob, squaring accounts with their old-time foes, the Jews, by whom they were oppressed? I answer just as decidedly that such an explanation of the Kishinev pogrom is one-sided, incorrect, and wholly artificial.

It cannot be denied that in the provinces included in the Jewish Pale of Settlement it is especially the Jews who were the victims of plunder and violence. The main cause of this is the special legislation facilitating the view that Jews are subjects beyond the law's full protection and dangerous to the state. Of course, it may be granted that some racial peculiarities and their religious exclusiveness place them, in certain cases, in contrast to other ethnic groups. It is necessary, however, to remark that the significance of this aloofness of the Jewish people is usually exaggerated by their enemies. There are also complaints of Jewish exploitation, though this complaint is much more often heard from those who merely observe this exploitation than from those exploited. But all these suggested causes do not suffice to originate pogroms. A more direct cause is necessary for the outburst of the mob's passions. A cause sufficient to start the Kishinev massacre could not be discovered. All the information once spread of a quarrel that broke out between Jews and Orthodox Christians on Chuflin Square proved false. But I must mention other factors attending the Kishinev pogrom of 1903.

A significant role in preparing for the pogrom was played by the press, this especially by Krushevan's [a local bigwig of Moldavian origin] local paper and the St. Petersburg publications of similar tendencies, shipped to Kishinev for distribution. Issues of these papers were filled with accusations against the Jews, as well as statements and arguments calculated to stir up the passions. Krushevan's authority, in the eyes of his readers, was to a certain degree supported by the open patronage of the chief bureau of the press censorship. The effect was that the local administration was powerless to temper his anti-Semitic zeal. The bureau officials proceeded against him perfunctorily, but Krushevan's complaints against the local censorship found their ready ear. I myself heard Senator Z——, head of the bureau, express the opinion that Krushevan's tendencies and activity had a sound basis, and that from the government's point of view it was undesirable to suspend his publication. Moreover, a local resident could not help noting the government's favorable attitude towards those who endeavored to develop their "Russian spirit," in patriotic garb, thus advancing their private interests.

The monstrous manifestations of this spirit, which later created the notorious leagues of "True Russians," are universally known. Most people free from bias doubtless noticed that these "patriotic bodies" include many persons of dubious antecedents, of unenviable reputation, and utter lack of scruple. Hatred of the Jews is one of their chief articles of faith. Among those of this notorious class at Kishinev were Pronin [a successful entrepreneur of Russian origin] and company, and these individuals openly boasted themselves the mainstay of the Russian government and the pioneers of Russian interests in an alien country. It cannot be doubted that such people did enjoy a certain degree of protection from a government that regarded them as a "sound foundation," a patriotic bulwark of the autocracy and Russian ethnicity. It was equally true that in this crowd could be found any number who were ready to beat and plunder the Jews in the name of the Orthodox Church, in defence of the Orthodox people, and for the glory of the autocratic Russian Tsar.

The connection of these Russians with the police, especially with the secret service, already existed at the time I describe. The Kishinev police, as probably the police in other cities where the Jewish population predominated, noted the spirit of the center and its manifestations in their vicinity. The police, therefore, thought that a hostile attitude towards the Jews was a sort of government watchword; that Jews might be oppressed not out of "fear," but as a matter of "conscience." In connection with this, the conviction grew among the ignorant masses that hostile acts against the Jews could be undertaken with impunity. Things went so far that a legend appeared among the people that the Tsar had ordered a three-day Jewish pogrom. Early on the morning of the third day of the Kishinev riot the police captain stopped at the Skulian toll-gate a crowd of peasants who had come a long way with a business-like air, and in full consciousness of performing their duty, "to beat the Jews by order of the Tsar." I emphasize this characteristic of the Kishinev massacre. The predominant motive actuating the rioters was neither hatred nor revenge, but the enforcement of such measures as, in the opinion of some, promoted the aims and intentions of the government or, in the opinion of others, were fully authorized; or were, according to popular wisdom, the fulfillment of the Tsar's order.

Thus, in my opinion, the central government cannot shake off its moral responsibility for the slaughter and plunder that went on at Kishinev. I consider our government guilty of encouraging the narrow, nationalistic tendencies. It inaugurated a short-sighted policy, coarse in its methods, with regard to the frontier country and the non-Russian population [inorodtsam]—a policy fostering among the several ethnic groups mutual distrust and hatred. Finally, the authorities connived at the militant chauvinism. Thus are indirectly encouraged those barbarous instincts that vanish the moment the government openly announces that a pogrom founded on national differences is a crime—a crime for which an administration that condones it in any way must be held responsible. This was demonstrated in the 1880s by the famous circular of Count Tolstoi, the Minister of the Interior. Thus I regard the charge of connivance lodged against the government as proven.

But can one fully exonerate the government of the suspicion that—at least through its secret agents—it did take a direct part in the pogrom? And can it be maintained that its immediate cause was of a natural, accidental character, and not the execution of "an order"? During my service at Kishinev, and long after, I did not admit the idea that the pogrom policy had its active adherents and secret inspirers in government circles. But various events . . . helped to change my original views. Those features of the Kishinev pogrom which, thus far incomprehensible and concealed, had puzzled me, I began to refer to wires pulled by those higher up. It is possible that Lewendal, the head of the Kishinev secret police, to whom rumor attributed the immediate engineering of the April pogrom, played a double part; that, having prepared the pogrom with one hand, with the other he wrote to the Department of State Police the report, which I saw when I looked up the case at the department, giving warning of possible disorders.

This supposition is all the more admissible because of the fact that Lewendal, as an officer of the gendarmerie on the one hand, was under the orders of the Department of State Police, while on the other he had to report to the commander of the local gendarmerie. This post was then occupied by the well-known General Wahl, formerly Prefect of Police of St. Petersburg. He enjoyed an unenviable reputation, was capable of anything to advance himself in the service, and hated the Jews, who had caused him trouble at Vilno when he was governor there.

Neither did Lewendal inspire any confidence. Two matters in relation to this individual were peculiarly suspicious and interesting in connection with the present question. These were his intimacy with Pronin, and the fact that, though he was called to explain a shortage of government money after his resignation, his career was not hurt by his failure to clear himself of the charges against him. He received, on the contrary, a good position in the bureau of the Governor-General of Kiev, Kliegel, who, like General Wahl, was a court dignitary of the type that combines military and police functions. One might, finally, look still higher for the backing and inspiration of the pogrom policy.

I do not care to pass my suppositions for facts. I only point out the way in which the anti-Semitism of Plehve, Minister of the Interior, possibly voiced by him as a mere matter of conviction, could be interpreted by his colleague Wahl, who was guided, in addition, by other extra-ministerial influences. These influences might well have suggested to him the desirability of trying the experiment of applying the pogrom policy. Moreover, I showed how this hint, rolling down the hierarchic incline of the gendarmerie corps, reached Lewendal in the guise of a *wish* on the part of the higher authorities, reached Pronin and Krushevan as a *call* for a patriotic deed, and reached the Moldavian rioters as an *order* of the Tsar. The pogrom trial lasted a very long time, and I did not continue in office at Kishinev until the end. To the best of my recollection, the number of men acquitted was approximately equal to the number of those convicted. The penalties meted out were, with rare exceptions, very lenient. The suits for damages were mostly left unsatisfied, as it was impossible to prove the extent of the damage done by any one of the defendants. However, the trial largely pacified the Jewish population, having given them something like moral satisfaction. No censure was cast on the court from Jewish sources. . . .

In the fall of 1903 I was invited by the Minister of the Interior [Plehve] to state my views relative to the condition of the Jews in Russia, and particularly in Bessarabia, and to submit my opinions as to what changes were advisable in the legislation then in force concerning the Jews. To carry out the task I had to formulate and systematize my observations and the scraps of information I possessed about the Bessarabian Jews. The conclusions I reached were at that time very daring on the surface, as they practically amounted to a condemnation of the Temporary Regulations of May 3, 1882, worked out, as is known, with the active participation of Plehve as director of the department of public police. Now, after the first Duma declared itself in favor of granting Jews full civil equality as a necessity, it is strange to recall the modest hopes entertained by our Jews in 1903 of the possibility of obtaining some extension of their rights in particular cases and some "privileges," as the Jews then termed the occasional nonenforcement of special restrictive and punitive legislation. Moreover, as the Council of Ministers, in answer to the Duma, has not offered any objection on the subject of granting equal rights to Jews, it is equally strange to recall the impression produced in St. Petersburg bureaus by my modest and moderate memorial, in which no mention was made either of abolishing the Pale of Settlement or of granting Jews the right to acquire estates or hold office. . . .

Inscrutable are the ways in which the Russian government has led the Russian Jews the last hundred and fifty years. If, on the one hand, as early as the eighteenth century a Russian empress [Elizabeth] did not expect any interesting profits from the "enemies of Christ," her successor [Catherine II] in the same century saw in the Jews the sort of middle-class people from whom the state expects "much good," directing them to turn to "commerce and industry."

Special Jewish legislation in the nineteenth century was an eddy created by the confluence of different currents, Russian Jewry now unexpectedly gaining various rights and now losing them without cause. Thus, for example, in the beginning of the nineteenth century Jews residing in the Pale of Settlement were allowed to engage in the business of distilling brandy and to lease from the government the sale of liquor—at first everywhere, then in the cities only, then again in the villages. In the middle of the century the liquor industries were again prohibited to Jews in villages, but subsequently an exception was made in favor of those Jews holding a liquor monopoly in certain provinces. After the lapse of fifteen years Jews received the right to engage in the sale of liquor under the general law and to lease distilleries. Eleven years later this right was restricted, and fifteen years later followed a prohibition practically shutting out the Jews entirely from the liquor trade.

It is also of interest that the Jews were first considered desirable as merchants and manufacturers, and, some time afterwards, as farmers and land-owners. At the beginning of the nineteenth century they were authorized to buy land. In the 1830s they were spurred on by great inducements to buy land—as, for instance, by exemption from military service, the soul tax, and so forth. But afterwards these lands were taken from them. The right granted the Jews, since 1862, to buy land and other properties belonging to manorial estates was followed by a decree enjoining them from buying such lands in nine provinces. In 1882 the execution of deeds of sale in lands within the Pale of Settlement was discontinued, and in 1903 Jews forfeited the right of buying lands outside of the Pale as well.

Here is another example. At the beginning of the nineteenth century a "special committee" guarding the people against Jews demanded their expulsion from villages. Five years later another committee came to the conclusion that Jews in rural localities, far from being injurious, were, on the contrary, useful, and declared itself strongly in favor leaving the Jews where they were. In the 1820s, however, Jews were expelled from villages in four provinces, and, though discontinued in the 1830s, the expulsions were resumed in the 1840s for "military" reasons. Then Jews residing in rural localities were no longer molested until the issue of the Regulations of 1882, prohibiting Jews from settling outside of cities and towns. The then Minister of the Interior justified his prohibition on the ground of desiring to guard the Jews against the Christians.

Passing to the present time, I will confine myself to the facts and observations that formed the materials for my memorial. I shall mention first that, in 1903, the Jewish population of Bessarabia was about two hundred and fifty thousand, or approximately eleven percent of the total population of the province. Fifty years ago the Jews in Bessarabia numbered about seventy-eight thousand, but the total population of the province did not exceed seven hundred and ten thousand. Thus the increase of the Jews in this case at least is proportionate to the total increase. Bessarabia forms a part of the so-called Pale of Jewish Settlement, embracing, besides Poland, about fifteen provinces in which Jews are permitted to live. It is therefore commonly claimed that Jewish complaints of being congested in the Pale are groundless, given the vast stretch of rich lands in southwestern Russia at their disposal.

This claim is untenable. Our Jews, in reality, are not only debarred from land valuable for agricultural and industrial purposes, but are confined within very narrow limits for purposes of residence and migration.

The Regulations of May 3, 1882, prohibit Jews from settling outside of cities and towns. After this date the Jews of Bessarabia particularly received the opportunity to choose for residential purposes only ten to twelve cities and about thirty towns. It would then be more correct to say that not the whole province, but an exceedingly small area of homestead land, limited strictly by city and town areas, forms the actual Pale of Settlement of the Bessarabian Jews.

But the process of forcing the Jews out of rural localities, and the tendency to make them "cook in their own juice," did not stop with these measures. The government set to work, in a systematic and persistent manner, to herd into the cities and towns those of the Jews whom the Regulations found in the villages. For this purpose a number of towns, one after the other, were renamed "villages," and the areas of the remaining cities and towns were subjected to artificial shrinkage. The natural increase in the population of the cities did not affect the Jews, as the new city line beyond the previously incorporated plan was considered a rural locality. The Senate once had to hear a case where a Jew had been evicted from a house one corner of which projected beyond the incorporated city line.

The authorities of one province doubted the right of deceased Jews to be interred in rural localities. The Regulations of May 3, as construed by them, did not grant the right of interment to deceased Jews outside the city limits. As cemeteries were not allowed in cities, the only alternative left in this case was to enlarge, by way of exception, the rights of Jews. A lively guerilla war was at the same time conducted by the provincial authorities against Jews living in villages. Police officers scattered all over the province were coached in the aims of this campaign. As many as possible of the Jews previously living in villages were to be made new settlers and then deported to their places of registration in accordance with the May laws. It was in Bessarabia especially that the most ingenious devices to carry out the above aims were resorted to. I shall therefore cite instances.

A soldier who had completed his term returned to his parents living in a village. As an alleged new settler he was deported from the village where he had been born and had passed his childhood and boyhood, and where his parents still lived without having left their place, and was sent to the city or town where he was registered. His brother, engaged to a girl in a Jewish family living in a neighboring village, stayed for some time after the wedding with his father-in-law. In view of this he was supposed to have forfeited his right to return home. Moreover, as at that time he had no right to live at the village with his new kin, the young couple were deported to the town. Then came the turn of his father. If the latter left the village on business so that his absence was noticed and the fact of his staying in town established by police records, he was debarred from returning to his village. He was allowed to return and take with him his household effects, on condition of immediately removing to the town where he was registered.

The above case, cited here as a striking illustration of how Jewish families were eradicated from the villages and country places, reflects the systematic and constant practice of the Bessarabian authorities as regards Jews. A reference to the digest of Senate decisions will bear out this view of the matter. If such reference discloses the fact that the Senate sometimes disagrees with the local authorities, and annuls their rulings in favor of the petitioners, it must not be assumed that this fact in any way puts a check on our local interpreters of the law. These Senate decisions, relatively very few in number, were handed down years after the Jews in question had lived in the places of their registration, and, besides, were rarely carried out. The evasion of these decisions was effected by a special stratagem devised by our provincial officials. A decision of the Senate, according to which the deportation of a Jew was illegal, was construed as establishing the error of the provincial administration. But the fact that the Jews had lived outside of the village during the time between this unlawful deportation and the receipt of the Senate's decree was taken as a new case, depriving the complainant, in the long run, of the right to return to his former position.

The province of Bessarabia is pear-shaped, with its oblong side skirting the river Pruth, which separates Russia from Austria and Romania. The whole border tract, fifty versts wide,[2] was for a long time past forbidden ground for Jewish settlement. As early as 1846 the Jews were ordered out of this tract into the interior of the province, and were allowed two years within which to sell their real estate. Although this measure did not answer its purpose and the Ministry of Finance demanded its recall, nevertheless the fifty-verst tract continued to be taboo for Jewish settlers even in my time in Bessarabia. This restricted the Jews' rights of residence still more.

This policy of the government with regard to the settlement of Jews, so promptly carried out and with such consistency and success, met, of course, with many an obstacle. Jews dodged deportation in every sort of way, and even managed sometimes to reappear in the villages and country places whence they had been deported. This illegal sojourn of the Jews was partly aided by the village people themselves, who willingly gave transient Jews shelter against the authorities; the police saw in this a constant, never-failing source of income; and, lastly, a certain amount of tolerance, from which even the powers that be are not free, sometimes forcibly brought to mind the fact that the persecuted Jews were human beings for all that, and not a sort of noxious weed of which the countryside must rid itself. Nevertheless, the aims of the government were, to a large extent, realized, and the congestion of Jews in cities and towns greatly increased.

The observer is struck by the number of Jewish signs in Bessarabian towns. The houses along second-rate and even back streets are occupied in unbroken succession by stores, big and small, shops of watch-makers, shoe-makers, locksmiths, tinsmiths, tailors, carpenters, and so on. All these workers were huddled together in nooks and lanes amid shocking poverty. They toil hard for a living so scanty that a rusty herring and a slice of onion is considered the tip-top of luxury and prosperity. There are scores of watch-makers in small towns where the townsfolk, as a rule, have no watches. It is hard to understand where all these artisans, frequently making up seventy-five percent of the total population of a city or town, get their orders and patrons. Competition cuts their earnings to the limit of bare subsistence. The struggle for mere bread breeds mutual hatred and informers, and compels many Jews to resort to the vilest methods to get rid of competitors and, as much as possible, to reduce the artificial overcrowding in the trades.

---

2. A Russian *versta* = 0.67 miles.—Ed.

It is self-evident that trades and commerce on anything like a paying basis, leaving a margin above the point of mere subsistence, are unthinkable in the cities and towns where Jewish destitution reigns supreme. The result is that in such communities there is a wholesale exodus of artisans and small merchants of other ethnic groups, and along with this comes the usual complaint against the invasion of the Jews into all branches of industry and commerce to the exclusion of everybody else. Anti-Jewish discontent grows in proportion to the increasing number of Jews, preparing in this way the ground on which pogroms have of late so richly bloomed. One cannot but think that the government's anxiety for the safety of the Jews as reflected in the May laws must, to say the least, be declared a failure.

Bessarabia is one of the six provinces where Jews, after the emancipation of the peasants [1861], were allowed the right to buy and lease land. The May laws did not invalidate this right, nor was it limited until the passage of the enactments of 1903. These laws suspended for a time the execution by Jews of sale deeds and mortgages, as well as the certification of land leases entered into by Jews. The inference would seem to be that the above prohibition referred only to the validation of deeds and the certification of agreements by the courts, but did not affect the right of the Jews themselves to acquire land (for example, by ten years' uncontested and undisturbed use), as also their right to lease land by private agreement. But the Aesopian language of the law-giver was not in this case construed completely in accordance with his implied intentions. The provincial authorities, therefore, even before the publication of the supplementary regulations explaining the true intent of the May laws, prosecuted bogus land transactions, including the lease of land by proxy on the part of the Jews. At any rate, the law prohibiting Jews from purchasing and leasing land was in force "temporarily" during the twenty-one years preceding the period I am now describing, and still continues in force. But besides those I mentioned, there are many other ways in which the rights of Jews are restricted. . . .

Jews have discharged military duty directly since 1827. At first they had to furnish twenty recruits for every two thousand of the population, while Christians furnished only seven recruits. Then Jews were compelled to furnish supplementary recruits as an extra contingent, to pay off arrears in taxes, and the famous "Cantonist" schools (where Jewish boys twelve years old were trained for the army) came into being. It was only with the accession of Alexander II [1855] that the enrollment of Jews was established on the general plan. However, the Jews did not very long enjoy this equality with regard to military duty. First, a set of restrictions debarred Jews from holding military appointments and from enrolling in the privileged branches of the army; then Jews were subjected to a whole array of restrictive regulations as regards exemptions due to the situation of the family, as regards examination on account of physical immaturity, and in respect to family registration lists; last came the provision according to which a Jewish family was to be held responsible to the extent of paying a fine of three hundred rubles in case any of its members subject to military duty failed to report. This responsibility held, even though the rest of the family proved that they could not in any way be instrumental in compelling the members in question to be present for military duty.

As a result, the Jews in Russia are required to give a greater quota of men for the army than are other Russian subjects. A comparison of the government's report with the data of the census of 1897 shows that in the enrollment lists of 1900 the number of Jewish recruits was 5.49 percent of the total Jewish population of the Empire, while the rate for other recruits was 4.13 percent.

All are familiar with the trite plea about the "systematic evasion of military duty on the part of the Jews" advanced every time the Jews and the army are in question. Indeed, the Jewish recruits unnerve their military examiners to the point of despair by the cunning devices to which they resort to secure exemption from military service. The Colonel in command of the regiment stationed at Kishinev, my fellow-member at the military board, once expressed to me his authoritative opinion on the subject. "No wonder," said the Colonel, "that the Jews dodge military duty. Their position in the army is very hard. Imagine a Jew from an Orthodox family of small means suddenly transported to our barracks. His manners, his dialect, his abashed awkwardness make him a laughing-stock. Everything about him is dreadfully strange, wild, and terrible. He is the object of strenuous efforts to 'break him in'; his habits and religious mode of life are unintentionally violated in the ordinary course of military life. Sometimes on the very first day of his soldier life he is compelled to gulp down cabbage soup with pork and be at drill on Saturday. His kin and friends think him polluted, and begin to shun him. He is forsaken and lonely, his spirits are dejected. We, on our part, to tell the truth, pay little attention to the condition of Jews in our army."

The Colonel might have added that the Jewish soldiers could not become sergeant-majors, serve in the [elite] guards or frontier troops, and only a percentage of them may serve on the musical staff of a regiment. Standing in line in defense of his country, the Jew continues to be a man divested of full civil rights. . . .

In Russia, as is well known, Jews, excepting physicians, are practically not admitted to government service. They are especially barred from the zemstvo assemblies and electoral meetings, from the mayorality, from membership on different boards elected by the zemstvos or the cities. A Jew cannot be presiding officer of the artisan boards, even where, as in Bessarabia, almost all the artisans are Jews. The number of Jewish members on boards of aldermen must not exceed one-tenth of the whole board, and these Jewish aldermen are appointed by the city council from a special list made up by the city executive board. The admission of Jews to committees of boards of trade, to merchants', burghers', and artisans' guilds, is subject to rigid restrictions.

At the beginning of the twentieth century we have entirely forgotten the dictum of the great Empress [Catherine II] enunciated at the close of the eighteenth century, that "if society sees fit to elect Jews to office, they cannot be hindered from entering upon the duties imposed upon them by these offices." But this is not all. Since about the middle of the 1880s the Ministry of the Interior, when incorporating private associations and stock companies, has required them to insert in their bylaws a section restricting or altogether prohibiting the participation of Jews in the direction of such corporations. It is worthy of mention that the tendency of the Ministry indicated in this order, counter to common-sense, became especially pronounced in the case of corporate undertakings where the shareholders were Jews.

The last fact, a curious example of the government's petty captiousness, is otherwise not very essential, as every association can easily secure a figure-head directorate consisting of Russians.

The Jews are far more handicapped in educational opportunities. The government long ago closed the official Jewish governmental schools of the first and second class, and replaced them by the Jewish elementary schools, grudgingly opened and meagerly equipped. This latter type affords an education only to a trifling percentage of the Jewish children of school age. The majority of such children get their elementary education in the traditional Jewish schools from Hebrew teachers. Owing to the lack of Jewish schools for training teachers, the teaching in Jewish primary schools is of a very low grade. Besides, Jewish teachers are forbidden to teach Russian to their pupils, so that reading and writing Russian is almost out of reach of most Jewish children of the lower classes. An investigation conducted in 1900 by a special commission appointed by the Odessa city board disclosed the fact that in Southern Russia only eleven percent of the Jewish population could read and write Russian. . . .

Indeed, many educational institutions, intermediate as well as higher, are entirely inaccessible to Jews. Jews are not admitted to teachers' seminaries, theatrical schools in the capitals, the St. Petersburg Electrotechnic Institute and the Institute of Ways and Communications, the Moscow Agricultural College, the Moscow College of Civil Engineers, the Medical Academy, the Kharkov Veterinary Institute, and other schools that need not be enumerated here. The admission of Jews to all the high schools and universities is limited to from two to ten percent. In connection with this it must be kept in mind that this quota is not the only obstacle to education with which the Jews have to contend; there are other difficulties, as will be seen from the case within my recollection that arose in Bessarabia in 1904. The son of a Kishinev Jew of small means, a very bright, industrious boy eleven years old, excellently prepared for admission to the second class of Kishinev Technical High School, was not admitted on account of the quota. His father, not sparing labor or expense in order to give his son an education, thought of sending him to the Technical High School located in the village of Kamrat. After strenuous intercession with the district board of education and the local school council, his boy was granted admission provided there was no opposition on the part of the administrative authorities to allow him to reside at Kamrat. Armed with this certificate, given by the director of the school, the father applied to the provincial authorities for permission to place his son at Kamrat, to room and board with one of the teachers, who agreed to take charge of him. The authorities refused to grant the permission asked for by the petitioner, on the ground that Kamrat was a rural locality situated at a distance less than fifty versts from the Romanian frontier. . . .

Jewish paupers, invalids, and cripples are denied state care and aid. All this, taken in connection with the general civil and political disability of the Jews, would be intelligible if they did not bear the burden of state and public taxation and duties in the same way as the rest of the Russian people. But far from enjoying any privilege in the matter of taxation, the Jews on the contrary have borne and bear now the burden of special taxes. As early as a century ago the Jews paid in taxes twice as much as did the Christians. The whole Jewish community was held account-able for arrears of Jewish taxpayers, and later Jewish merchants were made collec-tively responsible for the arrears of Jewish burghers. When the soul tax was abolished, and the Jews were put on an equal basis with the Christians in relation to state taxes, they still continued to pay special dues—the box tax and the candle tax—preserved up to the present time. The first tax is collected from every "kosher"-slaughtered beast or fowl, and from every pound of "kosher" meat; the second, from the candles lighted in the synagogue. . . .

The second charge brought against the Jews—indeed, the most prevalent one—is the so-called "exploitation of the people." It is regarded as an axiom that the Jews, by fair and foul means, drain the vitality of the people around them; that all the Jews do is get rich in violation of the law and at the expense of others; that they do not produce things of economic value, do not increase the national wealth, but only pocket the product of the toil of others. Jewish money bothers a great many people. This money is the object of many hands stretched out both at home and in the capital, in an attempt to divert, so far as possible, at least a part of the national wealth that found its way to the Jews back into circulation among the Russian people. As far as this is concerned, they are not mistaken who attribute to the Jews a "corrupting" influence upon their surroundings; most of the officials, especially the police, whose function it is to enforce the laws against Jews, are doubtless in close touch with the Jewish purse.

I should like to approach timidly the question of exploitation by Jews. I say timidly, not because I am afraid to advance an opinion not coinciding with the one in vogue, but because of the limited range of my observation along the lines in question, and because my acquaintance with the doings of the Jewish masses was of short duration. I shall endeavor to describe conscientiously what I saw and heard in Bessarabia for a year and a half. . . .

The Jews in Bessarabia did not show any tendency to acquire extensive land-holdings. In spite of the fact that they have enjoyed the right to acquire property in land for some decades past and its price has been very low, their total holdings in Bessarabia aggregate only sixty thousand desyatins out of the four million and sixty thousand desyatins making up the area of the province.[3] About three thousand desyatins of this land are owned by Jewish colonies, giving homes to five hundred and forty families. The rest is distributed among a few individual owners.

The estates of Bessarabian Jews are not in any way peculiar enough to make them stand out from the general run of landowners' estates. None of the Jewish estates seem to be especially noted for their methods of farming, nor, on the other hand, did I hear any complaints against the owners of such estates made by their peasant neighbors. Nothing in my time disturbed the peaceful, neighborly relations between Jewish land-owners and the working-class. Nor were any agrarian misunder-standings on that score reported to me in regard to the past. One could notice

---

3. A *desiatina* of land = 2.7 acres.—Ed.

rather the efforts of the Jewish land-owners to shield themselves from the reproach of exerting pressure on the peasants and workers. At any rate, it must be admitted that the Jewish land-owners did not furnish material to bear out the charge of exploitation and extortion of exceptional incomes. . . .

Jewish colonists have squatted on their land in Bessarabia since the 1730s. Their holdings average five and a half desyatins per farm, while the average size of a separate peasant farm in Bessarabia is about eight desyatins. These colonists cannot be given credit for any special service to the cause of the country's farming. Their preference, however, for crops requiring intensive soil culture—tobacco-growing, vineyards, and orchards—completely tallies with the local conditions of small holdings. In this line of farming, calling for punctual, constant labor, a certain grade of mental development and enterprise, the Jews can hardly be considered harmful. There would be no ground for apprehension even if Jews should receive the opportunity to own, for the same purpose, a greater amount of land in small allotments. Intensive cultivation of high-priced plants and fruits in Bessarabia is so far developing slowly, and needs, therefore, to be encouraged rather than restricted from fear of possible excessive competition.

Jewish landholding in Bessarabia is of so trifling and innocent a character that it does not give rise to censure even among the sworn enemies of Jews in general and of the Bessarabian Jews in particular. Far more grave and acute is the question of the leasing of large landed estates by Jews.

The conditions of Russian agriculture did not create in our country a class of stable land tenants engaged in farming by right of succession or by bequest. Our frequently changing tenant avoids investing his capital for making improvements on the land of another. He carries on his farming in a rapaciously wasteful manner, and at the expiration of his lease he returns the estate to its owner in an exceedingly ruined condition. Bessarabian land-owners very often lease their land for long terms without incommoding the tenant by making his tenure conditioned on his cultivating the land with his own stock, on the use of fertilizers, or, in general, on the adoption of any definite agricultural system. The Bessarabian tenant is therefore not so much a farmer as he is middleman and a responsible agent for subletting separate sections of the estate to the neighbors in need of land. His object is to get, during his lease-term, a maximum amount of differential rent from his peasant sublessees.

Such use of land on lease cannot deserve encouragement in any respect. The estates in such cases deteriorate, the relations with the neighbors become still worse, and, therefore, most cases of agrarian friction usually centre around lands held on long-term leases by separate persons.

A Jew wishing to go into the business of leasing estates has to stand a lot of trouble and spend a great deal of money. First, he has to find, for a consideration, a fictitious tenant to make for him the agreement with the land-owner, after which the actual tenant behind this straw man enters his service as a clerk. But such a comparatively simple method of getting hold of an estate is not always feasible, as the Jew usually has no right to live at the place where the estate leased by him is located. In such a case the Jew is compelled, in addition to the bogus tenant, to keep at his own expense a bona-fide agent who is to act for him under his control and instructions. This the tenant manages to do by frequently coming down to the estate as a "transient staying on business."

The above succession of maneuvres does not, of course, remain a secret, as the countryside does not brook concealment of any kind, and the Jew is therefore bound to become a tributary at the same time both of the local police and of the other powers—namely, the township and the village authorities. At stated times he pays in his tribute, sanctioned by custom and order, to ward off judicial prying into his illegal agreement, and to be secure against a chain of prosecutions that may embarrass and totally destroy all his farming ventures.

However, in spite of legal obstacles and additional onerous outlays, amounting to two rubles per desyatin for small estates, most of the estates leased in Bessarabia get into Jewish hands. There are persons who are convinced of the detrimental influence exerted by the Jews upon the rural population, and entertain no doubt as to the constant success achieved by Jews through their rapacious methods. To these persons the cause of the above anomaly is very clear, and it runs like this: "The Jews evidently know how to 'work' the neighboring population with such success, wring out the life-blood of their victims with such force, that the income they get is more than enough to cover all sorts of extra outlays." Such an explanation is very attractive on account of its simplicity, and completely tallies with the current notion of Jewish exploitation; but impartial and attentive investigations do not bear out such a hasty conclusion.

The question of the Jewish practice of leasing land by proxy attracted my attention at the very beginning of my career as Governor. I could not clearly explain to myself in what way Jews succeeded in inducing land-owners to agree to a practice absolutely forbidden by the law. I therefore used every opportunity to learn in detail the stipulations of such secret agreements. My information grew in proportion as the range of my acquaintance among land-owners widened, and I found that the majority of the local land-owners, including the most biased anti-Semites, always preferred a Jewish tenant to a Greek, Armenian, or Russian. Thus the K——s, a family well known to us in Kishinev, consisting of many separate and independent members, heartily abhor "those Jews in general." Their estates, however, they lease exclusively to Jews at fourteen rubles a desyatin, although tenants of other nationalities offered them sixteen rubles. I have known cases where land-owners, tempted by a high price, refused to lease to their old Jewish tenants, but afterwards regretting this seized the first opportunity to restore their former tenants.

If it were possible to start something like an investigation in St. Petersburg among the owners of estates located in the southwest the results obtained would prove still more curious. Members of the State Council, Senators, even Ministers, who have been instrumental in introducing restrictive Jewish legislation, stoop to leasehold by proxy. I say this not to their disparagement, as experience along this line had long ago proved the viciousness of the May laws. According to this view there can be nothing reprehensible in the fact that one person desires to lease his property to another ready to take it. It is conceded by most that Jewish tenants are remarkable for their faithful, exact payment of rent, and generally for their conscientious fulfillment of all the terms of the agreement. But what is considered still more valuable is their business methods. A Jewish tenant runs his farm business in such a way as to avoid any friction with neighbors, and affords no ground for litigation and disputes, endeavoring to settle every difficulty in a peaceful way, without resort to the courts or the authorities. A Jew will not collect his debts by such methods as seizing the grain in the stacks, selling his neighbor's property, and the like. He bides his time, jogs the debtor's memory, chooses the right occasion, and gets his bill without the aid of the police or the sheriff. He does not mar the mutual relations of owner and neighbor, and creates no basis for disputes and hostility. On account of all this, I have, for example, never received or heard any complaints from the people of the province against Jewish tenants, while we had some litigation in connection with difficulties in which either landowners themselves, or especially non-Jewish tenants, were principals. I think it entirely correct to say that Jewish land lease in Bessarabia is an evil in so far as it is land lease and not because it is Jewish. At any rate, this conclusion will not be questioned either by the land-owners or by the peasants of Bessarabia. . . .

I had many occasions to observe at Kishinev the easy-going Moldavian [peasant] hauling to market a wagon load of hay or grain, and then stretching out in the shade to smoke his pipe. The bustling, nimble Jew, fussy and fidgety, button-holed prospective customers praising the farm produce, ran the round of the stores with the samples, and finally, having found a customer and having agreed with him about the price, fairly dragged up his principal to have his accounts settled. Pocketing his money, the Moldavian, with an air of good-natured gravity, handed his agent a silver coin of fifteen or twenty copecks and went home.

Many people are ready to call—and, indeed, do call—such acts of Jews outrageous exploitation; but I fail to see where, in this case, the detrimental influence of the agent entered, so long as he did not pool his interest with the buyer and did not swindle the seller out of his price. It is impossible to watch over the country people to such an extreme degree as if they were feeble-minded children, and there is no ground for generalizing separate cases of deceit and fraud, and identifying them with hypothetical traits supposed to be specifically Jewish.

On my visits to the villages I tried to ascertain the part that Jews play in buying up the farm products on the spot, and spoke a good deal on this subject with the peasants. In such cases, I gathered from their repeated declarations, to debar such buyers from free access to the country places was of no advantage to the peasants; indeed, the seller derives more advantage from a sale made at home than under market conditions. In the first case, he has his grain in his granary or cellar, and is free to sell or bide his time; he is thus master of the situation. In the market he finds himself dependent upon a variety of conditions: fluctuations in price, accidental variations in shipment, weather and road conditions, and, finally, pooling of buyers. The persecutions, then, to which Jewish buyers driving around the country districts are subjected, on the plea of protecting the country people, seemed to me just as little intelligible as are a good many other things in the ill-fated Jewish question. . . .

In the above enumerated special lines of Jewish activity in Bessarabia I failed to find any facts that would invite the charge against the Jews of systematically robbing the people. With all my efforts to connect individual cases within my knowledge of abuse on the part of Jews, to reduce them to a system, to detect in them planned-out methods—so to speak, the "national mission" of the Jews—I was forced to the conclusion that the Bessarabian Jews, be they land-owners or tenants, merchants or agents, may eat their hard-earned bread with as unruffled a conscience as the rest of the people of our land. Besides, I convinced myself that the most fiery denunciation of Jewish exploiters is to be traced in Bessarabia to the ranks of those who had not taken the trouble to find out how the exploited themselves feel on the subject. Indeed, the alleged sufferers do not, in most cases, understand those who plead for them, and before the invariably negative answer as to the weight of Jewish oppression can be drawn from the peasants, it has to be made plain to them in what this traditional oppression is supposed to consist.

However, there are in Bessarabia lines of occupations that, being in themselves objectionable, constitute, as it were, a Jewish specialty. It must be conceded that the cases arising in connection with the smuggling business and complaints against usury are checkered with Jewish names.

I intentionally set these two questions apart from the whole number of occupations where Jews come under our observation, as they deal with acts that constitute crimes punishable by law. Besides, the activity of Jewish smugglers is detrimental to the state treasury, and not to the surrounding population, to whom such smuggling of goods is even profitable. . . .

Usury in Bessarabia is not, in my opinion, more extended than elsewhere in the Empire. I have not heard at Kishinev stories of fabulous exploits, of discounting loan shops and notorious pawnbrokers, who, as in Moscow, furnished themes for novels and tales. But still the practice of lending money at extortionate rates flourishes in Bessarabian towns and villages, and it must be admitted that the majority of the local usurers are, to judge by the opinion of the Bessarabian judiciary, of Jewish descent.

I was especially interested in illicit credit transactions carried on in the villages. I knew, from my experiences in the central provinces, that rural Russia, deprived of the facilities for obtaining small credit, is working out a special type of usurers who manage to get on short loans, in cash payments and in service, a yearly profit of over one hundred percent. . . . Essentially the same phenomenon I observed in Bessarabia, with the only difference that here the loan rates were more definitely fixed and the transactions were reduced to writing in the form of notes and bills. Jewish money-lenders are in the habit of taking duplicate notes, one of which bears the character of forfeit for breach of contract. The latter, in case of prompt payment of the debt, is returned to the debtor, and the interest is in this instance quite moderate. But the debt often becomes overdue, and the debtor fails to pay his creditor. It is, however, necessary to add that the local courts have long ago discounted this Jewish practice of taking double notes, and very willingly and easily nonsuit such claims when testimonial evidence or the court's opinion warrants it. I must notice in this connection that cases of collecting a debt on the duplicate note in case of accurate payment are extremely rare. As a rule, the forfeit note is returned without any objection in this regard. Jewish money-lenders, as admitted by all, strive to preserve the honor of the profession intact.

As a result the following may be said about money-lending in Bessarabia: Admitting that competition in this field has left the Jews to a great extent as conquerors, it is a matter of great regret that usury in general is so wide-spread and that the war against this evil is confined to court fines without passing into constructive effort to organize cheap rural credit. What the people would gain, however, if the majority of money-lenders of Bessarabia were Greeks or Armenians, remains unknown. . . .

One of the newest German philosophers, Dühring, has decided that Judaism is no religion, but a race, a tribe inimical to all civilized nations of the present day. Dühring finds that there is no possibility of abandoning Judaism and at the same time of preserving Christian traditions. He is of the opinion that "Christianity originated with the prophets of the Old Testament," and finds that a Christian cannot seriously be an anti-Semite. Hence he proposes abandoning the Christian religion in order to get rid of Judaism.

This last view will hardly meet with approval among the masses of the people in Russia. The ancient reproach of our people against the Jews, that they "crucified Christ," indicates the condemnation of this historical fact in Russian religious consciousness, but it does not justify the conclusion that the Russian people are religiously intolerant. On the other hand, we find in the mass of Russian Orthodox believers an instinctive fear of Judaism and that unaccountable hatred which comes from the realization of an ever-progressing, irrepressible victory on the part of a foreign and hostile force. The agitation against the Jews, which has grown stronger of late, and which travels from above to beneath, from the center to the periphery, from the palaces to the cottages, is firmly seized upon by the cottage population, who, filled with hatred, listen questioningly to the threatening warnings of their official protectors and worthy advocates. It can well be said that our people are not inclined to "idle gossip," that the thought of equal rights is as foreign to them as, for example, the equal rights of women, the suggestion of which in the Duma evoked despairing cries from the peasant deputies. It may even be admitted that the agrarian reform, which now holds the attention of the peasants, causes here and there a man to pay some attention to the voices of those who are taking pains to impress on the agricultural population the idea that the Jews are striving for a general distribution of land, so that they may gain possession of the best pieces for themselves. But this impression is only temporary, and I incline to the opinion that it is not a salient cause of the national opposition to projects of general political equality that provide, among other things, for the liberation of the Jews from the restrictions now laid upon them by the law.

For myself personally the Jewish question has become clear. . . . I am not so much appalled at the fate of the victims of some particular attitude of Russian officialdom towards the Jews as at the process of thought which has brought our average officials half-unconsciously to employ a special moral code against Jews, who are without legal rights. Less harmful for the Jews than for Russia is, in my opinion, this dulling of the moral sense which appears in the case of men appointed as guardians of the law, and which is regarded as a sure sign of a hopeful career and of proper qualities of subordination.

Is the dignity of the Russian army increased by the anti-Semitic propaganda favored by the military officials, and carried on by aid of the well-known brochures and appeals to safeguard the military reputation, and is the attitude of officers and soldiers during the Jewish pogroms in keeping with that military dignity?

Is it not more just to call those hate-envenomed sermons against the Jews, which the clerical authorities allow in the churches only because the civil authorities have likewise placed the Jews beyond the law, a decomposition of the Christian spirit?

Therefore the legal recognition of equal rights of the Jews does not shock me in the least. I see in it the possibility of freeing ourselves from the struggle against the Jews, which is ruining us. If we must struggle against the influence of the Jews, let the fight be on the road of peaceable competition and natural development. I am convinced that the Russian people will lose thereby neither its material possessions nor its spiritual wealth.

## FURTHER READING

I. Michael Aronson, *Troubled Waters: The Origins of the 1891 Anti-Jewish Pogroms in Russia* (1990)

Muriel Atkin, *Russia and Iran, 1780–1825* (1980)

Seymour Becker, *Russia's Protectorates in Central Asia: Bukhara and Khiva 1865–1924* (1968)

Norman Davies, *Heart of Europe: A Short History of Poland,* Chapter IV (1986)

George Demko, *Russian Colonization of Kazakhstan, 1896–1916* (1969)

James Forsyth, *A History of the Peoples of Siberia: Russia's North Asian Colony, 1581–1990* (1992)

James T. Flynn, "Uvarov and the 'Western Provinces': A Study of Russia's Polish Problem," *Slavonic and East European Review,* 64 (1986), 212–236

Dietrich Geyer, *Russian Imperialism: The Interaction of Domestic and Foreign Policy, 1860–1914,* trans. (from German) Bruce Little (1987)

Anders H. Henriksson, *The Tsar's Loyal Germans: The Riga German Community: Social Change and the Nationality Question, 1855–1905* (1983)

John Hiden and Patrick Salmon, *The Baltic Nations and Europe: Estonia, Latvia and Lithuania in the Twentieth Century* (1991)

John-Paul Himka, "Young Radicals and Independent Statehood: The Idea of a Ukrainian Nation-State, 1890–95," *Slavic Review,* 41 (1982), 219–235

Peter Hopkirk, *The Great Game: The Struggle for Empire in Central Asia* (1992)

Taras Hunczak, ed., *Russian Imperialism from Ivan the Great to the Revolution [1917]* (1974)

Charles and Barbara Jelavich, eds., *The Education of a Russian Statesman: The Memoirs of Nicholas Giers* (1962)

D. G. Kirby, ed., *Finland and Russia, 1808–1920: From Autonomy to Independence; A Selection of Documents* (1975)

John D. Klier, "The Jewish Question in the Reform Era Russian Press, 1855–65," *Russian Review,* 39 (1980), 301–319

———— and Shlomo Lamboza, eds., *Pogroms: Anti-Jewish Violence in Modern Russian History* (1991)

David MacKenzie, *The Lion of Tashkent: The Career of General M. G. Cherniaev* (1974)

————, "Turkestan's Significance to Russia", *The Russian Review*, 33 (1974), 167–168

Steven G. Marks, *Road to Power: The Trans-Siberian Railroad and the Colonization of Asian Russia, 1850–1917* (1991)

Anna T. Pienkos, *The Imperfect Autocrat: Grand Duke Constantine Pavlovich and the Polish Congress Kingdom* (1987)

Richard Pipes, "Catherine II and the Jews: The Origins of the Pale of Settlement," in Pipes, *Russia Observed: Collected Essays on Russian and Soviet History* (1989), 59–82

Alexis E. Pogorelskin, "*Vestnik Evropy* and the Polish Question in the Reign of Alexander II," *Slavic Review*, 46 (1987), 87–105

Toivo U. Raun, "The Latvian and Estonian National Movements, 1860–1914," *Slavonic and East European Review*, 64 (1986), 66–80

Anthony L. H. Rhinelander, *Prince Michael Vorontsov: Viceroy to the Tsar* (1990)

Hans Rogger, *Jewish Policies and Right-Wing Politics in Imperial Russia* (1986)

————, "Russian Ministers and the Jewish Question, 1881–1917," *California Slavic Studies*, 8 (1975), 15–76

Michael Rywkin, ed., *Russian Colonial Expansion to 1917* (1988)

S. Frederick Starr, ed., *Russia's American Colony* (1987)

Orest Subtelny, *Ukraine: A History*, Part Four (1988)

B. H. Sumner, *Russia and the Balkans, 1870–1880* (1937, 1962)

————, *Tsardom and Imperialism in the Far East and the Middle East, 1880–1914* (1940, 1968)

Ronald G. Suny, *The Making of the Georgian Nation: From Prehistory to Soviet Rule* (1989)

Edward C. Thaden, *Russia's Western Borderlands, 1710–1870* (1984)

————, ed., *Russification in the Baltic Provinces and Finland, 1855–1914* (1981)

Georg Von Rauch, *The Baltic States. The Years of Independence: Estonia, Latvia, Lithuania, 1917–1940*, trans. (from German) Gerald Onn (1974)

Wayne S. Vucinich, ed., *Russia and Asia: Essays on the Influence of Russia on the Asian Peoples* (1972)

Piotr S. Wandycz, *The Lands of Partitioned Poland, 1795–1918* (1974)

Alan Wood, ed., *The History of Siberia: From Russian Conquest to Revolution [1917]* (1991)

Steven J. Zipperstein, *The Jews of Odessa: A Cultural History, 1794–1881* (1986)

# Conclusion

The last tsar, Nicholas II, with his family in the Crimea.

# Industrialization

In the concluding Part IV of this book, various aspects of life in Russia during the last decades of the Imperial regime are examined. Chapters 11, 12, and 13 pay special attention to major economic and social developments which, while historically important in their own right, also contributed to the gathering political crisis that brought down the regime in 1917 (the subject of Chapter 14). Regrettably, there simply is not room here for a separate chapter on urbanization as such (see Further Reading, works by Bradley and others) and for another on the spread of education at both the elite and popular levels. Educational development in late Imperial Russia was an indispensable factor in the government's drive to industrialize. But it may also be considered an underlying cause of the growth of opposition to the regime, fueling as it did the political demands of a growing educated public while facilitating—through the printed word—communication between that elite and ordinary workers and peasants, increasing numbers of whom were learning how to read. (On this subject, see the essay by Victoria Bonnell below, and the books by Eklof, Brooks, and McReynolds listed in Further Reading, Chapter 12.)

## E S S A Y S

Industrialization was clearly the most important of the major economic and social developments occurring in the last decades of the Imperial regime in Russia. Essentially a process of large-scale economic modernization undertaken and directed by the Imperial government in order to ensure that Russia remained a Great Power, industrialization in Russia, as elsewhere, had widespread social and political consequences. It fostered urbanization and the growth of new social classes—an industrial proletariat and a new class of capitalists—in addition to the rapid economic growth that the government sought. It also fostered gross inequalities of wealth between the social classes as well as gross disparities in economic development among the Empire's various regions and ethnic groups (see the essay by Andreas Kappeler in Chapter 10). By the early years of the twentieth century the Russian Empire had become, by various measures, one of the foremost economic powers in the world. But within the Empire social, ethnic, regional, and attendant political tensions, which the government conspicuously failed to assuage, twice reached the breaking point. Industrialization, in short, was also an underlying cause of the revolutions of 1905 and 1917.

Industrialization in late Imperial Russia is discussed in the essays that follow, beginning with a penetrating critique of government policy by Arcadius Kahan, late professor of economics and history at the University of Chicago. Victoria E. Bonnell, who teaches sociology at the University of California, Berkeley, then describes Russia's new working class.

# The Government's Role

## ARCADIUS KAHAN

If we were to reconstruct a blueprint of the Russian government's goals and priorities for industrial development in the late nineteenth century, it would include the following: (1) development of a network of internal transportation, (2) stabilization of the ruble in foreign exchanges through convertibility and the building-up of an export surplus as a prerequisite for enabling the Russian government to borrow abroad, and (3) stimulation of the development of new industries in Russia and their protection [through high tariffs] in their "infancy." Given the relative success of Russia's industrialization during the end of the nineteenth and beginning of the twentieth centuries and the important role that the government played in this effort, there is no justification for outright rejection or condemnation of Russian government economic policies. There were, however, serious shortcomings in particular government policies, and the presumed effects that they had upon the industrialization process were not always desirable. This essay is a modest attempt to reexamine Russian government policies on the assumption that the industrialization of Russia was a continuing goal of the state . . . beginning with the 1880s and one of relatively high priority. The implication of the analysis is that if some of the defects of the state's policies had been avoided, the process of industrialization in Russia would have proceeded at least at as fast a pace and the economic costs to Russian society would probably have been smaller.

The following features of Russian economic policies have been selected for discussion: (1) fiscal policy and its impact upon the domestic demand for industrial goods in Russia; (2) government borrowings and their impact upon private investment in industry; (3) government tariff policy, its fiscal characteristics, its protective features, and the welfare loss to the consumers resulting from the tariff; and (4) monetary policy and the possible costs to the Russion economy. For the discussion of the first point data for the period 1885–1913 were used, for the second and third points the period 1880–1900 was examined, and for the fourth point the period 1897–1913 was pertinent.

From Arcadius Kahan in *The Journal of Economic History*, vol. 27 no. 4 (December 1967), pp. 460–77. Reprinted by permission of Cambridge University Press.

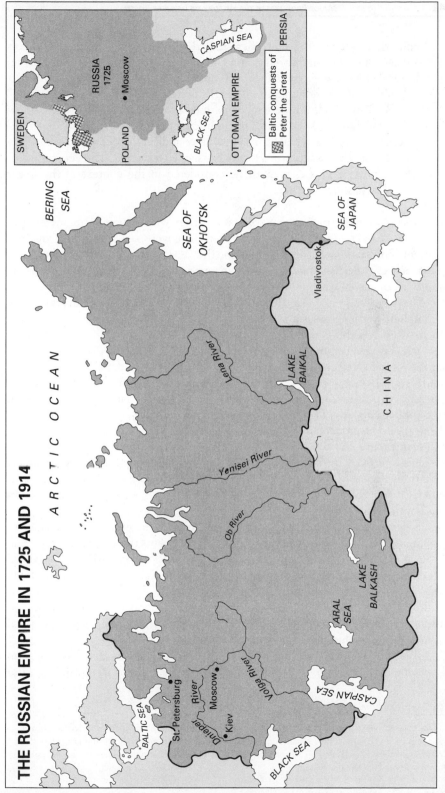

# THE RUSSIAN EMPIRE IN 1725 AND 1914

**ARCTIC OCEAN**

**BERING SEA**

**SEA OF OKHOTSK**

**SEA OF JAPAN**

Vladivostok

Lena River

LAKE BAIKAL

Yenisei River

Ob River

CHINA

ARAL SEA

LAKE BALKASH

CASPIAN SEA

BLACK SEA

St. Petersburg

Moscow

Kiev

Dnieper River

Volga River

BALTIC SEA

**Inset map:**

SWEDEN

POLAND

RUSSIA 1725

• Moscow

CASPIAN SEA

BLACK SEA

OTTOMAN EMPIRE

PERSIA

Baltic conquests of Peter the Great

Neil M. Heyman, *Russian History* (McGraw-Hill's College Core Handbook, 1993)

Implicitly perhaps it is assumed here that the underlying complicating factors and problems of Russian industrialization can be attributed to the state of Russian agriculture[1] and its slow progress in transforming and modernizing itself, and that state policies which were committed to the preservation of some "traditional" features of Russian agriculture were incompatible with a bold program of industrialization. Thus, whether right or wrong, the implicit assumption is that the industrialization process in Russia required a much more radical and constructive policy toward agriculture than was pursued by the Russian government. The very tentative conclusions drawn in this essay must be considered in the context of the larger issue raised by these assumptions.

The process of industrialization accelerates either when there is an increase of domestic demand for industrial goods or when the government conducts a vigorous policy of industrialization. In my opinion, the second alternative was chosen in Russia because the first was not given an opportunity to assert itself under the conditions of the existing political regime in Russia.

When one talks about an increase of domestic demand for industrial goods, one implicitly assumes a sustained rise in per capita incomes over a certain period, which stimulates the demand for goods with a relatively high income elasticity, although perhaps also with a substantial price elasticity. I assume that an increasing demand for industrial consumer goods would tend to stimulate their mass production; that this would be accompanied by a fall in their prices due to economies of scale; that import substitution would follow; and that as a secondary effect the demand for capital goods would increase. If the economy had any long-run comparative advantage in the production of these capital goods, their domestic production would tend to increase.

This type of industrialization, perhaps idealized and simplified in its "organic," gradual development, was not, however, permitted to be tried simply because government policies assigned higher priorities to fiscal revenues than to increases in consumption and the accumulation of personal savings.

Tables 1, 2, and 3 and the accompanying textual material are an attempt to estimate the size of government taxation which represents the volume of taxes paid to the government (except for other forms of taxation levied by various local government authorities, which constituted an additional 15 percent of the taxes paid to the government) and their changes over time.

In order to have some yardstick to judge the size and impact of taxation in Russia, we ought to compare it with two measures, that of per capita national income and the value of retail trade. . . .

Given the fact that the larger part of peasant incomes were still in the form of incomes in kind, mostly as agricultural products consumed within the farm

---

1. The most important economic issue in Russia, namely the agrarian problem, was left out of the discussion for two reasons: first, because its complexity does not permit a short summary; second, everyone interested . . . will find an admirable analysis in Professor Alexander Gerschenkron's essay [on the subject (see Further Reading)].

TABLE 1    Per Capita Taxation (in rubles)

| Year | Total Taxes | Excise Taxes |
|------|-------------|--------------|
| 1885 | 6.41 | 2.43 |
| 1890 | 7.12 | 2.83 |
| 1895 | 8.15 | 3.29 |
| 1900 | 8.83 | 4.10 |
| 1905 | 9.53 | 5.59 |
| 1910 | 11.79 | 6.69 |
| 1913 | 11.43 | 7.34 |

TABLE 2    Relationship Between Per Capita Taxes, National Income, and Value of Retail Trade

| Year | Taxes as Percent of National Income | Taxes as Percent of Retail Trade |
|------|-------------------------------------|----------------------------------|
| 1885 | 12.8 | — |
| 1899 | — | 25.9 |
| 1900 | 13.2 | 27.4 |
| 1905 | — | 27.6 |
| 1910 | — | 32.3 |
| 1913 | 12.85 | 27.4 |

households, and that local taxes ought to be added, the burden of taxation upon the majority of the population becomes more significant.

One should also not leave out of sight the skewness of the income distribution in Russia[2] as well as the fact that excise taxes [indirect taxes on consumption, etc.] constituted a large share of the total burden of taxation. Excise taxes of the "Russian type" were regressive in their nature and thereby intensified the burden upon the lower income groups.

Thus one would have to conclude that the burden of taxation left relatively little room for substantial increases in demand for goods and services of the type that would stimulate industrial development. This explains also why some Russian industries would frequently "hit the ceiling" of effective demand for their products, [given] the limitations upon the population's purchasing power.

The volume of taxes when compared with the gross value of output of Russian industry provides an interesting insight [into] the quantitative relationship of the two. Although it indicates a sharp decline in the ratio of taxes to the gross value

2. About 22 percent of the national income was accounted for in 1909–1910 by about 0.9 percent of the economically active population, according to the computation of the Ministry of Finance. . . .

TABLE 3     Taxes as a Percent of the Gross Value of
            Industrial Output

| Year | Ratio |
|------|-------|
| 1885 | 51.3 |
| 1890 | 46.2 |
| 1900 | 27.3 |
| 1905 | 29.2 |
| 1910 | 34.4 |
| 1913 | 25.5 |

of industrial output, nevertheless it does not decrease to a level at which the fiscal policies would have a minor effect upon the demand for industrial goods, as can be surmised from Table 3.

. . . [One] would have to acquiesce in the conclusion that it was the government which, by taxing the incomes of the consumers, deprived Russia of an alternative pattern of industrialization, thus usurping for itself the role of an active participant and stimulant of this process. It is therefore incumbent upon the economic historian to investigate the basic tendencies of government economic activity in order to detect the elements which facilitated or intensified the process of industrialization. The primacy of fiscal policies in the government's activities in Russia appears to be established beyond any reasonable doubt.

To expect that fiscal considerations would be overruled by long-run industrialization policies is too much to expect of most governments, and to expect it from the government of Tsarist [Imperial] Russia is to misinterpret the nature of this particular political regime, and thereby to have to assume that its subsequent fall was the work of a *deus ex machina*.

Nevertheless, historians tend often to disregard the existing features of the reality of government policy and to pass judgment on the basis of general pronouncements or misleading government statistics. Let me illustrate this contention by [an] example from the work of a generally respected historian of the period under consideration, Theodore Von Laue, who was victimized by his admiration for the Russian minister of finance [Sergei Witte, 1892–1903] and by his misreading of Russian budget reports.

How much the government spent for its various economic activities in these years may come as a surprise. Roughly totaled, the appropriations for all economic ministries (Finance, Agriculture, Communications) and the service of the government debt (contracted largely for railroad construction) amounted to over 52 percent of the combined ordinary and extraordinary budgets in 1894 and 55 percent in the following year. The army and navy combined claimed about half as much, nearly 29 percent in 1894, but only 22.5 percent in 1895. What was left went to the administrative agencies, the Ministry of Interior with its extensive organization and its police, diplomatic service, schools and universities, the Church, the courts of law, the Ministry of Justice and the Imperial household. Obviously the economy rather than defense was the beneficiary of Witte's financial management.[3]

A closer inspection of the data used by our historian reveals that the distribution which he constructs is grossly misleading, for two reasons. First, the official budget figures he uses include the gross expenditure of such public enterprises as the government railways, and later of the state-operated alcohol monopoly; these expenditures should obviously not be classed as expenditures embodying an economic policy. Second, Von Laue overlooks the fact that the category of expenditure on administration includes only a part of the overhead expenses of the government apparatus; much of the expenditure of the so-called "economic ministries" was for pure administration. The fallacy of Von Laue's method can be illustrated by the fact that, applied to the budgets of 1887 and 1888—before Witte assumed control of policy—it shows that respectively 52.5 and 52.2 percent of total government expenditure was on the economic ministries. The same method when applied to 1913 reduces the share of defense expenditures from 36 per cent of the total, to 24.4 percent of the total budget expenditures.

An official distribution of the 1903 government budget expenditures (still Witte's brainchld) gives the following shares of different expense categories:

| Category | Per cent |
| --- | --- |
| Economy and cultural expenses | 16.4 |
| Payment for the interest and redemption of the public debt | 22.2 |
| National defense | 36.0 |
| Administration | 25.3 |

One could probably also argue with Von Laue about whether railroad construction or various wars were primarily responsible for the growth of the national debt and its service charges.

In addition, the category labeled Economy and cultural expenses included for 15 years during the period 1892–1912 the large figure of a total of 691.7 million rubles of famine relief and food reserves purchases (of which 565.2 million was direct famine relief). How productive such an expense was from the point of view of industrialization is difficult to assess. It is, however, even more difficult to absolve the government of Russia and her fiscal and economic policies from coresponsibility for the necessity of such government expenses. There is no doubt that the total government spending in manufacturing and mining never even came close to the expenses of famine relief.[4]

The fiscal policy of the government would be justified from the point of view of the objectives of industrialization if the forced savings siphoned off by the fiscal

---

3. Theodore H. Von Laue, *Sergei Witte and the Industrialization of Russia* (1963), pp. 100–101.
4. As many as a million peasants died in the great famine of 1891: see Richard G. Robbins, Jr., *Famine in Russia 1891–92: The Imperial Government Responds to a Crisis* (1975).—Ed.

authorities had been used to a large extent to finance industrial investment. *The specific criticism which can be brought up against the Russian government is that only a minute part of its budget expenditures went directly for purposes of developing the industrial sector* [italics added].

The area of the heaviest financial support by the government was that of railroad construction. Major criticisms of the Russian railroad network as a form of social overhead pointed out that much of it was constructed to serve the needs of troop movements in case of war mobilization or actual war rather than the economic needs of freight and passenger service. Even in view of the recent attempts to revise downward the previously exaggerated claims of the magnitude of social savings by railroads, the Russian railroads beyond any doubt contributed to the process of economic and cultural transformation of the country.

However, when we analyze the sources of financing railroad construction, we find that borrowing abroad and internal borrowing were the overwhelming sources of financing railroad construction rather than straight budget financing. It is difficult to find one's way in the maze of Russian railroad statistics for a number of reasons, but the rough approximation for expenses in direct railroad construction and for subsidizing private railroad construction would not exceed by much the figure of a total of one billion rubles for the 1880s and 1890s. For a comparison, this corresponds very closely to the government custom revenue from imports of tea, coffee, alcoholic beverages, salt, and herring. If we take into account that the interest payments on railroad bonds were paid from the gross revenue of the government-operated railroads and certain surcharges for their services, the expenditures by the state budget proper were not excessive.

But while the expenditures for railroad construction were the government's single largest item for industrialization purposes, the direct subsidies to industrial entrepreneurs did not come to even a close second, within the total expenditures for "development of the economy," for the last two decades of the nineteenth century.

In addition, the substitution of government demand for goods and services from the industrial sector, as well as the flow of government investment, were highly irregular and uneven. This had an adverse effect upon the economy, which moved in an erratic fashion, intensifying in some instances the business cycle and adversely affecting business expectation in some crucial branches of industry. This created a situation in Russia by which the growth of the industrial capital and output was all but smooth; among its results were the peak of the late 1890s and the virtual industrial stagnation of 1900–1906.

One of the often voiced criticisms of the Russian pattern of investment, typical of many criticisms of less developed economies, and in the minds of the critics justifying strong government intervention, is the relative low preference on the part of the investors for providing funds for the industrial sector of the economy.

As in many criticisms of this type, there is a grain of truth in this observation which calls for further investigation. There are two phenomena requiring additional scrutiny. One is that a substantial part of the savings was provided by successful landowners under conditions of an imperfect money market and banking system.

This might explain, in part at least, the preference for investment in land mortgages, under conditions of rising land prices. The greater familiarity with the agricultural sector, the relative security of funds invested in mortgage loans, the favorable attitude of the government to this particular type of loans expressed by its interest in the working of the "Bank of the Nobility" and the "Peasant Bank," made this type of investment a powerful competitor to industrial investments. But one ought not to forget that during the period 1880–1900 the government was not a newcomer in the money market, but a competitor for investable funds of long standing.

Unfortunately we have very sketchy and imprecise estimates from which to judge the relative competitive situation of the demand for investment in industry. The data are insufficient even to state with any degree of certainty whether we are dealing with a unified market or with a few separated markets for investable funds. However, some available estimates will indicate the general trend . . . [and] we can roughly distribute the investment flow among three major claimants: (1) the government, (2) the land mortgage banks and companies, and (3) the corporations engaged in industrial, mercantile, and other nonagricultural activity. Although the third group is amorphous, we could assume that in broad categories the increase of the stock of capital of such enterprises and institutions was a favorable element for the process of industrialization. . . .

The role of the government as a competitor for savings appears very clearly from [these estimates]. While during 1882–1890 the government borrowed 784 million rubles, out of a total of 1,552 million, or 50.7 percent, during the subsequent period the government borrowed 505 million out of 2,907 million or only 17.4 percent. Therefore, one is inclined to believe that not only might the preference for gilt-edge government bonds in the domestic market have declined in favor of other types of securities, but that the decreased government demand for savings in the domestic capital market (which was in part substituted by heavy borrowings abroad) enabled the Russian industrial entrepreneurs to borrow more freely. As imperfect as the underlying estimates may be, they tend to indicate that the difficulties (real or alleged) encountered by industrial entrepreneurs in obtaining the capital funds for profitable investments depended to some extent not upon the presence, but upon the absence, of the government as a borrower in the domestic money market. That its stepping down as the major claimant of investable funds indirectly helped the industrial entrepreneurs is also hinted at by the imperfect data at our disposal.

Russian tariff policy was as much revenue- as protection-oriented, the upward tendency in tariff rates being sustained by fiscal needs as much as by the clamor for protection. Of course there were differences in the timing of both factors, as well as distinctions between the tariffs on various groups of commodities, but the general nature can be established without much difficulty.[5]

---

5. The fiscal motives for producing revenue were variously estimated as being responsible for from two-thirds to three-fifths of the total custom revenue.

Custom duties as a per cent of total direct and indirect taxes collected by the government increased from 18.2 percent in 1881 to an average of 27.8 percent for the years 1897–1900. The revenue features of the tariff were most clearly reflected in the rates of the tariff on imported foodstuffs, which increased during the same period from 30.3 percent of the value of imports in 1881 to 69.4 percent during 1897–1900. The chief sources of revenue among the foodstuffs were tea, coffee, alcoholic beverages, tobacco, salt, and herring, thus complementing the state revenues from the excise taxes. That the fiscal features of the tariff policies were not limited to the importation of foodstuffs becomes evident in view of the parallel upward tendency of tariff rates on raw materials and semimanufactured goods.

This of course represented a conflict between short-run fiscal interests and the objectives of industrialization, since the tariff tended to increase the costs of such raw materials, imported or domestically produced, like cotton, wool, iron, etc., to the domestic manufacturing industries. The rising costs in turn "justified" the increase in tariff rates for cotton yarn, woolen cloth, metal products, etc. The result of this chain reaction was that fiscal considerations of the tariff contributed to the raising of the protective umbrella over an increasing number of manufactured goods, tools, machinery, and capital goods in general not excluded.

Although the government stimulated the development of some capital goods industries (like locomotive and railroad equipment, shipbuilding, etc.) by direct placing of supply contracts, a tariff was levied on some capital goods imports, presumably in the expectation of establishment or expansion of domestic output. In the meantime, a period which in some cases lasted rather long, Russia's capital goods importers experienced the paradox of having to pay higher prices for the type of imports which were to foster industrialization. This lack of refinement and discrimination in tariff policies (and many examples can be cited to support this claim) cannot be attributed either to ignorance or to bureaucratic routine, but it resulted from the overriding priorities of the fiscal needs.

No one would deny that the Russian tariff had a number of stimulating effects upon the growth of domestic industrial output, employment, and incomes. This is indisputable. Very seldom, however, have economic historians asked the question, how much did it cost the Russian consumer, the ultimate payer of the tariff?

There are two ways of measuring the impact of the tariff. One is simply to assess the custom revenues and add them on to the costs of the consumers. From the point of view of economic theory, however, custom duties, being a government income, cannot be assumed to constitute a loss to the consumers' welfare.

Another method, however, allows us to make some estimates of consumers' welfare losses. The tariff levied upon foreign imported goods raised their cost to the Russian consumers and allowed the domestic producers to charge for domestic substitutes a price equal to the foreign price plus the tariff.

By artifically increasing the price of foreign imports to the consumers the tariff distorted the allocation of consumer expenditures (the consumption cost of the tariff); by providing a subsidy to domestic producers the tariff distorted the allocation of resources that would have taken place under the conditions of a free market (the production cost of the tariff).

TABLE 4    Consumption Cost and Custom Revenue
of Selected Commodities, 1897 (in millions
of rubles)

| Commodity | Consumption Cost | Custom Revenue |
|-----------|------------------|----------------|
| Pig iron | 44.1 | 2.6 |
| Iron | 18.6 | 15.5 |
| Steel | 17.5 | 3.4 |
| Cotton | 12.3 | 27.8 |
| Cotton yarn | 20.0 | 1.6 |
| Total | 112.5 | 50.9 |

The consumption costs may be estimated as follows. . . . The selection of the commodities for which consumer losses were calculated was dictated by the ready availability of data and the relative importance of the commodity for the process of industrialization.

The preliminary results of the calculation indicate that the consumption cost of the Russian tariff on coal was negligible for the period 1880–1900 but that the costs to the consumers of the products of the metal and cotton textile industries, the two major industries of Russia, were considerable. Table 4 summarizes the results of the calculation (in millions of rubles). These results should be compared with the custom revenue from the enumerated commodities for a particular year.

Even if one assumed that the estimates of consumption cost tend to have an upward bias—the foreign goods imported being of higher quality—because of the use of domestic prices in the calculation instead of the average between domestic and foreign prices, or because the actual demand elasticity was less than unity, it would still probably be correct to assume that in terms of the loss to the economy in the long run, consumers' losses exceeded the short-run benefits to the treasury. Despite benefits in the growth of industrial employment (which involves the wage differential between industrial wages and alternative, let us say, farm wages) one would suspect that for some industries, at least, the tendency would be for the consumption cost to increase.

With regard to the production cost, in 1906 the Russian economist N. N. Savvin estimated the cost of the tariff to the Russian consumers of manufactured goods in 1900. He estimated the custom duties for imported manufactured goods as 140.7 million rubles and the "excess payment" for domestically produced goods as 237.7 million rubles, or about 22.1 percent of the estimated net output of the Russian manufacturing industries in 1900. . . . Although no attempt was made to estimate the consumption or production costs of the tariff beyond 1900, the circumstantial evidence pertaining to both the metal industries and to some branches of the cotton textile industries would indicate that the continuing tariff protection during the decade to come did not succeed in bringing them nearer to a position of competitiveness. The first decade of the twentieth century was marked by a growth of monopolistic tendencies in the metal-producing industries.

Monopolistic-type activities, such as price-setting collusion and quota-setting for output, became widespread in the Russian iron and steel industries with the organization of such producers' associations as "Prodamet," "Krovlia," "Prodvagon," and "Provoloka." Although attempts were made to organize the cotton textile producers in order to maintain prices and to divide markets, they were less successful than in the case of the iron industries.

Thus the tariff policies of the government, by imposing losses upon the consumers, not only limited the demand for industrial goods, but in addition shielded the producers from real competition, which would have forced them to innovate and decrease production costs. By allowing the producers to engage in monopolistic practices, the government permitted them to inflict more losses upon the consumers.

As more data become available to the economic historian, it will perhaps become possible to calculate with greater precision the costs (direct and indirect) of the government's tariff policies. At the moment we can only state that the protective features of the tariff were a mixed blessing, interpretation of which requires a balance sheet that would record the benefits as well as the costs.

One of the goals of Russian economic policy was to achieve a state of convertibility of its currency into gold at a fixed price. After a number of years of accumulation of substantial gold reserves by the Treasury and the State Bank, a monetary reform was carried out in August 1897. The new notes of the State Bank were convertible in gold on demand at the rate of 66.67 gold copecks for a paper ruble. Under the new arrangement the gold reserves for the bank notes were set at 50 percent for the amount below 600 million rubles and at 100 percent for any sum above 600 million. In addition, the mint started to put into circulation an increasing volume of gold and high-value silver coins.

The benefits of the monetary reform, apart from the elimination of the fluctuating exchange rate, were basically a greater facility in foreign borrowing for the Russian government and an influx of private foreign capital into Russia.[6]

Many economists and historians have sung praises to the Russian government or to the architects of their monetary policy for the introduction of the gold standard in Russia. Very few, if any, have asked about the economic costs of the gold standard as it was applied in Russia during the subsequent 17 years. . . . During the period 1897–1913 on the average an excess of 443 million rubles in gold was held by the State Bank over and above the requirements of its statutes. In fact if one would take into account the fact that gold in coins and reserves increased from 1,131 million in 1897 to 2,185 million in 1913 . . . , or by over a billion rubles, one could perhaps question the wisdom of such policies.

---

6. One ought not to exaggerate and to attribute the net increase on both accounts solely to the monetary reform. It coincided with greater availability of capital in the international money market on the one hand, and with the strengthening of the French-Russian political alliance, which opened up the Paris money market for Russian government and private securities on the other. It was also due to the fact that relative to other countries interest rates in Russia still remained high, and the returns on Russian securities and on foreign investment in Russia were still higher than elsewhere.

However, if the Russian government had instead kept a gold reserve of 66.7 percent of the total currency in circulation, the average yearly holdings in gold could have been less by about 590 million rubles. If we assumed that variations in the note circulation within each year would require about 100 million rubles in gold as an internal reserve, and an additional hundred million rubles deposited in foreign banks to facilitate balance of payments problems, it would still leave us with an excess gold reserve of about 400 million rubles yearly on the average. When invested instead of kept as a reserve by the State Bank, even at a 5 percent rate of interest, the income yield during the 17 years of the existence of the gold standard would have been at least 340 million rubles, a sum which a country as capital-poor as Russia could not have ignored. Yet the price of 20 million rubles per annum was not an unacceptable price to pay for the convenience and stability of operating under the gold standard.

From the above discussion the following tentative conclusions may be drawn: (1) There existed an inherent conflict between the fiscal interests and demands of the Russian state and the requirements of a vigorous long-range policy of industrialization. In most cases when choices of substantial magnitude of resources were involved, the primacy of short-run fiscal interests seemed to prevail. (2) To resolve the conflict, at least in part, the Russian government attempted to obtain funds from abroad, both in the form of straight government borrowings and foreign investments in Russian industries. (3) As a means of facilitating borrowing from abroad the Russian government was willing to pay the price imposed by its conservative monetary policy and was probably correct in following this course. (4) The success of the effort to secure foreign capital relieved the government of dependence upon internal savings and allowed for a substantial increase in private funds for industrial development. (5) The tariff policy of the government had a very significant fiscal impact which could be added to the direct impact of excise taxes upon the majority of Russian consumers. (6) The losses in welfare to the Russian consumers imposed by the tariff were considerable in comparison with the employment effects and benefits enjoyed by the protected industries. (7) The burden of taxation to support the Russian political regime appears to have been the chief obstacle to a more vigorous industrial development of Russia.

# The Labor Force

## VICTORIA E. BONNELL

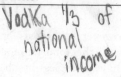

*Vodka 1/3 of national income*

The program of state-sponsored industrialization that got under way in Russia at the end of the nineteenth century brought about many changes in the nonagricultural economy, but none was so dramatic and fateful as the proliferation of factories and the appearance within them of a large and highly concentrated group of industrial workers.[1] As elsewhere in Europe at an earlier time, the advent of a factory system was inextricably connected to the expansion of two major industries: textiles and metalworking.

With more than half a million workers, the textile industry (cotton, silk, wool, and linen) was the largest single employer of factory labor in the Russian Empire in 1897. Textile mills could be found in many parts of Russia, but the industry was heavily concentrated in the cities and factory villages of the Central Industrial Region, an area encompassing six provinces in the heart of European Russia. Metalworking, the second largest employer of factory labor, accounted for about 414,000 workers at the end of the 1890s. This industry was centered in Petersburg province in the northwestern region of the country and, to a lesser extent, in Moscow province.

Both the textile and metalworking industries in Russia were distinguished by their unusually high concentration of workers per enterprise; in both branches there were many firms that employed more than one thousand workers. But here the similarities end, for the composition of the labor force in the two industries differed greatly. Whereas textile mills relied mainly on unskilled and semiskilled labor, there was a predominance of skilled workers in metalworking plants at the turn of the century. As many as four out of every five workers in some metalworking enterprises belonged to the ranks of skilled labor. Furthermore, the textile mills employed a large number of women and children; the labor force in metalworking, by contrast, was almost entirely male.

There were many differences between metal and textile workers—differences that are described in the selections that follow. Yet these two groups of workers shared one common characteristic that distinguished them from other segments of the urban laboring population. Most metal and textile workers were employed in enterprises that the government classified as "factories," and by the end of the

From Victoria E. Bonnell, ed. *Russian Worker: Life and Labor Under the Tsarist Regime*, excerpts from pages 3–17, 20–30. Copyright © 1983 The Regents of the University of California Press. Reprinted by permission of the University of California Press.

1. The precise definition and classification of the factory worker need not detain us here. Suffice it to note that before 1901 the government designated as a "factory" any manufacturing enterprise that employed fifteen or more workers or utilized engine-powered machinery. In 1901, the definition of a factory was changed to include only manufacturing enterprises with twenty or more workers, regardless of the type of machinery. These criteria were not, however, applied consistently by the government. . . .

nineteenth century factory workers were subject to a special set of laws and regulations setting them apart from the rest of the labor force.

As early as 1835, the tsarist [Imperial] government enacted legislation regulating the terms and conditions of factory employment, but implementation and enforcement of this law proved ineffectual. A similar fate befell the law of 1845, which banned factory night work for children under twelve years of age. In 1882, new legislation was promulgated restricting the work time of children and juveniles in factory enterprises. This law also established a Factory Inspectorate whose responsibilities included surveillance of firms to ensure compliance with government legislation. In 1885, additional laws were enacted prohibiting children under seventeen years of age and women from night work in cotton, linen, and wool mills. Further legislation the following year expanded government regulation of the labor contract, strengthened criminal sanctions for violations, and enlarged the role of the Factory Inspectorate.

A decade later, widespread labor unrest in St. Petersburg prompted the government to enact another major labor law. The legislation of June 2, 1897, restricted the length of the workday in factory enterprises to a maximum of eleven and a half hours for all adult workers on weekdays and to a maximum of ten hours on Saturdays and on the eves of holidays. Although overtime work was subsequently ruled permissible, this law—together with its predecessors—gave factory workers a degree of protection and regulation that was not extended to any other segment of the laboring population.

By the turn of the nineteenth century, factory workers, with their special juridical status, occupied a growing place in the manufacturing sector of the Russian economy. But in some branches of manufacturing, factories were still relatively undeveloped, and most production was carried on in small workshops based on traditional artisanal trades. Artisanal workers represented a broad and amorphous group in Russian cities around 1900. No official data are available on the total number of artisanal workers in the country as a whole, though in key cities they represented a very sizable and diverse group. Thus, in St. Petersburg around the turn of the century there were 150,709 artisanal workers compared with 161,924 in factory enterprises. In Moscow, the country's second largest urban and manufacturing center, artisanal workers (151,359) outnumbered the factory population (111,718).

Within the artisanal labor force, the largest single group was employed in the apparel trades. The 1897 census reported that there were 346,000 garment workers in the Russian Empire as a whole, nearly all of them employed in small firms that did not qualify as "factories" within the terms of government regulations. In cities such as St. Petersburg and Moscow, about one out of every three artisanal workers was employed in the apparel trades. Other large contingents of artisanal workers could be found in leather and shoemaking, woodworking, printing, metal and machine tool building, and in the skilled construction trades.

The large and variegated group of artisanal workers in urban Russia included many craftsmen who labored for long hours under sweatshop conditions in subcontracting shops and garrets, as well as a much smaller contingent employed in workshops that retained many of the features of preindustrial handicraft production.

Among the latter group were some craftsmen who still belonged to an artisanal guild at the beginning of the twentieth century.

Introduced into Russia in the early eighteenth century by Peter the Great, Russian guilds never attained extensive jurisdiction over production and distribution or the exclusive corporate privileges of their counterparts in Western Europe. When industrialization gathered momentum in the second half of the nineteenth century, Russian guilds maintained their juridical status but suffered a steady decline. By 1900, only 28 percent of the artisans in St. Petersburg still belonged to a guild, and a mere 16 percent in Moscow. For most handicraft workers at the turn of the century, therefore, guild organizations and regulations had little practical consequence.

Whereas the government regulated the terms and conditions of labor for factory workers, artisanal groups lacked comparable protection at the beginning of the twentieth century. This situation . . . had especially grave consequences for those employed in the large apparel industry where pressure for increased production led to the proliferation of subcontracting shops producing on a putting-out basis for wholesale and retail marketing firms.

Apart from the large segment of factory and artisanal workers there was a substantial group employed in sales and clerical occupations. These occupations can be divided into five major subgroups: salesclerks, cashiers, bookkeepers, clerks, and apprentices. Although their number in the Russian Empire cannot be ascertained on the basis of available data, in St. Petersburg there were more than 109,000 sales-clerical workers at the turn of the century and in Moscow about 86,000. Salesclerks represented the largest single category, with nearly 60,000 in St. Petersburg and more than 40,000 in Moscow. Thus, approximately one-half of the sales-clerical workers in these cities were employed as salesclerks in retail, wholesale, industrial, and cooperative firms. About 90 percent of them were male.

Toward the end of the nineteenth century, expansion of the economy led to a proliferation of commercial establishments. Just as there was a growing concentration of capital and labor in large factory enterprises, so the world of commerce witnessed the appearance of the first large retail establishments: department stores such as Muir and Merrilees. Similar trends can be discerned in other facets of commerce. But despite growing concentration, most transactions at the turn of the century still took place in small shops, sprawling public markets, street stalls, and by means of vendors and peddlers whose horse- and hand-drawn carts formed a colorful part of the urban landscape.

Around 1900, most Russian workers had been born in the countryside and had spent their early years in a village. The sojourn from the countryside to the city or factory was a familiar occurrence in European Russia. Rural poverty, overpopulation, and land scarcity drove peasants from their native villages in search of work; still others migrated in the hope of finding opportunities for a better life. Departure from the countryside frequently took place for the first time at an early age. [See the reminiscence of one such journey, by Kanatchikov, in Documents, Chapter 12.]

At the turn of the century, an apprenticeship system existed in virtually all skilled occupations, occupying a far more important place in working-class life than is generally acknowledged in the literature and exerting a formative influence over workers' conceptions of class and status in Russian society. Apprenticeship remained mandatory in virtually all artisanal trades and in numerous other skilled occupations carried on in a factory setting, in sales establishments, and in other sectors of the economy.

Many different types of workers served an apprenticeship in tsarist Russia, though the nature and conditions of this training were far from uniform. Kanatchikov's apprenticeship in patternmaking, like most craft training in a factory setting, proceeded on a more or less informal basis over a two-year period. . . .

Apprenticeship in apparel and other artisanal trades and in sales occupations generally began earlier in life than factory training and lasted for a longer term. . . . [It] was not unusual for ten-year-old boys and girls to serve an apprenticeship in workshops or commercial firms. An oral contract concluded between parents and the shop owner committed these children to the employer's tutelage and authority for a period normally lasting from three to five years. When this term had been completed, an individual was entitled to perform adult work. The traditional certification procedure in artisanal trades, involving a formal demonstration of craft skills, applied only to the small minority of guild members at the beginning of the twentieth century.

For tailors, salesclerks, and many other artisanal, commercial, and service occupations, the function of apprenticeship had undergone a subtle but important change in the closing decades of the nineteenth century. Shifts in production processes, an increasingly complex division of labor, and the spread of subcontracting and commercial activity induced many shop owners to rely increasingly on the unpaid labor of apprentices as a surrogate for adult labor while at the same time diminishing the instructional aspect of apprenticeship.

Whereas some peasant youths entered an apprenticeship when barely into their teens, there were many others between the age of twelve and fifteen who performed unskilled factory work without the prospect of advancing to a more skilled and specialized occupation. As in Western Europe, child labor was especially prevalent in the textile industry where many production tasks could easily be accomplished by boys and girls.

For youths recruited fresh from the countryside, early entry into the labor force had diverse effects. Those who entered an apprenticeship were more likely than others to find themselves inducted into the adult subculture of the factory or shop and to develop, albeit gradually and perhaps tenuously, a new self-image that corresponded to their growing skill as "a patternmaker," "a tailor," or "a salesclerk." To a far greater extent than child and juvenile laborers in factories and mills, young apprentices developed an awareness of their position as urban workers, a self-image still comparatively rare in Russia at the turn of the century. As a result of these experiences, youths such as Kanatchikov began to acquire a new identity as urban workers, in contrast to the peasantry from which most had come.

The process of identity formation was, of course, extremely complex in a society that officially discouraged the creation of a permanent stratum of urban workers, disengaged once and for all from their peasant roots. Thus, a great many workers maintained some connection with the countryside at the beginning of the twentieth century, and nearly all of them had to come to terms in one way or another with the vexing problem of their continuing ties to the village—its traditions, expectations, and social networks. The way in which a worker dealt with this problem depended, in large measure, on the position that he or she occupied in the *urban* work hierarchy.

Peasants entering the workplace for the first time encountered a highly stratified arrangement. Above them stood various authority figures. The factory director, as described by Pavlov [see Documents below], wielded vast power over his employees, controlling the destiny of hundreds or even thousands of individuals. The shop owner was no less powerful, however, and within the confines of the workshop or sales firm the employer could be a merciless tyrant. . . . In addition to bosses and managers, many firms (both large and small) employed intermediary figures of authority that included supervisors and technical personnel, foremen, assistant foremen, and work crew leaders. In a factory, the foreman occupied a unique place in the worker's everyday life. As [one worker put] it, "The foreman represents that lever . . . which presses on the worker the hardest." Workers were thus subordinated to many different types of direct and indirect authority at the workplace.

The labor force itself was highly stratified, primarily along the lines of skill and occupational specialization. Hierarchical subdivisions existed among various industries and trades. In St. Petersburg and Moscow, the sharpest contrast in the factory milieu was between the two major industrial groups: metalworkers and textile workers. . . . Status differences between the two groups were keenly discerned by contemporaries, as illustrated by the recollections of another Petersburg metal-worker, Aleksei Buzinov:

> Metalworking plants and textile mills were concentrated in our Nevskii district. At that time [about 1900], the difference between metal and textile workers was like the difference between the city and the countryside. . . . Metalworkers considered themselves aristocrats among other workers. Their occupations demanded more training and skill, and therefore they looked down on other workers, such as weavers and the like, as an inferior category, as country bumpkins: today he will be at the mill, but tomorrow he will be poking at the earth with his wooden plough. The superiority of the metal-worker and everything that it implied was appreciated by all.

Each industry or occupation also had an internal labor hierarchy. At the summit stood a small but highly skilled substratum such as metal patternmakers, fabric cutters in the garment industry, and clerks in fashionable retail stores catering to a prosperous and exclusive clientele. Below them were ranged a varity of skilled occupations—metalfitters, lathe operators, and smelters in metalworking, tailors employed in custom-made men's and women's tailoring shops, clerks in jewelry shops, and machinists in textile mills. They were followed by semiskilled and unskilled workers.

The labor force in skilled occupations was further subdivided into apprentices (*ucheniki*) and qualified adult workers. In artisanal trades, the latter group was further subdivided into journeymen (*podmaster'ia*) and master craftsmen (*mastera*). This arrangement still remained in effect at the turn of the century in both guild and nonguild workshops despite the fact that most journeymen could anticipate only lateral mobility and not vertical ascent into the ranks of workshop owners.

Prior to the 1880s, several designations for adult factory workers were utilized by the government, factory management, and the workers themselves. The term *masterovoi* (derived from the guild designation *master*) referred to the skilled worker whereas *rabochii* applied to semiskilled and unskilled workers alike. Among skilled metalworkers the word *rabochii* had such pejorative connotations that it was often used as a term of opprobrium.

Workers attached enormous importance to these designations and were bitterly opposed when factory management sought to alter them by eliminating the category of *masterovoi*, reclassifying skilled groups as *rabochie*, and applying the term *chernorabochie*[2] to the remainder. . . . [The] workers' preoccupation with matters of status differentiation [is clear, and social] interaction among individuals was determined, in large measure, by one's position in the status hierarchy. Thus, Kanatchikov recalls that when he was still a mere apprentice, the metalturner Rezvov would not condescend to socialize with him. This situation changed, however, when Kanatchikov himself became a fully qualified craftsman.

Highly attentive to nuances of difference among occupational specializations, Petersburg metalworkers responded to a 1908 survey with a list of more than one hundred separate occupational categories to identify their place in the industry. That workers keenly felt these differences can be documented from memoirs such as Buzinov's account of his apprenticeship at the Nevskii shipbuilding plant in St. Petersburg in the late 1890s:

> The more I grew into the factory family, the clearer became to me its heterogeneity, even within the boundaries of one plant. Soon I began to realize that workers in the machine shop—the metalfitters and lathe operators—looked down on me. After this, the inferior position of workers in the "hot" shops—the smelting, rolling, and blacksmith shops—became obvious. . . . I was especially struck by the absence of equality among workers. Now it seems a minor matter, something not even worth remembering. But at the time, it painfully wounded my pride. I didn't want to be worse than the others. I thought that if only I could master the skills of metalfitting and lathe operating, everything would fall into place.

The hierarchical subdivisions within the laboring population acquired particular significance for contemporaries in part because the minority of skilled workers stood out so sharply from their unskilled and semiskilled counterparts. In appearance and demeanor, skilled workers exhibited their differential status. Kanatchikov describes the urbanized patternmakers who wore fancy clothes and whose bearing conveyed their consciousness of their own worth. In a similar vein . . . tailoring shop workers and subcontract workers dressed quite differently. Whereas the former wore suits, stylish boots, and different coats according to the season, the subcontract workers could often be found wearing nothing but a calico shirt, faded pants, and long underwear.

The visibility of status differences shaped the ways workers thought of themselves and related to others, as well as their treatment by managerial personnel.

---

2. The prefix *cherno*, meaning "black," was affixed to the word *rabochii* to signify the lowest position within the ranks of workers.

The external appearance of the job applicant, [one worker] reports, affected the foreman's disposition. "His form of address will depend on your clothes. If you are well dressed, he might address you politely." There were many pressures on workers, moreover, to discard their peasant attire and to assume the clothing and demeanor of the urban milieu. A worker newly arriving in the city from the countryside could not fail to discern the status and dignity associated with an urbanized appearance. Kanatchikov recalls that "skilled workers looked down on me with scorn, pinched me by the ear, pulled me by the hair, called me a 'green country bumpkin' and other insulting names." Workers (including some skilled elements) who retained their peasant clothing—they "wore high boots, traditional cotton-print blouses girdled with a sash, had their hair cut 'under a pot,' and wore beards that were rarely touched by the barber's hand"—were called "gray devils" by their more urbane and sophisticated coworkers.

Even in the remote factory villages of the Central Industrial Region observed by Pavlov [see Documents below], workers were highly sensitive to exterior propriety and eager to purchase perfume, fine soap, fashionable jackets, and patent leather shoes. These pressures mounted in occupations that required regular contact with the general public. Thus, workers in sales and clerical jobs required attractive urban attire to obtain and maintain their employment, a situation that drove some women to seek supplementary income through prostitution.[3]

By the turn of the century, a growing group of workers in all sectors of the economy had succeeded in acquiring specialized skills and an appearance and demeanor that betokened their status and position in the world of the factory or shop. Yet a majority of these skilled and urbanized workers remained tied in various degrees to their native villages. The persistence of these ties represents a distinctive feature of the formative period in the development of the Russian working class.

The relation between the worker and the village assumed a variety of forms, ranging from permanent urban workers with no ties whatsoever to the countryside to semipeasant workers with ongoing ties to their native villages. In general, workers with the highest levels of occupational specialization and skill were the least likely to have continuing ties to the countryside.[4] Seasonal industries such as tailoring present a partial exception to this pattern since many skilled tailors departed annually for their villages when production subsided. Even here, however, the rate of seasonal return to the village was lower among the relatively more skilled retail tailoring shop workers than among subcontract workers.

The number of permanent urban workers was steadily increasing by the turn of the century. Data for Moscow show that Moscow-born workers comprised a minority of the labor force in 1902 (7 percent of the factory workers, 10 percent of the artisanal workers, and 20 percent of the sales-clerical employees). A considerably

---

3. On prostitution, see Richard Stites, *The Women's Liberation Movement in Russia: Feminism, Nihilism, and Bolshevism, 1860–1930* (1978), pp. 182–185.
4. By way of illustration, 65 percent of the highly skilled Moscow typesetters had no ties to the village in 1907. Among the less skilled lithographers and bindery workers, only 24 percent and 28 percent, respectively, had relinquished their connection to the village. . . .

larger group had migrated to Moscow and spent ten years or longer in the city (34 percent of factory workers, 37 percent of artisanal workers, and 34 percent of sales-clerical employees). Combining the two groups, we find that 41 percent of the factory workers, 47 percent of the artisans, and 54 percent of the sales-clerical employees either were permanent residents or had spent a decade or more living and working in Moscow by 1902.

Some of the workers, moreover, may have lived in more than one city. Kanatchikov is a case in point. After working for several years in Moscow, he moved to St. Petersburg, where he remained for fifteen months until illegal political activities led to his arrest and exile. There were numerous workers with a history of interurban migration, and though it is not possible to establish their exact number, these workers typically spent a prolonged period in various urban centers and had relinquished most of their ties to the countryside. De facto if not de jure, they had become a permanent part of the urban population.

Transitional workers with attenuated ties to the countryside comprised a very substantial group in the Russian labor force. Their involvement with rural life was limited to the possession of a house or parcel of land (cultivated by family members or rented out) and the provision of monetary assistance to family members in the countryside. They did not themselves engage in agricultural cultivation, and in many cases their immediate family lived in the city or the factory village. It was not unusual for such workers to work in a factory or shop for ten, twenty, or even thirty years while continuing to hold a rural passport and to pay taxes for land in the village.

. . . [Such] transitional workers frequently had an ambivalent attitude toward the village. Many skilled workers, for example, regarded their ties as an encumbrance and wanted to sever their connections to the village once and for all. But a variety of circumstances prevented them from doing so. Above all, the village served as a form of social security for workers in the absence of state or employer assistance for unemployment, illness, injury, and old age. Thus, even though skilled workers often felt that the village was more of a hindrance than a help, they nevertheless held onto a house or land or sent money to relatives in order to protect themselves against adversity. For transitional workers, contact with the village had been sharply curtailed but not yet ruptured altogether. After long years in a factory or shop, many of them belonged, for all practical purposes, to the urban working class and viewed themselves as such.

The semipeasant worker, by contrast, maintained close and continuing relations with the village. By 1900, only a small percentage of the factory labor force in St. Petersburg and Moscow returned seasonally to the countryside to participate in cultivation. Regular returns to the village were a more frequent occurrence among workers in seasonal occupations such as tailoring where the off-season coincided with the agricultural cycle. [A] survey conducted in 1910–1911 reveals that more than one-half of the tailoring shop workers and 78 percent of the subcontracting workers made three to five visits to their native village each year, remaining there for weeks or even months at a stretch.

The location of a worker's family was an important determinant of rural ties. Immediate family members (spouse and children) of male skilled workers were more likely to reside in the city than the family members of unskilled and semiskilled workers. In 1897, 69 percent of the married workers in the capital's metalworking industry maintained a wife and/or children in the countryside, whereas the corresponding figure for textile workers was 87 percent. The unskilled workers who predominated in industries such as textiles generally had insufficient earnings to support a family that had been transplanted from the village although, as Pavlov observes, entire families sometimes went to work in the mills, including children.

In sum, workers' relations with the countryside showed considerable variation. Some segments of the labor force remained closely tied to the village, "and their conversations," as Kanatchikov recalls, "were mostly about grain, land, the harvest, and livestock." In appearance, outlook, and family life they were still very much part of the rural environment. Gradually, however, some of these workers were becoming assimilated into the urban or factory milieu, with a corresponding attenuation of their links to the countryside. Finally, the urban workers—both city-born and those who had relinquished all connection to their native villages—comprised a small but growing group in Russian society. Kanatchikov eventually belonged to this category, as did many of his fellow patternmakers at the Gustave List factory who were "family men and were related to various petty bourgeois strata." So, too, were the female seamstresses in Moscow tailoring shops, nearly all of them city-born, together with many clerical employees and others. . . .

At the beginning of the twentieth century, many Russian workers depended upon their employer for housing. In artisanal, sales, and service occupations, workers frequently lived on the very premises where they labored during working hours. This situation was widespread among such groups as tailors . . . , bakers, shoemakers, and other urban craftsmen for whom the small workshop remained the characteristic unit of production. Salesclerks, too, sometimes lived in or adjacent to the shops where they worked, often sleeping on wooden planks in the kitchen or pantry. . . .

Workers obliged to live on the premises of the shop had to endure the continual surveillance of the employer, who often endeavored to control not only working hours but leisure time as well. In some small shops, employers locked the doors at the end of the workday to prevent workers from departing. Owners sometimes imposed curfews on workers and required regular church attendance. Thus, even during nonworking hours, the employees in these shops had little control over their lives.

The situation was scarcely better for factory workers living in employer-provided housing. In 1897, two out of every five factory workers in Russia still lived in a company dormitory or in barracks. This arrangement was more prevalent in factory villages—the large manufacturing centers in rural Russia—than in major urban centers. Nevertheless, Kanatchikov notes that the Mytishchensk railroad car factory, which opened in Moscow in 1896, included both little wooden houses and enormous barracks for bachelors. . . . Only 10 percent of the capital's [St. Petersburg's] factory workers occupied employer housing, however. Most of the workers in employer housing were in industries such as textiles where the labor force included many semipeasant elements.

In the factory villages of the Central Industrial Region, by contrast, about one-half of the workers were housed on company premises. A survey conducted in

Moscow province in 1904, for example, disclosed that 56 percent of the factory labor force occupied employer-provided lodging.[5] Another study of workers' budgets conducted in the Bogorodsk textile district of Moscow province in 1908 showed that married workers spent an average of 15 percent of their earnings on factory housing, whereas single workers spent an average of 3 percent. The latter group inhabited barracks of the type described by Pavlov, where rental charges were as minimal as the comfort and privacy they afforded. The workers in these rural factory districts who did not live in company housing either rented accommodations outside the factory gates or lived in their own cottages nearby.

The evidence indicates that many workers were far from satisfied with company housing. As Pavlov observes, factory lodgings usually resembled military barracks or a prison with their bleak uniformity, cramped conditions, lack of privacy, and regimentation. To be sure, some workers could recall even worse conditions in factories of an earlier decade, and for some peasants even the dismal dormitories and barracks represented an improvement over the peasant hovels they had left behind. Yet there were many others who longed for a cottage of their own, with a barn and garden beside it. Individual dwellings, as one worker put it to Pavlov, provided privacy and the freedom to do as one pleased.

Contemporary investigations confirm the impression conveyed by Pavlov that workers sought to flee company housing whenever possible and to move into the private sector. Those who rented private accommodations faced several options. Some joined an artel, a cooperative living arrangement. The artel was most frequently encountered among male workers from the same or neighboring districts in the countryside. United by a common bond as *zemliaki* (fellow countrymen), they pooled their resources to rent an apartment, purchase food, and prepare common meals. When Kanatchikov first arrived in Moscow to begin apprenticeship training, his father placed him in one such artel under the supervision of a fellow villager. . . . Once a worker became more fully and permanently integrated into the urban milieu, he generally withdrew from the artel and sought other types of housing that afforded greater privacy. Thus, the young Kanatchikov, after obtaining his first job as a fully qualified patternmaker, left the artel and moved into the apartment of a fellow worker and his wife.

In major urban centers, the housing supply failed to keep pace with the rapid growth of the laboring population, and accommodations for workers were scarce and costly. At the turn of the century, few workers could afford the luxury of a private apartment, and entire families often occupied a room or even half a room, while single workers commonly rented a corner of a room or merely a cot. A survey conducted in St. Petersburg in 1900 revealed that in the city as a whole, there were 1.7 persons per room in apartments, 3.2 people per room in one-room flats, and 3.4 people in cellars. Another survey taken in St. Petersburg in 1904 showed

---

5. Other surveys confirm this general trend. A survey conducted in 1897 in Vladimir province showed that 42 percent of the workers occupied company housing; a survey of the Bogorodsk district in Moscow province in 1899 showed that the proportion was 49 percent.

that it was not uncommon for six people to occupy a single room and for five or more people to share a bed.

Expenditures on housing generally represented one of the largest items in a worker's budget. St. Petersburg workers who rented lodging outside the factory or shop, for example, typically spent 21 percent of their earnings for this purpose if they were married, 15 percent if they were single. In exchange for their hard-earned money, however, workers usually found themselves housed in filthy slums that were overcrowded, damp, and cold. Mariia Pokrovskaia, a doctor who investigated housing conditions among Petersburg workers around the turn of the century, has summarized her findings:

> The general impression I had of the housing of Petersburg workers can be stated briefly. In these dwellings there is dampness, filth, darkness, foul air. Frequently there is no running water or flush toilets, which constitute an essential part of any comfortable dwelling. In the vast majority of cases, tenants use the primitive outhouses which contaminate the ground and spread stench in backyards and apartments.

Notwithstanding the deplorable conditions in workers' housing, those who lived outside the factory or shop enjoyed one important advantage: the freedom to dispose of their nonworking time as they pleased. Living in private lodgings gave workers considerably more contact with city life than they would have had in company housing and far greater discretion over their activities. In stores and taverns, on trams and in the crowded streets, workers came into contact with many different segments of the urban population. Some of them—typically the more skilled, literate, and prosperous workers with shorter hours and higher wages—took advantage of the cultural, recreational, and educational options available in a big city. But even in a factory village, workers who inhabited a cottage beyond the factory gates had certain freedoms and pleasures unavailable in the dormitory or company barracks. They often kept a garden and raised some livestock, and, most important of all, they could conduct themselves as they pleased, without submitting to onerous regulations or enduring the prying eyes of fellow workers.

Expenditures for food (excluding alcohol) represented the largest item in every worker's budget, consuming 31 to 48 percent of total earnings if the worker was single and 38 to 52 percent if married. Many workers—even some who did not live in employer-provided housing—depended on the employer to provide meals. In artisanal trades, shop owners often furnished meals, deducting the cost from workers' wages. This arrangement could be found in numerous subcontracting shops where . . . workers and the owner sometimes ate out of one large earthenware or enamel pot.

Some factories also served meals to employees, but this arrangement was encountered far less frequently than in workshops. A 1908 survey of Petersburg factory workers found that only 38 out of 632 respondents (6 percent) took their meals at the employer's facility. More commonly, factory workers had their main meal either at an artel, their place of residence, or in a local tavern or canteen. In still other cases, workers brought along food that was eaten cold on the premises of the firm. The type of arrangement depended, above all, on the distance between a worker's lodging and place of employment.

The midday meal break generally lasted one and a half hours, and by Russian custom this was the major meal of the day. Normally it was a hot meal that included soup as well as kasha or potatoes. Together with bread, these were the staples in the Russian worker's diet. One study of workers' budgets revealed that as much as one-half of the expenditures on food were allocated for starch; 9 to 19 percent of the food budget typically went for meat and meat products. The lack of sufficient meat in the diet sometimes gave rise to complaints by workers. [For example], striking tailors in 1911 demanded that their employer provide beef twice a week and that each worker be supplied with an individual plate.

Alcohol consumption was a major aspect of the Russian worker's daily life—both at the workplace, where it was an intrinsic part of many rituals and customs, and outside the workplace, where drinking was the inevitable accompaniment of social occasions and a convenient escape from the dreary and monotonous work routine. Expenditures on alcohol sometimes represented a considerable part of a worker's budget. Surveys conducted in St. Petersburg and the Central Industrial Region disclosed that textile workers spent 2 to 10 percent of their wages on alcohol. [A] study of Moscow tailors indicates that in some cases expenditures were far higher.

[There is much anecdotal evidence to] illustrate the ubiquitousness of alcohol consumption and widespread drunkenness among male workers. The communal aspects of drinking deserve special attention. There was scarcely an event in working-class life that did not culminate in communal drinking. By way of illustration, the new worker on the shop floor, the newly promoted foreman, and the newly elected shop elder were all expected to buy a round of drinks. On paydays (Saturdays), workers frequently went from the factory or shop to the local tavern. Still suffering from the aftereffects of protracted drinking when work resumed on Monday, many workers continued their carousing on the job.

. . . [V]arious explanations [have been offered] for the widespread consumption of alcohol. [Some] focus on the social pressure to participate in drinking bouts. [Others] emphasize the attractions of alcohol for workers with harsh, often confining, conditions in their daily lives. Pavlov draws attention to the lack of alternative forms of leisure time activities in factory villages. Boredom, he suggests, impelled many workers to turn to alcohol as a means of diversion from an otherwise monotonous and routine existence.[6]

The workday for most Russian workers lasted at least eleven hours and in some cases far longer. Typically, a worker was on the job six days a week, and some segments of the labor force—such as salesclerks—were required to work seven days a week. Yet despite the limited number of nonworking hours available for leisure time activities, workers found many different ways of occupying themselves when not at the workbench, the machine, or the sales counter.

------

6. And alcohol—vodka—had of course long been an integral part of Russian culture. See R. E. F. Smith and D. Christian, *Bread and Salt: A Social and Economic History of Food and Drink in Russia* (1984); and David Christian, *Living Water: Vodka and Russian Society on the Eve of Emancipation* (1990).—Ed.

. . . Visits to the local tavern provided, as [just noted], a widespread form of recreation, as did alcohol consumption generally. Many workers found relaxation in card games and various forms of gambling. Organizations, including clubs and mutual benefit societies, held social dances that enjoyed great popularity among younger workers. Kanatchikov's earnest efforts to acquire social graces and dance instruction from a "how-to" book reflect the mentality of young better-off worker-aristocrats in the urban labor force who were eager to emulate their social superiors.

Not all leisure time activities were frivolous, however. Kanatchikov recalls visiting museums in Moscow, and some workers attended theatrical performances and concerts as well. Church attendance was widespread among workers. An ethnographic study conducted in the 1920s reported that 70 percent of the male workers and 85 percent of the female workers who were interviewed had attended church prior to the 1917 revolution.

Some workers devoted their nonworking hours to self-improvement, including intellectual pursuits. In 1897, 74 percent of the male workers in St. Petersburg and 40 percent of the females were classified as literate. This was higher than in the Russian Empire as a whole where only 52 percent of the working population (both male and female) could claim basic literacy in that year. Literacy was correlated, above all, with skill and age. Industries and occupations with a high proportion of skilled workers, such as metalworking, showed a correspondingly high rate of literacy. In St. Petersburg, 73 percent of the metalworkers were literate compared with 44 percent in textiles.

Although no systematic data were collected on the proportion of literate workers in artisanal trades, we know that some trades made basic literacy a prerequisite for entry into apprenticeship. [A] study of Moscow tailors reveals that in tailoring shops, 89 percent of the male workers and 90 percent of the female workers were literate. . . . By contrast, only 73 percent of the men in subcontracting shops and 67 percent of the women were literate. Among salesclerks, literacy was often a requirement for the job, and according to [one source], nearly 88 percent of the country's clerks had attained literacy at the beginning of the twentieth century.

In assessing these data, it must be kept in mind that literacy often entailed little more than a very rudimentary ability to read. But if many literate workers were unable to read anything but the simplest text, there was a small but growing group of cultivated workers who sometimes attained a high level of intellectual development. Pavlov professes his amazement at discovering worker-intellectuals in the textile mill where he was employed in the 1890s. Such individuals were far more prevalent in other industries such as metalworking or printing. . . . [A] new type of worker-intelligentsia . . . was emerging in Russia at the beginning of the twentieth century.

Apart from a small stratum of worker-intellectuals, there was a far larger group of literate workers. They have been described by Jeffrey Brooks:

> Though their reading habits were in some respects similar to the peasants', the workers, concentrated in the cities with a high rate of literacy, formed the core of a new lower-class reading public for whom the written word was increasingly the dominant means of articulating social values and developing class consciousness. Unlike the countryside, the city was an environment filled with printed words. In the streets, in the shops, in places of work,

announcements, signs, newspapers and books beckoned those who were able to read. Workers had more money to spend than peasants and, small though their expenditures on "culture" were, they were still significant.[7]

The new working-class reading public was attracted to adventure and morality tales, much like their counterparts who remained behind in the countryside. Tales such as these were published both in book form and as serials in leading newspapers. Kanatchikov recalls that he and other members of his artel were fascinated by the lurid installments of stories published in *Moskovskii listok* (Moscow Sheet); they even shared a common subscription to the newspaper.

It was not until after the Revolution of 1905 that a new type of newspaper emerged, geared explicitly to the growing urban lower-class reading public. The so-called "copeck" newspapers first made an appearance in St. Petersburg and then spread to Moscow and other cities. Named for their low price, these newspapers swiftly acquired a huge circulation drawn mainly from the working population. A legal trade union and radical press appeared beginning in 1905, and it, too, was directed to a working-class audience. Although the circulation of these newspapers was far less impressive than that of the "copeck" papers, they nevertheless had considerable appeal among workers. Their emphasis on political topics, in many cases approached from a socialist perspective, attracted a readership among the more sophisticated and activist segments of the labor force.

[To conclude, I might] touch upon the issue of workers' aspirations, that is, their hopes and dreams and their visions of an alternative to the present. For some, this vision centered around a return to rural life, stripped of the painful features that had compelled many to flee the countryside for factories and shops. Others envisioned a blend of rural and factory life that combined the best features of both worlds. This image is illustrated by . . . the skilled and well-paid metalfitter in a textile mill who dreams of a factory village in which workers inhabit individual huts, each with a barn, a vegetable garden, livestock, pigs, and chickens.

For another group of workers, the primary aspiration was to achieve mobility and prosperity within the factory itself. For a blue-collar worker, there were several channels for upward mobility. Some workers advanced into the ranks of work crew leaders, assistant foremen, and even foremen. The foreman occupied the highest position a worker could attain in terms of wages, status, and responsibility within the enterprise. Consequently, . . . there were always workers who aspired to this position and who were prepared to take whatever steps were necessary to achieve it. If some aspired to join the ranks of low-level supervisory personnel, still others sought to advance from unskilled or semiskilled jobs to a skilled trade. As we have seen, the aspiration to become a *masterovoi* in the factory involved not only economic considerations but issues of status and dignity as well.

There were some, however, who sought to flee the bosses and to set themselves up as independent workers. In artisanal trades, garret-masters found a certain measure of independence from direct supervision when they began working at home,

7. Jeffrey Brooks, "Readers and Reading at the End of the Tsarist Era," in *Literature and Society in Imperial Russia 1800–1914*, ed. William Mills Todd III (1978), p. 142.

often with the aid of other family members. Enterprising artisans sometimes even set up shop as subcontractors or, more rarely, on a retail basis. The dream of becoming one's own master and owning a shop had not been entirely dissipated by the beginning of the twentieth century although in reality few artisanal workers could succeed in this endeavor.

Many salesclerks . . . harbored the vision of becoming shop owners. They came to believe early on that money would free them from the deprivation and humiliation they had known since childhood, making them master over others. Consequently, some clerks tried to accumulate sufficient savings to open a small stall or a shop of their own. By the end of the nineteenth century, however, large retail establishments and department stores intensified the competition for small firms, sharply curtailing the opportunities for independent entrepreneurship by working people.

One theme predominates in the discussions of workers' aspirations: the strong desire among workers to achieve more control over their lives, both at the workplace and outside it. In some cases, this meant the relative independence of the peasant proprietor. For others, it signified independent entrepreneurship or elevation into the ranks of managerial personnel. During the Revolution of 1905, another conception of the future gained currency among workers—the image of a new kind of society altogether. Partly under the influence of radical intellectuals, partly as a consequence of their own struggles with employers and the government, some workers began to envision an entirely new form of social organization in which they would attain dignity, civil and political rights, and the control over their everyday lives that most were denied under the prevailing order.

## D OCUMENTS

Sergei Witte (1849–1915), minister of finance from 1892 to 1903, was the key official directing the industrialization drive of late Imperial Russia. Indeed, Witte was emblematic of a new type that had risen to power in the Imperial system. Born in Tiflis, where his father—a man of Dutch descent—was a senior official, Witte was educated in the cosmopolitan Black Sea port of Odessa and graduated from Novorossiisk University (the University of New Russia) with a specialty in mathematics. After a period of study in western Europe, he returned to Odessa to take a position (1871) in the local, state-owned railroad. Soon, when the railroads were privatized, he resigned from the Imperial service to begin what proved to be a highly lucrative business career in the Southwestern Railway Company, of which he became the director. Attracted back into government service, he was appointed the first head of a new railway department of the Ministry of Finance in 1889, minister of transportation in 1892, and, later that year, minister of finance. From these prominent positions Witte was determined to advance the industrialization of Russia through active state intervention in the economy in support of private capitalism. To this end he promoted railroad construction (including the famous Trans-Siberian Railway), high tariffs (to protect Russia's new industries from foreign competition), and extensive foreign investment (to supply the large amounts of capital the Russian economy could not yet produce). To facilitate foreign investment and foster monetary stability, moreover, he insisted that Russia's money be based on the international gold standard. He also vigorously encouraged the development of technical and commercial education: during his ten years as minister of finance, some 175 technical and commercial schools were founded in the Empire.

In the first document, Witte's career as de facto chief minister of the Imperial government is reviewed by V. I. Gurko (1862–1927), himself a senior official who had ample opportunity to observe Witte in action. Gurko was from a noble Russian family distinguished in governmental and cultural affairs, and was deeply interested in agrarian matters (both he and his wife inherited landed estates). After resigning from state service in 1906, he settled on his estate near Tver, where he pursued a career in the local zemstvo; in 1912 he was elected to the State Council (now the upper house of Russia's parliament) by the local landowners. Gurko's background as a cultivated noble landlord and "zemstvo man" helps explain the animosity towards Witte evident in his account of Witte's career, which is excerpted from memoirs written in Paris in the 1920s. Gurko is especially critical, as will be seen, of Witte's neglect of agriculture—the immutable basis, as Gurko and many others saw it, of Russia's wealth.

Finally, Victoria Bonnell follows up her description of the new working class in Russia with a firsthand account of life in a giant textile mill in the 1890s. Its author was one Fedor Pavlovich Pavlov (pseudonym for A. N. Bykov), an engineer by training who spent six years working in textile mills in the Central Industrial Region before leaving in protest at how the workers were treated. His account is a composite of his experiences in the mills and formed part of a book on the subject that he published in Moscow in 1901.

## V. I. Gurko Recalls Sergei Witte's Years in Power, 1892–1906

In its influence upon state policy, the State Council [before 1906] was . . . above all a chamber of conciliation for arguing, and at times quarreling, ministers. It is easy to understand that under these conditions both the general trend of policy and the personal traits of individual ministers appeared in it in a particularly strong light in so far as they had anything to do with general state policies. Of the ministers the most important was S. Witte.

Witte's outstanding importance was due mostly to his influence and authority, and to some extent to his personality, for even when his position was more or less unstable his influence upon the decisions of the State Council remained unshaken. He was a discordant note in the orderly routine of the State Council. His huge rather burly figure; his enormous arms too long for his body; his rather expressionless, ordinary, homely face; his plain, unadorned, somewhat rough and uncultivated speech, with its pronounced Odessa accent; his utter disregard of the traditions of the [Council]—all these combined to produce an odd and not particularly favorable impression. He could not be termed an orator; his language was not adorned with the flowers of eloquence, nor was it always coherent and logical; yet when he spoke he managed to create a strong impression. Witte was obviously a master of

Reprinted from *Features and Figures of the Past* by V. I. Gurko, J. E. Wallace Sterling, Xenia Joukoff Eudin, and H. H. Fisher, and translated by Laura Matveev, pp. 52–61, 63–68 with the permission of the publishers, Stanford University Press. © 1939, 1967 by the Board of Trustees of the Leland Stanford Junior University.

psychology and, despite his apparent simplicity and artlessness of speech, he under-stood the men with whom he was dealing and put his arguments accordingly. He used flattery, at times quite openly, or, if the occasion called for it, he attacked his adversary with insinuations. If actual facts were not sufficient he sometimes resorted to fabrication.

By and large, Witte's attitude toward people was based on a deeply rooted contempt for all humanity. Yet he was kind and considerate by nature. He showed this clearly in his relations with his assistants and subordinates, whom he tried to assist and whose future he tried to arrange, even though sometimes such consider-ation was not deserved. A case in point is Maksimov, head of the Department of Railways, whose official career culminated in scandal.

Witte brought all these abilities and tactics into play in his relations with the State Council. He directed all his attention to the most important and influential members of a group and to assure himself of their assistance and particularly of freedom from their opposition, he used all sorts of methods which may be described by the blanket term—bribery. If flattery failed, he used—and this, alas, was usually the case—more material bribes. Witte had it in his power to confer material advantages. As Minister of Finance he controlled the disposal of a great number of remunerative positions; he also controlled state credit. He was in charge of the State Bank which made trade and industrial loans, of the Bank of the Nobility and of the Peasant Bank, which could purchase lands at almost any price.

Now and then, of course, Witte met with a sharp rebuff from those he was trying to win to his side. When he suggested to the newly appointed Minister of Foreign Affairs, Prince Lobanov-Rostovsky, that his salary might be raised to correspond to that of an ambassador (the difference being some 30,000 rubles yearly), the Prince answered: "Has anyone told you that I have applied for such an increase? If so, you have been misinformed."

But such sharp answers did not change Witte's customary policy. He nearly always succeeded in disarming a great number of influential adversaries; those whom he could not disarm he attacked directly; and sometimes he even terrorized them. Witte demonstrated the latter method in the State Council over the question of an additional assignment of some two million rubles for the founding of the St. Petersburg Polytechnic Institute. The preliminary scheme of erection and equip-ment called for about five million rubles, if I am not mistaken; and, later, two more appropriations of large sums were needed. With the last appropriation of two million, the cost of the Institute's organization would have reached almost ten million rubles. The State Comptroller, P. L. Lobko, considered this sum entirely too large and persisted in trying to have it reduced. In a meeting of one of the Council's departments Lobko sharply criticized the Ministry of Finance in connection with the estblishment of the Institute. Witte's retort was no less sharp and Lobko, offended by some of Witte's statements, could not constrain himself. He charged that the conduct of the Ministry of Finance in this affair could be judged by the fact that the land on which the Institute buildings at the Lesnoi were to be erected had been purchased by the Ministry for 200,000 rubles from a Mr. Segal, who had paid 30,000 rubles for it a few months before. The chairman sought to hush up the incident by saying that it was not the strict concern of the State Council, and as it was late (almost 6:00 P.M., the customary time of adjournment) he suggested that they vote on the matter. But he had not reckoned with Witte, who was not the man to allow such a challenge to pass unheeded. "We shall remain here until midnight," he announced, ignoring the rights of the chairman, "for, since one of you has chosen to engage in insinuations, I shall not remain silent." In a very brilliant improvisation Witte successfully opposed Lobko's ill-timed attack, and the appropriation was unanimously accepted—even Lobko himself voted for it.

Another incident is very typical of Witte. The State Council was debating the taxation on diocesan candle works. K. P. Pobedonostsev, [chief administrator] of the Holy Synod, was opposed to the measure, and his arguments were, as always, accorded great attention; for although he spoke infrequently he spoke well, and although he was not a creative thinker he had a keen analytic mind and was at his best as critic [see Documents, Chapter 9]. . . . Pobedonostsev was . . . extremely emaciated; his skin was like parchment; his face was that of an ascetic and was made more striking by a pair of large horn-rimmed glasses; he gave the appearance of a clerk or barrister of the [pre-Reform] courts who was versed in all the niceties of legal casuistry, as indeed he was. On those occasions when in his excitement he raised both arms and pictured the horrors awaiting the Empire if the measure he happened to be opposing should be adopted, he was something worth seeing. And now in opposition to the proposed tax, he held that there existed a sovereign ordinance exempting diocesan candle works from taxation. This roused Witte. "I cannot exhume all sovereign ordinances," he said. "I have no time to do so. And anyway, what do they matter?" Never had such a statement been heard by the State Council; yet coming from Witte it aroused no comment, so accustomed was his audience to his sallies.

By the time of the accession of Nicholas II [1894], Witte had had time to demonstrate his particular qualities: courage, determination, and a great deal of creative energy. He had established the government liquor monopoly, and he had gone through a customs war with Germany as a result of the tariff he had established on German industrial products. According to the commercial treaty of 1894 a tariff was retained; but it was a lower one, and Germany modified her tariff on Russian agricultural products. However, the most important accomplishment of Witte in the new reign was the establishment of a gold standard for Russia (1897).

When Witte was appointed Minister of Finance in 1892 he had only a vague understanding of finances and their practical management. By education he was a mathematician, and by profession a railway man; yet with characteristic self-assurance he undertook a series of most decisive reforms which broke all the established precedents of the Ministry of Finance. At the outset he did not contemplate the establishment of the gold standard; on the contrary, he planned, as a means of speeding up national economic progress, a "satiating of the shallowest channels of monetary exchange." This was to be accomplished by increasing the issue of new bank notes, a plan supported by Katkov,[1] who had helped Witte to

---

1. M. N. Katkov (1818–1887), a leading conservative, nationalist writer and editor.—Ed.

secure the appointment of Minister of Finance. This plan, together with Witte's scheme to support the building of the entire Trans-Siberian Railway with paper currency, had served to win him the appointment.

During the first years of his activities as Minister of Finance Witte subscribed so fully to this plan that he prevented the realization of certain measures for stabilizing our monetary unit, measures which had been projected and partially realized by his predecessors. . . .

Witte's first financial adviser was a former professor of Kiev University, Antonovich, whom Witte appointed as his assistant. Antonovich was strongly in favor of expanding trade and industry in Russia by increasing the amount of money in circulation within the country, and to this end revised the statutes concerning the State Bank. According to the new statutes, the Bank was expected to increase considerably its loans to industry. But the new statutes had hardly been put into effect when Witte completely changed his attitude both toward the question of an increased issue of banknotes and toward Professor Antonovich. Once he had succeeded in orienting himself in this unfamiliar field of finance he felt no hesitation in altering radically his course of action and in parting with Antonovich, who was supplanted as adviser on financial problems by Rothstein, a newcomer from Berlin and a director of the International Bank. With the close assistance of this banker Witte succeeded in passing a monetary reform and in stabilizing our monetary unit, although the State Council's opposition to this reform obliged him to carry his project through the Finance Committee and to have it confirmed by an Imperial [decree]. Witte's prestige was then (1897) at its height. His use of the unlimited authority of the Tsar to gain his end was not entirely without danger, for it not only made him solely responsible for his actions but also roused many influential persons and groups against him. But Witte was willing to run this risk. At that time he considered authority not as a goal in itself but as a means of carrying out his creative ideas, as a field in which to apply his remarkable talents.

The part Witte played in the development of Russian industry is well known. His influence in this direction was all the more remarkable since his measures were directed to the single end of creating a situation favorable to the development of Russian industry. Yet this situation had its dark side, and a rather important one. Some of the measures were artificial and consequently temporary; and when their practice was discontinued, some branches of industry began to weaken. This was especially true of the metallurgical industry, which had been developed mainly by large governmental orders designed to meet the needs of state railways. With the termination of railway construction, the factories engaged in supplying railway materials were left without a ready market for their products.

But with all his talent in matters of finance, Witte was not a statesman. Entire spheres of state organization remained a closed book to him to the end of his days. He had but a hazy understanding of Russia and of the Russian people, a fact which became particularly evident [after 1903] when he became head of the government [that is, chairman of the Committee of Ministers]. Although his business acumen guided him in the solution of those varied problems of the day with which he was faced, it did not give him that vision of the future which is the indispensable attribute of all true creators of public welfare and state power. Thus, Witte's economic policy was but a program to meet the current need and showed that simplicity of conception which was his distinctive trait. This policy was, in brief, the accumulation of funds in the state treasury and the accumulation of private capital in the country. Realizing that the best method of increasing state resources was to develop the country's economic life, he encouraged such development; but he considered that the only means to attain this end was to develop industry, heavy industry especially, since it was the source of all great private fortunes.

Witte's views on agriculture reflected those of Friedrich List,[2] on whose doctrine he had compiled a little treatise. Witte held that agriculture is but a limited field for the application of human labor, while industry, unconfined by material limitations, may develop indefinitely and thereby use an indefinite amount of labor. Agriculture to him was a necessary but purely subordinate branch of public economy; agriculture was necessary to feed the population, but could not serve as the sole source of its well-being. This explains his negative attitude toward all measures designed to improve the agricultural situation.

At first glance it is difficult to understand Witte's indifference toward the great fall in prices of agricultural products during the nineties [1890s] throughout Russia. These low prices, particularly for cereals, caused a severe agricultural crisis. Witte denied the existence of such a crisis when he exclaimed with mingled pathos and irony in his most humble report: "How strange that there should be such a crisis when the price of land is steadily increasing."

In making this statement, Witte did not take the trouble to find out whether or not the productivity of the land corresponded to its market value. To deny that there was an agricultural crisis . . . during the very time of Witte's activity as Minister of Finance would indeed be odd. Yet, when the price of rye in the Volga region and other central gubernias [provinces] fell . . . , Witte was content to engage a group of economists . . . to compile a series of articles. . . . These articles may be considered a code to Witte's policy. Their purpose was to silence press comment on the deplorable effects of low grain prices upon the lives of the agricultural elements of Russia, elements which made up eighty percent of the entire population. To the extent of several hundreds of pages and with tables of complicated statistics, these gentlemen expounded the theory that the Russian peasant was not really the producer but the consumer of the grain—at least of that part of it which finds its way to the market—and, therefore, a low price for this commodity could only be to his advantage. . . .

How could Witte, with his intelligence and practical perception, [be] indifferent to the fall in grain prices? Perhaps because he was unable to raise them. Yet, this is not so. It was, of course, beyond his power to influence world prices. All our export trade prices depended upon prices in Germany; export prices naturally influence domestic prices, and Witte was powerless to force Germany to lower the tariff on Russian grain. To accomplish this we should have had to make concessions

---

2. Friedrich List (1789–1846), a German economist who lived in the United States from 1825–1832, stressed the importance of government encouragement of industrialization in economically backward countries.—Ed.

in our protective tariff on German industrial products, which would have rendered our own industry utterly unable to compete with German industry even in our own domestic markets and would have wiped out many branches of Russian industry. Yet there was a method that might have been used to secure higher prices for Russian grain in foreign markets. Western Europe could not have done without Russian grain at that time. It would have been quite feasible to establish a network of grain elevators, to introduce a warrant system for the grain kept in them, to enlarge credit operations on grain, to guarantee the quality of exported grain, and so on. The low price of Russian grain was caused to a great extent by the fact that the producer lacked floating or any other kind of capital and was forced to dispose of all his crops immediately after the harvest at the existing price. This situation was exploited by grain traders and by exporters. Each year toward threshing time, when there was a reasonably good crop, domestic prices for grain declined sharply, then rose again in the spring. The measures mentioned above would have gone far to check such practices, and Witte was perfectly capable of conceiving them, the more so since he had been advised by a number of people to resort to such measures. Yet, if he put these measures into effect at all, it was on such a small scale that they were without significance and served only to enable him to say that he was making efforts in that direction but could not extend his undertakings because of the great expenditures entailed and because actual experience showed that they were not successful anyway.

What, then, was the real reason for his inexplicable attitude? Undoubtedly there was one: Witte, eager to develop Russian industry at any cost, saw the need of providing cheap labor for this industry. Lacking a rich and elastic domestic market, Russian industry could hope to compete with western Europe only if it had a ready supply of cheap labor. With inferior technical equipment and poorly trained workers, who had but recently been attracted to industrial occupations, Russian industry could not develop without such labor. At Russia's then economic level the cost of labor was almost directly dependent upon the cost of foodstuffs. Again, low profits in agriculture would have assured a continual influx of workers into factories. . . . The keeping of grain prices at a low level corresponded in every way to the grandiose plans of Witte, who repeatedly affirmed that in a few more years Russia would be the first industrial country of the world.

Here, in my opinion, lies the answer to the riddle of Witte's attitude toward agriculture, particularly as regards profit-yielding land-ownership. Admitting that fortunes in the form of ready capital could not be made from agriculture under any conditions, he considered that great agricultural development and extensive employment of high-priced labor would be a serious handicap to the development of our industry. Witte was but a son of his time; a fervent admirer of the capitalistic structure of society and of capitalism in general. But in his mind this capitalism was connected with trade and industry and not with agriculture. Nor must it be forgotten that Witte's paramount aim was not so much to bring happiness and prosperity to individual citizens of the country as to assure the greatness and might of the empire as a whole. To him different classes of society were so much building material with which to erect the edifice of a great state.

Witte's unconcern with agriculture, a result of his policy of industrialization, was greatly increased by the opposition he experienced from the agricultural element, an opposition which was not wholly disinterested. The criticisms directed at Witte because of his establishment of the gold standard and because of his tariff policy for the protection of our industry were mostly unfounded. Even so, it was natural that he should be disturbed by this critical attitude which threatened to undermine his position and frustrate his plans. Very soon, therefore, his indifference toward landowners changed to open animosity, and invariably he included in this class all landed gentry [nobility], whom he accused of furthering solely their own class interests.

Be it noted, however, that Witte's hatred was directed not at the landed magnates but at the small and average landowners whom he described as a ruined class living from hand to mouth. He treated the landed aristocracy altogether differently and endeavored to separate it from the mass of landed gentry and to interest it in industrial undertakings in order to break up its economic solidarity with the smaller landowners. Witte needed the support of this class of great landowners in order to strengthen his position with the throne—since the members of this class had access to the court—and in order to gratify his petty vanity. So that he might enter St. Petersburg's high society he ingratiated himself with their representatives and tried hard to gain their friendship. He arranged to sell state lands to some of them at moderate rates; to others he advanced considerable industrial loans and subsidies; from others he purchased land for the Peasant Bank at a nice price. Yet, after spending so much energy in tempting them, in his *Memoirs* Witte accuses them of currying favors and of boundless cupidity and avarice.[3]

Witte's malice toward the lesser landed gentry is reflected in his reminiscences of the Special Conference for the Affairs of the Nobility, which functioned from 1897 to 1902. Not without significance in his statement that this conference was organized primarily to find means to assist the small landed gentry, for neither the name nor the documents of this institution specify its purpose as such. It is true that the small and moderately well-to-do landed gentry were in severe economic straits, and any objection to supporting them as a class could have been only theoretical. In fact, this class included nearly all of the landowners who were fighting poverty. The agricultural crisis had dealt just as hard a blow to these owners as to the peasant population. They loved the land with a love developed through generations, yet they were often forced to abandon their traditional occupation and seek some other means of livelihood. They did not seek exceptional profits, but merely a chance to make both ends meet, to support their families, and to educate their children. These were the men whom Witte denounced for their cupidity, their class aspirations, and their desire to improve their own welfare at the expense of the rest of the population. As a matter of fact he was opposed to and even contemptu-

---

3. Witte's *Memoirs*, translated by A. Yarmolinsky, were published in New York in 1921 and, in his original Russian, in Berlin in 1922. For a new English edition, see Further Reading.—Ed.

ous of these people because of their poverty and their inability (due to circumstances quite beyond their control) to accumulate fortunes. Prominent financiers making millions, industrial magnates who had doubled their fortunes within a few years—these were the persons he respected and whose wishes he treated with utmost consideration. . . .

Witte's hostile attitude toward the agricultural elements and the representatives of the landed gentry was carried over from them to the zemstvo, which rested exclusively on these elements. In 1899 he made a report concerning the project to establish zemstvo institutions in the western gubernias [provinces], and in this report he tried to establish the idea that under an autocracy the zemstvo was an ineffective and dangerous administrative organization, and pronounced himself definitely for the curtailment of its activities. Witte further developed this latter idea in another report of the same period dealing with public education. In this he argued in favor of exempting all schools from the authority of the zemstvos and of transferring them to the authority of the Synod. Of the cultural role of the zemstvos, the importance of which no one has ever denied, Witte said not a word; on the contrary he insisted that the zemstvos were "overtaxing the peasantry."

But Witte's animosity to the zemstvos was caused by something more than his hostility to the landed gentry. The zemstvos enjoyed the privilege of levying their own taxes. As this did not accord with Witte's policy of directing the greatest possible amount of the public wealth into the state treasury, he endeavored to curtail this zemstvo privilege. It was to this end that he tried to deprive the zemstvos of their administration of public education. He affirmed in the report mentioned above that the zemstvos spent for educational purposes seven million rubles a year, a sum which the state could administer to far better advantage. But he went even farther in his attack on zemstvo privileges. In 1900 he, together with Minister of the Interior Sipiagin, submitted to the State Council a project which sought to limit the zemstvos' right of taxation. There was much discussion and some objection, and when the project was finally adopted it was in a much-moderated form. The limits set to the zemstvos' right of taxation were specified in the law itself and were not left to the discretion of the administration, as the original draft had stipulated. In practice this law had essentially no effect, yet it produced a most unfavorable impression. It was, in short, one of those pinpricks which undermined the prestige of the government and roused the dissatisfaction of the public.[4]

One of Witte's glaring inconsistencies is to be seen in a comparison of his attitude to the zemstvos on the one hand and to the municipal administrations on the other. The latter as well as the former had the right to levy taxes; and actually both organizations were anomalous in an autocratic regime. But Witte never opposed the municipal administration because he never opposed the industrial classes. Not only did he refrain from handicapping any sort of social organization allied to industry but often he endeavored to increase its strength. In 1899, for instance, it

---

4. The western provinces had not received zemstvo institutions in the local government reform of 1864. Six of these provinces—in Ukraine and Belorussia—were granted restricted zemstvos in 1903, expanded to full zemstvos in 1911.—Ed.

was decided on Witte's initiative to allow periodical conventions of representatives of the metallurgical and other industries and of the railway-construction shops and machine factories of the Northern and Baltic regions. Many of these conventions were later transformed into permanent organizations to further the interests of the industry they represented, and acquired much power and influence. Witte feared the privilege of the zemstvos indefinitely to raise the tax rate on real estate as one that might harm the interests of the industrial class whose property consisted of factories, was generally situated outside the city limits, and was subject to zemstvo taxation, although the representatives of the industrial class were always in the minority in the assemblies of the zemstvos.

Witte's opposition to local self-administration, evident in his report on the zemstvos, at first seems strange and even inexplicable. . . . But the fact remains that with Witte public opinion was one thing and public activities were another. By nature Witte was a very masterful man and, perhaps unwittingly, a rational absolutist. He was an ardent champion of public education; he strove impatiently and passionately to carry through reforms that would develop the country's general economic strength; but at the same time he was firmly persuaded that this end could be attained far more quickly by an autocratic power, unlimited and free from all interference, than by elected institutions, obliged to consider the shifting opinions of a democracy. Accordingly, public opinion was important to Witte not in itself, but as an indication of what course of action to follow, not as a factor of public life, but as a means of accomplishing his own definite ends. His sceptical attitude toward all humanity convinced him that the people ought to have no active part in government, and that the rulers, merely in order to strengthen their position and their power, should so present their measures as to gain public approval. . . . In Witte's position as Minister of Finance it was undoubtedly easier for him to act through an absolute authority; it is natural then that he should become its advocate and that public opinion should be for him an important but decidedly secondary factor in strengthening his position. . . .

But if Witte is to be criticized for his methods, it should also be said that in the pursuit of his plans he was confronted with great difficulties which were all the more disheartening and aggravating because they usually consisted of innumerable petty and hidden checks. In his efforts to overcome these obstacles Witte sought support wherever he could find it. . . . Under different circumstances Witte would undoubtedly have been more discriminating, but those with whom he had to contend were not famous for the scrupulousness of their methods; and Witte invariably acted on the motto that "To live with wolves one must howl like one of them." If his adaptability, powers of discernment, and innate lack of principle enabled him to become a veritable virtuoso in intrigue, that does not at all mean that his contemporaries and associates were without guilt in this regard. His *Memoirs* sometimes show partiality, but they also reveal that he hated his enemies with a bitter hatred and cherished no illusions about his friends. Witte had conceived of or initiated his most notable reforms under Alexander III, to whose memory he was unswervingly loyal and whose support had been all that was necessary to carry through a measure. When the death of Alexander III [1894] removed that support, Witte saw conditions change and was obliged to call upon all his resources and energy to carry out his plans. Afterward Witte used to say that if some of his measures were insufficiently worked out it was because he had had to hurry them through, as he was never quite sure what the situation would be on the morrow. As to selection of method, Witte was, as has been pointed out, an opportunist; he was facile also in shifting his opinion when he considered such shifts advisable. But his aim of promoting the economic development of Russia as a basis for political strength was steady and unswerving.

In summary, Witte's accomplishments as Minister of Finance reveal his great merit as an organizer of our state economy. He brought order into the state budget, avoided deficits, and achieved even a pronounced increase of revenues; he strengthened Russian finances as much by the introduction of the gold standard as by his successful conversion of state loans to a lower rate of interest, to four instead of six percent. He extended the network of our railways; he introduced and developed university and secondary technical education; he assembled a fine group of assistants and other officers in the Ministry of Finance; he organized the department of tax supervision; he most successfully introduced and organized the large-scale liquor monopoly. All these were the fruits of Witte's strenuous labor. Thanks to him our industry began to develop at an almost incredible speed and attracted a part of the population away from agricultural pursuits which could not absorb all the peasant labor as the population increased.

Had Witte used his outstanding abilities and capacity for work to further the development of agriculture, his activities would have been of even greater historical significance. If, in good time, he had directed his attention to the question of rural economy, he would have realized that the center of gravity lay in the formation of large peasant holdings which could supply the markets with produce; at the same time he would have preserved the gentry who owned profit-yielding farms and who were responsible for the development of Russian agriculture. Had Witte studied the peasant problem, he could have hastened the abolition of the communes[5] . . . . This last step would have tended to give free play to the country's economic forces, and would have furthered the transference of the land into the hands best fitted to make use of its productive forces. Such a policy would have strengthened industry by improving the domestic market; it would have raised the level of our rural economy; and, most important, it would have prevented Russia from slipping into that abyss into which she was pushed by the fanatics [Bolsheviks] that are still oppressing our country. They would have been opposed by an enriched and consequently better-educated peasantry, able to see that the well-being of the Russian tiller of the soil would be assured not simply by additions to his lot of tillable land but also by improvement in the methods of its cultivation.

But, alas, Witte could work with spirit only for that which depended upon him directly, that which was under his personal and unrestricted authority. Agriculture and rural economy were not in his sphere of activity, and he treated them at

---

5. A policy introduced by Prime Minister Peter Stolypin in 1906, after Witte had left the government.—Ed.

first with indifference and later, when their representatives opposed his policies, with open hostility. Still later, as Chairman of the Committee of Ministers and then [1905–1906] of the Council of Ministers, he seemed to take some interest in the peasant and land problems.[6] But really, to him the peasantry meant merely cheap labor for industry and the landowning peasant was to him not so much a source of national wealth as a taxpayer who paid his taxes mostly through his consumption of liquor.

For this onesided policy, which his successor, Stolypin, . . . tried in vain . . . to straighten out in order to avert the threatening catastrophe, Russia is now paying with her whole being. And the cataclysm has effaced all traces of Witte's great work.

It is to be hoped that this cruel lesson has not been in vain; that future rebuilders of the Russian state will realize that the foundation of the well-being of the Russian people consists in an organized and technically improved agriculture which uses the people's labor to the best advantage; that they will see that all this labor cannot be utilized for agriculture alone and that a part—a great part—must be attracted to a non-agricultural field of endeavor because the development of industry is just as important for Russia as the intensification of her agriculture.

## F. P. Pavlov Depicts Life in a Textile Mill, 1890s

Today is a holiday. Sitting with my samovar,[1] I feel especially content that there is no need to rush, that I can do as I please, and do not have to listen to the noise of the looms and other factory hubbub. Having finished my tea and turning to get a box of tobacco, I am unable to avert my eyes from the view outside my window. Beyond the fence that surrounds the small yard outside my house, I can see the enormous factory site, bound on one side by a river. Right now, all its imperfections, the ruts and the dirt, are concealed under a bright cover from the first snowfall. Even the piles of broken bricks, old logs, metal scraps, and other trash which for some reason have not been removed from the main yard since the spring, somehow look attractive under the cover of snow sparkling

---

6. In 1903, Witte was "promoted" by Nicholas II to the largely honorific post of chairman of the Committee of Ministers. In October 1905, having prevailed upon Nicholas II to issue the October Manifesto granting Russia a parliament, he was appointed chairman of the newly designated Council of Ministers, or prime minister (see Chapter 14). He resigned the latter position in April 1906.—Ed.

From Victoria E. Bonnell, ed. *Russian Worker: Life and Labor Under the Tsarist Regime*, excerpts from pages 115–123, 149–152. Copyright © 1983 The Regents of the University of California Press. Reprinted by permission of the University of California Press.

1. A samovar is a large metal urn used for making tea. It contains an internal tube into which hot coals are placed to heat the water. Usually a small pot of very strong tea is placed on top of the samovar. Hot water is then removed from the urn and used to dilute the strong tea.

in the last rays of the setting winter sun. The river has not frozen yet and seems especially dark between the white snowy banks. Behind the river, there is an ordinary central Russian winter landscape, which is always dear to the Russian heart: the white cloth of the meadow, a gently sloping hill with a few patches of green winter wheat, a village in the distance, and the blue bank of a forest on the horizon.

This picture is abruptly interrupted on the left by a massive five-story textile mill. Behind it, by the river, I can see the smokestack of the dye works, also part of our enterprise. Further to the left, on a hill above the factory, a row of dormitories begins. The factory is separated from the workers' dormitories by a wide road, which leads to a small grove. The church and the infirmary are here, set apart from the other buildings. The view to the right ends in an enormous garden, or rather three adjacent gardens. In front of me stands the small cottage of the factory director, surrounded by recently planted trees. Next to it is the garden and park of the owner's mansion which, except for the roof, is concealed by tall leafless trees. Still further, there is a small grove with a school building next to it. I complete this picture of the factory site by imagining other parts that are not directly in my view: whole streets of houses for the rest of the personnel, the club house, the tea house, the workers' library, the large grocery store, the slaughterhouses. These structures are situated behind the apartment buildings for technicians, and I am standing by a window in one of these apartments. . . .

This factory employs some 5,500 workers and nearly 250 clerical, technical, and managerial personnel. Not more than 750 workers live outside the factory gates. The rest of the workers, many of them with families, live in the factory complex which houses over 8,000 souls, if one counts the old men and children. According to the latest [1897] census, the whole of the Russian Empire can boast of only 138 towns with a population exceeding that of our factory. There is even one provincial capital, Iakutsk, with a population of only 2,000. The lives of these 8,000 inhabitants, not to mention several thousand of their relatives, are tied to the factory in the most intimate way. To me, this tie seems so powerful that I cannot help but ask whether there is an administrative or political power anywhere in the civilized world that can control an individual so completely, down to the last detail, as does the director of a Russian factory.

The director designs the rules and the schedule to which the worker must adhere. At the sound of the factory whistle the worker gets up, goes to work, has lunch and supper. The same director alone decides what living quarters to assign and determines the conditions for their use. For example, the director may require that workers return home by a specific hour and may also restrict the number of people allowed to gather for a social occasion in the room of a friend. It is true that all such rules are, to a certain extent, controlled by the Factory Inspectorate,[2]

---

2. As Professor Bonnell indicated in her essay above, the Factory Inspectorate was created by the Imperial government in 1882 to ensure that factory owners and managers complied with all relevant labor legislation.—Ed.

but, by necessity, this control is of a formal and therefore only negative nature. The inspector must make sure that the factory administration does not include anything in its regulations that would violate the law. The law, naturally, is only concerned with direct violations of a worker's rights. It does not protect him from a whole mass of regulations, sometimes necessary but often quite unnecessary, that are considered part of his contract. For example, if a worker's contract states that he must return home by ten o'clock at night, he will be subject to a fine if he returns at eleven. Or if a worker plays an accordion in his room longer than the regulations allow, he is also subject to a fine. It will not strain the reader's imagination to prolong this list almost indefinitely.

Apart from work and living quarters, the administration supplies the worker with almost everything that he needs for his existence. And if it chooses to do so, the factory administration can fulfill all his needs. The factory maintains a store where the worker receives the necessities: flour, sugar, a horsewhip, a kettle, boots, a shawl, firewood, and mittens. The quality and price of these products, even their availability, are completely controlled by the administration, and a worker has little chance of receiving credit anywhere but the factory store. Besides, the factory store is often the only place of this sort for miles around. Workers often spend up to 70 or 80 percent of their wages there.

The factory administration not only determines the extent to which a worker's material needs are satisfied; it also reigns supreme in the sphere of rational and spiritual needs. It is the owner who builds the church, and it is the same owner who decides whether to build a school and hire the teachers. Likewise, the administration decides which worker will send his children to the factory school and which children will be allowed to receive an education. Libraries and workers' reading rooms are also set up according to the administration's wishes, and even the tickets to an occasional play are distributed in a manner designed to reward the most productive workers. Needless to say, the power to enact all of these regulations is minor compared with the power that is inherent in the administration's right to deny a worker employment and income, no matter how much this right has been circumscribed by law.[3]

Consequently, each step, each hour of the worker's life and the life of his family can be controlled by the factory administration, which is headed by one omnipotent person who governs the factory—its director. The director is the single autonomous legislator, the judge and the executor of his own regulations. The fines that the director imposes on workers cannot be challenged or appealed if their amount does not exceed the legal limit.[4] Once the contract runs out, which happens

---

3. According to government factory legislation, the employer was required to give two weeks' notice in order to terminate a contract, except in cases of poor behavior such as unexcused absence from work, criminal activity, or insolence toward the factory administration.

4. Fines were imposed on workers by the factory administration for infractions such as lateness and poor workmanship. Before 1886, there was no legal limit on the amount of these fines. The labor law enacted in that year decreed that fines could not exceed one-third of a single worker's monthly wage or one-quarter of the monthly wage of a married worker.

no more than twice a year,[5] the law allows the director to take away a worker's living quarters, terminate his credit at the store, prevent his son from attending school, and, finally, deny him further employment, forcing him onto the job market and possibly to starvation.

The Factory Inspectorate, albeit only in a formal manner, controls to some extent the relationship between the director and the worker. As to the technical, clerical, and managerial personnel, especially the lower ranks, they are subject to the director's absolute power. With the exception of the chief accountant and the two or three chief managers presiding over our ant hill, the rest of us do not receive any regular contracts from the administration. As a result, we can all be dismissed on a day's notice without any opportunity for legal recourse.

I can easily picture the familiar figure of our director, a small man with broad shoulders and penetrating eyes. One has to do him justice: he is very intelligent, knowledgeable, and hard working. But how spoiled he is by his unlimited power over all of his subordinates! He can barely tolerate even minor disagreements, and a serious difference with him is tantamount, in his eyes, to committing a crime. The workers, of course, are worse off. They never actually resort to impertinence or rudeness, but the director considers even an insufficiently respectful tone to be a transgression meriting the maximum fine, if not a summary dismissal. I can only compare the discipline reigning at our factory with military discipline, and I believe that on the scales of authority, the power of our director will outweigh that of any commander of a brigade or regiment.

It is possible to tolerate such power if it happens to be combined with intelligence, knowledge, and diligence. The factory population, from the lowest worker to the highest-ranking manager, greatly values these qualities and always respects the man who possesses them, submitting to his will without resistance and easily forgetting an occasional grudge. But what can happen if such power falls into the hands of a man who is neither intelligent, experienced, nor honest? . . .

. . . [What] kind of *formal* requirements do you have to satisfy in order to become a factory director? Not a single one! An official letter, informing the Factory Inspectorate that the owner has appointed Mr. So-and-So to be the factory's director, is sufficient to entrust one individual with the power to decide the fate of a few thousand people. It would not even occur to anyone to question this man's literacy, not to mention his education. Quite incredible! However surprising, this is the true state of affairs.

It is reasonable to suppose that a desire for profit will prompt the owner to find a man who is both intelligent and an expert, and this supposition is borne out by experience more often than not. Nevertheless, we technicians know of factories with hundreds and sometimes thousands of employees that are run by directors who can barely sign their names. Besides, a factory owner is looking, at most, for someone with technical expertise and skills. But these attributes alone do not

5. Labor contracts were usually drawn up so as to expire twice a year, prior to the Easter holidays and on October 1.

qualify one to be the unchallenged ruler of a population numbering five or six thousand souls. Those of us with experience in the field are already familiar with the names of factory directors who, due to judicial reports on recent factory disorders, are gaining notoriety in all of Russia. These people, and particularly the foreigners among them, failed to take into account the customs, rights, and needs of Russian workers.[6] As a result, they precipitated incidents of a highly undesirable nature.

If an omnipotent director gives us such food for thought, his opposite, the "disenfranchised" director hired to serve as a figurehead, presents an even bleaker picture. In this case, it is the owner who runs the business while the legal responsibility belongs to this figurehead director, who must pay the fines imposed by the legal system out of his own pocket. He even bears the brunt of any criminal prosecution, including imprisonment, for which he is sure to receive appropriate remuneration from the owner. Yes, we even have directors of this sort in Russia. . . .

Last summer, the factory administration asked me to supervise the installation of central heating in the dormitories, and I had plenty of opportunity to observe the workers in their living quarters. Now, when I look at these buildings from afar, I no longer see them as the picturesque. . . . Before my eyes there now pass scenes and memories of that other, different life which I observed in those enormous dormitory buildings.

I clearly remember the gruesome feeling of nagging monotony that overtook me when I went inside the dormitory for the first time. All three of them were designed according to a single pattern, each of the four stories resembling the others in every minute detail. A long corridor separated the two rows of "cells," which are formed by thin partitions. Each small room measured 10.5 feet wide, [11.6] feet deep, and 11.7 feet high. It . . . could easily accommodate four people, given the legal requirements. "One cubic *sazhen'* per person," the factory owner used to say, distinctly pronouncing each word.[7] Our chief accountant, who remembers the old days, once assured me that they used to put eight people in a room of this size. Because the factory operated round the clock, the night-shift workers had occupied the room during the day and the day-shift workers at night. This way the owner saved on mattresses as well, since both shifts could sleep on the same mattress. But the factory owner laughed off this kind of calculation, saying that it was not for him and that he wished to provide his workers with decent living quarters.

It is true that our dormitories are decent compared with others. They are well ventilated and have other excellent facilities. The factory administration is relatively generous when it comes to keeping the dormitory in good order: the interior is painted once a year, the corridors, the kitchens, and the stairs are always well swept and generally clean. Nevertheless, each time I enter one of these buildings, I have the impression of entering either a military barracks or a prison. Monotony is

---

6. Following a massive strike of St. Petersburg textile workers in 1896, a government report stated that one reason for worker dissatisfaction was the prevalence of foreign factory managers who had little respect for Russian labor laws and social customs. . . .

7. A Russian *sazhen'* equals 2.13 meters, or just over 7 feet. Thus each "cell" here met the legal minimum cubic capacity for four people.—Ed.

everywhere. Each floor has a corridor 315 feet long. Each corridor is lined with thirty cubicles on one side and twenty on the other; the rest of the space is taken up by the staircase and those facilities that usually remain unmentioned in print.

Each building has a special annex in the middle containing an enormous stove heated by the central furnace. On the stove there are two rows of small burners, twenty-five altogether, one for every two rooms. Each room has two beds, one to the right and one to the left of the door, and there is a table surrounded by four stools by the window. If the rooms had not been numbered, I think the tenants themselves would have had difficulty finding their own quarters, because these fifty rooms on each of the four floors of each of the three buildings are so much alike. The only variety is in small details. In the rooms inhabited only by women workers, it is cleaner; when there are children, you can see cradles that make the already crowded space even more confined. The rooms occupied by weavers—workers who earn considerably more than the average wage at the mill—sometimes have curtains on the windows and a plant or two on the window sill.

The cheap prints covering the walls allow one to form an opinion about the aesthetic sensibility and intellectual potential of the inhabitants. Some rooms have religious themes; others have didactic prints such as "sayings in pictures" or the well-known "stages on life's way." For some reason, this product of a Nikolskaia Street[8] artist's imagination enjoys the most popularity. This strange picture depicts two sets of stairs meeting at the top. On one side there is an infant ascending the stairs who then turns into a youth, and then into a man with a stupid face wearing a top hat. This same man descends the stairs on the other side, finally reaching a coffin that is skillfully depicted in the lower right-hand corner. It is a rare room that does not have a print or two.

Unless the room is occupied by a single family—and most rooms have two— light curtains are all that shield the beds from each other. For some reason, I remember one of those curtains quite well: a cotton print with white specks against a red background. The first few times I went into those little rooms inhabited by two families, I was very surprised at the calm way the tenants accepted such close cohabitation, living a mere half dozen feet away from the other couple. Whenever I asked them whether they felt uncomfortable sharing such close quarters, the men usually replied, "We don't mind, only the women quarrel," or "No, sir, why should we? We're all from the same village, almost kin."

Sometimes the old men piped up, "You don't know how we lived before! Before we didn't even know what a room was like. We all slept together in one row."

"Do you like it better now?"

"How can you ask! Of course it's better!"

Yes, at least now in central and western Russia, those barracks where every-one—men, women, and children—slept in one place without any partitions between them are now part of the past. When we young technicians began our careers, such conditions had already ceased to be the order of the day. But even now one can get some idea of the old days by visiting the factory barracks for unmarried

---

8. Nikolskaia Street, located near the Kremlin, was known for the sale of religious artifacts.

workers. Today these barracks are divided according to sex and age, and most owners pay attention to ventilation and general hygiene.[9] Yet the basic features of the "common barracks," which I would rather call a common boxcar, remain unchanged. There is the same large, often enormous room. Depending on the width, it contains one or two uninterrupted rows of scaffolding raised less than one foot above the floor. The rows themselves, extending from one wall to the other, are about thirteen feet deep. A single beam, elevated some seven inches above the scaffolding, runs the whole length of the row. On both sides of it are filthy bags filled with straw which often serve as the only bedding. Dozens and dozens of people sleep on these bags, with their heads facing the dividing beam. In these so-called "living quarters" there are neither tables nor chairs. Apparently, this room is not meant for people to sit down, to relax, or to read something. By day, you work at the factory; at night, you sleep on the common plank bed; and in between, you eat in common dining rooms.

Once, at the very beginning of my career, I said in the director's presence that it would be a good idea to have carpenters make tables and stools for the common barracks. "And where are you going to put them?" the director asked. "Do not let the size of these halls mislead you," he went on. "According to our calculations their space has already been filled to capacity—one cubic *sazhen'* per person. There isn't any floor space for such frivolity." . . .

At first glance, it may appear that our workers are completely indifferent to their constant lack of privacy. They do not seem to care that they have to share their living quarters with strangers, be it in the common barracks or the less crowded dormitory cubicles. I thought so, too, until a chance incident changed my mind. This took place when the factory was under expansion. In the course of building new quarters for additional workers, the director decided to experiment by replacing the traditional dormitory with fifteen or so small cottages, each modeled after a simple peasant hut. The cottage was to be divided into two sections, each occupied by a single family. You should have seen the demand for those houses, and the impatience of the lucky few who had been selected to live in them, as they anxiously awaited the completion of construction. Our factory charged twenty-five copecks a month per person for lodging in the dormitory.[10] This is a very decent rent. At other factories a worker often paid four or five times more for the same accommodations. Our workers were willing to pay twice as much, and even more, to get one of the new cottages, which were finally allocated to workers who had been at the factory longest and to a few of the most privileged workers, selected by the administration. Unfortunately, this project was the last we saw of such experimentation. It turned out that the cottages cost the employer 40 percent more to construct than the more traditional dormitories.

---

9. As Pavlov implies here, conditions in factory barracks had once been much worse. Laws promulgated in the 1880s required factories to provide separate accommodations for unmarried men and women. Before that time, it was not uncommon for all workers to sleep together in a single room.
10. In 1901, the average monthly wage for a textile worker in Moscow Province was 14 rubles and 48 copecks. . . . Thus, lodging in a dormitory at this factory consumed roughly 1.7 percent of the average monthly wage.

As I have already mentioned, soon afterwards I was given an assignment to supervise furnace repairs in the workers' dormitories. At one point I asked some women gathered in the kitchen why they had all been so anxious to move into the new cottages.

"Of course, we all want to live there, that's why!" one very energetic weaver answered on everyone's behalf. "You've got freedom there, you can do what you please. And here, may the Lord forgive me, you can't even spit without everybody noticing it! All sorts of things happen between a husband and wife, but you can't even exchange a couple of words here—right away, the neighbors sharing your room will spread the news all over the corridor!"

"Don't listen to her, Fedor Pavlovich," an old woman interrupted, speaking in a sweet, ingratiating voice.[11] "All of us here like everything. We've got nothing to complain about. She's just saying that 'cause her husband gave her a good beating last week, and she didn't like it when we all found out, so she's smarting!"

"Shut up, old liar. You just envy me 'cause you've got nobody to beat you any more!" the angry textile weaver retorted. She slammed the damper on the stove, grabbed her pot, and ran out.

Later in the day, I discussed this conversation with the metalfitter Krasnov, who was working with me on the furnace.

"Why don't these women like the barracks?" I asked.

"They've already told you why, haven't they? Why should they like them? Fedor Pavlovich, let me tell you about the time I worked at a glass factory. There we had real quarters. It was really nice. We had a whole village of cottages, only they were bigger and better than the ones we have here. The big huts were divided in half and shared by two families, but a single family could have a smaller one all to itself. Each hut had a little barn for cattle, a vegetable garden, and the workers were allowed to mow the grass in the woods nearby and take their cattle there for grazing. Before you knew it, you already had a couple of pigs, chickens. . . . It means a lot to the working man to have something of his own. I don't understand why our factory isn't building more of these cottages. They say it takes up too much land, but our owner has 15,000 *desiatiny* [over 40,000 acres]. That's land enough! And if the village gets too big, you can have horse-drawn streetcars, like people say they have in Poland. Sure, it will cost more, but the worker will gladly pay for it. I wish we could have it so good! And what do we have now? Sure, it looks nice. The floor's asphalt, and there's ventilation if you please. But you can't tempt the worker with such things. Barracks are barracks, and that's that!"

True enough, barracks! I've heard that foreigners, and especially Frenchmen, find our barracks and dormitories too much like prisons. Individualists by nature, they thoroughly disapprove of our barracks. They maintain that the strict regimen our workers are subjected to, both on the job and during their free time, robs them of their individuality and has an enormously negative effect on their capacity for work. It is difficult to know for certain, but they may be right.

---

11. The old woman addresses Pavlov respectfully, using his first name and patronymic, "Fedor Pavlovich."—Ed.

You have to imagine every detail of dormitory living in order to see the potential power it has to influence workers. Take our factory, for example. Twenty-four hundred men and women occupy rooms which are as similar as peas in a pod. They all obey the same factory whistle. They all get up at the same time, as though by order, and every day they have to perform the same or nearly the same task at their workplace. Those wives who remain behind all start to cook simultaneously at the call of the same factory whistle. At seven o'clock in the evening, all twenty-four hundred workers anticipate the same moment when half of them will leave for home and the other half will take their place at work. It will be the same tomorrow and the day after tomorrow, year in and year out, with only holidays to interrupt the routine. And during all this time there is never a moment of privacy, never a chance to have something different from your neighbor. Add to this the fact that your room is assigned by the dormitory supervisor, who can ask you to move into a different one at any time. And then twice a year, at Easter and the Feast of the Intercession [Oct. 1], when contracts are renewed, you may be turned out of the dormitories altogether. Ponder this, and you will understand Krasnov's exclamation, "Barracks are barracks, and that's that!" . . .

. . . Workdays at the factory are uniformly boring. What are holidays like? Factory workers might go down to the river, but they have already been there. Yet they go a second time, without any purpose or goal, and a third time, and finally they have had enough. How, then, can they spend their leisure time?

Should they read?

The love of reading—I would even say infatuation with reading—has truly become more and more common. There is no doubt that at the present time the factory masses, at least as far as male workers are concerned, include a significant stratum of *intellectuals*. (I will leave it to the statisticians to find out how large this stratum is—whether it is 1, 2, or 3 percent.) I am talking about real intellectuals, the kind that did not exist among working-class people twenty or twenty-five years ago. Of course, then too there were more than a few intelligent, educated workers who liked to read. But they were scattered individuals, set apart from the crowd either by chance or by virtue of their special talent.

Today, one can sense the existence of a true *intelligentsia stratum* among workers—a stratum that includes intelligent people, people of average ability, and some who are not at all smart, as well as workers of different proclivities, temperaments, and views. All of these have received a certain amount of primary education and have developed a taste for reading and a striving for thought. Given their persistent work habits, these people—notwithstanding the primitive nature of their schooling—have developed a passion for reading, and are able to achieve remarkable results from time to time. Dissatisfied with *belles-lettres* [literature], they begin to devour books on history, economics, and philosophy. Darwin and Tyndall and Byron and Mill and Gladstone and Bismarck and dozens of other great European figures, not to speak of major Russian writers and public figures, are known to them, and not merely by name. Believing in science and appreciating the great service that knowledge can render, they thirst for enlightenment. Considering their serious attitude toward life, toward their studies and the printed word, they should not be considered inferior to our so-to-speak privileged intelligentsia.

Just as among other classes of society for whom reading has become a pressing need, this stratum of educated workers constitutes a small minority whose number diminishes in those branches of labor where wages are lower. If you go into a machine tool plant, you will find many more educated workers (yes, reader, I mean *educated*) than among spinners. But spinners are more cultivated than weavers, and unskilled workers cannot be considered on the same level as weavers. As to the leatherworkers and bricklayers, in terms of their intellectual interests they still occupy the same step on the ladder where they stood twenty-five or thirty years ago. In the latter groups, a well-read worker is even now—just as in the old days—an exception.

Reading undoubtedly plays an enormous role in the life of the worker-intelligentsia, but can the same be said about the masses as a whole? I have thought about this question more than once, but despite my desire to answer this question positively, I have to say no. For the mass of workers, just as for the mass of the middle class, books still serve, as a rule, merely as entertainment. And entertainment, for the majority to enjoy it, must of course be highly accessible. But how accessible are books to the workers?

How, from where, and by what means can a factory worker obtain a book? One can say with certainty that in four out of five cases the source is either a factory library or a reading room. The average worker who lives in a factory far away from the city is in this respect fully and directly dependent on the good will of the factory manager. One would look in vain in the vicinity of a factory for private libraries, reading rooms, or bookstores.

And let us suppose that a worker lays his hands on an interesting and meaningful book. Where will he read it? The library is not always convenient; not all libraries have a reading room and those that do make it difficult to use. It is open only at certain hours, and in order to go there the factory worker has to change clothes, since every worker, within the limits of his understanding and his custom, is highly sensitive to exterior propriety. Therefore, he is more likely than not to look for a place to read at home. But where at home? In the barracks, where space has been calculated at one cubic *sazhen'* per person, where there is neither a table nor a stool nor adequate evening lighting, and the only furniture consists of bunks intended for sleeping and not for reading? Or will he read in a little overcrowded room inhabited by two or sometimes three different families with children, where the atmosphere is stifling and women constantly quarrel and he has to encounter all the inconveniences of forced cohabitation?

So if you do not see genuine merriment among the holiday factory crowd, it is because the conditions of everyday life place a mass of obstacles and inconveniences in the path of reading, and physical exercise and sports have not become part of the custom, and aesthetic entertainment in the form of concerts, exhibitions, theater, and museums, such as open their doors to workers in Germany, England, and other Western European countries, are inaccessible to our Russian workers, and because communal activities, such as choral and mutual aid societies, do not exist in the factory milieu. Where, then, can the worker go? And how can he spend his rare day off?

Outside the windows of my apartment, workers wander around aimlessly, hour after hour, bored, sluggish, as though half asleep. On this gloomy autumn day I keep on thinking how much willpower and firmness of character a worker needs in order to avoid the temptations which, in the provinces, destroy thousands of people, even among the intelligentsia. I have in mind alcohol, cardplaying, and sexual promiscuity. Consequently, I am not surprised at the enormous quantities of vodka sold at the nearby taverns, nor at the reckless infatuation with cards and games of chance that is so prevalent among factory workers, or at the growing incidence of venereal disease and syphilis in the factory population.

## FURTHER READING

James H. Bater, *St. Petersburg: Industrialization and Change* (1976)

—— and R. A. French, *Studies in Russian Historical Geography*, vol. 2 (1983)

William L. Blackwell, *The Industrialization of Russia* (1970, 1982, 1994)

Joseph C. Bradley, *Muzhik and Muscovite: Urbanization in Late Imperial Russia* (1985)

Daniel R. Brower, *The Russian City between Tradition and Modernity, 1850–1900* (1990)

Jonathan Coopersmith, *The Electrification of Russia, 1880–1926* (1992)

Olga Crisp, *Studies in the Russian Economy before 1914* (1976)

Theodore H. Friedgut, *Iuzovka and Revolution*, vol. 1: *Life and Work in Russia's Donbass, 1869–1924* (1989)

Peter Gatrell, *The Tsarist Economy, 1850–1917* (1986)

Alexander Gerschenkron, "Russia: Agrarian Policies and Industrialization, 1861–1917," and "Russian Economic History before 1917," in Gerschenkron, *Continuity in History and Other Essays* (1968), 140–248, 409–69

Paul Gregory, *Russian National Income, 1885–1913* (1982)

Michael F. Hamm, ed., *The City in Late Imperial Russia* (1986)

Patricia Herlihy, *Odessa: A History, 1794–1914* (1986, 1990)

Arcadius Kahan, *Russian Economic History: The Nineteenth Century*, ed. Roger Weiss (1989)

Susan P. McCaffray, "The Association of Southern Coal and Steel Producers and the Problems of Industrial Progress in Tsarist Russia," *Slavic Review*, 47 (1988), 464–82

John P. McKay, *Pioneers for Profit: Foreign Entrepreneurship and Russian Industrialization, 1885–1913* (1970)

Thomas C. Owen, *The Corporation under Russian Law, 1800–1917: A Study in Tsarist Economic Policy* (1991)

Theodore H. Von Laue, "Russian Labor Between Field and Factory, 1892–1903," *California Slavic Studies*, 3 (1964), 33–65

——, *Sergei Witte and the Industrialization of Russia* (1963, 1969)

Sergei Witte, *The Memoirs of Count Witte*, ed. and trans. Sidney Harcave (1990)

CHAPTER 12

# Late Imperial Society

Previous chapters have shown how the vision of a society of self-regulating estates *(sosloviia)*, each with its privileges and obligations codified in law, and governed by an absolute monarch acting in the best interests of all, animated Russian rulers from Peter the Great to Alexander II. It also remained fixed in the minds of Russia's last two emperors, Alexander III and Nicholas II. But the vision, never fully realized in practice, was increasingly at odds with reality. Following Emancipation and the Great Reforms, and in the wake of rapid industrialization, a wide-ranging social transformation was under way in late Imperial Russia. Capitalism was coming to the countryside, profoundly affecting the lives of both landlords and peasants; impoverished or "surplus" peasants were leaving the land for the cities and other industrial sites; both an urban proletariat and a new class of industrialists were on the rise; and the class of educated and professional people—the intelligentsia—was growing rapidly in volume and variety. Increasing numbers of people of all estates and classes were participating in local government and asserting an ever greater say in public affairs. Trade unions sprang up along with business and professional associations, ethnic or national organizations, philanthropic foundations, and, at last, political parties. A Marxist Russian Social-Democratic Labor party was formed, clandestinely, in Minsk in 1898; in 1902, the party of Socialist Revolutionaries, blending Marxism with Russian populism, emerged—as did, among parties that were subsequently to play a major role in Russian politics, a liberal Constitutional Democratic party (1905). But the Imperial government remained unmoved. Wedded to its vision of autocracy and privileged nobility, and willing to resort to military force as well as a wide variety of police measures in suppressing any and all opposition, the government of Alexander III and, after 1894, of Nicholas II trudged relentlessly backwards into the future (the drive to industrialize, and fitful military modernization, being the major exceptions to this overall policy). Ignominious defeat in the Russo-Japanese War of 1904–1905 inevitably exacerbated the growing social, ethnic, regional, and political tensions; and a massive general strike in October 1905, bringing the country to a virtual standstill, forced Nicholas II to issue his October Manifesto, promising basic civil rights for all and an empire-wide parliament. The Revolution of 1905 had occurred.

# Essays

The Russian nobility, the Empire's privileged "First Estate," naturally was caught up in the great transformations taking place in late Imperial Russia. Never more than about 1 percent of the Empire's total population, its ethnically and economically diverse members were increasingly leaving the land (if they possessed any) and entering business and the professions as well as government service, the traditional career. Yet some 100,000 noble landowners remained a formidable presence in rural Russia, where in 1905 they held more than a third of all the land (the rest was divided among some 12,000,000 peasant households). In the first essay, Professor Gary M. Hamburg of Notre Dame University outlines the gradual politicization of this class and the growing "crisis" of the noble estate as a whole. Equally critical was the state of late Imperial Russia's "middle ranks" as portrayed in the essay by Alfred Rieber, who teaches Russian history at the University of Pennsylvania. And then there was Russia's nascent working class, described in the previous chapter by Victoria Bonnell. Here the special plight of women workers is depicted by Rose L. Glickman of the State University of New York at Buffalo. In doing so she makes frequent reference to the peasantry, the source of both men and women workers and still the mass social base of Imperial Russia.

Of course, these essays hardly exhaust the question of social reality and change in late Imperial Russia, and we might do well to remember, in particular, that huge and increasingly complex institution known as the Russian Orthodox church. Administered as it still was by officials of the Holy Synod and still both supported and oppressed by Imperial patronage, growing numbers of its clergy were nevertheless being educated to a high level (bringing about a theological renascence), monasticism had undergone a spiritual revival, major cultural figures (like the writer Dostoevsky) celebrated the church's national and moral role, and various of its leaders insisted on expanding its charitable mission. By 1912 or so the Russian Orthodox church, with well over 200,000 clergy, ran some 31,000 parishes and more than 1,000 monasteries and convents, some 37,000 primary schools as well as 57 seminaries and 4 university-level academies, along with thousands of orphanages, old people's homes, and hospitals. The church was, as Thomas Masaryk observed (Chapter 1), an inseparable component of Russian society, containing within it "the oldest and most genuine Russian life."

# The Nobility in Crisis

## Gary M. Hamburg

In the quarter-century between 1881 and 1905, members of the Russian landed nobility sought to reconcile the continued existence of the First Estate with a changing social and political environment. At first, in the wake of the terrorist campaign from 1878 to 1881, there were hopes for a political resolution of Russia's crisis that would have incorporated the nobility into the central government's decision-making apparatus. Zemstvo liberals called for the convocation of a *zemskii*

From *Politics of the Russian Nobility 1881–1905* by Gary M. Hamburg, pp. 225–28, 239–40. Copyright © 1984 by Rutgers, The State University. Reprinted by permission of Rutgers University Press.

*sobor* [council of the land: see Chapter 2] in which the Russian land would "merge closely with the Sovereign," but the zemtsy failed to press the government for a formal limitation of the autocrat's prerogatives. Meanwhile, the Holy Retinue [a semi-clandestine organization of nobles dedicated to preserving Russia's traditional order] posed as prospective guardian of the national interest. It demanded [1881–1882] that propertied elements of the nobility be given an advisory role in the fight against terrorism, a statutory right to sit on the State Council, and an undefined role in the *zemskii sobor*. When Alexander III's ministers recovered their courage after the regicide of 1 March, they disbanded the Holy Retinue and forbade zemstvos to raise sensitive political issues. This reassertion of the central government's traditional authority pushed liberalism and aristocratic-conservatism out of Petersburg political life for a generation.

The beginning of the Great Depression [1880s–1890s] turned the attention of the landowning nobility to the problem of economic survival. Indeed, the Great Depression, which seriously affected the estates of the noble political leadership, transformed economic issues into the preoccupation of noble assemblies until after the turn of the century. Thus, the politics of structural political change was displaced by the politics of economic interest.

In the initial stage of the Great Depression lasting until 1891, noble interest politics was animated by resistance to the market economy. In a phrase that might have been used by Karl Marx, Iu. D. Rodionov complained that "money is faceless." Rodionov and other marshals [elected leaders of the nobility] worried that faceless capital would drive nobles from their ancestral homes and replace them with greedy predators who, caring only for profit, would one day turn Russia into a desert. Concerned marshals from the blacksoil belt and southern steppes petitioned the government to create a Noble Land Bank that would avert the ruin of the First Estate by offering loans at rates of interest lower than private banks. Marshals from seventeen provinces also advocated the adoption of new entail legislation that would legally obstruct the sale of noble land to other social groups. Unfortunately for the nobility, the provincial advocates of these new laws failed to agree on a common version of the proposed changes, thus making it easier for opponents of change to water down the final legislation. . . .

By the late 1880s there were disturbing signs that noble resentment against the market and its surrogates might spill over into a frontal attack on government policy. In fact, that did occur during the second phase of the Great Depression after 1891, when some provincial nobles became convinced that economic pressures on the First Estate could not be alleviated without changes in existing government programs and agencies. Between 1891 and 1895 certain provincial marshals criticized the government's decisions to centralize the Noble Land Bank's operations and to run the bank as a competitive business charging high interest rates. In 1893 nobles from the central agricultural area and the Volga Basin became anxious over the government's new differential tariff policy, which facilitated export trade partly by attracting grain shipments from the eastern periphery and so allegedly threatened the ascendancy of central producers on the domestic market. These two issues led angry nobles to launch a general attack on the central government's agrarian policies, thus signaling the beginning of a struggle with Minister of Finance Witte over the fate of rural Russia [see Chapter 11].

From the tactical perspective this struggle was very interesting. Politically active nobles made a serious attempt to align themselves in a united front against Witte. The joint memorandum of January 1895, signed by eleven marshals and three private landowners from eight provinces, was the first example of concerted action. Then in early 1896, twenty-seven provincial marshals met in St. Petersburg and collaborated on a seventy-page memorandum concerning the needs of the nobility. From 1896 to 1902 nobles sat on government commissions formed to consider agrarian policies, among which the most notable were the Special Commission on the Nobility (1897–1899) and the Special Commission on the Needs of Agriculture. Despite the aggrieved nobles' attempts to coordinate their efforts and their use of new political forums, all the advantages in bureaucratic struggle lay with Witte. By his mastery of economic fact, the force of his office and personality, and his adroit political maneuvers, Witte divided his critics and took advantage of their disagreements. Although the government made minor adjustments in its bank and tariff policies, Witte managed to preserve intact the principles of differential tariffs and a centralized commercial Noble Land Bank. Despite the slow recovery of grain price levels following the nadir of the depression, Witte's victory in agrarian politics dashed the nobility's hopes for economic accommodation to the new order.

The turn of the century found Russian peasants in the blacksoil center and New [southern] Russia engaged in a serious struggle against local landlords. The 1902 uprisings in Poltava and Kharkov and the high level of tension elsewhere in southern and central Russia led to a complete reassessment of political assumptions. The patriarchal nobility, who formerly had granted the peasant question only a contingent status, now recognized the necessity of peasant reforms, especially the abolition of the commune. Those nobles who formerly had recognized the need for peasant reforms were driven to demand structural political changes either to accompany economic reform or to serve as a precondition for economic reform. Among the structural changes advocated were the granting of zemstvo autonomy, the equalization of peasant civil rights with those of other social groups, the abolition of legally delimited Estates, and the adoption of a constitution. Here was the end of economic accommodation and the climax of the nobility's confrontation with the central government.

With the support for the Russian liberation movement [see Chapter 13] by a substantial minority of provincial noble landowners and their allies in the intelligentsia, noble politics came full circle. After a quarter-century in which the politics of economic interest had displaced the advocacy of structural political change, the question of how Russia should be governed now returned to its rightful place on the national agenda. Yet there were important differences between the advocates of political change in 1881 and 1905. In 1881 both zemstvo liberals and the Holy Retinue portrayed themselves as saviors of the autocracy from terrorism. In 1905 liberal nobles joined with the intelligentsia and popular radicals in a united front against the autocracy. In 1881 political reform was not firmly connected with a concrete program of peasant reform; indeed, the Holy Retinue's bias was to preserve large landownership. In 1905 there was at least a temporary linkage between political and economic reform, although this linkage would later be broken. In 1881 the emphasis of zemstvo liberals was on the cooperation of social Estates in the zemstvo milieu; in 1905 liberals looked forward to the effacement of all legal barriers between

Estates and the building of an egalitarian society. For liberal nobles in 1905, an egalitarian civil order was the end of their identity as nobles and the beginning of their life as citizens—the culmination of a dream born with the Emancipation. As former Kozlov district marshal Alexander Ivanovich Novikov wrote in memoirs published in 1905: "I was able to kill off the man of *high life*, the landlord, the nobleman, and the land captain. I was able to become simply a human being, and there is nothing higher than that on this earth." . . .

That Russian noble politics was at once a variant of agrarianism and of Estate politics in a dying monarchy enables us to understand its historical peculiarities. The crisis of the Russian nobility at the end of the nineteenth century was a dual crisis: the question of the nobility's place in Russia's social and economic order and the question of the nobility's proper political role in the state were raised almost simultaneously. An economic and social crisis was superimposed on a political crisis. Agrarianism was the response to the social-economic crisis, but it was insufficient as an answer to the political crisis, hence the transcendence of narrow economic issues and mere status anxiety by global social and political issues after the turn of the century. In both the economic and political realms, the nobility's reaction to crisis was complex and contradictory rather than simple and consistent. An effective economic and political program to preserve the nobility never appeared in Russia because there was no noble class to save, only an Estate of nobles. In 1896 Novgorod's provincial marshal B. A. Vasilchikov explained to the Special Commission on the Nobility the characteristic problem of the nobility:

> Our Russian nobility encompasses persons so diverse in religious, national, economic, and territorial relations that it is impossible to unite them at the present time. The interests of each individual noble are closer to the interests of his profession than to the interests of the Estate as a whole. It is inconceivable that one should expect in the late nineteenth century the awakening of Estate consciousness and solidarity in this diverse mass.

## The Fragmented "Middle Ranks"

### Alfred J. Rieber

On the eve of the [Revolution of 1917] the middle ranks of Russian society were rapidly breaking up into smaller and smaller fragments. This process had been under way since the emancipation, but its beginnings can be traced to an even earlier period in Russian history. During the two centuries between Peter's reforms and the end of the Empire, social change had taken an irregular course. The merchantry, in particular, had not followed an ascending, linear progression from caste to middle class. The mere ownership of the means of production in a burgeoning capitalist society had been insufficient by itself to create a full-blown bourgeoisie. Over the course of two centuries no common social or political consciousness had emerged to bind together the merchants and entrepreneurial groups into a cohesive class striving for power and cultural supremacy. In the absence of a clear ideology, a unified organization, and a strong will, the divided merchants and entrepreneurs had not been able to rally around them the mass of small producers—the meshchanstvo and trading peasants—or even their economic dependents—the clerks and shop assistants. The very narrowness of their outlook had cut them off from the professional intelligentsia, including large numbers of engineers and technical personnel who had been deeply involved in the same productive process. It was this general aspect of Russia's peculiar social evolution that the populists seized upon as proof of the artificial nature of Russian captitalism and the unique quality of Russia's social structure.

But Russia was not a static society. By the turn of the century industrialization had weathered its transplanting from "the hothouse" to natural soil. If the "Asiatic mode of production" had ever existed there, it had been undermined in the eighteenth century and smashed in the nineteenth. Indigenous capitalists contributed as much to the great industrial spurt as did foreign entrepreneurs and the state. Economic differentiation had penetrated the countryside, and economic conflicts between workers and owners exhibited many features of the class struggle. Marxists seized upon this aspect of Russia's peculiar social evolution as proof of Russia's conformity to the West European model of socioeconomic development.

Both the populists and the Marxists constructed such a convincing case that the two positions have remained unreconciled to the present, and each continues to enroll partisans. But the contradiction between them is more apparent than real if one admits that there is a great deal of social space between the immobility of caste and the dynamism of class—and if one admits that there is no historical imperative to force an outright choice between them. In Russia social groups that normally composed the bourgeoisie in Western Europe moved into this space separately without giving any indication of joining together or moving forward at some future time. How they got there and why they could not get out has been one of [my] main themes.

Over two centuries of socioeconomic change in Imperial Russia one characteristic was remarkably persistent: the fragmentation and isolation of social groups. In Muscovite Russia a bewildering variety of duties, obligations, and privileges was attached to different elements of the population. Peter the Great tried his best in the little time allowed him after the Great Northern War to impose a new corporate structure upon Russian society, but his system of service classes was never fully realized and its built-in social mobility was subverted by the nobility. Catherine failed to endow the system with truly representative institutions of self-government. Nicholas [I] made it more rigid at a time when economic growth required that it be more flexible. Thus, sosloviia [estates] in Russia lacked the essential ingredients for the development of corporate rights and self-consciousness. Unlike Western Europe, Russia had not properly laid the foundations upon which to construct a genuine class society.

When the government finally acknowledged in 1861 that the soslovie [estate] system was bankrupt, it could not or would not abolish the sosloviia themselves. Theoretically, an all-class principle underlay the reforms of justice, local government, education, and the military draft. In reality, the new institutions were tainted by the residue of soslovie mentalities. The government preserved legal and status distinctions among the population for purposes of taxation, local government, the administration of justice, census taking, and, perhaps most important of all in its subtle way, the awarding of honors and decorations. Although the sense of social hierarchy was no longer so rigid as before, it was just as pervasive. It may be argued that the implications of social differences became more obvious as opportunities for social intercourse among the sosloviia increased in the postreform period. In any case, legal equality of the population remained as incomplete and inconsistent at the end of the nineteenth century as corporate rights and self-goverment had been in the earlier period.

The impact of bureaucratic centralization and the great industrial spurt in the 1890s failed to sweep away the remnants of the soslovie system. In fact, the attempt by the government, with the support of powerful elements in society, to preserve the traditional social structure while promoting modern administrative and economic policies created serious tensions within the country. The bureaucracy and the intelligentsia bear much of the responsibility for this anomalous situation. They believed that capitalism had to be tamed before it could be unleashed. Suspicion of any uncontrolled social progress was deep-seated in Russian political culture. Beginning with the Marxists, part of the intelligentsia finally accepted the coming of capitalism to Russia, but they, and many of the liberals as well, scorned the capitalists for their lack of social conscience. The bureaucrats feared that a free market and joint-stock companies would spawn autonomous social organizations and promote financial speculation and lead inevitably to political opposition and social instability. For these reasons the government piled up fresh obstacles to the formation of class consciousness among capitalists from different sosloviia and regions by limiting private associations and prohibiting all-Russian organizations. Even such a partisan of dynamic capitalism as Count Witte endorsed these controls. What Russia needed to enforce these restrictions was a strong and unified government, and that was sorely lacking.

Economic and social policies varied from reign to reign and from minister to minister, and bureaucratic infighting often crippled those that were adopted. Of all the government departments the Ministry of Finance and, later, the Ministry of Trade and Industry were most sympathetic to the needs of the merchants and entrepreneurs. Yet even they insisted on close surveillance and imposed strict controls over the whole range of economic activity, from railroad concessions to stock market regulations. Official ministerial representatives were prominent at the meetings of the representative associations of trade and industry and chaired the manufacturing and commercial councils. For all their sympathy they could not rid themselves of their conviction that the merchants were benighted and inert. Right down to the end of the empire the financial bureaucracy berated the merchants for their failure to organize, expand their markets, and compete with foreigners.

Other ministries were even more contemptuous of or openly hostile toward the merchants and entrepreneurs. The Ministry of Transportation, staffed by professional engineers, scorned private enterprise and favored a state-built and state-operated railroad system (except for a brief period in the 1870s). The ministries of Internal Affairs and Justice blamed the capitalists as much as the workers for strikes and disorders and devised dangerous schemes to patronize the working class in classical *Polizeistaat* [police state, in the eighteenth-century sense of enlightened absolutism] fashion. The Ministry of Agriculture, a stronghold of the landholding nobility, sought to protect handicrafts and cottage industries against big merchants and manufacturers. In the absence of true ministerial government the fragmentation of the bureaucracy matched that of the merchants and entrepreneurs, with tragic consequences for all.

No social group in the empire suffered a greater loss of identity and vitality in this unsystematic system that the merchantry. But its unhappy condition was not solely the work or responsibility of the state. Like other enfeebled sosloviia, but more pathetically, the merchantry failed to generate the intellectual vigor and collective action necessary to carry out its own emancipation and transformation. The explanations here are more complex.

The merchantry underwent many legal and administrative changes in the two centuries of its existence, but it also retained much of its traditional character. There was a greater turnover in the merchant population than in any other group, yet the newcomers did not effectively challenge the old ways. Mainly peasants, they tended to reinforce the patriarchal family customs and cautious business practices. The main exceptions were the Old Believers. In their case a deviant social position stimulated political awareness and economic enterprise. Nobles who joined the [merchant] guilds after the 1880s showed no inclination to alter its structure.

Besides its customary behavior and outlook the merchantry was characterized by internal differences in wealth, status, and rank. Membership in the first guild, the distinction of honored citizen, titles like commercial counsellor, decorations and orders, choice elective offices—all were the tangible signs of the pervostateinye [first-rank] merchants. Their lordly manner and high-handed treatment of lesser merchants were rarely balanced by qualities of leadership and independence toward their social superiors, the nobles and officials. This one-sided arrogance contributed to their lack of a popular following. . . .

A second kind of split in the ranks of the merchantry was cultural. By the end of the empire it was possible to distinguish three roughly defined horizontal strata among the merchants. Those who made up the largest layer, which included the mass of the merchantry, accommodated themselves as little as possible to the demands of a modern capitalist economy and, after 1905, a parliamentary government. They were very slow to shake off what [social anthropologist] Clifford Geertz had called "the nonrational pressures of institutional custom." Living mainly in the provincial towns of western and central Russia and throughout Siberia, but also to be found in the largest cities, these merchants were primarily engaged in retail trade, owned a shop or small factory, and belonged to the second guild. Wealth was not, however, an exact criterion. This layer also included first-guild merchants in the wholesale trade, mainly grain, timber, and leather goods. Resisting the adoption of foreign dress, formal schooling, and modern business practices, they clung to their patriarchal attitudes, their extended-family firms, their bazaar mentality, and their antiintellectual bias. They traded at the fairs or in one of the large urban markets, avoided the commercial exchanges, and conducted business in their shops or warehouses. They took little interest in secondary or higher education for their sons and daughters and even less in politics. Standing in awe of the tsar, they despised his officials. Deference to the nobility marked both their social life generally and their attitudes toward local governmental politics, except on occasion in Moscow. In 1905 their timid foray into national politics brought them little but humiliation. Thereafter, they constituted the bulk of the nonvoters in the second curia [merchant division] for the duma elections, forming the inert mass described by the provincial governors in 1916. At the turn of the century they numbered under a quarter of a million.

Merchants whose traditional lifestyle and values had undergone some important modifications during the previous half century, made up a second, much thinner layer. These men adopted European dress, gave their children formal schooling, traveled abroad, showed great interest in technological innovation, and carried out their commercial operations on the floors of the exchanges. Mainly first-guild merchants and honored citizens, they engaged in wholesale and foreign trade, light industry, and commercial banking. Vigorous defenders of merchant rights, they participated in government commissions and ran for office in the town dumas and, less frequently, in the provincial zemstvos. After 1905 they tended to vote Octobrist [the main, moderately conservative party], but they also gave support to the smaller parties of the center and, if they were members of national minorities that had no parties of their own, to the Kadets [the Constitutional Democratic Party]. But they retained their faith in the family firm, conceding to the need for greater capital only in the formation of partnerships. Residing in the merchant districts of the large towns and cities, they posed no challenge to the social domination of the nobility. On the contrary, eager for decorations and rank, they still aspired to noble status or at least to that of honored citizen. Before 1905 they were steadfastly loyal to the tsar and externally respectful of all state authority, while remaining suspicious of bureaucratic interference in business and asking only to be consulted on matters touching their material interests. Their number can be estimated by adding up the total membership in the exchanges of the main towns of Moscow, St. Petersburg, Odessa, Nizhnii-Novgorod, Kiev, and Warsaw, which was about two thousand.

The top stratum comprised the merchant members of the various entrepreneurial groups. Most of these were in Moscow, but a few resided in Petersburg and Kiev. . . . Strong supporters of the guilds and the commercial exchanges, they were proud of their status as merchants and scorned the scramble for ennoblement, though not the title of honored citizen or other civic distinctions. Fiercely nationalistic, they eagerly patronized Russian culture in whatever form it took, from the realism of the Peredvizhniki [populist artists concerned with depicting social reality] to the avant-garde journals the *World of Art* and the *Golden Fleece*. But beyond this they had also taken on the complex social roles of a modern industrial world. They were bankers and industrialists as well as traders. Having accumulated most of their capital in traditional economic activities like textiles, vodka, timber, and sugar beets, they invested in a wide variety of enterprises, including banks, railroads, newspapers, publishing houses, and foreign trade. They adopted new technologies and up-to-date business methods, opened new markets, and endowed technical schools, expositions, and museums, although they tried to maintain patriarchal or at least fraternal relations with their workers. In a word, they sought to russify industrialization, to avoid the horrors of mass secular culture and class conflict which they saw in the West. Of course, they meant to do all this without diminishing their profits or control over their enterprises.

This small group of merchants boldly plunged into mass politics. At times, they reached out to the professional intelligentsia, the rest of the merchantry, the Old Believer peasants, and, in 1916, even to the workers. While they criticized the bureaucracy openly, they remained nominally loyal to the monarchy. Their conversion to democratic institutions and civil rights came too late and was too shallow. Politically naive and elitist and personally contentious, they could not bridge the deep social cleavages within their soslovie or their region, to say nothing of the country at large. By the end of the empire they had fallen to quarreling among themselves. They numbered no more than one hundred families.

Cutting through these layers were vertical divisions based upon ethnic and regional loyalties. The vertical divisions in Imperial Russian society sliced more deeply through the merchantry than through any other soslovie. The ethnic encirclement of the Great Russian merchantry outlived the coming of the transportation revolution and finance capitalism, the decline of the fairs, and the creation of an all-Russian market. With it flourished various forms of anti-Semitism, polonophobia, and xenophobia, even though Russians frequently employed foreigners as agents, technicians, or managers in their enterprises. On the eve of the war it appeared to many merchants that German economic penetration was tightening the bands of ethnic encirclement. But the non-Russian merchants on the periphery were too closely tied to foreign trade and foreign capital to share these sentiments. Thus, it is small wonder that they were reluctant to join with the Great Russians in any strong empire-wide economic or political organization.

During times of crises, such as 1905 and 1917, merchants on the periphery associated themselves with local autonomist or national movements. In the former Kingdom of Poland, along the Tatar Volga, and in Central Asia, groups supported national parties in the duma. Jewish, Ukrainian, Baltic-German, and Armenian merchants confronted a more difficult choice. On the one hand, all of them resisted extreme russification. On the other hand, they equally opposed autonomous movements led by moderate socialist parties like the [Jewish] Bund, the Ukrainian Socialist Federalist party, and the [Armenian] Dashnaks. For the Baltic-Germans the enemy was the national movements of the Estonians, Latvians, and Lithuanians. The embattled merchants of this second group were the true advocates of a *Rossiiskaia imperiia*, a term which lacks a good English equivalent but comes close to the idea of cultural autonomy, which was favored more by the Kadets than by any other political party in Russia.

These vertical differences did not signify a complete absence of common aims among the merchantry. In areas like taxation, relations with bureaucratic agencies, and zemstvos, there was generally much agreement. But strong disagreements persisted over the tariff, railroad rates, trusts, and the labor question. It has been customary to mask these differences and to ignore the ethnic conflicts by calling each segment of the merchantry or, more loosely, of the trade and industry class a national bourgeoisie. But to add an ethnic or regional modifier like Tatar, Jewish, German, Ukrainian, Armenian, or Russian (to say nothing of Muscovite or Petersburg) to the term *bourgeoisie* simply deprives it of all meaning as a category of historical analysis. In such disguises bourgeoisie is at best an occupational description and at worst an utter confusion.

If the merchantry as a whole can be identified by reference to soslovie and ethnic composition, entrepreneurial interests groups must be defined by social role and economic region. The distinction between the two was not absolute: the Muscow enterpreneurial group, for example, was virtually synonymous with the top layer of the merchantry. But the members of the second generation of the Moscow entrepreneurs were the only genuine merchants to dominate an entrepreneurial group.

The other main entrepreneurial interest groups—the southern entrepreneurs, the Petersburg group, and the financial oligarchy—were made up of individuals from varied social backgrounds, mainly nobility who had cut their ties to the land and raznochintsy [persons of no estate] in the professions. Culturally, they were worlds apart from the merchantry—even from those in the Moscow entrepreneurial group. Their ethnic origins were mixed, with Russian, Jewish, German, and Polish predominating. In education, appearance, and manner they were thoroughly Europeanized. They resembled the merchants on the periphery in that they felt most comfortable in a cosmopolitan empire where ethnic nationalism was subordinated to loyalty to the tsar and the state. Although they were usually directors and managers of joint-stock enterprises, rather than the outright owners, they held stock and had a material stake in those firms. In many cases their investments were large and well distributed among the biggest banks, railroads, and industrial complexes in the empire.

They shared with the Moscow entrepreneurs the particular characteristics outlined [earlier]. To repeat these in somewhat different form, they occupied a new set of social roles free from the attachment to soslovie and characterized by technological innovation, economic risk taking, and political activism. As the leaders of the great industrial spurt in their regions, they perceived the necessity of constructing a solid economic infrastructure by establishing technical schools and credit and transportation facilities. They produced for a national market but organized on a regional basis. They sought to influence the government through propaganda, petitions, membership in official commissions, and personal influence in the corridors of power. Strongly opposed to bureaucratic interference in the work place as socially disruptive, they relied heavily on government loans, contracts, and protective tariffs for their economic well-being. This contradiction nourished an ambivalent attitude toward authority, stronger in Moscow perhaps but keenly felt in the south and northwest as well. Thus, their uncertain stand in 1905 and 1917 reflected more their interest in obtaining a free hand in their factories than in winning civil and political rights.

Their relationships with each other alternated between abortive attempts at alliances and bids by individual groups for hegemony over the others. After 1905 the southern entrepreneurs conspired to control the Permanent Advisory Office and then the Association of the Representatives of Trade and Industry. The financial oligarchy worked more obliquely through the trusts and then briefly and unsuccessfully through the special councils early in the war [World War I]. Moscow, too, waited until the war to hatch its schemes in the war industries committees and the Congress of Trade and Industry. If they joined the same all-Russian organizations or sent delegates to the same congresses, it was mainly to prevent their rivals from claiming to represent "all-Russia." It was impossible for them to join in supporting a single political party. The Moscow entrepreneurs were mainly Progressives, the Petersburg entrepreneurs and financial oligarchy voted Octobrist, and the southern entrepreneurs scattered their support from the Kadets to the Polish Kolo.

It is significant that the members of entrepreneurial groups never referred to themselves as a bourgeoisie or a middle class. . . . At most, they called themselves the trade and industry class. It is hard to avoid the conclusion that this was no quirk of language but a conscious choice. Like the merchants, the entrepreneurs knew full well that the idea of a bourgeoisie, no less than its existence, in Russia was extremely unpopular among officials, intellectuals, and the laboring masses of workers and peasants. The neutral occupational definition that they adopted could only be much safer.

By West European standards the entrepreneurs most nearly resembled a fully developed class in their economic interest, organization, and ideology, but each group remained a general staff without an army. Not by any stretch of the imagination can their small numbers be equated with the dimensions of a socioeconomic class, even when compared to Russia's underdeveloped urban population. Nor can they be regarded as merely the highest stratum of their class—a haute bourgeoisie. There are two compelling reasons why not. First, they may have dominated the economic life of their regions, but they did not achieve an equivalent degree of social preeminence. Despite their wealth and status they played an insignificant role in setting the norms of social behavior—the ethical and moral standards, the cultural values, the lifestyle—that must be expected of the top stratum of a class, even one *in statu ascendi* [on the rise]. Second, they made no significant contribution to the political orientation of the country; they neither produced important changes in its institutional life or its code of civic responsibility nor effected innovations on matters of economic policy. In a word, they did not stand at the summit of a hierarchical structure serving as a reference group for the aspirations of the social strata below them.

Even after the destruction of the old regime gave them a place in the Provisional Government [of February–October 1917,] the entrepreneurial groups did not coalesce into a ruling class. They expected, it appears, that in an open society their economic power would automatically confer upon them the respect and authority that they had vainly demanded in a closed one. They can hardly be blamed for thinking so because the European experience pointed in that direction and they had no other to guide them.

Social isolation as much as social division condemned both the merchantry and the entrepreneurial groups to languish between caste and class. In Russia the business and professional worlds enjoyed no close relationship. In other societies the lawyers, doctors, journalists, teachers, and engineers gave the bourgeoisie much of its ethical legitimacy and cultural panache. Their Russian counterparts displayed skepticism or hostility toward what they called "the narrow economic interests." They drew their ethical and political models from a tradition in Russia that went much deeper than the theories linking private property, free competition, and individual liberty. Even those . . . who made a fetish of capitalism as a civilizing force could not quite stomach the Russian merchant-capitalists. To be sure the professional intelligentsia was not composed only of socialists or revolutionaries. But even the moderates perceived themselves as the bearers of liberal and humanistic values against the ruthless pretensions of the traders and the factory owners. In every attempt to bridge the gap the results hardly justified the effort. The quest for a center party in 1905, the economic debates in 1909–1912, the Progressive party in 1912, the war industries committees and the Progressive bloc in 1915–1916—all ended in mutual frustration and recrimination. In a long history of failures, the first and last coalitions of the Provisional Government were simply the most spectacular examples.

The merchants and entrepreneurs also cut themselves off from their potential "class reserves." The uncompromising, patriarchal attitudes of the merchantry toward their shop assistants, clerks, [and] petty traders . . . were repaid with mistrust and fear. In city government, [any success] in forging a coalition among these elements [appears] almost unique. It was not so much a case of missed opportunities for the merchants as of political inertia and intellectual bankruptcy. Except for the Moscow group the entrepreneurial groups showed little inclination to get involved in urban affairs. At the national level they withdrew from mass politics to a safer refuge in the State Council, rather than appeal to a broader electorate. In the countryside the kulaks [better-off peasants] went their own way, seeing no reason to surrender their profitable monopoly of capitalism in the commune to the vagaries of a free market dominated by wholesale merchants or to the structures of a controlled one run by big bankers and industrialists.

If class identity means anything, it means consciousness of one's class enemy. In Russia the merchants and entrepreneurial groups held on to the myth of nonantagonistic social relations between owners and workers far beyond the point at which reasonable doubts might have been expected to set in. Most of the merchants, the Moscow entrepreneurs, and some of the southern group fostered patriarchal ties with the workers long after those relations were outmoded. As we have seen, the same spirit animated their attempts to distinguish themselves from a Western bourgeoisie. Their social myopia stemmed from their confused self-perceptions and their belief in Russia's uniqueness. The St. Petersburg entrepreneurs shook off this self-perception, but only at the cost of isolating themselves from the other entrepreneurs. The government did not help matters by arbitrarily intervening in the relations between the owners and workers. This often obscured the naked economic character of the conflict. To be sure, near unanimity prevailed among the employers over such issues as the length of the working day, factory discipline, and strikebearing. But there were disagreements over equally important questions, such as the workers' right to organize and participate in government commissions, boards of conciliation, and the war industries committees.

Only during periods of violent mass assaults upon their property did they abandon their illusions and grope toward unity of action. Yet even when confronted with imminent loss of control over the productive forces the capitalists exhibited little evidence of real class solidarity. They did not organize themselves on a national basis to deal with either the government or the workers on the labor question. In 1917 their confusion in the face of mass strikes, falling production, and a chaotic supply system contrasted sharply with the energy of the technical intelligentsia, though that, too, proved insufficient to check the slide toward ruin. They could not even agree on who should save them at the end, [General Lavr] Kornilov and the army or [Prime Minister Alexander] Kerensky and democracy. The denouement resembled less a two-sided class conflict as portrayed in the classical version of the end of the bourgeois epoch and more a multifaceted struggle waged on several levels by social groups strung out along the theoretical spectrum between caste and class. It is unlikely that this process of social fragmentation would have been reversed if the war and revolution had not happened when they did. As the government gained the means to regulate the economy, it lost the unity of purpose to apply them. As the economy grew more sophisticated, entrepreneurial interest groups proliferated. As Great Russian nationalism sharpened, ethnic loyalties became stronger.

It might be well to stop here, but another, broader conclusion may be in order. Social fragmentation and political disunity were not phenomena unique to the merchantry and the entrepreneurial groups. Recent studies have shown that the political parties were in various stages of factionalism and disintegration on the eve of the war, a process which accelerated right down to the revolution and beyond. Much less has been done on the condition of the large social formations like the peasantry, nobility, and meshchanstvo [small traders, artisans, laborers]. Yet even here the evidence suggests that as the old soslovie boundaries were breaking down, they were not being replaced by clear lines of class demarcation.

The nobles, for example, had no common economic interest. The main concern of landlords after 1907 was to defend themselves against the industrial monopolies and the skupshchiki (middlemen) who had ceased to be independent but who had become agents of big commercial banks and exchanges. In both cases the noble landlords found themselves facing noble industrialists, particularly in the Urals but also in the Donbass, and noble bankers, especially in St. Petersburg, who were taking over the wholesale grain trade from the local merchants. At the sixth congress of the United Nobility in 1910 a special report recommended a unified noble organization modeled on the Association of the Representatives of Trade and Industry to defend the economic position of the noble soslovie. But the delegates voted it down on the grounds that they were too divided by economic and regional interests to join a single organization.

Yet the noble capitalists, divided as they were among themselves, were unwilling to join with the merchants to create a powerful political or economic organization in defense of their joint interests. Like the merchantry, they were split by the contradiction between a hierarchical social structure buttressed by law, custom, and tradition and a dynamic economic process that rewarded mobility, initiative, and technical skills. It is conceivable, then, that in Russia, behind the facade of industrialization, bureaucratization, and social reform—that is, of modernization—another less visible process of social disintegration was taking place.

## Women Workers

### Rose L. Glickman

The factory woman in tsarist [Imperial] Russia shared with her male coworkers the travails, dislocations, poverty, and exploitation of early industrialization. Yet until the mid-1880's she was all but invisible to the public eye. To the extent that educated, moneyed, or official society noted her existence in the labor force, it was with the unquestioned assumption that she would work in the factory just as her peasant predecessor, or she herself, had worked in the village—the factory was simply a change of venue. The peasant economy had always been dependent on women's labor in the field. Though denied certain jobs by tradition (notably sowing and beekeeping), peasant women participated in mowing, reaping, and threshing, as well as in tending the vegetable garden. And women had full responsibility for certain agricultural tasks—for example, turning, raking, and baling the hay—and for all the household tasks, including child-raising. Yet a woman's reward was hardly commensurate with her contribution to the peasant family's survival. The rigidly patriarchal structure of the peasant world denied her full humanity; as a proverb put it, "a hen is not a bird and a woman is not a person." Ordinarily, she was forbidden to sit in the village councils that determined the economic and civic life of the commune. Within the family she had no voice in the allocation of economic resources, for these decisions were made by the male head of the household in consultation with other male family members. Married or unmarried, she had no rights of inheritance aside from her dowry and certain domestic utensils as long as a male relative lived. (The rare exceptions were widows, and even here attitudes varied considerably from one region to another.) Thus the fact that women were doing hard physical labor as factory workers, or indeed, as any kind of wage earners, rural or urban, was not considered especially noteworthy.

The burgeoning proportions of the labor problem from the 1880s and the growing number of women in the industrial labor force elicited some slow and selective cognizance of the Russian factory woman, although her importance in the labor force and the magnitude of her problems were never properly recognized.

In this essay I propose to review the position of women in industry between the 1880s and 1914, the conditions under which they lived and worked, the

From *Women in Russia*, edited by Dorothy Atkinson, Alexander Dallin, and Gail Warshofsky Lapidus, pp. 63–83 with the permission of the publishers, Stanford University Press. © 1977 by the Board of Trustees of the Leland Stanford Junior University.

responses of various groups to their problems, and, to a lesser extent, women's own attitudes toward their lives.

Women had participated in nonagricultural market production from the very origins of Russian industrialization. An ukase [decree] issued by Peter the Great in his desperation to provide a labor pool for existing or planned factories prescribed that women in Moscow and the provinces who had been convicted of various crimes were to serve out their sentences in factories. Subsequent decrees ordered that the streets be swept clean of vagrants, paupers, and prostitutes, and that they, too, be assigned to factory labor. In March 1762, the police were empowered to distribute to factories in St. Petersburg and its environs the idle, able-bodied wives of soldiers, sailors, and other service people. Later in the eighteenth century, however, women were increasingly recruited from "freely hired labor."[1]

Statistical data on factory workers for this period are sparse, and what figures exist are not broken down by sex. But we can be reasonably certain that within the textile industry—where the greatest numbers of women workers were to be found—about 18 percent of the labor force in the second half of the eighteenth century were women. Nor was it exceptional to find women in other areas of production—for example, in mining and metallurgy, which drew indiscriminately from the serf population, so that women came to dig ore and do heavy labor alongside men. By the middle of the nineteenth century, women worked only rarely and in insignificant numbers in heavy industry, but increasingly in textiles and other light industries. On the basis of official information gathered in 1859, we find that in the city and *uezd* (county) of St. Petersburg women constituted 20 percent of the total labor force; but they constituted 44.3 percent of workers in the cotton-spinning industry and 34.2 percent of workers in the tobacco industry, the two industries in which they were most highly represented.

Labor statistics, as students of Russian labor history are painfully aware, are flawed in many ways throughout the prerevolutionary period. For example, no one in the nineteenth century—or in the early twentieth century for that matter—could decide on the definition of a factory, so from one set of data to another the "factory" may vary from a small unmechanized workshop to an entreprise employing thousands of workers and utilizing sophisticated machines. Often the data do not address the same questions, so comparisons from one year to the next or between regions are impossible. The questions one might ask about women workers specifically are subject to further complications—it is often not clear, for example, whether the information pertains to all female workers, including children and adolescents, or only to adults. Nonetheless, from the mid-1880s there is sufficient qualitative and quantitative improvement in the data to construct a reasonably accurate and reliable picture for some areas of Russia and to discern unmistakable overall trends.

---

1. "Freely hired labor" refers to workers who were employed in factories on the basis of contracts concluded between the factories and individual workers, even though the workers might have been serfs.

TABLE 1    Percentages of Women Employed in Factories in
           European Russia in 1885, by Industry

| Okrug (with component gubernii) | % of Women Employed in Selected Industries | | | Total % of Women Employed in All Industries |
|---|---|---|---|---|
| | Textile | Paper | Tobacco | |
| Moscow (Moscow, Tver, Smolensk, Tula, Riazan, Kaluga) | 31.2% | 47.2% | 47.5% | 31.7% |
| Vladimir (Vladimir, Vologda, Kostroma, Nizhnii-Novgorod, Iaroslavl) | 25.0 | 41.5 | 10.2 | 36.3 |
| St. Petersburg (St. Petersburg, Olonets, Arkhagelsk, Lifliand, Pskov, Novgorod) | 45.6 | 28.8 | 84.3 | 36.5 |
| Kiev (Kiev, Volynia, Podolia, Kherson) | 32.2 | 27.4 | 22.7 | 10.1 |
| Kharkov (Kharkov, Poltava, Ekaterinoslav, Chernigov, Oblast Voiska Donskogo) | 54.7 | 27.3 | 56.9 | 22.6 |
| Kazan (Kazan, Perm, Viatka, Simbirsk, Ufa, Orenburg) | 40.0 | — | — | 5.2 |
| Voronezh (Voronezh, Penza, Samara, Saratov, Astrakhan, Kursk, Tambov, Orel) | 25.6 | 48.9 | 47.3 | 18.2 |
| Vilno (Vilno, Kovno, Grodno, Minsk, Mogilev, Kurliand, Vitebsk) | 39.0 | 30.0 | 59.4 | 16.3 |
| TOTAL | 36.7% | 35.9% | 46.9% | 22.1% |

Of course, as the picture becomes fuller, it also becomes more complicated. What is true of urban factories is not always true of rural ones. What can be said of one rural area with some concentration of industry often cannot be said of another, owing in part to differences in agricultural productivity, in the types of industries, and in the division between local and migrant labor in the two areas. These variables and others influence the numbers, age, and marital status of women workers, and help explain why and how women were drawn into the factories.

The first serious attempt to compile information about the factory population as a whole came with the establishment of a factory inspectorate in 1882. The 48 European Russian gubernii (provinces) were arranged into nine factory okrugi (districts), each one under the supervision of an inspector and a small staff of technical assistants; the results of the efforts of the first group of dedicated and quite extraordinary factory inspectors were published in 1886. I have given the percentages of women employed in factories in 1885 in Table 1. In European Russia (exclusive of the Kingdom of Poland), women constituted 22.1 percent of all factory workers. However, it is noteworthy that in the three most heavily industrialized okrugi, namely Moscow, Vladimir, and St. Petersburg, their percentage in the total industrial labor force was substantially greater than 22 percent. This was partly owing to the fact that Russia's major industry—textiles—was concentrated in these three areas and made great use of women workers. A glance at the first column in Table 1 shows that anywhere from a quarter to over half of all textile workers in Russia were women. Yet these averages do not reflect the considerable variations in female employment from factory to factory. In Kazan *okrug*, for example, where women were 40 percent of the textile workers, the Stepanov cloth factory employed 590 men and not one woman. Similar examples can be cited from Kiev *okrug*, where the percentage of women workers overall was relatively small: the records show some tobacco factories where women were more than half the work force and others where no women were employed.

Women were scarcely present at all in the metalworking industries, although again there are some interesting local variations, especially in areas with relatively little industry. In Vilno *okrug*, where metalworking was the third-largest industry after textiles and tobacco, no women were employed in the iron foundries; but in the manufacture of metal buttons and needles, women were as much as 89 percent of the work force. Another area of high female concentration in some factory districts was the manufacture of matches: in Moscow *okrug*, women were 42.6 percent of the work force in this industry; and the figures were higher for Kharkov and Vilno. In most other industries the fluctuations in the numbers of female workers were considerable; an analysis would require an intensive discussion of local conditions beyond the scope of this paper.

The government found the factory inspectors' reports of 1885 so critical of the conditions under which workers lived and labored that subsequent reports were not published until 1900. From 1900 to 1914 the reports were published again, but only as a *Svod*, or *Summary*, for all European Russia. The 1897 census, however, showed that the percentages of women working in textiles in the three major industrial *okrugi* had increased significantly since 1885. In Moscow *okrug* women went from 31.2 percent of the work force in textiles to 40.8 percent; in Vladimir *okrug* the increase was from 25.0 percent to a startling 42.9 percent; in St. Petersburg *okrug* the increase was from 45.6 percent to 46.2 percent. The *Svod* for 1901 calculated that women workers were 26.8 percent of the total factory work force, pointing out that in the highly industrialized *okrugi* (and therefore in textiles) they were considerably more. By 1909 the estimate was up to 30.9 percent. It was noted that there was a slow but consistent increase in the number of women working in industries where they previously had not been employed—for example, in the sugar, glass, rope, cement, and brick-making industries.

The factory inspectors from 1900 to 1914 responded to this trend with some alarm, for it appeared that the number of women workers was increasing at the expense of the male work force. From 1900 to 1901, the number of male workers decreased by 13,000 whereas the number of female workers increased by 12,000. In 1905 the senior factory inspector remarked hopefully that some of this increase might represent women replacing children and adolescents in the work force. But by 1909, the trend was unmistakable: since 1900 the labor force had shrunk in the absolute numbers as a result of economic crisis, the Russo-Japanese War, and the political disturbances of 1905; child labor had remained roughly the same; and employment of adolescent boys had increased slightly though with considerable variations from year to year. But the absolute numbers of women workers and their percentage in the labor force had steadily grown.

Throughout the nineteenth century, it was assumed both in Russia and in Western Europe that women and children worked in the factory because mechanization eliminated the sheer brawn previously necessary in many industrial processes; and as mechanization overtook handwork, it was expected that women would be ever more employed. To be sure, the generalization holds true for some industries. In textiles, even in 1885, women were employed in consistently greater numbers than men in weaving factories using mechanized looms. The greater the number of mechanized looms in a factory, the greater the number of women; and, conversely, the greater the number of handlooms, the more men. In Vilno *okrug*, for example, handloom weaving was done exclusively by men; but in factories with mechanized looms, women made up more than half the work force. In silk and velvet factories, all mechanized weaving was done by women. In Vladimir *okrug* women were 30 percent of the handloom weavers and 44.9 percent of the mechanized-loom weavers. However, once we look beyond weaving the generalization breaks down. Even within the textile industry we find women heavily represented in some of the preparatory processes—like wool cleaning—that required physical strength and endurance but little skill. The 1885 factory inspector's report for Kiev *okrug* noted that women accounted for 90 percent of the wool cleaners in the district; the report for Kharkov *okrug* cited a figure of 89 percent.

Nor does the generalization hold up outside the textile industry. The tobacco industry, for example, did not begin widespread conversion from hand to machine production until the 1890's (in 1890 only 13.2 percent of tobacco factories used machines). And factories relying entirely on hand production were still being built in the early years of the twentieth century. Yet this was an industry dominated by women workers throughout the period under consideration. Moreover, in every *okrug* some industries requiring no physical strength at all, such as wine distilleries, glove and perfume factories, and mineral water enterprises, employed few or no women workers. Thus although mechanization was without question a very important factor in the increasing employment of women in the factory, it was everywhere tempered by many other factors—by local economic conditions, by custom, and primarily by wages.

Throughout Russia, women's nominal wages were from one-half to two-thirds of men's in every industry and for every job—even where men and women did identical work, and even in industries or specialties where women predominated. Moreover, the de facto earnings of women workers could be, and often were, lower than these ratios suggest. After the prohibition of night work for women [1885], factory owners justified decreased daily wages for women on the grounds that night work was more demanding. Women were also highly susceptible to the system of fines by which employers were able to reduce a worker's nominal wage for numerous real or alleged errors in production. Women with children were particularly hard hit, for fines were levied against them—or bonuses were withheld—for various types of absenteeism over which they had little control, such as caring for sick children or taking time off to nurse infants. Where wages were based on piecework, the female worker was doubly penalized in these cases: she was fined for taking time off, and she was therefore less likely to make as many pieces.

The increasing employment of women followed from the fact that women were cheap labor, but the relationship was not clear to early observers—not even to the most lucid and sympathetic. In 1884, I. I. Ianzhul, factory inspector for the Moscow *okrug*, predicted that "the more men's wages rise in the future as the techniques of industry improve and hand labor is replaced by mechanical devices, the greater will be the demand in our factories for female and child labor. The demand for men's labor will drop correspondingly." However, it was not the case that the wages of men rose with mechanization; rather, mechanization made it possible to employ women in jobs that previously had been too difficult for them physically or that had demanded skills they had not acquired. The demand for cheap labor was nothing new, but as the tempo of industrialization quickened and as mechanization increased, it simply became increasingly possible to replace male and female labor. Moreover, women were hired with growing frequency to do unskilled, arduous hand labor. By the early years of the twentieth century, though, the factory inspectors were beginning to understand the importance of wages as a factor and were reporting that "substitution of women for men where possible is a positive preference on the part of factory administrations." Thus in 1908 the senior factory inspector of Moscow *guberniia* noted that "wallpaper factories that previously employed only men are now hiring women. The Azibera factory, which manufactures tin boxes, began hiring women in the soldering department, and now they are employed in other departments and even work at mechanized lathes. The substitution of female for male labor allows the factory to economize on wages."

The increasing prevalence of women workers stemmed not only from the fact that they would accept lower wages than men but also from the fact that since the promulgation of the factory legislation of 1882–1883 the employment of children—like women another source of cheap labor—was subject to strict regulation. Although the Factory Law of June 1, 1882, made no mention of women workers, its effects on them were considerable. It was designed to prohibit employment of children under the age of ten and to establish an eight-hour day for children aged ten to fifteen. Despite confusion and misunderstanding on the part of factory owners—not to mention deliberate evasions—the law soon produced perceptible results. Child workers were replaced by adolescents and women, who, as one factory inspector pointed out, received the wages of children. By 1885 in Moscow *okrug*, the number of children in factories was 32.5 percent of what it had been in 1882. Some of these child workers were not replaced at all, owing to the economic crisis of the first half of the 1880's; some were replaced by adolescent boys; but most were replaced by women. In cotton manufacture women went from 35.4 percent of the total work force in 1882 to 39.1 percent in 1885; in wool they went from 28.6 percent to 32.5 percent, and in tobacco they replaced child labor almost entirely. Since even by 1885 the news of the law had barely penetrated beyond Moscow *guberniia*, the rate of increase of women workers was greatest there. In the other *guberniia* of Moscow *okrug*, the rate of increase was in proportion to the level of comprehension of the law on the part of factory management. Subsequent child labor legislation further encouraged employment of female workers. As it became illegal—or at least more complicated (and therefore less profitable)—to hire children and adolescents, the employer's quest for the other cheap source of labor—women—quickened.

Closely related to the fact that women were cheaper to hire than men was the conviction on the part of factory owners that women were the "calmer, steadier element." Women workers were definitely less demanding than men, although, as we shall see, they were not entirely without initiative. Relevant here is that the demands of most concern to factory administrations were obviously demands for higher wages; and to the extent that factory owners had less to fear from women, women were more desirable as workers. As the *Svod* for 1907 noted, "The increase in female labor is especially marked in the cotton-weaving industry, where the woman weaver is forcing men out. The reasons are the same as before. They are more industrious, attentive, and restrained (they do not drink or smoke), as well as more submissive and less demanding regarding wages." These specific reasons for preferring women workers are not apparent before the 1890s, but with the great strikes of that decade and the events of 1905, factory administrations clearly perceived that their economic interests were best served by seeking out labor that promised to remain relatively docile, especially in demands for increased wages.

The conditions under which factory workers labored and lived in Russia are well known: they were deplorable not only in retrospect but even in comparison with conditions in other countries at comparable stages of industrialization. The absence of safety measures; the disregard for ventilation; the primitive sanitary conditions; the long hours of arduous labor; the almost complete absence of regular procedures for hiring, firing, and paying wages; the wretched living quarters; and the humiliating treatment were shared equally by men and women workers. But women workers suffered in ways specific to their sex. Women working in the most deleterious industrial processes were forced by economic necessity to work through pregnancy to the very last moment with neither hygienic nor sanitary safeguards, and without physical respite. All observers remarked on the tremendous pressure felt by the woman to continue working through pregnancy and to return to work almost immediately after childbirth. Obviously there was no question of payment of wages during her absence; rather, the issue was whether she would be rehired if she left her position for too long a time.

Once factory women had children, new domestic responsibilities and burdens were simply added to their already long hours and exhausting toil. There were basically three alternatives for factory women who could not stay at home with their children. The first was to send infants to relatives in the country, if possible, or to leave them in the care of an elderly female relative or an older child who lived with the family. The second, which was permitted only in exceptional cases, was to bring infants to the factory. This enabled the mother to breast-feed her child, although she was docked for the time she spent doing it. The last alternative, a practice that was observed in 1884 and that increased over the decades, was baby farming. This was an arrangement whereby elderly women near the factory or families in the country earned income by caring for as many children of factory workers as possible. The system usually had unfortunate consequences for the children farmed out since profits could be increased by economizing on the youngsters' food.

The single woman worker had her specific problems, too. Though the disparity in wages—both nominal and actual—between men and women was unjust for all women, it was hardest on the self-supporting factory woman. She had to survive on one-half to two-thirds the income of her male counterpart, and even men's wages barely sustained any but the highly skilled workman. When a single woman had children to support, the burden became tremendous. The undeviating consensus from various budget studies, as well as from more impressionistic observations, was that female workers consistently ate far less than male workers and that their food was of much poorer quality. From a study done by the sanitary section of the Moscow zemstvo in the early 1880s, it would appear that the male cotton-spinner spent one-third of his income on food and the female spinner two-thirds; yet she consumed only 71 percent of the protein and 65 percent of the fat that he did. There was no change in this situation over the years.

Single women working in urban industry, where housing was rarely provided by the factory, had the same problem with housing as with food. Because of their lower incomes, they spent a higher proportion of their earnings on housing than men did. More often than not, shelter for a single woman worker meant a corner in a room occupied by another family. Frequently, it was shared with a male lodger. In factories that provided housing (usually barracks), women shared with men cramped quarters, lack of privacy, poor ventilation, and primitive sanitary conditions. Many factories arranged for one bunk to be shared by several people, who slept in it by turns according to the shift they worked. The sensitivities of women were of little concern to the factory owner, who often installed single men and women in the same barracks room.

Another disadvantage that all factory women experienced was lack of access to literacy. The problem of literacy in this context is an extremely complex one that is beyond the scope of this study, but the rates of literacy of men and women factory workers are an interesting gauge of the relative deprivation of women workers. To be sure, more women workers than women in the total population of the Russian Empire were literate, just as more men workers than men in the total population were literate. In 1897, only 13.1 percent of all women in Russia were literate, whereas 21.3 percent of factory women were. The comparable figures for men in 1897 were 29.3 percent for the total population and 56.5 percent for the factory population, respectively. And despite the fact that the literacy rate for women in textiles rose to 37.5 percent by 1918, the level of literacy of women workers consistently lagged behind that of men workers to a very considerable extent. Consider, for example, the literacy rates for the cotton industry in 1908: 72.5 percent of the men in the industry were literate as compared to 25.3 percent of the women.

Official interest in the position of factory women was sporadic and inconsistent. Women and children were usually placed in the same category—useful but expendable—with the weight of sympathy, such as it was, on the side of children rather than women. The law of 1885 that prohibited night work for women (and adolescents) in the textile industry was enacted as much to ameliorate the severe economic crisis of the 1880s as to correct the inhumane conditions under which women worked.

The negotiations preceding passage of the law illuminate the mentality of both industrialists and the government. In response to a government initiative, a group of St. Petersburg textile manufacturers gathered to discuss ways of easing the economic crisis. As the lesser of several evils, they opted for abolition of night work for women and adolescents; this, they claimed, would mitigate the crisis by equalizing supply with demand. The current economic difficulties were blamed on the widespread use of night work in the central industrial region and resultant overproduction. Behind this argument, however, was the long-standing competition between St. Petersburg and the central industrial region. St. Petersburg manufacturers stood to gain by prohibiting night work because cheaper access to raw materials, greater mechanization, and higher work productivity had already made it nearly obsolete in St. Petersburg. The Moscow industrialists, on the other hand, felt dependent on women's night work in order to compete with St. Petersburg and were vehemently against the proposed law. The ensuing debate reflected this ongoing battle, each side mustering morality and compassion for women to prove its point. To St. Petersburg's claim that night work was "physically excessive" and "morally harmful" to women and adolescents, Moscow retorted that night work was no worse for workers than "the barracks and drinking establishments which existed for debauchery . . . and from which it is impossible to avert the working people." In the end, a few of the big Moscow industrialists who could afford to dispense with night work defected from the Moscow position and the law was approved. In its final form, the law prohibited night work (defined as work from 9 P.M. to 5 A.M.) for adolescents to age 17 and women in three industries—cotton, linen, and wool. The law might have had very positive effects for women workers, since the great majority of them worked precisely in those industries. However, evasions were difficult to uncover and punish, since the factory inspectorate entrusted with enforcement of the law was far too limited in numbers and financial resources to do an effective job. Subsequent legislation took away with one hand what it had given with the other: factory owners were permitted to hire women for night work in busy seasons and to fill rush orders; certain industries were exempted entirely from the night work prohibition; and night work was redefined to mean work from 10 P.M. to 4 A.M.

Between 1890 and 1899 a few *gubernii* attempted to regulate medical aid for pregnant women. In 1892, St. Petersburg *guberniia* required that a midwife be employed by factories where the number of women workers exceeded 100. Similar laws went into effect in several other *guberniia*. But, as a member of the medical profession pointed out, these laws were poorly defined; moreover, in the majority of cases, supervision for their execution was almost entirely lacking.

Until the late 1890s the people most concerned about the wretched lives of Russian women workers were the early factory inspectors, zemstvo sanitary officials, and doctors. These were highly trained, well-educated specialists who knew the conditions of Russian factories from years of study and first-hand observation and who were well acquainted with the literature on factories, labor legislation, and workers' living conditions in Western Europe as well. Though at one time or another most of them held official positions, it would be a distortion to characterize their views on labor problems as "official," for between the early 1870s (in some cases even earlier) and the late 1890s they carried on a losing battle against both government agencies and industrialists.

Their attitude toward women in the factory was a fascinating blend of pragmatism, sincere compassion, and traditional prejudices. This combination inspired them to suggest some very advanced solutions to the problems of the factory woman and to ignore other obvious ones. "If industry has such a ruinous effect on male workers, as we can see from the data, . . . then obviously the pernicious influence on women is far greater. In general women have more delicate, sensitive constitutions and are more weakly defended against illness than men. Therefore all the harmful conditions of factory life reflect more harshly on women workers than men."

Whether or not women are more delicate than men is a question that need not detain us here. What is important is that the people who knew the conditions of factory life from their own studies and observations perceived that these conditions—terrible for all workers—exacted a greater price from the woman worker than from the man because of her dual role as worker and mother. But the factory inspectors and other experts, unlike their Western counterparts, never proposed sending the factory woman back to some utopian rural bliss; they understood perfectly that women of the peasantry did hard physical labor and that this was appropriate to peasant conditions. They accepted the fact that women were indispensable participants in industrial labor, and felt that female factory labor was necessary for women, for industrialists, and for the well-being of the entire nation. What they sought was to ameliorate and humanize the working woman's life. As they hoped for nothing from industrialists, they looked to the government to pass appropriate legislation to safeguard the health and well-being of working women. They envisioned laws to end night work for all women, to regulate factory women's hours, to prohibit women from working in especially arduous and dangerous industries, and to make medical facilities available to all women, especially mothers. For mothers, too, they envisioned facilities for the care and education of young children. It should be noted that they were often in advance of their Western counterparts in these demands. And they were optimistic. As the Moscow *zemstvo* doctor F. F. Erisman wrote in 1890: "Between the factory owners' following their own personal interests [cheap labor] and the government which is morally obligated to protect the weak and defenseless, there will be a new struggle which will have the same character as the contemporary struggle over child labor; but it will be played out on other no less important grounds—on the soil of the protection of women's labor."

Unfortunately, such optimism was based on their own sense of justice, not on a realistic estimate of the forces ranged against the promulgation of such legislation. The anticipated battle for the protection of women in the factory never came to pass.

These dedicated, knowledgeable, and compassionate men were bound by the universal belief that primary to women was "the fulfillment of her maternal functions dictated by nature"; and though they had the facts and figures at their disposal to prove otherwise, they based all their analyses, predictions, and solutions on the assumption that all women were or would be married and would have children. In fact, one of the main reasons they felt it was important to protect the health of the factory woman was that "the sacrifice of women's strength and health affects the future generations of the working classes." Yet, in Moscow *guberniia* in 1885–1887, 59.4 percent of the 35,890 women workers were unmarried. To be sure, between the ages of 20 and 50 only 28.8 percent were unmarried. However, the statistics do not indicate how many women, married or unmarried, were the sole support of themselves and their children. And, the fact remains that most factory women were self-supporting at some time in their lives, and many were all of their lives. But nowhere in the proposals of the factory inspectors, medical experts, and *zemstvo* officials do we find a discussion of or a solution to the hardships of the single factory woman. Aside from the barbarous working and living conditions, the main obstacle to a decent life for the self-supporting factory woman was her indecently low wage. Nowhere is there the recognition that equal wages for equal work might be a just and tenable demand to make of either industrialists or government.

Educated and articulate women of the upper classes, conscious of the oppression of women in general, had very little to say about women in the factory before the mid-1880s. The *zhenskii vopros* ("woman question") debates were carried on solely by, and to suit the needs of, the intelligentsia. The factory woman's experience was so distant from their own that they barely noted her existence. Moreover, the major goal in the early stages of concern with the "woman question" was to find ways to release upper-class women from enforced idleness and economic dependence. To the extent that the intelligentsia was even aware of the woman in the factory, it seemed to them that she was already a step ahead—she, after all, already worked for her daily bread. One of the earliest journals devoted to women's problems, *Zhenskii Vestnik* [*Woman's Herald*] (1866–67), carried only one article on factory women.[2]

*Drug Zhenshchin* [*Women's Friend*], a journal published in the mid-1880s with the active collaboration of educated upper-class women, contained several serious articles on factory women, some of which were based on the most exhaustive data available. Typical was one that queried "Why does our peasant woman leave her deprived, laborious, but free peasant life in exchange for crowded, gloomy factories?" The answer was the growing number of mouths that could no longer be nourished from the meager peasant allotment. What were the consequences of this exchange? The factory woman's low wages, poor diet, wretched living conditions, and long hours of hard work were all carefully noted and lamented. But the most deleterious effect of the factory, in the author's opinion, was that it took the peasant woman away from her natural place by the domestic hearth, and was thus an "expression of the economic disintegration of the peasant family." It followed that the woman worker was doomed to moral degeneration: "The constant combination of both sexes [in the factory] in the absence of a moral regimen which provides people

---

2. This article, by the radical [P. N.] Tkachev, is long, complex, confused, and fascinating. His main point is that industrialization, which theoretically should have provided the working woman with the possibility of economic independence from men, was in fact a disaster for her.

with a settled domestic life with mutual, shared economic and family concerns cannot help but contribute to the degeneration of [women's] morals."

The practical results of this concern were minimal and were merely extensions of the episodic philanthropic activities that had been aimed at the urban poor since the 1860s. In 1897 the Society for the Care of Young Girls was formed in St. Petersburg to "protect young girls, primarily of the working class . . . from the influence of morally damaging conditions of life." The Society sponsored Sunday gatherings for women workers at which they were taught to sew and to read and write. They heard lectures on hygiene and religion, listened to concerts, and danced. About 200 young women came each week, mostly tobacco and textile workers, but some seamstresses from small workshops and a few domestic servants. The members of the Society wrung their hands in despair over the wretched lot of the St. Petersburg factory woman, but class condescension prevented them from seeing beyond the alleged immorality into which factory life led her. The goal of the Society was limited to providing a "bright and joyful moment" in the life of the factory woman in the hopes that it would contribute to her "spiritual well-being" and keep her from sin.

But alongside this philanthropic outlook, a broad and increasingly sophisticated feminism was emerging as a generation of professionally educated women perceived another dimension to women's problems. The most articulate representative of this generation was Mariia Ivanovna Pokrovskaia, a doctor who had a profound knowledge of and compassion for factory workers in general and women workers in particular. For many years she practiced among St. Petersburg's workers, making her own independent studies and expending vast amounts of energy to bring the realities of the factory woman's life to the attention of anyone who would listen—women of her own station, the medical profession, the government. She had too much experience practicing medicine in the countryside to have illusions about the life of the rural woman and fully accepted the inevitability of women in industry. She was a major influence in keeping alive some interest in working women within the feminist movement, which from its inception in the early years of the twentieth century to its demise in 1917 was mainly concerned with the problems of middle- and upper-class women. But as the feminist movement grew in size and sophistication, as it began to attract women who were touched by Pokrovskaia's broad perspective and especially as it became politicized after 1905, the woman in the factory became a consistent, if minor, concern. The journals representing the various women's political groups from 1904 to 1917—*Zhenskii Vestnik*, *Soiuz Zhenshchin* [*Union of Women*], and *Zhenskoe Delo* [*Women's Work*]—included many notes and articles, more informative than analytical, on women workers in Russia and abroad. The most conservative of the journals, *Soiuz Zhenshchin*, was "dedicated to questions connected with the struggle for feminine equality, mainly [women's] right to vote as the first necessary step on the road to emancipation," and was only minimally interested in factory women. *Zhenskii Vestnik*, on the other hand, edited by Pokrovskaia, reflected her approach and was more assiduous in the collection, publication, and analysis of information on the working woman. In varying degrees, all foresaw a women's political movement including women of all classes and felt that the vote would be the ultimate panacea for the oppression of women. In 1905 the feminists made their first concrete attempt to draw factory women into the struggle for political rights with the formation of four women's political clubs in St. Petersburg. The clubs functioned for almost two months before they were closed down by the police in 1906 after the dismissal of the First Duma.[3]

Until the last decade of the nineteenth century the radical tradition offered little more than the feminist movement did to the Russian factory woman. To be sure, in the early 1870s as part of a broad effort to reach the people, a few populist women assumed the identities of factory women and actually worked in the factories of Moscow and other cities. The exposure was terrifying. "I remember the Sunday night preceding Monday at 4 A.M., 1874, when Gravchevskii and I surrendered Betia Kaminskaia to the Moiseev factory. . . . It seemed to me as if we were leading this girl to some kind of terrible execution and that Subbotina wept as if foreseeing this execution." A week later, "We greeted Kaminskaia as if we had literally not seen her for years. And, in fact, she had changed markedly, as if years had passed. Before she was rosy-cheeked and fresh. Now she looked pale, thin, and exhausted."

The effort to contact factory women was fleeting, for the mass arrests of 1874 put an end to this phase of radical activity. Even before the arrests, however, there was dissension within the [populist] movement over the wisdom of subjecting populist women to the horrors of the factory. Though the history of radical attempts to work with women in the factory after these modest beginnings remains to be thoroughly explored, there is nothing to suggest that interest in awakening women workers to the possibility of radical or revolutionary action was programmatic. On the contrary, a common tactic of radical circles was to make initial and exploratory approaches to workers not in the factories but in the taverns—not a very likely place to run into women workers.

Most of these [radical] groups in the 1870s and 1880s fell somewhere on a blurred continuum between populist and proto-Marxist. As Marxist thinking penetrated Russia's radical oppositional movement, the importance of addressing propaganda and organizational efforts to factory women received a theoretical basis. The emancipation of women was an integral part of Marxist ideology. It clearly recognized the double oppression of working-class women—by virtue of their sex (which affected women of all classes) and by virtue of their exploited position as workers within a capitalist system. Moreover, it insisted on the absolute necessity of including working women in the revolutionary struggle, not only for their own emancipation, but for the success of the proletarian revolution as a whole. Thus, some Marxist circles of the 1890s made special efforts to reach factory women, usually with considerable success. Sometimes this was done by male organizers and sometimes by female social-democratic intellectuals. The method followed the traditional pattern for underground activity in the factory. An *intelligent* [member of the intelligentsia] made contact with a promising woman worker and exposed her to books, usually on a wide variety of topics. When she was considered sufficiently

---

3. The feminist movement in late Imperial Russia is further discussed in the essay by Richard Stites in Chapter 13.—Ed.

"developed," she was encouraged to assume a leading role in other groups. A number of women workers educated in this manner remained very active through the revolutionary ferment of the early twentieth century.

Like every European country with a Marxist movement of any significance, Russia before 1917 had Marxist women leaders fiercely dedicated to the emancipation of women workers. And in Russia, as elsewhere, these women had to struggle on two fronts—the ideological one, against what were considered the conceptual errors of the bourgeois feminist movement; and the practical one, against the indifference or even hostility toward women workers within the Marxist camp. For though there was no lack of rhetoric about, and no absence of compassion for, the plight of the woman worker, in practice women workers were always very low on the list of Marxist priorities.

The main reason for this was the pervasive and profoundly ingrained attitude toward women in general that the social-democratic leadership, worker or intelligentsia, shared with male workers. The experience of Vera Karelina, a woman worker active in the underground from the 1890's on and one of the social-democratic members of the Gapon [labor] organization, is typical. When she attempted to bring women workers to the attention of the organization (with Gapon's backing), she met with the following obstacles: "Then the masses of workers held the opinion that any social [public] activity was not a woman's business. She has her own business—at the factory, the machine; at home, the children, the diapers and the pots. I recall what I had to put up with when the question of female membership in the *Obshchestvo* [organization] was discussed. There was not a single mention of the woman worker, as if she were entirely nonexistent, as if she were some kind of appendage—despite the fact that there were industries in which the workers were exclusively women." Nonetheless, Karelina managed to form women's sections within the Gapon organization, to which women workers flocked. But she shouldered the burden alone: "A few times the attempt was made to attract women of the intelligentsia to this activity. But the same general alienation and hostility to working with women that existed in intelligentsia sections . . . was an obstacle."

The stormy events of 1905, the strike movement, and the tremendous outburst of union organization provide further evidence of how revolutionary parties and the industrial proletariat regarded women workers in practice. In principle, most unions—with a few exceptions—were not against including women workers, but very little energy was directed at organizing or educating them. The leaders of the Bolshevik-dominated textile unions of the Moscow region, for example, at their first regional conference in February 1906, noted that "in the textile industry women are a very significant part, at times the overwhelming majority of workers, and that women's labor increases day by day." They further considered that "the only solution to the problems of improving the position of the working class in general, and of women in particular, is organization of the proletariat." Given that "women, because of their economic and domestic situation, are much less capable of defending themselves against the bondage and exploitation of capital," the conference proposed that "all measures be taken to attract women on an equal basis with men into unions and all other workers' organizations." What these measures should be and how the proposal might be implemented were not discussed. Nor is it likely that the leaders of the unions, social-democratic or otherwise, had much more than a rhetorical interest in the problem. The strike literature of the 1905–1907 period clearly shows that—whatever lip service was paid to the importance of including women in strike and union activities—the exhortations to *action* were addressed to the "true *sons* of the army of labor whose name is proletariat." In a call to "*all* textile workers" of the Moscow region in 1907, the workers were asked to "Stop and look at your endless tortured labor, . . . at your constant unfulfilled needs, at your *wives*' tears" (emphases mine). In short, in real situations as opposed to paper ones, the workers called to action were envisaged as exclusively male. The examples are legion.

To be sure, actual strike demands throughout 1905–1907 more often than not reflected women workers' needs. There is scarcely a strike document—in industries employing women—that does not mention, in some form, demands for paid maternity leave (usually four weeks before and six weeks after childbirth), for time off for feeding infants, and for construction of nurseries at the factory.

But these kinds of demands, of course, were strictly related to the woman worker's maternal or domestic functions. In a 1907 textile strike in Ivanovo-Voznesensk, strikers even demanded that women be released for half a day to launder clothes. The demand for equal wages for men and women workers, though now heard with some frequency, was by no means universal. And there were cases where an explicit minimum wage was requested with lower rages for women than for men.

It is not surprising, then, that the number of women workers in unions was far less than the number of men; moreover, it was considerably less than the proportion of women in the industrial work force would lead us to expect. In Moscow in 1907, for example, women were only 4.4 percent of union members. They were somewhat better represented in the rest of the central industrial region and especially in St. Petersburg, but the percentages never reached impressive proportions.

It should be noted, however, that women workers were not always passive, that they did not invariably conform to the employers' stereotype of a "calmer, steadier element." In 1878 some 300 women tobacco workers from two St. Petersburg factories marched en masse to negotiate with the management over arbitrarily lowered piecework rates. When the management responded with curses and threats, the women returned to the factories to throw everything—tools and furniture—out the windows. The management accorded to their demands. From that time on there is ample evidence of women's participation in every type of workers' protest. Examples range from a rowdy strike initiated by women workers in the St. Petersburg tobacco factory of Laferm in 1895 to a massive strike, also in 1895, at a weaving factory in Ivanovo-Voznesensk where several women were among the 25 workers who negotiated with the factory management.

What this and other evidence suggests is that as long as protest was spontaneous, as long as it remained in a relatively unideological, unorganized stage and was therefore not "bureaucratized," women workers were capable of manifesting their discontent in concrete ways. But as soon as protests began to assume more organized forms, from the time of the formation of the Gapon organization [1903–1904] through the rest of the prerevolutionary period, women workers seemed unable to sustain consistent participation. This cannot simply be put down to the insensitivity of male-dominated unions and political groups toward working women, and to the unwillingness of male activists to solicit female support. To understand this development we must recognize the complex relationship between men's attitudes toward women workers and women's own image of themselves; and we must recall the low levels of female literacy, the low incomes of women vis-à-vis those of men, the double role of laboring women as both workers and mothers, and the general psychological makeup of women. Vera Karelina expressed the feelings of women workers toward participation in workers' groups: "Well, I do want to express myself, but then I think it over—so many people, they will all be looking at me and what if someone laughs at what I say. . . . I grow cold with these thoughts, I'm filled with terror. So—you sit silently, but your heart is enflamed."

[In sum:] From the mid-1880s the factory woman's existence began to penetrate public awareness and the hardships unique to her situation assumed the dimensions of a social problem. Yet, as a social problem she was treated as a minor appurtenance to some related issue. She was the occasional recipient of philanthropic sympathy directed at the urban poor in general. She was an appendage to a broader labor problem; amelioration of the conditions of her life was sometimes seen as a partial solution to the problems of labor unrest or as a way to insure future generations of healthy workers. From time to time populist activists caught a glimpse of her within the factory walls and made desultory efforts to include her in their tactical calculations. Concern for the factory woman grew somewhat more intense at the beginning of the twentieth century. First, official Russia, with some astonishment, began to take serious note of the growing numbers of women in the factory, partly because the increase was at the expense of male labor. Second, feminism evolved into a cohesive movement that maintained a peripheral but consistent solicitude for women workers. Third, the Marxist opponents of tsarist Russia, armed with an ideology that included women among the victims of capitalist exploitation, perceived women workers as important allies and attempted, at least sporadically, to draw them into revolutionary struggle. But throughout the period under consideration the woman worker remained a bas-relief [in the background] rather than a freestanding figure. Her full historical dimensions remain to be further investigated and revealed.

## DOCUMENTS

These two documents are excerpted from the memoirs of persons who were at the top and the bottom of late Imperial Russian society. The first is by Michael Ignatieff, a Canadian writer and trained historian who reconstructs with remarkable detachment the lives and memories of his grandfather Count Paul Ignatieff and grandmother Princess Natasha Mestchersky (spellings throughout are Michael Ignatieff's). In their separate family histories and in their life together, which ended in Canadian exile (1919), Count Paul and Princess Natasha embodied much of the character and experience of the higher Imperial elite in its last decades. Both families traced their nobility and landed wealth to service to the crown in the eighteenth and nineteenth centuries, a tradition they strove to fulfill to the end; and both families contained their share of amusing eccentrics and sad wastrels, heroes and charming dilettantes, exploiters and wistful survivors. In reconstructing his grandparents' extraordinarily privileged lives in late Imperial Russia, Michael Ignatieff drew on their own written memoirs and photograph albums along with extensive family interviews, straight historical research, and trips back to their homeland.

Ignatieff is followed by passages from the autobiography of Semën (Simon) Ivanovich Kanatchikov, nicknamed "Senka," which he published in Moscow between 1929 and 1934. Kanatchikov was born a peasant in the village of Gusevo, in the Volokolamsk (westernmost) district of Moscow province, in 1879; he died a middle-level Communist party official in Moscow in 1940 (it is not known whether he was a victim of Stalin's purges). In these initial passages from his book we learn of his childhood in the village, of his departure for Moscow at the age of sixteen (spring 1895), and of his life there and work in the List factory (as a painter and pattern-maker) until May 1896, when he witnessed a major disaster on the outskirts of the city connected with the coronation of Nicholas II. Along the way, recapitulating the experience of thousands of young Russians, Kanatchikov loses his peasant mentality and assumes the outlook and attitudes of a "conscious worker" and, eventually, a revolutionary activist.

## Michael Ignatieff Describes Life Among the High Nobility, 1880s–1890s

Summer mornings at the Mestchersky country estate in the 1880s began with the same ritual. Natasha [author's grandmother] and her sister Vera, already washed, combed and dressed by their nurse, would file into their mother's bedroom and kiss her good morning. Their mother would then sit up in bed and swallow a raw egg. The maid brought it in a glass on a silver tray and her mother would down it with a brisk, convulsive snort. The maid would then pour warm water from a ewer into a silver basin and Natasha's mother would wash her hands. Natasha and her sister Vera sat on the end of the bed and watched.

The silver ewer and basin are just about the only things that have survived from those mornings at Doughino, the family estate in the western Russian province of Smolensk. . . .

After the egg and the washing of the hands, the maid brought Natasha, Vera and their mother cups of Ceylon tea, with scalded cream from the estate dairy. While their mother's jet-black hair was being braided, piled in two tight buns above her ears, she fired questions at Natasha and Vera: had they said their prayers? Were they washed? Were they ready for their lessons? The two little girls in their pinafores held hands and replied in unison. It was a family joke that when spoken to they always chimed in together with voices like mice. Their mother beckoned them closer, straightened their pinafores, took Natasha's hair between her fingers: why did it never curl? Natasha must have another session with Miss Saunders's curling iron.

When the butler appeared with the morning's post on a tray, the two girls were dismissed with a peck on the forehead. From her bed their mother dictated her correspondence to a secretary and the girls went off to the schoolroom for their lessons with Miss Saunders and later with Mr. Sharples, the English tutor. They kept up English ways in the nursery—bread pudding with Lyle's Golden Syrup, Huntley & Palmer biscuits in square red tins from the English shops in Moscow.

Natasha was born Princess Mestchersky in August 1877, into a family of six girls and two boys: Katherine, Alexander (known as Sasha), Alexandra, Maria, Sonia, Peter, Vera and Natasha. She was the last, the little gawky one, a child of middle age. Her mother, Maria Panin, was a descendant of Nikita Panin, Catherine the Great's minister of foreign affairs, whose brother Peter had led the suppression of the uprising of the peasant bandit Pugachev in 1773–1774. Doughino, the family estate, was a gift to the Panins from the Empress. Natasha's father, Prince Nicolas Mestchersky, was rector of Moscow University.

Only one photograph remains of Natasha's mother and father. They are seated side by side on a couch at Doughino. He is thin, fine-boned and long in the face. His long white beard trails down the front of his frock coat. He is bending to graze his wife's hand with his lips. His eyes gaze at her devotedly. She does not spare him a glance. She stares out at the camera, massive, stout and ugly with highly polished black ankle boots poking out beneath her black taffeta dress. Her black hair is pulled back in a tight bun; her cheeks are heavy; her lidded eyes appraise the photographer with lofty amusement. The Panins had once been Panini and had come to Russia from Italy some time in the seventeenth century to make their fortune. From them, Natasha's mother had inherited the dark olive skin and a passion for argument. Her daughters said she had a "man's brain," she was impatient of the coy and innocent vagueness of the women of her time and class. Ugly and vivacious, imperious and argumentative, she ruled Doughino in the summers and the upper reaches of Moscow society in the winters. Together with Countess Sheremetieff and a Miss Tuitcheff, she made up a trio known as the "conseil des infallibles" ["council of the infallible ones"] in the Moscow society of the 1880s. They were the court of final instance on manners, deportment and marriages. She was famous in her heyday for the sharpness of her tongue. Once when old Prince Volkonsky took her hand at a dinner party and began to tell her unsavory Moscow gossip, she reached into her reticule, pulled out a small padlock and handed it to him, saying tartly in French that if he couldn't stop telling tales about his friends, he should keep his mouth shut. She dominated them all, husband, children, servants: every summer the married daughters were commanded to appear at Doughino with their husbands and children from the four corners of western Russia, with nurses and governesses, tutors and coachmen, to spend the summer together under her watchful and disapproving eye.

Natasha's father was a mild old gentleman of conventional opinions, ruled by his wife and his daughters. Natasha took after him in looks and temperament: high forehead, long straight nose, tall and thin-boned. His only apparent role in his children's upbringing was to line them up in his study every morning and administer a spoonful of cod-liver oil followed by a slice of black bread to take away the taste.

He was generous and absent-minded, always doling out money to the Moscow beggars when out on his morning walk to the university. Once when Natasha was with him, a beggar approached and when her father replied ruefully that he had forgotten to carry any change, the beggar replied that he had plenty; Natasha's father stood there smiling absently while the beggar took the ruble note and handed back enough copecks to make the transaction satisfactory to both sides. In matters of charity, as in matters of the home, Natasha's father was a patriarch ruled by others.

Natasha's father had a brother as scabrous as he was respectable. An anti-Semitic homosexual, always in the company of young Guards officers, he was known in Petersburg circles as the Prince of Sodom. He was also the editor of *The Citizen* (*Grazhdanin*), required reading for the reactionaries of his epoch. Because of Uncle Vladimir, "a certain kind of citizen" became the Mestchersky code-phrase for homosexuals. "Petty informer, tattler, toady, a creature of perverted sexual taste, pulp novelist, embezzler"—the gossips did not spare him. It was said his wife had caught him *in flagrante* with a trumpet player of the Guards. It was whispered the Prince also dressed up in women's clothes. Yet his morals apparently did not bother those who read him for his opinions. After the assassination of the Liberator Tsar [Alexander II] in 1881, Vladimir Mestchersky wrote an editorial in *The Citizen* which brayed out the master theme of a new epoch: "Everywhere one goes, only a single cry is heard from the people: Beat them! Beat them! In answer to this what do the authorities reply? Anything except the birch. What is the result of this contradiction? A terrible lack of discipline, the destruction of the father's authority within the family, drunkenness, crime and so on. . . ."

When the new Tsar, Alexander III, took the throne in 1881, there were few makers of opinion more to his taste than Prince Mestchersky. Natasha's father and mother refused to receive the old debaucher in their home, yet they seem to have shared most of his views, though in milder form.

The Mestcherskys were a family of highly strung hypochondriacs. Like most Russian families of the time, they called doctors at the slightest cough or fever. In their case, however, family anxieties about health had some foundation. Natasha's oldest sister, Katherine, had gone to a hotel in Ostend to take the sea air and had died of "galloping consumption" (tuberculosis) at the age of twenty; in their grief, Natasha's mother and father watched over their remaining children with obsessive attention. The third daughter, Maria, had been invalided by a riding accident and was taken on a round-the-world tour by her mother to recover. The older son, Sasha, a stooping giant six foot six inches tall, was a mild and gentle character whose passion was his mother's greenhouses: he grew carnations from cuttings and became a fanatic for the color green, wearing a suit of green baize with a green deerstalker hat and experimenting with all the variations of green orchids. His favorite dish was pea soup.

An English tutor was hired to turn this shy and peculiar boy into a gentleman fit for a career. No one ever knew quite what happened—Natasha's mother could not bear to discuss it—but the tutor took to beating Sasha for every mistake in lessons and for every bout of masturbation in bed. The boy would have silently endured this routine had he not succumbed to meningitis. When he recovered the truth came out, the tutor was dismissed, and the parents reconciled themselves to the fact that poor Sasha was happier after all devoting himself to his Malmaison carnations and the manageable world of the greenhouse.

Natasha thought Sasha was lovable but insipid and Peter, her younger brother, charming but weak; her sisters were "all good women, but none of them brilliant." The tall and elegant Sonia, with her chestnut hair, was a bit of a flirt before marriage and then too austere and serious-minded afterwards; Alexandra likewise was too earnest; Maria a bit of an invalid; poor Vera "very high strung" and the man she married, the worthy Baron Offenberg, a most dreadful bore. Natasha was as blunt as her mother in her estimation of the faults of her kin.

The winters of Natasha's childhood were spent in the Mestchersky house opposite the yellow and white buildings of Moscow University, just behind the Kremlin on the Nikitskaya [street]. The summers, from late May until the end of September, were spent at Doughino.

I take out Baedeker's guide to the Russian Empire, 1914 edition, and follow the railway lines 200 miles west from Moscow to the province of Smolensk and find the river Vasousa. The river flowed through the bottom of the estate. In spring it would burst its banks and the surrounding countryside would be flooded, with clumps of trees marooned in the sodden fields. When the Mestcherskys arrived from Moscow in these wet springs to begin their summer at the estate, they would have to be poled through the fields by their servants in flat-bottomed boats from the station. Carriages would be waiting on the high ground to take them up through the white-columned gates past the twin spires of the family chapel to the house on the hill.

It was a peach-colored two-story eighteenth-century mansion, garlanded with vines, with six huge marble columns supporting a classical Corinthian portico. Hothouse plants decorated the balconies over the entrance and there were two life-size marble lions on either side of the doorway. In the photographs I count thirty-four windows looking out onto the English garden. There were a hundred rooms, stables, greenhouses and acres of park laid out in boxwood, pines and floral beds; the sloping meadows down to the river at the foot of the garden used to burst with flowers in the spring. Wherever she was afterwards, Natasha could always guide her mind's eye through the vanished rooms, along the big entrance hall lined with oak benches, up the two flights of stairs, past the illustrations from La Fontaine's fables in the gilt frames, through her father's study, to the dancing hall, the dining room furnished in maplewood, past the china cabinets, to her mother's boudoir. There her memory moved to a portrait of her grandmother in a dark-brown velvet dress with frills, her sparkling eyes as brown as the wood of the frame.

Somewhere behind, there was a door to the library. All along the rows of maplewood shelves were lined the books of her ancestor Nicholas Karamzin, flagged with his slips, scribbled over with his annotations. It was from this store of books that he had written his history of Russia [see Documents, Chapter 7]. Through all the waystations of revolution and exile, Natasha was to insist on carrying the full three volumes of Karamzin's history of the Russian state, in their red leather bindings decorated with the family crest. Like her mother's basin and ewer, these volumes were her talismans: she held on to them to keep faith with all the other things she had left behind.

Above the library, there was a small theater under the eaves, where the children gave performances in the summer for their parents and guests. They were excused lessons for rehearsals. The hairdresser from the local town came on the day of the performance to make the children up. Everyone from the surrounding villages came and the servants watched from the doorway. Vera and Natasha sat very still in their costumes, while the hairdresser wet his finger with his tongue, dipped it in the pot of rouge and dabbed pink on their cheeks. In the candlelit mirror they watched themselves becoming women. . . .

On fair mornings at eleven Fidki the Cossack would wheel Natasha's mother in a wicker Bath chair through the gravel pathways of the parks and gardens. The gardener would lean forward to hear her orders, and *Hofmeister* Bertram the forester would also make an appearance. The Bertrams had served the family as far back as the old Count [Panin] himself. Brought from Germany in the 1780s to bring European order to the Count's Russian woods, father and son had succeeded each other, serving as both doctor to the trees and doctor to the family. When Natasha's mother called out the *Hofmeister* at night for the children's fevers, they would hear him stumping up the stairs damning *"diese verfluchte Familie"*—this accursed family—under his breath. Then he would be at their cots, bending over them and smelling of evergreen.

Gardening was her mother's passion, and the morning meetings with the *Hofmeister* and the gardener were as serious as a staff conference of generals. Natasha's mother would wave her stick about and the *Hofmeister* would grunt and bend over and look in the direction she was pointing. The new redwoods from California were to go there, there was to be a new alley of roses here, and what on earth were those dandelions doing on the English lawn? So seriously did she take her gardening that when her older son Sasha—in his only known gesture of defiance—said that when the estate was his he would like to cut down her favorite alley of cypresses, she disinherited him on the spot. The matter might have ended tragically. He spent weeks pleading with her that he had only been joking.

Natasha loved these tours of the garden with her mother, particularly the visit to the greenhouses: vast airy sheds with warm red earth underfoot and blowsy female statuary in the alcoves. In winter, the greenhouses were a lush corner of Crimea in northern Russia. Outside the lawns and trees were draped with snow; inside, peaches and lemons ripened, warm to her touch.

Between Natasha and her mother there was a screen of nurses, butlers, tutors and gardeners, and older brothers and sisters. Natasha always held back; only when the others had left to start their own families did she find her way to her mother's heart. She remembered herself as being painfully shy; "when scarcely out of baby age when meeting strangers I put up my arm to hide my face to the great indignation particularly of my eldest sister who assured me it was an affectation." Her shyness, she always said, was her great misfortune. Nonsense, said her aunt, your shyness shows your great self-love and pride. If you would realize once and for all you are not even noticed or looked upon all that shyness would be gone. But she could not help it. She hid behind the curtains watching the others play.

The last of the litter, the gawky awkward one, Natasha clung to her older sister, the elegant Sonia, and used to weep when she disappeared to the society balls in Moscow, grazing her little sister with a fragrant kiss. Her sisters crossed the divide into the world of stays and button shoes, corsages and women's problems and left her behind in girlhood. Natasha sat in their boudoirs while they dressed at night and then would be left upstairs, sitting on the topmost step, hidden from view, watching the dancers whirl by the open door of the downstairs dining room. Later, when she was older, while her sisters danced the polka and the quadrille, and the *dirigeur*, the leader of the dance, would bring them a succession of young officers as partners, she played the *bouquetière*, the flower girl, wheeling a small cart of posies around the dance floor, stopping before each table so that the officers could offer their ladies a bouquet. A picture was taken of Natasha standing before her cart in her green pinafore, with a pink cap with ribbons in her curls—and then they packed her up to bed, while the dances surged beneath her in the bright rooms below.

Most of the winter months of her childhood were spent within sight of the Kremlin wall in Moscow in a large house with several adjoining buildings in Nikitskaya [street] opposite the yellow and cream classical porticoes and domes of the university. In the faded photographs, there is an inner garden, laid down in grass, bisected by gravel pathways and on all sides the house rises around it, with awnings over the windows. In the gravel driveway outside a coachman in a full-length cream coat and a top hat sits on his box in the family brougham, holding on to the reins of a piebald mare. He is waiting for his master who is about to appear. The butler stands ready to open the door.

On the nights when all the lamps were lit and guests were expected for dinner, Natasha and Vera would slide down the banisters to the front door and ring the bell which the footman used to announce the arrival of visitors. Her father would appear at the head of the stairs and she and Vera would jump out to surprise him. Just before the visitors would arrive, the butler would go round the rooms with a long censer held on a stick. In the censer was a hot iron plate over which the butler would pour a perfume called Court Water. The sweet humid odor slipped along the hallways, under the doors, into the rooms and suffused the sheets on the beds. It would still be there, a fragrant ghost, when she tucked herself into bed.

On Easter Saturday night Natasha would sit in her best dress at the open window waiting for the Kremlin bells to sound. All day the cooks had been making *kulich* [special Easter cake] and *paskha* [Easter cream cheese] and the house smelled of sweet dough, raisins and almonds. By early evening, the Easter feast was ready in the dining room: the white dome of the *paskha* stood in the center of the long trestle table; there were bowls full of the dyed eggs with "хв"—for "Christ is Risen"—on each of them; and she had stained her hands green and blue from dipping the eggs in the dye in the pantry with her sister. At midnight the Kremlin bells would begin to boom out through the night air and the tolling and pealing would be taken up by church bells all around her, the white domed church at the top of the street where Pushkin had got married, the red brick one down the alley, the chapels in all the side streets, the sound rising to a crescendo of celebration. Then she would leap down from the window casement and run to the family chapel on the third floor where the choir—nuns from a neighboring convent, house servants, soloists from the Choudofskoy choir—and her older sisters were already singing. The butler came up the stairs spreading the Court Water and calling out on each floor, "Service is commencing," and the servants and governesses and sisters and brothers would rush to take their places. Behind the butler came the priest and his acolytes in a procession up the winding red-carpeted stairs. And when the clergy in their white robes had exclaimed, "Christ is risen, Christ is risen indeed," and everyone in the chapel had lit their candles and embraced each other three times, they went out in the dawn air, to feel the breath of spring and the promise of resurrection from winter. And then they were back inside the dining room to feast on *paskha* and *kulich* and taste the abundance of the Easter feast after the fasting of Lent. . . .

When Natasha was sixteen she spent her first winter in Nice with the family. She took her father's arm on the Promenade des Anglais during Carnival Week in February and they walked through the crowds, ducking the showers of confetti, watching the clowns, joining in the singing and then escaping the crowds to stand at the end of the promenade alone together to watch the black calm of the winter sea.

She was in Nice with her mother in the winter of 1894 when *Hofmeister* Bertram wired them to come home to Doughino immediately. The master was ill. She raced back through Paris and Dresden and Berlin to find her father twisting and turning on his bed in the last stages of a fatal urinary and kidney infection. Surgeons and nurses were brought from Moscow to the estate. They slept on divans outside his room and the daughters took shifts sitting with him. She had the night watch. Just before morning, after weeks of suffering, he seemed to awake and to look about. Before she had time to call her mother in the next room, he looked up at his daughter and closed his eyes for ever. . . .

All her sisters and brothers had begun their adult lives by then: Sasha had been sent to the lyceum and then to university, Peter to the regiment and the daughters to marriage: Natasha was at all family conferences when her sisters' suitors were mercilessly discussed and their antecedents checked, through the *Almanach de Gotha* [standard reference book on the European nobility]. She was at the engagement parties, raised her champagne glass to their happiness, buttoned them into their wedding dresses, held their bouquets at the step of the landau and waved them down the long driveway to their honeymoons. And then she was left alone with her mother, the aging autocrat in the Bath chair. Natasha became the dutiful daughter, reading Carlyle's *History of Frederick the Great* to her in the long summer afternoons; the one who pushed her Bath chair along the Promenade des Anglais [in Nice] in the weak winter light and who, when they were back at Doughino, accompanied her on the daily tour of the estate gardens, watching the old hands palpating the peaches in the greenhouse and tapping her beloved evergreens with her stick. When her mother complained of the cold, Fidki, the lazy Cossack, would turn the Bath chair on the gravel and wheel her back home and Natasha would follow behind.

She slept in the next room to her mother, ready to rise, to comfort, to listen to the groans and lamentations. There was a pain in the old woman's breast which would not go away. The quacks descended: one whose name was Blitz prescribed massage, but the pain grew worse and the lump in her breast began to swell. Finally it became impossible to deny what was happening. From Doughino, a wire was sent to a surgeon in Moscow. He arrived by train seven hours later, took one look at his patient and ordered that a mass be sung in the chapel and that a room be scrubbed down for an operation.

Her mother's oldest friend, Countess Sheremetieff, who had been a nurse in the Russo-Turkish War [1877–1878], held her head while the chloroformed gauze was passed over her face. Under the chloroform, Natasha's mother shouted frantically that the surgeon should give up medicine and become a teacher, where he could at least do humanity some good, instead of inflicting such torture. Natasha waited in the chloroform-filled passageway, saying her prayers, listening to her mother's babbling in the next room.

The operation brought them all several years' respite. Life resumed at Doughino: the peasant children brought berries to the pantry door and the cook bought them to make jam. In the early autumn, there were mushroom hunts with the peasant children in the damp piney places under the trees and the cook would bake them into mushroom pies. In the spring, they would make a drink from the sap of birch trees and another with new buds of blackcurrant, flavored with lemons and oranges, sugar and champagne. There were troika rides in summer, sleigh rides in the winter, muffled deep in furs. On the long summer afternoons, Natasha would take her nephews and nieces down to the meadow by the river while her sisters slept with their husbands upstairs in the bedrooms darkened against the heat.

The old woman's rule was drawing to a close but none of her daughters or sons-in-law dared disobey her. From June till September, she insisted the clan must be about her though she did not actually like to see them once they were there. On her morning walk, she forbade the sight of her grandchildren and if they heard the Bath chair crunching along the gravel they would scurry for cover behind the box hedges until the procession had gone by.

Doughino was a closed universe with the world held at the distance beyond the white gates. When the jangling bells of troikas were heard approaching in the park, Natasha and the servants would come running to see who the visitors might be. There was Chomiakoff, after 1905 one of the presidents of the Duma, a "queer man," Mongolian in appearance, always contradicting himself; and the elegant Ourousoffs, as delicate as moths, in their fawn riding clothes, recounting the latest gossip from the Riviera in a Russian flavored with a slight French accent. She remembered best Professor Rachinsky, an excitable little man, with a face like a squeezed-out lemon, yellow but full of life. An indefatigable eccentric, he arrived with tremendous bustle from his estate in Tver province and seemed to inspect every leaf in the garden, and quizzed the village priest about the state of the peasants' moral education. At his own estate, he ran a school for peasant children.

Natasha wondered whether Professor Rachinsky's philanthropy ever came to anything—one of his peasant children became a priest, another became an artist—but the rest returned to the soil, untouched by the Professor's lessons. She was generous enough herself, as her father had been, but she was unburdened by that Tolstoyan sense of guilt and responsibility for the peasants that drove the old Professor on his grinding round of benevolence.

There was another visitor who talked like Rachinsky, a typical Russian madcap of a doctor, who had handsome red hair and who used to sit and spill out all his Tolstoyan theories to Natasha after dinner in the study. She was attracted to him, though marriage with a young country doctor was out of the question, and she liked the look of Russian absorption which came over him when he talked of putting the country to rights. He told her that he liked her austerity, the plain black dresses, the simple unadorned meals at table, the frugality observed in this most splendid of old houses. He said it would prepare her well for whatever life had to offer. She found the compliment amusing: it was said so somberly, as if darkness lay ahead for both of them.

The subject of the peasantry always seemed to send the men at Doughino into that special mood of earnest self-importance which came over aristocratic Russians when they discussed a "social question." She herself had very few thoughts about the peasants. They were in another world beyond the gates. Only one photograph in her family album shows peasants in the frame. The picture was taken sometimes in the 1890s at the festival of St. Peter and St. Paul by the doorway of the family chapel at Doughino. Women in white kerchiefs crowd around the icons which are draped in white and carried by deacons with flowing black hair and vestments. The sea of faces is turned towards the icons, but one face—that of a woman in a white kerchief—is looking over her shoulder. Her back is broad and strong; there is an apron around her waist. She is staring at someone "from the big house," and her gaze is curious and unafraid.

In just twenty years these peasants were to burn Doughino to the ground and make the owner, mild stooping Sasha, sweep out the latrines in the prison yard at [nearby] Sichevka. This irony—that I know what is coming and Natasha could not—is one of the barriers between us. I have to forget what comes next. To share her past, I have to forget her future. . . .

# S. I. Kanatchikov Recounts His Adventures as a Peasant-Worker-Activist, 1879–1896

My early childhood was not accompanied by any particularly outstanding events, unless one counts the fact that I survived; I wasn't devoured by a pig, I wasn't butted by a cow, I didn't drown in a pool, and I didn't die of some infectious disease

Reprinted from A Radical Worker in Tsarist Russia, Translated and Edited by Reginald E. Zelnik, pp. 1–11, 27–37, 39–45 with the permission of the publishers, Stanford University Press. © 1986 by the Board of Trustees of the Leland Stanford Junior University.

the way thousands of peasant children perished in those days [1880s], abandoned without any care during the summer harvest season.

For a village child to survive in those times was a rare event. As evidence of this there is at least the fact that my own mother, according to some sources, brought eighteen children into this world—according to others the number was twelve—yet only four of us survived. It is clear from the two figures I have mentioned, even if we take only the second, that I had little choice but to view my presence on earth as a great stroke of fortune.

My father—and this was more than half a century before our era—belonged to the very large stratum of middle peasants. Of course I have no intention whatever of claiming that circumstance as a credit to either my father or me, for we can hardly assume the presence on his part of a carefully thought-out plan to remain a middle peasant all his life. Indeed, to the best of my judgment he had no desire whatever to remain at that rank and he endeavored throughout his life to enter the ranks of the kulaks: he tried to rent land, to engage in trade, and so on. But because he lacked the kulak's tightfisted grasp, because he was a simple peasant, honest and just to the core, he was always defeated in his kulak efforts.

My father's past, to the extent that I can picture it in my own mind on the basis of separate, fragmentary memories, looked something like this. During the days of serfdom, when still a young boy, he was sent to St. Petersburg to work as a servant. He was employed in various big hotels as a bellboy, a room-servant, a billiard-room assistant, and so on. He taught himself to read and write; he was very good at reading aloud but he wrote very poorly. Most of his life was passed "in freedom," that is, away from his home. Nevertheless, he was attached in various ways to his peasant household. He often sent money back to his village, money that he tore away from his scanty earnings; whenever he had the opportunity, he would try to go back to his village or would send for his mother to come visit him in the city. Around the age of 50, having completely ruined his health, he moved back to the village for good. He loved the land and he tried to implant that love in me. "Stick to the land, my son—the land is our provider with water and food," he would often repeat to me. Yet he was not capable of doing peasant work himself; in addition, he was short-winded and couldn't engage in hard work.

Our peasant household was actually managed by my older brother, who already had his own family. During the winter, when the field work was over, he too went off to a factory to earn money.

Our family consisted of nine or ten souls. There was no way we could live off the land alone, for our [land] allotments were very paltry and the winter earnings of my older brother were inadequate. My father tried to sow more flax and to get into commerce, but, as I said earlier, nothing came of these efforts: the land was exhausted, the price of flax was falling, and the commercial endeavor was shattered. In this way he continued to struggle, year in and year out, barely able to make ends meet.

When I was nine they sent me off to attend school in the nearest large village. During the winter, every day they would take us children there by sled, one at a time. For our generation the methods of school instruction in those days were very uncomplicated: the ruler, the birch rod, the teacher's belt, and the simple slap in the face. To be sure, there were also some more humane teachers at our school, teachers to whom the methods of modern pedagogy were not alien; these were the ones who would take us by the nose and put us in a corner on our knees or would make us go without lunch. In our school these teachers were replaced rather often. And, depending on the individual inclinations of the particular pedagogue, their methods of instruction changed as well. We looked upon all these methods as the unavoidable components of pedagogy, recalling the dictum: "Better one man who's been schooled [literally, "beaten"] than two who have not been."

Many amusing but at the same time unpleasant moments were provided to us by our religion instructor—an enormous, broad-shouldered, long-haired priest from the neighboring village, who was distinguished by his ferocity toward us and by his great love of horses. His lessons took place after lunch on Fridays, when he usually returned from the open-air market where he liked to wheel and deal; on his return trip he would stop at our school. A bit tight, speaking inarticulately, he would ask us to say the prayers and make us read the Gospels in Church Slavonic and translate them into Russian. After the lesson, which was always accompanied by a large number of thrashings, he would test our "knowledge" by asking his own rather peculiar kind of questions. They were distinguished by their extremely unpredictable quality, such as, for example, how many hands were on the icon called the "three-handed" Holy Mother of God, or, perhaps, does a calf have a soul? Two or three incorrect answers from the same pupil would again produce a thrashing. When the "lesson" was over, our religion instructor would get into his wagon, which was harnessed to a great bay stallion, and drive off madly to his own village until the following Friday.

Yet despite all this, my studies went rather well, which gave my father great pleasure. Often when I came home from school I would read to him aloud, on a long winter's evening, selections from *The Native Word* [a primer] or else recount from memory some of the entertaining stories from the Old Testament. He would caress my hair, praise me, and in his turn tell me stories of his life in St. Petersburg.

I can still remember individual episodes from those stories, such as how the former artisan-hatter Komissarov, Alexander II's "savior," who, during the attempt on the tsar's life [1866], while standing behind the "nahilist" Karakozov, had jolted the hand with which Karakozov was aiming his revolver at the tsar—how this same Komissarov had stayed at the hotel where my father worked. Alexander II had generously rewarded Komissarov and granted him noble status.

My father also told me stories about the execution of the "Jewess" Perovskaia and the "nahilist" Zheliabov.[1] When I asked him why they were executed, Father replied:

"They wanted to kill the tsar."

"But who were these nahilists?"

---

1. Both were executed for complicity in the assassination of Alexander II in 1881 (see Documents, Chapter 9).—Ed.

"Landowners and students, and they killed the Tsar-liberator [Alexander II] because he'd given freedom to the peasants. They are all 'Freemazons,' " he added, "they believe in neither God nor tsar."

Just what these "Freemazons" were, Father himself could not explain with any clarity. From time to time he used the word "pedagogues," which he was also unable to explain. Somehow he thought that this word too meant something akin to atheist and "nahilist."

At the age of thirteen I finished elementary school. My father was now faced with the question of what to do with me next. He lacked the resources to continue my education, and in any case my own heart wasn't in my studies. Nor did Father wish to "set me free" in the city of Moscow where, without paternal supervision, he feared I might cut myself off from our homestead and be corrupted. His real dream was to keep me in the village, to make me into a good peasant. But our peasant farmstead, with its small allotments of land, held no promise for the future. And so two years went by without any resolution of this problem. During that time I grew accustomed to peasant work: I tilled the soil, I harrowed, mowed, and threshed, and in the winter I went to the forest to gather wood.

My father was strict in disposition and despotic in character. He kept the entire family in mortal fright. We all feared him and did everything we could to please him.

There were times when he would "go on a binge," and when he was on a binge—as they'd say in our village—"he locks the gate." During his drinking bouts Father usually spent his time away from home, in the circle of his drinking companions and hangers-on. At such times he would become kind, merry, generous, and extravagant. Not infrequently he would drink to the point where he was seriously ill, and there were even occasions when he was close to death.

When his binges were over and he'd begun to recover, Father would become gloomy, morose, and demanding. A heavy silence reigned over our home, and everyone would tremble. To compensate for the money he'd squandered on drink, Father would introduce a regimen of economizing and would reduce the family's expenditures: instead of drinking tea twice a day, we'd drink it only once; Mother would stop baking pies and cakes on holidays, and so on.

But the biggest burden at times like this fell upon my unfortunate mother; my father was her deathblow. I loved my mother intensely and hated my father with an animal hate: I would become rude to him, insolent and disrespectful. I passionately took my mother's part and prevented him from beating her. This kind of interference usually ended with Father beating me up as well, unless I managed to dodge his blows in time and run away.

My older brother stood aside from these family tragedies and refused to get involved. Father disliked him very much and any attempt on his part to intervene might easily have led Father to cut him off.

In spite of all these defects, however, my father did have some positive features in his character. He was a religious believer, but he wasn't superstitious. He did not believe in demons, household spirits, or magic spells, he made fun of village wise women and healers, and he didn't like priests. He read many different books and once he even took out a subscription to a cheap newspaper. Observing him when, his iron eyeglasses atop his nose, he sat for days on end fixated on some book, I too developed a passion for reading. I would steal some money from my father and some eggs from my mother and purchase some popular illustrated books in the neighboring village.

When I reached the age of fourteen, a terrible misfortune beset me—my mother took ill with an inflammation of the lungs and died. Before she died we summoned a priest to her, gathered around her, and administered the last sacrament; then she quietly passed away.

For whole nights through, holding a waxen candle over the corpse of my deeply beloved mother, I read aloud from the Psalter, hoping to help her to migrate to the "heavenly kingdom." According to the popular belief of those times, you had to read the entire Psalter forty times over in order to achieve this goal. Great were my bitterness and suffering when, at the twenty-eighth reading of the Psalter, exhausted, worn out by the sleepless nights, I began to fall asleep and stopped reading.

My life in the village was becoming unbearable. I wanted to rid myself of the monotony of village life as quickly as possible, to free myself from my father's despotism and tutelage, to begin to live a self-reliant, independent life. It was not long before the opportunity presented itself, and Father, after long arguments and discussions, decided to let me go to Moscow. My joy and delight were boundless!

My departure was invested with a certain solemnity. In the morning Father gathered the entire family in the cottage and lit the icon lamps in front of the images of the saints. Everyone sat on the benches in solemn silence and waited. Then Father arose and began to pray to the icon. The entire family followed his example. When the prayer was over, Father addressed me with his parting words, once more reminding me not to forget God, to honor my superiors, to serve my employer honestly, and, above all else, to be mindful of our home.

In the spring of 1895, when I was sixteen years old, Father drove me to Moscow where he placed me into apprenticeship at the "Gustav List" engineering works.[2] Since there was no place in the pattern shop, I began in the painting shop.

## In the "Artel"

I remember what a stunning impression Moscow made on me. My father and I, sitting in our cart, walked our gray horse along the brightly lighted streets. Huge multistoried houses—most of them with lighted windows—stores, shops, taverns, beer halls, horse-drawn carriages going by, a horse-drawn tramway—and all around us crowds of bustling people, rushing to unknown destinations for unknown reasons. I was not even able to read the signboards. What struck me most was the abundance of stores and shops: for every house, there was one store after another.

---

2. The List factory, founded in 1863, was a moderately large machine-construction plant (in the 1890s, 500–800 workers were employed).

"Who buys all these goods?" I asked my father. "Why, there are more stores here than there are people!"

"Mother Moscow, she feeds all of Russia. Our tradesmen also come here for merchandise," Father responded, coughing and moaning from shortness of breath.

Compared with our village hovels, what struck me about the houses of Moscow was their grandiose appearance, their luxury.

"Am I to live in a house like that?" I asked with delight.

"You'll find out in due course."

And sure enough our gray horse soon turned into a side street, and the wagon entered the gates of a huge stone house with a courtyard that looked like a large stone well. Wet linens dangled from taut clotheslines all along the upper stories. The courtyard had an acrid stench of carbolic acid. Throughout the courtyard were dirty puddles of water and discarded vegetables. In the apartments and all around the courtyard people were crowding, making noise, yelling, cursing.

My delight was beginning to turn into depression, into some kind of inexplicable terror before the grandiose appearance and cold indifference of my surroundings. I felt like a small insignificant grain of sand, lost in the unfamiliar and hostile sea of people that surrounded me.

On the evening of the same day, my father and I, together with our countryman [zemliak] Korovin, who had arranged my job at the factory, went to a tavern. Father ordered tea for three, with rolls and a pint of vodka.

Korovin—tall, round-shouldered, sporting a goatee, in a faded, knitted jacket worn over his shirt—adopted the strict, preceptorial attitude of a teacher with me. But when the pint had taken effect, he began to brag about his closeness to the foreman, his knowledge of his craft, his high wage, and his plan to build a two-story house in the village.

Father sat quietly, nodding his head in approval, occasionally offering advice on the building of the house. At the end of the evening Father asked Korovin to treat me strictly, to keep me from consorting and getting into mischief with the wrong kind of people. And he again admonished me to be obedient to my bosses and superiors and have faith in God.

On the following day, early in the morning, Father departed for the village, and I remained alone. Two feelings were struggling in my soul. I longed for the village, for the meadows, the brook, the bright country sun, the free clear air of the fields, and for the people who were near and dear to me. Here, in the hostile world of Moscow, I felt lonely, abandoned, needed by no one. While at work in the painting shop to which I'd been temporarily assigned, and which smelled of paint and turpentine, I would remember pictures of our village life, tears would come to my eyes, and it was only with great effort that I could keep from crying. But there was another, more powerful feeling that provided me with courage and steadfastness: my awareness of my independence, my longing to make contact with people, to become independent and proud, to live in accordance with my own wishes, and not by the caprice and will of my father.

Awkward, sluggish, with long hair that had been cut under a round bowl, wearing heavy boots with horseshoes, I was a typical village youth. The skilled workers looked down on me with scorn, pinched me by the ear, pulled me by the hair, called me a "green country bumpkin" and other insulting names.

One workday at the factory lasted eleven and a half hours, plus a one-and-a-half-hour lunch break. In the beginning I would grow terribly tired so that as soon as I got home from work and ate dinner, I would fall into my filthy, hard, straw-filled sack and sleep like a dead man, despite the myriad bedbugs and fleas.

I roomed and boarded not far from the factory, in a large, smelly house inhabited by all kinds of poor folk—peddlers, cabmen, casual laborers, and the like. We rented the apartment communally, as an artel of about fifteen men. Some were bachelors, others had wives who lived in the village and ran their households. I was put in a tiny, dark, windowless corner room; it was dirty and stuffy, with many bedbugs and fleas and the strong stench of "humanity." The room contained two wooden cots. One belonged to Korovin, my countryman and guardian; the other I shared with Korovin's son Vanka [Ivan], who was also an apprentice and worked in the factory's pattern shop.

Our food and the woman who prepared it were also paid for communally. The food was purchased on credit at a shop; our individual shares were assessed twice monthly. Every day at noon, as soon as the factory's lunch bell rang, we would hurry back to the apartment and sit down at the table, where a huge basin full of cabbage soup was already steaming.

All fifteen men ate from a common bowl with wooden spoons. The cabbage soup contained little pieces of meat. First, they would ladle out only the soup; then, when the soup was almost all gone, everyone tensely awaited a signal. A moment later someone would bang his spoon against the edge of the soup basin and say the words we were waiting for: "Dig in!" Then began the furious hunt of the spoons for the floating morsels of meat. The more dexterous would come up with the most.

Avdotia, the cook, her sleeves tucked up and the hem of her calico-print dress pulled back, would look steadfastly at the bottom of the soup basin, saying:

"Is there anything left, fellows, to dig out of there?"

"Go ahead, Duniakha [diminutive of Avdotia], dig away!" several voices would sing out in unison.

Avdotia would carry the basin to the oven, refill it with cabbage soup, and return it to the table. After the soup came either buckwheat gruel with lard or fried potatoes. Everyone was hungry as a wolf; they ate quickly, greedily.

After lunch everyone—except the youngsters—would throw himself on a cot to rest without removing his boots or workshirt.

Twice a week—on Wednesday and Friday—Avdotia would prepare the fast-day food: cabbage soup with a fishhead and gruel with vegetable oil.[3]

Twice a month, on the Saturday paydays, our artel indulged in wild carousing. Some, as soon as they had collected their pay, would go directly from the factory

---

3. According to strict Russian Orthodox observance, believers were expected to eat no meat or dairy products on Wednesdays (the day of the betrayal of Christ) and Fridays (the day of the Crucifixion).

to beer halls, taverns, or to some grassy spot, whereas others—the somewhat more dandified types—first went back to the apartment to change clothes.

Somber, cross, often bruised, and in some cases still in a state of undiluted intoxication, the inhabitants of our artel would return home late at night or on Sunday morning.

Korovin was a passionate fisherman; therefore every Saturday he would wind up the line on his fishing rod while Vanka and I prepared his worms, which we gathered at night from other people's gardens at the risk of our lives. Then off he'd go to fish all nights in the Moscow River.

Korovin usually returned from his fishing on Sunday morning. Sometimes he brought back two or three grunters or shiners, and usually he came back with nothing at all, but he unfailingly came back smelling of vodka. His goatee would be disheveled, his face inflamed, sweaty, his thinning hair stuck to his forehead.

On Monday he would still be out of sorts—cross, somber, and ill-tempered. Although he normally had little interest in the condition of our intellects, at moments like this he would summon Vanka and me and begin to recite his moral-pedagogical teachings.

"Where did you little pigs go yesterday?" he would begin in a severe voice.

If our conduct had stayed within the confines of our prescribed program we responded truthfully, but if we had gone beyond it we would lie.

"Did you go to mass?"

"We went to the Cathedral of St. Basil the Blessed, and for the early morning service we went to 'St. Nicholas on the Drops' [small local church]."

"You probably fooled around more than you prayed, and ogled the girls."

"By the word of God, papa, we stayed through the entire service," Vanka swore.

"And which deacon held the service?" Korovin continued to interrogate us suspiciously.

"The same one again—the big one, with curly hair and a red beard and a bass voice."

Korovin knew the Moscow deacons backwards and forwards. It was hard to fool him.

"Did you see Stogov?"

"No, we didn't."

"Don't you dare get involved with that awful Stogov when I'm not around. He'll take you to the Khitrovka [a notorious market]."

This was virtually the entire range of Korovin's moral instruction. After a final threat to "pull our hair," he let us go in peace.

Ivan Stogov, the man whom Korovin had cautioned us to avoid, was a copper smelter by trade and a close relative of Korovin's. I remember his appearance. He was blond, with his hair in a brush cut, of average height, with a worn, emaciated face and gray, thoughtful eyes. At the time I saw him he was about 25 years old. He worked for the so-called "graters" (the owners of tiny workshops operating on subcontract), and often changed employers. As a craftsman he was unusually talented. Even Korovin acknowledged this, saying: "His hands are golden, but his mouth is foul."

He suffered from heavy drinking and during such periods would disappear, no one knew where. People would encounter him at the Khitrov market, in all-night teahouses, in flophouses. From time to time he would be sent back to his home village under police escort. Stogov lived in our artel and paid two and a half rubles a month for his cot, but he rarely showed up. He only appeared at those times when, having spent everything he had on drink, he would divest himself of all his possessions—there was nothing to sell or to hock, and as everyone knows, when he's out of money even a good drunkard gives up drinking. Then he would suddenly show up in our apartment.

At such moments his appearance would be picturesque. Rags of some indescribable color would hang from his body; on his feet were something resembling old worn-out footwear or the high shoes worn by women, trodden down at the heels, with rubbers. Agitated and sullen, he would silently sit down on his cot and remain there for hours without moving. The compassionate Avdotia would serve him some soup with a hunk of bread and tenderly try to scold him. . . .

In the wintertime, when the Moscow River was frozen, we would go to the wall of the dike and have fistfights with workers from the Butikov factory. In the evening we would return home with our black eyes and our broken bloody noses.

But we also had our "cultural" amusements. The artel subscribed to the boulevard newspaper *Moscow Sheet,* in which what interested us the most were the chronicle of criminal cases and the "feuilletons." At that time the paper was running a long, serialized novel called *Bogdan Khmelnitsky,* in which the entire artel became engrossed.[4]

On Sundays we sometimes went to look at the pictures at the Tretiakov Gallery and the Rumiantsev Museum.

In addition, we never missed a Moscow fire, and no matter how tired, we would run at breakneck speed to see these free spectacles.

Once a year, on a winter Sunday, my employer would organize a public prayer meeting at the factory. In the enormous machine shop, a large rostrum was erected which was ascended by all the authorities of the factory: the owner, the director, the chief engineer, the foremen of the various shops, and the clergymen in their gilded sacerdotal holiday robes. Through the dense crowd of workers, the older workers elbowed their way forward and took their places at the tribune, under the eyes of the authorities. They crossed themselves with fervor, kneeled, and bowed down to the ground, especially when the priest prayed for the long life of the factory owner. When the prayers were over, the priest delivered an emotional, moralizing sermon about a negligent slave and a zealous lord. Then we came up to the priest and kissed the cross. . . .

---

4. Khmelnitsky was a renowned cossack leader who led Ukrainians in a series of uprisings against their Polish landlords in the mid-seventeenth century.

## THE BEGINNING OF MY APOSTASY

The Gustav List machine-building factory never held a ranking position in the struggle of the working class for its emancipation. Neither yesterday nor today has a single outstanding event in the annals of revolutionary history been linked to its name. And yet at the same time the factory had not been a backward one. It has always participated in all the notable events, and the role of individual List workers in those events has been far from insignificant.

In those days [1890s], however, it was the Gopper factory that was considered really advanced. Even in those early years strikes had already taken place there. The leading role in that factory was played by the pattern shop, some of whose pattern-makers had already spent time in exile or under police surveillance. The workers in the pattern shop at my factory used to call the Gopper pattern-makers "students"—that is, people who are against the tsar and do not believe in God—and they were somewhat afraid of them.

My own conception of these "students" was extremely confused. My only encounters with them were on the streets, and my feeling toward them was always one of great admiration mingled with fear and terror. I feared them because they didn't believe in God and might be able to shake my faith as well, which could have resulted in eternal hellish torments in the next world—"not for a hundred years, not for a thousand years, but for eternity without end," where there will be "weeping and the gnashing of teeth"—I often recalled the words of some divine revelation. But I admitted them because they were so free, so independent, so well-informed about everything, and because there was nobody and nothing on earth that they feared.

The only thing that amazed me was that they were walking freely on the streets instead of being imprisoned in the Peter-and-Paul Fortress. Such tolerance on the part of the authorities was incomprehensible to me.

How great were my surprise and curiosity when I learned one fine day that a pattern-maker from the Gopper factory had joined our workshop.

Just three benches away from mine a thin, sinewy man of medium height, with curly, light-colored hair and huge blue eyes, was fidgeting about. His shirt was tucked in and he wore his trousers outside his boots. In short, his outward appearance was no different from that of most of our pattern-makers. But he struck me as being particularly impetuous and fidgety.

My acquaintance with him began on the very first day.

"Well, my boy, how about giving me a hand with this cabinet," he said, beckoning me with his finger. "What's your name?"

"Semën."

"Have you been working here long?"

"This is my second year."

"I guess you already chase the girls, right?"

I grinned and, to cover my embarrassment, began to lift the heavy cabinet filled with tools.

"Hey, wait a second, watch out or you'll break your back! I have so many tools in there that even two of us can't lift it."

With enormous effort we managed to lift the cabinet. Then he took a brush out of it, brushed the wood shavings off his workbench, tested the stability of its longitudinal screw, and began to lay out his tools while continuing to chat with me.

"What district are you from?"

"Volokolamsk."

"Your father's probably ready to get you married, right?"

"I'm not going to marry until I've done my military service," I replied.

This person was definitely beginning to appeal to me. I was won over by his comradely, jocular tone, a tone that other adult workers assumed with me only rarely.

"What if he has approached me in this roundabout manner in order to convert me to his godless faith?" I cautioned myself.

Other workers too approached him carefully, with a mixture of suspicion and curiosity.

Merry, sociable, and thoroughly skilled in our trade, he quickly overcame the normal workshop hostility with which the old-timers always treat the newcomer. Whenever the foreman left the shop, people would gather around his workbench. Jokes and wisecracks would fly about, anecdotes would be told, and at times a loud, infectious burst of laughter would resound. Obscenities were almost never heard.

Not infrequently, fierce and bitter political or theological arguments would be launched.

In the stories and anecdotes, however, it was always the priests who were given pride of place. Even the older workers listened indulgently to tales about the adventures of priests. But when the talk began to turn to the saints or to God, the mood would change completely: then there would be no end of noise, shouting, and mutual insults. Savinov (that was the newcomer's name) was particularly fond of making sport of the sacred things of Moscow. He would refer to the Iversky icon of the Mother of God, which at the time was being carried about in a carriage harnessed to a team of six horses, as "a priest's tool for gaining money"; he'd refer to monks as "parasites," to priests as a "breed of horses," to Ioann of Kronstadt [a popular holy man] as "Vaniukha," and so forth.

"Well all right, let's say that the priests really are greedy, dissolute parasites; there's still no point in your sneering at miracles and the relics of saints, Savinov," the venerable and respectable-looking old worker Smirnov, a dogmatist and church-goer, would say, losing his patience. "Why at the Monastery of the Caves in Kiev I saw with my own eyes how they tended to this very sick man—he couldn't use his legs at all, couldn't take a step—and how they brought the holy relics to his lips. Well no sooner had he kissed the relics and said his prayers than he was up on his feet. He just walked out of the monastery as if nothing had happened! So, what do you say to that?"

"But why do you call that a miracle? If, say, he had no legs at all and you'd seen his legs grow back with your own eyes, then that would be a real miracle," Savinov would reply calmly, his irony barely perceptible. "What you described was simply the effect of hypnotism. Why in the town of Babye they say there's a hypnotist whose miracles are much greater. I've been told of occasions when they brought him people who not only couldn't walk but who were completely paralyzed, and they left his place fully restored. And he can cure people of diseases like alcoholism and female hysteria as with a touch. . . . As for your relics, Smirnov, they're just a priest's trick, and nothing more. What I'd like to hear from you is how many lazy, good-for-nothing monks and priests hang around those relics like parasites, looking for suckers!"

"I suppose you think that relics that never decay are also a trick?" Smirnov would intone passionately, shaking his gray beard as he stepped closer to Savinov. "There's a saint who has been lying in the earth for 300 years. Then he appears in the dream of a truly pious man. So they go to dig up his grave and they find him lying there looking alive and well, as if they'd only buried him yesterday. Why he even smells good. Now could that ever happen to an ordinary sinner?"

"Certainly it could. You just go visit the Historical Museum, old fellow, and take a look around. You'll find Egyptian mummies there, lying under glass. Each one is more than a thousand years old. These people were alive before the birth of Christ and yet they've been preserved to this very day—and with their hair intact. Yet the Egyptians were idol-worshipers. Surely you wouldn't call them saints, would you?" Savinov would parry with a smile, sensing his superiority. "Let's take another example. Not long ago our tsar, Alexander III, died of drink. They took out his intestines and embalmed him. Now they say he can lie there like that for 300 years without decaying. In 300 years will he be taken out and used as relics too?"

"Well, master, does this mean you don't even believe in hell?" Sushchy [another worker] would inquire meekly, in his quiet voice, his tobacco pouch in his hands, while he pushed in a pinch of snuff out of agitation.

"What in the world do you need hell for? A worker spends his whole life in the torment of hell. If you want to see for yourself just go visit the foundry some evening, when they're carrying the pots filled with castings. Not even a priest could invent a hell like that."

"Does that mean we'll receive no retribution in the next world for the sins we commit on earth?" Sushchy would meekly continue his inquiry.

"Our only retribution is our conscience, inside of us. It punishes us for our bad deeds. Retribution in the next world is something the priests have invented for simple people who aren't conscious. Meanwhile the rich can live here as if they were in paradise, enjoy themselves to their hearts' content, and pay the priests to prepare a paradise for them in the world to come."

After arguments like that were over the older workers would sigh sorrowfully as they dispersed, shake their heads, and whisper to each other: "What a hopeless man: he doesn't believe in God, he's against the tsar, he stirs up the Orthodox faithful, the people. He'll never escape the prison wagon, that's for sure!"

"When I lived in St. Petersburg lots of troublemakers like that got caught," old Smirnov would say. "They'd take the guy away—he'd disappear, no one knew where—without telling his parents, relatives, or anyone else. They wasted no words there: they'd lock him up in a prison-fortress, grind him up in a mill—I've heard there's a mill in every cell—and throw the remains in the Neva River."

The younger workers, on the other hand, listened to Savinov's talk with enthusiasm and interest. Often they would turn to him with questions and requests for clarification. Nevertheless, it wasn't easy for him to overcome their suspicion—rooted in them from early childhood—of everything that was new, hard to grasp, or unfamiliar.

There were times when I was deeply angered and pained by Savinov's words. Questions that I had long since resolved, so I thought, and which had raised no doubts in my mind, would suddenly begin to drill themselves slowly and steadily into my brain, as if a piece of thin cold steel was being thrust into it. My beliefs, my views of the surrounding world, the moral foundations with which I had lived and grown up so nicely, peacefully, comfortably—suddenly began to shake. Even that which I'd thought to be most solid—the earth itself—was spinning beneath our feet, as Savinov put it, while we, like cockroaches on a flywheel, went crawling along it. Shivers ran up my spine—I became cold and terrified, as if I were preparing to leap across some abyss. But at the same time I felt light and free when I remembered that together with the old principles would also disappear that terrible nightmare that threatened me with the tortures of hell "not for a hundred years, not for a thousand years, but for eternity without end."

Having mastered my rage and indignation over his insulting remarks about "sacred" things, I timidly, cautiously began to get into arguments with Savinov. Despite what to me was the obvious correctness of my positions, my arguments with Savinov invariably ended in defeat. I would be seized with passion, rage, and indignation, but I had at my disposal neither the facts, the logical arguments, nor the appropriate words with which to refute his convictions.

"You say there is no hell, there is no heaven, no holy relics, no saint; then are you also saying there is no God?" I inquired, my heart already sinking in anticipation of his answer.

"No God? Of course there's a God, only not the kind that's conjured up by the priests," Savinov answered evasively, alerted by my passion.

"Then in your opinion who created the first man?"

"Why did he have to be created? He developed by himself. Those are just fairy tales in the Bible that tell you how God created man from clay, when the fact is that he was created by nature. I can prove it to you with an example, my little friend," Savinov continued, staring fixedly at me with his dreamy blue eyes.

I was taken aback by surprise. "How can he possibly prove it to me with an example? Could he be some kind of sorcerer or magician, or perhaps the devil himself in the form of a man?" Ideas like this flashed in my head.

"What's wrong? Don't you believe me?"

"Of course I can't believe such nonsense."

"All right, then do this: find yourself a little box, say, and fill it with earth. Take a good close look at the earth, to be sure there's nothing in it. Then put the box in a warm place for about two weeks, and you'll see that without fail worms or little insects will begin to appear there."

"And then what happens?"

"And then other creatures will begin to develop from the insects, and so on. . . . And, in the course of four, five, or may even ten thousand years, man himself will emerge."

At the time this example seemed so convincing to me that later, when I had already become "conscious," I still used those little "worms" and "insects" for many years as one of the most convincing arguments in my debates.

So the ice had been broken. My talks with Savinov became more frequent, more prolonged and detailed. His confidence in me was apparently increasing.

He told me many interesting things about the "Dukhobors" [a religious sect], who "would not oppose evil with violent means," and who preached true evangelical love of humanity.

"The tsarist officials want to make them serve in the army, but they refuse to go. They are given guns, but they fling them to the ground. 'We will not make war,' they say, 'we have no enemies; all men are brothers. We wish to live by the gospel,'" Savinov recounted with admiration. "What wonderful human beings!"

Savinov was only about 27, but he had already managed to roam the length and breadth of Russia, wherever he could find work. He had been to Warsaw, had worked in the metallurgical factories of the Ural Mountains and in the South, but he never stayed anywhere very long.

"It bores me to stay in one place, Semën," he would say to me. "I don't like the grass to grow under my feet. So whenever spring comes along, I long to head for new places. I need to look at new people, to see other ways of doing things. But I'll tell you one thing that's for sure: everywhere you go life is just as bad for the worker, who always lives in pitch-black darkness. The only place I haven't worked is Petersburg. They say the people there are much more conscious than our people here. I'll be heading there next year, no question about it."

One evening, as I was approaching my workbench, Savinov stealthily and cautiously thrust some kind of disheveled, grease-stained little book under my bench.

"Read it, Semën, and don't show it to anyone else," he whispered to me.

Tormented by curiosity and fear, I could barely wait for the bell. I finished the book in two sittings. It was Hauptmann's *The Weavers*.[5] At the time it was still an illegal publication. The book made a rather strong impression on me. I soon learned the "song of the weavers" by heart and would recite it to the other apprentices of my age group in the workshop. The words kept echoing again and again in my ears:

So merciful and upright, the court in our land:
To the worker it shows scorn, honor to the gentleman!
Our workers are tormented, as in a torture cell,
They plunder, starve, oppress us, but you are silent, silent! . . .

---

5. Russian translation of a German play depicting a bloody uprising in 1844 of exploited linen weavers.

The book had a very disturbing effect on me, stirring up my animosity toward the rich and my pity for the oppressed and awakening many new, previously unknown emotions, yet it did not really satisfy me. It failed to answer the questions that were tormenting me: how should I live and what should I do? It had nothing to contribute to the formulation of my world outlook.

That task was to be accomplished by yet another little book that I read, also passed on to me by Savinov: *What Should Every Worker Know and Remember?* I don't remember the author's name.[6] Clearly written, in a popular but passionate style, this book produced a total transformation in my ideas. A complete revelation for me was the elegant exposition of its views of the socialist society of the future. Factories, workshops, the land, the forests, the mines—everything would become the common property of the toilers! The organized struggle of the working class against the capitalists, the landowners, and the tsar—that was the meaning of life and work for every conscious worker.

For an entire week I was in a state of virtual ecstasy, as if I were standing up high on some tall stilts, from where all other people appeared to me like some kind of bugs, like beetles rummaging in dung, while I alone had grasped the mechanics and the meaning of existence. My past life seemed completely boring, dull, uninteresting. Every day had been identical, just like clockwork—late to bed and early to rise, again and again, day after day. That was "eternity without end"!

The next book I read was G. Plekhanov's *The Russian Worker in the Revolutionary Movement*, after which many aspects of my father's old stories about the "nahilists" became clear and comprehensible to me.[7] Now my emancipation from my old prejudices moved forward at an accelerated tempo.

I now withdrew from my artel and settled in a separate room with one of my comrades. I stopped going to the priest for "confession," no longer attended church, and began to eat "forbidden" food during Lenten fast days. However, for a long time to come I didn't abandon the habit of crossing myself, especially when I returned to the village for holidays.

Noticing my blatant "apostasy," Korovin made several attempts to lecture me on morality:

"Don't you listen to that heretic Savinov, Senka," he would say. "He's not going to do you any good. They'll kick you out of the factory, and you haven't even learned to do the work properly yet. Where will you go then? Some student you turned out to be! Why the milk on your lips still isn't dry and you're already mixing with wiseacres. I think I'll write to your father; let him burn your back with 25 strokes!"

"But I'm not doing anything illegal, am I?" I replied in self-justification.

---

6. Illegal Russian translation of a Polish pamphlet widely used to propagandize workers and frequently confiscated by the police.
7. Georgy V. Plekhanov (1857–1918), often called the father of Russian Marxism, first published this pamphlet in Geneva in 1892. Plekhanov, disillusioned with populism, had left Russia in 1880 and settled in Switzerland, where with other exiled radicals he founded the Group for the Emancipation of Labor, which was dedicated to disseminating Marxism in Russia.—Ed.

"I know just what you've been doing! They're going to put a necktie made of hemp around your neck—you'll hang there with your feet jerking."

However, these admonitions failed to impress me.

Then Korovin would write letters about my apostasy to my father. Alarmed, Father would insist on each occasion that I return to the village for the holidays to hear his parental admonitions. In the intervals between holidays he would write me edifying letters, in which he advised me to say my prayers, attend church, and call on the reigning Mother of God and St. Nicholas for assistance, that they might guard me from atheism and every other horror.

During my visits to the village on holidays, Father and I would quickly get entangled in theological arguments. Because I was already quite well versed in these questions by then I almost always emerged the victor from these arguments with my father. To be sure, not wishing to cause him great pain, I wouldn't pose the question of the "non-existence" of God very sharply and I gladly agreed to grant His existence as a possibility.

Father would then calm down somewhat and would even be proud of me. But this never lasted very long. As soon as I left for Moscow Father was on his own once more and, when he began to receive disturbing letters from Korovin, Father's edifying letters to me would resume.

But none of this was considered by Father to be all that terrible. There was only one thing he was unable to come to terms with—the fact that I was so indifferent to our home and to our peasant farmstead. Once during one of my visits Father summoned me to the barn, where, three years earlier, he had already prepared himself a good hollow coffin, which in the meantime was used to store oats, cabbages, firewood for the winter, and so on.

"I would like to have a serious talk with you," said my father.

"Fine, let's talk."

"As you know," he began in a sad voice, "I'm already growing old and might die quite soon. I've made myself a coffin and there's really nothing more I need, just seven feet of earth. But for me to die in peace I would like to see you settled down."

"But I am already settled down. I'm working at a factory and I'll soon be earning a good wage," I replied, pretending not to understand what Father was getting at.

"No, that's not what I'm talking about. . . . As you know, I don't get along well with your brother. I want to give him a separate property settlement and to have you get married while I'm still alive, so that the house will mean more to you and you'll be better off while you're still young, since if you wait until you're older you won't even marry."

"No, I don't want to marry until I've done my military service; when I'm a civilian again, then I'll get married," I answered fairly decisively.

"But I'll be dead by then."

"Well, I will get married on my own," I declared firmly.

Father, understanding that there was no chance of persuading me, gave up the fight and said with sadness:

"Well, God be with you! Live according to your own lights!"

## Khodynka

Well before the coronation of the new tsar,[8] the authorities had begun to "purge" Moscow of all unreliable elements. In houses inhabited by all kinds of poor people the janitors began to check on the apartments more often than usual; they would verify passports, examine registration forms more closely, and so on. Spies and stool pigeons of all varieties made their way stealthily through the city's outlying neighborhoods, through the working-class quarters, listening attentively for talk that might sound excessive. In our factory rumors abounded that all "suspicious" persons would be banished from the city. But just who these suspicious persons were, no one could say with any precision. However, everyone said: "Now is the time to hold one's tongue." There were stories going round about people who worm themselves into all kinds of places, eavesdrop, play the simpleton, deliberately elicit derogatory comments about the tsar, even get people drunk with vodka and beer— and then, as soon as you weaken, as soon as you begin to chatter, this nice fellow, who turns out to be a detective, grabs you and hauls you off to jail. In short, a tense atmosphere of suspicion and pursuit could be felt everywhere. . . .

The coronation ceremonies were held in Moscow during the first half of May. The weather was unusually warm and sunny. The entire city was illuminated and decorated with a multitude of flags. The Sofia embankment near the "Gustav List" factory was lined with guns, which from time to time fired off deafening ceremonial volleys, causing the air to vibrate. You could hear the sounds of glass breaking in the nearby houses. In the evenings Moscow glowed with the light of millions of electric lamps while multicolored fireworks soared high into the sky. For three days the streets near the Kremlin were blocked off by the celebrating public. The Alexander Garden was in an absolute uproar. It was flooded with townspeople, artisans, and other workers; tall, handsome hussars and cuirassiers in picturesque costumes, their sparkling swords dragging along the ground, would emerge proudly and pompously with "the ladies of their hearts" while shelling little seeds. House-maids, cooks, seamstresses, milliners—in those days all the women were the virtual prisoners of the dashing Petersburg guard officers.

"There isn't any female nourishment left for the working man," the skirt-chasers from our factory would complain angrily.

All around the Alexander Garden crowds of people were gathered to enjoy themselves. Some were singing in chorus, songs like "Down Along the Mother Volga," others danced the Kamarinskaia to the shrill sounds of an accordion, and in still another group people were telling entertaining stories. . . . In a word, the people were making merry. The uniformed police were nowhere to be seen.

At our factory, the director announced that during the three days of celebration in honor of the coronation the workers would work only eight hours a day, with a one-hour break for lunch. Our joy was unbounded! In the course of those three days we came to understand for the first time just how sweet was the taste of the eight-hour day and to feel the full weight of eleven and a half hours of work.

---

8. Nicholas II had become Emperor on the unexpected death of his father, Alexander III, in the fall of 1894; but his coronation, to be held, as always, in Moscow, was scheduled for May 1896.—Ed.

After eight hours of work, we still had so much time left over that we didn't even know how to fill our remaining hours: we strolled along the streets and boulevards, gazed at the reveling holiday crowd, attempted to cut through to the front rows and "get a glimpse of the tsar." Admittedly, we tried to do this not out of respect or admiration for the tsar, but from simple curiosity to see royal luxury, the royal suite, and so on. Moreover, we looked upon this business as a kind of sport. Vanka Korovin and I would get all stirred up whenever someone asked us in a tone of surprise:

"Do you mean you still haven't seen the tsar?"

We would reply with embarrassment that we had not.

"But how is that possible! Why, I've already seen him three times. . . . You boys should get up a little earlier in the morning and find a good place to stand," someone would instruct us at the end of such dialogues.

After repeated and persistent attempts to "get a glimpse of the tsar," the last in our series of efforts ended very sadly: when we tried to force our way through the front rows, Cossack troops drove us back with their whips, hurting us, even tearing apart Vanka's jacket. We ran home with a feeling of shame and disgrace, and never again attempted to "get a glimpse of the tsar."

"Well, boys, eat up and let's go try to see the tsar"—these words continued to resound around us in the workshop for quite some time.

Either on the 14th or 15th of May, a big public celebration was announced, to be held on the Khodynka field.[9] It was said that during the festivities little bundles filled with sausages, rolls, a mug bearing the emblem of the tsar, and a half-ruble piece would be distributed to everyone from special booths. No one could say with any accuracy just what kind of mug it would be: some said copper, others said tin or porcelain.

On the day before the celebration, Krasnitsky, the master mechanic at our factory, gathered together the foremen of all the shops to announce that, in order to avoid the big crush, all our workers were to start off for Khodynka at eight in the morning in a single group led by him, Krasnitsky; the workers shouldn't be worried, since special gifts from the tsar were being prepared for everyone at our factory.

That evening the most contradictory, ominous rumors were already being spread in the house where we lived. Huge masses of people had begun to gather on the Khodynka field on the eve of the celebration. Several people from our house were among them. We began to grow agitated and to speak rudely about the master mechanic, fearing that by the time we got to the field all the gifts would already be distributed. Some of the men proposed to leave immediately and spend the night there. Vanka and I were fully prepared to go in the evening, but Korovin, who had complete faith in Krasnitsky's promises, would not allow it.

It is a clear and sunny morning. Commanded by master mechanic Krasnitsky, we march in a long file to the Khodynka field. The morning air is bracing, the sun

---

9. Khodynka field, soon to be the site of catastrophe, was a parade ground with barracks located on the northwest outskirts of Moscow.

shines brightly, there is laughter, joking, animated talk, and, at the end of our path, crowds of joyful people making merry, puppet shows, music, folkdancing, singing, the brash, endless sounds of the accordion, and so on. And then, suddenly . . . .

As we approach the vicinity of Khondynka, we encounter a cabman. In his cab a young woman is tossing about and screaming something incomprehensible at the top of her lungs.

"Nervous hysteria, most likely," we decide, and we continue our procession.

The master mechanic led us to a place that was still pretty far from the celebration and then went off on his own to find out about our gifts. We settled down to await his return. However, we soon began to disperse in different directions.

Then some people approached our group, shouting: "Oh my God, oh my God! How many people have been crushed! They're taking away the corpses by cartloads!"

"Who!? How were they crushed?"

"You can't imagine how many people fell into the wells! There's this deep, deep well; people kept falling into it even when it was already packed," others told us. "They say the wells were left open on purpose!"

"There was this enormous crowd there, swaying from side to side, moving like waves in the sea," says another, "and you could see the steam from the stuffy air hovering over the crowd. And all the people standing there, just as if everyone was still alive, but when the crowd finally gives way, suddenly they fall to the ground by the hundreds: their crushed bodies had been standing up."

"The only reason I'm still alive is because I managed to make my way through by practically climbing over everyone's head. A kind person came by and put me down on a safe, high spot," said a small, skinny man in a visored cap.

We never received our gifts and we were certainly in no mood for them anyway. We were happy and thankful that we hadn't left for the field in the evening and hadn't ended up in that mess ourselves. On the way back home, now and then we would run into military wagons piled with corpses covered with bast mats; arms, legs, and heads could be seen dangling out from under the mats. . . . It was terrifying.

On the following day the crush at Khodynka was the only thing discussed at our factory. The newspapers were beginning to publish lists of the victims. Some of the workers found the names of their friends. A low murmur began to arise. The atmosphere grew tense. The lists that appeared in the papers clearly underestimated the number of victims, placing it at two or three hundred, I can't remember exactly. This evoked enormous outrage.

"The papers are lying. They crushed thirty thousand, not three hundred, the dogs!" the old worker Smirnov, whose friend or relative had been killed, said angrily. "Have you ever heard of anything like it? Thousands of people are crushed to death and they don't even find the guilty party!"[10]

---

10. The number of deaths and injuries during the coronation festivities at Khodynka has never been precisely calculated; but the official estimate of 1,400 dead and 1,300 injured was clearly much too low.

"And who, sir, is the guilty party? Why, we're the guilty ones ourselves. We coveted those gifts, we didn't maintain order, and, well, we crushed one another," Sushchy responded in a meek, sweet voice.

"It's a gift to the tsar, the little father, that's what it is!" Savinov interjected bitterly.

Sushchy remained silent. We were afraid to stay with this theme very long.

Mikhail Afanesev [a pattern-maker suspected of being a police spy], who had turned a bit pale, lowered his tone and attempted to focus the other workers' attention on the tsar's promise to "compensate" the widows and orphans of those who had perished at Khodynka. Of course that promise was of little consolation to us, but no one would contradict Afanasev. It felt as if each new day contained some new secret, and somehow we all withdrew into ourselves and awaited something.

Little by little our lives began to return to their ordinary daily routines, but for a long time we were unable to forget the pleasure of the eight-hour day, which often served us as a topic of conversation. We still continued to await something and we all hoped that important changes in our life would somehow come about on their own.

One payday Savinov took up some kind of a collection among the pattern-makers. They apparently contributed very enthusiastically, for Savinov was very pleased with the results. But the destination and purpose of these collections were unknown to me. On one such occasion, however, my fellow countryman Novikov—a loud-mouthed drunkard—having used his pay to get himself drunk, began to reproach Savinov for these collections.

"You've been treating us like fools," Novikov blurted out, "you collect money from us and nobody even knows who or what it's for! Maybe you spent it all on drink. . . . Some clever guy you turned out to be!"

At first Savinov shrugged this off lightly, but then, having lost patience over the last remark, he rushed toward Novikov's workbench, grabbed some object along the way, and would have just about massacred him if the neighboring workers hadn't intervened in time.

"You drunkard! You stupid animal! Here, you can choke on your money!" Whereupon Savinov, his hands trembling with rage, hurled some silver coins at Novikov's bench, the coins clattering as they rolled along it.

Evidently Novikov had not anticipated such a stormy protest; suddenly taken aback, he calmed down and stood there in silence, having completely lost heart. His intoxication instantly seemed to vanish.

"Well, all right. . . . That's enough of that! I suppose I've been drinking too much," he said with embarrassment.

At that time I had the impression that Savinov's "collections" were directly connected with the strike of the Petersburg weavers. It seems that shortly after the scene with Novikov that I described above, during one of lunch breaks, a triumphant Mikhail Afanasev arrived in our workshop carrying a copy of the [liberal] newspaper Russian News. A group of pattern-makers quickly formed near his workbench and he loudly and clearly read them an article about the strike of the Petersburg weavers. Although the article recounted those events in a dry, bureaucratic style, for us it was a complete revelation; we appropriated everything in the article that was related to our daily life and work. Thenceforth the words "strike" and "combination," which were mentioned in the article, would assume a real meaning for us, would truly come alive. Heroic though it was, the unequal struggle of lone individuals—of "students"—who were imprisoned and "ground up in mills," was now transformed into a struggle of the working masses. The terrifying legends that had had such a hold on the workers' imaginations were now losing all their significance. As a practical matter, it was impossible to imprison 30,000 Petersburg weavers in the Peter-and-Paul Fortress and put them through the mill!

Shortly after these events our factory changed from an eleven-and-a-half-hour workday to ten hours. We could now breathe more freely and we immediately felt that an enormous burden had been lifted from our shoulders. Granted, in those years there were few of us who knew how to organize and exploit our free time in a rational manner. Yet it was already a wonderful thing that we were now able merely to rest physically and to think about subjects that were unrelated to our work. For our generation this in itself was a great conquest. From here on in it would become much easier for us to engage in organizational work, propaganda, and agitation among the broad masses of workers.

Over thirty years have since passed, but at that time, when my understanding of political questions was still very weak, I could already sense that these three events—Khodynka, the Petersburg weavers' strike, and the shift to the ten-hour day—were closely connected to one another and somehow stood in a state of causal interdependency.

Although it had no direct relation to the shop-floor interests of the workers of our factory, the Khodynka catastrophe greatly weakened the authority of our rulers and undermined the old blind faith in the tsar, even among the older men. What aroused people's indignation most of all was the irresponsibility, the impunity of the authorities who had destroyed thousands of lives.

"Why did these Christian souls have to perish?" one worker would ask.

"For the benefit of tsarist circles."

Remarks and anecdotes like this circulated widely among the workers.

On November 14, the occasion of the half-year anniversary of the Khodynka catastrophe, the students of Moscow University organized a memorial service for the victims that turned into a demonstration. The students were surrounded by the police and driven into the riding academy [training ground for cavalry]. This incident had great agitational significance at our factory. Previously, the mass of workers had looked upon students as restless rioters, as atheists who attacked the tsar for obscure reasons and, in any case, stood at a very great distance from the workers' day-to-day interests. But now many workers were beginning to speak sympathetically of students who, unafraid of punishment, "seek after justice."

# FURTHER READING

Roger Bartlett, ed., *Land Commune and Peasant Community in Russia: Communal Forms in [Late] Imperial and Early Soviet Society* (1990)

Seymour Becker, *Nobility and Privilege in Late Imperial Russia* (1985)

I. S. Belliustin, *Description of the Clergy in Rural Russia: The Memoir of a Nineteenth-Century Parish Priest*, ed. and trans. Gregory L. Freeze (1985)

Jeffrey Brooks, "Readers and Reading at the End of the Tsarist Era," in William Mills Todd III, ed., *Literature and Society in Imperial Russia, 1800–1914* (1978)

———, *When Russia Learned to Read: Literacy and Popular Literature, 1861–1914* (1985)

Daniel R. Brower, *Training the Nihilists: Education and Radicalism in Tsarist Russia* (1975)

William C. Brumfield and Milos M. Velimirovic, eds., *Christianity and the Arts in Russia* (1991)

Barbara Evans Clements, Barbara Alpern Engel, and Christine D. Worobec, eds., *Russia's Women: Accommodation, Resistance, Transformation* (1991)

Edith W. Clowes, Samuel D. Kassow, and James L. West, eds., *Between Tsar and People: Educated Society and the Quest for Public Identity in Late Imperial Russia* (1991)

Ben Eklof, *Russian Peasant Schools: Officialdom, Village Culture, and Popular Pedagogy, 1861–1914* (1986)

——— and Stephen P. Frank, eds., *The World of the Russian Peasant: Post-Emancipation Culture and Society* (1990)

Beatrice Farnsworth and Lynne Viola, eds., *Russian Peasant Women*, Part I (1992)

Anne L. Fitzpatrick, *The Great Russian Fair: Nizhnii Novgorod, 1840–90* (1990)

Nancy Frieden, *Russian Physicians in an Era of Reform and Revolution, 1856–1905* (1981)

Cathy A. Frierson, *Peasant Icons: Representations of Rural People in Late Nineteenth-Century Russia* (1993)

Rose L. Glickman, *Russian Factory Women: Workplace and Society, 1880–1914* (1984)

Patricia Herlihy, "Joy of Rus': Rites and Rituals of Russian Drinking," *The Russian Review*, 50 (1991), 131–47

John F. Hutchinson, *Politics and Public Health in Revolutionary Russia, 1890–1918* (1990)

Mikhail P. Iroshnikov, et al., *Before the Revolution: St. Petersburg in Photographs, 1890–1914* (1992)

Robert E. Johnson, *Peasant and Proletarian: The Working Class of Moscow in the Late Nineteenth Century* (1979)

Esther Kingston-Mann and Timothy Mixter, eds., *Peasant Economy, Culture, and Politics of European Russia, 1800–1921* (1991)

W. Bruce Lincoln, *In War's Dark Shadow: The Russians before the Great War [1914]* (1983)

Louise McReynolds, *The News under Russia's Old Regime* (1991)

Robert J. Nichols and Theofanis G. Stavrou, eds., *Russian Orthodoxy under the Old Regime* (1978)

Chloe Obolensky, *The Russian Empire: A Portrait in Photographs* (1979)

Thomas C. Owen, *Capitalism and Politics in Russia: A Social History of the Moscow Merchants, 1855–1905* (1981)

David L. Ransel, ed., *The Family in Imperial Russia* (1978)

Jo Ann Ruckman, *The Moscow Business Elite: A Social and Cultural Portrait of Two Generations, 1840–1905* (1984)

Susan Gross Solomon and John F. Hutchinson, *Health and Society in Pre-Revolutionary Russia* (1990)

Henri Troyat, *Daily Life in Russia Under the Last Tsar*, trans. (from French) Malcolm Barnes (1961, 1979)

Wayne S. Vucinich, ed., *The Peasant in Nineteenth-Century Russia* (1968)

Christine D. Worobec, *Peasant Russia: Family and Community in the Post-Emancipation Period* (1991)

Reginald E. Zelnik, *Labor and Society in Tsarist Russia: The Factory Workers of St. Petersburg, 1855–1870* (1971)

# CHAPTER 13

# Opposition to the Imperial Regime

The issue of opposition to the Imperial regime in Russia has risen frequently in this book. In Chapter 5, indeed, both the popular rebellion against Catherine II led by Pugachev and the intellectual critique written by Radishchev were discussed (and the latter quoted) at length; and these two events—the one representing the opposition of ordinary people and the other, that of an intellectual elite—may be taken as the paradigm of opposition to the Imperial regime throughout its remaining history. Radishchev and fellow critics of the age of Catherine would be followed, most notably, by the Decembrists of 1825; by assorted westerners, populists, and socialists of the 1840s and the era of the Great Reforms; and by the various liberals, radicals, and revolutionaries of the ensuing era of reaction and counter-reform. In the meantime, while peasant uprisings and, later, industrial strikes were common down through the nineteenth century, mass popular rebellion did not occur again (such was the repressive strength and prestige of the Imperial regime) until 1905. And now the great question was, could the disaffected elite's demands somehow be joined with mass discontent to force the government into fundamental, systemic change? That seemed to be happening, at last, in the revolutionary years 1905–1907, when a broadly based "liberation movement" publicly emerged, political parties became active, and an empire-wide State Duma (lower house of parliament) with real legislative authority was elected—albeit in a complex, indirect way—on the basis of nearly universal manhood suffrage. The opposition in all its variety now had a national forum in which it could express its opinions and help make the Empire's laws.

The Revolution of 1905, in other words, ushered in a quasi-constitutional period in Russian history: only "quasi-" because, under the revised Fundamental Laws (constitution) granted by Nicholas II in April 1906, the Emperor retained enormous powers, including command of the armed forces and sole power to declare war and make peace, exclusive management of the Empire's foreign policy, and the right to appoint—and dismiss—the ministers who together formed the government. Moreover, virtually from the outset Nicholas II and his ministers seem to have been determined to subvert the new order by any and all means—including dissolution of the First and Second

Dumas after they had met only for a few weeks (April 27–July 9, 1906; February 20–June 3, 1907). And by his electoral "reform" of June 3, 1907, Nicholas's newly appointed prime minister, Peter Stolypin, drastically restricted the franchise, in effect granting a political monopoly in the Third and Fourth Dumas to some 30,000 landed noblemen. These nobles already dominated the State Council, or upper house of parliament, up to half of whose members were appointed by the Emperor and the rest chosen by special constituencies. Thus, Stolypin's manifesto of June 3, 1907, dissolving the Second Duma and proclaiming the new electoral law, has been described by historians as a virtual coup d'état; and the consequent reassertion of autocratic government through the bureaucracy and police has been called the "Third of June System."

# E S S A Y S

Most historical scholarship in English dealing with the opposition to the Imperial regime during its last decades concentrates on the revolutionary movement and the emergence of the revolutionary parties—chiefly the Social Democrats, who in 1903 split into the Bolshevik and Menshevik factions, and the Socialist Revolutionaries, who also were divided into various factions. But until 1917 these parties played only a minor role in the Empire's politics; or rather, they played an essentially negative role, goading the government by their revolutionary agitation and rhetoric and by their subversive activities (including political assassination) into taking repressive measures which in turn helped to radicalize the rest of society. Mindful, therefore, of our strict space limitations, the two essays chosen for inclusion here deal with less familiar, less studied aspects of the opposition to the Imperial regime during its last decades—leaving the revolutionary movement to speak in various Documents (Breshkovskaia and Lenin, below; also Figner, Chapter 9, and Kanatchikov, Chapter 12).

In the first essay, Professor Terence Emmons of Stanford University traces the evolution of constitutional reform in Russia down to the creation of the Duma, and then assesses the fate of the parliamentary movement in the ensuing Duma period. Emmons pays particular attention to the First and Second Dumas—the more truly representative of the four Dumas, given the much broader franchise on which they were elected—and to the fate of the Constitutional Democratic (Kadet) party led by Paul Miliukov (1859–1943), which can be considered the standard-bearer of the constitutional movement. The second essay, excerpted from Richard Stites's pioneering work on the struggle for women's liberation in Russia, describes the feminist movement of the time, showing how no other protest movement or opposition group encountered such hostility from all sides, or such indifference: traditional patriarchalism, it seems, remained dominant throughout Russian society, not just among the peasantry. Stites is professor of Russian history at Georgetown University.

# The Constitutional Movement

TERENCE EMMONS

Russian civil society (*obshchestvo*) at the turn of the century was not only small as a proportion of the total population, but its capacity for action independent of the state, not to mention in opposition to the state, appeared to be extremely limited because of its links to privileged noble status, its dependence on the state for employment, and its lack of control over major economic processes.

Nevertheless, the main constituent elements of civil society were mobilized in opposition to the regime coincidentally with the emergence of an urban mass movement, which was spearheaded by the still small but partially politicized and strategically located industrial labor force, and by widespread spontaneous peasant disorders in the countryside. Through this unique concatenation of events, Russian obshchestvo was able to extract from the autocracy in October 1905 the promise of constitutional reform, including an elected parliament with legislative authority and, for the first time in the country's long history, toleration of open political-party activity.

A constitutional-reform movement and a socialist revolutionary movement had coexisted in Russia since the 1860s, when the state itself had undermined the foundations of the old order by abolishing serfdom and instituting a number of other reforms. Both movements from the beginning consciously drew on the European revolutionary tradition in their challenges to the legitimacy of the old [Imperial] regime. The constitutional-reform movement was gotten under way by representatives of the landed nobility in their confrontation with the government over the issue of emancipation and how it was to be carried out, and was then carried over into the zemstvos, the organs of limited local self-administration that were brought into existence in 1864; they were generally dominated, especially at the provincial level, by nobles. Although support for constitutional reform in the zemstvos fluctuated over time, it remained a minority movement there until the end of the nineteenth century.

The Russian revolutionary movement took its inspiration more or less directly from the European revolutionary left of 1848. The first attempts to organize for revolutionary action came in the reform era [period of the Great Reforms], in anticipation that the government's conservatively motivated, cautious reforms would set off a broad popular movement, if not a peasant rebellion. It was sustained at first by intelligentsia youth, mostly of noble origin, in and around the universities.

For the first two decades, the reformers and the revolutionaries essentially went their separate ways. Until the assassination of Alexander II in 1881, the Russian left was generally negatively disposed toward "mere" political reforms (a lesson drawn, in part, from the experience of the left in the revolutions of 1848) and

Reprinted by permission of the publishers from *The Formation of Political Parties and the First National Elections in Russia*, pp. 4–17, 353, 355–66, 368–76, by Terence Emmons, Cambridge, Mass.: Harvard University Press, Copyright © 1983 by the President and Fellows of Harvard College.

tended to associate constitutionalism with "capitalism" and "the bourgeoisie," toward whose specters the peasantophile radical intelligentsia youth, who were already reading Marx after their own fashion, were as inhospitably disposed as they were toward the realities of the autocracy.

Following the failure of the populists' terrorist strategy, which culminated in the assassination of Alexander II and the onset of a prolonged period of political reaction instead of the regime's capitulation to direct popular sovereignty for which they had naively hoped, the idea of uniting revolutionaries and reformers in a struggle for the limited goal of constitutional reform gradually gained ground among the remnants of the revolutionary movement surviving in European emigration, especially with the spread among them of the influence of orthodox Marxism (orthodox in the sense that Marx's views on the past and future development of European society were held to be applicable in their essentials to Russia as well). The influence of Marxism became very widespread in Russian intellectual circles in the mid-1890s, when the advent of rapid industrial development seemed to confirm that Russia's was not to be a separate path of development as the populists had hoped. By this time, even the keepers of the populist faith in exile in London began to propagate the idea of a joint effort with the reformers for a constitution as a necessary precondition for advancement toward changes in the social and economic spheres.

Inside Russia this confluence of opinion led to the formation in the mid-1890s of the short-lived "People's Rights party," which brought together old revolutionaries returned from exile and younger intellectuals of various ideological persuasions (primarily Marxist and populist) for the purpose of uniting all oppositionist groups in the country for the overthrow of autocracy and the establishment of a constitutionalist regime.

A stimulus to this convergence of opinion about the possibility of such a movement was the growing perception toward the end of the century, as Leopold Haimson has observed, of the emergence of an independent civil society (obshchestvo) which was generally hostile toward the existing regime.[1] The reality behind this perception was the consolidation by about this time of a rudimentary professional middle class (the product of the regime's considerable investment in higher education over the preceding decades and of the country's economic development) and the pressure for political participation that naturally accompanied it; simultaneously, there developed a general trend in state policy, set under way after the death of Alexander II and continuing through the reign of Alexander III (1881–1894) and the first decade of the reign of Nicholas II, that was hostile not only toward expansion of political participation but also toward manifestations of public initiative in a wide range of ostensibly nonpolitical areas of culture, education, and popular welfare. A crucial, but by no means the exclusive, bone of contention between

---

1. Leopold Haimson, "The Parties and the State: The Evolution of Political Attitudes," in Cyril Black, ed., *The Transformation of Russian Society: Aspects of Social Change Since 1861* (1967), pp. 110–145.

most of the emergent civil society and the state bureaucracy was the latter's industrialization policies, directed since 1892 by Sergei Witte, minister of finance. With their concentration of state resources, largely derived from taxation of the agrarian sector, on heavy industrial development, these policies were widely opposed in educated society, from populist intellectuals at one extreme to large landowners at the other. The tax pressure exerted on the peasantry by these policies was very widely blamed for setting off the famine and cholera epidemic in east-central Russia in 1891–1892, the major public scandal of the 1890s.

The industrial downturn that set in at the turn of the century (1900–1903) and then, in 1902, the first large-scale peasant disturbances since the 1870s (in Poltava and Kharkov provinces) accelerated the sense of urgency and broadened the ranks of the discontented to include, among others, many formerly passive noble landowners.

Considering the conditions prevailing in Russia prior to 1905, it is not surprising that it was the most radical opponents of the regime who were first to organize for the political struggle—clandestinely and, in the beginning, for the most part abroad. By definition, only "professional revolutionaries" could take the risk and time required for such activity. By the time the crisis of the old regime was sufficiently advanced to propel significant numbers of "nonprofessionals" into political action, the revolutionary organizations were already relatively well established, at least in their leadership groups and programs.

After an abortive first attempt as early as 1898, the Marxist Social Democratic party was established shortly after the turn of the century by pioneers of the Russian Marxist movement together with those converts of the 1890s who were devoted to mobilizing the working class for revolutionary action. They were stimulated to organize by the appearance in 1896–1897 of the first manifestations of mass working-class strike activity, and by the simultaneous development of revisionist views among other Marxist intellectuals. The populist Socialist Revolutionaries (SRs) founded their party in short order (they first proclaimed the existence of a party at the end of 1901), partly in reaction to the organizing activity of the Social Democrats (SDs) and, by 1902, under the stimulus of the revival of peasant activity. Because of the necessarily underground and elitist character of their activities and their doctrinal stances, neither of the revolutionary parties was able to attract more than a small portion of the intelligentsia with socialist sympathies, let alone the broader ranks of the educated minority, which were now too numerous and ideologically differentiated for any single party, or two parties, to encompass.

These circumstances gave rise to a new and unique organization (modeled nevertheless to a considerable extent on the revolutionary parties), the Union of Liberation, which set itself the task of mobilizing into the struggle against the autocratic regime the widest range possible of civil society—from the socialist-oriented "democratic intelligentsia" on the left to the gentry [noble] zemstvo constitutionalists on the right. Lacking any narrow ideological program, or rather desisting from the elaboration of one because of the ideological diversity of its membership, the Union of Liberation had succeeded to a remarkable extent in its task by early 1905, stimulating organized demands for constitutional reform in the zemstvos and among the professional intelligentsia; and the united-front strategy of the Liberationists was accepted, although not without reservations and concern for their own organizational and ideological independence, by the revolutionary parties. A sort of concord on first political objectives was reached, with the result that a considerable part of Russian obshchestvo was now mobilized to press the demand for constitutional reform.

Under the stimulus of this broad, if irregular, movement on the one hand, and the increasingly evident inability of the regime either to prosecute the war with Japan into which it had stumbled in January 1904 or to deal with mounting urban and rural violence at home, by the early months of 1905 even traditionally conservative Russian industrialists and the provincial noble corporations had been at least partially mobilized into the opposition. The culmination of the "liberation movement" came with massive strike activity beginning in September 1905, which yielded by the second week of October the country's first general strike, in which virtually all of industry, the communications and service sectors, the professions, the schools, and even many government offices were closed down.

Faced with the nearly unanimous opposition of civil society, a working-class strike movement that supported society's political demands (in addition to pressing its own economic demands), and an unprecedented level of peasant disorders in the countryside (which had also begun to accelerate rapidly in September in response to the breakdown of order in the urban centers); demoralized by the humiliation of defeat in the war with Japan, which had been terminated in August by a negotiated peace; and unsure of the loyalty of the armed forces at his disposal because of recent (albeit isolated) rebellions in the army and navy, Nicholas II at last promised in the imperial manifesto issued on October 17, 1905, to introduce civil and political liberties and to summon a legislative assembly elected on a broad franchise [the October Manifesto].

Plans for including an element of public representation in government did not of course originate during the October crisis. Various schemes for consultative representation had been under discussion intermittently in government circles ever since the introduction of a European-style system of ministerial-bureaucratic government in the early years of the reign of Alexander I (1801–1825). Indeed, the first well-known plan, which already contained the element that was to appear in almost all future plans elaborated in government circles until 1905—representation from permanent bodies of local self-administration rather than by means of special elections—was the work of the architect of the new ministerial system, M. M. Speransky [see Chapter 7, essay by Raeff]. Others followed. The first to adapt that principle to the institutions of elective local self-administration created in the 1860s, the zemstvos, was actually drawn up before they were in operation, by the then minister of internal affairs, P. A. Valuev, in a draft submitted to the tsar in 1863. Valuev correctly foresaw that the zemstvos would become the focus of constitutionalist aspirations and proposed forestalling them by institutionalizing at the outset central representation from the zemstvos in an anodyne appendage to the State Council, the empire's supreme consultative-legislative organ, which until 1906 was composed entirely of high officials appointed by the emperor. Most later plans borrowed heavily from the Valuev project.

Several such plans were considered in the ensuing years of Alexander II's reign (1855–1881), and although Alexander himself was not disposed to the idea of public representation, there was a nearly general assumption among his advisers that sooner or later, as part of the country's advancement toward the status of a modern European polity, representative institutions would be introduced in Russia. During the political crisis created by the revolutionary terrorist campaign, in fact just a few days before it took his life, Alexander came around to approving a first step toward introduction of a considerably diluted version of the Valuev plan in a draft presented by his de facto prime minister, General Loris-Melikov [see Chapter 9, introduction]. That was the last time serious consideration was to be given to plans for representative institutions before the onset of the final crisis period of the old regime, although the government did continue, as earlier, to consult on an ad hoc basis with various groups of "public men"—representatives of the zemstvos, town councils, the noble corporations [assemblies], and so on.

In the early stages of the general crisis, which came during V. K. Plehve's tenure as minister of internal affairs (1902–1904), the regime attempted to use repression as the main method of dealing with the growing demands for political reform. The reversal of this trend came with Plehve's assassination on July 15, 1904, in the midst of the Russo-Japanese War. After a month's hiatus, the vacated office was assumed by Prince P. D. Sviatopolk-Mirsky, who turned to the strategy of conciliation that led eventually to constitutional reform.

Mirsky's basic plan was to win over the more tractable members of the opposition, the zemstvo liberals who had been brought to a high point of discontent by the Plehve administration's punitive measures against the zemstvos, by resurrecting the scheme for consultative representation from the zemstvos and town dumas. The only direct product of Mirsky's plans for political concessions during his tenure was the ukaz [decree] of December 12, 1904, which promised improvements in regard to civil liberties and limitation of arbitrary actions by government officials, but made no mention of public representation. That point in Mirsky's draft had been struck out at the last moment by Nicholas II.

The vague promises of the December 12 ukaz did nothing to impede the momentum of the political opposition, and following the tragic Petersburg workers' demonstration on January 9, "Bloody Sunday," when about 130 peaceful demonstrators and innocent bystanders were killed by government troops, the question of representation was again raised in government circles (the petition drawn up by Father Gapon's Workingmen's Assembly, which the workers had tried to deliver to the tsar on January 9, included a request for constitutional reform [see Documents, Gapon]). To internal pressure for reform there was now added external pressure in the form of warnings from French financial circles that Russia would be unable to secure further French loans in the absence of significant political reforms. By early February the Council of Ministers had come around, with the tsar's approval, to conceding the necessity of some kind of public representation, and on February 18 a rescript to the new minister of internal affairs, A. G. Bulygin, was issued announcing the tsar's intention to summon elected representatives to participate in "preliminary elaboration and discussion of legislative proposals." The rescript authorized creation of a special conference under Bulygin for working out the means for implementing this very generally stated intention. Although it was accompanied by a manifesto that called on the population to pray for "the greater strengthening of true autocracy," it was still an unprecedented concession of principle.

The fundamental structure of the representative system called for in the rescript was worked up in the chancery of Bulygin's ministry by the same official, S. E. Kryzhanovsky, who had earlier drafted Mirsky's proposals. Significant modifications were later introduced in the Council of Ministers and then in the special conference called for in the rescript, but they did not affect the basic system first advanced by the ministry.

The Mirsky proposals had skirted the issue of whether to convene a separate representative assembly or to attach public representatives to the State Council (the more time-honored variant), although Mirsky had expressed preference for the latter. In the tradition of government-generated plans, they had designated representation from the provincial zemstvos, the "crowning of the edifice," rather than by special elections. The ministry's [Ministry of the Interior] new draft on the State Duma, as the representative chamber was thereafter to be called, went considerably beyond the Mirsky proposals in some respects, while retaining much that was by now traditional in government schemes.

The issue of a separate institution versus attachment of an elected element to the State Council was now decided in favor of the former, on the grounds that the principal function of public representation—to give the main social groups and regions of the country the sense that their views were being consulted—would require a much larger body than a mere satellite of the State Council. The competency of the Duma was considerably greater than anything seen or implied in earlier government plans. Although the Duma was explicitly identified as a consultative body in the manifesto accompanying the publication of the final legislation on August 6, 1905, and its recommendations were not to be binding on the sovereign, a broad range of legislative and budgetary matters would have had to be submitted to its consideration, in parity with the State Council. Moreover, the Duma was granted the right of interpellation of government ministers, and it could initiate legislation: amendments of existing laws or new laws, not extending, however, to the Fundamental Laws defining the basic structures of the governmental system. If the Duma could gain the concurrence of the State Council in rejecting proposals put to them, no government-sponsored bill could become law. However—and this was the essential provision that justified designation of the Duma as *consultative*—the Duma alone could not prevent passage of government-sponsored bills; at least the implication of the lapidary statutes on the Duma was that the government could promulgate legislation with the approval of the State Council alone.

Although the statutes framing the competency of the Duma were the subject of considerable discussion in the several instances through which the draft legislation passed, it was the electoral system for the Duma that was given the most prolonged scrutiny and went through the most substantial changes from the original draft to the final form it took in the "Bulygin constitution" published on August 6.

The traditional scheme, representation from the zemstvos, did not survive the first reviews of the draft within the ministry, although Kryzhanovsky preferred it and continued to believe it was the best system all the while he was elaborating schemes on demand for special elections in succeeding months and years; it was rejected by Bulygin on the grounds that it would lead to politicization of the zemstvos, and that it would be too restrictive of the franchise in regard to both social groups (primarily the peasantry) and territory (the zemstvos existed in only thirty-four of the fifty-one provinces of European Russia).

Neither of the two extreme possible bases for special elections—universal suffrage or election by the traditional estates—was given serious consideration: the former was simply too radical a departure, whose results, except for the certainty that propertied elements would be buried in the popular vote, were impossible of prediction; the latter faced a coalescence of opposition from various viewpoints, but it was generally accepted that the estate system no longer accurately reflected social realities.

By an inertial process of elimination the government planners settled on the multistaged curial system already in use for elections to the zemstvos and town administrations. This system would be easy to implement, since the zemstvo and town voter-qualification records could be used, and its results could be more or less accurately anticipated. As in the original zemstvo system (certain changes introduced in 1890 were bypassed), the electorate was divided into three categories: private landowners; a curia of owners of industrial and commercial enterprises and other urban property; and the peasantry. The system was "class-based," with individual economic status as the criterion for enfranchisement, except for the peasant curia, which simply encompassed the peasants living in village communities. District assemblies for each curial group were to choose electors; the electors from all the curiae would then gather together in a provincial assembly for election of deputies to the Duma.

As in the zemstvo system, holders of full property qualification in the first two curiae could participate personally in the district assemblies, while owners of less than a full *cens* could gather in preliminary assemblies and send one delegate per full cens to the district assemblies. Peasant representation was to pass through two stages preliminary to the district assembly: election by the peasant village community of delegates to a volost' assembly, and election there of delegates to the district assembly.

The provincial assembly of electors from the three curiae was to elect by majority vote the number of Duma deputies allotted to the province. That number was to be based on a general population ratio (1 : 250,000; a higher ratio was later introduced for the borderlands), while the distribution of elector's seats among the curiae in the provincial assembly was to be based on the total value of property owned within each curial group. Finally, separate representation, also based on the property-qualification system of the 1892 statutes of urban self-administration, was to be accorded the largest cities of the empire.

Although the general outlines of the ministerial draft on the electoral system emerged intact in the August 6 law, its content was subjected to considerable correctives in the course of its discussion in the State Council and the special conference. These included a number of adjustments designed to extend the suffrage to a few groups and territories that were not included in the early scheme, and to reduce the level of representation from the borderlands; the basis of curial representation was shifted, for facility's sake, from direct property assessment to amount of zemstvo taxes paid, and so on. But the main target of the critics of the ministry scheme in these meetings was the weight it allotted to the peasants and the landowners, respectively, in the electoral system.

Kryzhanovsky and Bulygin had anticipated that the curial system would produce a Duma that would look very much like a provincial zemstvo assembly—a body dominated by noble landowners with an interest in public affairs—and they were generally concerned to keep peasant representation in the Duma at the lowest possible level commensurate with the foundations of the system. In their view, a Duma with large numbers of unlettered and politically inexperienced peasants would be incapable of serious work. Kryzhanovsky aimed to ensure the appropriate composition of the provincial assemblies through the election of provincial electors by *general* district assemblies of voters and delegates from all three curiae—the same system that had produced the predominantly noble provincial zemstvo assemblies. Although the majority of the State Council apparently had no quarrel with Kryzhanovsky's aim, it nevertheless struck out the provision for general district assemblies, thereby assuring that the distribution of electors among the curiae in the provincial assemblies would be fixed. This was essentially a concession to the argument that the ministry plan provided insufficient guarantee of adequate representation from the peasantry, although apparently no one but Kryzhanovsky realized that its result would be provincial assemblies radically different in composition from the zemstvo assemblies that had served as the ministry's model.

In the special conference, which was drawn from a broader and more heterogeneous group of dignitaries than that allowed by the professional-bureaucratic milieu of the ministry and State Council, arguments were heard for reviving the estate principle so as to produce a Duma with a fixed proportion of deputies from each order. Although these arguments were rejected, a compromise in the form of having the peasant electors select a separate deputy from their midst in each of the fifty-one assemblies of European Russia was supported by the advocates of the estates idea, mostly conservative nobles. The latter were joined by bureaucrats who questioned the loyalty of the nobility to the throne, pointing to widespread noble participation in the zemstvo constitutionalist movement, and believed the rank-and-file peasantry would be more likely to provide conservative support for the regime. (In keeping with the same view of peasant conservatism, the literacy requirement for election to the Duma was also removed.)

No changes were made, however, in the relative weight of the curiae in the provincial assemblies. According to the ministry's calculations, these stood in the aggregate at:

| Curia | Percent of provincial electors |
| --- | --- |
| Peasant | 43 |
| Landowners | 34 |
| Urban | 23 |

Aside from the highly disproportionate ratios of representation for the different groups of the enfranchised population, significant social groups would have gone entirely unrepresented in this system, including the industrial workers, small private (mostly peasant) landowners, and the great mass of the urban population without significant property or business affairs, which included the bulk of the intelligentsia.

Here matters stood until October 17, at least in regard to the Duma and its electoral system. Then came the October Manifesto [see Documents below]. The manifesto was the work of Sergei Witte and his assistants, Witte having been given the leading role . . . as the figure generally recognized in the government to be best suited to deal with the mounting crisis situation. Although Witte had apparently come to the conclusion in the weeks immediately preceding the general strike [Oct. 7–17] that preservation of autocracy was a lost cause and the time for a parliamentary order had arrived, his immediate aim was to split up the opposition and gain time for the government; and in this, at least for the short term, he succeeded in adequate measure. The manifesto was accordingly addressed primarily to the liberal opposition, and its concessions, though far-reaching in principle, were stated abstractly enough to allow for considerable flexibility in their realization.

The manifesto's concessions were embodied in three points: the first promised to honor the right of habeas corpus and freedom of conscience, speech, assembly, and association.

The second point promised to extend the franchise for elections to the Duma so as to include "those classes of the population that are now completely deprived of electoral rights," without suspending the established timetable for elections (January 1906), and leaving "the further development of the principle of general suffrage" to be worked out in the new legislative system.

The third and final point stated that "no law may go into effect without the approval of the State Duma," and assured that the Duma would be given a "genuine part" in monitoring the legality of the actions of government officials. The principle of representative government had at last been recognized by the regime, if only in the most general terms.

The issue of electoral reform was engaged immediately by Witte, who, as of October 19, when the law creating a united ministry (that is, a cabinet system of government) was published, officially became the country's first prime minister. The basic scheme for carrying out the promise of point two of the manifesto was readied in a few days (once again by Kryzhanovsky): a mechanical increase in the electorate by significantly lowering qualification levels in the two property-based curiae (in the process, property in the strict sense in fact ceased to be a prerequisite for qualification), and the creation of a separate workers' curia, analogous to that of the peasant curia.

The aim of the revisions was clearly stated in the conference Witte called immediately after issuing the manifesto: to satisfy the demands for participation in the elections by "those classes of the population which have been most aroused by deprivation of electoral rights; namely, the workers and persons living by intellectual labor." It appears that the admission to the polls of a much wider group of smallholders in the landowners' curia and of the petty bourgeoisie in the urban curia flowed more or less automatically from the decision to expand the franchise to the working class and the intelligentsia.

The decision to give the workers a separate curia was linked to the general system: short of instituting universal suffrage, it was the only way the workers could be given a more or less visible role in the elections. Unlike the peasants, however, the workers were not given a special allotment of deputies in the Duma; their delegates would simply join the others in the provincial assemblies and large-city assemblies.

The December law [law of Dec. 11, 1905], greatly expanded the size and character of the electorate in the urban and landowners' curiae. The peasant curia was not affected by the December 11 revisions. The relative weight of the curiae was also left essentially unchanged: the workers' delegates would occupy only 2.5 percent of the electors' seats in the provincial assemblies of European Russia.

With the convocation of a parliament armed with considerable legislative authority in the offing, the government moved, at the same time it was broadening the suffrage system, to alter other structures of the central government so as to better deal with, and control, the new element of public representation. The first items on the agenda, both in fact under consideration before October in connection with the projected Bulygin Duma, were the creation of a united ministry, or cabinet system, which had long been contemplated but never realized in Russia, where each minister had traditionally dealt directly with the sovereign; and the reform of the State Council into an upper house with powers equal to those of the Duma. The united ministry, though flawed in important ways (the prime minister could not control appointments of the other ministers and generally lacked control over the internal operations of the individual ministries), was made law immediately after issuance of the October Manifesto. The reform of the State Council, which in contrast to the introduction of the cabinet system constituted an obvious encroachment on the October promise concerning the power of the Duma, was made the subject of a special law defining its composition, competence, and operations, issued simultaneously with a law defining the details of the competence and operations of the Duma, on February 20, 1906. Finally, a new version of the Fundamental Laws of the Russian Empire, accommodating all these changes, was issued on April 23, 1906, a scant three days before the convening of the first State Duma.

These laws followed upon lengthy discussions, extensive searches through the constitutions of the European monarchies, lengthy debate about whether or not Russia had become a constitutional monarchy, and numerous redactions, which cannot be dwelt on here, although a general idea of their content is necessary for understanding the political context in which the new parties operated and the elections were held. The ultimate structures of these institutions were not predestined, and in fact remained uncertain until the final acts were published, although there was to be observed a general tendency as their preparation progressed to mold them into conservative restraints on the new public representation. Moreover, Witte was clearly motivated by the idea of forestalling the Duma's preoccupation with constituent functions—the avowed aim of most of the political groups that were preparing to take part in the elections—by presenting the Duma with a fait accompli in regard to the political constitution. (It should be noted that there was very little questioning in government circles of the regime's right to elaborate the political constitution prior to convocation of the Duma; the government had not ceded any constituent functions to the Duma on October 17.)

Renovation of the State Council consisted of two related parts: expansion of its sphere of activities to include legislative authority; that is, its assumption of the status of an upper chamber with legislative parity with the Duma-to-be, and alteration of its composition. The council was to serve as a conservative counterweight to the Duma, making it unnecessary for the sovereign to expose himself to the accusation that he was operating against the popular will by frequently vetoing Duma measures. This transformation in the functions of the State Council necessitated reform of its composition, in order to enhance its autonomy: in its old composition—mostly superannuated career bureaucrats and generals—the council could hardly be taken seriously as an independent element in the political constitution. It was accordingly decided to introduce elective representatives from "responsible groups" of the population into the council. After much debate, it was decided that the elected portion of the council would be no less than half the total, and would be filled by corporate elections from the clergy, the provincial zemstvo assemblies, the provincial corporations of nobility, the Academy of Sciences and the universities, and the organizations of trade and industry. In effect, more than two thirds of the elected deputies were to be provided by the landed nobility: the provincial zemstvo assemblies and the noble corporations were allotted three fourths of the ninety-eight elected seats on the council.

The "Institution of the State Duma," published the same day as the law reforming the State Council [Feb. 20, 1906], incorporated the promise of the October Manifesto that no law would go into effect without the Duma's consent. At the same time, it established that no measures issuing from the Duma could take effect without the approval of the State Council and the emperor. Bills could be initiated by the executive branch or by either chamber of the legislative branch. However, prior to taking legislative initiative, the Duma was required to inform the appropriate ministry and to attend upon it for one month, so that the ministry could prepare a bill of its own or otherwise respond to the Duma's expression of need for new legislation in the area in question.

The law likewise honored the second part of point three of the October Manifesto, concerning supervision of the actions of government officials, by providing that the Duma had the right of interpellation [right to question official policy]. This right was hedged, however, by the provision (article 40) that ministers could refuse to respond to calls for interpellations "on subjects that, for considerations of state security, should not be made public." It also provided that ministers could send their assistants to respond to interpellations, and, most significantly, it explicitly stated that the right of legislative initiative of the Duma did not extend to the Fundamental Laws; that was the prerogative of the monarch alone. In addition to matters of legislative initiative and review, the law enumerated the other areas of Duma competence, mainly having to do with examination and approval of the state budget and other financial activities of the government.

Finally, the law stipulated that the Duma, which was ordinarily to be convened for a five-year term, could be prorogued [dissolved] by order of the emperor, with the stipulation that the order was to call for new elections and set the date for convening a new Duma. And, in the manifesto that accompanied the publication of the laws on the State Council and the Duma, the emperor proclaimed that the executive could institute emergency provisional "measures" that ordinarily required legislative review prior to their implementation. These "measures" would have to be submitted for the approval of the Duma within the first two months after its reconvocation, however, if they were to remain in effect. The Fundamental Laws and the laws concerning the institutions of the Duma and the State Council were ruled outside the sphere of application of this procedure.

Revision of the Fundamental Laws was required by the changes in the political constitution brought about by the October Manifesto and the succeeding laws on the State Council and the Duma. The document [revision] issued on April 23 might have been significantly more liberal in regard to such matters as the definition of civil rights and the circumscription of the power of the Crown had its preparation not taken place within the context of a power struggle between Witte and I. L. Goremykin (soon to succeed Witte as prime minister); the two vied for Nicholas's favor by proposing revisions in the text of the Fundamental Laws in the direction of minimizing the concessions of political power made on October 17. However, the foundations of the new political constitution had already been enunciated in the February 20 laws and the accompanying manifesto. The central significance of the new rendition of the Fundamental Laws lay in the fact that by at once incorporating the main provisions of the laws on the Duma and proclaiming that changes in the Fundamental Laws were the sole prerogative of the emperor, they formally excluded the possibility of the Duma legally occupying itself with changes in its own structure or competence.

The first article of the first chapter of the Fundamental Laws proclaimed: "Supreme autocratic authority belongs to the All-Russian EMPEROR. God himself ordains submission to HIS authority, not only from fear, but also as a matter of conscience." Nicholas II, in the last Tsarskoe Selo [Imperial palace] conference held in April 1906 to discuss the draft of the new Fundamental Laws, tried to persuade his advisers to restore to the traditional formula on the autocratic authority of the emperor the qualifying adjective "unlimited"; but with two exceptions (one of them, significantly, his next choice for prime minister) they all objected that this would be both untruthful and unpolitic, and Nicholas reluctantly conceded the point.

At the beginning of the twentieth century Russia was just starting to confront the political-institutional issues arising from the conflicting concepts of the old regime and popular sovereignty. These issues were those that had already been dominating the political life of most West European countries for at least half a century: the questions of the form of central government and of the relations between central and local government, of civil and political rights and control over the bureaucracy, of suffrage, public representation, and the formation of political parties for organizing public participation in constitutional government. The fact alone that when these issues were finally engaged in Russia they were still being contested in western and central Europe promised that the transition from autocracy to a new political-institutional order would not be easily or rapidly accomplished.

The Manifesto of October 17, 1905, set the stage for the open struggle of political concepts and institutions: it conceded the principle of effective public participation in government, but the circumstances surrounding its promulgation and subsequent planning for institutional change in high places revealed that the ruling elite expected that the new institutions could be molded in such a way as to allow them to remain in control.

In estate terms the first Duma was dominated by peasants and nobles, with 231 and 180 deputies respectively out of a total of just under 500. Better than half the nobles were landowners, although many of these had other occupations as well, and not quite half the peasants were cultivators: there were just over 100 in each group. Representatives of the intelligentsia professions, mostly deputies from those same estate categories, were present in about the same number (108). In descending order, men in trade and industry (67), salaried employees (45), workers (25), and clergy (17) constituted most of the remaining deputies. . . .

Just under 60 percent of the deputies (265 of the 448 respondents to [a] questionnaire) were Great Russians. The next most numerous ethnic-national groups were the Ukrainians, with 13.8 percent (62) of the deputies, and the Poles, with 11.3 percent (51). No other nationalities provided more than 3 percent of the deputies. By confession, 75.6 percent of the deputies were identified as Russian Orthodox, and 14 percent as Catholics.

In terms of political affiliations, the first Duma was in a constant state of flux from its first day [April 27] to its dissolution seventy-two days later on July 9 as a result of the combined processes of ongoing party formation and the continual arrival of new deputies from distant regions of the empire. . . . [Yet] once constituted[,] the general proportions of the larger political groupings did not change radically during the course of the Duma's existence.

The Kadets sent about 130 established party members to the first Duma from the elections in European Russia, and this number grew to somewhere between 170 and 180 by the end of the Duma session, mainly through the arrival of deputies from the Caucasus, central Asia, and Siberia. They constituted more than a third of all the deputies assembled.

The second largest formation in the first Duma, the Trudovik [Laborite] fraction, began to take shape in Petersburg just before the opening of the Duma, as a few deputies-elect who were veterans of the Peasant Union took it upon themselves to unite the peasant deputies as they arrived from the provinces—first the not insignificant number who were known to have had connections with the Peasant Union, and then, through them, other peasant deputies-elect who were thought to be sympathetic to the union. A sort of orientation club for arriving peasant deputies was set up for this purpose near the Nikolaevskii railway station.

The Trudovik organizers at first planned to create an exclusively peasant organization, mainly for fear that the presence of nonpeasants would scare off the politically uncommitted peasant deputies whom they hoped to keep away from the Kadets or other parties and to mobilize for the left. The artificiality of maintaining an exclusively peasant fraction soon became apparent, however, to the group's main initiators. . . . Although elected from the peasant curia, they were all intelligenty who had, in the words of the party's historian, "long since ceased to share [the peasants'] perception of the world and way of life." And more like them were arriving daily. After the arrival of the Saratov delegation, most of whose members shared these characteristics, it was agreed that the fraction would be open to "all who stand for the laboring people, who live by their own labor, and are capable of defending the interests of the laboring people." The group grew rapidly to about 130 members, and then shrank to just over 100; about 80 percent of the members were of peasant origin, but only some 40 percent were peasant cultivators.

Although there was a considerable variety of political orientations and related differences over such concrete issues as the agrarian and nationalities questions among the Trudoviki, it was the populist Peasant Union group that took the lead and generally set the tone of the fraction.

Virtually identical in size to the Trudovik group was the nonparty group, which was not really a disciplined fraction but a kind of political way station. One hundred five deputies, nearly two-thirds of them Russian land-working peasants, identified themselves as nonparty for the May questionnaire. Some of them appear to have been sympathetic toward the Kadets and other parties of the opposition but stayed out of the fractions for fear of retaliation from local authorities. The remainder were mostly Russian nobles from the landowners' curia who were generally conservative in their views but apparently did not wish to associate themselves openly in the Duma with the defeated monarchist organizations.

The next largest formation to take shape in the Duma was the Autonomist group, to which sixty-three deputies without other party affiliations belonged at the time of the May questionnaire; these were predominantly Poles from the Kingdom of Poland and the western provinces. . . .

The other western nationalities did not organize separate fractions in the first Duma. With the consolidation of the Polish groups, whose members numbered together about forty-five, the remaining deputies who had initially identified themselves as Autonomists joined one or another of the large fractions, primarily the Kadets or the Trudoviki; a few remained in the nonparty group.

There were no other groups of comparable size in the first Duma, although an interesting attempt was made there to consolidate a large centrist fraction by bringing together the few Octobrists [moderately conservative supporters of the October Manifesto], right-wing Kadet deputies, and peasants. The upshot of this attempt was the disappearance of a separate Octobrist fraction and the formation of the Peaceful Renewal group (PR), which eventually grew to twenty-six members, the same number that had entered the Duma as candidates of the Octobrist bloc. It included most of the original Octobrist-bloc deputies, two right-wing Kadets, one member of the Party of Democratic Reforms, and one of the two Trade-Industry party members who had been elected to the Duma. All but one of them were landowners. The new fraction was formed on the initiative of the Octobrist deputies Count Geiden and M. M. Stakhovich, who persuaded their fellow Octobrists in the Duma to abandon the Octobrist label and endorse a more radical program of land reform, which in its essentials differed little from the Kadet program. Their proclaimed long-range aim (whence came their justification for dropping the unpopular name and changing the agrarian program) was to create a party based on cooperation between the landowning gentry and the peasants. . . .

The appearance of Peaceful Renewal was a test of the cohesiveness of both the Octobrist and Kadet organizations, and both withstood the test without major losses. The Octobrist organization remained by and large with Guchkov,[2] approving his tactic of supporting the government's actions for the restoration of order without repudiating the union's constitutionalist commitment in principle. And the Kadet organization survived the crisis caused in its ranks by the Vyborg appeal [reaction to the dissolution of the Duma on July 9] through the efforts of Miliukov and other centrist leaders who arranged a compromise position for the party on Vyborg: approving the manifesto condemning the government for having dissolved the Duma, but abstaining from implementation of its call for acts of civil disobedience.

With the arrival of the five Caucasian deputies who had been elected as candidates of the SD party (Mensheviks), and in keeping with the Menshevik-sponsored resolution taken at the SD congress in late April, a separate Social-Democratic fraction was formed in the first Duma. The Caucasian SDs were joined by another late-arriving SD deputy from Akmolinsk and by deputies already present, mostly workers from a special workers' group in the Trudovik fraction. Together they brought the fraction to a total membership of seventeen or eighteen. The three or four successful candidates of the business parties joined after mid-May with another eight or nine deputies in a "progressive group," which Borodin [contemporary reporter] described as the "extreme right" of the Duma. The smallest fraction in the first Duma at the time of its dissolution, with six members, was the Party of Democratic Reforms led by M. M. Kovalevsky and V. D. Kuzmin-Karavaev. In most respects the Democratic Reform fraction operated as an appendage of the Kadet party in the first Duma.

The overall effect of the Kadets' unexpected success in the elections was to reenforce substantially their commitment to the tactical resolutions on the Duma that had been adopted at the second party congress in January [1906] and, more generally, to heighten the anticipation that the Duma would become an "organ of struggle" with the government over the still unresolved issue of whether or not Russia was to be transformed into a proper parliamentary regime. This commitment was made even stronger at the third party congress, which was held on the eve of the Duma's convocation [April 27]. There was much heavier representation at the third congress than in the previous congresses from radically oriented provincial groups, whose delegates appeared flush with victory in the elections, irritated with their conflicts with the local bureaucracy, and little informed about the situation in Petersburg. Feeling was widespread at the congress that the party had ridden to victory on a wave of popular revolutionary sentiment; that the party's deputies-elect accordingly had the responsibility of representing not only the party but this general revolutionary mood. The prevailing combative mood was further reenforced by the regime's recent efforts to forestall "constituent" action by the Duma: the promulgation of the statutes on the Duma and the State Council on February 20. The government's floating of a large loan from France in order to withstand financial pressure from the Duma further reenforced anticipation of confrontation.

---

2. A. I. Guchkov (1862–1936), respected leader of the Octobrists; see Documents, Chapter 14.—Ed.

There was much indecisive debate at the Kadet congress over programmatic issues, especially the agrarian question. The constituency of the congress and the heightened atmosphere in which it was working made consensus on specific programmatic issues even less likely than at the second congress. In the end, the third congress passed the issues on, in the form of the recommendations of the several program committees, to the party's parliamentary delegation. There may have been cool heads present, especially among the central committee members, but the debates on tactics tended to be over whether to adopt radical or more radical resolutions: the concluding statement of the resolution on Duma tactics proposed by the central committee, which enjoined the Kadet deputies to defend "the people's demands as formulated by the party . . . even to the point of an open break with the government," or that introduced by the radical leader of the Viatka party group, I. N. Ovchinnikov, which asserted that the "progressive majority" of the Duma would uncompromisingly fulfill the people's will and would turn directly to the people for support if they were to run into obstacles set by the "dying regime, in the form either of the bureaucratic government or the State Council." After two inconclusive ballotings on these versions, a third gave a majority of 119 to 73 for the central committee's text.

The unanticipated publication of the Fundamental Laws on the penultimate day of the congress only increased the sense of righteous outrage and made conflict seem more likely than before. A special resolution was issued, condemning that act as a violation of the rights of the people, an attempt to transform the Duma into "the handmaiden of the bureaucratic government," and ending with the declaration that "no obstacles set up by the government shall restrain the people's representatives from carrying out the tasks set them by the people." "This was already the style of the first Duma," Miliukov recalled in his memoirs, "the conflict had, in reality, begun before it opened."

There were differences of opinion in party councils and within the Kadet Duma delegation, but the prevailing view on the eve of the Duma's convocation was that the party's chances of winning the struggle for shifting the center of political power from bureaucracy to parliament were good, that the government would not dare withstand the Duma. Thirty-three years later, Miliukov ruefully recalled the stormy applause that had greeted Kizevetter's [a delegate] ringing words at the third congress: "If they dissolve the Duma, that will be the government's last act, after which it will cease to exist."

The party's tactic for the first Duma, elaborated as usual mainly by Miliukov, endorsed by the central committee, and accepted essentially intact by the third party congress, was to confine the conflict with the regime insofar as possible to the Duma, to keep the struggle for power, as Miliukov characteristically put it, "within civilized limits," and to let the burden of breaking those limits, should things come to that, lie with the government. This tactic required accepting the institutional framework created by the February 20 statutes on the Duma and the State Council. Work could be done within that framework, in the Duma, on the two fundamental popular mandates expressed in the elections and already embodied in the second party congress resolutions: revision of the electoral law to universal suffrage, and agrarian reform including expropriation of private land. The first order of work in the Duma was to introduce bills on these subjects. The formal resolutions adopted by the third congress added as subjects for early legislative initiative the issues of civil rights, national rights, political amnesty, and the abolition of capital punishment. It also called for appointment of a parliamentary committee for investigation of illegal actions committed by government officials since October 17.

The stance taken by the Kadets in the first Duma was influenced by their need to maintain a coalition with the Trudoviki, whom they by and large recognized as representing the mood of the masses (even if they did not know how to properly defend the masses' interests in parliament) and without whose support the Kadets could not have maintained a reliable majority in the Duma. In any case, for the Kadets, who for the most part controlled the first Duma's procedures, as much as for the Trudoviki leaders and the Social Democrats to their left, the first Duma was first and foremost the scene of a struggle with the government for political power; its aim, as Petrunkevich [a Kadet] put it, was to "break the power of the bureaucracy." Many of the speeches made by Kadets on the floor of the Duma left nothing in their stridency and radicalism to those of the most fiery SD and Trudovik leaders. The distinction between themselves and the far left on which the Kadet leaders insisted—that the Kadets were committed to waging the struggle in parliament and generally within the bounds of the Fundamental Laws and that the Duma was "more than just a means to them," whereas the leftists looked on the Duma purely as a means for discrediting the regime and appealing for popular support—must have been small comfort to the government under attack, although some members of it were certainly aware of these differences and had hopes of splitting the Kadets away from the opposition by coopting them into the government.

The atmosphere of conflict led in short order to a state of paralysis in the relations between the Duma and the Goremykin government. Following the emperor's greeting to the members of the Duma and the State Council, the Duma, on the initiative of the Kadets, produced a reply to the speech from the throne (as they chose to interpret Nicholas's greeting), in which the general goals of the Duma majority were laid out—both those principal goals that could be advanced by legislative initiative in the Duma and those that would demand exercise of the royal [Imperial] prerogative under the Fundamental Laws. The reply, which contained in generally stated terms all the points of the Kadet tactical program, was adopted unanimously by the Duma, with Count Geiden and ten other moderates absenting themselves from the chambers during the roll call.

The emperor refused to receive the Duma delegation selected to present the reply, and on May 13, Prime Minister Goremykin delivered the government's answer to the reply, which rejected all its points out of hand, making no distinction between questions on which the Duma had the right to prepare legislation and those that required exercise of the royal prerogative. The rejection of the Duma's agrarian-reform plan, and of its provision for expropriation in particular, was given especially detailed refutation. The response was taken as an outrage by the Duma majority; the minister's anticipatory rejection of the measures within the Duma's competence was declared a violation of the constitution; and a formal vote of nonconfidence and a demand for the government's resignation was passed by a large majority in the Duma.

At this point relations between the government and the Duma essentially broke down. On the government side, the ministers ceased attending Duma sessions, generally sending their assistants to answer Duma interpellations (if responding at all), and during the first month of the Duma's existence they presented no legislation for the Duma's consideration, with the exception of two bills prepared in the Ministry of Enlightenment [Education] concerning the establishment of certain private courses of instruction and funds for construction of a greenhouse and a laundry at Iurev University. Demands for the Duma's dismissal were being made in the Council of Ministers even before the Duma's formal adoption of its reply, and the view was widespread there that cooperation with the Duma was out of the question; it would have to be dismissed and the electoral law revised to produce a Duma not dominated by the opposition. It was decided, however, to await an appropriate occasion: immediate dismissal without sufficient provocation would probably produce repercussions in the country (reports that the Duma had wide popular support, that great hopes were attached to it, and that the provincial governmental institutions were widely discredited were coming in from the governors and were being communicated to the tsar by Stolypin [now minister of the interior] and Goremykin).

The Duma, on its side, proceeded directly to the preparation of its own legislative bills, principally based on the drafts that the Kadet central committee subcommittees had been at work on since their second congress, ignoring in the process the spirit, if not the letter, of the Fundamental Laws. The first area of substantive legislation begun by the Duma was agrarian reform, with draft bills sent to committee by the Kadets and by the Trudovik fraction. Both, of course, provided for large-scale expropriation of private estates, with the Trudovik plan going considerably further in that regard than that of the Kadets. Although it may be an exaggeration to say that the Duma simply ignored the bills of some substance that began to be submitted to it by the ministries in June, it is true that most of them were never put on the agenda, let alone sent to committee, before the Duma's dissolution, and only one, a bill for supplementary famine relief funds, was approved by the first Duma.

At the same time, the Duma used its right of interpellation very extensively in order to carry on a running inquiry into current administrative practices, including an inquiry into complicity by government officials in the Belostok pogrom, which occurred while the Duma was in session. Special investigating committees for inquiries in the field were appointed, and a general Duma committee for the investigation of criminal actions by government officials after October 17 was set up at the end of May. In all, there were nearly 400 interpellations introduced in the two months of the Duma's existence, and on the few occasions when ministry officials appeared to respond to them, they were often booed and insulted from the floor and, on at least one occasion, not even allowed to speak.

Faced with the hostility of the Duma and yet reluctant to dismiss it, a number of highly placed persons, including several ministers in the Goremykin government, explored over the second half of June various combinations for altering the composition of the government so as to make coexistence with the Duma possible. One of the combinations proposed, the only one that could have succeeded in significantly altering relations with the Duma, was the creation of a Kadet ministry; that is, a government de facto responsible to the Duma majority. Although none of the more powerful ministers in the Goremykin government supported this solution, which would have entailed their removal from power, it was given serious consideration in circles near the throne and, apparently, by Nicholas II himself. This solution would have been acceptable to the Kadet leaders, several of whom (principally Miliukov and Muromtsev) were approached by administration figures at the time, and it is clear that some of them, including Miliukov, believed for a time that there was a strong possibility of their being summoned to power.

It is not clear when the alternative of forming a ministry from the parliamentary majority was ruled out in government circles by the consolidation against it of the principal ministers and other officials who would have been the first to lose their positions in the event. In any case, the campaign for dissolving the Duma and creating a new but entirely "bureaucratic" ministry under his leadership was decisively joined by the energetic minister of internal affairs, P. A. Stolypin, toward the end of June. It appears that Goremykin took the decision to proceed directly to dissolve the Duma on July 2, and in the next two or three days the plan was elaborated and sanctioned in principle by the tsar. Sometime between July 3 and July 5, the final decision was taken by the tsar to dissolve the Duma on July 9 and to replace Goremykin by Stolypin, whose decisiveness in the preparations for dissolution had apparently convinced Nicholas that he was the man to take charge under the new political conditions.

The occasion for dismissal presented itself to Stolypin in the "Declaration to the People" issued by the Duma in response to a public communiqué of June 20 by the Council of Ministers on the agrarian question. This communiqué, which laid out the government's alternative to the agrarian reforms proposed by the Duma majority, was apparently made in anticipation of the impending dissolution of the Duma. According to the advice given the tsar by one of the most persistent advocates of dissolution, State Comptroller P. K. Shvanebakh, a move against the Duma should be preceded by a proclamation for the peasants, "explaining the complete impracticality of the Duma's agrarian projects and laying out the ensemble of the government's measures for meeting the peasants' needs." The aim was to combat the idea that the Duma had been martyred for its defense of peasant interests, and it was executed with rather impressive demagogic skill.

In the Duma the government communiqué was generally taken as a threat to the Duma's legislative authority, and it was soon decided (on the proposal of the moderate Kuzmin-Karavaev) to answer with the Duma's own public statement on the agrarian question. Following stormy debate a declaration restating the Duma's agrarian-reform plans, pointing out that the government communiqué did not have the force of law, and calling on the population to wait for solution of the agrarian problem by the Duma was passed by the Kadets alone on July 6: the other fractions to right and left either abstaining or voting against it for their several reasons. As Miliukov remarked in his memoirs, the Kadets were put in the unenviable position of simultaneously taking the step that would serve as the pretext for the Duma's dissolution and revealing that they could not in fact command the solid majority on which a Kadet ministry could rely.

In the early hours of Sunday, July 9, the doors of the Tauride Palace were locked, a guard mounted, and the imperial order dissolving the Duma and calling for new elections and convening of a new Duma in seven months was posted on the doors. Led by the Kadets, about a third of the deputies repaired to Vyborg just across the Finnish border, where they proceeded to sign and publish the next day a manifesto "to the citizens of all Russia." The Vyborg manifesto described the dissolution of the Duma as a violation of the people's right of representation, explained the government's action as the result of its wish to stop the Duma from carrying out its reform program, particularly the agrarian reform, and warned that the government would act arbitrarily in the seven months intervening before the summoning of a new Duma, using all means at its disposal to acquire election of a servile Duma (implied here was an arbitrary revision of the electoral law), and might not reconvene the Duma at all. In its second part the manifesto called on the people to engage in passive resistance or civil disobedience—by refusing to pay taxes or submit to military recruitment—in order to compel the government to summon a new Duma promptly.

The Kadet chronicler of the Vyborg manifesto [M. M. Vinaver] would later claim that it had accomplished its main aim: the next Duma was called on schedule and was elected under the same suffrage law as the first Duma. But the fact was that neither the dissolution of the Duma nor the Vyborg appeal elicited any significant response among the population. One of the casualties of this experience was any illusions entertained in the Kadet leadership about the utility of the party network they had built up around the country for any purpose other than competing in elections. It had in fact become clear to the Kadet leaders very early that the party groups that had sprung up around the country to take part in the first [Duma] elections did not constitute a stable network of political communication. As already noted, many of these groups never bothered to respond to central committee inquiries, and the party secretariat's repeated efforts to collect the minimal dues that were a formal condition of membership were almost entirely unsuccessful: from the beginning the expenses of the central party organs and the capital press were met by contributions from a few wealthy members. And despite the party leader's earnest injunctions to local delegates at the third party congress to go on working at building up the party in the postelection period precisely in anticipation of the need to mobilize popular support for the Duma in its struggle with the government, central committee inquiries showed that many party groups had vanished by the second half of 1906. The absence of solid organization was particularly felt in the wake of the Vyborg appeal, when the party leaders tried to mobilize local party groups to effect its implementation: not only the public at large, but the party itself failed to respond to the manifesto.

During the course of the summer the Kadets retreated from the idea of trying to implement the second part of the Vyborg manifesto and turned toward preparing for the next elections. In his tactical speech to the fourth party congress (September 24–28, 1906) Miliukov relegated the manifesto to the status of a "historical document." This marked the end of the party's uncharacteristic venture into illegal action.

The revival of party activity in the second election campaign [fall 1906] confirmed that a good deal of Kadet party organization consisted essentially of temporary election-campaign committees. The second elections also prove, however, that the

Kadets' strong showing in the first elections was not a fluke, not merely the result, as it is usually explained, of the revolutionary parties' boycott of the first elections, which left the Kadets as the most radical party in the elections amidst a radically minded electorate. To be sure, the Kadets' strength was considerably diminished in the second Duma, but they remained the largest party in the Duma, and an analysis of the second elections, held in February 1907, shows that reduced representation in the Duma was not the result of a dramatic shift of voter support away from the Kadets to the left parties, which were all now participating in the elections.

Although there are difficulties in comparing party-affiliation figures for the two Dumas, . . . [the available data show] a remarkable swelling of the two extremes of the political spectrum in the Duma.[3] This shift took place only partially at the expense, so to speak, of the center, and of the Kadets in particular, for the greatest dislocation was out of the nonparty groups. . . .

The data on the political orientation of provincial electors in European Russia demonstrate that by and large the gains of the extreme parties in the Duma, and of the left in particular, did not take place as a result of the Kadets' having lost ground numerically among the electors in the provincial assemblies. . . . Kadet representation among peasant delegates, although remaining modest, was actually larger than it had been in the first two elections. In the landowners' curia Kadet representation was reduced noticeably (from 11.5 to 8.9 percent), but in the urban curia the Kadets accounted for considerably more of the electors than in the first elections (this is partly attributable to the highly incomplete character of the data on the first elections; but even if one compares the data of the two elections in strictly proportional terms, Kadet representation falls by only a fraction of a percent). As a percentage function of total provincial electors accounted for in each election, the Kadets actually increased their strength slightly: from 14.1 percent to 14.3 percent. . . .

This is not to say that there was no attrition in the popular vote for the Kadets. That there was attrition is clear from an examination of the returns in the urban curia, which had been and remained the main source of Kadet strength. And here the attrition was mainly to the benefit of the socialist parties, as was made particularly clear in the cities with special elections, where the correspondence between the popular vote and the party affiliation of the Duma deputies elected was closest. This time Kadets were elected in only nine instead of nineteen of these special elections in European Russia, and took fifteen instead of twenty-six deputies there. As nearly as can be judged, about 58 percent of the electors chosen in these elections were Kadets, as compared to 83 percent in the first elections; the remainder were split almost evenly between electors to the left of the Kadets and those to their right.

Where the Kadets ran alone in the second elections—in about half the urban elections, apparently—they generally collected about as many popular votes as the

---

3. Of a total of 474 deputies elected to the Second Duma, 108 were Kadets (with adherents) whereas 175 were socialists or other leftists (including Trudoviki) and 72 were of the extreme right. These figures compare respectively with 185 Kadets (with adherents), 111 socialists and other leftists; and 0 (none) from the extreme right among the 478 deputies to the First Duma.—Ed.

parties to their left and right combined. Of 307,733 popular votes accounted for in sixteen towns (including the capitals), the Kadets took 138,039, or about 45 percent. Where left, right, and center all ran separate candidates, the Octobrists did nearly as well, in the ensemble, as the socialist parties in collecting popular votes, and together with the extreme right generally attracted more popular votes than did the parties to the left of the Kadets.[4]

The Kadets emerged victorious once again in both capitals, now running alone, and although their recorded popular vote was lower than in 1906 (more noticeably so, as might have been expected, in Petersburg than in Moscow), the Kadets showed altogether impressive strength, considering that their vote was now much more nearly a truly partisan one than in the bloc voting of 1906. In Petersburg the number of votes cast in 1906 for the Kadet bloc in the twelve precincts had been 39,657; in 1907 it was 28,698. A precinct-by-precinct count shows that in most cases the number of votes lost by the Kadets was quite close to the number of votes taken by the left bloc (SDs, SRs, PSP, and Trudoviki; in all, the left bloc took about 25 percent of the popular vote).

In Moscow, attrition of the Kadet popular vote was on the order of 10 percent (from about 65 percent to 55 percent); correspondingly, the left bloc there took about 13 percent of the vote. (The vote to the right of the Kadets was about one third the total in Moscow; about 20 percent in Petersburg.)

In view of the more competitive atmosphere prevailing in the provincial assemblies in the second elections, it is not surprising that there were considerably fewer Kadets in the deputations sent to the second Duma from those provincial assemblies where they had earlier either dominated the elections or shared the deputies' seats with predominantly nonparty peasants. In the first case, this result suggests that in those provinces where there was already a high level of mobilized opposition in the first elections, and the right was weak, the end of the boycott by the socialist parties gave vent to the expression of political sympathies that had been blocked in the first elections. The supporters of the left in these provinces made their weight felt. In the second case, the results were more complex. In Viatka the left bloc took all the seats, and Kadet weight was seriously undercut by the left in Samara and Ekaterinoslav provinces, although what they essentially meant in several of these provinces was that the formerly nonpartisan peasant partners in the coalition had in the meantime acquired leftist political labels. And in two such provinces—Poltava and Smolensk—what appears to have happened is that the nonpeasant Kadets were displaced by nonpeasant deputies politically to their right.

There were some dramatic changes in the assemblies that had sent up politically mixed delegations to the first Duma, but the Kadets held their own in this group (the Kadets now sent twenty-four deputies to the Duma, as compared to the twenty-five they had sent to the first Duma). Losses were mainly to the right, through the landowners' curia, but the dissipation of Kadet strength by the left in the urban curia was also a significant factor.

---

4. The number of Octobrist and other moderately conservative deputies rose from 13 in the First Duma to 31 in the Second.—Ed.

Kadet attrition was proportionally greatest in the West, except for the Baltic provinces, where the returns remained virtually identical to those in 1906. The number of Kadet-bloc deputies from the western provinces (the Baltic excluded) fell from twenty-five to five. With the exception of the contribution of the Kiev assembly—which, as could have been expected from the strength of the left and the generally high level of political mobilization obtaining already at the time of the first elections, produced a predominantly left-oriented and almost exclusively peasant delegation to the second Duma—the Kadet losses in the West were mostly to the right. They were displaced by Polish National Democrats in the Vitebsk elections; by Octobrists and Monarchists in Minsk; by one Monarchist and two "progressives" in Grodno; and by Monarchists in Mogilev. With the exception of one or two "progressives," these were landowners or professional men, mostly Russian, elected together with peasants who were also mostly on the right according to the press reports. Moderate or conservative landowners and peasants now predominated where liberal Jewish-urban, Polish-landowner, and nonparty peasant coalitions had earlier been victorious: in Minsk the Jewish-Polish coalition was replaced by one of "Russian" landowners and peasants, the groups that had demonstrated against them in the first elections; in Mogilev the Jewish-Polish-peasant bloc which had been dominated by peasants was replaced by a conservative landowner-peasant coalition in which the landowners predominated; essentially the same pattern prevailed in Vitebsk; and in Grodno the Jewish-peasant delegation was replaced by one of "Russians" and peasants. Only in Kovno in the Northwest did the Jewish-peasant bloc apparently survive, electing three peasant adherents of the "Jewish-Lithuanian party" and two Jewish lawyers—both Kadets—to the Duma. The Vilno elections were dominated by the Polish National Democrats.

Conservative mobilization of landowners was a major factor in the second elections especially in those western borderland areas where Russian landowners must have felt particularly vulnerable to threats to their status but still were able to carry heavy weight in the provincial assemblies. In several provinces the independent consolidation of the Polish vote behind the National Democrats also contributed to the breakdown of the Kadet bloc. The National Democrats were more conservative than the Kadets in social policy, and in particular objected to the opposition's plans for expropriation of estate lands.

The elections to the second Duma demonstrated that the Constitutional Democrats could attract a considerable vote in their own right in competition with the socialist left, particularly among the urban population. This urban support came not only from professional and intelligentsia elements but extended fairly deeply into the ranks of salaried employees, shopkeepers, and the like: the "petty bourgeoisie." Much of this support, of course (as party leaders were the first to recognize), did not extend beyond the ballot box, but it proved to be remarkably stable.

From the perspective of the second elections it can be seen that the Kadets' strength in the first Duma, which was quite out of proportion to their popular support or even their representation in the provincial assemblies, was the product of a particular historical moment, two of the most salient features of which were the relatively low degree of political mobilization still obtaining among the electorate, especially the peasantry, and the structure of the electoral system. The importance of the electoral system may be judged by the fact that the Kadets still did extremely well in the second elections.

Would they have done as well had the first elections been held on the basis of universal, *direct* suffrage [italics added], as the Kadets and all parties to their left wished? Ironically, the answer is almost certainly not. It is not easy to imagine how elections by universal, direct suffrage would have functioned at that time, given the state of literacy and communications prevailing in the country, and specifically in the absence of a system for the preliminary identification of a limited number of candidates by generally known political labels, but, because of these very conditions, it is extremely unlikely that any single party could have taken more than a small minority of the Duma seats. It is more likely that the Duma would have been quite variegated politically, with a considerable number of deputies being associated with the local cadre or patronage parties that had sprung up in profusion before the first elections.

Without entering into a detailed discussion of the coup d'état of June 3, 1907, it can be seen how the character of the first two elections contributed to that momentous event in the history of the Russian state and were reflected in it.

The circumstances of the Kadets' remarkable success in the elections explain a great deal about their behavior in the first two Dumas, the subject of much mutual recrimination between former party members after 1917 which has been carried over into the historical literature. More generally speaking, these circumstances explain much about the conflict between the Duma and the government that issued in the coup d'état of June 3. The Kadets' dependence on peasant support reinforced the populist sentiments that ran deep in party circles, and with them their commitment to a program of radical land reform that could not be accommodated to the government's emerging plan for conservative agrarian reform, based on dissolution of communal tenure and encouragement of small private farming, which was introduced as interim legislation in November 1906. In the background lay the paramount issues of the nature of the new order and the distribution of power in it; but in the foreground, as the most important substantive issue at stake in the conflict that led to the "Third of June System," lay the agrarian question.

By the same token, the Kadets found their most reliable support in the Dumas, particularly in the second Duma, among the national minority groups. Some of them, like the large Polish delegation, were not enthusiastic about the Kadet agrarian program but supported it because of the party's nationalities program. In this way the agrarian and nationalities questions were inseparably intertwined in the first two Dumas.

It was hardly accidental that the two groups whose representation was most drastically undercut by the revision of the electoral law of June 3, 1907, were precisely the peasants and the Poles (along with diverse other national minorities). June 3 marked the real end of the "Revolution of 1905." With the waning of the mass movement, agents of the imperial bureaucracy led by Stolypin were gearing up for sweeping reforms (most of them elaborated in the Ministry of Internal Affairs even before 1905). The regime was moving into a pattern of response to threats to its power and stability that had been repeated several times over in the nearly two hundred years of the empire's existence; the situation bore particular similarities to the period of great reforms that followed the Russian defeat in the Crimean War sixty years earlier [see Chapter 8].

The Duma, whose plans for agrarian and political-administrative reforms were far more radical than the government's, stood in the way; therefore the Duma, as a broadly representative assembly, was removed. This act was at once a dramatic reassertion of the government's authority and an admission that the reforming bureaucracy's plans were incompatible with more or less democratic public representation. The two main aims of the electoral law promulgated on June 3, 1907, were to increase the weight of the propertied strata, especially the large landowners, and to increase representation of the "Russian element": the new Duma, declared Stolypin's manifesto of June 3, would become "Russian in spirit." The most important feature of the new electoral law was its radical redistribution of the weight of the curiae in the provincial assemblies. . . . [The] landowners' curia, now largely purgued of peasant smallholders (the Senate clarification of October 7, 1906, was enlarged upon in several ways, making it impossible for any member of a peasant village community to vote in that curia), was greatly increased in weight. Now the landowners would enjoy an absolute majority in twenty-seven of European Russia's fifty-one provinces, half the vote in four others, and a plurality closely approaching half almost everywhere else.

The additional weight of the landowners came primarily at the expense of peasant representation, which was halved in the aggregate. The peasant curia no longer enjoyed a majority or plurality in any provincial assembly. Aside from the arithmetic adjustment of the curiae, other restrictions were placed on the peasant curia, beginning with the incorporation of the Senate clarification restricting voting to actual heads of peasant households and ending with the removal of the peasants' earlier exclusive privilege of electing a separate deputy in each provincial assembly: now seats were also set aside for landowners and urban electors in virtually all the provinces, and for a variety of other categories in a few, with the result that 194 of the 442 deputies' seats [in the Third Duma] were predetermined so far as curia was concerned; and all were to be elected by the provincial assemblies at large. This scheme meant that in most provinces the large landowners could greatly influence, if not dictate, the identity of the peasant-curia deputy.

Although the aggregate weight of urban representation in the provincial assemblies was not reduced (it was in fact very slightly increased), the character of that representation was significantly affected by the new law. In the first place, the privilege of separate representation was removed from all but seven cities of the empire: Petersburg, Moscow, Odessa, Riga, Kiev, Warsaw, and Lodz. Second, the urban electorate was subdivided into two curiae, with a very small part of the electorate, possessors of sizable business enterprises or other urban property, grouped into a first urban curia with more than half of the electors allotted to it; and the remainder, the vast majority of the urban electorate, in the second.

Finally, the law drastically curtailed representation for Russia's borderlands: the total number of deputies from the borderlands was halved, while separate representation for the Orthodox population in these areas was markedly increased.

The overall decrease in the statutory number of Duma deputies from 524 to 442 came almost entirely at the expense of the borderlands.

In general, the results of the third elections must have been encouraging to the government, especially since the illegal promulgation of the new electoral law produced no untoward public reaction. Although there are as usual no firm figures on the political orientations of the Duma deputies, it is clear that the opposition had been more than halved, from more than two thirds to less than one-third. S. N. Harper [an American historian] gave the following figures (the labels are his):

| | |
|---|---|
| Extreme rightists | 76 |
| Rightists | 40 |
| Octobrists | 155 |
| Progressivists | 52 |
| Constitutional Democrats | 46 |
| Leftists (including the national groups) | 35 |
| Extreme leftists and socialists | 28 |

And A. Ia. Avrekh [a Soviet historian] used the following figures in his work:

| | |
|---|---|
| Rights | 50 |
| Moderate right and National group | 97 |
| Octobrists and adherents | 154 |
| Progressives | 28 |
| Kadets | 54 |
| Muslim group | 8 |
| Polish Kolo [Nationalists] | 18 |
| Trudoviki | 13 |
| Social Democrats | 20 |

As can be seen, the familiar party groups (with the exception of the Russian National group) are still there, but in radically changed proportions.

It appeared that Stolypin had found the kind of representative system he needed in order to proceed with his reforms: one that would not only desist from open confrontation with the government but would provide support for his program against its numerous opponents in the bureaucracy, at court, and in noble circles. As in Prussia in 1849, it appeared that monarchy and aristocracy had combined successfully to defeat the democratic revolution.

History, however, is full of paradoxes and unintended consequences. By the commencement of the Duma's third session, some fifteen months after its initial convocation [November 1907], Stolypin's Octobrist-led majority was beginning to disintegrate and it had become clear that all his ministry's major reform plans, with the exception of the agrarian legislation, were confronting powerful resistance. Eventually—during the fourth Duma session in November 1913—the Octobrist fraction would collapse entirely, splitting into three separate groups; and well before his death at an assassin's hand in the Kiev Opera House on September 1, 1911, Stolypin had been forced to abandon virtually all the main elements of his reform plans except the agrarian legislation.

With regard to the system of representation, the "Third of June System," as it came to be called, was in the first place a wager on the provincial nobility; it involved a wager on the strong yeoman peasant only as a matter of political futures. This short-term gamble on the nobility was linked to a long-term strategy based to a considerable extent on the conclusion that the role of the nobility in local affairs had already declined and would continue to do so, necessitating the cultivation of new bases of support in rural Russia. The nobility, in effect, was being asked to use its newly acquired voice in affairs at the center in order to assist in the emasculation of its established status and authority in the provinces. Therein lay the basis for the conflict between Stolypin and the noble organizations and the main social dimension of the struggle that ensued over the implementation of the bureaucratic reform program. Although there is little direct evidence that would demonstrate a decisive role for the groups representing conversative noble interests in the defeat of Stolypin's local-reform plans, their actions undoubtedly tended to reinforce opposition to his policies in the imperial bureaucracy and at court. At the very least, it is clear that Stolypin failed to find among the noble landowners whose voting power he had so generously increased the kind of support he needed for success.

One of the most ominous developments for the fortunes of Russian constitution-alism in the period after June 3 was the rapid disintegration of the extraparliamentary organizations of the two major constitutionalist parties, the Kadets and the Oc-tobrists. The atrophy of the Kadet party network cannot be measured precisely, but it is clearly reflected in the records of its central committee. By 1908 party lead-ers were talking of having to start the entire process of party building over again, beginning with the old network of zemstvo acquaintances. A central-committee survey in early 1908 revealed that Kadet committees were still active in only eight provinces and had completely disbanded in all but twelve others; and theses adopted at a party conference in November 1909 explicitly recognized "the isolation of the party from the population." With the collapse of the party network in the country came a reduction in the activities of the party's central organs: in 1910 the Petersburg and Moscow branches of the Kadet central committee met only five times each, and not a single plenary session was held. The failure of the Kadets to build a strong organization left them ill-prepared to engage in the politics of mass mobilization in 1917. . . .

# The Feminist Movement

## RICHARD STITES

Although the issue of women's emancipation had occupied the attention of the Russian public for some fifty years before 1905, there was no genuine women's movement until that year. And then, true to the ways of Russian social history, two separate movements for women appeared almost at once: a feminist women's suffrage movement, and a socialist one opposed to it. Both had a pre-history beginning in the 1890s, but were largely unknown to each other until 1905. The feminists before 1905 continued and expanded the traditions of social activity laid down in the 1860s and 1870s. After 1905, when the women's suffrage movement arose, the older feminists persisted in their stress upon the non-political aspects of the women's struggle and either rejected the political movement altogether or made up its conservative wing. The difference in outlook and behavior between them and the new generation of 1905 was certainly great; and many in both groups would have spurned the use of the word "feminist" either for themselves or for the movement as a whole. But, while allowing these differences, we must not permit ourselves to violate the useful conventions of comparative history by stressing only the unique. And there is sufficient unity in the efforts of the non-socialist women's rights activists for us to speak unhesitatingly of a feminist tradition running from 1860 up to the Revolution of 1917.

A very proper women's manual of 1901, *Woman in Family and Social Life*, offered charity and education as the only appropriate public activities for the lady outside the home. These remained, indeed, the principal concerns of the older feminists. There were of course "charity ladies" of the purer sort, quite alien to feminism, who pursued philanthropic activities either out of a genuine concern for the poor, a desire for social prominence, or both. They could be found on the council of the very undemocratic Union of Charitable Organizations and Leaders, hobnobbing with the Dowager Empress [Empress Maria Fedorovna, Mother of Nicholas II] and other prominent figures, and "promoting charity as a way of life." But some charity enterprises catered particularly to women. In 1896 a *Dom Trudliubiia* (best rendered as "Center to Promote Diligence") for "educated women" was added to the seven others that served as workhouses for orphans and the poor in Petersburg. Founded on the principle that "the only rational form of charity is to provide the needy with *paid employment*," the Center was located in a fairly well-to-do quarter and catered to middle-class high school or institute graduates unable to make a decent living. The Society for Assisting Young Girls, by contrast, was designed specifically for servants, shopgirls, and working women, with the aim of protecting them from the harmful moral atmosphere of their natural milieu. By

From Stites, Richard *The Women's Liberation Movement in Russia: Feminism, Nihilism, and Bolshevism, 1860–1930*, pp. 191–210. Copyright © 1978 by Princeton University Press. Reprinted by permission of Princeton University Press.

1906, some 2,000 women and girls were regularly visiting the nine Petersburg chapters of the Society to receive lessons in reading, stitching, and religion.

The most important of the strictly charitable enterprises for women was the Russian Society for the Protection of Women founded in 1900. Headed alternately by two princesses, Evgeniia Oldenburgskaia and Elena Saksen-Altenburgskaia, it was well staffed by titled patricians and by wealthy philanthropists like Baron Gintsburg, Countess Panina, and the Tereshchenkos of Kiev, as well as representatives of the intelligentsia, the world of culture, the professions, and a number of feminists. The Society's headquarters on Nadezhdinskaia Street, as well as the homes of many of its members, lay in that enchanted triangle of Petersburg north of Nevsky Prospect [Avenue]. The central budget, which was strictly managed, drew the bulk of its income from church and personal contributions and disbursed various sums to its branches in the capital and eight other cities. Like most such organizations, the Society was designed to be run efficiently rather than democratically, and though a general meeting of its 250 members was to take place twice a year, it was usually faced with a fixed and concise agenda.

After 1905 the Society became one of the chief lobbyists against prostitution. But its political tactics, not to mention the substance of its reform program, remained exceedingly cautious. For instance in 1913 the Society agreed that when a project was being considered by the State Council, it ought not to bother itself with independent and parallel deliberation of the project.

Opportunities for women in philanthropy abounded in pre-revolutionary [late Imperial] Russia. Charities, public and private, mutual aid societies, funds and scholarship committees sprang up at the beginning of the century as educational and professional opportunities for women expanded. All provided a modicum of training in organization and finance. But the energetic flurry of women so engaged by no means attracted universal approval.

> We watch the meetings of boards, where speeches are delivered, and the committees where men and women sit wearied and indifferent, ignorant of affairs, discussing regulations and paragraphs; we read reports prepared by paid officials, we hear the magniloquent verdicts of self-appointed pedagogues on systems of instruction; we attend, O height of hypocrisy! the charity bazaar, where the lady stall-keepers, who sacrificed not a penny, are dressed in costumes costing double the profit of their sales. And these we call the works of Christian charity!

These are the words not of some sardonic Social Democrat, but of Pobedonostsev, a powerful government official and the patron of a number of charities [see Documents, Chapter 9]; and his nebulous but decidedly negative view of "charity ladies" was certainly shared by many in all ranks of society. That many women held it as well was to become apparent within a few years of Pobedonostsev's remark.

By 1900 almost all of the original feminists of the 1860s had left the scene. [Maria] Trubnikova, beset by illness and economic difficulties, had withdrawn from feminist activities after 1881, spent some time in a mental hospital, and died in 1897. Nadezhda Stasova busied herself helping women students up to the day she died in 1897. [Anna] Engelhardt had also withdrawn from active work and Maria

Tsebrikova was in exile for her brash letter to the Tsar.[1] Only Anna Filosofova remained to greet the new century. Like most of her generation, she had given up civic pursuits in the 1880s. But with the death of her husband and the revival of women's education in the 1890s, she became active again in the last of the pre-1905 feminist organizations, the Mutual Philanthropic Society. Filosofova devoted her remaining years to uniting all women's clubs in Russia and affiliating them to a feminist international organization. As a result, the political struggle largely bypassed her (she was out of the country in the crucial years 1905–1906) and her last major act was the decorative one of presiding over Russia's own Women's Congress of 1908. When she died in 1912, she was widely honored.

. . . Anna Filosofova was, like many of her feminist colleagues, essentially a "woman of the 1860s" and had no understanding either of Marx or of Nietzsche. Upon symbolism, decadence, and Saninism—indeed upon the whole new world of ethical and aesthetic values being shaped before her very eyes by Dmitry Filosofov and Sergei Diaghilev (her son and nephew)—she gazed with embarrassed incomprehension. Hers were the simple and vibrant moral ideals of the 1860s; and to her, Tolstoyanism, with all its vagueness and contradictions, appeared to be the only intellectual system that contained them. For Marxism she had no use, and in fact looked upon all political parties as "a herd of bison" almost indistinguishable from one another. Although she joined the Kadets [Constitutional Democratic Party] as a concession to modernity, she left politics wholly to her closest associate Anna Shabanova, expending her own energy on good works and the job of unifying Russian women. In her last years, at odds with the times, she sought further spiritual solace in Theosophy.

Filosofova's chief collaborator in the Philanthropic Society and a myriad of other activities was Anna Nikitichna Shabanova (a somewhat older contemporary of [Vera] Figner, [Sofia] Perovskaia, and [Vera] Zasulich [revolutionaries of the 1870s and 1880s]. Like them she was gentry, well educated, and possessed a police record for political activities—in her case as a member of the Ivanova Dressmaking Workshop. But unlike them Shabanova walked a path from radicalism through medicine to charity and feminism. After six months in prison she was cured of radicalism forever and pursued medical studies in Helsinki and then at the new Women's Medical Academy from which she graduated as one of the first class. Her teaching, writing, and clinical work on children's diseases put her into contact with the philanthropist, Princess Oldenburgskaia, and thus into the world of the feminists. In 1895 she helped to found the Mutual Philanthropic Society and became its real leader, though always tactfully sharing the honors with Filosofova. In 1905, she established the Society's Electoral Department that addressed itself to women's suffrage. After Filosofova's death, Shabanova became the sole leader of the Society until its demise after the October [Bolshevik] Revolution. She was the first of a

---

1. In 1890 Tsebrikova wrote to Alexander III denouncing the stupid, inhumane, and corrupt "bureaucratic anarchism" of his reign.

number of women doctors to take up a commanding post in the feminist movement, showing, if nothing else, that medicine could lead as naturally to feminism as it could to radicalism.

The Mutual Philanthropic Society was by far the most important feminist institution prior to 1905 and marked the transition between the older feminism of the nineteenth century and the suffrage movement of the twentieth. It was to be modeled on the American club "for the intellectual and moral improvement of women" and unencumbered by the presence of men. But a women's club, properly speaking, was not acceptable to the Ministry of Interior that licensed all private organizations and could close them at will, so the founders had to content themselves with the clumsy title of Russian Women's Mutual Philanthropic Society. Difficulties plagued the early years of the Society. At its birth, cartoons, anonymous letters, and dirty stories circulated about its members, while its first headquarters on Pushkinskaia [street] . . . was nicknamed The Terem [the women's quarters in the palace of the Muscovite tsars] and Bald Mountain (the witch's haunt of Russian legend). Then its first years were marked by internal strife, petty squabbles, and "egoism" as Shabanova herself called it. The main cause of this, we know from other sources, was the resentment of certain "democratic feminists" toward what they took to be the autocratic manner of the leadership.

In spite of its limiting title and government strictures, the Society managed to function as a genuine women's club, concerned at first with charity, organization of women, education, and culture, then later with a broad spectrum of political and social problems. Its organization was standard for the time: a General Meeting elected by the members at large; a Council (sovet) chosen by it with regular and candidate members; and various special commissions for charter revision, budget, and so on. And its actual functioning, undescribed in any charter, was also standard: self-perpetuating leadership, cooptation, flow of initiative and control mostly from the top. Assisting Shabanova and Filosofova were gentry women (though no titled ones), widows of medium-high officials, intelligentki, and professionals. The Charity Division maintained a network of day nurseries, shelters, dormitories, and cheap eating places for educated and professional women tied down by children or in financial doldrums. Such eminently practical activity must account for some of the prestige which the Society, in spite of its political conservatism, continued to enjoy among the female intelligentsia.

Much of Shabanova's, and all of Filosofova's, attention came to be riveted on the growth of a conservative world feminist organization, the International Council of Women (ICW). Founded in Chicago in 1893, the ICW held congresses every few years in the major cities of Europe. It was largely based on the Anglo-American idea that women's charity and benevolent groups throughout the world ought to organize and communicate with each other. Political and economic issues were ignored. When Lili Braun of the German Socialist Party challenged this narrow focus and raised the problem of protection of women's labor, the ICW leaders countered with a resolution on "complete freedom of work" and neglected to invite socialist delegates to their next congress. In fact the program of the ICW became so laden with trivia (the joys of gardening, pocket money, and luxurious breakfasts at Windsor Castle) that by 1904 the more political non-socialist women formed their own International Women's Suffrage Association (IWSA). These two groups plus the women's division of the Second (socialist) International constituted the three women's internationals of the pre-war period. Russian women were to affiliate with all three and their choice of affiliation is a key to their position on the ideological spectrum of Russian feminism.

When the Mutual Philanthropic Society leaders began displaying an interest in international affiliation, the ICW was the only important world-wide women's group in existence. Shabanova and others attended the early congresses as guests and their glowing description of Filosofova's great pioneering work over the past generation led the ICW to appoint her Honorary Vice President and to invite her to form a National Women's Council in Russia. Such a council could only be recognized if it was elected by all the women's groups in the country. Typical of a national council in a small European state was the Danske [Danish] Kvinders Nationalraad formed in 1899 of fifty-five women's organizations with some 80,000 members. By 1908, there were twenty-three such councils, including ones from tiny new nations like Bulgaria, sending delegates regularly to the ICW congresses. Filosofova maintained a constant stream of petitions to the Ministry of Interior for permission to form a national council. Personal vanity was probably at stake here too; one guesses from her correspondence that the old lady's dream was to host a congress of the ICW in St. Petersburg and take Lady Aberdeen (its President) to a reception at the Winter Palace. The government consistently refused. A national network of women formed "without distinction of religion or nationality" and with foreign connections was not the kind of idea that tsarist [Imperial] bureaucrats could swallow. When Filosofova died, Shabanova continued the fruitless campaign. But Russia remained formally outside the ICW, though bound closely by mutual sympathy and regular communication.

Other public causes that attracted the feminist-minded woman may be summed up quickly. First among them was Temperance. An uneasy combination of hostility to alcoholism (Alexander III) and a thirst for more state revenue (Witte) led to the gradual imposition of a government vodka monopoly in the years 1890–1901. But drunkenness did not slacken and its growth alarmed every element of society from the socialist to the priest. Government and Church responded with a network of tearooms and lecturers called Guardians of Public Sobriety. Feminists followed this pattern with their own temperance societies. Mme. Chebysheva-Dmitrieva, a colleague of Shabanova's in the Mutual Philanthropic Society, established a Society for the Struggle Against Alcohol, and proclaimed that alcohol was the chief obstacle to women's emancipation and happiness. Mme. Baudouin de Courtenay, a Polish resident of St. Petersburg, founded her own temperance organization as a part of the Ethical-Social Movement. Her circle of 170 men and women maintained a tearoom, but when soldiers began invading the premises and insulting the teetotalers, the government closed the circle on a formal pretext. By 1913 half the state budget was generated from vodka sales and the problem was only solved (temporarily) by the Tsar's 1914 prohibition decree.

Health and dress reform had less attraction for Russian women than it seemed to for those of the West, though physical culture clubs like the Women's Health Preservation Society did appear occasionally. Dress reform programs, like the assault on the bone corset, aroused no enthusiasm; nor did the bicycle. In any case, nihilist austerity had been the fashion for decades among the female intelligentsia. On the more serious side, each new year saw the birth of societies for winning and protecting the rights of women in the various professions. Scholarship committees appeared in the wake of each newly opened women's educational institution, the oldest of these celebrating its twenty-fifth anniversary in 1903. Thus in every major city and in many towns, women's committees, *ad hoc* groups, and charities sprang up to serve as schools of organization, finance, and communication. No central body and no journal served as a hub for these. The only common reading matter for feminist minded people was the annual *First Women's Calendar* (1899–1915?), a mish-mash of useful information edited by Praskoviia Ariian, the energetic organizer of women's engineering courses.

The young, sensitive, intelligent—and basically man-hating—student [Elizabeth] Diakonova, who gave freely to narrow feminist causes, perceived that this impressive looking array of organization was hardly sufficient to free woman as long as she lacked political power. She despised "the official barracks atmosphere which men with such needless artificiality introduce everywhere" and recognized that power, connections, and the chance for a brilliant future belonged only to them. Without political power, she wrote, women must remain hopelessly shunted along fenced roads, slaves, squirrels on a treadmill. It was precisely this feeling of inadequacy and frustration that would push women of the younger generation into a struggle for political rights within a few years.

In 1904, on the eve of a revolution, Alexander Amfiteatrov observed that ten years earlier only a few hundred Russian women dreamed of equality, while at the time of his writing there were tens of thousands. If the first part of his statement was an understatement, events were soon to bear out the truth of the second. The Russian women's movement synchronized closely with the rhythm of the nation's social history. In times of general apathy, the feminists languished in charity work and internal dialogues; in times of stress they were galvanized into political activity. In the winter of 1904–1905, the ingredients for such a burst of activity were present: the organizational skills and self-confidence developed over the years by the old feminists; and the dissatisfaction of the new generation of feminists with mere organization and philanthropy. Close at hand was a stirring example—the suffrage movement in Finland. There the history of women's emancipation had followed the general continental [European] pattern: philosophical probing in the literature of the 1840s, educational victories in the 1870s, "social work" at the end of the century. The conservative Finnish Women's Association (from 1884) and the more militant Women's Rights Union (from 1892) differed in their stress on votes for women but, because of the unusual turbulence of the Finnish nationalist movement in 1898–1906, a large degree of unanimity among women was achieved. Their solidarity was expressed in a resolution on women's suffrage adopted by a congress of women on November 8, 1904, and their continued agitation led to their enfranchisement in a year and a half. This display of solidarity and agitational skill was not lost on the Russian feminists who awaited only an opportunity. It came in January 1905.

During the winter, the Union of Liberation and other liberal groups invited women to their political banquets, though sometimes only as decoration. A month after Bloody Sunday [January 9, 1905], a large group of women, 468 members of "Moscow society" published in *Russian News* a lament for the violence in St. Petersburg and for the bloodshed in the Far East [Russo-Japanese War]. At the end of the same month, some 30 women liberals of Moscow declared the formation of a national women's political organization, The All-Russian Union for Women's Equality, whose general aim was "freedom and equality before the law without regard to sex." Its first act was to petition the [Moscow] City Duma and the local zemstvo for voting rights in those bodies. Next it formed branches all over Russia and within a month a solid organization had arisen in Petersburg that then became its center. The leaders lived in both capitals and were mostly women journalists, notably Zinaida Mirovich-Ivanova and Anna Kalmanovich from Moscow, Liubov Gurevich and Maria Chekhova from St. Petersburg. Their ranks were strengthened by the presence of two female members of the circles that became the Kadet Party—Anna Miliukova and Ariadna Tyrkova. Perceiving that "the old order was in disarray," the Union called the first political meeting for women in Russian history on April 10 in the capital. It attracted about 1,000 visitors, including some hostile socialists and workers, and laid the groundwork for the Union's first congress.

By May, twenty-six local chapters had sent 70 delegates to the congress which was held in Moscow, May 7–10. Miliukova presided over the 300 recognized delegates who included some of the older feminists from the Mutual Philanthropic Society as well as some who would later break away to establish their own group. The charter adopted by the congress provided for an elected central bureau, autonomous local chapters, and special committees for politics, education, labor, and organization. The program of the Union, specific and far-reaching, demanded: immediate convocation of a constituent assembly elected by the so-called seven-tailed suffrage (equal, direct, secret, and universal, without distinction of nationality, religion, or sex); national autonomy; equality of the sexes before the law; equal rights of peasant women in any land reforms; laws for the welfare, insurance, and protection of women workers; equal opportunity for women; co-education at every level; reform of laws relating to prostitution; abolition of the death penalty. The crucial question of whether to adhere to the narrow struggle for female suffrage exclusively or to join in the liberation movement was thus resolved emphatically by this program and by the Union's official declaration: "a change in women's status is impossible without the general political liberation of our country."

The Women's Union now set out energetically to win support from the professional and trade unions which were then joining forces in the Union of Unions. The women were invited to join the Union on the basis of their program, but when they appeared at one of its meetings, members of its central bureau exclaimed in surprise: "But there must be some misunderstanding." The women continued to attend meetings and to bombard the members with their propaganda until at last in July 1905, the Union of Unions agreed to endorse the Women's Union as one of its own. One of the few who voted against the proposal was the future Kadet leader, Paul Miliukov. The Women's Union also asked the City Duma and zemstvo organizations to be allowed to vote in local elections and later, when the word "parliament" was in the air, sought their support on the national suffrage issue. In at least three dozen cities women organized meetings, signed petitions, and presented them to various political and public bodies throughout the spring and summer. In response to all this—often sincerely and spontaneously—local ruling bodies (especially urban ones) passed resolutions endorsing women's suffrage. But the usually liberal congresses of zemstvo and city leaders resisted. In April they simply received the petition without comment or action, though some delegates privately voiced hostility or amused contempt. The next congress in July was more polite: its bureau replied to inquiries from the Women's Union that it supported the *principle* of women's suffrage but not as a practical issue at the moment. This was an opinion widely shared by Russian liberals and it came to be their favorite argument against putting women's suffrage in their programs.

The word "inopportune" became a hated one among the feminists, and some of them were never able to forgive the liberals for what they took to be paternalistic cant. The notion of tactical timing in the emancipation of this or that rightless segment of the population was hardly unique to Russian liberals—or to liberals in general. In Europe one could always find figures even on the far left offering the same argument against enfranchisement campaigns for women until after "bigger" things were settled. This infuriated the Women's Union, which asked, in a stiffly worded note, what guarantees women had that the urban-zemstvo leaders would ever try to realize such a principle as women's rights. Monarchs and privileged orders, they said, always urged the underprivileged to be patient. But if the next congress did not support women's suffrage, the letter warned in angry cadences, the Union would have to look for support among the extreme parties of the working class. The Women's Union soon learned through a questionnaire that other fears were at work: fear of peasant women voters, of female conservatism, and of the unnerving effects of politics upon the gentle sex. But the delegates to the next congress of City and zemstvo government, unnerved perhaps themselves by the unrelenting barrage from women lobbyists, finally gave in and approved a project giving both sexes the right to vote and hold office. In the end, the Union and most other feminists found themselves in the liberal camp even though many disliked the sour taste of male liberalism in action.

The Union for Women's Equality, though unquestionably the largest and most vigorous feminist group operating in 1905, was not the only one. In April 1905, Anna Shabanova steered the Mutual Philanthropic Society into Russian politics. She called on the membership to work for women's participation in any national assembly that might be convoked by the government, explaining that men could not be trusted to look after the rights of women in the future political order. Throughout the year she and her colleagues unleashed a blizzard of paper upon official Russia, ignoring the parties, the unions, and the liberation groups, and concentrating their persuasive techniques upon those in power. Before the year was out Shabanova's words had reached the Premier (Witte), the State Council, all the Ministers, fifty-one Governors, forty-six Marshals of the Nobility, scores of other officials, hundreds of *zemstva* and City Dumas, and thousands of private and public organizations. Her requests and questionnaires all dealt with the possibility of women receiving the vote. But her efforts were futile, and the Society, though caught in the spirit of the times, remained pretty much on the margin of the active suffrage struggle for the next two years.

In December the third and last of the feminist groups of 1905–1907 was born under the leadership of Dr. Maria Ivanovna Pokrovskaia of St. Petersburg. An 1882 graduate of the women's medical courses, Pokrovskaia, like many of her colleagues, had been drawn to the problem of women's inequality through her social-medical work with children, the poor, and prostitutes. In 1904 she had founded a journal, *The Women's Messenger*, which devoted itself to these problems. As a member of the Mutual Philanthropic Society, Pokrovskaia found the tactics of the Women's Union too militant and those of the Society too apolitical, so at the December 15 meeting of the latter body she introduced the idea of a women's political party. Finding no support among the leaders there, she and a handful of supporters established a Women's Progressive Party that held its first meeting early in the following year and adopted a broad political platform: a "democratic constitutional monarchy" with the usual civil rights; family equality in financial and parental matters; liberalization of divorce and legitimacy laws; abolition of state-licensed prostitution; labor reforms; equal rights to land for peasant women; co-education; and an end to militarism.

The broad sweep of this program was opposed by some of the "purer" feminists whose views had been voiced earlier by Praskoviia Ariian in *Women's Messenger*: "Many people think that women's interests are too narrow," she wrote, "and so would like to see women in the ranks of those who fight for general [human] interests. But such people fail to see that the private struggle of small groups with their own demands, aspirations, and ideals of society and humanity really contribute to the realization of common ideals." But Pokrovskaia's wider view prevailed and the Progressive Party, like the Women's Union, subscribed to the "liberation" movement—at least in theory. Unlike the Union, however, which admitted and cooperated with men, Pokrovskaia's party excluded them. "Supporters of united action with men in the struggle for women's rights lose sight of the fact that in many resolutions and projects of the future political order, women's rights are completely omitted," wrote one of Pokrovskaia's adherents. And she herself warned members of the new party that cooperation with men would mean advantages for men alone. The question of a united front of the sexes was to become one of the major issues of Russian feminism.

Politically, the Women's Progressive Party stood about midway between the effervescent militance of the Union for Women's Equality and the cautious conservatism of the Mutual Philanthropic Society. Always impeccably legal in its activities, the Party repudiated revolution and violence and adhered to the tactic of rapid, but peaceful, improvement through lawful means. But it boasted a social dimension as well. Dr. Pokrovskaia herself believed in a vague kind of socialism compounded of the European principles of 1789 and the Russian traditions of the 1860s, though she wore this "socialism" as lightly as did the Western feminists their Christianity, and in practice was opposed to strikes. Yet the Party differed from its "bourgeois" counterparts in the West by the detailed attention that it gave to women workers, calling not only for general factory reform but specifically for women factory inspectors, a ten-month fully paid pregnancy leave, nursing facilities in the factories, and equal wages for equal work. The Women's Progressive Party was one of those Russian liberal groups whose outlook was far more social than their presumed opposite numbers in Europe.

In the Manifesto of October 17, the Tsar had made a qualified promise to give the vote to those previously deprived of it, and many women had hoped that they would be among the favored. The mood of disappointment was deep when, on December 11, 1905, the government announced that the electorate for the new parliament (the Duma) would not include "persons of the female sex." But since the Manifesto had also suggested that the new Duma would take up the question of broadening the suffrage, the feminists now set to work to find out where the new political parties stood on the issue. These ranged from Tolstoyans and anarchists on one side to the extreme monarchist groups on the other. Of them, only three of the major parties mentioned women's suffrage: the Social Democrats (Bolshevik and Menshevik), the Socialist Revolutionaries, and the Constitutional Democrats. The Marxist parties endorsed women's suffrage as a matter of principle along with universal suffrage, and never as a separate issue. But both the Socialist Revolutionaries and the Kadets had some initial problems over the issue.

The Socialist Revolutionary Party, established some [three] years earlier by Dr. Gershuni, Viktor Chernov, [Katerina] Breshkovskaia [see Documents, below], and others, saw itself as the heir of the *narodnik* [populist] traditions, and it looked with hostility upon sexual discrimination. When Chernov finally set down the first draft of the Socialist Revolutionary program in 1904, he included a clause on universal suffrage "without distinction of sex" as a matter of socialist principle. However at the congresses of the Peasant Unions—upon whose constituency the Socialist Revolutionaries heavily relied—some voices of opposition were heard. A few insisted on giving village women only "active" rights (i.e., the right to vote and *not* to be elected). Proponents of full equality for women exhibited an impressive array of evidence that village women were competent members of the village community. At one of the congresses, several peasant women appeared as delegates, decked out colorfully in national costumes. In the end, the Peasant Union joined the intellectual-led Socialist Revolutionary Party in endorsing political equality for women. This explains the fact that the Trudoviki [Laborites], independent Socialist Revolutionaries or non-party socialists in the Duma who held Socialist Revolutionary views, became the first champions for women's rights in that body.

The Kadets were more deeply divided and owed their eventual adoption of a women's suffrage clause largely to the efforts of two women, Anna Miliukova and Ariadna Tyrkova. Miliukova (née Smirnova) was the daughter of the rector of the Moscow Theological Academy. Her struggle to study and to escape the life of a priest's wife led to a family drama reminiscent of the 1860s. She studied history at the Guerrier Courses [a private school] and there met [Paul] Miliukov whom she married. Miliukova acquired her interest in the woman question from a circle of Bulgarian feminists whom she met when her husband was teaching in Sofia. At the first congress of the Kadet Party—much to the chagrin of her husband and the amusement of the delegates—she led the forces favoring women's suffrage. Miliukov was strongly opposed on the grounds that it would alienate peasant voters. . . . Miliukova's resolution to include the words "regardless of sex" in the appropriate place in the platform won by two votes. Her husband won approval for a footnote which explained that support of women's suffrage was not binding on members.

Tyrkova came late to the cause of women's emancipation. She was born in St. Petersburg in 1869 to an old Novgorod landowning family and was a cousin of the revolutionary, Sofia Loschern von Herzfeldt. But her childhood, though filled with heroic "daydreams" and admiration for the Girondistes [radicals of the French Revolution], betrayed no deep radical commitment. Frustrated in her plans to become a doctor by the closing of the women's medical courses, she enrolled in the Bestuzhev Courses [a private school]. At the same time, she married and divorced soon afterward; she subsequently married the English journalist, Harold Williams. Tyrkova always remained cold to Marxism, though as she tells us, all her closest school friends were married to sometime Marxists, [including] Nadia Krupskaia to Lenin. Through Williams, Struve, and Prince Shakhovskoi, she was drawn eventually to liberalism and had several brushes with the police for appearing in demonstrations and smuggling in *Liberation* [a liberal Russian newspaper published in Stuttgart] from Europe. But up to 1906, Tyrkova showed no sympathy for the women's cause as such because, as she tells us, she considered herself equal to men already. A meeting of the Women's Union left her unimpressed, and when practically commanded by her acquaintance Olga Volkenstein to join, she refused.

Tyrkova's view of things quickly changed, however, when at the second (first legal) Kadet congress in January 1906 she learned that she and other women were not considered equals by their political colleagues. Miliukov, in a serious effort to erase the offending clause inserted by his wife at the last congress, made another speech, this time alluding to the low cultural level of peasant women. He was strongly seconded by a Kazan Tatar who informed the delegates that Muslim women did not want the vote. Tyrkova, who had never read a thing on the woman question, rose to her feet and instinctively presented the standard counter-arguments. She was followed by Miliukova and then by the gentle and esteemed Professor Petrazhitsky whose support of the women's suffrage clause won the day for the feminists. But the Kadet Party remained divided on the issue until after the First Duma. The four other tiny liberal parties, while evincing an interest in legal and educational equality, made no mention of female suffrage in their programs. Tyrkova now joined Miliukova in her work, both as voice for the feminists among the Kadets and as an agent for the Kadets among the feminists. It was at least partly due to them that the women's suffrage movement became largely Kadet in its sympathies.

The Octobrists clearly opposed women's equality, though their program was silent on the issue.[2] When Zinaida Mirovich, a pro-Kadet member of the Women's Union, asked permission to speak on women's suffrage at one of their meetings, the Octobrists flatly refused. The party also circulated an anti-Kadet brochure accusing liberals of Jesuitical manipulation of women for political purposes. The brochure also spoke of the deep psychological gulf between sexes, and of the special

---

2. The Octobrist party, formed in the wake of Nicholas II's October Manifesto of 1905, was moderately conservative—as noted in the previous essay, by Terence Emmons.—Ed.

female capacity for great love and for great cruelty. When confronted with the issue individually, according to Mirovich, Octobrists usually offered the more chivalrous explanation: "Europe does not have it yet." Of the seven other moderate conservative parties clustered around the Octobrists, only one, The Union of Peaceful Reconstruction, demanded equality of sexes before the law. Three mentioned improvement of working conditions for women; the other three said nothing at all. None mentioned the suffrage question. These parties and all those to the right of them had no female members.

The program of the ultra right Russian Assembly whose motto was "For Faith, Tsar, and Fatherland," was too cluttered with praise for autocracy, church, and gentry and with attacks upon the Jews to leave any space for comments on women. The same thing held for the Russian Narodnik [Populist] Non-Class Union. The Monarchist-Constitutionalists (Tsarists) opposed the four-tailed suffrage as "absolutely impossible" for Russia. The Fatherland Union refused to believe that all Russians, even males, possessed any understanding of politics, and for good measure added that the schools should teach respect for the family as well as for church, country, and law. Thus stood the Russian parties [in 1906] on the eve of the election to the Duma.

The suffragists were not happy with the small base of party support for their program. The Union soon found itself torn between the socialists and the Kadets. In the heat of the revolutionary upsurge of spring and summer, it had wooed the "liberation movement" and all opposition parties. But the autumn shattering of the nation-wide united front of public opinion affected the feminists as well. A schism arose in early October. The question of whether or not to support the so-called Bulygin Duma with its narrowly restricted suffrage divided the assembly into "boycotters" and "burrowers," the latter hoping to use any kind of parliament as a means for further extension of the suffrage. After the October Manifesto widened the suffrage for the new Duma, the two wings revealed a deeper difference and became transmuted into pro-socialists and pro-liberals. "If our Union wishes to remain close to life and to the struggle, and if it wishes to be a women's rather than a ladies' organization, it must learn how to broaden its efforts and it must encounter the woman worker directly," proclaimed the new program hammered out by the pro-socialist wing. It also passed a resolution forbidding Union members to join any party that did not demand women's suffrage. Until January 1906, with the revision of the Kadet program, this meant only the Socialist Revolutionaries and the Marxist groups. After the Kadets made the support of women's suffrage binding on their membership, many Unionists turned to them in relief, while the left wing of the Union chose the Trudoviki as their champions in the Duma. Pokrovskaia and Shabanova were even less inclined to support the socialists, and their groups endorsed the Kadets as the least radical of the pro-feminist parties.

The troublesome issue decided, the suffragists threw themselves energetically into the election campaign and deluged Russia with books and brochures on the woman question. Female volunteers supported candidates and agitated alongside them in the hustings. They organized meetings, raised money, and helped count returns. The suffragists and their allies regained the verbal militance that had been theirs in the previous summer. Some factory women, having caught the spirit, appeared at the polls and demanded the right to vote and interfered with the voting. In the provinces, some enterprising women even managed to vote in place of men.

On election day, March 16, 1906, the Moscow branch of the Women's Union issued the following statement:

> Citizens! We the women of Russia, who chance to be living in this great epoch of Russia's renewal, and who have more than once demonstrated our undying love for the Fatherland, feel at this moment with special intensity the bitterness of being without rights, and we warmly protest being excluded from taking part in decisions which concern us. Though bearing full responsibility and liability before the law for our actions, we are deprived of our rights. Therefore we appeal to your conscience and honor and demand—not request—recognition of civil and political rights equal to yours.

The quotation is revealing in a number of ways. It repeats, in a more frenetic and expectant context, what Mme. Destunis and other Russian women had said on the eve of serf emancipation five decades earlier. Indeed it voices the very feeling that had given the first vigorous impulses to feminists almost everywhere in Europe two or three generations before: a fear of being left behind, floating in the wake of "great events"; and the urgent desire to "play a role" in society and to be taken aboard the swiftly moving ship of state. Less obvious, but audible enough behind the sharply imperious tones of the demand, is also the theme of loyalty-in-return-for-rights that would become the dominant theme—played fortissimo—in the feminist patriotism of World War I.

After the election the feminists kept the pressure on through the work of the Agitational Commission of the Women's Union. . . . It drafted appeals to public leaders, Duma deputies, and party officials; it secured endorsements from literary and cultural leaders; and in general it endeavored to give the impression to all who could read that women's suffrage was one of the foremost issues of the times. But the Union went beyond the limited appeal of the printed word. In the capital it established four women's political clubs, one of which became a meeting place for feminists, workers, trade union people, and socialist politicians. Even more impressive was the sending of agents into the villages to agitate among peasant women. Neither the Populists nor the famine volunteers and other village social workers of recent years had been able to make much contact with peasant women. Now feminists from the city arrived to agitate among them and to persuade their husbands to support equality for their wives. And they met with a surprisingly successful response. From the provinces of Tambov, Tula, Iaroslavl and Tver came reports of village women insisting on equal political representation.

Some feminists invaded the cloakroom of the Duma itself, adding a festive air to the scene, and acting as though they owned the Tauride Palace [where the Duma met]—at least according to Tyrkova who, as a Duma reporter, felt perhaps somewhat superior. Bernard Pares, who was transparently hostile to them, recalled how one day the lobby was "raided by suffragettes, short-haired young ladies in spectacles, most of them very puny looking." One of them cornered a peasant deputy from Tambov and queried him about women's suffrage. " 'Give us a little time,' he answered, 'we have only just got here ourselves, and when we have had time to find our feet, we'll give you some rights.' 'Give?' said the young lady indignantly: 'we mean to take them.'" The peasant then disclosed his deeper sentiments and replied ("kindly" according to Pares): "'Look here, let me give you a piece of advice. You get married: then you'll have a husband and he'll look after you altogether.' The lady was furious but speechless."[3]

As hopes for a women's suffrage bill from the Duma began to fade, the feminists strove for unity at a meeting of members of the Union, the Women's Progressive Party, and the Mutual Philanthropic Society. But this meeting (May 1906) was punctuated by quarrels. Pokrovskaia advised the feminists to punish the Kadets by withdrawing from the party if it did not mount a suffrage bill. Von Rutzen, titular head of the Union, vigorously supported the Kadets. The socialist women present heaped ridicule on the entire issue, yelling "We don't need paper resolutions." Feminists with socialist sympathies had to defend feminism itself against "the smirks and guffaws" of the Social Democrats and at the same time had to ward off the proposals of the "narrow feminists" who wanted to abandon the general struggle in favor of a purely women's effort.

What was happening in the Duma? The first item of business of the new body was to draft a response to the Address from the Throne.[4] Drafted in committee by Kadet deputies, it dealt with the abolition of archaic privileges and the establishment of equality before the law. When it was reported out on May 2, the Trudovik, Ryzhkov, moved to amend by including a demand for women's suffrage in the Response. "We have forgotten," he said, "that a son of a slave-woman cannot be a citizen." In this he was echoed by a half-dozen more Trudoviki and one Kadet. But three other Kadets opposed, one on the grounds that the Duma could not know whether or not all Russia really wanted women's suffrage. The non-party peasant Kruglikov put it more bluntly: "Our women are not concerned with universal suffrage; our women look after the household, the children, and the cooking." The motion was defeated. The Response was amended in committee, however by adding the words italicized in the following clause: "Abolition of all disabilities and privileges occasioned by class, nationality, religion, *and sex.*" Even this was challenged by a Kadet deputy from Minsk, but the revised passage and the Response passed.

On May 15 a group of 111 deputies signed a declaration concerning the equalization of rights of peasants, nationalities, underprivileged classes, and women. The eminent Polish jurist, Lev Petrazhitsky, an ardent adherent of sexual equality, headed a subcommittee on women's rights that was eagerly assisted by lobbyists from the Women's Union and the Mutual Philanthropic Society. During the June debates on this issue, Petrazhitsky gave the main report, speaking eloquently in support of civil, economic, educational, and political equality for women. His main opponents, aside from the silent, sneering deputies on the right benches, were Count Geiden of the Octobrists, who opposed the project on "practical" grounds, and Maxim Kovalevsky, a brilliant scholar, who could find no better argument

---

3. Bernard Pares, *My Russian Memoirs* (1931), p. 113. Pares (1867–1949) was a distinguished English journalist and scholar who devoted his professional life to Russia.—Ed.
4. The Address was delivered by Nicholas II at the opening of the First Duma on April 27, 1906.—Ed.

than the suggestion that Russia would have to draft women into the army if they insisted on equality. The droll Kruglikov, whose previous remarks had evoked a sharp letter to the Duma from Samara peasant women, amused the deputies with his homespun wit. "The peasant lives, ye see, by God's law," he said. "And the Lord made Eve to be Adam's helper and not his equal. And Paul said 'Let the wife fear her husband' (Laughter and applause)." Petrazhitsky's project was referred back to committee for more work. A month later, the Women's Union presented him with an elaborately worked out legislative project. But the Duma was dissolved [by Nicholas II] two days later.

The suffragists largely marked time for the next seven months and then repeated their efforts of the previous year. After the election of the Second Duma in February 1907, the Women's Union mounted an intensive lobbying campaign among Kadets, Trudoviki, Social Democrats, Socialist Revolutionaries, and even Muslims whose Duma fractions were lobbied by teams of Unionists. The Kadets promised to support "the sacred cause"; so did the Trudoviki, the Socialist Revolutionaries (who had boycotted the first Duma), and some Muslims who favored votes for non-Muslim women. The Social Democrats, however, were indifferent. "The woman question," said the Bolshevik deputy Aleksinsky, "will be resolved only with the final victory of the proletariat."

The Russian feminists, like their counterparts elsewhere, had an inordinate faith in the power of petition and spent much of their energies in gathering signatures. In this they were extremely successful, both in numbers and in variety of signatories. Petition forms were mass-mailed, placed in journals, and passed out to thousands of women and men. Young peasant women gathered names in their villages; a Petersburg carter filled a large sheet with names of [fellow male and female workers] from his own courtyard; another worker obtained the signatures of eighty-four laundresses. In all, the monster petition presented to the Trudoviki contained over 26,000 names. But once again, the Duma was dismissed [June 1907] before the substance of the petition could reach the floor.

In terms of concrete results, the Revolution of 1905–1907 had brought precious little to Russian women, except consciousness and organizational activity. "Her legal position had not changed one iota," observed Anna Shabanova. "She was neither recognized as a citizen nor granted a human right, but remained as of old at the washtub while the golden fish concealed herself in the depths of the blue sea." The reference to Pushkin's wonder-granting golden fish was not merely poetic. The friends of feminism were to be largely absent from the next [conservative Third] Duma [1907–1912]; and many enthusiasts for women's suffrage lost interest after the curtain of political reaction descended upon Russia. Nothing fails like failure, and the suffragists themselves retreated glumly into rhetoric. Not until 1917, when it was far too late, would the suffrage movement reach such a level of activity as it had reached in these years. . . .

# DOCUMENTS

The October Manifesto (Manifesto of October 17, 1905) referred to repeatedly in the preceding pages is the first of the primary sources printed here. It was drafted by Sergei

Witte, the architect of Russia's industrialization drive (Chapter 11), who in 1903 had fallen out of favor with Nicholas II for his opposition to policies that had precipitated Russia's disastrous war against Japan. Nicholas now turned to Witte, just home (September 1905) from successfully negotiating the Treaty of Portsmouth formally ending the Russo-Japanese War, as the deepening domestic crisis in Russia was turning into revolution. Never himself a constitutionalist or a democrat, Witte believed rather in autocracy—that is, enlightened bureaucratic absolutism—as the necessary instrument of economic modernization in Russia (from which, someday, would flow social and political modernization). Nevertheless, he had become convinced that only by granting universal civil liberties and some sort of broadly representative legislature could the monarchy itself, and the whole Imperial regime, be saved. Hence the Manifesto which Nicholas II finally issued on October 17, 1905, the tenth day of the massive general strike. On October 19, with the promulgation of the law creating a Council of Ministers, Witte became its chairman: a "united ministry" or cabinet system of government had been established, as Professor Emmons noted above, and Witte had become in effect Russia's first prime minister. He resigned this position in April 1906, having once more lost Nicholas's favor, in part because of his aggressive advocacy of the new system.

If the October Manifesto, with its promise of a new era of civil liberty and limited representative government in Russia, marked the high point of the 1905 Revolution, "Bloody Sunday"—January 9, 1905—surely marked its violent beginning. On that day thousands of striking workers and their families converged on the center of St. Petersburg, bearing church banners and led by a priest, Father George (Georgy) Gapon, to petition their "Little Father," Nicholas II, for a redress of their grievances—only to be met by troops with orders to disperse them. In the ensuing melee at least 130 people were killed, many more were wounded, and thousands were scandalized; indeed the shock of Bloody Sunday, conveyed by telegram and photograph, produced horrified reactions around the world. There was, as usual, no positive response from the Emperor—who was not even in the capital on the day of the massacre. But he had been warned of impending demonstrations and had been sent a copy of the workers' petition by Father Gapon.

Gapon was born to peasants in 1870, trained for the priesthood at the Orthodox seminary in Poltava, in his native Ukraine, and studied at the elite St. Petersburg Ecclesiastical Academy (1898–1903). There he conceived a vocation to serve the industrial workers of the city, and while working as a prison chaplain he organized, with police cooperation, a workers' association aimed at diverting them from the path of socialism and revolution into supporting a more moderate program of reform. Apparently sincere in his desire to improve worker conditions and outraged at government inaction, he led the petition drive and "procession" to the tsar on January 9. Forced by the bloody events of that day to go into hiding and then into exile abroad, Gapon wrote an account of his experiences (excerpted below) that was instantly published in London and elsewhere in the West. He returned to Russia early in 1906, taking advantage of the newly proclaimed civil liberties, and agreed to work again for the police, this time by spying on a terrorist faction of the Socialist Revolutionary party. He was soon exposed as a police spy and secretly executed by order of a revolutionary tribunal (March 1906): a bizarre and tragic end that can be understood only in the context of the bizarre politics of late Imperial Russia and Gapon's own naive monarchism—his almost mystical belief, once widely shared in Russia, that only scoundrels and bureaucrats stood between a loving reconciliation of tsar and people. His autobiography, written in the aftermath of Bloody Sunday, tells another—and remarkably prophetic—tale. This excerpt is followed by the English translation of the workers' petition of January 9 appended to Gapon's autobiography. It should be noted that most of the demands enumerated in the petition were subsequently either granted by the Emperor, however grudgingly, or enacted by the Duma. Also to be noted is the naive monarchism expressed in the petition.

Another, quite different reaction to Bloody Sunday and the political crisis engulfing Russia was that of V. I. Lenin, leader of the Bolshevik faction of the Social Democratic party (SDs). Lenin—the revolutionary pseudonym of Vladimir Ilyich Ulianov (1870–1924)—was in Switzerland when he got news of Bloody Sunday; a few days later he wrote the article reprinted below for publication in his party's newspaper. In it, and unlike Father Gapon, Lenin positively welcomes the prospect of a violent overthrow of the Imperial regime while giving a decidedly Marxist spin to his account of events. He went back to Russia late in 1905 but played only a minor role in ensuing developments before going abroad again in November 1907. Lenin would not return to Russia until April 1917, when a revolution once again was under way.

Still another voice of radical opposition in late Imperial Russia was that of Katerina Breshkovskaia (1844–1934). Daughter of enlightened serf-owning parents, Breshkov- skaia early devoted herself to educational and social work among the peasantry and for her pains was arrested, tried (the notorious trial of 193 populists in January 1878), and sentenced to hard labor in Siberia—the first woman to be thus condemned. In Siberia she was visited (1885) by the American journalist George Kennan (see Pipes essay, Chapter 9), whose published account of her sufferings made her internationally famous. Allowed to return to Russia proper in 1896, she helped organize the Socialist Revolutionary party (SRs)—whose orientation, in contrast to the proletarian bias of Lenin and his Bolsheviks, was definitely toward the peasantry. The SRs became the most widely supported of the populist organizations until, badly split into Center, Left, and Right factions, their party was destroyed in the wake of the Bolshevik coup of October 1917. Breshkovskaia herself, who had been arrested again in 1907 and banished to Siberia, was opposed to the Bolsheviks on both theoretical and practical grounds. Thus in spite of her long and distinguished revolutionary career—on her return from Siberia in 1917 she was hailed as the "Grandmother of the Russian Revolution"—she was forced to emigrate in 1918. In 1920 she settled in Prague, where she promptly completed the memoirs excerpted here. They convey well the revolutionary idealism of her times, peasant rage against the system, and the extent of the SRs' grass-roots organization—an organization so conspicuously lacking, as Professor Emmons pointed out, in Miliukov's Constitutional Democratic party.

# The October Manifesto
# of Nicholas II, 1905

By the Grace of God, We, Nicholas II, Emperor and All-Russian Autocrat, King [Tsar] of Poland, Grand Prince of Finland, etc., etc., etc., proclaim to all Our loyal subjects:

Rioting and disturbances in the capitals and in many localities of Our Empire fill Our heart with great and heavy grief. The well-being of the Russian sovereign is inseparable from the well-being of the people; and the people's sorrow is His

From *PSZ*, 3rd series, vol. 25 part 1 (St. Petersburg, 1906), no. 26,803. Translated by James Cracraft.

sorrow. The present disturbances could cause grave disorder among the people and endanger the integrity and unity of Our state.

We are obliged by Our great vow of royal service to use all Our resources of wisdom and authority to bring a speedy end to this dangerous unrest. We have ordered the responsible officials to take measures to terminate direct manifestations of disorder, lawlessness, and violence, and to protect peaceful persons quietly seeking to do their duty. More effectively to fulfill the general measures designed by Us to pacify public life, We believe it necessary to unify the operations of the higher government.

We therefore enjoin the government to execute this, Our inflexible will:

1. To grant the people the inviolable foundations of civic freedom based on the principles of genuine personal inviolability [habeas corpus], freedom of conscience, speech, assembly, and association.

2. To admit to participation in the State Duma [created by decree of August 6], so far as practicable, all those classes of the population that are now completely deprived of electoral rights, leaving the further development of the principle of universal suffrage to the future legislative order.

3. To establish it as an inviolable rule that no law may go into effect without the approval of the State Duma, and that the elected representatives of the people shall have a genuine part in monitoring the legality of actions taken by the officials We appoint.

We summon all loyal sons of Russia to remember their duty to their Fatherland, to assist in terminating this unprecedented unrest, and to make every effort together with Us to restore peace and tranquility in Our native Land.

Given at Peterhof [palace] on October 17 of the year of Our Lord 1905 and of Our reign the eleventh.

[signed] NICHOLAS

## Father George Gapon Describes Bloody Sunday, 1905

[O]n leaving Russia after Bloody Sunday] I visited in turn Switzerland, Paris, London. Everywhere I found an atmosphere of liberty, allowing the peaceful development of the mass of the people, and making impossible any such events as those in which I had taken part during the last few weeks. I was living now in a new world, but only in order to work for the transformation of the old world which I had left behind. Twice I had escaped from death—the first time from the bullets of the soldiers at the Narva Gate [in St. Petersburg, on Bloody Sunday]; the second

From Father George Gapon, *The Story of My Life*, 2nd Edn. (London: Chapman & Hall, Ltd., 1906), pp. 247–61.

time by evading an arrest which would have certainly finished cruelly for me in the dungeons of St. Peter and St. Paul, or Schlusselburg [fortress-prisons in and near St. Petersburg]. But I felt now more than ever that my life belonged to my people, and that I must devote all my energies to preparing for the moment when I should be able to return to my workmen, and lead them with certainty on the path toward liberty and welfare.

Several months have passed, bringing this day nearer. The massacres of January were a revelation which brought about a complete change in the mind of the nation. This act of the Tsar's Government proved to be a finishing stroke to the many years of educational work which had been carried on at so much sacrifice by the revolutionary parties, by the many years of misrule and its sequel of misery and suffering, and last, but not least, by the criminal and senseless [Russo-Japanese] war, which was as much hated by the whole people as it was harmful to them. The despotism of the last century has made famine a national institution among us; it has brought the State finances to the verge of bankruptcy; it has destroyed the very foundation of peasant agriculture; it has ruined thousands upon thousands of the best lives of our youth. At the moment when the whole nation was clamoring for a change of policy, for a respite, at least, from the baneful oppression to which it had been so long subjected, at this moment the paternal Government of the Tsar had found nothing better to do than to waste millions on the building of railways, fortresses, and war-ships in foreign lands, and then to begin a war which was unprecedented, as well by its military disasters as the degree of corruption and incapacity it revealed.

I say that the events of January 9 were the finishing stroke by which the true meaning of these things was brought home to the minds of the people. It was a definite and irrevocable lesson, as everything that has followed proves beyond doubt. With unexampled solidarity, one town after another responded to the shouts of horror of the workmen of the capital, and struck work or the performance of their professional duties—teachers, barristers, journalists, as well as skilled and unskilled laborers, beginning with Moscow and Riga, and rolling southward to the industrial regions of the west, the steppes of the Black Sea, and even into the mountains of the Caucasus.

To appreciate rightly this movement, one must take into account the amount of suffering which such strikes entail. Remember that the immense majority of Russian workmen have no savings, that they live from hand to mouth, and rarely have clothing or furniture that can be pawned or sold. These strikes have often lasted for weeks, and even months, amid the cries of famished children and the sobs of heartbroken mothers. Soon the peasants joined the revolt. An agrarian war broke out in numerous districts, especially in the Baltic and Central provinces, around Odessa, and in the Caucasus; and, after being extinguished with bloodshed in one place, broke out in another, always more fiercely than before, and on a larger scale. Here, too, the Government has done everything to increase the horrors of the situation. By order of Ministers and of the superior heads of the Orthodox priesthood, the village policeman and priests have incited the peasants against the "intellectuals," the doctors who nursed and the students who helped them in famine years, against those of the landlords who were too good or liberal. In many places, the higher administration of the provinces has organized bands of hooligans, whom we call "black hundreds," who call themselves "Russian men"; and these they have incited to attacks on the educated classes and on all non-Orthodox peoples, especially the Jews and Armenians, telling them that these people have been bought by Japanese or English gold to ruin their country. As a result, many of the landlords have fled from their domains into the towns; and, not finding safety even there, they too have been forced to procure arms for themselves, and to organize secret defense committees.

This agrarian crisis is one of the reasons why the Zemstvo movement has gained so much strength, and why many of the more liberal nobles have taken a bolder part in it. The Jews, Poles, and Armenians have shown still greater energy. The wholesale massacre of these unhappy races is arranged by the Government in a systematic, almost a scientific, way. The massacres of the Armenians in Baku, Batoum, Tiflis, and other towns, to which I have referred; the massacres of Jews, reports of which we receive almost daily now; the wholesale slaughter of Poles and Jews in Lodz, where the people actually rose in open insurrection;—these crimes have established already a sporadic civil war throughout the length of Russia.

And yet this is only the beginning. Forcing every class of the Russian nation and every race inhabiting the country to train themselves for military resistance, and making a question of life and death of it, the Government has done its best to produce a revolution before which the great French Revolution will appear as a game of Lilliputians. For what have the Tsar and the bureaucracy done to alleviate the horrors of the crisis? Absolutely nothing. Every decree of reform that has been issued has been at once spoiled by some trick, and always by the fact that its realization was confided to the same agents whose crimes are crying to Heaven for vengeance. Thus the Tsar granted in February last a decree of religious toleration. But this does not permit freedom of religious discussion; it does not touch at all six millions of Jews and many millions of Mohammedans [Muslims] and other non-Christian peoples; and such partial freedom as is granted to the Christian creeds was, in numberless cases, reduced to a dead letter by the local officials not having received instructions. Who, indeed, could force them to apply the decree, when all publicity was forbidden? Again, the Elective Assembly [State Duma] which the Tsar granted in August was a shameless mockery of real Parliamentary institutions, as well as of the national demand for constitutional government. It did not confide to the people any rights at all, and left the Assembly to be constructed in such a way as to form a new weapon to strengthen the Throne and the bureaucracy.

And now, as I write [late 1905], the news reaches me that the crops have failed in the larger half of the Empire through the lack of labor and cultivation, and that vast tracts of the country are threatened with famine. Who will come to the help of the twenty millions of peasants who are already beginning to starve in many districts? And whence can the salvation of my people come, if the nation will not rise, armed as best it may, and determined to chase away the blasphemous Tsar and his satraps, at any price of blood it may cost?

Fortunately, this price may be less than might be expected some time ago. There are already numerous signs that the forces of the Government are getting more and more sick of the task of killing their brethren. The mutiny of the [crews of certain Russian warships] and practically, though perhaps less openly, of the whole of the fleet, has already deprived the Tsar of one mighty arm; and now every day there are more and more numerous signs that the second and still more formidable weapon, the army, is beginning to yield to the atmosphere of revolt by which it is enveloped. If not in the towns, at least in the villages, the soldiers fraternize with the people; and in this way the agrarian war of which I have spoken will have a fatal influence on them. It is, of course, impossible to expect that the general outbreak will wait till the whole army mutinies. It is an elemental force which gets stronger the more often it is repressed, and grows in its very exercise. The only thing that the leaders of the revolutionary movement can do is to organize this elemental force so as to deal the blow more quickly, to take the duration of the struggle shorter, to avoid innocent bloodshed, to achieve an effect as decisive and as favorable to the masses as circumstances permit.

It is to these ends that I have directed my activity since I left Russia.

Before I end my story I may be asked how long this contest may continue, and what are the chances of the classes in which I am most interested—the workmen and the peasants. If the Tsar would promptly display some wisdom, of which during his reign there has as yet been no sign, and if, instead of vague promises, undefined and unguaranteed, he would immediately grant the Russian people the fullest freedom to work out their own destinies, the dynasty might possibly be saved to enjoy the position of a limited monarchy. But what reason have we to hope for such a manly and intelligent act on the part of the Tsar? He has never hitherto succeeded in getting free from the influence of Pobedonostsev [see Documents, Chapter 9] and such ruthless oppressors as Plehve and Trepoff [the well-known reactionary officials]. There is, in fact, none, because such an act would mean not only the limitation of the autocracy; its sequel in publicity and Parliamentary control would inevitably put an end to the career of the official criminals under whom we are now suffering. Against such a course the bureaucrats will find pretexts, even if the Tsar were personally inclined for it.

There might be another possibility. If the Tsar would not give by one decisive act full political freedom to all his subjects, he might discriminate and devolve a part of his power upon the upper classes on condition of receiving an indemnity for himself and his former servants; and he might differentiate between the various classes by a skillful gradation of rights and privileges. By such measures, as well as by real agrarian reforms, by the lessening of taxation that falls upon the peasants, by lowering the protectionist tariff, and by reforming the whole administration, he might weaken very much the forces of the Opposition. In this way the support of the upper and middle classes might be won, and, for a time, the bitterness of the peasants softened. But even so, the revolution would be only adjourned for a few years. It would be in no way destroyed, because the chief support of the revolutionary movement lies in the industrial classes, who would go on agitating with as much energy as ever. The agrarian reforms would soon prove hollow, because a Parliament composed mainly of landlords and merchants would frustrate any real attempt in this direction. Apart from this consideration, such a policy would require a mature sense of statesmanship, real courage, and skill. The so-called Constitution which the Tsar promised on August 6, and again on October 17, shows no traces of these qualities.

I may say, therefore, with certainty, that the struggle is quickly approaching its inevitable climax; that Nicholas II is preparing for himself the fate which befell a certain English King [Charles I, beheaded in 1649] and a certain French King [Louis XVI, guillotined in 1793] long ago, and that such members of his dynasty as escape unhurt from the throes of the revolution may, on some day in the not very distant future, find themselves exiles upon some Western shore.

## THE ST. PETERSBURG WORKMEN'S PETITION
## TO THE TSAR, JANUARY 9, 1905.

SIRE,—

We working men of St. Petersburg, our wives and children, and our parents, helpless, aged men and women, have come to you, O Tsar, in quest of justice and protection. We have been beggared, oppressed, over-burdened with excessive toil, treated with contumely. We are not recognized as normal human beings, but are dealt with as slaves who have to bear their bitter lot in silence. Patiently we endured this; but now we are being thrust deeper into the slough of rightlessness and ignorance, are being suffocated by despotism and arbitrary whims, and now, O Tsar, we have no strength left. The awful moment has come when death is better than the prolongation of our unendurable tortures. Therefore, we have left work, and informed our employers that we shall not resume it until they have fulfilled our demands. What we have asked is little, consisting solely of that without which our life is not life, but hell and eternal torture.

Our first petition was that our employers should investigate our needs together with ourselves, and even that has been refused. The very right of discussing our wants has been withheld from us on the ground that the law does not recognize any such right, and our demand for an eight-hours day has been dismissed as illegal. To fix the prices of our labor in concert with ourselves, to adjudge upon misunderstandings between us and the lower administration of the factories, to raise the wages of unskilled work men and women up to a ruble a day, to abolish overtime, to take better care of the sick, to instruct without insulting us, to arrange the workshops so that we might work there without encountering death through drafts, rain, and snow: all these requests have been condemned by our employers as unlawful, and our very petition treated as a crime, while the wish to better our condition is regarded as a piece of insolence towards the employers.

O Emperor, there are more than three hundred thousand of us here, yet we are all of us human beings only in appearance and outwardly, while in reality we are deemed devoid of a single human right, even that of speaking, thinking, and meeting to talk over our needs, and of taking measures to better our condition. Any one of us who should dare lift his voice in defense of the working class is thrown into prison or banished. The possession of a kindly heart, of a sensitive soul, is punished in us as a crime. Fellow-feeling for a forlorn, maltreated human being who is bereft of his rights is consequently a heinous crime. O Tsar, is this in accordance with God's commandments, in virtue of which you are now reigning? Is life under such laws worth living? Would it not be better for all of us working people in Russia to die, leaving capitalists and officials to live and enjoy existence?

Such is the future which confronts us, Sire, and therefore we are gathered together before your palace walls. Here we await the last available means of rescue. Refuse not to help your people out of the gulf of rightlessness, misery, and ignorance. Give them a chance of accomplishing their destiny. Deliver them from the intolerable oppression of the bureaucracy. Demolish the wall between yourself and the people, and let them govern the country in conjunction with yourself. You have been sent to lead the people to happiness; but happiness is snatched from us by the officials, who leave us only sorrow and humiliation. Consider our demands attentively and without anger. They have been uttered not for evil, but for good; for our good, Sire, and yours. It is not insolence that speaks in us, but the consciousness of the general necessity of escaping from the present intolerable state of things. Russia is too vast, her wants too manifold, to admit of bureaucrats alone governing her. It is absolutely necessary that the people should assist, because only they know their own hardships.

Refuse not to succor your people; give orders without delay to representatives of all classes in the land to meet together. Let capitalists and workmen be present; let officials, priests, physicians, and teachers all come and choose their own delegates. Let all be free to elect whom they will, and for this purpose let the elections to the Constituent Assembly [or State Duma] be organized on the principle of universal suffrage. This is our principal request, on which everything else depends. It is the best and only plaster for our open wounds, without which they will ever remain open and hurry us on to death. There is no one panacea for all our ills; many are needed, and we now proceed to enumerate them, speaking plainly and candidly to you, Sire, as to a father. The following measures are indispensable.

In the first section are those which are directed against the ignorance and disfranchisement of the Russian people. They include—

1. Freedom and inviolability of the person, liberty of speech, of the press, of association, of conscience in matters of religion, and separation of Church and State.
2. General and obligatory education by the State.
3. The responsibility of Ministers to the nation, and guarantees for the legality of administrative methods.
4. Equality of all persons, without exception, before the law.
5. The immediate recall of all who have suffered for their convictions.

In the second section are measures against the poverty of the nation.

1. The repeal of indirect taxation, and the substitution of a direct progressive income-tax.
2. Repeal of the land redemption tax. Cheap credit, and a gradual transfer of the land to the people.

The third section comprises measures against the crushing of labor by capital.

1. Protection of labor by the law.

2. Freedom of working men's associations for co-operative and professional purposes.

3. An eight-hour working day and the limitation of overtime.

4. The freedom of the struggle between labor and capital.

5. The participation of representatives of the working classes in the elaboration of a bill dealing with the State insurance of workmen.

6. A normal working wage.

Those, Sire, constitute our principal needs, which we come to lay before you. Give orders and swear that they shall be fulfilled, and you will render Russia happy and glorious, and will impress your name on our hearts and on the hearts of our children, and our children's children for all time. But if you withhold the word, if you are not responsive to our petition, we will die here on this square before your palace, for we have nowhere else to go to and no reason to repair elsewhere. For us there are but two roads, one leading to liberty and happiness, the other to the tomb. Point, Sire, to either of them; we will take it, even though it lead to death. Should our lives serve as a holocaust of agonizing Russia, we will not grudge these sacrifices; we gladly offer them up.

Signed by GEORGE GAPON and about 135,000 workmen.

## V. I. Lenin Exhorts the Proletariat to Revolution, 1905

Events of the greatest historical significance are developing in Russia. The proletariat has risen against tsarism. The proletariat was driven to revolt by the government. There can hardly be any doubt now that the government deliberately allowed the strike movement to develop and a wide demonstration to be started more or less without hindrance in order to bring matters to a point where military force could be used. Its maneuver was successful. Thousands of killed and wounded—such is the toll of Bloody Sunday, January 9, in St. Petersburg. The army defeated unarmed workers, women, and children. The army vanquished the enemy by shooting prostrate workers. "We have taught them a good lesson!" the tsar's henchmen and their European flunkeys from among the conservative bourgeoisie say with consummate cynicism.

Yes, it was a great lesson, one which the Russian proletariat will not forget. The most uneducated, backward sections of the working class, who naively trusted the tsar and sincerely wished to put peacefully before "the tsar himself" the petition of a tormented people, were all taught a lesson by the troops led by the tsar or his uncle, the Grand Duke Vladimir.

From V. I. Lenin, *Selected Works*, 3 vols. (New York: International Publishers, 1967), vol. 1, pp. 450–53.

The working class has received a momentous lesson in civil war; the revolutionary education of the proletariat made more progress in one day than it could have made in months and years of drab, humdrum, wretched existence. The slogan of the heroic St. Petersburg proletariat, "Death or freedom!" is reverberating throughout Russia. Events are developing with astonishing rapidity. The general strike in St. Petersburg is spreading. All industrial, public and political activities are paralysed. On Monday, January 10, still more violent clashes occurred between the workers and the military. Contrary to the mendacious government reports, blood is flowing in many parts of the capital. The workers of Kolpino are rising. The proletariat is arming itself and the people. The workers are said to have seized the Sestroretsk Arsenal. They are providing themselves with revolvers, forging their tools into weapons, and procuring bombs for a desperate bid for freedom. The general strike is spreading to the provinces. Ten thousand have already ceased work in Moscow, and a general strike has been called there for tomorrow (Thursday, January 13). An uprising has broken out in Riga. The workers are demonstrating in Lodz, an uprising is being prepared in Warsaw, proletarian demonstrations are taking place in Helsingfors [Helsinki]. Unrest is growing among the workers and the strike is spreading in Baku, Odessa, Kiev, Kharkov, Kovno, and Vilno. In Sevastopol, the naval stores and arsenals are ablaze, and the troops refuse to shoot at the mutineers. Strikes in Revel and in Saratov. Workers and reservists clash with the troops in Radom.

The revolution is spreading. The government is beginning to lose its head. From the policy of bloody repression it is attempting to change over to economic concessions and to save itself by throwing a sop to the workers or promising the nine-hour day. But the lesson of Bloody Sunday cannot be forgotten. The demand of the insurgent St. Petersburg workers—the immediate convocation of a constituent assembly on the basis of universal, direct, and equal suffrage by secret ballot—must become the demand of all the striking workers. Immediate overthrow of the government—this was the slogan with which even the St. Petersburg workers who had believed in the tsar answered the massacre of January 9; they answered through their leader, the priest George Gapon, who declared after that bloody day: "We no longer have a tsar. A river of blood divides the tsar from the people. Long live the fight for freedom!"

Long live the revolutionary proletariat! say we. The general strike is rousing and rallying increasing masses of the working class and the urban poor. The arming of the people is becoming an immediate task of the revolutionary moment.

Only an armed people can be the real bulwark of popular liberty. The sooner the proletariat succeeds in arming, and the longer it holds its fighting positions as striker and revolutionary, the sooner will the army begin to waver; more and more soldiers will at last begin to realize what they are doing and they will join sides with the people against the fiends, against the tyrant, against the murderers of defenseless workers and of their wives and children. No matter what the outcome of the present uprising in St. Petersburg may be, it will, in any case, be the first step to a wider, more conscious, better organized uprising. The government may possibly succeed in putting off the day of reckoning, but the postponement will only make the next step of the revolutionary onset more stupendous. This will only mean that the Social Democrats will take advantage of this postponement to rally the organized fighters and spread the news about the start made by the St. Petersburg workers. The proletariat will join in the struggle, it will quit mill and factory and will prepare arms for itself. The slogans of the struggle for freedom will be carried more and more widely into the midst of the urban poor and of the millions of peasants. Revolutionary committees will be set up at every factory, in every city district, in every large village. The people in revolt will overthrow all the government institutions of the tsarist autocracy and proclaim the immediate convocation of a constituent assembly.

The immediate arming of the workers and of all citizens in general, the preparation and organization of the revolutionary forces for overthrowing the government authorities and institutions—this is the practical basis on which revolutionaries of every variety can and must unite to strike the common blow. The proletariat must always pursue its own independent path, never weakening its connection with the Social Democratic Party, always bearing in mind its great, ultimate objective, which is to rid mankind of all exploitation. But this independence of the Social Democratic proletarian party will never cause us to forget the importance of a common revolutionary onset at the moment of actual revolution. We Social Democrats can and must act independently of the bourgeois-democratic revolutionaries and guard the class independence of the proletariat. But we must go hand in hand with them during the uprising, when direct blows are being struck at tsarism, when resistance is offered the troops, when the bastilles of the accursed enemy of the entire Russian people are stormed.

The proletariat of the whole world is now looking eagerly towards the proletariat of Russia. The overthrow of tsarism in Russia, so valiantly begun by our working class, will be the turning-point in the history of all countries; it will facilitate the task of the workers of all nations, in all states, in all parts of the globe. Let, therefore, every Social Democrat, every class-conscious worker bear in mind the immense tasks of the broad popular struggle that now rest upon his shoulders. Let him not forget that he represents also the needs and interests of the whole peasantry, of all who toil, of all who are exploited, of the whole people against their enemy. The proletarian heroes of St. Petersburg now stand as an example to all.

Long live the revolution!

Long live the insurgent proletariat!

*Geneva, January 12, 1905.*

## Katerina Breshkovskaia Evokes
## the Struggle to Liberate
## the Peasantry, 1896–1917

When I returned [from Siberia to Russia proper, in 1896] I found agriculture in an almost unbelievable state. The cows and horses were very small because of lack of pasturage. There were no fowls except chickens. The peasants had stopped growing flax, because there was barely enough land for grain. The population had multiplied, and the patches of land owned by the peasants were too small to support it. There was no way that the peasant could work for a living. There were hardly any factories in the provinces and only a few peasant industries. The peasant could do nothing except go to the landlord or the *kulak* [relatively rich peasant]. The peasants regarded the landlords and *kulaks* alike as enemies.

As I observed all this, the theory of the proletarization of the peasant [advanced by Lenin] seemed to me to be absurd. Into what worse slavery could the peasant be driven? He had no land and no freedom. In spite of everything I found that the peasant had made a step forward intellectually. The general Westernization of the Russian state had affected him. The villagers, seeking ways and means for a decent living, had become interested in political and economic questions. There were frequent clashes with local officials. In such cases the higher authorities used the intelligentsia as go-betweens, and the peasants found them to be unselfish and sympathetic. They ceased to be suspicious of town clothes, and in some places even wore them themselves.

From the first days of my return to Russia I had to live as an outlaw, only occasionally at first, but permanently after two years, for the police were suspicious of my interest in the villages. In order to reorganize the Socialist-Revolutionary Party, I had to visit many governments [provinces] in order to find out who among the intelligentsia and peasants could be trusted for our work. In some towns I found remnants of the old [People's Will] party, experienced and mature men and women, who had served their terms in prison and in exile and were now working in county and municipal educational institutions. Severe trials had left their mark upon these people, but in their souls the old fire burned, ready to leap into flame at the touch of a current of fresh air. Their fears had been roused by the militant propaganda of Marxism, but these subsided at the prospect of once more being able to come into contact with the masses. These experienced workers were very useful to us. They were the nuclei of local party organizations and the leaders of government and district committees. The local young people and village leaders grouped themselves about them.

Reprinted from *Hidden Springs of the Russian Revolution: Personal Memoirs of Katerina Breshkovskaia*, edited by Lincoln Hutchinson, pp. 277–84, 286–91 with the permission of the publishers, Stanford University Press. © 1931 by the Board of Trustees of the Leland Stanford Junior University. Copyright renewed 1959 by James S. Hutchinson.

During the first seven years of my life as an outlaw (from 1896 to 1903) I visited many governments [provinces] as an organizer. . . . I often had to repeat my visits several times, especially in the Volga districts. I lived in each of these places for from a fortnight to a month. My advanced age and modest dress induced the peasants to speak to me frankly. I realized that their social condition was as bad as it had ever been. The few reforms, grudgingly given, had not covered the growing needs. The townspeople were adopting Marxism, because they wanted a definite doctrine on which to base their hopes. Except for the insignificant *tiers-état* ["third estate"]—the schoolmasters and under-secretaries—and the few of our group who had managed to escape arrest, there was no one among the educated people who had the slightest interest in the problems of the people. If the landlords ever through the Zemstvos gave the peasants a few crumbs from their table, the higher authorities objected. Nicholas II, commenting on a report which contained a mention of a certain sum which had been assigned to country schools, wrote the memorable words, "A little less energy in this direction."

The peasants intensely desired education for their children, for they realized that this was the only way in which they could escape the slavery they themselves had endured. In the villages I sometimes met a self-educated peasant who was familiar with such scientific works as Buckle, Draper, and Darwin. The contrast between the intellectual development of such a man and his home surroundings was startling. A hut with four walls and an earthen floor was his home. His furniture consisted of an oven, which occupied one-fourth of the space of the hut, a log of wood for a chair, and a carpenter's bench for a table. I would find the master of the house working at the bench while his wife and daughters were diligently weaving. After the first awkwardness was over he would draw a box from underneath the bench and show me his treasure—books. I had many discussions with such men on any matter under the sun and found them to have a fine understanding on many matters and regretful that they could not obtain books on the subjects that interested them the most. Such men cherished one wish above all others—a university education for their children.

Such types were, to be sure, not frequent, but there was a general craving for knowledge among the peasants. The schools could accommodate only one-tenth of those who wished to attend. When our party began to print appeals to the people with hectographs and mimeographs, the peasants learned how to do it and multiplied them for us at home. Sometimes they even wrote leaflets themselves, printed them, and sent them to our committee for distribution.

Organization and propaganda did not by any means progress equally well in all governments. Much depended on the revolutionary traditions which had been preserved among the population as well as on the amount of energy that had been devoted to propaganda there by the teachers of socialism and the preachers of revolution. The peasants along the Volga responded readily to our propaganda. Neither the local printing-presses nor those at a distance were able to supply enough literature to satisfy them. They learned to form their own committees, to organize meetings, and to establish communications with distant centers. Saratov was rich in experienced and able organizers, recruited from among our best intelligentsia. The governments of Chernigov, Poltava, Kharkov, Kiev, Kursk, and Voronezh were also easily aroused. Their ardor was felt in 1902, when the so-called "disorders in Poltava and Kharkov" broke out.

During the winter of 1901–1902 a group of Socialist Revolutionary students worked in Kiev and in a wide area surrounding the city. Their proclamations were energetic protests against the political and financial oppression of the peasant population and laid particular emphasis on the peasants' right to the land. They did not by a single word urge the peasants to rebellion, but their propaganda had a surprising result. The peasants in the central governments suffered particularly from lack of land. Those in the rich black-soil region were in dire poverty. They were at the end of their patience and ready to listen with approval to all agitators.

In less than a month of such work, in the spring of 1901, the peasants of Poltava and the adjoining districts began to turn the landlords off their estates and to distribute the land and implements among themselves. It was done in this way: The householders of the village would go up to the master's house and tell him that an order had been issued that he give his land to the peasants, that he himself was to go to town and enter the service of the state, that his house was to be made into a school, and that everything else belonged to the peasants. The peasants would then harness the horses, take possession of the keys of all the buildings, and invite the landlord and his family to take with them all that they could carry and go to the town and remain there. The peasants committed no rude or offensive acts, because they believed sincerely that what they were doing was perfectly legal. It all happened so suddenly and so generally that the police were unable to stop it. The peasants acted quietly and consistently. They were sure that at last they were to see the day when justice would reign on the earth.

Encouraged by their quiet assurance, the adjoining districts began to turn out their landlords in the same quiet fashion, fearing neither punishment nor prohibition. They felt no anger toward the landlord, for they thought that since their acts were lawful he would make no attempt to return. This is the movement known officially as "the disorders in Kharkov and Poltava."

Unfortunately, the authorities did not appreciate the fairness with which the peasants had acted but took advantage of their peaceful attitude to swoop down upon them with all the cruelty of which they were capable. Prince Obolensky, the governor of Kharkov, sent military detachments who behaved as if they were in a barbarous, conquered country. The peasants were flogged until they were almost dead. Sometimes they did die. The householders were forced to return twice the amount of the products they had taken from the estates and to pay enormous fines for rioting and huge sums to the landlords as compensation for imaginary losses. Kharkov and Poltava were ruined. The nobility cried "Victory," but their triumph was only apparent. The attempt on the life of Prince Obolensky by a member of the Socialist Revolutionary Party drew attention to his methods of suppression and aroused much criticism. Also the boldness of the peasants made a great impression throughout southern and central Russia.

There was wide publicity of the events and of the trial that followed. "Did you hear what happened in Kharkov and Poltava?" was a frequent question in railway cars and on the country roads, in the tea-rooms and market-places. The people did not consider it a defeat. They only thought of the bravery of the participants and held them up as examples to the whole peasant world.

The landlords complained loudly that they could not control their peasants. Contractors cried that the price of labor had doubled and trebled, that the peasants refused to discuss the situation. "The peasant is lolling in the market-place with outstretched feet. There is an inscription in chalk on the soles of his boots. 'Three rubles a day!' He will not deign to speak; the price is there; there is no use for words." When the peasant was abused by the officials, he would reply, "You forget what has happened in Kharkov and Poltava."

The officials' reply would be the same remark. But the peasant would only retort, "Very well. But we shall see what happens next time."

Peasant discussions of the events usually led to this conclusion: "It was foolish to leave the nests [landlord houses] intact; we should have burned them down. We left them their homes, and they have come back. If we had destroyed them, they would have had to stay in town."

These comments may seem naive and silly, but they express in simple words the general outlook of the peasant. The Russian peasant is not bloodthirsty. He hates "soul murder." He is capable of cruelty and violence only in cases of extreme anger or when he is carried away by mob impulse.

This movement among the peasants of Kharkov and Poltava, almost forgotten now, played an important part in rousing the revolutionary spirit in Russia. A demand for literature, for propagandists, and for organization increased rapidly. The Socialist Revolutionary Party printed hundreds of thousands of pamphlets which were eagerly read by young and old in all parts of the country. . . .

The year 1905 marked a high point in the struggle for freedom. The tragic end of the [Russo-Japanese] war and the shameful way in which it had been conducted had so discredited the government that the noisy meetings of protest held by the revolutionary parties caught the general interest and approval of the people. The strike of the railway employees inspired the peasants and filled them with hope and exultant energy. Russia was celebrating a spiritual victory over tyranny, over centuries of moral and intellectual oppression. Hope had revived. The political exiles, with complete faith in the amnesty of Nicholas, returned from Siberia and from abroad. They took an active part in meetings and party conferences. I personally did not trust the amnesty and did not alter my outlaw status. At the time when the manifesto promising a constitution was issued [October 17] I was in Simbirsk and was connected with the local village revolutionary groups. . . . It is interesting that on that same night a telegram from Samara warned me that the gendarmes were looking for me. I left the town and moved on to a small Tatar village where I had a good opportunity to discuss the situation with the peasants. The Tatars took a lively part in our talks. Sometimes *mullahs* [Muslim clerics] appeared with proclamations that had been translated and printed by the students of the Clerical [Ecclesiastical] Seminary at Kazan. I talked also to the Cheremiss and the Mordva. All these tribes were in complete sympathy with the general movement and followed the course of events with interest, although they were cautious and left the leadership to Russians. At the secret meetings they accepted the resolutions drawn up by the Socialist Revolutionary Party. If one traces the spread of our political propaganda on a map and compares it with the progress of the revolutionary movement among the peasants, one finds a remarkable coincidence between the two.

The center of propaganda on the Volga was Saratov. A considerable number of political exiles and old revolutionaries lived in this town. Their leader was the cautious, severe Leonid Petrovich Bulakov, an old man of wide experience. He loved young people and knew how to train them into valuable party workers. He directed the revolutionary affairs of the governments of Saratov, Simbirsk, Samara, Penza, Tambov, Voronezh, and Kazan. Such activities included the management of printing-offices and copying devices of all kinds, the appointment of committees, the calling of conferences, and the distribution of literature, ciphers, and codes. Bulakov's name was kept secret by the Party. He also had adult helpers, the greatest among them being the never-to-be-forgotten Pavel Pavlovich Kraft. Other reliable workers were Milashevsky, his wife, Maria Ivanovna, and Alexander Vassilievich Panov, the son of a poor peasant woman of Olonets. Panov was responsible for much of the revolutionary activity in Nizhnii-Novgorod. He had been a brilliant student while at school, and after he had finished the [Kazan Ecclesiastical] Academy had devoted himself to literature and science. Although he suffered much persecution, he always managed as the gendarmes drove him from place to place to take his excellent library with him. With the help of this library he educated hundreds of young people. He sent his pupils into the villages and in this way established communications with the entire government of Nizhnii-Novgorod and parts of Vladimir and Iaroslav. He was continually being arrested, but this did not discourage him. He died, while still young, from tuberculosis which he had contracted in prison.

A good many active workers joined our party through the influence of Katcharovsky. He was preparing statistics on the peasant land communities and was able to visit all the towns with statistical archives. He took gifted young people with him as helpers. At Smolensk he formed a noteworthy group of reliable young women, among whom was Mastasia Bitsentzo. Chernigov, Poltava, and Kiev also produced many remarkable workers. It was easy to agitate in the period from 1903 to 1906. The soil was thoroughly prepared and seeds germinated readily. The sprouts that developed were so strong that mass deportations, floggings, prison, and any other inventions of the gendarmes could not crush them.

Our enemies thought that our activity had been stopped. Had they not hanged enough, shot enough, flogged enough to have wiped us out forever? There were not enough trains to transport the exiles. Of schoolteachers alone twenty thousand were exiled. From 1906 to 1909 the school buildings were empty except at night when they were opened for secret revolutionary meetings.

The people knew by this time that it was useless to expect benevolence from the government. It was not only the events of January 9 [Bloody Sunday] but the whole history of the policy of the administration that showed them clearly that those in authority, from the Tsar down to the village policeman, were opposed to any system that would bring equality of rights to the peasants. They were in a dangerous state of mind. By 1907 the older ones realized that the revolution had been a failure and that their masters were trying to deprive them of those concessions which had been promised them by the government in its first fright. They had again lost all hope of getting the land. They were weary; they were full of grief and dismay, although they had not lost confidence in revolution as a remedy. They believed that they had failed because the movement had not been general enough, that not enough governments [provinces] had been involved.

The young people thought differently. They wanted to try again. They had seen the results of their three years of careful preparation. They had seen their mothers and sisters violated. They had seen their fathers' beards torn out. Their cattle had been stolen. Whole villages had been burned. Beloved leaders had been imprisoned. Entire families had been exiled. The young people had seen it all, and they were bitter.

The years from 1908 to 1910 had filled Siberia and Northern Russia with exiles from the lower classes. Peasants, laborers, soldiers, and sailors were there. Most of the peasants were elderly people who had been separated from their families. They were in extreme poverty, but bore the hard conditions of exile well in spite of it. They continually discussed the Revolution and made prediction for the future in such remarks as this: "Next time it will be different. It is terrible to think about. The young people all carry knives in their boots. When they next attack the landlords there will be no pity. Kindness does not work. We have tried that. We thought they would not come back, but we were wrong. They came bringing with them gendarmes and Cossacks who flogged us. We won't be silly another time. Our young people will make it hot for them."

The laborers, soldiers, and sailors were also sure that the next revolution would be a bloody one. No one doubted that it would come again and soon. They knew that events had been stopped midway and that it would be quite easy to bring them to completion. Many of these exiles tried to escape in order to continue the work of organization. They were frequently caught and sent back, but they usually tried it again.

They were all determined not to fail in the next revolution, and followed closely the revolutionary progress of the laborers in the cities and read the speeches in the Duma carefully. They laughed at the government because it thought that the revolutionists had been intimidated by its repressive measures. The bourgeoisie did not seem to be aware of the situation. . . .

There were tens of thousands of exiles in every government [province]. The district of Kirensk, which was as large as France, a thinly populated area covered with *taiga* [scrubby evergreens], had, during the years from 1908 to 1910 and from 1911 to 1913, when I was there again, several thousand political exiles. A great many of the young comrades visited my hut, and I always knew of their plans to escape. They were all anxious to return to European Russia, and all had the definite intention of taking up their revolutionary work again as soon as possible. When I myself returned in 1917 I met a great many of them again and found that they were not in sympathy with the Bolsheviks. . . .

In the revolutionary meetings of 1917 I could see a great difference between those people who had had training in the revolutionary organizations of 1904 to 1906 and the new ones who had been under the influence of the Bolsheviks from the beginning of their activity. They [the latter] had not had time to develop well-formed opinions and were quite ready to support madmen and traitors. In the struggle between the two currents the mob was the victor. Worn out, half-starved, embittered by the disappointments of 1905, the mob knew that humility, patience, and prayer would bring them nothing. They had seen that the peasants of Kharkov and Poltava had tried to act honestly and had been cruelly punished for it. The repressions after the outbreak of 1905 goaded them to despair. The short-sighted treatment of the peasants by the privileged classes was the thing that made Bolshevism possible in Russia.

## FURTHER READING

Abraham Ascher, *The Revolution of 1905*, 2 vols. (1988, 1993)

Victoria E. Bonnell, *Roots of Rebellion: Workers' Politics and Organization in St. Petersburg and Moscow, 1900–1914* (1983)

Daniel R. Brower, "Labor Violence in Russia in the Late Nineteenth Century," *Slavic Review* 41 (1982), 417–453

John Bushnell, *Mutiny amid Repression: Russian Soldiers in the Revolution of 1905–1906* (1985)

Olga Crisp and Linda Edmondson, eds., *Civil Rights in Imperial Russia* (1989)

Robert Edelman, *Proletarian Peasants: The Revolution of 1905 in Russia's Southwest* (1987)

Linda Harriet Edmondson, *Feminism in Russia, 1900–1917* (1984)

Terence Emmons, *The Formation of Political Parties and the First National Elections in Russia* (1983)

Barbara Alpern Engel, *Mothers and Daughters: Woman of the Intelligentsia in Nineteenth-Century Russia* (1983)

Laura Engelstein, *Moscow 1905: Working-Class Organization and Political Conflict* (1982)

George Fischer, *Russian Liberalism: From Gentry to Intelligentsia* (1958)

Gregory L. Freeze, ed. and trans., *From Supplication to Revolution: A Documentary Social History of Imperial Russia*, Part Three (1988)

Klaus Frohlich, *The Emergence of Russian Constitutionalism, 1900–1904* (1981)

Shmuel Galai, *The Liberation Movement in Russia, 1900–1905* (1973)

Leopold H. Haimson, *The Russian Marxists and the Origins of Bolshevism* (1955)

Sidney Harcave, *The Russian Revolution of 1905* (1970)

Neil Harding, ed., *Marxism in Russia: Key Documents, 1879–1906* (1983)

Hannu Immonen, *The Agrarian Program of the Russian Socialist Revolutionary Party, 1900–1914* (1988)

John L. H. Keep, *The Rise of Social Democracy in Russia* (1963)

Howard D. Mehlinger and John M. Thompson, *Count Witte and the Tsarist Government in the 1905 Revolution* (1972)

Michael Melancon, "The Socialist Revolutionaries from 1902 to 1907: Peasant and Workers' Party," *Russian History* 12 (1985), 2–47

Paul N. Miliukov, *Political Memoirs, 1905–1917*, trans. C. Goldberg, ed. Arthur P. Mendel (1967)

Maureen P. Perrie, *The Agrarian Policy of the Russian Socialist-Revolutionary Party: From Its Origins through the Revolution of 1905–1907* (1976)

————, "The Peasant Movement [1905–1907]," *Past and Present; A Journal of Historical Studies* 57 (1972), 123–155

Richard Pipes, ed., *The Russian Intelligentsia* (1961)

————, *Struve: Liberal on the Left, 1870–1905* (1970)

————, *Struve: Liberal on the Right, 1905–1944* (1980)

Philip Pomper, *The Russian Revolutionary Intelligentsia*, 2d ed. (1993)

Don C. Rawson, "Rightist Politics in the Revolution of 1905: The Case of Tula Province," *Slavic Review* 51 (1992), 99–116

Henry Reichman, *Railwaymen and Revolution: Russia, 1905* (1987)

Thomas Riha, *A Russian European: Paul Miliukov in Russian Politics* (1969)

Walter Sablinsky, *The Road to Bloody Sunday: Father Gapon and the St. Petersburg Massacre of 1905* (1976)

Jonathan Sanders, "Lessons from the Periphery: Saratov, January 1905," *Slavic Review* 46 (1987), 229–244

Jeremiah Schneiderman, *Sergei Zubatov and Revolutionary Marxism: The Struggle for the Working Class in Tsarist Russia* (1976)

Scott J. Seregny, *Russian Teachers and Peasant Revolution: The Politics of Education in 1905* (1989)

Robert Service, *Lenin: A Political Life*, vol. 1 (1985)

Teodor Shanin, *Russia, 1905–1907: Revolution as a Moment of Truth* (1986)

Richard Stites, *The Women's Liberation Movement in Russia: Feminism, Nihilism, and Bolshevism, 1860–1930* (1978, 1991)

Gerald D. Surh, *1905 in St. Petersburg: Labor, Society, and Revolution* (1989)

————, "Petersburg's First Mass Labor Organization: The Assembly of Russian Workers and Father Gapon," *Russian Review* 40 (1981), 241–262, 412–441

Geoffrey Swain, *Russian Social Democracy and the Legal Labor Movement, 1906–1914* (1988)

Charles Timberlake, ed., *Essays on Russian Liberalism* (1972)

Henry J. Tobias, *The Jewish Bund in Russia: From Its Origins to 1905* (1972)

Donald Treadgold, *Lenin and His Rivals: The Struggle for Russia's Future, 1898–1906* (1955)

Franco Venturi, *Roots of Revolution: A History of the Populist and Socialist Movements in Nineteenth-Century Russia*, trans. (from Italian) Francis Haskell (1960, 1983)

Andrew M. Verner, *The Crisis of Russian Autocracy: Nicholas II and the 1905 Revolution* (1990)

Andrzej Walicki, *Legal Philosophies of Russian Liberalism* (1987)

Robert C. Williams, *The Other Bolsheviks: Lenin and His Critics, 1904–1914* (1986)

Charters S. Wynn, *Workers, Strikes, and Pogroms: The Donbass-Dnepr Bend in Late Imperial Russia, 1870–1905* (1992)

Avrahm Yarmolinsky, *Road to Revolution: A Century of Russian Radicalism* (1957, 1986)

Judith Zimmerman, "Russian Liberal Theory, 1900–1917," *Canadian-American Slavic Studies* 14 (1980), 1–20

CHAPTER **14**

# Crisis and Collapse

The fall of the Russian Empire, like its rise, may be attributed in considerable measure to the fortunes of war: in the earlier case, to Peter I's heroic victory over Sweden in the Great Northern War (1700–1721); in the latter, to Nicholas II's gross mismanagement of Russia's wars first against Japan (1904–1905) and then against Germany, in World War I (1914–1918). Yet, as we have seen, the Imperial regime in its last decades was beset by internal difficulties, too, including growing ethnic tension, intensifying social conflict, and recurring political violence. In part these difficulties resulted from the regime's determination to industrialize Russia and maintain the Empire as a great power; in part, from its persistent inability or refusal to respond to the needs and demands of its ever diverse, still largely impoverished, but increasingly educated subjects. Dramatic public reversals—not only the humiliating military defeats by feared or hated foreign enemies, but such domestic catastrophes as the Khodynka tragedy of 1896 (see Kanatchikov document, Chapter 12) and Bloody Sunday in 1905—severely weakened the autocracy's prestige, opening the door to withering attacks by its liberal and revolutionary opponents. Reflecting the widening social and political ferment was Imperial Russia's last great cultural splurge, known as the Silver Age: a heady, even apocalyptic movement of bold artistic experimentation, intense religious searching, sexual license, and philosophical innovation that all but eclipsed the intelligentsia's fascination with Marxism.

Most historians date the onset of Imperial Russia's terminal crisis to 1905. And it is against this background of spreading crisis—political and social, economic and cultural—that the wartime collapse of the Imperial regime should be seen.

## E SSAYS

Peter A. Stolypin (1862–1911) is generally considered the last really capable government minister of Imperial Russia. A true son of the Imperial elite, he entered government service (1885) after graduating from St. Petersburg University and then served (1889–1902) as marshal of the local nobility while managing his own estate—and developing a close interest in agricultural reform—in Kovno Province (in Lithuania). In 1902 he was appointed governor of Grodno Province (in Belorussia) and shortly thereafter, governor of the Volga province of Saratov, where he again delved into agrarian problems and confronted peasant radicalism. His success in quelling the revolutionary outbreak in Saratov in 1905 attracted the attention of St. Petersburg, and in April 1906 the current prime minister, Goremykin, nominated him minister of the interior. In July Nicholas II appointed Stolypin prime minister as well. In this position he pursued, until assassinated in 1911, the controversial policy of reform appraised in the trenchant essay, reprinted below, by the late Leonard Schapiro, a distinguished Russianist who taught for many years at the London School of Economics. This is followed by a masterful summary of events between July 1914 and February 1917 by Professor Hans Rogger of the University of California at Los Angeles. Rogger describes the military disasters and innumerable casualties, the intense political maneuvering, the general war-weariness and sharpening peasant unrest, the workers' strikes, soldiers' mutinies, and women's demonstrations that culminated in the February Revolution and the collapse of the Imperial regime. Regarding events of international significance, it will be noted, Rogger gives dates according to both the Old Style calendar (used in Russia until February 1918, and throughout this book) and the New Style (in general use in Europe and beyond, then as now).

## Stolypin

### Leonard Schapiro

Peter Arkadievich Stolypin was the Prime Minister who dominated Russia's short constitutional period. Appointed on July 7, 1906, he was shot by an assassin on September 1, 1911, and died a few days later. Probably no other figure in the modern history of Russia has aroused so much controversy. By the left he is generally dismissed as the savage butcher who hanged [revolutionary] peasants and workers. (A monument to him erected in Kiev in 1912 was destroyed in 1917.) To the extreme right he became an odious figure, whose policy of reform and attempt to work with the Duma, or parliament, were a threat to the sacred principle of autocracy (which the right continued to pretend still subsisted, in spite of the constitutional regime inaugurated in 1906). For his many admirers he has posthumously become the wisest statesman that Russia ever had, who could, had he been given time, have saved Russia from war and revolution, and have effected a peaceful transformation of the country on moderate and modern lines. His ministerial colleagues, and others who knew him, have recorded that he was a man of great courage, sincerity, and absolute integrity. . . .

The First Duma to come into being as the result of the Imperial Manifesto of October 17, 1905, and the new Fundamental State Laws of April 23, 1906, was elected on a wide franchise, which produced a turbulent and radical body, determined from the start not to cooperate with the government, or with any government not responsible to it. Stolypin, who had been appointed Minister of the Interior a day before the Duma met, on April 26, 1906, showed that he was better able to stand up to the barrage of hostile abuse which the government faced than the weak Prime Minister, Goremykin. It soon became obvious that no common ground could be found between the government and the Duma (historians will, no doubt, long debate the question whose fault this was), so the Duma was dissolved on July 9, with an announcement that it would reconvene [after new elections] on February 20, 1907. Just before the dissolution, Stolypin was appointed Prime Minister.

Stolypin faced the Second Duma with a vast program, which had been set out in detail in a government communiqué in August 1906. The omens for any kind of harmonious cooperation between the government and the still radical (if somewhat chastened) Second Duma were not good. Efforts to persuade some of the liberal leaders to come into the government had failed. Moreover, the country was in a state of revolutionary turmoil: for example, 3,000 deaths were caused by terrorists in 1907. In August 1906 a terrorist bomb had exploded in Stolypin's house, wounding his children. The government retaliated with strong measures, including numerous executions by sentence of courts martial which succeeded in breaking the wave of terrorism, but shocked and antagonized radical and liberal opinion. But Stolypin's policy, as the communiqué made clear, and as he told the Second Duma, was based on the belief that for the government to call a halt to necessary reforms and to devote all its energies to the suppression of terrorism, was wrong. He therefore envisaged a comprehensive program of reforms, aimed at ultimately removing the causes of social discontent. Apart from the land reform, which occupied Stolypin in the Third Duma, the program included the following: reform of civil rights; improvement of workers' conditions of life; extension and improvement of local government administration; reform of local courts; reform of secondary education; and reform of the police. Not included in the program of reforms submitted to the Second Duma was a proposal, which Stolypin had persuaded the Council of Ministers to accept in October 1906, for the removal of a great number of restrictions from which the Jews suffered. The Emperor refused to approve the proposal in response, as he put it, to "an inner voice (which) keeps on insisting more and more." The hostile reaction of the Duma astonished even Stolypin's critics—indeed, as one of the Kadet leaders later noted, it would have been incomprehensible to an Englishman. The social democratic leader Tsereteli actually spoke of "tossing us a few scraps of reforms . . . incapable of satisfying anyone."

What was central to the entire program, in Stolypin's view, was putting an end to the separate legal status of the peasants, derived from the survival of communal ownership of land. Unless the majority of the population could be given equal status with the rest, and relieved of its legal *apartheid*, all the other reforms in his view would be no more than "cosmetics on a corpse"—to quote the graphic phrase which he used in conversation with a colleague. Unless this fundamental belief of Stolypin is understood . . . his political conduct in 1907, which aroused severe controversy, cannot be seen in perspective.

Since there was no hope of passing a complicated and comprehensive law which would enable the peasants to leave the commune and to become individual, legally protected owners of land with the cooperation of the Second Duma, a way had to be found of doing it without this cooperation. Professor Seton-Watson is probably right when he observes that Stolypin "was in favor of cooperating with the elected representatives of the people, provided that they did what he wanted. But when his policies met with opposition, he had no respect either for the electorate or the law."[1] At any rate, this is what happened in June 1907.

Article 87 of the Fundamental State Laws provided that "while the Duma is not in session" the Council of Ministers could submit an urgently required legislative proposal for the Emperor to approve. But a bill had to be introduced for the endorsement of the Duma within the first two months of the next Duma session; and the proposed measure could not alter the laws governing elections to the Duma. In defiance of this last provision, Stolypin persuaded his cabinet not only to dissolve the Second Duma (on June 3, 1907) so as to enable him to introduce his agrarian reforms by decree, but also substantially to alter the rules and system of election to the Duma, so as to ensure that the Third Duma would be dominated by more conservative and moderate delegates than the Second. This *coup d'état*, as it is usually described . . . , was vociferously condemned by the more radical liberals, for many of whom the Duma became "tainted." On the other hand, there was not the remotest possibility of passing the agrarian laws in the Second Duma, or in any Duma elected on a similar franchise. It is, at all events, arguable that in a country in which constitutional practice is still in its infancy the slow process of learning this subtle art must be helped along by the occasional rough jolt. But there were many moderate and responsible men who rejected this argument, and who is to say that they were wrong in maintaining that a result, however desirable, can never be achieved by illegal means? This issue became even more acute in the Western zemstvo crisis referred to later.

The famous land reform was embodied in three decrees, of October 5, November 9, and November 15, 1907, which were debated at great length both in the Duma and in the State Council, and were eventually passed into law on June 14, 1910. This did not leave Stolypin much time for his other reforms, before his life was cut short. Dr. Tokmakoff deals in a somewhat pedestrian manner with the debates in both chambers.[2] I suspect that the omissions from his accounts of the debates (and inclusion of much of little interest) are to be explained by the fact that he does not really appreciate the main idea underlying Stolypin's land reform—the transformation of millions of peasants from the status of subjects of public law to that of subjects of private law; or, in other words, from persons whose needs are protected by the state by means of communal rights, to persons whose rights are rights of individual property, governed by the civil law.

There is, to take one of several examples of such an omission, no mention of Count Olsufiev's argument in the State Council (which was typical of the patriarchal attitude to the peasants which was still common among landowners) that the Russian peasant had no real sense of or desire for private ownership—in other words, the traditional populist and Slavophile image of the peasant. The fallaciousness of

---

1. Quoting Hugh Seton-Watson, *The Russian Empire, 1801–1917* (1967), p. 631.—Ed.
2. Referring to George Tokmakoff, *P. A. Stolypin and the Third Duma: An Appraisal of the Three Major Issues* (1981).—Ed.

this view, which was widely held by opponents of the Stolypin reforms, was established beyond doubt, with a mass of evidence, by the late Dr. V. Leontovitsch.[3] Another argument omitted is that of Kropotov, the Trudovik (agrarian socialist) deputy in the Duma, that the effect of the reform was to deprive a member of the commune of his traditional right, embodied in decisions of the Senate, to have land allocated to him for his subsistence. This argument, true in itself, which was left without a reply by the government, went to the very heart of the Stolypin reforms, which were precisely designed to replace a right under public law by a private law right of ownership.

According to Stolypin in 1910, given ten years of peace Russia would be "unrecognizable." Of course, there were only four years of peace left. Even so, most critics of the Stolypin reforms concede them a measure of success in revitalizing Russian agriculture—and it is often forgotten that Stolypin's concern for peasant welfare was genuine, and that he was not merely motivated in putting through his reforms to effect a "wager on the strong," and to remove a powerful source of revolutionary unrest. By 1916, the last years of the old regime, nearly two and a half million households, or around twenty-four percent of the total number of households in forty provinces of European Russia, had obtained individual proprietorship, and there were nearly three quarters of a million applications pending. With the aid of the Land Bank, nearly ten million hectares were purchased by the peasants from the landed gentry [nobility] between 1906 and 1915. Resettlement in Siberia, which was a part of the Stolypin land reform, was also successful, and resulted in the creation in new areas of a prosperous and independent-minded peasantry. The "wager on the strong" was well under way when the war interrupted it. Even Lenin was forced to concede that the effect of Stolypin's policy might make it necessary for the social democrats to discard hopes of rallying the peasant mass to their side and to rely on the wage laborers on the land alone. Yet, while it is true that, given some more years of peace, the prospects of revolution in Russia might well have receded, the effect of the Stolypin reforms, uncompleted as they were, perhaps made the collapse in 1917 the more likely. For revolutions seem to occur where growth and high expectation are combined, and where an unyielding political order stands in the way of demands.

The so-called Western zemstvo crisis was an even more extreme example of Stolypin's indifference to constitutional niceties. Expanding the scope and activity of the local elected councils was an integral part of his program, and many restrictions on their powers were removed on his initiative in 1906. The question of introducing the zemstvo system to the six western provinces was complicated by the fact that, unless modifications were made to the existing system of elections, the better educated and economically stronger Polish inhabitants would predominate in the resulting councils at the expense of the Russian population. The matter was debated in 1910 and 1911. The bill was eventually passed in the Duma, but ran into strong

3. See his *Geschichte des Liberalismus in Russland [A History of Liberalism in Russia]* (1957), pp. 168–176.

opposition in the State Council which, combined with a right-wing intrigue to oust Stolypin from power, resulted in its defeat.

Dr. Tokmakoff devotes a detailed and useful chapter to an analysis of this crisis. Once again Stolypin resorted to Article 87 to get the bill passed, but, although he had taken this action in the interests of a policy approved by the Duma, his flouting of the normal constitutional process alienated all his former supporters in the Duma, and led to a severe decline of his political influence. Moreover, his intemperate action on this occasion, which had less justification perhaps than the resort to Article 87 in 1907, was a reaction against underhand intrigue by leaders of the right in the State Council and of the ambivalent behavior of the Emperor.

Six months later Stolypin was dead, shot in the presence of the Emperor at a performance in the Kiev opera house. His assassin was both a former police agent and a one-time revolutionary: the question whether the murder was plotted by the police at the instigation of right extremists, or was the act of a penitent revolutionary, has never been resolved—though Dr. Tokmakoff inclines to the latter view. In any case, the murder was symbolic of the way in which those who reject all-encompassing doctrines and systems as the solution for all ills—and such political actors have been rare in Russia—incur the enmity of both the extremes, the right and the left.

The classification of Stolypin by the late Professor Leontovitsch as a "conservative liberal" is probably not far off the mark, though the view has won few adherents. This is no doubt because those who find it hard to apply the term "liberal" to a man who was both a repressive upholder of order and one who achieved reform by defiance of the constitution, have not paused to reflect on Leontovitsch's detailed analysis of the whole concept of liberalism. This . . . sees the essence of liberalism as both preserving an existing type of government or social order, and developing and perfecting its features in the direction of liberty by dismantling institutions which hamper such liberty. Above all, liberalism does not consist of the replacement of one type by another, which was the aim of the main Russian liberal party, the Kadets, and of course of the revolutionary parties.

The policy of Stolypin lay precisely in completing the process started by the emancipation of the serfs by granting them the legal equality which the reform of 1861 had failed to provide. This lack of legal equality—of a status in private law as distinct from the protection of public law—Stolypin saw as the main obstacle to the development of legal order in Russia, which he often stated, and no doubt believed to be, his main aim. Can legal order be achieved by illegal acts? Unfortunately the change in the status of the peasants had not gone far enough by the time the collapse [revolution of 1917] came for this question to be answered.

# The Last Act

## Hans Rogger

On June 15/28, 1914, a member of the secret Serbian society "Union or
. . . Death"—which had for several years engaged in terror, sabotage, and
propaganda against Austria[1]—assassinated the Archduke Francis Ferdinand, heir
to the Habsburg throne, in the Bosnian city of Sarajevo. Austria blamed the Serbian
government and after receiving firm promises of German support, presented the
Serbians with an ultimatum. To its harsh and bullying demands the Serbians gave
a conciliatory reply which the German emperor thought had removed all reasons
for war. The Austrians, feeling that they must seize what might be their last chance
to pluck the Serbian thorn from their side, thought otherwise. On July 15/28 they
declared war on Serbia. All efforts to localize the conflict failed. To demonstrate
her resolve and prevent the annihilation of Serbia, Russia mobilized. Germany
demanded that Russia rescind her preparations and when she failed to do so,
declared war on Russia (July 19/August 1) and two days later on France. The
German invasion of Belgium, dictated by the necessity of striking quickly at France
before Russian forces could assemble in strength, brought England into the conflict
on the side of Russia and France.

The circumstances of Russia's involvement in the war [World War I] and the
fact that she would fight it alongside the Western democracies helped to win
acceptance for it in broad circles of Russian society. In Russia, as elsewhere, there
was a surge of patriotic enthusiasm all across the political spectrum and a closing
of ranks behind the government. The Duma politicians who had only yesterday
deplored its recalcitrance and incompetence seemed almost relieved to be rescued
from the impasse in which their isolation and irresolution had landed them. They
welcomed the tsar's wish "to be at one with his people in defence of Russia and
her Slav brothers against an insolent foe" and greeted the unity of purpose war
made necessary as a portent of lasting collaboration and mutual trust. The war,
commented a liberal review, had brought the nation to its senses. "What had
appeared unattainable in time of peace, was achieved."

The achievement was, in fact, the government's alone. It became even less
dependent on the goodwill of society and freed itself for most of the war from
Duma criticism and control by summoning that body for only brief periods and
adjourning it when it became an inconvenience or an embarrassment. During the
one-day session of July 26, the majority of its members practically invited the
administration to ignore them and exacted no promises or concessions for their
loyal support. The Duma's Octobrist president, [M. V.] Rodzianko, told a minister,

---

From Hans Rogger, *Russia in the Age of Modernisation and Revolution, 1881–1917* (London, New
York: Longman, 1983), pp. 255–269. Reprinted with the permission of the Longman Group UK Ltd.

1. "Austria" refers to the dual monarchy of Austria-Hungary, ruled by the Habsburg dynasty of king-
emperors; like the Russian and German empires, it too collapsed in World War I.—Ed.

"We shall only hinder you; it is better, therefore, to dismiss us altogether until the end of hostilities." The Kadet leader [Paul] Miliukov asked his party's friends and followers to suspend their quarrels with the government and to remember that their first duty was to preserve Russia one and indivisible and to defend her position as a great power. "In this struggle we are all as one; we present no conditions or demands; we simply throw upon the scales of battle our firm determination to overcome the aggressor."

Only the minuscule deputations of the Left—5 Bolsheviks, 6 Mensheviks, and 10 Trudoviki—refused to issue the government a blank check and denounced the ruling classes of all countries for the suffering and bloodshed they had brought upon workers and peasants. They did not, however, call for the defeat of tsarism as the lesser evil, as Lenin would shortly do. Their spokesmen—[Alexander] Kerensky for the Trudoviki and V. I. Khaustov for the Social Democrats—vowed that the Russian democracy and proletariat would defend the native land from any attacks, whatever their source; and having defended it, would set it free. When the Duma voted approval of the government's actions and credits for the war, the leftists, perhaps to avoid accusations of disloyalty if they opposed them, walked out or abstained. Even if they had been determined to "make war on war," they could not have been sure that the people would follow them. Mobilization went off smoothly, for the most part; there was little resistance to it either in the villages or the cities where strikes ceased almost completely for nearly a year.

Some of the most famous figures of the revolutionary movement—including the grand old men of anarchism and Marxism, [P. A.] Kropotkin and [George] Plekhanov—called upon their comrades to make the defeat of German militarism their first duty. There had been nothing like it in the Japanese war but, with Germany the enemy, it was different. Lenin might fume but even among his Bolsheviks patriotism—or "defensism"—took its toll. The story among the Socialist Revolutionaries was much the same. What remained of uncompromising defeatism, pacifism, or internationalism was silent or barely managed to survive abroad.

That the patriotic intoxication might be neither deep nor lasting, least of all among the masses who would bear the brunt of the burdens of war, was apparent to fearful conservatives even before hostilities began. In February 1914, P. N. Durnovo, now a member of the Council of State, pleaded with the emperor for an accommodation with Germany in order to avoid war. He predicted social revolution, the disintegration of the army, and hopeless anarchy in the likely event of military setbacks. N. A. Maklakov, the reactionary minister of interior, feared a repetition of what had happened in 1905. When he was brought the mobilization order for his signature he said: "War cannot be popular among the broad masses of the people who are more receptive to ideas of revolution than of victory over Germany." V. I. Gurko, an ex-assistant minister of interior, was close to the mark with his observation that although the war aroused neither patriotism nor indignation among peasants or workers, it deeply stirred the patriotic sentiments of the educated classes.

The reverses suffered by the armies in the opening months of the war were not yet so grave as to exhaust the sturdy endurance of the soldiers or the goodwill articulate society had extended the country's leaders. The great battles at Tannenberg and the Masurian Lakes of August and September [1914], which caused the

Russians to be driven out of East Prussia at a loss of 170,000 men in prisoners and casualties, were not decisive. They proved to be costly to the victorious Germans; they served to weaken the German front in the West, where Paris may have been saved by the shifting of troops to meet the unexpectedly rapid Russian onslaught; and they were balanced by the successes which Russian forces scored over the Austrians in Galicia and Bukovina, advancing as far as Cracow and northern Hungary by the beginning of November.

Yet victories and defeats alike revealed defects and created problems which reached an unprecedented magnitude with the offensives launched by the Central Powers in April 1915.[2] When the Russians ended their retreat in September and were able to stabilize their defenses on a line running from just west of Riga in Livland [Latvia] south to Czernowitz (Chernovtsy) in Bukovina, they had given up not only the conquests of the previous year, Galicia and Bukovina, but also all of Poland, with its industries and coalmines, as well as Courland, Lithuania, and much of White Russia [Belorussia]. And against the Turks, who had entered the war in October 1914, the Russian high command had to send twenty-two badly needed divisions to the Caucasian front.

The vaunted Russian steamroller, the nightmare of an endless flood of men which had haunted the German General Staff, turned out to be neither unstoppable nor inexhaustible. During the five months of the Great Retreat of 1915 there were almost a million dead and wounded and another million taken prisoner. In the campaigns of 1914 the losses had been nearly as great. The rate at which trained conscripts and reserves had then been expended contributed to the later debacle and to the manpower crisis in a country which put fewer men into uniform than did Germany and barely more than France with their much smaller populations. Of the nearly 15 million men who served in the [Russian] forces during three years of the war, about half were eliminated by enemy action: 2.4 million prisoners; 2.8 million wounded and sick; 1.8 million killed.

The reasons for this carnage and Russia's failure to make better use of her human resources are many, and they have been examined in detail in two studies which are indispensable to an understanding of events at and behind the eastern front.[3] Before the war lack of money restricted the annual intake of conscripts to about one-third of the available manpower; as a result much less of it was trained than in Germany or France. The shortage of officers and noncoms was another factor keeping that proportion down and it got worse when high casualty rates among the regulars caused them to be replaced by inexperienced men who were often as disaffected as the soldiers they were supposed to lead, yet rarely gained their respect. Difficulties of supply and support services over great distances, poor roads and railways, also limited the number of troops who could be put into the front lines when and where they were needed.

---

2. The Central Powers: Germany, Austria-Hungary, Bulgaria, Turkey. They were opposed by the Allies—principally Britain and France as well as Russia and, after April 1917, the United States.—Ed.
3. Norman Stone, *The Eastern Front, 1914–1917* (1975); Allan K. Wildman, *The End of the Russian Imperial Army* (1980).

An erratic and inequitable system of exemptions and deferments allowed many to escape conscription which was, in any case, unable to reach into every corner of the vast empire. And what a more determined effort at mobilization could lead to among people who were indifferent or hostile to the Russian war effort was shown in the Central Asian revolt of 1916. Thus, technical constraints and prudence made less of Russia's manpower available as trained combat soldiers than mere numbers would suggest. The deficiency became critical because the extraordinary wastage of men and *matériel* had not been anticipated. No country was prepared for the kind of bloodletting or for the enormous expenditure of weapons and ammunition that occurred. But Russia faced more and greater obstacles in repairing the material, moral, and political damage those losses inflicted.

The shortages of artillery, machineguns, rifles, shells, and bullets that caused such havoc and demoralization—although poor generalship bears a large part of the blame for the defeats and casualties of 1914 and 1915—were remedied most easily. By the end of 1916 the Russians were at least as well provided as their adversaries, perhaps better. Industry, and especially the larger and more modern firms which had not used their full capacity before the war, was able to supply most of the army's needs. Allied help, previously blocked by Turkey's barring of the Straits, began to arrive by way of newly built or expanded rail lines to White Sea and Pacific ports and could be expected to increase in 1917.

In spite of the fact that Russian industry performed better than has generally been thought—[Norman] Stone attributes its problems to rapid modernization, not backwardness—there were economic as well as non-economic limits to the maintenance and even more to the bettering of its performance. Whether it could have continued to meet the demands of the military as well as other essential requirements is far from certain. Output in such important sectors as iron ore and coal, pig iron and steel, began to drop in 1916, before the catastrophic declines of revolutionary 1917. Scarcities of fuel and raw material were aggravated by the disruption of foreign trade and domestic transport, the latter caused by the disrepair of rolling stock and the loss of key railways in enemy-occupied territory. Labor productivity declined with the employment of unskilled hands, including large numbers of women. Not until 1915, when it was too late for many of them, were workers in critical occupations exempted from conscription. With 80 percent of the labor force engaged in war production, little if any improvement could be obtained by adding to it and further cutting back the manufacture of consumer goods which were already in short supply.

Industry's impressive record in supplying the armies was achieved by guaranteeing huge profits and neglecting needs which turned out to be as imperative as those of the military. By the end of 1915 the production of agricultural machinery had fallen by half; together with the requisitioning of horses and the cessation of imports, this had obvious and predictable consequence for the ability of agriculture to feed workers and soldiers and keep food prices from soaring. The lack of machinery (as of chemical fertilizer) was much less damaging, however, for the bulk of the peasantry than for the owners of estates and prosperous farms who were the chief users and purchasers of both. With the virtual ending of shipments abroad and the introduction of prohibition in 1914, there should have been enough grain for the armies and cities.

Peasant producers were, in fact, able to better their output and incomes, thanks to good weather, the relative abundance of labor, state payments for soldiers' dependents and requisitions, and the expansion of ploughland. If the marketed share of harvests declined from 25 percent pre-war to 15 percent in 1916/17, the explanation lies once again in the disorganization of transport, but more importantly in the failure of industry to produce common items of consumption—such as tools, boots, cloth, and nails—in quantities and at prices that would have induced the peasants to part with their grain. Since the "scissor" . . . between what they had to pay and what they received was constantly widening, the peasants preferred to eat their produce themselves, to feed it to their animals, or to withhold it in expectation of better terms of trade. Profiteers and speculators made matters worse, while neither the state's fixing of uniform grain prices in September 1916 nor the setting of allotment and delivery quotas in November improved them. By that time the cities, their populations swollen with six million newcomers, were getting less than half the foodstuffs they required. In the last two weeks of January 1917 food shipments to Moscow fell 60 percent short of need; the northern capital, renamed Petrograd in 1914, had only a few days' grain reserves when bread riots broke out in February.

The army was beginning to feel the pinch as well. At the end of 1916 the bread ration was cut from three to two pounds and then to one. Soldiers so thoroughly detested the lentils which were issued to supplement it that they "can almost be accounted as a major cause of the Revolution."[4] There were, of course, others of equal or greater importance and the revolution did not start at the fronts, which were holding, but in the rear. The grumbling about poor food—what kind of government was it that could not assure its fighting men of enough coarse rye bread to fill their stomachs?—was only one manifestation of the discontent which had been growing among the troops from the very beginning of hostilities.

The obvious superiority of the German enemy in the skills and engines of war, the devastating casualties he inflicted, and the woeful inadequacy of their medical and supply services robbed the men of what little patriotic fervor there was among them. They very quickly became convinced that . . . the war could not be won, and that even if it could, they would not survive it. Whether they blamed incompetent generals, cowardly and cruel officers, greedy landlords, Jewish spies, or German influences at court and in government, they deserted it physically.

That the armies had more and better weapons in 1916, that dressing stations and field hospitals were much improved thanks to the Unions of Towns and Zemstvos, made little difference to men who feared that the slaughter would only be prolonged. The Russian offensives of 1916 on the northern, south-western, and Turkish fronts, and in particular the spectacular advance of General A. A. Brusilov against the Austrians in Volynia, Galicia, and Bukovina proved them right; they cost another million casualties and brought no lasting or decisive gains. Brusilov's advance was stopped with the aid of fifteen German divisions brought from France. The Rumanians, who had been encouraged by his success to enter the war on

4. Wildman, p. 108.

Russia's side in August, were hard pressed by the Central Powers and instead of relieving the Russians, needed their help.

Towards the end of 1915 there had already been conscription riots in several cities and attacks on the police who did not have to serve. A year later mutinies involving several combat regiments were reported. Such incidents were still few and they were quickly dealt with, but more passive and subtle forms of insubordination were widespread: from the sullen and half-hearted execution of orders to malingering, voluntary capture, individual desertions to the rear, and self-mutilation, the so-called "finger wounds." They gave clear warning that the front-line units, whose ranks were being replenished with hastily trained raw youths and angry family men in their forties, were not immune from the war-weariness and disgruntlement that infected the garrison towns of the rear. The unwilling warriors who filled them—replacements, trainees, and recovering wounded—represented half the army's strength in 1916 and proved to be its weakest link in 1917.

The letters and rumors that reached the soldiers in the field telling of conditions at home contributed to their demoralization and the feeling that it was they and their worker and peasant families who suffered most of the privations. There were, it is true, jobs to be had as well as higher wages in the burgeoning war industries, on the railroads, in mines, and on landowners' estates to make up for the closing of many cottage and consumer goods industries and the earnings of men who had gone to war. But for much of the unskilled labor which replaced them there was also lower pay, compulsory overtime, the lifting of restrictions on night work for women and children, and beginning in 1915 the inflation which soon wiped out the gains even of favored workers in defense plants. The scarcity of consumer goods and food and the government's fiscal policy combined to make Russia's inflation worse than that of other warring countries. In the second half of 1916 the price index was almost three times above the level of 1913; by the beginning of 1917 the paper ruble had lost two-thirds of its pre-war value. High rents and prices, long lines for food and fuel, and terrible crowding in the working-class quarters of the urban centers led to the revival of the strike movement, which in 1916 approached the scope of the immediate pre-war period. In Petrograd the first case of soldiers refusing to fire on strikers occurred in October. A month later 5,000 troops demonstrated in sympathy with striking workers in a Ukrainian town.

Efforts to control prices and guarantee the provisioning of the cities were late and ineffective. The sporadic rationing of certain commodities did not begin until the autumn of 1916 when sugar cards were introduced in Moscow. The measure did not fill the stores which issued them: it drove up prices in the open market to which supplies were now diverted, and it heightened anxieties. The rationing of flour and bread in Moscow on February 20, 1917, caused panic buying, shortages, and rumors of worse to come which spread to Petrograd and led to riots there. It was beyond the capacity of the government to enforce or win acceptance for a comprehensive and equitable system of rationing, price controls, and procurements. The millions of suspicious peasants who had reverted to a subsistence or barter economy would hardly be affected by it and the larger producers and traders successfully opposed it by threatening, more or less openly, to withhold deliveries unless they could be sure of what they considered an adequate return.

The minister of agriculture, who happened also to be a leader of the United Nobility, an agrarian pressure group, justified the raising of grain prices in September 1916 by saying, not incorrectly, that without such an inducement production would decline. A state project for the procurement of coal at fixed prices and its planned distribution was turned down by a solid front of mine owners and other industrialists as an unwarranted infringement of the freedom of enterprise. Fiscal policy was similarly hampered by considerations of feasibility and politics. To pay for the war and to make up for lost income from the liquor monopoly, railways, and customs duties, indirect taxes were raised; but there were limits to what the sorely tried consumer could be made to pay. Income and excess profits taxes, finally adopted in 1916, were kept ridiculously low to avoid drying up sources of capital and alienating its owners; they yielded little revenue and were useless as demonstrations that the rich were paying a fair share of the war's costs. These had to be met for the most part by loans and recourse to the printing press with the inflationary results already described.

The liberality the government thought it wise or necessary to extend to powerful economic interests was not matched in the political arena. It served, on the contrary, to divide and weaken an opposition which was beginning to revive in 1915. In that desperate year, as news of military bungling and disasters reached the public, small gestures of goodwill and the sacrifice of unpopular ministers were offered to society and answered their purpose of forestalling a concerted assault on the regime. In January [1915] the recall of the Duma appeased for a time the increasingly restive politicians who were allowed to reaffirm their unity with the government in the prosecution of the war and, as agreed in advance, to pass its budget. With Mensheviks and Trudoviki abstaining—the Bolshevik deputies, in violation of their parliamentary immunity, had been arrested—there was no opposition. After three days the Duma was recessed; its members dispersed without protesting, at least in public. During the session only Kerensky and a Progressive deputy questioned the wisdom of their uncritical and undemanding compliance.

The worsening situation at the fronts and pressure from their constituents made it impossible for the leaders of the moderate parties to continue their silent endorsement of the administration. It was now proving what had been feared all along—that the bureaucracy was incapable of organizing itself for war. Tacitly admitting its inadequacy, it allowed a larger role to organizations and individuals it had previously kept at arm's length.

The Unions of Towns and Zemstvos, formed in 1914 for war relief, were suspect because of their liberal leanings and tolerated rather than welcomed. In June 1915 they were [nonetheless] permitted to join forces in Zemgor to enlist light industries and rural artisans in the filling of state orders for army supplies. A Central War Industries Committees, headed by [A. I.] Guchkov, was established at the same time to coordinate the activities of larger enterprises. Both organizations were represented on the Special Councils for Defense, Food, Fuel and Transportation set up in August where they sat side by side with deputies of the Duma and State Council and representatives of the ministries who were in the majority.

The economic importance of the voluntary or public organizations was modest; their share of war production, it has been estimated, was no more than 5 percent of the total, the rest being furnished by state-owned firms (15 percent) or the giants of heavy industry and the syndicates (80 percent) which the government found less troublesome and more efficient. They did, however, contribute to the rising chorus of demands that the regime show greater trust in society and seek its help by recalling the Duma. Nicholas was persuaded of the advisability of doing so by the moderate members of his cabinet. In order to avoid an open confrontation with the legislature, he parted with four of the more offensive of their colleagues, including [I. V.] Shcheglovitov (Justice), whose name was connected with the shameful Beilis affair,[5] and Maklakov (Interior) who insisted to the last that the Duma posed a threat to the emperor's power and should become a purely consultative organ. But the retention of Goremykin as head of the cabinet [prime minister, 1914–1916] spelled trouble, as did the politicians' realization that their continued silence would be interpreted as surrender.

Six weeks after it was convened on July 19, 1915, the Duma was prorogued (September 3). A few weeks later the tsar refused to receive a delegation of the Unions of Towns and Zemstvos on the grounds that they were political in nature; his wife urged him to get rid of Guchkov and the War Industries Committee. There had obviously been no change of heart, only a cosmetic correction of course that was reversed when the Duma and especially the public organizations proved to be less tractable than expected and to have allies in the cabinet and at army headquarters.

The Duma had, in fact, offered very reasonable terms for its collaboration in hopes of prolonging its own life and keeping more militant forces from supplanting it. A Nationalist [party] resolution, adopted on the first day of the session and calling for a ministry enjoying the confidence of the nation (instead of the Progressives' "ministry responsible to the Duma"), became the basis on which a broad spectrum of some 300 out of 430 members joined with a group from the State Council to form the Progressive Bloc.

In late August [1915] confident that their numbers, their moderation, the sympathy of most ministers, and the government's loss of popularity would convince the tsar to accept it, they presented the Bloc's program. It asked for no structural changes in the institutions of state, merely for a united cabinet able and willing to cooperate with the legislature and to gain its confidence and that of the country by a strict observance of legality in its dealings with society. To unify the nation for victory a number of immediate conciliatory steps, as well as agreement on future legislation, were deemed essential: imperial clemency for persons charged with or exiled for religious and political offences; an end to the persecution of religious groups and workers' organizations; submission of bills for Polish autonomy and of a program "beginning the abolition of restrictions on the rights of Jews"; relief for Finns and Ukrainians; equalization of peasants' rights with those of other classes; the introduction of zemstvos in the [peasant] volosts, Siberia, and the Caucasus, and a lessening of bureaucratic control over all organs of local government.

---

5. Shcheglovitov's Ministry of Justice had tried for two years to prove that Mendel Beilis, a Jewish clerk, was guilty of the ritual murder of a Christian boy (actually killed by a gang of thieves). At his trial in Kiev in 1913 Beilis was acquitted.—Ed.

Goremykin, who was a prime target of the Bloc, which would not have found him acceptable in a reformed ministry, easily persuaded Nicholas to reject its overtures and to adjourn the Duma. Dismissals of several ministers favorable to the Bloc followed in short order. They, indeed the entire cabinet with the exception of Goremykin and the service ministers, had already incurred the emperor's displeasure by a collective plea (and tender of resignation) that he reverse his decision of taking the place of the Grand Duke Nikolai Nikolaevich as commander of the armies at headquarters (*Stavka*) in Western Russia. They feared that henceforth the monarch and the monarchy would be held directly responsible for military reverses; that the emperor's absence from the capital would only compound the existing confusion and conflicts of authority between Stavka and government, generals and ministers, front and rear; and that the empress's meddling in high politics against the Duma and its ministerial allies would get worse, as it did.

"Had you given in now in these different questions," [Empress] Alexandra wrote to her husband [Nicholas II], "they would have dragged out yet more of you." Judging by their reactions, neither the ministers nor the leaders of the Bloc were likely to do so. The former, told by the emperor to stay at their posts and follow his and Goremykin's orders, obediently awaited their dismissals; the latter, although stunned and angered by the unexpected turn of events, carried out none of their threats of boycotting the war effort, appealing to the tsar, or taking their case to the country. Failure, the lack of any response, would advertise their impotence, as had happened with the futile Vyborg Appeal after the dissolution of the First Duma. Success would transfer the battle from parliament into the streets. That would defeat one of the chief purposes of the Bloc, the very one which had given it such broad support. As expressed by the Nationalist deputy V. V. Shulgin, it was "to replace the discontent of the masses, which might easily turn into revolution, with the discontent of the Duma." Shulgin and others were beginning to wonder whether they were not fanning rather than dampening the fires of revolution and the thought kept them from pressing their attack.

The dilemma of the moderates was most pronounced and painful for the liberal wing of the Bloc which was torn and ultimately paralyzed by contrary pulls to left and right. On the one side, favored by the Progressives and Left Kadets, there lay common action with radical groups, mass movements, and the more militant of the public organizations towards a seizure of power; on the other, preservation of the Bloc and of the alliance with its conservative members, pressure on the government to mend its ways, and the maintenance of social peace, for revolution invited defeat. If organizing Russia for victory required organizing her for revolution, the Kadet leader Miliukov told a special session of the Duma in March 1916, he would wish to leave her as she was, unorganized, while the war lasted.

By November 1916, with victory nowhere in sight, with Goremykin replaced (in January) by the inept B. V. Sturmer who was close to the empress and Rasputin[6] and wrongly suspected of pro-German leanings, Miliukov accused the government

---

6. Grigory Novykh (1872–1916), adopted surname Rasputin (from Russian for "libertine"), the notorious hypnotist and faith healer who had worked his way into the Empress's confidence.—Ed.

of claiming that to organize the country meant to organize a revolution. He charged that it preferred chaos and disorganization to joining forces with society and asked, "What is this, stupidity or treason?"—repeating the question each time he listed one of the administration's sins of omission or commission. The implication of sinister and treacherous influences working behind the scenes for a separate peace with Germany gained credibility from Sturmer's name and the empress's German birth. Miliukov's speech, which the censor deleted from press accounts of the Duma sitting, circulated in mimeographed and typewritten copies, inflaming popular hatred of "that German woman" and more vaguely all who were held responsible for the miseries of war, from ministers to policemen.

Intemperate and offensive as his language had been, Miliukov had not departed from constitutional propriety. He had asked for no more than what the Bloc had demanded for over a year: the replacement of a cabinet which he called incapable and ill-intentioned by one acceptable to the Duma majority. His denunciations did not achieve even that limited goal, although they were echoed all across the house to the benches of the far right. They merely persuaded the tsar, over the objections of his wife, to part with Sturmer and to entrust the chairmanship of the Council of Ministers to A. F. Trepov, minister of transport. The mentally unbalanced and universally detested A. D. Protopopov, a protege of Alexandra and Rasputin, retained the ministry of interior to the very end. Until the next round of "ministerial leapfrog" only one other portfolio, that of agriculture, changed hands.

Trepov had been chosen because he had better relations with the Duma than Sturmer; having secured its quiet adjournment on December 17 to February 14, 1917—even Miliukov did not really want to rouse a storm lest it "break out in a form we do not desire"—he was asked by Nicholas to resign after six weeks in office. His successor was an outsider to government, Prince N. D. Golitsyn, who had no political experience, influence, or ambitions. He was the last occupant of the post which he had accepted with the utmost reluctance and held for only two months.

The specters of a mass rising and a lost war which Miliukov had hoped to banish by his verbal attack drove other men to still more desperate strategems. Guchkov [see Documents below] had come to feel that the only way to save the country and the monarchy was to remove the monarch. In August 1916 he began to lay the groundwork for a plot which would with the help of a group of young cavalry officers and elements of the Petrograd garrison depose Nicholas and install a new government. Some generals were sympathetic but unwilling to commit themselves in advance. Guchkov's illness delayed preparations for the coup, planned for the middle of March, until it was too late. Its success would not, in all probability, have changed the course of history profoundly.

The murder on December 16–17 [1916] of Rasputin, the supposed author of Russia's misfortunes, had little impact on the course of events. He fell victim to a conspiracy which three men had entered to rid the dynasty of its evil genius: Grand Duke Dmitry Pavlovich, Prince Iusupov (a nephew by marriage of the tsar), and the head of the proto-fascist Union of the Archangel Michael, Purishkevich, who had denounced Rasputin in the Duma as a "filthy, vicious, and venal muzhik." Their deed had no political effects and if it was welcomed by some citizens; others, ever ready to believe the worst of their "masters," were sure he had been done in because he was a simple peasant who worked for peace.

All three attempts to improve the nation's chances for victory by changes of personnel at the heights of power betrayed an inability to recognize or admit how wide was the gulf in late 1916 between the mass of ordinary Russians and respectable society—all those who would soon be categorized as the bourgeoisie. The former were no longer interested in victory, if they had ever been, and more and more often they blamed society, represented in the Duma and the voluntary organizations, as much as the tsar and his officials, for prolonging their hardships. Hostility to the war had grown so much among the workers that their representatives at a December conference of War Industries Committees (WICs) felt compelled to voice it by criticizing the Duma for its refusal to discuss German peace feelers.

The Workers Groups of the Central WIC at Petrograd and of its provincial branches were the only legal channels, with the closely watched exception of factory sick benefit and insurance funds, for the expression of labor's views and wants. They were virtually its only channels, and a privileged one at that, because the police had disrupted the work of the trade unions and the radical parties. In order to secure the collaboration of the workers and the support of their leaders, Guchkov and the industrialists of the WICs had in the summer of 1915 obtained the grudging assent of the government to the election of worker delegates to the committees. The first group, chosen in the factories of Petrograd in November 1915, was followed by others and by May 1916 worker representatives had been elected to 20 regional and 98 district WICs. Their uniquely protected status allowed them not only to defend the workers' material interests and to encourage their organization; they also made use of their access to the factories to raise political issues bearing on the conduct and goals of the war.

Anti-war socialists—Bolsheviks, Maximalist SRs, and Internationalist Mensheviks—, although they differed over the tactics to be followed in resisting the imperialist conflict, denounced collaboration with the bourgeoisie as treason to the working class and "social chauvinism." They were unable, however, to overcome the arguments of defensist or pragmatic Mensheviks and SRs that membership in the WICs offered unique opportunities for organizing the working class, protecting its rights, and articulating its political demands. The Mensheviks in particular saw the Workers' Groups as the nucleus of a broad-based labor movement which could, in guarded cooperation with the liberal bourgeoisie, fight a reactionary regime for the democratization of the political order and capital for the satisfaction of workers' needs.

That their entry into the WICs did not mean cooptation by the bourgeoisie, or wholehearted support of the war, the workers' representatives made clear from the very beginning. They declared that an irresponsible government had taken Russia into a war for capitalist markets—a far cry from making Prussian militarism the chief culprit; that this government was making war on its own people; and that it bore the guilt, in which Duma politicians shared, for all the disasters which had befallen the country. A constituent assembly elected by universal suffrage; the immediate granting of full civil and religious liberty; the right of self-determination for the non-Russian nationalities; comprehensive social legislation, the eight-hour day, and land for the peasants were the most important demands put forward by the Petrograd Workers' Group in November 1915. It also embraced the central tenet of "revolutionary defensism," which Kerensky and the Menshevik N. S. Chkheidze had advanced in the Duma in August: a democratic peace without annexations or indemnities.

Yet for a year the Workers' Group urged caution upon the proletariat of the capital, warning against premature and isolated strikes, and recommending common action with other classes against the tsarist government. By the end of 1916 the workers' impatience and the competition of a growing number of Bolshevik and other militants made such restraint appear inadvisable, and the Workers' Group joined in a strike call for the anniversary of Bloody Sunday on January 9, 1917. It was answered by 140,000 or 40 percent of Petrograd's workers and was followed on February 14 by another strike of 84,000 which the Workers' Group had called for the reopening of the Duma. By that time its leaders had been arrested (January 27) and the strike movement, sometimes egged on, sometimes held back for tactical reasons by the militants, had assumed a life of its own. Strikes were still confined to individual shops and plants, moving from one to another without becoming general, and still concerned, for the most part, with wages, hours, and food supplies.

But on Thursday, February 23, which was International Women's Day, there began the unplanned and unforeseen transformation of uncoordinated strike action into a revolutionary rising. A week later it had led to the abdication of Nicholas (March 2) and the end of the Romanov dynasty when his brother, the Grand Duke Michael, renounced the throne (March 3). What distinguished the events of the first day of the Second [1917] Russian Revolution from those immediately preceding it was the determination of the strikers to take their grievances beyond the workplace to the center of the capital. Their purpose was to enlist its citizens in demonstrations which demanded on this and more insistently on subsequent days not only bread or even peace but the overthrow of the government and of autocracy.

As the strikes and marches gained momentum, they were aided by agitators and organizers of all socialist factions making the round of the factories—from members of the Worker's Group who were still at liberty to a thousand or more militant anti-war Mensheviks, SRs, and some 3,000 Bolsheviks. The demonstrators' biggest accretion of strength, however, came from the women of Petrograd and the soldiers of its garrison. The former, exasperated by hours of mostly futile waiting in bread lines, took to smashing bakeries and food shops; the latter followed them into open defiance of authority from which there was no turning back. The soldiers' sympathies were with the crowds, not with those who were going to send them to the front to be maimed or killed.

The soldiers' revolt was decisive in converting the workers' and women's angry protests into revolution. It was precipitated by an order Nicholas issued from GHQ (Stavka) on the night of February 25. Told for the first time of the extent of the disorders and of the general strike which had paralyzed Petrograd that day, he instructed the authorities, who hoped until then to confine the disturbances to the factory districts, to put them down with whatever force was required. When troops were ordered to fire on the demonstrators on the 26th and 27th [of February], their occasional disregard of officers' commands on previous days became a full-fledged mutiny, with soldiers joining the crowds in attacks on the hated police who were disarmed and went into hiding if they were not beaten or killed. By the 28th, Petrograd was in full insurrection and there were no longer any substantial units of loyal troops in the capital or in the nation's second city, Moscow, which fell to the insurgents on March 1.

There was, in fact, no longer a government in Russia. Late on the 27th the members of the cabinet, in their own timid version of mutiny or desertion, had resigned their posts. Knowing that the situation was out of control and that their lives were in danger, they covered their retreat by recommending to Nicholas that he appoint the Grand Duke Michael as temporary dictator. The tsar rejecting their suggestion as well as their resignation. The ministers chose discretion over obedience to their sovereign and so, in a matter of days, did the commanders of the armed forces in the field and at GHQ. They abandoned plans to march on the insurgent capital, backed the Duma leaders' demand for the abdication of Nicholas, and acquiesced in the demise of the monarchy because they were unsure whether it would help to preserve the loyalty of their men or be the cause of further disaffection.

The generals were also held back from an immediate commitment to counter-revolution by the misleading assurances they received from the president of the Duma, Rodzianko, that he and the politicians of the Progressive Bloc could control the revolution, halt the disintegration of army and country, and save the dynasty if the tsar appointed a responsible ministry chosen from their midst. When Nicholas acceded, it was already too late, as Rodzianko, the politicians, the generals, and the emperor himself quickly realized. The mood of the masses was so implacably anti-monarchist that the removal of Nicholas became a necessity and his replacement by Michael, either as regent for the young tsarevich [Crown Prince Aleksei, or Alexis] or as tsar in his own right, an impossibility. The moderates were thus deprived of the symbol of authority, continuity, and legitimacy they craved and thought necessary for the nation's acceptance of their rule and the return of stability.

Formation on February 27 by leaders of the Progressive Bloc of a Temporary Duma Committee to "re-establish order in the capital and for liaison with persons and institutions," was their first hesitant step towards the assumption of governmental responsibility. It was taken in response to the prorogation of the Duma, which had been the last premier's last act on [February 26], and to the revolution of the streets which the Bloc's members had neither wanted nor made. Yet it was to them, meeting unofficially and in the greatest perplexity in the Duma's Tauride Palace, that much of the city's populace looked for leadership when the agencies of the tsar's government ceased to function or were no longer obeyed. Although it had been elected [in 1912] on a most restricted franchise and was felt to represent property and privilege, the Duma was the only established institution which enjoyed a measure of public respect because it had been critical of the regime of which it was a part. The mere fact that some of its members continued to meet after prorogation was taken as an act of defiance which ranged them on the side of revolution.

The leaderless soldiers who came to pledge support for the Temporary Committee and thereby to gain approval for their rebellion also found installed in the

Tauride Palace the Executive Committee of the Petrograd Soviet [Council] of Workers' and (subsequently) Soldiers' Deputies which had been formed almost simultaneously with the Duma Committee. It was the creation of socialist intellectuals and politicians, for the most part Mensheviks and members of the Workers' Group released from prison by the crowds, who appealed to workers and soldiers to send delegates from their factories and units to the Soviet's first session to be held on the evening of the 27th. That meeting, at which there were as yet few worker and soldier delegates, elected the Menshevik Duma deputy Chkheidze as chairman of the Soviet, Kerensky and another socialist Duma member (M. I. Skobelev) as vice-chairmen, and a regular Executive Committee on which all the socialist parties were represented.

In spite of the fact that the Soviet claimed to speak for the "Russian democracy," the revolutionary masses, and although it organized district committees, a workers' militia, and a military commission, it did not lay claim to sole leadership of the revolution or the state. The Soviet's leaders were not setting up an alternative government to the one they expected the bourgeoisie to establish but an organ for watching over it and for defending and deepening the gains of the revolution.

The moderates none the less perceived the Soviet as a competitor for power, which at this time only a few of the most radical socialists wished it to be. Fear of the Soviet and of the growing anarchy finally pushed even the most reluctant members of the Temporary Committee of the Duma to form a Provisional Government on March 2 and to announce it to the country on the next day. They did so as the presumptive legatees of the Duma which had ceased to function, without the stamp of continuity and legality that a ruler or regent might have supplied, but with the half-hearted agreement of the Soviet to accept the new government in so far as it continued to struggle against the old regime and acted to realize the reforms it had promised.

These included an immediate and complete amnesty, the full range of civil liberties, the abolition of all national and religious restrictions, and the "immediate preparation for the convocation of the Constituent Assembly . . . which will determine the form of government and the constitution of the country."

The complexion of the new government—it contained six Kadets, two Progressives, two Octobrists, one non-party liberal and one nominal socialist—was to the left of the Duma Committee and the Progressive Bloc. Its make-up reflected an awareness of how far the moderate opposition had been left behind by the radicalization of the masses. Yet in their eyes the cabinet, with the exception of Kerensky (who now declared himself a Socialist Revolutionary), was still too closely identified with the old order and the upper classes. G. E. Lvov, the non-party liberal who had been head of the Union of Zemstvos, became premier and minister of interior; he was a large landowner and bore the unfortunate title of prince. There were two wealthy industrialists among the ministers, A. I. Konovalov and M. I. Tereshchenko; Guchkov, the minister of war and navy, was suspect because of his monarchism and because he, like Miliukov at the Foreign Ministry, was known to favor the vigorous prosecution of the war. Whether a government committed to that end, however it was composed, would be able to maintain the quiet which was gradually returning to the streets of Petrograd remained to be seen.[7]

# DOCUMENTS

Alexander I. Guchkov (1862–1936) was born in Moscow, the scion of a wealthy industrialist family of peasant Old Believer origins. After graduating from Moscow University (1885) he studied in Germany, traveled the world, and acquired a reputation as something of a swashbuckler; Bernard Pares, the contemporary English specialist on Russia, compared him with Winston Churchill—against whom Guchkov fought in the Boer War, in South Africa, in 1900: an ardent Russian nationalist, he had been eager to fight the British Empire personally. His career as a "public man" began in Moscow city politics; in 1905, in response to Nicholas II's October Manifesto, he helped found the Union of October 17, or Octobrist party. The Octobrists were committed to realizing in practice the constitutional monarchy promised in the manifesto, with its guaranteed civil liberties for all and representative legislature (Duma) based on general (but not direct) manhood suffrage. Their party, dominated by landowners and businessmen, achieved very limited success in the elections to the first two Dumas, but with Stolypin's electoral "reform" of June 1907 they became the largest single party bloc—or "fraction"—in the Third and Fourth Dumas. Guchkov, elected a deputy to the Third Duma from Moscow, led the Octobrist fraction, supported Stolypin (also an Octobrist), and became head of the Duma's Defense Commission, where he ardently championed military modernization. In a famous speech in May 1908 he denounced the continued meddling in military affairs by highly placed amateurs, mentioning several grand dukes by name; for this he earned Nicholas II's lasting enmity. In 1910 he was elected chairman of the Third Duma but resigned in March 1911 when Stolypin prorogued the Duma in order to pass by Imperial decree his Western zemstvo bill (see Schapiro essay above)—a sign of the splintering of the Octobrist party and of the intensifying legislative stalemate. With Stolypin's assassination (1911) Guchkov began a public campaign against the "dark forces" in general, Rasputin in particular, whose influence at court, he and much of the Duma thought, was blocking the achievement of constitutionalism and necessary reform. These and other alarms are sounded in the notably prescient speech, reprinted below, that he delivered to a conference of the Octobrist party in St. Petersburg on November 8, 1913.

With the outbreak of World War I Guchkov resumed his earlier Red Cross connections and went to the front. In despair at the course of events, he went so far in 1916 as to plan the coup against Nicholas II described above by Professor Rogger; his role in Nicholas's abdication is mentioned in the second of these documents. Guchkov was named minister of war and marine in the first Provisional Government (March 2, 1917), but by the end of April he felt compelled to resign amid rising antiwar and "anti-bourgeois" pressures. With the Bolshevik takeover of the revolution in October, which he vigorously opposed, Guchkov left Russia to settle first in Berlin and then in Paris.

---

7. The determination of the Provisional Government to fight the war to the finish is considered by historians a major reason for its fall to the Bolsheviks in October 1917.—Ed.

The second document gives an eyewitness account of the abdication of Nicholas II, an event that may be taken to mark the end of the Imperial period of Russian history. Its author, Nicolas de Basily (N. A. Vazily, 1883–1963), was educated (1897–1903) at the Imperial Alexander Lycée located at Tsarskoe Selo near St. Petersburg, site of the Emperor's principal residence (built by Empress Elizabeth, extensively remodeled by Catherine the Great); the purpose of the school, founded by Alexander I, was to train sons of noblemen for careers in state service. Basily was the third generation of his family—of Balkan and French descent—to serve in the Imperial diplomatic service, where his father had risen to the top and also been appointed chamberlain of the Emperor's court. Young Basily's senior thesis at the Alexander Lycée, devoted to the constitutional projects of Michael Speransky (Raeff essay, Chapter 7), won first prize "in spite of the fact," as he says in his memoirs, "that we were still living under an autocratic regime." Notwithstanding the school's prevailing monarchism, fueled by the Emperor's annual visit, his courses chiefly in law and modern languages "usually had a certain liberal air to them," and his teachers included known liberals and socialists. On his father's death in 1902 he inherited the family estate in southern Russia, farmed by German Mennonite immigrants; in 1903, the year he entered the diplomatic service, he imported an Oldsmobile from the United States, one of the first cars seen in Russia. Such details of his life, taken from his memoirs, reflect the variety of influences shaping the Imperial elite in what proved to be its last generation—an elite that was devoted to serving, and preserving, the Empire founded by Peter the Great.

In February 1917 Basily was serving as director of the Diplomatic Chancellery at Imperial Army headquarters (Stavka) in Mogilev (Belorussia). This position put him in direct contact with the Emperor (since September 1915 acting as commander-in-chief of the armed forces), with General Mikhail Alekseev (Alexeev), the army chief of staff, and other senior officers; with government officials in Petrograd, and, as the political crisis in the capital deepened, with leaders of the Duma. He was the only official at Stavka with legal training and capable therefore of giving legal advice and drafting legal documents. His description of the abdication is taken from his memoirs, which were written in exile (in French) with the aid of a large cache of papers that he took with him from Russia in 1919 and that are now in the archives of the Hoover Institution in Stanford, California.


## A. I. Guchkov Warns of Impending Disaster, 1913

The chief aim of our [Octobrist Party] Conference is not to revise our political *credo*, our program. There is nothing in the program for us to renounce; and for the present, unfortunately, there is nothing to add to it. The first stage which we marked out has not yet been traversed, and it is still early to set up further landmarks along the same route. If our program had been carried out, we should now see our country completely regenerated. And here we may note a curious

From *The Russian Review* (University of Liverpool, England; London, Thomas Nelson and Sons), vol. 3 no. 1 (1914), pp. 141–58.

feature in our history. Our program is for us a normal one, but at the time when it was drafted [1905] it was condemned from the standpoint of orthodox radicalism as heretical, as extravagantly moderate and retrograde. Now it has penetrated into the consciousness of broader circles and has become a minimum program even for more radical parties.

The burning question of the hour is not one of principle, or of the general objects which the Octobrist Party has in view, but one of the ways and means by which these principles may be put into effect and these objects attained—in a word, the question of tactics. This question has been placed in the forefront by the course of events during the last few years, and by the general political situation at the present moment. What should the tactics of the Party be? What attitude should it take up toward the other factors in the political life of the nation, more especially toward the government and to other political parties? A practical examination of this question has already begun. A process of evolution in our tactics has already set in—a *process* which has perhaps not always been realized, and in any case has not been systematised and clearly formulated.

To find and verify this formula, to affirm it as the categorical imperative of further political work for all organs of our party, this is the first and most important task of our Conference. This will be at once an important act of our own political consciousness and an event of very great significance in the political life of the country at large. It is natural, accordingly, that public attention should be focused, as it now is, on the question we are discussing, as to the further tactics of the Union [Party], and the position it is to adopt.

Octobrism had its origin in the heart of that liberal Opposition which grew up around the Zemstvo in the struggle against the reactionary policy adopted by the government about the end of the sixties [1860s], and was maintained, with accidental and temporary digressions, until the time of disorders in the early years of the present century. This Opposition did what cultural work it could within the narrow limits and under the unfavorable conditions imposed by the general political situation, but it never lost sight of the necessity of making fundamental political reforms based on national representation as the headstone of the corner. The nucleus of Octobrists who in November, 1905, founded the Octobrist Party, was formed out of the minority in the Zemstvo Congresses. This minority joined in the general demand for broad liberal reforms in all departments of life and for a transition from the obsolete forms of unlimited autocracy to a constitutional system; but it set its face against the passion for unbridled radicalism and against socialistic experiments which threatened to bring in their train grave political and social disturbances. The men who formed the Octobrist Party from the first marked themselves off sharply from those revolutionary elements which thought to take advantage of the embarrassment of the government in order to effect a violent seizure of power. In the struggle with sedition at a moment of mortal danger for the Russian State, the Octobrists resolutely took the side of the government, which, in a series of solemn assurances emanating from the Sovereign himself, had declared itself ready for the broadest liberal reforms. A series of acts of State, from the [decree] to the Governing Senate of December 12, 1904, to the Manifesto of October 17, 1905, contained an extensive program of reform suited to the mature needs of the country and promising the fulfillment of hopes and dreams which the Russian public has long cherished. These acts were a triumph for Russian Liberalism; for the principles contained in them were the watchwords in the name of which Russian Liberals had been fighting for half a century.

Such was the political environment in which Octobrism came into being. In fact, it was bound to come into being. Octobrism was a tacit but solemn contract between that government, on the one hand, which was the product of the whole course of Russian history, and the Russian public on the other—a contract of loyalty, of mutual loyalty. The Manifesto of October 17 was, so it seemed, an act of confidence in the nation on the part of the Sovereign; Octobrism was the nation's answer; it was an act of faith in the Sovereign.

But the contract contained obligations for both sides; and collaboration with the government meant joint effort in the work of carrying out the broad program of reforms that had been outlined. Primarily it meant joint action for the purpose of strengthening and developing the principles of the constitutional system. Only by means of combined and friendly effort on the part of the government and of the public could this task be accomplished. A situation was created which is rare in Russian life, a situation the like of which had not been seen since the beginning of the sixties. Two forces which had been constantly, and as it seemed irreconcilably, hostile to each other—the government and the public—came together and pursued a common path. The public began to believe in the government; the government keenly realized the need of support from the public. In this act of reconciliation a prominent part was played by Mr. Stolypin, who represented a wholly exceptional combination of the qualities required at that particular moment. His charming personality, the lofty qualities of his intellect and character changed the hate and suspicion that formerly prevailed into an atmosphere of public goodwill and confidence in the government.

In the third Imperial Duma, Octobrism was able to take its place as an important factor in political life. History will give a juster estimate of the significance of the third Duma than that given by contemporaries. It will give it due credit for having passed a number of important legislative measures in the spheres of finance, land reform, public instruction, and justice, for having practically laid the bases—firm bases, as it seemed—of the new constitutional system, and most of all for having by its even temper and its tranquil labors exercised a profound educative influence on the Russian public. In the gradual calming and sobering process that has been noticeable in the public temper during the last five years, the third Imperial Duma played a very important part. History will duly appreciate those difficulties, both internal and external, which the young representative assembly had to face. It seemed as though unprecedentedly favorable conditions had been established for carrying out the proposed [Stolypin] reforms—reforms which promised regeneration in all departments of life. The severe lesson of the recent past had, it seemed, irrevocably condemned the policy which had brought Russia to disaster, almost to the verge of ruin. The revolutionary movement and the political terror that accompanied it, had been suppressed; the public sympathy in which they formerly flourished had been withdrawn from them. With the disappearance of revolutionary excesses, the excesses of the government had lost their former justification. The government, so it seemed, had attained clearness of vision and could count in its reforming work on the support of wide and influential circles of society. In a word, a new era was opening.

But side by side with this tendency, parallel to it, but in a reverse direction, proceeded an evolution of another character. In proportion as tranquillity was restored, in proportion as the public laid down its arms and the danger of revolution receded into the distance, those elements which in former epochs and in all countries have been distinguished for the shortness of their memory, raised their heads. These were the forces that held the fate of Russia in their hands in the pre-emancipation epoch, and determined the policy which brought a great empire to unprecedented depths of humiliation. At the moment when danger threatened, before what seemed to be the inevitable hour of stern expiation of their sins and crimes, they effaced themselves, disappeared, as it were, from the surface of Russian life, abandoning their posts in mortal fear for their personal safety. Now they have crawled out of their crevices—these "saviors of the country"—but where were they then? They were not to be found in the government, at any rate in the government of Stolypin's time. It was among [representatives] of the obsolete political system, among the Court *camarilla*, among those suspicious characters who huddled and warmed themselves around the festering sores of Russian life, among those whom the new political system mercilessly threw overboard—it was among these that the reviving reaction recruited its forces. And among these well-known and only too familiar figures—new, unexpected, strange shapes, stragglers, as it were, from some entirely different epoch of civilization—appeared as important factors in our political life.[1] Those irresponsible, ex-governmental, super-governmental and in the present case anti-governmental tendencies which were organically bound up with the forms of Russian absolutism quickly recovered, under the new order, their hold on the positions that had been taken from them and abandoned by them. The man who bravely fought with them and fell under their onslaught, Mr. Stolypin, made the following melancholy admission in conversation with a Russian journalist: "It is a mistake to think," he said, "that the Russian Cabinet even in its present form is the government. It is only a reflection of the government. It is necessary to know that impact of pressure and influence under the weight of which it has to work."

It was, as you know, the right wing of the Council of the Empire [State Council] and the Organization of the United Gentry [Nobility] that became the official bulwarks of reaction. It would be wrong to consider these bodies as in any way faithful indicators of the temper prevailing among the Russian gentry and the higher Russian bureaucracy. Consistent, artificial selection was needed to make them what they are. The Russian gentry, who with their own hands carried out the great civilizing mission of the Zemstvo, are, undoubtedly—an overwhelming majority of them at any rate—an element of progress. Moreover, the legend of the isolation of the Russian bureaucracy, of its estrangement from the public temper and public

---

1. A reference, no doubt, to Rasputin.—Ed.

needs, is greatly exaggerated. In those rare moments of illumination when the government has entered on the path of broad creative effort, it has found among its bureaucracy not a few gifted men who gladly brought their immense political experience to the service of the great tasks opening out before them. Thus, for instance, at a happy moment in our history, the new Russian judicial system came into being [1864] as a result of the creative effort of our bureaucracy.

The third Imperial Duma, at the moment when it first met [November 1907] found dominant in the Council of the Empire the so-called group of the Center. This group was by no means homogeneous in its composition, but it was united by a common recognition of the Manifesto of October 17 and other decrees promulgated by the Sovereign during the epoch of liberation [1905–1907] as determining bases for the forthcoming work of reform.

On this group, which constituted together with the left wing a decisive majority, the government could rely in carrying out its program of reforms. Between this group and the Duma Center, which was also made up of various elements and constituted a majority in the Duma, there existed, in spite of all differences of political temper, common ground, a common language, a possibility of establishing agreement by means of mutual concessions. A series of new appointments, made consistently year after year in a definite direction, gradually but decisively transferred the center of gravity in the Council of the Empire to the right wing.[2] The right wing was not merely mechanically or numerically strengthened. The very character of the appointments showed what political tendency was in favor at the moment. And this circumstance naturally could not fail to influence those unstable elements which had long been in the habit of adjusting their policy to prevailing tendencies.

The effect was one of painful ambiguity. On the one hand, the general position seemed to be unchanged; the Manifesto had not been repealed, the promises given had not been withdrawn, the government, with the permission of the Monarch, continued to draft and to bring into the legislative bodies bills containing references to the acts of the epoch of liberation, bills bearing very definitely the stamp of that epoch. On the other hand, also with the Sovereign's permission, certain elements were consistently strengthened. These elements did not attempt to conceal their irreconcilable hostility to the new political system and to those representatives of the government who were on its side; they regarded the Manifesto of October 17 and kindred acts of the Monarch as frivolous and timid concessions wrung out either by force or deception; they made it their object to urge the Sovereign to effect a *coup d'état*, and gladly offered their services for this purpose.

The chief efforts of the reaction were directed at first not so much against the representative assembly as against the Prime Minister [Stolypin], who was a firm supporter of the new political system. A characteristic moment in this struggle was the memorable episode of the bill for the estimates of the Marine [Navy] General Staff.[3] This was a trial of strength. The blow was skillfully prepared and cleverly

---

2. We note again that up to half the members of the State Council were appointed by the Emperor. For the Council, see D. C. B. Lieven, *Russia's Rulers under the Old Regime* (1989).—Ed.
3. This bill, designed to professionalize the Navy as well as pay for it, was vetoed by Nicholas II in April 1909 on the grounds that it infringed on his prerogative. Thereafter the minister of war was

calculated. It was aimed at a vital point; the question of Imperial Defense touches every Russian statesman to the quick.

The dangerous man [Stolypin] was beaten and broken. It was necessary to repeat the blow. And blows were showered on him. You remember the complicated intrigue that arose over the question of establishing Zemstva in the Western Provinces. You remember the fatal mistake Mr. Stolypin allowed himself to make; his ephemeral victory was turned into final defeat.[4] The campaign conducted against this eminent statesman whose services to the Empire and the Monarchy were immense, found inspiration and support in those irresponsible, extra-governmental tendencies which rightly saw in him an irreconcilable and most dangerous opponent. The political center of gravity moved more and more to their side. Individuals were promoted or degraded, important events occurred in the life of the State without the participation of the government and with the aid of other, secret, but more powerful factors. The government gradually lost that tinge of constitutionalism which is implied in the idea of a united cabinet. We returned to the traditions of a personal *régime* with its worst accessories.

Stolypin's struggle with these reactionary tendencies which he considered ruinous for Russia and for the Monarchy, ended in his defeat. Long before his physical death his mortal political agony had set in. And the catastrophe in Kiev [where Stolypin was assassinated in 1911] evoked a feeling of joy, or, at any rate, of relief, not only in those revolutionary circles from which the shot was fired; not only in the camp of the Russian radicals was the death of this splendid fighting man regarded as a gain and as removing a dangerous opponent. It is certain that if there were some who aimed the treacherous shot there were others who did not hinder it. The senatorial revision [investigation] and its results only confirmed the suspicions and surmises that arose in this connection.

Stolypin's successors naturally proved unequal to the struggle in which such a giant as he succumbed. In fact, they hardly made any attempt to continue it; the fate of their predecessor was an only too sharp and threatening warning. You must crouch and belittle yourself, was the feeling; it is dangerous to oppose, and heaven forbid that we should be the wall of defense. Only at such a price was it possible to remain in power—at the price of self-effacement. And the government effaced itself, the government capitulated all along the line. . . .

The results of the success attained by the reaction very soon made themselves felt. Political productiveness came to an end. The government was fast bound in a paralysis; it had neither Imperial aims nor a broadly conceived plan, nor a common will. Instead there were a conflict of personal intrigues and aspirations, a continual attempt to settle personal accounts, and dissensions between various departments. The ship of state has lost its course, and is aimlessly tossing on the waves. Never has the authority of the Imperial Government sunk so low. Not only has the government failed to arouse sympathy or confidence; it is incapable of inspiring even fear. Even the harm that it does, it sometimes does without ill-will, very often

---

forbidden to appear in the Duma, thus frustrating Guchkov and many other deputies who believed the Duma had a right to supervise, and approve, military expenditures.—Ed.
4. The Western zemstvo crisis is explained in the essay above by Leonard Schapiro.—Ed.

it does it unintelligently, in the way of reflex, spasmodic movements. Only the comic element was lacking. And this touch, too, the government has managed to introduce, making all Russia roar with laughter, with tragic laughter.

True, there are some Ministries which by inertia or through the chance of favorable circumstances continue working on the plan that was drafted under other conditions; but even these meet at best with cool indifference on the part of the central government, and at worst with ill-will and opposition. True, on solemn occasions the old, familiar words are sometimes uttered, but no one believes them now—neither speakers nor hearers.

The collapse of the central government naturally finds its reflection in a complete disorganization of local administration. A kind of administrative decentralization has actually been effected, but it is a caricature on the very idea of decentralization. On the strength of this peculiar type of autonomy the local authorities, confident in their impunity and guessing, so to speak, at the views of the central government, have developed the arbitrary exercise of authority to an incredible degree, sometimes to the point of sheer ruffianism.

It is wholly natural that in such circumstances the government should find itself solitary, abandoned by all. As a matter of fact, reaction in its various forms has no roots anywhere in the country, unless we count those political organizations which have been fattened at the Treasury's expense and which try to hide under flags and banners their impotence and insignificance. The public sympathy and confidence which the government in the time of Stolypin attracted to itself at the cost of great toil and effort, receded in one moment from the government of his successors. The honeymoon is over.

But the paralysis of the government has made itself felt not only in internal collapse. Events of world-wide, immense, historical importance have occurred. Broad horizons opened up before Russia, new and unprecedentedly favourable international combinations arose. The historical traditions of Russia, her real political interests, her honor and her profit demanded of her that she, as the great Slavic power, should play a decisive part in this world-wide crisis. Russia, a vigorous, powerful, healthy Russia, loyal to her history and confident in her future, a Russia like this would have done her duty. But that state of prostration and marasm which numbed our political organism at home, fettered our movements and paralyzed our will abroad. Our timid and incapable foreign policy let slip all those advantages which opened out before Russia through no merit of our own; but through the efforts of others and by the will of a fortune that had at last turned in our favor. But it also lost even the positions won in previous reigns by incalculable sacrifices on the part of the Russian people. We must not shut our eyes to the fact that those bloodless but shameful defeats which Russia suffered during the Balkan crisis[5] had an enormous effect on the popular temper, especially among the masses of the people and those sections of the educated classes who, like the people, regard the

---

5. Guchkov alludes to Russia's unsuccessful efforts in 1912–1913 to lead an alliance of Balkan states against Turkey for control of the Dardanelles, permitting Russian warships free access from the Black Sea to the Mediterranean.—Ed.

question of Russia's *rôle* as a Great Power as the chief article of their political faith, outweighing in importance all questions as to defects in the conduct of internal affairs.

What is to be the issue of the grave crisis through which we are now [November 1913] passing? What does the encroachment of reaction bring with it? Whither is the government policy, or rather lack of policy, carrying us?

Towards an inevitable and grave catastrophe! In this general forecast all are agreed; people of the most sharply opposed political views, of the most varied social groups, all agree with a rare, an unprecedented unanimity. Even representatives of the government, of that government which is the chief offender against the Russian people, are prepared to agree to this forecast, and their official and obligatory optimism ill conceals their inward alarm.

When will the catastrophe take effect? What forms will it assume? Who can foretell? Some scan the horizon with joyful anticipation, others with dread. But greatly do those err who calculate that on the ruins of the demolished system will arise that order which corresponds to their particular political and social views. In those forces that seem likely to come to the top in the approaching struggle, I do not see stable elements that would guarantee any kind of permanent political order. Are we not rather in danger of being plunged into a period of protracted, chronic anarchy which will lead to the dissolution of the Empire? Shall we not again pass through a Time of Trouble,[6] only under new and more dangerous international conditions? . . .

We are, in fact, now confronted with an entirely new political situation, one that has practically nothing in common with that which prevailed when our party was formed and our tactics were determined. The government with which we are now face to face is not the government with which we made our contract. Formerly, in spite of all defects in the reform work of the government, the country had no ground for anxiety in respect to the main acquisition of the epoch of liberation, namely, the representative assembly [Duma] with which all the future of Russia is bound up. But in the present policy of the government we cannot fail to recognize a direct menace to the constitutional system, and the beginning of a liquidation of the era of reforms. We know that the question of the system under which Russia is to be governed has been raised, if not by the government itself, at any rate in those extra-governmental circles that are stronger than the government. . . .

What must the Russian public do in view of this danger which menaces not particular reforms but reform itself and its vital center, the idea of national representation? What is to be done by those political parties who have made it their object to bring about the renewal of Russia on the bases of those principles of political liberty and social justice which found expression in the decrees of the Sovereign during the epoch of liberation? What can and what should be done by

6. Reference is to the period of political disintegration and social upheaval in Russia between 1598 and 1613.—Ed.

the Imperial Duma, that body which has been charged by the people to guard the permanence of the political system?

True, at the price of meekness, faint-hearted concession, humiliating compacts the representative assembly might succeed in gaining a respite, on condition that it confined itself to petty, humdrum work and refrained from touching on great problems of state. And then it might be hoped that when the dark days pass and the horizon brightens, it would be found to have safely survived this gloomy time and to have held its place in the apparatus of the State and so would be able once again to occupy a commanding position in the political system and to work broadly and productively. But would the Duma really maintain its existence even at such a price? And would not this be tantamount to the political suicide of the representative assembly, the wreck of the very idea of national representation in the mind of the people? And in the meantime, in our political organism the process of dissolution would rage unchecked, mortifying the vital tissues and accumulating the elements of death and corruption.

For an Imperial Duma faithful to its duty to the Emperor and the Empire, there is only one way. If other organs of authority take refuge in timorous connivance, or it may be are themselves criminal accomplices, the Imperial Duma must take up the defense of the cause of Russian liberty and of the integrity of our political system. It must devote to this cause all the instruments of its powers, all the strength of its authority. The weapons of warfare at the disposal of the representative assembly, however limited their number may seem, have not all been made use of to the fullest extent. In the name of a long looked-for political liberty, in defense of the constitutional principle, in the struggle for reforms, all legal forms of parliamentary combat must be employed—parliamentary freedom of speech, the authority of the parliamentary tribune, the right of rejecting bills, and, first and foremost, the Duma's budget rights, the right of refusing votes of money. . . .

And it is upon us, Octobrists, that this duty primarily lies. Once in the days of the people's madness [1905] we raised our sobering voice against the excesses of radicalism. In the days of the madness of the government it is we who should speak to the government a grave word of warning. We once believed and invited others to believe; we patiently waited. Now we must declare that our patience is exhausted, and with our patience our faith; at such a moment as this we must not leave to the professional Opposition, to the radical and socialist parties, the monopoly of opposing the government and the ruinous policy it has adopted; for in so doing we should create the dangerous illusion that the government is combating radical utopias and social experiments,—whereas it is opposing the satisfaction of the most moderate and elementary demands of public opinion, demands that at one time were admitted by the government itself. Before the approaching catastrophe it is we who should make the final attempt to bring the government to reason, to open its eyes, to awaken in it the alarm that we so strongly feel. For we are the representatives of those propertied classes, all the vital interests of which are bound up with the peaceful evolution of the State, and on which in case of disaster the first blow will fall. . . .

Will our voice be heard? Will our cry of warning reach the heights where the fate of Russia is decided? Shall we succeed in communicating to the government our own alarm? Shall we awaken it from the lethargy that envelops it? We should be glad to think so. In any case, this is our last opportunity of securing a peaceful issue from the crisis. Let those in power make no mistake about the temper of the people; let them not take outward indications of prosperity as a pretext for lulling themselves into security. Never were those revolutionary organizations which aim at a violent upheaval so broken and impotent as they are now,[7] and never were the Russian public and the Russian people so profoundly revolutionized by the actions of the government, for day by day faith in the government is steadily waning, and with it is waning faith in the possibility of a peaceful issue from the crisis.

The danger at the present moment lies, in fact, not in the revolutionary parties, not in anti-monarchical propaganda, not in anti-religious teaching, not in the dissemination of the ideas of socialism and anti-militarism, not in the agitation of anarchists against the government. The historical drama through which we are now passing lies in the fact that we are compelled to uphold the monarchy against those who are the natural defenders of the monarchical principle, we are compelled to defend the Church against the ecclesiastical hierarchy, the army against its leaders, the authority of the government against the government itself. We seemed to have sunk into a state of public despondency and apathy, a passive condition. But thence it is only one step to despair, which is an active force of tremendously destructive quality. May God avert from our country the danger that overshadows it.

## Nicolas de Basily Recounts the Abdication of Nicholas II, 1917

The Interallied [War] Conference in Petrograd came to an end on February 8, 1917, and the foreign delegates departed, certainly anxious about the future of Russia but far from realizing the gravity of the situation.

During the conference General Vasily Gurko occupied a room in the Hotel d'Europe in Petrograd. One day when I went to see him—it must have been February 6 or 7—our attention was attracted by noise in the streets, and we saw a crowd, largely composed of women, parading on Nevsky Prospect [Avenue] and demonstrating against high prices and the shortage of food. We exchanged remarks expressing our anxiety.

---

7. Evidently true: for example, Social Democratic Party membership (Bolshevik and Menshevik) had reached 150,000 in early 1907; by 1910, the total was down to 10,000.—Ed.

Reprinted with minor modifications for consistency from *Nicolas de Basily Memoirs: Diplomat of Imperial Russia, 1903–1917* by Nicolas de Basily, pp. 103–26, 132–33, 135–37, 140–41, 145–46, with permission of Hoover Institution Press. Copyright 1973 by the Board of Trustees of the Leland Stanford Junior University.

After the close of the Interallied Conference I remained several days in Petrograd, then returned to the Stavka, as the Russians called the General Headquarters. There I found General Mikhail V. Alekseev, who had just returned to Mogilev on February 18. I was most pleased to see him again, but would have been more pleased had he been in better physical condition. He had considered it his duty to return to his functions as chief of staff of the High Command before completely recovering from an illness, and at night he still sometimes suffered attacks of high fever. On February 23, Emperor Nicholas came to Mogilev. As usual, we went to the railway station to await his arrival.

The rush of events had accelerated. Rumors reached us that strikes had occurred in the big factories of Petrograd, the Putilov metallurgic works. On February 25 we learned through telegrams from the minister of war, Beliaev, and from General Khabalov, commander of the Petrograd Military District, that disorders had broken out in the capital.

The following day, the news was even more alarming. Khabalov informed us that 240,000 workmen had stopped work, that their movement had transformed itself into an uprising rallying to the cry "Down with war!" and that troops had fired on a crowd amassed in Nevsky Prospect.

The disorders had been provoked in Petrograd by a shortage of food supplies, especially of bread. The war had forced the railroads to make an effort beyond their capacity and the result was a growing disorganization of transportation. The inept administration of the minister of the interior, Alexander D. Protopopov, had not been able to resolve the problem of food supply so important in maintaining order in the capital. This serious fault had been exacerbated by another. At the beginning of the war all regiments of the guard had been sent to the front, and not one unit of well-trained troops was left in Petrograd. On the other hand, a large number of new recruits and reservists—about 160,000 men—had been concentrated in the capital, where they were receiving military instruction. This mass of soldiers, as yet little disciplined, was commanded by reserve officers who were insufficient in number and lacking in necessary authority. Under these conditions the garrison of the capital not only did not constitute an effective guarantee for maintaining order, but could easily become a source of grave danger.

On the morning of February 27 we learned at the Stavka that the troops in Petrograd had refused to use their arms against the crowds, that they had arrested or killed their officers and joined the rebellion. Generals Mikhail A. Beliaev and Sergei S. Khabalov demanded that reliable support troops be sent to Petrograd from the front.

My consternation grew still greater when I learned that in obedience to an order of the Emperor, the president of the Council [prime minister], Prince Nikolai Golitsyn, had decreed the prorogation of the Duma. There was no longer any doubt in my mind: suddenly we found ourselves faced with a popular uprising. For some time we had known it to be inevitable, but we had not thought it so near at hand, and we dreaded it with our whole being. Yet the Emperor persisted in his blindness and imprudently rejected the support that the Duma would have been happy to give him had he been willing to pay attention to its counsel.

In face of the gravity of the situation, I expressed to General Alekseev my profound conviction that this was the very last opportunity the Emperor would have to rally the opinion of the country—or at least to attempt to do so—and for that it was necessary for him to declare immediately and solemnly his decision to dismiss his incompetent, discredited ministers and to surround himself from then on with collaborators possessing the public confidence. One cannot govern if one has lost the support of both the elite and the masses.

My venerable chief shook his head sadly and showed me a telegram he had received during the night from the president of the Duma, Mikhail Rodzianko. The message was written in anguished terms:

> The disturbances are assuming threatening and irreducible proportions. . . . The public authorities have lost all credit and are incapable of pulling the country out of its tragic situation. . . . It is urgent to appoint a government of men who have the confidence of the public. . . . In this terrible hour there is no other solution, and I entreat you to intercede in this sense with His Majesty in order to avoid a catastrophe. Any delay is equivalent to suicide.

General Alekseev added: "This morning I submitted this telegram to the Emperor. Again, I did everything possible to convince him to take the road to salvation at last. Again, I ran against a wall."

Unwilling to doubt the fidelity of seasoned troops, the Emperor gave orders that some regiments be taken from the front and dispatched to Petrograd to put down the riots. Would these troops agree to fire against the insurgents? I no longer had many illusions on this subject, and I was convinced that first the mood of the country must be calmed by an assurance that things were going to change. In reality, the morale of the army no longer had the same solidity as before. The ranks of the career officers as well as of the noncommissioned officers had been decimated. The losses had been filled by reservists who were far from presenting the same guarantees of obedience as the cadres of professional military men. The recruits, freshly arrived from their villages, were even less stable. The profound disturbance that had taken hold of people all over the country could not have failed to extend to the Army, where the disappointment caused by military reverses was felt even more deeply than among the civilians. The military shared the discontent of the home front over the economic difficulties of all kinds resulting from the prolongation of the war. Moreover the soldiers, who mostly came from the countryside, expected that their sacrifices would be recompensed by greater consideration for their desire for land, but the preference accorded in high places to the reactionary nobility did not encourage them to hope for a breakup of the large estates.

The obvious incompetence of the ministers chosen by the Emperor tended to convert many officers to liberal, or even radical, ideas. Moreover imprudent speeches pronounced in the Duma against the government had had great repercussions throughout the country and had helped considerably to undermine the authority of the establishment. Finally, the Army was aroused, as was the rest of the country, by rumors of the confidence the sovereigns had placed in the corrupt Rasputin. What was still worse, they dared—in the Army as well as at the rear—to suspect the Empress of serving the interests of Germany, which in fact was pure calumny. The traditional prestige of the Tsar was too greatly shaken for soldiers already fatigued by war to accept fighting against their brothers in order to defend the tottering authority of the unfortunate sovereign.

So it was not astonishing that during the day of February 27 General Nikolai V. Ruzsky, commander in chief of the Northern Army Group, telegraphed to the Emperor that measures of repression would only aggravate the situation, and that it was a matter of the greatest urgency that the population be calmed and its confidence in him restored.

More and more alarming news arrived at the Stavka. The soldiers were fraternizing with the workmen. The crowd and the insurgent troops were marching to the Duma and expecting it to lead them. Thus contrary to its expectations and its will, the Duma became for a time the center of a movement it was far from having initiated. It was evident to us that, at any price, this moment must be seized to reconstitute power by supporting it on that prestige which the Duma still possessed. The monarchy had yet a chance to be conciliated with the moderate elements. To let this occasion escape was to lose irremediably all control over the development of events and to play into the hands of the parties of the extreme left. Would the liberals who desired an orderly transformation of the country be put aside or even crushed by those for whom progress must begin with the destruction of all the heritage of the past? In short, if the internal struggle were to be prolonged and to spread, the war would necessarily terminate in defeat and failure in our obligations toward our allies. Even should the monarchy accept defeat, the people would not forgive it.

Preoccupied by these somber thoughts, I took advantage of a moment of liberty to visit my friends of the Navy Staff. For years we had had the most confident relations, and our way of looking at things was often the same. These naval officers were cultivated men, liberal and generally well informed, and mostly on an intellectual level superior to that of the Army men. They were in communication by direct wire with the Admiralty in Petrograd and received news from the capital continuously. Since the disturbances of 1905 the Navy had proved particularly vulnerable to revolutionary propaganda. If the agitation won over the fleet, the officers certainly ran the greatest risks of being assassinated. I found my friends most anxious, and as desirous as I to see an eleventh-hour understanding between the monarch and the Duma.

On the evening of this same day, February 27, I dined with the Emperor. The guests were nervous but made an effort not to appear so, and most of the time they chatted about unimportant subjects. They also spoke of the health of the sovereign's daughters and son, who were ill with measles in Tsarskoe Selo. The Emperor, as usual, appeared calm and impassive. He spoke a great deal with his aide-de-camp General Nikolai Ivanov, who sat at his left. About a year earlier, Ivanov, a small man with big white sideburns, had been relieved of his functions as commander in chief of the Southern Army Group. At the beginning of the war he had inflicted a crushing defeat on the Austrians, which had given him a certain prestige. We knew, however, that his successes were due chiefly to the fact that he had then had General Alekseev as his chief of staff. Though not a man of great ability,

General Ivanov had a crafty, subtle mind and knew well how to make his way. Since his retirement from command he had been attached to the person of the Emperor and had lived, without doing much of anything, in a special railway carriage at the Mogilev station.

During dinner my table companions explained to me that the sovereign had just appointed Ivanov commander in chief of the Petrograd district, with ample powers to suppress the insurrection, and that he would leave for the capital the next day with the Saint George Battalion, which was stationed at the General Staff Headquarters. This unit was composed of soldiers who had displayed exemplary conduct on the battlefield and had been decorated with the Cross of Saint George.

In 1914 I had had some difference with Ivanov over the clumsy policies practiced in Russian-occupied Galicia. Therefore I was much surprised when, after dinner, he asked me to visit him that same evening in his railway carriage at the station. He gave the same invitation to one of my good friends of the Navy Staff, Captain Bubnov.

When Bubnov and I joined General Ivanov in his railway carriage, he asked us to tell him very frankly what we thought of his mission. We told him that once on the spot he would see whether it was still possible to crush the rebellion with a decisive blow, but that we feared it was already too late. In any case, it seemed to us certain that, in view of the state of mind now prevalent in Russia, there was no chance that the troops could be used against the Duma, and that if the Duma was really at the head of the movement, the expedition was doomed beforehand to failure. We concluded that it would be infinitely preferable to seek some ground of understanding with the Duma and thus separate the relatively moderate elements from the extremist parties. It was necessary at any price to avoid the spread of a civil war with all its disastrous consequences, as well for the monarchy as for the pursuit of the war and the future of the country. The old general replied that he was not far from sharing our point of view. I thought it my duty to repeat the next morning to General Alekseev what I had just said to Ivanov.

We left General Ivanov toward midnight, and on route to our destination we met an officer who confided to us that he had serious reason to believe that the soldiers of the Saint George Battalion would not fire on the insurgents. And this was an elite unit, thought to be reliable under all circumstances.

I accompanied my friend Bubnov to the offices of the Navy Staff. The chief of staff there, Admiral Russin, had just received a telegram from Petrograd informing him that the troops in ever increasing numbers were joining the insurrection, that anarchy was growing in the city, and that, on the demand of the insurgents, the Duma had formed a provisional committee with the purpose of restoring order in the capital, as far as possible.

While I was returning to my offices at about one o'clock in the morning, two automobiles passed me on Dnieprovskii Prospect, moving at high speed toward the station. I immediately recognized the imperial limousines. The Emperor, then, had decided to leave the Stavka.

The next morning I had the explanation for the monarch's hurried departure. In the afternoon of February 27 he had made up his mind to rejoin his family in Tsarskoe Selo and to leave the following day, but a telephone conversation he had with the Empress during the evening had caused him to hasten his departure. General Alekseev had implored him not to enter the Petrograd zone, where he risked falling into the hands of the insurgents, and not to leave at such a moment the center of command of his armies, where he remained in communication with the whole empire and would be in a better position to make decisions. The Emperor did not yield to these arguments. He was first of all an excellent husband and a good father. In these moments of anguish he was anxious about his family and desired above all to be with them.

During the morning of February 28, in the offices of General Alekseev, I also learned of the latest messages received by the Emperor, and of the last dispositions taken by him before his departure. In the afternoon of February 27 he had been given a telegram from the president of the Duma, Rodzianko, written in terms still more pressing than the one addressed twelve hours earlier to General Alekseev. Rodzianko told the Tsar that civil war had begun and was spreading, that the government was powerless, that it was urgent that the management of affairs be given to people who enjoyed popularity and that the Duma be reconvened. He ended his appeal with these dramatic words: "The hour has come which will decide your fate and that of our country. Tomorrow it may be too late." Thus Rodzianko, who had struggled so hard to renovate the Russian monarchical system, was striving to the last hour to save the monarchy and the person of the sovereign.

Rodzianko's telegram was followed several hours later by a message from the president of the Council of Ministers, Nikolai D. Golitsyn. This worthy old dignitary, ineffectual and inexperienced, had also finally concluded that the cabinet was unable to fulfill its task: he implored Nicholas II to dismiss his ministers and to appoint either Prince George Lvov or Rodzianko to form a new ministry. He added that the presence of Protopopov in the government had provoked general exasperation.

That evening the Grand Duke Michael, brother of the Emperor, had a conversation by direct wire with General Alekseev and asked him to insist with the Emperor that he follow the advice of Golitsyn immediately. General Alekseev, who had had an attack of fever that night, left his bed to go and plead with the Emperor to yield at last to the wise counsels lavished upon him. To add more weight to his supplications, the good general is said to have gone down on his knees before his sovereign (this detail was told me by one of his officers, to whom the general had described the scene). The Emperor retreated as usual into intransigence. He left Rodzianko's telegram without reply and shortly before his departure from Mogilev telegraphed Golitsyn that under the present conditions he considered any change in the cabinet inadmissible. It was the utmost degree of blindness, and those of us who were informed of this message were filled with despair.

The Emperor's train did not leave the Mogilev station until five o'clock in the morning. He was conferring there with General Ivanov when a telegram from General Khabalov was delivered to him. The commander of the Petrograd Military District informed Nicholas II that he was in no position to execute the instructions received and to restore order in the capital because most of the troops had refused to obey orders and the greater part of the city had fallen into the hands of the insurgents. Obviously, it would be impossible to prevent the repercussions this news would necessarily have on the troops at the front. From then on, the preservation of order and unity in the army, as well as the maintenance of transportation, became the principal preoccupation of General Alekseev. He immediately sent an account of the events to all the commanders of army groups and reminded them of their sacred duty to keep the troops faithful to the oaths they had sworn to Emperor and to country.

The news received during the day of February 28 was of extreme gravity. The revolutionaries had become masters of the whole capital, and no faithful troops remained in Petrograd. Toward evening the struggle ended and the situation in the city became more calm. The Committee of the Duma was striving to induce the disbanded soldiers to return to the barracks in order to get them away from the influence of extreme left agitators and to place them once again under the authority of their officers. The railroads' delegate in the Duma, Alexander A. Bublikov, a moderate man whom I knew well, sent out an ardent appeal to the patriotic sentiments of the railwaymen asking them to do their utmost to reestablish proper operation of the railways.

The situation seemed to be taking a new turn. General Alekseev concluded that he must immediately adapt his action accordingly. During the night of February 28–March 1, he sent a telegram to General Ivanov at Tsarskoe Selo, where the latter was to arrive in the morning. In this telegram Alekseev expressed hope for an understanding with the Duma and recommended the avoidance of force.

In the meantime, the Navy Staff notified us that the socialists were intensifying their action and that it was to be feared that the workers' organizations would "raise the banner of socialism and crush the Duma."

That prophetic phrase was written by my naval friends on the very same day that the Petrograd Soviet of 1917 was to meet for the first time (during the night of February 28–March 1, in the palace of the Duma). The Soviet had already appeared during the disturbances of 1905 and set itself up as the center of revolutionary action of the socialist parties, but at that time it was composed only of factory delegates. It was now revived on a wider base with the addition of delegates from the Petrograd regiments, thus becoming the "workers' and soldiers' Soviet." If in the first moment of disorder the masses had turned toward the Duma, it remained evident to us that the latter lacked deep roots in the lower strata of the population. Indeed, had this assembly not become in the eyes of the masses "the Duma of great landowners" since June 1907, when Nicholas II had, on the advice of Stolypin, modified the electoral system? The number of deputies elected by the peasants was at that time arbitrarily reduced in order to prevent them from getting the Duma to accept a division in their favor of the great landed properties still belonging to the nobility. In thus taking sides against the peasants, the Tsar had in one blow undermined the prestige of both the crown and the popular representation. The "professional revolutionaries" grouped within the Soviet—sincere socialists and demagogues alike—found their task greatly facilitated. Were we not now about to pay the price of these errors?

The train carrying General Ivanov and the Saint George Battalion left Mogilev on February 28 toward noon and took the Kiev-Petrograd line passing through Vitebsk, Dno, and Vyritsa. The general arrived safely the following morning in

Tsarskoe Selo, but without the battalion, which was prevented by railway workers from proceeding to its destination.

Not wishing to hinder the movement of the troops, the Emperor decided to set out for Tsarskoe Selo via Orsha, Viazma, and Likhoslav and then take the main Moscow-Petrograd line through Bologoe and Malaia Vychera. As usual the Emperor's journey was ensured, for greater security, by two trains, one following the other. The monarch and his immediate suite occupied one of the trains; the other, called "the service train," was reserved for various military personnel and civilians who accompanied the sovereign, and for his military escort.

In the evening of February 28 the Stavka lost all contact with the imperial trains, and we were seized with great anxiety for the fate of the Emperor. Our first fear was that he had fallen into the hands of the insurgents. But even if such an eventuality was avoided, misfortune had willed that there was no longer any means of communicating with the Emperor at a time when he alone could make the necessary decisions to put an end to the anarchy.

At last, on the morning of March 1, we were able to locate the imperial trains. They had been able to reach Malaia Vychera but could go no farther, the revolutionaries having blocked the line between there and Petrograd. The Emperor was obliged to turn back through Bologoe to Dno. We thought at first that he was trying to continue his journey to Tsarskoe Selo by another line, but in the afternoon we learned that he was on his way to Pskov, where the headquarters of the Northern Army Group, commanded by General Ruzsky, was installed. Evidently the monarch did not wish to go too far from his family and at the same time desired to be in a big military center provided with all means of communication. Pskov was the nearest place connected by direct telegraph with the General Head-quarters in Mogilev, and this fact contributed greatly to the Emperor's decision to go there.

Meanwhile, during the day of March 1, the revolutionary movement spread beyond the capital. Since the day before, work had been stopped in all the Moscow factories. Now, twenty-four hours later, Moscow was in full revolution, with the troops no longer obeying their officers and going over to the rebels. The other large cities also were beginning to give way to the revolutionary fever. We learned that the big naval base at Kronstadt, situated near the capital, had revolted and that the commander of the port had been assassinated. To avoid a general slaughter of the officers, Admiral Adrian I. Nepenin had been obliged to put the Baltic fleet under orders of the Committee of the Duma. In Petrograd, all the ministers had been relieved of their functions by the revolutionaries and the Provisional Committee of the Duma had undertaken the management of the governmental institutions [the formation of the first Provisional Government]. Rodzianko notified the Stavka of these developments that afternoon. However—as a telegram from Count Kapnist of the Naval Staff emphasized—beside the Duma there loomed the growing menace of the parties of the extreme left grouped around the Soviet of Workers' and Soldiers' Deputies. In order to spread the revolution, these parties had just sent emissaries to the armies. Their arrival on the northern front in the region of Pskov had already been reported.

Under the impress of this news, in the afternoon of March 1 Alekseev, in his fine, regular handwriting, wrote a telegram to the Emperor to put him face to face with his responsibilities. He said, in substance, that the disorganization at the rear would deprive the army of its supplies, that it was not possible to ask it to fight the enemy if a revolution was spreading behind the front; under the conditions prevailing, repression of the unrest by force would present great danger and would lead Russia and the army to their ruin; if the sovereign did not decide immediately to make concessions susceptible of restoring tranquillity, power would pass tomorrow to the extremist elements and Russia would suffer all the horrors of revolution.

General Alekseev's initiative was immediately supported by messages to the Emperor from his first cousin, the Grand Duke Sergei Mikhailovich, general inspector of the artillery, and by General Aleksei Brusilov, commander of the Southwestern front.

In order to move the Emperor to make the decision so long awaited, it was necessary to submit to him the text of a declaration which he could sign for publication. Remarking that General Alekseev was tired and ailing, I offered to assist him and proposed writing a draft manifesto and an explanatory telegram to the Emperor. Alekseev asked me to do so, and some time later I brought him the following text:

> From one moment to the next, anarchy threatens to spread throughout the country. The disintegration of the Army is becoming an ever more pressing danger. Under these conditions the continuation of the war would no longer be possible. The situation requires the immediate publication of an imperial act that might still be able to restore calm. But this result can be obtained only by the constitution of a responsible ministry whose formation would be entrusted to the president of the Duma. Present intelligence permits us to hope that the members of the Duma, led by Rodzianko, are still capable of halting the general collapse, and that it will be possible to work with them. Each hour that is lost, however, diminishes the chances of maintaining and reestablishing order and facilitates a seizure of power by extreme left elements. For this reason, I beg Your Imperial Majesty to authorize immediate publication by General Headquarters of the following manifesto:

> > We declare the following to all our faithful subjects. The ferocious and powerful enemy is gathering his last forces for the struggle against our fatherland. The decisive hour approaches. The destiny of Russia, the honor of our heroic Army, the well-being of the people, all the future of our dear fatherland demand that at any price the war be pursued to a victorious end. Wishing to solidify all the forces of the nation in order to hasten the victory, I consider it my duty to appoint a ministry responsible to the representatives of the people, and to entrust the president of the Duma, Rodzianko, to form it with the help of persons possessing the confidence of all Russia.

> > I firmly hope that all the faithful sons of Russia will unite closely around the throne and the national representation, and will give to our valiant Army their fervent support for the achievement of its glorious task. In the name of our beloved country, I appeal to all Russians to fulfill their sacred duty toward Russia, in order to prove once again that she remains as firm as ever, and that no effort of her enemies can destroy her.

> > May God help us.

Alekseev showed this text to General Lukomsky, the quartermaster general, who made two minor word alterations, and the telegram was dispatched on March

1 at ten o'clock in the evening to Pskov, where Nicholas II had arrived at seven o'clock in the evening.

This telegram proposed changes much more profound than those which had been contemplated until then. In fact, only a few days before—outside the extremist parties—it had been generally accepted that in order to redress the situation it would suffice for the Emperor to call into the government men known for their honor and their liberal ideas, without however renouncing the right of choosing his ministers. An intimate collaboration between the government and the national representation had seemed clearly indispensable, but that did not necessarily imply the responsibility of the cabinet before the chamber, that is to say a parliamentary system, which Russia did not seem to be in condition to adopt before a period of political apprenticeship. But again the Emperor had delayed too long and now, to recover lost time, it was in all evidence necessary to go ahead with concessions. Moreover, the text proposed to the Emperor contemplated that the cabinet would thenceforth be placed under the control of the Duma.

Alas, events had gone so fast that even this concession, however important it seemed to us at that moment, could no longer suffice to calm the minds of the people. The excitement of the crowd had taken on such proportions that only sweeping measures could appease it. We did not have to wait long to see this confirmed.

During that night of March 1–2 all our attention was turned toward Pskov, where the Emperor was. At a very late hour, General Ruzskii had a long conversation by direct wire with the president of the Duma. The general informed Rodzianko of the Emperor's decision to appoint a new cabinet responsible to the Duma and to entrust its formation to him. Rodzianko replied that evidently neither the Emperor nor the generals realized what was happening, that one of the most terrible revolutions was developing and that he himself, as president of the Duma, was far from being able to contain the rage of the people. The Empress was the object of increasing hatred. A change of ministers and the introduction of ministerial responsibility would have been acceptable on February 27, but now the position of the sovereign himself had become untenable. On all sides rose the demand for the abdication of the Emperor Nicholas in favor of his son Aleksei, with a regency of the Grand Duke Michael, brother of the Emperor. Rodzianko added that it had been necessary to announce a recall of the troops sent from the front to Petrograd. They had, moreover, been stopped on the way by the revolutionaries.

My friend General Iury Danilov immediately transmitted a resumé of this conversation from Pskov to Alekseev. General Danilov's communication very clearly confirmed my feeling that there was not one minute to be lost. It was more and more obvious that solutions acceptable one day became impossible the next. On the morning of March 2, I suggested to General Alekseev that he summon the president of the Duma immediately for a direct-line conversation with the purpose of reaching a mutual understanding concerning ways to end the progress of the revolutionary movement. The decisions made would be submitted at once to the chiefs of the armies for their approval, and then, in the name of the Duma and the Army, presented to the Emperor for his acceptance. The general did not wish to accelerate events, and he did not sign the draft of a telegram to Rodzianko written by me to this effect. On the contrary, he asked me to prepare for him a short legal brief on the problems that would arise with a possible abdication of Emperor Nicholas.

I consulted the lawbooks to refresh my memory and immediately drew up the brief the general had requested. I explained that the Fundamental Laws of the Empire did not foresee the abandonment of power by a reigning monarch; however these laws did authorize members of the imperial family so desiring to renounce their rights of succession in expectation of a situation whereby they might be called upon to ascend the throne. There was no reason to refuse that right of renunciation to a member of the reigning family already invested with power. As for the succession to the throne, it was regulated in the strictest manner by the Fundamental Laws. They stipulated that if the reigning monarch had a son or several sons, it would be this son or the eldest of these sons, minor or not, who should necessarily succeed him on the throne. This order of succession could not be modified by Emperor Nicholas.

In fact, like his predecessors, Nicholas had at the time of his accession solemnly pledged to respect the manner of succession established by the Fundamental Laws. Only an amendment of these laws could introduce a change in the order of succession to the throne. Furthermore, since the reforms of 1906, no change could be made in the Fundamental Laws without the approval of the legislative chambers, that is, the State Council and the Duma. But no Fundamental Law had been enacted to modify the provisions relative to the order of succession. Thus Nicholas II could legally abdicate only in favor of his legitimate heir, his young son Aleksei. Since the latter was then only twelve and a half years old, a regency would be required until he reached majority. As for the person of the regent, the Fundamental Laws left Emperor Nicholas free to choose whomever he wished. When I handed this memorandum to General Alekseev he said to me: "Your conclusions confirm what I had thought."

In spite of the extreme gravity of the situation, Alekseev kept his usual calm and equilibrium, but for anyone who knew him well it was easy to see that the worthy general felt to the highest degree the burden of responsibility that weighed upon him. How often had he warned the Emperor against the disastrous conse-quences of his erroneous decisions. The obstinacy of the monarch in persevering on the way to disaster had often filled his heart with despair. As a faithful soldier, however, he had never failed in his loyalty to his sovereign and supreme commander. Except for a few very intimate associates, no one could know his discontent and his bitterness. It was also extremely painful for him to have to prevail on the Emperor to renounce the crown. It cost him even more because he had a clear foreboding of the perturbation that any disturbance of the imperial power would cause in the country, and he wished with all his heart to avoid such commotion in a time of war. Nevertheless, Alekseev realized immediately that no other solution remained but the abdication of Nicholas II, and he supported it with the full weight of his authority. To oppose it would have been to add civil war to the external war.

The fears that a change of monarch inspired were somewhat attenuated by the fact that the abdication of Nicholas II in favor of his son Aleksei would bring about a number of favorable conditions. This solution would safeguard the legitimacy. Because a minor could not renounce his rights, it would create a situation that could not be legally modified—at least not for several years. There was a great chance that the people and the Army would accept the elevation to the throne of a charming child against whom no grievances could exist and whose illness [hemophilia] would naturally draw sympathy. All this permitted the hope of maintaining the monarchy and thereby lessened the risks of a leap into the unknown.

Once his decision was taken, the first concern of General Alekseev was to ensure the solidarity of the military commanders and to avoid all peril of disunity in the armed forces. Toward eleven o'clock in the morning he sent identical messages to the commanders of the Army groups, Generals Evert, Brusilov, and Sakharov, and to the Grand Duke Nicholas Nikolaevich, commander in chief on the Caucasian front. General Ruzsky was not consulted because his favorable attitude toward the abdication was already known from the communications exchanged with him. In his telegram Alekseev stated that the functioning of the railways and the provisions for the Army were in fact already in the hands of the new powers set up in Petrograd. To preserve the Army and prevent its being contaminated by the internal struggle, the general saw in the existing situation no other solution than the abdication of Nicholas II. If the military commanders shared his views, Alekseev urged them to submit their recommendations in this sense to the Emperor, without delay. All of them replied immediately, entreating the sovereign to renounce the throne. At half past two in the afternoon their telegrams were transmitted to Pskov to be presented to Nicholas II together with a message from Alekseev. The general's message appealed to the ardent patriotism of Nicholas II and implored him to "make the decision that God would inspire in him" for the salvation of Russia.

The Emperor answered Alekseev immediately that he would make any sacrifice for the welfare of the country. At the same time we learned that the Committee of the Duma had sent [an] elective member of the State Council, Alexander Guchkov, and the conservative Duma deputy [V. V.] Shulgin to Pskov to confer with the Emperor, and that they were expected to arrive there that evening.

Alekseev then asked me to draw up the act of abdication. "Put all your heart into it," he added. I shut myself up in my office, and one hour later I returned with the following text:

> In the days of great struggle with an external foe who has been striving for almost three years to enslave our native land, it has been God's will to visit upon Russia a new grievous trial. The internal disturbances which have begun among the people threaten to have a calamitous effect on the future conduct of a hard-fought war. The destiny of Russia, the honor of our heroic Army, the welfare of the people, the whole future of our beloved fatherland demand that the war be carried to a victorious conclusion no matter what the cost. The cruel foe is straining his last resources and the time is already close at hand when our valiant Army, together with our glorious allies, will be able to crush the foe completely. In these decisive days in the life of Russia, We have deemed it Our duty in conscience to help Our people to draw closer together and to unite all the forces of the nation for a speedier attainment

of victory, and, in agreement with the State Duma, We have judged it right to abdicate the Throne of the Russian State and to lay down the Supreme Power. In conformance with the order established by the Fundamental Laws, We hand over Our succession to Our beloved Son, the Tsar Successor Tsarevich and Grand Duke Aleksei Nicholaevich, and bless Him on his accession to the Throne of the Russian State. We entrust to Our brother, the Grand Duke Michael Alexandrovich, the duty of Regent of the Empire until the coming of age of Our Son. We enjoin Our Son, and also until His coming of age the Regent of the Empire, to conduct the affairs of the state in complete and inviolable union with the representatives of the people in the legislative bodies on the principles to be established by them. In the name of the dearly beloved native land, We call upon all true sons of the Fatherland to fulfill their sacred duty to it by their obedience to the Tsar at this hour of national trial and to help Him, together with the people's representatives, to lead the Russian State onto the path of victory, prosperity, and glory. May the Lord God help Russia!

This text was approved without change by General Alekseev, as well as by General Lukomsky and the Grand Duke Sergei Mikhailovich, cousin of the Emperor. I then took it to the chief telegraph operator for Pskov, where it was transmitted that evening toward half past seven.

I spent the evening awaiting the Emperor's reply with the Grand Duke Sergei and a few officers. We had gathered together in the room of the officer on duty, just below Alekseev's office and next to the room housing the Hughes telegraphic apparatus belonging to the General Staff. The little group was nervous, smoking a great deal and exchanging impressions of the situation. The Grand Duke and some of the rest of us were seated on a green rep-covered sofa which together with a few chairs and a large mirror constituted the furnishings of the small room. From time to time General Lukomsky looked in to see if there was any news. Toward half past one in the morning—it was the night of March 2–3—we were advised that a communication would be transmitted from Pskov. We rushed to the telegraph. My eyes never left the ribbon of paper covered with Russian print emerging from the machine. I immediately recognized my text of the abdication manifesto. At first I saw no change, then suddenly I was stupefied to see that the name of the Emperor's son, the young Aleksei, had been replaced by that of the Grand Duke Michael, brother of Nicholas II. All mention of the regency was omitted. The rest of the manifesto had undergone no change, except that at the end of the second paragraph of my text, after the words, "on the bases established by them" (that is, by the legislative assemblies), the following words had been added in Pskov: "and to swear an inviolable oath to that effect in the name of the beloved country." In the case of little Prince Aleksei there would have been no reason for that addition, as a minor cannot take an oath.

The abdication of Nicholas II in favor of his brother instead of his son was for us a crushing blow indeed. The Grand Duke [Sergei] collapsed on the green sofa, exclaiming: "This is the end!" Those words seemed to answer the question which at that moment filled us all with anguish: Could [Grand Duke Michael] face the situation and maintain his place on the throne, or would this be the fall of the monarchy? Legally, the [Grand Duke's] claim to the crown was not beyond dispute.

Very modest, a man of a gentle nature who preferred to remain in the shadows, he had acquired no personal prestige and was not known to the people. General Alekseev was overwhelmed. If Nicholas II had not left the Stavka, Alekseev would have had an opportunity to defend and perhaps to bring about the only solution that to him seemed practicable—the accession of the legitimate heir, the young Aleksei. Why had this solution been set aside? We all asked ourselves this question—without comprehending.

It was not until the following day, when I spoke with the Emperor, that I had the key to the enigma. But for the moment I could not turn my thoughts from the terrible drama Nicholas II had lived through in Pskov, alone, far from his family. I thought of the humiliation, the suffering he must have endured in signing his total failure before the man he considered his greatest enemy—Alexander Guchkov. We knew how the Empress [Alexandra] had turned her husband against Guchkov after the latter had unhesitatingly attacked what he considered to be an abuse of the imperial prerogatives. Since then Alexandra, wounded by Guchkov's criticisms, had never acknowledged his firm attachment to the monarchy, his profound patriotism, and his absolute integrity. . . .

. . . General Alekseev had scarcely had time to recover from the shock of the abdication of Nicholas II in favor of his brother when, on March 3 at six o'clock in the morning, he was called to the Hughes apparatus by Rodzianko, who had asked to confer with him. The president of the Duma first requested that the general stop publication to the Army of the manifesto signed by Nicholas II. Rodzianko explained that the accession of the young Aleksei under the regency of the Grand Duke Mikhail would probably have been accepted, but that the elevation to the throne of the latter would meet with insurmountable opposition.

As a matter of fact, on the afternoon of March 2, resentment against the fallen regime had provoked a frightful revolt among the undisciplined soldiers of the Petrograd garrison, with cries of "Down with the Romanovs!" "Down with the officers!" "Land and liberty!" Many officers had been massacred. Crowds of workmen had joined the soldiers. Under these conditions, to announce the accession of the Grand Duke Michael to the throne would only add fuel to the fire of revolt. These passions had subsided only after laborious negotiations during the night, when the Committee of the Duma was able to come to a mutual understanding with the leaders of the Soviet. A Constituent Assembly, to be elected by direct and universal suffrage, would be convoked at the earliest possible time. That assembly would decide the future form of government in Russia. In the meantime the country would be ruled by a Provisional Government formed by the Duma Committee. Having no forces to support them in subduing the insurgents, the moderate elements of the Duma found no other solution but a compromise with the Soviet. This was the sole means of retaining any power in their own hands and keeping the door open for an eventual reestablishment of the monarchy. Rodzianko concluded on an optimistic note. He expressed the conviction that the solution they had adopted would provoke a powerful wave of patriotic enthusiasm and would assure tranquillity to the country and lead to victory. . . .

Toward three o'clock in the afternoon (still March 3), General Alekseev had me called and requested that I go to meet the imperial train and inform the Emperor of the latest events. A locomotive and a railway car were immediately prepared, and at half past three I left the Mogilev station. I carried with me a small notebook bound in black leather, in which I had made a resumé, day by day, of the principal communications received at the Stavka, or sent by the Stavka, since the outbreak of the revolution. The sun was sinking, and the snow on the fields and the trees of the forests glittered in its light.

At a little before six o'clock we reached Orsha, and the chief of my convoy came to tell me that we would wait there for the imperial train, which had already been announced. I had time to take only a few steps on the deserted platform of that little station when I caught sight of the gold-trimmed blue cars of the imperial train slowly approaching. General Count Grabbe, commander of the Tsar's escort, was at the door of one of the carriages and invited me to enter as soon as the train had stopped. Colonel Anatoly A. Mordvinov, the Emperor's aide-de-camp then on duty, announced me immediately to the sovereign. In his memoirs, Mordvinov relates that I looked utterly defeated and that, to all evidence, I was horror-stricken at what was happening. My emotion was increased still more by my misgivings about seeing the Emperor again in such painful circumstances.

As soon as I was in the Emperor's presence, his own self-control revived me. Nicholas II received me in a small compartment which served as an office. A mahogany writing table stood under the window, and beside it was a sofa covered with green fabric.

The Emperor came forward amiably to meet me, and I explained to him the reason for my visit. He motioned me to a small desk armchair in front of the table and seated himself on the sofa. He was dressed in the gray plastun uniform of a Caucasian infantry regiment. His face and his small beard were as carefully groomed as ever. His expression was absolutely calm, and betrayed no trace of emotion. The look in his fine blue eyes was affable as always.

Referring to the notes in my small notebook, I summed up for him, as briefly as possible, the news that had reached us during the last few days describing a situation that was becoming more and more desperate. Everything was collapsing. The capital had refused to accept the succession of the Grand Duke Michael to the throne. The dynasty was in danger of falling; the country was adrift.

The Emperor listened, impassive. Each time I finished giving him some piece of information, he would say, "But yes, naturally,"[1] in the most quiet voice. I was stupefied by the calm of his replies, by his extraordinary self-possession. I could not believe my eyes, or my ears. This "but yes, naturally," repeated itself like a refrain all during my report, and the restrained sound of his voice repeating those words remains forever engraved in my memory. He manifested no astonishment at the

---

1. In Russian, *"Nu da, konechno."*

turn that events had taken in so short a time. One would even have thought he expected it. The Emperor's extraordinarily calm attitude permitted me to tell him, at the end of my report, how distressed we were that he had not followed General Alekseev's suggestion and abdicated in favor of his son. He replied very simply: "You know that my son is ill. I could not separate myself from him."

At the end of the interview the Emperor rose and shook my hand. Then, after a moment of hesitation, he asked me: "Do you wish to return to Mogilev in your train, or do you prefer to go back with me?" Did the Emperor, with his innate delicacy, already fear to compromise in the eyes of the new power the persons who remained with him? This thought was very painful to me, and I replied to the Emperor that I would be infinitely happy to accompany him. Nicholas II smiled amiably.

I left him filled with admiration for his dignity, for his stoicism in the face of adversity. He had been virtually deposed without anyone's lifting a hand to defend him. He spoke of it as of a thing that did not touch him. He accepted fate without the least revolt, without the least show of anger or ill humor, without the least reproach to anyone. This man, who on so many occasions had seemed to us to lack will, had made his decision with great courage and dignity, without hesitation. Now that his destiny demanded the sacrifice, he accepted it with all his heart, with real grandeur. According to the English expression, he knew how to lose. . . .

The imperial train reached Mogilev at twenty minutes past eight in the evening [March 3]. The personnel of the Stavka with General Alekseev at their head, as well as the Grand Dukes Sergei Mikhailovich and Boris Vladimirovich, were assembled at the railway station to meet the Emperor. I immediately took my place among the chiefs of services of the General Headquarters.

Nicholas II approached General Alekseev and embraced him, then he slowly walked among the persons present. In silence he saluted each one of us with a handshake, looking into our eyes. All were greatly moved, and stifled sobs could be heard. The Emperor kept his apparent calm. From time to time he threw back his head in a movement customary to him. A few tears formed in the corners of his eyes and he brushed them away with a gesture of his hand.

The emotions that shook the witnesses of this scene derived from a throng of sentiments. We had so often deplored the poor judgment of Nicholas II, so many times we had criticized his blindness, and yet we could not judge him too harshly for his errors knowing that the responsibility for his unfortunate decisions rested primarily with the Empress Alexandra. We pitied the Emperor's weakness in the face of his wife, the unconscious factor of his failure. Was not Nicholas II, in the manner of the heroes of the Greek tragedies, the predestined victim of an implacable fate? It was preordained that the woman he married—a German princess, grand-daughter of Queen Victoria of England—should embrace the cause of Russian autocracy with such fervor that she inspired in her husband a firm will to resist any attack on the imperial prerogatives. Fate also decreed that a kind of monk, the false and debauched Grigory Rasputin, who in some mysterious manner twice arrested near-fatal hemophilia crises for the Grand Duke Aleksei, should appear in the eyes of the anguished, mystical Empress as a "man of God" and thereby acquire such influence in the affairs of state that he became the grave-digger of the tsarist

[Imperial] regime. Had not some of us, facing the danger which menaced the monarchy, reproached ourselves at times for having remained loyal to our sovereign when a coup d'état to replace him on the throne by another member of the dynasty might perhaps have averted the catastrophe? In spite of his faults as a sovereign, Nicholas II as a man had never inspired in us anything other than sympathy and even affection. All his life he had sought to do what he considered to be his duty. As a private individual he would have been a model of virtue. And then, for almost twenty-five years he had been the symbol of our country, as his ancestors, the builders of the Russian Empire, had been. Without the Tsar what would Russia become? We had served Nicholas II to the best of our ability, and yet not one of us, and no one in Russia, had attempted to defend his crown. It was obvious that all intervention in this sense would have been not only useless but disastrous. All these thoughts came to our minds as we bowed before our Emperor, a man fallen yet grown in stature through the moral courage he gave proof of in adversity. . . .

The Grand Duke Michael's act of abdication was signed early in the afternoon of March 3 and published during the night, at the same time as that of Emperor Nicholas II. The renunciation of the Grand Duke Michael to the succession of his brother was formulated in these terms:

> A heavy burden has been laid on me by my brother, who has passed over to me the imperial throne of Russia at a time of unprecedented war and popular disturbances.
>
> Animated by the thought which is in the minds of all, that the good of the State is above other considerations, I have decided to accept the supreme power only if that be the desire of our great people, expressed at a general election for their representatives to the Constituent Assembly, which should determine the form of government and lay down the fundamental laws of the Russian Empire.
>
> With a prayer to God for His blessings, I beseech all citizens of the Empire to subject themselves to the Provisional Government, which is created by and invested with full power by the State Duma until the summoning, at the earliest possible moment, of a Constituent Assembly, selected by universal, direct, equal, and secret ballot, which shall establish a government in accordance with the will of the people.
>
> March 3, 1917                                                              Michael

A few days later one of the authors of this text, my old friend Baron Boris Nolde, explained to me that the phrase "I beseech all the citizens of the Empire to subject themselves to the Provisional Government, which is created by and invested with full power by the State Duma" was written in order not only to establish the transfer of supreme power to the new government but also to endow that government with the right to issue laws. Obviously this was a weak legal formulation, but one had to be content with it, having nothing better. Its purpose of assuring at least a semblance of continuity between the powers of the monarchy and those of the Provisional Government corresponded well with the state of mind of the Provisional Government's members. They did not wish to owe their power to the rebellion, to the street, and were concerned with legality, whereas the

Petrograd Soviet boasted of its purely revolutionary origin and in moving toward the triumph of socialism rejected all ties with the past.

# FURTHER READING

Richard Abraham, *Alexander Kerensky: The First Love of the Revolution* (1987)

Dorothy Atkinson, *The End of the Russian Land Commune, 1905–1930* (1983)

Michael Brainerd, "The Octobrists and the Gentry in the Russian Social Crisis of 1913–1914," *Russian Review* 38 (1979), 160–179

E. N. Burdzhalov, *Russia's Second Revolution: The February 1917 Uprising in Petrograd,* ed. and trans. Donald J. Raleigh (1987)

Mary Shaeffer Conroy, *Peter Arkad'evich Stolypin: Practical Politics in Late Tsarist Russia* (1976)

Ben Eklof, "Worlds in Conflict: Patriarchal Authority, Discipline, and the Russian School, 1861–1914," *Slavic Review* 50 (1991), 792–806

John D. Elsworth, ed., *The Silver Age in Russian Literature* (1992)

Laura Engelstein, *The Keys to Happiness: Sex and the Search for Modernity in Fin-de-Siècle Russia* (1992)

Marc Ferro, *Nicholas II: The Last of the Tsars,* trans. (from French) Brian Pearce (1993)

Michael T. Florinsky, *The End of the Russian Empire* (1931, 1979)

William C. Fuller, Jr., *Civil-Military Conflict in Imperial Russia, 1881–1914* (1985)

Graeme J. Gill, *Peasants and Government in the Russian Revolution* (1979)

Leopold H. Haimson, ed., *The Politics of Rural Russia, 1905–1914* (1979)

——, "The Problem of Social Stability in Urban Russia, 1905–1917," *Slavic Review* 23 (1964), 619–642; 24 (1965), 1–22

Tsuyoshi Hasegawa, *The February Revolution: Petrograd 1917* (1981)

Geoffrey A. Hosking, *The Russian Constitutional Experiment: Government and Duma, 1907–1914* (1973)

Samuel D. Kassow, *Students, Professors, and the State in Tsarist Russia* (1989)

George Katkov, *Russia 1917: The February Revolution* (1967)

John L. H. Keep, *The Russian Revolution: A Study in Mass Mobilization* (1976)

George F. Kennan, *The Fateful Alliance: France, Russia, and the Coming of the First World War* (1984)

Diane P. Koenker, *Moscow Workers and the 1917 Revolution* (1981)

Alfred Levin, "Peter Arkad'evich Stolypin: A Political Appraisal," *Journal of Modern History* 37 (1965), 445–463

Dominic C. B. Lieven, *Russia and the Origins of the First World War* (1983)

——, *Russia's Rulers under the Old Regime [the State Council, 1894–1914]* (1989)

W. Bruce Lincoln, *Passage Through Armageddon: The Russians In War and Revolution, 1914–1918* (1986)

Tim McDaniel, *Autocracy, Capitalism, and Revolution in Russia* (1988)

David M. McDonald, *United Government and Foreign Policy in Russia, 1900–1914* (1992)

Robert B. McKean, *St. Petersburg Between the Revolutions: Workers and Revolutionaries, June 1907–February 1917* (1990)

M. David Mandel, *Petrograd Workers and the Fall of the Old Regime* (1983)

Louis Menashe, " 'A Liberal with Spurs': Alexander Guchkov, A Russian Bourgeois in Politics," *Russian Review,* 26 (1967), 38–53

Paul N. Miliukov, *The Russian Revolution,* ed. and trans. Richard Stites (1978)

Judith Pallot, "Modernization from Above: The Stolypin Land Reform," in Judith Pallot and Denis J. B. Shaw, *Landscape and Settlement in Romanov Russia, 1613–1917* (1990), 164–192

Alexander Pasternak, *A Vanished Present: The Memoirs of Alexander Pasternak [1893–1982]*, ed. and trans. Ann Pasternak Slater (1984)

Ben-Cion Pinchuk, *The Octobrists in the Third Duma, 1907–1912* (1974)

Richard Pipes, *The Russian Revolution* (1990)

Raymond Pearson, *The Russian Moderates and the Crisis of Tsarism, 1914–1917* (1977)

Carl Proffer and Eilendea Proffer, eds., *The Silver Age of Russian Culture* (1975)

George F. Putnam, *Russian Alternatives to Marxism: Christian Socialism and Idealistic Liberalism in [Early] Twentieth-Century Russia* (1977)

Christopher Read, *Religion, Revolution and the Russian Intelligentsia, 1900–1912: The Vekhi Debate and Its Intellectual Background* (1980)

Richard G. Robbins, Jr., *The Tsar's Viceroys: Russian Provincial Governors in the Last Years of the Empire* (1987)

William G. Rosenberg, *Liberals in the Russian Revolution: The Constitutional Democratic Party, 1917–1921* (1974)

Robert Service, *Lenin: A Political Life*, vol. 2 (1991)

Norman E. Saul, *Sailors in Revolt: The Russian Baltic Fleet in 1917* (1978)

Marshall S. Shatz and Judith E. Zimmerman, eds. and trans., *Signposts: A Collection of Articles [1909] on the Russian Intelligentsia* (1986)

V. V. Shulgin, *Days of the Russian Revolution: Memoirs from the Right, 1905–1917*, ed. and trans. Bruce F. Adams (1990)

Lewis H. Siegelbaum, *The Politics of Industrial Mobilization in Russia, 1914–1917: A Study of the War-Industries Committees* (1983)

S. A. Smith, *Red Petrograd: Revolution in the Factories, 1917–1918* (1983)

Richard Stites, *Revolutionary Dreams: Utopian Vision and Experimental Life in the Russian Revolution* (1988)

———, *Russian Popular Culture: Entertainment and Society Since 1900* (1992)

Norman Stone, *The Eastern Front, 1914–1917* (1975)

Robert W. Thurston, *Liberal City, Conservative State: Moscow and Russia's Urban Crisis, 1906–1914* (1987)

George Vernadsky *et al.*, eds. and trans., *A Source Book for Russian History from Early Times to 1917*, vol. 3 (1972)

Rex A. Wade and Scott J. Seregny, eds., *Politics and Society in Provincial Russia: Saratov, 1590[1860]–1917* (1989)

Francis W. Wcislo, *Reforming Rural Russia: State, Local Society, and National Politics, 1855–1914* (1990)

Neil B. Weissman, *Reform in Tsarist Russia: The State Bureaucracy and Local Government, 1900–1914* (1981)

J. N. Westwood, *Russia against Japan, 1904–1905: A New Look at the Russo-Japanese War* (1986)

Allan K. Wildman, *The End of the Russian Imperial Army: The Old Army and the Soldiers' Revolt (March–April 1917)* (1980)